Arnold Bennett, Collection no

In this book:
How to Live on 24 Hours a
The Human Machine
The Old Wives' Tale
The Card, A Story Of Adventure In The Five Towns
The Grand Babylon Hotel
Anna of the Five Towns

Enoch Arnold Bennett (27 May 1867 – 27 March 1931) was an English writer. He is best known as a novelist, but he also worked in other fields such as journalism, propaganda and film. One of his most popular non-fiction works, which is still read to this day, is the self-help book How to Live on 24 Hours a Day.

In 1908 The Old Wives' Tale was published and was an immediate success throughout the English-speaking world. After a visit to America in 1911, where he had been publicized and acclaimed as no other visiting writer since Charles Dickens, he returned to England where Old Wives' Tale was reappraised and hailed as a masterpiece.

In this book:

How to Live on 24 Hours a Day
PREFACE TO THIS EDITION

This preface, though placed at the beginning, as a preface must be, should be read at the end of the book.

I have received a large amount of correspondence concerning this small work, and many reviews of it—some of them nearly as long as the book itself—have been printed. But scarcely any of the comment has been adverse. Some people have objected to a frivolity of tone; but as the tone is not, in my opinion, at all frivolous, this objection did not impress me; and had no weightier reproach been put forward I might almost have been persuaded that the volume was flawless! A more serious stricture has, however, been offered—not in the press, but by sundry obviously sincere correspondents—and I must deal with it. A reference to page 43 will show that I anticipated and feared this disapprobation. The sentence against which protests have been made is as follows:—"In the majority of instances he [the typical man] does not precisely feel a passion for his business; at best he does not dislike it. He begins his business functions with some reluctance, as late as he can, and he ends them with joy, as early as he can. And his engines, while he is engaged in his business, are seldom at their full 'h.p.'"

I am assured, in accents of unmistakable sincerity, that there are many business men—not merely those in high positions or with fine prospects, but modest subordinates with no hope of ever being much better off—who do enjoy their business functions, who do not shirk them, who do not arrive at the office as late as possible and depart as early as possible, who, in a word, put the whole of their force into their day's work and are genuinely fatigued at the end thereof.

I am ready to believe it. I do believe it. I know it. I always knew it. Both in London and in the provinces it has been my lot to spend long years in subordinate situations of business; and the fact did not escape me that a certain proportion of my peers showed what amounted to an honest passion for their duties, and that while engaged in those duties they were really *living* to the fullest extent of which they were capable. But I remain convinced that these fortunate and happy individuals (happier perhaps than they guessed) did not and do not constitute a majority, or anything like a majority. I remain convinced that the majority of decent average conscientious men of business (men with aspirations and ideals) do not as a rule go home of a night genuinely tired. I remain convinced that they put not as much but as little of themselves as they conscientiously can into the earning of a livelihood, and that their vocation bores rather than interests them.

Nevertheless, I admit that the minority is of sufficient importance to merit attention, and that I ought not to have ignored it so completely as I did do. The whole difficulty of the hard-working minority was put in a single colloquial sentence by one of my correspondents. He wrote: "I am just as keen as anyone on doing something to 'exceed my programme,' but allow me to tell you that when I get home at six thirty p.m. I am not anything like so fresh as you seem to imagine."

Now I must point out that the case of the minority, who throw themselves with passion and gusto into their daily business task, is infinitely less deplorable than the case of the majority, who go half-heartedly and feebly through their official day. The former are less in need of advice "how to live." At any rate during their official day of, say, eight hours they are really alive; their engines are giving the full indicated "h.p." The other eight working hours of their day may be badly organised, or even frittered away; but it is less disastrous to waste eight hours a day than sixteen hours a day; it is better to have lived a bit than never to have lived at all. The real tragedy is the tragedy of the man who is braced to effort neither in the office nor out of it, and to this man this book is primarily addressed. "But," says the other and more fortunate man, "although my ordinary programme is bigger than his, I want to exceed my programme too! I am living a bit; I want to live more. But I really can't do another day's work on the top of my official day."

The fact is, I, the author, ought to have foreseen that I should appeal most strongly to those who already had an interest in existence. It is always the man who has tasted life who demands more of it. And it is always the man who never gets out of bed who is the most difficult to rouse.

Well, you of the minority, let us assume that the intensity of your daily money-getting will not allow you to carry out quite all the suggestions in the following pages. Some of the suggestions may yet stand. I admit that you may not be able to use the time spent on the journey home at night; but the suggestion for the journey to the office in the morning is as practicable for you as for anybody. And that weekly interval of forty hours, from Saturday to Monday, is yours just as much as the other man's, though a slight accumulation of fatigue may prevent you from employing the whole of your "h.p." upon it. There remains, then, the important portion of the three or more evenings a week. You tell me flatly that you are too tired to do anything outside your programme at night. In reply to which I tell you flatly that if your ordinary day's work is thus exhausting, then the balance of your life is wrong and must be adjusted. A man's powers ought not to be monopolised by his ordinary day's work. What, then, is to be done?

The obvious thing to do is to circumvent your ardour for your ordinary day's work by a ruse. Employ your engines in something beyond the programme before, and not after, you employ them on the programme itself. Briefly, get up earlier in the morning. You say you cannot. You say it is impossible for you to go earlier to bed of a night—to do so would upset the entire household. I do not think it is quite impossible to go to bed earlier at night. I think that if you persist in rising earlier, and the consequence is insufficiency of sleep, you will soon find a way of going to bed earlier. But my impression is that the consequences of rising earlier will not be an insufficiency of sleep. My impression, growing stronger every year, is that sleep is partly a matter of habit—and of slackness. I am convinced that most people sleep as long as they do because they are at a loss for any other diversion. How much sleep do you think is daily obtained by the powerful healthy man who daily rattles up your street in charge of Carter Patterson's van? I have consulted a doctor on this point. He is a doctor who for twenty-four years has had a large general practice in a large flourishing suburb of London, inhabited by exactly such people as you and me. He is a curt man, and his answer was curt:

"Most people sleep themselves stupid."

He went on to give his opinion that nine men out of ten would have better health and more fun out of life if they spent less time in bed.

Other doctors have confirmed this judgment, which, of course, does not apply to growing youths.

Rise an hour, an hour and a half, or even two hours earlier; and—if you must—retire earlier when you can. In the matter of exceeding programmes, you will accomplish as much in one morning hour as in two evening hours. "But," you say, "I couldn't begin without some food, and servants." Surely, my dear sir, in an age when an excellent spirit-lamp (including a saucepan) can be bought for less than a shilling, you are not going to allow your highest welfare to depend upon the precarious immediate co-operation of a fellow creature! Instruct the fellow creature, whoever she may be, at night. Tell her to put a tray in a suitable position over night. On that tray two biscuits, a cup and saucer, a box of matches and a spirit-lamp; on the lamp, the saucepan; on the saucepan, the lid—but turned the wrong way up; on the reversed lid, the small teapot, containing a minute quantity of tea leaves. You will then have to strike a match—that is all. In three minutes the water boils, and you pour it into the teapot (which is already warm). In three more minutes the tea is infused. You can begin your day while drinking it. These details may seem trivial to the foolish, but to the thoughtful they will not seem trivial. The proper, wise balancing of one's whole life may depend upon the feasibility of a cup of tea at an unusual hour.

A. B.

THE DAILY MIRACLE

"Yes, he's one of those men that don't know how to manage. Good situation. Regular income. Quite enough for luxuries as well as needs. Not really extravagant. And yet the fellow's always in difficulties. Somehow he gets nothing out of his money. Excellent flat—half empty! Always looks as if he'd had the brokers in. New suit—old hat! Magnificent necktie—baggy trousers! Asks you to dinner: cut glass—bad mutton, or Turkish coffee—cracked cup! He can't understand it. Explanation simply is that he fritters his income away. Wish I had the half of it! I'd show him—"

So we have most of us criticised, at one time or another, in our superior way.

We are nearly all chancellors of the exchequer: it is the pride of the moment. Newspapers are full of articles explaining how to live on such-and-such a sum, and these articles provoke a correspondence whose violence proves the interest they excite. Recently, in a daily organ, a battle raged round the question whether a woman can exist nicely in the country on L85 a year. I have seen an essay, "How to live on eight shillings a week." But I have never seen an essay, "How to live on twenty-four hours a day." Yet it has been said that time is money. That proverb understates the case. Time is a great deal more than money. If you have time you can obtain money—usually. But though you have the wealth of a cloak-room attendant at the Carlton Hotel, you cannot buy yourself a minute more time than I have, or the cat by the fire has.

Philosophers have explained space. They have not explained time. It is the inexplicable raw material of everything. With it, all is possible; without it, nothing. The supply of time is truly a daily miracle, an affair genuinely astonishing when one examines it. You wake up in the morning, and lo! your purse is magically filled with twenty-four hours of the unmanufactured tissue of the universe of your life! It is yours. It is the most precious of possessions. A highly singular commodity, showered upon you in a manner as singular as the commodity itself!

For remark! No one can take it from you. It is unstealable. And no one receives either more or less than you receive.

Talk about an ideal democracy! In the realm of time there is no aristocracy of wealth, and no aristocracy of intellect. Genius is never rewarded by even an extra hour a day. And there is no punishment. Waste your infinitely precious commodity as much as you will, and the supply will never be withheld from you. No mysterious power will say:—"This man is a fool, if not a knave. He does not deserve time; he shall be cut off at the meter." It is more certain than consols, and payment of income is not affected by Sundays. Moreover, you cannot draw on the future. Impossible to get into debt! You can only waste the passing moment. You cannot waste to-morrow; it is kept for you. You cannot waste the next hour; it is kept for you.

I said the affair was a miracle. Is it not?

You have to live on this twenty-four hours of daily time. Out of it you have to spin health, pleasure, money, content, respect, and the evolution of your immortal soul. Its right use, its most effective use, is a matter of the highest urgency and of the most thrilling actuality. All depends on that. Your happiness—the elusive prize that you are all clutching for, my friends!—depends on that. Strange that the newspapers, so enterprising and up-to-date as they are, are not full of "How to live on a given income of time," instead of "How to live on a given income of money"! Money is far commoner than time. When one reflects, one perceives that money is just about the commonest thing there is. It encumbers the earth in gross heaps.

If one can't contrive to live on a certain income of money, one earns a little more—or steals it, or advertises for it. One doesn't necessarily muddle one's life because one can't quite manage on a thousand pounds a year; one braces the muscles and makes it guineas, and balances the budget. But if one cannot arrange that an income of twenty-four hours a day shall exactly cover all proper items of expenditure, one does muddle one's life definitely. The supply of time, though gloriously regular, is cruelly restricted.

Which of us lives on twenty-four hours a day? And when I say "lives," I do not mean exists, nor "muddles through." Which of us is free from that uneasy feeling that the "great spending departments" of his daily life are not managed as they ought to be? Which of us is quite sure that his fine suit is not surmounted by a shameful hat, or that in attending to the crockery he has forgotten the quality of the food? Which of us is not saying to himself—which of us has not been saying to himself all his life: "I shall alter that when I have a little more time"?

We never shall have any more time. We have, and we have always had, all the time there is. It is the realisation of this profound and neglected truth (which, by the way, I have not discovered) that has led me to the minute practical examination of daily time-expenditure.

II
THE DESIRE TO EXCEED ONE'S PROGRAMME

"But," someone may remark, with the English disregard of everything except the point, "what is he driving at with his twenty-four hours a day? I have no difficulty in living on twenty-four hours a day. I do all that I want to do, and still find time to go in for newspaper competitions. Surely it is a simple affair, knowing that one has only twenty-four hours a day, to content one's self with twenty-four hours a day!"

To you, my dear sir, I present my excuses and apologies. You are precisely the man that I have been wishing to meet for about forty years. Will you kindly send me your name and address, and state your charge for telling me how you do it? Instead of me talking to you, you ought to be talking to me. Please come forward. That you exist, I am convinced, and that I have not yet encountered you is my loss. Meanwhile, until you appear, I will continue to chat with my companions in distress—that innumerable band of souls who are haunted, more or less painfully, by the feeling that the years slip by, and slip by, and slip by, and that they have not yet been able to get their lives into proper working order.

If we analyse that feeling, we shall perceive it to be, primarily, one of uneasiness, of expectation, of looking forward, of aspiration. It is a source of constant discomfort, for it behaves like a skeleton at the feast of all our enjoyments. We go to the theatre and laugh; but between the acts it raises a skinny finger at us. We rush violently for the last train, and while we are cooling a long age on the platform waiting for the last train, it promenades its bones up and down by our side and inquires: "O man, what hast thou done with thy youth? What art thou doing with thine age?" You may urge that this feeling of continuous looking forward, of aspiration, is part of life itself, and inseparable from life itself. True!

But there are degrees. A man may desire to go to Mecca. His conscience tells him that he ought to go to Mecca. He fares forth, either by the aid of Cook's, or unassisted; he may probably never reach Mecca; he may drown before he gets to Port Said; he may perish ingloriously on the coast of the Red Sea; his desire may remain eternally frustrate. Unfulfilled aspiration may always trouble him. But he will not be tormented in the same way as the man who, desiring to reach Mecca, and harried by the desire to reach Mecca, never leaves Brixton.

It is something to have left Brixton. Most of us have not left Brixton. We have not even taken a cab to Ludgate Circus and inquired from Cook's the price of a conducted tour. And our excuse to ourselves is that there are only twenty-four hours in the day.

If we further analyse our vague, uneasy aspiration, we shall, I think, see that it springs from a fixed idea that we ought to do something in addition to those things which we are loyally and morally obliged to do. We are obliged, by various codes written and unwritten, to maintain ourselves and our families (if any) in health and comfort, to pay our debts, to save, to increase our prosperity by increasing our efficiency. A task sufficiently difficult! A task which very few of us achieve! A task often beyond our skill! Yet, if we succeed in it, as we sometimes do, we are not satisfied; the skeleton is still with us.

And even when we realise that the task is beyond our skill, that our powers cannot cope with it, we feel that we should be less discontented if we gave to our powers, already overtaxed, something still further to do.

And such is, indeed, the fact. The wish to accomplish something outside their formal programme is common to all men who in the course of evolution have risen past a certain level.

Until an effort is made to satisfy that wish, the sense of uneasy waiting for something to start which has not started will remain to disturb the peace of the soul. That wish has been called by many names. It is one form of the universal desire for knowledge. And it is so strong that men whose whole lives have been given to the systematic acquirement of knowledge have been driven by it to overstep the limits of their programme in search of still more knowledge. Even Herbert Spencer, in my opinion the greatest mind that ever lived, was often forced by it into agreeable little backwaters of inquiry.

I imagine that in the majority of people who are conscious of the wish to live—that is to say, people who have intellectual curiosity—the aspiration to exceed formal programmes takes a literary shape. They would like to embark on a course of reading. Decidedly the British people are becoming more and more literary. But I would point out that literature by no means comprises the whole field of knowledge, and that the disturbing thirst to improve one's self—to increase one's knowledge—may well be slaked quite apart from literature. With the various ways of slaking I shall deal later. Here I merely point out to those who have no natural sympathy with literature that literature is not the only well.

III
PRECAUTIONS BEFORE BEGINNING

Now that I have succeeded (if succeeded I have) in persuading you to admit to yourself that you are constantly haunted by a suppressed dissatisfaction with your own arrangement of your daily life; and that the primal cause of that inconvenient dissatisfaction is the feeling that you are every day leaving undone something which you would like to do, and which, indeed, you are always hoping to do when you have "more time"; and now that I have drawn your attention to the glaring, dazzling truth that you never will have "more time," since you already have all the time there is—you expect me to let you into some wonderful secret by which you may at any rate approach the ideal of a perfect arrangement of the day, and by which, therefore, that haunting, unpleasant, daily disappointment of things left undone will be got rid of!

I have found no such wonderful secret. Nor do I expect to find it, nor do I expect that anyone else will ever find it. It is undiscovered. When you first began to gather my drift, perhaps there was a resurrection of hope in your breast. Perhaps you said to yourself, "This man will show me an easy, unfatiguing way of doing what I have so long in vain wished to do." Alas, no! The fact is that there is no easy way, no royal road. The path to Mecca is extremely hard and stony, and the worst of it is that you never quite get there after all.

The most important preliminary to the task of arranging one's life so that one may live fully and comfortably within one's daily budget of twenty-four hours is the calm realisation of the extreme difficulty of the task, of the sacrifices and the endless effort which it demands. I cannot too strongly insist on this.

If you imagine that you will be able to achieve your ideal by ingeniously planning out a time-table with a pen on a piece of paper, you had better give up hope at once. If you are not prepared for discouragements and disillusions; if you will not be content with a small result for a big effort, then do not begin. Lie down again and resume the uneasy doze which you call your existence.

It is very sad, is it not, very depressing and sombre? And yet I think it is rather fine, too, this necessity for the tense bracing of the will before anything worth doing can be done. I rather like it myself. I feel it to be the chief thing that differentiates me from the cat by the fire.

"Well," you say, "assume that I am braced for the battle. Assume that I have carefully weighed and comprehended your ponderous remarks; how do I begin?" Dear sir, you simply begin. There is no magic method of beginning. If a man standing on the edge of a swimming-bath and wanting to jump into the cold water should ask you, "How do I begin to jump?" you would merely reply, "Just jump. Take hold of your nerves, and jump."

As I have previously said, the chief beauty about the constant supply of time is that you cannot waste it in advance. The next year, the next day, the next hour are lying ready for you, as perfect, as unspoilt, as if you had never wasted or misapplied a single moment in all your career. Which fact is very gratifying and reassuring. You can turn over a new leaf every hour if you choose. Therefore no object is served in waiting till next week, or even until to-morrow. You may fancy that the water will be warmer next week. It won't. It will be colder.

But before you begin, let me murmur a few words of warning in your private ear.

Let me principally warn you against your own ardour. Ardour in well-doing is a misleading and a treacherous thing. It cries out loudly for employment; you can't satisfy it at first; it wants more and more; it is eager to move mountains and divert the course of rivers. It isn't content till it perspires. And then, too often, when it feels the perspiration on its brow, it wearies all of a sudden and dies, without even putting itself to the trouble of saying, "I've had enough of this."

Beware of undertaking too much at the start. Be content with quite a little. Allow for accidents. Allow for human nature, especially your own.

A failure or so, in itself, would not matter, if it did not incur a loss of self-esteem and of self-confidence. But just as nothing succeeds like success, so nothing fails like failure. Most people who are ruined are ruined by attempting too much. Therefore, in setting out on the immense enterprise of living fully and comfortably within the narrow limits of twenty-four hours a day, let us avoid at any cost the risk of an early failure. I will not agree that, in this business at any rate, a glorious failure is better than a petty success. I am all for the petty success. A glorious failure leads to nothing; a petty success may lead to a success that is not petty.

So let us begin to examine the budget of the day's time. You say your day is already full to overflowing. How? You actually spend in earning your livelihood—how much? Seven hours, on the average? And in actual sleep, seven? I will add two hours, and be generous. And I will defy you to account to me on the spur of the moment for the other eight hours.

IV
THE CAUSE OF THE TROUBLES

In order to come to grips at once with the question of time-expenditure in all its actuality, I must choose an individual case for examination. I can only deal with one case, and that case cannot be the average case, because there is no such case as the average case, just as there is no such man as the average man. Every man and every man's case is special.

But if I take the case of a Londoner who works in an office, whose office hours are from ten to six, and who spends fifty minutes morning and night in travelling between his house door and his office door, I shall have got as near to the average as facts permit. There are men who have to work longer for a living, but there are others who do not have to work so long.

Fortunately the financial side of existence does not interest us here; for our present purpose the clerk at a pound a week is exactly as well off as the millionaire in Carlton House-terrace.

Now the great and profound mistake which my typical man makes in regard to his day is a mistake of general attitude, a mistake which vitiates and weakens two-thirds of his energies and interests. In the majority of instances he does not precisely feel a passion for his business; at best he does not dislike it. He begins his business functions with reluctance, as late as he can, and he ends them with joy, as early as he can. And his engines while he is engaged in his business are seldom at their full "h.p." (I know that I shall be accused by angry readers of traducing the city worker; but I am pretty thoroughly acquainted with the City, and I stick to what I say.)

Yet in spite of all this he persists in looking upon those hours from ten to six as "the day," to which the ten hours preceding them and the six hours following them are nothing but a prologue and epilogue. Such an attitude, unconscious though it be, of course kills his interest in the odd sixteen hours, with the result that, even if he does not waste them, he does not count them; he regards them simply as margin.

This general attitude is utterly illogical and unhealthy, since it formally gives the central prominence to a patch of time and a bunch of activities which the man's one idea is to "get through" and have "done with." If a man makes two-thirds of his existence subservient to one-third, for which admittedly he has no absolutely feverish zest, how can he hope to live fully and completely? He cannot.

If my typical man wishes to live fully and completely he must, in his mind, arrange a day within a day. And this inner day, a Chinese box in a larger Chinese box, must begin at 6 p.m. and end at 10 a.m. It is a day of sixteen hours; and during all these sixteen hours he has nothing whatever to do but cultivate his body and his soul and his fellow men. During those sixteen hours he is free; he is not a wage-earner; he is not preoccupied with monetary cares; he is just as good as a man with a private income. This must be his attitude. And his attitude is all important. His success in life (much more important than the amount of estate upon what his executors will have to pay estate duty) depends on it.

What? You say that full energy given to those sixteen hours will lessen the value of the business eight? Not so. On the contrary, it will assuredly increase the value of the business eight. One of the chief things which my typical man has to learn is that the mental faculties are capable of a continuous hard activity; they do not tire like an arm or a leg. All they want is change—not rest, except in sleep.

I shall now examine the typical man's current method of employing the sixteen hours that are entirely his, beginning with his uprising. I will merely indicate things which he does and which I think he ought not to do, postponing my suggestions for "planting" the times which I shall have cleared—as a settler clears spaces in a forest.

In justice to him I must say that he wastes very little time before he leaves the house in the morning at 9.10. In too many houses he gets up at nine, breakfasts between 9.7 and 9.9 1/2, and then bolts. But immediately he bangs the front door his mental faculties, which are tireless, become idle. He walks to the station in a condition of mental coma. Arrived there, he usually has to wait for the train. On hundreds of suburban stations every morning you see men calmly strolling up and down platforms while railway companies unblushingly rob them of time, which is more than money. Hundreds of thousands of hours are thus lost every day simply because my typical man thinks so little of time that it has never occurred to him to take quite easy precautions against the risk of its loss.

He has a solid coin of time to spend every day—call it a sovereign. He must get change for it, and in getting change he is content to lose heavily.

Supposing that in selling him a ticket the company said, "We will change you a sovereign, but we shall charge you three halfpence for doing so," what would my typical man exclaim? Yet that is the equivalent of what the company does when it robs him of five minutes twice a day.

You say I am dealing with minutiae. I am. And later on I will justify myself.

Now will you kindly buy your paper and step into the train?

V

TENNIS AND THE IMMORTAL SOUL

You get into the morning train with your newspaper, and you calmly and majestically give yourself up to your newspaper. You do not hurry. You know you have at least half an hour of security in front of you. As your glance lingers idly at the advertisements of shipping and of songs on the outer pages, your air is the air of a leisured man, wealthy in time, of a man from some planet where there are a hundred and twenty-four hours a day instead of twenty-four. I am an impassioned reader of newspapers. I read five English and two French dailies, and the news-agents alone know how many weeklies, regularly. I am obliged to mention this personal fact lest I should be accused of a prejudice against newspapers when I say that I object to the reading of newspapers in the morning train. Newspapers are produced with rapidity, to be read with rapidity. There is no place in my daily programme for newspapers. I read them as I may in odd moments. But I do read them. The idea of devoting to them thirty or forty consecutive minutes of wonderful solitude (for nowhere can one more perfectly immerse one's self in one's self than in a compartment full of silent, withdrawn, smoking males) is to me repugnant. I cannot possibly allow you to scatter priceless pearls of time with such Oriental lavishness. You are not the Shah of time. Let me respectfully remind you that you have no more time than I have. No newspaper reading in trains! I have already "put by" about three-quarters of an hour for use.

Now you reach your office. And I abandon you there till six o'clock. I am aware that you have nominally an hour (often in reality an hour and a half) in the midst of the day, less than half of which time is given to eating. But I will leave you all that to spend as you choose. You may read your newspapers then.

I meet you again as you emerge from your office. You are pale and tired. At any rate, your wife says you are pale, and you give her to understand that you are tired. During the journey home you have been gradually working up the tired feeling. The tired feeling hangs heavy over the mighty suburbs of London like a virtuous and melancholy cloud, particularly in winter. You don't eat immediately on your arrival home. But in about an hour or so you feel as if you could sit up and take a little nourishment. And you do. Then you smoke, seriously; you see friends; you potter; you play cards; you flirt with a book; you note that old age is creeping on; you take a stroll; you caress the piano.... By Jove! a quarter past eleven. You then devote quite forty minutes to thinking about going to bed; and it is conceivable that you are acquainted with a genuinely good whisky. At last you go to bed, exhausted by the day's work. Six hours, probably more, have gone since you left the office—gone like a dream, gone like magic, unaccountably gone!

That is a fair sample case. But you say: "It's all very well for you to talk. A man *is* tired. A man must see his friends. He can't always be on the stretch." Just so. But when you arrange to go to the theatre (especially with a pretty woman) what happens? You rush to the suburbs; you spare no toil to make yourself glorious in fine raiment; you rush back to town in another train; you keep yourself on the stretch for four hours, if not five; you take her home; you take yourself home. You don't spend three-quarters of an hour in "thinking about" going to bed. You go. Friends and fatigue have equally been forgotten, and the evening has seemed so exquisitely long (or perhaps too short)! And do you remember that time when you were persuaded to sing in the chorus of the amateur operatic society, and slaved two hours every other night for three months? Can you deny that when you have something definite to look forward to at eventide, something that is to employ all your energy—the thought of that something gives a glow and a more intense vitality to the whole day?

What I suggest is that at six o'clock you look facts in the face and admit that you are not tired (because you are not, you know), and that you arrange your evening so that it is not cut in the middle by a meal. By so doing you will have a clear expanse of at least three hours. I do not suggest that you should employ three hours every night of your life in using up your mental energy. But I do suggest that you might, for a commencement, employ an hour and a half every other evening in some important and consecutive cultivation of the mind. You will still be left with three evenings for friends, bridge, tennis, domestic scenes, odd reading, pipes, gardening, pottering, and prize competitions. You will still have the terrific wealth of forty-five hours between 2 p.m. Saturday and 10 a.m. Monday. If you persevere you will soon want to pass four evenings, and perhaps five, in some sustained endeavour to be genuinely alive. And you will fall out of that habit of muttering to yourself at 11.15 p.m., "Time to be thinking about going to bed." The man who begins to go to bed forty minutes before he opens his bedroom door is bored; that is to say, he is not living.

But remember, at the start, those ninety nocturnal minutes thrice a week must be the most important minutes in the ten thousand and eighty. They must be sacred, quite as sacred as a dramatic rehearsal or a tennis match. Instead of saying, "Sorry I can't see you, old chap, but I have to run off to the tennis club," you must say, "...but I have to work." This, I admit, is intensely difficult to say. Tennis is so much more urgent than the immortal soul.

VI

REMEMBER HUMAN NATURE

I have incidentally mentioned the vast expanse of forty-four hours between leaving business at 2 p.m. on Saturday and returning to business at 10 a.m. on Monday. And here I must touch on the point whether the week should consist of six days or of seven. For many years—in fact, until I was approaching forty—my own week consisted of seven days. I was constantly being informed by older and wiser people that more work, more genuine living, could be got out of six days than out of seven.

And it is certainly true that now, with one day in seven in which I follow no programme and make no effort save what the caprice of the moment dictates, I appreciate intensely the moral value of a weekly rest.

Nevertheless, had I my life to arrange over again, I would do again as I have done. Only those who have lived at the full stretch seven days a week for a long time can appreciate the full beauty of a regular recurring idleness. Moreover, I am ageing. And it is a question of age. In cases of abounding youth and exceptional energy and desire for effort I should say unhesitatingly: Keep going, day in, day out.

But in the average case I should say: Confine your formal programme (super-programme, I mean) to six days a week. If you find yourself wishing to extend it, extend it, but only in proportion to your wish; and count the time extra as a windfall, not as regular income, so that you can return to a six-day programme without the sensation of being poorer, of being a backslider.

Let us now see where we stand. So far we have marked for saving out of the waste of days, half an hour at least on six mornings a week, and one hour and a half on three evenings a week. Total, seven hours and a half a week.

I propose to be content with that seven hours and a half for the present. "What?" you cry. "You pretend to show us how to live, and you only deal with seven hours and a half out of a hundred and sixty-eight! Are you going to perform a miracle with your seven hours and a half?" Well, not to mince the matter, I am—if you will kindly let me! That is to say, I am going to ask you to attempt an experience which, while perfectly natural and explicable, has all the air of a miracle. My contention is that the full use of those seven-and-a-half hours will quicken the whole life of the week, add zest to it, and increase the interest which you feel in even the most banal occupations. You practise physical exercises for a mere ten minutes morning and evening, and yet you are not astonished when your physical health and strength are beneficially affected every hour of the day, and your whole physical outlook changed. Why should you be astonished that an average of over an hour a day given to the mind should permanently and completely enliven the whole activity of the mind?

More time might assuredly be given to the cultivation of one's self. And in proportion as the time was longer the results would be greater. But I prefer to begin with what looks like a trifling effort.

It is not really a trifling effort, as those will discover who have yet to essay it. To "clear" even seven hours and a half from the jungle is passably difficult. For some sacrifice has to be made. One may have spent one's time badly, but one did spend it; one did do something with it, however ill-advised that something may have been. To do something else means a change of habits.

And habits are the very dickens to change! Further, any change, even a change for the better, is always accompanied by drawbacks and discomforts. If you imagine that you will be able to devote seven hours and a half a week to serious, continuous effort, and still live your old life, you are mistaken. I repeat that some sacrifice, and an immense deal of volition, will be necessary. And it is because I know the difficulty, it is because I know the almost disastrous effect of failure in such an enterprise, that I earnestly advise a very humble beginning. You must safeguard your self-respect. Self-respect is at the root of all purposefulness, and a failure in an enterprise deliberately planned deals a desperate wound at one's self-respect. Hence I iterate and reiterate: Start quietly, unostentatiously.

When you have conscientiously given seven hours and a half a week to the cultivation of your vitality for three months—then you may begin to sing louder and tell yourself what wondrous things you are capable of doing.

Before coming to the method of using the indicated hours, I have one final suggestion to make. That is, as regards the evenings, to allow much more than an hour and a half in which to do the work of an hour and a half. Remember the chance of accidents. Remember human nature. And give yourself, say, from 9 to 11.30 for your task of ninety minutes.

VII
CONTROLLING THE MIND

People say: "One can't help one's thoughts." But one can. The control of the thinking machine is perfectly possible. And since nothing whatever happens to us outside our own brain; since nothing hurts us or gives us pleasure except within the brain, the supreme importance of being able to control what goes on in that mysterious brain is patent. This idea is one of the oldest platitudes, but it is a platitude whose profound truth and urgency most people live and die without realising. People complain of the lack of power to concentrate, not witting that they may acquire the power, if they choose.

And without the power to concentrate—that is to say, without the power to dictate to the brain its task and to ensure obedience—true life is impossible. Mind control is the first element of a full existence.

Hence, it seems to me, the first business of the day should be to put the mind through its paces. You look after your body, inside and out; you run grave danger in hacking hairs off your skin; you employ a whole army of individuals, from the milkman to the pig-killer, to enable you to bribe your stomach into decent behaviour. Why not devote a little attention to the far more delicate machinery of the mind, especially as you will require no extraneous aid? It is for this portion of the art and craft of living that I have reserved the time from the moment of quitting your door to the moment of arriving at your office.

"What? I am to cultivate my mind in the street, on the platform, in the train, and in the crowded street again?" Precisely. Nothing simpler! No tools required! Not even a book. Nevertheless, the affair is not easy.

When you leave your house, concentrate your mind on a subject (no matter what, to begin with). You will not have gone ten yards before your mind has skipped away under your very eyes and is larking round the corner with another subject.

Bring it back by the scruff of the neck. Ere you have reached the station you will have brought it back about forty times. Do not despair. Continue. Keep it up. You will succeed. You cannot by any chance fail if you persevere. It is idle to pretend that your mind is incapable of concentration. Do you not remember that morning when you received a disquieting letter which demanded a very carefully-worded answer? How you kept your mind steadily on the subject of the answer, without a second's intermission, until you reached your office; whereupon you instantly sat down and wrote the answer? That was a case in which *you* were roused by circumstances to such a degree of vitality that you were able to dominate your mind like a tyrant. You would have no trifling. You insisted that its work should be done, and its work was done.

By the regular practice of concentration (as to which there is no secret—save the secret of perseverance) you can tyrannise over your mind (which is not the highest part of *you*) every hour of the day, and in no matter what place. The exercise is a very convenient one. If you got into your morning train with a pair of dumb-bells for your muscles or an encyclopaedia in ten volumes for your learning, you would probably excite remark. But as you walk in the street, or sit in the corner of the compartment behind a pipe, or "strap-hang" on the Subterranean, who is to know that you are engaged in the most important of daily acts? What asinine boor can laugh at you?

I do not care what you concentrate on, so long as you concentrate. It is the mere disciplining of the thinking machine that counts. But still, you may as well kill two birds with one stone, and concentrate on something useful. I suggest—it is only a suggestion—a little chapter of Marcus Aurelius or Epictetus.

Do not, I beg, shy at their names. For myself, I know nothing more "actual," more bursting with plain common-sense, applicable to the daily life of plain persons like you and me (who hate airs, pose, and nonsense) than Marcus Aurelius or Epictetus. Read a chapter—and so short they are, the chapters!—in the evening and concentrate on it the next morning. You will see.

Yes, my friend, it is useless for you to try to disguise the fact. I can hear your brain like a telephone at my ear. You are saying to yourself: "This fellow was doing pretty well up to his seventh chapter. He had begun to interest me faintly. But what he says about thinking in trains, and concentration, and so on, is not for me. It may be well enough for some folks, but it isn't in my line."

It is for you, I passionately repeat; it is for you. Indeed, you are the very man I am aiming at.

Throw away the suggestion, and you throw away the most precious suggestion that was ever offered to you. It is not my suggestion. It is the suggestion of the most sensible, practical, hard-headed men who have walked the earth. I only give it you at second-hand. Try it. Get your mind in hand. And see how the process cures half the evils of life—especially worry, that miserable, avoidable, shameful disease—worry!

The exercise of concentrating the mind (to which at least half an hour a day should be given) is a mere preliminary, like scales on the piano. Having acquired power over that most unruly member of one's complex organism, one has naturally to put it to the yoke. Useless to possess an obedient mind unless one profits to the furthest possible degree by its obedience. A prolonged primary course of study is indicated.

Now as to what this course of study should be there cannot be any question; there never has been any question. All the sensible people of all ages are agreed upon it. And it is not literature, nor is it any other art, nor is it history, nor is it any science. It is the study of one's self. Man, know thyself. These words are so hackneyed that verily I blush to write them. Yet they must be written, for they need to be written. (I take back my blush, being ashamed of it.) Man, know thyself. I say it out loud. The phrase is one of those phrases with which everyone is familiar, of which everyone acknowledges the value, and which only the most sagacious put into practice. I don't know why. I am entirely convinced that what is more than anything else lacking in the life of the average well-intentioned man of to-day is the reflective mood.

We do not reflect. I mean that we do not reflect upon genuinely important things; upon the problem of our happiness, upon the main direction in which we are going, upon what life is giving to us, upon the share which reason has (or has not) in determining our actions, and upon the relation between our principles and our conduct.

And yet you are in search of happiness, are you not? Have you discovered it?

The chances are that you have not. The chances are that you have already come to believe that happiness is unattainable. But men have attained it. And they have attained it by realising that happiness does not spring from the procuring of physical or mental pleasure, but from the development of reason and the adjustment of conduct to principles.

I suppose that you will not have the audacity to deny this. And if you admit it, and still devote no part of your day to the deliberate consideration of your reason, principles, and conduct, you admit also that while striving for a certain thing you are regularly leaving undone the one act which is necessary to the attainment of that thing.

Now, shall I blush, or will you?

Do not fear that I mean to thrust certain principles upon your attention. I care not (in this place) what your principles are. Your principles may induce you to believe in the righteousness of burglary. I don't mind. All I urge is that a life in which conduct does not fairly well accord with principles is a silly life; and that conduct can only be made to accord with principles by means of daily examination, reflection, and resolution. What leads to the permanent sorrowfulness of burglars is that their principles are contrary to burglary. If they genuinely believed in the moral excellence of burglary, penal servitude would simply mean so many happy years for them; all martyrs are happy, because their conduct and their principles agree.

As for reason (which makes conduct, and is not unconnected with the making of principles), it plays a far smaller part in our lives than we fancy. We are supposed to be reasonable but we are much more instinctive than reasonable. And the less we reflect, the less reasonable we shall be. The next time you get cross with the waiter because your steak is over-cooked, ask reason to step into the cabinet-room of your mind, and consult her. She will probably tell you that the waiter did not cook the steak, and had no control over the cooking of the steak; and that even if he alone was to blame, you accomplished nothing good by getting cross; you merely lost your dignity, looked a fool in the eyes of sensible men, and soured the waiter, while producing no effect whatever on the steak.

The result of this consultation with reason (for which she makes no charge) will be that when once more your steak is over-cooked you will treat the waiter as a fellow-creature, remain quite calm in a kindly spirit, and politely insist on having a fresh steak. The gain will be obvious and solid.

In the formation or modification of principles, and the practice of conduct, much help can be derived from printed books (issued at sixpence each and upwards). I mentioned in my last chapter Marcus Aurelius and Epictetus. Certain even more widely known works will occur at once to the memory. I may also mention Pascal, La Bruyere, and Emerson. For myself, you do not catch me travelling without my Marcus Aurelius. Yes, books are valuable. But not reading of books will take the place of a daily, candid, honest examination of what one has recently done, and what one is about to do—of a steady looking at one's self in the face (disconcerting though the sight may be).

When shall this important business be accomplished? The solitude of the evening journey home appears to me to be suitable for it. A reflective mood naturally follows the exertion of having earned the day's living. Of course if, instead of attending to an elementary and profoundly important duty, you prefer to read the paper (which you might just as well read while waiting for your dinner) I have nothing to say. But attend to it at some time of the day you must. I now come to the evening hours.

IX
INTEREST IN THE ARTS

Many people pursue a regular and uninterrupted course of idleness in the evenings because they think that there is no alternative to idleness but the study of literature; and they do not happen to have a taste for literature. This is a great mistake.

Of course it is impossible, or at any rate very difficult, properly to study anything whatever without the aid of printed books. But if you desire to understand the deeper depths of bridge or of boat-sailing you would not be deterred by your lack of interest in literature from reading the best books on bridge or boat-sailing. We must, therefore, distinguish between literature, and books treating of subjects not literary. I shall come to literature in due course.

Let me now remark to those who have never read Meredith, and who are capable of being unmoved by a discussion as to whether Mr. Stephen Phillips is or is not a true poet, that they are perfectly within their rights. It is not a crime not to love literature. It is not a sign of imbecility. The mandarins of literature will order out to instant execution the unfortunate individual who does not comprehend, say, the influence of Wordsworth on Tennyson. But that is only their impudence. Where would they be, I wonder, if requested to explain the influences that went to make Tschaikowsky's "Pathetic Symphony"?

There are enormous fields of knowledge quite outside literature which will yield magnificent results to cultivators. For example (since I have just mentioned the most popular piece of high-class music in England to-day), I am reminded that the Promenade Concerts begin in August. You go to them. You smoke your cigar or cigarette (and I regret to say that you strike your matches during the soft bars of the "Lohengrin" overture), and you enjoy the music. But you say you cannot play the piano or the fiddle, or even the banjo; that you know nothing of music.

What does that matter? That you have a genuine taste for music is proved by the fact that, in order to fill his hall with you and your peers, the conductor is obliged to provide programmes from which bad music is almost entirely excluded (a change from the old Covent Garden days!).

Now surely your inability to perform "The Maiden's Prayer" on a piano need not prevent you from making yourself familiar with the construction of the orchestra to which you listen a couple of nights a week during a couple of months! As things are, you probably think of the orchestra as a heterogeneous mass of instruments producing a confused agreeable mass of sound. You do not listen for details because you have never trained your ears to listen to details.

If you were asked to name the instruments which play the great theme at the beginning of the C minor symphony you could not name them for your life's sake. Yet you admire the C minor symphony. It has thrilled you. It will thrill you again. You have even talked about it, in an expansive mood, to that lady—you know whom I mean. And all you can positively state about the C minor symphony is that Beethoven composed it and that it is a "jolly fine thing."

Now, if you have read, say, Mr. Krehbiel's "How to Listen to Music" (which can be got at any bookseller's for less than the price of a stall at the Alhambra, and which contains photographs of all the orchestral instruments and plans of the arrangement of orchestras) you would next go to a promenade concert with an astonishing intensification of interest in it. Instead of a confused mass, the orchestra would appear to you as what it is—a marvellously balanced organism whose various groups of members each have a different and an indispensable function. You would spy out the instruments, and listen for their respective sounds. You would know the gulf that separates a French horn from an English horn, and you would perceive why a player of the hautboy gets higher wages than a fiddler, though the fiddle is the more difficult instrument. You would *live* at a promenade concert, whereas previously you had merely existed there in a state of beatific coma, like a baby gazing at a bright object.

The foundations of a genuine, systematic knowledge of music might be laid. You might specialise your inquiries either on a particular form of music (such as the symphony), or on the works of a particular composer. At the end of a year of forty-eight weeks of three brief evenings each, combined with a study of programmes and attendances at concerts chosen out of your increasing knowledge, you would really know something about music, even though you were as far off as ever from jangling "The Maiden's Prayer" on the piano.

"But I hate music!" you say. My dear sir, I respect you.

What applies to music applies to the other arts. I might mention Mr. Clermont Witt's "How to Look at Pictures," or Mr. Russell Sturgis's "How to Judge Architecture," as beginnings (merely beginnings) of systematic vitalising knowledge in other arts, the materials for whose study abound in London.

"I hate all the arts!" you say. My dear sir, I respect you more and more.

I will deal with your case next, before coming to literature.

X
NOTHING IN LIFE IS HUMDRUM

Art is a great thing. But it is not the greatest. The most important of all perceptions is the continual perception of cause and effect—in other words, the perception of the continuous development of the universe—in still other words, the perception of the course of evolution. When one has thoroughly got imbued into one's head the leading truth that nothing happens without a cause, one grows not only large-minded, but large-hearted.

It is hard to have one's watch stolen, but one reflects that the thief of the watch became a thief from causes of heredity and environment which are as interesting as they are scientifically comprehensible; and one buys another watch, if not with joy, at any rate with a philosophy that makes bitterness impossible. One loses, in the study of cause and effect, that absurd air which so many people have of being always shocked and pained by the curiousness of life. Such people live amid human nature as if human nature were a foreign country full of awful foreign customs. But, having reached maturity, one ought surely to be ashamed of being a stranger in a strange land!

The study of cause and effect, while it lessens the painfulness of life, adds to life's picturesqueness. The man to whom evolution is but a name looks at the sea as a grandiose, monotonous spectacle, which he can witness in August for three shillings third-class return. The man who is imbued with the idea of development, of continuous cause and effect, perceives in the sea an element which in the day-before-yesterday of geology was vapour, which yesterday was boiling, and which to-morrow will inevitably be ice.

He perceives that a liquid is merely something on its way to be solid, and he is penetrated by a sense of the tremendous, changeful picturesqueness of life. Nothing will afford a more durable satisfaction than the constantly cultivated appreciation of this. It is the end of all science.

Cause and effect are to be found everywhere. Rents went up in Shepherd's Bush. It was painful and shocking that rents should go up in Shepherd's Bush. But to a certain point we are all scientific students of cause and effect, and there was not a clerk lunching at a Lyons Restaurant who did not scientifically put two and two together and see in the (once) Two-penny Tube the cause of an excessive demand for wigwams in Shepherd's Bush, and in the excessive demand for wigwams the cause of the increase in the price of wigwams.

"Simple!" you say, disdainfully. Everything—the whole complex movement of the universe—is as simple as that—when you can sufficiently put two and two together. And, my dear sir, perhaps you happen to be an estate agent's clerk, and you hate the arts, and you want to foster your immortal soul, and you can't be interested in your business because it's so humdrum.

Nothing is humdrum.

The tremendous, changeful picturesqueness of life is marvellously shown in an estate agent's office. What! There was a block of traffic in Oxford Street; to avoid the block people actually began to travel under the cellars and drains, and the result was a rise of rents in Shepherd's Bush! And you say that isn't picturesque!

15

Suppose you were to study, in this spirit, the property question in London for an hour and a half every other evening. Would it not give zest to your business, and transform your whole life?

You would arrive at more difficult problems. And you would be able to tell us why, as the natural result of cause and effect, the longest straight street in London is about a yard and a half in length, while the longest absolutely straight street in Paris extends for miles. I think you will admit that in an estate agent's clerk I have not chosen an example that specially favours my theories.

You are a bank clerk, and you have not read that breathless romance (disguised as a scientific study), Walter Bagehot's "Lombard Street"? Ah, my dear sir, if you had begun with that, and followed it up for ninety minutes every other evening, how enthralling your business would be to you, and how much more clearly you would understand human nature.

You are "penned in town," but you love excursions to the country and the observation of wild life—certainly a heart-enlarging diversion. Why don't you walk out of your house door, in your slippers, to the nearest gas lamp of a night with a butterfly net, and observe the wild life of common and rare moths that is beating about it, and co-ordinate the knowledge thus obtained and build a superstructure on it, and at last get to know something about something?

You need not be devoted to the arts, not to literature, in order to live fully.

The whole field of daily habit and scene is waiting to satisfy that curiosity which means life, and the satisfaction of which means an understanding heart.

I promised to deal with your case, O man who hates art and literature, and I have dealt with it. I now come to the case of the person, happily very common, who does "like reading."

XI
SERIOUS READING

Novels are excluded from "serious reading," so that the man who, bent on self-improvement, has been deciding to devote ninety minutes three times a week to a complete study of the works of Charles Dickens will be well advised to alter his plans. The reason is not that novels are not serious—some of the great literature of the world is in the form of prose fiction—the reason is that bad novels ought not to be read, and that good novels never demand any appreciable mental application on the part of the reader. It is only the bad parts of Meredith's novels that are difficult. A good novel rushes you forward like a skiff down a stream, and you arrive at the end, perhaps breathless, but unexhausted. The best novels involve the least strain. Now in the cultivation of the mind one of the most important factors is precisely the feeling of strain, of difficulty, of a task which one part of you is anxious to achieve and another part of you is anxious to shirk; and that feeling cannot be got in facing a novel. You do not set your teeth in order to read "Anna Karenina." Therefore, though you should read novels, you should not read them in those ninety minutes.

Imaginative poetry produces a far greater mental strain than novels. It produces probably the severest strain of any form of literature. It is the highest form of literature. It yields the highest form of pleasure, and teaches the highest form of wisdom. In a word, there is nothing to compare with it. I say this with sad consciousness of the fact that the majority of people do not read poetry.

I am persuaded that many excellent persons, if they were confronted with the alternatives of reading "Paradise Lost" and going round Trafalgar Square at noonday on their knees in sack-cloth, would choose the ordeal of public ridicule. Still, I will never cease advising my friends and enemies to read poetry before anything.

If poetry is what is called "a sealed book" to you, begin by reading Hazlitt's famous essay on the nature of "poetry in general." It is the best thing of its kind in English, and no one who has read it can possibly be under the misapprehension that poetry is a mediaeval torture, or a mad elephant, or a gun that will go off by itself and kill at forty paces. Indeed, it is difficult to imagine the mental state of the man who, after reading Hazlitt's essay, is not urgently desirous of reading some poetry before his next meal. If the essay so inspires you I would suggest that you make a commencement with purely narrative poetry.

There is an infinitely finer English novel, written by a woman, than anything by George Eliot or the Brontes, or even Jane Austen, which perhaps you have not read. Its title is "Aurora Leigh," and its author E.B.

Browning. It happens to be written in verse, and to contain a considerable amount of genuinely fine poetry. Decide to read that book through, even if you die for it. Forget that it is fine poetry. Read it simply for the story and the social ideas. And when you have done, ask yourself honestly whether you still dislike poetry. I have known more than one person to whom "Aurora Leigh" has been the means of proving that in assuming they hated poetry they were entirely mistaken.

Of course, if, after Hazlitt, and such an experiment made in the light of Hazlitt, you are finally assured that there is something in you which is antagonistic to poetry, you must be content with history or philosophy. I shall regret it, yet not inconsolably. "The Decline and Fall" is not to be named in the same day with "Paradise Lost," but it is a vastly pretty thing; and Herbert Spencer's "First Principles" simply laughs at the claims of poetry and refuses to be accepted as aught but the most majestic product of any human mind. I do not suggest that either of these works is suitable for a tyro in mental strains. But I see no reason why any man of average intelligence should not, after a year of continuous reading, be fit to assault the supreme masterpieces of history or philosophy. The great convenience of masterpieces is that they are so astonishingly lucid.

I suggest no particular work as a start. The attempt would be futile in the space of my command. But I have two general suggestions of a certain importance. The first is to define the direction and scope of your efforts. Choose a limited period, or a limited subject, or a single author. Say to yourself: "I will know something about the French Revolution, or the rise of railways, or the works of John Keats." And during a given period, to be settled beforehand, confine yourself to your choice. There is much pleasure to be derived from being a specialist.

The second suggestion is to think as well as to read. I know people who read and read, and for all the good it does them they might just as well cut bread-and-butter. They take to reading as better men take to drink. They fly through the shires of literature on a motor-car, their sole object being motion. They will tell you how many books they have read in a year.

Unless you give at least forty-five minutes to careful, fatiguing reflection (it is an awful bore at first) upon what you are reading, your ninety minutes of a night are chiefly wasted. This means that your pace will be slow.

Never mind.

Forget the goal; think only of the surrounding country; and after a period, perhaps when you least expect it, you will suddenly find yourself in a lovely town on a hill.

XII
DANGERS TO AVOID

I cannot terminate these hints, often, I fear, too didactic and abrupt, upon the full use of one's time to the great end of living (as distinguished from vegetating) without briefly referring to certain dangers which lie in wait for the sincere aspirant towards life. The first is the terrible danger of becoming that most odious and least supportable of persons—a prig. Now a prig is a pert fellow who gives himself airs of superior wisdom. A prig is a pompous fool who has gone out for a ceremonial walk, and without knowing it has lost an important part of his attire, namely, his sense of humour. A prig is a tedious individual who, having made a discovery, is so impressed by his discovery that he is capable of being gravely displeased because the entire world is not also impressed by it. Unconsciously to become a prig is an easy and a fatal thing.

Hence, when one sets forth on the enterprise of using all one's time, it is just as well to remember that one's own time, and not other people's time, is the material with which one has to deal; that the earth rolled on pretty comfortably before one began to balance a budget of the hours, and that it will continue to roll on pretty comfortably whether or not one succeeds in one's new role of chancellor of the exchequer of time. It is as well not to chatter too much about what one is doing, and not to betray a too-pained sadness at the spectacle of a whole world deliberately wasting so many hours out of every day, and therefore never really living. It will be found, ultimately, that in taking care of one's self one has quite all one can do.

Another danger is the danger of being tied to a programme like a slave to a chariot. One's programme must not be allowed to run away with one. It must be respected, but it must not be worshipped as a fetish. A programme of daily employ is not a religion.

This seems obvious. Yet I know men whose lives are a burden to themselves and a distressing burden to their relatives and friends simply because they have failed to appreciate the obvious. "Oh, no," I have heard the martyred wife exclaim, "Arthur always takes the dog out for exercise at eight o'clock and he always begins to read at a quarter to nine. So it's quite out of the question that we should..." etc., etc. And the note of absolute finality in that plaintive voice reveals the unsuspected and ridiculous tragedy of a career.

On the other hand, a programme is a programme. And unless it is treated with deference it ceases to be anything but a poor joke. To treat one's programme with exactly the right amount of deference, to live with not too much and not too little elasticity, is scarcely the simple affair it may appear to the inexperienced.

And still another danger is the danger of developing a policy of rush, of being gradually more and more obsessed by what one has to do next. In this way one may come to exist as in a prison, and one's life may cease to be one's own. One may take the dog out for a walk at eight o'clock, and meditate the whole time on the fact that one must begin to read at a quarter to nine, and that one must not be late.

And the occasional deliberate breaking of one's programme will not help to mend matters. The evil springs not from persisting without elasticity in what one has attempted, but from originally attempting too much, from filling one's programme till it runs over. The only cure is to reconstitute the programme, and to attempt less.

But the appetite for knowledge grows by what it feeds on, and there are men who come to like a constant breathless hurry of endeavour. Of them it may be said that a constant breathless hurry is better than an eternal doze.

In any case, if the programme exhibits a tendency to be oppressive, and yet one wishes not to modify it, an excellent palliative is to pass with exaggerated deliberation from one portion of it to another; for example, to spend five minutes in perfect mental quiescence between chaining up the St. Bernard and opening the book; in other words, to waste five minutes with the entire consciousness of wasting them.

The last, and chiefest danger which I would indicate, is one to which I have already referred—the risk of a failure at the commencement of the enterprise.

I must insist on it.

A failure at the commencement may easily kill outright the newborn impulse towards a complete vitality, and therefore every precaution should be observed to avoid it. The impulse must not be over-taxed. Let the pace of the first lap be even absurdly slow, but let it be as regular as possible.

And, having once decided to achieve a certain task, achieve it at all costs of tedium and distaste. The gain in self-confidence of having accomplished a tiresome labour is immense.

Finally, in choosing the first occupations of those evening hours, be guided by nothing whatever but your taste and natural inclination.

It is a fine thing to be a walking encyclopaedia of philosophy, but if you happen to have no liking for philosophy, and to have a like for the natural history of street-cries, much better leave philosophy alone, and take to street-cries.

The Human Machine

There are men who are capable of loving a machine more deeply than they can love a woman. They are among the happiest men on earth. This is not a sneer meanly shot from cover at women. It is simply a statement of notorious fact. Men who worry themselves to distraction over the perfecting of a machine are indubitably blessed beyond their kind. Most of us have known such men. Yesterday they were constructing motorcars. But to-day aeroplanes are in the air—or, at any rate, they ought to be, according to the inventors. Watch the inventors. Invention is not usually their principal business. They must invent in their spare time. They must invent before breakfast, invent in the Strand between Lyons's and the office, invent after dinner, invent on Sundays. See with what ardour they rush home of a night! See how they seize a half-holiday, like hungry dogs a bone! They don't want golf, bridge, limericks, novels, illustrated magazines, clubs, whisky, starting-prices, hints about neckties, political meetings, yarns, comic songs, anturic salts, nor the smiles that are situate between a gay corsage and a picture hat. They never wonder, at a loss, what they will do next. Their evenings never drag—are always too short. You may, indeed, catch them at twelve o'clock at night on the flat of their backs; but not in bed! No, in a shed, under a machine, holding a candle (whose paths drop fatness) up to the connecting-rod that is strained, or the wheel that is out of centre. They are continually interested, nay, enthralled. They have a machine, and they are perfecting it. They get one part right, and then another goes wrong; and they get that right, and then another goes wrong, and so on. When they are quite sure they have reached perfection, forth issues the machine out of the shed—and in five minutes is smashed up, together with a limb or so of the inventors, just because they had been quite sure too soon. Then the whole business starts again. They do not give up—that particular wreck was, of course, due to a mere oversight; the whole business starts again. For they have glimpsed perfection; they have the gleam of perfection in their souls. Thus their lives run away. 'They will never fly!' you remark, cynically. Well, if they don't? Besides, what about Wright? With all your cynicism, have you never envied them their machine and their passionate interest in it?

You know, perhaps, the moment when, brushing in front of the glass, you detected your first grey hair. You stopped brushing; then you resumed brushing, hastily; you pretended not to be shocked, but you were. Perhaps you know a more disturbing moment than that, the moment when it suddenly occurred to you that you had 'arrived' as far as you ever will arrive; and you had realised as much of your early dream as you ever will realise, and the realisation was utterly unlike the dream; the marriage was excessively prosaic and eternal, not at all what you expected it to be; and your illusions were dissipated; and games and hobbies had an unpleasant core of tedium and futility; and the ideal tobacco-mixture did not exist; and one literary masterpiece resembled another; and all the days that are to come will more or less resemble the present day, until you die; and in an illuminating flash you understood what all those people were driving at when they wrote such unconscionably long letters to the *Telegraph* as to life being worth living or not worth living; and there was naught to be done but face the grey, monotonous future, and pretend to be cheerful with the worm of *ennui* gnawing at your heart! In a word, the moment when it occurred to you that yours is 'the common lot.' In that moment have you not wished—do you not continually wish—for an exhaustless machine, a machine that you could never get to the end of? Would you not give your head to be lying on the flat of your back, peering with a candle, dirty, foiled, catching cold—but absorbed in the pursuit of an object? Have you not gloomily regretted that you were born without a mechanical turn, because there is really something about a machine...?

It has never struck you that you do possess a machine! Oh, blind! Oh, dull! It has never struck you that you have at hand a machine wonderful beyond all mechanisms in sheds, intricate, delicately adjustable, of astounding and miraculous possibilities, interminably interesting! That machine is yourself. 'This fellow is preaching. I won't have it!' you exclaim resentfully. Dear sir, I am not preaching, and, even if I were, I think you *would* have it. I think I can anyhow keep hold of your button for a while, though you pull hard. I am not preaching. I am simply bent on calling your attention to a fact which has perhaps wholly or partially escaped

19

you—namely, that you are the most fascinating bit of machinery that ever was. You do yourself less than justice. It is said that men are only interested in themselves. The truth is that, as a rule, men are interested in every mortal thing except themselves. They have a habit of taking themselves for granted, and that habit is responsible for nine-tenths of the boredom and despair on the face of the planet.

A man will wake up in the middle of the night (usually owing to some form of delightful excess), and his brain will be very active indeed for a space ere he can go to sleep again. In that candid hour, after the exaltation of the evening and before the hope of the dawn, he will see everything in its true colours—except himself. There is nothing like a sleepless couch for a clear vision of one's environment. He will see all his wife's faults and the hopelessness of trying to cure them. He will momentarily see, though with less sharpness of outline, his own faults. He will probably decide that the anxieties of children outweigh the joys connected with children. He will admit all the shortcomings of existence, will face them like a man, grimly, sourly, in a sturdy despair. He will mutter: 'Of course I'm angry! Who wouldn't be? Of course I'm disappointed! Did I expect this twenty years ago? Yes, we ought to save more. But we don't, so there you are! I'm bound to worry! I know I should be better if I didn't smoke so much. I know there's absolutely no sense at all in taking liqueurs. Absurd to be ruffled with her when she's in one of her moods. I don't have enough exercise. Can't be regular, somehow. Not the slightest use hoping that things will be different, because I know they won't. Queer world! Never really what you may call happy, you know. Now, if things were different ...' He loses consciousness.

Observe: he has taken himself for granted, just glancing at his faults and looking away again. It is his environment that has occupied his attention, and his environment—'things'—that he would wish to have 'different,' did he not know, out of the fulness of experience, that it is futile to desire such a change? What he wants is a pipe that won't put itself into his mouth, a glass that won't leap of its own accord to his lips, money that won't slip untouched out of his pocket, legs that without asking will carry him certain miles every day in the open air, habits that practise themselves, a wife that will expand and contract according to his humours, like a Wernicke bookcase, always complete but never finished. Wise man, he perceives at once that he can't have these things. And so he resigns himself to the universe, and settles down to a permanent, restrained discontent. No one shall say he is unreasonable.

You see, he has given no attention to the machine. Let us not call it a flying-machine. Let us call it simply an automobile. There it is on the road, jolting, screeching, rattling, perfuming. And there he is, saying: 'This road ought to be as smooth as velvet. That hill in front is ridiculous, and the descent on the other side positively dangerous. And it's all turns—I can't see a hundred yards in front.' He has a wild idea of trying to force the County Council to sand-paper the road, or of employing the new Territorial Army to remove the hill. But he dismisses that idea—he is so reasonable. He accepts all. He sits clothed in reasonableness on the machine, and accepts all. 'Ass!' you exclaim. 'Why doesn't he get down and inflate that tyre, for one thing? Anyone can see the sparking apparatus is wrong, and it's perfectly certain the gear-box wants oil.'

Why doesn't he—?' I will tell you why he doesn't. Just because he isn't aware that he is on a machine at all. He has never examined what he is on. And at the back of his consciousness is a dim idea that he is perched on a piece of solid, immutable rock that runs on castors.

II
AMATEURS IN THE ART OF LIVING

Considering that we have to spend the whole of our lives in this human machine, considering that it is our sole means of contact and compromise with the rest of the world, we really do devote to it very little attention. When I say 'we,' I mean our inmost spirits, the instinctive part, the mystery within that exists. And when I say 'the human machine' I mean the brain and the body—and chiefly the brain. The expression of the soul by means of the brain and body is what we call the art of 'living.' We certainly do not learn this art at school to any appreciable extent. At school we are taught that it is necessary to fling our arms and legs to and fro for so many hours per diem. We are also shown, practically, that our brains are capable of performing certain useful tricks, and that if we do not compel our brains to perform those tricks we shall suffer. Thus one day we run home and proclaim to our delighted parents that eleven twelves are 132. A feat of the brain! So it goes on until our parents begin to look up to us because we can chatter of cosines or sketch the foreign policy of Louis XIV.

Good! But not a word about the principles of the art of living yet! Only a few detached rules from our parents, to be blindly followed when particular crises supervene. And, indeed, it would be absurd to talk to a schoolboy about the expression of his soul. He would probably mutter a monosyllable which is not 'mice.'

Of course, school is merely a preparation for living; unless one goes to a university, in which case it is a preparation for university. One is supposed to turn one's attention to living when these preliminaries are over—say at the age of about twenty. Assuredly one lives then; there is, however, nothing new in that, for one has been living all the time, in a fashion; all the time one has been using the machine without understanding it. But does one, school and college being over, enter upon a study of the machine? Not a bit. The question then becomes, not how to live, but how to obtain and retain a position in which one will be able to live; how to get minute portions of dead animals and plants which one can swallow, in order not to die of hunger; how to acquire and constantly renew a stock of other portions of dead animals and plants in which one can envelop oneself in order not to die of cold; how to procure the exclusive right of entry into certain huts where one may sleep and eat without being rained upon by the clouds of heaven. And so forth. And when one has realised this ambition, there comes the desire to be able to double the operation and do it, not for oneself alone, but for oneself and another. Marriage! But no scientific sustained attention is yet given to the real business of living, of smooth intercourse, of self-expression, of conscious adaptation to environment—in brief, to the study of the machine. At thirty the chances are that a man will understand better the draught of a chimney than his own respiratory apparatus—to name one of the simple, obvious things—and as for understanding the working of his own brain—what an idea! As for the skill to avoid the waste of power involved by friction in the business of living, do we give an hour to it in a month? Do we ever at all examine it save in an amateurish and clumsy fashion? A young lady produces a water-colour drawing. 'Very nice!' we say, and add, to ourselves, 'For an amateur.' But our living is more amateurish than that young lady's drawing; though surely we ought every one of us to be professionals at living!

When we have been engaged in the preliminaries to living for about fifty-five years, we begin to think about slacking off. Up till this period our reason for not having scientifically studied the art of living—the perfecting and use of the finer parts of the machine—is not that we have lacked leisure (most of us have enormous heaps of leisure), but that we have simply been too absorbed in the preliminaries, have, in fact, treated the preliminaries to the business as the business itself. Then at fifty-five we ought at last to begin to live our lives with professional skill, as a professional painter paints pictures. Yes, but we can't. It is too late then. Neither painters, nor acrobats, nor any professionals can be formed at the age of fifty-five. Thus we finish our lives amateurishly, as we have begun them. And when the machine creaks and sets our teeth on edge, or refuses to obey the steering-wheel and deposits us in the ditch, we say: 'Can't be helped!' or 'Doesn't matter! It will be all the same a hundred years hence!' or: 'I must make the best of things.' And we try to believe that in accepting the *status quo* we have justified the *status quo*, and all the time we feel our insincerity.

You exclaim that I exaggerate. I do. To force into prominence an aspect of affairs usually overlooked, it is absolutely necessary to exaggerate. Poetic licence is one name for this kind of exaggeration. But I exaggerate very little indeed, much less than perhaps you think. I know that you are going to point out to me that vast numbers of people regularly spend a considerable portion of their leisure in striving after self-improvement. Granted! And I am glad of it. But I should be gladder if their strivings bore more closely upon the daily business of living, of self-expression without friction and without futile desires. See this man who regularly studies every evening of his life! He has genuinely understood the nature of poetry, and his taste is admirable. He recites verse with true feeling, and may be said to be highly cultivated. Poetry is a continual source of pleasure to him. True! But why is he always complaining about not receiving his deserts in the office? Why is he worried about finance? Why does he so often sulk with his wife? Why does he persist in eating more than his digestion will tolerate? It was not written in the book of fate that he should complain and worry and sulk and suffer. And if he was a professional at living he would not do these things. There is no reason why he should do them, except the reason that he has never learnt his business, never studied the human machine as a whole, never really thought rationally about living. Supposing you encountered an automobilist who was swerving and grinding all over the road, and you stopped to ask what was the matter, and he replied: 'Never mind what's the matter. Just look at my lovely acetylene lamps, how they shine, and how I've polished them!' You would not regard him as a Clifford-Earp, or even as an entirely sane man. So with our student of poetry. It is indubitable that a large amount of what is known as self-improvement is simply self-indulgence—a form of pleasure which only incidentally improves a particular part of the machine, and even that to the neglect of far more important parts.

21

My aim is to direct a man's attention to himself as a whole, considered as a machine, complex and capable of quite extraordinary efficiency, for travelling through this world smoothly, in any desired manner, with satisfaction not only to himself but to the people he meets *en route*, and the people who are overtaking him and whom he is overtaking. My aim is to show that only an inappreciable fraction of our ordered and sustained efforts is given to the business of actual living, as distinguished from the preliminaries to living.

III
THE BRAIN AS A GENTLEMAN-AT-LARGE

It is not as if, in this business of daily living, we were seriously hampered by ignorance either as to the results which we ought to obtain, or as to the general means which we must employ in order to obtain them. With all our absorption in the mere preliminaries to living, and all our carelessness about living itself, we arrive pretty soon at a fairly accurate notion of what satisfactory living is, and we perceive with some clearness the methods necessary to success. I have pictured the man who wakes up in the middle of the night and sees the horrid semi-fiasco of his life. But let me picture the man who wakes up refreshed early on a fine summer morning and looks into his mind with the eyes of hope and experience, not experience and despair. That man will pass a delightful half-hour in thinking upon the scheme of the universe as it affects himself. He is quite clear that contentment depends on his own acts, and that no power can prevent him from performing those acts. He plans everything out, and before he gets up he knows precisely what he must and will do in certain foreseen crises and junctures. He sincerely desires to live efficiently—who would wish to make a daily mess of existence?—and he knows the way to realise the desire.

And yet, mark me! That man will not have been an hour on his feet on this difficult earth before the machine has unmistakably gone wrong: the machine which was designed to do this work of living, which is capable of doing it thoroughly well, but which has not been put into order! What is the use of consulting the map of life and tracing the itinerary, and getting the machine out of the shed, and making a start, if half the nuts are loose, or the steering pillar is twisted, or there is no petrol in the tank? (Having asked this question, I will drop the mechanico-vehicular comparison, which is too rough and crude for the delicacy of the subject.) Where has the human machine gone wrong? It has gone wrong in the brain. What, is he 'wrong in the head'? Most assuredly, most strictly. He knows—none better—that when his wife employs a particular tone containing ten grains of asperity, and he replies in a particular tone containing eleven grains, the consequences will be explosive. He knows, on the other hand, that if he replies in a tone containing only one little drop of honey, the consequences may not be unworthy of two reasonable beings. He knows this. His brain is fully instructed. And lo! his brain, while arguing that women are really too absurd (as if that was the point), is sending down orders to the muscles of the throat and mouth which result in at least eleven grains of asperity, and conjugal relations are endangered for the day. He didn't want to do it. His desire was not to do it. He despises himself for doing it. But his brain was not in working order. His brain ran away—'raced'—on its own account, against reason, against desire, against morning resolves—and there he is!

That is just one example, of the simplest and slightest. Examples can be multiplied. The man may be a young man whose immediate future depends on his passing an examination—an examination which he is capable of passing 'on his head,' which nothing can prevent him from passing if only his brain will not be so absurd as to give orders to his legs to walk out of the house towards the tennis court instead of sending them upstairs to the study; if only, having once safely lodged him in the study, his brain will devote itself to the pages of books instead of dwelling on the image of a nice girl—not at all like other girls. Or the man may be an old man who will live in perfect comfort if only his brain will not interminably run round and round in a circle of grievances, apprehensions, and fears which no amount of contemplation can destroy or even ameliorate.

The brain, the brain—that is the seat of trouble! 'Well,' you say, 'of course it is. We all know that!' We don't act as if we did, anyway. 'Give us more brains, Lord!' ejaculated a great writer. Personally, I think he would have been wiser if he had asked first for the power to keep in order such brains as we have. We indubitably possess quite enough brains, quite as much as we can handle. The supreme muddlers of living are often people of quite remarkable intellectual faculty, with a quite remarkable gift of being wise for others. The pity is that our brains have a way of 'wandering,' as it is politely called. Brain-wandering is indeed now recognised as a specific disease. I wonder what you, O business man with an office in Ludgate Circus, would say to your office-boy, whom you had dispatched on an urgent message to Westminster, and whom you found larking around Euston Station when you rushed to catch your week-end train. 'Please, sir, I started to go to Westminster, but there's something funny in my limbs that makes me go up all manner of streets. I can't help it, sir!' 'Can't you?' you would say. 'Well, you had better go and be somebody else's office-boy.' Your brain is something worse than that office-boy, something more insidiously potent for evil.

I conceive the brain of the average well-intentioned man as possessing the tricks and manners of one of those gentlemen-at-large who, having nothing very urgent to do, stroll along and offer their services gratis to some shorthanded work of philanthropy. They will commonly demoralise and disorganise the business conduct of an affair in about a fortnight. They come when they like; they go when they like. Sometimes they are exceedingly industrious and obedient, but then there is an even chance that they will shirk and follow their own sweet will. And they mustn't be spoken to, or pulled up—for have they not kindly volunteered, and are they not giving their days for naught! These persons are the bane of the enterprises in which they condescend to meddle. Now, there is a vast deal too much of the gentleman-at-large about one's brain. One's brain has no right whatever to behave as a gentleman-at-large: but it in fact does. It forgets; it flatly ignores orders; at the critical moment when pressure is highest, it simply lights a cigarette and goes out for a walk. And we meekly sit down under this behaviour! 'I didn't feel like stewing,' says the young man who, against his wish, will fail in his examination. 'The words were out of my mouth before I knew it,' says the husband whose wife is a woman. 'I couldn't get any inspiration to-day,' says the artist. 'I can't resist Stilton,' says the fellow who is dying of greed. 'One can't help one's thoughts,' says the old worrier. And this last really voices the secret excuse of all five.

And you all say to me: 'My brain is myself. How can I alter myself? I was born like that.' In the first place you were not born 'like that,' you have lapsed to that. And in the second place your brain is not yourself. It is only a part of yourself, and not the highest seat of authority. Do you love your mother, wife, or children with your brain? Do you desire with your brain? Do you, in a word, ultimately and essentially *live* with your brain? No. Your brain is an instrument. The proof that it is an instrument lies in the fact that, when extreme necessity urges, *you* can command your brain to do certain things, and it does them. The first of the two great principles which underlie the efficiency of the human machine is this: *The brain is a servant, exterior to the central force of the Ego.* If it is out of control the reason is not that it is uncontrollable, but merely that its discipline has been neglected. The brain can be trained, as the hand and eye can be trained; it can be made as obedient as a sporting dog, and by similar methods. In the meantime the indispensable preparation for brain discipline is to form the habit of regarding one's brain as an instrument exterior to one's self, like a tongue or a foot.

IV
THE FIRST PRACTICAL STEP

The brain is a highly quaint organism. Let me say at once, lest I should be cannonaded by physiologists, psychologists, or metaphysicians, that by the 'brain' I mean the faculty which reasons and which gives orders to the muscles. I mean exactly what the plain man means by the brain. The brain is the diplomatist which arranges relations between our instinctive self and the universe, and it fulfils its mission when it provides for the maximum of freedom to the instincts with the minimum of friction. It argues with the instincts. It takes them on one side and points out the unwisdom of certain performances. It catches them by the coat-tails when they are about to make fools of themselves. 'Don't drink all that iced champagne at a draught,' it says to one instinct; 'we may die of it.' 'Don't catch that rude fellow one in the eye,' it says to another instinct; 'he is more powerful than us.' It is, in fact, a majestic spectacle of common sense. And yet it has the most extraordinary lapses. It is just like that man—we all know him and consult him—who is a continual fount of excellent, sagacious advice on everything, but who somehow cannot bring his sagacity to bear on his own personal career.

In the matter of its own special activities the brain is usually undisciplined and unreliable. We never know what it will do next. We give it some work to do, say, as we are walking along the street to the office. Perhaps it has to devise some scheme for making £150 suffice for £200, or perhaps it has to plan out the heads of a very important letter. We meet a pretty woman, and away that undisciplined, sagacious brain runs after her, dropping the scheme or the draft letter, and amusing itself with aspirations or regrets for half an hour, an hour, sometimes a day. The serious part of our instinctive self feebly remonstrates, but without effect. Or it may be that we have suffered a great disappointment, which is definite and hopeless. Will the brain, like a sensible creature, leave that disappointment alone, and instead of living in the past live in the present or the future? Not it! Though it knows perfectly well that it is wasting its time and casting a very painful and utterly unnecessary gloom over itself and us, it can so little control its unhealthy morbid appetite that no expostulations will induce it to behave rationally. Or perhaps, after a confabulation with the soul, it has been decided that when next a certain harmful instinct comes into play the brain shall firmly interfere. 'Yes,' says the brain, 'I really will watch that.' But when the moment arrives, is the brain on the spot? The brain has probably forgotten the affair entirely, or remembered it too late; or sighs, as the victorious instinct knocks it on the head: 'Well, *next* time!'

All this, and much more that every reader can supply from his own exciting souvenirs, is absurd and ridiculous on the part of the brain. It is a conclusive proof that the brain is out of condition, idle as a nigger, capricious as an actor-manager, and eaten to the core with loose habits. Therefore the brain must be put into training. It is the most important part of the human machine by which the soul expresses and develops itself, and it must learn good habits. And primarily it must be taught obedience. Obedience can only be taught by imposing one's will, by the sheer force of volition. And the brain must be mastered by will-power. The beginning of wise living lies in the control of the brain by the will; so that the brain may act according to the precepts which the brain itself gives. With an obedient disciplined brain a man may live always right up to the standard of his best moments.

To teach a child obedience you tell it to do something, and you see that that something is done. The same with the brain. Here is the foundation of an efficient life and the antidote for the tendency to make a fool of oneself. It is marvellously simple. Say to your brain: 'From 9 o'clock to 9.30 this morning you must dwell without ceasing on a particular topic which I will give you.' Now, it doesn't matter what this topic is—the point is to control and invigorate the brain by exercise—but you may just as well give it a useful topic to think over as a futile one. You might give it this: 'My brain is my servant. I am not the play-thing of my brain.' Let it concentrate on these statements for thirty minutes. 'What?' you cry. 'Is this the way to an efficient life? Why, there's nothing in it!' Simple as it may appear, this *is* the way, and it is the only way. As for there being nothing in it, try it. I guarantee that you will fail to keep your brain concentrated on the given idea for thirty seconds—let alone thirty minutes. You will find your brain conducting itself in a manner which would be comic were it not tragic. Your first experiments will result in disheartening failure, for to exact from the brain, at will and by will, concentration on a given idea for even so short a period as half an hour is an exceedingly difficult feat—and a fatiguing! It needs perseverance. It needs a terrible obstinacy on the part of the will. That brain of yours will be hopping about all over the place, and every time it hops you must bring it back by force to its original position. You must absolutely compel it to ignore every idea except the one which you have selected for its attention. You cannot hope to triumph all at once. But you can hope to triumph. There is no royal road to the control of the brain. There is no patent dodge about it, and no complicated function which a plain person may not comprehend. It is simply a question of: 'I will, *I* will, and I *will*.' (Italics here are indispensable.)

Let me resume. Efficient living, living up to one's best standard, getting the last ounce of power out of the machine with the minimum of friction: these things depend on the disciplined and vigorous condition of the brain. The brain can be disciplined by learning the habit of obedience. And it can learn the habit of obedience by the practice of concentration. Disciplinary concentration, though nothing could have the air of being simpler, is the basis of the whole structure. This fact must be grasped imaginatively; it must be seen and felt. The more regularly concentration is practised, the more firmly will the imagination grasp the effects of it, both direct and indirect. After but a few days of honest trying in the exercise which I have indicated, you will perceive its influence. You will grow accustomed to the idea, at first strange in its novelty, of the brain being external to the supreme force which is *you*, and in subjection to that force. You will, as a not very distant possibility, see yourself in possession of the power to switch your brain on and off in a particular subject as you switch electricity on and off in a particular room. The brain will get used to the straight paths of obedience. And—a remarkable phenomenon—it will, by the mere practice of obedience, become less forgetful and more effective. It will not so frequently give way to an instinct that takes it by surprise. In a word, it will have received a general tonic. With a brain that is improving every day you can set about the perfecting of the machine in a scientific manner.

V
HABIT-FORMING BY CONCENTRATION

As soon as the will has got the upper hand of the brain—as soon as it can say to the brain, with a fair certainty of being obeyed: 'Do this. Think along these lines, and continue to do so without wandering until I give you leave to stop'—then is the time arrived when the perfecting of the human machine may be undertaken in a large and comprehensive spirit, as a city council undertakes the purification and reconstruction of a city. The tremendous possibilities of an obedient brain will be perceived immediately we begin to reflect upon what we mean by our 'character.' Now, a person's character is, and can be, nothing else but the total result of his habits of thought. A person is benevolent because he habitually thinks benevolently. A person is idle because his thoughts dwell habitually on the instant pleasures of idleness. It is true that everybody is born with certain predispositions, and that these predispositions influence very strongly the early formation of habits of thought. But the fact remains that the character is built by long-continued habits of thought. If the mature edifice of character usually shows in an exaggerated form the peculiarities of the original predisposition, this merely indicates a probability that the slow erection of the edifice has proceeded at haphazard, and that reason has not presided over it. A child may be born with a tendency to bent shoulders. If nothing is done, if on the contrary he becomes a clerk and abhors gymnastics, his shoulders will develop an excessive roundness, entirely through habit. Whereas, if his will, guided by his reason, had compelled the formation of a corrective physical habit, his shoulders might have been, if not quite straight, nearly so. Thus a physical habit! The same with a mental habit.

The more closely we examine the development of original predispositions, the more clearly we shall see that this development is not inevitable, is not a process which works itself out independently according to mysterious, ruthless laws which we cannot understand. For instance, the effect of an original predisposition may be destroyed by an accidental shock. A young man with an inherited tendency to alcohol may develop into a stern teetotaller through the shock caused by seeing his drunken father strike his mother; whereas, if his father had chanced to be affectionate in drink, the son might have ended in the gutter. No ruthless law here! It is notorious, also, that natures are sometimes completely changed in their development by chance momentary contact with natures stronger than themselves. 'From that day I resolved—' etc. You know the phrase. Often the resolve is not kept; but often it is kept. A spark has inflamed the will. The burning will has tyrannised over the brain. New habits have been formed. And the result looks just like a miracle.

Now, if these great transformations can be brought about by accident, cannot similar transformations be brought about by a reasonable design? At any rate, if one starts to bring them about, one starts with the assurance that transformations are not impossible, since they have occurred. One starts also in the full knowledge of the influence of habit on life. Take any one of your own habits, mental or physical. You will be able to recall the time when that habit did not exist, or if it did exist it was scarcely perceptible. And you will discover that nearly all your habits have been formed unconsciously, by daily repetitions which bore no relation to a general plan, and which you practised not noticing. You will be compelled to admit that your 'character,' as it is to-day, is a structure that has been built almost without the aid of an architect; higgledy-piggledy, anyhow. But occasionally the architect did step in and design something. Here and there among your habits you will find one that you consciously and of deliberate purpose initiated and persevered with—doubtless owing to some happy influence. What is the difference between that conscious habit and the unconscious habits? None whatever as regards its effect on the sum of your character. It may be the strongest of all your habits. The only quality that differentiates it from the others is that it has a definite object (most likely a good object), and that it wholly or partially fulfils that object. There is not a man who reads these lines but has, in this detail or that, proved in himself that the will, forcing the brain to repeat the same action again and again, can modify the shape of his character as a sculptor modifies the shape of damp clay.

But if a grown man's character is developing from day to day (as it is), if nine-tenths of the development is due to unconscious action and one-tenth to conscious action, and if the one-tenth conscious is the most satisfactory part of the total result; why, in the name of common sense, henceforward, should not nine-tenths, instead of one-tenth, be due to conscious action? What is there to prevent this agreeable consummation? There is nothing whatever to prevent it—except insubordination on the part of the brain. And insubordination of the brain can be cured, as I have previously shown. When I see men unhappy and inefficient in the craft of *living*, from sheer, crass inattention to their own development; when I see misshapen men building up businesses and empires, and never stopping to build up themselves; when I see dreary men expending precisely the same energy on teaching a dog to walk on its hind-legs as would brighten the whole colour of their own lives, I feel as if I wanted to give up the ghost, so ridiculous, so fatuous does the spectacle seem! But, of course, I do not give up the ghost. The paroxysm passes. Only I really must cry out: 'Can't you see what you're missing? Can't you see that you're missing the most interesting thing on earth, far more interesting than businesses, empires, and dogs? Doesn't it strike you how clumsy and short-sighted you are—working always with an inferior machine when you might have a smooth-gliding perfection? Doesn't it strike you how badly you are treating yourself?'

Listen, you confirmed grumbler, you who make the evening meal hideous with complaints against destiny—for it is you I will single out. Are you aware what people are saying about you behind your back? They are saying that you render yourself and your family miserable by the habit which has grown on you of always grumbling. 'Surely it isn't as bad as that?' you protest. Yes, it is just as bad as that. You say: 'The fact is, I know it's absurd to grumble. But I'm like that. I've tried to stop it, and I can't!' How have you tried to stop it? 'Well, I've made up my mind several times to fight against it, but I never succeed. This is strictly between ourselves. I don't usually admit that I'm a grumbler.' Considering that you grumble for about an hour and a half every day of your life, it was sanguine, my dear sir, to expect to cure such a habit by means of a solitary intention, formed at intervals in the brain and then forgotten. No! You must do more than that. If you will daily fix your brain firmly for half an hour on the truth (you know it to be a truth) that grumbling is absurd and futile, your brain will henceforward begin to form a habit in that direction; it will begin to be moulded to the idea that grumbling is absurd and futile. In odd moments, when it isn't thinking of anything in particular, it will suddenly remember that grumbling is absurd and futile. When you sit down to the meal and open your mouth to say: 'I can't think what my ass of a partner means by—' it will remember that grumbling is absurd and futile, and will alter the arrangement of your throat, teeth, and tongue, so that you will say: 'What fine weather we're having!' In brief, it will remember involuntarily, by a new habit. All who look into their experience will admit that the failure to replace old habits by new ones is due to the fact that at the critical moment the brain does not remember; it simply forgets. The practice of concentration will cure that. All depends on regular concentration. This grumbling is an instance, though chosen not quite at hazard.

VI
LORD OVER THE NODDLE

Having proved by personal experiment the truth of the first of the two great principles which concern the human machine—namely, that the brain is a servant, not a master, and can be controlled—we may now come to the second. The second is more fundamental than the first, but it can be of no use until the first is understood and put into practice. The human machine is an apparatus of brain and muscle for enabling the Ego to develop freely in the universe by which it is surrounded, without friction. Its function is to convert the facts of the universe to the best advantage of the Ego. The facts of the universe are the material with which it is its business to deal—not the facts of an ideal universe, but the facts of this universe. Hence, when friction occurs, when the facts of the universe cease to be of advantage to the Ego, the fault is in the machine. It is not the solar system that has gone wrong, but the human machine. Second great principle, therefore: '*In case of friction, the machine is always at fault.*'

You can control nothing but your own mind. Even your two-year-old babe may defy you by the instinctive force of its personality. But your own mind you can control. Your own mind is a sacred enclosure into which nothing harmful can enter except by your permission. Your own mind has the power to transmute every external phenomenon to its own purposes. If happiness arises from cheerfulness, kindliness, and rectitude (and who will deny it?), what possible combination of circumstances is going to make you unhappy so long as the machine remains in order? If self-development consists in the utilisation of one's environment (not utilisation of somebody else's environment), how can your environment prevent you from developing? You would look rather foolish without it, anyway. In that noddle of yours is everything necessary for development, for the maintaining of dignity, for the achieving of happiness, and you are absolute lord over the noddle, will you but exercise the powers of lordship. Why worry about the contents of somebody else's noddle, in which you can be nothing but an intruder, when you may arrive at a better result, with absolute certainty, by confining your activities to your own? 'Look within.' 'The Kingdom of Heaven is within you.' 'Oh, yes!' you protest. 'All that's old. Epictetus said that. Marcus Aurelius said that. Christ said that.' They did. I admit it readily. But if you were ruffled this morning because your motor-omnibus broke down, and you had to take a cab, then so far as you are concerned these great teachers lived in vain. You, calling yourself a reasonable man, are going about dependent for your happiness, dignity, and growth, upon a thousand things over which you have no control, and the most exquisitely organised machine for ensuring happiness, dignity, and growth, is rusting away inside you. And all because you have a sort of notion that a saying said two thousand years ago cannot be practical.

You remark sagely to your child: 'No, my child, you cannot have that moon, and you will accomplish nothing by crying for it. Now, here is this beautiful box of bricks, by means of which you may amuse yourself while learning many wonderful matters and improving your mind. You must try to be content with what you have, and to make the best of it. If you had the moon you wouldn't be any happier.' Then you lie awake half the night repining because the last post has brought a letter to the effect that 'the Board cannot entertain your application for,' etc. You say the two cases are not alike. They are not. Your child has never heard of Epictetus. On the other hand, justice *is* the moon. At your age you surely know that. 'But the Directors *ought* to have granted my application,' you insist. Exactly! I agree. But we are not in a universe of *oughts*. You have a special apparatus within you for dealing with a universe where *oughts* are flagrantly disregarded. And you are not using it. You are lying awake, keeping your wife awake, injuring your health, injuring hers, losing your dignity and your cheerfulness. Why? Because you think that these antics and performances will influence the Board? Because you think that they will put you into a better condition for dealing with your environment to-morrow? Not a bit. Simply because the machine is at fault.

In certain cases we do make use of our machines (as well as their sad condition of neglect will allow), but in other cases we behave in an extraordinarily irrational manner. Thus if we sally out and get caught in a heavy shower we do not, unless very far gone in foolishness, sit down and curse the weather. We put up our umbrella, if we have one, and if not we hurry home. We may grumble, but it is not serious grumbling; we accept the shower as a fact of the universe, and control ourselves. Thus also, if by a sudden catastrophe we lose somebody who is important to us, we grieve, but we control ourselves, recognising one of those hazards of destiny from which not even millionaires are exempt. And the result on our Ego is usually to improve it in essential respects. But there are other strokes of destiny, other facts of the universe, against which we protest as a child protests when deprived of the moon.

Take the case of an individual with an imperfect idea of honesty. Now, that individual is the consequence of his father and mother and his environment, and his father and mother of theirs, and so backwards to the single-celled protoplasm. That individual is a result of the cosmic order, the inevitable product of cause and effect. We know that. We must admit that he is just as much a fact of the universe as a shower of rain or a storm at sea that swallows a ship. We freely grant in the abstract that there must be, at the present stage of evolution, a certain number of persons with unfair minds. We are quite ready to contemplate such an individual with philosophy—until it happens that, in the course of the progress of the solar system, he runs up against ourselves. Then listen to the outcry! Listen to the continual explosions of a righteous man aggrieved! The individual may be our clerk, cashier, son, father, brother, partner, wife, employer. We are ill-used! We are being treated unfairly! We kick; we scream. We nourish the inward sense of grievance that eats the core out of content. We sit down in the rain. We decline to think of umbrellas, or to run to shelter.

We care not that that individual is a fact which the universe has been slowly manufacturing for millions of years. Our attitude implies that we want eternity to roll back and begin again, in such wise that we at any rate shall not be disturbed. Though we have a machine for the transmutation of facts into food for our growth, we do not dream of using it. But, we say, he is doing us harm! Where? In our minds. He has robbed us of our peace, our comfort, our happiness, our good temper. Even if he has, we might just as well inveigh against a shower. But has he? What was our brain doing while this naughty person stepped in and robbed us of the only possessions worth having? No, no! It is not that he has done us harm—the one cheerful item in a universe of stony facts is that no one can harm anybody except himself—it is merely that we have been silly, precisely as silly as if we had taken a seat in the rain with a folded umbrella by our side.... The machine is at fault. I fancy we are now obtaining glimpses of what that phrase really means.

It is in intercourse—social, sentimental, or business—with one's fellows that the qualities and the condition of the human machine are put to the test and strained. That part of my life which I conduct by myself, without reference—or at any rate without direct reference—to others, I can usually manage in such a way that the gods do not positively weep at the spectacle thereof. My environment is simpler, less puzzling, when I am alone, my calm and my self-control less liable to violent fluctuations. Impossible to be disturbed by a chair! Impossible that a chair should get on one's nerves! Impossible to blame a chair for not being as reasonable, as archangelic as I am myself! But when it comes to people!... Well, that is 'living,' then! The art of life, the art of extracting all its power from the human machine, does not lie chiefly in processes of bookish-culture, nor in contemplations of the beauty and majesty of existence. It lies chiefly in keeping the peace, the whole peace, and nothing but the peace, with those with whom one is 'thrown.' Is it in sitting ecstatic over Shelley, Shakespeare, or Herbert Spencer, solitary in my room of a night, that I am 'improving myself' and learning to live? Or is it in watching over all my daily human contacts? Do not seek to escape the comparison by insinuating that I despise study, or by pointing out that the eternal verities are beyond dailiness. Nothing of the kind! I am so 'silly' about books that merely to possess them gives me pleasure. And if the verities are good for eternity they ought to be good for a day. If I cannot exchange them for daily coin—if I can't buy happiness for a single day because I've nothing less than an eternal verity about me and nobody has sufficient change—then my eternal verity is not an eternal verity. It is merely an unnegotiable bit of glass (called a diamond), or even a note on the Bank of Engraving.

I can say to myself when I arise in the morning: 'I am master of my brain. No one can get in there and rage about like a bull in a china shop. If my companions on the planet's crust choose to rage about they cannot affect *me*! I will not let them. I have power to maintain my own calm, and I will. No earthly being can force me to be false to my principles, or to be blind to the beauty of the universe, or to be gloomy, or to be irritable, or to complain against my lot. For these things depend on the brain; cheerfulness, kindliness, and honest thinking are all within the department of the brain. The disciplined brain can accomplish them. And my brain is disciplined, and I will discipline it more and more as the days pass. I am, therefore, independent of hazard, and I will back myself to conduct all intercourse as becomes a rational creature.' ... I can say this. I can ram this argument by force of will into my brain, and by dint of repeating it often enough I shall assuredly arrive at the supreme virtues of reason. I should assuredly conquer—the brain being such a machine of habit—even if I did not take the trouble to consider in the slightest degree what manner of things my fellow-men are—by acting merely in my own interests. But the way of perfection (I speak relatively) will be immensely shortened and smoothed if I do consider, dispassionately, the case of the other human machines. Thus:—

The truth is that my attitude towards my fellows is fundamentally and totally wrong, and that it entails on my thinking machine a strain which is quite unnecessary, though I may have arranged the machine so as to withstand the strain successfully. The secret of smooth living is a calm cheerfulness which will leave me always in full possession of my reasoning faculty—in order that I may live by reason instead of by instinct and momentary passion. The secret of calm cheerfulness is kindliness; no person can be consistently cheerful and calm who does not consistently think kind thoughts. But how can I be kindly when I pass the major portion of my time in blaming the people who surround me—who are part of my environment? If I, blaming, achieve some approach to kindliness, it is only by a great and exhausting effort of self-mastery. The inmost secret, then, lies in not blaming, in not judging and emitting verdicts. Oh! I do not blame by word of mouth! I am far too advanced for such a puerility. I keep the blame in my own breast, where it festers. I am always privately forgiving, which is bad for me. Because, you know, there is nothing to forgive. I do not have to forgive bad weather; nor, if I found myself in an earthquake, should I have to forgive the earthquake.

All blame, uttered or unexpressed, is wrong. I do not blame myself. I can explain myself to myself. I can invariably explain myself. If I forged a friend's name on a cheque I should explain the affair quite satisfactorily to myself. And instead of blaming myself I should sympathise with myself for having been driven into such an excessively awkward corner. Let me examine honestly my mental processes, and I must admit that my attitude towards others is entirely different from my attitude towards myself. I must admit that in the seclusion of my mind, though I say not a word, I am constantly blaming others because I am not happy. Whenever I bump up against an opposing personality and my smooth progress is impeded, I secretly blame the opposer. I act as though I had shouted to the world: 'Clear out of the way, every one, for I am coming!' Every one does not clear out of the way. I did not really expect every one to clear out of the way. But I act, within, as though I had so expected. I blame. Hence kindliness, hence cheerfulness, is rendered vastly more difficult for me.

What I ought to do is this! I ought to reflect again and again, and yet again, that the beings among whom I have to steer, the living environment out of which I have to manufacture my happiness, are just as inevitable in the scheme of evolution as I am myself; have just as much right to be themselves as I have to be myself; are precisely my equals in the face of Nature; are capable of being explained as I am capable of being explained; are entitled to the same latitude as I am entitled to, and are no more responsible for their composition and their environment than I for mine. I ought to reflect again and again, and yet again, that they all deserve from me as much sympathy as I give to myself. Why not? Having thus reflected in a general manner, I ought to take one by one the individuals with whom I am brought into frequent contact, and seek, by a deliberate effort of the imagination and the reason, to understand them, to understand why they act thus and thus, what their difficulties are, what their 'explanation' is, and how friction can be avoided. So I ought to reflect, morning after morning, until my brain is saturated with the cases of these individuals. Here is a course of discipline. If I follow it I shall gradually lose the preposterous habit of blaming, and I shall have laid the foundations of that quiet, unshakable self-possession which is the indispensable preliminary of conduct according to reason, of thorough efficiency in the machine of happiness. But something in me, something distinctly base, says: 'Yes. The put-yourself-in-his-place business over again! The do-unto-others business over again!' Just so! Something in me is ashamed of being 'moral.' (You all know the feeling!) Well, morals are naught but another name for reasonable conduct; a higher and more practical form of egotism—an egotism which, while freeing others, frees myself. I have tried the lower form of egotism. And it has failed. If I am afraid of being moral, if I prefer to cut off my nose to spite my face, well, I must accept the consequences. But truth will prevail.

VIII
THE DAILY FRICTION

It is with common daily affairs that I am now dealing, not with heroic enterprises, ambitions, martyrdoms. Take the day, the ordinary day in the ordinary house or office. Though it comes seven times a week, and is the most banal thing imaginable, it is quite worth attention. How does the machine get through it? Ah! the best that can be said of the machine is that it does get through it, somehow. The friction, though seldom such as to bring matters to a standstill, is frequent—the sort of friction that, when it occurs in a bicycle, is just sufficient to annoy the rider, but not sufficient to make him get off the machine and examine the bearings. Occasionally the friction is very loud; indeed, disturbing, and at rarer intervals it shrieks, like an omnibus brake out of order. You know those days when you have the sensation that life is not large enough to contain the household or the office-staff, when the business of intercourse may be compared to the manoeuvres of two people who, having awakened with a bad headache, are obliged to dress simultaneously in a very small bedroom. 'After you with that towel!' in accents of bitter, grinding politeness. 'If you could kindly move your things off this chair!' in a voice that would blow brains out if it were a bullet. I venture to say that you know those days. 'But,' you reply, 'such days are few. Usually...!' Well, usually, the friction, though less intense, is still proceeding. We grow accustomed to it. We scarcely notice it, as a person in a stuffy chamber will scarcely notice the stuffiness. But the deteriorating influence due to friction goes on, even if unperceived. And one morning we perceive its ravages—and write a letter to the *Telegraph* to inquire whether life is worth living, or whether marriage is a failure, or whether men are more polite than women. The proof that friction, in various and varying degrees, is practically conscious in most households lies in the fact that when we chance on a household where there is no friction we are startled. We can't recover from the phenomenon. And in describing this household to our friends, we say: 'They get on so well together,' as if we were saying: 'They have wings and can fly! Just fancy! Did you ever hear of such a thing?'

Ninety per cent. of all daily friction is caused by tone—mere tone of voice. Try this experiment. Say: 'Oh, you little darling, you sweet pet, you entirely charming creature!' to a baby or a dog; but roar these delightful epithets in the tone of saying: 'You infernal little nuisance! If I hear another sound I'll break every bone in your body!' The baby will infallibly whimper, and the dog will infallibly mouch off. True, a dog is not a human being, neither is a baby. They cannot understand. It is precisely because they cannot understand and articulate words that the experiment is valuable; for it separates the effect of the tone from the effect of the word spoken. He who speaks, speaks twice. His words convey his thought, and his tone conveys his mental attitude towards the person spoken to. And certainly the attitude, so far as friction goes, is more important than the thought. Your wife may say to you: 'I shall buy that hat I spoke to you about.' And you may reply, quite sincerely, 'As you please.' But it will depend on your tone whether you convey: 'As you please. I am sympathetically anxious that your innocent caprices should be indulged.' Or whether you convey: 'As you please. Only don't bother me with hats. I am above hats. A great deal too much money is spent in this house on hats. However, I'm helpless!' Or whether you convey: 'As you please, heart of my heart, but if you would like to be a nice girl, go gently. We're rather tight.' I need not elaborate. I am sure of being comprehended.

As tone is the expression of attitude, it is, of course, caused by attitude. The frictional tone is chiefly due to that general attitude of blame which I have already condemned as being absurd and unjustifiable. As, by constant watchful discipline, we gradually lose this silly attitude of blame, so the tone will of itself gradually change. But the two ameliorations can proceed together, and it is a curious thing that an agreeable tone, artificially and deliberately adopted, will influence the mental attitude almost as much as the mental attitude will influence the tone. If you honestly feel resentful against some one, but, having understood the foolishness of fury, intentionally mask your fury under a persuasive tone, your fury will at once begin to abate. You will be led into a rational train of thought; you will see that after all the object of your resentment has a right to exist, and that he is neither a doormat nor a scoundrel, and that anyhow nothing is to be gained, and much is to be lost, by fury. You will see that fury is unworthy of you.

Do you remember the gentleness of the tone which you employed after the healing of your first quarrel with a beloved companion? Do you remember the persuasive tone which you used when you wanted to obtain something from a difficult person on whom your happiness depended? Why should not your tone always combine these qualities? Why should you not carefully school your tone? Is it beneath you to ensure the largest possible amount of your own 'way' by the simplest means? Or is there at the back of your mind that peculiarly English and German idea that politeness, sympathy, and respect for another immortal soul would imply deplorable weakness on your part? You say that your happiness does not depend on every person whom you happen to speak to. Yes, it does. Your happiness is always dependent on just that person. Produce friction, and you suffer. Idle to argue that the person has no business to be upset by your tone! You have caused avoidable friction, simply because your machine for dealing with your environment was suffering from pride, ignorance, or thoughtlessness. You say I am making a mountain out of a mole-hill. No! I am making a mountain out of ten million mole-hills. And that is what life does. It is the little but continuous causes that have great effects. I repeat: Why not deliberately adopt a gentle, persuasive tone—just to see what the results are? Surely you are not ashamed to be wise. You may smile superiorly as you read this. Yet you know very well that more than once you *have* resolved to use a gentle and persuasive tone on all occasions, and that the sole reason why you had that fearful shindy yesterday with your cousin's sister-in-law was that you had long since failed to keep your resolve. But you were of my mind once, and more than once.

What you have to do is to teach the new habit to your brain by daily concentration on it; by forcing your brain to think of nothing else for half an hour of a morning. After a time the brain will begin to remember automatically. For, of course, the explanation of your previous failures is that your brain, undisciplined, merely forgot at the critical moment. The tone was out of your mouth before your brain had waked up. It is necessary to watch, as though you were a sentinel, not only against the wrong tone, but against the other symptoms of the attitude of blame. Such as the frown. It is necessary to regard yourself constantly, and in minute detail. You lie in bed for half an hour and enthusiastically concentrate on this beautiful new scheme of the right tone. You rise, and because you don't achieve a proper elegance of necktie at the first knotting, you frown and swear and clench your teeth! There is a symptom of the wrong attitude towards your environment. You are awake, but your brain isn't. It is in such a symptom that you may judge yourself. And not a trifling symptom either! If you will frown at a necktie, if you will use language to a necktie which no gentleman should use to a necktie, what will you be capable of to a responsible being?... Yes, it is very difficult. But it can be done.

IX
'FIRE!'

In this business of daily living, of ordinary usage of the machine in hourly intercourse, there occurs sometimes a phenomenon which is the cause of a great deal of trouble, and the result of a very ill-tended machine. It is a phenomenon impossible to ignore, and yet, so shameful is it, so degrading, so shocking, so miserable, that I hesitate to mention it. For one class of reader is certain to ridicule me, loftily saying: 'One really doesn't expect to find this sort of thing in print nowadays!' And another class of reader is certain to get angry. Nevertheless, as one of my main objects in the present book is to discuss matters which 'people don't talk about,' I shall discuss this matter. But my diffidence in doing so is such that I must approach it deviously, describing it first by means of a figure.

Imagine that, looking at a man's house, you suddenly perceive it to be on fire. The flame is scarcely perceptible. You could put it out if you had a free hand. But you have not got a free hand. It is his house, not yours. He may or may not know that his house is burning. You are aware, by experience, however, that if you directed his attention to the flame, the effect of your warning would be exceedingly singular, almost incredible. For the effect would be that he would instantly begin to strike matches, pour on petroleum, and fan the flame, violently resenting interference. Therefore you can only stand and watch, hoping that he will notice the flames before they are beyond control, and extinguish them. The probability is, however, that he will notice the flames too late. And powerless to avert disaster, you are condemned, therefore, to watch the damage of valuable property. The flames leap higher and higher, and they do not die down till they have burned themselves out. You avert your gaze from the spectacle, and until you are gone the owner of the house pretends that nothing has occurred. When alone he curses himself for his carelessness.

The foregoing is meant to be a description of what happens when a man passes through the incendiary experience known as 'losing his temper.' (There! the cat of my chapter is out of the bag!) A man who has lost his temper is simply being 'burnt out.' His constitutes one of the most curious and (for everybody) humiliating spectacles that life offers. It is an insurrection, a boiling over, a sweeping storm. Dignity, common sense, justice are shrivelled up and destroyed. Anarchy reigns. The devil has broken his chain. Instinct is stamping on the face of reason. And in that man civilisation has temporarily receded millions of years. Of course, the thing amounts to a nervous disease, and I think it is almost universal. You at once protest that you never lose your temper—haven't lost your temper for ages! But do you not mean that you have not smashed furniture for ages? These fires are of varying intensities. Some of them burn very dully. Yet they burn. One man loses his temper; another is merely 'ruffled.' But the event is the same in kind. When you are 'ruffled,' when you are conscious of a resentful vibration that surprises all your being, when your voice changes, when you notice a change in the demeanour of your companion, who sees that he has 'touched a tender point,' you may not go to the length of smashing furniture, but you have had a fire, and your dignity is damaged. You admit it to yourself afterwards. I am sure you know what I mean. And I am nearly sure that you, with your courageous candour, will admit that from time to time you suffer from these mysterious 'fires.'

'Temper,' one of the plagues of human society, is generally held to be incurable, save by the vague process of exercising self-control—a process which seldom has any beneficial results. It is regarded now as smallpox used to be regarded—as a visitation of Providence, which must be borne. But I do not hold it to be incurable. I am convinced that it is permanently curable. And its eminent importance as a nuisance to mankind at large deserves, I think, that it should receive particular attention. Anyhow, I am strongly against the visitation of Providence theory, as being unscientific, primitive, and conducive to unashamed *laissez-aller*. A man can be master in his own house. If he cannot be master by simple force of will, he can be master by ruse and wile. I would employ cleverness to maintain the throne of reason when it is likely to be upset in the mind by one of these devastating and disgraceful insurrections of brute instinct.

It is useless for a man in the habit of losing or mislaying his temper to argue with himself that such a proceeding is folly, that it serves no end, and does nothing but harm. It is useless for him to argue that in allowing his temper to stray he is probably guilty of cruelty, and certainly guilty of injustice to those persons who are forced to witness the loss. It is useless for him to argue that a man of uncertain temper in a house is like a man who goes about a house with a loaded revolver sticking from his pocket, and that all considerations of fairness and reason have to be subordinated in that house to the fear of the revolver, and that such peace as is maintained in that house is often a shameful and an unjust peace. These arguments will not be strong enough to prevail against one of the most powerful and capricious of all habits. This habit must be met and conquered (and it *can* be!) by an even more powerful quality in the human mind; I mean the universal human horror of looking ridiculous. The man who loses his temper often thinks he is doing something rather fine and majestic. On the contrary, so far is this from being the fact, he is merely making an ass of himself. He is merely parading himself as an undignified fool, as that supremely contemptible figure—a grown-up baby. He may intimidate a feeble companion by his raging, or by the dark sullenness of a more subdued flame, but in the heart of even the weakest companion is a bedrock feeling of contempt for him. The way in which a man of uncertain temper is treated by his friends proves that they despise him, for they do not treat him as a reasonable being. How should they treat him as a reasonable being when the tenure of his reason is so insecure? And if only he could hear what is said of him behind his back!...

The invalid can cure himself by teaching his brain the habit of dwelling upon his extreme fatuity. Let him concentrate regularly, with intense fixation, upon the ideas: 'When I lose my temper, when I get ruffled, when that mysterious vibration runs through me, I am making a donkey of myself, a donkey, and a donkey! You understand, a preposterous donkey! I am behaving like a great baby. I look a fool. I am a spectacle bereft of dignity. Everybody despises me, smiles at me in secret, disdains the idiotic ass with whom it is impossible to reason.'

Ordinarily the invalid disguises from himself this aspect of his disease, and his brain will instinctively avoid it as much as it can. But in hours of calm he can slowly and regularly force his brain, by the practice of concentration, to familiarise itself with just this aspect, so that in time its instinct will be to think first, and not last, of just this aspect. When he has arrived at that point he is saved. No man who, at the very inception of the fire, is visited with a clear vision of himself as an arrant ass and pitiable object of contempt, will lack the volition to put the fire out. But, be it noted, he will not succeed until he can do it at once. A fire is a fire, and the engines must gallop by themselves out of the station instantly. This means the acquirement of a mental habit. During the preliminary stages of the cure he should, of course, avoid inflammable situations. This is a perfectly simple thing to do, if the brain has been disciplined out of its natural forgetfulness.

X
MISCHIEVOUSLY OVERWORKING IT

I have dealt with the two general major causes of friction in the daily use of the machine. I will now deal with a minor cause, and make an end of mere dailiness. This minor cause—and after all I do not know that its results are so trifling as to justify the epithet 'minor'—is the straining of the machine by forcing it to do work which it was never intended to do. Although we are incapable of persuading our machines to do effectively that which they are bound to do somehow, we continually overburden them with entirely unnecessary and inept tasks. We cannot, it would seem, let things alone.

For example, in the ordinary household the amount of machine horse-power expended in fighting for the truth is really quite absurd. This pure zeal for the establishment and general admission of the truth is usually termed 'contradictoriness.' But, of course, it is not that; it is something higher. My wife states that the Joneses have gone into a new flat, of which the rent is £165 a year. Now, Jones has told me personally that the rent of his new flat is £156 a year. I correct my wife. Knowing that she is in the right, she corrects me. She cannot bear that a falsehood should prevail. It is not a question of £9, it is a question of truth. Her enthusiasm for truth excites my enthusiasm for truth. Five minutes ago I didn't care twopence whether the rent of the Joneses' new flat was £165 or £156 or £1056 a year. But now I care intensely that it is £156. I have formed myself into a select society for the propagating of the truth about the rent of the Joneses' new flat, and my wife has done the same. In eloquence, in argumentative skill, in strict supervision of our tempers, we each of us squander enormous quantities of that h.-p. which is so precious to us. And the net effect is naught.

Now, if one of us two had understood the elementary principles of human engineering, that one would have said (privately): 'Truth is indestructible. Truth will out. Truth is never in a hurry. If it doesn't come out to-day it will come out to-morrow or next year. It can take care of itself. Ultimately my wife (or my husband) will learn the essential cosmic truth about the rent of the Joneses' new flat. I already know it, and the moment when she (or he) knows it also will be the moment of my triumph. She (or he) will not celebrate my triumph openly, but it will be none the less real. And my reputation for accuracy and calm restraint will be consolidated. If, by a rare mischance, I am in error, it will be vastly better for me in the day of my undoing that I have not been too positive now. Besides, nobody has appointed me sole custodian of the great truth concerning the rent of the Joneses' new flat. I was not brought into the world to be a safe-deposit, and more urgent matters summon me to effort.' If one of us had meditated thus, much needless friction would have been avoided and power saved; *amour-propre* would not have been exposed to risks; the sacred cause of truth would not in the least have suffered; and the rent of the Joneses' new flat would anyhow have remained exactly what it is.

In addition to straining the machine by our excessive anxiety for the spread of truth, we give a very great deal too much attention to the state of other people's machines. I cannot too strongly, too sarcastically, deprecate this astonishing habit. It will be found to be rife in nearly every household and in nearly every office. We are most of us endeavouring to rearrange the mechanism in other heads than our own. This is always dangerous and generally futile. Considering the difficulty we have in our own brains, where our efforts are sure of being accepted as well-meant, and where we have at any rate a rough notion of the machine's construction, our intrepidity in adventuring among the delicate adjustments of other brains is remarkable. We are cursed by too much of the missionary spirit. We must needs voyage into the China of our brother's brain, and explain there that things are seriously wrong in that heathen land, and make ourselves unpleasant in the hope of getting them put right. We have all our own brain and body on which to wreak our personality, but this is not enough; we must extend our personality further, just as though we were a colonising world-power intoxicated by the idea of the 'white man's burden.'

One of the central secrets of efficient daily living is to leave our daily companions alone a great deal more than we do, and attend to ourselves. If a daily companion is conducting his life upon principles which you know to be false, and with results which you feel to be unpleasant, the safe rule is to keep your mouth shut. Or if, out of your singular conceit, you are compelled to open it, open it with all precautions, and with the formal politeness you would use to a stranger. Intimacy is no excuse for rough manners, though the majority of us seem to think it is. You are not in charge of the universe; you are in charge of yourself. You cannot hope to manage the universe in your spare time, and if you try you will probably make a mess of such part of the universe as you touch, while gravely neglecting yourself. In every family there is generally some one whose meddlesome interest in other machines leads to serious friction in his own. Criticise less, even in the secrecy of your chamber. And do not blame at all. Accept your environment and adapt yourself to it in silence, instead of noisily attempting to adapt your environment to yourself. Here is true wisdom. You have no business trespassing beyond the confines of your own individuality. In so trespassing you are guilty of impertinence. This is obvious. And yet one of the chief activities of home-life consists in prancing about at random on other people's private lawns. What I say applies even to the relation between parents and children. And though my precept is exaggerated, it is purposely exaggerated in order effectively to balance the exaggeration in the opposite direction.

All individualities, other than one's own, are part of one's environment. The evolutionary process is going on all right, and they are a portion of it. Treat them as inevitable. To assert that they are inevitable is not to assert that they are unalterable. Only the alteration of them is not primarily your affair; it is theirs. Your affair is to use them, as they are, without self-righteousness, blame, or complaint, for the smooth furtherance of your own ends. There is no intention here to rob them of responsibility by depriving them of free-will while saddling *you* with responsibility as a free agent. As your environment they must be accepted as inevitable, because they *are* inevitable. But as centres themselves they have their own responsibility: which is not yours. The historic question: 'Have we free-will, or are we the puppets of determinism?' enters now. As a question it is fascinating and futile. It has never been, and it never will be, settled. The theory of determinism cannot be demolished by argument. But in his heart every man, including the most obstinate supporter of the theory, demolishes it every hour of every day. On the other hand, the theory of free-will can be demolished by ratiocination! So much the worse for ratiocination! *If we regard ourselves as free agents, and the personalities surrounding us as the puppets of determinism*, we shall have arrived at the working compromise from which the finest results of living can be obtained. The philosophic experience of centuries, if it has proved anything, has proved this. And the man who acts upon it in the common, banal contracts and collisions of the difficult experiment which we call daily life, will speedily become convinced of its practical worth.

For ten chapters you have stood it, but not without protest. I know the feeling which is in your minds, and which has manifested itself in numerous criticisms of my ideas. That feeling may be briefly translated, perhaps, thus: 'This is all very well, but it isn't true, not a bit! It's only a fairy-tale that you have been telling us. Miracles don't happen,' etc. I, on my part, have a feeling that unless I take your feeling in hand at once, and firmly deal with it, I had better put my shutters up, for you will have got into the way of regarding me simply as a source of idle amusement. Already I can perceive, from the expressions of some critics, that, so far as they are concerned, I might just as well not have written a word. Therefore at this point I pause, in order to insist once more upon what I began by saying.

The burden of your criticism is: 'Human nature is always the same. I know my faults. But it is useless to tell me about them. I can't alter them. I was born like that.' The fatal weakness of this argument is, first, that it is based on a complete falsity; and second, that it puts you in an untenable position. Human nature *does* change. Nothing can be more unscientific, more hopelessly mediæval, than to imagine that it does not. It changes like everything else. You can't see it change. True! But then you can't see the grass growing—not unless you arise very early.

Is human nature the same now as in the days of Babylonian civilisation, when the social machine was oiled by drenchings of blood? Is it the same now as in the days of Greek civilisation, when there was no such thing as romantic love between the sexes? Is it the same now as it was during the centuries when constant friction had to provide its own cure in the shape of constant war? Is it the same now as it was on 2nd March 1819, when the British Government officially opposed a motion to consider the severity of the criminal laws (which included capital punishment for cutting down a tree, and other sensible dodges against friction), and were defeated by a majority of only nineteen votes? Is it the same now as in the year 1883, when the first S.P.C.C. was formed in England?

If you consider that human nature is still the same you should instantly go out and make a bonfire of the works of Spencer, Darwin, and Wallace, and then return to enjoy the purely jocular side of the present volume. If you admit that it has changed, let me ask you how it has changed, unless by the continual infinitesimal efforts, *upon themselves*, of individual men, like you and me. Did you suppose it was changed by magic, or by Acts of Parliament, or by the action of groups on persons, and not of persons on groups? Let me tell you that human nature has changed since yesterday. Let me tell you that to-day reason has a more powerful voice in the directing of instinct than it had yesterday. Let me tell you that to-day the friction of the machines is less screechy and grinding than it was yesterday.

'You were born like that, and you can't alter yourself, and so it's no use talking.' If you really believe this, why make any effort at all? Why not let the whole business beautifully slide and yield to your instincts? What object can there be in trying to control yourself in any manner whatever if you are unalterable? Assert yourself to be unalterable, and you assert yourself a fatalist. Assert yourself a fatalist, and you free yourself from all moral responsibility—and other people, too. Well, then, act up to your convictions, if convictions they are. If you can't alter yourself, I can't alter myself, and supposing that I come along and bash you on the head and steal your purse, you can't blame me. You can only, on recovering consciousness, affectionately grasp my hand and murmur: 'Don't apologise, my dear fellow; we can't alter ourselves.'

This, you say, is absurd. It is. That is one of my innumerable points. The truth is, you do not really believe that you cannot alter yourself. What is the matter with you is just what is the matter with me—sheer idleness. You hate getting up in the morning, and to excuse your inexcusable indolence you talk big about Fate. Just as 'patriotism is the last refuge of a scoundrel,' so fatalism is the last refuge of a shirker. But you deceive no one, least of all yourself. You have not, rationally, a leg to stand on. At this juncture, because I have made you laugh, you consent to say: 'I do try, all I can. But I can only alter myself a very little. By constitution I am mentally idle. I can't help that, can I?' Well, so long as you are not the only absolutely unchangeable thing in a universe of change, I don't mind. It is something for you to admit that you can alter yourself even a very little. The difference between our philosophies is now only a question of degree.

In the application of any system of perfecting the machine, no two persons will succeed equally. From the disappointed tone of some of your criticisms it might be fancied that I had advertised a system for making archangels out of tailors' dummies. Such was not my hope. I have no belief in miracles. But I know that when a thing is thoroughly well done it often has the air of being a miracle. My sole aim is to insist that every man shall perfect his machine to the best of *his* powers, not to the best of somebody else's powers. I do not indulge in any hope that a man can be better than his best self. I am, however, convinced that every man fails to be his best self a great deal oftener than he need fail—for the reason that his will-power, be it great or small, is not directed according to the principles of common sense.

Common sense will surely lead a man to ask the question: 'Why did my actions yesterday contradict my reason?' The reply to this question will nearly always be: 'Because at the critical moment I forgot.' The supreme explanation of the abortive results of so many efforts at self-alteration, the supreme explanation of our frequent miserable scurrying into a doctrine of fatalism, is simple forgetfulness. It is not force that we lack, but the skill to remember exactly what our reason would have us do or think at the moment itself. How is this skill to be acquired? It can only be acquired, as skill at games is acquired, by practice; by the training of the organ involved to such a point that the organ acts rightly by instinct instead of wrongly by instinct. There are degrees of success in this procedure, but there is no such phenomenon as complete failure.

Habits which increase friction can be replaced by habits which lessen friction. Habits which arrest development can be replaced by habits which encourage development. And as a habit is formed naturally, so it can be formed artificially, by imitation of the unconscious process, by accustoming the brain to the new idea. Let me, as an example, refer again to the minor subject of daily friction, and, within that subject, to the influence of tone. A man employs a frictional tone through habit. The frictional tone is an instinct with him. But if he had a quarter of an hour to reflect before speaking, and if during that quarter of an hour he could always listen to arguments against the frictional tone, his use of the frictional tone would rapidly diminish; his reason would conquer his instinct. As things are, his instinct conquers his reason by a surprise attack, by taking it unawares. Regular daily concentration of the brain, for a certain period, upon the non-frictional tone, and the immense advantages of its use, will gradually set up in the brain a new habit of thinking about the non-frictional tone; until at length the brain, disciplined, turns to the correct act before the old, silly instinct can capture it; and ultimately a new sagacious instinct will supplant the old one.

This is the rationale. It applies to all habits. Any person can test its efficiency in any habit. I care not whether he be of strong or weak will—he can test it. He will soon see the tremendous difference between merely 'making a good resolution'—(he has been doing that all his life without any very brilliant consequences)—and concentrating the brain for a given time exclusively upon a good resolution. Concentration, the efficient mastery of the brain—all is there!

XII
AN INTEREST IN LIFE

After a certain period of mental discipline, of deliberate habit-forming and habit-breaking, such as I have been indicating, a man will begin to acquire at any rate a superficial knowledge, a nodding acquaintance, with that wonderful and mysterious affair, his brain, and he will also begin to perceive how important a factor in daily life is the control of his brain. He will assuredly be surprised at the miracles which lie between his collar and his hat, in that queer box that he calls his head. For the effects that can be accomplished by mere steady, persistent thinking must appear to be miracles to apprentices in the practice of thought. When once a man, having passed an unhappy day because his clumsy, negligent brain forgot to control his instincts at a critical moment, has said to his brain: 'I will force you, by concentrating you on that particular point, to act efficiently the next time similar circumstances arise,' and when he has carried out his intention, and when the awkward circumstances have recurred, and his brain, disciplined, has done its work, and so prevented unhappiness—then that man will regard his brain with a new eye. 'By Jove!' he will say; 'I've stopped one source of unhappiness, anyway. There was a time when I should have made a fool of myself in a little domestic crisis such as to-day's. But I have gone safely through it. I am all right. She is all right. The atmosphere is not dangerous with undischarged electricity! And all because my brain, being in proper condition, watched firmly over my instincts! I must keep this up.' He will peer into that brain more and more. He will see more and more of its possibilities. He will have a new and a supreme interest in *life*. A garden is a fairly interesting thing. But the cultivation of a garden is as dull as cold mutton compared to the cultivation of a brain; and wet weather won't interfere with digging, planting, and pruning in the box.

In due season the man whose hobby is his brain will gradually settle down into a daily routine, with which routine he will start the day. The idea at the back of the mind of the ordinary man (by the ordinary man I mean the man whose brain is not his hobby) is almost always this: 'There are several things at present hanging over me—worries, unfulfilled ambitions, unrealised desires. As soon as these things are definitely settled, then I shall begin to live and enjoy myself.' That is the ordinary man's usual idea. He has it from his youth to his old age. He is invariably waiting for something to happen before he really begins to live. I am sure that if you are an ordinary man (of course, you aren't, I know) you will admit that this is true of you; you exist in the hope that one day things will be sufficiently smoothed out for you to begin to live. That is just where you differ from the man whose brain is his hobby. His daily routine consists in a meditation in the following vein: 'This day is before me. The circumstances of this day are my environment; they are the material out of which, by means of my brain, I have to live and be happy and to refrain from causing unhappiness in other people. It is the business of my brain to make use of *this* material. My brain is in its box for that sole purpose. Not to-morrow! Not next year! Not when I have made my fortune! Not when my sick child is out of danger! Not when my wife has returned to her senses! Not when my salary is raised! Not when I have passed that examination! Not when my indigestion is better! But *now!* To-day, exactly as to-day is! The facts of to-day, which in my unregeneracy I regarded primarily as anxieties, nuisances, impediments, I now regard as so much raw material from which my brain has to weave a tissue of life that is comely.'

And then he foresees the day as well as he can. His experience teaches him where he will have difficulty, and he administers to his brain the lessons of which it will have most need. He carefully looks the machine over, and arranges it specially for the sort of road which he knows that it will have to traverse. And especially he readjusts his point of view, for his point of view is continually getting wrong. He is continually seeing worries where he ought to see material. He may notice, for instance, a patch on the back of his head, and he wonders whether it is the result of age or of disease, or whether it has always been there. And his wife tells him he must call at the chemist's and satisfy himself at once. Frightful nuisance! Age! The endless trouble of a capillary complaint! Calling at the chemist's will make him late at the office! etc. etc. But then his skilled, efficient brain intervenes: 'What peculiarly interesting material this mean and petty circumstance yields for the practice of philosophy and right living!' And again: 'Is *this* to ruffle you, O my soul? Will it serve any end whatever that I should buzz nervously round this circumstance instead of attending to my usual business?'

I give this as an example of the necessity of adjusting the point of view, and of the manner in which a brain habituated by suitable concentration to correct thinking will come to the rescue in unexpected contingencies. Naturally it will work with greater certainty in the manipulation of difficulties that are expected, that can be 'seen coming '; and preparation for the expected is, fortunately, preparation for the unexpected. The man who commences his day by a steady contemplation of the dangers which the next sixteen hours are likely to furnish, and by arming himself specially against those dangers, has thereby armed himself, though to a less extent, against dangers which he did not dream of. But the routine must be fairly elastic. It may be necessary to commence several days in succession—for a week or for months, even—with disciplining the brain in one particular detail, to the temporary neglect of other matters. It is astonishing how you can weed every inch of a garden path and keep it in the most meticulous order, and then one morning find in the very middle of it a lusty, full-grown plant whose roots are positively mortised in granite! All gardeners are familiar with such discoveries.

But a similar discovery, though it entails hard labour on him, will not disgust the man whose hobby is his brain. For the discovery in itself is part of the material out of which he has to live. If a man is to turn everything whatsoever into his own calm, dignity, and happiness, he must make this use even of his own failures. He must look at them as phenomena of the brain in that box, and cheerfully set about taking measures to prevent their repetition. All that happens to him, success or check, will but serve to increase his interest in the contents of that box. I seem to hear you saying: 'And a fine egotist he'll be!' Well, he'll be the right sort of egotist. The average man is not half enough of an egotist. If egotism means a terrific interest in one's self, egotism is absolutely essential to efficient living. There is no getting away from that. But if egotism means selfishness, the serious student of the craft of daily living will not be an egotist for more than about a year. In a year he will have proved the ineptitude of egotism.

I am sadly aware that these brief chapters will be apt to convey, especially to the trustful and enthusiastic reader, a false impression; the impression of simplicity; and that when experience has roughly corrected this impression, the said reader, unless he is most solemnly warned, may abandon the entire enterprise in a fit of disgust, and for ever afterwards maintain a cynical and impolite attitude towards all theories of controlling the human machine. Now, the enterprise is not a simple one. It is based on one simple principle—the conscious discipline of the brain by selected habits of thought—but it is just about as complicated as anything well could be. Advanced golf is child's play compared to it. The man who briefly says to himself: 'I will get up at 8, and from 8.30 to 9 I will examine and control my brain, and so my life will at once be instantly improved out of recognition'—that man is destined to unpleasant surprises. Progress will be slow. Progress may appear to be quite rapid at first, and then a period of futility may set in, and the would-be vanquisher of his brain may suffer a series of the most deadly defeats. And in his pessimism he may imagine that all his pains have gone for nothing, and that the unserious loungers in exhibition gardens and readers of novels in parlours are in the right of it after all. He may even feel rather ashamed of himself for having been, as he thinks, taken in by specious promises, like the purchaser of a quack medicine.

The conviction that great effort has been made and no progress achieved is the chief of the dangers that affront the beginner in machine-tending. It is, I will assert positively, in every case a conviction unjustified by the facts, and usually it is the mere result of reaction after fatigue, encouraged by the instinct for laziness. I do not think it will survive an impartial examination; but I know that a man, in order to find an excuse for abandoning further effort, is capable of convincing himself that past effort has yielded no fruit at all. So curious is the human machine. I beg every student of himself to consider this remark with all the intellectual honesty at his disposal. It is a grave warning.

When the machine-tender observes that he is frequently changing his point of view; when he notices that what he regarded as the kernel of the difficulty yesterday has sunk to a triviality to-day, being replaced by a fresh phenomenon; when he arises one morning and by means of a new, unexpected glimpse into the recesses of the machine perceives that hitherto he has been quite wrong and must begin again; when he wonders how on earth he could have been so blind and so stupid as not to see what now he sees; when the new vision is veiled by new disappointments and narrowed by continual reservations; when he is overwhelmed by the complexity of his undertaking—then let him unhearten himself, for he is succeeding. The history of success in any art—and machine-tending is an art—is a history of recommencements, of the dispersal and reforming of doubts, of an ever-increasing conception of the extent of the territory unconquered, and an ever-decreasing conception of the extent of the territory conquered.

It is remarkable that, though no enterprise could possibly present more diverse and changeful excitements than the mastering of the brain, the second great danger which threatens its ultimate success is nothing but a mere drying-up of enthusiasm for it! One would have thought that in an affair which concerned him so nearly, in an affair whose results might be in a very strict sense vital to him, in an affair upon which his happiness and misery might certainly turn, a man would not weary from sheer tedium. Nevertheless, it is so. Again and again I have noticed the abandonment, temporary or permanent, of this mighty and thrilling enterprise from simple lack of interest. And I imagine that, in practically all cases save those in which an exceptional original force of will renders the enterprise scarcely necessary, the interest in it will languish unless it is regularly nourished from without. Now, the interest in it cannot be nourished from without by means of conversation with other brain-tamers. There are certain things which may not be discussed by sanely organised people; and this is one. The affair is too intimate, and it is also too moral. Even after only a few minutes' vocalisation on this subject a deadly infection seems to creep into the air—the infection of priggishness. (Or am I mistaken, and do I fancy this horror? No; I cannot believe that I am mistaken.)

Hence the nourishment must be obtained by reading; a little reading every day. I suppose there are some thousands of authors who have written with more or less sincerity on the management of the human machine. But the two which, for me, stand out easily above all the rest are Marcus Aurelius Antoninus and Epictetus. Not much has been discovered since their time. 'The perfecting of life is a power residing in the soul,' wrote Marcus Aurelius in the ninth book of *To Himself*, over seventeen hundred years ago. Marcus Aurelius is assuredly regarded as the greatest of writers in the human machine school, and not to read him daily is considered by many to be a bad habit. As a confession his work stands alone. But as a practical 'Bradshaw' of existence, I would put the discourses of Epictetus before M. Aurelius. Epictetus is grosser; he will call you a blockhead as soon as look at you; he is witty, he is even humorous, and he never wanders far away from the incidents of daily life. He is brimming over with actuality for readers of the year 1908. He was a freed slave. M. Aurelius was an emperor, and he had the morbidity from which all emperors must suffer. A finer soul than Epictetus, he is not, in my view, so useful a companion. Not all of us can breathe freely in his atmosphere. Nevertheless, he is of course to be read, and re-read continually. When you have gone through Epictetus—a single page or paragraph per day, well masticated and digested, suffices—you can go through M. Aurelius, and then you can return to Epictetus, and so on, morning by morning, or night by night, till your life's end. And they will conserve your interest in yourself.

In the matter of concentration, I hesitate to recommend Mrs. Annie Besant's *Thought Power*, and yet I should be possibly unjust if I did not recommend it, having regard to its immense influence on myself. It is not one of the best books of this astounding woman. It is addressed to theosophists, and can only be completely understood in the light of theosophistic doctrines. (To grasp it all I found myself obliged to study a much larger work dealing with theosophy as a whole.) It contains an appreciable quantity of what strikes me as feeble sentimentalism, and also a lot of sheer dogma. But it is the least unsatisfactory manual of the brain that I have met with. And if the profane reader ignores all that is either Greek or twaddle to him, there will yet remain for his advantage a vast amount of very sound information and advice. All these three books are cheap.

XIV
A MAN AND HIS ENVIRONMENT

I now come to an entirely different aspect of the whole subject. Hitherto I have dealt with the human machine as a contrivance for adapting the man to his environment. My aim has been to show how much depends on the machine and how little depends on the environment, and that the essential business of the machine is to utilise, for making the stuff of life, the particular environment in which it happens to find itself—and no other! All this, however, does not imply that one must accept, fatalistically and permanently and passively, any preposterous environment into which destiny has chanced to throw us. If we carry far enough the discipline of our brains, we can, no doubt, arrive at surprisingly good results in no matter what environment. But it would not be 'right reason' to expend an excessive amount of will-power on brain-discipline when a slighter effort in a different direction would produce consequences more felicitous. A man whom fate had pitched into a canal might accomplish miracles in the way of rendering himself amphibian; he might stagger the world by the spectacle of his philosophy under amazing difficulties; people might pay sixpence a head to come and see him; but he would be less of a nincompoop if he climbed out and arranged to live definitely on the bank.

The advantage of an adequate study of the control of the machine, such as I have outlined, is that it enables the student to judge, with some certainty, whether the unsatisfactoriness of his life is caused by a disordered machine or by an environment for which the machine is, in its fundamental construction, unsuitable. It does help him to decide justly whether, in the case of a grave difference between them, he, or the rest of the universe, is in the wrong. And also, if he decides that he is not in the wrong, it helps him to choose a new environment, or to modify the old, upon some scientific principle. The vast majority of people never know, with any precision, why they are dissatisfied with their sojourn on this planet. They make long and fatiguing excursions in search of precious materials which all the while are concealed in their own breasts. They don't know what they want; they only know that they want something. Or, if they contrive to settle in their own minds what they do want, a hundred to one the obtaining of it will leave them just as far off contentment as they were at the beginning! This is a matter of daily observation: that people are frantically engaged in attempting to get hold of things which, by universal experience, are hideously disappointing to those who have obtained possession of them. And still the struggle goes on, and probably will go on. All because brains are lying idle! 'It is no trifle that is at stake,' said Epictetus as to the question of control of instinct by reason. '*It means, Are you in your senses or are you not?*' In this significance, indubitably the vast majority of people are not in their senses; otherwise they would not behave as they do, so vaguely, so happy-go-luckily, so blindly. But the man whose brain is in working order emphatically *is* in his senses.

And when a man, by means of the efficiency of his brain, has put his reason in definite command over his instincts, he at once sees things in a truer perspective than was before possible, and therefore he is able to set a just value upon the various parts which go to make up his environment. If, for instance, he lives in London, and is aware of constant friction, he will be led to examine the claims of London as a Mecca for intelligent persons. He may say to himself: 'There is something wrong, and the seat of trouble is not in the machine. London compels me to tolerate dirt, darkness, ugliness, strain, tedious daily journeyings, and general expensiveness. What does London give me in exchange?' And he may decide that, as London offers him nothing special in exchange except the glamour of London and an occasional seat at a good concert or a bad play, he may get a better return for his expenditure of brains, nerves, and money in the provinces. He may perceive, with a certain French novelist, that 'most people of truly distinguished mind prefer the provinces.' And he may then actually, in obedience to reason, quit the deceptions of London with a tranquil heart, sure of his diagnosis. Whereas a man who had not devoted much time to the care of his mental machinery could not screw himself up to the step, partly from lack of resolution, and partly because he had never examined the sources of his unhappiness. A man who, not having full control of his machine, is consistently dissatisfied with his existence, is like a man who is being secretly poisoned and cannot decide with what or by whom. And so he has no middle course between absolute starvation and a continuance of poisoning.

As with the environment of place, so with the environment of individuals. Most friction between individuals is avoidable friction; sometimes, however, friction springs from such deep causes that no skill in the machine can do away with it. But how is the man whose brain is not in command of his existence to judge whether the unpleasantness can be cured or not, whether it arises in himself or in the other? He simply cannot judge. Whereas a man who keeps his brain for use and not for idle amusement will, when he sees that friction persists in spite of his brain, be so clearly impressed by the advisability of separation as the sole cure that he will steel himself to the effort necessary for a separation. One of the chief advantages of an efficient brain is that an efficient brain is capable of acting with firmness and resolution, partly, of course, because it has been toned up, but more because its operations are not confused by the interference of mere instincts.

Thirdly, there is the environment of one's general purpose in life, which is, I feel convinced, far more often hopelessly wrong and futile than either the environment of situation or the environment of individuals. I will be bold enough to say that quite seventy per cent. of ambition is never realised at all, and that ninety-nine per cent. of all realised ambition is fruitless. In other words, that a gigantic sacrifice of the present to the future is always going on. And here again the utility of brain-discipline is most strikingly shown. A man whose first business it is every day to concentrate his mind on the proper performance of that particular day, must necessarily conserve his interest in the present. It is impossible that his perspective should become so warped that he will devote, say, fifty-five years of his career to problematical preparations for his comfort and his glory during the final ten years. A man whose brain is his servant, and not his lady-help or his pet dog, will be in receipt of such daily content and satisfaction that he will early ask himself the question: 'As for this ambition that is eating away my hours, what will it give me that I have not already got?' Further, the steady development of interest in the hobby (call it!) of common-sense daily living will act as an automatic test of any ambition. If an ambition survives and flourishes on the top of that daily cultivation of the machine, then the owner of the ambition may be sure that it is a genuine and an invincible ambition, and he may pursue it in full faith; his developed care for the present will prevent him from making his ambition an altar on which the whole of the present is to be offered up.

I shall be told that I want to do away with ambition, and that ambition is the great motive-power of existence, and that therefore I am an enemy of society and the truth is not in me. But I do not want to do away with ambition. What I say is that current ambitions usually result in disappointment, that they usually mean the complete distortion of a life. This is an incontestable fact, and the reason of it is that ambitions are chosen either without knowledge of their real value or without knowledge of what they will cost. A disciplined brain will at once show the unnecessariness of most ambitions, and will ensure that the remainder shall be conducted with reason. It will also convince its possessor that the ambition to live strictly according to the highest common sense during the next twenty-four hours is an ambition that needs a lot of beating.

Anybody who really wishes to talk simple truth about money at the present time is confronted by a very serious practical difficulty. He must put himself in opposition to the overwhelming body of public opinion, and resign himself to being regarded either as a *poseur*, a crank, or a fool. The public is in search of happiness now, as it was a million years ago. Money is not the principal factor in happiness. It may be argued whether, as a factor in happiness, money is of twentieth-rate importance or fiftieth-rate importance. But it cannot be argued whether money, in point of fact, does or does not of itself bring happiness. There can be no doubt whatever that money does not bring happiness. Yet, in face of this incontrovertible and universal truth, the whole public behaves exactly as if money were the sole or the principal preliminary to happiness. The public does not reason, and it will not listen to reason; its blood is up in the money-hunt, and the philosopher might as well expostulate with an earthquake as try to take that public by the button-hole and explain. If a man sacrifices his interest under the will of some dead social tyrant in order to marry whom he wishes, if an English minister of religion declines twenty-five thousand dollars a year to go into exile and preach to New York millionaires, the phenomenon is genuinely held to be so astounding that it at once flies right round the world in the form of exclamatory newspaper articles! In an age when such an attitude towards money is sincere, it is positively dangerous—I doubt if it may not be harmful—to persist with loud obstinacy that money, instead of being the greatest, is the least thing in the world. In times of high military excitement a man may be ostracised if not lynched for uttering opinions which everybody will accept as truisms a couple of years later, and thus the wise philosopher holds his tongue—lest it should be cut out. So at the zenith of a period when the possession of money in absurd masses is an infallible means to the general respect, I have no intention either of preaching or of practising quite all that I privately in the matter of riches.

It was not always thus. Though there have been previous ages as lustful for wealth and ostentation as our own, there have also been ages when money-getting and millionaire-envying were not the sole preoccupations of the average man. And such an age will undoubtedly succeed to ours. Few things would surprise me less, in social life, than the upspringing of some anti-luxury movement, the formation of some league or guild among the middling classes (where alone intellect is to be found in quantity), the members of which would bind themselves to stand aloof from all the great, silly, banal, ugly, and tedious *luxe*-activities of the time and not to spend more than a certain sum per annum on eating, drinking, covering their bodies, and being moved about like parcels from one spot of the earth's surface to another. Such a movement would, and will, help towards the formation of an opinion which would condemn lavish expenditure on personal satisfactions as bad form. However, the shareholders of grand hotels, restaurants, and race-courses of all sorts, together with popular singers and barristers, etc., need feel no immediate alarm. The movement is not yet.

As touching the effect of money on the efficient ordering of the human machine, there is happily no necessity to inform those who have begun to interest themselves in the conduct of their own brains that money counts for very little in that paramount affair. Nothing that really helps towards perfection costs more than is within the means of every person who reads these pages. The expenses connected with daily meditation, with the building-up of mental habits, with the practice of self-control and of cheerfulness, with the enthronement of reason over the rabble of primeval instincts—these expenses are really, you know, trifling. And whether you get that well-deserved rise of a pound a week or whether you don't, you may anyhow go ahead with the machine; it isn't a motor-car, though I started by comparing it to one. And even when, having to a certain extent mastered, through sensible management of the machine, the art of achieving a daily content and dignity, you come to the embroidery of life—even the best embroidery of life is not absolutely ruinous. Meat may go up in price—it has done—but books won't. Admission to picture galleries and concerts and so forth will remain quite low. The views from Richmond Hill or Hindhead, or along Pall Mall at sunset, the smell of the earth, the taste of fruit and of kisses—these things are unaffected by the machinations of trusts and the hysteria of stock exchanges. Travel, which after books is the finest of all embroideries (and which is not to be valued by the mile but by the quality), is decidedly cheaper than ever it was. All that is required is ingenuity in one's expenditure. And much ingenuity with a little money is vastly more profitable and amusing than much money without ingenuity.

And all the while as you read this you are saying, with your impatient sneer: 'It's all very well; it's all very fine talking, *but* ...' In brief, you are not convinced. You cannot deracinate that wide-rooted dogma within your soul that more money means more joy. I regret it. But let me put one question, and let me ask you to answer it honestly. Your financial means are greater now than they used to be. Are you happier or less discontented than you used to be? Taking your existence day by day, hour by hour, judging it by the mysterious *feel* (in the chest) of responsibilities, worries, positive joys and satisfactions, are you genuinely happier than you used to be?

I do not wish to be misunderstood. The financial question cannot be ignored. If it is true that money does not bring happiness, it is no less true that the lack of money induces a state of affairs in which efficient living becomes doubly difficult. These two propositions, superficially perhaps self-contradictory, are not really so. A modest income suffices for the fullest realisation of the Ego in terms of content and dignity; but you must live within it. You cannot righteously ignore money. A man, for instance, who cultivates himself and instructs a family of daughters in everything except the ability to earn their own livelihood, and then has the impudence to die suddenly without leaving a penny—that man is a scoundrel. Ninety—or should I say ninety-nine?—per cent. of all those anxieties which render proper living almost impossible are caused by the habit of walking on the edge of one's income as one might walk on the edge of a precipice. The majority of Englishmen have some financial worry or other continually, everlastingly at the back of their minds. The sacrifice necessary to abolish this condition of things is more apparent than real. All spending is a matter of habit.

Speaking generally, a man can contrive, out of an extremely modest income, to have all that he needs—unless he needs the esteem of snobs. Habit may, and habit usually does, make it just as difficult to keep a family on two thousand a year as on two hundred. I suppose that for the majority of men the suspension of income for a single month would mean either bankruptcy, the usurer, or acute inconvenience. Impossible, under such circumstances, to be in full and independent possession of one's immortal soul! Hence I should be inclined to say that the first preliminary to a proper control of the machine is the habit of spending decidedly less than one earns or receives. The veriest automaton of a clerk ought to have the wherewithal of a whole year as a shield against the caprices of his employer. It would be as reasonable to expect the inhabitants of an unfortified city in the midst of a plain occupied by a hostile army to apply themselves successfully to the study of logarithms or metaphysics, as to expect a man without a year's income in his safe to apply himself successfully to the true art of living.

And the whole secret of relative freedom from financial anxiety lies not in income, but in expenditure. I am ashamed to utter this antique platitude. But, like most aphorisms of unassailable wisdom, it is completely ignored. You say, of course, that it is not easy to leave a margin between your expenditure and your present income. I know it. I fraternally shake your hand. Still it is, in most cases, far easier to lessen one's expenditure than to increase one's income without increasing one's expenditure. The alternative is before you. However you decide, be assured that the foundation of philosophy is a margin, and that the margin can always be had.

XVI
REASON, REASON!

In conclusion, I must insist upon several results of what I may call the 'intensive culture' of the reason. The brain will not only grow more effectively powerful in the departments of life where the brain is supposed specially to work, but it will also enlarge the circle of its activities. It will assuredly interfere in everything. The student of himself must necessarily conduct his existence more and more according to the views of his brain. This will be most salutary and agreeable both for himself and for the rest of the world. You object. You say it will be a pity when mankind refers everything to reason. You talk about the heart. You envisage an entirely reasonable existence as a harsh and callous existence. Not so. When the reason and the heart come into conflict the heart is invariably wrong. I do not say that the reason is always entirely right, but I do say that it is always less wrong than the heart. The empire of the reason is not universal, but within its empire reason is supreme, and if other forces challenge it on its own soil they must take the consequences. Nearly always, when the heart opposes the brain, the heart is merely a pretty name which we give to our idleness and our egotism.

We pass along the Strand and see a respectable young widow standing in the gutter, with a baby in her arms and a couple of boxes of matches in one hand. We know she is a widow because of her weeds, and we know she is respectable by her clothes. We know she is not begging because she is selling matches. The sight of her in the gutter pains our heart. Our heart weeps and gives the woman a penny in exchange for a halfpenny box of matches, and the pain of our heart is thereby assuaged. Our heart has performed a good action. But later on our reason (unfortunately asleep at the moment) wakes up and says: 'That baby was hired; the weeds and matches merely a dodge. The whole affair was a spectacle got up to extract money from a fool like you. It is as mechanical as a penny in the slot. Instead of relieving distress you have simply helped to perpetuate an infamous system. You ought to know that you can't do good in that offhand way.' The heart gives pennies in the street. The brain runs the Charity Organisation Society. Of course, to give pennies in the street is much less trouble than to run the C.O.S. As a method of producing a quick, inexpensive, and pleasing effect on one's egotism the C.O.S. is simply not in it with this dodge of giving pennies at random, without inquiry. Only— which of the two devices ought to be accused of harshness and callousness? Which of them is truly kind? I bring forward the respectable young widow as a sample case of the Heart v. Brain conflict. All other cases are the same. The brain is always more kind than the heart; the brain is always more willing than the heart to put itself to a great deal of trouble for a very little reward; the brain always does the difficult, unselfish thing, and the heart always does the facile, showy thing. Naturally the result of the brain's activity on society is always more advantageous than the result of the heart's activity.

Another point. I have tried to show that, if the reason is put in command of the feelings, it is impossible to assume an attitude of blame towards any person whatsoever for any act whatsoever. The habit of blaming must depart absolutely. It is no argument against this statement that it involves anarchy and the demolition of society. Even if it did (which emphatically it does not), that would not affect its truth. All great truths have been assailed on the ground that to accept them meant the end of everything. As if that mattered! As I make no claim to be the discoverer of this truth I have no hesitation in announcing it to be one of the most important truths that the world has yet to learn. However, the real reason why many people object to this truth is not because they think it involves the utter demolition of society (fear of the utter demolition of society never stopped any one from doing or believing anything, and never will), but because they say to themselves that if they can't blame they can't praise. And they do so like praising! If they are so desperately fond of praising, it is a pity that they don't praise a little more! There can be no doubt that the average man blames much more than he praises. His instinct is to blame. If he is satisfied he says nothing; if he is not, he most illogically kicks up a row. So that even if the suppression of blame involved the suppression of praise the change would certainly be a change for the better. But I can perceive no reason why the suppression of blame should involve the suppression of praise. On the contrary, I think that the habit of praising should be fostered. (I do not suggest the occasional use of trowels, but the regular use of salt-spoons.) Anyhow, the triumph of the brain over the natural instincts (in an ideally organised man the brain and the natural instincts will never have even a tiff) always means the ultimate triumph of kindness.

And, further, the culture of the brain, the constant disciplinary exercise of the reasoning faculty, means the diminution of misdeeds. (Do not imagine I am hinting that you are on the verge of murdering your wife or breaking into your neighbour's house. Although you personally are guiltless, there is a good deal of sin still committed in your immediate vicinity.) Said Balzac in *La Cousine Bette*, 'A crime is in the first instance a defect of reasoning powers.' In the appreciation of this truth, Marcus Aurelius was, as usual, a bit beforehand with Balzac. M. Aurelius said, 'No soul wilfully misses truth.' And Epictetus had come to the same conclusion before M. Aurelius, and Plato before Epictetus. All wrong-doing is done in the sincere belief that it is the best thing to do. Whatever sin a man does he does either for his own benefit or for the benefit of society. At the moment of doing it he is convinced that it is the only thing to do. He is mistaken. And he is mistaken because his brain has been unequal to the task of reasoning the matter out. Passion (the heart) is responsible for all crimes. Indeed, crime is simply a convenient monosyllable which we apply to what happens when the brain and the heart come into conflict and the brain is defeated. That transaction of the matches was a crime, you know.

Lastly, the culture of the brain must result in the habit of originally examining all the phenomena of life and conduct, to see what they really are, and to what they lead. The heart hates progress, because the dear old thing always wants to do as has always been done. The heart is convinced that custom is a virtue. The heart of the dirty working man rebels when the State insists that he shall be clean, for no other reason than that it is his custom to be dirty. Useless to tell his heart that, clean, he will live longer! He has been dirty and he will be. The brain alone is the enemy of prejudice and precedent, which alone are the enemies of progress. And this habit of originally examining phenomena is perhaps the greatest factor that goes to the making of personal dignity; for it fosters reliance on one's self and courage to accept the consequences of the act of reasoning. Reason is the basis of personal dignity.

I finish. I have said nothing of the modifications which the constant use of the brain will bring about in the *general value of existence*. Modifications slow and subtle, but tremendous! The persevering will discover them. It will happen to the persevering that their whole lives are changed—texture and colour, too! Naught will happen to those who do not persevere.

The Old Wives' Tale

BOOK I
MRS. BAINES
CHAPTER I
THE SQUARE
I

Those two girls, Constance and Sophia Baines, paid no heed to the manifold interest of their situation, of which, indeed, they had never been conscious. They were, for example, established almost precisely on the fifty-third parallel of latitude. A little way to the north of them, in the creases of a hill famous for its religious orgies, rose the river Trent, the calm and characteristic stream of middle England. Somewhat further northwards, in the near neighbourhood of the highest public-house in the realm, rose two lesser rivers, the Dane and the Dove, which, quarrelling in early infancy, turned their backs on each other, and, the one by favour of the Weaver and the other by favour of the Trent, watered between them the whole width of England, and poured themselves respectively into the Irish Sea and the German Ocean. What a county of modest, unnoticed rivers! What a natural, simple county, content to fix its boundaries by these tortuous island brooks, with their comfortable names—Trent, Mease, Dove, Tern, Dane, Mees, Stour, Tame, and even hasty Severn! Not that the Severn is suitable to the county! In the county excess is deprecated. The county is happy in not exciting remark. It is content that Shropshire should possess that swollen bump, the Wrekin, and that the exaggerated wildness of the Peak should lie over its border. It does not desire to be a pancake like Cheshire. It has everything that England has, including thirty miles of Watling Street; and England can show nothing more beautiful and nothing uglier than the works of nature and the works of man to be seen within the limits of the county. It is England in little, lost in the midst of England, unsung by searchers after the extreme; perhaps occasionally somewhat sore at this neglect, but how proud in the instinctive cognizance of its representative features and traits!

Constance and Sophia, busy with the intense preoccupations of youth, recked not of such matters. They were surrounded by the county. On every side the fields and moors of Staffordshire, intersected by roads and lanes, railways, watercourses and telegraph-lines, patterned by hedges, ornamented and made respectable by halls and genteel parks, enlivened by villages at the intersections, and warmly surveyed by the sun, spread out undulating. And trains were rushing round curves in deep cuttings, and carts and waggons trotting and jingling on the yellow roads, and long, narrow boats passing in a leisure majestic and infinite over the surface of the stolid canals; the rivers had only themselves to support, for Staffordshire rivers have remained virgin of keels to this day. One could imagine the messages concerning prices, sudden death, and horses, in their flight through the wires under the feet of birds. In the inns Utopians were shouting the universe into order over beer, and in the halls and parks the dignity of England was being preserved in a fitting manner. The villages were full of women who did nothing but fight against dirt and hunger, and repair the effects of friction on clothes. Thousands of labourers were in the fields, but the fields were so broad and numerous that this scattered multitude was totally lost therein. The cuckoo was much more perceptible than man, dominating whole square miles with his resounding call. And on the airy moors heath-larks played in the ineffaceable mule-tracks that had served centuries before even the Romans thought of Watling Street. In short, the usual daily life of the county was proceeding with all its immense variety and importance; but though Constance and Sophia were in it they were not of it.

The fact is, that while in the county they were also in the district; and no person who lives in the district, even if he should be old and have nothing to do but reflect upon things in general, ever thinks about the county. So far as the county goes, the district might almost as well be in the middle of the Sahara. It ignores the county, save that it uses it nonchalantly sometimes as leg-stretcher on holiday afternoons, as a man may use his back garden. It has nothing in common with the county; it is richly sufficient to itself. Nevertheless, its self-sufficiency and the true salt savour of its life can only be appreciated by picturing it hemmed in by county. It lies on the face of the county like an insignificant stain, like a dark Pleiades in a green and empty sky. And

Hanbridge has the shape of a horse and its rider, Bursley of half a donkey, Knype of a pair of trousers, Longshaw of an octopus, and little Turnhill of a beetle. The Five Towns seem to cling together for safety. Yet the idea of clinging together for safety would make them laugh. They are unique and indispensable. From the north of the county right down to the south they alone stand for civilization, applied science, organized manufacture, and the century—until you come to Wolverhampton. They are unique and indispensable because you cannot drink tea out of a teacup without the aid of the Five Towns; because you cannot eat a meal in decency without the aid of the Five Towns. For this the architecture of the Five Towns is an architecture of ovens and chimneys; for this its atmosphere is as black as its mud; for this it burns and smokes all night, so that Longshaw has been compared to hell; for this it is unlearned in the ways of agriculture, never having seen corn except as packing straw and in quartern loaves; for this, on the other hand, it comprehends the mysterious habits of fire and pure, sterile earth; for this it lives crammed together in slippery streets where the housewife must change white window-curtains at least once a fortnight if she wishes to remain respectable; for this it gets up in the mass at six a.m., winter and summer, and goes to bed when the public-houses close; for this it exists—that you may drink tea out of a teacup and toy with a chop on a plate. All the everyday crockery used in the kingdom is made in the Five Towns—all, and much besides. A district capable of such gigantic manufacture, of such a perfect monopoly—and which finds energy also to produce coal and iron and great men—may be an insignificant stain on a county, considered geographically, but it is surely well justified in treating the county as its back garden once a week, and in blindly ignoring it the rest of the time.

Even the majestic thought that whenever and wherever in all England a woman washes up, she washes up the product of the district; that whenever and wherever in all England a plate is broken the fracture means new business for the district—even this majestic thought had probably never occurred to either of the girls. The fact is, that while in the Five Towns they were also in the Square, Bursley and the Square ignored the staple manufacture as perfectly as the district ignored the county. Bursley has the honours of antiquity in the Five Towns. No industrial development can ever rob it of its superiority in age, which makes it absolutely sure in its conceit. And the time will never come when the other towns—let them swell and bluster as they may—will not pronounce the name of Bursley as one pronounces the name of one's mother. Add to this that the Square was the centre of Bursley's retail trade (which scorned the staple as something wholesale, vulgar, and assuredly filthy), and you will comprehend the importance and the self-isolation of the Square in the scheme of the created universe. There you have it, embedded in the district, and the district embedded in the county, and the county lost and dreaming in the heart of England!

The Square was named after St. Luke. The Evangelist might have been startled by certain phenomena in his square, but, except in Wakes Week, when the shocking always happened, St. Luke's Square lived in a manner passably saintly—though it contained five public-houses. It contained five public-houses, a bank, a barber's, a confectioner's, three grocers', two chemists', an ironmonger's, a clothier's, and five drapers'. These were all the catalogue. St. Luke's Square had no room for minor establishments. The aristocracy of the Square undoubtedly consisted of the drapers (for the bank was impersonal); and among the five the shop of Baines stood supreme. No business establishment could possibly be more respected than that of Mr. Baines was respected. And though John Baines had been bedridden for a dozen years, he still lived on the lips of admiring, ceremonious burgesses as 'our honoured fellow-townsman.' He deserved his reputation.

The Baines's shop, to make which three dwellings had at intervals been thrown into one, lay at the bottom of the Square. It formed about one-third of the south side of the Square, the remainder being made up of Critchlow's (chemist), the clothier's, and the Hanover Spirit Vaults. ("Vaults" was a favourite synonym of the public-house in the Square. Only two of the public-houses were crude public-houses: the rest were "vaults.") It was a composite building of three storeys, in blackish-crimson brick, with a projecting shop-front and, above and behind that, two rows of little windows. On the sash of each window was a red cloth roll stuffed with sawdust, to prevent draughts; plain white blinds descended about six inches from the top of each window. There were no curtains to any of the windows save one; this was the window of the drawing-room, on the first floor at the corner of the Square and King Street. Another window, on the second storey, was peculiar, in that it had neither blind nor pad, and was very dirty; this was the window of an unused room that had a separate staircase to itself, the staircase being barred by a door always locked. Constance and Sophia had lived in continual expectation of the abnormal issuing from that mysterious room, which was next to their own. But they were disappointed. The room had no shameful secret except the incompetence of the architect who had made one house out of three; it was just an empty, unemployable room. The building had also a considerable frontage on King Street, where, behind the shop, was sheltered the parlour, with a large window and a door that led directly by two steps into the street. A strange peculiarity of the shop was that it bore no signboard.

45

Once it had had a large signboard which a memorable gale had blown into the Square. Mr. Baines had decided not to replace it. He had always objected to what he called "puffing," and for this reason would never hear of such a thing as a clearance sale. The hatred of "puffing" grew on him until he came to regard even a sign as "puffing." Uninformed persons who wished to find Baines's must ask and learn. For Mr. Baines, to have replaced the sign would have been to condone, yea, to participate in, the modern craze for unscrupulous self-advertisement. This abstention of Mr. Baines's from indulgence in signboards was somehow accepted by the more thoughtful members of the community as evidence that the height of Mr. Baines's principles was greater even than they had imagined.

Constance and Sophia were the daughters of this credit to human nature.

He had no other children.

II

They pressed their noses against the window of the show-room, and gazed down into the Square as perpendicularly as the projecting front of the shop would allow. The show-room was over the millinery and silken half of the shop. Over the woollen and shirting half were the drawing-room and the chief bedroom. When in quest of articles of coquetry, you mounted from the shop by a curving stair, and your head gradually rose level with a large apartment having a mahogany counter in front of the window and along one side, yellow linoleum on the floor, many cardboard boxes, a magnificent hinged cheval glass, and two chairs. The window-sill being lower than the counter, there was a gulf between the panes and the back of the counter, into which important articles such as scissors, pencils, chalk, and artificial flowers were continually disappearing: another proof of the architect's incompetence.

The girls could only press their noses against the window by kneeling on the counter, and this they were doing. Constance's nose was snub, but agreeably so. Sophia had a fine Roman nose; she was a beautiful creature, beautiful and handsome at the same time. They were both of them rather like racehorses, quivering with delicate, sensitive, and luxuriant life; exquisite, enchanting proof of the circulation of the blood; innocent, artful, roguish, prim, gushing, ignorant, and miraculously wise. Their ages were sixteen and fifteen; it is an epoch when, if one is frank, one must admit that one has nothing to learn: one has learnt simply everything in the previous six months.

"There she goes!" exclaimed Sophia.

Up the Square, from the corner of King Street, passed a woman in a new bonnet with pink strings, and a new blue dress that sloped at the shoulders and grew to a vast circumference at the hem. Through the silent sunlit solitude of the Square (for it was Thursday afternoon, and all the shops shut except the confectioner's and one chemist's) this bonnet and this dress floated northwards in search of romance, under the relentless eyes of Constance and Sophia. Within them, somewhere, was the soul of Maggie, domestic servant at Baines's. Maggie had been at the shop since before the creation of Constance and Sophia. She lived seventeen hours of each day in an underground kitchen and larder, and the other seven in an attic, never going out except to chapel on Sunday evenings, and once a month on Thursday afternoons. "Followers" were most strictly forbidden to her; but on rare occasions an aunt from Longshaw was permitted as a tremendous favour to see her in the subterranean den. Everybody, including herself, considered that she had a good "place," and was well treated. It was undeniable, for instance, that she was allowed to fall in love exactly as she chose, provided she did not "carry on" in the kitchen or the yard. And as a fact, Maggie had fallen in love. In seventeen years she had been engaged eleven times. No one could conceive how that ugly and powerful organism could softly languish to the undoing of even a butty-collier, nor why, having caught a man in her sweet toils, she could ever be imbecile enough to set him free. There are, however, mysteries in the souls of Maggies. The drudge had probably been affianced oftener than any woman in Bursley. Her employers were so accustomed to an interesting announcement that for years they had taken to saying naught in reply but 'Really, Maggie!' Engagements and tragic partings were Maggie's pastime. Fixed otherwise, she might have studied the piano instead.

"No gloves, of course!" Sophia criticized.

"Well, you can't expect her to have gloves," said Constance.

Then a pause, as the bonnet and dress neared the top of the Square.

"Supposing she turns round and sees us?" Constance suggested.

"I don't care if she does," said Sophia, with a haughtiness almost impassioned; and her head trembled slightly.

There were, as usual, several loafers at the top of the Square, in the corner between the bank and the "Marquis of Granby." And one of these loafers stepped forward and shook hands with an obviously willing Maggie. Clearly it was a rendezvous, open, unashamed. The twelfth victim had been selected by the virgin of forty, whose kiss would not have melted lard! The couple disappeared together down Oldcastle Street.

"WELL!" cried Constance. "Did you ever see such a thing?"

While Sophia, short of adequate words, flushed and bit her lip.

With the profound, instinctive cruelty of youth, Constance and Sophia had assembled in their favourite haunt, the show-room, expressly to deride Maggie in her new clothes. They obscurely thought that a woman so ugly and soiled as Maggie was had no right to possess new clothes. Even her desire to take the air of a Thursday afternoon seemed to them unnatural and somewhat reprehensible. Why should she want to stir out of her kitchen? As for her tender yearnings, they positively grudged these to Maggie. That Maggie should give rein to chaste passion was more than grotesque; it was offensive and wicked. But let it not for an instant be doubted that they were nice, kind-hearted, well-behaved, and delightful girls! Because they were. They were not angels.

"It's too ridiculous!" said Sophia, severely. She had youth, beauty, and rank in her favour. And to her it really was ridiculous.

"Poor old Maggie!" Constance murmured. Constance was foolishly good-natured, a perfect manufactory of excuses for other people; and her benevolence was eternally rising up and overpowering her reason.

"What time did mother say she should be back?" Sophia asked.

"Not until supper."

"Oh! Hallelujah!" Sophia burst out, clasping her hands in joy. And they both slid down from the counter just as if they had been little boys, and not, as their mother called them, "great girls."

"Let's go and play the Osborne quadrilles," Sophia suggested (the Osborne quadrilles being a series of dances arranged to be performed on drawing-room pianos by four jewelled hands).

"I couldn't think of it," said Constance, with a precocious gesture of seriousness. In that gesture, and in her tone, was something which conveyed to Sophia: "Sophia, how can you be so utterly blind to the gravity of our fleeting existence as to ask me to go and strum the piano with you?" Yet a moment before she had been a little boy.

"Why not?" Sophia demanded.

"I shall never have another chance like to-day for getting on with this," said Constance, picking up a bag from the counter.

She sat down and took from the bag a piece of loosely woven canvas, on which she was embroidering a bunch of roses in coloured wools. The canvas had once been stretched on a frame, but now, as the delicate labour of the petals and leaves was done, and nothing remained to do but the monotonous background, Constance was content to pin the stuff to her knee. With the long needle and several skeins of mustard-tinted wool, she bent over the canvas and resumed the filling-in of the tiny squares. The whole design was in squares—the gradations of red and greens, the curves of the smallest buds—all was contrived in squares, with a result that mimicked a fragment of uncompromising Axminster carpet. Still, the fine texture of the wool, the regular and rapid grace of those fingers moving incessantly at back and front of the canvas, the gentle sound of the wool as it passed through the holes, and the intent, youthful earnestness of that lowered gaze, excused and invested with charm an activity which, on artistic grounds, could not possibly be justified. The canvas was destined to adorn a gilt firescreen in the drawing-room, and also to form a birthday gift to Mrs. Baines from her elder daughter. But whether the enterprise was as secret from Mrs. Baines as Constance hoped, none save Mrs. Baines knew.

"Con," murmured Sophia, "you're too sickening sometimes."

"Well," said Constance, blandly, "it's no use pretending that this hasn't got to be finished before we go back to school, because it has." Sophia wandered about, a prey ripe for the Evil One. "Oh," she exclaimed joyously—even ecstatically—looking behind the cheval glass, "here's mother's new skirt! Miss Dunn's been putting the gimp on it! Oh, mother, what a proud thing you will be!" Constance heard swishings behind the glass. "What are you doing, Sophia?"

"Nothing."

"You surely aren't putting that skirt on?"

"Why not?"

"You'll catch it finely, I can tell you!"

Without further defence, Sophia sprang out from behind the immense glass. She had already shed a notable part of her own costume, and the flush of mischief was in her face. She ran across to the other side of the room and examined carefully a large coloured print that was affixed to the wall.

This print represented fifteen sisters, all of the same height and slimness of figure, all of the same age—about twenty-five or so, and all with exactly the same haughty and bored beauty. That they were in truth sisters was clear from the facial resemblance between them; their demeanour indicated that they were princesses, offspring of some impossibly prolific king and queen. Those hands had never toiled, nor had those features ever relaxed from the smile of courts. The princesses moved in a landscape of marble steps and verandahs, with a bandstand and strange trees in the distance. One was in a riding-habit, another in evening attire, another dressed for tea, another for the theatre; another seemed to be ready to go to bed. One held a little girl by the hand; it could not have been her own little girl, for these princesses were far beyond human passions. Where had she obtained the little girl? Why was one sister going to the theatre, another to tea, another to the stable, and another to bed? Why was one in a heavy mantle, and another sheltering from the sun's rays under a parasol? The picture was drenched in mystery, and the strangest thing about it was that all these highnesses were apparently content with the most ridiculous and out-moded fashions. Absurd hats, with veils flying behind; absurd bonnets, fitting close to the head, and spotted; absurd coiffures that nearly lay on the nape; absurd, clumsy sleeves; absurd waists, almost above the elbow's level; absurd scolloped jackets! And the skirts! What a sight were those skirts! They were nothing but vast decorated pyramids; on the summit of each was stuck the upper half of a princess. It was astounding that princesses should consent to be so preposterous and so uncomfortable. But Sophia perceived nothing uncanny in the picture, which bore the legend: "Newest summer fashions from Paris. Gratis supplement to Myra's Journal." Sophia had never imagined anything more stylish, lovely, and dashing than the raiment of the fifteen princesses.

For Constance and Sophia had the disadvantage of living in the middle ages. The crinoline had not quite reached its full circumference, and the dress-improver had not even been thought of. In all the Five Towns there was not a public bath, nor a free library, nor a municipal park, nor a telephone, nor yet a board-school. People had not understood the vital necessity of going away to the seaside every year. Bishop Colenso had just staggered Christianity by his shameless notions on the Pentateuch. Half Lancashire was starving on account of the American war. Garroting was the chief amusement of the homicidal classes. Incredible as it may appear, there was nothing but a horse-tram running between Bursley and Hanbridge—and that only twice an hour; and between the other towns no stage of any kind! One went to Longshaw as one now goes to Pekin. It was an era so dark and backward that one might wonder how people could sleep in their beds at night for thinking about their sad state.

Happily the inhabitants of the Five Towns in that era were passably pleased with themselves, and they never even suspected that they were not quite modern and quite awake. They thought that the intellectual, the industrial, and the social movements had gone about as far as these movements could go, and they were amazed at their own progress. Instead of being humble and ashamed, they actually showed pride in their pitiful achievements. They ought to have looked forward meekly to the prodigious feats of posterity; but, having too little faith and too much conceit, they were content to look behind and make comparisons with the past. They did not foresee the miraculous generation which is us. A poor, blind, complacent people! The ludicrous horse-car was typical of them. The driver rang a huge bell, five minutes before starting, that could be heard from the Wesleyan Chapel to the Cock Yard, and then after deliberations and hesitations the vehicle rolled off on its rails into unknown dangers while passengers shouted good-bye. At Bleakridge it had to stop for the turnpike, and it was assisted up the mountains of Leveson Place and Sutherland Street (towards Hanbridge) by a third horse, on whose back was perched a tiny, whip-cracking boy; that boy lived like a shuttle on the road between Leveson Place and Sutherland Street, and even in wet weather he was the envy of all other boys. After half an hour's perilous transit the car drew up solemnly in a narrow street by the Signal office in Hanbridge, and the ruddy driver, having revolved many times the polished iron handle of his sole brake, turned his attention to his passengers in calm triumph, dismissing them with a sort of unsung doxology. And this was regarded as the last word of traction! A whip-cracking boy on a tip horse! Oh, blind, blind! You could not foresee the hundred and twenty electric cars that now rush madly bumping and thundering at twenty miles an hour through all the main streets of the district!

So that naturally Sophia, infected with the pride of her period, had no misgivings whatever concerning the final elegance of the princesses. She studied them as the fifteen apostles of the ne plus ultra; then, having taken some flowers and plumes out of a box, amid warnings from Constance, she retreated behind the glass, and presently emerged as a great lady in the style of the princesses. Her mother's tremendous new gown ballooned about her in all its fantastic richness and expensiveness. And with the gown she had put on her mother's importance—that mien of assured authority, of capacity tested in many a crisis, which characterized Mrs. Baines, and which Mrs. Baines seemed to impart to her dresses even before she had regularly worn them. For it was a fact that Mrs. Baines's empty garments inspired respect, as though some essence had escaped from her and remained in them.

"Sophia!"

Constance stayed her needle, and, without lifting her head, gazed, with eyes raised from the wool-work, motionless at the posturing figure of her sister. It was sacrilege that she was witnessing, a prodigious irreverence. She was conscious of an expectation that punishment would instantly fall on this daring, impious child. But she, who never felt these mad, amazing impulses, could nevertheless only smile fearfully. "Sophia!" she breathed, with an intensity of alarm that merged into condoning admiration. "Whatever will you do next?"

Sophia's lovely flushed face crowned the extraordinary structure like a blossom, scarcely controlling its laughter. She was as tall as her mother, and as imperious, as crested, and proud; and in spite of the pigtail, the girlish semi-circular comb, and the loose foal-like limbs, she could support as well as her mother the majesty of the gimp-embroidered dress. Her eyes sparkled with all the challenges of the untried virgin as she minced about the showroom. Abounding life inspired her movements. The confident and fierce joy of youth shone on her brow. "What thing on earth equals me?" she seemed to demand with enchanting and yet ruthless arrogance. She was the daughter of a respected, bedridden draper in an insignificant town, lost in the central labyrinth of England, if you like; yet what manner of man, confronted with her, would or could have denied her naive claim to dominion? She stood, in her mother's hoops, for the desire of the world. And in the innocence of her soul she knew it! The heart of a young girl mysteriously speaks and tells her of her power long ere she can use her power. If she can find nothing else to subdue, you may catch her in the early years subduing a gate-post or drawing homage from an empty chair. Sophia's experimental victim was Constance, with suspended needle and soft glance that shot out from the lowered face.

Then Sophia fell, in stepping backwards; the pyramid was overbalanced; great distended rings of silk trembled and swayed gigantically on the floor, and Sophia's small feet lay like the feet of a doll on the rim of the largest circle, which curved and arched above them like a cavern's mouth. The abrupt transition of her features from assured pride to ludicrous astonishment and alarm was comical enough to have sent into wild uncharitable laughter any creature less humane than Constance. But Constance sprang to her, a single embodied instinct of benevolence, with her snub nose, and tried to raise her.

"Oh, Sophia!" she cried compassionately—that voice seemed not to know the tones of reproof—"I do hope you've not messed it, because mother would be so—"

The words were interrupted by the sound of groans beyond the door leading to the bedrooms. The groans, indicating direst physical torment, grew louder. The two girls stared, wonder-struck and afraid, at the door, Sophia with her dark head raised, and Constance with her arms round Sophia's waist. The door opened, letting in a much-magnified sound of groans, and there entered a youngish, undersized man, who was frantically clutching his head in his hands and contorting all the muscles of his face. On perceiving the sculptural group of two prone, interlocked girls, one enveloped in a crinoline, and the other with a wool-work bunch of flowers pinned to her knee, he jumped back, ceased groaning, arranged his face, and seriously tried to pretend that it was not he who had been vocal in anguish, that, indeed, he was just passing as a casual, ordinary wayfarer through the showroom to the shop below. He blushed darkly; and the girls also blushed.

"Oh, I beg pardon, I'm sure!" said this youngish man suddenly; and with a swift turn he disappeared whence he had come.

He was Mr. Povey, a person universally esteemed, both within and without the shop, the surrogate of bedridden Mr. Baines, the unfailing comfort and stand-by of Mrs. Baines, the fount and radiating centre of order and discipline in the shop; a quiet, diffident, secretive, tedious, and obstinate youngish man, absolutely faithful, absolutely efficient in his sphere; without brilliance, without distinction; perhaps rather little-minded, certainly narrow-minded; but what a force in the shop! The shop was inconceivable without Mr. Povey. He was under twenty and not out of his apprenticeship when Mr. Baines had been struck down, and he had at once proved his worth. Of the assistants, he alone slept in the house. His bedroom was next to that of his employer; there was a door between the two chambers, and the two steps led down from the larger to the less. The girls regained their feet, Sophia with Constance's help. It was not easy to right a capsized crinoline. They both began to laugh nervously, with a trace of hysteria.

"I thought he'd gone to the dentist's," whispered Constance.

Mr. Povey's toothache had been causing anxiety in the microcosm for two days, and it had been clearly understood at dinner that Thursday morning that Mr. Povey was to set forth to Oulsnam Bros., the dentists at Hillport, without any delay. Only on Thursdays and Sundays did Mr. Povey dine with the family. On other days he dined later, by himself, but at the family table, when Mrs. Baines or one of the assistants could "relieve" him in the shop. Before starting out to visit her elder sister at Axe, Mrs. Baines had insisted to Mr. Povey that he had eaten practically nothing but "slops" for twenty-four hours, and that if he was not careful she would have him on her hands. He had replied in his quietest, most sagacious, matter-of-fact tone—the tone that carried weight with all who heard it—that he had only been waiting for Thursday afternoon, and should of course go instantly to Oulsnams' and have the thing attended to in a proper manner. He had even added that persons who put off going to the dentist's were simply sowing trouble for themselves.

None could possibly have guessed that Mr. Povey was afraid of going to the dentist's. But such was the case. He had not dared to set forth. The paragon of commonsense, pictured by most people as being somehow unliable to human frailties, could not yet screw himself up to the point of ringing a dentist's door-bell.

"He did look funny," said Sophia. "I wonder what he thought. I couldn't help laughing!"

Constance made no answer; but when Sophia had resumed her own clothes, and it was ascertained beyond doubt that the new dress had not suffered, and Constance herself was calmly stitching again, she said, poising her needle as she had poised it to watch Sophia:

"I was just wondering whether something oughtn't to be done for Mr. Povey."

"What?" Sophia demanded.

"Has he gone back to his bedroom?"

"Let's go and listen," said Sophia the adventuress.

They went, through the showroom door, past the foot of the stairs leading to the second storey, down the long corridor broken in the middle by two steps and carpeted with a narrow bordered carpet whose parallel lines increased its apparent length. They went on tiptoe, sticking close to one another. Mr. Povey's door was slightly ajar. They listened; not a sound.

"Mr. Povey!" Constance coughed discreetly.

No reply. It was Sophia who pushed the door open. Constance made an elderly prim plucking gesture at Sophia's bare arm, but she followed Sophia gingerly into the forbidden room, which was, however, empty. The bed had been ruffled, and on it lay a book, "The Harvest of a Quiet Eye."

"Harvest of a quiet tooth!" Sophia whispered, giggling very low.

"Hsh!" Constance put her lips forward.

From the next room came a regular, muffled, oratorical sound, as though some one had begun many years ago to address a meeting and had forgotten to leave off and never would leave off. They were familiar with the sound, and they quitted Mr. Povey's chamber in fear of disturbing it. At the same moment Mr. Povey reappeared, this time in the drawing-room doorway at the other extremity of the long corridor. He seemed to be trying ineffectually to flee from his tooth as a murderer tries to flee from his conscience.

"Oh, Mr. Povey!" said Constance quickly—for he had surprised them coming out of his bedroom; "we were just looking for you."

"To see if we could do anything for you," Sophia added.

"Oh no, thanks!" said Mr. Povey.

Then he began to come down the corridor, slowly.

"You haven't been to the dentist's," said Constance sympathetically.

"No, I haven't," said Mr. Povey, as if Constance was indicating a fact which had escaped his attention. "The truth is, I thought it looked like rain, and if I'd got wet—you see—"

Miserable Mr. Povey!

"Yes," said Constance, "you certainly ought to keep out of draughts. Don't you think it would be a good thing if you went and sat in the parlour? There's a fire there."

"I shall be all right, thank you," said Mr. Povey. And after a pause:

"Well, thanks, I will."

III

50

The girls made way for him to pass them at the head of the twisting stairs which led down to the parlour. Constance followed, and Sophia followed Constance.

"Have father's chair," said Constance.

There were two rocking-chairs with fluted backs covered by antimacassars, one on either side of the hearth. That to the left was still entitled "father's chair," though its owner had not sat in it since long before the Crimean war, and would never sit in it again.

"I think I'd sooner have the other one," said Mr. Povey, "because it's on the right side, you see." And he touched his right cheek.

Having taken Mrs. Baines's chair, he bent his face down to the fire, seeking comfort from its warmth. Sophia poked the fire, whereupon Mr. Povey abruptly withdrew his face. He then felt something light on his shoulders. Constance had taken the antimacassar from the back of the chair, and protected him with it from the draughts. He did not instantly rebel, and therefore was permanently barred from rebellion. He was entrapped by the antimacassar. It formally constituted him an invalid, and Constance and Sophia his nurses. Constance drew the curtain across the street door. No draught could come from the window, for the window was not 'made to open.' The age of ventilation had not arrived. Sophia shut the other two doors. And, each near a door, the girls gazed at Mr. Povey behind his back, irresolute, but filled with a delicious sense of responsibility.

The situation was on a different plane now. The seriousness of Mr. Povey's toothache, which became more and more manifest, had already wiped out the ludicrous memory of the encounter in the showroom. Looking at these two big girls, with their short-sleeved black frocks and black aprons, and their smooth hair, and their composed serious faces, one would have judged them incapable of the least lapse from an archangelic primness; Sophia especially presented a marvellous imitation of saintly innocence. As for the toothache, its action on Mr. Povey was apparently periodic; it gathered to a crisis like a wave, gradually, the torture increasing till the wave broke and left Mr. Povey exhausted, but free for a moment from pain. These crises recurred about once a minute. And now, accustomed to the presence of the young virgins, and having tacitly acknowledged by his acceptance of the antimacassar that his state was abnormal, he gave himself up frankly to affliction. He concealed nothing of his agony, which was fully displayed by sudden contortions of his frame, and frantic oscillations of the rocking-chair. Presently, as he lay back enfeebled in the wash of a spent wave, he murmured with a sick man's voice:

"I suppose you haven't got any laudanum?"

The girls started into life. "Laudanum, Mr. Povey?"

"Yes, to hold in my mouth."

He sat up, tense; another wave was forming. The excellent fellow was lost to all self-respect, all decency.

"There's sure to be some in mother's cupboard," said Sophia.

Constance, who bore Mrs. Baines's bunch of keys at her girdle, a solemn trust, moved a little fearfully to a corner cupboard which was hung in the angle to the right of the projecting fireplace, over a shelf on which stood a large copper tea-urn. That corner cupboard, of oak inlaid with maple and ebony in a simple border pattern, was typical of the room. It was of a piece with the deep green "flock" wall paper, and the tea-urn, and the rocking-chairs with their antimacassars, and the harmonium in rosewood with a Chinese paper-mache tea-caddy on the top of it; even with the carpet, certainly the most curious parlour carpet that ever was, being made of lengths of the stair-carpet sewn together side by side. That corner cupboard was already old in service; it had held the medicines of generations. It gleamed darkly with the grave and genuine polish which comes from ancient use alone. The key which Constance chose from her bunch was like the cupboard, smooth and shining with years; it fitted and turned very easily, yet with a firm snap. The single wide door opened sedately as a portal.

The girls examined the sacred interior, which had the air of being inhabited by an army of diminutive prisoners, each crying aloud with the full strength of its label to be set free on a mission.

"There it is!" said Sophia eagerly.

And there it was: a blue bottle, with a saffron label, "Caution.

POISON. Laudanum. Charles Critchlow, M.P.S. Dispensing Chemist. St.

Luke's Square, Bursley."

Those large capitals frightened the girls. Constance took the bottle as she might have taken a loaded revolver, and she glanced at Sophia. Their omnipotent, all-wise mother was not present to tell them what to do. They, who had never decided, had to decide now. And Constance was the elder. Must this fearsome stuff, whose very name was a name of fear, be introduced in spite of printed warnings into Mr. Povey's mouth? The responsibility was terrifying.

"Perhaps I'd just better ask Mr. Critchlow," Constance faltered.

The expectation of beneficent laudanum had enlivened Mr. Povey, had already, indeed, by a sort of suggestion, half cured his toothache.

"Oh no!" he said. "No need to ask Mr. Critchlow … Two or three drops in a little water." He showed impatience to be at the laudanum.

The girls knew that an antipathy existed between the chemist and Mr. Povey.

"It's sure to be all right," said Sophia. "I'll get the water."

With youthful cries and alarms they succeeded in pouring four mortal dark drops (one more than Constance intended) into a cup containing a little water. And as they handed the cup to Mr. Povey their faces were the faces of affrighted comical conspirators. They felt so old and they looked so young.

Mr. Povey imbibed eagerly of the potion, put the cup on the mantelpiece, and then tilted his head to the right so as to submerge the affected tooth. In this posture he remained, awaiting the sweet influence of the remedy. The girls, out of a nice modesty, turned away, for Mr. Povey must not swallow the medicine, and they preferred to leave him unhampered in the solution of a delicate problem. When next they examined him, he was leaning back in the rocking-chair with his mouth open and his eyes shut.

"Has it done you any good, Mr. Povey?"

"I think I'll lie down on the sofa for a minute," was Mr. Povey's strange reply; and forthwith he sprang up and flung himself on to the horse-hair sofa between the fireplace and the window, where he lay stripped of all his dignity, a mere beaten animal in a grey suit with peculiar coat-tails, and a very creased waistcoat, and a lapel that was planted with pins, and a paper collar and close-fitting paper cuffs.

Constance ran after him with the antimacassar, which she spread softly on his shoulders; and Sophia put another one over his thin little legs, all drawn up.

They then gazed at their handiwork, with secret self-accusations and the most dreadful misgivings.

"He surely never swallowed it!" Constance whispered.

"He's asleep, anyhow," said Sophia, more loudly.

Mr. Povey was certainly asleep, and his mouth was very wide open—like a shop-door. The only question was whether his sleep was not an eternal sleep; the only question was whether he was not out of his pain for ever. Then he snored—horribly; his snore seemed a portent of disaster.

Sophia approached him as though he were a bomb, and stared, growing bolder, into his mouth.

"Oh, Con," she summoned her sister, "do come and look! It's too droll!"

In an instant all their four eyes were exploring the singular landscape of Mr. Povey's mouth. In a corner, to the right of that interior, was one sizeable fragment of a tooth, that was attached to Mr. Povey by the slenderest tie, so that at each respiration of Mr. Povey, when his body slightly heaved and the gale moaned in the cavern, this tooth moved separately, showing that its long connection with Mr. Povey was drawing to a close.

"That's the one," said Sophia, pointing. "And it's as loose as anything. Did you ever see such a funny thing?"

The extreme funniness of the thing had lulled in Sophia the fear of Mr. Povey's sudden death.

"I'll see how much he's taken," said Constance, preoccupied, going to the mantelpiece.

"Why, I do believe—" Sophia began, and then stopped, glancing at the sewing-machine, which stood next to the sofa.

It was a Howe sewing-machine. It had a little tool-drawer, and in the tool-drawer was a small pair of pliers. Constance, engaged in sniffing at the lees of the potion in order to estimate its probable deadliness, heard the well-known click of the little tool-drawer, and then she saw Sophia nearing Mr. Povey's mouth with the pliers.

"Sophia!" she exclaimed, aghast. "What in the name of goodness are you doing?"

"Nothing," said Sophia.

The next instant Mr. Povey sprang up out of his laudanum dream.

"It jumps!" he muttered; and, after a reflective pause, "but it's much better." He had at any rate escaped death. Sophia's right hand was behind her back.

Just then a hawker passed down King Street, crying mussels and cockles.

"Oh!" Sophia almost shrieked. "Do let's have mussels and cockles for tea!" And she rushed to the door, and unlocked and opened it, regardless of the risk of draughts to Mr. Povey.

In those days people often depended upon the caprices of hawkers for the tastiness of their teas; but it was an adventurous age, when errant knights of commerce were numerous and enterprising. You went on to your doorstep, caught your meal as it passed, withdrew, cooked it and ate it, quite in the manner of the early Briton. Constance was obliged to join her sister on the top step. Sophia descended to the second step.

"Fresh mussels and cockles all alive oh!" bawled the hawker, looking across the road in the April breeze. He was the celebrated Hollins, a professional Irish drunkard, aged in iniquity, who cheerfully saluted magistrates in the street, and referred to the workhouse, which he occasionally visited, as the Bastile.

Sophia was trembling from head to foot.

"What ARE you laughing at, you silly thing?" Constance demanded.

Sophia surreptitiously showed the pliers, which she had partly thrust into her pocket. Between their points was a most perceptible, and even recognizable, fragment of Mr. Povey.

This was the crown of Sophia's career as a perpetrator of the unutterable.

"What!" Constance's face showed the final contortions of that horrified incredulity which is forced to believe. Sophia nudged her violently to remind her that they were in the street, and also quite close to Mr. Povey.

"Now, my little missies," said the vile Hollins. "Three pence a pint, and how's your honoured mother to-day? Yes, fresh, so help me God!"

CHAPTER II

THE TOOTH
I

The two girls came up the unlighted stone staircase which led from Maggie's cave to the door of the parlour. Sophia, foremost, was carrying a large tray, and Constance a small one. Constance, who had nothing on her tray but a teapot, a bowl of steaming and balmy-scented mussels and cockles, and a plate of hot buttered toast, went directly into the parlour on the left. Sophia had in her arms the entire material and apparatus of a high tea for two, including eggs, jam, and toast (covered with the slop-basin turned upside down), but not including mussels and cockles. She turned to the right, passed along the corridor by the cutting-out room, up two steps into the sheeted and shuttered gloom of the closed shop, up the showroom stairs, through the showroom, and so into the bedroom corridor. Experience had proved it easier to make this long detour than to round the difficult corner of the parlour stairs with a large loaded tray. Sophia knocked with the edge of the tray at the door of the principal bedroom. The muffled oratorical sound from within suddenly ceased, and the door was opened by a very tall, very thin, black-bearded man, who looked down at Sophia as if to demand what she meant by such an interruption.

"I've brought the tea, Mr. Critchlow," said Sophia.

And Mr. Critchlow carefully accepted the tray.

"Is that my little Sophia?" asked a faint voice from the depths of the bedroom.

"Yes, father," said Sophia.

But she did not attempt to enter the room. Mr. Critchlow put the tray on a white-clad chest of drawers near the door, and then he shut the door, with no ceremony. Mr. Critchlow was John Baines's oldest and closest friend, though decidedly younger than the draper. He frequently "popped in" to have a word with the invalid; but Thursday afternoon was his special afternoon, consecrated by him to the service of the sick. From two o'clock precisely till eight o'clock precisely he took charge of John Baines, reigning autocratically over the bedroom. It was known that he would not tolerate invasions, nor even ambassadorial visits. No! He gave up his weekly holiday to this business of friendship, and he must be allowed to conduct the business in his own way. Mrs. Baines herself avoided disturbing Mr. Critchlow's ministrations on her husband. She was glad to do so; for Mr. Baines was never to be left alone under any circumstances, and the convenience of being able to rely upon the presence of a staid member of the Pharmaceutical Society for six hours of a given day every week outweighed the slight affront to her prerogatives as wife and house-mistress. Mr. Critchlow was an extremely peculiar man, but when he was in the bedroom she could leave the house with an easy mind. Moreover, John Baines enjoyed these Thursday afternoons. For him, there was 'none like Charles Critchlow.' The two old friends experienced a sort of grim, desiccated happiness, cooped up together in the bedroom, secure from women and fools generally. How they spent the time did not seem to be certainly known, but the impression was that politics occupied them. Undoubtedly Mr. Critchlow was an extremely peculiar man. He was a man of habits. He must always have the same things for his tea. Black-currant jam, for instance. (He called it "preserve.") The idea of offering Mr. Critchlow a tea which did not comprise black-currant jam was inconceivable by the intelligence of St. Luke's Square. Thus for years past, in the fruit-preserving season, when all the house and all the shop smelt richly of fruit boiling in sugar, Mrs. Baines had filled an extra number of jars with black-currant jam, 'because Mr. Critchlow wouldn't TOUCH any other sort.'

So Sophia, faced with the shut door of the bedroom, went down to the parlour by the shorter route. She knew that on going up again, after tea, she would find the devastated tray on the doormat.

Constance was helping Mr. Povey to mussels and cockles. And Mr. Povey still wore one of the antimacassars. It must have stuck to his shoulders when he sprang up from the sofa, woollen antimacassars being notoriously parasitic things. Sophia sat down, somewhat self-consciously. The serious Constance was also perturbed. Mr. Povey did not usually take tea in the house on Thursday afternoons; his practice was to go out into the great, mysterious world. Never before had he shared a meal with the girls alone. The situation was indubitably unexpected, unforeseen; it was, too, piquant, and what added to its piquancy was the fact that Constance and Sophia were, somehow, responsible for Mr. Povey. They felt that they were responsible for him. They had offered the practical sympathy of two intelligent and well-trained young women, born nurses by reason of their sex, and Mr. Povey had accepted; he was now on their hands. Sophia's monstrous, sly operation in Mr. Povey's mouth did not cause either of them much alarm, Constance having apparently recovered from the first shock of it. They had discussed it in the kitchen while preparing the teas; Constance's extraordinarily severe and dictatorial tone in condemning it had led to a certain heat. But the success of the impudent wrench justified it despite any irrefutable argument to the contrary. Mr. Povey was better already, and he evidently remained in ignorance of his loss.

"Have some?" Constance asked of Sophia, with a large spoon hovering over the bowl of shells.

"Yes, PLEASE," said Sophia, positively.

Constance well knew that she would have some, and had only asked from sheer nervousness.

"Pass your plate, then."

Now when everybody was served with mussels, cockles, tea, and toast, and Mr. Povey had been persuaded to cut the crust off his toast, and Constance had, quite unnecessarily, warned Sophia against the deadly green stuff in the mussels, and Constance had further pointed out that the evenings were getting longer, and Mr. Povey had agreed that they were, there remained nothing to say. An irksome silence fell on them all, and no one could lift it off. Tiny clashes of shell and crockery sounded with the terrible clearness of noises heard in the night. Each person avoided the eyes of the others. And both Constance and Sophia kept straightening their bodies at intervals, and expanding their chests, and then looking at their plates; occasionally a prim cough was discharged. It was a sad example of the difference between young women's dreams of social brilliance and the reality of life. These girls got more and more girlish, until, from being women at the administering of laudanum, they sank back to about eight years of age—perfect children—at the tea-table.

The tension was snapped by Mr. Povey. "My God!" he muttered, moved by a startling discovery to this impious and disgraceful oath (he, the pattern and exemplar—and in the presence of innocent girlhood too!). "I've swallowed it!"

"Swallowed what, Mr. Povey?" Constance inquired.

The tip of Mr. Povey's tongue made a careful voyage of inspection all round the right side of his mouth.

"Oh yes!" he said, as if solemnly accepting the inevitable. "I've swallowed it!"

Sophia's face was now scarlet; she seemed to be looking for some place to hide it. Constance could not think of anything to say.

"That tooth has been loose for two years," said Mr. Povey, "and now
I've swallowed it with a mussel."

"Oh, Mr. Povey!" Constance cried in confusion, and added, "There's one good thing, it can't hurt you any more now."

"Oh!" said Mr. Povey. "It wasn't THAT tooth that was hurting me. It's an old stump at the back that's upset me so this last day or two. I wish it had been."

Sophia had her teacup close to her red face. At these words of Mr. Povey her cheeks seemed to fill out like plump apples. She dashed the cup into its saucer, spilling tea recklessly, and then ran from the room with stifled snorts.

"Sophia!" Constance protested.

"I must just——" Sophia incoherently spluttered in the doorway. "I shall be all right. Don't——"

Constance, who had risen, sat down again.

II

Sophia fled along the passage leading to the shop and took refuge in the cutting-out room, a room which the astonishing architect had devised upon what must have been a backyard of one of the three constituent houses. It was lighted from its roof, and only a wooden partition, eight feet high, separated it from the passage. Here Sophia gave rein to her feelings; she laughed and cried together, weeping generously into her handkerchief and wildly giggling, in a hysteria which she could not control. The spectacle of Mr. Povey mourning for a tooth which he thought he had swallowed, but which in fact lay all the time in her pocket, seemed to her to be by far the most ridiculous, side-splitting thing that had ever happened or could happen on earth. It utterly overcame her. And when she fancied that she had exhausted and conquered its surpassing ridiculousness, this ridiculousness seized her again and rolled her anew in depths of mad, trembling laughter.

Gradually she grew calmer. She heard the parlour door open, and Constance descend the kitchen steps with a rattling tray of tea-things. Tea, then, was finished, without her! Constance did not remain in the kitchen, because the cups and saucers were left for Maggie to wash up as a fitting coda to Maggie's monthly holiday. The parlour door closed. And the vision of Mr. Povey in his antimacassar swept Sophia off into another convulsion of laughter and tears. Upon this the parlour door opened again, and Sophia choked herself into silence while Constance hastened along the passage. In a minute Constance returned with her woolwork, which she had got from the showroom, and the parlour received her. Not the least curiosity on the part of Constance as to what had become of Sophia!

At length Sophia, a faint meditative smile being all that was left of the storm in her, ascended slowly to the showroom, through the shop. Nothing there of interest! Thence she wandered towards the drawing-room, and encountered Mr. Critchlow's tray on the mat. She picked it up and carried it by way of the showroom and shop down to the kitchen, where she dreamily munched two pieces of toast that had cooled to the consistency of leather. She mounted the stone steps and listened at the door of the parlour. No sound! This seclusion of Mr. Povey and Constance was really very strange. She roved right round the house, and descended creepingly by the twisted house-stairs, and listened intently at the other door of the parlour. She now detected a faint regular snore. Mr. Povey, a prey to laudanum and mussels, was sleeping while Constance worked at her fire-screen! It was now in the highest degree odd, this seclusion of Mr. Povey and Constance; unlike anything in Sophia's experience! She wanted to go into the parlour, but she could not bring herself to do so. She crept away again, forlorn and puzzled, and next discovered herself in the bedroom which she shared with Constance at the top of the house; she lay down in the dusk on the bed and began to read "The Days of Bruce;" but she read only with her eyes.

Later, she heard movements on the house-stairs, and the familiar whining creak of the door at the foot thereof. She skipped lightly to the door of the bedroom.

"Good-night, Mr. Povey. I hope you'll be able to sleep."

Constance's voice!

"It will probably come on again."

Mr. Povey's voice, pessimistic!

Then the shutting of doors. It was almost dark. She went back to the bed, expecting a visit from Constance. But a clock struck eight, and all the various phenomena connected with the departure of Mr. Critchlow occurred one after another. At the same time Maggie came home from the land of romance. Then long silences! Constance was now immured with her father, it being her "turn" to nurse; Maggie was washing up in her cave, and Mr. Povey was lost to sight in his bedroom. Then Sophia heard her mother's lively, commanding knock on the King Street door. Dusk had definitely yielded to black night in the bedroom. Sophia dozed and dreamed. When she awoke, her ear caught the sound of knocking. She jumped up, tiptoed to the landing, and looked over the balustrade, whence she had a view of all the first-floor corridor. The gas had been lighted; through the round aperture at the top of the porcelain globe she could see the wavering flame. It was her mother, still bonneted, who was knocking at the door of Mr. Povey's room. Constance stood in the doorway of her parents' room. Mrs. Baines knocked twice with an interval, and then said to Constance, in a resonant whisper that vibrated up the corridor——

55

"He seems to be fast asleep. I'd better not disturb him."

"But suppose he wants something in the night?"

"Well, child, I should hear him moving. Sleep's the best thing for him."

Mrs. Baines left Mr. Povey to the effects of laudanum, and came along the corridor. She was a stout woman, all black stuff and gold chain, and her skirt more than filled the width of the corridor. Sophia watched her habitual heavy mounting gesture as she climbed the two steps that gave variety to the corridor. At the gas-jet she paused, and, putting her hand to the tap, gazed up into the globe.

"Where's Sophia?" she demanded, her eyes fixed on the gas as she lowered the flame.

"I think she must be in bed, mother," said Constance, nonchalantly.

The returned mistress was point by point resuming knowledge and control of that complicated machine—her household.

Then Constance and her mother disappeared into the bedroom, and the door was shut with a gentle, decisive bang that to the silent watcher on the floor above seemed to create a special excluding intimacy round about the figures of Constance and her father and mother. The watcher wondered, with a little prick of jealousy, what they would be discussing in the large bedroom, her father's beard wagging feebly and his long arms on the counterpane, Constance perched at the foot of the bed, and her mother walking to and fro, putting her cameo brooch on the dressing-table or stretching creases out of her gloves. Certainly, in some subtle way, Constance had a standing with her parents which was more confidential than Sophia's.

III

When Constance came to bed, half an hour later, Sophia was already in bed. The room was fairly spacious. It had been the girls' retreat and fortress since their earliest years. Its features seemed to them as natural and unalterable as the features of a cave to a cave-dweller. It had been repapered twice in their lives, and each papering stood out in their memories like an epoch; a third epoch was due to the replacing of a drugget by a resplendent old carpet degraded from the drawing-room. There was only one bed, the bedstead being of painted iron; they never interfered with each other in that bed, sleeping with a detachment as perfect as if they had slept on opposite sides of St. Luke's Square; yet if Constance had one night lain down on the half near the window instead of on the half near the door, the secret nature of the universe would have seemed to be altered. The small fire-grate was filled with a mass of shavings of silver paper; now the rare illnesses which they had suffered were recalled chiefly as periods when that silver paper was crammed into a large slipper-case which hung by the mantelpiece, and a fire of coals unnaturally reigned in its place—the silver paper was part of the order of the world. The sash of the window would not work quite properly, owing to a slight subsidence in the wall, and even when the window was fastened there was always a narrow slit to the left hand between the window and its frame; through this slit came draughts, and thus very keen frosts were remembered by the nights when Mrs. Baines caused the sash to be forced and kept at its full height by means of wedges—the slit of exposure was part of the order of the world.

They possessed only one bed, one washstand, and one dressing-table; but in some other respects they were rather fortunate girls, for they had two mahogany wardrobes; this mutual independence as regards wardrobes was due partly to Mrs. Baines's strong commonsense, and partly to their father's tendency to spoil them a little. They had, moreover, a chest of drawers with a curved front, of which structure Constance occupied two short drawers and one long one, and Sophia two long drawers. On it stood two fancy work-boxes, in which each sister kept jewellery, a savings-bank book, and other treasures, and these boxes were absolutely sacred to their respective owners. They were different, but one was not more magnificent than the other. Indeed, a rigid equality was the rule in the chamber, the single exception being that behind the door were three hooks, of which Constance commanded two.

"Well," Sophia began, when Constance appeared. "How's darling Mr. Povey?" She was lying on her back, and smiling at her two hands, which she held up in front of her.

"Asleep," said Constance. "At least mother thinks so. She says sleep is the best thing for him."

"'It will probably come on again,'" said Sophia.

"What's that you say?" Constance asked, undressing.

"'It will probably come on again.'"

These words were a quotation from the utterances of darling Mr. Povey on the stairs, and Sophia delivered them with an exact imitation of Mr. Povey's vocal mannerism.

56

"Sophia," said Constance, firmly, approaching the bed, "I wish you wouldn't be so silly!" She had benevolently ignored the satirical note in Sophia's first remark, but a strong instinct in her rose up and objected to further derision. "Surely you've done enough for one day!" she added.

For answer Sophia exploded into violent laughter, which she made no attempt to control. She laughed too long and too freely while Constance stared at her.

"*I* don't know what's come over you!" said Constance.

"It's only because I can't look at it without simply going off into fits!" Sophia gasped out. And she held up a tiny object in her left hand.

Constance started, flushing. "You don't mean to say you've kept it!" she protested earnestly. "How horrid you are, Sophia! Give it me at once and let me throw it away. I never heard of such doings. Now give it me!"

"No," Sophia objected, still laughing. "I wouldn't part with it for worlds. It's too lovely."

She had laughed away all her secret resentment against Constance for having ignored her during the whole evening and for being on such intimate terms with their parents. And she was ready to be candidly jolly with Constance.

"Give it me," said Constance, doggedly.

Sophia hid her hand under the clothes. "You can have his old stump, when it comes out, if you like. But not this. What a pity it's the wrong one!"

"Sophia, I'm ashamed of you! Give it me."

Then it was that Sophia first perceived Constance's extreme seriousness. She was surprised and a little intimidated by it. For the expression of Constance's face, usually so benign and calm, was harsh, almost fierce. However, Sophia had a great deal of what is called "spirit," and not even ferocity on the face of mild Constance could intimidate her for more than a few seconds. Her gaiety expired and her teeth were hidden.

"I've said nothing to mother——" Constance proceeded.

"I should hope you haven't," Sophia put in tersely.

"But I certainly shall if you don't throw that away," Constance finished.

"You can say what you like," Sophia retorted, adding contemptuously a term of opprobrium which has long since passed out of use: "Cant!"

"Will you give it me or won't you?"

"No!"

It was a battle suddenly engaged in the bedroom. The atmosphere had altered completely with the swiftness of magic. The beauty of Sophia, the angelic tenderness of Constance, and the youthful, naive, innocent charm of both of them, were transformed into something sinister and cruel. Sophia lay back on the pillow amid her dark-brown hair, and gazed with relentless defiance into the angry eyes of Constance, who stood threatening by the bed. They could hear the gas singing over the dressing-table, and their hearts beating the blood wildly in their veins. They ceased to be young without growing old; the eternal had leapt up in them from its sleep. Constance walked away from the bed to the dressing-table and began to loose her hair and brush it, holding back her head, shaking it, and bending forward, in the changeless gesture of that rite. She was so disturbed that she had unconsciously reversed the customary order of the toilette. After a moment Sophia slipped out of bed and, stepping with her bare feet to the chest of drawers, opened her work-box and deposited the fragment of Mr. Povey therein; she dropped the lid with an uncompromising bang, as if to say, "We shall see if I am to be trod upon, miss!" Their eyes met again in the looking-glass. Then Sophia got back into bed.

Five minutes later, when her hair was quite finished, Constance knelt down and said her prayers. Having said her prayers, she went straight to Sophia's work-box, opened it, seized the fragment of Mr. Povey, ran to the window, and frantically pushed the fragment through the slit into the Square.

"There!" she exclaimed nervously.

She had accomplished this inconceivable transgression of the code of honour, beyond all undoing, before Sophia could recover from the stupefaction of seeing her sacred work-box impudently violated. In a single moment one of Sophia's chief ideals had been smashed utterly, and that by the sweetest, gentlest creature she had ever known. It was a revealing experience for Sophia—and also for Constance. And it frightened them equally. Sophia, staring at the text, "Thou God seest me," framed in straw over the chest of drawers, did not stir. She was defeated, and so profoundly moved in her defeat that she did not even reflect upon the obvious inefficacy of illuminated texts as a deterrent from evil-doing. Not that she eared a fig for the fragment of Mr. Povey! It was the moral aspect of the affair, and the astounding, inexplicable development in Constance's character, that staggered her into silent acceptance of the inevitable.

Constance, trembling, took pains to finish undressing with dignified deliberation. Sophia's behaviour under the blow seemed too good to be true; but it gave her courage. At length she turned out the gas and lay down by Sophia. And there was a little shuffling, and then stillness for a while.

"And if you want to know," said Constance in a tone that mingled amicableness with righteousness, "mother's decided with Aunt Harriet that we are BOTH to leave school next term."

CHAPTER III

A BATTLE
I

The day sanctioned by custom in the Five Towns for the making of pastry is Saturday. But Mrs. Baines made her pastry on Friday, because Saturday afternoon was, of course, a busy time in the shop. It is true that Mrs. Baines made her pastry in the morning, and that Saturday morning in the shop was scarcely different from any other morning. Nevertheless, Mrs. Baines made her pastry on Friday morning instead of Saturday morning because Saturday afternoon was a busy time in the shop. She was thus free to do her marketing without breath-taking flurry on Saturday morning.

On the morning after Sophia's first essay in dentistry, therefore, Mrs. Baines was making her pastry in the underground kitchen. This kitchen, Maggie's cavern-home, had the mystery of a church, and on dark days it had the mystery of a crypt. The stone steps leading down to it from the level of earth were quite unlighted. You felt for them with the feet of faith, and when you arrived in the kitchen, the kitchen, by contrast, seemed luminous and gay; the architect may have considered and intended this effect of the staircase. The kitchen saw day through a wide, shallow window whose top touched the ceiling and whose bottom had been out of the girls' reach until long after they had begun to go to school. Its panes were small, and about half of them were of the "knot" kind, through which no object could be distinguished; the other half were of a later date, and stood for the march of civilization. The view from the window consisted of the vast plate-glass windows of the newly built Sun vaults, and of passing legs and skirts. A strong wire grating prevented any excess of illumination, and also protected the glass from the caprices of wayfarers in King Street. Boys had a habit of stopping to kick with their full strength at the grating.

Forget-me-nots on a brown field ornamented the walls of the kitchen. Its ceiling was irregular and grimy, and a beam ran across it; in this beam were two hooks; from these hooks had once depended the ropes of a swing, much used by Constance and Sophia in the old days before they were grown up. A large range stood out from the wall between the stairs and the window. The rest of the furniture comprised a table—against the wall opposite the range—a cupboard, and two Windsor chairs. Opposite the foot of the steps was a doorway, without a door, leading to two larders, dimmer even than the kitchen, vague retreats made visible by whitewash, where bowls of milk, dishes of cold bones, and remainders of fruit-pies, reposed on stillages; in the corner nearest the kitchen was a great steen in which the bread was kept. Another doorway on the other side of the kitchen led to the first coal-cellar, where was also the slopstone and tap, and thence a tunnel took you to the second coal-cellar, where coke and ashes were stored; the tunnel proceeded to a distant, infinitesimal yard, and from the yard, by ways behind Mr. Critchlow's shop, you could finally emerge, astonished, upon Brougham Street. The sense of the vast-obscure of those regions which began at the top of the kitchen steps and ended in black corners of larders or abruptly in the common dailiness of Brougham Street, a sense which Constance and Sophia had acquired in infancy, remained with them almost unimpaired as they grew old.

Mrs. Baines wore black alpaca, shielded by a white apron whose string drew attention to the amplitude of her waist. Her sleeves were turned up, and her hands, as far as the knuckles, covered with damp flour. Her ageless smooth paste-board occupied a corner of the table, and near it were her paste-roller, butter, some pie-dishes, shredded apples, sugar, and other things. Those rosy hands were at work among a sticky substance in a large white bowl.

"Mother, are you there?" she heard a voice from above.

"Yes, my chuck."

Footsteps apparently reluctant and hesitating clinked on the stairs, and Sophia entered the kitchen.

"Put this curl straight," said Mrs. Baines, lowering her head slightly and holding up her floured hands, which might not touch anything but flour. "Thank you. It bothered me. And now stand out of my light. I'm in a hurry. I must get into the shop so that I can send Mr. Povey off to the dentist's. What is Constance doing?"

"Helping Maggie to make Mr. Povey's bed."

"Oh!"

Though fat, Mrs. Baines was a comely woman, with fine brown hair, and confidently calm eyes that indicated her belief in her own capacity to accomplish whatever she could be called on to accomplish. She looked neither more nor less than her age, which was forty-five. She was not a native of the district, having been culled by her husband from the moorland town of Axe, twelve miles off. Like nearly all women who settle in a strange land upon marriage, at the bottom of her heart she had considered herself just a trifle superior to the strange land and its ways. This feeling, confirmed by long experience, had never left her. It was this feeling which induced her to continue making her own pastry—with two thoroughly trained "great girls" in the house! Constance could make good pastry, but it was not her mother's pastry. In pastry-making everything can be taught except the "hand," light and firm, which wields the roller. One is born with this hand, or without it. And if one is born without it, the highest flights of pastry are impossible. Constance was born without it. There were days when Sophia seemed to possess it; but there were other days when Sophia's pastry was uneatable by any one except Maggie. Thus Mrs. Baines, though intensely proud and fond of her daughters, had justifiably preserved a certain condescension towards them. She honestly doubted whether either of them would develop into the equal of their mother.

"Now you little vixen!" she exclaimed. Sophia was stealing and eating slices of half-cooked apple. "This comes of having no breakfast! And why didn't you come down to supper last night?"

"I don't know. I forgot."

Mrs. Baines scrutinized the child's eyes, which met hers with a sort of diffident boldness. She knew everything that a mother can know of a daughter, and she was sure that Sophia had no cause to be indisposed. Therefore she scrutinized those eyes with a faint apprehension.

"If you can't find anything better to do," said she, "butter me the inside of this dish. Are your hands clean? No, better not touch it."

Mrs. Baines was now at the stage of depositing little pats of butter in rows on a large plain of paste. The best fresh butter! Cooking butter, to say naught of lard, was unknown in that kitchen on Friday mornings. She doubled the expanse of paste on itself and rolled the butter in—supreme operation!

"Constance has told you—about leaving school?" said Mrs. Baines, in the vein of small-talk, as she trimmed the paste to the shape of a pie-dish.

"Yes," Sophia replied shortly. Then she moved away from the table to the range. There was a toasting-fork on the rack, and she began to play with it.

"Well, are you glad? Your aunt Harriet thinks you are quite old enough to leave. And as we'd decided in any case that Constance was to leave, it's really much simpler that you should both leave together."

"Mother," said Sophia, rattling the toasting-fork, "what am I going to do after I've left school?"

"I hope," Mrs. Baines answered with that sententiousness which even the cleverest of parents are not always clever enough to deny themselves, "I hope that both of you will do what you can to help your mother—and father," she added.

"Yes," said Sophia, irritated. "But what am I going to DO?"

"That must be considered. As Constance is to learn the millinery, I've been thinking that you might begin to make yourself useful in the underwear, gloves, silks, and so on. Then between you, you would one day be able to manage quite nicely all that side of the shop, and I should be—"

"I don't want to go into the shop, mother."

This interruption was made in a voice apparently cold and inimical. But Sophia trembled with nervous excitement as she uttered the words. Mrs. Baines gave a brief glance at her, unobserved by the child, whose face was towards the fire. She deemed herself a finished expert in the reading of Sophia's moods; nevertheless, as she looked at that straight back and proud head, she had no suspicion that the whole essence and being of Sophia was silently but intensely imploring sympathy.

"I wish you would be quiet with that fork," said Mrs. Baines, with the curious, grim politeness which often characterized her relations with her daughters.

The toasting-fork fell on the brick floor, after having rebounded from the ash-tin. Sophia hurriedly replaced it on the rack.

"Then what SHALL you do?" Mrs. Baines proceeded, conquering the annoyance caused by the toasting-fork. "I think it's me that should ask you instead of you asking me. What shall you do? Your father and I were both hoping you would take kindly to the shop and try to repay us for all the—"

Mrs. Baines was unfortunate in her phrasing that morning. She happened to be, in truth, rather an exceptional parent, but that morning she seemed unable to avoid the absurd pretensions which parents of those days assumed quite sincerely and which every good child with meekness accepted.

Sophia was not a good child, and she obstinately denied in her heart the cardinal principle of family life, namely, that the parent has conferred on the offspring a supreme favour by bringing it into the world. She interrupted her mother again, rudely.

"I don't want to leave school at all," she said passionately.

"But you will have to leave school sooner or later," argued Mrs. Baines, with an air of quiet reasoning, of putting herself on a level with Sophia. "You can't stay at school for ever, my pet, can you? Out of my way!" She hurried across the kitchen with a pie, which she whipped into the oven, shutting the iron door with a careful gesture.

"Yes," said Sophia. "I should like to be a teacher. That's what I want to be."

The tap in the coal-cellar, out of repair, could be heard distinctly and systematically dropping water into a jar on the slopstone.

"A school-teacher?" inquired Mrs. Baines.

"Of course. What other kind is there?" said Sophia, sharply. "With Miss Chetwynd."

"I don't think your father would like that," Mrs. Baines replied. "I'm sure he wouldn't like it."

"Why not?"

"It wouldn't be quite suitable."

"Why not, mother?" the girl demanded with a sort of ferocity. She had now quitted the range. A man's feet twinkled past the window.

Mrs. Baines was startled and surprised. Sophia's attitude was really very trying; her manners deserved correction. But it was not these phenomena which seriously affected Mrs. Baines; she was used to them and had come to regard them as somehow the inevitable accompaniment of Sophia's beauty, as the penalty of that surpassing charm which occasionally emanated from the girl like a radiance. What startled and surprised Mrs. Baines was the perfect and unthinkable madness of Sophia's infantile scheme. It was a revelation to Mrs. Baines. Why in the name of heaven had the girl taken such a notion into her head? Orphans, widows, and spinsters of a certain age suddenly thrown on the world—these were the women who, naturally, became teachers, because they had to become something. But that the daughter of comfortable parents, surrounded by love and the pleasures of an excellent home, should wish to teach in a school was beyond the horizons of Mrs. Baines's common sense. Comfortable parents of to-day who have a difficulty in sympathizing with Mrs. Baines, should picture what their feelings would be if their Sophias showed a rude desire to adopt the vocation of chauffeur.

"It would take you too much away from home," said Mrs. Baines, achieving a second pie.

She spoke softly. The experience of being Sophia's mother for nearly sixteen years had not been lost on Mrs. Baines, and though she was now discovering undreamt-of dangers in Sophia's erratic temperament, she kept her presence of mind sufficiently well to behave with diplomatic smoothness. It was undoubtedly humiliating to a mother to be forced to use diplomacy in dealing with a girl in short sleeves. In HER day mothers had been autocrats. But Sophia was Sophia.

"What if it did?" Sophia curtly demanded.

"And there's no opening in Bursley," said Mrs. Baines.

"Miss Chetwynd would have me, and then after a time I could go to her sister."

"Her sister? What sister?"

"Her sister that has a big school in London somewhere."

Mrs. Baines covered her unprecedented emotions by gazing into the oven at the first pie. The pie was doing well, under all the circumstances. In those few seconds she reflected rapidly and decided that to a desperate disease a desperate remedy must be applied.

London! She herself had never been further than Manchester. London, 'after a time'! No, diplomacy would be misplaced in this crisis of Sophia's development!

"Sophia," she said, in a changed and solemn voice, fronting her daughter, and holding away from her apron those floured, ringed hands, "I don't know what has come over you. Truly I don't! Your father and I are prepared to put up with a certain amount, but the line must be drawn. The fact is, we've spoilt you, and instead of getting better as you grow up, you're getting worse. Now let me hear no more of this, please. I wish you would imitate your sister a little more. Of course if you won't do your share in the shop, no one can make you. If you choose to be an idler about the house, we shall have to endure it. We can only advise you for your own good. But as for this …" She stopped, and let silence speak, and then finished: "Let me hear no more of it."

It was a powerful and impressive speech, enunciated clearly in such a tone as Mrs. Baines had not employed since dismissing a young lady assistant five years ago for light conduct.

"But, mother—"

A commotion of pails resounded at the top of the stone steps. It was Maggie in descent from the bedrooms. Now, the Baines family passed its life in doing its best to keep its affairs to itself, the assumption being that Maggie and all the shop-staff (Mr. Povey possibly excepted) were obsessed by a ravening appetite for that which did not concern them. Therefore the voices of the Baineses always died away, or fell to a hushed, mysterious whisper, whenever the foot of the eavesdropper was heard.

Mrs. Baines put a floured finger to her double chin. "That will do," said she, with finality.

Maggie appeared, and Sophia, with a brusque precipitation of herself, vanished upstairs.

II

"Now, really, Mr. Povey, this is not like you," said Mrs. Baines, who, on her way into the shop, had discovered the Indispensable in the cutting-out room.

It is true that the cutting-out room was almost Mr. Povey's sanctum, whither he retired from time to time to cut out suits of clothes and odd garments for the tailoring department. It is true that the tailoring department flourished with orders, employing several tailors who crossed legs in their own homes, and that appointments were continually being made with customers for trying-on in that room. But these considerations did not affect Mrs. Baines's attitude of disapproval.

"I'm just cutting out that suit for the minister," said Mr. Povey.

The Reverend Mr. Murley, superintendent of the Wesleyan Methodist circuit, called on Mr. Baines every week. On a recent visit Mr. Baines had remarked that the parson's coat was ageing into green, and had commanded that a new suit should be built and presented to Mr. Murley. Mr. Murley, who had a genuine mediaeval passion for souls, and who spent his money and health freely in gratifying the passion, had accepted the offer strictly on behalf of Christ, and had carefully explained to Mr. Povey Christ's use for multifarious pockets.

"I see you are," said Mrs. Baines tartly. "But that's no reason why you should be without a coat—and in this cold room too. You with toothache!"

The fact was that Mr. Povey always doffed his coat when cutting out.

Instead of a coat he wore a tape-measure.

"My tooth doesn't hurt me," said he, sheepishly, dropping the great scissors and picking up a cake of chalk.

"Fiddlesticks!" said Mrs. Baines.

This exclamation shocked Mr. Povey. It was not unknown on the lips of Mrs. Baines, but she usually reserved it for members of her own sex. Mr. Povey could not recall that she had ever applied it to any statement of his. "What's the matter with the woman?" he thought. The redness of her face did not help him to answer the question, for her face was always red after the operations of Friday in the kitchen.

"You men are all alike," Mrs. Baines continued. "The very thought of the dentist's cures you. Why don't you go in at once to Mr. Critchlow and have it out—like a man?"

Mr. Critchlow extracted teeth, and his shop sign said "Bone-setter and chemist." But Mr. Povey had his views.

"I make no account of Mr. Critchlow as a dentist," said he.

"Then for goodness' sake go up to Oulsnam's."

"When? I can't very well go now, and to-morrow is Saturday."

"Why can't you go now?"

"Well, of course, I COULD go now," he admitted.

"Let me advise you to go, then, and don't come back with that tooth in your head. I shall be having you laid up next. Show some pluck, do!"

"Oh! pluck—!" he protested, hurt.

At that moment Constance came down the passage singing.

"Constance, my pet!" Mrs. Baines called.

"Yes, mother." She put her head into the room. "Oh!" Mr. Povey was assuming his coat.

"Mr. Povey is going to the dentist's."

"Yes, I'm going at once," Mr. Povey confirmed.

"Oh! I'm so GLAD!" Constance exclaimed. Her face expressed a pure sympathy, uncomplicated by critical sentiments. Mr. Povey rapidly bathed in that sympathy, and then decided that he must show himself a man of oak and iron.

"It's always best to get these things done with," said he, with stern detachment. "I'll just slip my overcoat on."

"Here it is," said Constance, quickly. Mr. Povey's overcoat and hat were hung on a hook immediately outside the room, in the passage. She gave him the overcoat, anxious to be of service.

"I didn't call you in here to be Mr. Povey's valet," said Mrs. Baines to herself with mild grimness; and aloud: "I can't stay in the shop long, Constance, but you can be there, can't you, till Mr. Povey comes back? And if anything happens run upstairs and tell me."

"Yes, mother," Constance eagerly consented. She hesitated and then turned to obey at once.

"I want to speak to you first, my pet," Mrs. Baines stopped her. And her tone was peculiar, charged with import, confidential, and therefore very flattering to Constance.

"I think I'll go out by the side-door," said Mr. Povey. "It'll be nearer."

This was truth. He would save about ten yards, in two miles, by going out through the side-door instead of through the shop. Who could have guessed that he was ashamed to be seen going to the dentist's, afraid lest, if he went through the shop, Mrs. Baines might follow him and utter some remark prejudicial to his dignity before the assistants? (Mrs. Baines could have guessed, and did.)

"You won't want that tape-measure," said Mrs. Baines, dryly, as Mr. Povey dragged open the side-door. The ends of the forgotten tape-measure were dangling beneath coat and overcoat.

"Oh!" Mr. Povey scowled at his forgetfulness.

"I'll put it in its place," said Constance, offering to receive the tape-measure.

"Thank you," said Mr. Povey, gravely. "I don't suppose they'll be long over my bit of a job," he added, with a difficult, miserable smile.

Then he went off down King Street, with an exterior of gay briskness and dignified joy in the fine May morning. But there was no May morning in his cowardly human heart.

"Hi! Povey!" cried a voice from the Square.

But Mr. Povey disregarded all appeals. He had put his hand to the plough, and he would not look back.

"Hi! Povey!"

Useless!

Mrs. Baines and Constance were both at the door. A middle-aged man was crossing the road from Boulton Terrace, the lofty erection of new shops which the envious rest of the Square had decided to call "showy." He waved a hand to Mrs. Baines, who kept the door open.

"It's Dr. Harrop," she said to Constance. "I shouldn't be surprised if that baby's come at last, and he wanted to tell Mr. Povey."

Constance blushed, full of pride. Mrs. Povey, wife of "our Mr. Povey's" renowned cousin, the high-class confectioner and baker in Boulton Terrace, was a frequent subject of discussion in the Baines family, but this was absolutely the first time that Mrs. Baines had acknowledged, in presence of Constance, the marked and growing change which had characterized Mrs. Povey's condition during recent months. Such frankness on the part of her mother, coming after the decision about leaving school, proved indeed that Constance had ceased to be a mere girl.

"Good morning, doctor."

The doctor, who carried a little bag and wore riding-breeches (he was the last doctor in Bursley to abandon the saddle for the dog-cart), saluted and straightened his high, black stock.

"Morning! Morning, missy! Well, it's a boy."

"What? Yonder?" asked Mrs. Baines, indicating the confectioner's.

Dr. Harrop nodded. "I wanted to inform him," said he, jerking his shoulder in the direction of the swaggering coward.

"What did I tell you, Constance?" said Mrs. Baines, turning to her daughter.

Constance's confusion was equal to her pleasure. The alert doctor had halted at the foot of the two steps, and with one hand in the pocket of his "full-fall" breeches, he gazed up, smiling out of little eyes, at the ample matron and the slender virgin.

"Yes," he said. "Been up most of th' night. Difficult! Difficult!"

"It's all RIGHT, I hope?"

"Oh yes. Fine child! Fine child! But he put his mother to some trouble, for all that. Nothing fresh?" This time he lifted his eyes to indicate Mr. Baines's bedroom.

"No," said Mrs. Baines, with a different expression.

"Keeps cheerful?"

"Yes."

"Good! A very good morning to you."

He strode off towards his house, which was lower down the street.

"I hope she'll turn over a new leaf now," observed Mrs. Baines to Constance as she closed the door. Constance knew that her mother was referring to the confectioner's wife; she gathered that the hope was slight in the extreme.

"What did you want to speak to me about, mother?" she asked, as a way out of her delicious confusion.

"Shut that door," Mrs. Baines replied, pointing to the door which led to the passage; and while Constance obeyed, Mrs. Baines herself shut the staircase-door. She then said, in a low, guarded voice—

"What's all this about Sophia wanting to be a school-teacher?"

"Wanting to be a school-teacher?" Constance repeated, in tones of amazement.

"Yes. Hasn't she said anything to you?"

"Not a word!"

"Well, I never! She wants to keep on with Miss Chetwynd and be a teacher." Mrs. Baines had half a mind to add that Sophia had mentioned London. But she restrained herself. There are some things which one cannot bring one's self to say. She added, "Instead of going into the shop!"

"I never heard of such a thing!" Constance murmured brokenly, in the excess of her astonishment. She was rolling up Mr. Povey's tape-measure.

"Neither did I!" said Mrs. Baines.

"And shall you let her, mother?"

"Neither your father nor I would ever dream of it!" Mrs. Baines replied, with calm and yet terrible decision. "I only mentioned it to you because I thought Sophia would have told you something."

"No, mother!"

As Constance put Mr. Povey's tape-measure neatly away in its drawer under the cutting-out counter, she thought how serious life was—what with babies and Sophias. She was very proud of her mother's confidence in her; this simple pride filled her ardent breast with a most agreeable commotion. And she wanted to help everybody, to show in some way how much she sympathized with and loved everybody. Even the madness of Sophia did not weaken her longing to comfort Sophia.

III

That afternoon there was a search for Sophia, whom no one had seen since dinner. She was discovered by her mother, sitting alone and unoccupied in the drawing-room. The circumstance was in itself sufficiently peculiar, for on weekdays the drawing-room was never used, even by the girls during their holidays, except for the purpose of playing the piano. However, Mrs. Baines offered no comment on Sophia's geographical situation, nor on her idleness.

"My dear," she said, standing at the door, with a self-conscious effort to behave as though nothing had happened, "will you come and sit with your father a bit?"

"Yes, mother," answered Sophia, with a sort of cold alacrity.

"Sophia is coming, father," said Mrs. Baines at the open door of the bedroom, which was at right-angles with, and close to, the drawing-room door. Then she surged swishing along the corridor and went into the showroom, whither she had been called.

Sophia passed to the bedroom, the eternal prison of John Baines. Although, on account of his nervous restlessness, Mr. Baines was never left alone, it was not a part of the usual duty of the girls to sit with him. The person who undertook the main portion of the vigils was a certain Aunt Maria—whom the girls knew to be not a real aunt, not a powerful, effective aunt like Aunt Harriet of Axe—but a poor second cousin of John Baines; one of those necessitous, pitiful relatives who so often make life difficult for a great family in a small town. The existence of Aunt Maria, after being rather a "trial" to the Baineses, had for twelve years past developed into something absolutely "providential" for them. (It is to be remembered that in those days Providence was still busying himself with everybody's affairs, and foreseeing the future in the most extraordinary manner. Thus, having foreseen that John Baines would have a "stroke" and need a faithful, tireless nurse, he had begun fifty years in advance by creating Aunt Maria, and had kept her carefully in misfortune's way, so that at the proper moment she would be ready to cope with the stroke. Such at least is the only theory which will explain the use by the Baineses, and indeed by all thinking Bursley, of the word "providential" in connection with Aunt Maria.) She was a shrivelled little woman, capable of sitting twelve hours a day in a bedroom and thriving on the regime. At nights she went home to her little cottage in Brougham Street; she had her Thursday afternoons and generally her Sundays, and during the school vacations she was supposed to come only when she felt inclined, or when the cleaning of her cottage permitted her to come. Hence, in holiday seasons, Mr. Baines weighed more heavily on his household than at other times, and his nurses relieved each other according to the contingencies of the moment rather than by a set programme of hours.

The tragedy in ten thousand acts of which that bedroom was the scene, almost entirely escaped Sophia's perception, as it did Constance's. Sophia went into the bedroom as though it were a mere bedroom, with its majestic mahogany furniture, its crimson rep curtains (edged with gold), and its white, heavily tasselled counterpane. She was aged four when John Baines had suddenly been seized with giddiness on the steps of his shop, and had fallen, and, without losing consciousness, had been transformed from John Baines into a curious and pathetic survival of John Baines. She had no notion of the thrill which ran through the town on that night when it was known that John Baines had had a stroke, and that his left arm and left leg and his right eyelid were paralyzed, and that the active member of the Local Board, the orator, the religious worker, the very life of the town's life, was permanently done for. She had never heard of the crisis through which her mother, assisted by Aunt Harriet, had passed, and out of which she had triumphantly emerged. She was not yet old enough even to suspect it. She possessed only the vaguest memory of her father before he had finished with the world. She knew him simply as an organism on a bed, whose left side was wasted, whose eyes were often inflamed, whose mouth was crooked, who had no creases from the nose to the corners of the mouth like other people, who experienced difficulty in eating because the food would somehow get between his gums and his cheek, who slept a great deal but was excessively fidgety while awake, who seemed to hear what was said to him a long time after it was uttered, as if the sense had to travel miles by labyrinthine passages to his brain, and who talked very, very slowly in a weak, trembling voice.

And she had an image of that remote brain as something with a red spot on it, for once Constance had said: "Mother, why did father have a stroke?" and Mrs. Baines had replied: "It was a haemorrhage of the brain, my dear, here"—putting a thimbled finger on a particular part of Sophia's head.

Not merely had Constance and Sophia never really felt their father's tragedy; Mrs. Baines herself had largely lost the sense of it—such is the effect of use. Even the ruined organism only remembered fitfully and partially that it had once been John Baines. And if Mrs. Baines had not, by the habit of years, gradually built up a gigantic fiction that the organism remained ever the supreme consultative head of the family; if Mr. Critchlow had not obstinately continued to treat it as a crony, the mass of living and dead nerves on the rich Victorian bedstead would have been of no more account than some Aunt Maria in similar case. These two persons, his wife and his friend, just managed to keep him morally alive by indefatigably feeding his importance and his dignity. The feat was a miracle of stubborn self-deceiving, splendidly blind devotion, and incorrigible pride.

When Sophia entered the room, the paralytic followed her with his nervous gaze until she had sat down on the end of the sofa at the foot of the bed. He seemed to study her for a long time, and then he murmured in his slow, enfeebled, irregular voice:

"Is that Sophia?"

"Yes, father," she answered cheerfully.

And after another pause, the old man said: "Ay! It's Sophia."

And later: "Your mother said she should send ye."

Sophia saw that this was one of his bad, dull days. He had, occasionally, days of comparative nimbleness, when his wits seized almost easily the meanings of external phenomena.

Presently his sallow face and long white beard began to slip down the steep slant of the pillows, and a troubled look came into his left eye. Sophia rose and, putting her hands under his armpits, lifted him higher in the bed. He was not heavy, but only a strong girl of her years could have done it.

"Ay!" he muttered. "That's it. That's it."

64

And, with his controllable right hand, he took her hand as she stood by the bed. She was so young and fresh, such an incarnation of the spirit of health, and he was so far gone in decay and corruption, that there seemed in this contact of body with body something unnatural and repulsive. But Sophia did not so feel it.

"Sophia," he addressed her, and made preparatory noises in his throat while she waited.

He continued after an interval, now clutching her arm, "Your mother's been telling me you don't want to go in the shop."

She turned her eyes on him, and his anxious, dim gaze met hers. She nodded.

"Nay, Sophia," he mumbled, with the extreme of slowness. "I'm surprised at ye… Trade's bad, bad! Ye know trade's bad?" He was still clutching her arm.

She nodded. She was, in fact, aware of the badness of trade, caused by a vague war in the United States. The words "North" and "South" had a habit of recurring in the conversation of adult persons. That was all she knew, though people were starving in the Five Towns as they were starving in Manchester.

"There's your mother," his thought struggled on, like an aged horse over a hilly road. "There's your mother!" he repeated, as if wishful to direct Sophia's attention to the spectacle of her mother. "Working hard! Con— Constance and you must help her…. Trade's bad! What can I do … lying here?"

The heat from his dry fingers was warming her arm. She wanted to move, but she could not have withdrawn her arm without appearing impatient. For a similar reason she would not avert her glance. A deepening flush increased the lustre of her immature loveliness as she bent over him. But though it was so close he did not feel that radiance. He had long outlived a susceptibility to the strange influences of youth and beauty.

"Teaching!" he muttered. "Nay, nay! I canna' allow that."

Then his white beard rose at the tip as he looked up at the ceiling above his head, reflectively.

"You understand me?" he questioned finally.

She nodded again; he loosed her arm, and she turned away. She could not have spoken. Glittering tears enriched her eyes. She was saddened into a profound and sudden grief by the ridiculousness of the scene. She had youth, physical perfection; she brimmed with energy, with the sense of vital power; all existence lay before her; when she put her lips together she felt capable of outvying no matter whom in fortitude of resolution. She had always hated the shop. She did not understand how her mother and Constance could bring themselves to be deferential and flattering to every customer that entered. No, she did not understand it; but her mother (though a proud woman) and Constance seemed to practise such behaviour so naturally, so unquestioningly, that she had never imparted to either of them her feelings; she guessed that she would not be comprehended. But long ago she had decided that she would never "go into the shop." She knew that she would be expected to do something, and she had fixed on teaching as the one possibility. These decisions had formed part of her inner life for years past. She had not mentioned them, being secretive and scarcely anxious for unpleasantness. But she had been slowly preparing herself to mention them. The extraordinary announcement that she was to leave school at the same time as Constance had taken her unawares, before the preparations ripening in her mind were complete—before, as it were, she had girded up her loins for the fray. She had been caught unready, and the opposing forces had obtained the advantage of her. But did they suppose she was beaten?

No argument from her mother! No hearing, even! Just a curt and haughty 'Let me hear no more of this'! And so the great desire of her life, nourished year after year in her inmost bosom, was to be flouted and sacrificed with a word! Her mother did not appear ridiculous in the affair, for her mother was a genuine power, commanding by turns genuine love and genuine hate, and always, till then, obedience and the respect of reason. It was her father who appeared tragically ridiculous; and, in turn, the whole movement against her grew grotesque in its absurdity. Here was this antique wreck, helpless, useless, powerless—merely pathetic— actually thinking that he had only to mumble in order to make her 'understand'! He knew nothing; he perceived nothing; he was a ferocious egoist, like most bedridden invalids, out of touch with life,—and he thought himself justified in making destinies, and capable of making them! Sophia could not, perhaps, define the feelings which overwhelmed her; but she was conscious of their tendency. They aged her, by years. They aged her so that, in a kind of momentary ecstasy of insight, she felt older than her father himself.

"You will be a good girl," he said. "I'm sure o' that."

It was too painful. The grotesqueness of her father's complacency humiliated her past bearing. She was humiliated, not for herself, but for him. Singular creature! She ran out of the room.

Fortunately Constance was passing in the corridor, otherwise Sophia had been found guilty of a great breach of duty.

"Go to father," she whispered hysterically to Constance, and fled upwards to the second floor.

65

At supper, with her red, downcast eyes, she had returned to sheer girlishness again, overawed by her mother. The meal had an unusual aspect. Mr. Povey, safe from the dentist's, but having lost two teeth in two days, was being fed on 'slops'—bread and milk, to wit; he sat near the fire. The others had cold pork, half a cold apple-pie, and cheese; but Sophia only pretended to eat; each time she tried to swallow, the tears came into her eyes, and her throat shut itself up. Mrs. Baines and Constance had a too careful air of eating just as usual. Mrs. Baines's handsome ringlets dominated the table under the gas.

"I'm not so set up with my pastry to-day," observed Mrs. Baines, critically munching a fragment of pie-crust. She rang a little hand-bell. Maggie appeared from the cave. She wore a plain white bib-less apron, but no cap.

"Maggie, will you have some pie?"

"Yes, if you can spare it, ma'am."

This was Maggie's customary answer to offers of food.

"We can always spare it, Maggie," said her mistress, as usual. "Sophia, if you aren't going to use that plate, give it to me."

Maggie disappeared with liberal pie.

Mrs. Baines then talked to Mr. Povey about his condition, and in particular as to the need for precautions against taking cold in the bereaved gum. She was a brave and determined woman; from start to finish she behaved as though nothing whatever in the household except her pastry and Mr. Povey had deviated that day from the normal. She kissed Constance and Sophia with the most exact equality, and called them 'my chucks' when they went up to bed.

Constance, excellent kind heart, tried to imitate her mother's tactics as the girls undressed in their room. She thought she could not do better than ignore Sophia's deplorable state.

"Mother's new dress is quite finished, and she's going to wear it on Sunday," said she, blandly.

"If you say another word I'll scratch your eyes out!" Sophia turned on her viciously, with a catch in her voice, and then began to sob at intervals. She did not mean this threat, but its utterance gave her relief. Constance, faced with the fact that her mother's shoes were too big for her, decided to preserve her eyesight.

Long after the gas was out, rare sobs from Sophia shook the bed, and they both lay awake in silence.

"I suppose you and mother have been talking me over finely to-day?"

Sophia burst forth, to Constance's surprise, in a wet voice.

"No," said Constance soothingly. "Mother only told me."

"Told you what?"

"That you wanted to be a teacher."

"And I will be, too!" said Sophia, bitterly.

"You don't know mother," thought Constance; but she made no audible comment.

There was another detached, hard sob. And then, such is the astonishing talent of youth, they both fell asleep. The next morning, early, Sophia stood gazing out of the window at the Square. It was Saturday, and all over the Square little stalls, with yellow linen roofs, were being erected for the principal market of the week. In those barbaric days Bursley had a majestic edifice, black as basalt, for the sale of dead animals by the limb and rib—it was entitled 'the Shambles'—but vegetables, fruit, cheese, eggs, and pikelets were still sold under canvas. Eggs are now offered at five farthings apiece in a palace that cost twenty-five thousand pounds. Yet you will find people in Bursley ready to assert that things generally are not what they were, and that in particular the romance of life has gone. But until it has gone it is never romance. To Sophia, though she was in a mood which usually stimulates the sense of the romantic, there was nothing of romance in this picturesque tented field. It was just the market. Holl's, the leading grocer's, was already open, at the extremity of the Square, and a boy apprentice was sweeping the pavement in front of it. The public-houses were open, several of them specializing in hot rum at 5.30 a.m. The town-crier, in his blue coat with red facings, crossed the Square, carrying his big bell by the tongue. There was the same shocking hole in one of Mrs. Povey's (confectioner's) window-curtains—a hole which even her recent travail could scarcely excuse. Such matters it was that Sophia noticed with dull, smarting eyes.

"Sophia, you'll take your death of cold standing there like that!"

She jumped. The voice was her mother's. That vigorous woman, after a calm night by the side of the paralytic, was already up and neatly dressed. She carried a bottle and an egg-cup, and a small quantity of jam in a table-spoon.

"Get into bed again, do! There's a dear! You're shivering."

White Sophia obeyed. It was true; she was shivering. Constance awoke. Mrs. Baines went to the dressing-table and filled the egg-cup out of the bottle.

"Who's that for, mother?" Constance asked sleepily.

"It's for Sophia," said Mrs. Baines, with good cheer. "Now, Sophia!" and she advanced with the egg-cup in one hand and the table-spoon in the other.

"What is it, mother?" asked Sophia, who well knew what it was.

"Castor-oil, my dear," said Mrs. Baines, winningly.

The ludicrousness of attempting to cure obstinacy and yearnings for a freer life by means of castor-oil is perhaps less real than apparent. The strange interdependence of spirit and body, though only understood intelligently in these intelligent days, was guessed at by sensible mediaeval mothers. And certainly, at the period when Mrs. Baines represented modernity, castor-oil was still the remedy of remedies. It had supplanted cupping. And, if part of its vogue was due to its extreme unpleasantness, it had at least proved its qualities in many a contest with disease. Less than two years previously old Dr. Harrop (father of him who told Mrs. Baines about Mrs. Povey), being then aged eighty-six, had fallen from top to bottom of his staircase. He had scrambled up, taken a dose of castor-oil at once, and on the morrow was as well as if he had never seen a staircase. This episode was town property and had sunk deep into all hearts.

"I don't want any, mother," said Sophia, in dejection. "I'm quite well."

"You simply ate nothing all day yesterday," said Mrs. Baines. And she added, "Come!" As if to say, "There's always this silly fuss with castor-oil. Don't keep me waiting."

"I don't WANT any," said Sophia, irritated and captious.

The two girls lay side by side, on their backs. They seemed very thin and fragile in comparison with the solidity of their mother. Constance wisely held her peace.

Mrs. Baines put her lips together, meaning: "This is becoming tedious.
I shall have to be angry in another moment!"

"Come!" said she again.

The girls could hear her foot tapping on the floor.

"I really don't want it, mamma," Sophia fought. "I suppose I ought to know whether I need it or not!" This was insolence.

"Sophia, will you take this medicine, or won't you?"

In conflicts with her children, the mother's ultimatum always took the formula in which this phrase was cast. The girls knew, when things had arrived at the pitch of 'or won't you' spoken in Mrs. Baines's firmest tone, that the end was upon them. Never had the ultimatum failed.

There was a silence.

"And I'll thank you to mind your manners," Mrs. Baines added.

"I won't take it," said Sophia, sullenly and flatly; and she hid her face in the pillow.

It was a historic moment in the family life. Mrs. Baines thought the last day had come. But still she held herself in dignity while the apocalypse roared in her ears.

"OF COURSE I CAN'T FORCE YOU TO TAKE IT," she said with superb evenness, masking anger by compassionate grief. "You're a big girl and a naughty girl. And if you will be ill you must."

Upon this immense admission, Mrs. Baines departed.

Constance trembled.

Nor was that all. In the middle of the morning, when Mrs. Baines was pricing new potatoes at a stall at the top end of the Square, and Constance choosing threepennyworth of flowers at the same stall, whom should they both see, walking all alone across the empty corner by the Bank, but Sophia Baines! The Square was busy and populous, and Sophia was only visible behind a foreground of restless, chattering figures. But she was unmistakably seen. She had been beyond the Square and was returning. Constance could scarcely believe her eyes. Mrs. Baines's heart jumped. For let it be said that the girls never under any circumstances went forth without permission, and scarcely ever alone. That Sophia should be at large in the town, without leave, without notice, exactly as if she were her own mistress, was a proposition which a day earlier had been inconceivable. Yet there she was, and moving with a leisureliness that must be described as effrontery!

Red with apprehension, Constance wondered what would happen. Mrs. Baines said nought of her feelings, did not even indicate that she had seen the scandalous, the breath-taking sight. And they descended the Square laden with the lighter portions of what they had bought during an hour of buying. They went into the house by the King Street door; and the first thing they heard was the sound of the piano upstairs. Nothing happened.

Mr. Povey had his dinner alone; then the table was laid for them, and the bell rung, and Sophia came insolently downstairs to join her mother and sister. And nothing happened. The dinner was silently eaten, and Constance having rendered thanks to God, Sophia rose abruptly to go.

"Sophia!"

"Yes, mother."

"Constance, stay where you are," said Mrs. Baines suddenly to Constance, who had meant to flee. Constance was therefore destined to be present at the happening, doubtless in order to emphasize its importance and seriousness.

"Sophia," Mrs. Baines resumed to her younger daughter in an ominous voice. "No, please shut the door. There is no reason why everybody in the house should hear. Come right into the room—right in! That's it. Now, what were you doing out in the town this morning?"

Sophia was fidgeting nervously with the edge of her little black apron, and worrying a seam of the carpet with her toes. She bent her head towards her left shoulder, at first smiling vaguely. She said nothing, but every limb, every glance, every curve, was speaking. Mrs. Baines sat firmly in her own rocking-chair, full of the sensation that she had Sophia, as it were, writhing on the end of a skewer. Constance was braced into a moveless anguish.

"I will have an answer," pursued Mrs. Baines. "What were you doing out in the town this morning?"

"I just went out," answered Sophia at length, still with eyes downcast, and in a rather simpering tone.

"Why did you go out? You said nothing to me about going out. I heard Constance ask you if you were coming with us to the market, and you said, very rudely, that you weren't."

"I didn't say it rudely," Sophia objected.

"Yes you did. And I'll thank you not to answer back."

"I didn't mean to say it rudely, did I, Constance?" Sophia's head turned sharply to her sister. Constance knew not where to look.

"Don't answer back," Mrs. Baines repeated sternly. "And don't try to drag Constance into this, for I won't have it."

"Oh, of course Constance is always right!" observed Sophia, with an irony whose unparalleled impudence shook Mrs. Baines to her massive foundations.

"Do you want me to have to smack you, child?"

Her temper flashed out and you could see ringlets vibrating under the provocation of Sophia's sauciness. Then Sophia's lower lip began to fall and to bulge outwards, and all the muscles of her face seemed to slacken.

"You are a very naughty girl," said Mrs. Baines, with restraint. ("I've got her," said Mrs. Baines to herself. "I may just as well keep my temper.")

And a sob broke out of Sophia. She was behaving like a little child. She bore no trace of the young maiden sedately crossing the Square without leave and without an escort.

("I knew she was going to cry," said Mrs. Baines, breathing relief.)

"I'm waiting," said Mrs. Baines aloud.

A second sob. Mrs. Baines manufactured patience to meet the demand.

"You tell me not to answer back, and then you say you're waiting," Sophia blubbered thickly.

"What's that you say? How can I tell what you say if you talk like that?" (But Mrs. Baines failed to hear out of discretion, which is better than valour.)

"It's of no consequence," Sophia blurted forth in a sob. She was weeping now, and tears were ricocheting off her lovely crimson cheeks on to the carpet; her whole body was trembling.

"Don't be a great baby," Mrs. Baines enjoined, with a touch of rough persuasiveness in her voice.

"It's you who make me cry," said Sophia, bitterly. "You make me cry and then you call me a great baby!" And sobs ran through her frame like waves one after another. She spoke so indistinctly that her mother now really had some difficulty in catching her words.

"Sophia," said Mrs. Baines, with god-like calm, "it is not I who make you cry. It is your guilty conscience makes you cry. I have merely asked you a question, and I intend to have an answer."

"I've told you." Here Sophia checked the sobs with an immense effort.

"What have you told me?"

"I just went out."

"I will have no trifling," said Mrs. Baines. "What did you go out for, and without telling me? If you had told me afterwards, when I came in, of your own accord, it might have been different. But no, not a word! It is I who have to ask! Now, quick! I can't wait any longer."

("I gave way over the castor-oil, my girl," Mrs. Baines said in her own breast. "But not again! Not again!")

"I don't know," Sophia murmured.

"What do you mean—you don't know?"

The sobbing recommenced tempestuously. "I mean I don't know. I just went out." Her voice rose; it was noisy, but scarcely articulate. "What if I did go out?"

"Sophia, I am not going to be talked to like this. If you think because you're leaving school you can do exactly as you like—"

"Do I want to leave school?" yelled Sophia, stamping. In a moment a hurricane of emotion overwhelmed her, as though that stamping of the foot had released the demons of the storm. Her face was transfigured by uncontrollable passion. "You all want to make me miserable!" she shrieked with terrible violence. "And now I can't even go out! You are a horrid, cruel woman, and I hate you! And you can do what you like! Put me in prison if you like! I know you'd be glad if I was dead!"

She dashed from the room, banging the door with a shock that made the house rattle. And she had shouted so loud that she might have been heard in the shop, and even in the kitchen. It was a startling experience for Mrs. Baines. Mrs. Baines, why did you saddle yourself with a witness? Why did you so positively say that you intended to have an answer?

"Really," she stammered, pulling her dignity about her shoulders like a garment that the wind has snatched off. "I never dreamed that poor girl had such a dreadful temper! What a pity it is, for her OWN sake!" It was the best she could do.

Constance, who could not bear to witness her mother's humiliation, vanished very quietly from the room. She got halfway upstairs to the second floor, and then, hearing the loud, rapid, painful, regular intake of sobbing breaths, she hesitated and crept down again.

This was Mrs. Baines's first costly experience of the child thankless for having been brought into the world. It robbed her of her profound, absolute belief in herself. She had thought she knew everything in her house and could do everything there. And lo! she had suddenly stumbled against an unsuspected personality at large in her house, a sort of hard marble affair that informed her by means of bumps that if she did not want to be hurt she must keep out of the way.

V

On the Sunday afternoon Mrs. Baines was trying to repose a little in the drawing-room, where she had caused a fire to be lighted. Constance was in the adjacent bedroom with her father. Sophia lay between blankets in the room overhead with a feverish cold. This cold and her new dress were Mrs. Baines's sole consolation at the moment. She had prophesied a cold for Sophia, refuser of castor-oil, and it had come. Sophia had received, for standing in her nightdress at a draughty window of a May morning, what Mrs. Baines called 'nature's slap in the face.' As for the dress, she had worshipped God in it, and prayed for Sophia in it, before dinner; and its four double rows of gimp on the skirt had been accounted a great success. With her lace-bordered mantle and her low, stringed bonnet she had assuredly given a unique lustre to the congregation at chapel. She was stout; but the fashions, prescribing vague outlines, broad downward slopes, and vast amplitudes, were favourable to her shape. It must not be supposed that stout women of a certain age never seek to seduce the eye and trouble the meditations of man by other than moral charms. Mrs. Baines knew that she was comely, natty, imposing, and elegant; and the knowledge gave her real pleasure. She would look over her shoulder in the glass as anxious as a girl: make no mistake.

She did not repose; she could not. She sat thinking, in exactly the same posture as Sophia's two afternoons previously. She would have been surprised to hear that her attitude, bearing, and expression powerfully recalled those of her reprehensible daughter. But it was so. A good angel made her restless, and she went idly to the window and glanced upon the empty, shuttered Square. She too, majestic matron, had strange, brief yearnings for an existence more romantic than this; shootings across her spirit's firmament of tailed comets; soft, inexplicable melancholies. The good angel, withdrawing her from such a mood, directed her gaze to a particular spot at the top of the square.

She passed at once out of the room—not precisely in a hurry, yet without wasting time. In a recess under the stairs, immediately outside the door, was a box about a foot square and eighteen inches deep covered with black American cloth. She bent down and unlocked this box, which was padded within and contained the Baines silver tea-service. She drew from the box teapot, sugar-bowl, milk-jug, sugar-tongs, hot-water jug, and cake-stand (a flattish dish with an arching semicircular handle)—chased vessels, silver without and silver-gilt within; glittering heirlooms that shone in the dark corner like the secret pride of respectable families. These she put on a tray that always stood on end in the recess. Then she looked upwards through the banisters to the second floor.

"Maggie!" she piercingly whispered.

"Yes, mum," came a voice.

"Are you dressed?"

"Yes, mum. I'm just coming."

"Well, put on your muslin." "Apron," Mrs. Baines implied.

Maggie understood.

"Take these for tea," said Mrs. Baines when Maggie descended. "Better rub them over. You know where the cake is—that new one. The best cups. And the silver spoons."

They both heard a knock at the side-door, far off, below.

"There!" exclaimed Mrs. Baines. "Now take these right down into the kitchen before you open."

"Yes, mum," said Maggie, departing.

Mrs. Baines was wearing a black alpaca apron. She removed it and put on another one of black satin embroidered with yellow flowers, which, by merely inserting her arm into the chamber, she had taken from off the chest of drawers in her bedroom. Then she fixed herself in the drawing-room.

Maggie returned, rather short of breath, convoying the visitor.

"Ah! Miss Chetwynd," said Mrs. Baines, rising to welcome. "I'm sure I'm delighted to see you. I saw you coming down the Square, and I said to myself, 'Now, I do hope Miss Chetwynd isn't going to forget us.'"

Miss Chetwynd, simpering momentarily, came forward with that self-conscious, slightly histrionic air, which is one of the penalties of pedagogy. She lived under the eyes of her pupils. Her life was one ceaseless effort to avoid doing anything which might influence her charges for evil or shock the natural sensitiveness of their parents. She had to wind her earthly way through a forest of the most delicate susceptibilities—fern-fronds that stretched across the path, and that she must not even accidentally disturb with her skirt as she passed. No wonder she walked mincingly! No wonder she had a habit of keeping her elbows close to her sides, and drawing her mantle tight in the streets! Her prospectus talked about 'a sound and religious course of training,' 'study embracing the usual branches of English, with music by a talented master, drawing, dancing, and calisthenics.' Also 'needlework plain and ornamental;' also 'moral influence;' and finally about terms, 'which are very moderate, and every particular, with references to parents and others, furnished on application.' (Sometimes, too, without application.) As an illustration of the delicacy of fern-fronds, that single word 'dancing' had nearly lost her Constance and Sophia seven years before!

She was a pinched virgin, aged forty, and not 'well off;' in her family the gift of success had been monopolized by her elder sister. For these characteristics Mrs. Baines, as a matron in easy circumstances, pitied Miss Chetwynd. On the other hand, Miss Chetwynd could choose ground from which to look down upon Mrs. Baines, who after all was in trade. Miss Chetwynd had no trace of the local accent; she spoke with a southern refinement which the Five Towns, while making fun of it, envied. All her O's had a genteel leaning towards 'ow,' as ritualism leans towards Romanism. And she was the fount of etiquette, a wonder of correctness; in the eyes of her pupils' parents not so much 'a perfect LADY' as 'a PERFECT lady.' So that it was an extremely nice question whether, upon the whole, Mrs. Baines secretly condescended to Miss Chetwynd or Miss Chetwynd to Mrs. Baines. Perhaps Mrs. Baines, by virtue of her wifehood, carried the day.

Miss Chetwynd, carefully and precisely seated, opened the conversation by explaining that even if Mrs. Baines had not written she should have called in any case, as she made a practice of calling at the home of her pupils in vacation time: which was true. Mrs. Baines, it should be stated, had on Friday afternoon sent to Miss Chetwynd one of her most luxurious notes—lavender-coloured paper with scalloped edges, the selectest mode of the day—to announce, in her Italian hand, that Constance and Sophia would both leave school at the end of the next term, and giving reasons in regard to Sophia.

Before the visitor had got very far, Maggie came in with a lacquered tea-caddy and the silver teapot and a silver spoon on a lacquered tray. Mrs. Baines, while continuing to talk, chose a key from her bunch, unlocked the tea-caddy, and transferred four teaspoonfuls of tea from it to the teapot and relocked the caddy.

"Strawberry," she mysteriously whispered to Maggie; and Maggie disappeared, bearing the tray and its contents.

"And how is your sister? It is quite a long time since she was down here," Mrs. Baines went on to Miss Chetwynd, after whispering "strawberry."

The remark was merely in the way of small-talk—for the hostess felt a certain unwilling hesitation to approach the topic of daughters—but it happened to suit the social purpose of Miss Chetwynd to a nicety. Miss Chetwynd was a vessel brimming with great tidings.

"She is very well, thank you," said Miss Chetwynd, and her expression grew exceedingly vivacious. Her face glowed with pride as she added, "Of course everything is changed now."

"Indeed?" murmured Mrs. Baines, with polite curiosity.

"Yes," said Miss Chetwynd. "You've not heard?"

"No," said Mrs. Baines. Miss Chetwynd knew that she had not heard.

"About Elizabeth's engagement? To the Reverend Archibald Jones?"

It is the fact that Mrs. Baines was taken aback. She did nothing indiscreet; she did not give vent to her excusable amazement that the elder Miss Chetwynd should be engaged to any one at all, as some women would have done in the stress of the moment. She kept her presence of mind.

"This is really MOST interesting!" said she.

It was. For Archibald Jones was one of the idols of the Wesleyan Methodist Connexion, a special preacher famous throughout England. At 'Anniversaries' and 'Trust sermons,' Archibald Jones had probably no rival. His Christian name helped him; it was a luscious, resounding mouthful for admirers. He was not an itinerant minister, migrating every three years. His function was to direct the affairs of the 'Book Room,' the publishing department of the Connexion. He lived in London, and shot out into the provinces at week-ends, preaching on Sundays and giving a lecture, tinctured with bookishness, 'in the chapel' on Monday evenings. In every town he visited there was competition for the privilege of entertaining him. He had zeal, indefatigable energy, and a breezy wit. He was a widower of fifty, and his wife had been dead for twenty years. It had seemed as if women were not for this bright star. And here Elizabeth Chetwynd, who had left the Five Towns a quarter of a century before at the age of twenty, had caught him! Austere, moustached, formidable, desiccated, she must have done it with her powerful intellect! It must be a union of intellects! He had been impressed by hers, and she by his, and then their intellects had kissed. Within a week fifty thousand women in forty counties had pictured to themselves this osculation of intellects, and shrugged their shoulders, and decided once more that men were incomprehensible. These great ones in London, falling in love like the rest! But no! Love was a ribald and voluptuous word to use in such a matter as this. It was generally felt that the Reverend Archibald Jones and Miss Chetwynd the elder would lift marriage to what would now be termed an astral plane.

After tea had been served, Mrs. Baines gradually recovered her position, both in her own private esteem and in the deference of Miss Aline Chetwynd.

"Yes," said she. "You can talk about your sister, and you can call HIM Archibald, and you can mince up your words. But have you got a tea-service like this? Can you conceive more perfect strawberry jam than this? Did not my dress cost more than you spend on your clothes in a year? Has a man ever looked at you? After all, is there not something about my situation … in short, something…?"

She did not say this aloud. She in no way deviated from the scrupulous politeness of a hostess. There was nothing in even her tone to indicate that Mrs. John Baines was a personage. Yet it suddenly occurred to Miss Chetwynd that her pride in being the prospective sister-in-law of the Rev. Archibald Jones would be better for a while in her pocket. And she inquired after Mr. Baines. After this the conversation limped somewhat.

"I suppose you weren't surprised by my letter?" said Mrs. Baines.

"I was and I wasn't," answered Miss Chetwynd, in her professional manner and not her manner of a prospective sister-in-law. "Of course I am naturally sorry to lose two such good pupils, but we can't keep our pupils for ever." She smiled; she was not without fortitude—it is easier to lose pupils than to replace them. "Still"—a pause—"what you say of Sophia is perfectly true, perfectly. She is quite as advanced as Constance. Still"—another pause and a more rapid enunciation—"Sophia is by no means an ordinary girl."

"I hope she hasn't been a very great trouble to you?"

"Oh NO!" exclaimed Miss Chetwynd. "Sophia and I have got on very well together. I have always tried to appeal to her reason. I have never FORCED her … Now, with some girls … In some ways I look on Sophia as the most remarkable girl—not pupil—but the most remarkable—what shall I say?—individuality, that I have ever met with." And her demeanour added, "And, mind you, this is something—from me!"

"Indeed!" said Mrs. Baines. She told herself, "I am not your common foolish parent. I see my children impartially. I am incapable of being flattered concerning them."

Nevertheless she was flattered, and the thought shaped itself that really Sophia was no ordinary girl.

"I suppose she has talked to you about becoming a teacher?" asked Miss

Chetwynd, taking a morsel of the unparalleled jam.

She held the spoon with her thumb and three fingers. Her fourth finger, in matters of honest labour, would never associate with the other three; delicately curved, it always drew proudly away from them.

"Has she mentioned that to you?" Mrs. Baines demanded, startled.

"Oh yes!" said Miss Chetwynd. "Several times. Sophia is a very secretive girl, very—but I think I may say I have always had her confidence. There have been times when Sophia and I have been very near each other. Elizabeth was much struck with her. Indeed, I may tell you that in one of her last letters to me she spoke of Sophia and said she had mentioned her to Mr. Jones, and Mr. Jones remembered her quite well."

Impossible for even a wise, uncommon parent not to be affected by such an announcement!

"I dare say your sister will give up her school now," observed Mrs.

Baines, to divert attention from her self-consciousness.

"Oh NO!" And this time Mrs. Baines had genuinely shocked Miss Chetwynd.

"Nothing would induce Elizabeth to give up the cause of education.

Archibald takes the keenest interest in the school. Oh no! Not for

worlds!"

"THEN YOU THINK SOPHIA WOULD MAKE A GOOD TEACHER?" asked Mrs. Baines with apparent inconsequence, and with a smile. But the words marked an epoch in her mind. All was over.

"I think she is very much set on it and—"

"That wouldn't affect her father—or me," said Mrs. Baines quickly.

"Certainly not! I merely say that she is very much set on it. Yes, she would, at any rate, make a teacher far superior to the average." ("That girl has got the better of her mother without me!" she reflected.) "Ah! Here is dear Constance!"

Constance, tempted beyond her strength by the sounds of the visit and the colloquy, had slipped into the room.

"I've left both doors open, mother," she excused herself for quitting her father, and kissed Miss Chetwynd. She blushed, but she blushed happily, and really made a most creditable debut as a young lady. Her mother rewarded her by taking her into the conversation. And history was soon made.

So Sophia was apprenticed to Miss Aline Chetwynd. Mrs. Baines bore herself greatly. It was Miss Chetwynd who had urged, and her respect for Miss Chetwynd … Also somehow the Reverend Archibald Jones came into the cause.

Of course the idea of Sophia ever going to London was ridiculous, ridiculous! (Mrs. Baines secretly feared that the ridiculous might happen; but, with the Reverend Archibald Jones on the spot, the worst could be faced.) Sophia must understand that even the apprenticeship in Bursley was merely a trial. They would see how things went on. She had to thank Miss Chetwynd.

"I made Miss Chetwynd come and talk to mother," said Sophia magnificently one night to simple Constance, as if to imply, 'Your Miss Chetwynd is my washpot.'

To Constance, Sophia's mere enterprise was just as staggering as her success. Fancy her deliberately going out that Saturday morning, after her mother's definite decision, to enlist Miss Chetwynd in her aid!

There is no need to insist on the tragic grandeur of Mrs. Baines's renunciation—a renunciation which implied her acceptance of a change in the balance of power in her realm. Part of its tragedy was that none, not even Constance, could divine the intensity of Mrs. Baines's suffering. She had no confidant; she was incapable of showing a wound. But when she lay awake at night by the organism which had once been her husband, she dwelt long and deeply on the martyrdom of her life. What had she done to deserve it? Always had she conscientiously endeavoured to be kind, just, patient. And she knew herself to be sagacious and prudent. In the frightful and unguessed trials of her existence as a wife, surely she might have been granted consolations as a mother! Yet no; it had not been! And she felt all the bitterness of age against youth—youth egotistic, harsh, cruel, uncompromising; youth that is so crude, so ignorant of life, so slow to understand! She had Constance. Yes, but it would be twenty years before Constance could appreciate the sacrifice of judgment and of pride which her mother had made, in a sudden decision, during that rambling, starched, simpering interview with Miss Aline Chetwynd. Probably Constance thought that she had yielded to Sophia's passionate temper! Impossible to explain to Constance that she had yielded to nothing but a perception of Sophia's complete inability to hear reason and wisdom. Ah! Sometimes as she lay in the dark, she would, in fancy, snatch her heart from her bosom and fling it down before Sophia, bleeding, and cry: "See what I carry about with me, on your account!" Then she would take it back and hide it again, and sweeten her bitterness with wise admonitions to herself.

All this because Sophia, aware that if she stayed in the house she would be compelled to help in the shop, chose an honourable activity which freed her from the danger. Heart, how absurd of you to bleed!

CHAPTER IV

ELEPHANT

I

"Sophia, will you come and see the elephant? Do come!" Constance entered the drawing-room with this request on her eager lips.

"No," said Sophia, with a touch of condescension. "I'm far too busy for elephants."

Only two years had passed; but both girls were grown up now; long sleeves, long skirts, hair that had settled down in life; and a demeanour immensely serious, as though existence were terrific in its responsibilities; yet sometimes childhood surprisingly broke through the crust of gravity, as now in Constance, aroused by such things as elephants, and proclaimed with vivacious gestures that it was not dead after all. The sisters were sharply differentiated. Constance wore the black alpaca apron and the scissors at the end of a long black elastic, which indicated her vocation in the shop. She was proving a considerable success in the millinery department. She had learnt how to talk to people, and was, in her modest way, very self-possessed. She was getting a little stouter. Everybody liked her. Sophia had developed into the student. Time had accentuated her reserve. Her sole friend was Miss Chetwynd, with whom she was, having regard to the disparity of their ages, very intimate. At home she spoke little. She lacked amiability; as her mother said, she was 'touchy.' She required diplomacy from others, but did not render it again. Her attitude, indeed, was one of half-hidden disdain, now gentle, now coldly bitter. She would not wear an apron, in an age when aprons were almost essential to decency. No! She would not wear an apron, and there was an end of it. She was not so tidy as Constance, and if Constance's hands had taken on the coarse texture which comes from commerce with needles, pins, artificial flowers, and stuffs, Sophia's fine hands were seldom innocent of ink. But Sophia was splendidly beautiful. And even her mother and Constance had an instinctive idea that that face was, at any rate, a partial excuse for her asperity.

"Well," said Constance, "if you won't, I do believe I shall ask mother if she will."

Sophia, bending over her books, made no answer. But the top of her head said: "This has no interest for me whatever."

Constance left the room, and in a moment returned with her mother.

"Sophia," said her mother, with gay excitement, "you might go and sit with your father for a bit while Constance and I just run up to the playground to see the elephant. You can work just as well in there as here. Your father's asleep."

"Oh, very, well!" Sophia agreed haughtily. "Whatever is all this fuss about an elephant? Anyhow, it'll be quieter in your room. The noise here is splitting." She gave a supercilious glance into the Square as she languidly rose.

It was the morning of the third day of Bursley Wakes; not the modern finicking and respectable, but an orgiastic carnival, gross in all its manifestations of joy. The whole centre of the town was given over to the furious pleasures of the people. Most of the Square was occupied by Wombwell's Menagerie, in a vast oblong tent, whose raging beasts roared and growled day and night. And spreading away from this supreme attraction, right up through the market-place past the Town Hall to Duck Bank, Duck Square and the waste land called the 'playground' were hundreds of booths with banners displaying all the delights of the horrible. You could see the atrocities of the French Revolution, and of the Fiji Islands, and the ravages of unspeakable diseases, and the living flesh of a nearly nude human female guaranteed to turn the scale at twenty-two stone, and the skeletons of the mysterious phantoscope, and the bloody contests of champions naked to the waist (with the chance of picking up a red tooth as a relic). You could try your strength by hitting an image of a

73

fellow-creature in the stomach, and test your aim by knocking off the heads of other images with a wooden ball. You could also shoot with rifles at various targets. All the streets were lined with stalls loaded with food in heaps, chiefly dried fish, the entrails of animals, and gingerbread. All the public-houses were crammed, and frenzied jolly drunkards, men and women, lunged along the pavements everywhere, their shouts vying with the trumpets, horns, and drums of the booths, and the shrieking, rattling toys that the children carried.

It was a glorious spectacle, but not a spectacle for the leading families. Miss Chetwynd's school was closed, so that the daughters of leading families might remain in seclusion till the worst was over. The Baineses ignored the Wakes in every possible way, choosing that week to have a show of mourning goods in the left-hand window, and refusing to let Maggie outside on any pretext. Therefore the dazzling social success of the elephant, which was quite easily drawing Mrs. Baines into the vortex, cannot imaginably be over-estimated. On the previous night one of the three Wombwell elephants had suddenly knelt on a man in the tent; he had then walked out of the tent and picked up another man at haphazard from the crowd which was staring at the great pictures in front, and tried to put this second man into his mouth. Being stopped by his Indian attendant with a pitchfork, he placed the man on the ground and stuck his tusk through an artery of the victim's arm. He then, amid unexampled excitement, suffered himself to be led away. He was conducted to the rear of the tent, just in front of Baines's shuttered windows, and by means of stakes, pulleys, and ropes forced to his knees. His head was whitewashed, and six men of the Rifle Corps were engaged to shoot at him at a distance of five yards, while constables kept the crowd off with truncheons. He died instantly, rolling over with a soft thud. The crowd cheered, and, intoxicated by their importance, the Volunteers fired three more volleys into the carcase, and were then borne off as heroes to different inns. The elephant, by the help of his two companions, was got on to a railway lorry and disappeared into the night. Such was the greatest sensation that has ever occurred, or perhaps will ever occur, in Bursley. The excitement about the repeal of the Corn Laws, or about Inkerman, was feeble compared to that excitement. Mr. Critchlow, who had been called on to put a hasty tourniquet round the arm of the second victim, had popped in afterwards to tell John Baines all about it. Mr. Baines's interest, however, had been slight. Mr. Critchlow succeeded better with the ladies, who, though they had witnessed the shooting from the drawing-room, were thirsty for the most trifling details.

The next day it was known that the elephant lay near the playground, pending the decision of the Chief Bailiff and the Medical Officer as to his burial. And everybody had to visit the corpse. No social exclusiveness could withstand the seduction of that dead elephant. Pilgrims travelled from all the Five Towns to see him.

"We're going now," said Mrs. Baines, after she had assumed her bonnet and shawl.

"All right," said Sophia, pretending to be absorbed in study, as she sat on the sofa at the foot of her father's bed.

And Constance, having put her head in at the door, drew her mother after her like a magnet.

Then Sophia heard a remarkable conversation in the passage.

"Are you going up to see the elephant, Mrs. Baines?" asked the voice of Mr. Povey.

"Yes. Why?"

"I think I had better come with you. The crowd is sure to be very rough." Mr. Povey's tone was firm; he had a position.

"But the shop?"

"We shall not be long," said Mr. Povey.

"Oh yes, mother," Constance added appealingly.

Sophia felt the house thrill as the side-door banged. She sprang up and watched the three cross King Street diagonally, and so plunge into the Wakes. This triple departure was surely the crowning tribute to the dead elephant! It was simply astonishing. It caused Sophia to perceive that she had miscalculated the importance of the elephant. It made her regret her scorn of the elephant as an attraction. She was left behind; and the joy of life was calling her. She could see down into the Vaults on the opposite side of the street, where working men—potters and colliers—in their best clothes, some with high hats, were drinking, gesticulating, and laughing in a row at a long counter.

She noticed, while she was thus at the bedroom window, a young man ascending King Street, followed by a porter trundling a flat barrow of luggage. He passed slowly under the very window. She flushed. She had evidently been startled by the sight of this young man into no ordinary state of commotion. She glanced at the books on the sofa, and then at her father. Mr. Baines, thin and gaunt, and acutely pitiable, still slept. His brain had almost ceased to be active now; he had to be fed and tended like a bearded baby, and he would sleep for hours at a stretch even in the daytime. Sophia left the room. A moment later she ran into the shop, an apparition that amazed the three young lady assistants. At the corner near the window on the fancy side a little nook had been formed by screening off a portion of the counter with large flower-boxes placed end-up. This corner had come to be known as "Miss Baines's corner." Sophia hastened to it, squeezing past a young lady assistant in the narrow space between the back of the counter and the shelf-lined wall. She sat down in Constance's chair and pretended to look for something. She had examined herself in the cheval-glass in the showroom, on her way from the sick-chamber. When she heard a voice near the door of the shop asking first for Mr. Povey and then for Mrs. Baines, she rose, and seizing the object nearest to her, which happened to be a pair of scissors, she hurried towards the showroom stairs as though the scissors had been a grail, passionately sought and to be jealously hidden away. She wanted to stop and turn round, but something prevented her. She was at the end of the counter, under the curving stairs, when one of the assistants said:

"I suppose you don't know when Mr. Povey or your mother are likely to be back, Miss Sophia? Here's—"

It was a divine release for Sophia.

"They're—I—" she stammered, turning round abruptly. Luckily she was still sheltered behind the counter. The young man whom she had seen in the street came boldly forward.

"Good morning, Miss Sophia," said he, hat in hand. "It is a long time since I had the pleasure of seeing you." Never had she blushed as she blushed then. She scarcely knew what she was doing as she moved slowly towards her sister's corner again, the young man following her on the customer's side of the counter.

II

She knew that he was a traveller for the most renowned and gigantic of all Manchester wholesale firms—Birkinshaws. But she did not know his name, which was Gerald Scales. He was a rather short but extremely well-proportioned man of thirty, with fair hair, and a distinguished appearance, as became a representative of Birkinshaws. His broad, tight necktie, with an edge of white collar showing above it, was particularly elegant. He had been on the road for Birkinshaws for several years; but Sophia had only seen him once before in her life, when she was a little girl, three years ago. The relations between the travellers of the great firms and their solid, sure clients in small towns were in those days often cordially intimate. The traveller came with the lustre of a historic reputation around him; there was no need to fawn for orders; and the client's immense and immaculate respectability made him the equal of no matter what ambassador. It was a case of mutual esteem, and of that confidence-generating phenomenon, "an old account." The tone in which a commercial traveller of middle age would utter the phrase "an old account" revealed in a flash all that was romantic, prim, and stately in mid-Victorian commerce. In the days of Baines, after one of the elaborately engraved advice-circulars had arrived ('Our Mr. —— will have the pleasure of waiting upon you on ——day next, the —— inst.') John might in certain cases be expected to say, on the morning of ——day, 'Missis, what have ye gotten for supper to-night?'

Mr. Gerald Scales had never been asked to supper; he had never even seen John Baines; but, as the youthful successor of an aged traveller who had had the pleasure of St. Luke's Square, on behalf of Birkinshaws, since before railways, Mrs. Baines had treated him with a faint agreeable touch of maternal familiarity; and, both her daughters being once in the shop during his visit, she had on that occasion commanded the gawky girls to shake hands with him.

Sophia had never forgotten that glimpse. The young man without a name had lived in her mind, brightly glowing, as the very symbol and incarnation of the masculine and the elegant.

The renewed sight of him seemed to have wakened her out of a sleep. Assuredly she was not the same Sophia. As she sat in her sister's chair in the corner, entrenched behind the perpendicular boxes, playing nervously with the scissors, her beautiful face was transfigured into the ravishingly angelic. It would have been impossible for Mr. Gerald Scales, or anybody else, to credit, as he gazed at those lovely, sensitive, vivacious, responsive features, that Sophia was not a character of heavenly sweetness and perfection. She did not know what she was doing; she was nothing but the exquisite expression of a deep instinct to attract and charm. Her soul itself emanated from her in an atmosphere of allurement and acquiescence. Could those laughing lips hang in a heavy pout? Could that delicate and mild voice be harsh? Could those burning eyes be coldly inimical? Never! The idea was inconceivable! And Mr. Gerald Scales, with his head over the top of the boxes, yielded to the spell. Remarkable that Mr. Gerald Scales, with all his experience, should have had to come to Bursley to find the pearl, the paragon, the ideal! But so it was. They met in an equal abandonment; the only difference between them was that Mr. Scales, by force of habit, kept his head.

"I see it's your wakes here," said he.

He was polite to the wakes; but now, with the least inflection in the world, he put the wakes at its proper level in the scheme of things as a local unimportance! She adored him for this; she was athirst for sympathy in the task of scorning everything local.

"I expect you didn't know," she said, implying that there was every reason why a man of his mundane interests should not know.

"I should have remembered if I had thought," said he. "But I didn't think. What's this about an elephant?"

"Oh!" she exclaimed. "Have you heard of that?"

"My porter was full of it."

"Well," she said, "of course it's a very big thing in Bursley."

As she smiled in gentle pity of poor Bursley, he naturally did the same. And he thought how much more advanced and broad the younger generation was than the old! He would never have dared to express his real feelings about Bursley to Mrs. Baines, or even to Mr. Povey (who was, however, of no generation); yet here was a young woman actually sharing them.

She told him all the history of the elephant.

"Must have been very exciting," he commented, despite himself.

"Do you know," she replied, "it WAS."

After all, Bursley was climbing in their opinion.

"And mother and my sister and Mr. Povey have all gone to see it. That's why they're not here."

That the elephant should have caused both Mr. Povey and Mrs. Baines to forget that the representative of Birkinshaws was due to call was indeed a final victory for the elephant.

"But not you!" he exclaimed.

"No," she said. "Not me."

"Why didn't you go too?" He continued his flattering investigations with a generous smile.

"I simply didn't care to," said she, proudly nonchalant.

"And I suppose you are in charge here?"

"No," she answered. "I just happened to have run down here for these scissors. That's all."

"I often see your sister," said he. "'Often' do I say?—that is, generally, when I come; but never you."

"I'm never in the shop," she said. "It's just an accident to-day."

"Oh! So you leave the shop to your sister?"

"Yes." She said nothing of her teaching.

Then there was a silence. Sophia was very thankful to be hidden from the curiosity of the shop. The shop could see nothing of her, and only the back of the young man; and the conversation had been conducted in low voices. She tapped her foot, stared at the worn, polished surface of the counter, with the brass yard-measure nailed along its edge, and then she uneasily turned her gaze to the left and seemed to be examining the backs of the black bonnets which were perched on high stands in the great window. Then her eyes caught his for an important moment.

"Yes," she breathed. Somebody had to say something. If the shop missed the murmur of their voices the shop would wonder what had happened to them.

Mr. Scales looked at his watch. "'I dare say if I come in again about two—" he began.

"Oh yes, they're SURE to be in then," she burst out before he could finish his sentence.

He left abruptly, queerly, without shaking hands (but then it would have been difficult—she argued—for him to have put his arm over the boxes), and without expressing the hope of seeing her again. She peeped through the black bonnets, and saw the porter put the leather strap over his shoulders, raise the rear of the barrow, and trundle off; but she did not see Mr. Scales. She was drunk; thoughts were tumbling about in her brain like cargo loose in a rolling ship. Her entire conception of herself was being altered; her attitude towards life was being altered. The thought which knocked hardest against its fellows was, "Only in these moments have I begun to live!"

And as she flitted upstairs to resume watch over her father she sought to devise an innocent-looking method by which she might see Mr. Scales when he next called. And she speculated as to what his name was.

III

76

When Sophia arrived in the bedroom, she was startled because her father's head and beard were not in their accustomed place on the pillow. She could only make out something vaguely unusual sloping off the side of the bed. A few seconds passed—not to be measured in time—and she saw that the upper part of his body had slipped down, and his head was hanging, inverted, near the floor between the bed and the ottoman. His face, neck, and hands were dark and congested; his mouth was open, and the tongue protruded between the black, swollen, mucous lips; his eyes were prominent and coldly staring. The fact was that Mr. Baines had wakened up, and, being restless, had slid out partially from his bed and died of asphyxia. After having been unceasingly watched for fourteen years, he had, with an invalid's natural perverseness, taken advantage of Sophia's brief dereliction to expire. Say what you will, amid Sophia's horror, and her terrible grief and shame, she had visitings of the idea: he did it on purpose!

She ran out of the room, knowing by intuition that he was dead, and shrieked out, "Maggie," at the top of her voice; the house echoed.

"Yes, miss," said Maggie, quite close, coming out of Mr. Povey's chamber with a slop-pail.

"Fetch Mr. Critchlow at once. Be quick. Just as you are. It's father—"

Maggie, perceiving darkly that disaster was in the air, and instantly filled with importance and a sort of black joy, dropped her pail in the exact middle of the passage, and almost fell down the crooked stairs. One of Maggie's deepest instincts, always held in check by the stern dominance of Mrs. Baines, was to leave pails prominent on the main routes of the house; and now, divining what was at hand, it flamed into insurrection.

No sleepless night had ever been so long to Sophia as the three minutes which elapsed before Mr. Critchlow came. As she stood on the mat outside the bedroom door she tried to draw her mother and Constance and Mr. Povey by magnetic force out of the wakes into the house, and her muscles were contracted in this strange effort. She felt that it was impossible to continue living if the secret of the bedroom remained unknown one instant longer, so intense was her torture, and yet that the torture which could not be borne must be borne. Not a sound in the house! Not a sound from the shop! Only the distant murmur of the wakes!

"Why did I forget father?" she asked herself with awe. "I only meant to tell him that they were all out, and run back. Why did I forget father?" She would never be able to persuade anybody that she had literally forgotten her father's existence for quite ten minutes; but it was true, though shocking.

Then there were noises downstairs.

"Bless us! Bless us!" came the unpleasant voice of Mr. Critchlow as he bounded up the stairs on his long legs; he strode over the pail. "What's amiss?" He was wearing his white apron, and he carried his spectacles in his bony hand.

"It's father—he's—" Sophia faltered.

She stood away so that he should enter the room first. He glanced at her keenly, and as it were resentfully, and went in. She followed, timidly, remaining near the door while Mr. Critchlow inspected her handiwork. He put on his spectacles with strange deliberation, and then, bending his knees outwards, thus lowered his body so that he could examine John Baines point-blank. He remained staring like this, his hands on his sharp apron-covered knees, for a little space; and then he seized the inert mass and restored it to the bed, and wiped those clotted lips with his apron.

Sophia heard loud breathing behind her. It was Maggie. She heard a huge, snorting sob; Maggie was showing her emotion.

"Go fetch doctor!" Mr. Critchlow rasped. "And don't stand gaping there!"

"Run for the doctor, Maggie," said Sophia.

"How came ye to let him fall?" Mr. Critchlow demanded.

"I was out of the room. I just ran down into the shop—"

"Gallivanting with that young Scales!" said Mr. Critchlow, with devilish ferocity. "Well, you've killed yer father; that's all!"

He must have been at his shop door and seen the entry of the traveller! And it was precisely characteristic of Mr. Critchlow to jump in the dark at a horrible conclusion, and to be right after all. For Sophia Mr. Critchlow had always been the personification of malignity and malevolence, and now these qualities in him made him, to her, almost obscene. Her pride brought up tremendous reinforcements, and she approached the bed.

"Is he dead?" she asked in a quiet tone. (Somewhere within a voice was whispering, "So his name is Scales.")

"Don't I tell you he's dead?"

"Pail on the stairs!"

This mild exclamation came from the passage. Mrs. Baines, misliking the crowds abroad, had returned alone; she had left Constance in charge of Mr. Povey. Coming into her house by the shop and showroom, she had first noted the phenomenon of the pail—proof of her theory of Maggie's incurable untidiness.

"Been to see the elephant, I reckon!" said Mr. Critchlow, in fierce sarcasm, as he recognized Mrs. Baines's voice.

Sophia leaped towards the door, as though to bar her mother's entrance.

But Mrs. Baines was already opening the door.

"Well, my pet—" she was beginning cheerfully.

Mr. Critchlow confronted her. And he had no more pity for the wife than for the daughter. He was furiously angry because his precious property had been irretrievably damaged by the momentary carelessness of a silly girl. Yes, John Baines was his property, his dearest toy! He was convinced that he alone had kept John Baines alive for fourteen years, that he alone had fully understood the case and sympathized with the sufferer, that none but he had been capable of displaying ordinary common sense in the sick-room. He had learned to regard John Baines as, in some sort, his creation. And now, with their stupidity, their neglect, their elephants, between them they had done for John Baines. He had always known it would come to that, and it had come to that.

"She let him fall out o' bed, and ye're a widow now, missis!" he announced with a virulence hardly conceivable. His angular features and dark eyes expressed a murderous hate for every woman named Baines.

"Mother!" cried Sophia, "I only ran down into the shop to—to—"

She seized her mother's arm in frenzied agony.

"My child!" said Mrs. Baines, rising miraculously to the situation with a calm benevolence of tone and gesture that remained for ever sublime in the stormy heart of Sophia, "do not hold me." With infinite gentleness she loosed herself from those clasping hands. "Have you sent for the doctor?" she questioned Mr. Critchlow.

The fate of her husband presented no mysteries to Mrs. Baines. Everybody had been warned a thousand times of the danger of leaving the paralytic, whose life depended on his position, and whose fidgetiness was thereby a constant menace of death to him. For five thousand nights she had wakened infallibly every time he stirred, and rearranged him by the flicker of a little oil lamp. But Sophia, unhappy creature, had merely left him. That was all.

Mr. Critchlow and the widow gazed, helplessly waiting, at the pitiable corpse, of which the salient part was the white beard. They knew not that they were gazing at a vanished era. John Baines had belonged to the past, to the age when men really did think of their souls, when orators by phrases could move crowds to fury or to pity, when no one had learnt to hurry, when Demos was only turning in his sleep, when the sole beauty of life resided in its inflexible and slow dignity, when hell really had no bottom, and a gilt-clasped Bible really was the secret of England's greatness. Mid-Victorian England lay on that mahogany bed. Ideals had passed away with John Baines. It is thus that ideals die; not in the conventional pageantry of honoured death, but sorrily, ignobly, while one's head is turned—

And Mr. Povey and Constance, very self-conscious, went and saw the dead elephant, and came back; and at the corner of King Street, Constance exclaimed brightly—

"Why! who's gone out and left the side-door open?"

For the doctor had at length arrived, and Maggie, in showing him upstairs with pious haste, had forgotten to shut the door.

And they took advantage of the side-door, rather guiltily, to avoid the eyes of the shop. They feared that in the parlour they would be the centre of a curiosity half ironical and half reproving; for had they not accomplished an escapade? So they walked slowly.

The real murderer was having his dinner in the commercial room up at the Tiger, opposite the Town Hall.

IV

Several shutters were put up in the windows of the shop, to indicate a death, and the news instantly became known in trading circles throughout the town. Many people simultaneously remarked upon the coincidence that Mr. Baines should have died while there was a show of mourning goods in his establishment. This coincidence was regarded as extremely sinister, and it was apparently felt that, for the sake of the mind's peace, one ought not to inquire into such things too closely. From the moment of putting up the prescribed shutters, John Baines and his funeral began to acquire importance in Bursley, and their importance grew rapidly almost from hour to hour. The wakes continued as usual, except that the Chief Constable, upon representations being made to him by Mr. Critchlow and other citizens, descended upon St. Luke's Square and forbade the activities of Wombwell's orchestra. Wombwell and the Chief Constable differed as to the justice of the decree, but every well-minded person praised the Chief Constable, and he himself considered that he had enhanced the town's reputation for a decent propriety. It was noticed, too, not without a shiver of the uncanny, that that night the lions and tigers behaved like lambs, whereas on the previous night they had roared the whole Square out of its sleep.

The Chief Constable was not the only individual enlisted by Mr. Critchlow in the service of his friend's fame. Mr. Critchlow spent hours in recalling the principal citizens to a due sense of John Baines's past greatness. He was determined that his treasured toy should vanish underground with due pomp, and he left nothing undone to that end. He went over to Hanbridge on the still wonderful horse-car, and saw the editor-proprietor of the Staffordshire Signal (then a two-penny weekly with no thought of Football editions), and on the very day of the funeral the Signal came out with a long and eloquent biography of John Baines. This biography, giving details of his public life, definitely restored him to his legitimate position in the civic memory as an ex-chief bailiff, an ex-chairman of the Burial Board, and of the Five Towns Association for the Advancement of Useful Knowledge, and also as a "prime mover" in the local Turnpike Act, in the negotiations for the new Town Hall, and in the Corinthian facade of the Wesleyan Chapel; it narrated the anecdote of his courageous speech from the portico of the Shambles during the riots of 1848, and it did not omit a eulogy of his steady adherence to the wise old English maxims of commerce and his avoidance of dangerous modern methods. Even in the sixties the modern had reared its shameless head. The panegyric closed with an appreciation of the dead man's fortitude in the terrible affliction with which a divine providence had seen fit to try him; and finally the Signal uttered its absolute conviction that his native town would raise a cenotaph to his honour. Mr. Critchlow, being unfamiliar with the word "cenotaph," consulted Worcester's Dictionary, and when he found that it meant "a sepulchral monument to one who is buried elsewhere," he was as pleased with the Signal's language as with the idea, and decided that a cenotaph should come to pass.

The house and shop were transformed into a hive of preparation for the funeral. All was changed. Mr. Povey kindly slept for three nights on the parlour sofa, in order that Mrs. Baines might have his room. The funeral grew into an obsession, for multitudinous things had to be performed and done sumptuously and in strict accordance with precedent. There were the family mourning, the funeral repast, the choice of the text on the memorial card, the composition of the legend on the coffin, the legal arrangements, the letters to relations, the selection of guests, and the questions of bell-ringing, hearse, plumes, number of horses, and grave-digging. Nobody had leisure for the indulgence of grief except Aunt Maria, who, after she had helped in the laying-out, simply sat down and bemoaned unceasingly for hours her absence on the fatal morning. "If I hadn't been so fixed on polishing my candle-sticks," she weepingly repeated, "he mit ha' been alive and well now." Not that Aunt Maria had been informed of the precise circumstances of the death; she was not clearly aware that Mr. Baines had died through a piece of neglect. But, like Mr. Critchlow, she was convinced that there had been only one person in the world truly capable of nursing Mr. Baines. Beyond the family, no one save Mr. Critchlow and Dr. Harrop knew just how the martyr had finished his career. Dr. Harrop, having been asked bluntly if an inquest would be necessary, had reflected a moment and had then replied: "No." And he added, "Least said soonest mended—mark me!" They had marked him. He was commonsense in breeches.

As for Aunt Maria, she was sent about her snivelling business by Aunt Harriet. The arrival in the house of this genuine aunt from Axe, of this majestic and enormous widow whom even the imperial Mrs. Baines regarded with a certain awe, set a seal of ultimate solemnity on the whole event. In Mr. Povey's bedroom Mrs. Baines fell like a child into Aunt Harriet's arms and sobbed:

"If it had been anything else but that elephant!"

Such was Mrs. Baines's sole weakness from first to last.

Aunt Harriet was an exhaustless fountain of authority upon every detail concerning interments. And, to a series of questions ending with the word "sister," and answers ending with the word "sister," the prodigious travail incident to the funeral was gradually and successfully accomplished. Dress and the repast exceeded all other matters in complexity and difficulty. But on the morning of the funeral Aunt Harriet had the satisfaction of beholding her younger sister the centre of a tremendous cocoon of crape, whose slightest pleat was perfect. Aunt Harriet seemed to welcome her then, like a veteran, formally into the august army of relicts. As they stood side by side surveying the special table which was being laid in the showroom for the repast, it appeared inconceivable that they had reposed together in Mr. Povey's limited bed. They descended from the showroom to the kitchen, where the last delicate dishes were inspected. The shop was, of course, closed for the day, but

Mr. Povey was busy there, and in Aunt Harriet's all-seeing glance he came next after the dishes. She rose from the kitchen to speak with him.

"You've got your boxes of gloves all ready?" she questioned him.

"Yes, Mrs. Maddack."

"You'll not forget to have a measure handy?"

"No, Mrs. Maddack."

"You'll find you'll want more of seven-and-three-quarters and eights than anything."

"Yes. I have allowed for that."

"If you place yourself behind the side-door and put your boxes on the harmonium, you'll be able to catch every one as they come in."

"That is what I had thought of, Mrs. Maddack."

She went upstairs. Mrs. Baines had reached the showroom again, and was smoothing out creases in the white damask cloth and arranging glass dishes of jam at equal distances from each other.

"Come, sister," said Mrs. Maddack. "A last look."

And they passed into the mortuary bedroom to gaze at Mr. Baines before he should be everlastingly nailed down. In death he had recovered some of his earlier dignity; but even so he was a startling sight. The two widows bent over him, one on either side, and gravely stared at that twisted, worn white face all neatly tucked up in linen.

"I shall fetch Constance and Sophia," said Mrs. Maddack, with tears in her voice. "Do you go into the drawing-room, sister."

But Mrs. Maddack only succeeded in fetching Constance.

Then there was the sound of wheels in King Street. The long rite of the funeral was about to begin. Every guest, after having been measured and presented with a pair of the finest black kid gloves by Mr. Povey, had to mount the crooked stairs and gaze upon the carcase of John Baines, going afterwards to the drawing-room to condole briefly with the widow. And every guest, while conscious of the enormity of so thinking, thought what an excellent thing it was that John Baines should be at last dead and gone. The tramping on the stairs was continual, and finally Mr. Baines himself went downstairs, bumping against corners, and led a cortege of twenty vehicles.

The funeral tea was not over at seven o'clock, five hours after the commencement of the rite. It was a gigantic and faultless meal, worthy of John Baines's distant past. Only two persons were absent from it—John Baines and Sophia. The emptiness of Sophia's chair was much noticed; Mrs. Maddack explained that Sophia was very high-strung and could not trust herself. Great efforts were put forth by the company to be lugubrious and inconsolable, but the secret relief resulting from the death would not be entirely hidden. The vast pretence of acute sorrow could not stand intact against that secret relief and the lavish richness of the food.

To the offending of sundry important relatives from a distance, Mr. Critchlow informally presided over that assemblage of grave men in high stocks and crinolined women. He had closed his shop, which had never before been closed on a weekday, and he had a great deal to say about this extraordinary closure. It was due as much to the elephant as to the funeral. The elephant had become a victim to the craze for souvenirs. Already in the night his tusks had been stolen; then his feet disappeared for umbrella-stands, and most of his flesh had departed in little hunks. Everybody in Bursley had resolved to participate in the elephant. One consequence was that all the chemists' shops in the town were assaulted by strings of boys. 'Please a pennorth o' alum to tak' smell out o' a bit o' elephant.' Mr. Critchlow hated boys.

"'I'll alum ye!' says I, and I did. I alummed him out o' my shop with a pestle. If there'd been one there'd been twenty between opening and nine o'clock. 'George,' I says to my apprentice, 'shut shop up. My old friend John Baines is going to his long home to-day, and I'll close. I've had enough o' alum for one day.'"

The elephant fed the conversation until after the second relay of hot muffins. When Mr. Critchlow had eaten to his capacity, he took the Signal importantly from his pocket, posed his spectacles, and read the obituary all through in slow, impressive accents. Before he reached the end Mrs. Baines began to perceive that familiarity had blinded her to the heroic qualities of her late husband. The fourteen years of ceaseless care were quite genuinely forgotten, and she saw him in his strength and in his glory. When Mr. Critchlow arrived at the eulogy of the husband and father, Mrs. Baines rose and left the showroom. The guests looked at each other in sympathy for her. Mr. Critchlow shot a glance at her over his spectacles and continued steadily reading. After he had finished he approached the question of the cenotaph.

Mrs. Baines, driven from the banquet by her feelings, went into the drawing-room. Sophia was there, and Sophia, seeing tears in her mother's eyes, gave a sob, and flung herself bodily against her mother, clutching her, and hiding her face in that broad crape, which abraded her soft skin.

"Mother," she wept passionately, "I want to leave the school now. I want to please you. I'll do anything in the world to please you. I'll go into the shop if you'd like me to!" Her voice lost itself in tears.

"Calm yourself, my pet," said Mrs. Baines, tenderly, caressing her. It was a triumph for the mother in the very hour when she needed a triumph.

CHAPTER V

THE TRAVELLER
I

'Equisite, 1s. 11d.'

These singular signs were being painted in shiny black on an unrectangular parallelogram of white cardboard by Constance one evening in the parlour. She was seated, with her left side to the fire and to the fizzing gas, at the dining-table, which was covered with a checked cloth in red and white. Her dress was of dark crimson; she wore a cameo brooch and a gold chain round her neck; over her shoulders was thrown a white knitted shawl, for the weather was extremely cold, the English climate being much more serious and downright at that day than it is now. She bent low to the task, holding her head slightly askew, putting the tip of her tongue between her lips, and expending all the energy of her soul and body in an intense effort to do what she was doing as well as it could be done.

"Splendid!" said Mr. Povey.

Mr. Povey was fronting her at the table; he had his elbows on the table, and watched her carefully, with the breathless and divine anxiety of a dreamer who is witnessing the realization of his dream. And Constance, without moving any part of her frame except her head, looked up at him and smiled for a moment, and he could see her delicious little nostrils at the end of her snub nose.

Those two, without knowing or guessing it, were making history—the history of commerce. They had no suspicion that they were the forces of the future insidiously at work to destroy what the forces of the past had created, but such was the case. They were conscious merely of a desire to do their duty in the shop and to the shop; probably it had not even occurred to them that this desire, which each stimulated in the breast of the other, had assumed the dimensions of a passion. It was ageing Mr. Povey, and it had made of Constance a young lady tremendously industrious and preoccupied.

Mr. Povey had recently been giving attention to the question of tickets. It is not too much to say that Mr. Povey, to whom heaven had granted a minimum share of imagination, had nevertheless discovered his little parcel of imagination in the recesses of being, and brought it effectively to bear on tickets. Tickets ran in conventional grooves. There were heavy oblong tickets for flannels, shirting, and other stuffs in the piece; there were smaller and lighter tickets for intermediate goods; and there were diamond-shaped tickets (containing nothing but the price) for bonnets, gloves, and flimflams generally. The legends on the tickets gave no sort of original invention. The words 'lasting,' 'durable,' 'unshrinkable,' 'latest,' 'cheap,' 'stylish,' 'novelty,' 'choice' (as an adjective), 'new,' and 'tasteful,' exhausted the entire vocabulary of tickets. Now Mr. Povey attached importance to tickets, and since he was acknowledged to be the best window-dresser in Bursley, his views were entitled to respect. He dreamed of other tickets, in original shapes, with original legends. In brief, he achieved, in regard to tickets, the rare feat of ridding himself of preconceived notions, and of approaching a subject with fresh, virginal eyes. When he indicated the nature of his wishes to Mr. Chawner, the wholesale stationer who supplied all the Five Towns with shop-tickets, Mr. Chawner grew uneasy and worried; Mr. Chawner was indeed shocked. For Mr. Chawner there had always been certain well-defined genera of tickets, and he could not conceive the existence of other genera. When Mr. Povey suggested circular tickets—tickets with a blue and a red line round them, tickets with legends such as 'unsurpassable,' 'very dainty,' or 'please note,' Mr. Chawner hummed and hawed, and finally stated that it would be impossible to manufacture these preposterous tickets, these tickets which would outrage the decency of trade.

If Mr. Povey had not happened to be an exceedingly obstinate man, he might have been defeated by the crass Toryism of Mr. Chawner. But Mr. Povey was obstinate, and he had resources of ingenuity which Mr. Chawner little suspected. The great, tramping march of progress was not to be impeded by Mr. Chawner. Mr. Povey began to make his own tickets. At first he suffered as all reformers and inventors suffer. He used the internal surface of collar-boxes and ordinary ink and pens, and the result was such as to give customers the idea that Baineses were too poor or too mean to buy tickets like other shops. For bought tickets had an ivory-tinted gloss, and the ink was black and glossy, and the edges were very straight and did not show yellow between two layers of white. Whereas Mr. Povey's tickets were of a bluish-white, without gloss; the ink was neither black nor shiny, and the edges were amateurishly rough: the tickets had an unmistakable air of having been 'made out of something else'; moreover, the lettering had not the free, dashing style of Mr. Chawner's tickets.

And did Mrs. Baines encourage him in his single-minded enterprise on behalf of HER business? Not a bit! Mrs. Baines's attitude, when not disdainful, was inimical! So curious is human nature, so blind is man to his own advantage! Life was very complex for Mr. Povey. It might have been less complex had Bristol board and Chinese ink been less expensive; with these materials he could have achieved marvels to silence all prejudice and stupidity; but they were too costly. Still, he persevered, and Constance morally supported him; he drew his inspiration and his courage from Constance. Instead of the internal surface of collar-boxes, he tried the external surface, which was at any rate shiny. But the ink would not 'take' on it. He made as many experiments as Edison was to make, and as many failures. Then Constance was visited by a notion for mixing sugar with ink. Simple, innocent creature—why should providence have chosen her to be the vessel of such a sublime notion? Puzzling enigma, which, however, did not exercise Mr. Povey! He found it quite natural that she should save him. Save him she did. Sugar and ink would 'take' on anything, and it shone like a 'patent leather' boot. Further, Constance developed a 'hand' for lettering which outdid Mr. Povey's. Between them they manufactured tickets by the dozen and by the score—tickets which, while possessing nearly all the smartness and finish of Mr. Chawner's tickets, were much superior to these in originality and strikingness. Constance and Mr. Povey were delighted and fascinated by them. As for Mrs. Baines, she said little, but the modern spirit was too elated by its success to care whether she said little or much. And every few days Mr. Povey thought of some new and wonderful word to put on a ticket.

His last miracle was the word 'exquisite.' 'Exquisite,' pinned on a piece of broad tartan ribbon, appeared to Constance and Mr. Povey as the finality of appropriateness. A climax worthy to close the year! Mr. Povey had cut the card and sketched the word and figures in pencil, and Constance was doing her executive portion of the undertaking. They were very happy, very absorbed, in this strictly business matter. The clock showed five minutes past ten. Stern duty, a pure desire for the prosperity of the shop, had kept them at hard labour since before eight o'clock that morning!

The stairs-door opened, and Mrs. Baines appeared, in bonnet and furs and gloves, all clad for going out. She had abandoned the cocoon of crape, but still wore weeds. She was stouter than ever.

"What!" she cried. "Not ready! Now really!"

"Oh, mother! How you made me jump!" Constance protested. "What time is it? It surely isn't time to go yet!"

"Look at the clock!" said Mrs. Baines, drily.

"Well, I never!" Constance murmured, confused.

"Come, put your things together, and don't keep me waiting," said Mrs. Baines, going past the table to the window, and lifting the blind to peep out. "Still snowing," she observed. "Oh, the band's going away at last! I wonder how they can play at all in this weather. By the way, what was that tune they gave us just now? I couldn't make out whether it was 'Redhead,' or—"

"Band?" questioned Constance—the simpleton!

Neither she nor Mr. Povey had heard the strains of the Bursley Town Silver Prize Band which had been enlivening the season according to its usual custom. These two practical, duteous, commonsense young and youngish persons had been so absorbed in their efforts for the welfare of the shop that they had positively not only forgotten the time, but had also failed to notice the band! But if Constance had had her wits about her she would at least have pretended that she had heard it.

"What's this?" asked Mrs. Baines, bringing her vast form to the table and picking up a ticket.

Mr. Povey said nothing. Constance said: "Mr. Povey thought of it to-day. Don't you think it's very good, mother?"

"I'm afraid I don't," Mrs. Baines coldly replied.

She had mildly objected already to certain words; but 'exquisite' seemed to her silly; it seemed out of place; she considered that it would merely bring ridicule on her shop. 'Exquisite' written upon a window-ticket! No! What would John Baines have thought of 'exquisite'?

"'Exquisite!'" She repeated the word with a sarcastic inflection, putting the accent, as every one put it, on the second syllable. "I don't think that will quite do."

"But why not, mother?"

"It's not suitable, my dear."

She dropped the ticket from her gloved hand. Mr. Povey had darkly flashed. Though he spoke little, he was as sensitive as he was obstinate. On this occasion he said nothing. He expressed his feelings by seizing the ticket and throwing it into the fire.

The situation was extremely delicate. Priceless employes like Mr. Povey cannot be treated as machines, and Mrs. Baines of course instantly saw that tact was needed.

"Go along to my bedroom and get ready, my pet," said she to Constance.

"Sophia is there. There's a good fire. I must just speak to Maggie."

She tactfully left the room.

Mr. Povey glanced at the fire and the curling red remains of the ticket. Trade was bad; owing to weather and war, destitution was abroad; and he had been doing his utmost for the welfare of the shop; and here was the reward!

Constance's eyes were full of tears. "Never mind!" she murmured, and went upstairs.

It was all over in a moment.

II

In the Wesleyan Methodist Chapel on Duck Bank there was a full and influential congregation. For in those days influential people were not merely content to live in the town where their fathers had lived, without dreaming of country residences and smokeless air—they were content also to believe what their fathers had believed about the beginning and the end of all. There was no such thing as the unknowable in those days. The eternal mysteries were as simple as an addition sum; a child could tell you with absolute certainty where you would be and what you would be doing a million years hence, and exactly what God thought of you. Accordingly, every one being of the same mind, every one met on certain occasions in certain places in order to express the universal mind. And in the Wesleyan Methodist Chapel, for example, instead of a sparse handful of persons disturbingly conscious of being in a minority, as now, a magnificent and proud majority had collected, deeply aware of its rightness and its correctness.

And the minister, backed by minor ministers, knelt and covered his face in the superb mahogany rostrum; and behind him, in what was then still called the 'orchestra' (though no musical instruments except the grand organ had sounded in it for decades), the choir knelt and covered their faces; and all around in the richly painted gallery and on the ground-floor, multitudinous rows of people, in easy circumstances of body and soul, knelt in high pews and covered their faces. And there floated before them, in the intense and prolonged silence, the clear vision of Jehovah on a throne, a God of sixty or so with a moustache and a beard, and a non-committal expression which declined to say whether or not he would require more bloodshed; and this God, destitute of pinions, was surrounded by white-winged creatures that wafted themselves to and fro while chanting; and afar off was an obscene monstrosity, with cloven hoofs and a tail very dangerous and rude and interfering, who could exist comfortably in the middle of a coal-fire, and who took a malignant and exhaustless pleasure in coaxing you by false pretences into the same fire; but of course you had too much sense to swallow his wicked absurdities. Once a year, for ten minutes by the clock, you knelt thus, in mass, and by meditation convinced yourself that you had too much sense to swallow his wicked absurdities. And the hour was very solemn, the most solemn of all the hours.

Strange that immortal souls should be found with the temerity to reflect upon mundane affairs in that hour! Yet there were undoubtedly such in the congregation; there were perhaps many to whom the vision, if clear, was spasmodic and fleeting. And among them the inhabitants of the Baines family pew! Who would have supposed that Mr. Povey, a recent convert from Primitive Methodism in King Street to Wesleyan Methodism on Duck Bank, was dwelling upon window-tickets and the injustice of women, instead of upon his relations with Jehovah and the tailed one? Who would have supposed that the gentle-eyed Constance, pattern of daughters, was risking her eternal welfare by smiling at the tailed one, who, concealing his tail, had assumed the image of Mr. Povey? Who would have supposed that Mrs. Baines, instead of resolving that Jehovah and not the tailed one should have ultimate rule over her, was resolving that she and not Mr. Povey should have ultimate rule over her house and shop? It was a pew-ful that belied its highly satisfactory appearance. (And possibly there were other pew-fuls equally deceptive.)

Sophia alone, in the corner next to the wall, with her beautiful stern face pressed convulsively against her hands, was truly busy with immortal things. Turbulent heart, the violence of her spiritual life had made her older! Never was a passionate, proud girl in a harder case than Sophia! In the splendour of her remorse for a fatal forgetfulness, she had renounced that which she loved and thrown herself into that which she loathed. It was her nature so to do. She had done it haughtily, and not with kindness, but she had done it with the whole force of her will. Constance had been compelled to yield up to her the millinery department, for Sophia's fingers had a gift of manipulating ribbons and feathers that was beyond Constance. Sophia had accomplished miracles in the millinery. Yes, and she would be utterly polite to customers; but afterwards, when the customers were gone, let mothers, sisters, and Mr. Poveys beware of her fiery darts!

But why, when nearly three months had elapsed after her father's death, had she spent more and more time in the shop, secretly aflame with expectancy? Why, when one day a strange traveller entered the shop and announced himself the new representative of Birkinshaws—why had her very soul died away within her and an awful sickness seized her? She knew then that she had been her own deceiver. She recognized and admitted, abasing herself lower than the lowest, that her motive in leaving Miss Chetwynd's and joining the shop had been, at the best, very mixed, very impure. Engaged at Miss Chetwynd's, she might easily have never set eyes on Gerald Scales again. Employed in the shop, she could not fail to meet him. In this light was to be seen the true complexion of the splendour of her remorse. A terrible thought for her! And she could not dismiss it. It contaminated her existence, this thought! And she could confide in no one. She was incapable of showing a wound. Quarter had succeeded quarter, and Gerald Scales was no more heard of. She had sacrificed her life for worse than nothing. She had made her own tragedy. She had killed her father, cheated and shamed herself with a remorse horribly spurious, exchanged content for misery and pride for humiliation—and with it all, Gerald Scales had vanished! She was ruined.

She took to religion, and her conscientious Christian virtues, practised with stern inclemency, were the canker of the family. Thus a year and a half had passed.

And then, on this last day of the year, the second year of her shame and of her heart's widowhood, Mr. Scales had reappeared. She had gone casually into the shop and found him talking to her mother and Mr. Povey. He had come back to the provincial round and to her. She shook his hand and fled, because she could not have stayed. None had noticed her agitation, for she had held her body as in a vice. She knew the reason neither of his absence nor of his return. She knew nothing. And not a word had been said at meals. And the day had gone and the night come; and now she was in chapel, with Constance by her side and Gerald Scales in her soul! Happy beyond previous conception of happiness! Wretched beyond an unutterable woe! And none knew! What was she to pray for? To what purpose and end ought she to steel herself? Ought she to hope, or ought she to despair? "O God, help me!" she kept whispering to Jehovah whenever the heavenly vision shone through the wrack of her meditation. "O God, help me!" She had a conscience that, when it was in the mood for severity, could be unspeakably cruel to her.

And whenever she looked, with dry, hot eyes, through her gloved fingers, she saw in front of her on the wall a marble tablet inscribed in gilt letters, the cenotaph! She knew all the lines by heart, in their spacious grandiloquence; lines such as:

EVER READY WITH HIS TONGUE HIS PEN AND HIS PURSE TO HELP THE CHURCH OF HIS FATHERS IN HER HE LIVED AND IN HER HE DIED CHERISHING A DEEP AND ARDENT AFFECTION FOR HIS BELOVED FAITH AND CREED.

And again:

HIS SYMPATHIES EXTENDED BEYOND HIS OWN COMMUNITY HE WAS ALWAYS TO THE FORE IN GOOD WORKS AND HE SERVED THE CIRCUIT THE TOWN AND THE DISTRICT WITH GREAT ACCEPTANCE AND USEFULNESS.

Thus had Mr. Critchlow's vanity been duly appeased.

As the minutes sped in the breathing silence of the chapel the emotional tension grew tighter; worshippers sighed heavily, or called upon Jehovah for a sign, or merely coughed an invocation. And then at last the clock in the middle of the balcony gave forth the single stroke to which it was limited; the ministers rose, and the congregation after them; and everybody smiled as though it was the millennium, and not simply the new year, that had set in. Then, faintly, through walls and shut windows, came the sound of bells and of steam syrens and whistles. The superintendent minister opened his hymn-book, and the hymn was sung which had been sung in Wesleyan Chapels on New Year's morn since the era of John Wesley himself. The organ finished with a clanguor of all its pipes; the minister had a few last words with Jehovah, and nothing was left to do except to persevere in well-doing. The people leaned towards each other across the high backs of the pews.

"A happy New Year!"

"Eh, thank ye! The same to you!"

"Another Watch Night service over!"

"Eh, yes!" And a sigh.

Then the aisles were suddenly crowded, and there was a good-humoured, optimistic pushing towards the door. In the Corinthian porch occurred a great putting-on of cloaks, ulsters, goloshes, and even pattens, and a great putting-up of umbrellas. And the congregation went out into the whirling snow, dividing into several black, silent-footed processions, down Trafalgar Road, up towards the playground, along the market-place, and across Duck Square in the direction of St. Luke's Square.

Mr. Povey was between Mrs. Baines and Constance.

"You must take my arm, my pet," said Mrs. Baines to Sophia.

Then Mr. Povey and Constance waded on in front through the drifts. Sophia balanced that enormous swaying mass, her mother. Owing to their hoops, she had much difficulty in keeping close to her. Mrs. Baines laughed with the complacent ease of obesity, yet a fall would have been almost irremediable for her; and so Sophia had to laugh too. But, though she laughed, God had not helped her. She did not know where she was going, nor what might happen to her next.

"Why, bless us!" exclaimed Mrs. Baines, as they turned the corner into

King Street. "There's some one sitting on our door-step!"

There was: a figure swathed in an ulster, a maud over the ulster, and a high hat on the top of all. It could not have been there very long, because it was only speckled with snow. Mr. Povey plunged forward.

"It's Mr. Scales, of all people!" said Mr. Povey.

"Mr. Scales!" cried Mrs. Baines.

And, "Mr. Scales!" murmured Sophia, terribly afraid.

Perhaps she was afraid of miracles. Mr. Scales sitting on her mother's doorstep in the middle of the snowy night had assuredly the air of a miracle, of something dreamed in a dream, of something pathetically and impossibly appropriate—'pat,' as they say in the Five Towns. But he was a tangible fact there. And years afterwards, in the light of further knowledge of Mr. Scales, Sophia came to regard his being on the doorstep as the most natural and characteristic thing in the world. Real miracles never seem to be miracles, and that which at the first blush resembles one usually proves to be an instance of the extremely prosaic.

III

"Is that you, Mrs. Baines?" asked Gerald Scales, in a half-witted voice, looking up, and then getting to his feet. "Is this your house? So it is! Well, I'd no idea I was sitting on your doorstep."

He smiled timidly, nay, sheepishly, while the women and Mr. Povey surrounded him with their astonished faces under the light of the gas-lamp. Certainly he was very pale.

"But whatever is the matter, Mr. Scales?" Mrs. Baines demanded in an anxious tone. "Are you ill? Have you been suddenly—"

"Oh no," said the young man lightly. "It's nothing. Only I was set on just now, down there,"—he pointed to the depths of King Street.

"Set on!" Mrs. Baines repeated, alarmed.

"That makes the fourth case in a week, that we KNOW of!" said Mr.

Povey. "It really is becoming a scandal."

The fact was that, owing to depression of trade, lack of employment, and rigorous weather, public security in the Five Towns was at that period not as perfect as it ought to have been. In the stress of hunger the lower classes were forgetting their manners—and this in spite of the altruistic and noble efforts of their social superiors to relieve the destitution due, of course, to short-sighted improvidence. When (the social superiors were asking in despair) will the lower classes learn to put by for a rainy day? (They might have said a snowy and a frosty day.) It was 'really too bad' of the lower classes, when everything that could be done was being done for them, to kill, or even attempt to kill, the goose that lays the golden eggs! And especially in a respectable town! What, indeed, were things coming to? Well, here was Mr. Gerald Scales, gentleman from Manchester, a witness and victim to the deplorable moral condition of the Five Towns. What would he think of the Five Towns? The evil and the danger had been a topic of discussion in the shop for a week past, and now it was brought home to them.

"I hope you weren't—" said Mrs. Baines, apologetically and sympathetically.

"Oh no!" Mr. Scales interrupted her quite gaily. "I managed to beat them off. Only my elbow—"

Meanwhile it was continuing to snow.

"Do come in!" said Mrs. Baines.

"I couldn't think of troubling you," said Mr. Scales. "I'm all right now, and I can find my way to the Tiger."

"You must come in, if it's only for a minute," said Mrs. Baines, with decision. She had to think of the honour of the town.

"You're very kind," said Mr. Scales.

The door was suddenly opened from within, and Maggie surveyed them from the height of the two steps.

"A happy New Year, mum, to all of you."

"Thank you, Maggie," said Mrs. Baines, and primly added:

"The same to you!" And in her own mind she said that Maggie could best prove her desire for a happy new year by contriving in future not to 'scamp her corners,' and not to break so much crockery.

Sophia, scarce knowing what she did, mounted the steps.

"Mr. Scales ought to let our New Year in, my pet," Mrs. Baines stopped her.

"Oh, of course, mother!" Sophia concurred with, a gasp, springing back nervously.

Mr. Scales raised his hat, and duly let the new year, and much snow, into the Baines parlour. And there was a vast deal of stamping of feet, agitating of umbrellas, and shaking of cloaks and ulsters on the doormat in the corner by the harmonium. And Maggie took away an armful of everything snowy, including goloshes, and received instructions to boil milk and to bring 'mince.' Mr. Povey said "B-r-r-r!" and shut the door (which was bordered with felt to stop ventilation); Mrs. Baines turned up the gas till it sang, and told Sophia to poke the fire, and actually told Constance to light the second gas.

Excitement prevailed.

The placidity of existence had been agreeably disturbed (yes, agreeably, in spite of horror at the attack on Mr. Scales's elbow) by an adventure. Moreover, Mr. Scales proved to be in evening-dress. And nobody had ever worn evening-dress in that house before.

Sophia's blood was in her face, and it remained there, enhancing the vivid richness of her beauty. She was dizzy with a strange and disconcerting intoxication. She seemed to be in a world of unrealities and incredibilities. Her ears heard with indistinctness, and the edges of things and people had a prismatic colouring. She was in a state of ecstatic, unreasonable, inexplicable happiness. All her misery, doubts, despair, rancour, churlishness, had disappeared. She was as softly gentle as Constance. Her eyes were the eyes of a fawn, and her gestures delicious in their modest and sensitive grace. Constance was sitting on the sofa, and, after glancing about as if for shelter, she sat down on the sofa by Constance's side. She tried not to stare at Mr. Scales, but her gaze would not leave him. She was sure that he was the most perfect man in the world. A shortish man, perhaps, but a perfect. That such perfection could be was almost past her belief. He excelled all her dreams of the ideal man. His smile, his voice, his hand, his hair—never were such! Why, when he spoke—it was positively music! When he smiled—it was heaven! His smile, to Sophia, was one of those natural phenomena which are so lovely that they make you want to shed tears. There is no hyperbole in this description of Sophia's sensations, but rather an under-statement of them. She was utterly obsessed by the unique qualities of Mr. Scales. Nothing would have persuaded her that the peer of Mr. Scales existed among men, or could possibly exist. And it was her intense and profound conviction of his complete pre-eminence that gave him, as he sat there in the rocking-chair in her mother's parlour, that air of the unreal and the incredible.

"I stayed in the town on purpose to go to a New Year's party at Mr. Lawton's," Mr. Scales was saying.

"Ah! So you know Lawyer Lawton!" observed Mrs. Baines, impressed, for Lawyer Lawton did not consort with tradespeople. He was jolly with them, and he did their legal business for them, but he was not of them. His friends came from afar.

"My people are old acquaintances of his," said Mr. Scales, sipping the milk which Maggie had brought.

"Now, Mr. Scales, you must taste my mince. A happy month for every tart you eat, you know," Mrs. Baines reminded him.

He bowed. "And it was as I was coming away from there that I got into difficulties." He laughed.

Then he recounted the struggle, which had, however, been brief, as the assailants lacked pluck. He had slipped and fallen on his elbow on the kerb, and his elbow might have been broken, had not the snow been so thick. No, it did not hurt him now; doubtless a mere bruise. It was fortunate that the miscreants had not got the better of him, for he had in his pocket-book a considerable sum of money in notes—accounts paid! He had often thought what an excellent thing it would be if commercials could travel with dogs, particularly in winter. There was nothing like a dog.

"You are fond of dogs?" asked Mr. Povey, who had always had a secret but impracticable ambition to keep a dog.

"Yes," said Mr. Scales, turning now to Mr. Povey.

"Keep one?" asked Mr. Povey, in a sporting tone.

"I have a fox-terrier bitch," said Mr. Scales, "that took a first at Knutsford; but she's getting old now."

The sexual epithet fell queerly on the room. Mr. Povey, being a man of the world, behaved as if nothing had happened; but Mrs. Baines's curls protested against this unnecessary coarseness. Constance pretended not to hear. Sophia did not understandingly hear. Mr. Scales had no suspicion that he was transgressing a convention by virtue of which dogs have no sex. Further, he had no suspicion of the local fame of Mrs. Baines's mince-tarts. He had already eaten more mince-tarts than he could enjoy, before beginning upon hers, and Mrs. Baines missed the enthusiasm to which she was habituated from consumers of her pastry.

Mr. Povey, fascinated, proceeded in the direction of dogs, and it grew more and more evident that Mr. Scales, who went out to parties in evening dress, instead of going in respectable broad-cloth to watch night-services, who knew the great ones of the land, and who kept dogs of an inconvenient sex, was neither an ordinary commercial traveller nor the kind of man to which the Square was accustomed. He came from a different world.

"Lawyer Lawton's party broke up early—at least I mean, considering—"

Mrs. Baines hesitated.

After a pause Mr. Scales replied, "Yes, I left immediately the clock struck twelve. I've a heavy day to-morrow—I mean to-day."

It was not an hour for a prolonged visit, and in a few minutes Mr. Scales was ready again to depart. He admitted a certain feebleness ('wankiness,' he playfully called it, being proud of his skill in the dialect), and a burning in his elbow; but otherwise he was quite well—thanks to Mrs. Baines's most kind hospitality … He really didn't know how he came to be sitting on her doorstep. Mrs. Baines urged him, if he met a policeman on his road to the Tiger, to furnish all particulars about the attempted highway robbery, and he said he decidedly would.

He took his leave with distinguished courtliness.

"If I have a moment I shall run in to-morrow morning just to let you know I'm all right," said he, in the white street.

"Oh, do!" said Constance. Constance's perfect innocence made her strangely forward at times.

"A happy New Year and many of them!"

"Thanks! Same to you! Don't get lost."

"Straight up the Square and first on the right," called the commonsense of Mr. Povey.

Nothing else remained to say, and the visitor disappeared silently in the whirling snow. "Brrr!" murmured Mr. Povey, shutting the door. Everybody felt: "What a funny ending of the old year!"

"Sophia, my pet," Mrs. Baines began.

But Sophia had vanished to bed.

"Tell her about her new night-dress," said Mrs. Baines to Constance.

"Yes, mother."

"I don't know that I'm so set up with that young man, after all," Mrs. Baines reflected aloud.

"Oh, mother!" Constance protested. "I think he's just lovely."

"He never looks you straight in the face," said Mrs. Baines.

"Don't tell ME!" laughed Constance, kissing her mother good night. "You're only on your high horse because he didn't praise your mince. *I* noticed it."

IV

"If anybody thinks I'm going to stand the cold in this showroom any longer, they're mistaken," said Sophia the next morning loudly, and in her mother's hearing. And she went down into the shop carrying bonnets. She pretended to be angry, but she was not. She felt, on the contrary, extremely joyous, and charitable to all the world. Usually she would take pains to keep out of the shop; usually she was preoccupied and stern. Hence her presence on the ground-floor, and her demeanour, excited interest among the three young lady assistants who sat sewing round the stove in the middle of the shop, sheltered by the great pile of shirtings and linseys that fronted the entrance.

Sophia shared Constance's corner. They had hot bricks under their feet, and fine-knitted wraps on their shoulders. They would have been more comfortable near the stove, but greatness has its penalties. The weather was exceptionally severe. The windows were thickly frosted over, so that Mr. Povey's art in dressing them was quite wasted. And—rare phenomenon!—the doors of the shop were shut. In the ordinary way they were not merely open, but hidden by a display of 'cheap lines.' Mr. Povey, after consulting Mrs. Baines, had decided to close them, foregoing the customary display. Mr. Povey had also, in order to get a little warmth into his limbs, personally assisted two casual labourers to scrape the thick frozen snow off the pavement; and he wore his kid mittens. All these things together proved better than the evidence of barometers how the weather nipped.

Mr. Scales came about ten o'clock. Instead of going to Mr. Povey's counter, he walked boldly to Constance's corner, and looked over the boxes, smiling and saluting. Both the girls candidly delighted in his visit. Both blushed; both laughed—without knowing why they laughed. Mr. Scales said he was just departing and had slipped in for a moment to thank all of them for their kindness of last night—'or rather this morning.' The girls laughed again at this witticism. Nothing could have been more simple than his speech. Yet it appeared to them magically attractive. A customer entered, a lady; one of the assistants rose from the neighbourhood of the stove, but the daughters of the house ignored the customer; it was part of the etiquette of the shop that customers, at any rate chance customers, should not exist for the daughters of the house, until an assistant had formally drawn attention to them. Otherwise every one who wanted a pennyworth of tape would be expecting to be served by Miss Baines, or Miss Sophia, if Miss Sophia were there. Which would have been ridiculous. Sophia, glancing sidelong, saw the assistant parleying with the customer; and then the assistant came softly behind the counter and approached the corner.

"Miss Constance, can you spare a minute?" the assistant whispered discreetly.

Constance extinguished her smile for Mr. Scales, and, turning away, lighted an entirely different and inferior smile for the customer.

"Good morning, Miss Baines. Very cold, isn't it?"

"Good morning, Mrs. Chatterley. Yes, it is. I suppose you're getting anxious about those—" Constance stopped.

Sophia was now alone with Mr. Scales, for in order to discuss the unnameable freely with Mrs. Chatterley her sister was edging up the counter. Sophia had dreamed of a private conversation as something delicious and impossible. But chance had favoured her. She was alone with him. And his neat fair hair and his blue eyes and his delicate mouth were as wonderful to her as ever. He was gentlemanly to a degree that impressed her more than anything had impressed her in her life. And all the proud and aristocratic instinct that was at the base of her character sprang up and seized on his gentlemanliness like a famished animal seizing on food.

"The last time I saw you," said Mr. Scales, in a new tone, "you said you were never in the shop."

"What? Yesterday? Did I?"

"No, I mean the last time I saw you alone," said he.

"Oh!" she exclaimed. "It's just an accident."

"That's exactly what you said last time."

"Is it?"

Was it his manner, or what he said, that flattered her, that intensified her beautiful vivacity?

"I suppose you don't often go out?" he went on.

"What? In this weather?"

"Any time."

"I go to chapel," said she, "and marketing with mother." There was a little pause. "And to the Free Library."

"Oh yes. You've got a Free Library here now, haven't you?"

"Yes. We've had it over a year."

"And you belong to it? What do you read?"

"Oh, stories, you know. I get a fresh book out once a week."

"Saturdays, I suppose?"

"No," she said. "Wednesdays." And she smiled. "Usually."

"It's Wednesday to-day," said he. "Not been already?"

She shook her head. "I don't think I shall go to-day. It's too cold. I don't think I shall venture out to-day."

"You must be very fond of reading," said he.

Then Mr. Povey appeared, rubbing his mittened hands. And Mrs. Chatterley went.

"I'll run and fetch mother," said Constance.

Mrs. Baines was very polite to the young man. He related his interview with the police, whose opinion was that he had been attacked by stray members of a gang from Hanbridge. The young lady assistants, with ears cocked, gathered the nature of Mr. Scales's adventure, and were thrilled to the point of questioning Mr. Povey about it after Mr. Scales had gone. His farewell was marked by much handshaking, and finally Mr. Povey ran after him into the Square to mention something about dogs.

At half-past one, while Mrs. Baines was dozing after dinner, Sophia wrapped herself up, and with a book under her arm went forth into the world, through the shop. She returned in less than twenty minutes. But her mother had already awakened, and was hovering about the back of the shop. Mothers have supernatural gifts. Sophia nonchalantly passed her and hurried into the parlour where she threw down her muff and a book and knelt before the fire to warm herself.

Mrs. Baines followed her. "Been to the Library?" questioned Mrs. Baines.

"Yes, mother. And it's simply perishing."

"I wonder at your going on a day like to-day. I thought you always went on Thursdays?"

"So I do. But I'd finished my book."

"What is this?" Mrs. Baines picked up the volume, which was covered with black oil-cloth.

She picked it up with a hostile air. For her attitude towards the Free Library was obscurely inimical. She never read anything herself except The Sunday at Home, and Constance never read anything except The Sunday at Home. There were scriptural commentaries, Dugdale's Gazetteer, Culpepper's Herbal, and works by Bunyan and Flavius Josephus in the drawing-room bookcase; also Uncle Tom's Cabin. And Mrs. Baines, in considering the welfare of her daughters, looked askance at the whole remainder of printed literature. If the Free Library had not formed part of the Famous Wedgwood Institution, which had been opened with immense eclat by the semi-divine Gladstone; if the first book had not been ceremoniously 'taken out' of the Free Library by the Chief Bailiff in person—a grandfather of stainless renown—Mrs. Baines would probably have risked her authority in forbidding the Free Library.

"You needn't be afraid," said Sophia, laughing. "It's Miss Sewell's Experience of Life."

"A novel, I see," observed Mrs. Baines, dropping the book.

Gold and jewels would probably not tempt a Sophia of these days to read Experience of Life; but to Sophia Baines the bland story had the piquancy of the disapproved.

The next day Mrs. Baines summoned Sophia into her bedroom.

"Sophia," said she, trembling, "I shall be glad if you will not walk about the streets with young men until you have my permission."

The girl blushed violently. "I—I—"

"You were seen in Wedgwood Street," said Mrs. Baines.

"Who's been gossiping—Mr. Critchlow, I suppose?" Sophia exclaimed scornfully.

"No one has been 'gossiping,'" said Mrs. Baines. "Well, if I meet some one by accident in the street I can't help it, can I?" Sophia's voice shook.

"You know what I mean, my child," said Mrs. Baines, with careful calm.

Sophia dashed angrily from the room.

"I like the idea of him having 'a heavy day'!" Mrs. Baines reflected ironically, recalling a phrase which had lodged in her mind. And very vaguely, with an uneasiness scarcely perceptible, she remembered that 'he,' and no other, had been in the shop on the day her husband died.

CHAPTER VI

ESCAPADE

I

The uneasiness of Mrs. Baines flowed and ebbed, during the next three months, influenced by Sophia's moods. There were days when Sophia was the old Sophia—the forbidding, difficult, waspish, and even hedgehog Sophia. But there were other days on which Sophia seemed to be drawing joy and gaiety and goodwill from some secret source, from some fount whose nature and origin none could divine. It was on these days that the uneasiness of Mrs. Baines waxed. She had the wildest suspicions; she was almost capable of accusing Sophia of carrying on a clandestine correspondence; she saw Sophia and Gerald Scales deeply and wickedly in love; she saw them with their arms round each other's necks.... And then she called herself a middle-aged fool, to base such a structure of suspicion on a brief encounter in the street and on an idea, a fancy, a curious and irrational notion! Sophia had a certain streak of pure nobility in that exceedingly heterogeneous thing, her character. Moreover, Mrs. Baines watched the posts, and she also watched Sophia— she was not the woman to trust to a streak of pure nobility—and she came to be sure that Sophia's sinfulness, if any, was not such as could be weighed in a balance, or collected together by stealth and then suddenly placed before the girl on a charger.

Still, she would have given much to see inside Sophia's lovely head. Ah! Could she have done so, what sleep-destroying wonders she would have witnessed! By what bright lamps burning in what mysterious grottoes and caverns of the brain would her mature eyes have been dazzled! Sophia was living for months on the exhaustless ardent vitality absorbed during a magical two minutes in Wedgwood Street. She was living chiefly on the flaming fire struck in her soul by the shock of seeing Gerald Scales in the porch of the Wedgwood Institution as she came out of the Free Library with Experience Of Life tucked into her large astrakhan muff. He had stayed to meet her, then: she knew it! "After all," her heart said, "I must be very beautiful, for I have attracted the pearl of men!" And she remembered her face in the glass. The value and the power of beauty were tremendously proved to her. He, the great man of the world, the handsome and elegant man with a thousand strange friends and a thousand interests far remote from her, had remained in Bursley on the mere chance of meeting her! She was proud, but her pride was drowned in bliss. "I was just looking at this inscription about Mr. Gladstone." "So you decided to come out as usual!" "And may I ask what book you have chosen?" These were the phrases she heard, and to which she responded with similar phrases. And meanwhile a miracle of ecstasy had opened—opened like a flower. She was walking along Wedgwood Street by his side, slowly, on the scraped pavements, where marble bulbs of snow had defied the spade and remained. She and he were exactly of the same height, and she kept looking into his face and he into hers. This was all the miracle. Except that she was not walking on the pavement—she was walking on the intangible sward of paradise! Except that the houses had receded and faded, and the passers-by were subtilized into unnoticeable ghosts! Except that her mother and Constance had become phantasmal beings existing at an immense distance!

What had happened? Nothing! The most commonplace occurrence! The eternal cause had picked up a commercial traveller (it might have been a clerk or curate, but it in fact was a commercial traveller), and endowed him with all the glorious, unique, incredible attributes of a god, and planted him down before Sophia in order to produce the eternal effect. A miracle performed specially for Sophia's benefit! No one else in Wedgwood Street saw the god walking along by her side. No one else saw anything but a simple commercial traveller. Yes, the most commonplace occurrence!

Of course at the corner of the street he had to go. "Till next time!" he murmured. And fire came out of his eyes and lighted in Sophia's lovely head those lamps which Mrs. Baines was mercifully spared from seeing. And he had shaken hands and raised his hat. Imagine a god raising his hat! And he went off on two legs, precisely like a dashing little commercial traveller.

And, escorted by the equivocal Angel of Eclipses, she had turned into King Street, and arranged her face, and courageously met her mother. Her mother had not at first perceived the unusual; for mothers, despite their reputation to the contrary, really are the blindest creatures. Sophia, the naive ninny, had actually supposed that her walking along a hundred yards of pavement with a god by her side was not going to excite remark! What a delusion! It is true, certainly, that no one saw the god by direct vision. But Sophia's cheeks, Sophia's eyes, the curve of Sophia's neck as her soul yearned towards the soul of the god—these phenomena were immeasurably more notable than Sophia guessed. An account of them, in a modified form to respect Mrs. Baines's notorious dignity, had healed the mother of her blindness and led to that characteristic protest from her, "I shall be glad if you will not walk about the streets with young men," etc.

When the period came for the reappearance of Mr. Scales, Mrs. Baines outlined a plan, and when the circular announcing the exact time of his arrival was dropped into the letter-box, she formulated the plan in detail. In the first place, she was determined to be indisposed and invisible herself, so that Mr. Scales might be foiled in any possible design to renew social relations in the parlour. In the second place, she flattered Constance with a single hint—oh, the vaguest and briefest!—and Constance understood that she was not to quit the shop on the appointed morning. In the third place, she invented a way of explaining to Mr. Povey that the approaching advent of Gerald Scales must not be mentioned. And in the fourth place, she deliberately made appointments for Sophia with two millinery customers in the showroom, so that Sophia might be imprisoned in the showroom.

Having thus left nothing to chance, she told herself that she was a foolish woman full of nonsense. But this did not prevent her from putting her lips together firmly and resolving that Mr. Scales should have no finger in the pie of HER family. She had acquired information concerning Mr. Scales, at secondhand, from Lawyer Pratt. More than this, she posed the question in a broader form—why should a young girl be permitted any interest in any young man whatsoever? The everlasting purpose had made use of Mrs. Baines and cast her off, and, like most persons in a similar situation, she was, unconsciously and quite honestly, at odds with the everlasting purpose.

II

On the day of Mr. Scales's visit to the shop to obtain orders and money on behalf of Birkinshaws, a singular success seemed to attend the machinations of Mrs. Baines. With Mr. Scales punctuality was not an inveterate habit, and he had rarely been known, in the past, to fulfil exactly the prophecy of the letter of advice concerning his arrival. But that morning his promptitude was unexampled. He entered the shop, and by chance Mr. Povey was arranging unshrinkable flannels in the doorway. The two youngish little men talked amiably about flannels, dogs, and quarter-day (which was just past), and then Mr. Povey led Mr. Scales to his desk in the dark corner behind the high pile of twills, and paid the quarterly bill, in notes and gold—as always; and then Mr. Scales offered for the august inspection of Mr. Povey all that Manchester had recently invented for the temptation of drapers, and Mr. Povey gave him an order which, if not reckless, was nearer 'handsome' than 'good.' During the process Mr. Scales had to go out of the shop twice or three times in order to bring in from his barrow at the kerb-stone certain small black boxes edged with brass. On none of these excursions did Mr. Scales glance wantonly about him in satisfaction of the lust of the eye. Even if he had permitted himself this freedom he would have seen nothing more interesting than three young lady assistants seated round the stove and sewing with pricked fingers from which the chilblains were at last deciding to depart. When Mr. Scales had finished writing down the details of the order with his ivory-handled stylo, and repacked his boxes, he drew the interview to a conclusion after the manner of a capable commercial traveller; that is to say, he implanted in Mr. Povey his opinion that Mr. Povey was a wise, a shrewd and an upright man, and that the world would be all the better for a few more like him. He inquired for Mrs. Baines, and was deeply pained to hear of her indisposition while finding consolation in the assurance that the Misses Baines were well. Mr. Povey was on the point of accompanying the pattern of commercial travellers to the door, when two customers simultaneously came in—ladies. One made straight for Mr. Povey, whereupon Mr. Scales parted from him at once, it being a universal maxim in shops that even the most distinguished commercial shall not hinder the business of even the least distinguished customer. The other customer had the effect of causing Constance to pop up from her cloistral corner. Constance had been there all the time, but of course, though she heard the remembered voice, her maidenliness had not permitted that she should show herself to Mr. Scales. Now, as he was leaving, Mr. Scales saw her, with her agreeable snub nose and her kind, simple eyes. She was requesting the second customer to mount to the showroom, where was Miss Sophia. Mr. Scales hesitated a moment, and in that moment Constance, catching his eye, smiled upon him, and nodded. What else could she do? Vaguely aware though she was that her mother was not 'set up' with Mr. Scales, and even feared the possible influence of the young man on Sophia, she could not exclude him from her general benevolence towards the universe. Moreover, she liked him; she liked him very much and thought him a very fine specimen of a man.

He left the door and went across to her. They shook hands and opened a conversation instantly; for Constance, while retaining all her modesty, had lost all her shyness in the shop, and could chatter with anybody. She sidled towards her corner, precisely as Sophia had done on another occasion, and Mr. Scales put his chin over the screening boxes, and eagerly prosecuted the conversation.

There was absolutely nothing in the fact of the interview itself to cause alarm to a mother, nothing to render futile the precautions of Mrs. Baines on behalf of the flower of Sophia's innocence. And yet it held danger for Mrs. Baines, all unconscious in her parlour. Mrs. Baines could rely utterly on Constance not to be led away by the dandiacal charms of Mr. Scales (she knew in what quarter sat the wind for Constance); in her plan she had forgotten nothing, except Mr. Povey; and it must be said that she could not possibly have foreseen the effect on the situation of Mr. Povey's character.

Mr. Povey, attending to his customer, had noticed the bright smile of Constance on the traveller, and his heart did not like it. And when he saw the lively gestures of a Mr. Scales in apparently intimate talk with a Constance hidden behind boxes, his uneasiness grew into fury. He was a man capable of black and terrible furies. Outwardly insignificant, possessing a mind as little as his body, easily abashed, he was none the less a very susceptible young man, soon offended, proud, vain, and obscurely passionate. You might offend Mr. Povey without guessing it, and only discover your sin when Mr. Povey had done something too decisive as a result of it.

The reason of his fury was jealousy. Mr. Povey had made great advances since the death of John Baines. He had consolidated his position, and he was in every way a personage of the first importance. His misfortune was that he could never translate his importance, or his sense of his importance, into terms of outward demeanour. Most people, had they been told that Mr. Povey was seriously aspiring to enter the Baines family, would have laughed. But they would have been wrong. To laugh at Mr. Povey was invariably wrong. Only Constance knew what inroads he had effected upon her.

The customer went, but Mr. Scales did not go. Mr. Povey, free to reconnoitre, did so. From the shadow of the till he could catch glimpses of Constance's blushing, vivacious face. She was obviously absorbed in Mr. Scales. She and he had a tremendous air of intimacy. And the murmur of their chatter continued. Their chatter was nothing, and about nothing, but Mr. Povey imagined that they were exchanging eternal vows. He endured Mr. Scales's odious freedom until it became insufferable, until it deprived him of all his self-control; and then he retired into his cutting-out room. He meditated there in a condition of insanity for perhaps a minute, and excogitated a device. Dashing back into the shop, he spoke up, half across the shop, in a loud, curt tone: "Miss Baines, your mother wants you at once."

He was launched on the phrase before he noticed that, during his absence, Sophia had descended from the showroom and joined her sister and Mr. Scales. The danger and scandal were now less, he perceived, but he was glad he had summoned Constance away, and he was in a state to despise consequences.

The three chatterers, startled, looked at Mr. Povey, who left the shop abruptly. Constance could do nothing but obey the call.

She met him at the door of the cutting-out room in the passage leading to the parlour.

"Where is mother? In the parlour?" Constance inquired innocently.

There was a dark flush on Mr. Povey's face. "If you wish to know," said he in a hard voice, "she hasn't asked for you and she doesn't want you."

He turned his back on her, and retreated into his lair.

"Then what—?" she began, puzzled.

He fronted her. "Haven't you been gabbling long enough with that jackanapes?" he spit at her. There were tears in his eyes.

Constance, though without experience in these matters, comprehended. She comprehended perfectly and immediately. She ought to have put Mr. Povey into his place. She ought to have protested with firm, dignified finality against such a ridiculous and monstrous outrage as that which Mr. Povey had committed. Mr. Povey ought to have been ruined for ever in her esteem and in her heart. But she hesitated.

"And only last Sunday—afternoon," Mr. Povey blubbered.

(Not that anything overt had occurred, or been articulately said, between them last Sunday afternoon. But they had been alone together, and had each witnessed strange and disturbing matters in the eyes of the other.)

Tears now fell suddenly from Constance's eyes. "You ought to be ashamed—" she stammered.

Still, the tears were in her eyes, and in his too. What he or she merely said, therefore, was of secondary importance.

Mrs. Baines, coming from the kitchen, and hearing Constance's voice, burst upon the scene, which silenced her. Parents are sometimes silenced. She found Sophia and Mr. Scales in the shop.

III

That afternoon Sophia, too busy with her own affairs to notice anything abnormal in the relations between her mother and Constance, and quite ignorant that there had been an unsuccessful plot against her, went forth to call upon Miss Chetwynd, with whom she had remained very friendly: she considered that she and Miss Chetwynd formed an aristocracy of intellect, and the family indeed tacitly admitted this. She practised no secrecy in her departure from the shop; she merely dressed, in her second-best hoop, and went, having been ready at any moment to tell her mother, if her mother caught her and inquired, that she was going to see Miss Chetwynd. And she did go to see Miss Chetwynd, arriving at the house-school, which lay amid trees on the road to Turnhill, just beyond the turnpike, at precisely a quarter-past four. As Miss Chetwynd's pupils left at four o'clock, and as Miss Chetwynd invariably took a walk immediately afterwards, Sophia was able to contain her surprise upon being informed that Miss Chetwynd was not in. She had not intended that Miss Chetwynd should be in.

She turned off to the right, up the side road which, starting from the turnpike, led in the direction of Moorthorne and Red Cow, two mining villages. Her heart beat with fear as she began to follow that road, for she was upon a terrific adventure. What most frightened her, perhaps, was her own astounding audacity. She was alarmed by something within herself which seemed to be no part of herself and which produced in her curious, disconcerting, fleeting impressions of unreality.

In the morning she had heard the voice of Mr. Scales from the showroom—that voice whose even distant murmur caused creepings of the skin in her back. And she had actually stood on the counter in front of the window in order to see down perpendicularly into the Square; by so doing she had had a glimpse of the top of his luggage on a barrow, and of the crown of his hat occasionally when he went outside to tempt Mr. Povey. She might have gone down into the shop—there was no slightest reason why she should not; three months had elapsed since the name of Mr. Scales had been mentioned, and her mother had evidently forgotten the trifling incident of New Year's Day—but she was incapable of descending the stairs! She went to the head of the stairs and peeped through the balustrade—and she could not get further. For nearly a hundred days those extraordinary lamps had been brightly burning in her head; and now the light-giver had come again, and her feet would not move to the meeting; now the moment had arrived for which alone she had lived, and she could not seize it as it passed! "Why don't I go downstairs?" she asked herself. "Am I afraid to meet him?"

The customer sent up by Constance had occupied the surface of her life for ten minutes, trying on hats; and during this time she was praying wildly that Mr. Scales might not go, and asserting that it was impossible he should go without at least asking for her. Had she not counted the days to this day? When the customer left Sophia followed her downstairs, and saw Mr. Scales chatting with Constance. All her self-possession instantly returned to her, and she joined them with a rather mocking smile. After Mr. Povey's strange summons had withdrawn Constance from the corner, Mr. Scales's tone had changed; it had thrilled her. "You are YOU," it had said, "there is you—and there is the rest of the universe!" Then he had not forgotten; she had lived in his heart; she had not for three months been the victim of her own fancies! ... She saw him put a piece of folded white paper on the top edge of the screening box and flick it down to her. She blushed scarlet, staring at it as it lay on the counter. He said nothing, and she could not speak.... He had prepared that paper, then, beforehand, on the chance of being able to give it to her! This thought was exquisite but full of terror. "I must really go," he had said, lamely, with emotion in his voice, and he had gone—like that! And she put the piece of paper into the pocket of her apron, and hastened away. She had not even seen, as she turned up the stairs, her mother standing by the till—that spot which was the conning-tower of the whole shop. She ran, ran, breathless to the bedroom.

"I am a wicked girl!" she said quite frankly, on the road to the rendezvous. "It is a dream that I am going to meet him. It cannot be true. There is time to go back. If I go back I am safe. I have simply called at Miss Chetwynd's and she wasn't in, and no one can say a word. But if I go on—if I'm seen! What a fool I am to go on!"

And she went on, impelled by, amongst other things, an immense, naive curiosity, and the vanity which the bare fact of his note had excited. The Loop railway was being constructed at that period, and hundreds of navvies were at work on it between Bursley and Turnhill. When she came to the new bridge over the cutting, he was there, as he had written that he would be.

They were very nervous, they greeted each other stiffly and as though they had met then for the first time that day. Nothing was said about his note, nor about her response to it. Her presence was treated by both of them as a basic fact of the situation which it would be well not to disturb by comment. Sophia could not hide her shame, but her shame only aggravated the stinging charm of her beauty. She was wearing a hard Amazonian hat, with a lifted veil, the final word of fashion that spring in the Five Towns; her face, beaten by the fresh breeze, shone rosily; her eyes glittered under the dark hat, and the violent colours of her Victorian frock— green and crimson—could not spoil those cheeks. If she looked earthwards, frowning, she was the more adorable so. He had come down the clayey incline from the unfinished red bridge to welcome her, and when the salutations were over they stood still, he gazing apparently at the horizon and she at the yellow marl round the edges of his boots. The encounter was as far away from Sophia's ideal conception as Manchester from Venice.

"So this is the new railway!" said she.

"Yes," said he. "This is your new railway. You can see it better from the bridge."

"But it's very sludgy up there," she objected with a pout.

"Further on it's quite dry," he reassured her.

From the bridge they had a sudden view of a raw gash in the earth; and hundreds of men were crawling about in it, busy with minute operations, like flies in a great wound. There was a continuous rattle of picks, resembling a muffled shower of hail, and in the distance a tiny locomotive was leading a procession of tiny waggons.

"And those are the navvies!" she murmured.

The unspeakable doings of the navvies in the Five Towns had reached even her: how they drank and swore all day on Sundays, how their huts and houses were dens of the most appalling infamy, how they were the curse of a God-fearing and respectable district! She and Gerald Scales glanced down at these dangerous beasts of prey in their yellow corduroys and their open shirts revealing hairy chests. No doubt they both thought how inconvenient it was that railways could not be brought into existence without the aid of such revolting and swinish animals. They glanced down from the height of their nice decorum and felt the powerful attraction of similar superior manners. The manners of the navvies were such that Sophia could not even regard them, nor Gerald Scales permit her to regard them, without blushing.

In a united blush they turned away, up the gradual slope. Sophia knew no longer what she was doing. For some minutes she was as helpless as though she had been in a balloon with him.

"I got my work done early," he said; and added complacently, "As a matter of fact I've had a pretty good day." She was reassured to learn that he was not neglecting his duties. To be philandering with a commercial traveller who has finished a good day's work seemed less shocking than dalliance with a neglecter of business; it seemed indeed, by comparison, respectable.

"It must be very interesting," she said primly.

"What, my trade?"

"Yes. Always seeing new places and so on."

"In a way it is," he admitted judicially. "But I can tell you it was much more agreeable being in Paris."

"Oh! Have you been to Paris?"

"Lived there for nearly two years," he said carelessly. Then, looking at her, "Didn't you notice I never came for a long time?"

"I didn't know you were in Paris," she evaded him.

"I went to start a sort of agency for Birkinshaws," he said.

"I suppose you talk French like anything."

94

"Of course one has to talk French," said he. "I learnt French when I was a child from a governess—my uncle made me—but I forgot most of it at school, and at the Varsity you never learn anything—precious little, anyhow! Certainly not French!"

She was deeply impressed. He was a much greater personage than she had guessed. It had never occurred to her that commercial travellers had to go to a university to finish their complex education. And then, Paris! Paris meant absolutely nothing to her but pure, impossible, unattainable romance. And he had been there! The clouds of glory were around him. He was a hero, dazzling. He had come to her out of another world. He was her miracle. He was almost too miraculous to be true.

She, living her humdrum life at the shop! And he, elegant, brilliant, coming from far cities! They together, side by side, strolling up the road towards the Moorthorne ridge! There was nothing quite like this in the stories of Miss Sewell.

"Your uncle…?" she questioned vaguely.

"Yes, Mr. Boldero. He's a partner in Birkinshaws."

"Oh!"

"You've heard of him? He's a great Wesleyan."

"Oh yes," she said. "When we had the Wesleyan Conference here, he—"

"He's always very great at Conferences," said Gerald Scales.

"I didn't know he had anything to do with Birkinshaws."

"He isn't a working partner of course," Mr. Scales explained. "But he means me to be one. I have to learn the business from the bottom. So now you understand why I'm a traveller."

"I see," she said, still more deeply impressed.

"I'm an orphan," said Gerald. "And Uncle Boldero took me in hand when I was three."

"I SEE!" she repeated.

It seemed strange to her that Mr. Scales should be a Wesleyan—just like herself. She would have been sure that he was 'Church.' Her notions of Wesleyanism, with her notions of various other things, were sharply modified.

"Now tell me about you," Mr. Scales suggested.

"Oh! I'm nothing!" she burst out.

The exclamation was perfectly sincere. Mr. Scales's disclosures concerning himself, while they excited her, discouraged her.

"You're the finest girl I've ever met, anyhow," said Mr. Scales with gallant emphasis, and he dug his stick into the soft ground.

She blushed and made no answer.

They walked on in silence, each wondering apprehensively what might happen next.

Suddenly Mr. Scales stopped at a dilapidated low brick wall, built in a circle, close to the side of the road.

"I expect that's an old pit-shaft," said he.

"Yes, I expect it is."

He picked up a rather large stone and approached the wall.

"Be careful!" she enjoined him.

"Oh! It's all right," he said lightly. "Let's listen. Come near and listen."

She reluctantly obeyed, and he threw the stone over the dirty ruined wall, the top of which was about level with his hat. For two or three seconds there was no sound. Then a faint reverberation echoed from the depths of the shaft. And on Sophia's brain arose dreadful images of the ghosts of miners wandering for ever in subterranean passages, far, far beneath. The noise of the falling stone had awakened for her the secret terrors of the earth. She could scarcely even look at the wall without a spasm of fear.

"How strange," said Mr. Scales, a little awe in his voice, too, "that that should be left there like that! I suppose it's very deep."

"Some of them are," she trembled.

"I must just have a look," he said, and put his hands on the top of the wall.

"Come away!" she cried.

"Oh! It's all right!" he said again, soothingly. "The wall's as firm as a rock." And he took a slight spring and looked over.

She shrieked loudly. She saw him at the distant bottom of the shaft, mangled, drowning. The ground seemed to quake under her feet. A horrible sickness seized her. And she shrieked again. Never had she guessed that existence could be such pain.

95

He slid down from the wall, and turned to her. "No bottom to be seen!" he said. Then, observing her transformed face, he came close to her, with a superior masculine smile. "Silly little thing!" he said coaxingly, endearingly, putting forth all his power to charm.

He perceived at once that he had miscalculated the effects of his action. Her alarm changed swiftly to angry offence. She drew back with a haughty gesture, as if he had intended actually to touch her. Did he suppose, because she chanced to be walking with him, that he had the right to address her familiarly, to tease her, to call her 'silly little thing' and to put his face against hers? She resented his freedom with quick and passionate indignation.

She showed him her proud back and nodding head and wrathful skirts; and hurried off without a word, almost running. As for him, he was so startled by unexpected phenomena that he did nothing for a moment—merely stood looking and feeling foolish.

Then she heard him in pursuit. She was too proud to stop or even to reduce her speed.

"I didn't mean to—" he muttered behind her.

No recognition from her.

"I suppose I ought to apologize," he said.

"I should just think you ought," she answered, furious.

"Well, I do!" said he. "Do stop a minute."

"I'll thank you not to follow me, Mr. Scales." She paused, and scorched him with her displeasure. Then she went forward. And her heart was in torture because it could not persuade her to remain with him, and smile and forgive, and win his smile.

"I shall write to you," he shouted down the slope.

She kept on, the ridiculous child. But the agony she had suffered as he clung to the frail wall was not ridiculous, nor her dark vision of the mine, nor her tremendous indignation when, after disobeying her, he forgot that she was a queen. To her the scene was sublimely tragic. Soon she had recrossed the bridge, but not the same she! So this was the end of the incredible adventure!

When she reached the turnpike she thought of her mother and of Constance. She had completely forgotten them; for a space they had utterly ceased to exist for her.

IV

"You've been out, Sophia?" said Mrs. Baines in the parlour, questioningly. Sophia had taken off her hat and mantle hurriedly in the cutting-out room, for she was in danger of being late for tea; but her hair and face showed traces of the March breeze. Mrs. Baines, whose stoutness seemed to increase, sat in the rocking-chair with a number of The Sunday at Home in her hand. Tea was set.

"Yes, mother. I called to see Miss Chetwynd."

"I wish you'd tell me when you are going out."

"I looked all over for you before I started."

"No, you didn't, for I haven't stirred from this room since four o'clock…. You should not say things like that," Mrs. Baines added in a gentler tone.

Mrs. Baines had suffered much that day. She knew that she was in an irritable, nervous state, and therefore she said to herself, in her quality of wise woman, "I must watch myself. I mustn't let myself go." And she thought how reasonable she was. She did not guess that all her gestures betrayed her; nor did it occur to her that few things are more galling than the spectacle of a person, actuated by lofty motives, obviously trying to be kind and patient under what he considers to be extreme provocation.

Maggie blundered up the kitchen stairs with the teapot and hot toast; and so Sophia had an excuse for silence. Sophia too had suffered much, suffered excruciatingly; she carried at that moment a whole tragedy in her young soul, unaccustomed to such burdens. Her attitude towards her mother was half fearful and half defiant; it might be summed up in the phrase which she had repeated again and again under her breath on the way home, "Well, mother can't kill me!"

Mrs. Baines put down the blue-covered magazine and twisted her rocking-chair towards the table.

"You can pour out the tea," said Mrs. Baines.

"Where's Constance?"

"She's not very well. She's lying down."

"Anything the matter with her?"

"No."

This was inaccurate. Nearly everything was the matter with Constance, who had never been less Constance than during that afternoon. But Mrs. Baines had no intention of discussing Constance's love-affairs with Sophia. The less said to Sophia about love, the better! Sophia was excitable enough already!

They sat opposite to each other, on either side of the fire—the monumental matron whose black bodice heavily overhung the table, whose large rounded face was creased and wrinkled by what seemed countless years of joy and disillusion; and the young, slim girl, so fresh, so virginal, so ignorant, with all the pathos of an unsuspecting victim about to be sacrificed to the minotaur of Time! They both ate hot toast, with careless haste, in silence, preoccupied, worried, and outwardly nonchalant.

"And what has Miss Chetwynd got to say?" Mrs. Baines inquired.

"She wasn't in."

Here was a blow for Mrs. Baines, whose suspicions about Sophia, driven off by her certainties regarding Constance, suddenly sprang forward in her mind, and prowled to and fro like a band of tigers.

Still, Mrs. Baines was determined to be calm and careful. "Oh! What time did you call?"

"I don't know. About half-past four." Sophia finished her tea quickly, and rose. "Shall I tell Mr. Povey he can come?"

(Mr. Povey had his tea after the ladies of the house.)

"Yes, if you will stay in the shop till I come. Light me the gas before you go."

Sophia took a wax taper from a vase on the mantelpiece, stuck it in the fire and lit the gas, which exploded in its crystal cloister with a mild report.

"What's all that clay on your boots, child?" asked Mrs. Baines.

"Clay?" repeated Sophia, staring foolishly at her boots.

"Yes," said Mrs. Baines. "It looks like marl. Where on earth have you been?"

She interrogated her daughter with an upward gaze, frigid and unconsciously hostile, through her gold-rimmed glasses.

"I must have picked it up on the roads," said Sophia, and hastened to the door.

"Sophia!"

"Yes, mother."

"Shut the door."

Sophia unwillingly shut the door which she had half opened.

"Come here."

Sophia obeyed, with falling lip.

"You are deceiving me, Sophia," said Mrs. Baines, with fierce solemnity. "Where have you been this afternoon?"

Sophia's foot was restless on the carpet behind the table. "I haven't been anywhere," she murmured glumly.

"Have you seen young Scales?"

"Yes," said Sophia with grimness, glancing audaciously for an instant at her mother. ("She can't kill me: She can't kill me," her heart muttered. And she had youth and beauty in her favour, while her mother was only a fat middle-aged woman. "She can't kill me," said her heart, with the trembling, cruel insolence of the mirror-flattered child.)

"How came you to meet him?"

No answer.

"Sophia, you heard what I said!"

Still no answer. Sophia looked down at the table. ("She can't kill me.")

"If you are going to be sullen, I shall have to suppose the worst," said Mrs. Baines.

Sophia kept her silence.

"Of course," Mrs. Baines resumed, "if you choose to be wicked, neither your mother nor any one else can stop you. There are certain things I CAN do, and these I SHALL do … Let me warn you that young Scales is a thoroughly bad lot. I know all about him. He has been living a wild life abroad, and if it hadn't been that his uncle is a partner in Birkinshaws, they would never have taken him on again." A pause. "I hope that one day you will be a happy wife, but you are much too young yet to be meeting young men, and nothing would ever induce me to let you have anything to do with this Scales. I won't have it. In future you are not to go out alone. You understand me?"

Sophia kept silence.

"I hope you will be in a better frame of mind to-morrow. I can only hope so. But if you aren't, I shall take very severe measures. You think you can defy me. But you never were more mistaken in your life. I don't want to see any more of you now. Go and tell Mr. Povey; and call Maggie for the fresh tea. You make me almost glad that your father died even as he did. He has, at any rate, been spared this."

Those words 'died even as he did' achieved the intimidation of Sophia. They seemed to indicate that Mrs. Baines, though she had magnanimously never mentioned the subject to Sophia, knew exactly how the old man had died. Sophia escaped from the room in fear, cowed. Nevertheless, her thought was, "She hasn't killed me. I made up my mind I wouldn't talk, and I didn't."

In the evening, as she sat in the shop primly and sternly sewing at hats—while her mother wept in secret on the first floor, and Constance remained hidden on the second—Sophia lived over again the scene at the old shaft; but she lived it differently, admitting that she had been wrong, guessing by instinct that she had shown a foolish mistrust of love. As she sat in the shop, she adopted just the right attitude and said just the right things. Instead of being a silly baby she was an accomplished and dazzling woman, then. When customers came in, and the young lady assistants unobtrusively turned higher the central gas, according to the regime of the shop, it was really extraordinary that they could not read in the heart of the beautiful Miss Baines the words which blazed there; "YOU'RE THE FINEST GIRL I EVER MET," and "I SHALL WRITE TO YOU." The young lady assistants had their notions as to both Constance and Sophia, but the truth, at least as regarded Sophia, was beyond the flight of their imaginations. When eight o'clock struck and she gave the formal order for dust-sheets, the shop being empty, they never supposed that she was dreaming about posts and plotting how to get hold of the morning's letters before Mr. Povey.

CHAPTER VII

A DEFEAT

I

It was during the month of June that Aunt Harriet came over from Axe to spend a few days with her little sister, Mrs. Baines. The railway between Axe and the Five Towns had not yet been opened; but even if it had been opened Aunt Harriet would probably not have used it. She had always travelled from Axe to Bursley in the same vehicle, a small waggonette which she hired from Bratt's livery stables at Axe, driven by a coachman who thoroughly understood the importance, and the peculiarities, of Aunt Harriet.

Mrs. Baines had increased in stoutness, so that now Aunt Harriet had very little advantage over her, physically. But the moral ascendency of the elder still persisted. The two vast widows shared Mrs. Baines's bedroom, spending much of their time there in long, hushed conversations—interviews from which Mrs. Baines emerged with the air of one who has received enlightenment and Aunt Harriet with the air of one who has rendered it. The pair went about together, in the shop, the showroom, the parlour, the kitchen, and also into the town, addressing each other as 'Sister,' 'Sister.' Everywhere it was 'sister,' 'sister,' 'my sister,' 'your dear mother,' 'your Aunt Harriet.' They referred to each other as oracular sources of wisdom and good taste. Respectability stalked abroad when they were afoot. The whole Square wriggled uneasily as though God's eye were peculiarly upon it. The meals in the parlour became solemn collations, at which shone the best silver and the finest diaper, but from which gaiety and naturalness seemed to be banished. (I say 'seemed' because it cannot be doubted that Aunt Harriet was natural, and there were moments when she possibly considered herself to be practising gaiety—a gaiety more desolating than her severity.) The younger generation was extinguished, pressed flat and lifeless under the ponderosity of the widows.

Mr. Povey was not the man to be easily flattened by ponderosity of any kind, and his suppression was a striking proof of the prowess of the widows; who, indeed, went over Mr. Povey like traction-engines, with the sublime unconsciousness of traction-engines, leaving an inanimate object in the road behind them, and scarce aware even of the jolt. Mr. Povey hated Aunt Harriet, but, lying crushed there in the road, how could he rebel? He felt all the time that Aunt Harriet was adding him up, and reporting the result at frequent intervals to Mrs. Baines in the bedroom. He felt that she knew everything about him—even to those tears which had been in his eyes. He felt that he could hope to do nothing right for Aunt Harriet, that absolute perfection in the performance of duty would make no more impression on her than a caress on the fly-wheel of a traction-engine. Constance, the dear Constance, was also looked at askance. There was nothing in Aunt Harriet's demeanour to her that you could take hold of, but there was emphatically something that you could not take hold of—a hint, an inkling, that insinuated to Constance, "Have a care, lest peradventure you become the second cousin of the scarlet woman."

Sophia was petted. Sophia was liable to be playfully tapped by Aunt Harriet's thimble when Aunt Harriet was hemming dusters (for the elderly lady could lift a duster to her own dignity). Sophia was called on two separate occasions, 'My little butterfly.' And Sophia was entrusted with the trimming of Aunt Harriet's new summer bonnet. Aunt Harriet deemed that Sophia was looking pale. As the days passed, Sophia's pallor was emphasized by Aunt Harriet until it developed into an article of faith, to which you were compelled to subscribe on pain of excommunication. Then dawned the day when Aunt Harriet said, staring at Sophia as an affectionate aunt may: "That child would do with a change." And then there dawned another day when Aunt Harriet, staring at Sophia compassionately, as a devoted aunt may, said: "It's a pity that child can't have a change." And Mrs. Baines also stared—and said: "It is."

And on another day Aunt Harriet said: "I've been wondering whether my little Sophia would care to come and keep her old aunt company a while."

There were few things for which Sophia would have cared less. The girl swore to herself angrily that she would not go, that no allurement would induce her to go. But she was in a net; she was in the meshes of family correctness. Do what she would, she could not invent a reason for not going. Certainly she could not tell her aunt that she merely did not want to go. She was capable of enormities, but not of that. And then began Aunt Harriet's intricate preparations for going. Aunt Harriet never did anything simply. And she could not be hurried. Seventy-two hours before leaving she had to commence upon her trunk; but first the trunk had to be wiped by Maggie with a damp cloth under the eye and direction of Aunt Harriet. And the liveryman at Axe had to be written to, and the servants at Axe written to, and the weather prospects weighed and considered. And somehow, by the time these matters were accomplished, it was tacitly understood that Sophia should accompany her kind aunt into the bracing moorland air of Axe. No smoke at Axe! No stuffiness at Axe! The spacious existence of a wealthy widow in a residential town with a low death-rate and famous scenery! "Have you packed your box, Sophia?" No, she had not. "Well, I will come and help you."

Impossible to bear up against the momentum of a massive body like Aunt Harriet's! It was irresistible.

The day of departure came, throwing the entire household into a commotion. Dinner was put a quarter of an hour earlier than usual so that Aunt Harriet might achieve Axe at her accustomed hour of tea. After dinner Maggie was the recipient of three amazing muslin aprons, given with a regal gesture. And the trunk and the box were brought down, and there was a slight odour of black kid gloves in the parlour. The waggonette was due and the waggonette appeared ("I can always rely upon Bladen!" said Aunt Harriet), and the door was opened, and Bladen, stiff on his legs, descended from the box and touched his hat to Aunt Harriet as she filled up the doorway.

"Have you baited, Bladen?" asked she.

"Yes'm," said he, assuringly.

Bladen and Mr. Povey carried out the trunk and the box, and Constance charged herself with parcels which she bestowed in the corners of the vehicle according to her aunt's prescription; it was like stowing the cargo of a vessel.

"Now, Sophia, my chuck!" Mrs. Baines called up the stairs. And Sophia came slowly downstairs. Mrs. Baines offered her mouth. Sophia glanced at her.

"You needn't think I don't see why you're sending me away!" exclaimed Sophia in a hard, furious voice, with glistening eyes. "I'm not so blind as all that!" She kissed her mother—nothing but a contemptuous peck. Then, as she turned away she added: "But you let Constance do just as she likes!"

This was her sole bitter comment on the episode, but into it she put all the profound bitterness accumulated during many mutinous nights.

Mrs. Baines concealed a sigh. The explosion certainly disturbed her.

She had hoped that the smooth surface of things would not be ruffled.

Sophia bounced out. And the assembly, including several urchins, watched with held breath while Aunt Harriet, after having bid majestic good-byes, got on to the step and introduced herself through the doorway of the waggonette into the interior of the vehicle; it was an operation like threading a needle with cotton too thick. Once within, her hoops distended in sudden release, filling the waggonette. Sophia followed, agilely.

As, with due formalities, the equipage drove off, Mrs. Baines gave another sigh, one of relief. The sisters had won. She could now await the imminent next advent of Mr. Gerald Scales with tranquillity.

II

Those singular words of Sophia's, 'But you let Constance do just as she likes,' had disturbed Mrs. Baines more than was at first apparent. They worried her like a late fly in autumn. For she had said nothing to any one about Constance's case, Mrs. Maddack of course excepted. She had instinctively felt that she could not show the slightest leniency towards the romantic impulses of her elder daughter without seeming unjust to the younger, and she had acted accordingly. On the memorable morn of Mr. Povey's acute jealousy, she had, temporarily at any rate, slaked the fire, banked it down, and hidden it; and since then no word had passed as to the state of Constance's heart. In the great peril to be feared from Mr. Scales, Constance's heart had been put aside as a thing that could wait; so one puts aside the mending of linen when earthquake shocks are about. Mrs. Baines was sure that Constance had not chattered to Sophia concerning Mr. Povey. Constance, who understood her mother, had too much commonsense and too nice a sense of propriety to do that—and yet here was Sophia exclaiming, 'But you let Constance do just as she likes.' Were the relations between Constance and Mr. Povey, then, common property? Did the young lady assistants discuss them?

As a fact, the young lady assistants did discuss them; not in the shop—for either one of the principal parties, or Mrs. Baines herself, was always in the shop, but elsewhere. They discussed little else, when they were free; how she had looked at him to-day, and how he had blushed, and so forth interminably. Yet Mrs. Baines really thought that she alone knew. Such is the power of the ineradicable delusion that one's own affairs, and especially one's own children, are mysteriously different from those of others.

After Sophia's departure Mrs. Baines surveyed her daughter and her manager at supper-time with a curious and a diffident eye. They worked, talked, and ate just as though Mrs. Baines had never caught them weeping together in the cutting-out room. They had the most matter-of-fact air. They might never have heard whispered the name of love. And there could be no deceit beneath that decorum; for Constance would not deceive. Still, Mrs. Baines's conscience was unruly. Order reigned, but nevertheless she knew that she ought to do something, find out something, decide something; she ought, if she did her duty, to take Constance aside and say: "Now, Constance, my mind is freer now. Tell me frankly what has been going on between you and Mr. Povey. I have never understood the meaning of that scene in the cutting-out room. Tell me." She ought to have talked in this strain. But she could not. That energetic woman had not sufficient energy left. She wanted rest, rest—even though it were a coward's rest, an ostrich's tranquillity—after the turmoil of apprehensions caused by Sophia. Her soul cried out for peace. She was not, however, to have peace.

On the very first Sunday after Sophia's departure, Mr. Povey did not go to chapel in the morning, and he offered no reason for his unusual conduct. He ate his breakfast with appetite, but there was something peculiar in his glance that made Mrs. Baines a little uneasy; this something she could not seize upon and define. When she and Constance returned from chapel Mr. Povey was playing "Rock of Ages" on the harmonium—again unusual! The serious part of the dinner comprised roast beef and Yorkshire pudding—the pudding being served as a sweet course before the meat. Mrs. Baines ate freely of these things, for she loved them, and she was always hungry after a sermon. She also did well with the Cheshire cheese. Her intention was to sleep in the drawing-room after the repast. On Sunday afternoons she invariably tried to sleep in the drawing-room, and she did not often fail. As a rule the girls accompanied her thither from the table, and either 'settled down' likewise or crept out of the room when they perceived the gradual sinking of the majestic form into the deep hollows of the easy-chair. Mrs. Baines was anticipating with pleasure her somnolent Sunday afternoon.

Constance said grace after meat, and the formula on this particular occasion ran thus—

"Thank God for our good dinner, Amen.—Mother, I must just run upstairs to my room." ('MY room'-Sophia being far away.)

And off she ran, strangely girlish.

"Well, child, you needn't be in such a hurry," said Mrs. Baines, ringing the bell and rising.

She hoped that Constance would remember the conditions precedent to sleep.

"I should like to have a word with you, if it's all the same to you,

Mrs. Baines," said Mr. Povey suddenly, with obvious nervousness. And his tone struck a rude unexpected blow at Mrs. Baines's peace of mind.

It was a portentous tone.

"What about?" asked she, with an inflection subtly to remind Mr. Povey what day it was.

"About Constance," said the astonishing man.

"Constance!" exclaimed Mrs. Baines with a histrionic air of bewilderment.

Maggie entered the room, solely in response to the bell, yet a thought jumped up in Mrs. Baines's brain, "How prying servants are, to be sure!" For quite five seconds she had a grievance against Maggie. She was compelled to sit down again and wait while Maggie cleared the table. Mr. Povey put both his hands in his pockets, got up, went to the window, whistled, and generally behaved in a manner which foretold the worst. At last Maggie vanished, shutting the door.

"What is it, Mr. Povey?"

"Oh!" said Mr. Povey, facing her with absurd nervous brusqueness, as though pretending: "Ah, yes! We have something to say—I was forgetting!" Then he began: "It's about Constance and me."

Yes, they had evidently plotted this interview. Constance had evidently taken herself off on purpose to leave Mr. Povey unhampered. They were in league. The inevitable had come. No sleep! No repose! Nothing but worry once more!

"I'm not at all satisfied with the present situation," said Mr. Povey, in a tone that corresponded to his words.

"I don't know what you mean, Mr. Povey," said Mrs. Baines stiffly. This was a simple lie.

"Well, really, Mrs. Baines!" Mr. Povey protested, "I suppose you won't deny that you know there is something between me and Constance? I suppose you won't deny that?"

"What is there between you and Constance? I can assure you I—"

"That depends on you," Mr. Povey interrupted her. When he was nervous his manners deteriorated into a behaviour that resembled rudeness. "That depends on you!" he repeated grimly.

"But—"

"Are we to be engaged or are we not?" pursued Mr. Povey, as though Mrs. Baines had been guilty of some grave lapse and he was determined not to spare her. "That's what I think ought to be settled, one way or the other. I wish to be perfectly open and aboveboard—in the future, as I have been in the past."

"But you have said nothing to me at all!" Mrs. Baines remonstrated, lifting her eyebrows. The way in which the man had sprung this matter upon her was truly too audacious.

Mr. Povey approached her as she sat at the table, shaking her ringlets and looking at her hands.

"You know there's something between us!" he insisted.

"How should I know there is something between you? Constance has never said a word to me. And have you?"

"Well," said he. "We've hidden nothing."

"What is there between you and Constance? If I may ask!"

"That depends on you," said he again.

"Have you asked her to be your wife?"

"No. I haven't exactly asked her to be my wife." He hesitated. "You see—"

Mrs. Baines collected her forces. "Have you kissed her?" This in a cold voice.

Mr. Povey now blushed. "I haven't exactly kissed her," he stammered, apparently shocked by the inquisition. "No, I should not say that I had kissed her."

It might have been that before committing himself he felt a desire for Mrs. Baines's definition of a kiss.

"You are very extraordinary," she said loftily. It was no less than the truth.

"All I want to know is—have you got anything against me?" he demanded roughly. "Because if so—"

"Anything against you, Mr. Povey? Why should I have anything against you?"

"Then why can't we be engaged?"

She considered that he was bullying her. "That's another question," said she.

"Why can't we be engaged? Ain't I good enough?"

The fact was that he was not regarded as good enough. Mrs. Maddack had certainly deemed that he was not good enough. He was a solid mass of excellent qualities; but he lacked brilliance, importance, dignity. He could not impose himself. Such had been the verdict.

And now, while Mrs. Baines was secretly reproaching Mr. Povey for his inability to impose himself, he was most patently imposing himself on her—and the phenomenon escaped her! She felt that he was bullying her, but somehow she could not perceive his power. Yet the man who could bully Mrs. Baines was surely no common soul!

"You know my very high opinion of you," she said.

Mr. Povey pursued in a mollified tone. "Assuming that Constance is willing to be engaged, do I understand you consent?"

"But Constance is too young."

"Constance is twenty. She is more than twenty."

"In any case you won't expect me to give you an answer now."

"Why not? You know my position."

She did. From a practical point of view the match would be ideal: no fault could be found with it on that side. But Mrs. Baines could not extinguish the idea that it would be a 'come-down' for her daughter. Who, after all, was Mr. Povey? Mr. Povey was nobody.

"I must think things over," she said firmly, putting her lips together.

"I can't reply like this. It is a serious matter."

"When can I have your answer? To-morrow?"

"No—really—"

"In a week, then?"

"I cannot bind myself to a date," said Mrs. Baines, haughtily. She felt that she was gaining ground.

"Because I can't stay on here indefinitely as things are," Mr. Povey burst out, and there was a touch of hysteria in his tone.

"Now, Mr. Povey, please do be reasonable."

"That's all very well," he went on. "That's all very well. But what I say is that employers have no right to have male assistants in their houses unless they are prepared to let their daughters marry! That's what I say! No RIGHT!"

Mrs. Baines did not know what to answer.

The aspirant wound up: "I must leave if that's the case."

"If what's the case?" she asked herself. "What has come over him?" And aloud: "You know you would place me in a very awkward position by leaving, and I hope you don't want to mix up two quite different things. I hope you aren't trying to threaten me."

"Threaten you!" he cried. "Do you suppose I should leave here for fun? If I leave it will be because I can't stand it. That's all. I can't stand it. I want Constance, and if I can't have her, then I can't stand it. What do you think I'm made of?"

"I'm sure—" she began.

"That's all very well!" he almost shouted.

"But please let me speak,' she said quietly.

"All I say is I can't stand it. That's all…. Employers have no right…. We have our feelings like other men." He was deeply moved. He might have appeared somewhat grotesque to the strictly impartial observer of human nature. Nevertheless he was deeply and genuinely moved, and possibly human nature could have shown nothing more human than Mr. Povey at the moment when, unable any longer to restrain the paroxysm which had so surprisingly overtaken him, he fled from the parlour, passionately, to the retreat of his bedroom.

"That's the worst of those quiet calm ones," said Mrs. Baines to herself. "You never know if they won't give way. And when they do, it's awful—awful…. What did I do, what did I say, to bring it on? Nothing! Nothing!"

And where was her afternoon sleep? What was going to happen to her daughter? What could she say to Constance? How next could she meet Mr. Povey? Ah! It needed a brave, indomitable woman not to cry out brokenly: "I've suffered too much. Do anything you like; only let me die in peace!" And so saying, to let everything indifferently slide!

III

Neither Mr. Povey nor Constance introduced the delicate subject to her again, and she was determined not to be the first to speak of it. She considered that Mr. Povey had taken advantage of his position, and that he had also been infantile and impolite. And somehow she privately blamed Constance for his behaviour. So the matter hung, as it were, suspended in the ether between the opposing forces of pride and passion.

Shortly afterwards events occurred compared to which the vicissitudes of Mr. Povey's heart were of no more account than a shower of rain in April. And fate gave no warning of them; it rather indicated a complete absence of events. When the customary advice circular arrived from Birkinshaws, the name of 'our Mr. Gerald

Scales' was replaced on it by another and an unfamiliar name. Mrs. Baines, seeing the circular by accident, experienced a sense of relief, mingled with the professional disappointment of a diplomatist who has elaborately provided for contingencies which have failed to happen. She had sent Sophia away for nothing; and no doubt her maternal affection had exaggerated a molehill into a mountain. Really, when she reflected on the past, she could not recall a single fact that would justify her theory of an attachment secretly budding between Sophia and the young man Scales! Not a single little fact! All she could bring forward was that Sophia had twice encountered Scales in the street.

She felt a curious interest in the fate of Scales, for whom in her own mind she had long prophesied evil, and when Birkinshaws' representative came she took care to be in the shop; her intention was to converse with him, and ascertain as much as was ascertainable, after Mr. Povey had transacted business. For this purpose, at a suitable moment, she traversed the shop to Mr. Povey's side, and in so doing she had a fleeting view of King Street, and in King Street of a familiar vehicle. She stopped, and seemed to catch the distant sound of knocking. Abandoning the traveller, she hurried towards the parlour, in the passage she assuredly did hear knocking, angry and impatient knocking, the knocking of someone who thinks he has knocked too long.

"Of course Maggie is at the top of the house!" she muttered sarcastically.

She unchained, unbolted, and unlocked the side-door.

"At last!" It was Aunt Harriet's voice, exacerbated. "What! You, sister? You're soon up. What a blessing!" The two majestic and imposing creatures met on the mat, craning forward so that their lips might meet above their terrific bosoms.

"What's the matter?" Mrs. Baines asked, fearfully.

"Well, I do declare!" said Mrs. Maddack. "And I've driven specially over to ask you!"

"Where's Sophia?" demanded Mrs. Baines.

"You don't mean to say she's not come, sister?" Mrs. Maddack sank down on to the sofa.

"Come?" Mrs. Baines repeated. "Of course she's not come! What do you mean, sister?"

"The very moment she got Constance's letter yesterday, saying you were ill in bed and she'd better come over to help in the shop, she started. I got Bratt's dog-cart for her."

Mrs. Baines in her turn also sank down on to the sofa.

"I've not been ill," she said. "And Constance hasn't written for a week! Only yesterday I was telling her—"

"Sister—it can't be! Sophia had letters from Constance every morning. At least she said they were from Constance. I told her to be sure and write me how you were last night, and she promised faithfully she would. And it was because I got nothing by this morning's post that I decided to come over myself, to see if it was anything serious."

"Serious it is!" murmured Mrs. Baines.

"What—"

"Sophia's run off. That's the plain English of it!" said Mrs. Baines with frigid calm.

"Nay! That I'll never believe. I've looked after Sophia night and day as if she was my own, and—"

"If she hasn't run off, where is she?"

Mrs. Maddack opened the door with a tragic gesture.

"Bladen," she called in a loud voice to the driver of the waggonette, who was standing on the pavement.

"Yes'm."

"It was Pember drove Miss Sophia yesterday, wasn't it?"

"Yes'm."

She hesitated. A clumsy question might enlighten a member of the class which ought never to be enlightened about one's private affairs.

"He didn't come all the way here?"

"No'm. He happened to say last night when he got back as Miss Sophia had told him to set her down at Knype Station."

"I thought so!" said Mrs. Maddack, courageously.

"Yes'm."

"Sister!" she moaned, after carefully shutting the door.

They clung to each other.

The horror of what had occurred did not instantly take full possession of them, because the power of credence, of imaginatively realizing a supreme event, whether of great grief or of great happiness, is ridiculously finite. But every minute the horror grew more clear, more intense, more tragically dominant over them. There were many things that they could not say to each other,—from pride, from shame, from the inadequacy of words.

Neither could utter the name of Gerald Scales. And Aunt Harriet could not stoop to defend herself from a possible charge of neglect; nor could Mrs. Baines stoop to assure her sister that she was incapable of preferring such a charge. And the sheer, immense criminal folly of Sophia could not even be referred to: it was unspeakable. So the interview proceeded, lamely, clumsily, inconsequently, leading to naught. Sophia was gone. She was gone with Gerald Scales.

That beautiful child, that incalculable, untamable, impossible creature, had committed the final folly; without pretext or excuse, and with what elaborate deceit! Yes, without excuse! She had not been treated harshly; she had had a degree of liberty which would have astounded and shocked her grandmothers; she had been petted, humoured, spoilt. And her answer was to disgrace the family by an act as irrevocable as it was utterly vicious. If among her desires was the desire to humiliate those majesties, her mother and Aunt Harriet, she would have been content could she have seen them on the sofa there, humbled, shamed, mortally wounded! Ah, the monstrous Chinese cruelty of youth!

What was to be done? Tell dear Constance? No, this was not, at the moment, an affair for the younger generation. It was too new and raw for the younger generation. Moreover, capable, proud, and experienced as they were, they felt the need of a man's voice, and a man's hard, callous ideas. It was a case for Mr. Critchlow. Maggie was sent to fetch him, with a particular request that he should come to the side-door. He came expectant, with the pleasurable anticipation of disaster, and he was not disappointed. He passed with the sisters the happiest hour that had fallen to him for years. Quickly he arranged the alternatives for them. Would they tell the police, or would they take the risks of waiting? They shied away, but with fierce brutality he brought them again and again to the immediate point of decision.... Well, they could not tell the police! They simply could not. Then they must face another danger.... He had no mercy for them. And while he was torturing them there arrived a telegram, despatched from Charing Cross, "I am all right, Sophia." That proved, at any rate, that the child was not heartless, not merely careless.

Only yesterday, it seemed to Mrs. Baines, she had borne Sophia; only yesterday she was a baby, a schoolgirl to be smacked. The years rolled up in a few hours. And now she was sending telegrams from a place called Charing Cross! How unlike was the hand of the telegram to Sophia's hand! How mysteriously curt and inhuman was that official hand, as Mrs. Baines stared at it through red, wet eyes!

Mr. Critchlow said some one should go to Manchester, to ascertain about Scales. He went himself, that afternoon, and returned with the news that an aunt of Scales had recently died, leaving him twelve thousand pounds, and that he had, after quarrelling with his uncle Boldero, abandoned Birkinshaws at an hour's notice and vanished with his inheritance.

"It's as plain as a pikestaff," said Mr. Critchlow. "I could ha' warned ye o' all this years ago, even since she killed her father!"

Mr. Critchlow left nothing unsaid.

During the night Mrs. Baines lived through all Sophia's life, lived through it more intensely than ever Sophia had done.

The next day people began to know. A whisper almost inaudible went across the Square, and into the town: and in the stillness every one heard it. "Sophia Baines run off with a commercial!"

In another fortnight a note came, also dated from London.

"Dear Mother, I am married to Gerald Scales. Please don't worry about me. We are going abroad. Your affectionate Sophia. Love to Constance." No tear-stains on that pale blue sheet! No sign of agitation!

And Mrs. Baines said: "My life is over." It was, though she was scarcely fifty. She felt old, old and beaten. She had fought and been vanquished. The everlasting purpose had been too much for her. Virtue had gone out of her—the virtue to hold up her head and look the Square in the face. She, the wife of John Baines! She, a Syme of Axe!

Old houses, in the course of their history, see sad sights, and never forget them! And ever since, in the solemn physiognomy of the triple house of John Baines at the corner of St. Luke's Square and King Street, have remained the traces of the sight it saw on the morning of the afternoon when Mr. and Mrs. Povey returned from their honeymoon—the sight of Mrs. Baines getting into the waggonette for Axe; Mrs. Baines, encumbered with trunks and parcels, leaving the scene of her struggles and her defeat, whither she had once come as slim as a wand, to return stout and heavy, and heavy-hearted, to her childhood; content to live with her grandiose sister until such time as she should be ready for burial! The grimy and impassive old house perhaps heard her heart saying: "Only yesterday they were little girls, ever so tiny, and now—" The driving-off of a waggonette can be a dreadful thing.

BOOK II

CONSTANCE

CHAPTER I

REVOLUTION
I

"Well," said Mr. Povey, rising from the rocking-chair that in a previous age had been John Baines's, "I've got to make a start some time, so I may as well begin now!"

And he went from the parlour into the shop. Constance's eye followed him as far as the door, where their glances met for an instant in the transient gaze which expresses the tenderness of people who feel more than they kiss.

It was on the morning of this day that Mrs. Baines, relinquishing the sovereignty of St. Luke's Square, had gone to live as a younger sister in the house of Harriet Maddack at Axe. Constance guessed little of the secret anguish of that departure. She only knew that it was just like her mother, having perfectly arranged the entire house for the arrival of the honeymoon couple from Buxton, to flit early away so as to spare the natural blushing diffidence of the said couple. It was like her mother's commonsense and her mother's sympathetic comprehension. Further, Constance did not pursue her mother's feelings, being far too busy with her own. She sat there full of new knowledge and new importance, brimming with experience and strange, unexpected aspirations, purposes, yes—and cunnings! And yet, though the very curves of her cheeks seemed to be mysteriously altering, the old Constance still lingered in that frame, an innocent soul hesitating to spread its wings and quit for ever the body which had been its home; you could see the timid thing peeping wistfully out of the eyes of the married woman.

Constance rang the bell for Maggie to clear the table; and as she did so she had the illusion that she was not really a married woman and a house-mistress, but only a kind of counterfeit. She did most fervently hope that all would go right in the house—at any rate until she had grown more accustomed to her situation.

The hope was to be disappointed. Maggie's rather silly, obsequious smile concealed but for a moment the ineffable tragedy that had lain in wait for unarmed Constance.

"If you please, Mrs. Povey," said Maggie, as she crushed cups together on the tin tray with her great, red hands, which always looked like something out of a butcher's shop; then a pause, "Will you please accept of this?"

Now, before the wedding Maggie had already, with tears of affection, given Constance a pair of blue glass vases (in order to purchase which she had been obliged to ask for special permission to go out), and Constance wondered what was coming now from Maggie's pocket. A small piece of folded paper came from Maggie's pocket. Constance accepted of it, and read: "I begs to give one month's notice to leave. Signed Maggie. June 10, 1867."

"Maggie!" exclaimed the old Constance, terrified by this incredible occurrence, ere the married woman could strangle her.

"I never give notice before, Mrs. Povey," said Maggie, "so I don't know as I know how it ought for be done—not rightly. But I hope as you'll accept of it, Mrs. Povey."

"Oh! of course," said Mrs. Povey, primly, just as if Maggie was not the central supporting pillar of the house, just as if Maggie had not assisted at her birth, just as if the end of the world had not abruptly been announced, just as if St. Luke's Square were not inconceivable without Maggie. "But why—"

"Well, Mrs. Povey, I've been a-thinking it over in my kitchen, and I said to myself: 'If there's going to be one change there'd better be two,' I says. Not but what I wouldn't work my fingers to the bone for ye, Miss Constance."

Here Maggie began to cry into the tray.

Constance looked at her. Despite the special muslin of that day she had traces of the slatternliness of which Mrs. Baines had never been able to cure her. She was over forty, big, gawky. She had no figure, no charms of

105

any kind. She was what was left of a woman after twenty-two years in the cave of a philanthropic family. And in her cave she had actually been thinking things over! Constance detected for the first time, beneath the dehumanized drudge, the stirrings of a separate and perhaps capricious individuality. Maggie's engagements had never been real to her employers. Within the house she had never been, in practice, anything but 'Maggie'—an organism. And now she was permitting herself ideas about changes!

"You'll soon be suited with another, Mrs. Povey," said Maggie. "There's many a—many a—" She burst into sobs.

"But if you really want to leave, what are you crying for, Maggie?" asked Mrs. Povey, at her wisest. "Have you told mother?"

"No, miss," Maggie whimpered, absently wiping her wrinkled cheeks with ineffectual muslin. "I couldn't seem to fancy telling your mother. And as you're the mistress now, I thought as I'd save it for you when you come home. I hope you'll excuse me, Mrs. Povey."

"Of course I'm very sorry. You've been a very good servant. And in these days—"

The child had acquired this turn of speech from her mother. It did not appear to occur to either of them that they were living in the sixties.

"Thank ye, miss."

"And what are you thinking of doing, Maggie? You know you won't get many places like this."

"To tell ye the truth, Mrs. Povey, I'm going to get married mysen."

"Indeed!" murmured Constance, with the perfunctoriness of habit in replying to these tidings.

"Oh! but I am, mum," Maggie insisted. "It's all settled. Mr. Hollins, mum."

"Not Hollins, the fish-hawker!"

"Yes, mum. I seem to fancy him. You don't remember as him and me was engaged in '48. He was my first, like. I broke it off because he was in that Chartist lot, and I knew as Mr. Baines would never stand that. Now he's asked me again. He's been a widower this long time."

"I'm sure I hope you'll be happy, Maggie. But what about his habits?"

"He won't have no habits with me, Mrs. Povey."

A woman was definitely emerging from the drudge.

When Maggie, having entirely ceased sobbing, had put the folded cloth in the table-drawer and departed with the tray, her mistress became frankly the girl again. No primness about her as she stood alone there in the parlour; no pretence that Maggie's notice to leave was an everyday document, to be casually glanced at—as one glances at an unpaid bill! She would be compelled to find a new servant, making solemn inquiries into character, and to train the new servant, and to talk to her from heights from which she had never addressed Maggie. At that moment she had an illusion that there were no other available, suitable servants in the whole world. And the arranged marriage? She felt that this time—the thirteenth or fourteenth time—the engagement was serious and would only end at the altar. The vision of Maggie and Hollins at the altar shocked her. Marriage was a series of phenomena, and a general state, very holy and wonderful—too sacred, somehow, for such creatures as Maggie and Hollins. Her vague, instinctive revolt against such a usage of matrimony centred round the idea of a strong, eternal smell of fish. However, the projected outrage on a hallowed institution troubled her much less than the imminent problem of domestic service.

She ran into the shop—or she would have run if she had not checked her girlishness betimes—and on her lips, ready to be whispered importantly into a husband's astounded ear, were the words, "Maggie has given notice! Yes! Truly!" But Samuel Povey was engaged. He was leaning over the counter and staring at an outspread paper upon which a certain Mr. Yardley was making strokes with a thick pencil. Mr. Yardley, who had a long red beard, painted houses and rooms. She knew him only by sight. In her mind she always associated him with the sign over his premises in Trafalgar Road, "Yardley Bros., Authorised plumbers. Painters. Decorators. Paper-hangers. Facia writers." For years, in childhood, she had passed that sign without knowing what sort of things 'Bros,' and 'Facia' were, and what was the mysterious similarity between a plumber and a version of the Bible. She could not interrupt her husband, he was wholly absorbed; nor could she stay in the shop (which appeared just a little smaller than usual), for that would have meant an unsuccessful endeavour to front the young lady-assistants as though nothing in particular had happened to her. So she went sedately up the showroom stairs and thus to the bedroom floors of the house—her house! Mrs. Povey's house! She even climbed to Constance's old bedroom; her mother had stripped the bed—that was all, except a slight diminution of this room, corresponding to that of the shop! Then to the drawing-room. In the recess outside the drawing-room door the black box of silver plate still lay. She had expected her mother to take it; but no! Assuredly her mother was one to do things handsomely—when she did them. In the drawing-room, not a tassel of an antimacassar touched! Yes, the fire-screen, the luscious bunch of roses on an expanse of mustard, which Constance had worked for her mother years ago, was gone! That her mother should have clung to just that one souvenir, out of all the heavy opulence of the drawing-room, touched Constance intimately. She perceived that if she could not talk to her husband she must write to her mother. And she sat down at the oval table and wrote, "Darling mother, I am sure you will be very surprised to hear…. She means it…. I think she is making a serious mistake. Ought I to put an advertisement in the Signal, or will it do if…. Please write by return. We are back and have enjoyed ourselves very much. Sam says he enjoys getting up late…." And so on to the last inch of the fourth scolloped page.

She was obliged to revisit the shop for a stamp, stamps being kept in Mr. Povey's desk in the corner—a high desk, at which you stood. Mr. Povey was now in earnest converse with Mr. Yardley at the door, and twilight, which began a full hour earlier in the shop than in the Square, had cast faint shadows in corners behind counters.

"Will you just run out with this to the pillar, Miss Dadd?"

"With pleasure, Mrs. Povey."

"Where are you going to?" Mr. Povey interrupted his conversation to stop the flying girl.

"She's just going to the post for me," Constance called out from the region of the till.

"Oh! All right!"

A trifle! A nothing! Yet somehow, in the quiet customerless shop, the episode, with the scarce perceptible difference in Samuel's tone at his second remark, was delicious to Constance. Somehow it was the REAL beginning of her wifehood. (There had been about nine other real beginnings in the past fortnight.)

Mr. Povey came in to supper, laden with ledgers and similar works which Constance had never even pretended to understand. It was a sign from him that the honeymoon was over. He was proprietor now, and his ardour for ledgers most justifiable. Still, there was the question of her servant.

"Never!" he exclaimed, when she told him all about the end of the world. A 'never' which expressed extreme astonishment and the liveliest concern!

But Constance had anticipated that he would have been just a little more knocked down, bowled over, staggered, stunned, flabbergasted. In a swift gleam of insight she saw that she had been in danger of forgetting her role of experienced, capable married woman.

"I shall have to set about getting a fresh one," she said hastily, with an admirable assumption of light and easy casualness.

Mr. Povey seemed to think that Hollins would suit Maggie pretty well. He made no remark to the betrothed when she answered the final bell of the night.

He opened his ledgers, whistling.

"I think I shall go up, dear," said Constance. "I've a lot of things to put away."

"Do," said he. "Call out when you've done."

II

"Sam!" she cried from the top of the crooked stairs.

No answer. The door at the foot was closed.

"Sam!"

"Hello?" Distantly, faintly.

"I've done all I'm going to do to-night."

And she ran back along the corridor, a white figure in the deep gloom, and hurried into bed, and drew the clothes up to her chin.

In the life of a bride there are some dramatic moments. If she has married the industrious apprentice, one of those moments occurs when she first occupies the sacred bed-chamber of her ancestors, and the bed on which she was born. Her parents' room had always been to Constance, if not sacred, at least invested with a certain moral solemnity. She could not enter it as she would enter another room. The course of nature, with its succession of deaths, conceptions, and births, slowly makes such a room august with a mysterious quality which interprets the grandeur of mere existence and imposes itself on all. Constance had the strangest sensations in that bed, whose heavy dignity of ornament symbolized a past age; sensations of sacrilege and trespass, of being a naughty girl to whom punishment would accrue for this shocking freak. Not since she was quite tiny had she slept in that bed—one night with her mother, before her father's seizure, when he had been away. What a limitless, unfathomable bed it was then! Now it was just a bed—so she had to tell herself—like any other bed. The tiny child that, safely touching its mother, had slept in the vast expanse, seemed to her now a pathetic little thing; its image made her feel melancholy. And her mind dwelt on sad events: the death of her father, the flight of darling Sophia; the immense grief, and the exile, of her mother. She esteemed that she knew what life was, and that it was grim. And she sighed. But the sigh was an affectation, meant partly to convince herself that she was grown-up, and partly to keep her in countenance in the intimidating bed. This melancholy was factitious, was less than transient foam on the deep sea of her joy. Death and sorrow and sin were dim shapes to her; the ruthless egoism of happiness blew them away with a puff, and their wistful faces vanished. To see her there in the bed, framed in mahogany and tassels, lying on her side, with her young glowing cheeks, and honest but not artless gaze, and the rich curve of her hip lifting the counterpane, one would have said that she had never heard of aught but love.

Mr. Povey entered, the bridegroom, quickly, firmly, carrying it off rather well, but still self-conscious. "After all," his shoulders were trying to say, "what's the difference between this bedroom and the bedroom of a boarding-house? Indeed, ought we not to feel more at home here? Besides, confound it, we've been married a fortnight!"

"Doesn't it give you a funny feeling, sleeping in this room? It does me," said Constance. Women, even experienced women, are so foolishly frank. They have no decency, no self-respect.

"Really?" replied Mr. Povey, with loftiness, as who should say: "What an extraordinary thing that a reasonable creature can have such fancies! Now to me this room is exactly like any other room." And he added aloud, glancing away from the glass, where he was unfastening his necktie: "It's not a bad room at all." This, with the judicial air of an auctioneer.

Not for an instant did he deceive Constance, who read his real sensations with accuracy. But his futile poses did not in the slightest degree lessen her respect for him. On the contrary, she admired him the more for them; they were a sort of embroidery on the solid stuff of his character. At that period he could not do wrong for her. The basis of her regard for him was, she often thought, his honesty, his industry, his genuine kindliness of act, his grasp of the business, his perseverance, his passion for doing at once that which had to be done. She had the greatest admiration for his qualities, and he was in her eyes an indivisible whole; she could not admire one part of him and frown upon another. Whatever he did was good because he did it. She knew that some people were apt to smile at certain phases of his individuality; she knew that far down in her mother's heart was a suspicion that she had married ever so little beneath her. But this knowledge did not disturb her. She had no doubt as to the correctness of her own estimate.

Mr. Povey was an exceedingly methodical person, and he was also one of those persons who must always be 'beforehand' with time. Thus at night he would arrange his raiment so that in the morning it might be reassumed in the minimum of minutes. He was not a man, for example, to leave the changing of studs from one shirt to another till the morrow. Had it been practicable, he would have brushed his hair the night before. Constance already loved to watch his meticulous preparations. She saw him now go into his old bedroom and return with a paper collar, which he put on the dressing-table next to a black necktie. His shop-suit was laid out on a chair.

"Oh, Sam!" she exclaimed impulsively, "you surely aren't going to begin wearing those horrid paper collars again!" During the honeymoon he had worn linen collars.

Her tone was perfectly gentle, but the remark, nevertheless, showed a lack of tact. It implied that all his life Mr. Povey had been enveloping his neck in something which was horrid. Like all persons with a tendency to fall into the ridiculous, Mr. Povey was exceedingly sensitive to personal criticisms. He flushed darkly.

"I didn't know they were 'horrid,'" he snapped. He was hurt and angry.

Anger had surprised him unawares.

Both of them suddenly saw that they were standing on the edge of a chasm, and drew back. They had imagined themselves to be wandering safely in a flowered meadow, and here was this bottomless chasm! It was most disconcerting.

Mr. Povey's hand hovered undecided over the collar. "However—" he muttered.

She could feel that he was trying with all his might to be gentle and pacific. And she was aghast at her own stupid clumsiness, she so experienced!

"Just as you like, dear," she said quickly. "Please!"

"Oh no!" And he did his best to smile, and went off gawkily with the collar and came back with a linen one.

Her passion for him burned stronger than ever. She knew then that she did not love him for his good qualities, but for something boyish and naive that there was about him, an indescribable something that occasionally, when his face was close to hers, made her dizzy.

The chasm had disappeared. In such moments, when each must pretend not to have seen or even suspected the chasm, small-talk is essential.

"Wasn't that Mr. Yardley in the shop to-night?" began Constance.

"Yes."

"What did he want?"

"I'd sent for him. He's going to paint us a signboard."

Useless for Samuel to make-believe that nothing in this world is more ordinary than a signboard.

"Oh!" murmured Constance. She said no more, the episode of the paper collar having weakened her self-confidence.

But a signboard!

What with servants, chasms, and signboards, Constance considered that her life as a married woman would not be deficient in excitement. Long afterwards, she fell asleep, thinking of Sophia.

III

A few days later Constance was arranging the more precious of her wedding presents in the parlour; some had to be wrapped in tissue and in brown paper and then tied with string and labelled; others had special cases of their own, leather without and velvet within. Among the latter was the resplendent egg-stand holding twelve silver-gilt egg-cups and twelve chased spoons to match, presented by Aunt Harriet. In the Five Towns' phrase, 'it must have cost money.' Even if Mr. and Mrs. Povey had ten guests or ten children, and all the twelve of them were simultaneously gripped by a desire to eat eggs at breakfast or tea—even in this remote contingency Aunt Harriet would have been pained to see the egg-stand in use; such treasures are not designed for use. The presents, few in number, were mainly of this character, because, owing to her mother's heroic cession of the entire interior, Constance already possessed every necessary. The fewness of the presents was accounted for by the fact that the wedding had been strictly private and had taken place at Axe. There is nothing like secrecy in marriage for discouraging the generous impulses of one's friends. It was Mrs. Baines, abetted by both the chief parties, who had decided that the wedding should be private and secluded. Sophia's wedding had been altogether too private and secluded; but the casting of a veil over Constance's (whose union was irreproachable) somehow justified, after the event, the circumstances of Sophia's, indicating as it did that Mrs. Baines believed in secret weddings on principle. In such matters Mrs. Baines was capable of extraordinary subtlety.

And while Constance was thus taking her wedding presents with due seriousness, Maggie was cleaning the steps that led from the pavement of King Street to the side-door, and the door was ajar. It was a fine June morning.

Suddenly, over the sound of scouring, Constance heard a dog's low growl and then the hoarse voice of a man:

"Mester in, wench?"

"Happen he is, happen he isn't," came Maggie's answer. She had no fancy for being called wench.

Constance went to the door, not merely from curiosity, but from a feeling that her authority and her responsibilities as house-mistress extended to the pavement surrounding the house.

The famous James Boon, of Buck Row, the greatest dog-fancier in the Five Towns, stood at the bottom of the steps: a tall, fat man, clad in stiff, stained brown and smoking a black clay pipe less than three inches long. Behind him attended two bull-dogs.

"Morning, missis!" cried Boon, cheerfully. "I've heerd tell as th' mister is looking out for a dog, as you might say."

"I don't stay here with them animals a-sniffing at me—no, that I don't!" observed Maggie, picking herself up.

"Is he?" Constance hesitated. She knew that Samuel had vaguely referred to dogs; she had not, however, imagined that he regarded a dog as aught but a beautiful dream. No dog had ever put paw into that house, and it seemed impossible that one should ever do so. As for those beasts of prey on the pavement…!

"Ay!" said James Boon, calmly.

"I'll tell him you're here," said Constance. "But I don't know if he's at liberty. He seldom is at this time of day. Maggie, you'd better come in."

She went slowly to the shop, full of fear for the future.

"Sam," she whispered to her husband, who was writing at his desk, "here's a man come to see you about a dog."

Assuredly he was taken aback. Still, he behaved with much presence of mind.

"Oh, about a dog! Who is it?"

"It's that Jim Boon. He says he's heard you want one."

The renowned name of Jim Boon gave him pause; but he had to go through with the affair, and he went through with it, though nervously. Constance followed his agitated footsteps to the side-door.

"Morning, Boon."

"Morning, master."

They began to talk dogs, Mr. Povey, for his part, with due caution.

"Now, there's a dog!" said Boon, pointing to one of the bull-dogs, a miracle of splendid ugliness.

"Yes," responded Mr. Povey, insincerely. "He is a beauty. What's it worth now, at a venture?"

"I'll tak' a hundred and twenty sovereigns for her," said Boon. "Th' other's a bit cheaper—a hundred."

"Oh, Sam!" gasped Constance.

And even Mr. Povey nearly lost his nerve. "That's more than I want to give," said he timidly.

"But look at her!" Boon persisted, roughly snatching up the more expensive animal, and displaying her cannibal teeth.

Mr. Povey shook his head. Constance glanced away.

"That's not quite the sort of dog I want," said Mr. Povey.

"Fox-terrier?"

"Yes, that's more like," Mr. Povey agreed eagerly.

"What'll ye run to?"

"Oh," said Mr. Povey, largely, "I don't know."

"Will ye run to a tenner?"

"I thought of something cheaper."

"Well, hoo much? Out wi' it, mester."

"Not more than two pounds," said Mr. Povey. He would have said one pound had he dared. The prices of dogs amazed him.

"I thowt it was a dog as ye wanted!" said Boon. "Look 'ere, mester.

Come up to my yard and see what I've got."

"I will," said Mr. Povey.

"And bring missis along too. Now, what about a cat for th' missis? Or a gold-fish?"

The end of the episode was that a young lady aged some twelve months entered the Povey household on trial. Her exiguous legs twinkled all over the parlour, and she had the oddest appearance in the parlour. But she was so confiding, so affectionate, so timorous, and her black nose was so icy in that hot weather, that Constance loved her violently within an hour. Mr. Povey made rules for her. He explained to her that she must never, never go into the shop. But she went, and he whipped her to the squealing point, and Constance cried an instant, while admiring her husband's firmness.

The dog was not all.

On another day Constance, prying into the least details of the parlour, discovered a box of cigars inside the lid of the harmonium, on the keyboard. She was so unaccustomed to cigars that at first she did not realize what the object was. Her father had never smoked, nor drunk intoxicants; nor had Mr. Critchlow. Nobody had ever smoked in that house, where tobacco had always been regarded as equally licentious with cards, 'the devil's playthings.' Certainly Samuel had never smoked in the house, though the sight of the cigar-box reminded Constance of an occasion when her mother had announced an incredulous suspicion that Mr. Povey, fresh from an excursion into the world on a Thursday evening, 'smelt of smoke.'

She closed the harmonium and kept silence.

That very night, coming suddenly into the parlour, she caught Samuel at the harmonium. The lid went down with a resonant bang that awoke sympathetic vibrations in every corner of the room.

"What is it?" Constance inquired, jumping.

"Oh, nothing!" replied Mr. Povey, carelessly. Each was deceiving the other: Mr. Povey hid his crime, and Constance hid her knowledge of his crime. False, false! But this is what marriage is.

And the next day Constance had a visit in the shop from a possible new servant, recommended to her by Mr. Holl, the grocer.

"Will you please step this way?" said Constance, with affable primness, steeped in the novel sense of what it is to be the sole responsible mistress of a vast household. She preceded the girl to the parlour, and as they passed the open door of Mr. Povey's cutting-out room, Constance had the clear vision and titillating odour of her husband smoking a cigar. He was in his shirt-sleeves, calmly cutting out, and Fan (the lady companion), at watch on the bench, yapped at the possible new servant.

"I think I shall try that girl," said she to Samuel at tea. She said nothing as to the cigar; nor did he.

On the following evening, after supper, Mr. Povey burst out:

"I think I'll have a weed! You didn't know I smoked, did you?"

Thus Mr. Povey came out in his true colours as a blood, a blade, and a gay spark.

But dogs and cigars, disconcerting enough in their degree, were to the signboard, when the signboard at last came, as skim milk is to hot brandy. It was the signboard that, more startlingly than anything else, marked the dawn of a new era in St. Luke's Square. Four men spent a day and a half in fixing it; they had ladders, ropes, and pulleys, and two of them dined on the flat lead roof of the projecting shop-windows. The signboard was thirty-five feet long and two feet in depth; over its centre was a semicircle about three feet in radius; this semicircle bore the legend, judiciously disposed, "S. Povey. Late." All the sign-board proper was devoted to the words, "John Baines," in gold letters a foot and a half high, on a green ground.

The Square watched and wondered; and murmured: "Well, bless us! What next?"

It was agreed that in giving paramount importance to the name of his late father-in-law, Mr. Povey had displayed a very nice feeling.

Some asked with glee: "What'll the old lady have to say?"

Constance asked herself this, but not with glee. When Constance walked down the Square homewards, she could scarcely bear to look at the sign; the thought of what her mother might say frightened her. Her mother's first visit of state was imminent, and Aunt Harriet was to accompany her. Constance felt almost sick as the day approached. When she faintly hinted her apprehensions to Samuel, he demanded, as if surprised—

"Haven't you mentioned it in one of your letters?"

"Oh NO!"

"If that's all," said he, with bravado, "I'll write and tell her myself."

IV

So that Mrs. Baines was duly apprised of the signboard before her arrival. The letter written by her to Constance after receiving Samuel's letter, which was merely the amiable epistle of a son-in-law anxious to be a little more than correct, contained no reference to the signboard. This silence, however, did not in the least allay Constance's apprehensions as to what might occur when her mother and Samuel met beneath the signboard itself. It was therefore with a fearful as well as an eager, loving heart that Constance opened her side-door and ran down the steps when the waggonette stopped in King Street on the Thursday morning of the great visit of the sisters. But a surprise awaited her. Aunt Harriet had not come. Mrs. Baines explained, as she soundly kissed her daughter, that at the last moment Aunt Harriet had not felt well enough to undertake the journey. She sent her fondest love, and cake. Her pains had recurred. It was these mysterious pains which had prevented the sisters from coming to Bursley earlier. The word "cancer"—the continual terror of stout women—had been on their lips, without having been actually uttered; then there was a surcease, and each was glad that she had refrained from the dread syllables. In view of the recurrence, it was not unnatural that Mrs. Baines's vigorous cheerfulness should be somewhat forced.

"What is it, do you think?" Constance inquired.

Mrs. Baines pushed her lips out and raised her eyebrows—a gesture which meant that the pains might mean God knew what.

"I hope she'll be all right alone," observed Constance. "Of course," said Mrs. Baines, quickly. "But you don't suppose I was going to disappoint you, do you?" she added, looking round as if to defy the fates in general.

This speech, and its tone, gave intense pleasure to Constance; and, laden with parcels, they mounted the stairs together, very content with each other, very happy in the discovery that they were still mother and daughter, very intimate in an inarticulate way.

Constance had imagined long, detailed, absorbing, and highly novel conversations between herself and her mother upon this their first meeting after her marriage. But alone in the bedroom, and with a clear half-hour to dinner, they neither of them seemed to have a great deal to impart.

111

Mrs. Baines slowly removed her light mantle and laid it with precautions on the white damask counterpane. Then, fingering her weeds, she glanced about the chamber. Nothing was changed. Though Constance had, previous to her marriage, envisaged certain alterations, she had determined to postpone them, feeling that one revolutionist in a house was enough.

"Well, my chick, you all right?" said Mrs. Baines, with hearty and direct energy, gazing straight into her daughter's eyes.

Constance perceived that the question was universal in its comprehensiveness, the one unique expression that the mother would give to her maternal concern and curiosity, and that it condensed into six words as much interest as would have overflowed into a whole day of the chatter of some mothers. She met the candid glance, flushing.

"Oh YES!" she answered with ecstatic fervour. "Perfectly!"

And Mrs. Baines nodded, as if dismissing THAT. "You're stouter," said she, curtly. "If you aren't careful you'll be as big as any of us."

"Oh, mother!"

The interview fell to a lower plane of emotion. It even fell as far as Maggie. What chiefly preoccupied Constance was a subtle change in her mother. She found her mother fussy in trifles. Her manner of laying down her mantle, of smoothing out her gloves, and her anxiety that her bonnet should not come to harm, were rather trying, were perhaps, in the very slightest degree, pitiable. It was nothing; it was barely perceptible, and yet it was enough to alter Constance's mental attitude to her mother. "Poor dear!" thought Constance. "I'm afraid she's not what she was." Incredible that her mother could have aged in less than six weeks! Constance did not allow for the chemistry that had been going on in herself.

The encounter between Mrs. Baines and her son-in-law was of the most satisfactory nature. He was waiting in the parlour for her to descend. He made himself exceedingly agreeable, kissing her, and flattering her by his evidently sincere desire to please. He explained that he had kept an eye open for the waggonette, but had been called away. His "Dear me!" on learning about Aunt Harriet lacked nothing in conviction, though both women knew that his affection for Aunt Harriet would never get the better of his reason. To Constance, her husband's behaviour was marvellously perfect. She had not suspected him to be such a man of the world. And her eyes said to her mother, quite unconsciously: "You see, after all, you didn't rate Sam as high as you ought to have done. Now you see your mistake."

As they sat waiting for dinner, Constance and Mrs. Baines on the sofa, and Samuel on the edge of the nearest rocking-chair, a small scuffling noise was heard outside the door which gave on the kitchen steps, the door yielded to pressure, and Fan rushed importantly in, deranging mats. Fan's nose had been hinting to her that she was behind the times, not up-to-date in the affairs of the household, and she had hurried from the kitchen to make inquiries. It occurred to her en route that she had been washed that morning. The spectacle of Mrs. Baines stopped her. She stood, with her legs slightly out-stretched, her nose lifted, her ears raking forward, her bright eyes blinking, and her tail undecided. "I was sure I'd never smelt anything like that before," she was saying to herself, as she stared at Mrs. Baines.

And Mrs. Baines, staring at Fan, had a similar though not the same sentiment. The silence was terrible. Constance took on the mien of a culprit, and Sam had obviously lost his easy bearing of a man of the world. Mrs. Baines was merely thunderstruck.

A dog!

Suddenly Fan's tail began to wag more quickly; and then, having looked in vain for encouragement to her master and mistress, she gave one mighty spring and alighted in Mrs. Baines's lap. It was an aim she could not have missed. Constance emitted an "Oh, FAN!" of shocked terror, and Samuel betrayed his nervous tension by an involuntary movement. But Fan had settled down into that titanic lap as into heaven. It was a greater flattery than Mr. Povey's.

"So your name's Fan!" murmured Mrs. Baines, stroking the animal. "You are a dear!"

"Yes, isn't she?" said Constance, with inconceivable rapidity.

The danger was past. Thus, without any explanation, Fan became an accepted fact.

The next moment Maggie served the Yorkshire pudding.

"Well, Maggie," said Mrs. Baines. "So you are going to get married this time? When is it?"

"Sunday, ma'am."

"And you leave here on Saturday?"

"Yes, ma'am."

"Well, I must have a talk with you before I go."

During the dinner, not a word as to the signboard! Several times the conversation curved towards that signboard in the most alarming fashion, but invariably it curved away again, like a train from another train when two trains are simultaneously leaving a station. Constance had frights, so serious as to destroy her anxiety about the cookery. In the end she comprehended that her mother had adopted a silently disapproving attitude. Fan was socially very useful throughout the repast.

After dinner Constance was on pins lest Samuel should light a cigar. She had not requested him not to do so, for though she was entirely sure of his affection, she had already learned that a husband is possessed by a demon of contrariety which often forces him to violate his higher feelings. However, Samuel did not light a cigar. He went off to superintend the shutting-up of the shop, while Mrs. Baines chatted with Maggie and gave her L5 for a wedding present. Then Mr. Critchlow called to offer his salutations.

A little before tea Mrs. Baines announced that she would go out for a short walk by herself.

"Where has she gone to?" smiled Samuel, superiorly, as with Constance at the window he watched her turn down King Street towards the church.

"I expect she has gone to look at father's grave," said Constance.

"Oh!" muttered Samuel, apologetically.

Constance was mistaken. Before reaching the church, Mrs. Baines deviated to the right, got into Brougham Street and thence, by Acre Lane, into Oldcastle Street, whose steep she climbed. Now, Oldcastle Street ends at the top of St. Luke's Square, and from the corner Mrs. Baines had an excellent view of the signboard. It being Thursday afternoon, scarce a soul was about. She returned to her daughter's by the same extraordinary route, and said not a word on entering. But she was markedly cheerful.

The waggonette came after tea, and Mrs. Baines made her final preparations to depart. The visit had proved a wonderful success; it would have been utterly perfect if Samuel had not marred it at the very door of the waggonette. Somehow, he contrived to be talking of Christmas. Only a person of Samuel's native clumsiness would have mentioned Christmas in July.

"You know you'll spend Christmas with us!" said he into the waggonette.

"Indeed I shan't!" replied Mrs. Baines. "Aunt Harriet and I will expect you at Axe. We've already settled that."

Mr. Povey bridled. "Oh no!" he protested, hurt by this summariness.

Having had no relatives, except his cousin the confectioner, for many years, he had dreamt of at last establishing a family Christmas under his own roof, and the dream was dear to him.

Mrs. Baines said nothing. "We couldn't possibly leave the shop," said
Mr. Povey.

"Nonsense!" Mrs. Baines retorted, putting her lips together. "Christmas
Day is on a Monday."

The waggonette in starting jerked her head towards the door and set all her curls shaking. No white in those curls yet, scarcely a touch of grey!

"I shall take good care we don't go there anyway," Mr. Povey mumbled, in his heat, half to himself and half to Constance.

He had stained the brightness of the day.

CHAPTER II

CHRISTMAS AND THE FUTURE
I

Mr. Povey was playing a hymn tune on the harmonium, it having been decided that no one should go to chapel. Constance, in mourning, with a white apron over her dress, sat on a hassock in front of the fire; and near her, in a rocking-chair, Mrs. Baines swayed very gently to and fro. The weather was extremely cold. Mr. Povey's mittened hands were blue and red; but, like many shopkeepers, he had apparently grown almost insensible to vagaries of temperature. Although the fire was immense and furious, its influence, owing to the fact that the mediaeval grate was designed to heat the flue rather than the room, seemed to die away at the borders of the fender. Constance could not have been much closer to it without being a salamander. The era of good old-fashioned Christmases, so agreeably picturesque for the poor, was not yet at an end.

Yes, Samuel Povey had won the battle concerning the locus of the family Christmas. But he had received the help of a formidable ally, death. Mrs. Harriet Maddack had passed away, after an operation, leaving her house and her money to her sister. The solemn rite of her interment had deeply affected all the respectability of the town of Axe, where the late Mr. Maddack had been a figure of consequence; it had even shut up the shop in St. Luke's Square for a whole day. It was such a funeral as Aunt Harriet herself would have approved, a tremendous ceremonial which left on the crushed mind an ineffaceable, intricate impression of shiny cloth, crape, horses with arching necks and long manes, the drawl of parsons, cake, port, sighs, and Christian submission to the inscrutable decrees of Providence. Mrs. Baines had borne herself with unnatural calmness until the funeral was over: and then Constance perceived that the remembered mother of her girlhood existed no longer. For the majority of human souls it would have been easier to love a virtuous principle, or a mountain, than to love Aunt Harriet, who was assuredly less a woman than an institution. But Mrs. Baines had loved her, and she had been the one person to whom Mrs. Baines looked for support and guidance. When she died, Mrs. Baines paid the tribute of respect with the last hoarded remains of her proud fortitude, and weepingly confessed that the unconquerable had been conquered, the inexhaustible exhausted; and became old with whitening hair.

She had persisted in her refusal to spend Christmas in Bursley, but both Constance and Samuel knew that the resistance was only formal. She soon yielded. When Constance's second new servant took it into her head to leave a week before Christmas, Mrs. Baines might have pointed out the finger of Providence at work again, and this time in her favour. But no! With amazing pliancy she suggested that she should bring one of her own servants to 'tide Constance over' Christmas. She was met with all the forms of loving solicitude, and she found that her daughter and son-in-law had 'turned out of' the state bedroom in her favour. Intensely flattered by this attention (which was Mr. Povey's magnanimous idea), she nevertheless protested strongly. Indeed she 'would not hear of it.'

"Now, mother, don't be silly," Constance had said firmly. "You don't expect us to be at all the trouble of moving back again, do you?" And Mrs. Baines had surrendered in tears.

Thus had come Christmas. Perhaps it was fortunate that, the Axe servant being not quite the ordinary servant, but a benefactor where a benefactor was needed, both Constance and her mother thought it well to occupy themselves in household work, 'sparing' the benefactor as much as possible. Hence Constance's white apron.

"There he is!" said Mr. Povey, still playing, but with his eye on the street.

Constance sprang up eagerly. Then there was a knock on the door. Constance opened, and an icy blast swept into the room. The postman stood on the steps, his instrument for knocking (like a drumstick) in one hand, a large bundle of letters in the other, and a yawning bag across the pit of his stomach.

"Merry Christmas, ma'am!" cried the postman, trying to keep warm by cheerfulness.

Constance, taking the letters, responded, while Mr. Povey, playing the harmonium with his right hand, drew half a crown from his pocket with the left.

"Here you are!" he said, giving it to Constance, who gave it to the postman.

Fan, who had been keeping her muzzle warm with the extremity of her tail on the sofa, jumped down to superintend the transaction.

"Brrr!" vibrated Mr. Povey as Constance shut the door.

"What lots!" Constance exclaimed, rushing to the fire. "Here, mother!

Here, Sam!"

The girl had resumed possession of the woman's body.

Though the Baines family had few friends (sustained hospitality being little practised in those days) they had, of course, many acquaintances, and, like other families, they counted their Christmas cards as an Indian counts scalps. The tale was satisfactory. There were between thirty and forty envelopes. Constance extracted Christmas cards rapidly, reading their contents aloud, and then propping them up on the mantelpiece. Mrs. Baines assisted. Fan dealt with the envelopes on the floor. Mr. Povey, to prove that his soul was above toys and gewgaws, continued to play the harmonium.

"Oh, mother!" Constance murmured in a startled, hesitant voice, holding an envelope.

"What is it, my chuck?"

"It's——"

The envelope was addressed to "Mrs. and Miss Baines" in large, perpendicular, dashing characters which Constance instantly recognised as Sophia's. The stamps were strange, the postmark 'Paris.' Mrs. Baines leaned forward and looked.

"Open it, child," she said.

The envelope contained an English Christmas card of a common type, a spray of holly with greetings, and on it was written, "I do hope this will reach you on Christmas morning. Fondest love." No signature, nor address. Mrs. Baines took it with a trembling hand, and adjusted her spectacles.

She gazed at it a long time.

"And it has done!" she said, and wept.

She tried to speak again, but not being able to command herself, held forth the card to Constance and jerked her head in the direction of Mr. Povey. Constance rose and put the card on the keyboard of the harmonium. "Sophia!" she whispered.

Mr. Povey stopped playing. "Dear, dear!" he muttered.

Fan, perceiving that nobody was interested in her feats, suddenly stood still.

Mrs. Baines tried once more to speak, but could not. Then, her ringlets shaking beneath the band of her weeds, she found her feet, stepped to the harmonium, and, with a movement almost convulsive, snatched the card from Mr. Povey, and returned to her chair.

Mr. Povey abruptly left the room, followed by Fan. Both the women were in tears, and he was tremendously surprised to discover a dangerous lump in his own throat. The beautiful and imperious vision of Sophia, Sophia as she had left them, innocent, wayward, had swiftly risen up before him and made even him a woman too! Yet he had never liked Sophia. The awful secret wound in the family pride revealed itself to him as never before, and he felt intensely the mother's tragedy, which she carried in her breast as Aunt Harriet had carried a cancer.

At dinner he said suddenly to Mrs. Baines, who still wept: "Now, mother, you must cheer up, you know."

"Yes, I must," she said quickly. And she did do.

Neither Samuel nor Constance saw the card again. Little was said. There was nothing to say. As Sophia had given no address she must be still ashamed of her situation. But she had thought of her mother and sister. She … she did not even know that Constance was married … What sort of a place was Paris? To Bursley, Paris was nothing but the site of a great exhibition which had recently closed.

Through the influence of Mrs. Baines a new servant was found for Constance in a village near Axe, a raw, comely girl who had never been in a 'place.' And through the post it was arranged that this innocent should come to the cave on the thirty-first of December. In obedience to the safe rule that servants should never be allowed to meet for the interchange of opinions, Mrs. Baines decided to leave with her own servant on the thirtieth. She would not be persuaded to spend the New Year in the Square. On the twenty-ninth poor Aunt Maria died all of a sudden in her cottage in Brougham Street. Everybody was duly distressed, and in particular Mrs. Baines's demeanour under this affliction showed the perfection of correctness. But she caused it to be understood that she should not remain for the funeral. Her nerves would be unequal to the ordeal; and, moreover, her servant must not stay to corrupt the new girl, nor could Mrs. Baines think of sending her servant to Axe in advance, to spend several days in idle gossip with her colleague.

This decision took the backbone out of Aunt Maria's funeral, which touched the extreme of modesty: a hearse and a one-horse coach. Mr. Povey was glad, because he happened to be very busy. An hour before his mother-in-law's departure he came into the parlour with the proof of a poster.

"What is that, Samuel?" asked Mrs. Baines, not dreaming of the blow that awaited her.

"It's for my first Annual Sale," replied Mr. Povey with false tranquillity.

Mrs. Baines merely tossed her head. Constance, happily for Constance, was not present at this final defeat of the old order. Had she been there, she would certainly not have known where to look.

II

"Forty next birthday!" Mr. Povey exclaimed one day, with an expression and in a tone that were at once mock-serious and serious. This was on his thirty-ninth birthday.

Constance was startled. She had, of course, been aware that they were getting older, but she had never realized the phenomenon. Though customers occasionally remarked that Mr. Povey was stouter, and though when she helped him to measure himself for a new suit of clothes the tape proved the fact, he had not changed for her.

She knew that she too had become somewhat stouter; but for herself, she remained exactly the same Constance. Only by recalling dates and by calculations could she really grasp that she had been married a little over six years and not a little over six months. She had to admit that, if Samuel would be forty next birthday, she would be twenty-seven next birthday. But it would not be a real twenty-seven; nor would Sam's forty be a real forty, like other people's twenty-sevens and forties. Not long since she had been in the habit of regarding a man of forty as senile, as practically in his grave.

She reflected, and the more she reflected the more clearly she saw that after all the almanacs had not lied. Look at Fan! Yes, it must be five years since the memorable morning when doubt first crossed the minds of Samuel and Constance as to Fan's moral principles. Samuel's enthusiasm for dogs was equalled by his ignorance of the dangers to which a young female of temperament may be exposed, and he was much disturbed as doubt developed into certainty. Fan, indeed, was the one being who did not suffer from shock and who had no fears as to the results. The animal, having a pure mind, was bereft of modesty. Sundry enormities had she committed, but none to rank with this one! The result was four quadrupeds recognizable as fox-terriers. Mr. Povey breathed again. Fan had had more luck than she deserved, for the result might have been simply anything. Her owners forgave her and disposed of these fruits of iniquity, and then married her lawfully to a husband who was so high up in the world that he could demand a dowry. And now Fan was a grandmother, with fixed ideas and habits, and a son in the house, and various grandchildren scattered over the town. Fan was a sedate and disillusioned dog. She knew the world as it was, and in learning it she had taught her owners above a bit.

Then there was Maggie Hollins. Constance could still vividly recall the self-consciousness with which she had one day received Maggie and the heir of the Hollinses; but it was a long time ago. After staggering half the town by the production of this infant (of which she nearly died) Maggie allowed the angels to waft it away to heaven, and everybody said that she ought to be very thankful—at her age. Old women dug up out of their minds forgotten histories of the eccentricities of the goddess Lucina. Mrs. Baines was most curiously interested; she talked freely to Constance, and Constance began to see what an incredible town Bursley had always been—and she never suspected it! Maggie was now mother of other children, and the draggled, lame mistress of a drunken home, and looked sixty. Despite her prophecy, her husband had conserved his 'habits.' The Poveys ate all the fish they could, and sometimes more than they enjoyed, because on his sober days Hollins invariably started his round at the shop, and Constance had to buy for Maggie's sake. The worst of the worthless husband was that he seldom failed to be cheery and polite. He never missed asking after the health of Mrs. Baines. And when Constance replied that her mother was 'pretty well considering,' but that she would not come over to Bursley again until the Axe railway was opened, as she could not stand the drive, he would shake his grey head and be sympathetically gloomy for an instant.

All these changes in six years! The almanacs were in the right of it.

But nothing had happened to her. Gradually she had obtained a sure ascendency over her mother, yet without seeking it, merely as the outcome of time's influences on her and on her mother respectively. Gradually she had gained skill and use in the management of her household and of her share of the shop, so that these machines ran smoothly and effectively and a sudden contretemps no longer frightened her. Gradually she had constructed a chart of Samuel's individuality, with the submerged rocks and perilous currents all carefully marked, so that she could now voyage unalarmed in those seas. But nothing happened. Unless their visits to Buxton could be called happenings! Decidedly the visit to Buxton was the one little hill that rose out of the level plain of the year. They had formed the annual habit of going to Buxton for ten days. They had a way of saying: "Yes, we always go to Buxton. We went there for our honeymoon, you know." They had become confirmed Buxtonites, with views concerning St. Anne's Terrace, the Broad Walk and Peel's Cavern. They could not dream of deserting their Buxton. It was the sole possible resort. Was it not the highest town in England? Well, then! They always stayed at the same lodgings, and grew to be special favourites of the landlady, who whispered of them to all her other guests as having come to her house for their honeymoon, and as never missing a year, and as being most respectable, superior people in quite a large way of business. Each year they walked out of Buxton station behind their luggage on a truck, full of joy and pride because they knew all the landmarks, and the lie of all the streets, and which were the best shops.

At the beginning, the notion of leaving the shop to hired custody had seemed almost fantastic, and the preparations for absence had been very complicated. Then it was that Miss Insull had detached herself from the other young lady assistants as a creature who could be absolutely trusted. Miss Insull was older than Constance; she had a bad complexion, and she was not clever, but she was one of your reliable ones. The six years had witnessed the slow, steady rise of Miss Insull. Her employers said 'Miss Insull' in a tone quite different from that in which they said 'Miss Hawkins,' or 'Miss Dadd.' 'Miss Insull' meant the end of a discussion. 'Better tell Miss Insull.' 'Miss Insull will see to that.' 'I shall ask Miss Insull.' Miss Insull slept in the house ten nights every year. Miss Insull had been called into consultation when it was decided to engage a fourth hand in the shape of an apprentice.

Trade had improved in the point of excellence. It was now admitted to be good—a rare honour for trade! The coal-mining boom was at its height, and colliers, in addition to getting drunk, were buying American organs and expensive bull-terriers. Often they would come to the shop to purchase cloth for coats for their dogs. And they would have good cloth. Mr. Povey did not like this. One day a butty chose for his dog the best cloth of Mr. Povey's shop—at 12s. a yard. "Will ye make it up? I've gotten th' measurements," asked the collier. "No, I won't!" said Mr. Povey, hotly. "And what's more, I won't sell you the cloth either! Cloth at 12s. a yard on a dog's back indeed! I'll thank you to get out of my shop!" The incident became historic, in the Square. It finally established that Mr. Povey was a worthy son-in-law and a solid and successful man. It vindicated the old pre-eminence of "Baines's." Some surprise was expressed that Mr. Povey showed no desire nor tendency towards entering the public life of the town. But he never would, though a keen satirical critic of the Local Board in private. And at the chapel he remained a simple private worshipper, refusing stewardships and trusteeships.

III

Was Constance happy? Of course there was always something on her mind, something that had to be dealt with, either in the shop or in the house, something to employ all the skill and experience which she had acquired. Her life had much in it of laborious tedium—tedium never-ending and monotonous. And both she and Samuel worked consistently hard, rising early, 'pushing forward,' as the phrase ran, and going to bed early from sheer fatigue; week after week and month after month as season changed imperceptibly into season. In June and July it would happen to them occasionally to retire before the last silver of dusk was out of the sky. They would lie in bed and talk placidly of their daily affairs. There would be a noise in the street below. "Vaults closing!" Samuel would say, and yawn. "Yes, it's quite late," Constance would say. And the Swiss clock would rapidly strike eleven on its coil of resonant wire. And then, just before she went to sleep, Constance might reflect upon her destiny, as even the busiest and smoothest women do, and she would decide that it was kind. Her mother's gradual decline and lonely life at Axe saddened her. The cards which came now and then at extremely long intervals from Sophia had been the cause of more sorrow than joy. The naive ecstasies of her girlhood had long since departed—the price paid for experience and self-possession and a true vision of things. The vast inherent melancholy of the universe did not exempt her. But as she went to sleep she would be conscious of a vague contentment. The basis of this contentment was the fact that she and Samuel comprehended and esteemed each other, and made allowances for each other. Their characters had been tested and had stood the test. Affection, love, was not to them a salient phenomenon in their relations. Habit had inevitably dulled its glitter. It was like a flavouring, scarce remarked; but had it been absent, how they would have turned from that dish!

Samuel never, or hardly ever, set himself to meditate upon the problem whether or not life had come up to his expectations. But he had, at times, strange sensations which he did not analyze, and which approached nearer to ecstasy than any feeling of Constance's. Thus, when he was in one of his dark furies, molten within and black without, the sudden thought of his wife's unalterable benignant calm, which nothing could overthrow, might strike him into a wondering cold. For him she was astoundingly feminine. She would put flowers on the mantelpiece, and then, hours afterwards, in the middle of a meal, ask him unexpectedly what he thought of her 'garden;' and he gradually divined that a perfunctory reply left her unsatisfied; she wanted a genuine opinion; a genuine opinion mattered to her. Fancy calling flowers on a mantelpiece a 'garden'! How charming, how childlike! Then she had a way, on Sunday mornings, when she descended to the parlour all ready for chapel, of shutting the door at the foot of the stairs with a little bang, shaking herself, and turning round swiftly as if for his inspection, as if saying: "Well, what about this? Will this do?" A phenomenon always associated in his mind with the smell of kid gloves! Invariably she asked him about the colours and cut of her dresses. Would he prefer this, or that? He could not take such questions seriously until one day he happened to hint, merely hint, that he was not a thorough-going admirer of a certain new dress—it was her first new dress after the definite abandonment of crinolines. She never wore it again. He thought she was not serious at first, and remonstrated against a joke being carried too far. She said: "It's not a bit of use you talking, I shan't wear it again." And then he so far appreciated her seriousness as to refrain, by discretion, from any comment. The

117

incident affected him for days. It flattered him; it thrilled him; but it baffled him. Strange that a woman subject to such caprices should be so sagacious, capable, and utterly reliable as Constance was! For the practical and commonsense side of her eternally compelled his admiration. The very first example of it—her insistence that the simultaneous absence of both of them from the shop for half an hour or an hour twice a day would not mean the immediate downfall of the business—had remained in his mind ever since. Had she not been obstinate—in her benevolent way—against the old superstition which he had acquired from his employers, they might have been eating separately to that day. Then her handling of her mother during the months of the siege of Paris, when Mrs. Baines was convinced that her sinful daughter was in hourly danger of death, had been extraordinarily fine, he considered. And the sequel, a card for Constance's birthday, had completely justified her attitude.

Sometimes some blundering fool would jovially exclaim to them:

"What about that baby?"

Or a woman would remark quietly: "I often feel sorry you've no children."

And they would answer that really they did not know what they would do if there was a baby. What with the shop and one thing or another…! And they were quite sincere.

IV

It is remarkable what a little thing will draw even the most regular and serious people from the deep groove of their habits. One morning in March, a boneshaker, an affair on two equal wooden wheels joined by a bar of iron, in the middle of which was a wooden saddle, disturbed the gravity of St. Luke's Square. True, it was probably the first boneshaker that had ever attacked the gravity of St. Luke's Square. It came out of the shop of Daniel Povey, the confectioner and baker, and Samuel Povey's celebrated cousin, in Boulton Terrace. Boulton Terrace formed nearly a right angle with the Baines premises, and at the corner of the angle Wedgwood Street and King Street left the Square. The boneshaker was brought forth by Dick Povey, the only son of Daniel, now aged eleven years, under the superintendence of his father, and the Square soon perceived that Dick had a natural talent for breaking-in an untrained boneshaker. After a few attempts he could remain on the back of the machine for at least ten yards, and his feats had the effect of endowing St. Luke's Square with the attractiveness of a circus. Samuel Povey watched with candid interest from the ambush of his door, while the unfortunate young lady assistants, though aware of the performance that was going on, dared not stir from the stove. Samuel was tremendously tempted to sally out boldly, and chat with his cousin about the toy; he had surely a better right to do so than any other tradesman in the Square, since he was of the family; but his diffidence prevented him from moving. Presently Daniel Povey and Dick went to the top of the Square with the machine, opposite Holl's, and Dick, being carefully installed in the saddle, essayed to descend the gentle paven slopes of the Square. He failed time after time; the machine had an astonishing way of turning round, running uphill, and then lying calmly on its side. At this point of Dick's life-history every shop-door in the Square was occupied by an audience. At last the boneshaker displayed less unwillingness to obey, and lo! in a moment Dick was riding down the Square, and the spectators held their breath as if he had been Blondin crossing Niagara. Every second he ought to have fallen off, but he contrived to keep upright. Already he had accomplished twenty yards—thirty yards! It was a miracle that he was performing! The transit continued, and seemed to occupy hours. And then a faint hope rose in the breast of the watchers that the prodigy might arrive at the bottom of the Square. His speed was increasing with his 'nack.' But the Square was enormous, boundless. Samuel Povey gazed at the approaching phenomenon, as a bird at a serpent, with bulging, beady eyes. The child's speed went on increasing and his path grew straighter. Yes, he would arrive; he would do it! Samuel Povey involuntarily lifted one leg in his nervous tension. And now the hope that Dick would arrive became a fear, as his pace grew still more rapid. Everybody lifted one leg, and gaped. And the intrepid child surged on, and, finally victorious, crashed into the pavement in front of Samuel at the rate of quite six miles an hour.

Samuel picked him up, unscathed. And somehow this picking up of Dick invested Samuel with importance, gave him a share in the glory of the feat itself.

Daniel Povey same running and joyous. "Not so bad for a start, eh?" exclaimed the great Daniel. Though by no means a simple man, his pride in his offspring sometimes made him a little naive.

Father and son explained the machine to Samuel, Dick incessantly repeating the exceedingly strange truth that if you felt you were falling to your right you must turn to your right and vice versa. Samuel found himself suddenly admitted, as it were, to the inner fellowship of the boneshaker, exalted above the rest of the Square. In another adventure more thrilling events occurred. The fair-haired Dick was one of those dangerous, frenzied madcaps who are born without fear. The secret of the machine had been revealed to him in his recent transit, and he was silently determining to surpass himself. Precariously balanced, he descended the Square again, frowning hard, his teeth set, and actually managed to swerve into King Street. Constance, in the parlour, saw an incomprehensible winged thing fly past the window. The cousins Povey sounded an alarm and protest and ran in pursuit; for the gradient of King Street is, in the strict sense, steep. Half-way down King Street Dick was travelling at twenty miles an hour, and heading straight for the church, as though he meant to disestablish it and perish. The main gate of the churchyard was open, and that affrighting child, with a lunatic's luck, whizzed safely through the portals into God's acre. The cousins Povey discovered him lying on a green grave, clothed in pride. His first words were: "Dad, did you pick my cap up?" The symbolism of the amazing ride did not escape the Square; indeed, it was much discussed.

This incident led to a friendship between the cousins. They formed a habit of meeting in the Square for a chat. The meetings were the subject of comment, for Samuel's relations with the greater Daniel had always been of the most distant. It was understood that Samuel disapproved of Mrs. Daniel Povey even, more than the majority of people disapproved of her. Mrs. Daniel Povey, however, was away from home; probably, had she not been, Samuel would not even have gone to the length of joining Daniel on the neutral ground of the open Square. But having once broken the ice, Samuel was glad to be on terms of growing intimacy with his cousin. The friendship flattered him, for Daniel, despite his wife, was a figure in a world larger than Samuel's; moreover, it consecrated his position as the equal of no matter what tradesman (apprentice though he had been), and also he genuinely liked and admired Daniel, rather to his own astonishment.

Every one liked Daniel Povey; he was a favourite among all ranks. The leading confectioner, a member of the Local Board, and a sidesman at St. Luke's, he was, and had been for twenty-five years, very prominent in the town. He was a tall, handsome man, with a trimmed, greying beard, a jolly smile, and a flashing, dark eye. His good humour seemed to be permanent. He had dignity without the slightest stiffness; he was welcomed by his equals and frankly adored by his inferiors. He ought to have been Chief Bailiff, for he was rich enough; but there intervened a mysterious obstacle between Daniel Povey and the supreme honour, a scarcely tangible impediment which could not be definitely stated. He was capable, honest, industrious, successful, and an excellent speaker; and if he did not belong to the austerer section of society, if, for example, he thought nothing of dropping into the Tiger for a glass of beer, or of using an oath occasionally, or of telling a facetious story—well, in a busy, broad-minded town of thirty thousand inhabitants, such proclivities are no bar whatever to perfect esteem. But—how is one to phrase it without wronging Daniel Povey? He was entirely moral; his views were unexceptionable. The truth is that, for the ruling classes of Bursley, Daniel Povey was just a little too fanatical a worshipper of the god Pan. He was one of the remnant who had kept alive the great Pan tradition from the days of the Regency through the vast, arid Victorian expanse of years. The flighty character of his wife was regarded by many as a judgment upon him for the robust Rabelaisianism of his more private conversation, for his frank interest in, his eternal preoccupation with, aspects of life and human activity which, though essential to the divine purpose, are not openly recognized as such—even by Daniel Poveys. It was not a question of his conduct; it was a question of the cast of his mind. If it did not explain his friendship with the rector of St. Luke's, it explained his departure from the Primitive Methodist connexion, to which the Poveys as a family had belonged since Primitive Methodism was created in Turnhill in 1807.

Daniel Povey had a way of assuming that every male was boiling over with interest in the sacred cult of Pan. The assumption, though sometimes causing inconvenience at first, usually conquered by virtue of its inherent truthfulness. Thus it fell out with Samuel. Samuel had not suspected that Pan had silken cords to draw him. He had always averted his eyes from the god—that is to say, within reason. Yet now Daniel, on perhaps a couple of fine mornings a week, in full Square, with Fan sitting behind on the cold stones, and Mr. Critchlow ironic at his door in a long white apron, would entertain Samuel Povey for half an hour with Pan's most intimate lore, and Samuel Povey would not blench. He would, on the contrary, stand up to Daniel like a little man, and pretend with all his might to be, potentially, a perfect arch-priest of the god. Daniel taught him a lot; turned over the page of life for him, as it were, and, showing the reverse side, seemed to say: "You were missing all that." Samuel gazed upwards at the handsome long nose and rich lips of his elder cousin, so experienced, so agreeable, so renowned, so esteemed, so philosophic, and admitted to himself that he had lived to the age of forty in a state of comparative boobyism. And then he would gaze downwards at the faint patch of flour on Daniel's right leg, and conceive that life was, and must be, life.

Not many weeks after his initiation into the cult he was startled by Constance's preoccupied face one evening. Now, a husband of six years' standing, to whom it has not happened to become a father, is not easily startled by such a face as Constance wore. Years ago he had frequently been startled, had frequently lived in suspense for a few days. But he had long since grown impervious to these alarms. And now he was startled again—but as a man may be startled who is not altogether surprised at being startled. And seven endless days passed, and Samuel and Constance glanced at each other like guilty things, whose secret refuses to be kept. Then three more days passed, and another three. Then Samuel Povey remarked in a firm, masculine, fact-fronting tone: "Oh, there's no doubt about it!"

And they glanced at each other like conspirators who have lighted a fuse and cannot take refuge in flight.

Their eyes said continually, with a delicious, an enchanting mixture of ingenuous modesty and fearful joy: "Well, we've gone and done it!"

There it was, the incredible, incomprehensible future—coming!

Samuel had never correctly imagined the manner of its heralding. He had imagined in his early simplicity that one day Constance, blushing, might put her mouth to his ear and whisper—something positive. It had not occurred in the least like that. But things are so obstinately, so incurably unsentimental.

"I think we ought to drive over and tell mother, on Sunday," said Constance.

His impulse was to reply, in his grand, offhand style: "Oh, a letter will do!"

But he checked himself and said, with careful deference: "You think that will be better than writing?"

All was changed. He braced every fibre to meet destiny, and to help Constance to meet it.

The weather threatened on Sunday. He went to Axe without Constance. His cousin drove him there in a dog-cart, and he announced that he should walk home, as the exercise would do him good. During the drive Daniel, in whom he had not confided, chattered as usual, and Samuel pretended to listen with the same attitude as usual; but secretly he despised Daniel for a man who has got something not of the first importance on the brain. His perspective was truer than Daniel's.

He walked home, as he had decided, over the wavy moorland of the county dreaming in the heart of England. Night fell on him in mid-career, and he was tired. But the earth, as it whirled through naked space, whirled up the moon for him, and he pressed on at a good speed. A wind from Arabia wandering cooled his face. And at last, over the brow of Toft End, he saw suddenly the Five Towns a-twinkle on their little hills down in the vast amphitheatre. And one of those lamps was Constance's lamp—one, somewhere. He lived, then. He entered into the shadow of nature. The mysteries made him solemn. What! A boneshaker, his cousin, and then this! "Well, I'm damned! Well, I'm damned!" he kept repeating, he who never swore.

CHAPTER III

CYRIL

I

Constance stood at the large, many-paned window in the parlour. She was stouter. Although always plump, her figure had been comely, with a neat, well-marked waist. But now the shapeliness had gone; the waist-line no longer existed, and there were no more crinolines to create it artificially. An observer not under the charm of her face might have been excused for calling her fat and lumpy. The face, grave, kind, and expectant, with its radiant, fresh cheeks, and the rounded softness of its curves, atoned for the figure. She was nearly twenty-nine years of age.

It was late in October. In Wedgwood Street, next to Boulton Terrace, all the little brown houses had been pulled down to make room for a palatial covered market, whose foundations were then being dug. This destruction exposed a vast area of sky to the north-east. A great dark cloud with an untidy edge rose massively out of the depths and curtained off the tender blue of approaching dusk; while in the west, behind Constance, the sun was setting in calm and gorgeous melancholy on the Thursday hush of the town. It was one of those afternoons which gather up all the sadness of the moving earth and transform it into beauty.

Samuel Povey turned the corner from Wedgwood Street, and crossed King Street obliquely to the front-door, which Constance opened. He seemed tired and anxious.

"Well?" demanded Constance, as he entered.

"She's no better. There's no getting away from it, she's worse. I should have stayed, only I knew you'd be worrying. So I caught the three-fifty."

"How is that Mrs. Gilchrist shaping as a nurse?"

"She's very good," said Samuel, with conviction. "Very good!"

"What a blessing! I suppose you didn't happen to see the doctor?"

"Yes, I did."

"What did he say to you?"

Samuel gave a deprecating gesture. "Didn't say anything particular.

With dropsy, at that stage, you know ..."

Constance had returned to the window, her expectancy apparently unappeased.

"I don't like the look of that cloud," she murmured.

"What! Are they out still?" Samuel inquired, taking off his overcoat.

"Here they are!" cried Constance. Her features suddenly transfigured, she sprang to the door, pulled it open, and descended the steps.

A perambulator was being rapidly pushed up the slope by a breathless girl.

"Amy," Constance gently protested, "I told you not to venture far."

"I hurried all I could, mum, soon as I seed that cloud," the girl puffed, with the air of one who is seriously thankful to have escaped a great disaster.

Constance dived into the recesses of the perambulator and extricated from its cocoon the centre of the universe, and scrutinized him with quiet passion, and then rushed with him into the house, though not a drop of rain had yet fallen.

"Precious!" exclaimed Amy, in ecstasy, her young virginal eyes following him till he disappeared. Then she wheeled away the perambulator, which now had no more value nor interest than an egg-shell. It was necessary to take it right round to the Brougham Street yard entrance, past the front of the closed shop.

Constance sat down on the horsehair sofa and hugged and kissed her prize before removing his bonnet.

"Here's Daddy!" she said to him, as if imparting strange and rapturous tidings. "Here's Daddy come back from hanging up his coat in the passage! Daddy rubbing his hands!" And then, with a swift transition of voice and features: "Do look at him, Sam!"

Samuel, preoccupied, stooped forward. "Oh, you little scoundrel! Oh, you little scoundrel!" he greeted the baby, advancing his finger towards the baby's nose.

The baby, who had hitherto maintained a passive indifference to external phenomena, lifted elbows and toes, blew bubbles from his tiny mouth, and stared at the finger with the most ravishing, roguish smile, as though saying: "I know that great sticking-out limb, and there is a joke about it which no one but me can see, and which is my secret joy that you shall never share."

"Tea ready?" Samuel asked, resuming his gravity and his ordinary pose.

"You must give the girl time to take her things off," said Constance. "We'll have the table drawn, away from the fire, and baby can lie on his shawl on the hearthrug while we're having tea." Then to the baby, in rapture: "And play with his toys; all his nice, nice toys!"

"You know Miss Insull is staying for tea?"

Constance, her head bent over the baby, who formed a white patch on her comfortable brown frock, nodded without speaking.

Samuel Povey, walking to and fro, began to enter into details of his hasty journey to Axe. Old Mrs. Baines, having beheld her grandson, was preparing to quit this world. Never again would she exclaim, in her brusque tone of genial ruthlessness: 'Fiddlesticks!' The situation was very difficult and distressing, for Constance could not leave her baby, and she would not, until the last urgency, run the risks of a journey with him to Axe. He was being weaned. In any case Constance could not have undertaken the nursing of her mother. A nurse had to be found. Mr. Povey had discovered one in the person of Mrs. Gilchrist, the second wife of a farmer at Malpas in Cheshire, whose first wife had been a sister of the late John Baines. All the credit of Mrs. Gilchrist was due to Samuel Povey. Mrs. Baines fretted seriously about Sophia, who had given no sign of life for a very long time. Mr. Povey went to Manchester and ascertained definitely from the relatives of Scales that nothing was known of the pair. He did not go to Manchester especially on this errand. About once in three weeks, on Tuesdays, he had to visit the Manchester warehouses; but the tracking of Scales's relative cost him so much trouble and time that, curiously, he came to believe that he had gone to Manchester one Tuesday for no other end. Although he was very busy indeed in the shop, he flew over to Axe and back whenever he possibly could, to the neglect of his affairs. He was glad to do all that was in his power; even if he had not done it graciously his sensitive, tyrannic conscience would have forced him to do it. But nevertheless he felt rather virtuous, and worry and fatigue and loss of sleep intensified this sense of virtue.

"So that if there is any sudden change they will telegraph," he finished, to Constance.

She raised her head. The words, clinching what had led up to them, drew her from her dream and she saw, for a moment, her mother in an agony.

"But you don't surely mean—?" she began, trying to disperse the painful vision as unjustified by the facts.

"My dear girl," said Samuel, with head singing, and hot eyes, and a consciousness of high tension in every nerve of his body, "I simply mean that if there's any sudden change they will telegraph."

While they had tea, Samuel sitting opposite to his wife, and Miss Insull nearly against the wall (owing to the moving of the table), the baby rolled about on the hearthrug, which had been covered with a large soft woollen shawl, originally the property of his great-grandmother. He had no cares, no responsibilities. The shawl was so vast that he could not clearly distinguish objects beyond its confines. On it lay an indiarubber ball, an indiarubber doll, a rattle, and fan. He vaguely recollected all four items, with their respective properties. The fire also was an old friend. He had occasionally tried to touch it, but a high bright fence always came in between. For ten months he had never spent a day without making experiments on this shifting universe in which he alone remained firm and stationary. The experiments were chiefly conducted out of idle amusement, but he was serious on the subject of food. Lately the behaviour of the universe in regard to his food had somewhat perplexed him, had indeed annoyed him. However, he was of a forgetful, happy disposition, and so long as the universe continued to fulfil its sole end as a machinery for the satisfaction, somehow, of his imperious desires, he was not inclined to remonstrate. He gazed at the flames and laughed, and laughed because he had laughed. He pushed the ball away and wriggled after it, and captured it with the assurance of practice. He tried to swallow the doll, and it was not until he had tried several times to swallow it that he remembered the failure of previous efforts and philosophically desisted. He rolled with a fearful shock, arms and legs in air, against the mountainous flank of that mammoth Fan, and clutched at Fan's ear. The whole mass of Fan upheaved and vanished from his view, and was instantly forgotten by him. He seized the doll and tried to swallow it, and repeated the exhibition of his skill with the ball. Then he saw the fire again and laughed. And so he existed for centuries: no responsibilities, no appetites; and the shawl was vast. Terrific operations went on over his head. Giants moved to and fro. Great vessels were carried off and great books were brought and deep voices rumbled regularly in the spaces beyond the shawl. But he remained oblivious. At last he became aware that a face was looking down at his. He recognized it, and immediately an uncomfortable sensation in his stomach disturbed him; he tolerated it for fifty years or so, and then he gave a little cry. Life had resumed its seriousness.

"Black alpaca. B quality. Width 20, t.a. 22 yards," Miss Insull read out of a great book. She and Mr. Povey were checking stock.

And Mr. Povey responded, "Black alpaca B quality. Width 20, t.a. 22 yards. It wants ten minutes yet." He had glanced at the clock.

"Does it?" said Constance, well knowing that it wanted ten minutes.

The baby did not guess that a high invisible god named Samuel Povey, whom nothing escaped, and who could do everything at once, was controlling his universe from an inconceivable distance. On the contrary, the baby was crying to himself, There is no God.

His weaning had reached the stage at which a baby really does not know what will happen next. The annoyance had begun exactly three months after his first tooth, such being the rule of the gods, and it had grown more and more disconcerting. No sooner did he accustom himself to a new phenomenon than it mysteriously ceased, and an old one took its place which he had utterly forgotten. This afternoon his mother nursed him, but not until she had foolishly attempted to divert him from the seriousness of life by means of gewgaws of which he was sick. Still; once at her rich breast, he forgave and forgot all. He preferred her simple natural breast to more modern inventions. And he had no shame, no modesty. Nor had his mother. It was an indecent carouse at which his father and Miss Insull had to assist. But his father had shame. His father would have preferred that, as Miss Insull had kindly offered to stop and work on Thursday afternoon, and as the shop was chilly, the due rotation should have brought the bottle round at half-past five o'clock, and not the mother's breast. He was a self-conscious parent, rather apologetic to the world, rather apt to stand off and pretend that he had nothing to do with the affair; and he genuinely disliked that anybody should witness the intimate scene of HIS wife feeding HIS baby. Especially Miss Insull, that prim, dark, moustached spinster! He would not have called it an outrage on Miss Insull, to force her to witness the scene, but his idea approached within sight of the word.

Constance blandly offered herself to the child, with the unconscious primitive savagery of a young mother, and as the baby fed, thoughts of her own mother flitted to and fro ceaselessly like vague shapes over the deep sea of content which filled her mind. This illness of her mother's was abnormal, and the baby was now, for the first time perhaps, entirely normal in her consciousness. The baby was something which could be disturbed, not something which did disturb. What a change! What a change that had seemed impossible until its full accomplishment!

For months before the birth, she had glimpsed at nights and in other silent hours the tremendous upset. She had not allowed herself to be silly in advance; by temperament she was too sagacious, too well balanced for that; but she had had fitful instants of terror, when solid ground seemed to sink away from her, and imagination shook at what faced her. Instants only! Usually she could play the comedy of sensible calmness to almost perfection. Then the appointed time drew nigh. And still she smiled, and Samuel smiled. But the preparations, meticulous, intricate, revolutionary, belied their smiles. The intense resolve to keep Mrs. Baines, by methods scrupulous or unscrupulous, away from Bursley until all was over, belied their smiles. And then the first pains, sharp, shocking, cruel, heralds of torture! But when they had withdrawn, she smiled, again, palely. Then she was in bed, full of the sensation that the whole house was inverted and disorganized, hopelessly. And the doctor came into the room. She smiled at the doctor apologetically, foolishly, as if saying: "We all come to it. Here I am." She was calm without. Oh, but what a prey of abject fear within! "I am at the edge of the precipice," her thought ran; "in a moment I shall be over." And then the pains—not the heralds but the shattering army, endless, increasing in terror as they thundered across her. Yet she could think, quite clearly: "Now I'm in the middle of it. This is it, the horror that I have not dared to look at. My life's in the balance. I may never get up again. All has at last come to pass. It seemed as if it would never come, as if this thing could not happen to me. But at last it has come to pass!"

Ah! Some one put the twisted end of a towel into her hand again—she had loosed it; and she pulled, pulled, enough to break cables. And then she shrieked. It was for pity. It was for some one to help her, at any rate to take notice of her. She was dying. Her soul was leaving her. And she was alone, panic-stricken, in the midst of a cataclysm a thousand times surpassing all that she had imagined of sickening horror. "I cannot endure this," she thought passionately. "It is impossible that I should be asked to endure this!" And then she wept; beaten, terrorized, smashed and riven. No commonsense now! No wise calmness now! No self-respect now! Why, not even a woman now! Nothing but a kind of animalized victim! And then the supreme endless spasm, during which she gave up the ghost and bade good-bye to her very self.

She was lying quite comfortable in the soft bed; idle, silly: happiness forming like a thin crust over the lava of her anguish and her fright. And by her side was the soul that had fought its way out of her, ruthlessly; the secret disturber revealed to the light of morning. Curious to look at! Not like any baby that she had ever seen; red, creased, brutish! But—for some reason that she did not examine—she folded it in an immense tenderness.

Sam was by the bed, away from her eyes. She was so comfortable and silly that she could not move her head nor even ask him to come round to her eyes. She had to wait till he came.

In the afternoon the doctor returned, and astounded her by saying that hers had been an ideal confinement. She was too weary to rebuke him for a senseless, blind, callous old man. But she knew what she knew. "No one will ever guess," she thought, "no one ever can guess, what I've been through! Talk as you like. I KNOW, now."

Gradually she had resumed cognizance of her household, perceiving that it was demoralized from top to bottom, and that when the time came to begin upon it she would not be able to settle where to begin, even supposing that the baby were not there to monopolize her attention. The task appalled her. Then she wanted to get up. Then she got up. What a blow to self-confidence! She went back to bed like a little scared rabbit to its hole, glad, glad to be on the soft pillows again. She said: "Yet the time must come when I shall be downstairs, and walking about and meeting people, and cooking and superintending the millinery." Well, it did come— except that she had to renounce the millinery to Miss Insull—but it was not the same. No, different! The baby pushed everything else on to another plane. He was a terrific intruder; not one minute of her old daily life was left; he made no compromise whatever. If she turned away her gaze from him he might pop off into eternity and leave her.

And now she was calmly and sensibly giving him suck in presence of Miss Insull. She was used to his importance, to the fragility of his organism, to waking twice every night, to being fat. She was strong again. The convulsive twitching that for six months had worried her repose, had quite disappeared. The state of being a mother was normal, and the baby was so normal that she could not conceive the house without him. All in ten months!

When the baby was installed in his cot for the night, she came downstairs and found Miss Insull and Samuel still working, and Larder than ever, but at addition sums now. She sat down, leaving the door open at the foot of the stairs. She had embroidery in hand: a cap. And while Miss Insull and Samuel combined pounds, shillings, and pence, whispering at great speed, she bent over the delicate, intimate, wasteful handiwork, drawing the needle with slow exactitude. Then she would raise her head and listen.

"Excuse me," said Miss Insull, "I think I hear baby crying."

"And two are eight and three are eleven. He must cry," said Mr. Povey, rapidly, without looking up.

The baby's parents did not make a practice of discussing their domestic existence even with Miss Insull; but Constance had to justify herself as a mother.

"I've made perfectly sure he's comfortable," said Constance. "He's only crying because he fancies he's neglected. And we think he can't begin too early to learn."

"How right you are!" said Miss Insull. "Two and carry three."

That distant, feeble, querulous, pitiful cry continued obstinately. It continued for thirty minutes. Constance could not proceed with her work. The cry disintegrated her will, dissolved her hard sagacity.

Without a word she crept upstairs, having carefully deposed the cap on her rocking-chair.

Mr. Povey hesitated a moment and then bounded up after her, startling Fan. He shut the door on Miss Insull, but Fan was too quick for him. He saw Constance with her hand on the bedroom door.

"My dear girl," he protested, holding himself in. "Now what ARE you going to do?"

"I'm just listening," said Constance.

"Do be reasonable and come downstairs."

He spoke in a low voice, scarcely masking his nervous irritation, and tiptoed along the corridor towards her and up the two steps past the gas-burner. Fan followed, wagging her tail expectant.

"Suppose he's not well?" Constance suggested.

"Pshaw!" Mr. Povey exclaimed contemptuously. "You remember what happened last night and what you said!"

They argued, subduing their tones to the false semblance of good-will, there in the closeness of the corridor. Fan, deceived, ceased to wag her tail and then trotted away. The baby's cry, behind the door, rose to a mysterious despairing howl, which had such an effect on Constance's heart that she could have walked through fire to reach the baby. But Mr. Povey's will held her. And she rebelled, angry, hurt, resentful. Commonsense, the ideal of mutual forbearance, had winged away from that excited pair. It would have assuredly ended in a quarrel, with Samuel glaring at her in black fury from the other side of a bottomless chasm, had not Miss Insull most surprisingly burst up the stairs.

Mr. Povey turned to face her, swallowing his emotion.

"A telegram!" said Miss Insull. "The postmaster brought it down himself—"

"What? Mr. Derry?" asked Samuel, opening the telegram with an affectation of majesty.

"Yes. He said it was too late for delivery by rights. But as it seemed very important …"

Samuel scanned it and nodded gravely; then gave it to his wife. Tears came into her eyes.

"I'll get Cousin Daniel to drive me over at once," said Samuel, master of himself and of the situation.

"Wouldn't it be better to hire?" Constance suggested. She had a prejudice against Daniel.

Mr. Povey shook his head. "He offered," he replied. "I can't refuse his offer."

"Put your thick overcoat on, dear," said Constance, in a dream, descending with him.

"I hope it isn't—" Miss Insull stopped.

"Yes it is, Miss Insull," said Samuel, deliberately.

In less than a minute he was gone.

Constance ran upstairs. But the cry had ceased. She turned the door-knob softly, slowly, and crept into the chamber. A night-light made large shadows among the heavy mahogany and the crimson, tasselled rep in the close-curtained room. And between the bed and the ottoman (on which lay Samuel's newly-bought family Bible) the cot loomed in the shadows. She picked up the night-light and stole round the bed. Yes, he had decided to fall asleep. The hazard of death afar off had just defeated his devilish obstinacy. Fate had bested him. How marvellously soft and delicate that tear-stained cheek! How frail that tiny, tiny clenched hand! In Constance grief and joy were mystically united.

II

The drawing-room was full of visitors, in frocks of ceremony. The old drawing-room, but newly and massively arranged with the finest Victorian furniture from dead Aunt Harriet's house at Axe; two "Canterburys," a large bookcase, a splendid scintillant table solid beyond lifting, intricately tortured chairs and armchairs! The original furniture of the drawing-room was now down in the parlour, making it grand. All the house breathed opulence; it was gorged with quiet, restrained expensiveness; the least considerable objects, in the most modest corners, were what Mrs. Baines would have termed 'good.' Constance and Samuel had half of all Aunt Harriet's money and half of Mrs. Baines's; the other half was accumulating for a hypothetical Sophia, Mr. Critchlow being the trustee. The business continued to flourish. People knew that Samuel Povey was buying houses. Yet Samuel and Constance had not made friends; they had not, in the Five Towns phrase, 'branched out socially,' though they had very meetly branched out on subscription lists. They kept themselves to themselves (emphasizing the preposition). These guests were not their guests; they were the guests of Cyril. He had been named Samuel because Constance would have him named after his father, and Cyril because his father secretly despised the name of Samuel; and he was called Cyril; 'Master Cyril,' by Amy, definite successor to Maggie. His mother's thoughts were on Cyril as long as she was awake. His father, when not planning Cyril's welfare, was earning money whose unique object could be nothing but Cyril's welfare. Cyril was the pivot of the house; every desire ended somewhere in Cyril. The shop existed now solely for him. And those houses that Samuel bought by private treaty, or with a shamefaced air at auctions—somehow they were aimed at Cyril. Samuel and Constance had ceased to be self-justifying beings; they never thought of themselves save as the parents of Cyril.

They realized this by no means fully. Had they been accused of monomania they would have smiled the smile of people confident in their commonsense and their mental balance. Nevertheless, they were monomaniacs. Instinctively they concealed the fact as much as possible; They never admitted it even to themselves. Samuel, indeed, would often say: "That child is not everybody. That child must be kept in his place." Constance was always teaching him consideration for his father as the most important person in the household. Samuel was always teaching him consideration for his mother as the most important person in the household. Nothing was left undone to convince him that he was a cipher, a nonentity, who ought to be very glad to be alive. But he knew all about his importance. He knew that the entire town was his. He knew that his parents were deceiving themselves. Even when he was punished he well knew that it was because he was so important. He never imparted any portion of this knowledge to his parents; a primeval wisdom prompted him to retain it strictly in his own bosom.

He was four and a half years old, dark, like his father; handsome like his aunt, and tall for his age; not one of his features resembled a feature of his mother's, but sometimes he 'had her look.' From the capricious production of inarticulate sounds, and then a few monosyllables that described concrete things and obvious desires, he had gradually acquired an astonishing idiomatic command over the most difficult of Teutonic languages; there was nothing that he could not say. He could walk and run, was full of exact knowledge about God, and entertained no doubt concerning the special partiality of a minor deity called Jesus towards himself. Now, this party was his mother's invention and scheme. His father, after flouting it, had said that if it was to be done at all, it should be done well, and had brought to the doing all his organizing skill. Cyril had accepted it at first—merely accepted it; but, as the day approached and the preparations increased in magnitude, he had come to look on it with favour, then with enthusiasm. His father having taken him to Daniel Povey's opposite, to choose cakes, he had shown, by his solemn and fastidious waverings, how seriously he regarded the affair. Of course it had to occur on a Thursday afternoon. The season was summer, suitable for pale and fragile toilettes. And the eight children who sat round Aunt Harriet's great table glittered like the sun. Not Constance's specially provided napkins could hide that wealth and profusion of white lace and stitchery. Never in after-life are the genteel children of the Five Towns so richly clad as at the age of four or five years. Weeks of labour, thousands of cubic feet of gas, whole nights stolen from repose, eyesight, and general health, will disappear into the manufacture of a single frock that accidental jam may ruin in ten seconds. Thus it was in those old days; and thus it is to-day. Cyril's guests ranged in years from four to six; they were chiefly older than their

125

host; this was a pity, it impaired his importance; but up to four years a child's sense of propriety, even of common decency, is altogether too unreliable for a respectable party.

Round about the outskirts of the table were the elders, ladies the majority; they also in their best, for they had to meet each other. Constance displayed a new dress, of crimson silk; after having mourned for her mother she had definitely abandoned the black which, by reason of her duties in the shop, she had constantly worn from the age of sixteen to within a few months of Cyril's birth; she never went into the shop now, except casually, on brief visits of inspection. She was still fat; the destroyer of her figure sat at the head of the table. Samuel kept close to her; he was the only male, until Mr. Critchlow astonishingly arrived; among the company Mr. Critchlow had a grand-niece. Samuel, if not in his best, was certainly not in his everyday suit. With his large frilled shirt-front, and small black tie, and his little black beard and dark face over that, he looked very nervous and self-conscious. He had not the habit of entertaining. Nor had Constance; but her benevolence ever bubbling up to the calm surface of her personality made self-consciousness impossible for her. Miss Insull was also present, in shop-black, 'to help.' Lastly there was Amy, now as the years passed slowly assuming the character of a faithful retainer, though she was only twenty-three. An ugly, abrupt, downright girl, with convenient notions of pleasure! For she would rise early and retire late in order to contrive an hour to go out with Master Cyril; and to be allowed to put Master Cyril to bed was, really, her highest bliss.

All these elders were continually inserting arms into the fringe of fluffy children that surrounded the heaped table; removing dangerous spoons out of cups into saucers, replacing plates, passing cakes, spreading jam, whispering consolations, explanations, and sage counsel. Mr. Critchlow, snow-white now but unbent, remarked that there was 'a pretty cackle,' and he sniffed. Although the window was slightly open, the air was heavy with the natural human odour which young children transpire. More than one mother, pressing her nose into a lacy mass, to whisper, inhaled that pleasant perfume with a voluptuous thrill.

Cyril, while attending steadily to the demands of his body, was in a mood which approached the ideal. Proud and radiant, he combined urbanity with a certain fine condescension. His bright eyes, and his manner of scraping up jam with a spoon, said: "I am the king of this party. This party is solely in my honour. I know that. We all know it. Still, I will pretend that we are equals, you and I." He talked about his picture-books to a young woman on his right named Jennie, aged four, pale, pretty, the belle in fact, and Mr. Critchlow's grand-niece. The boy's attractiveness was indisputable; he could put on quite an aristocratic air. It was the most delicious sight to see them, Cyril and Jennie, so soft and delicate, so infantile on their piles of cushions and books, with their white socks and black shoes dangling far distant from the carpet; and yet so old, so self-contained! And they were merely an epitome of the whole table. The whole table was bathed in the charm and mystery of young years, of helpless fragility, gentle forms, timid elegance, unshamed instincts, and waking souls. Constance and Samuel were very satisfied; full of praise for other people's children, but with the reserve that of course Cyril was hors concours. They both really did believe, at that moment, that Cyril was, in some subtle way which they felt but could not define, superior to all other infants.

Some one, some officious relative of a visitor, began to pass a certain cake which had brown walls, a roof of cocoa-nut icing, and a yellow body studded with crimson globules. Not a conspicuously gorgeous cake, not a cake to which a catholic child would be likely to attach particular importance; a good, average cake! Who could have guessed that it stood, in Cyril's esteem, as the cake of cakes? He had insisted on his father buying it at Cousin Daniel's, and perhaps Samuel ought to have divined that for Cyril that cake was the gleam that an ardent spirit would follow through the wilderness. Samuel, however, was not a careful observer, and seriously lacked imagination. Constance knew only that Cyril had mentioned the cake once or twice. Now by the hazard of destiny that cake found much favour, helped into popularity as it was by the blundering officious relative who, not dreaming what volcano she was treading on, urged its merits with simpering enthusiasm. One boy took two slices, a slice in each hand; he happened to be the visitor of whom the cake-distributor was a relative, and she protested; she expressed the shock she suffered. Whereupon both Constance and Samuel sprang forward and swore with angelic smiles that nothing could be more perfect than the propriety of that dear little fellow taking two slices of that cake. It was this hullaballoo that drew Cyril's attention to the evanescence of the cake of cakes. His face at once changed from calm pride to a dreadful anxiety. His eyes bulged out. His tiny mouth grew and grew, like a mouth in a nightmare. He was no longer human; he was a cake-eating tiger being balked of his prey. Nobody noticed him. The officious fool of a woman persuaded Jennie to take the last slice of the cake, which was quite a thin slice.

Then every one simultaneously noticed Cyril, for he gave a yell. It was not the cry of a despairing soul who sees his beautiful iridescent dream shattered at his feet; it was the cry of the strong, masterful spirit, furious.

126

He turned upon Jennie, sobbing, and snatched at her cake. Unaccustomed to such behaviour from hosts, and being besides a haughty put-you-in-your-place beauty of the future, Jennie defended her cake. After all, it was not she who had taken two slices at once. Cyril hit her in the eye, and then crammed most of the slice of cake into his enormous mouth. He could not swallow it, nor even masticate it, for his throat was rigid and tight. So the cake projected from his red lips, and big tears watered it. The most awful mess you can conceive! Jennie wept loudly, and one or two others joined her in sympathy, but the rest went on eating tranquilly, unmoved by the horror which transfixed their elders.

A host to snatch food from a guest! A host to strike a guest! A gentleman to strike a lady!

Constance whipped up Cyril from his chair and flew with him to his own room (once Samuel's), where she smacked him on the arm and told him he was a very, very naughty boy and that she didn't know what his father would say. She took the food out of his disgusting mouth—or as much of it as she could get at—and then she left him, on the bed. Miss Jennie was still in tears when, blushing scarlet and trying to smile, Constance returned to the drawing-room. Jennie would not be appeased. Happily Jennie's mother (being about to present Jennie with a little brother—she hoped) was not present. Miss Insull had promised to see Jennie home, and it was decided that she should go. Mr. Critchlow, in high sardonic spirits, said that he would go too; the three departed together, heavily charged with Constance's love and apologies. Then all pretended, and said loudly, that what had happened was naught, that such things were always happening at children's parties. And visitors' relatives asseverated that Cyril was a perfect darling and that really Mrs. Povey must not …

But the attempt to keep up appearance was a failure.

The Methuselah of visitors, a gaping girl of nearly eight years, walked across the room to where Constance was standing, and said in a loud, confidential, fatuous voice:

"Cyril HAS been a rude boy, hasn't he, Mrs. Povey?"

The clumsiness of children is sometimes tragic.

Later, there was a trickling stream of fluffy bundles down the crooked
stairs and through the parlour and so out into King Street. And
Constance received many compliments and sundry appeals that darling
Cyril should be forgiven.

"I thought you said that boy was in his bedroom," said Samuel to Constance, coming into the parlour when the last guest had gone. Each avoided the other's eyes.

"Yes, isn't he?"

"No."

"The little jockey!" ("Jockey," an essay in the playful, towards making light of the jockey's sin!) "I expect he's been in search of Amy."

She went to the top of the kitchen stairs and called out: "Amy, is
Master Cyril down there?"

"Master Cyril? No, mum. But he was in the parlour a bit ago, after the first and second lot had gone. I told him to go upstairs and be a good boy."

Not for a few moments did the suspicion enter the minds of Samuel and Constance that Cyril might be missing, that the house might not contain Cyril. But having once entered, the suspicion became a certainty. Amy, cross-examined, burst into sudden tears, admitting that the side-door might have been open when, having sped 'the second lot,' she criminally left Cyril alone in the parlour in order to descend for an instant to her kitchen. Dusk was gathering. Amy saw the defenceless innocent wandering about all night in the deserted streets of a great city. A similar vision with precise details of canals, tramcar-wheels, and cellar-flaps, disturbed Constance. Samuel said that anyhow he could not have got far, that some one was bound to remark and recognize him, and restore him. "Yes, of course," thought sensible Constance. "But supposing—"

They all three searched the entire house again. Then, in the drawing-room (which was in a sad condition of anticlimax) Amy exclaimed:

"Eh, master! There's town-crier crossing the Square. Hadn't ye better have him cried?"

"Run out and stop him," Constance commanded.

And Amy flew.

Samuel and the aged town-crier parleyed at the side door, the women in the background.

"I canna' cry him without my bell," drawled the crier, stroking his shabby uniform. "My bell's at wum (home). I mun go and fetch my bell. Yo' write it down on a bit o' paper for me so as I can read it, and I'll foot off for my bell. Folk wouldna' listen to me if I hadna' gotten my bell."

Thus was Cyril cried.

127

"Amy," said Constance, when she and the girl were alone, "there's no use in you standing blubbering there. Get to work and clear up that drawing-room, do! The child is sure to be found soon. Your master's gone out, too."

Brave words! Constance aided in the drawing-room and kitchen. Theirs was the woman's lot in a great crisis. Plates have always to be washed.

Very shortly afterwards, Samuel Povey came into the kitchen by the underground passage which led past the two cellars to the yard and to Brougham Street. He was carrying in his arms an obscene black mass.

This mass was Cyril, once white.

Constance screamed. She was at liberty to give way to her feelings, because Amy happened to be upstairs.

"Stand away!" cried Mr. Povey. "He isn't fit to touch."

And Mr. Povey made as if to pass directly onward, ignoring the mother.

"Wherever did you find him?"

"I found him in the far cellar," said Mr. Povey, compelled to stop, after all. "He was down there with me yesterday, and it just occurred to me that he might have gone there again."

"What! All in the dark?"

"He'd lighted a candle, if you please! I'd left a candle-stick and a box of matches handy because I hadn't finished that shelving."

"Well!" Constance murmured. "I can't think how ever he dared go there all alone!"

"Can't you?" said Mr. Povey, cynically. "I can. He simply did it to frighten us."

"Oh, Cyril!" Constance admonished the child. "Cyril!"

The child showed no emotion. His face was an enigma. It might have hidden sullenness or mere callous indifference, or a perfect unconsciousness of sin.

"Give him to me," said Constance.

"I'll look after him this evening," said Samuel, grimly.

"But you can't wash him," said Constance, her relief yielding to apprehension.

"Why not?" demanded Mr. Povey. And he moved off.

"But Sam—"

"I'll look after him, I tell you!" Mr. Povey repeated, threateningly.

"But what are you going to do?" Constance asked with fear.

"Well," said Mr. Povey, "has this sort of thing got to be dealt with, or hasn't it?" He departed upstairs.

Constance overtook him at the door of Cyril's bedroom.

Mr. Povey did not wait for her to speak. His eyes were blazing.

"See here!" he admonished her cruelly. "You get away downstairs, mother!"

And he disappeared into the bedroom with his vile and helpless victim.

A moment later he popped his head out of the door. Constance was disobeying him. He stepped into the passage and shut the door so that Cyril should not hear.

"Now please do as I tell you," he hissed at his wife. "Don't let's have a scene, please."

She descended, slowly, weeping. And Mr. Povey retired again to the place of execution.

Amy nearly fell on the top of Constance with a final tray of things from the drawing-room. And Constance had to tell the girl that Cyril was found. Somehow she could not resist the instinct to tell her also that the master had the affair in hand. Amy then wept.

After about an hour Mr. Povey at last reappeared. Constance was trying to count silver teaspoons in the parlour.

"He's in bed now," said Mr. Povey, with a magnificent attempt to be nonchalant. "You mustn't go near him."

"But have you washed him?" Constance whimpered.

"I've washed him," replied the astonishing Mr. Povey.

"What have you done to him?"

"I've punished him, of course," said Mr. Povey, like a god who is above human weaknesses. "What did you expect me to do? Someone had to do it."

Constance wiped her eyes with the edge of the white apron which she was wearing over her new silk dress. She surrendered; she accepted the situation; she made the best of it. And all the evening was spent in dismally and horribly pretending that their hearts were beating as one. Mr. Povey's elaborate, cheery kindliness was extremely painful.

They went to bed, and in their bedroom Constance, as she stood close to Samuel, suddenly dropped the pretence, and with eyes and voice of anguish said:

"You must let me look at him."

They faced each other. For a brief instant Cyril did not exist for Constance. Samuel alone obsessed her, and yet Samuel seemed a strange, unknown man. It was in Constance's life one of those crises when the human soul seems to be on the very brink of mysterious and disconcerting cognitions, and then, the wave recedes as inexplicably as it surged up.

"Why, of course!" said Mr. Povey, turning away lightly, as though to imply that she was making tragedies out of nothing.

She gave an involuntary gesture of almost childish relief.

Cyril slept calmly. It was a triumph for Mr. Povey.

Constance could not sleep. As she lay darkly awake by her husband, her secret being seemed to be a-quiver with emotion. Not exactly sorrow; not exactly joy; an emotion more elemental than these! A sensation of the intensity of her life in that hour; troubling, anxious, yet not sad! She said that Samuel was quite right, quite right. And then she said that the poor little thing wasn't yet five years old, and that it was monstrous. The two had to be reconciled. And they never could be reconciled. Always she would be between them, to reconcile them, and to be crushed by their impact. Always she would have to bear the burden of both of them. There could be no ease for her, no surcease from a tremendous preoccupation and responsibility. She could not change Samuel; besides, he was right! And though Cyril was not yet five, she felt that she could not change Cyril either. He was just as unchangeable as a growing plant. The thought of her mother and Sophia did not present itself to her; she felt, however, somewhat as Mrs. Baines had felt on historic occasions; but, being more softly kind, younger, and less chafed by destiny, she was conscious of no bitterness, conscious rather of a solemn blessedness.

CHAPTER IV

CRIME

I

"Now, Master Cyril," Amy protested, "will you leave that fire alone?

It's not you that can mend my fires."

A boy of nine, great and heavy for his years, with a full face and very short hair, bent over the smoking grate. It was about five minutes to eight on a chilly morning after Easter. Amy, hastily clad in blue, with a rough brown apron, was setting the breakfast table. The boy turned his head, still bending.

"Shut up, Ame," he replied, smiling. Life being short, he usually called her Ame when they were alone together. "Or I'll catch you one in the eye with the poker."

"You ought to be ashamed of yourself," said Amy. "And you know your mother told you to wash your feet this morning, and you haven't done. Fine clothes is all very well, but—"

"Who says I haven't washed my feet?" asked Cyril, guiltily.

Amy's mention of fine clothes referred to the fact that he was that morning wearing his Sunday suit for the first time on a week-day.

"I say you haven't," said Amy.

She was more than three times his age still, but they had been treating each other as intellectual equals for years.

"And how do you know?" asked Cyril, tired of the fire.

"I know," said Amy.

"Well, you just don't, then!" said Cyril. "And what about YOUR feet? I should be sorry to see your feet, Ame."

Amy was excusably annoyed. She tossed her head. "My feet are as clean as yours any day," she said. "And I shall tell your mother."

But he would not leave her feet alone, and there ensued one of those endless monotonous altercations on a single theme which occur so often between intellectual equals when one is a young son of the house and the other an established servant who adores him. Refined minds would have found the talk disgusting, but the sentiment of disgust seemed to be unknown to either of the wranglers. At last, when Amy by superior tactics had cornered him, Cyril said suddenly:

"Oh, go to hell!"

Amy banged down the spoon for the bacon gravy. "Now I shall tell your mother. Mark my words, this time I SHALL tell your mother."

Cyril felt that in truth he had gone rather far. He was perfectly sure that Amy would not tell his mother. And yet, supposing that by some freak of her nature she did! The consequences would be unutterable; the consequences would more than extinguish his private glory in the use of such a dashing word. So he laughed, a rather silly, giggling laugh, to reassure himself.

"You daren't," he said.

"Daren't I?" she said grimly. "You'll see. *I* don't know where you learn! It fair beats me. But it isn't Amy Bates as is going to be sworn at. As soon as ever your mother comes into this room!"

The door at the foot of the stairs creaked and Constance came into the room. She was wearing a dress of majenta merino, and a gold chain descended from her neck over her rich bosom. She had scarcely aged in five years. It would have been surprising if she had altered much, for the years had passed over her head at an incredible rate. To her it appeared only a few months since Cyril's first and last party.

"Are you all ready, my pet? Let me look at you." Constance greeted the boy with her usual bright, soft energy.

Cyril glanced at Amy, who averted her head, putting spoons into three saucers.

"Yes, mother," he replied in a new voice.

"Did you do what I told you?"

"Yes, mother," he said simply.

"That's right."

Amy made a faint noise with her lips, and departed.

He was saved once more. He said to himself that never again would he permit his soul to be disturbed by any threat of old Ame's.

Constance's hand descended into her pocket and drew out a hard paper packet, which she clapped on to her son's head.

"Oh, mother!" He pretended that she had hurt him, and then he opened the packet. It contained Congleton butterscotch, reputed a harmless sweetmeat.

"Good!" he cried, "good! Oh! Thanks, mother."

"Now don't begin eating them at once."

"Just one, mother."

"No! And how often have I told you to keep your feet off that fender.
See how it's bent. And it's nobody but you."

"Sorry."

"It's no use being sorry if you persist in doing it."

"Oh, mother, I had such a funny dream!"

They chatted until Amy came up the stairs with tea and bacon. The fire had developed from black to clear red.

"Run and tell father that breakfast is ready."

After a little delay a spectacled man of fifty, short and stoutish, with grey hair and a small beard half grey and half black, entered from the shop. Samuel had certainly very much aged, especially in his gestures, which, however, were still quick. He sat down at once—his wife and son were already seated—and served the bacon with the rapid assurance of one who needs not to inquire about tastes and appetites. Not a word was said, except a brief grace by Samuel. But there was no restraint. Samuel had a mild, benignant air. Constance's eyes were a fountain of cheerfulness. The boy sat between them and ate steadily.

Mysterious creature, this child, mysteriously growing and growing in the house! To his mother he was a delicious joy at all times save when he disobeyed his father. But now for quite a considerable period there had been no serious collision. The boy seemed to be acquiring virtue as well as sense. And really he was charming. So big, truly enormous (every one remarked on it), and yet graceful, lithe, with a smile that could ravish. And he was distinguished in his bearing. Without depreciating Samuel in her faithful heart, Constance saw plainly the singular differences between Samuel and the boy. Save that he was dark, and that his father's 'dangerous look' came into those childish eyes occasionally, Cyril had now scarcely any obvious resemblance to his father. He was a Baines. This naturally deepened Constance's family pride. Yes, he was mysterious to Constance, though probably not more so than any other boy to any other parent. He was equally mysterious to Samuel, but otherwise Mr. Povey had learned to regard him in the light of a parcel which he was always attempting to wrap up in a piece of paper imperceptibly too small. When he successfully covered the parcel at one corner it burst out at another, and this went on for ever, and he could never get the string on. Nevertheless, Mr. Povey had unabated confidence in his skill as a parcel-wrapper. The boy was strangely subtle at times, but then at times he was astoundingly ingenuous, and then his dodges would not deceive the dullest. Mr. Povey knew himself more than a match for his son. He was proud of him because he regarded him as not an ordinary boy; he took it as a matter of course that his boy should not be an ordinary boy. He never, or very rarely, praised Cyril. Cyril thought of his father as a man who, in response to any request, always began by answering with a thoughtful, serious 'No, I'm afraid not.'

"So you haven't lost your appetite!" his mother commented.

Cyril grinned. "Did you expect me to, mother?"

"Let me see," said Samuel, as if vaguely recalling an unimportant fact.

"It's to-day you begin to go to school, isn't it?"

"I wish father wouldn't be such a chump!" Cyril reflected. And, considering that this commencement of school (real school, not a girls' school, as once) had been the chief topic in the house for days, weeks; considering that it now occupied and filled all hearts, Cyril's reflection was excusable.

"Now, there's one thing you must always remember, my boy," said Mr. Povey. "Promptness. Never be late either in going to school or in coming home. And in order that you may have no excuse"—Mr. Povey pressed on the word 'excuse' as though condemning Cyril in advance—"here's something for you!" He said the last words quickly, with a sort of modest shame.

It was a silver watch and chain.

Cyril was staggered. So also was Constance, for Mr. Povey could keep his own counsel. At long intervals he would prove, thus, that he was a mighty soul, capable of sublime deeds. The watch was the unique flowering of Mr. Povey's profound but harsh affection. It lay on the table like a miracle. This day was a great day, a supremely exciting day in Cyril's history, and not less so in the history of his parents.

The watch killed its owner's appetite dead.

Routine was ignored that morning. Father did not go back into the shop. At length the moment came when father put on his hat and overcoat to take Cyril, and Cyril's watch and satchel, to the Endowed School, which had quarters in the Wedgwood Institution close by. A solemn departure, and Cyril could not pretend by his demeanour that it was not! Constance desired to kiss him, but refrained. He would not have liked it. She watched them from the window. Cyril was nearly as tall as his father; that is to say, not nearly as tall, but creeping up his father's shoulder. She felt that the eyes of the town must be on the pair. She was very happy, and nervous.

At dinner-time a triumph seemed probable, and at tea-time, when Cyril came home under a mortar-board hat and with a satchel full of new books and a head full of new ideas, the triumph was actually and definitely achieved. He had been put into the third form, and he announced that he should soon be at the top of it. He was enchanted with the life of school; he liked the other boys, and it appeared that the other boys liked him. The fact was that, with a new silver watch and a packet of sweets, he had begun his new career in the most advantageous circumstances. Moreover, he possessed qualities which ensure success at school. He was big, and easy, with a captivating smile and a marked aptitude to learn those things which boys insist on teaching to their new comrades. He had muscle, a brave demeanour, and no conceit.

During tea the parlour began, to accustom itself to a new vocabulary, containing such words as 'fellows,' 'kept in,'m' lines,' 'rot,' 'recess,' 'jolly.' To some of these words the parents, especially Mr. Povey, had an instinct to object, but they could not object, somehow they did not seem to get an opportunity to object; they were carried away on the torrent, and after all, their excitement and pleasure in the exceeding romantic novelty of existence were just as intense and nearly as ingenuous as their son's.

He demonstrated that unless he was allowed to stay up later than aforetime he would not be able to do his home-work, and hence would not keep that place in the school to which his talents entitled him. Mr. Povey suggested, but only with half a heart, that he should get up earlier in the morning. The proposal fell flat. Everybody knew and admitted that nothing save the scorpions of absolute necessity, or a tremendous occasion such as that particular morning's, would drive Cyril from his bed until the smell of bacon rose to him from the kitchen. The parlour table was consecrated to his lessons. It became generally known that 'Cyril was doing his lessons.' His father scanned the new text-books while Cyril condescendingly explained to him that all others were superseded and worthless. His father contrived to maintain an air of preserving his mental equilibrium, but not his mother; she gave it up, she who till that day had under his father's direction taught him nearly all that he knew, and Cyril passed above her into regions of knowledge where she made no pretence of being able to follow him.

When the lessons were done, and Cyril had wiped his fingers on bits of blotting-paper, and his father had expressed qualified approval and had gone into the shop, Cyril said to his mother, with that delicious hesitation which overtook him sometimes:

"Mother."

"Well, my pet."

"I want you to do something for me."

"Well, what is it?"

"No, you must promise."

"I'll do it if I can."

"But you CAN. It isn't doing. It's NOT doing."

"Come, Cyril, out with it."

"I don't want you to come in and look at me after I'm asleep any more."

"But, you silly boy, what difference can it make to you if you're asleep?"

"I don't want you to. It's like as if I was a baby. You'll have to stop doing it some day, and so you may as well stop now."

It was thus that he meant to turn his back on his youth.

She smiled. She was incomprehensibly happy. She continued to smile.

"Now you'll promise, won't you, mother?"

She rapped him on the head with her thimble, lovingly. He took the gesture for consent.

"You are a baby," she murmured.

"Now I shall trust you," he said, ignoring this. "Say 'honour bright.'"

"Honour bright."

With what a long caress her eyes followed him, as he went up to bed on his great sturdy legs! She was thankful that school had not contaminated her adorable innocent. If she could have been Ame for twenty-four hours, she perhaps would not have hesitated to put butter into his mouth lest it should melt.

Mr. Povey and Constance talked late and low that night. They could neither of them sleep; they had little desire to sleep. Constance's face said to her husband: "I've always stuck up for that boy, in spite of your severities, and you see how right I was!" And Mr. Povey's face said: "You see now the brilliant success of my system. You see how my educational theories have justified themselves. Never been to a school before, except that wretched little dame's school, and he goes practically straight to the top of the third form—at nine years of age!" They discussed his future. There could be no sign of lunacy in discussing his future up to a certain point, but each felt that to discuss the ultimate career of a child nine years old would not be the act of a sensible parent; only foolish parents would be so fond. Yet each was dying to discuss his ultimate career. Constance yielded first to the temptation, as became her. Mr. Povey scoffed, and then, to humour Constance, yielded also. The matter was soon fairly on the carpet. Constance was relieved to find that Mr. Povey had no thought whatever of putting Cyril in the shop. No; Mr. Povey did not desire to chop wood with a razor. Their son must and would ascend. Doctor! Solicitor! Barrister! Not barrister—barrister was fantastic. When they had argued for about half an hour Mr. Povey intimated suddenly that the conversation was unworthy of their practical commonsense, and went to sleep.

II

Nobody really thought that this almost ideal condition of things would persist: an enterprise commenced in such glory must surely traverse periods of difficulty and even of temporary disaster. But no! Cyril seemed to be made specially for school. Before Mr. Povey and Constance had quite accustomed themselves to being the parents of 'a great lad,' before Cyril had broken the glass of his miraculous watch more than once, the summer term had come to an end and there arrived the excitations of the prize-giving, as it was called; for at that epoch the smaller schools had not found the effrontery to dub the breaking-up ceremony a 'speech-day.' This prize-giving furnished a particular joy to Mr. and Mrs. Povey. Although the prizes were notoriously few in number—partly to add to their significance, and partly to diminish their cost (the foundation was poor)—Cyril won a prize, a box of geometrical instruments of precision; also he reached the top of his form, and was marked for promotion to the formidable Fourth. Samuel and Constance were bidden to the large hall of the Wedgwood Institution of a summer afternoon, and they saw the whole Board of Governors raised on a rostrum, and in the middle, in front of what he referred to, in his aristocratic London accent, as 'a beggarly array of rewards,' the aged and celebrated Sir Thomas Wilbraham Wilbraham, ex-M.P., last respectable member of his ancient line. And Sir Thomas gave the box of instruments to Cyril, and shook hands with him. And everybody was very well dressed. Samuel, who had never attended anything but a National School, recalled the simple rigours of his own boyhood, and swelled. For certainly, of all the parents present, he was among the richest. When, in the informal promiscuities which followed the prize distribution, Cyril joined his father and mother, sheepishly, they duly did their best to make light of his achievements, and failed. The walls of the hall were covered with specimens of the pupils' skill, and the headmaster was observed to direct the attention of the mighty to a map done by Cyril. Of course it was a map of Ireland, Ireland being the map chosen by every map-drawing schoolboy who is free to choose. For a third-form boy it was considered a masterpiece. In the shading of mountains Cyril was already a prodigy. Never, it was said, had the Macgillycuddy Reeks been indicated by a member of that school with a more amazing subtle refinement than by the young Povey. From a proper pride in themselves, from a proper fear lest they should be secretly accused of ostentation by other parents, Samuel and Constance did not go near that map. For the rest, they had lived with it for weeks, and Samuel (who, after all, was determined not to be dirt under his son's feet) had scratched a blot from it with a completeness that defied inquisitive examination.

The fame of this map, added to the box of compasses and Cyril's own desire, pointed to an artistic career. Cyril had always drawn and daubed, and the drawing-master of the Endowed School, who was also headmaster of the Art School, had suggested that the youth should attend the Art School one night a week. Samuel, however, would not listen to the idea; Cyril was too young. It is true that Cyril was too young, but Samuel's real objection was to Cyril's going out alone in the evening. On that he was adamant.

The Governors had recently made the discovery that a sports department was necessary to a good school, and had rented a field for cricket, football, and rounders up at Bleakridge, an innovation which demonstrated that the town was moving with the rapid times. In June this field was open after school hours till eight p.m. as well as on Saturdays. The Squire learnt that Cyril had a talent for cricket, and Cyril wished to practise in the evenings, and was quite ready to bind himself with Bible oaths to rise at no matter what hour in the morning for the purpose of home lessons. He scarcely expected his father to say 'Yes' as his father never did say 'Yes,' but he was obliged to ask. Samuel nonplussed him by replying that on fine evenings, when he could spare time from the shop, he would go up to Bleakridge with his son. Cyril did not like this in the least. Still, it might be tried. One evening they went, actually, in the new steam-car which had superseded the old horse-cars, and which travelled all the way to Longshaw, a place that Cyril had only heard of. Samuel talked of the games played in the Five Towns in his day, of the Titanic sport of prison-bars, when the team of one 'bank' went forth to the challenge of another 'bank,' preceded by a drum-and-fife band, and when, in the heat of the chase, a man might jump into the canal to escape his pursuer; Samuel had never played at cricket.

Samuel, with a very young grandson of Fan (deceased), sat in dignity on the grass and watched his cricketer for an hour and a half (while Constance kept an eye on the shop and superintended its closing). Samuel then conducted Cyril home again. Two days later the father of his own accord offered to repeat the experience. Cyril refused. Disagreeable insinuations that he was a baby in arms had been made at school in the meantime. Nevertheless, in other directions Cyril sometimes surprisingly conquered. For instance, he came home one day with the information that a dog that was not a bull-terrier was not worth calling a dog. Fan's grandson had been carried off in earliest prime by a chicken-bone that had pierced his vitals, and Cyril did indeed persuade his father to buy a bull-terrier. The animal was a superlative of forbidding ugliness, but father and son vied with each other in stern critical praise of his surpassing beauty, and Constance, from good nature, joined in the pretence. He was called Lion, and the shop, after one or two untoward episodes, was absolutely closed to him. But the most striking of Cyril's successes had to do with the question of the annual holiday. He spoke of the sea soon after becoming a schoolboy. It appeared that his complete ignorance of the sea prejudicially affected him at school. Further, he had always loved the sea; he had drawn hundreds of three-masted ships with studding-sails set, and knew the difference between a brig and a brigantine. When he first said: "I say, mother, why can't we go to Llandudno instead of Buxton this year?" his mother thought he was out of his senses. For the idea of going to any place other than Buxton was inconceivable! Had they not always been to Buxton? What would their landlady say? How could they ever look her in the face again? Besides … well…! They went to Llandudno, rather scared, and hardly knowing how the change had come about. But they went. And it was the force of Cyril's will, Cyril the theoretic cypher, that took them.

III

The removal of the Endowed School to more commodious premises in the shape of Shawport Hall, an ancient mansion with fifty rooms and five acres of land round about it, was not a change that quite pleased Samuel or Constance. They admitted the hygienic advantages, but Shawport Hall was three-quarters of a mile distant from St. Luke's Square—in the hollow that separates Bursley from its suburb of Hillport; whereas the Wedgwood Institution was scarcely a minute away. It was as if Cyril, when he set off to Shawport Hall of a morning, passed out of their sphere of influence. He was leagues off, doing they knew not what. Further, his dinner-hour was cut short by the extra time needed for the journey to and fro, and he arrived late for tea; it may be said that he often arrived very late for tea; the whole machinery of the meal was disturbed. These matters seemed to Samuel and Constance to be of tremendous import, seemed to threaten the very foundations of existence. Then they grew accustomed to the new order, and wondered sometimes, when they passed the Wedgwood Institution and the insalubrious Cock Yard—once sole playground of the boys—that the school could ever have 'managed' in the narrow quarters once allotted to it.

Cyril, though constantly successful at school, a rising man, an infallible bringer-home of excellent reports, and a regular taker of prizes, became gradually less satisfactory in the house. He was 'kept in' occasionally, and although his father pretended to hold that to be kept in was to slur the honour of a spotless family, Cyril continued to be kept in; a hardened sinner, lost to shame. But this was not the worst. The worst undoubtedly was that Cyril was 'getting rough.' No definite accusation could be laid against him; the offence was general, vague, everlasting; it was in all he did and said, in every gesture and movement. He shouted, whistled, sang, stamped, stumbled, lunged. He omitted such empty rites as saying 'Yes' or 'Please,' and wiping his nose. He replied gruffly and nonchalantly to polite questions, or he didn't reply until the questions were repeated, and even then with a 'lost' air that was not genuine. His shoelaces were a sad sight, and his finger-nails no sight at all for a decent woman; his hair was as rough as his conduct; hardly at the pistol's point could he be forced to put oil on it. In brief, he was no longer the nice boy that he used to be. He had unmistakably deteriorated. Grievous! But what can you expect when YOUR boy is obliged, month after month and year after year, to associate with other boys? After all, he was a GOOD boy, said Constance, often to herself and now and then to Samuel. For Constance, his charm was eternally renewed. His smile, his frequent ingenuousness, his funny self-conscious gesture when he wanted to 'get round' her—these characteristics remained; and his pure heart remained; she could read that in his eyes. Samuel was inimical to his tastes for sports and his triumphs therein. But Constance had pride in all that. She liked to feel him and to gaze at him, and to smell that faint, uncleanly odour of sweat that hung in his clothes.

In this condition he reached the advanced age of thirteen. And his parents, who despite their notion of themselves as wide-awake parents were a simple pair, never suspected that his heart, conceived to be still pure, had become a crawling, horrible mass of corruption.

One day the head-master called at the shop. Now, to see a head-master walking about the town during school-hours is a startling spectacle, and is apt to give you the same uncanny sensation as when, alone in a room, you think you see something move which ought not to move. Mr. Povey was startled. Mr. Povey had a thumping within his breast as he rubbed his hands and drew the head-master to the private corner where his desk was. "What can I do for you to-day?" he almost said to the head-master. But he did not say it. The boot was emphatically not on that leg. The head-master talked to Mr. Povey, in tones carefully low, for about a quarter of an hour, and then he closed the interview. Mr. Povey escorted him across the shop, and the head-master said with ordinary loudness: "Of course it's nothing. But my experience is that it's just as well to be on the safe side, and I thought I'd tell you. Forewarned is forearmed. I have other parents to see." They shook hands at the door. Then Mr. Povey stepped out on to the pavement and, in front of the whole Square, detained an unwilling head-master for quite another minute.

His face was deeply flushed as he returned into the shop. The assistants bent closer over their work. He did not instantly rush into the parlour and communicate with Constance. He had dropped into a way of conducting many operations by his own unaided brain. His confidence in his skill had increased with years. Further, at the back of his mind, there had established itself a vision of Mr. Povey as the seat of government and of Constance and Cyril as a sort of permanent opposition. He would not have admitted that he saw such a vision, for he was utterly loyal to his wife; but it was there. This unconfessed vision was one of several causes which had contributed to intensify his inherent tendency towards Machiavellianism and secretiveness. He said nothing to Constance, nothing to Cyril; but, happening to encounter Amy in the showroom, he was inspired to interrogate her sharply. The result was that they descended to the cellar together, Amy weeping. Amy was commanded to hold her tongue. And as she went in mortal fear of Mr. Povey she did hold her tongue. Nothing occurred for several days. And then one morning—it was Constance's birthday: children are nearly always horribly unlucky in their choice of days for sin—Mr. Povey, having executed mysterious movements in the shop after Cyril's departure to school, jammed his hat on his head and ran forth in pursuit of Cyril, whom he intercepted with two other boys, at the corner of Oldcastle Street and Acre Passage.

Cyril stood as if turned into salt. "Come back home!" said Mr. Povey, grimly; and for the sake of the other boys: "Please."

"But I shall be late for school, father," Cyril weakly urged.

"Never mind."

They passed through the shop together, causing a terrific concealed emotion, and then they did violence to Constance by appearing in the parlour. Constance was engaged in cutting straws and ribbons to make a straw-frame for a water-colour drawing of a moss-rose which her pure-hearted son had given her as a birthday present.

"Why—what—?" she exclaimed. She said no more at the moment because she was sure, from the faces of her men, that the time was big with fearful events.

"Take your satchel off," Mr. Povey ordered coldly. "And your mortar-board," he added with a peculiar intonation, as if glad thus to prove that Cyril was one of those rude boys who have to be told to take their hats off in a room.

"Whatever's amiss?" Constance murmured under her breath, as Cyril obeyed the command. "Whatever's amiss?"

Mr. Povey made no immediate answer. He was in charge of these proceedings, and was very anxious to conduct them with dignity and with complete effectiveness. Little fat man over fifty, with a wizened face, grey-haired and grey-bearded, he was as nervous as a youth. His heart beat furiously. And Constance, the portly matron who would never see forty again, was just as nervous as a girl. Cyril had gone very white. All three felt physically sick.

"What money have you got in your pockets?" Mr. Povey demanded, as a commencement.

Cyril, who had had no opportunity to prepare his case, offered no reply.

"You heard what I said," Mr. Povey thundered.

"I've got three-halfpence," Cyril murmured glumly, looking down at the floor. His lower lip seemed to hang precariously away from his gums.

"Where did you get that from?"

"It's part of what mother gave me," said the boy.

"I did give him a threepenny bit last week," Constance put in guiltily.

"It was a long time since he had had any money."

"If you gave it him, that's enough," said Mr. Povey, quickly, and to the boy: "That's all you've got?"

"Yes, father," said the boy.

"You're sure?"

"Yes, father."

Cyril was playing a hazardous game for the highest stakes, and under grave disadvantages; and he acted for the best. He guarded his own interests as well as he could.

Mr. Povey found himself obliged to take a serious risk. "Empty your pockets, then."

Cyril, perceiving that he had lost that particular game, emptied his pockets.

"Cyril," said Constance, "how often have I told you to change your handkerchiefs oftener! Just look at this!"

Astonishing creature! She was in the seventh hell of sick apprehension, and yet she said that!

After the handkerchief emerged the common schoolboy stock of articles useful and magic, and then, last, a silver florin!

Mr. Povey felt relief.

"Oh, Cyril!" whimpered Constance.

"Give it your mother," said Mr. Povey.

The boy stepped forward awkwardly, and Constance, weeping, took the coin.

"Please look at it, mother," said Mr. Povey. "And tell me if there's a cross marked on it."

135

Constance's tears blurred the coin. She had to wipe her eyes.

"Yes," she whispered faintly. "There's something on it."

"I thought so," said Mr. Povey. "Where did you steal it from?" he demanded.

"Out of the till," answered Cyril.

"Have you ever stolen anything out of the till before?"

"Yes."

"Yes, what."

"Yes, father."

"Take your hands out of your pockets and stand up straight, if you can.
How often?"

"I—I don't know, father."

"I blame myself," said Mr. Povey, frankly. "I blame myself. The till ought always to be locked. All tills ought always to be locked. But we felt we could trust the assistants. If anybody had told me that I ought not to trust you, if anybody had told me that my own son would be the thief, I should have—well, I don't know what I should have said!"

Mr. Povey was quite justified in blaming himself. The fact was that the functioning of that till was a patriarchal survival, which he ought to have revolutionized, but which it had never occurred to him to revolutionize, so accustomed to it was he. In the time of John Baines, the till, with its three bowls, two for silver and one for copper (gold had never been put into it), was invariably unlocked. The person in charge of the shop took change from it for the assistants, or temporarily authorized an assistant to do so. Gold was kept in a small linen bag in a locked drawer of the desk. The contents of the till were never checked by any system of book-keeping, as there was no system of book-keeping; when all transactions, whether in payment or receipt, are in cash—the Baineses never owed a penny save the quarterly wholesale accounts, which were discharged instantly to the travellers—a system of book-keeping is not indispensable. The till was situate immediately at the entrance to the shop from the house; it was in the darkest part of the shop, and the unfortunate Cyril had to pass it every day on his way to school. The thing was a perfect device for the manufacture of young criminals.

"And how have you been spending this money?" Mr. Povey inquired.

Cyril's hands slipped into his pockets again. Then, noticing the lapse, he dragged them out.

"Sweets," said he.

"Anything else?"

"Sweets and things."

"Oh!" said Mr. Povey. "Well, now you can go down into the cinder-cellar and bring up here all the things there are in that little box in the corner. Off you go!"

And off went Cyril. He had to swagger through the kitchen.

"What did I tell you, Master Cyril?" Amy unwisely asked of him. "You've copped it finely this time."

'Copped' was a word which she had learned from Cyril.

"Go on, you old bitch!" Cyril growled.

As he returned from the cellar, Amy said angrily:

"I told you I should tell your father the next time you called me that, and I shall. You mark my words."

"Cant! cant!" he retorted. "Do you think I don't know who's been canting? Cant! cant!"

Upstairs in the parlour Samuel was explaining the matter to his wife. There had been a perfect epidemic of smoking in the school. The head-master had discovered it and, he hoped, stamped it out. What had disturbed the head-master far more than the smoking was the fact that a few boys had been found to possess somewhat costly pipes, cigar-holders, or cigarette-holders. The head-master, wily, had not confiscated these articles; he had merely informed the parents concerned. In his opinion the articles came from one single source, a generous thief; he left the parents to ascertain which of them had brought a thief into the world.

Further information Mr. Povey had culled from Amy, and there could remain no doubt that Cyril had been providing his chums with the utensils of smoking, the till supplying the means. He had told Amy that the things which he secreted in the cellar had been presented to him by blood-brothers. But Mr. Povey did not believe that. Anyhow, he had marked every silver coin in the till for three nights, and had watched the till in the mornings from behind the merino-pile; and the florin on the parlour-table spoke of his success as a detective.

Constance felt guilty on behalf of Cyril. As Mr. Povey outlined his case she could not free herself from an entirely irrational sensation of sin; at any rate of special responsibility. Cyril seemed to be her boy and not Samuel's boy at all. She avoided her husband's glance. This was very odd.

Then Cyril returned, and his parents composed their faces and he deposited, next to the florin, a sham meerschaum pipe in a case, a tobacco-pouch, a cigar of which one end had been charred but the other not cut, and a half-empty packet of cigarettes without a label.

Nothing could be hid from Mr. Povey. The details were distressing.

"So Cyril is a liar and a thief, to say nothing of this smoking!" Mr. Povey concluded.

He spoke as if Cyril had invented strange and monstrous sins. But deep down in his heart a little voice was telling him, as regards the smoking, that HE had set the example. Mr. Baines had never smoked. Mr. Critchlow never smoked. Only men like Daniel smoked.

Thus far Mr. Povey had conducted the proceedings to his own satisfaction. He had proved the crime. He had made Cyril confess. The whole affair lay revealed. Well—what next? Cyril ought to have dissolved in repentance; something dramatic ought to have occurred. But Cyril simply stood with hanging, sulky head, and gave no sign of proper feeling.

Mr. Povey considered that, until something did happen, he must improve the occasion.

"Here we have trade getting worse every day," said he (it was true), "and you are robbing your parents to make a beast of yourself, and corrupting your companions! I wonder your mother never smelt you!"

"I never dreamt of such a thing!" said Constance, grievously.

Besides, a young man clever enough to rob a till is usually clever enough to find out that the secret of safety in smoking is to use cachous and not to keep the stuff in your pockets a minute longer than you can help.

"There's no knowing how much money you have stolen," said Mr. Povey. "A thief!"

If Cyril had stolen cakes, jam, string, cigars, Mr. Povey would never have said 'thief' as he did say it. But money! Money was different. And a till was not a cupboard or a larder. A till was a till. Cyril had struck at the very basis of society.

"And on your mother's birthday!" Mr. Povey said further.

"There's one thing I can do!" he said. "I can burn all this. Built on lies! How dared you?"

And he pitched into the fire—not the apparatus of crime, but the water-colour drawing of a moss-rose and the straws and the blue ribbon for bows at the corners.

"How dared you?" he repeated.

"You never gave me any money," Cyril muttered.

He thought the marking of coins a mean trick, and the dragging-in of bad trade and his mother's birthday roused a familiar devil that usually slept quietly in his breast.

"What's that you say?" Mr. Povey almost shouted.

"You never gave any money," the devil repeated in a louder tone than Cyril had employed.

(It was true. But Cyril 'had only to ask' and he would have received all that was good for him.)

Mr. Povey sprang up. Mr. Povey also had a devil. The two devils gazed at each other for an instant; and then, noticing that Cyril's head was above Mr. Povey's, the elder devil controlled itself. Mr. Povey had suddenly had as much drama as he wanted.

"Get away to bed!" said he with dignity.

Cyril went, defiantly.

"He's to have nothing but bread and water, mother," Mr. Povey finished.

He was, on the whole, pleased with himself.

Later in the day Constance reported, tearfully, that she had been up to Cyril and that Cyril had wept. Which was to Cyril's credit. But all felt that life could never be the same again. During the remainder of existence this unspeakable horror would lift its obscene form between them. Constance had never been so unhappy.

Occasionally, when by herself, she would rebel for a brief moment, as one rebels in secret against a mummery which one is obliged to treat seriously. "After all," she would whisper, "suppose he HAS taken a few shillings out of the till! What then? What does it matter?" But these moods of moral insurrection against society and Mr. Povey were very transitory. They were come and gone in a flash.

CHAPTER V

ANOTHER CRIME
I

One night—it was late in the afternoon of the same year, about six months after the tragedy of the florin—Samuel Povey was wakened up by a hand on his shoulder and a voice that whispered: "Father!"

The thief and the liar was standing in his night-shirt by the bed.

Samuel's sleepy eyes could just descry him in the thick gloom.

"What—what?" questioned the father, gradually coming to consciousness.

"What are you doing there?"

"I didn't want to wake mother up," the boy whispered. "There's someone been throwing dirt or something at our windows, and has been for a long time."

"Eh, what?"

Samuel stared at the dim form of the thief and liar. The boy was tall, not in the least like a little boy; and yet, then, he seemed to his father as quite a little boy, a little 'thing' in a night-shirt, with childish gestures and childish inflections, and a childish, delicious, quaint anxiety not to disturb his mother, who had lately been deprived of sleep owing to an illness of Amy's which had demanded nursing. His father had not so perceived him for years. In that instant the conviction that Cyril was permanently unfit for human society finally expired in the father's mind. Time had already weakened it very considerably. The decision that, be Cyril what he might, the summer holiday must be taken as usual, had dealt it a fearful blow. And yet, though Samuel and Constance had grown so accustomed to the companionship of a criminal that they frequently lost memory of his guilt for long periods, nevertheless the convention of his leprosy had more or less persisted with Samuel until that moment: when it vanished with strange suddenness, to Samuel's conscious relief.

There was a rain of pellets on the window.

"Hear that?" demanded Cyril, whispering dramatically. "And it's been like that on my window too."

Samuel arose. "Go back to your room!" he ordered in the same dramatic whisper; but not as father to son—rather as conspirator to conspirator.

Constance slept. They could hear her regular breathing.

Barefooted, the elderly gowned figure followed the younger, and one after the other they creaked down the two steps which separated Cyril's room from his parents'.

"Shut the door quietly!" said Samuel.

Cyril obeyed.

And then, having lighted Cyril's gas, Samuel drew the blind, unfastened the catch of the window, and began to open it with many precautions of silence. All the sashes in that house were difficult to manage. Cyril stood close to his father, shivering without knowing that he shivered, astonished only that his father had not told him to get back into bed at once. It was, beyond doubt, the proudest hour of Cyril's career. In addition to the mysterious circumstances of the night, there was in the situation that thrill which always communicates itself to a father and son when they are afoot together upon an enterprise unsuspected by the woman from whom their lives have no secrets.

Samuel put his head out of the window.

A man was standing there.

"That you, Samuel?" The voice came low.

"Yes," replied Samuel, cautiously. "It's not Cousin Daniel, is it?"

"I want ye," said Daniel Povey, curtly.

Samuel paused. "I'll be down in a minute," he said.

Cyril at length received the command to get back into bed at once.

"Whatever's up, father?" he asked joyously.

"I don't know. I must put some things on and go and see."

He shut down the window on all the breezes that were pouring into the room.

"Now quick, before I turn the gas out!" he admonished, his hand on the gas-tap.

"You'll tell me in the morning, won't you, father?"

"Yes," said Mr. Povey, conquering his habitual impulse to say 'No.'

He crept back to the large bedroom to grope for clothes.

When, having descended to the parlour and lighted the gas there, he opened the side-door, expecting to let Cousin Daniel in, there was no sign of Cousin Daniel. Presently he saw a figure standing at the corner of the Square. He whistled—Samuel had a singular faculty of whistling, the envy of his son—and Daniel beckoned to him. He nearly extinguished the gas and then ran out, hatless. He was wearing most of his clothes, except his linen collar and necktie, and the collar of his coat was turned up.

Daniel advanced before him, without waiting, into the confectioner's shop opposite. Being part of the most modern building in the Square, Daniel's shop was provided with the new roll-down iron shutter, by means of which you closed your establishment with a motion similar to the winding of a large clock, instead of putting up twenty separate shutters one by one as in the sixteenth century. The little portal in the vast sheet of armour was ajar, and Daniel had passed into the gloom beyond. At the same moment a policeman came along on his beat, cutting off Mr. Povey from Daniel.

"Good-night, officer! Brrr!" said Mr. Povey, gathering his dignity about him and holding himself as though it was part of his normal habit to take exercise bareheaded and collarless in St. Luke's Square on cold November nights. He behaved so because, if Daniel had desired the services of a policeman, Daniel would of course have spoken to this one.

"Goo' night, sir," said the policeman, after recognizing him.

"What time is it?" asked Samuel, bold.

"A quarter-past one, sir."

The policeman, leaving Samuel at the little open door, went forward across the lamplit Square, and Samuel entered his cousin's shop.

Daniel Povey was standing behind the door, and as Samuel came in he shut the door with a startling sudden movement. Save for the twinkle of gas, the shop was in darkness. It had the empty appearance which a well-managed confectioner's and baker's always has at night. The large brass scales near the flour-bins glinted; and the glass cake-stands, with scarce a tart among them, also caught the faint flare of the gas.

"What's the matter, Daniel? Anything wrong?" Samuel asked, feeling boyish as he usually did in the presence of Daniel.

The well-favoured white-haired man seized him with one hand by the shoulder in a grip that convicted Samuel of frailty.

"Look here, Sam'l," said he in his low, pleasant voice, somewhat altered by excitement. "You know as my wife drinks?"

He stared defiantly at Samuel.

"N—no," said Samuel. "That is—no one's ever SAID——"

This was true. He did not know that Mrs. Daniel Povey, at the age of fifty, had definitely taken to drink. There had been rumours that she enjoyed a glass with too much gusto; but 'drinks' meant more than that.

"She drinks," Daniel Povey continued. "And has done this last two year!"

"I'm very sorry to hear it," said Samuel, tremendously shocked by this brutal rending of the cloak of decency. Always, everybody had feigned to Daniel, and Daniel had feigned to everybody, that his wife was as other wives. And now the man himself had torn to pieces in a moment the veil of thirty years' weaving.

"And if that was the worst!" Daniel murmured reflectively, loosening his grip.

Samuel was excessively disturbed. His cousin was hinting at matters which he himself, at any rate, had never hinted at even to Constance, so abhorrent were they; matters unutterable, which hung like clouds in the social atmosphere of the town, and of which at rare intervals one conveyed one's cognizance, not by words, but by something scarce perceptible in a glance, an accent. Not often is a town such as Bursley starred with such a woman as Mrs. Daniel Povey.

"But what's wrong?" Samuel asked, trying to be firm.

And, "What is wrong?" he asked himself. "What does all this mean, at after one o'clock in the morning?"

"Look here, Sam'l," Daniel recommenced, seizing his shoulder again. "I went to Liverpool corn market to-day, and missed the last train, so I came by mail from Crewe. And what do I find? I find Dick sitting on the stairs in the dark pretty high naked."

"Sitting on the stairs? Dick?"

"Ay! This is what I come home to!"

"But—"

"Hold on! He's been in bed a couple of days with a feverish cold, caught through lying in damp sheets as his mother had forgot to air. She brings him no supper to-night. He calls out. No answer. Then he gets up to go down-stairs and see what's happened, and he slips on th' stairs and breaks his knee, or puts it out or summat. Sat there hours, seemingly! Couldn't walk neither up nor down."

"And was your—wife—was Mrs.—?"

"Dead drunk in the parlour, Sam'l."

"But the servant?"

"Servant!" Daniel Povey laughed. "We can't keep our servants. They won't stay. YOU know that."

He did. Mrs. Daniel Povey's domestic methods and idiosyncrasies could at any rate be freely discussed, and they were.

"And what have you done?"

"Done? Why, I picked him up in my arms and carried him upstairs again. And a fine job I had too! Here! Come here!"

Daniel strode impulsively across the shop—the counterflap was up—and opened a door at the back. Samuel followed. Never before had he penetrated so far into his cousin's secrets. On the left, within the doorway, were the stairs, dark; on the right a shut door; and in front an open door giving on to a yard. At the extremity of the yard he discerned a building, vaguely lit, and naked figures strangely moving in it.

"What's that? Who's there?" he asked sharply.

"That's the bakehouse," Daniel replied, as if surprised at such a question. "It's one of their long nights."

Never, during the brief remainder of his life, did Samuel eat a mouthful of common bread without recalling that midnight apparition. He had lived for half a century, and thoughtlessly eaten bread as though loaves grew ready-made on trees.

"Listen!" Daniel commanded him.

He cocked his ear, and caught a feeble, complaining wail from an upper floor.

"That's Dick! That is!" said Daniel Povey.

It sounded more like the distress of a child than of an adventurous young man of twenty-four or so.

"But is he in pain? Haven't you fetched the doctor?"

"Not yet," answered Daniel, with a vacant stare.

Samuel gazed at him closely for a second. And Daniel seemed to him very old and helpless and pathetic, a man unequal to the situation in which he found himself; and yet, despite the dignified snow of his age, wistfully boyish. Samuel thought swiftly: "This has been too much for him. He's almost out of his mind. That's the explanation. Some one's got to take charge, and I must." And all the courageous resolution of his character braced itself to the crisis. Being without a collar, being in slippers, and his suspenders imperfectly fastened anyhow,—these things seemed to be a part of the crisis.

"I'll just run upstairs and have a look at him," said Samuel, in a matter-of-fact tone.

Daniel did not reply.

There was a glimmer at the top of the stairs. Samuel mounted, found the gas-jet, and turned it on full. A dingy, dirty, untidy passage was revealed, the very antechamber of discomfort. Guided by the moans, Samuel entered a bedroom, which was in a shameful condition of neglect, and lighted only by a nearly expired candle. Was it possible that a house-mistress could so lose her self-respect? Samuel thought of his own abode, meticulously and impeccably 'kept,' and a hard bitterness against Mrs. Daniel surged up in his soul.

"Is that you, doctor?" said a voice from the bed; the moans ceased.

Samuel raised the candle.

Dick lay there, his face, on which was a beard of several days' growth, distorted by anguish, sweating; his tousled brown hair was limp with sweat.

"Where the hell's the doctor?" the young man demanded brusquely. Evidently he had no curiosity about Samuel's presence; the one thing that struck him was that Samuel was not the doctor.

"He's coming, he's coming," said Samuel, soothingly.

"Well, if he isn't here soon I shall be damn well dead," said Dick, in feeble resentful anger. "I can tell you that."

Samuel deposited the candle and ran downstairs. "I say, Daniel," he said, roused and hot, "this is really ridiculous. Why on earth didn't you fetch the doctor while you were waiting for me? Where's the missis?"

Daniel Povey was slowly emptying grains of Indian corn out of his jacket-pocket into one of the big receptacles behind the counter on the baker's side of the shop. He had provisioned himself with Indian corn as ammunition for Samuel's bedroom window; he was now returning the surplus.

"Are ye going for Harrop?" he questioned hesitatingly.

"Why, of course!" Samuel exclaimed. "Where's the missis?"

"Happen you'd better go and have a look at her," said Daniel Povey.

"She's in th' parlour."

He preceded Samuel to the shut door on the right. When he opened it the parlour appeared in full illumination. "Here! Go in!" said Daniel.

Samuel went in, afraid. In a room as dishevelled and filthy as the bedroom, Mrs. Daniel Povey lay stretched awkwardly on a worn horse-hair sofa, her head thrown back, her face discoloured, her eyes bulging, her mouth wet and yawning: a sight horribly offensive. Samuel was frightened; he was struck with fear and with disgust. The singing gas beat down ruthlessly on that dreadful figure. A wife and mother! The lady of a house! The centre of order! The fount of healing! The balm for worry, and the refuge of distress! She was vile. Her scanty yellow-grey hair was dirty, her hollowed neck all grime, her hands abominable, her black dress in decay. She was the dishonour of her sex, her situation, and her years. She was a fouler obscenity than the inexperienced Samuel had ever conceived. And by the door stood her husband, neat, spotless, almost stately, the man who for thirty years had marshalled all his immense pride to suffer this woman, the jolly man who had laughed through thick and thin! Samuel remembered when they were married. And he remembered when, years after their marriage, she was still as pretty, artificial, coquettish, and adamantine in her caprices as a young harlot with a fool at her feet. Time and the slow wrath of God had changed her.

He remained master of himself and approached her; then stopped.

"But—" he stammered.

"Ay, Sam'l, lad!" said the old man from the door. "I doubt I've killed her! I doubt I've killed her! I took and shook her. I got her by the neck. And before I knew where I was, I'd done it. She'll never drink brandy again. This is what it's come to!"

He moved away.

All Samuel's flesh tingled as a heavy wave of emotion rolled through his being. It was just as if some one had dealt him a blow unimaginably tremendous. His heart shivered, as a ship shivers at the mountainous crash of the waters. He was numbed. He wanted to weep, to vomit, to die, to sink away. But a voice was whispering to him: "You will have to go through with this. You are in charge of this." He thought of HIS wife and child, innocently asleep in the cleanly pureness of HIS home. And he felt the roughness of his coat-collar round his neck and the insecurity of his trousers. He passed out of the room, shutting the door. And across the yard he had a momentary glimpse of those nude nocturnal forms, unconsciously attitudinizing in the bakehouse. And down the stairs came the protests of Dick, driven by pain into a monotonous silly blasphemy.

"I'll fetch Harrop," he said, melancholily, to his cousin.

The doctor's house was less than fifty yards off, and the doctor had a night-bell, which, though he was a much older man than his father had been at his age, he still answered promptly. No need to bombard the doctor's premises with Indian corn! While Samuel was parleying with the doctor through a window, the question ran incessantly through his mind: "What about telling the police?"

But when, in advance of old Harrop, he returned to Daniel's shop, lo! the policeman previously encountered had returned upon his beat, and Daniel was talking to him in the little doorway. No other soul was about. Down King Street, along Wedgwood Street, up the Square, towards Brougham Street, nothing but gaslamps burning with their everlasting patience, and the blind facades of shops. Only in the second storey of the Bank Building at the top of the Square a light showed mysteriously through a blind. Somebody ill there!

The policeman was in a high state of nervous excitement. That had happened to him which had never happened to him before. Of the sixty policemen in Bursley, just he had been chosen by fate to fit the socket of destiny. He was startled.

"What's this, what's this, Mr. Povey?" he turned hastily to Samuel.

"What's this as Mr. Councillor Povey is a-telling me?"

"You come in, sergeant," said Daniel.

"If I come in," said the policeman to Samuel, "you mun' go along Wedgwood Street, Mr. Povey, and bring my mate. He should be on Duck Bank, by rights."

It was astonishing, when once the stone had begun to roll, how quickly it ran. In half an hour Samuel had actually parted from Daniel at the police-office behind the Shambles, and was hurrying to rouse his wife so that she could look after Dick Povey until he might be taken off to Pirehill Infirmary, as old Harrop had instantly, on seeing him, decreed.

"Ah!" he reflected in the turmoil of his soul: "God is not mocked!" That was his basic idea: God is not mocked! Daniel was a good fellow, honourable, brilliant; a figure in the world. But what of his licentious tongue? What of his frequenting of bars? (How had he come to miss that train from Liverpool? How?) For many years he, Samuel, had seen in Daniel a living refutation of the authenticity of the old Hebrew menaces. But he had been wrong, after all! God is not mocked! And Samuel was aware of a revulsion in himself towards that strict codified godliness from which, in thought, he had perhaps been slipping away.

And with it all he felt, too, a certain officious self-importance, as he woke his wife and essayed to break the news to her in a manner tactfully calm. He had assisted at the most overwhelming event ever known in the history of the town.

II

"Your muffler—I'll get it," said Constance. "Cyril, run upstairs and get father's muffler. You know the drawer."

Cyril ran. It behoved everybody, that morning, to be prompt and efficient.

"I don't need any muffler, thank you," said Samuel, coughing and smothering the cough.

"Oh! But, Sam—" Constance protested.

"Now please don't worry me!" said Samuel with frigid finality. "I've got quite enough—!" He did not finish. Constance sighed as her husband stepped, nervous and self-important, out of the side-door into the street. It was early, not yet eight o'clock, and the shop still unopened.

"Your father couldn't wait," Constance said to Cyril when he had thundered down the stairs in his heavy schoolboy boots. "Give it to me." She went to restore the muffler to its place.

The whole house was upset, and Amy still an invalid! Existence was disturbed; there vaguely seemed to be a thousand novel things to be done, and yet she could think of nothing whatever that she needed to do at that moment; so she occupied herself with the muffler. Before she reappeared Cyril had gone to school, he who was usually a laggard. The truth was that he could no longer contain within himself a recital of the night, and in particular of the fact that he had been the first to hear the summons of the murderer on the window-pane. This imperious news had to be imparted to somebody, as a preliminary to the thrilling of the whole school; and Cyril had issued forth in search of an appreciative and worthy confidant. He was scarcely five minutes after his father.

In St. Luke's Square was a crowd of quite two hundred persons, standing moveless in the November mud. The body of Mrs. Daniel Povey had already been taken to the Tiger Hotel, and young Dick Povey was on his way in a covered wagonette to Pirehill Infirmary on the other side of Knype. The shop of the crime was closed, and the blinds drawn at the upper windows of the house. There was absolutely nothing to be seen, not even a policeman. Nevertheless the crowd stared with an extraordinary obstinate attentiveness at the fatal building in Boulton Terrace. Hypnotized by this face of bricks and mortar, it had apparently forgotten all earthly ties, and, regardless of breakfast and a livelihood, was determined to stare at it till the house fell down or otherwise rendered up its secret. Most of its component individuals wore neither overcoats nor collars, but were kept warm by a scarf round the neck and by dint of forcing their fingers into the furthest inch of their pockets. Then they would slowly lift one leg after the other. Starers of infirm purpose would occasionally detach themselves from the throng and sidle away, ashamed of their fickleness. But reinforcements were continually arriving. And to these new-comers all that had been said in gossip had to be repeated and repeated: the same questions, the same answers, the same exclamations, the same proverbial philosophy, the same prophecies recurred in all parts of the Square with an uncanny iterance. Well-dressed men spoke to mere professional loiterers; for this unparalleled and glorious sensation, whose uniqueness grew every instant more impressive, brought out the essential brotherhood of mankind. All had a peculiar feeling that the day was neither Sunday nor week-day, but some eighth day of the week. Yet in the St. Luke's Covered Market close by, the stall-keepers were preparing their stalls just as though it were Saturday, just as though a Town Councillor had not murdered his wife—at last! It was stated, and restated infinitely, that the Povey baking had been taken over by Brindley, the second-best baker and confectioner, who had a stall in the market. And it was asserted, as a philosophical truth, and reasserted infinitely, that there would have been no sense in wasting good food.

Samuel's emergence stirred the multitude. But Samuel passed up the Square with a rapt expression; he might have been under an illusion, caused by the extreme gravity of his preoccupations, that he was crossing a deserted Square. He hurried past the Bank and down the Turnhill Road, to the private residence of 'Young Lawton,' son of the deceased 'Lawyer Lawton.' Young Lawton followed his father's profession; he was, as his father had been, the most successful solicitor in the town (though reputed by his learned rivals to be a fool),

142

but the custom of calling men by their occupations had died out with horse-cars. Samuel caught young Lawton at his breakfast, and presently drove with him, in the Lawton buggy, to the police-station, where their arrival electrified a crowd as large as that in St. Luke's Square. Later, they drove together to Hanbridge, informally to brief a barrister; and Samuel, not permitted to be present at the first part of the interview between the solicitor and the barrister, was humbled before the pomposity of legal etiquette.

It seemed to Samuel a game. The whole rigmarole of police and police-cells and formalities seemed insincere. His cousin's case was not like any other case, and, though formalities might be necessary, it was rather absurd to pretend that it was like any other case. In what manner it differed from other cases Samuel did not analytically inquire. He thought young Lawton was self-important, and Daniel too humble, in the colloquy of these two, and he endeavoured to indicate, by the dignity of his own demeanour, that in his opinion the proper relative tones had not been set. He could not understand Daniel's attitude, for he lacked imagination to realize what Daniel had been through. After all, Daniel was not a murderer; his wife's death was due to accident, was simply a mishap.

But in the crowded and stinking court-room of the Town Hall, Samuel began to feel qualms. It occurred that the Stipendiary Magistrate was sitting that morning at Bursley. He sat alone, as not one of the Borough Justices cared to occupy the Bench while a Town Councillor was in the dock. The Stipendiary, recently appointed, was a young man, from the southern part of the county; and a Town Councillor of Bursley was no more to him than a petty tradesman to a man of fashion. He was youthfully enthusiastic for the majesty and the impartiality of English justice, and behaved as though the entire responsibility for the safety of that vast fabric rested on his shoulders. He and the barrister from Hanbridge had had a historic quarrel at Cambridge, and their behaviour to each other was a lesson to the vulgar in the art of chill and consummate politeness. Young Lawton, having been to Oxford, secretly scorned the pair of them, but, as he had engaged counsel, he of course was precluded from adding to the eloquence, which chagrined him. These three were the aristocracy of the court-room; they knew it; Samuel Povey knew it; everybody knew it, and felt it. The barrister brought an unexceptionable zeal to the performance of his duties; be referred in suitable terms to Daniel's character and high position in the town, but nothing could hide the fact that for him too his client was a petty tradesman accused of simple murder. Naturally the Stipendiary was bound to show that before the law all men are equal—the Town Councillor and the common tippler; he succeeded. The policeman gave his evidence, and the Inspector swore to what Daniel Povey had said when charged. The hearing proceeded so smoothly and quickly that it seemed naught but an empty rite, with Daniel as a lay figure in it. The Stipendiary achieved marvellously the illusion that to him a murder by a Town Councillor in St. Luke's Square was quite an everyday matter. Bail was inconceivable, and the barrister, being unable to suggest any reason why the Stipendiary should grant a remand—indeed, there was no reason—Daniel Povey was committed to the Stafford Assizes for trial. The Stipendiary instantly turned to the consideration of an alleged offence against the Factory Acts by a large local firm of potters. The young magistrate had mistaken his vocation. With his steely calm, with his imperturbable detachment from weak humanity, he ought to have been a General of the Order of Jesuits.

Daniel was removed—he did not go: he was removed, by two bare-headed constables. Samuel wanted to have speech with him, and could not. And later, Samuel stood in the porch of the Town Hall, and Daniel appeared out of a corridor, still in the keeping of two policemen, helmeted now. And down below at the bottom of the broad flight of steps, up which passed dancers on the nights of subscription balls, was a dense crowd, held at bay by other policemen; and beyond the crowd a black van. And Daniel—to his cousin a sort of Christ between thieves—was hurried past the privileged loafers in the corridor, and down the broad steps. A murmuring wave agitated the crowd. Unkempt idlers and ne'er-do-wells in corduroy leaped up like tigers in the air, and the policemen fought them back furiously. And Daniel and his guardians shot through the little living lane. Quick! Quick! For the captive is more sacred even than a messiah. The law has him in charge! And like a feat of prestidigitation Daniel disappeared into the blackness of the van. A door slammed loudly, triumphantly, and a whip cracked. The crowd had been balked. It was as though the crowd had yelled for Daniel's blood and bones, and the faithful constables had saved him from their lust.

Yes, Samuel had qualms. He had a sickness in the stomach.

The aged Superintendent of Police walked by, with the aged Rector. The Rector was Daniel's friend. Never before had the Rector spoken to the Nonconformist Samuel, but now he spoke to him; he squeezed his hand.

"Ah, Mr. Povey!" he ejaculated grievously.

"I—I'm afraid it's serious!" Samuel stammered. He hated to admit that it was serious, but the words came out of his mouth.

He looked at the Superintendent of Police, expecting the Superintendent to assure him that it was not serious; but the Superintendent only raised his small white-bearded chin, saying nothing. The Rector shook his head, and shook a senile tear out of his eye.

After another chat with young Lawton, Samuel, on behalf of Daniel, dropped his pose of the righteous man to whom a mere mishap has occurred, and who is determined, with the lofty pride of innocence, to indulge all the whims of the law, to be more royalist than the king. He perceived that the law must be fought with its own weapons, that no advantage must be surrendered, and every possible advantage seized. He was truly astonished at himself that such a pose had ever been adopted. His eyes were opened; he saw things as they were.

He returned home through a Square that was more interested than ever in the facade of his cousin's house. People were beginning to come from Hanbridge, Knype, Longshaw, Turnhill, and villages such as Moorthorne, to gaze at that facade. And the fourth edition of the Signal, containing a full report of what the Stipendiary and the barrister had said to each other, was being cried.

In his shop he found customers, as absorbed in the trivialities of purchase as though nothing whatever had happened. He was shocked; he resented their callousness.

"I'm too busy now," he said curtly to one who accosted him.

"Sam!" his wife called him in a low voice. She was standing behind the till.

"What is it?" He was ready to crush, and especially to crush indiscreet babble in the shop. He thought she was going to vent her womanly curiosity at once.

"Mr. Huntbach is waiting for you in the parlour," said Constance.

"Mr. Huntbach?"

"Yes, from Longshaw." She whispered, "It's Mrs. Povey's cousin. He's come to see about the funeral and so on, the—the inquest, I suppose."

Samuel paused. "Oh, has he!" said he defiantly. "Well, I'll see him. If he WANTS to see me, I'll see him."

That evening Constance learned all that was in his mind of bitterness against the memory of the dead woman whose failings had brought Daniel Povey to Stafford gaol and Dick to the Pirehill Infirmary. Again and again, in the ensuing days, he referred to the state of foul discomfort which he had discovered in Daniel's house. He nursed a feud against all her relatives, and when, after the inquest, at which he gave evidence full of resentment, she was buried, he vented an angry sigh of relief, and said: "Well, SHE'S out of the way!" Thenceforward he had a mission, religious in its solemn intensity, to defend and save Daniel. He took the enterprise upon himself, spending the whole of himself upon it, to the neglect of his business and the scorn of his health. He lived solely for Daniel's trial, pouring out money in preparation for it. He thought and spoke of nothing else. The affair was his one preoccupation. And as the weeks passed, he became more and more sure of success, more and more sure that he would return with Daniel to Bursley in triumph after the assize. He was convinced of the impossibility that 'anything should happen' to Daniel; the circumstances were too clear, too overwhelmingly in Daniel's favour.

When Brindley, the second-best baker and confectioner, made an offer for Daniel's business as a going concern, he was indignant at first. Then Constance, and the lawyer, and Daniel (whom he saw on every permitted occasion) between them persuaded him that if some arrangement was not made, and made quickly, the business would lose all its value, and he consented, on Daniel's behalf, to a temporary agreement under which Brindley should reopen the shop and manage it on certain terms until Daniel regained his freedom towards the end of January. He would not listen to Daniel's plaintive insistence that he would never care to be seen in Bursley again. He pooh-poohed it. He protested furiously that the whole town was seething with sympathy for Daniel; and this was true. He became Daniel's defending angel, rescuing Daniel from Daniel's own weakness and apathy. He became, indeed, Daniel.

One morning the shop-shutter was wound up, and Brindley, inflated with the importance of controlling two establishments, strutted in and out under the sign of Daniel Povey. And traffic in bread and cakes and flour was resumed. Apparently the sea of time had risen and covered Daniel and all that was his; for his wife was under earth, and Dick lingered at Pirehill, unable to stand, and Daniel was locked away. Apparently, in the regular flow of the life of the Square, Daniel was forgotten. But not in Samuel Povey's heart was he forgotten! There, before an altar erected to the martyr, the sacred flame of a new faith burned with fierce consistency. Samuel, in his greying middle-age, had inherited the eternal youth of the apostle.

144

On the dark winter morning when Samuel set off to the grand assize, Constance did not ask his views as to what protection he would adopt against the weather. She silently ranged special underclothing, and by the warmth of the fire, which for days she had kept ablaze in the bedroom, Samuel silently donned the special underclothing. Over that, with particular fastidious care, he put his best suit. Not a word was spoken. Constance and he were not estranged, but the relations between them were in a state of feverish excitement. Samuel had had a cold on his flat chest for weeks, and nothing that Constance could invent would move it. A few days in bed or even in one room at a uniform temperature would have surely worked the cure. Samuel, however, would not stay in one room: he would not stay in the house, nor yet in Bursley. He would take his lacerating cough on chilly trains to Stafford. He had no ears for reason; he simply could not listen; he was in a dream. After Christmas a crisis came. Constance grew desperate. It was a battle between her will and his that occurred one night when Constance, marshalling all her forces, suddenly insisted that he must go out no more until he was cured. In the fight Constance was scarcely recognizable. She deliberately gave way to hysteria; she was no longer soft and gentle; she flung bitterness at him like vitriol; she shrieked like a common shrew. It seems almost incredible that Constance should have gone so far; but she did. She accused him, amid sobs, of putting his cousin before his wife and son, of not caring whether or not she was left a widow as the result of this obstinacy. And she ended by crying passionately that she might as well talk to a post. She might just as well have talked to a post. Samuel answered quietly and coldly. He told her that it was useless for her to put herself about, as he should act as he thought fit. It was a most extraordinary scene, and quite unique in their annals. Constance was beaten. She accepted the defeat, gradually controlling her sobs and changing her tone to the tone of the vanquished. She kissed him in bed, kissing the rod. And he gravely kissed her.

Henceforward she knew, in practice, what the inevitable, when you have to live with it, may contain of anguish wretched and humiliating. Her husband was risking his life, so she was absolutely convinced, and she could do nothing; she had come to the bed-rock of Samuel's character. She felt that, for the time being, she had a madman in the house, who could not be treated according to ordinary principles. The continual strain aged her. Her one source of relief was to talk with Cyril. She talked to him without reserve, and the words 'your father,' 'your father,' were everlastingly on her complaining tongue. Yes, she was utterly changed. Often she would weep when alone.

Nevertheless she frequently forgot that she had been beaten. She had no notion of honourable warfare. She was always beginning again, always firing under a flag of truce; and thus she constituted a very inconvenient opponent. Samuel was obliged, while hardening on the main point, to compromise on lesser questions. She too could be formidable, and when her lips took a certain pose, and her eyes glowed, he would have put on forty mufflers had she commanded. Thus it was she who arranged all the details of the supreme journey to Stafford. Samuel was to drive to Knype, so as to avoid the rigours of the Loop Line train from Bursley and the waiting on cold platforms. At Knype he was to take the express, and to travel first-class.

After he was dressed on that gas-lit morning, he learnt bit by bit the extent of her elaborate preparations. The breakfast was a special breakfast, and he had to eat it all. Then the cab came, and he saw Amy put hot bricks into it. Constance herself put goloshes over his boots, not because it was damp, but because indiarubber keeps the feet warm. Constance herself bandaged his neck, and unbuttoned his waistcoat and stuck an extra flannel under his dickey. Constance herself warmed his woollen gloves, and enveloped him in his largest overcoat. Samuel then saw Cyril getting ready to go out. "Where are you off?" he demanded.

"He's going with you as far as Knype," said Constance grimly. "He'll see you into the train and then come back here in the cab."

She had sprung this indignity upon him. She glared. Cyril glanced with timid bravado from one to the other. Samuel had to yield.

Thus in the winter darkness—for it was not yet dawn—Samuel set forth to the trial, escorted by his son. The reverberation of his appalling cough from the cab was the last thing that Constance heard.

During most of the day Constance sat in 'Miss Insull's corner' in the shop. Twenty years ago this very corner had been hers. But now, instead of large millinery-boxes enwrapped in brown paper, it was shut off from the rest of the counter by a rich screen of mahogany and ground-glass, and within the enclosed space all the apparatus necessary to the activity of Miss Insull had been provided for. However, it remained the coldest part of the whole shop, as Miss Insull's fingers testified. Constance established herself there more from a desire to do something, to interfere in something, than from a necessity of supervising the shop, though she had said to

Samuel that she would keep an eye on the shop. Miss Insull, whose throne was usurped, had to sit by the stove with less important creatures; she did not like it, and her underlings suffered accordingly.

It was a long day. Towards tea-time, just before Cyril was due from school, Mr. Critchlow came surprisingly in. That is to say, his arrival was less of a surprise to Miss Insull and the rest of the staff than to Constance. For he had lately formed an irregular habit of popping in at tea-time, to chat with Miss Insull. Mr. Critchlow was still defying time. He kept his long, thin figure perfectly erect. His features had not altered. His hair and beard could not have been whiter than they had been for years past. He wore his long white apron, and over that a thick reefer jacket. In his long, knotty fingers he carried a copy of the Signal.

Evidently he had not expected to find the corner occupied by Constance.

She was sewing.

"So it's you!" he said, in his unpleasant, grating voice, not even glancing at Miss Insull. He had gained the reputation of being the rudest old man in Bursley. But his general demeanour expressed indifference rather than rudeness. It was a manner that said: "You've got to take me as I am. I may be an egotist, hard, mean, and convinced; but those who don't like it can lump it. I'm indifferent."

He put one elbow on the top of the screen, showing the Signal.

"Mr. Critchlow!" said Constance, primly; she had acquired Samuel's dislike of him.

"It's begun!" he observed with mysterious glee.

"Has it?" Constance said eagerly. "Is it in the paper already?"

She had been far more disturbed about her husband's health than about the trial of Daniel Povey for murder, but her interest in the trial was of course tremendous. And this news, that it had actually begun, thrilled her.

"Ay!" said Mr. Critchlow. "Didn't ye hear the Signal boy hollering just now all over the Square?"

"No," said Constance. For her, newspapers did not exist. She never had the idea of opening one, never felt any curiosity which she could not satisfy, if she could satisfy it at all, without the powerful aid of the press. And even on this day it had not occurred to her that the Signal might be worth opening.

"Ay!" repeated Mr. Critchlow. "Seemingly it began at two o'clock—or thereabouts." He gave a moment of his attention to a noisy gas-jet, which he carefully lowered.

"What does it say?"

"Nothing yet!" said Mr. Critchlow; and they read the few brief sentences, under their big heading, which described the formal commencement of the trial of Daniel Povey for the murder of his wife. "There was some as said," he remarked, pushing up his spectacles, "that grand jury would alter the charge, or summat!" He laughed, grimly tolerant of the extreme absurdity. "Ah!" he added contemplatively, turning his head to see if the assistants were listening. They were. It would have been too much, on such a day, to expect a strict adherence to the etiquette of the shop.

Constance had been hearing a good deal lately of grand juries, but she had understood nothing, nor had she sought to understand.

"I'm very glad it's come on so soon," she said. "In a sense, that is! I was afraid Sam might be kept at Stafford for days. Do you think it will last long?"

"Not it!" said Mr. Critchlow, positively. "There's naught in it to spin out."

Then a silence, punctuated by the sound of stitching.

Constance would really have preferred not to converse with the old man; but the desire for reassurance, for the calming of her own fears, forced her to speak, though she knew well that Mr. Critchlow was precisely the last man in the town to give moral assistance if he thought it was wanted.

"I do hope everything will be all right!" she murmured.

"Everything'll be all right!" he said gaily. "Everything'll be all right. Only it'll be all wrong for Dan."

"Whatever do you mean, Mr. Critchlow?" she protested.

Nothing, she reflected, could rouse pity in that heart, not even a tragedy like Daniel's. She bit her lip for having spoken.

"Well," he said in loud tones, frankly addressing the girls round the stove as much as Constance. "I've met with some rare good arguments this new year, no mistake! There's been some as say that Dan never meant to do it. That's as may be. But if it's a good reason for not hanging, there's an end to capital punishment in this country. 'Never meant'! There's a lot of 'em as 'never meant'! Then I'm told as she was a gallivanting woman and no housekeeper, and as often drunk as sober. I'd no call to be told that. If strangling is a right punishment for a wife as spends her time in drinking brandy instead of sweeping floors and airing sheets, then Dan's safe. But I don't seem to see Judge Lindley telling the jury as it is. I've been a juryman under Judge Lindley myself—and more than once—and I don't seem to see him, like!" He paused with his mouth open. "As for all them nobs," he continued, "including th' rector, as have gone to Stafford to kiss the book and swear that Dan's reputation is second to none—if they could ha' sworn as Dan wasn't in th' house at all that night, if they could ha' sworn he was in Jericho, there'd ha' been some sense in their going. But as it is, they'd ha' done better to stop at home and mind their business. Bless us! Sam wanted ME to go!"

He laughed again, in the faces of the horrified and angry women.

"I'm surprised at you, Mr. Critchlow! I really am!" Constance exclaimed.

And the assistants inarticulately supported her with vague sounds. Miss Insull got up and poked the stove. Every soul in the establishment was loyally convinced that Daniel Povey would be acquitted, and to breathe a doubt on the brightness of this certainty was a hideous crime. The conviction was not within the domain of reason; it was an act of faith; and arguments merely fretted, without in the slightest degree disturbing it.

"Ye may be!" Mr. Critchlow gaily concurred. He was very content.

Just as he shuffled round to leave the shop, Cyril entered.

"Good afternoon, Mr. Critchlow," said Cyril, sheepishly polite.

Mr. Critchlow gazed hard at the boy, then nodded his head several times rapidly, as though to say: "Here's another fool in the making! So the generations follow one another!" He made no answer to the salutation, and departed.

Cyril ran round to his mother's corner, pitching his bag on to the showroom stairs as he passed them. Taking off his hat, he kissed her, and she unbuttoned his overcoat with her cold hands.

"What's old Methuselah after?" he demanded.

"Hush!" Constance softly corrected him. "He came in to tell me the trial had started."

"Oh, I knew that! A boy bought a paper and I saw it. I say, mother, will father be in the paper?" And then in a different tone: "I say, mother, what is there for tea?"

When his stomach had learnt exactly what there was for tea, the boy began to show an immense and talkative curiosity in the trial. He would not set himself to his home-lessons. "It's no use, mother," he said, "I can't."

They returned to the shop together, and Cyril would go every moment to the door to listen for the cry of a newsboy. Presently he hit upon the idea that perhaps newsboys might be crying the special edition of the Signal in the market-place, in front of the Town Hall, to the neglect of St. Luke's Square. And nothing would satisfy him but he must go forth and see. He went, without his overcoat, promising to run. The shop waited with a strange anxiety. Cyril had created, by his restless movements to and fro, an atmosphere of strained expectancy. It seemed now as if the whole town stood with beating heart, fearful of tidings and yet burning to get them. Constance pictured Stafford, which she had never seen, and a court of justice, which she had never seen, and her husband and Daniel in it. And she waited.

Cyril ran in. "No!" he announced breathlessly. "Nothing yet."

"Don't take cold, now you're hot," Constance advised.

But he would keep near the door. Soon he ran off again.

And perhaps fifteen seconds after he had gone, the strident cry of a Signal boy was heard in the distance, faint and indistinct at first, then clearer and louder.

"There's a paper!" said the apprentice.

"Sh!" said Constance, listening.

"Sh!" echoed Miss Insull.

"Yes, it is!" said Constance. "Miss Insull, just step out and get a paper. Here's a halfpenny."

The halfpenny passed quickly from one thimbled hand to another. Miss Insull scurried.

She came in triumphantly with the sheet, which Constance tremblingly took. Constance could not find the report at first. Miss Insull pointed to it, and read—

"'Summing up!' Lower down, lower down! 'After an absence of thirty-five minutes the jury found the prisoner guilty of murder, with a recommendation to mercy. The judge assumed the black cap and pronounced sentence of death, saying that he would forward the recommendation to the proper quarter.'"

Cyril returned. "Not yet!" he was saying—when he saw the paper lying on the counter. His crest fell.

Long after the shop was shut, Constance and Cyril waited in the parlour for the arrival of the master of the house. Constance was in the blackest despair. She saw nothing but death around her. She thought: misfortunes never come singly. Why did not Samuel come? All was ready for him, everything that her imagination could suggest, in the way of food, remedies, and the means of warmth. Amy was not allowed to go to bed, lest she might be needed. Constance did not even hint that Cyril should go to bed. The dark, dreadful minutes ticked themselves off on the mantelpiece until only five minutes separated Constance from the moment when she would not know what to do next. It was twenty-five minutes past eleven. If at half-past Samuel did not appear, then he could not come that night, unless the last train from Stafford was inconceivably late.

The sound of a carriage! It ceased at the door. Mother and son sprang up.

Yes, it was Samuel! She beheld him once more. And the sight of his condition, moral and physical, terrified her. His great strapping son and Amy helped him upstairs. "Will he ever come down those stairs again?" This thought lanced Constance's heart. The pain was come and gone in a moment, but it had surprised her tranquil commonsense, which was naturally opposed to, and gently scornful of, hysterical fears. As she puffed, with her stoutness, up the stairs, that bland cheerfulness of hers cost her an immense effort of will. She was profoundly troubled; great disasters seemed to be slowly approaching her from all quarters.

Should she send for the doctor? No. To do so would only be a concession to the panic instinct. She knew exactly what was the matter with Samuel: a severe cough persistently neglected, no more. As she had expressed herself many times to inquirers, "He's never been what you may call ill." Nevertheless, as she laid him in bed and possetted him, how frail and fragile he looked! And he was so exhausted that he would not even talk about the trial.

"If he's not better to-morrow I shall send for the doctor!" she said to herself. As for his getting up, she swore she would keep him in bed by force if necessary.

IV

The next morning she was glad and proud that she had not yielded to a scare. For he was most strangely and obviously better. He had slept heavily, and she had slept a little. True that Daniel was condemned to death! Leaving Daniel to his fate, she was conscious of joy springing in her heart. How absurd to have asked herself: "Will he ever come down those stairs again?"!

A message reached her from the forgotten shop during the morning, that Mr. Lawton had called to see Mr. Povey. Already Samuel had wanted to arise, but she had forbidden it in the tone of a woman who is dangerous, and Samuel had been very reasonable. He now said that Mr. Lawton must be asked up. She glanced round the bedroom. It was 'done'; it was faultlessly correct as a sick chamber. She agreed to the introduction into it of the man from another sphere, and after a preliminary minute she left the two to talk together. This visit of young Lawton's was a dramatic proof of Samuel's importance, and of the importance of the matter in hand. The august occasion demanded etiquette, and etiquette said that a wife should depart from her husband when he had to transact affairs beyond the grasp of a wife.

The idea of a petition to the Home Secretary took shape at this interview, and before the day was out it had spread over the town and over the Five Towns, and it was in the Signal. The Signal spoke of Daniel Povey as 'the condemned man.' And the phrase startled the whole district into an indignant agitation for his reprieve. The district woke up to the fact that a Town Councillor, a figure in the world, an honest tradesman of unspotted character, was cooped solitary in a little cell at Stafford, waiting to be hanged by the neck till he was dead. The district determined that this must not and should not be. Why! Dan Povey had actually once been Chairman of the Bursley Society for the Prosecution of Felons, that association for annual eating and drinking, whose members humorously called each other 'felons'! Impossible, monstrous, that an ex-chairman of the 'Felons' should be a sentenced criminal!

However, there was nothing to fear. No Home Secretary would dare to run counter to the jury's recommendation and the expressed wish of the whole district. Besides, the Home Secretary's nephew was M.P. for the Knype division. Of course a verdict of guilty had been inevitable. Everybody recognized that now. Even Samuel and all the hottest partisans of Daniel Povey recognized it. They talked as if they had always foreseen it, directly contradicting all that they had said on only the previous day. Without any sense of any inconsistency or of shame, they took up an absolutely new position. The structure of blind faith had once again crumbled at the assault of realities, and unhealthy, un-English truths, the statement of which would have meant ostracism twenty-four hours earlier, became suddenly the platitudes of the Square and the market-place.

Despatch was necessary in the affair of the petition, for the condemned man had but three Sundays. But there was delay at the beginning, because neither young Lawton nor any of his colleagues was acquainted with the proper formula of a petition to the Home Secretary for the reprieve of a criminal condemned to death. No such petition had been made in the district within living memory. And at first, young Lawton could not get sight or copy of any such petition anywhere, in the Five Towns or out of them. Of course there must exist a proper formula, and of course that formula and no other could be employed. Nobody was bold enough to suggest that young Lawton should commence the petition, "To the Most Noble the Marquis of Welwyn, K.C.B., May it please your Lordship," and end it, "And your petitioners will ever pray!" and insert between those phrases a simple appeal for the reprieve, with a statement of reasons. No! the formula consecrated by tradition must be found. And, after Daniel had arrived a day and a half nearer death, it was found. A lawyer at Alnwick had the draft of a petition which had secured for a murderer in Northumberland twenty years' penal servitude instead of sudden death, and on request he lent it to young Lawton. The prime movers in the petition felt that Daniel Povey was now as good as saved. Hundreds of forms were printed to receive signatures, and these forms, together with copies of the petition, were laid on the counters of all the principal shops, not merely in Bursley, but in the other towns. They were also to be found at the offices of the Signal, in railway waiting-rooms, and in the various reading-rooms; and on the second of Daniel's three Sundays they were exposed in the porches of churches and chapels. Chapel-keepers and vergers would come to Samuel and ask with the heavy inertia of their stupidity: "About pens and ink, sir?" These officials had the air of audaciously disturbing the sacrosanct routine of centuries in order to confer a favour.

Samuel continued to improve. His cough shook him less, and his appetite increased. Constance allowed him to establish himself in the drawing-room, which was next to the bedroom, and of which the grate was particularly efficient. Here, in an old winter overcoat, he directed the vast affair of the petition, which grew daily to vaster proportions. Samuel dreamed of twenty thousand signatures. Each sheet held twenty signatures, and several times a day he counted the sheets; the supply of forms actually failed once, and Constance herself had to hurry to the printers to order more. Samuel was put into a passion by this carelessness of the printers. He offered Cyril sixpence for every sheet of signatures which the boy would obtain. At first Cyril was too shy to canvass, but his father made him blush, and in a few hours Cyril had developed into an eager canvasser. One whole day he stayed away from school to canvas. Altogether he earned over fifteen shillings, quite honestly except that he got a companion to forge a couple of signatures with addresses lacking at the end of a last sheet, generously rewarding him with sixpence, the value of the entire sheet.

When Samuel had received a thousand sheets with twenty thousand signatures, he set his heart on twenty-five thousand signatures. And he also announced his firm intention of accompanying young Lawton to London with the petition. The petition had, in fact, become one of the most remarkable petitions of modern times. So the Signal said. The Signal gave a daily account of its progress, and its progress was astonishing. In certain streets every householder had signed it. The first sheets had been reserved for the signatures of members of Parliament, ministers of religion, civic dignitaries, justices of the peace, etc. These sheets were nobly filled. The aged Rector of Bursley signed first of all; after him the Mayor of Bursley, as was right; then sundry M.P.'s.

Samuel emerged from the drawing-room. He went into the parlour, and, later, into the shop; and no evil consequence followed. His cough was nearly, but not quite, cured. The weather was extraordinarily mild for the season. He repeated that he should go with the petition to London; and he went; Constance could not validly oppose the journey. She, too, was a little intoxicated by the petition. It weighed considerably over a hundredweight. The crowning signature, that of the M.P. for Knype, was duly obtained in London, and Samuel's one disappointment was that his hope of twenty-five thousand signatures had fallen short of realization—by only a few score. The few score could have been got had not time urgently pressed. He returned from London a man of mark, full of confidence; but his cough was worse again.

His confidence in the power of public opinion and the inherent virtue of justice might have proved to be well placed, had not the Home Secretary happened to be one of your humane officials. The Marquis of Welwyn was celebrated through every stratum of the governing classes for his humane instincts, which were continually fighting against his sense of duty. Unfortunately his sense of duty, which he had inherited from several centuries of ancestors, made havoc among his humane instincts on nearly every occasion of conflict. It was reported that he suffered horribly in consequence. Others also suffered, for he was never known to advise a remission of a sentence of flogging. Certain capital sentences he had commuted, but he did not commute Daniel Povey's. He could not permit himself to be influenced by a wave of popular sentiment, and assuredly not by his own nephew's signature. He gave to the case the patient, remorseless examination which he gave to every case. He spent a sleepless night in trying to discover a reason for yielding to his humane instincts, but without success. As Judge Lindley remarked in his confidential report, the sole arguments in favour of Daniel were provocation and his previous high character; and these were no sort of an argument. The provocation was utterly inadequate, and the previous high character was quite too ludicrously beside the point. So once more the Marquis's humane instincts were routed and he suffered horribly.

149

On the Sunday morning after the day on which the Signal had printed the menu of Daniel Povey's supreme breakfast, and the exact length of the 'drop' which the executioner had administered to him, Constance and Cyril stood together at the window of the large bedroom. The boy was in his best clothes; but Constance's garments gave no sign of the Sabbath. She wore a large apron over an old dress that was rather tight for her. She was pale and looked ill.

"Oh, mother!" Cyril exclaimed suddenly. "Listen! I'm sure I can hear the band."

She checked him with a soundless movement of her lips; and they both glanced anxiously at the silent bed, Cyril with a gesture of apology for having forgotten that he must make no noise.

The strains of the band came from down King Street, in the direction of St. Luke's Church. The music appeared to linger a long time in the distance, and then it approached, growing louder, and the Bursley Town Silver Prize Band passed under the window at the solemn pace of Handel's "Dead March." The effect of that requiem, heavy with its own inherent beauty and with the vast weight of harrowing tradition, was to wring the tears from Constance's eyes; they fell on her aproned bosom, and she sank into a chair. And though, the cheeks of the trumpeters were puffed out, and though the drummer had to protrude his stomach and arch his spine backwards lest he should tumble over his drum, there was majesty in the passage of the band. The boom of the drum, desolating the interruptions of the melody, made sick the heart, but with a lofty grief; and the dirge seemed to be weaving a purple pall that covered every meanness.

The bandsmen were not all in black, but they all wore crape on their sleeves and their instruments were knotted with crape. They carried in their hats a black-edged card. Cyril held one of these cards in his hands. It ran thus:

SACRED TO THE MEMORY OF DANIEL POVEY A TOWN COUNCILLOR OF THIS TOWN JUDICIALLY MURDERED AT 8 O'CLOCK IN THE MORNING 8TH FEBRUARY 1888 "HE WAS MORE SINNED AGAINST THAN SINNING."

In the wake of the band came the aged Rector, bare-headed, and wearing a surplice over his overcoat; his thin white hair was disarranged by the breeze that played in the chilly sunshine; his hands were folded on a gilt-edged book. A curate, churchwardens, and sidesmen followed. And after these, tramping through the dark mud in a procession that had apparently no end, wound the unofficial male multitude, nearly all in mourning, and all, save the more aristocratic, carrying the memorial card in their hats. Loafers, women, and children had collected on the drying pavements, and a window just opposite Constance was ornamented with the entire family of the landlord of the Sun Vaults. In the great bar of the Vaults a barman was craning over the pitchpine screen that secured privacy to drinkers. The procession continued without break, eternally rising over the verge of King Street 'bank,' and eternally vanishing round the corner into St. Luke's Square; at intervals it was punctuated by a clergyman, a Nonconformist minister, a town crier, a group of foremen, or a few Rifle Volunteers. The watching crowd grew as the procession lengthened. Then another band was heard, also playing the march from Saul. The first band had now reached the top of the Square, and was scarcely audible from King Street. The reiterated glitter in the sun of memorial cards in hats gave the fanciful illusion of an impossible whitish snake that was straggling across the town. Three-quarters of an hour elapsed before the tail of the snake came into view, and a rabble of unkempt boys closed in upon it, filling the street.

"I shall go to the drawing-room window, mother," said Cyril.

She nodded. He crept out of the bedroom.

St. Luke's Square was a sea of hats and memorial cards. Most of the occupiers of the Square had hung out flags at half-mast, and a flag at half-mast was flying over the Town Hall in the distance. Sightseers were at every window. The two bands had united at the top of the Square; and behind them, on a North Staffordshire Railway lorry, stood the white-clad Rector and several black figures. The Rector was speaking; but only those close to the lorry could hear his feeble treble voice.

Such was the massive protest of Bursley against what Bursley regarded as a callous injustice. The execution of Daniel Povey had most genuinely excited the indignation of the town. That execution was not only an injustice; it was an insult, a humiliating snub. And the worst was that the rest of the country had really discovered no sympathetic interest in the affair. Certain London papers, indeed, in commenting casually on the execution, had slurred the morals and manners of the Five Towns, professing to regard the district as notoriously beyond the realm of the Ten Commandments. This had helped to render furious the townsmen. This, as much as anything, had encouraged the spontaneous outburst of feeling which had culminated in a St.

Luke's Square full of people with memorial cards in their hats. The demonstration had scarcely been organized; it had somehow organized itself, employing the places of worship and a few clubs as centres of gathering. And it proved an immense success. There were seven or eight thousand people in the Square, and the pity was that England as a whole could not have had a glimpse of the spectacle. Since the execution of the elephant, nothing had so profoundly agitated Bursley. Constance, who left the bedroom momentarily for the drawing-room, reflected that the death and burial of Cyril's honoured grandfather, though a resounding event, had not caused one-tenth of the stir which she beheld. But then John Baines had killed nobody.

The Rector spoke too long; every one felt that. But at length he finished. The bands performed the Doxology, and the immense multitudes began to disperse by the eight streets that radiate from the Square. At the same time one o'clock struck, and the public-houses opened with their customary admirable promptitude. Respectable persons, of course, ignored the public-houses and hastened homewards to a delayed dinner. But in a town of over thirty thousand souls there are sufficient dregs to fill all the public-houses on an occasion of ceremonial excitement. Constance saw the bar of the Vaults crammed with individuals whose sense of decent fitness was imperfect. The barman and the landlord and the principal members of the landlord's family were hard put to it to quench that funereal thirst. Constance, as she ate a little meal in the bedroom, could not but witness the orgy. A bandsman with his silver instrument was prominent at the counter. At five minutes to three the Vaults spewed forth a squirt of roysterers who walked on the pavement as on a tight-rope; among them was the bandsman, his silver instrument only half enveloped in its bag of green serge. He established an equilibrium in the gutter. It would not have mattered so seriously if he had not been a bandsman. The barman and the landlord pushed the ultimate sot by force into the street and bolted the door (till six o'clock) just as a policeman strolled along, the first policeman of the day. It became known that similar scenes were enacting at the thresholds of other inns. And the judicious were sad.

VI

When the altercation between the policeman and the musician in the gutter was at its height, Samuel Povey became restless; but since he had scarcely stirred through the performances of the bands, it was probably not the cries of the drunkard that had aroused him.

He had shown very little interest in the preliminaries of the great demonstration. The flame of his passion for the case of Daniel Povey seemed to have shot up on the day before the execution, and then to have expired. On that day he went to Stafford in order, by permit of the prison governor, to see his cousin for the last time. His condition then was undoubtedly not far removed from monomania. 'Unhinged' was the conventional expression which frequently rose in Constance's mind as a description of the mind of her husband; but she fought it down; she would not have it; it was too crude—with its associations. She would only admit that the case had 'got on' his mind. A startling proof of this was that he actually suggested taking Cyril with him to see the condemned man. He wished Cyril to see Daniel; he said gravely that he thought Cyril ought to see him. The proposal was monstrous, inexplicable—or explicable only by the assumption that his mind, while not unhinged, had temporarily lost its balance. Constance opposed an absolute negative, and Samuel being in every way enfeebled, she overcame. As for Cyril, he was divided between fear and curiosity. On the whole, perhaps Cyril regretted that he would not be able to say at school that he had had speech with the most celebrated killer of the age on the day before his execution.

Samuel returned hysterical from Stafford. His account of the scene, which he gave in a very loud voice, was a most absurd and yet pathetic recital, obviously distorted by memory. When he came to the point of the entrance of Dick Povey, who was still at the hospital, and who had been specially driven to Stafford and carried into the prison, he wept without restraint. His hysteria was painful in a very high degree.

He went to bed—of his own accord, for his cough had improved again. And on the following day, the day of the execution, he remained in bed till the afternoon. In the evening the Rector sent for him to the Rectory to discuss the proposed demonstration. On the next day, Saturday, he said he should not get up. Icy showers were sweeping the town, and his cough was worse after the evening visit to the Rector. Constance had no apprehensions about him. The most dangerous part of the winter was over, and there was nothing now to force him into indiscretions. She said to herself calmly that he should stay in bed as long as he liked, that he could not have too much repose after the cruel fatigues, physical and spiritual, which he had suffered. His cough was short, but not as troublesome as in the past; his face flushed, dusky, and settled in gloom; and he was slightly feverish, with quick pulse and quick breathing—the symptoms of a renewed cold. He passed a wakeful night, broken by brief dreams in which he talked. At dawn he had some hot food, asked what day it was, frowned, and seemed to doze off at once. At eleven o'clock he had refused food. And he had intermittently dozed during the progress of the demonstration and its orgiastic sequel.

Constance had food ready for his waking, and she approached the bed and leaned over him. The fever had increased somewhat, the breathing was more rapid, and his lips were covered with tiny purple pimples. He feebly shook his head, with a disgusted air, at her mention of food. It was this obstinate refusal of food which first alarmed her. A little uncomfortable suspicion shot up in her: Surely there's nothing the MATTER with him?

Something—impossible to say what—caused her to bend still lower, and put her ear to his chest. She heard within that mysterious box a rapid succession of thin, dry, crackling sounds: sounds such as she would have produced by rubbing her hair between her fingers close to her ear. The crepitation ceased, then recommenced, and she perceived that it coincided with the intake of his breath. He coughed; the sounds were intensified; a spasm of pain ran over his face; and he put his damp hand to his side.

"Pain in my side!" he whispered with difficulty.

Constance stepped into the drawing-room, where Cyril was sketching by the fire.

"Cyril," she said, "go across and ask Dr. Harrop to come round at once.

And if he isn't in, then his new partner."

"Is it for father?"

"Yes."

"What's the matter?"

"Now do as I say, please," said Constance, sharply, adding: "I don't know what's the matter. Perhaps nothing. But I'm not satisfied."

The venerable Harrop pronounced the word 'pneumonia.' It was acute double pneumonia that Samuel had got. During the three worst months of the year, he had escaped the fatal perils which await a man with a flat chest and a chronic cough, who ignores his condition and defies the weather. But a journey of five hundred yards to the Rectory had been one journey too many. The Rectory was so close to the shop that he had not troubled to wrap himself up as for an excursion to Stafford. He survived the crisis of the disease and then died of toxsemia, caused by a heart that would not do its duty by the blood. A casual death, scarce noticed in the reaction after the great febrile demonstration! Besides, Samuel Povey never could impose himself on the burgesses. He lacked individuality. He was little. I have often laughed at Samuel Povey. But I liked and respected him. He was a very honest man. I have always been glad to think that, at the end of his life, destiny took hold of him and displayed, to the observant, the vein of greatness which runs through every soul without exception. He embraced a cause, lost it, and died of it.

CHAPTER VI

THE WIDOW
I

Constance, alone in the parlour, stood expectant by the set tea-table. She was not wearing weeds; her mother and she, on the death of her father, had talked of the various disadvantages of weeds; her mother had worn them unwillingly, and only because a public opinion not sufficiently advanced had intimidated her. Constance had said: "If ever I'm a widow I won't wear them," positively, in the tone of youth; and Mrs. Baines had replied: "I hope you won't, my dear." That was over twenty years ago, but Constance perfectly remembered. And now, she was a widow! How strange and how impressive was life! And she had kept her word; not positively, not without hesitations; for though times were changed, Bursley was still Bursley; but she had kept it.

This was the first Monday after Samuel's funeral. Existence in the house had been resumed on the plane which would henceforth be the normal plane. Constance had put on for tea a dress of black silk with a jet brooch of her mother's. Her hands, just meticulously washed, had that feeling of being dirty which comes from roughening of the epidermis caused by a day spent in fingering stuffs. She had been 'going through'

Samuel's things, and her own, and ranging all anew. It was astonishing how little the man had collected, of 'things,' in the course of over half a century. All his clothes were contained in two long drawers and a short one. He had the least possible quantity of haberdashery and linen, for he invariably took from the shop such articles as he required, when he required them, and he would never preserve what was done with. He possessed no jewellery save a set of gold studs, a scarf-ring, and a wedding-ring; the wedding-ring was buried with him. Once, when Constance had offered him her father's gold watch and chain, he had politely refused it, saying that he preferred his own—a silver watch (with a black cord) which kept excellent time; he had said later that she might save the gold watch and chain for Cyril when he was twenty-one. Beyond these trifles and a half-empty box of cigars and a pair of spectacles, he left nothing personal to himself. Some men leave behind them a litter which takes months to sift and distribute. But Samuel had not the mania for owning. Constance put his clothes in a box to be given away gradually (all except an overcoat and handkerchiefs which might do for Cyril); she locked up the watch and its black cord, the spectacles and the scarf-ring; she gave the gold studs to Cyril; she climbed on a chair and hid the cigar-box on the top of her wardrobe; and scarce a trace of Samuel remained!

By his own wish the funeral had been as simple and private as possible. One or two distant relations, whom Constance scarcely knew and who would probably not visit her again until she too was dead, came—and went. And lo! the affair was over. The simple celerity of the funeral would have satisfied even Samuel, whose tremendous self-esteem hid itself so effectually behind such externals that nobody had ever fully perceived it. Not even Constance quite knew Samuel's secret opinion of Samuel. Constance was aware that he had a ridiculous side, that his greatest lack had been a lack of spectacular dignity. Even in the coffin, where nevertheless most people are finally effective, he had not been imposing—with his finicky little grey beard persistently sticking up.

The vision of him in his coffin—there in the churchyard, just at the end of King Street!—with the lid screwed down on that unimportant beard, recurred frequently in the mind of the widow, as something untrue and misleading. She had to say to herself: "Yes, he is really there! And that is why I have this particular feeling in my heart." She saw him as an object pathetic and wistful, not majestic. And yet she genuinely thought that there could not exist another husband quite so honest, quite so just, quite so reliable, quite so good, as Samuel had been. What a conscience he had! How he would try, and try, to be fair with her! Twenty years she could remember, of ceaseless, constant endeavour on his part to behave rightly to her! She could recall many an occasion when he had obviously checked himself, striving against his tendency to cold abruptness and to sullenness, in order to give her the respect due to a wife. What loyalty was his! How she could depend on him! How much better he was than herself (she thought with modesty)!

His death was an amputation for her. But she faced it with calmness. She was not bowed with sorrow. She did not nurse the idea that her life was at an end; on the contrary, she obstinately put it away from her, dwelling on Cyril. She did not indulge in the enervating voluptuousness of grief. She had begun in the first hours of bereavement by picturing herself as one marked out for the blows of fate. She had lost her father and her mother, and now her husband. Her career seemed to be punctuated by interments. But after a while her gentle commonsense came to insist that most human beings lose their parents, and that every marriage must end in either a widower or a widow, and that all careers are punctuated by interments. Had she not had nearly twenty-one years of happy married life? (Twenty-one years—rolled up! The sudden thought of their naive ignorance of life, hers and his, when they were first married, brought tears into her eyes. How wise and experienced she was now!) And had she not Cyril? Compared to many women, she was indeed very fortunate.

The one visitation which had been specially hers was the disappearance of Sophia. And yet even that was not worse than the death outright of Sophia, was perhaps not so bad. For Sophia might return out of the darkness. The blow of Sophia's flight had seemed unique when it was fresh, and long afterwards; had seemed to separate the Baines family from all other families in a particular shame. But at the age of forty-three Constance had learnt that such events are not uncommon in families, and strange sequels to them not unknown. Thinking often of Sophia, she hoped wildly and frequently.

She looked at the clock; she had a little spasm of nervousness lest Cyril might fail to keep his word on that first day of their new regular life together. And at the instant he burst into the room, invading it like an armed force, having previously laid waste the shop in his passage.

"I'm not late, mother! I'm not late!" he cried proudly.

She smiled warmly, happy in him, drawing out of him balm and solace. He did not know that in that stout familiar body before him was a sensitive, trembling soul that clutched at him ecstatically as the one reality in the universe. He did not know that that evening meal, partaken of without hurry after school had released him to her, was to be the ceremonial sign of their intimate unity and their interdependence, a tender and delicious proof that they were 'all in all to each other': he saw only his tea, for which he was hungry—just as hungry as though his father were not scarcely yet cold in the grave.

But he saw obscurely that the occasion demanded something not quite ordinary, and so exerted himself to be boyishly charming to his mother. She said to herself 'how good he was.' He felt at ease and confident in the future, because he detected beneath her customary judicial, impartial mask a clear desire to spoil him.

After tea, she regretfully left him, at his home-lessons, in order to go into the shop. The shop was the great unsolved question. What was she to do with the shop? Was she to continue the business or to sell it? With the fortunes of her father and her aunt, and the economies of twenty years, she had more than sufficient means. She was indeed rich, according to the standards of the Square; nay, wealthy! Therefore she was under no material compulsion to keep the shop. Moreover, to keep it would mean personal superintendence and the burden of responsibility, from which her calm lethargy shrank. On the other hand, to dispose of the business would mean the breaking of ties and leaving the premises: and from this also she shrank. Young Lawton, without being asked, had advised her to sell. But she did not want to sell. She wanted the impossible: that matters should proceed in the future as in the past, that Samuel's death should change nothing save in her heart.

In the meantime Miss Insull was priceless. Constance thoroughly understood one side of the shop; but Miss Insull understood both, and the finance of it also. Miss Insull could have directed the establishment with credit, if not with brilliance. She was indeed directing it at that moment. Constance, however, felt jealous of Miss Insull; she was conscious of a slight antipathy towards the faithful one. She did not care to be in the hands of Miss Insull.

There were one or two customers at the millinery counter. They greeted her with a deplorable copiousness of tact. Most tactfully they avoided any reference to Constance's loss; but by their tone, their glances, at Constance and at each other, and their heroically restrained sighs, they spread desolation as though they had been spreading ashes instead of butter on bread. The assistants, too, had a special demeanour for the poor lone widow which was excessively trying to her. She wished to be natural, and she would have succeeded, had they not all of them apparently conspired together to make her task impossible.

She moved away to the other side of the shop, to Samuel's desk, at which he used to stand, staring absently out of the little window into King Street while murmurously casting figures. She lighted the gas-jet there, arranged the light exactly to suit her, and then lifted the large flap of the desk and drew forth some account books.

"Miss Insull!" she called, in a low, clear voice, with a touch of haughtiness and a touch of command in it. The pose, a comical contradiction of Constance's benevolent character, was deliberately adopted; it illustrated the effects of jealousy on even the softest disposition.

Miss Insull responded. She had no alternative but to respond. And she gave no sign of resenting her employer's attitude. But then Miss Insull seldom did give any sign of being human.

The customers departed, one after another, obsequiously sped by the assistants, who thereupon lowered the gases somewhat, according to secular rule; and in the dim eclipse, as they restored boxes to shelves, they could hear the tranquil, regular, half-whispered conversation of the two women at the desk, discussing accounts; and then the chink of gold.

Suddenly there was an irruption. One of the assistants sprang instinctively to the gas; but on perceiving that the disturber of peace was only a slatternly girl, hatless and imperfectly clean, she decided to leave the gas as it was, and put on a condescending, suspicious demeanour.

"If you please, can I speak to the missis?" said the girl, breathlessly.

She seemed to be about eighteen years of age, fat and plain. Her blue frock was torn, and over it she wore a rough brown apron, caught up at one corner to the waist. Her bare forearms were of brick-red colour.

"What is it?" demanded the assistant.

Miss Insull looked over her shoulder across the shop. "It must be Maggie's—Mrs. Hollins's daughter!" said Miss Insull under her breath.

"What can she want?" said Constance, leaving the desk instantly; and to the girl, who stood sturdily holding her own against the group of assistants: "You are Mrs. Hollins's daughter, aren't you?"

"Yes, mum."

"What's your name?"

"Maggie, mum. And, if you please, mother's sent me to ask if you'll kindly give her a funeral card."

154

"A funeral card?"

"Yes. Of Mr. Povey. She's been expecting of one, and she thought as how perhaps you'd forgotten it, especially as she wasn't asked to the funeral."

The girl stopped.

Constance perceived that by mere negligence she had seriously wounded the feelings of Maggie, senior. The truth was, she had never thought of Maggie. She ought to have remembered that funeral cards were almost the sole ornamentation of Maggie's abominable cottage.

"Certainly," she replied after a pause. "Miss Insull, there are a few cards left in the desk, aren't there? Please put me one in an envelope for Mrs. Hollins."

She gave the heavily bordered envelope to the ruddy wench, who enfolded it in her apron, and with hurried, shy thanks ran off.

"Tell your mother I send her a card with pleasure," Constance called after the girl.

The strangeness of the hazards of life made her thoughtful. She, to whom Maggie had always seemed an old woman, was a widow, but Maggie's husband survived as a lusty invalid. And she guessed that Maggie, vilely struggling in squalor and poverty, was somehow happy in her frowsy, careless way.

She went back to the accounts, dreaming.

II

When the shop had been closed, under her own critical and precise superintendence, she extinguished the last gas in it and returned to the parlour, wondering where she might discover some entirely reliable man or boy to deal with the shutters night and morning. Samuel had ordinarily dealt with the shutters himself, and on extraordinary occasions and during holidays Miss Insull and one of her subordinates had struggled with their unwieldiness. But the extraordinary occasion had now become ordinary, and Miss Insull could not be expected to continue indefinitely in the functions of a male. Constance had a mind to engage an errand-boy, a luxury against which Samuel had always set his face. She did not dream of asking the herculean Cyril to open and shut shop.

He had apparently finished his home-lessons. The books were pushed aside, and he was sketching in lead-pencil on a drawing-block. To the right of the fireplace, over the sofa, there hung an engraving after Landseer, showing a lonely stag paddling into a lake. The stag at eve had drunk or was about to drink his fill, and Cyril was copying him. He had already indicated a flight of birds in the middle distance; vague birds on the wing being easier than detailed stags, he had begun with the birds.

Constance put a hand on his shoulder. "Finished your lessons?" she murmured caressingly.

Before speaking, Cyril gazed up at the picture with a frowning, busy expression, and then replied in an absent-minded voice:

"Yes." And after a pause: "Except my arithmetic. I shall do that in the morning before breakfast."

"Oh, Cyril!" she protested.

It had been a positive ordinance, for a long time past, that there should be no sketching until lessons were done. In his father's lifetime Cyril had never dared to break it.

He bent over his block, feigning an intense absorption. Constance's hand slipped from his shoulder. She wanted to command him formally to resume his lessons. But she could not. She feared an argument; she mistrusted herself. And, moreover, it was so soon after his father's death!

"You know you won't have time to-morrow morning!" she said weakly.

"Oh, mother!" he retorted superiorly. "Don't worry." And then, in a cajoling tone: "I've wanted to do that stag for ages."

She sighed and sat down in her rocking-chair. He went on sketching, rubbing out, and making queer expostulatory noises against his pencil, or against the difficulties needlessly invented by Sir Edwin Landseer. Once he rose and changed the position of the gas-bracket, staring fiercely at the engraving as though it had committed a sin.

Amy came to lay the supper. He did not acknowledge that she existed.

"Now, Master Cyril, after you with that table, if you please!" She announced herself brusquely, with the privilege of an old servant and a woman who would never see thirty again.

"What a nuisance you are, Amy!" he gruffly answered. "Look here, mother, can't Amy lay the cloth on that half of the table? I'm right in the middle of my drawing. There's plenty of room there for two."

He seemed not to be aware that, in the phrase 'plenty of room for two,' he had made a callous reference to their loss. The fact was, there WAS plenty of room for two.

Constance said quickly: "Very well, Amy. For this once."

Amy grunted, but obeyed.

Constance had to summon him twice from art to nourishment. He ate with rapidity, frequently regarding the picture with half-shut, searching eyes. When he had finished, he refilled his glass with water, and put it next to his sketching-block.

"You surely aren't thinking of beginning to paint at this time of night!" Constance exclaimed, astonished.

"Oh YES, mother!" he fretfully appealed. "It's not late."

Another positive ordinance of his father's had been that there should be nothing after supper except bed. Nine o'clock was the latest permissible moment for going to bed. It was now less than a quarter to.

"It only wants twelve minutes to nine," Constance pointed out.

"Well, what if it does?"

"Now, Cyril," she said, "I do hope you are going to be a good boy, and not cause your mother anxiety." But she said it too kindly.

He said sullenly: "I do think you might let me finish it. I've begun it. It won't take me long."

She made the mistake of leaving the main point. "How can you possibly choose your colours properly by gas-light?" she said.

"I'm going to do it in sepia," he replied in triumph.

"It mustn't occur again," she said.

He thanked God for a good supper, and sprang to the harmonium, where his paint-box was. Amy cleared away. Constance did crochet-work. There was silence. The clock struck nine, and it also struck half-past nine. She warned him repeatedly. At ten minutes to ten she said persuasively:

"Now, Cyril, when the clock strikes ten I shall really put the gas out."

The clock struck ten.

"Half a mo, half a mo!" he cried. "I've done! I've done!"

Her hand was arrested.

Another four minutes elapsed, and then he jumped up. "There you are!" he said proudly, showing her the block. And all his gestures were full of grace and cajolery.

"Yes, it's very good," Constance said, rather indifferently.

"I don't believe you care for it!" he accused her, but with a bright smile.

"I care for your health," she said. "Just look at that clock!"

He sat down in the other rocking-chair, deliberately.

"Now, Cyril!"

"Well, mother, I suppose you'll let me take my boots off!" He said it with teasing good-humour.

When he kissed her good night, she wanted to cling to him, so affectionate was his kiss; but she could not throw off the habits of restraint which she had been originally taught and had all her life practised. She keenly regretted the inability.

In her bedroom, alone, she listened to his movements as he undressed. The door between the two rooms was unlatched. She had to control a desire to open it ever so little and peep at him. He would not have liked that. He could have enriched her heart beyond all hope, and at no cost to himself; but he did not know his power. As she could not cling to him with her hands, she clung to him with that heart of hers, while moving sedately up and down the room, alone. And her eyes saw him through the solid wood of the door. At last she got heavily into bed. She thought with placid anxiety, in the dark: "I shall have to be firm with Cyril." And she thought also, simultaneously: "He really must be a good boy. He MUST." And clung to him passionately, without shame! Lying alone there in the dark, she could be as unrestrained and girlish as her heart chose. When she loosed her hold she instantly saw the boy's father arranged in his coffin, or flitting about the room. Then she would hug that vision too, for the pleasure of the pain it gave her.

III

She was reassured as to Cyril during the next few days. He did not attempt to repeat his ingenious naughtiness of the Monday evening, and he came directly home for tea; moreover he had, as a kind of miracle performed to dazzle her, actually arisen early on the Tuesday morning and done his arithmetic. To express her satisfaction she had manufactured a specially elaborate straw-frame for the sketch after Sir Edwin Landseer, and had hung it in her bedroom: an honour which Cyril appreciated. She was as happy as a woman suffering from a recent amputation can be; and compared with the long nightmare created by Samuel's monomania and illness, her existence seemed to be now a beneficent calm.

Cyril, she thought, had realized the importance in her eyes of tea, of that evening hour and that companionship which were for her the flowering of the day. And she had such confidence in his goodness that she would pour the boiling water on the Horniman tea-leaves even before he arrived: certainty could not be more sure. And then, on the Friday of the first week, he was late! He bounded in, after dark, and the state of his clothes indicated too clearly that he had been playing football in the mud that was a grassy field in summer.

"Have you been kept in, my boy?" she asked, for the sake of form.

"No, mother," he said casually. "We were just kicking the ball about a bit. Am I late?"

"Better go and tidy yourself," she said, not replying to his question.

"You can't sit down in that state. And I'll have some fresh tea made. This is spoilt."

"Oh, very well!"

Her sacred tea—the institution which she wanted to hallow by long habit, and which was to count before everything with both of them—had been carelessly sacrificed to the kicking of a football in mud! And his father buried not ten days! She was wounded: a deep, clean, dangerous wound that would not bleed. She tried to be glad that he had not lied; he might easily have lied, saying that he had been detained for a fault and could not help being late. No! He was not given to lying; he would lie, like any human being, when a great occasion demanded such prudence, but he was not a liar; he might fairly be called a truthful boy. She tried to be glad, and did not succeed. She would have preferred him to have lied.

Amy, grumbling, had to boil more water.

When he returned to the parlour, superficially cleaned, Constance expected him to apologize in his roundabout boyish way; at any rate to woo and wheedle her, to show by some gesture that he was conscious of having put an affront on her. But his attitude was quite otherwise. His attitude was rather brusque and overbearing and noisy. He ate a very considerable amount of jam, far too quickly, and then asked for more, in a tone of a monarch who calls for his own. And ere tea was finished he said boldly, apropos of nothing:

"I say, mother, you'll just have to let me go to the School of Art after Easter."

And stared at her with a fixed challenge in his eyes.

He meant, by the School of Art, the evening classes at the School of Art. His father had decided absolutely against the project. His father had said that it would interfere with his lessons, would keep him up too late at night, and involve absence from home in the evening. The last had always been the real objection. His father had not been able to believe that Cyril's desire to study art sprang purely from his love of art; he could not avoid suspecting that it was a plan to obtain freedom in the evenings—that freedom which Samuel had invariably forbidden. In all Cyril's suggestions Samuel had been ready to detect the same scheme lurking. He had finally said that when Cyril left school and took to a vocation, then he could study art at night if he chose, but not before.

"You know what your father said!" Constance replied.

"But, mother! That's all very well! I'm sure father would have agreed. If I'm going to take up drawing I ought to do it at once. That's what the drawing-master says, and I suppose he ought to know." He finished on a tone of insolence.

"I can't allow you to do it yet," said Constance, quietly. "It's quite out of the question. Quite!"

He pouted and then he sulked. It was war between them. At times he was the image of his Aunt Sophia. He would not leave the subject alone; but he would not listen to Constance's reasoning. He openly accused her of harshness. He asked her how she could expect him to get on if she thwarted him in his most earnest desires. He pointed to other boys whose parents were wiser.

"It's all very fine of you to put it on father!" he observed sarcastically.

He gave up his drawing entirely.

When she hinted that if he attended the School of Art she would be condemned to solitary evenings, he looked at her as though saying: "Well, and if you are—?" He seemed to have no heart.

After several weeks of intense unhappiness she said: "How many evenings do you want to go?"

The war was over.

He was charming again. When she was alone she could cling to him again. And she said to herself: "If we can be happy together only when I give way to him, I must give way to him." And there was ecstasy in her

yielding. "After all," she said to herself, "perhaps it's very important that he should go to the School of Art."
She solaced herself with such thoughts on three solitary evenings a week, waiting for him to come home.

CHAPTER VII

BRICKS AND MORTAR
I

In the summer of that year the occurrence of a white rash of posters on hoardings and on certain houses and shops, was symptomatic of organic change in the town. The posters were iterations of a mysterious announcement and summons, which began with the august words: "By Order of the Trustees of the late William Clews Mericarp, Esq." Mericarp had been a considerable owner of property in Bursley. After a prolonged residence at Southport, he had died, at the age of eighty-two, leaving his property behind. For sixty years he had been a name, not a figure; and the news of his death, which was assuredly an event, incited the burgesses to gossip, for they had come to regard him as one of the invisible immortals. Constance was shocked, though she had never seen Mericarp. ("Everybody dies nowadays!" she thought.) He owned the Baines-Povey shop, and also Mr. Critchlow's shop. Constance knew not how often her father and, later, her husband, had renewed the lease of those premises that were now hers; but from her earliest recollections rose a vague memory of her father talking to her mother about 'Mericarp's rent,' which was and always had been a hundred a year. Mericarp had earned the reputation of being 'a good landlord.' Constance said sadly: "We shall never have another as good!" When a lawyer's clerk called and asked her to permit the exhibition of a poster in each of her shop-windows, she had misgivings for the future; she was worried; she decided that she would determine the lease next year, so as to be on the safe side; but immediately afterwards she decided that she could decide nothing.
The posters continued: "To be sold by auction, at the Tiger Hotel at six-thirty for seven o'clock precisely." What six-thirty had to do with seven o'clock precisely no one knew. Then, after stating the name and credentials of the auctioneer, the posters at length arrived at the objects to be sold: "All those freehold messuages and shops and copyhold tenements namely." Houses were never sold by auction in Bursley. At moments of auction burgesses were reminded that the erections they lived in were not houses, as they had falsely supposed, but messuages. Having got as far as 'namely' the posters ruled a line and began afresh: "Lot I. All that extensive and commodious shop and messuage with the offices and appurtenances thereto belonging situate and being No. 4 St. Luke's Square in the parish of Bursley in the County of Stafford and at present in the occupation of Mrs. Constance Povey widow under a lease expiring in September 1889." Thus clearly asserting that all Constance's shop was for sale, its whole entirety, and not a fraction or slice of it merely, the posters proceeded: "Lot 2. All that extensive and commodious shop and messuage with the offices and appurtenances thereto belonging situate and being No. 3 St. Luke's Square in the parish of Bursley in the County of Stafford and at present in the occupation of Charles Critchlow chemist under an agreement for a yearly tenancy." The catalogue ran to fourteen lots. The posters, lest any one should foolishly imagine that a non-legal intellect could have achieved such explicit and comprehensive clarity of statement, were signed by a powerful firm of solicitors in Hanbridge. Happily in the Five Towns there were no metaphysicians; otherwise the firm might have been expected to explain, in the 'further particulars and conditions' which the posters promised, how even a messuage could 'be' the thing at which it was 'situate.'
Within a few hours of the outbreak of the rash, Mr. Critchlow abruptly presented himself before Constance at the millinery counter; he was waving a poster.
"Well!" he exclaimed grimly. "What next, eh?"
"Yes, indeed!" Constance responded.
"Are ye thinking o' buying?" he asked. All the assistants, including
Miss Insull, were in hearing, but he ignored their presence.
"Buying!" repeated Constance. "Not me! I've got quite enough house property as it is."
Like all owners of real property, she usually adopted towards her possessions an attitude implying that she would be willing to pay somebody to take them from her.

"Shall you?" she added, with Mr. Critchlow's own brusqueness.

"Me! Buy property in St. Luke's Square!" Mr. Critchlow sneered. And then left the shop as suddenly as he had entered it.

The sneer at St. Luke's Square was his characteristic expression of an opinion which had been slowly forming for some years. The Square was no longer what it had been, though individual businesses might be as good as ever. For nearly twelve months two shops had been to let in it. And once, bankruptcy had stained its annals. The tradesmen had naturally searched for a cause in every direction save the right one, the obvious one; and naturally they had found a cause. According to the tradesmen, the cause was 'this football.' The Bursley Football Club had recently swollen into a genuine rival of the ancient supremacy of the celebrated Knype Club. It had transformed itself into a limited company, and rented a ground up the Moorthorne Road, and built a grand stand. The Bursley F.C. had 'tied' with the Knype F.C. on the Knype ground—a prodigious achievement, an achievement which occupied a column of the Athletic News one Monday morning! But were the tradesmen civically proud of this glory? No! They said that 'this football' drew people out of the town on Saturday afternoons, to the complete abolition of shopping. They said also that people thought of nothing but 'this football;' and, nearly in the same breath, that only roughs and good-for-nothings could possibly be interested in such a barbarous game. And they spoke of gate-money, gambling, and professionalism, and the end of all true sport in England. In brief, something new had come to the front and was submitting to the ordeal of the curse.

The sale of the Mericarp estate had a particular interest for respectable stake-in-the-town persons. It would indicate to what extent, if at all, 'this football' was ruining Bursley. Constance mentioned to Cyril that she fancied she might like to go to the sale, and as it was dated for one of Cyril's off-nights Cyril said that he fancied he might like to go too. So they went together; Samuel used to attend property sales, but he had never taken his wife to one. Constance and Cyril arrived at the Tiger shortly after seven o'clock, and were directed to a room furnished and arranged as for a small public meeting of philanthropists. A few gentlemen were already present, but not the instigating trustees, solicitors, and auctioneers. It appeared that 'six-thirty for seven o'clock precisely' meant seven-fifteen. Constance took a Windsor chair in the corner nearest the door, and motioned Cyril to the next chair; they dared not speak; they moved on tiptoe; Cyril inadvertently dragged his chair along the floor, and produced a scrunching sound; he blushed, as though he had desecrated a church, and his mother made a gesture of horror. The remainder of the company glanced at the corner, apparently pained by this negligence. Some of them greeted Constance, but self-consciously, with a sort of shamed air; it might have been that they had all nefariously gathered together there for the committing of a crime. Fortunately Constance's widowhood had already lost its touching novelty, so that the greetings, if self-conscious, were at any rate given without unendurable commiseration and did not cause awkwardness.

When the official world arrived, fussy, bustling, bearing documents and a hammer, the general feeling of guilty shame was intensified. Useless for the auctioneer to try to dissipate the gloom by means of bright gestures and quick, cheerful remarks to his supporters! Cyril had an idea that the meeting would open with a hymn, until the apparition of a tapster with wine showed him his error. The auctioneer very particularly enjoined the tapster to see to it that no one lacked for his thirst, and the tapster became self-consciously energetic. He began by choosing Constance for service. In refusing wine, she blushed; then the fellow offered a glass to Cyril, who went scarlet, and mumbled 'No' with a lump in his throat; when the tapster's back was turned, he smiled sheepishly at his mother. The majority of the company accepted and sipped. The auctioneer sipped and loudly smacked, and said: "Ah!"

Mr. Critchlow came in.

And the auctioneer said again: "Ah! I'm always glad when the tenants come. That's always a good sign."

He glanced round for approval of this sentiment. But everybody seemed too stiff to move. Even the auctioneer was self-conscious.

"Waiter! Offer wine to Mr. Critchlow!" he exclaimed bullyingly, as if saying: "Man! what on earth are you thinking of, to neglect Mr. Critchlow?"

"Yes, sir; yes, sir," said the waiter, who was dispensing wine as fast as a waiter can.

The auction commenced.

Seizing the hammer, the auctioneer gave a short biography of William Clews Mericarp, and, this pious duty accomplished, called upon a solicitor to read the conditions of sale. The solicitor complied and made a distressing exhibition of self-consciousness. The conditions of sale were very lengthy, and apparently composed in a foreign tongue; and the audience listened to this elocution with a stoical pretence of breathless interest.

Then the auctioneer put up all that extensive and commodious messuage and shop situate and being No. 4, St. Luke's Square. Constance and Cyril moved their limbs surreptitiously, as though being at last found out. The auctioneer referred to John Baines and to Samuel Povey, with a sense of personal loss, and then expressed his pleasure in the presence of 'the ladies;' he meant Constance, who once more had to blush.

"Now, gentlemen," said the auctioneer, "what do you say for these famous premises? I think I do not exaggerate when I use the word 'famous.'"

Some one said a thousand pounds, in the terrorized voice of a delinquent.

"A thousand pounds," repeated the auctioneer, paused, sipped, and smacked.

"Guineas," said another voice self-accused of iniquity.

"A thousand and fifty," said the auctioneer.

Then there was a long interval, an interval that tightened the nerves of the assembly.

"Now, ladies and gentlemen," the auctioneer adjured.

The first voice said sulkily: "Eleven hundred."

And thus the bids rose to fifteen hundred, lifted bit by bit, as it were, by the magnetic force of the auctioneer's personality. The man was now standing up, in domination. He bent down to the solicitor's head; they whispered together.

"Gentlemen," said the auctioneer, "I am happy to inform you that the sale is now open." His tone translated better than words his calm professional beatitude. Suddenly in a voice of wrath he hissed at the waiter: "Waiter, why don't you serve these gentlemen?"

"Yes, sir; yes, sir."

The auctioneer sat down and sipped at leisure, chatting with his clerk and the solicitor and the solicitor's clerk. When he rose it was as a conqueror. "Gentlemen, fifteen hundred is bid. Now, Mr. Critchlow."

Mr. Critchlow shook his head. The auctioneer threw a courteous glance at Constance, who avoided it. After many adjurations, he reluctantly raised his hammer, pretended to let it fall, and saved it several times. And then Mr. Critchlow said: "And fifty."

"Fifteen hundred and fifty is bid," the auctioneer informed the company, electrifying the waiter once more. And when he had sipped he said, with feigned sadness: "Come, gentlemen, you surely don't mean to let this magnificent lot go for fifteen hundred and fifty pounds?"

But they did mean that.

The hammer fell, and the auctioneer's clerk and the solicitor's clerk took Mr. Critchlow aside and wrote with him.

Nobody was surprised when Mr. Critchlow bought Lot No. 2, his own shop.

Constance whispered then to Cyril that she wished to leave. They left, with unnatural precautions, but instantly regained their natural demeanour in the dark street.

"Well, I never! Well, I never!" she murmured outside, astonished and disturbed.

She hated the prospect of Mr. Critchlow as a landlord. And yet she could not persuade herself to leave the place, in spite of decisions.

The sale demonstrated that football had not entirely undermined the commercial basis of society in Bursley; only two Lots had to be withdrawn.

II

On Thursday afternoon of the same week the youth whom Constance had ended by hiring for the manipulation of shutters and other jobs unsuitable for fragile women, was closing the shop. The clock had struck two. All the shutters were up except the last one, in the midst of the doorway. Miss Insull and her mistress were walking about the darkened interior, putting dust-sheets well over the edges of exposed goods; the other assistants had just left. The bull-terrier had wandered into the shop as he almost invariably did at closing time—for he slept there, an efficient guard—and had lain down by the dying stove; though not venerable, he was stiffening into age.

"You can shut," said Miss Insull to the youth.

But as the final shutter was ascending to its position, Mr. Critchlow appeared on the pavement.

"Hold on, young fellow!" Mr. Critchlow commanded, and stepped slowly, lifting up his long apron, over the horizontal shutter on which the perpendicular shutters rested in the doorway.

160

"Shall you be long, Mr. Critchlow?" the youth asked, posing the shutter. "Or am I to shut?"

"Shut, lad," said Mr. Critchlow, briefly. "I'll go out by th' side door."

"Here's Mr. Critchlow!" Miss Insull called out to Constance, in a peculiar tone. And a flush, scarcely perceptible, crept very slowly over her dark features. In the twilight of the shop, lit only by a few starry holes in the shutters, and by the small side-window, not the keenest eye could have detected that flush.

"Mr. Critchlow!" Constance murmured the exclamation. She resented his future ownership of her shop. She thought he was come to play the landlord, and she determined to let him see that her mood was independent and free, that she would as lief give up the business as keep it. In particular she meant to accuse him of having deliberately deceived her as to his intentions on his previous visit.

"Well, missis!" the aged man greeted her. "We've made it up between us. Happen some folk'll think we've taken our time, but I don't know as that's their affair."

His little blinking eyes had a red border. The skin of his pale small face was wrinkled in millions of minute creases. His arms and legs were marvellously thin and sharply angular. The corners of his heliotrope lips were turned down, as usual, in a mysterious comment on the world; and his smile, as he fronted Constance with his excessive height, crowned the mystery.

Constance stared, at a loss. It surely could not after all be true, the substance of the rumours that had floated like vapours in the Square for eight years and more!

"What…?" she began.

"Me, and her!" He jerked his head in the direction of Miss Insull.

The dog had leisurely strolled forward to inspect the edges of the fiance's trousers. Miss Insull summoned the animal with a noise of fingers, and then bent down and caressed it. A strange gesture proving the validity of Charles Critchlow's discovery that in Maria Insull a human being was buried!

Miss Insull was, as near as any one could guess, forty years of age. For twenty-five years she had served in the shop, passing about twelve hours a day in the shop; attending regularly at least three religious services at the Wesleyan Chapel or School on Sundays, and sleeping with her mother, whom she kept. She had never earned more than thirty shillings a week, and yet her situation was considered to be exceptionally good. In the eternal fusty dusk of the shop she had gradually lost such sexual characteristics and charms as she had once possessed. She was as thin and flat as Charles Critchlow himself. It was as though her bosom had suffered from a prolonged drought at a susceptible period of development, and had never recovered. The one proof that blood ran in her veins was the pimply quality of her ruined complexion, and the pimples of that brickish expanse proved that the blood was thin and bad. Her hands and feet were large and ungainly; the skin of the fingers was roughened by coarse contacts to the texture of emery-paper. On six days a week she wore black; on the seventh a kind of discreet half-mourning. She was honest, capable, and industrious; and beyond the confines of her occupation she had no curiosity, no intelligence, no ideas. Superstitions and prejudices, deep and violent, served her for ideas; but she could incomparably sell silks and bonnets, braces and oilcloth; in widths, lengths, and prices she never erred; she never annoyed a customer, nor foolishly promised what could not be performed, nor was late nor negligent, nor disrespectful. No one knew anything about her, because there was nothing to know. Subtract the shop-assistant from her, and naught remained. Benighted and spiritually dead, she existed by habit.

But for Charles Critchlow she happened to be an illusion. He had cast eyes on her and had seen youth, innocence, virginity. During eight years the moth Charles had flitted round the lamp of her brilliance, and was now singed past escape. He might treat her with what casualness he chose; he might ignore her in public; he might talk brutally about women; he might leave her to wonder dully what he meant, for months at a stretch: but there emerged indisputable from the sum of his conduct the fact that he wanted her. He desired her; she charmed him; she was something ornamental and luxurious for which he was ready to pay—and to commit follies. He had been a widower since before she was born; to him she was a slip of a girl. All is relative in this world. As for her, she was too indifferent to refuse him. Why refuse him? Oysters do not refuse.

"I'm sure I congratulate you both," Constance breathed, realizing the import of Mr. Critchlow's laconic words. "I'm sure I hope you'll be happy."

"That'll be all right," said Mr. Critchlow.

"Thank you, Mrs. Povey," said Maria Insull.

Nobody seemed to know what to say next. "It's rather sudden," was on Constance's tongue, but did not achieve utterance, being patently absurd.

"Ah!" exclaimed Mr. Critchlow, as though himself contemplating anew the situation.

Miss Insull gave the dog a final pat.

"So that's settled," said Mr. Critchlow. "Now, missis, ye want to give up this shop, don't ye?"

"I'm not so sure about that," Constance answered uneasily.

"Don't tell me!" he protested. "Of course ye want to give up the shop."

"I've lived here all my life," said Constance.

"Ye've not lived in th' shop all ye're life. I said th' shop. Listen here!" he continued. "I've got a proposal to make to you. You can keep on the house, and I'll take the shop off ye're hands. Now?" He looked at her inquiringly.

Constance was taken aback by the brusqueness of the suggestion, which, moreover, she did not understand. "But how—" she faltered.

"Come here," said Mr. Critchlow, impatiently, and he moved towards the house-door of the shop, behind the till.

"Come where? What do you want?" Constance demanded in a maze.

"Here!" said Mr. Critchlow, with increasing impatience. "Follow me, will ye?"

Constance obeyed. Miss Insull sidled after Constance, and the dog after Miss Insull. Mr. Critchlow went through the doorway and down the corridor, past the cutting-out room to his right. The corridor then turned at a right-angle to the left and ended at the parlour door, the kitchen steps being to the left.

Mr. Critchlow stopped short of the kitchen steps, and extended his arms, touching the walls on either side. "Here!" he said, tapping the walls with his bony knuckles. "Here! Suppose I brick ye this up, and th' same upstairs between th' showroom and th' bedroom passage, ye've got your house to yourself. Ye say ye've lived here all your life. Well, what's to prevent ye finishing up here? The fact is," he added, "it would only be making into two houses again what was two houses to start with, afore your time, missis."

"And what about the shop?" cried Constance.

"Ye can sell us th' stock at a valuation."

Constance suddenly comprehended the scheme. Mr. Critchlow would remain the chemist, while Mrs. Critchlow became the head of the chief drapery business in the town. Doubtless they would knock a hole through the separating wall on the other side, to balance the bricking-up on this side. They must have thought it all out in detail. Constance revolted.

"Yes!" she said, a little disdainfully. "And my goodwill? Shall you take that at a valuation too?"

Mr. Critchlow glanced at the creature for whom he was ready to scatter thousands of pounds. She might have been a Phryne and he the infatuated fool. He glanced at her as if to say: "We expected this, and this is where we agreed it was to stop."

"Ay!" he said to Constance. "Show me your goodwill. Lap it up in a bit of paper and hand it over, and I'll take it at a valuation. But not afore, missis! Not afore! I'm making ye a very good offer. Twenty pound a year, I'll let ye th' house for. And take th' stock at a valuation. Think it over, my lass."

Having said what he had to say, Charles Critchlow departed, according to his custom. He unceremoniously let himself out by the side door, and passed with wavy apron round the corner of King Street into the Square and so to his own shop, which ignored the Thursday half-holiday. Miss Insull left soon afterwards.

III

Constance's pride urged her to refuse the offer. But in truth her sole objection to it was that she had not thought of the scheme herself. For the scheme really reconciled her wish to remain where she was with her wish to be free of the shop.

"I shall make him put me in a new window in the parlour—one that will open!" she said positively to Cyril, who accepted Mr. Critchlow's idea with fatalistic indifference.

After stipulating for the new window, she closed with the offer. Then there was the stock-taking, which endured for weeks. And then a carpenter came and measured for the window. And a builder and a mason came and inspected doorways, and Constance felt that the end was upon her. She took up the carpet in the parlour and protected the furniture by dustsheets. She and Cyril lived between bare boards and dustsheets for twenty days, and neither carpenter nor mason reappeared. Then one surprising day the old window was removed by the carpenter's two journeymen, and late in the afternoon the carpenter brought the new window, and the three men worked till ten o'clock at night, fixing it. Cyril wore his cap and went to bed in his cap, and Constance wore a Paisley shawl. A painter had bound himself beyond all possibility of failure to paint the window on the morrow. He was to begin at six a.m.; and Amy's alarm-clock was altered so that she might be up and dressed to admit him. He came a week later, administered one coat, and vanished for another ten days. Then two masons suddenly came with heavy tools, and were shocked to find that all was not prepared for them. (After three carpetless weeks Constance had relaid her floors.) They tore off wall-paper, sent cascades of plaster down the kitchen steps, withdrew alternate courses of bricks from the walls, and, sated with destruction, hastened away. After four days new red bricks began to arrive, carried by a quite guiltless hodman who had not visited the house before. The hodman met the full storm of Constance's wrath. It was not a vicious wrath, rather a good-humoured wrath; but it impressed the hodman. "My house hasn't been fit to live in for a month," she said in fine. "If these walls aren't built to-morrow, upstairs AND down—to-morrow, mind!—don't let any of you dare to show your noses here again, for I won't have you. Now you've brought your bricks. Off with you, and tell your master what I say!"

It was effective. The next day subdued and plausible workmen of all sorts awoke the house with knocking at six-thirty precisely, and the two doorways were slowly bricked up. The curious thing was that, when the barrier was already a foot high on the ground-floor Constance remembered small possessions of her own which she had omitted to remove from the cutting-out room. Picking up her skirts, she stepped over into the region that was no more hers, and stepped back with the goods. She had a bandanna round her head to keep the thick dust out of her hair. She was very busy, very preoccupied with nothings. She had no time for sentimentalities. Yet when the men arrived at the topmost course and were at last hidden behind their own erection, and she could see only rough bricks and mortar, she was disconcertingly overtaken by a misty blindness and could not even see bricks and mortar. Cyril found her, with her absurd bandanna, weeping in a sheet-covered rocking-chair in the sacked parlour. He whistled uneasily, remarked: "I say, mother, what about tea?" and then, hearing the heavy voices of workmen above, ran with relief upstairs. Tea had been set in the drawing-room, he was glad to learn that from Amy, who informed him also that she should 'never get used to them there new walls,' not as long as she lived.

He went to the School of Art that night. Constance, alone, could find nothing to do. She had willed that the walls should be built, and they had been built; but days must elapse before they could be plastered, and after the plaster still more days before the papering. Not for another month, perhaps, would her house be free of workmen and ripe for her own labours. She could only sit in the dust-drifts and contemplate the havoc of change, and keep her eyes as dry as she could. The legal transactions were all but complete; little bills announcing the transfer of the business lay on the counters in the shop at the disposal of customers. In two days Charles Critchlow would pay the price of a desire realized. The sign was painted out and new letters sketched thereon in chalk. In future she would be compelled, if she wished to enter the shop, to enter it as a customer and from the front. Yes, she saw that, though the house remained hers, the root of her life had been wrenched up.

And the mess! It seemed inconceivable that the material mess could ever be straightened away!

Yet, ere the fields of the county were first covered with snow that season, only one sign survived of the devastating revolution, and that was a loose sheet of wall-paper that had been too soon pasted on to new plaster and would not stick. Maria Insull was Maria Critchlow. Constance had been out into the Square and seen the altered sign, and seen Mrs. Critchlow's taste in window-curtains, and seen—most impressive sight of all—that the grimy window of the abandoned room at the top of the abandoned staircase next to the bedroom of her girlhood, had been cleaned and a table put in front of it. She knew that the chamber, which she herself had never entered, was to be employed as a storeroom, but the visible proof of its conversion so strangely affected her that she had not felt able to go boldly into the shop, as she had meant to do, and make a few purchases in the way of friendliness. "I'm a silly woman!" she muttered. Later, she did venture, timidly abrupt, into the shop, and was received with fitting state by Mrs. Critchlow (as desiccated as ever), who insisted on allowing her the special trade discount. And she carried her little friendly purchases round to her own door in King Street. Trivial, trivial event! Constance, not knowing whether to laugh or cry, did both. She accused herself of developing a hysterical faculty in tears, and strove sagely against it.

CHAPTER VIII

THE PROUDEST MOTHER
I

In the year 1893 there was a new and strange man living at No. 4, St. Luke's Square. Many people remarked on the phenomenon. Very few of his like had ever been seen in Bursley before. One of the striking things about him was the complex way in which he secured himself by means of glittering chains. A chain stretched across his waistcoat, passing through a special button-hole, without a button, in the middle. To this cable were firmly linked a watch at one end and a pencil-case at the other; the chain also served as a protection against a thief who might attempt to snatch the fancy waistcoat entire. Then there were longer chains, beneath the waistcoat, partly designed, no doubt, to deflect bullets, but serving mainly to enable the owner to haul up penknives, cigarette-cases, match-boxes, and key-rings from the profundities of hip-pockets. An essential portion of the man's braces, visible sometimes when he played at tennis, consisted of chain, and the upper and nether halves of his cuff-links were connected by chains. Occasionally he was to be seen chained to a dog. A reversion, conceivably, to a mediaeval type! Yes, but also the exemplar of the excessively modern! Externally he was a consequence of the fact that, years previously, the leading tailor in Bursley had permitted his son to be apprenticed in London. The father died; the son had the wit to return and make a fortune while creating a new type in the town, a type of which multiple chains were but one feature, and that the least expensive if the most salient. For instance, up to the historic year in which the young tailor created the type, any cap was a cap in Bursley, and any collar was a collar. But thenceforward no cap was a cap, and no collar was a collar, which did not exactly conform in shape and material to certain sacred caps and collars guarded by the young tailor in his back shop. None knew why these sacred caps and collars were sacred, but they were; their sacredness endured for about six months, and then suddenly—again none knew why—they fell from their estate and became lower than offal for dogs, and were supplanted on the altar. The type brought into existence by the young tailor was to be recognized by its caps and collars, and in a similar manner by every other article of attire, except its boots. Unfortunately the tailor did not sell boots, and so imposed on his creatures no mystical creed as to boots. This was a pity, for the boot-makers of the town happened not to be inflamed by the type-creating passion as the tailor was, and thus the new type finished abruptly at the edges of the tailor's trousers.

The man at No. 4, St. Luke's Square had comparatively small and narrow feet, which gave him an advantage; and as he was endowed with a certain vague general physical distinction he managed, despite the eternal untidiness of his hair, to be eminent among the type. Assuredly the frequent sight of him in her house flattered the pride of Constance's eye, which rested on him almost always with pleasure. He had come into the house with startling abruptness soon after Cyril left school and was indentured to the head-designer at "Peel's," that classic earthenware manufactory. The presence of a man in her abode disconcerted Constance at the beginning; but she soon grew accustomed to it, perceiving that a man would behave as a man, and must be expected to do so. This man, in truth, did what he liked in all things. Cyril having always been regarded by both his parents as enormous, one would have anticipated a giant in the new man; but, queerly, he was slim, and little above the average height. Neither in enormity nor in many other particulars did he resemble the Cyril whom he had supplanted. His gestures were lighter and quicker; he had nothing of Cyril's ungainliness; he had not Cyril's limitless taste for sweets, nor Cyril's terrific hatred of gloves, barbers, and soap. He was much more dreamy than Cyril, and much busier. In fact, Constance only saw him at meal-times. He was at Peel's in the day and at the School of Art every night. He would dream during a meal, even; and, without actually saying so, he gave the impression that he was the busiest man in Bursley, wrapped in occupations and preoccupations as in a blanket—a blanket which Constance had difficulty in penetrating.

Constance wanted to please him; she lived for nothing but to please him; he was, however, exceedingly difficult to please, not in the least because he was hypercritical and exacting, but because he was indifferent. Constance, in order to satisfy her desire of pleasing, had to make fifty efforts, in the hope that he might chance to notice one. He was a good man, amazingly industrious—when once Constance had got him out of bed in the morning; with no vices; kind, save when Constance mistakenly tried to thwart him; charming, with a curious strain of humour that Constance only half understood. Constance was unquestionably vain about him, and she could honestly find in him little to blame. But whereas he was the whole of her universe, she was merely a dim figure in the background of his. Every now and then, with his gentle, elegant raillery, he would apparently rediscover her, as though saying: "Ah! You're still there, are you?" Constance could not meet him on the plane where his interests lay, and he never knew the passionate intensity of her absorption in that minor part of his life which moved on her plane. He never worried about her solitude, or guessed that in throwing her a smile and a word at supper he was paying her meagrely for three hours of lone rocking in a rocking-chair.

The worst of it was that she was quite incurable. No experience would suffice to cure her trick of continually expecting him to notice things which he never did notice. One day he said, in the midst of a silence: "By the way, didn't father leave any boxes of cigars?" She had the steps up into her bedroom and reached down from the dusty top of the wardrobe the box which she had put there after Samuel's funeral. In handing him the box she was doing a great deed. His age was nineteen and she was ratifying his precocious habit of smoking by this solemn gift. He entirely ignored the box for several days. She said timidly: "Have you tried those cigars?" "Not yet," he replied. "I'll try 'em one of these days." Ten days later, on a Sunday when he chanced not to have gone out with his aristocratic friend Matthew Peel-Swynnerton, he did at length open the box and take out a cigar. "Now," he observed roguishly, cutting the cigar, "we shall see, Mrs. Plover!" He often called her Mrs. Plover, for fun. Though she liked him to be sufficiently interested in her to tease her, she did not like being called Mrs. Plover, and she never failed to say: "I'm not Mrs. Plover." He smoked the cigar slowly, in the rocking-chair, throwing his head back and sending clouds to the ceiling. And afterwards he remarked: "The old man's cigars weren't so bad." "Indeed!" she answered tartly, as if maternally resenting this easy patronage. But in secret she was delighted. There was something in her son's favourable verdict on her husband's cigars that thrilled her.

And she looked at him. Impossible to see in him any resemblance to his father! Oh! He was a far more brilliant, more advanced, more complicated, more seductive being than his homely father! She wondered where he had come from. And yet…! If his father had lived, what would have occurred between them? Would the boy have been openly smoking cigars in the house at nineteen?

She laboriously interested herself, so far as he would allow, in his artistic studies and productions. A back attic on the second floor was now transformed into a studio—a naked apartment which smelt of oil and of damp clay. Often there were traces of clay on the stairs. For working in clay he demanded of his mother a smock, and she made a smock, on the model of a genuine smock which she obtained from a country-woman who sold eggs and butter in the Covered Market. Into the shoulders of the smock she put a week's fancy-stitching, taking the pattern from an old book of embroidery. One day when he had seen her stitching morn, noon, and afternoon, at the smock, he said, as she rocked idly after supper: "I suppose you haven't forgotten all about the smock I asked you for, have you, mater?" She knew that he was teasing her; but, while perfectly realizing how foolish she was, she nearly always acted as though his teasing was serious; she picked up the smock again from the sofa. When the smock was finished he examined it intently; then exclaimed with an air of surprise: "By Jove! That's beautiful! Where did you get this pattern?" He continued to stare at it, smiling in pleasure. He turned over the tattered leaves of the embroidery-book with the same naive, charmed astonishment, and carried the book away to the studio. "I must show that to Swynnerton," he said. As for her, the epithet 'beautiful' seemed a strange epithet to apply to a mere piece of honest stitchery done in a pattern, and a stitch with which she had been familiar all her life. The fact was she understood his 'art' less and less. The sole wall decoration of his studio was a Japanese print, which struck her as being entirely preposterous, considered as a picture. She much preferred his own early drawings of moss-roses and picturesque castles—things that he now mercilessly contemned. Later, he discovered her cutting out another smock. "What's that for?" he inquired. "Well," she said, "you can't manage with one smock. What shall you do when that one has to go to the wash?" "Wash!" he repeated vaguely. "There's no need for it to go to the wash." "Cyril," she replied, "don't try my patience! I was thinking of making you half-a-dozen." He whistled. "With all that stitching?" he questioned, amazed at the undertaking. "Why not?" she said. In her young days, no seamstress ever made fewer than half-a-dozen of anything, and it was usually a dozen; it was sometimes half-a-dozen dozen. "Well," he murmured, "you have got a nerve! I'll say that." Similar things happened whenever he showed that he was pleased. If he said of a dish, in the local tongue: "I could do a bit of that!" or if he simply smacked his lips over it, she would surfeit him with that dish.

II

On a hot day in August, just before they were to leave Bursley for a month in the Isle of Man, Cyril came home, pale and perspiring, and dropped on to the sofa. He wore a grey alpaca suit, and, except his hair, which in addition to being very untidy was damp with sweat, he was a masterpiece of slim elegance, despite the heat. He blew out great sighs, and rested his head on the antimacassared arm of the sofa.

"Well, mater," he said, in a voice of factitious calm, "I've got it."

He was looking up at the ceiling.

165

"Got what?"

"The National Scholarship. Swynnerton says it's a sheer fluke. But I've got it. Great glory for the Bursley School of Art!"

"National Scholarship?" she said. "What's that? What is it?"

"Now, mother!" he admonished her, not without testiness. "Don't go and say I've never breathed a word about it!"

He lit a cigarette, to cover his self-consciousness, for he perceived that she was moved far beyond the ordinary.

Never, in fact, not even by the death of her husband, had she received such a frightful blow as that which the dreamy Cyril had just dealt her.

It was not a complete surprise, but it was nearly a complete surprise. A few months previously he certainly had mentioned, in his incidental way, the subject of a National Scholarship. Apropos of a drinking-cup which he had designed, he had said that the director of the School of Art had suggested that it was good enough to compete for the National, and that as he was otherwise qualified for the competition he might as well send the cup to South Kensington. He had added that Peel-Swynnerton had laughed at the notion as absurd. On that occasion she had comprehended that a National Scholarship involved residence in London. She ought to have begun to live in fear, for Cyril had a most disturbing habit of making a mere momentary reference to matters which he deemed very important and which occupied a large share of his attention. He was secretive by nature, and the rigidity of his father's rule had developed this trait in his character. But really he had spoken of the competition with such an extreme casualness that with little effort she had dismissed it from her anxieties as involving a contingency so remote as to be negligible. She had, genuinely, almost forgotten it. Only at rare intervals had it wakened in her a dull transitory pain—like the herald of a fatal malady. And, as a woman in the opening stage of disease, she had hastily reassured herself: "How silly of me! This can't possibly be anything serious!"

And now she was condemned. She knew it. She knew there could be no appeal. She knew that she might as usefully have besought mercy from a tiger as from her good, industrious, dreamy son.

"It means a pound a week," said Cyril, his self-consciousness intensified by her silence and by the dreadful look on her face. "And of course free tuition."

"For how long?" she managed to say.

"Well," said he, "that depends. Nominally for a year. But if you behave yourself it's always continued for three years." If he stayed for three years he would never come back: that was a certainty.

How she rebelled, furious and despairing, against the fortuitous cruelty of things! She was sure that he had not, till then, thought seriously of going to London. But the fact that the Government would admit him free to its classrooms and give him a pound a week besides, somehow forced him to go to London. It was not the lack of means that would have prevented him from going. Why, then, should the presence of means induce him to go? There was no logical reason. The whole affair was disastrously absurd. The art-master at the Wedgwood Institution had chanced, merely chanced, to suggest that the drinking-cup should be sent to South Kensington. And the result of this caprice was that she was sentenced to solitude for life! It was too monstrously, too incredibly wicked!

With what futile and bitter execration she murmured in her heart the word 'If.' If Cyril's childish predilections had not been encouraged! If he had only been content to follow his father's trade! If she had flatly refused to sign his indenture at Peel's and pay the premium! If he had not turned from, colour to clay! If the art-master had not had that fatal 'idea'! If the judges for the competition had decided otherwise! If only she had brought Cyril up in habits of obedience, sacrificing temporary peace to permanent security!

For after all he could not abandon her without her consent. He was not of age. And he would want a lot more money, which he could obtain from none but her. She could refuse....

No! She could not refuse. He was the master, the tyrant. For the sake of daily pleasantness she had weakly yielded to him at the start! She had behaved badly to herself and to him. He was spoiled. She had spoiled him. And he was about to repay her with lifelong misery, and nothing would deflect him from his course. The usual conduct of the spoilt child! Had she not witnessed it, and moralized upon it, in other families?

"You don't seem very chirpy over it, mater!" he said.

She went out of the room. His joy in the prospect of departure from the Five Towns, from her, though he masked it, was more manifest than she could bear.

The Signal, the next day, made a special item of the news. It appeared that no National Scholarship had been won in the Five Towns for eleven years. The citizens were exhorted to remember that Mr. Povey had gained his success in open competition with the cleverest young students of the entire kingdom—and in a branch of art which he had but recently taken up; and further, that the Government offered only eight scholarships each year. The name of Cyril Povey passed from lip to lip. And nobody who met Constance, in street or shop, could refrain from informing her that she ought to be a proud mother, to have such a son, but that truly they were not surprised … and how proud his poor father would have been! A few sympathetically hinted that maternal pride was one of those luxuries that may cost too dear.

III

The holiday in the Isle of Man was of course ruined for her. She could scarcely walk because of the weight of a lump of lead that she carried in her bosom. On the brightest days the lump of lead was always there. Besides, she was so obese. In ordinary circumstances they might have stayed beyond the month. An indentured pupil is not strapped to the wheel like a common apprentice. Moreover, the indentures were to be cancelled. But Constance did not care to stay. She had to prepare for his departure to London. She had to lay the faggots for her own martyrdom.

In this business of preparation she showed as much silliness, she betrayed as perfect a lack of perspective, as the most superior son could desire for a topic of affectionate irony. Her preoccupation with petty things of no importance whatever was worthy of the finest traditions of fond motherhood. However, Cyril's careless satire had no effect on her, save that once she got angry, thereby startling him; he quite correctly and sagely laid this unprecedented outburst to the account of her wrought nerves, and forgave it. Happily for the smoothness of Cyril's translation to London, young Peel-Swynnerton was acquainted with the capital, had a brother in Chelsea, knew of reputable lodgings, was, indeed, an encyclopaedia of the town, and would himself spend a portion of the autumn there. Otherwise, the preliminaries which his mother would have insisted on by means of tears and hysteria might have proved fatiguing to Cyril.

The day came when on that day week Cyril would be gone. Constance steadily fabricated cheerfulness against the prospect. She said:

"Suppose I come with you?"

He smiled in toleration of this joke as being a passable quality of joke. And then she smiled in the same sense, hastening to agree with him that as a joke it was not a bad joke.

In the last week he was very loyal to his tailor. Many a young man would have commanded new clothes after, not before, his arrival in London. But Cyril had faith in his creator.

On the day of departure the household, the very house itself, was in a state of excitement. He was to leave early. He would not listen to the project of her accompanying him as far as Knype, where the Loop Line joined the main. She might go to Bursley Station and no further. When she rebelled he disclosed the merest hint of his sullen-churlish side, and she at once yielded. During breakfast she did not cry, but the aspect of her face made him protest.

"Now, look here, mater! Just try to remember that I shall be back for

Christmas. It's barely three months." And he lit a cigarette.

She made no reply.

Amy lugged a Gladstone bag down the crooked stairs. A trunk was already close to the door; it had wrinkled the carpet and deranged the mat.

"You didn't forget to put the hair-brush in, did you, Amy?" he asked.

"N—no, Mr. Cyril," she blubbered.

"Amy!" Constance sharply corrected her, as Cyril ran upstairs, "I wonder you can't control yourself better than that."

Amy weakly apologized. Although treated almost as one of the family, she ought not to have forgotten that she was a servant. What right had she to weep over Cyril's luggage? This question was put to her in Constance's tone.

The cab came. Cyril tumbled downstairs with exaggerated carelessness, and with exaggerated carelessness he joked at the cabman.

"Now, mother!" he cried, when the luggage was stowed. "Do you want me to miss this train?" But he knew that the margin of time was ample. It was his fun!

"Nay, I can't be hurried!" she said, fixing her bonnet. "Amy, as soon as we are gone you can clear this table." She climbed heavily into the cab.

"That's it! Smash the springs!" Cyril teased her.

The horse got a stinging cut to recall him to the seriousness of life. It was a fine, bracing autumn morning, and the driver felt the need of communicating his abundant energy to some one or something. They drove off, Amy staring after them from the door. Matters had been so marvellously well arranged that they arrived at the station twenty minutes before the train was due.

"Never mind!" Cyril mockingly comforted his mother. "You'd rather be twenty minutes too soon than one minute too late, wouldn't you?"

His high spirits had to come out somehow.

Gradually the minutes passed, and the empty slate-tinted platform became dotted with people to whom that train was nothing but a Loop Line train, people who took that train every week-day of their lives and knew all its eccentricities.

And they heard the train whistle as it started from Turnhill. And Cyril had a final word with the porter who was in charge of the luggage. He made a handsome figure, and he had twenty pounds in his pocket. When he returned to Constance she was sniffing, and through her veil he could see that her eyes were circled with red. But through her veil she could see nothing. The train rolled in, rattling to a standstill. Constance lifted her veil and kissed him; and kissed her life out. He smelt the odour of her crape. He was, for an instant, close to her, close; and he seemed to have an overwhelmingly intimate glimpse into her secrets; he seemed to be choked in the sudden strong emotion of that crape. He felt queer.

"Here you are, sir! Second smoker!" called the porter.

The daily frequenters of the train boarded it with their customary disgust.

"I'll write as soon as ever I get there!" said Cyril, of his own accord. It was the best he could muster.

With what grace he raised his hat!

A sliding-away; clouds of steam; and she shared the dead platform with milk-cans, two porters, and Smith's noisy boy!

She walked home, very slowly and painfully. The lump of lead was heavier than ever before. And the townspeople saw the proudest mother in Bursley walking home.

"After all," she argued with her soul angrily, petulantly, "could you expect the boy to do anything else? He is a serious student, he has had a brilliant success, and is he to be tied to your apron-strings? The idea is preposterous. It isn't as if he was an idler, or a bad son. No mother could have a better son. A nice thing, that he should stay all his life in Bursley simply because you don't like being left alone!"

Unfortunately one might as well argue with a mule as with one's soul. Her soul only kept on saying monotonously: "I'm a lonely old woman now. I've nothing to live for any more, and I'm no use to anybody. Once I was young and proud. And this is what my life has come to! This is the end!"

When she reached home, Amy had not touched the breakfast things; the carpet was still wrinkled, and the mat still out of place. And, through the desolating atmosphere of reaction after a terrific crisis, she marched directly upstairs, entered his plundered room, and beheld the disorder of the bed in which he had slept.

BOOK III

SOPHIA

CHAPTER I

THE ELOPEMENT
I

Her soberly rich dress had a countrified air, as she waited, ready for the streets, in the bedroom of the London hotel on the afternoon of the first of July, 1866; but there was nothing of the provincial in that beautiful face, nor in that bearing at once shy and haughty; and her eager heart soared beyond geographical boundaries.

It was the Hatfield Hotel, in Salisbury Street, between the Strand and the river. Both street and hotel are now gone, lost in the vast foundations of the Savoy and the Cecil; but the type of the Hatfield lingers with ever-increasing shabbiness in Jermyn Street. In 1866, with its dark passages and crooked stairs, its candles, its carpets and stuffs which had outlived their patterns, its narrow dining-room where a thousand busy flies ate together at one long table, its acrid stagnant atmosphere, and its disturbing sensation of dirt everywhere concealing itself, it stood forth in rectitude as a good average modern hotel. The patched and senile drabness of the bedroom made an environment that emphasized Sophia's flashing youth. She alone in it was unsullied. There was a knock at the door, apparently gay and jaunty. But she thought, truly: "He's nearly as nervous as I am!" And in her sick nervousness she coughed, and then tried to take full possession of herself. The moment had at last come which would divide her life as a battle divides the history of a nation. Her mind in an instant swept backwards through an incredible three months.

The schemings to obtain and to hide Gerald's letters at the shop, and to reply to them! The far more complex and dangerous duplicity practised upon her majestic aunt at Axe! The visits to the Axe post-office! The three divine meetings with Gerald at early morning by the canal-feeder, when he had told her of his inheritance and of the harshness of his uncle Boldero, and with a rush of words had spread before her the prospect of eternal bliss! The nights of fear! The sudden, dizzy acquiescence in his plan, and the feeling of universal unreality which obsessed her! The audacious departure from her aunt's, showering a cascade of appalling lies! Her dismay at Knype Station! Her blush as she asked for a ticket to London! The ironic, sympathetic glance of the porter, who took charge of her trunk! And then the thunder of the incoming train! Her renewed dismay when she found that it was very full, and her distracted plunge into a compartment with six people already in it! And the abrupt reopening of the carriage-door and that curt inquisition from an inspector: "Where for, please? Where for? Where for?" Until her turn was reached: "Where for, miss?" and her weak little reply: "Euston"! And more violent blushes! And then the long, steady beating of the train over the rails, keeping time to the rhythm of the unanswerable voice within her breast: "Why are you here? Why are you here?" And then Rugby; and the awful ordeal of meeting Gerald, his entry into the compartment, the rearrangement of seats, and their excruciatingly painful attempts at commonplace conversation in the publicity of the carriage! (She had felt that that part of the enterprise had not been very well devised by Gerald.) And at last London; the thousands of cabs, the fabulous streets, the general roar, all dream-surpassing, intensifying to an extraordinary degree the obsession of unreality, the illusion that she could not really have done what she had done, that she was not really doing what she was doing!

Supremely and finally, the delicious torture of the clutch of terror at her heart as she moved by Gerald's side through the impossible adventure! Who was this rash, mad Sophia? Surely not herself!

The knock at the door was impatiently repeated.

"Come in," she said timidly.

Gerald Scales came in. Yes, beneath that mien of a commercial traveller who has been everywhere and through everything, he was very nervous. It was her privacy that, with her consent, he had invaded. He had engaged the bedroom only with the intention of using it as a retreat for Sophia until the evening, when they were to resume their travels. It ought not to have had any disturbing significance. But the mere disorder on the washstand, a towel lying on one of the cane chairs, made him feel that he was affronting decency, and so increased his jaunty nervousness. The moment was painful; the moment was difficult beyond his skill to handle it naturally.

Approaching her with factitious ease, he kissed her through her veil, which she then lifted with an impulsive movement, and he kissed her again, more ardently, perceiving that her ardour was exceeding his. This was the first time they had been alone together since her flight from Axe. And yet, with his worldly experience, he was naive enough to be surprised that he could not put all the heat of passion into his embrace, and he wondered why he was not thrilled at the contact with her! However, the powerful clinging of her lips somewhat startled his senses, and also delighted him by its silent promise. He could smell the stuff of her veil, the sarsenet of her bodice, and, as it were wrapped in these odours as her body was wrapped in its clothes, the faint fleshly perfume of her body itself. Her face, viewed so close that he could see the almost imperceptible down on those fruit-like cheeks, was astonishingly beautiful; the dark eyes were exquisitely misted; and he could feel the secret loyalty of her soul ascending to him. She was very slightly taller than her lover; but somehow she hung from him, her body curved backwards, and her bosom pressed against his, so that instead of looking up at her gaze he looked down at it. He preferred that; perfectly proportioned though he was, his stature was a delicate point with him. His spirits rose by the uplift of his senses. His fears slipped away; he began to be very satisfied with himself. He was the inheritor of twelve thousand pounds, and he had won this unique creature. She was his capture; he held her close, permittedly scanning the minutiae of her skin, permittedly crushing her flimsy silks. Something in him had forced her to lay her modesty on the altar of his desire. And the sun brightly shone. So he kissed her yet more ardently, and with the slightest touch of a victor's condescension; and her burning response more than restored the self-confidence which he had been losing.

"I've got no one but you now," she murmured in a melting voice.

She fancied in her ignorance that the expression of this sentiment would please him. She was not aware that a man is usually rather chilled by it, because it proves to him that the other is thinking about his responsibilities and not about his privileges. Certainly it calmed Gerald, though without imparting to him her sense of his responsibilities. He smiled vaguely. To Sophia his smile was a miracle continually renewed; it mingled dashing gaiety with a hint of wistful appeal in a manner that never failed to bewitch her. A less innocent girl than Sophia might have divined from that adorable half-feminine smile that she could do anything with Gerald except rely on him. But Sophia had to learn.

"Are you ready?" he asked, placing his hands on her shoulders and holding her away from him.

"Yes," she said, nerving herself. Their faces were still very near together.

"Well, would you like to go and see the Dore pictures?"

A simple enough question! A proposal felicitous enough! Dore was becoming known even in the Five Towns, not, assuredly, by his illustrations to the Contes Drolatiques of Balzac—but by his shuddering Biblical conceits. In pious circles Dore was saving art from the reproach of futility and frivolity. It was indubitably a tasteful idea on Gerald's part to take his love of a summer's afternoon to gaze at the originals of those prints which had so deeply impressed the Five Towns. It was an idea that sanctified the profane adventure.

Yet Sophia showed signs of affliction. Her colour went and came; her throat made the motion of swallowing; there was a muscular contraction over her whole body. And she drew herself from him. Her glance, however, did not leave him, and his eyes fell before hers.

"But what about the—wedding?" she breathed.

That sentence seemed to cost all her pride; but she was obliged to utter it, and to pay for it.

"Oh," he said lightly and quickly, just as though she had reminded him of a detail that might have been forgotten, "I was just going to tell you. It can't be done here. There's been some change in the rules. I only found out for certain late last night. But I've ascertained that it'll be as simple as ABC before the English Consul at Paris; and as I've got the tickets for us to go over to-night, as we arranged …" He stopped.

She sat down on the towel-covered chair, staggered. She believed what he said. She did not suspect that he was using the classic device of the seducer. It was his casualness that staggered her. Had it really been his intention to set off on an excursion and remark as an afterthought: "BY THE WAY, we can't be married as I told you at half-past two to-day"? Despite her extreme ignorance and innocence, Sophia held a high opinion of her own commonsense and capacity for looking after herself, and she could scarcely believe that he was expecting her to go to Paris, and at night, without being married. She looked pitiably young, virgin, raw, unsophisticated; helpless in the midst of dreadful dangers. Yet her head was full of a blank astonishment at being mistaken for a simpleton! The sole explanation could be that Gerald, in some matters, must himself be a confiding simpleton. He had not reflected. He had not sufficiently realized the immensity of her sacrifice in flying with him even to London. She felt sorry for him. She had the woman's first glimpse of the necessity for some adjustment of outlook as an essential preliminary to uninterrupted happiness.

"It'll be all right!" Gerald persuasively continued.

He looked at her, as she was not looking at him. She was nineteen. But she seemed to him utterly mature and mysterious. Her face baffled him; her mind was a foreign land. Helpless in one sense she might be; yet she, and not he, stood for destiny; the future lay in the secret and capricious workings of that mind.

"Oh no!" she exclaimed curtly. "Oh no!"

"Oh no what?"

"We can't possibly go like that," she said.

"But don't I tell you it'll be all right?" he protested. "If we stay here and they come after you…! Besides, I've got the tickets and all."

"Why didn't you tell me sooner?" she demanded.

"But how could I?" he grumbled. "Have we had a single minute alone?"

This was nearly true. They could not have discussed the formalities of marriage in the crowded train, nor during the hurried lunch with a dozen cocked ears at the same table. He saw himself on sure ground here. "Now, could we?" he pressed.

170

"And you talk about going to see pictures!" was her reply.

Undoubtedly this had been a grave error of tact. He recognized that it was a stupidity. And so he resented it, as though she had committed it and not he.

"My dear girl," he said, hurt, "I acted for the best. It isn't my fault if rules are altered and officials silly."

"You ought to have told me before," she persisted sullenly.

"But how could I?"

He almost believed in that moment that he had really intended to marry her, and that the ineptitudes of red-tape had prevented him from achieving his honourable purpose. Whereas he had done nothing whatever towards the marriage.

"Oh no! Oh no!" she repeated, with heavy lip and liquid eye. "Oh no!"

He gathered that she was flouting his suggestion of Paris.

Slowly and nervously he approached her. She did not stir nor look up.

Her glance was fixed on the washstand. He bent down and murmured:

"Come, now. It'll be all right. You'll travel in the ladies' saloon on the steam-packet."

She did not stir. He bent lower and touched the back of her neck with his lips. And she sprang up, sobbing and angry. Because she was mad for him she hated him furiously. All tenderness had vanished.

"I'll thank you not to touch me!" she said fiercely. She had given him her lips a moment ago, but now to graze her neck was an insult.

He smiled sheepishly. "But really you must be reasonable," he argued.

"What have I done?"

"It's what you haven't done, I think!" she cried. "Why didn't you tell me while we were in the cab?"

"I didn't care to begin worrying you just then," he replied: which was exactly true.

The fact was, he had of course shirked telling her that no marriage would occur that day. Not being a professional seducer of young girls, he lacked skill to do a difficult thing simply.

"Now come along, little girl," he went on, with just a trifle of impatience. "Let's go out and enjoy ourselves. I assure you that everything will be all right in Paris."

"That's what you said about coming to London," she retorted sarcastically through her sobs. "And look at you!"

Did he imagine for a single instant that she would have come to London with him save on the understanding that she was to be married immediately upon arrival? This attitude of an indignant question was not to be reconciled with her belief that his excuses for himself were truthful. But she did not remark the discrepancy. Her sarcasm wounded his vanity.

"Oh, very well!" he muttered. "If you don't choose to believe what I say!" He shrugged his shoulders.

She said nothing; but the sobs swept at intervals through her frame, shaking it.

Reading hesitation in her face, he tried again. "Come along, little girl. And wipe your eyes." And he approached her. She stepped back.

"No, no!" she denied him, passionately. He had esteemed her too cheaply. And she did not care to be called 'little girl.'

"Then what shall you do?" he inquired, in a tone which blended mockery and bullying. She was making a fool of him.

"I can tell you what I shan't do," she said. "I shan't go to Paris."

Her sobs were less frequent.

"That's not my question," he said icily. "I want to know what you will do."

There was now no pretence of affectionateness either on her part or on his. They might, to judge from their attitudes, have been nourished from infancy on mutual hatred.

"What's that got to do with you?" she demanded.

"It's got everything to do with me," he said.

"Well, you can go and find out!" she said.

It was girlish; it was childish; it was scarcely according to the canons for conducting a final rupture; but it was not the less tragically serious. Indeed, the spectacle of this young girl absurdly behaving like one, in a serious crisis, increased the tragicalness of the situation even if it did not heighten it. The idea that ran through Gerald's brain was the ridiculous folly of having anything to do with young girls. He was quite blind to her beauty.

"'Go'?" he repeated her word. "You mean that?"

"Of course I mean it," she answered promptly.

171

The coward in him urged him to take advantage of her ignorant, helpless pride, and leave her at her word. He remembered the scene she had made at the pit shaft, and he said to himself that her charm was not worth her temper, and that he was a fool ever to have dreamed that it was, and that he would be doubly a fool now not to seize the opportunity of withdrawing from an insane enterprise.

"I am to go?" he asked, with a sneer.

She nodded.

"Of course if you order me to leave you, I must. Can I do anything for you?"

She signified that he could not,

"Nothing? You're sure?"

She frowned.

"Well, then, good-bye." He turned towards the door.

"I suppose you'd leave me here without money or anything?" she said in a cold, cutting voice. And her sneer was far more destructive than his. It destroyed in him the last trace of compassion for her.

"Oh, I beg pardon!" he said, and swaggeringly counted out five sovereigns on to a chest of drawers.

She rushed at them. "Do you think I'll take your odious money?" she snarled, gathering the coins in her gloved hand.

Her first impulse was to throw them in his face; but she paused and then flung them into a corner of the room. "Pick them up!" she commanded him.

"No, thanks," he said briefly; and left, shutting the door.

Only a very little while, and they had been lovers, exuding tenderness with every gesture, like a perfume!

Only a very little while, and she had been deciding to telegraph condescendingly to her mother that she was 'all right'! And now the dream was utterly dissolved. And the voice of that hard commonsense which spake to her in her wildest moods grew loud in asserting that the enterprise could never have come to any good, that it was from its inception an impossible enterprise, unredeemed by the slightest justification. An enormous folly! Yes, an elopement; but not like a real elopement; always unreal! She had always known that it was only an imitation of an elopement, and must end in some awful disappointment. She had never truly wanted to run away; but something within her had pricked her forward in spite of her protests. The strict notions of her elderly relatives were right after all. It was she who had been wrong. And it was she who would have to pay. "I've been a wicked girl," she said to herself grimly, in the midst of her ruin.

She faced the fact. But she would not repent; at any rate she would never sit on that stool. She would not exchange the remains of her pride for the means of escape from the worst misery that life could offer. On that point she knew herself. And she set to work to repair and renew her pride.

Whatever happened she would not return to the Five Towns. She could not, because she had stolen money from her Aunt Harriet. As much as she had thrown back at Gerald, she had filched from her aunt, but in the form of a note. A prudent, mysterious instinct had moved her to take this precaution. And she was glad. She would never have been able to dart that sneer at Gerald about money if she had really needed money. So she rejoiced in her crime; though, since Aunt Harriet would assuredly discover the loss at once, the crime eternally prevented her from going back to her family. Never, never would she look at her mother with the eyes of a thief!

(In truth Aunt Harriet did discover the loss, and very creditably said naught about it to anybody. The knowledge of it would have twisted the knife in the maternal heart.)

Sophia was also glad that she had refused to proceed to Paris. The recollection of her firmness in refusing flattered her vanity as a girl convinced that she could take care of herself. To go to Paris unmarried would have been an inconceivable madness. The mere thought of the enormity did outrage to her moral susceptibilities. No, Gerald had most perfectly mistaken her for another sort of girl; as, for instance, a shop-assistant or a barmaid!

With this the catalogue of her satisfactions ended. She had no idea at all as to what she ought to do, or could do. The mere prospect of venturing out of the room intimidated her. Had Gerald left her trunk in the hall? Of course he had. What a question! But what would happen to her? London … London had merely dazed her. She could do nothing for herself. She was as helpless as a rabbit in London. She drew aside the window-curtain and had a glimpse of the river. It was inevitable that she should think of suicide; for she could not suppose that any girl had ever got herself into a plight more desperate than hers. "I could slip out at night and drown myself," she thought seriously. "A nice thing that would be for Gerald!"

Then loneliness, like a black midnight, overwhelmed her, swiftly wasting her strength, disintegrating her pride in its horrid flood. She glanced about for support, as a woman in the open street who feels she is going to faint, and went blindly to the bed, falling on it with the upper part of her body, in an attitude of abandonment. She wept, but without sobbing.

II

Gerald Scales walked about the Strand, staring up at its high narrow houses, crushed one against another as though they had been packed, unsorted, by a packer who thought of nothing but economy of space. Except by Somerset House, King's College, and one or two theatres and banks, the monotony of mean shops, with several storeys unevenly perched over them, was unbroken, Then Gerald encountered Exeter Hall, and examined its prominent facade with a provincial's eye; for despite his travels he was not very familiar with London. Exeter Hall naturally took his mind back to his Uncle Boldero, that great and ardent Nonconformist, and his own godly youth. It was laughable to muse upon what his uncle would say and think, did the old man know that his nephew had run away with a girl, meaning to seduce her in Paris. It was enormously funny! However, he had done with all that. He was well out of it. She had told him to go, and he had gone. She had money to get home; she had nothing to do but use the tongue in her head. The rest was her affair. He would go to Paris alone, and find another amusement. It was absurd to have supposed that Sophia would ever have suited him. Not in such a family as the Baineses could one reasonably expect to discover an ideal mistress. No! there had been a mistake. The whole business was wrong. She had nearly made a fool of him. But he was not the man to be made a fool of. He had kept his dignity intact.

So he said to himself. Yet all the time his dignity, and his pride also, were bleeding, dropping invisible blood along the length of the Strand pavements.

He was at Salisbury Street again. He pictured her in the bedroom. Damn her! He wanted her. He wanted her with an excessive desire. He hated to think that he had been baulked. He hated to think that she would remain immaculate. And he continued to picture her in the exciting privacy of that cursed bedroom.

Now he was walking down Salisbury Street. He did not wish to be walking down Salisbury Street; but there he was!

"Oh, hell!" he murmured. "I suppose I must go through with it."

He felt desperate. He was ready to pay any price in order to be able to say to himself that he had accomplished what he had set his heart on.

"My wife hasn't gone out, has she?" he asked of the hall-porter.

"I'm not sure, sir; I think not," said the hall-porter.

The fear that Sophia had already departed made him sick. When he noticed her trunk still there, he took hope and ran upstairs.

He saw her, a dark crumpled, sinuous piece of humanity, half on and half off the bed, silhouetted against the bluish-white counterpane; her hat was on the floor, with the spotted veil trailing away from it. This sight seemed to him to be the most touching that he had ever seen, though her face was hidden. He forgot everything except the deep and strange emotion which affected him. He approached the bed. She did not stir. Having heard the entry and knowing that it must be Gerald who had entered, Sophia forced herself to remain still. A wild, splendid hope shot up in her. Constrained by all the power of her will not to move, she could not stifle a sob that had lain in ambush in her throat.

The sound of the sob fetched tears to the eyes of Gerald.

"Sophia!" he appealed to her.

But she did not stir. Another sob shook her.

"Very well, then," said Gerald. "We'll stay in London till we can be married. I'll arrange it. I'll find a nice boarding-house for you, and I'll tell the people you're my cousin. I shall stay on at this hotel, and I'll come and see you every day."

A silence.

"Thank you!" she blubbered. "Thank you!"

He saw that her little gloved hand was stretching out towards him, like a feeler; and he seized it, and knelt down and took her clumsily by the waist. Somehow he dared not kiss her yet.

An immense relief surged very slowly through them both.

"I—I—really—" She began to say something, but the articulation was lost in her sobs.

"What? What do you say, dearest?" he questioned eagerly.

And she made another effort. "I really couldn't have gone to Paris with you without being married," she succeeded at last. "I really couldn't."

"No, no!" he soothed her. "Of course you couldn't. It was I who was wrong. But you didn't know how I felt…. Sophia, it's all right now, isn't it?"

She sat up and kissed him fairly.

It was so wonderful and startling that he burst openly into tears. She saw in the facile intensity of his emotion a guarantee of their future happiness. And as he had soothed her, so now she soothed him. They clung together, equally surprised at the sweet, exquisite, blissful melancholy which drenched them through and through. It was remorse for having quarrelled, for having lacked faith in the supreme rightness of the high adventure. Everything was right, and would be right; and they had been criminally absurd. It was remorse; but it was pure bliss, and worth the quarrel! Gerald resumed his perfection again in her eyes! He was the soul of goodness and honour! And for him she was again the ideal mistress, who would, however, be also a wife. As in his mind he rapidly ran over the steps necessary to their marriage, he kept saying to himself, far off in some remote cavern of the brain: "I shall have her! I shall have her!" He did not reflect that this fragile slip of the Baines stock, unconsciously drawing upon the accumulated strength of generations of honest living, had put a defeat upon him.

After tea, Gerald, utterly content with the universe, redeemed his word and found an irreproachable boarding-house for Sophia in Westminster, near the Abbey. She was astonished at the glibness of his lies to the landlady about her, and about their circumstances generally. He also found a church and a parson, close by, and in half an hour the formalities preliminary to a marriage were begun. He explained to her that as she was now resident in London, it would be simpler to recommence the business entirely. She sagaciously agreed. As she by no means wished to wound him again, she made no inquiry about those other formalities which, owing to red-tape, had so unexpectedly proved abortive! She knew she was going to be married, and that sufficed. The next day she carried out her filial idea of telegraphing to her mother.

CHAPTER II

SUPPER

I

They had been to Versailles and had dined there. A tram had sufficed to take them out; but for the return, Gerald, who had been drinking champagne, would not be content with less than a carriage. Further, he insisted on entering Paris by way of the Bois and the Arc de Triomphe. Thoroughly to appease his conceit, it would have been necessary to swing open the gates of honour in the Arc and allow his fiacre to pass through; to be forced to drive round the monument instead of under it hurt the sense of fitness which champagne engenders. Gerald was in all his pride that day. He had been displaying the wonders to Sophia, and he could not escape the cicerone's secret feeling: that he himself was somehow responsible for the wonders. Moreover, he was exceedingly satisfied with the effect produced by Sophia.

Sophia, on arriving in Paris with the ring on her triumphant finger, had timidly mentioned the subject of frocks. None would have guessed from her tone that she was possessed by the desire for French clothes as by a devil. She had been surprised and delighted by the eagerness of Gerald's response. Gerald, too, was possessed by a devil. He thirsted to see her in French clothes. He knew some of the shops and ateliers in the Rue de la Paix, the Rue de la Chaussee d'Antin, and the Palais Royal. He was much more skilled in the lore of frocks than she, for his previous business in Paris had brought him into relations with the great firms; and Sophia suffered a brief humiliation in the discovery that his private opinion of her dresses was that they were not dresses at all. She had been aware that they were not Parisian, nor even of London; but she had thought them pretty good. It healed her wound, however, to reflect that Gerald had so marvellously kept his own counsel in order to spare her self-love. Gerald had taken her to an establishment in the Chaussee d'Antin. It was not one of what Gerald called les grandes maisons, but it was on the very fringe of them, and the real haute couture was practised therein; and Gerald was remembered there by name.

Sophia had gone in trembling and ashamed, yet in her heart courageously determined to emerge uncompromisingly French. But the models frightened her. They surpassed even the most fantastic things that she had seen in the streets. She recoiled before them and seemed to hide for refuge in Gerald, as it were appealing to him for moral protection, and answering to him instead of to the saleswoman when the saleswoman offered remarks in stiff English. The prices also frightened her. The simplest trifle here cost sixteen pounds; and her mother's historic 'silk,' whose elaborateness had cost twelve pounds, was supposed to have approached the inexpressible! Gerald said that she was not to think about prices. She was, however, forced by some instinct to think about prices—she who at home had scorned the narrowness of life in the Square. In the Square she was understood to be quite without commonsense, hopelessly imprudent; yet here, a spring of sagacity seemed to be welling up in her all the time, a continual antidote against the general madness in which she found herself. With extraordinary rapidity she had formed a habit of preaching moderation to Gerald. She hated to 'see money thrown away,' and her notion of the boundary line between throwing money away and judiciously spending it was still the notion of the Square.

Gerald would laugh. But she would say, piqued and blushing, but self-sure: "You can laugh!" It was all deliciously agreeable.

On this evening she wore the first of the new costumes. She had worn it all day. Characteristically she had chosen something which was not too special for either afternoon or evening, for either warm or cold weather. It was of pale blue taffetas striped in a darker blue, with the corsage cut in basques, and the underskirt of a similar taffetas, but unstriped. The effect of the ornate overskirt falling on the plain underskirt with its small double volant was, she thought, and Gerald too, adorable. The waist was higher than any she had had before, and the crinoline expansive. Tied round her head with a large bow and flying blue ribbons under the chin, was a fragile flat capote like a baby's bonnet, which allowed her hair to escape in front and her great chignon behind. A large spotted veil flew out from the capote over the chignon. Her double skirts waved amply over Gerald's knees in the carriage, and she leaned back against the hard cushions and put an arrogant look into her face, and thought of nothing but the intense throbbing joy of life, longing with painful ardour for more and more pleasure, then and for ever.

As the carriage slipped downwards through the wide, empty gloom of the Champs Elysees into the brilliant Paris that was waiting for them, another carriage drawn by two white horses flashed upwards and was gone in dust. Its only occupant, except the coachman and footman, was a woman. Gerald stared after it.

"By Jove!" he exclaimed. "That's Hortense!"

It might have been Hortense, or it might not. But he instantly convinced himself that it was. Not every evening did one meet Hortense driving alone in the Champs Elysees, and in August too!

"Hortense?" Sophia asked simply.

"Yes. Hortense Schneider."

"Who is she?"

"You've never heard of Hortense Schneider?"

"No!"

"Well! Have you ever heard of Offenbach?"

"I—I don't know. I don't think so."

He had the mien of utter incredulity. "You don't mean to say you've never heard of Bluebeard?"

"I've heard of Bluebeard, of course," said she. "Who hasn't?"

"I mean the opera—Offenbach's."

She shook her head, scarce knowing even what an opera was.

"Well, well! What next?"

He implied that such ignorance stood alone in his experience. Really he was delighted at the cleanness of the slate on which he had to write. And Sophia was not a bit alarmed. She relished instruction from his lips. It was a pleasure to her to learn from that exhaustless store of worldly knowledge. To the world she would do her best to assume omniscience in its ways, but to him, in her present mood, she liked to play the ignorant, uninitiated little thing.

"Why," he said, "the Schneider has been the rage since last year but one. Absolutely the rage."

"I do wish I'd noticed her!" said Sophia.

"As soon as the Varietes reopens we'll go and see her," he replied, and then gave his detailed version of the career of Hortense Schneider.

More joys for her in the near future! She had yet scarcely penetrated the crust of her bliss. She exulted in the dazzling destiny which comprised freedom, fortune, eternal gaiety, and the exquisite Gerald.

175

As they crossed the Place de la Concorde, she inquired, "Are we going back to the hotel?"

"No," he said. "I thought we'd go and have supper somewhere, if it isn't too early."

"After all that dinner?"

"All what dinner? You ate about five times as much as me, anyhow!"

"Oh, I'm ready!" she said.

She was. This day, because it was the first day of her French frock, she regarded as her debut in the dizzy life of capitals. She existed in a rapture of bliss, an ecstasy which could feel no fatigue, either of body or spirit.

II

It was after midnight when they went into the Restaurant Sylvain; Gerald, having decided not to go to the hotel, had changed his mind and called there, and having called there, had remained a long time: this of course! Sophia was already accustoming herself to the idea that, with Gerald, it was impossible to predict accurately more than five minutes of the future.

As the chasseur held open the door for them to enter, and Sophia passed modestly into the glowing yellow interior of the restaurant, followed by Gerald in his character of man-of-the-world, they drew the attention of Sylvain's numerous and glittering guests. No face could have made a more provocative contrast to the women's faces in those screened rooms than the face of Sophia, so childlike between the baby's bonnet and the huge bow of ribbon, so candid, so charmingly conscious of its own pure beauty and of the fact that she was no longer a virgin, but the equal in knowledge of any woman alive. She saw around her, clustered about the white tables, multitudes of violently red lips, powdered cheeks, cold, hard eyes, self-possessed arrogant faces, and insolent bosoms. What had impressed her more than anything else in Paris, more even than the three-horsed omnibuses, was the extraordinary self-assurance of all the women, their unashamed posing, their calm acceptance of the public gaze. They seemed to say: "We are the renowned Parisiennes." They frightened her: they appeared to her so corrupt and so proud in their corruption. She had already seen a dozen women in various situations of conspicuousness apply powder to their complexions with no more ado than if they had been giving a pat to their hair. She could not understand such boldness. As for them, they marvelled at the phenomena presented in Sophia's person; they admired; they admitted the style of the gown; but they envied neither her innocence nor her beauty; they envied nothing but her youth and the fresh tint of her cheeks. "Encore des Anglais!" said some of them, as if that explained all.

Gerald had a very curt way with waiters; and the more obsequious they were, the haughtier he became; and a head-waiter was no more to him than a scullion. He gave loud-voiced orders in French of which both he and Sophia were proud, and a table was laid for them in a corner near one of the large windows. Sophia settled herself on the bench of green velvet, and began to ply the ivory fan which Gerald had given her. It was very hot; all the windows were wide open, and the sounds of the street mingled clearly with the tinkle of the supper-room. Outside, against a sky of deepest purple, Sophia could discern the black skeleton of a gigantic building; it was the new opera house.

"All sorts here!" said Gerald, contentedly, after he had ordered iced soup and sparkling Moselle. Sophia did not know what Moselle was, but she imagined that anything would be better than champagne.

Sylvain's was then typical of the Second Empire, and particularly famous as a supper-room. Expensive and gay, it provided, with its discreet decorations, a sumptuous scene where lorettes, actresses, respectable women, and an occasional grisette in luck, could satisfy their curiosity as to each other. In its catholicity it was highly correct as a resort; not many other restaurants in the centre could have successfully fought against the rival attractions of the Bois and the dim groves of the Champs Elysees on a night in August. The complicated richness of the dresses, the yards and yards of fine stitchery, the endless ruching, the hints, more or less incautious, of nether treasures of embroidered linen; and, leaping over all this to the eye, the vivid colourings of silks and muslins, veils, plumes and flowers, piled as it were pell-mell in heaps on the universal green cushions to the furthest vista of the restaurant, and all multiplied in gilt mirrors—the spectacle intoxicated Sophia. Her eyes gleamed. She drank the soup with eagerness, and tasted the wine, though no desire on her part to like wine could make her like it; and then, seeing pineapples on a large table covered with fruits, she told Gerald that she should like some pineapple, and Gerald ordered one.

She gathered her self-esteem and her wits together, and began to give Gerald her views on the costumes. She could do so with impunity, because her own was indubitably beyond criticism. Some she wholly condemned, and there was not one which earned her unreserved approval. All the absurd fastidiousness of her schoolgirlish provinciality emerged in that eager, affected torrent of remarks. However, she was clever enough to read, after a time, in Gerald's tone and features, that she was making a tedious fool of herself. And she adroitly shifted her criticism from the taste to the WORK—she put a strong accent on the word—and pronounced that to be miraculous beyond description. She reckoned that she knew what dressmaking and millinery were, and her little fund of expert knowledge caused her to picture a whole necessary cityful of girls stitching, stitching, and stitching day and night. She had wondered, during the few odd days that they had spent in Paris, between visits to Chantilly and other places, at the massed luxury of the shops; she had wondered, starting with St. Luke's Square as a standard, how they could all thrive. But now in her first real glimpse of the banal and licentious profusion of one among a hundred restaurants, she wondered that the shops were so few. She thought how splendid was all this expensiveness for trade. Indeed, the notions chasing each other within that lovely and foolish head were a surprising medley.

"Well, what do you think of Sylvain's?" Gerald asked, impatient to be assured that his Sylvain's had duly overwhelmed her.

"Oh, Gerald!" she murmured, indicating that speech was inadequate. And she just furtively touched his hand with hers.

The ennui due to her critical disquisition on the shortcomings of
Parisian costume cleared away from Gerald's face.

"What do you suppose those people there are talking about?" he said with a jerk of the head towards a chattering group of three gorgeous lorettes and two middle-aged men at the next table but one.

"What are they talking about?"

"They're talking about the execution of the murderer Rivain that takes place at Auxerre the day after to-morrow. They're arranging to make up a party and go and see it."

"Oh, what a horrid idea!" said Sophia.

"Guillotine, you know!" said Gerald.

"But can people see it?"

"Yes, of course."

"Well, I think it's horrible."

"Yes, that's why people like to go and see it. Besides, the man isn't an ordinary sort of criminal at all. He's very young and good-looking, and well connected. And he killed the celebrated Claudine…."

"Claudine?"

"Claudine Jacquinot. Of course you wouldn't know. She was a tremendous—er—wrong 'un here in the forties. Made a lot of money, and retired to her native town."

Sophia, in spite of her efforts to maintain the role of a woman who has nothing to learn, blushed.

"Then she was older than he is."

"Thirty-five years older, if a day."

"What did he kill her for?"

"She wouldn't give him enough money. She was his mistress—or rather one of 'em. He wanted money for a young lady friend, you see. He killed her and took all the jewels she was wearing. Whenever he went to see her she always wore all her best jewels—and you may bet a woman like that had a few. It seems she had been afraid for a long time that he meant to do for her."

"Then why did she see him? And why did she wear her jewels?"

"Because she liked being afraid, goose! Some women only enjoy themselves when they're terrified. Queer, isn't it?"

Gerald insisted on meeting his wife's gaze as he finished these revelations. He pretended that such stories were the commonest things on earth, and that to be scandalized by them was infantile. Sophia, thrust suddenly into a strange civilization perfectly frank in its sensuality and its sensuousness, under the guidance of a young man to whom her half-formed intelligence was a most diverting toy—Sophia felt mysteriously uncomfortable, disturbed by sinister, flitting phantoms of ideas which she only dimly apprehended. Her eyes fell. Gerald laughed self-consciously. She would not eat any more pineapple.

Immediately afterwards there came into the restaurant an apparition which momentarily stopped every conversation in the room. It was a tall and mature woman who wore over a dress of purplish-black silk a vast flowing sortie de bal of vermilion velvet, looped and tasselled with gold. No other costume could live by the side of that garment, Arab in shape, Russian in colour, and Parisian in style. It blazed. The woman's heavy coiffure was bound with fillets of gold braid and crimson rosettes. She was followed by a young Englishman in evening dress and whiskers of the most exact correctness. The woman sailed, a little breathlessly, to a table next to Gerald's, and took possession of it with an air of use, almost of tedium. She sat down, threw the cloak from her majestic bosom, and expanded her chest. Seeming to ignore the Englishman, who superciliously assumed the seat opposite to her, she let her large scornful eyes travel round the restaurant, slowly and imperiously meeting the curiosity which she had evoked. Her beauty had undoubtedly been dazzling, it was still effulgent; but the blossom was about to fall. She was admirably rouged and powdered; her arms were glorious; her lashes were long. There was little fault, save the excessive ripeness of a blonde who fights in vain against obesity. And her clothes combined audacity with the propriety of fashion. She carelessly deposed costly trinkets on the table, and then, having intimidated the whole company, she accepted the menu from the head-waiter and began to study it.

"That's one of 'em!" Gerald whispered to Sophia.

"One of what?" Sophia whispered.

Gerald raised his eyebrows warningly, and winked. The Englishman had overheard; and a look of frigid displeasure passed across his proud face. Evidently he belonged to a rank much higher than Gerald's; and Gerald, though he could always comfort himself by the thought that he had been to a university with the best, felt his own inferiority and could not hide that he felt it. Gerald was wealthy; he came of a wealthy family; but he had not the habit of wealth. When he spent money furiously, he did it with bravado, too conscious of grandeur and too conscious of the difficulties of acquiring that which he threw away. For Gerald had earned money. This whiskered Englishman had never earned money, never known the value of it, never imagined himself without as much of it as he might happen to want. He had the face of one accustomed to give orders and to look down upon inferiors. He was absolutely sure of himself. That his companion chiefly ignored him did not appear to incommode him in the least. She spoke to him in French. He replied in English, very briefly; and then, in English, he commanded the supper. As soon as the champagne was served he began to drink; in the intervals of drinking he gently stroked his whiskers. The woman spoke no more.

Gerald talked more loudly. With that aristocratic Englishman observing him, he could not remain at ease. And not only did he talk more loudly; he brought into his conversation references to money, travels, and worldly experiences. While seeking to impress the Englishman, he was merely becoming ridiculous to the Englishman; and obscurely he was aware of this. Sophia noticed and regretted it. Still, feeling very unimportant herself, she was reconciled to the superiority of the whiskered Englishman as to a natural fact. Gerald's behaviour slightly lowered him in her esteem. Then she looked at him—at his well-shaped neatness, his vivacious face, his excellent clothes, and decided that he was much to be preferred to any heavy-jawed, long-nosed aristocrat alive.

The woman whose vermilion cloak lay around her like a fortification spoke to her escort. He did not understand. He tried to express himself in French, and failed. Then the woman recommenced, talking at length. When she had done he shook his head. His acquaintance with French was limited to the vocabulary of food.

"Guillotine!" he murmured, the sole word of her discourse that he had understood.

"Oui, oui! Guillotine. Enfin…!" cried the woman excitedly. Encouraged by her success in conveying even one word of her remarks, she began a third time.

"Excuse me," said Gerald. "Madame is talking about the execution at Auxerre the day after to-morrow. N'est-ce-pas, madame, que vous parliez de Rivain?"

The Englishman glared angrily at Gerald's officious interruption. But the woman smiled benevolently on Gerald, and insisted on talking to her friend through him. And the Englishman had to make the best of the situation.

"There isn't a restaurant in Paris to-night where they aren't talking about that execution," said Gerald on his own account.

"Indeed!" observed the Englishman.

Wine affected them in different ways.

Now a fragile, short young Frenchman, with an extremely pale face ending in a thin black imperial, appeared at the entrance. He looked about, and, recognizing the woman of the scarlet cloak, very discreetly saluted her. Then he saw Gerald, and his worn, fatigued features showed a sudden, startled smile. He came rapidly forward, hat in hand, seized Gerald's palm and greeted him effusively.

"My wife," said Gerald, with the solemn care of a man who is determined to prove that he is entirely sober. The young man became grave and excessively ceremonious. He bowed low over Sophia's hand and kissed it. Her impulse was to laugh, but the gravity of the young man's deference stopped her. She glanced at Gerald, blushing, as if to say: "This comedy is not my fault." Gerald said something, the young man turned to him and his face resumed its welcoming smile.

"This is Monsieur Chirac," Gerald at length completed the introduction, "a friend of mine when I lived in Paris."

He was proud to have met by accident an acquaintance in a restaurant. It demonstrated that he was a Parisian, and improved his standing with the whiskered Englishman and the vermilion cloak.

"It is the first time you come Paris, madame?" Chirac addressed himself to Sophia, in limping, timorous English.

"Yes," she giggled. He bowed again.

Chirac, with his best compliments, felicitated Gerald upon his marriage.

"Don't mention it!" said the humorous Gerald in English, amused at his own wit; and then: "What about this execution?"

"Ah!" replied Chirac, breathing out a long breath, and smiling at Sophia. "Rivain! Rivain!" He made a large, important gesture with his hand.

It was at once to be seen that Gerald had touched the topic which secretly ravaged the supper-world as a subterranean fire ravages a mine.

"I go!" said Chirac, with pride, glancing at Sophia, who smiled self-consciously.

Chirac entered upon a conversation with Gerald in French. Sophia comprehended that Gerald was surprised and impressed by what Chirac told him and that Chirac in turn was surprised. Then Gerald laboriously found his pocket-book, and after some fumbling with it handed it to Chirac so that the latter might write in it.

"Madame!" murmured Chirac, resuming his ceremonious stiffness in order to take leave. "Alors, c'est entendu, mon cher ami!" he said to Gerald, who nodded phlegmatically. And Chirac went away to the next table but one, where were the three lorettes and the two middle-aged men. He was received there with enthusiasm.

Sophia began to be teased by a little fear that Gerald was not quite his usual self. She did not think of him as tipsy. The idea of his being tipsy would have shocked her. She did not think clearly at all. She was lost and dazed in the labyrinth of new and vivid impressions into which Gerald had led her. But her prudence was awake.

"I think I'm tired," she said in a low voice.

"You don't want to go, do you?" he asked, hurt.

"Well—"

"Oh, wait a bit!"

The owner of the vermilion cloak spoke again to Gerald, who showed that he was flattered. While talking to her he ordered a brandy-and-soda. And then he could not refrain from displaying to her his familiarity with Parisian life, and he related how he had met Hortense Schneider behind a pair of white horses. The vermilion cloak grew even more sociable at the mention of this resounding name, and chattered with the most agreeable vivacity. Her friend stared inimically.

"Do you hear that?" Gerald explained to Sophia, who was sitting silent. "About Hortense Schneider—you know, we met her to-night. It seems she made a bet of a louis with some fellow, and when he lost he sent her the louis set in diamonds worth a hundred thousand francs. That's how they go on here."

"Oh!" cried Sophia, further than ever in the labyrinth.

"'Scuse me," the Englishman put in heavily. He had heard the words 'Hortense Schneider,' 'Hortense Schneider,' repeating themselves in the conversation, and at last it had occurred to him that the conversation was about Hortense Schneider. "'Scuse me," he began again. "Are you—do you mean Hortense Schneider?"

"Yes," said Gerald. "We met her to-night."

"She's in Trouville," said the Englishman, flatly.

Gerald shook his head positively.

"I gave a supper to her in Trouville last night," said the Englishman.

"And she plays at the Casino Theatre to-night."

Gerald was repulsed but not defeated. "What is she playing in to-night?

Tell me that!" he sneered.

"I don't see why I sh'd tell you."

"Hm!" Gerald retorted. "If what you say is true, it's a very strange thing I should have seen her in the Champs Elysees to-night, isn't it?"

The Englishman drank more wine. "If you want to insult me, sir—" he began coldly.

"Gerald!" Sophia urged in a whisper.

"Be quiet!" Gerald snapped.

A fiddler in fancy costume plunged into the restaurant at that moment and began to play wildly. The shock of his strange advent momentarily silenced the quarrel; but soon it leaped up again, under the shelter of the noisy music,—the common, tedious, tippler's quarrel. It rose higher and higher. The fiddler looked askance at it over his fiddle. Chirac cautiously observed it. Instead of attending to the music, the festal company attended to the quarrel. Three waiters in a group watched it with an impartial sporting interest. The English voices grew more menacing.

Then suddenly the whiskered Englishman, jerking his head towards the door, said more quietly:

"Hadn't we better settle thish outside?"

"At your service!" said Gerald, rising.

The owner of the vermilion cloak lifted her eyebrows to Chirac in fatigued disgust, but she said nothing. Nor did Sophia say anything. Sophia was overcome by terror.

The swain of the cloak, dragging his coat after him across the floor, left the restaurant without offering any apology or explanation to his lady.

"Wait here for me," said Gerald defiantly to Sophia. "I shall be back in a minute."

"But, Gerald!" She put her hand on his sleeve.

He snatched his arm away. "Wait here for me, I tell you," he repeated.

The doorkeeper obsequiously opened the door to the two unsteady carousers, for whom the fiddler drew back, still playing.

Thus Sophia was left side by side with the vermilion cloak. She was quite helpless. All the pride of a married woman had abandoned her. She stood transfixed by intense shame, staring painfully at a pillar, to avoid the universal assault of eyes. She felt like an indiscreet little girl, and she looked like one. No youthful radiant beauty of features, no grace and style of a Parisian dress, no certificate of a ring, no premature initiation into the mysteries, could save her from the appearance of a raw fool whose foolishness had been her undoing. Her face changed to its reddest, and remained at that, and all the fundamental innocence of her nature, which had been overlaid by the violent experiences of her brief companionship with Gerald, rose again to the surface with that blush. Her situation drew pity from a few hearts and a careless contempt from the rest. But since once more it was a question of ces Anglais, nobody could be astonished.

Without moving her head, she twisted her eyes to the clock: half-past two. The fiddler ceased his dance and made a collection in his tasselled cap. The vermilion cloak threw a coin into the cap. Sophia stared at it moveless, until the fiddler, tired of waiting, passed to the next table and relieved her agony. She had no money at all. She set herself to watch the clock; but its fingers would not stir.

With an exclamation the lady of the cloak got up and peered out of the window, chatted with waiters, and then removed herself and her cloak to the next table, where she was received with amiable sympathy by the three lorettes, Chirac, and the other two men. The party surreptitiously examined Sophia from time to time. Then Chirac went outside with the head-waiter, returned, consulted with his friends, and finally approached Sophia. It was twenty minutes past three.

He renewed his magnificent bow. "Madame," he said carefully, "will you allow me to bring you to your hotel?"

He made no reference to Gerald, partly, doubtless, because his English was treacherous on difficult ground. Sophia had not sufficient presence of mind to thank her saviour.

"But the bill?" she stammered. "The bill isn't paid."

He did not instantly understand her. But one of the waiters had caught the sound of a familiar word, and sprang forward with a slip of paper on a plate.

"I have no money," said Sophia, with a feeble smile.

"Je vous arrangerai ca," he said. "What name of the hotel? Meurice, is it not?"

"Hotel Meurice," said Sophia. "Yes."

He spoke to the head-waiter about the bill, which was carried away like something obscene; and on his arm, which he punctiliously offered and she could not refuse, Sophia left the scene of her ignominy. She was so distraught that she could not manage her crinoline in the doorway. No sign anywhere outside of Gerald or his foe!

He put her into an open carriage, and in five minutes they had clattered down the brilliant silence of the Rue de la Paix, through the Place Vendome into the Rue de Rivoli; and the night-porter of the hotel was at the carriage-step.

"I tell them at the restaurant where you gone," said Chirac, bare-headed under the long colonnade of the street. "If your husband is there, I tell him. Till to-morrow…!"

His manners were more wonderful than any that Sophia had ever imagined. He might have been in the dark Tuileries on the opposite side of the street, saluting an empress, instead of taking leave of a raw little girl, who was still too disturbed even to thank him.

She fled candle in hand up the wide, many-cornered stairs; Gerald might be already in the bedroom, … drunk! There was a chance. But the gilt-fringed bedroom was empty. She sat down at the velvet-covered table amid the shadows cast by the candle that wavered in the draught from the open window. And she set her teeth and a cold fury possessed her in the hot and languorous night. Gerald was an imbecile. That he should have allowed himself to get tipsy was bad enough, but that he should have exposed her to the horrible situation from which Chirac had extricated her, was unspeakably disgraceful. He was an imbecile. He had no common sense. With all his captivating charm, he could not be relied upon not to make himself and her ridiculous, tragically ridiculous. Compare him with Mr. Chirac! She leaned despairingly on the table. She would not undress. She would not move. She had to realize her position; she had to see it.

Folly! Folly! Fancy a commercial traveller throwing a compromising piece of paper to the daughter of his customer in the shop itself: that was the incredible folly with which their relations had begun! And his mad gesture at the pit-shaft! And his scheme for bringing her to Paris unmarried! And then to-night! Monstrous folly! Alone in the bedroom she was a wise and a disillusioned woman, wiser than any of those dolls in the restaurant.

And had she not gone to Gerald, as it were, over the dead body of her father, through lies and lies and again lies? That was how she phrased it to herself…. Over the dead body of her father! How could such a venture succeed? How could she ever have hoped that it would succeed? In that moment she saw her acts with the terrible vision of a Hebrew prophet.

She thought of the Square and of her life there with her mother and Sophia. Never would her pride allow her to return to that life, not even if the worst happened to her that could happen. She was one of those who are prepared to pay without grumbling for what they have had.

There was a sound outside. She noticed that the dawn had begun. The door opened and disclosed Gerald. They exchanged a searching glance, and Gerald shut the door. Gerald infected the air, but she perceived at once that he was sobered. His lip was bleeding.

"Mr. Chirac brought me home," she said.

"So it seems," said Gerald, curtly. "I asked you to wait for me. Didn't I say I should come back?"

He was adopting the injured magisterial tone of the man who is ridiculously trying to conceal from himself and others that he has recently behaved like an ass.

She resented the injustice. "I don't think you need talk like that," she said.

"Like what?" he bullied her, determined that she should be in the wrong.

And what a hard look on his pretty face!

Her prudence bade her accept the injustice. She was his. Rapt away from her own world, she was utterly dependent on his good nature.

"I knocked my chin against the damned balustrade, coming upstairs," said Gerald, gloomily.

She knew that was a lie. "Did you?" she replied kindly. "Let me bathe it."

CHAPTER III

AN AMBITION SATISFIED
I

She went to sleep in misery. All the glory of her new life had been eclipsed. But when she woke up, a few hours later, in the large, velvety stateliness of the bedroom for which Gerald was paying so fantastic a price per day, she was in a brighter mood, and very willing to reconsider her verdicts. Her pride induced her to put Gerald in the right and herself in the wrong, for she was too proud to admit that she had married a charming

181

and irresponsible fool. And, indeed, ought she not to put herself in the wrong? Gerald had told her to wait, and she had not waited. He had said that he should return to the restaurant, and he had returned. Why had she not waited? She had not waited because she had behaved like a simpleton. She had been terrified about nothing. Had she not been frequenting restaurants now for a month past? Ought not a married woman to be capable of waiting an hour in a restaurant for her lawful husband without looking a ninny? And as for Gerald's behaviour, how could he have acted differently? The other Englishman was obviously a brute and had sought a quarrel. His contradiction of Gerald's statements was extremely offensive. On being invited by the brute to go outside, what could Gerald do but comply? Not to have complied might have meant a fight in the restaurant, as the brute was certainly drunk. Compared to the brute, Gerald was not at all drunk, merely a little gay and talkative. Then Gerald's fib about his chin was natural; he simply wished to minimize the fuss and to spare her feelings. It was, in fact, just like Gerald to keep perfect silence as to what had passed between himself and the brute. However, she was convinced that Gerald, so lithe and quick, had given that great brute with his supercilious ways as good as he received, if not better.

And if she were a man and had asked her wife to wait in a restaurant, and the wife had gone home under the escort of another man, she would most assuredly be much more angry than Gerald had been. She was very glad that she had controlled herself and exercised a meek diplomacy. A quarrel had thus been avoided. Yes, the finish of the evening could not be called a quarrel; after her nursing of his chin, nothing but a slight coolness on his part had persisted.

She arose silently and began to dress, full of a determination to treat Gerald as a good wife ought to treat a husband. Gerald did not stir; he was an excellent sleeper: one of those organisms that never want to go to bed and never want to get up. When her toilet was complete save for her bodice, there was a knock at the door. She started.

"Gerald!" She approached the bed, and leaned her nude bosom over her husband, and put her arms round his neck. This method of being brought back to consciousness did not displease him.

The knock was repeated. He gave a grunt.

"Some one's knocking at the door," she whispered.

"Then why don't you open it?" he asked dreamily.

"I'm not dressed, darling."

He looked at her. "Stick something on your shoulders, girl!" said he.

"What does it matter?"

There she was, being a simpleton again, despite her resolution!

She obeyed, and cautiously opened the door, standing behind it.

A middle-aged whiskered servant, in a long white apron, announced matters in French which passed her understanding. But Gerald had heard from the bed, and he replied.

"Bien, monsieur!" The servant departed, with a bow, down the obscure corridor.

"It's Chirac," Gerald explained when she had shut the door. "I was forgetting I asked him to come and have lunch with us, early. He's waiting in the drawing-room. Just put your bodice on, and go and talk to him till I come."

He jumped out of bed, and then, standing in his night-garb, stretched himself and terrifically yawned.

"Me?" Sophia questioned.

"Who else?" said Gerald, with that curious satiric dryness which he would sometimes import into his tone.

"But I can't speak French!" she protested.

"I didn't suppose you could," said Gerald, with an increase of dryness; "but you know as well as I do that he can speak English."

"Oh, very well, then!" she murmured with agreeable alacrity.

Evidently Gerald had not yet quite recovered from his legitimate displeasure of the night. He minutely examined his mouth in the glass of the Louis Philippe wardrobe. It showed scarcely a trace of battle.

"I say!" he stopped her, as, nervous at the prospect before her, she was leaving the room. "I was thinking of going to Auxerre to-day."

"Auxerre?" she repeated, wondering under what circumstances she had recently heard that name. Then she remembered: it was the place of execution of the murderer Rivain.

"Yes," he said. "Chirac has to go. He's on a newspaper now. He was an architect when I knew him. He's got to go and he thinks himself jolly lucky. So I thought I'd go with him."

The truth was that he had definitely arranged to go.

"Not to see the execution?" she stammered.

"Why not? I've always wanted to see an execution, especially with the guillotine. And executions are public in France. It's quite the proper thing to go to them."

"But why do you want to see an execution?"

"It just happens that I do want to see an execution. It's a fancy of mine, that's all. I don't know that any reason is necessary," he said, pouring out water into the diminutive ewer.

She was aghast. "And shall you leave me here alone?"

"Well," said he, "I don't see why my being married should prevent me from doing something that I've always wanted to do. Do you?"

"Oh NO!" she eagerly concurred.

"That's all right," he said. "You can do exactly as you like. Either stay here, or come with me. If you go to Auxerre there's no need at all for you to see the execution. It's an interesting old town—cathedral and so on. But of course if you can't bear to be in the same town as a guillotine, I'll go alone. I shall come back to-morrow."

It was plain where his wish lay. She stopped the phrases that came to her lips, and did her best to dismiss the thoughts which prompted them.

"Of course I'll go," she said quietly. She hesitated, and then went up to the washstand and kissed a part of his cheek that was not soapy. That kiss, which comforted and somehow reassured her, was the expression of a surrender whose monstrousness she would not admit to herself.

In the rich and dusty drawing-room, Chirac and Chirac's exquisite formalities awaited her. Nobody else was there.

"My husband …" she began, smiling and blushing. She liked Chirac.

It was the first time she had had the opportunity of using that word to other than a servant. It soothed her and gave her confidence. She perceived after a few moments that Chirac did genuinely admire her; more, that she inspired him with something that resembled awe. Speaking very slowly and distinctly she said that she should travel with her husband to Auxerre; as he saw no objection to that course; implying that if he saw no objection she was perfectly satisfied. Chirac was concurrence itself. In five minutes it seemed to be the most natural and proper thing in the world that, on her honeymoon, she should be going with her husband to a particular town because a notorious murderer was about to be decapitated there in public.

"My husband has always wanted to see an execution," she said, later.

"It would be a pity to …"

"As psychological experience," replied Chirac, pronouncing the p of the adjective, "it will be very interessant…. To observe one's self, in such circumstances …" He smiled enthusiastically.

She thought how strange even nice Frenchmen were. Imagine going to an execution in order to observe yourself!

II

What continually impressed Sophia as strange, in the behaviour not only of Gerald but of Chirac and other people with whom she came into contact, was its quality of casualness. She had all her life been accustomed to see enterprises, even minor ones, well pondered and then carefully schemed beforehand. In St. Luke's Square there was always, in every head, a sort of time-table of existence prepared at least one week in advance. But in Gerald's world nothing was prearranged. Elaborate affairs were decided in a moment and undertaken with extraordinary lightness. Thus the excursion to Auxerre! During lunch scarcely a word was said as to it; the conversation, in English for Sophia's advantage, turning, as usual under such circumstances, upon the difficulty of languages and the differences between countries. Nobody would have guessed that any member of the party had any preoccupation whatever for the rest of the day. The meal was delightful to Sophia; not merely did she find Chirac comfortingly kind and sincere, but Gerald was restored to the perfection of his charm and his good humour. Then suddenly, in the midst of coffee, the question of trains loomed up like a swift crisis. In five minutes Chirac had departed—whether to his office or his home Sophia did not understand, and within a quarter of an hour she and Gerald were driving rapidly to the Gare de Lyon, Gerald stuffing into his pocket a large envelope full of papers which he had received by registered post. They caught the train by about a minute, and Chirac by a few seconds. Yet neither he nor Gerald seemed to envisage the risk of inconvenience and annoyance which they had incurred and escaped. Chirac chattered through the window with another journalist in the next compartment. When she had leisure to examine him,

Sophia saw that he must have called at his home to put on old clothes. Everybody except herself and Gerald seemed to travel in his oldest clothes.

The train was hot, noisy, and dusty. But, one after another, all three of them fell asleep and slept heavily, calmly, like healthy and exhausted young animals. Nothing could disturb them for more than a moment. To Sophia it appeared to be by simple chance that Chirac aroused himself and them at Laroche and sleepily seized her valise and got them all out on the platform, where they yawned and smiled, full of the deep, half-realized satisfaction of repose. They drank nectar from a wheeled buffet, drank it eagerly, in thirsty gulps, and sighed with pleasure and relief, and Gerald threw down a coin, refusing change with a lord's gesture. The local train to Auxerre was full, and with a varied and sinister cargo. At length they were in the zone of the waiting guillotine. The rumour ran that the executioner was on the train. No one had seen him; no one was sure of recognizing him, but everyone hugged the belief that he was on the train. Although the sun was sinking the heat seemed not to abate. Attitudes grew more limp, more abandoned. Soot and prickly dust flew in unceasingly at the open windows. The train stopped at Bonnard, Chemilly, and Moneteau, each time before a waiting crowd that invaded it. And at last, in the great station at Auxerre, it poured out an incredible mass of befouled humanity that spread over everything like an inundation. Sophia was frightened. Gerald left the initiative to Chirac, and Chirac took her arm and led her forward, looking behind him to see that Gerald followed with the valise. Frenzy seemed to reign in Auxerre.

The driver of a cab demanded ten francs for transporting them to the Hotel de l'Epee.

"Bah!" scornfully exclaimed Chirac, in his quality of experienced Parisian who is not to be exploited by heavy-witted provincials.

But the driver of the next cab demanded twelve francs.

"Jump in," said Gerald to Sophia. Chirac lifted his eyebrows.

At the same moment a tall, stout man with the hard face of a flourishing scoundrel, and a young, pallid girl on his arm, pushed aside both Gerald and Chirac and got into the cab with his companion.

Chirac protested, telling him that the cab was already engaged.

The usurper scowled and swore, and the young girl laughed boldly.

Sophia, shrinking, expected her escort to execute justice heroic and final; but she was disappointed.

"Brute!" murmured Chirac, and shrugged his shoulders, as the carriage drove off, leaving them foolish on the kerb.

By this time all the other cabs had been seized. They walked to the Hotel de l'Epee, jostled by the crowd, Sophia and Chirac in front, and Gerald following with the valise, whose weight caused him to lean over to the right and his left arm to rise. The avenue was long, straight, and misty with a floating dust. Sophia had a vivid sense of the romantic. They saw towers and spires, and Chirac talked to her slowly and carefully of the cathedral and the famous churches. He said that the stained glass was marvellous, and with much care he catalogued for her all the things she must visit. They crossed a river. She felt as though she was stepping into the middle age. At intervals Gerald changed the valise from hand to hand; obstinately, he would not let Chirac touch it. They struggled upwards, through narrow curving streets.

"Voila!" said Chirac.

They were in front of the Hotel de l'Epee. Across the street was a cafe crammed with people. Several carriages stood in front. The Hotel de l'Epee had a reassuring air of mellow respectability, such as Chirac had claimed for it. He had suggested this hotel for Madame Scales because it was not near the place of execution. Gerald had said, "Of course! Of course!" Chirac, who did not mean to go to bed, required no room for himself.

The Hotel de l'Epee had one room to offer, at the price of twenty-five francs.

Gerald revolted at the attempted imposition. "A nice thing!" he grumbled, "that ordinary travellers can't get a decent room at a decent price just because some one's going to be guillotined to-morrow! We'll try elsewhere!"

His features expressed disgust, but Sophia fancied that he was secretly pleased.

They swaggered out of the busy stir of the hotel, as those must who, having declined to be swindled, wish to preserve their importance in the face of the world. In the street a cabman solicited them, and filled them with hope by saying that he knew of a hotel that might suit them and would drive them there for five francs. He furiously lashed his horse. The mere fact of being in a swiftly moving carriage which wayfarers had to avoid nimbly, maintained their spirits. They had a near glimpse of the cathedral. The cab halted with a bump, in a small square, in front of a repellent building which bore the sign, 'Hotel de Vezelay.' The horse was bleeding. Gerald instructed Sophia to remain where she was, and he and Chirac went up four stone steps into the hotel.

Sophia, stared at by loose crowds that were promenading, gazed about her, and saw that all the windows of the square were open and most of them occupied by people who laughed and chattered. Then there was a shout: Gerald's voice. He had appeared at a window on the second floor of the hotel with Chirac and a very fat woman. Chirac saluted, and Gerald laughed carelessly, and nodded.

"It's all right," said Gerald, having descended.

"How much do they ask?" Sophia inquired indiscreetly.

Gerald hesitated, and looked self-conscious. "Thirty-five francs," he said. "But I've had enough of driving about. It seems we're lucky to get it even at that."

And Chirac shrugged his shoulders as if to indicate that the situation and the price ought to be accepted philosophically. Gerald gave the driver five francs. He examined the piece and demanded a pourboire.

"Oh! Damn!" said Gerald, and, because he had no smaller change, parted with another two francs.

"Is any one coming out for this damned valise?" Gerald demanded, like a tyrant whose wrath would presently fall if the populace did not instantly set about minding their p's and q's.

But nobody emerged, and he was compelled to carry the bag himself.

The hotel was dark and malodorous, and every room seemed to be crowded with giggling groups of drinkers.

"We can't both sleep in this bed, surely," said Sophia when, Chirac having remained downstairs, she faced Gerald in a small, mean bedroom.

"You don't suppose I shall go to bed, do you?" said Gerald, rather brusquely. "It's for you. We're going to eat now. Look sharp."

III

It was night. She lay in the narrow, crimson-draped bed. The heavy crimson curtains had been drawn across the dirty lace curtains of the window, but the lights of the little square faintly penetrated through chinks into the room. The sounds of the square also penetrated, extraordinarily loud and clear, for the unabated heat had compelled her to leave the window open. She could not sleep. Exhausted though she was, there was no hope of her being able to sleep.

Once again she was profoundly depressed. She remembered the dinner with horror. The long, crowded table, with semi-circular ends, in the oppressive and reeking dining-room lighted by oil-lamps! There must have been at least forty people at that table. Most of them ate disgustingly, as noisily as pigs, with the ends of the large coarse napkins tucked in at their necks. All the service was done by the fat woman whom she had seen at the window with Gerald, and a young girl whose demeanour was candidly brazen. Both these creatures were slatterns. Everything was dirty. But the food was good. Chirac and Gerald were agreed that the food was good, as well as the wine. "Remarquable!" Chirac had said, of the wine. Sophia, however, could neither eat nor drink with relish. She was afraid. The company shocked her by its gestures alone. It was very heterogeneous in appearance, some of the diners being well dressed, approaching elegance, and others shabby. But all the faces, to the youngest, were brutalized, corrupt, and shameless. The juxtaposition of old men and young women was odious to her, especially when those pairs kissed, as they did frequently towards the end of the meal. Happily she was placed between Chirac and Gerald. That situation seemed to shelter her even from the conversation. She would have comprehended nothing of the conversation, had it not been for the presence of a middle-aged Englishman who sat at the opposite end of the table with a youngish, stylish Frenchwoman whom she had seen at Sylvain's on the previous night. The Englishman was evidently under a promise to teach English to the Frenchwoman. He kept translating for her into English, slowly and distinctly, and she would repeat the phrases after him, with strange contortions of the mouth.

Thus Sophia gathered that the talk was exclusively about assassinations, executions, criminals, and executioners. Some of the people there made a practice of attending every execution. They were fountains of interesting gossip, and the lions of the meal. There was a woman who could recall the dying words of all the victims of justice for twenty years past. The table roared with hysteric laughter at one of this woman's anecdotes. Sophia learned that she had related how a criminal had said to the priest who was good-naturedly trying to screen the sight of the guillotine from him with his body: "Stand away now, parson. Haven't I paid to see it?" Such was the Englishman's rendering. The wages of the executioners and their assistants were discussed, and differences of opinions led to ferocious arguments. A young and dandiacal fellow told, as a fact which he was ready to vouch for with a pistol, how Cora Pearl, the renowned English courtesan, had through her influence over a prefect of police succeeded in visiting a criminal alone in his cell during the night preceding his execution, and had only quitted him an hour before the final summons. The tale won the honours of the dinner. It was regarded as truly impressive, and inevitably it led to the general inquiry: what could the highest personages in the empire see to admire in that red-haired Englishwoman? And of course Rivain himself, the handsome homicide, the centre and hero of the fete, was never long out of the conversation. Several of the diners had seen him; one or two knew him and could give amazing details of his prowess as a man of pleasure. Despite his crime, he seemed to be the object of sincere idolatry. It was said positively that a niece of his victim had been promised a front place at the execution.

Apropos of this, Sophia gathered, to her intense astonishment and alarm, that the prison was close by and that the execution would take place at the corner of the square itself in which the hotel was situated. Gerald must have known; he had hidden it from her. She regarded him sideways, with distrust. As the dinner finished, Gerald's pose of a calm, disinterested, scientific observer of humanity gradually broke down. He could not maintain it in front of the increasing license of the scene round the table. He was at length somewhat ashamed of having exposed his wife to the view of such an orgy; his restless glance carefully avoided both Sophia and Chirac. The latter, whose unaffected simplicity of interest in the affair had more than anything helped to keep Sophia in countenance, observed the change in Gerald and Sophia's excessive discomfort, and suggested that they should leave the table without waiting for the coffee. Gerald agreed quickly. Thus had Sophia been released from the horror of the dinner. She did not understand how a man so thoughtful and kindly as Chirac—he had bidden her good night with the most distinguished courtesy—could tolerate, much less pleasurably savour, the gluttonous, drunken, and salacious debauchery of the Hotel de Vezelay; but his theory was, so far as she could judge from his imperfect English, that whatever existed might be admitted and examined by serious persons interested in the study of human nature. His face seemed to say: "Why not?" His face seemed to say to Gerald and to herself: "If this incommodes you, what did you come for?"

Gerald had left her at the bedroom door with a self-conscious nod. She had partly undressed and lain down, and instantly the hotel had transformed itself into a kind of sounding-box. It was as if, beneath and within all the noises of the square, every movement in the hotel reached her ears through cardboard walls: distant shoutings and laughter below; rattlings of crockery below; stampings up and down stairs; stealthy creepings up and down stairs; brusque calls; fragments of song, whisperings; long sighs suddenly stifled; mysterious groans as of torture, broken by a giggle; quarrels and bickering,—she was spared nothing in the strangely resonant darkness.

Then there came out of the little square a great uproar and commotion, with shrieks, and under the shrieks a confused din. In vain she pressed her face into the pillow and listened to the irregular, prodigious noise of her eyelashes as they scraped the rough linen. The thought had somehow introduced itself into her head that she must arise and go to the window and see all that was to be seen. She resisted. She said to herself that the idea was absurd, that she did not wish to go to the window. Nevertheless, while arguing with herself, she well knew that resistance to the thought was useless and that ultimately her legs would obey its command.

When ultimately she yielded to the fascination and went to the window and pulled aside one of the curtains, she had a feeling of relief. The cool, grey beginnings of dawn were in the sky, and every detail of the square was visible. Without exception all the windows were wide open and filled with sightseers. In the background of many windows were burning candles or lamps that the far distant approach of the sun was already killing. In front of these, on the frontier of two mingling lights, the attentive figures of the watchers were curiously silhouetted. On the red-tiled roofs, too, was a squatted population. Below, a troop of gendarmes, mounted on caracoling horses stretched in line across the square, was gradually sweeping the entire square of a packed, gesticulating, cursing crowd. The operation of this immense besom was very slow. As the spaces of the square were cleared they began to be dotted by privileged persons, journalists or law officers or their friends, who walked to and fro in conscious pride; among them Sophia descried Gerald and Chirac, strolling arm-in-arm and talking to two elaborately clad girls, who were also arm-in-arm.

Then she saw a red reflection coming from one of the side streets of which she had a vista; it was the swinging lantern of a waggon drawn by a gaunt grey horse. The vehicle stopped at the end of the square from which the besom had started, and it was immediately surrounded by the privileged, who, however, were soon persuaded to stand away. The crowd amassed now at the principal inlets of the square, gave a formidable cry and burst into the refrain—

"Le voila! Nicolas! Ah! Ah! Ah!"

The clamour became furious as a group of workmen in blue blouses drew piece by piece all the components of the guillotine from the waggon and laid them carefully on the ground, under the superintendence of a man in a black frock-coat and a silk hat with broad flat brims; a little fussy man of nervous gestures. And presently

186

the red columns had risen upright from the ground and were joined at the top by an acrobatic climber. As each part was bolted and screwed to the growing machine the man in the high hat carefully tested it. In a short time that seemed very long, the guillotine was finished save for the triangular steel blade which lay shining on the ground, a cynosure. The executioner pointed to it, and two men picked it up and slipped it into its groove, and hoisted it to the summit of the machine. The executioner peered at it interminably amid a universal silence. Then he actuated the mechanism, and the mass of metal fell with a muffled, reverberating thud. There were a few faint shrieks, blended together, and then an overpowering racket of cheers, shouts, hootings, and fragments of song. The blade was again lifted, instantly reproducing silence, and again it fell, liberating a new bedlam. The executioner made a movement of satisfaction. Many women at the windows clapped enthusiastically, and the gendarmes had to fight brutally against the fierce pressure of the crowd. The workmen doffed their blouses and put on coats, and Sophia was disturbed to see them coming in single file towards the hotel, followed by the executioner in the silk hat.

IV

There was a tremendous opening of doors in the Hotel de Vezelay, and much whispering on thresholds, as the executioner and his band entered solemnly. Sophia heard them tramp upstairs; they seemed to hesitate, and then apparently went into a room on same landing as hers. A door banged. But Sophia could hear the regular sound of new voices talking, and then the rattling of glasses on a tray. The conversation which came to her from the windows of the hotel now showed a great increase of excitement. She could not see the people at these neighbouring windows without showing her own head, and this she would not do. The boom of a heavy bell striking the hour vibrated over the roofs of the square; she supposed that it might be the cathedral clock. In a corner of the square she saw Gerald talking vivaciously alone with one of the two girls who had been together. She wondered vaguely how such a girl had been brought up, and what her parents thought—or knew! And she was conscious of an intense pride in herself, of a measureless haughty feeling of superiority. Her eye caught the guillotine again, and was held by it. Guarded by gendarmes, that tall and simple object did most menacingly dominate the square with its crude red columns. Tools and a large open box lay on the ground beside it. The enfeebled horse in the waggon had an air of dozing on his twisted legs. Then the first rays of the sun shot lengthwise across the square at the level of the chimneys; and Sophia noticed that nearly all the lamps and candles had been extinguished. Many people at the windows were yawning; they laughed foolishly after they had yawned. Some were eating and drinking. Some were shouting conversations from one house to another. The mounted gendarmes were still pressing back the feverish crowds that growled at all the inlets to the square. She saw Chirac walking to and fro alone. But she could not find Gerald. He could not have left the square. Perhaps he had returned to the hotel and would come up to see if she was comfortable or if she needed anything. Guiltily she sprang back into bed. When last she had surveyed the room it had been dark; now it was bright and every detail stood clear. Yet she had the sensation of having been at the window only a few minutes.

She waited. But Gerald did not come. She could hear chiefly the steady hum of the voices of the executioner and his aids. She reflected that the room in which they were must be at the back. The other sounds in the hotel grew less noticeable. Then, after an age, she heard a door open, and a low voice say something commandingly in French, and then a 'Oui, monsieur,' and a general descent of the stairs. The executioner and his aids were leaving. "You," cried a drunken English voice from an upper floor—it was the middle-aged Englishman translating what the executioner had said—"you, you will take the head." Then a rough laugh, and the repeating voice of the Englishman's girl, still pursuing her studies in English: "You will take ze 'ead. Yess, sair." And another laugh. At length quiet reigned in the hotel. Sophia said to herself: "I won't stir from this bed till it's all over and Gerald comes back!"

She dozed, under the sheet, and was awakened by a tremendous shrieking, growling, and yelling: a phenomenon of human bestiality that far surpassed Sophia's narrow experiences. Shut up though she was in a room, perfectly secure, the mad fury of that crowd, balked at the inlets to the square, thrilled and intimidated her. It sounded as if they would be capable of tearing the very horses to pieces. "I must stay where I am," she murmured. And even while saying it she rose and went to the window again and peeped out. The torture involved was extreme, but she had not sufficient force within her to resist the fascination. She stared greedily into the bright square. The first thing she saw was Gerald coming out of a house opposite, followed after a few seconds by the girl with whom he had previously been talking. Gerald glanced hastily up at the facade of the hotel, and then approached as near as he could to the red columns, in front of which were now drawn a line of gendarmes with naked swords. A second and larger waggon, with two horses, waited by the side of the other one. The racket beyond the square continued and even grew louder. But the couple of hundred persons within the cordons, and all the inhabitants of the windows, drunk and sober, gazed in a fixed and sinister enchantment at the region of the guillotine, as Sophia gazed. "I cannot stand this!" she told herself in horror, but she could not move; she could not move even her eyes.

At intervals the crowd would burst out in a violent staccato—

"Le voila! Nicholas! Ah! Ah! Ah!"

And the final 'Ah' was devilish.

Then a gigantic passionate roar, the culmination of the mob's fierce savagery, crashed against the skies. The line of maddened horses swerved and reared, and seemed to fall on the furious multitude while the statue-like gendarmes rocked over them. It was a last effort to break the cordon, and it failed.

From the little street at the rear of the guillotine appeared a priest, walking backwards, and holding a crucifix high in his right hand, and behind him came the handsome hero, his body all crossed with cords, between two warders, who pressed against him and supported him on either side. He was certainly very young. He lifted his chin gallantly, but his face was incredibly white. Sophia discerned that the priest was trying to hide the sight of the guillotine from the prisoner with his body, just as in the story which she had heard at dinner. Except the voice of the priest, indistinctly rising and falling in the prayer for the dying, there was no sound in the square or its environs. The windows were now occupied by groups turned to stone with distended eyes fixed on the little procession. Sophia had a tightening of the throat, and the hand trembled by which she held the curtain. The central figure did not seem to her to be alive; but rather a doll, a marionette wound up to imitate the action of a tragedy. She saw the priest offer the crucifix to the mouth of the marionette, which with a clumsy unhuman shoving of its corded shoulders butted the thing away. And as the procession turned and stopped she could plainly see that the marionette's nape and shoulders were bare, his shirt having been slit. It was horrible. "Why do I stay here?" she asked herself hysterically. But she did not stir. The victim had disappeared now in the midst of a group of men. Then she perceived him prone under the red column, between the grooves. The silence was now broken only by the tinkling of the horses' bits in the corners of the square. The line of gendarmes in front of the scaffold held their swords tightly and looked over their noses, ignoring the privileged groups that peered almost between their shoulders.

And Sophia waited, horror-struck. She saw nothing but the gleaming triangle of metal that was suspended high above the prone, attendant victim. She felt like a lost soul, torn too soon from shelter, and exposed for ever to the worst hazards of destiny. Why was she in this strange, incomprehensible town, foreign and inimical to her, watching with agonized glance this cruel, obscene spectacle? Her sensibilities were all a bleeding mass of wounds. Why? Only yesterday, and she had been, an innocent, timid creature in Bursley, in Axe, a foolish creature who deemed the concealment of letters a supreme excitement. Either that day or this day was not real. Why was she imprisoned alone in that odious, indescribably odious hotel, with no one to soothe and comfort her, and carry her away?

The distant bell boomed once. Then a monosyllabic voice sounded, sharp, low, nervous; she recognized the voice of the executioner, whose name she had heard but could not remember. There was a clicking noise. She shrank down to the floor in terror and loathing, and hid her face, and shuddered. Shriek after shriek, from various windows, rang on her ears in a fusillade; and then the mad yell of the penned crowd, which, like herself, had not seen but had heard, extinguished all other noise. Justice was done. The great ambition of Gerald's life was at last satisfied.

Later, amid the stir of the hotel, there came a knock at her door, impatient and nervous. Forgetting, in her tribulation, that she was without her bodice, she got up from the floor in a kind of miserable dream, and opened. Chirac stood on the landing, and he had Gerald by the arm. Chirac looked worn out, curiously fragile and pathetic; but Gerald was the very image of death. The attainment of ambition had utterly destroyed his equilibrium; his curiosity had proved itself stronger than his stomach. Sophia would have pitied him had she in that moment been capable of pity. Gerald staggered past her into the room, and sank with a groan on to the bed. Not long since he had been proudly conversing with impudent women. Now, in swift collapse, he was as flaccid as a sick hound and as disgusting as an aged drunkard.

"He is some little souffrant," said Chirac, weakly.

Sophia perceived in Chirac's tone the assumption that of course her present duty was to devote herself to the task of restoring her shamed husband to his manly pride.

"And what about me?" she thought bitterly.

The fat woman ascended the stairs like a tottering blancmange, and began to gabble to Sophia, who understood nothing whatever.

"She wants sixty francs," Chirac said, and in answer to Sophia's startled question, he explained that Gerald had agreed to pay a hundred francs for the room, which was the landlady's own—fifty francs in advance and the fifty after the execution. The other ten was for the dinner. The landlady, distrusting the whole of her clientele, was collecting her accounts instantly on the completion of the spectacle.

Sophia made no remark as to Gerald's lie to her. Indeed, Chirac had heard it. She knew Gerald for a glib liar to others, but she was naively surprised when he practised upon herself.

"Gerald! Do you hear?" she said coldly.

The amateur of severed heads only groaned.

With a movement of irritation she went to him and felt in his pockets for his purse; he acquiesced, still groaning. Chirac helped her to choose and count the coins.

The fat woman, appeased, pursued her way.

"Good-bye, madame!" said Chirac, with his customary courtliness, transforming the landing of the hideous hotel into some imperial antechamber.

"Are you going away?" she asked, in surprise. Her distress was so obvious that it tremendously flattered him. He would have stayed if he could. But he had to return to Paris to write and deliver his article.

"To-morrow, I hope!" he murmured sympathetically, kissing her hand. The gesture atoned somewhat for the sordidness of her situation, and even corrected the faults of her attire. Always afterwards it seemed to her that Chirac was an old and intimate friend; he had successfully passed through the ordeal of seeing 'the wrong side' of the stuff of her life.

She shut the door on him with a lingering glance, and reconciled herself to her predicament.

Gerald slept. Just as he was, he slept heavily.

This was what he had brought her to, then! The horrors of the night, of the dawn, and of the morning! Ineffable suffering and humiliation; anguish and torture that could never be forgotten! And after a fatuous vigil of unguessed license, he had tottered back, an offensive beast, to sleep the day away in that filthy chamber! He did not possess even enough spirit to play the role of roysterer to the end. And she was bound to him; far, far from any other human aid; cut off irrevocably by her pride from those who perhaps would have protected her from his dangerous folly. The deep conviction henceforward formed a permanent part of her general consciousness that he was simply an irresponsible and thoughtless fool! He was without sense. Such was her brilliant and godlike husband, the man who had given her the right to call herself a married woman! He was a fool. With all her ignorance of the world she could see that nobody but an arrant imbecile could have brought her to the present pass. Her native sagacity revolted. Gusts of feeling came over her in which she could have thrashed him into the realization of his responsibilities.

Sticking out of the breast-pocket of his soiled coat was the packet which he had received on the previous day. If he had not already lost it, he could only thank his luck. She took it. There were English bank-notes in it for two hundred pounds, a letter from a banker, and other papers. With precautions against noise she tore the envelope and the letter and papers into small pieces, and then looked about for a place to hide them. A cupboard suggested itself. She got on a chair, and pushed the fragments out of sight on the topmost shelf, where they may well be to this day. She finished dressing, and then sewed the notes into the lining of her skirt. She had no silly, delicate notions about stealing. She obscurely felt that, in the care of a man like Gerald, she might find herself in the most monstrous, the most impossible dilemmas. Those notes, safe and secret in her skirt, gave her confidence, reassured her against the perils of the future, and endowed her with independence. The act was characteristic of her enterprise and of her fundamental prudence. It approached the heroic. And her conscience hotly defended its righteousness.

She decided that when he discovered his loss, she would merely deny all knowledge of the envelope, for he had not spoken a word to her about it. He never mentioned the details of money; he had a fortune. However, the necessity for this untruth did not occur. He made no reference whatever to his loss. The fact was, he thought he had been careless enough to let the envelope be filched from him during the excesses of the night. All day till evening Sophia sat on a dirty chair, without food, while Gerald slept. She kept repeating to herself, in amazed resentment: "A hundred francs for this room! A hundred francs! And he hadn't the pluck to tell me!" She could not have expressed her contempt.

Long before sheer ennui forced her to look out of the window again, every sign of justice had been removed from the square. Nothing whatever remained in the heavy August sunshine save gathered heaps of filth where the horses had reared and caracoled.

189

CHAPTER IV

A CRISIS FOR GERALD
I

For a time there existed in the minds of both Gerald and Sophia the remarkable notion that twelve thousand pounds represented the infinity of wealth, that this sum possessed special magical properties which rendered it insensible to the process of subtraction. It seemed impossible that twelve thousand pounds, while continually getting less, could ultimately quite disappear. The notion lived longer in the mind of Gerald than in that of Sophia; for Gerald would never look at a disturbing fact, whereas Sophia's gaze was morbidly fascinated by such phenomena. In a life devoted to travel and pleasure Gerald meant not to spend more than six hundred a year, the interest on his fortune. Six hundred a year is less than two pounds a day, yet Gerald never paid less than two pounds a day in hotel bills alone. He hoped that he was living on a thousand a year, had a secret fear that he might be spending fifteen hundred, and was really spending about two thousand five hundred. Still, the remarkable notion of the inexhaustibility of twelve thousand pounds always reassured him. The faster the money went, the more vigorously this notion flourished in Gerald's mind. When twelve had unaccountably dwindled to three, Gerald suddenly decided that he must act, and in a few months he lost two thousand on the Paris Bourse. The adventure frightened him, and in his panic he scattered a couple of hundred in a frenzy of high living.

But even with only twenty thousand francs left out of three hundred thousand, he held closely to the belief that natural laws would in his case somehow be suspended. He had heard of men who were once rich begging bread and sweeping crossings, but he felt quite secure against such risks, by simple virtue of the axiom that he was he. However, he meant to assist the axiom by efforts to earn money. When these continued to fail, he tried to assist the axiom by borrowing money; but he found that his uncle had definitely done with him. He would have assisted the axiom by stealing money, but he had neither the nerve nor the knowledge to be a swindler; he was not even sufficiently expert to cheat at cards.

He had thought in thousands. Now he began to think in hundreds, in tens, daily and hourly. He paid two hundred francs in railway fares in order to live economically in a village, and shortly afterwards another two hundred francs in railway fares in order to live economically in Paris. And to celebrate the arrival in Paris and the definite commencement of an era of strict economy and serious search for a livelihood, he spent a hundred francs on a dinner at the Maison Doree and two balcony stalls at the Gymnase. In brief, he omitted nothing— no act, no resolve, no self-deception—of the typical fool in his situation; always convinced that his difficulties and his wisdom were quite exceptional.

In May, 1870, on an afternoon, he was ranging nervously to and fro in a three-cornered bedroom of a little hotel at the angle of the Rue Fontaine and the Rue Laval (now the Rue Victor Masse), within half a minute of the Boulevard de Clichy. It had come to that—an exchange of the 'grand boulevard' for the 'boulevard exterieur'! Sophia sat on a chair at the grimy window, glancing down in idle disgust of life at the Clichy-Odeon omnibus which was casting off its tip-horse at the corner of the Rue Chaptal. The noise of petty, hurried traffic over the bossy paving stones was deafening. The locality was not one to correspond with an ideal. There was too much humanity crowded into those narrow hilly streets; humanity seemed to be bulging out at the windows of the high houses. Gerald healed his pride by saying that this was, after all, the real Paris, and that the cookery was as good as could be got anywhere, pay what you would. He seldom ate a meal in the little salons on the first floor without becoming ecstatic upon the cookery. To hear him, he might have chosen the hotel on its superlative merits, without regard to expense. And with his air of use and custom, he did indeed look like a connoisseur of Paris who knew better than to herd with vulgar tourists in the pens of the Madeleine quarter. He was dressed with some distinction; good clothes, when put to the test, survive a change of fortune, as a Roman arch survives the luxury of departed empire. Only his collar, large V-shaped front, and wristbands, which bore the ineffaceable signs of cheap laundering, reflected the shadow of impending disaster.

He glanced sideways, stealthily, at Sophia. She, too, was still dressed with distinction; in the robe of black faille, the cashmere shawl, and the little black hat with its falling veil, there was no apparent symptom of beggary. She would have been judged as one of those women who content themselves with few clothes but good, and, greatly aided by nature, make a little go a long way. Good black will last for eternity; it discloses no secrets of modification and mending, and it is not transparent.

At last Gerald, resuming a suspended conversation, said as it were doggedly:

"I tell you I haven't got five francs altogether! and you can feel my pockets if you like," added the habitual liar in him, fearing incredulity.

"Well, and what do you expect me to do?" Sophia inquired.

The accent, at once ironic and listless, in which she put this question, showed that strange and vital things had happened to Sophia in the four years which had elapsed since her marriage. It did really seem to her, indeed, that the Sophia whom Gerald had espoused was dead and gone, and that another Sophia had come into her body: so intensely conscious was she of a fundamental change in herself under the stress of continuous experience. And though this was but a seeming, though she was still the same Sophia more fully disclosed, it was a true seeming. Indisputably more beautiful than when Gerald had unwillingly made her his legal wife, she was now nearly twenty-four, and looked perhaps somewhat older than her age. Her frame was firmly set, her waist thicker, neither slim nor stout. The lips were rather hard, and she had a habit of tightening her mouth, on the same provocation as sends a snail into its shell. No trace was left of immature gawkiness in her gestures or of simplicity in her intonations. She was a woman of commanding and slightly arrogant charm, not in the least degree the charm of innocence and ingenuousness. Her eyes were the eyes of one who has lost her illusions too violently and too completely. Her gaze, coldly comprehending, implied familiarity with the abjectness of human nature. Gerald had begun and had finished her education. He had not ruined her, as a bad professor may ruin a fine voice, because her moral force immeasurably exceeded his; he had unwittingly produced a masterpiece, but it was a tragic masterpiece. Sophia was such a woman as, by a mere glance as she utters an opinion, will make a man say to himself, half in desire and half in alarm lest she reads him too: "By Jove! she must have been through a thing or two. She knows what people are!"

The marriage was, of course, a calamitous folly. From the very first, from the moment when the commercial traveller had with incomparable rash fatuity thrown the paper pellet over the counter, Sophia's awakening commonsense had told her that in yielding to her instinct she was sowing misery and shame for herself; but she had gone on, as if under a spell. It had needed the irretrievableness of flight from home to begin the breaking of the trance. Once fully awakened out of the trance, she had recognized her marriage for what it was. She had made neither the best nor the worst of it. She had accepted Gerald as one accepts a climate. She saw again and again that he was irreclaimably a fool and a prodigy of irresponsibleness. She tolerated him, now with sweetness, now bitterly; accepting always his caprices, and not permitting herself to have wishes of her own. She was ready to pay the price of pride and of a moment's imbecility with a lifetime of self-repression. It was high, but it was the price. She had acquired nothing but an exceptionally good knowledge of the French language (she soon learnt to scorn Gerald's glib maltreatment of the tongue), and she had conserved nothing but her dignity. She knew that Gerald was sick of her, that he would have danced for joy to be rid of her; that he was constantly unfaithful; that he had long since ceased to be excited by her beauty. She knew also that at bottom he was a little afraid of her; here was her sole moral consolation. The thing that sometimes struck her as surprising was that he had not abandoned her, simply and crudely walked off one day and forgotten to take her with him.

They hated each other, but in different ways. She loathed him, and he resented her.

"What do I expect you to do?" he repeated after her. "Why don't you write home to your people and get some money out of them?"

Now that he had said what was in his mind, he faced her with a bullying swagger. Had he been a bigger man he might have tried the effect of physical bullying on her. One of his numerous reasons for resenting her was that she was the taller of the two.

She made no reply.

"Now you needn't turn pale and begin all that fuss over again. What I'm suggesting is a perfectly reasonable thing. If I haven't got money I haven't got it. I can't invent it."

She perceived that he was ready for one of their periodical tempestuous quarrels. But that day she felt too tired and unwell to quarrel. His warning against a repetition of 'fuss' had reference to the gastric dizziness from which she had been suffering for two years. It would take her usually after a meal. She did not swoon, but her head swam and she could not stand. She would sink down wherever she happened to be, and, her face alarmingly white, murmur faintly: "My salts." Within five minutes the attack had gone and left no trace. She had been through one just after lunch. He resented this affection. He detested being compelled to hand the smelling-bottle to her, and he would have avoided doing so if her pallor did not always alarm him. Nothing but this pallor convinced him that the attacks were not a deep ruse to impress him. His attitude invariably implied that she could cure the malady if she chose, but that through obstinacy she did not choose.

"Are you going to have the decency to answer my question, or aren't you?"

"What question?" Her vibrating voice was low and restrained.

"Will you write to your people?"

"For money?"

The sarcasm of her tone was diabolic. She could not have kept the sarcasm out of her tone; she did not attempt to keep it out. She cared little if it whipped him to fury. Did he imagine, seriously, that she would be capable of going on her knees to her family? She? Was he unaware that his wife was the proudest and the most obstinate woman on earth; that all her behaviour to him was the expression of her pride and her obstinacy? Ill and weak though she felt, she marshalled together all the forces of her character to defend her resolve never, never to eat the bread of humiliation. She was absolutely determined to be dead to her family. Certainly, one December, several years previously, she had seen English Christmas cards in an English shop in the Rue de Rivoli, and in a sudden gush of tenderness towards Constance, she had despatched a coloured greeting to Constance and her mother. And having initiated the custom, she had continued it. That was not like asking a kindness; it was bestowing a kindness. But except for the annual card, she was dead to St. Luke's Square. She was one of those daughters who disappear and are not discussed in the family circle. The thought of her immense foolishness, the little tender thoughts of Constance, some flitting souvenir, full of unwilling admiration, of a regal gesture of her mother,—these things only steeled her against any sort of resurrection after death.

And he was urging her to write home for money! Why, she would not even have paid a visit in splendour to St. Luke's Square. Never should they know what she had suffered! And especially her Aunt Harriet, from whom she had stolen!

"Will you write to your people?" he demanded yet again, emphasizing and separating each word.

"No," she said shortly, with terrible disdain.

"Why not?"

"Because I won't." The curling line of her lips, as they closed on each other, said all the rest; all the cruel truths about his unspeakable, inane, coarse follies, his laziness, his excesses, his lies, his deceptions, his bad faith, his truculence, his improvidence, his shameful waste and ruin of his life and hers. She doubted whether he realized his baseness and her wrongs, but if he could not read them in her silent contumely, she was too proud to recite them to him. She had never complained, save in uncontrolled moments of anger.

"If that's the way you're going to talk—all right!" he snapped, furious. Evidently he was baffled.

She kept silence. She was determined to see what he would do in the face of her inaction.

"You know, I'm not joking," he pursued. "We shall starve."

"Very well," she agreed. "We shall starve."

She watched him surreptitiously, and she was almost sure that he really had come to the end of his tether. His voice, which never alone convinced, carried a sort of conviction now. He was penniless. In four years he had squandered twelve thousand pounds, and had nothing to show for it except an enfeebled digestion and a tragic figure of a wife. One small point of satisfaction there was—and all the Baines in her clutched at it and tried to suck satisfaction from it—their manner of travelling about from hotel to hotel had made it impossible for Gerald to run up debts. A few debts he might have, unknown to her, but they could not be serious.

So they looked at one another, in hatred and despair. The inevitable had arrived. For months she had fronted it in bravado, not concealing from herself that it lay in waiting. For years he had been sure that though the inevitable might happen to others it could not happen to him. There it was! He was conscious of a heavy weight in his stomach, and she of a general numbness, enwrapping her fatigue. Even then he could not believe that it was true, this disaster. As for Sophia she was reconciling herself with bitter philosophy to the eccentricities of fate. Who would have dreamed that she, a young girl brought up, etc? Her mother could not have improved the occasion more uncompromisingly than Sophia did—behind that disdainful mask.

"Well—if that's it…!" Gerald exploded at length, puffing. And he puffed out of the room and was gone in a second.

II

She languidly picked up a book, the moment Gerald had departed, and tried to prove to herself that she was sufficiently in command of her nerves to read. For a long time reading had been her chief solace. But she could not read. She glanced round the inhospitable chamber, and thought of the hundreds of rooms—some splendid and some vile, but all arid in their unwelcoming aspect—through which she had passed in her progress from mad exultation to calm and cold disgust. The ceaseless din of the street annoyed her jaded ears. And a great wave of desire for peace, peace of no matter what kind, swept through her. And then her deep distrust of Gerald reawakened; in spite of his seriously desperate air, which had a quality of sincerity quite new in her experience of him, she could not be entirely sure that, in asserting utter penury, he was not after all merely using a trick to get rid of her.

She sprang up, threw the book on the bed, and seized her gloves. She would follow him, if she could. She would do what she had never done before—she would spy on him. Fighting against her lassitude, she descended the long winding stairs, and peeped forth from the doorway into the street. The ground floor of the hotel was a wine-shop; the stout landlord was lightly flicking one of the three little yellow tables that stood on the pavement. He smiled with his customary benevolence, and silently pointed in the direction of the Rue Notre Dame de Lorette. She saw Gerald down there in the distance. He was smoking a cigar.

He seemed to be a little man without a care. The smoke of the cigar came first round his left cheek and then round his right, sailing away into nothing. He walked with a gay spring, but not quickly, flourishing his cane as freely as the traffic of the pavement would permit, glancing into all the shop windows and into the eyes of all the women under forty. This was not at all the same man as had a moment ago been spitting angry menaces at her in the bedroom of the hotel. It was a fellow of blithe charm, ripe for any adventurous joys that destiny had to offer.

Supposing he turned round and saw her?

If he turned round and saw her and asked her what she was doing there in the street, she would tell him plainly: "I'm following you, to find out what you do."

But he did not turn. He went straight forward, deviating at the church, where the crowd became thicker, into the Rue du Faubourg Montmartre, and so to the boulevard, which he crossed. The whole city seemed excited and vivacious. Cannons boomed in slow succession, and flags were flying. Sophia had no conception of the significance of those guns, for, though she read a great deal, she never read a newspaper; the idea of opening a newspaper never occurred to her. But she was accustomed to the feverish atmosphere of Paris. She had lately seen regiments of cavalry flashing and prancing in the Luxembourg Gardens, and had much admired the fine picture. She accepted the booming as another expression of the high spirits that had to find vent somehow in this feverish empire. She so accepted it and forgot it, using all the panorama of the capital as a dim background for her exacerbated egoism.

She was obliged to walk slowly, because Gerald walked slowly. A beautiful woman, or any woman not positively hag-like or venerable, who walks slowly in the streets of Paris becomes at once the cause of inconvenient desires, as representing the main objective on earth, always transcending in importance politics and affairs. Just as a true patriotic Englishman cannot be too busy to run after a fox, so a Frenchman is always ready to forsake all in order to follow a woman whom he has never before set eyes on. Many men thought twice about her, with her romantic Saxon mystery of temperament, and her Parisian clothes; but all refrained from affronting her, not in the least out of respect for the gloom in her face, but from an expert conviction that those rapt eyes were fixed immovably on another male. She walked unscathed amid the frothing hounds as though protected by a spell.

On the south side of the boulevard, Gerald proceeded down the Rue Montmartre, and then turned suddenly into the Rue Croissant. Sophia stopped and asked the price of some combs which were exposed outside a little shop. Then she went on, boldly passing the end of the Rue Croissant. No shadow of Gerald! She saw the signs of newspapers all along the street, Le Bien Public, La Presse Libre, La Patrie. There was a creamery at the corner. She entered it, asked for a cup of chocolate and sat down. She wanted to drink coffee, but every doctor had forbidden coffee to her, on account of her attacks of dizziness. Then, having ordered chocolate, she felt that, on this occasion, when she had need of strength in her great fatigue, only coffee could suffice her, and she changed the order. She was close to the door, and Gerald could not escape her vigilance if he emerged at that end of the street. She drank the coffee with greedy satisfaction, and waited in the creamery till she began to feel conspicuous there. And then Gerald went by the door, within six feet of her. He turned the corner and continued his descent of the Rue Montmartre. She paid for her coffee and followed the chase. Her blood seemed to be up. Her lips were tightened, and her thought was: "Wherever he goes, I'll go, and I don't care what happens." She despised him. She felt herself above him. She felt that somehow, since quitting the hotel, he had been gradually growing more and more vile and meet to be exterminated. She imagined infamies as to the Rue Croissant. There was no obvious ground for this intensifying of her attitude towards him; it was merely the result of the chase. All that could be definitely charged against him was the smoking of a cigar.

193

He stepped into a tobacco-shop, and came out with a longer cigar than the first one, a more expensive article, stripped off its collar and lighted it as a millionaire might have lighted it. This was the man who swore that he did not possess five francs.

She tracked him as far as the Rue de Rivoli, and then lost him. There were vast surging crowds in the Rue de Rivoli, and much bunting, and soldiers and gesticulatory policemen. The general effect of the street was that all things were brightly waving in the breeze. She was caught in the crowd as in the current of a stream, and when she tried to sidle out of it into a square, a row of smiling policemen barred her passage; she was a part of the traffic that they had to regulate. She drifted till the Louvre came into view. After all, Gerald had only strolled forth to see the sight of the day, whatever it might be! She knew not what it was. She had no curiosity about it. In the middle of all that thickening mass of humanity, staring with one accord at the vast monument of royal and imperial vanities, she thought, with her characteristic grimness, of the sacrifice of her whole career as a school-teacher for the chance of seeing Gerald once a quarter in the shop. She gloated over that, as a sick appetite will gloat over tainted food. And she saw the shop, and the curve of the stairs up to the showroom, and the pier-glass in the showroom.

Then the guns began to boom again, and splendid carriages swept one after another from under a majestic archway and glittered westward down a lane of spotless splendid uniforms. The carriages were laden with still more splendid uniforms, and with enchanting toilets. Sophia, in her modestly stylish black, mechanically noticed how much easier it was for attired women to sit in a carriage now that crinolines had gone. That was the sole impression made upon her by this glimpse of the last fete of the Napoleonic Empire. She knew not that the supreme pillars of imperialism were exhibiting themselves before her; and that the eyes of those uniforms and those toilettes were full of the legendary beauty of Eugenie, and their ears echoing to the long phrases of Napoleon the Third about his gratitude to his people for their confidence in him as shown by the plebiscite, and about the ratification of constitutional reforms guaranteeing order, and about the empire having been strengthened at its base, and about showing force by moderation and envisaging the future without fear, and about the bosom of peace and liberty, and the eternal continuance of his dynasty.

She just wondered vaguely what was afoot.

When the last carriage had rolled away, and the guns and acclamations had ceased, the crowd at length began to scatter. She was carried by it into the Place du Palais Royal, and in a few moments she managed to withdraw into the Rue des Bons Enfants and was free.

The coins in her purse amounted to three sous, and therefore, though she felt exhausted to the point of illness, she had to return to the hotel on foot. Very slowly she crawled upwards in the direction of the Boulevard, through the expiring gaiety of the city. Near the Bourse a fiacre overtook her, and in the fiacre were Gerald and a woman. Gerald had not seen her; he was talking eagerly to his ornate companion. All his body was alive. The fiacre was out of sight in a moment, but Sophia judged instantly the grade of the woman, who was evidently of the discreet class that frequented the big shops of an afternoon with something of their own to sell.

Sophia's grimness increased. The pace of the fiacre, her fatigued body, Gerald's delightful, careless vivacity, the attractive streaming veil of the nice, modest courtesan—everything conspired to increase it.

III

Gerald returned to the bedroom which contained his wife and all else that he owned in the world at about nine o'clock that evening. Sophia was in bed. She had been driven to bed by weariness. She would have preferred to sit up to receive her husband, even if it had meant sitting up all night, but her body was too heavy for her spirit. She lay in the dark. She had eaten nothing. Gerald came straight into the room. He struck a match, which burned blue, with a stench, for several seconds, and then gave a clear, yellow flame. He lit a candle; and saw his wife.

"Oh!" he said; "you're there, are you?"

She offered no reply.

"Won't speak, eh?" he said. "Agreeable sort of wife! Well, have you made up your mind to do what I told you? I've come back especially to know."

She still did not speak.

He sat down, with his hat on, and stuck out his feet, wagging them to and fro on the heels.

"I'm quite without money," he went on. "And I'm sure your people will be glad to lend us a bit till I get some. Especially as it's a question of you starving as well as me. If I had enough to pay your fares to Bursley I'd pack you off. But I haven't."

She could only hear his exasperating voice. The end of the bed was between her eyes and his.

"Liar!" she said, with uncompromising distinctness. The word reached him barbed with all the poison of her contempt and disgust.

There was a pause.

"Oh! I'm a liar, am I? Thanks. I lied enough to get you, I'll admit. But you never complained of that. I remember be-ginning the New Year well with a thumping lie just to have a sight of you, my vixen. But you didn't complain then. I took you with only the clothes on your back. And I've spent every cent I had on you. And now I'm spun, you call me a liar."

She said nothing.

"However," he went on, "this is going to come to an end, this is!"

He rose, changed the position of the candle, putting it on a chest of drawers, and then drew his trunk from the wall, and knelt in front of it.

She gathered that he was packing his clothes. At first she did not comprehend his reference to beginning the New Year. Then his meaning revealed itself. That story to her mother about having been attacked by ruffians at the bottom of King Street had been an invention, a ruse to account plausibly for his presence on her mother's doorstep! And she had never suspected that the story was not true. In spite of her experience of his lying, she had never suspected that that particular statement was a lie. What a simpleton she was!

There was a continual movement in the room for about a quarter of an hour. Then a key turned in the lock of the trunk.

His head popped up over the foot of the bed. "This isn't a joke, you know," he said.

She kept silence.

"I give you one more chance. Will you write to your mother—or Constance if you like—or won't you?"

She scorned to reply in any way.

"I'm your husband," he said. "And it's your duty to obey me, particularly in an affair like this. I order you to write to your mother."

The corners of her lips turned downwards.

Angered by her mute obstinacy, he broke away from the bed with a sudden gesture.

"You do as you like," he cried, putting on his overcoat, "and I shall do as I like. You can't say I haven't warned you. It's your own deliberate choice, mind you! Whatever happens to you you've brought on yourself." He lifted and shrugged his shoulders to get the overcoat exactly into place on his shoulders.

She would not speak a word, not even to insist that she was indisposed.

He pushed his trunk outside the door, and returned to the bed.

"You understand," he said menacingly; "I'm off."

She looked up at the foul ceiling.

"Hm!" he sniffed, bringing his reserves of pride to combat the persistent silence that was damaging his dignity. And he went off, sticking his head forward like a pugilist.

"Here!" she muttered. "You're forgetting this."

He turned.

She stretched her hand to the night-table and held up a red circlet.

"What is it?"

"It's the bit of paper off the cigar you bought in the Rue Montmartre this afternoon," she answered, in a significant tone.

He hesitated, then swore violently, and bounced out of the room. He had made her suffer, but she was almost repaid for everything by that moment of cruel triumph. She exulted in it, and never forgot it.

Five minutes later, the gloomy menial in felt slippers and alpaca jacket, who seemed to pass the whole of his life flitting in and out of bedrooms like a rabbit in a warren, carried Gerald's trunk downstairs. She recognized the peculiar tread of his slippers.

Then there was a knock at the door. The landlady entered, actuated by a legitimate curiosity.

"Madame is suffering?" the landlady began.

Sophia refused offers of food and nursing.

"Madame knows without doubt that monsieur has gone away?"

195

"Has he paid the bill?" Sophia asked bluntly.

"But yes, madame, till to-morrow. Then madame has want of nothing?"

"If you will extinguish the candle," said Sophia.

He had deserted her, then!

"All this," she reflected, listening in the dark to the ceaseless rattle of the street, "because mother and Constance wanted to see the elephant, and I had to go into father's room! I should never have caught sight of him from the drawing-room window!"

IV

She passed a night of physical misery, exasperated by the tireless rattling vitality of the street. She kept saying to herself: "I'm all alone now, and I'm going to be ill. I am ill." She saw herself dying in Paris, and heard the expressions of facile sympathy and idle curiosity drawn forth by the sight of the dead body of this foreign woman in a little Paris hotel. She reached the stage, in the gradual excruciation of her nerves, when she was obliged to concentrate her agonized mind on an intense and painful expectancy of the next new noise, which when it came increased her torture and decreased her strength to support it. She went through all the interminable dilatoriness of the dawn, from the moment when she could scarcely discern the window to the moment when she could read the word 'Bock' on the red circlet of paper which had tossed all night on the sea of the counterpane. She knew she would never sleep again. She could not imagine herself asleep; and then she was startled by a sound that seemed to clash with the rest of her impressions. It was a knocking at the door. With a start she perceived that she must have been asleep.

"Enter," she murmured.

There entered the menial in alpaca. His waxen face showed a morose commiseration. He noiselessly approached the bed—he seemed to have none of the characteristics of a man, but to be a creature infinitely mysterious and aloof from humanity—and held out to Sophia a visiting card in his grey hand.

It was Chirac's card.

"Monsieur asked for monsieur," said the waiter. "And then, as monsieur had gone away he demanded to see madame. He says it is very important."

Her heart jumped, partly in vague alarm, and partly with a sense of relief at this chance of speaking to some one whom she knew. She tried to reflect rationally.

"What time is it?" she inquired.

"Eleven o'clock, madame."

This was surprising. The fact that it was eleven o'clock destroyed the remains of her self-confidence. How could it be eleven o'clock, with the dawn scarcely finished?

"He says it is very important," repeated the waiter, imperturbably and solemnly. "Will madame see him an instant?"

Between resignation and anticipation she said: "Yes."

"It is well, madame," said the waiter, disappearing without a sound.

She sat up and managed to drag her matinee from a chair and put it around her shoulders. Then she sank back from weakness, physical and spiritual. She hated to receive Chirac in a bedroom, and particularly in that bedroom. But the hotel had no public room except the dining-room, which began to be occupied after eleven o'clock. Moreover, she could not possibly get up. Yes, on the whole she was pleased to see Chirac. He was almost her only acquaintance, assuredly the only being whom she could by any stretch of meaning call a friend, in the whole of Europe. Gerald and she had wandered to and fro, skimming always over the real life of nations, and never penetrating into it. There was no place for them, because they had made none. With the exception of Chirac, whom an accident of business had thrown, into Gerald's company years before, they had no social relations. Gerald was not a man to make friends; he did not seem to need friends, or at any rate to feel the want of them. But, as chance had given him Chirac, he maintained the connection whenever they came to Paris. Sophia, of course, had not been able to escape from the solitude imposed by existence in hotels. Since her marriage she had never spoken to a woman in the way of intimacy. But once or twice she had approached intimacy with Chirac, whose wistful admiration for her always aroused into activity her desire to charm.

Preceded by the menial, he came into the room hurriedly, apologetically, with an air of acute anxiety. And as he saw her lying on her back, with flushed features, her hair disarranged, and only the grace of the silk ribbons of her matinee to mitigate the melancholy repulsiveness of her surroundings, that anxiety seemed to deepen. "Dear madame," he stammered, "all my excuses!" He hastened to the bedside and kissed her hand—a little peek according to his custom. "You are ill?"

"I have my migraine," she said. "You want Gerald?"

"Yes," he said diffidently. "He had promised——"

"He has left me," Sophia interrupted him in her weak and fatigued voice. She closed her eyes as she uttered the words.

"Left you?" He glanced round to be sure that the waiter had retired.

"Quitted me! Abandoned me! Last night!"

"Not possible!" he breathed.

She nodded. She felt intimate with him. Like all secretive persons, she could be suddenly expansive at times.

"It is serious?" he questioned.

"All that is most serious," she replied.

"And you ill! Ah, the wretch! Ah, the wretch! That, for example!" He waved his hat about.

"What is it you want, Chirac?" she demanded, in a confidential tone.

"Eh, well," said Chirac. "You do not know where he has gone?"

"No. What do you want?" she insisted.

He was nervous. He fidgetted. She guessed that, though warm with sympathy for her plight, he was preoccupied by interests and apprehensions of his own. He did not refuse her request temporarily to leave the astonishing matter of her situation in order to discuss the matter of his visit.

"Eh, well! He came to me yesterday afternoon in the Rue Croissant to borrow some money."

She understood then the object of Gerald's stroll on the previous afternoon.

"I hope you didn't lend him any," she said.

"Eh, well! It was like this. He said he ought to have received five thousand francs yesterday morning, but that he had had a telegram that it would not arrive till to-day. And he had need of five hundred francs at once. I had not five hundred francs"—he smiled sadly, as if to insinuate that he did not handle such sums—"but I borrowed it from the cashbox of the journal. It is necessary, absolutely, that I should return it this morning." He spoke with increased seriousness. "Your husband said he would take a cab and bring me the money immediately on the arrival of the post this morning—about nine o'clock. Pardon me for deranging you with such a——"

He stopped. She could see that he really was grieved to 'derange' her, but that circumstances pressed.

"At my paper," he murmured, "it is not so easy as that to—in fine——!"

Gerald had genuinely been at his last francs. He had not lied when she thought he had lied. The nakedness of his character showed now. Instantly upon the final and definite cessation of the lawful supply of money, he had set his wits to obtain money unlawfully. He had, in fact, simply stolen it from Chirac, with the ornamental addition of endangering Chirac's reputation and situation—as a sort of reward to Chirac for the kindness! And, further, no sooner had he got hold of the money than it had intoxicated him, and he had yielded to the first fatuous temptation. He had no sense of responsibility, no scruple. And as for common prudence—had he not risked permanent disgrace and even prison for a paltry sum which he would certainly squander in two or three days? Yes, it was indubitable that he would stop at nothing, at nothing whatever.

"You did not know that he was coming to me?" asked Chirac, pulling his short, silky brown beard.

"No," Sophia answered.

"But he said that you had charged him with your friendlinesses to me!" He nodded his head once or twice, sadly but candidly accepting, in his quality of a Latin, the plain facts of human nature—reconciling himself to them at once.

Sophia revolted at this crowning detail of the structure of Gerald's rascality.

"It is fortunate that I can pay you," she said.

"But——" he tried to protest.

"I have quite enough money."

She did not say this to screen Gerald, but merely from amour-propre. She would not let Chirac think that she was the wife of a man bereft of all honour. And so she clothed Gerald with the rag of having, at any rate, not left her in destitution as well as in sickness. Her assertion seemed a strange one, in view of the fact that he had abandoned her on the previous evening—that is to say, immediately after the borrowing from Chirac. But Chirac did not examine the statement.

"Perhaps he has the intention to send me the money. Perhaps, after all, he is now at the offices——"

"No," said Sophia. "He is gone. Will you go downstairs and wait for me. We will go together to Cook's office. It is English money I have."

"Cook's?" he repeated. The word now so potent had then little significance. "But you are ill. You cannot——"

"I feel better."

She did. Or rather, she felt nothing except the power of her resolve to remove the painful anxiety from that wistful brow. The shame of the trick played on Chirac awakened new forces in her. She dressed in a physical torment which, however, had no more reality than a nightmare. She searched in a place where even an inquisitive husband would not think of looking, and then, painfully, she descended the long stairs, holding to the rail, which swam round and round her, carrying the whole staircase with it. "After all," she thought, "I can't be seriously ill, or I shouldn't have been able to get up and go out like this. I never guessed early this morning that I could do it! I can't possibly be as ill as I thought I was!"

And in the vestibule she encountered Chirac's face, lightening at the sight of her, which proved to him that his deliverance was really to be accomplished.

"Permit me——"

"I'm all right," she smiled, tottering. "Get a cab." It suddenly occurred to her that she might quite as easily have given him the money in English notes; he could have changed them. But she had not thought. Her brain would not operate. She was dreaming and waking together.

He helped her into the cab.

V

In the bureau de change there was a little knot of English, people, with naive, romantic, and honest faces, quite different from the faces outside in the street. No corruption in those faces, but a sort of wondering and infantile sincerity, rather out of its element and lost in a land too unsophisticated, seeming to belong to an earlier age! Sophia liked their tourist stare, and their plain and ugly clothes. She longed to be back in England, longed for a moment with violence, drowning in that desire.

The English clerk behind his brass bars took her notes, and carefully examined them one by one. She watched him, not entirely convinced of his reality, and thought vaguely of the detestable morning when she had abstracted the notes from Gerald's pocket. She was filled with pity for the simple, ignorant Sophia of those days, the Sophia who still had a few ridiculous illusions concerning Gerald's character. Often, since, she had been tempted to break into the money, but she had always withstood the temptation, saying to herself that an hour of more urgent need would come. It had come. She was proud of her firmness, of the force of will which had enabled her to reserve the fund intact. The clerk gave her a keen look, and then asked her how she would take the French money. And she saw the notes falling down one after another on to the counter as the clerk separated them with a snapping sound of the paper.

Chirac was beside her.

"Does that make the count?" she said, having pushed towards him five hundred-franc notes.

"I should not know how to thank you," he said, accepting the notes.

"Truly—"

His joy was unmistakably eager. He had had a shock and a fright, and he now saw the danger past. He could return to the cashier of his newspaper, and fling down the money with a lordly and careless air, as if to say: "When it is a question of these English, one can always be sure!" But first he would escort her to the hotel. She declined—she did not know why, for he was her sole point of moral support in all France. He insisted. She yielded. So she turned her back, with regret, on that little English oasis in the Sahara of Paris, and staggered to the fiacre.

And now that she had done what she had to do, she lost control of her body, and reclined flaccid and inert. Chirac was evidently alarmed. He did not speak, but glanced at her from time to time with eyes full of fear. The carriage appeared to her to be swimming amid waves over great depths. Then she was aware of a heavy weight against her shoulder; she had slipped down upon Chirac, unconscious.

CHAPTER V

FEVER

I

Then she was lying in bed in a small room, obscure because it was heavily curtained; the light came through the inner pair of curtains of ecru lace, with a beautiful soft silvery quality. A man was standing by the side of the bed—not Chirac.

"Now, madame," he said to her, with kind firmness, and speaking with a charming exaggerated purity of the vowels. "You have the mucous fever. I have had it myself. You will be forced to take baths, very frequently. I must ask you to reconcile yourself to that, to be good."

She did not reply. It did not occur to her to reply. But she certainly thought that this doctor—he was probably a doctor—was overestimating her case. She felt better than she had felt for two days. Still, she did not desire to move, nor was she in the least anxious as to her surroundings. She lay quiet.

A woman in a rather coquettish deshabille watched over her with expert skill.

Later, Sophia seemed to be revisiting the sea on whose waves the cab had swum; but now she was under the sea, in a watery gulf, terribly deep; and the sounds of the world came to her through the water, sudden and strange. Hands seized her and forced her from the subaqueous grotto where she had hidden into new alarms. And she briefly perceived that there was a large bath by the side of the bed, and that she was being pushed into it. The water was icy cold. After that her outlook upon things was for a time clearer and more precise. She knew from fragments of talk which she heard that she was put into the cold bath by her bed every three hours, night and day, and that she remained in it for ten minutes. Always, before the bath, she had to drink a glass of wine, and sometimes another glass while she was in the bath. Beyond this wine, and occasionally a cup of soup, she took nothing, had no wish to take anything. She grew perfectly accustomed to these extraordinary habits of life, to this merging of night and day into one monotonous and endless repetition of the same rite amid the same circumstances on exactly the same spot. Then followed a period during which she objected to being constantly wakened up for this annoying immersion. And she fought against it even in her dreams. Long days seemed to pass when she could not be sure whether she had been put into the bath or not, when all external phenomena were disconcertingly interwoven with matters which she knew to be merely fanciful. And then she was overwhelmed by the hopeless gravity of her state. She felt that her state was desperate. She felt that she was dying. Her unhappiness was extreme, not because she was dying, but because the veils of sense were so puzzling, so exasperating, and because her exhausted body was so vitiated, in every fibre, by disease. She was perfectly aware that she was going to die. She cried aloud for a pair of scissors. She wanted to cut off her hair, and to send part of it to Constance and part of it to her mother, in separate packages. She insisted upon separate packages. Nobody would give her a pair of scissors. She implored, meekly, haughtily, furiously, but nobody would satisfy her. It seemed to her shocking that all her hair should go with her into her coffin while Constance and her mother had nothing by which to remember her, no tangible souvenir of her beauty. Then she fought for the scissors. She clutched at some one—always through those baffling veils— who was putting her into the bath by the bedside, and fought frantically. It appeared to her that this some one was the rather stout woman who had supped at Sylvain's with the quarrelsome Englishman, four years ago. She could not rid herself of this singular conceit, though she knew it to be absurd....

A long time afterwards—it seemed like a century—she did actually and unmistakably see the woman sitting by her bed, and the woman was crying.

"Why are you crying?" Sophia asked wonderingly.

And the other, younger, woman, who was standing at the foot of the bed, replied:

"You do well to ask! It is you who have hurt her, in your delirium, when you so madly demanded the scissors."

The stout woman smiled with the tears on her cheeks; but Sophia wept, from remorse. The stout woman looked old, worn, and untidy. The other one was much younger. Sophia did not trouble to inquire from them who they were.

That little conversation formed a brief interlude in the delirium, which overtook her again and distorted everything. She forgot, however, that she was destined to die.

One day her brain cleared. She could be sure that she had gone to sleep in the morning and not wakened till the evening. Hence she had not been put into the bath.

"Have I had my baths?" she questioned.

It was the doctor who faced her.

"No," he said, "the baths are finished."

She knew from his face that she was out of danger. Moreover, she was conscious of a new feeling in her body, as though the fount of physical energy within her, long interrupted, had recommenced to flow—but very slowly, a trickling. It was a rebirth. She was not glad, but her body itself was glad; her body had an existence of its own.

She was now often left by herself in the bedroom. To the right of the foot of the bed was a piano in walnut, and to the left a chimney-piece with a large mirror. She wanted to look at herself in the mirror. But it was a very long way off. She tried to sit up, and could not. She hoped that one day she would be able to get as far as the mirror. She said not a word about this to either of the two women.

Often they would sit in the bedroom and talk without ceasing. Sophia learnt that the stout woman was named Foucault, and the other Laurence. Sometimes Laurence would address Madame Foucault as Aimee, but usually she was more formal. Madame Foucault always called the other Laurence.

Sophia's curiosity stirred and awoke. But she could not obtain any very exact information as to where she was, except that the house was in the Rue Breda, off the Rue Notre Dame de Lorette. She recollected vaguely that the reputation of the street was sinister. It appeared that, on the day when she had gone out with Chirac, the upper part of the Rue Notre Dame de Lorette was closed for repairs—(this she remembered)—and that the cabman had turned up the Rue Breda in order to make a detour, and that it was just opposite to the house of Madame Foucault that she had lost consciousness. Madame Foucault happened to be getting into a cab at the moment; but she had told Chirac nevertheless to carry Sophia into the house, and a policeman had helped. Then, when the doctor came, it was discovered that she could not be moved, save to a hospital, and both Madame Foucault and Laurence were determined that no friend of Chirac's should be committed to the horrors of a Paris hospital. Madame Foucault had suffered in one as a patient, and Laurence had been a nurse in another....

Chirac was now away. The women talked loosely of a war.

"How kind you have been!" murmured Sophia, with humid eyes.

But they silenced her with gestures. She was not to talk. They seemed to have nothing further to tell her. They said Chirac would be returning perhaps soon, and that she could talk to him. Evidently they both held Chirac in affection. They said often that he was a charming boy.

Bit by bit Sophia comprehended the length and the seriousness of her illness, and the immense devotion of the two women, and the terrific disturbance of their lives, and her own debility. She saw that the women were strongly attached to her, and she could not understand why, as she had never done anything for them, whereas they had done everything for her. She had not learnt that benefits rendered, not benefits received, are the cause of such attachments.

All the time she was plotting, and gathering her strength to disobey orders and get as far as the mirror. Her preliminary studies and her preparations were as elaborate as those of a prisoner arranging to escape from a fortress. The first attempt was a failure. The second succeeded. Though she could not stand without support, she managed by clinging to the bed to reach a chair, and to push the chair in front of her until it approached the mirror. The enterprise was exciting and terrific. Then she saw a face in the glass: white, incredibly emaciated, with great, wild, staring eyes; and the shoulders were bent as though with age. It was a painful, almost a horrible sight. It frightened her, so that in her alarm she recoiled from it. Not attending sufficiently to the chair, she sank to the ground. She could not pick herself up, and she was caught there, miserably, by her angered jailers. The vision of her face taught her more efficiently than anything else the gravity of her adventure. As the women lifted her inert, repentant mass into the bed, she reflected, "How queer my life is!" It seemed to her that she ought to have been trimming hats in the showroom instead of being in that curtained, mysterious, Parisian interior.

II

One day Madame Foucault knocked at the door of Sophia's little room (this ceremony of knocking was one of the indications that Sophia, convalescent, had been reinstated in her rights as an individual), and cried:

"Madame, one is going to leave you all alone for some time."

"Come in," said Sophia, who was sitting up in an armchair, and reading.

Madame Foucault opened the door. "One is going to leave you all alone for some time," she repeated in a low, confidential voice, sharply contrasting with her shriek behind the door.

Sophia nodded and smiled, and Madame Foucault also nodded and smiled.

But Madame Foucault's face quickly resumed its anxious expression.

"The servant's brother marries himself to-day, and she implored me to accord her two days—what would you? Madame Laurence is out. And I must go out. It is four o'clock. I shall re-enter at six o'clock striking. Therefore ..."

"Perfectly," Sophia concurred.

She looked curiously at Madame Foucault, who was carefully made up and arranged for the street, in a dress of yellow tussore with blue ornaments, bright lemon-coloured gloves, a little blue bonnet, and a little white parasol not wider when opened than her shoulders. Cheeks, lips, and eyes were heavily charged with rouge, powder, or black. And that too abundant waist had been most cunningly confined in a belt that descended beneath, instead of rising above, the lower masses of the vast torso. The general effect was worthy of the effort that must have gone to it. Madame Foucault was not rejuvenated by her toilette, but it almost procured her pardon for the crime of being over forty, fat, creased, and worn out. It was one of those defeats that are a triumph.

"You are very chic," said Sophia, uttering her admiration.

"Ah!" said Madame Foucault, shrugging the shoulders of disillusion.

"Chic! What does that do?"

But she was pleased.

The front-door banged. Sophia, by herself for the first time in the flat into which she had been carried unconscious and which she had never since left, had the disturbing sensation of being surrounded by mysterious rooms and mysterious things. She tried to continue reading, but the sentences conveyed nothing to her. She rose—she could walk now a little—and looked out of the window, through the interstices of the pattern of the lace curtains. The window gave on the courtyard, which was about sixteen feet below her. A low wall divided the courtyard from that of the next house. And the windows of the two houses, only to be distinguished by the different tints of their yellow paint, rose tier above tier in level floors, continuing beyond Sophia's field of vision. She pressed her face against the glass, and remembered the St. Luke's Square of her childhood; and just as there from the showroom window she could not even by pressing her face against the glass see the pavement, so here she could not see the roof; the courtyard was like the bottom of a well. There was no end to the windows; six storeys she could count, and the sills of a seventh were the limit of her view. Every window was heavily curtained, like her own. Some of the upper ones had green sunblinds. Scarcely any sound! Mysteries brooded without as well as within the flat of Madame Foucault. Sophia saw a bodiless hand twitch at a curtain and vanish. She noticed a green bird in a tiny cage on a sill in the next house. A woman whom she took to be the concierge appeared in the courtyard, deposited a small plant in the track of a ray of sunshine that lighted a corner for a couple of hours in the afternoon, and disappeared again. Then she heard a piano—somewhere. That was all. The feeling that secret and strange lives were being lived behind those baffling windows, that humanity was everywhere intimately pulsing around her, oppressed her spirit yet not quite unpleasantly. The environment softened her glance upon the spectacle of existence, insomuch that sadness became a voluptuous pleasure. And the environment threw her back on herself, into a sensuous contemplation of the fundamental fact of Sophia Scales, formerly Sophia Baines.

She turned to the room, with the marks of the bath on the floor by the bed, and the draped piano that was never opened, and her two trunks filling up the corner opposite the door. She had the idea of thoroughly examining those trunks, which Chirac or somebody else must have fetched from the hotel. At the top of one of them was her purse, tied up with old ribbon and ostentatiously sealed! How comical these French people were when they deemed it necessary to be serious! She emptied both trunks, scrutinizing minutely all her goods, and thinking of the varied occasions upon which she had obtained them. Then she carefully restored them, her mind full of souvenirs newly awakened.

She sighed as she straightened her back. A clock struck in another room. It seemed to invite her towards discoveries. She had been in no other room of the flat. She knew nothing of the rest of the flat save by sound. For neither of the other women had ever described it, nor had it occurred to them that Sophia might care to leave her room though she could not leave the house.

She opened her door, and glanced along the dim corridor, with which she was familiar. She knew that the kitchen lay next to her little room, and that next to the kitchen came the front-door. On the opposite side of the corridor were four double-doors. She crossed to the pair of doors facing her own little door, and quietly turned the handle, but the doors were locked; the same with the next pair. The third pair yielded, and she was in a large bedroom, with three windows on the street. She saw that the second pair of doors, which she had failed to unfasten, also opened into this room. Between the two pairs of doors was a wide bed. In front of the central window was a large dressing-table. To the left of the bed, half hiding the locked doors, was a large screen. On the marble mantelpiece, reflected in a huge mirror, that ascended to the ornate cornice, was a gilt-and-basalt clock, with pendants to match. On the opposite side of the room from this was a long wide couch. The floor was of polished oak, with a skin on either side of the bed. At the foot of the bed was a small writing-table, with a penny bottle of ink on it. A few coloured prints and engravings—representing, for example, Louis Philippe and his family, and people perishing on a raft—broke the tedium of the walls. The first impression on Sophia's eye was one of sombre splendour. Everything had the air of being richly ornamented, draped, looped, carved, twisted, brocaded into gorgeousness. The dark crimson bed-hangings fell from massive rosettes in majestic folds. The counterpane was covered with lace. The window-curtains had amplitude beyond the necessary, and they were suspended from behind fringed and pleated valances. The green sofa and its sateen cushions were stiff with applied embroidery. The chandelier hanging from the middle of the ceiling, modelled to represent cupids holding festoons, was a glittering confusion of gilt and lustres; the lustres tinkled when Sophia stood on a certain part of the floor. The cane-seated chairs were completely gilded. There was an effect of spaciousness. And the situation of the bed between the two double-doors, with the three windows in front and other pairs of doors communicating with other rooms on either hand, produced in addition an admirable symmetry.

But Sophia, with the sharp gaze of a woman brought up in the traditions of a modesty so proud that it scorns ostentation, quickly tested and condemned the details of this chamber that imitated every luxury. Nothing in it, she found, was 'good.' And in St. Luke's Square 'goodness' meant honest workmanship, permanence, the absence of pretence. All the stuffs were cheap and showy and shabby; all the furniture was cracked, warped, or broken. The clock showed five minutes past twelve at five o'clock. And further, dust was everywhere, except in those places where even the most perfunctory cleaning could not have left it. In the obscurer pleatings of draperies it lay thick. Sophia's lip curled, and instinctively she lifted her peignoir. One of her mother's phrases came into her head: 'a lick and a promise.' And then another: "If you want to leave dirt, leave it where everybody can see it, not in the corners."

She peeped behind the screen, and all the horrible welter of a cabinet de toilette met her gaze: a repulsive medley of foul waters, stained vessels and cloths, brushes, sponges, powders, and pastes. Clothes were hung up in disorder on rough nails; among them she recognized a dressing-gown of Madame Foucault's, and, behind affairs of later date, the dazzling scarlet cloak in which she had first seen Madame Foucault, dilapidated now. So this was Madame Foucault's room! This was the bower from which that elegance emerged, the filth from which had sprung the mature blossom!

She passed from that room direct to another, of which the shutters were closed, leaving it in twilight. This room too was a bedroom, rather smaller than the middle one, and having only one window, but furnished with the same dubious opulence. Dust covered it everywhere, and small footmarks were visible in the dust on the floor. At the back was a small door, papered to match the wall, and within this door was a cabinet de toilette, with no light and no air; neither in the room nor in the closet was there any sign of individual habitation. She traversed the main bedroom again and found another bedroom to balance the second one, but open to the full light of day, and in a state of extreme disorder; the double-pillowed bed had not even been made: clothes and towels draped all the furniture: shoes were about the floor, and on a piece of string tied across the windows hung a single white stocking, wet. At the back was a cabinet de toilette, as dark as the other one, a vile malodorous mess of appliances whose familiar forms loomed vague and extraordinarily sinister in the dense obscurity. Sophia turned away with the righteous disgust of one whose preparations for the gaze of the world are as candid and simple as those of a child. Concealed dirt shocked her as much as it would have shocked her mother; and as for the trickeries of the toilet table, she contemned them as harshly as a young saint who has never been tempted contemns moral weakness. She thought of the strange flaccid daily life of those two women, whose hours seemed to slip unprofitably away without any result of achievement. She had actually witnessed nothing; but since the beginning of her convalescence her ears had heard, and she could piece the evidences together. There was never any sound in the flat, outside the kitchen, until noon. Then vague noises and smells would commence. And about one o'clock Madame Foucault, disarrayed, would come to inquire if the servant had attended to the needs of the invalid. Then the odours of cookery would accentuate themselves; bells rang; fragments of conversations escaped through doors ajar; occasionally a man's voice or a heavy step; then the fragrance of coffee; sometimes the sound of a kiss, the banging of the front door, the noise of

202

brushing, or of the shaking of a carpet, a little scream as at some trifling domestic contretemps. Laurence, still in a dressing-gown, would lounge into Sophia's room, dirty, haggard, but polite with a curious stiff ceremony, and would drink her coffee there. This wandering in peignoirs would continue till three o'clock, and then Laurence might say, as if nerving herself to an unusual and immense effort: "I must be dressed by five o'clock. I have not a moment." Often Madame Foucault did not dress at all; on such days she would go to bed immediately after dinner, with the remark that she didn't know what was the matter with her, but she was exhausted. And then the servant would retire to her seventh floor, and there would be silence until, now and then, faint creepings were heard at midnight or after. Once or twice, through the chinks of her door, Sophia had seen a light at two o'clock in the morning, just before the dawn.

Yet these were the women who had saved her life, who between them had put her into a cold bath every three hours night and day for weeks! Surely it was impossible after that to despise them for shiftlessness and talkative idling in peignoirs; impossible to despise them for anything whatever! But Sophia, conscious of her inheritance of strong and resolute character, did despise them as poor things. The one point on which she envied them was their formal manners to her, which seemed to become more dignified and graciously distant as her health improved. It was always 'Madame,' 'Madame,' to her, with an intonation of increasing deference. They might have been apologizing to her for themselves.

She prowled into all the corners of the flat; but she discovered no more rooms, nothing but a large cupboard crammed with Madame Foucault's dresses. Then she went back to the large bedroom, and enjoyed the busy movement and rattle of the sloping street, and had long, vague yearnings for strength and for freedom in wide, sane places. She decided that on the morrow she would dress herself 'properly,' and never again wear a peignoir; the peignoir and all that it represented, disgusted her. And while looking at the street she ceased to see it and saw Cook's office and Chirac helping her into the carriage. Where was he? Why had he brought her to this impossible abode? What did he mean by such conduct? But could he have acted otherwise? He had done the one thing that he could do…. Chance! … Chance! And why an impossible abode? Was one place more impossible than another? All this came of running away from home with Gerald. It was remarkable that she seldom thought of Gerald. He had vanished from her life as he had come into it—madly, preposterously. She wondered what the next stage in her career would be. She certainly could not forecast it. Perhaps Gerald was starving, or in prison … Bah! That exclamation expressed her appalling disdain of Gerald and of the Sophia who had once deemed him the paragon of men. Bah!

A carriage stopping in front of the house awakened her from her meditation. Madame Foucault and a man very much younger than Madame Foucault got out of it. Sophia fled. After all, this prying into other people's rooms was quite inexcusable. She dropped on to her own bed and picked up a book, in case Madame Foucault should come in.

III

In the evening, just after night had fallen, Sophia on the bed heard the sound of raised and acrimonious voices in Madame Foucault's room. Nothing except dinner had happened since the arrival of Madame Foucault and the young man. These two had evidently dined informally in the bedroom on a dish or so prepared by Madame Foucault, who had herself served Sophia with her invalid's repast. The odours of cookery still hung in the air.

The noise of virulent discussion increased and continued, and then Sophia could hear sobbing, broken by short and fierce phrases from the man. Then the door of the bedroom opened brusquely. "J'en ai soupé!" exclaimed the man, in tones of angry disgust. "Laisse-moi, je te prie!" And then a soft muffled sound, as of a struggle, a quick step, and the very violent banging of the front door. After that there was a noticeable silence, save for the regular sobbing. Sophia wondered when it would cease, that monotonous sobbing.

"What is the matter?" she called out from her bed.

The sobbing grew louder, like the sobbing of a child who has detected an awakening of sympathy and instinctively begins to practise upon it. In the end Sophia arose and put on the peignoir which she had almost determined never to wear again. The broad corridor was lighted by a small, smelling oil-lamp with a crimson globe. That soft, transforming radiance seemed to paint the whole corridor with voluptuous luxury: so much so that it was impossible to believe that the smell came from the lamp. Under the lamp lay Madame Foucault on the floor, a shapeless mass of lace, frilled linen, and corset; her light brown hair was loose and spread about the floor. At the first glance, the creature abandoned to grief made a romantic and striking picture, and Sophia thought for an instant that she had at length encountered life on a plane that would correspond to her dreams of romance. And she was impressed, with a feeling somewhat akin to that of a middling commoner when confronted with a viscount. There was, in the distance, something imposing and sensational about that prone, trembling figure. The tragic works of love were therein apparently manifest, in a sort of dignified beauty. But when Sophia bent over Madame Foucault, and touched her flabbiness, this illusion at once vanished; and instead of being dramatically pathetic the woman was ridiculous. Her face, especially as damaged by tears, could not support the ordeal of inspection; it was horrible; not a picture, but a palette; or like the coloured design of a pavement artist after a heavy shower. Her great, relaxed eyelids alone would have rendered any face absurd; and there were monstrous details far worse than the eyelids. Then she was amazingly fat; her flesh seemed to be escaping at all ends from a corset strained to the utmost limit. And above her boots—she was still wearing dainty, high-heeled, tightly laced boots—the calves bulged suddenly out.

As a woman of between forty and fifty, the obese sepulchre of a dead vulgar beauty, she had no right to passions and tears and homage, or even the means of life; she had no right to expose herself picturesquely beneath a crimson glow in all the panoply of ribboned garters and lacy seductiveness. It was silly; it was disgraceful. She ought to have known that only youth and slimness have the right to appeal to the feelings by indecent abandonments.

Such were the thoughts that mingled with the sympathy of the beautiful and slim Sophia as she bent down to Madame Foucault. She was sorry for her landlady, but at the same time she despised her, and resented her woe.

"What is the matter?" she asked quietly.

"He has chucked me!" stammered Madame Foucault. "And he's the last. I have no one now!"

She rolled over in the most grotesque manner, kicking up her legs, with a fresh outburst of sobs. Sophia felt quite ashamed for her.

"Come and lie down. Come now!" she said, with a touch of sharpness.

"You musn't lie there like that."

Madame Foucault's behaviour was really too outrageous. Sophia helped her, morally rather than physically, to rise, and then persuaded her into the large bedroom. Madame Foucault fell on the bed, of which the counterpane had been thrown over the foot. Sophia covered the lower part of her heaving body with the counterpane.

"Now, calm yourself, please!"

This room too was lit in crimson, by a small lamp that stood on the night-table, and though the shade of the lamp was cracked, the general effect of the great chamber was incontestably romantic. Only the pillows of the wide bed and a small semi-circle of floor were illuminated, all the rest lay in shadow. Madame Foucault's head had dropped between the pillows. A tray containing dirty plates and glasses and a wine-bottle was speciously picturesque on the writing-table.

Despite her genuine gratitude to Madame Foucault for astounding care during her illness, Sophia did not like her landlady, and the present scene made her coldly wrathful. She saw the probability of having another's troubles piled on the top of her own. She did not, in her mind, actively object, because she felt that she could not be more hopelessly miserable than she was; but she passively resented the imposition. Her reason told her that she ought to sympathize with this ageing, ugly, disagreeable, undignified woman; but her heart was reluctant; her heart did not want to know anything at all about Madame Foucault, nor to enter in any way into her private life.

"I have not a single friend now," stammered Madame Foucault.

"Oh, yes, you have," said Sophia, cheerfully. "You have Madame Laurence."

"Laurence—that is not a friend. You know what I mean."

"And me! I am your friend!" said Sophia, in obedience to her conscience.

"You are very kind," replied Madame Foucault, from the pillow. "But you know what I mean."

The fact was that Sophia did know what she meant. The terms of their intercourse had been suddenly changed. There was no pretentious ceremony now, but the sincerity that disaster brings. The vast structure of make-believe, which between them they had gradually built, had crumbled to nothing.

"I never treated badly any man in my life," whimpered Madame Foucault. "I have always been a—good girl. There is not a man who can say I have not been a good girl. Never was I a girl like the rest. And every one has said so. Ah! when I tell you that once I had a hotel in the Avenue de la Reine Hortense. Four horses … I have sold a horse to Madame Musard…. You know Madame Musard…. But one cannot make economies.

Impossible to make economies! Ah! In 'fifty-six I was spending a hundred thousand francs a year. That cannot last. Always I have said to myself: 'That cannot last.' Always I had the intention…. But what would you? I installed myself here, and borrowed money to pay for the furniture. There did not remain to me one jewel. The men are poltroons, all! I could let three bedrooms for three hundred and fifty francs a month, and with serving meals and so on I could live."

"Then that," Sophia interrupted, pointing to her own bedroom across the corridor, "is your room?"

"Yes," said Madame Foucault. "I put you in it because at the moment all these were let. They are so no longer. Only one—Laurence—and she does not pay me always. What would you? Tenants—that does not find itself at the present hour…. I have nothing, and I owe. And he quits me. He chooses this moment to quit me! And why? For nothing. For nothing. That is not for his money that I regret him. No, no! You know, at his age—he is twenty-five—and with a woman like me—one is not generous! No. I loved him. And then a man is a moral support, always. I loved him. It is at my age, mine, that one knows how to love. Beauty goes always, but not the temperament! Ah, that—No! … I loved him. I love him."

Sophia's face tingled with a sudden emotion caused by the repetition of those last three words, whose spell no usage can mar. But she said nothing.

"Do you know what I shall become? There is nothing but that for me. And I know of such, who are there already. A charwoman! Yes, a charwoman! More soon or more late. Well, that is life. What would you? One exists always." Then in a different tone: "I demand your pardon, madame, for talking like this. I ought to have shame."

And Sophia felt that in listening she also ought to be ashamed. But she was not ashamed. Everything seemed very natural, and even ordinary. And, moreover, Sophia was full of the sense of her superiority over the woman on the bed. Four years ago, in the Restaurant Sylvain, the ingenuous and ignorant Sophia had shyly sat in awe of the resplendent courtesan, with her haughty stare, her large, easy gestures, and her imperturbable contempt for the man who was paying. And now Sophia knew that she, Sophia, knew all that was to be known about human nature. She had not merely youth, beauty, and virtue, but knowledge—knowledge enough to reconcile her to her own misery. She had a vigorous, clear mind, and a clean conscience. She could look any one in the face, and judge every one too as a woman of the world. Whereas this obscene wreck on the bed had nothing whatever left. She had not merely lost her effulgent beauty, she had become repulsive. She could never have had any commonsense, nor any force of character. Her haughtiness in the day of glory was simply fatuous, based on stupidity. She had passed the years in idleness, trailing about all day in stuffy rooms, and emerging at night to impress nincompoops; continually meaning to do things which she never did, continually surprised at the lateness of the hour, continually occupied with the most foolish trifles. And here she was at over forty writhing about on the bare floor because a boy of twenty-five (who MUST be a worthless idiot) had abandoned her after a scene of ridiculous shoutings and stampings. She was dependent on the caprices of a young scamp, the last donkey to turn from her with loathing! Sophia thought: "Goodness! If I had been in her place I shouldn't have been like that. I should have been rich. I should have saved like a miser. I wouldn't have been dependent on anybody at that age. If I couldn't have made a better courtesan than this pitiable woman, I would have drowned myself."

In the harsh vanity of her conscious capableness and young strength she thought thus, half forgetting her own follies, and half excusing them on the ground of inexperience.

Sophia wanted to go round the flat and destroy every crimson lampshade in it. She wanted to shake Madame Foucault into self-respect and sagacity. Moral reprehension, though present in her mind, was only faint. Certainly she felt the immense gulf between the honest woman and the wanton, but she did not feel it as she would have expected to feel it. "What a fool you have been!" she thought; not: "What a sinner!" With her precocious cynicism, which was somewhat unsuited to the lovely northern youthfulness of that face, she said to herself that the whole situation and their relative attitudes would have been different if only Madame Foucault had had the wit to amass a fortune, as (according to Gerald) some of her rivals had succeeded in doing.

And all the time she was thinking, in another part of her mind: "I ought not to be here. It's no use arguing. I ought not to be here. Chirac did the only thing for me there was to do. But I must go now."

Madame Foucault continued to recite her woes, chiefly financial, in a weak voice damp with tears; she also continued to apologize for mentioning herself. She had finished sobbing, and lay looking at the wall, away from Sophia, who stood irresolute near the bed, ashamed for her companion's weakness and incapacity.

"You must not forget," said Sophia, irritated by the unrelieved darkness of the picture drawn by Madame Foucault, "that at least I owe you a considerable sum, and that I am only waiting for you to tell me how much it is. I have asked you twice already, I think."

"Oh, you are still suffering!" said Madame Foucault.

"I am quite well enough to pay my debts," said Sophia.

"I do not like to accept money from you," said Madame Foucault.

"But why not?"

"You will have the doctor to pay."

"Please do not talk in that way," said Sophia. "I have money, and I can pay for everything, and I shall pay for everything."

She was annoyed because she was sure that Madame Foucault was only making a pretence of delicacy, and that in any case her delicacy was preposterous. Sophia had remarked this on the two previous occasions when she had mentioned the subject of bills. Madame Foucault would not treat her as an ordinary lodger, now that the illness was past. She wanted, as it were, to complete brilliantly what she had begun, and to live in Sophia's memory as a unique figure of lavish philanthropy. This was a sentiment, a luxury that she desired to offer herself: the thought that she had played providence to a respectable married lady in distress; she frequently hinted at Sophia's misfortunes and helplessness. But she could not afford the luxury. She gazed at it as a poor woman gazes at costly stuffs through the glass of a shop-window. The truth was, she wanted the luxury for nothing. For a double reason Sophia was exasperated: by Madame Foucault's absurd desire, and by a natural objection to the role of a subject for philanthropy. She would not admit that Madame Foucault's devotion as a nurse entitled her to the satisfaction of being a philanthropist when there was no necessity for philanthropy.

"How long have I been here?" asked Sophia.

"I don't know." murmured Madame Foucault. "Eight weeks—or is it nine?"

"Suppose we say nine," said Sophia.

"Very well," agreed Madame Foucault, apparently reluctant.

"Now, how much must I pay you per week?"

"I don't want anything—I don't want anything! You are a friend of Chirac's. You——"

"Not at all!" Sophia interrupted, tapping her foot and biting her lip.

"Naturally I must pay."

Madame Foucault wept quietly.

"Shall I pay you seventy-five francs a week?" said Sophia, anxious to end the matter.

"It is too much!" Madame Foucault protested, insincerely.

"What? For all you have done for me?"

"I speak not of that," Madame Foucault modestly replied.

If the devotion was not to be paid for, then seventy-five francs a week was assuredly too much, as during more than half the time Sophia had had almost no food. Madame Foucault was therefore within the truth when she again protested, at sight of the bank-notes which Sophia brought from her trunk:

"I am sure that it is too much."

"Not at all!" Sophia repeated. "Nine weeks at seventy-five. That makes six hundred and seventy-five. Here are seven hundreds."

"I have no change," said Madame Foucault. "I have nothing."

"That will pay for the hire of the bath," said Sophia.

She laid the notes on the pillow. Madame Foucault looked at them gluttonously, as any other person would have done in her place. She did not touch them. After an instant she burst into wild tears.

"But why do you cry?" Sophia asked, softened.

"I—I don't know!" spluttered Madame Foucault. "You are so beautiful. I am so content that we saved you." Her great wet eyes rested on Sophia.

It was sentimentality. Sophia ruthlessly set it down as sentimentality. But she was touched. She was suddenly moved. Those women, such as they were in their foolishness, probably had saved her life—and she a stranger! Flaccid as they were, they had been capable of resolute perseverance there. It was possible to say that chance had thrown them upon an enterprise which they could not have abandoned till they or death had won. It was possible to say that they hoped vaguely to derive advantage from their labours. But even then? Judged by an ordinary standard, those women had been angels of mercy. And Sophia was despising them, cruelly taking their motives to pieces, accusing them of incapacity when she herself stood a supreme proof of their capacity in, at any rate, one direction! In a rush of emotion she saw her hardness and her injustice.

She bent down. "Never can I forget how kind you have been to me. It is incredible! Incredible!" She spoke softly, in tones loaded with genuine feeling. It was all she said. She could not embroider on the theme. She had no talent for thanksgiving.

Madame Foucault made the beginning of a gesture, as if she meant to kiss Sophia with those thick, marred lips; but refrained. Her head sank back, and then she had a recurrence of the fit of nervous sobbing.

Immediately afterwards there was the sound of a latchkey in the front-door of the flat; the bedroom door was open. Still sobbing very violently, she cocked her ear, and pushed the bank-notes under the pillow.

Madame Laurence—as she was called: Sophia had never heard her surname—came straight into the bedroom, and beheld the scene with astonishment in her dark twinkling eyes. She was usually dressed in black, because people said that black suited her, and because black was never out of fashion; black was an expression of her idiosyncrasy. She showed a certain elegance, and by comparison with the extreme disorder of Madame Foucault and the deshabille of Sophia her appearance, all fresh from a modish restaurant, was brilliant; it gave her an advantage over the other two—that moral advantage which ceremonial raiment always gives.

"What is it that passes?" she demanded.

"He has chucked me, Laurence!" exclaimed Madame Foucault, in a sort of hysteric scream which seemed to force its way through her sobs. From the extraordinary freshness of Madame Foucault's woe, it might have been supposed that her young man had only that instant strode out.

Laurence and Sophia exchanged a swift glance; and Laurence, of course, perceived that Sophia's relations with her landlady and nurse were now of a different, a more candid order. She indicated her perception of the change by a single slight movement of the eyebrows.

"But listen, Aimee," she said authoritatively. "You must not let yourself go like that. He will return."

"Never!" cried Madame Foucault. "It is finished. And he is the last!"

Laurence, ignoring Madame Foucault, approached Sophia. "You have an air very fatigued," she said, caressing Sophia's shoulder with her gloved hand. "You are pale like everything. All this is not for you. It is not reasonable to remain here, you still suffering! At this hour! Truly not reasonable!"

Her hands persuaded Sophia towards the corridor. And, in fact, Sophia did then notice her own exhaustion. She departed from the room with the ready obedience of physical weakness, and shut her door.

After about half an hour, during which she heard confused noises and murmurings, her door half opened.

"May I enter, since you are not asleep?" It was Laurence's voice.

Twice, now, she had addressed Sophia without adding the formal 'madame.'

"Enter, I beg you," Sophia called from the bed. "I am reading."

Laurence came in. Sophia was both glad and sorry to see her. She was eager to hear gossip which, however, she felt she ought to despise. Moreover, she knew that if they talked that night they would talk as friends, and that Laurence would ever afterwards treat her with the familiarity of a friend. This she dreaded. Still, she knew that she would yield, at any rate, to the temptation to listen to gossip.

"I have put her to bed," said Laurence, in a whisper, as she cautiously closed the door. "The poor woman! Oh, what a charming bracelet! It is a true pearl, naturally?"

Her roving eye had immediately, with an infallible instinct, caught sight of a bracelet which, in taking stock of her possessions, Sophia had accidentally left on the piano. She picked it up, and then put it down again.

"Yes," said Sophia. She was about to add: "It's nearly all the jewellery I possess;" but she stopped.

Laurence moved towards Sophia's bed, and stood over it as she had often done in her quality as nurse. She had taken off her gloves, and she made a piquant, pretty show, with her thirty years, and her agreeable, slightly roguish face, in which were mingled the knowingness of a street boy and the confidence of a woman who has ceased to be surprised at the influence of her snub nose on a highly intelligent man.

"Did she tell you what they had quarrelled about?" Laurence inquired abruptly. And not only the phrasing of the question, but the assured tone in which it was uttered, showed that Laurence meant to be the familiar of Sophia.

"Not a word!" said Sophia.

In this brief question and reply, all was crudely implied that had previously been supposed not to exist. The relations between the two women were altered irretrievably in a moment.

"It must have been her fault!" said Laurence. "With men she is insupportable. I have never understood how that poor woman has made her way. With women she is charming. But she seems to be incapable of not treating men like dogs. Some men adore that, but they are few. Is it not?"

Sophia smiled.

"I have told her! How many times have I told her! But it is useless. It is stronger than she is, and if she finishes on straw one will be able to say that it was because of that. But truly she ought not to have asked him here! Truly that was too much! If he knew…!"

"Why not?" asked Sophia, awkwardly. The answer startled her.

"Because her room has not been disinfected."

"But I thought all the flat had been disinfected?"

"All except her room."

"But why not her room?"

Laurence shrugged her shoulders. "She did not want to disturb her things! Is it that I know, I? She is like that. She takes an idea—and then, there you are!"

"She told me every room had been disinfected."

"She told the same to the police and the doctor."

"Then all the disinfection is useless?"

"Perfectly! But she is like that. This flat might be very remunerative; but with her, never! She has not even paid for the furniture—after two years!"

"But what will become of her?" Sophia asked.

"Ah—that!" Another shrug of the shoulders. "All that I know is that it will be necessary for me to leave here. The last time I brought Monsieur Cerf here, she was excessively rude to him. She has doubtless told you about Monsieur Cerf?"

"No. Who is Monsieur Cerf?"

"Ah! She has not told you? That astonishes me. Monsieur Cerf, that is my friend, you know."

"Oh!" murmured Sophia.

"Yes," Laurence proceeded, impelled by a desire to impress Sophia and to gossip at large. "That is my friend. I knew him at the hospital. It was to please him that I left the hospital. After that we quarrelled for two years; but at the end he gave me right. I did not budge. Two years! It is long. And I had left the hospital. I could have gone back. But I would not. That is not a life, to be nurse in a Paris hospital! No, I drew myself out as well as I could … He is the most charming boy you can imagine! And rich now; that is to say, relatively. He has a cousin infinitely more rich than he. I dined with them both to-night at the Maison Doree. For a luxurious boy, he is a luxurious boy—the cousin I mean. It appears that he has made a fortune in Canada."

"Truly!" said Sophia, with politeness. Laurence's hand was playing on the edge of the bed, and Sophia observed for the first time that it bore a wedding-ring.

"You remark my ring?" Laurence laughed. "That is he—the cousin. 'What!' he said, 'you do not wear an alliance? An alliance is more proper. We are going to arrange that after dinner.' I said that all the jewellers' shops would be closed. 'That is all the same to me,' he said. 'We will open one.' And in effect … it passed like that. He succeeded! Is it not beautiful?" She held forth her hand.

"Yes," said Sophia. "It is very beautiful."

"Yours also is beautiful," said Laurence, with an extremely puzzling intonation.

"It is just the ordinary English wedding-ring," said Sophia. In spite of herself she blushed.

"Now I have married you. It is I, the cure, said he—the cousin—when he put the ring on my finger. Oh, he is excessively amusing! He pleases me much. And he is all alone. He asked me whether I knew among my friends a sympathetic, pretty girl, to make four with us three for a picnic. I said I was not sure, but I thought not. Whom do I know? Nobody. I'm not a woman like the rest. I am always discreet. I do not like casual relations…. But he is very well, the cousin. Brown eyes…. It is an idea—will you come, one day? He speaks English. He loves the English. He is all that is most correct, the perfect gentleman. He would arrange a dazzling fete. I am sure he would be enchanted to make your acquaintance. Enchanted! … As for my Charles, happily he is completely mad about me—otherwise I should have fear."

She smiled, and in her smile was a genuine respect for Sophia's face.

"I fear I cannot come," said Sophia. She honestly endeavoured to keep out of her reply any accent of moral superiority, but she did not quite succeed. She was not at all horrified by Laurence's suggestion. She meant simply to refuse it; but she could not do so in a natural voice.

"It is true you are not yet strong enough," said the imperturbable Laurence, quickly, and with a perfect imitation of naturalness. "But soon you must make a little promenade." She stared at her ring. "After all, it is more proper," she observed judicially. "With a wedding-ring one is less likely to be annoyed. What is curious is that the idea never before came to me. Yet …"

"You like jewellery?" said Sophia.

"If I like jewellery!" with a gesture of the hands.

"Will you pass me that bracelet?"

Laurence obeyed, and Sophia clasped it round the girl's wrist.

"Keep it," Sophia said.

"For me?" Laurence exclaimed, ravished. "It is too much."

"It is not enough," said Sophia. "And when you look at it, you must remember how kind you were to me, and how grateful I am."

"How nicely you say that!" Laurence said ecstatically.

And Sophia felt that she had indeed said it rather nicely. This giving of the bracelet, souvenir of one of the few capricious follies that Gerald had committed for her and not for himself, pleased Sophia very much.

"I am afraid your nursing of me forced you to neglect Monsieur Cerf," she added.

"Yes, a little!" said Laurence, impartially, with a small pout of haughtiness. "It is true that he used to complain. But I soon put him straight. What an idea! He knows there are things upon which I do not joke. It is not he who will quarrel a second time! Believe me!"

Laurence's absolute conviction of her power was what impressed Sophia. To Sophia she seemed to be a vulgar little piece of goods, with dubious charm and a glance that was far too brazen. Her movements were vulgar. And Sophia wondered how she had established her empire and upon what it rested.

"I shall not show this to Aimee," whispered Laurence, indicating the bracelet.

"As you wish," said Sophia.

"By the way, have I told you that war is declared?" Laurence casually remarked.

"No," said Sophia. "What war?"

"The scene with Aimee made me forget it … With Germany. The city is quite excited. An immense crowd in front of the new Opera. They say we shall be at Berlin in a month—or at most two months."

"Oh!" Sophia muttered. "Why is there a war?"

"Ah! It is I who asked that. Nobody knows. It is those Prussians."

"Don't you think we ought to begin again with the disinfecting?" Sophia asked anxiously. "I must speak to Madame Foucault."

Laurence told her not to worry, and went off to show the bracelet to Madame Foucault. She had privately decided that this was a pleasure which, after all, she could not deny herself.

IV

About a fortnight later—it was a fine Saturday in early August—Sophia, with a large pinafore over her dress, was finishing the portentous preparations for disinfecting the flat. Part of the affair was already accomplished, her own room and the corridor having been fumigated on the previous day, in spite of the opposition of Madame Foucault, who had taken amiss Laurence's tale-bearing to Sophia. Laurence had left the flat—under exactly what circumstances Sophia knew not, but she guessed that it must have been in consequence of a scene elaborating the tiff caused by Madame Foucault's resentment against Laurence. The brief, factitious friendliness between Laurence and Sophia had gone like a dream, and Laurence had gone like a dream. The servant had been dismissed; in her place Madame Foucault employed a charwoman each morning for two hours. Finally, Madame Foucault had been suddenly called away that morning by a letter to her sick father at St. Mammes-sur-Seine. Sophia was delighted at the chance. The disinfecting of the flat had become an obsession with Sophia—the obsession of a convalescent whose perspective unconsciously twists things to the most wry shapes. She had had trouble on the day before with Madame Foucault, and she was expecting more serious trouble when the moment arrived for ejecting Madame Foucault as well as all her movable belongings from Madame Foucault's own room. Nevertheless, Sophia had been determined, whatever should happen, to complete an honest fumigation of the entire flat. Hence the eagerness with which, urging Madame Foucault to go to her father, Sophia had protested that she was perfectly strong and could manage by herself for a couple of days. Owing to the partial suppression of the ordinary railway services in favour of military needs, Madame Foucault could not hope to go and return on the same day. Sophia had lent her a louis.

Pans of sulphur were mysteriously burning in each of the three front rooms, and two pairs of doors had been pasted over with paper, to prevent the fumes from escaping. The charwoman had departed. Sophia, with brush, scissors, flour-paste, and news-sheets, was sealing the third pair of doors, when there was a ring at the front door.

She had only to cross the corridor in order to open.

It was Chirac. She was not surprised to see him. The outbreak of the war had induced even Sophia and her landlady to look through at least one newspaper during the day, and she had in this way learnt, from an article signed by Chirac, that he had returned to Paris after a mission into the Vosges country for his paper.

He started on seeing her. "Ah!" He breathed out the exclamation slowly.

And then smiled, seized her hand, and kissed it.

The sight of his obvious extreme pleasure in meeting her again was the sweetest experience that had fallen to Sophia for years.

"Then you are cured?"

"Quite."

He sighed. "You know, this is an enormous relief to me, to know, veritably, that you are no longer in danger. You gave me a fright … but a fright, my dear madame!"

She smiled in silence.

As he glanced inquiringly up and down the corridor, she said—

"I'm all alone in the flat. I'm disinfecting it."

"Then that is sulphur that I smell?"

She nodded. "Excuse me while I finish this door," she said.

He closed the front-door. "But you seem to be quite at home here!" he observed.

"I ought to be," said she.

He glanced again inquiringly up and down the corridor. "And you are really all alone now?" he asked, as though to be doubly sure.

She explained the circumstances.

"I owe you my most sincere excuses for bringing you here," he said confidentially.

"But why?" she replied, looking intently at her door. "They have been most kind to me. Nobody could have been kinder. And Madame Laurence being such a good nurse——"

"It is true," said he. "That was a reason. In effect they are both very good-natured little women.… You comprehend, as journalist it arrives to me to know all kinds of people …" He snapped his fingers … "And as we were opposite the house. In fine, I pray you to excuse me."

"Hold me this paper," she said. "It is necessary that every crack should be covered; also between the floor and the door."

"You English are wonderful," he murmured, as he took the paper. "Imagine you doing that! Then," he added, resuming the confidential tone, "I suppose you will leave the Foucault now, hein?"

"I suppose so," she said carelessly.

"You go to England?"

She turned to him, as she patted the creases out of a strip of paper with a duster, and shook her head.

"Not to England?"

"No."

"If it is not indiscreet, where are you going?"

"I don't know," she said candidly.

And she did not know. She was without a plan. Her brain told her that she ought to return to Bursley, or, at the least, write. But her pride would not hear of such a surrender. Her situation would have to be far more desperate than it was before she could confess her defeat to her family even in a letter. A thousand times no! That was a point which she had for ever decided. She would face any disaster, and any other shame, rather than the shame of her family's forgiving reception of her.

"And you?" she asked. "How does it go? This war?"

He told her, in a few words, a few leading facts about himself. "It must not be said," he added of the war, "but that will turn out ill! I—I know, you comprehend."

"Truly?" she answered with casualness.

"You have heard nothing of him?" Chirac asked.

"Who? Gerald?"

He gave a gesture.

"Nothing! Not a word! Nothing!"

"He will have gone back to England!"

"Never!" she said positively.

"But why not?"

"Because he prefers France. He really does like France. I think it is the only real passion he ever had."

"It is astonishing," reflected Chirac, "how France is loved! And yet…! But to live, what will he do? Must live!"

Sophia merely shrugged her shoulders.

"Then it is finished between you two?" he muttered awkwardly.

She nodded. She was on her knees, at the lower crack of the doors.

"There!" she said, rising. "It's well done, isn't it? That is all."

She smiled at him, facing him squarely, in the obscurity of the untidy and shabby corridor. Both felt that they had become very intimate. He was intensely flattered by her attitude, and she knew it.

"Now," she said, "I will take off my pinafore. Where can I niche you? There is only my bedroom, and I want that. What are we to do?"

"Listen," he suggested diffidently. "Will you do me the honour to come for a drive? That will do you good. There is sunshine. And you are always very pale."

"With pleasure," she agreed cordially.

While dressing, she heard him walking up and down the corridor; occasionally they exchanged a few words. Before leaving, Sophia pulled off the paper from one of the key-holes of the sealed suite of rooms, and they peered through, one after the other, and saw the green glow of the sulphur, and were troubled by its uncanniness. And then Sophia refixed the paper.

In descending the stairs of the house she felt the infirmity of her knees; but in other respects, though she had been out only once before since her illness, she was conscious of a sufficient strength. A disinclination for any enterprise had prevented her from taking the air as she ought to have done, but within the flat she had exercised her limbs in many small tasks. The little Chirac, nervously active and restless, wanted to take her arm, but she would not allow it.

The concierge and part of her family stared curiously at Sophia as she passed under the archway, for the course of her illness had excited the interest of the whole house. Just as the carriage was driving off, the concierge came across the pavement and paid her compliments, and then said:

"You do not know by hazard why Madame Foucault has not returned for lunch, madame?"

"Returned for lunch!" said Sophia. "She will not come back till to-morrow."

The concierge made a face. "Ah! How curious it is! She told my husband that she would return in two hours. It is very grave! Question of business."

"I know nothing, madame," said Sophia. She and Chirac looked at each other. The concierge murmured thanks and went off muttering indistinctly.

The fiacre turned down the Rue Laferriere, the horse slipping and sliding as usual over the cobblestones. Soon they were on the boulevard, making for the Champs Elysees and the Bois de Boulogne.

The fresh breeze and bright sunshine and the large freedom of the streets quickly intoxicated Sophia— intoxicated her, that is to say, in quite a physical sense. She was almost drunk, with the heady savour of life itself. A mild ecstasy of well-being overcame her. She saw the flat as a horrible, vile prison, and blamed herself for not leaving it sooner and oftener. The air was medicine, for body and mind too. Her perspective was instantly corrected. She was happy, living neither in the past nor in the future, but in and for that hour. And beneath her happiness moved a wistful melancholy for the Sophia who had suffered such a captivity and such woes. She yearned for more and yet more delight, for careless orgies of passionate pleasure, in the midst of which she would forget all trouble. Why had she refused the offer of Laurence? Why had she not rushed at once into the splendid fire of joyous indulgence, ignoring everything but the crude, sensuous instinct? Acutely aware as she was of her youth, her beauty, and her charm, she wondered at her refusal. She did not regret her refusal. She placidly observed it as the result of some tremendously powerful motive in herself, which could not be questioned or reasoned with—which was, in fact, the essential HER.

"Do I look like an invalid?" she asked, leaning back luxuriously in the carriage among the crowd of other vehicles.

Chirac hesitated. "My faith! Yes!" he said at length. "But it becomes you. If I did not know that you have little love for compliments, I—"

"But I adore compliments!" she exclaimed. "What made you think that?"

"Well, then," he youthfully burst out, "you are more ravishing than ever."

She gave herself up deliciously to his admiration.

After a silence, he said: "Ah! if you knew how disquieted I was about you, away there…! I should not know how to tell you. Veritably disquieted, you comprehend! What could I do? Tell me a little about your illness."

She recounted details.

As the fiacre entered the Rue Royale, they noticed a crowd of people in front of the Madeleine shouting and cheering.

The cabman turned towards them. "It appears there has been a victory!" he said.

"A victory! If only it was true!" murmured Chirac, cynically.

In the Rue Royale people were running frantically to and fro, laughing and gesticulating in glee. The customers in the cafes stood on their chairs, and even on tables, to watch, and occasionally to join in, the sudden fever. The fiacre was slowed to a walking pace. Flags and carpets began to show from the upper storeys of houses. The crowd grew thicker and more febrile. "Victory! Victory!" rang hoarsely, shrilly, and hoarsely again in the air.

"My God!" said Chirac, trembling. "It must be a true victory! We are saved! We are saved! … Oh yes, it is true!"

"But naturally it is true! What are you saying?" demanded the driver.

At the Place de la Concorde the fiacre had to stop altogether. The immense square was a sea of white hats and flowers and happy faces, with carriages anchored like boats on its surface. Flag after flag waved out from neighbouring roofs in the breeze that tempered the August sun. Then hats began to go up, and cheers rolled across the square like echoes of firing in an enclosed valley. Chirac's driver jumped madly on to his seat, and cracked his whip.

"Vive la France!" he bawled with all the force of his lungs.

A thousand throats answered him.

Then there was a stir behind them. Another carriage was being slowly forced to the front. The crowd was pushing it, and crying, "Marseillaise! Marseillaise!" In the carriage was a woman alone; not beautiful, but distinguished, and with the assured gaze of one who is accustomed to homage and multitudinous applause.

"It is Gueymard!" said Chirac to Sophia. He was very pale. And he too shouted, "Marseillaise!" All his features were distorted.

The woman rose and spoke to her coachman, who offered his hand and she climbed to the box seat, and stood on it and bowed several times.

"Marseillaise!" The cry continued. Then a roar of cheers, and then silence spread round the square like an inundation. And amid this silence the woman began to sing the Marseillaise. As she sang, the tears ran down her cheeks. Everybody in the vicinity was weeping or sternly frowning. In the pauses of the first verse could be heard the rattle of horses' bits, or a whistle of a tug on the river. The refrain, signalled by a proud challenging toss of Gueymard's head, leapt up like a tropical tempest, formidable, overpowering. Sophia, who had had no warning of the emotion gathering within her, sobbed violently. At the close of the hymn Gueymard's carriage was assaulted by worshippers. All around, in the tumult of shouting, men were kissing and embracing each other; and hats went up continually in fountains. Chirac leaned over the side of the carriage and wrung the hand of a man who was standing by the wheel.

"Who is that?" Sophia asked, in an unsteady voice, to break the inexplicable tension within her.

"I don't know," said Chirac. He was weeping like a child. And he sang out: "Victory! To Berlin! Victory!"

V

Sophia walked alone, with tired limbs, up the damaged oak stairs to the flat. Chirac had decided that, in the circumstances of the victory, he would do well to go to the offices of his paper rather earlier than usual. He had brought her back to the Rue Breda. They had taken leave of each other in a sort of dream or general enchantment due to their participation in the vast national delirium which somehow dominated individual feelings. They did not define their relations. They had been conscious only of emotion.

212

The stairs, which smelt of damp even in summer, disgusted Sophia. She thought of the flat with horror and longed for green places and luxury. On the landing were two stoutish, ill-dressed men, of middle age, apparently waiting. Sophia found her key and opened the door.

"Pardon, madame!" said one of the men, raising his hat, and they both pushed into the flat after her. They stared, puzzled, at the strips of paper pasted on the doors.

"What do you want?" she asked haughtily. She was very frightened. The extraordinary interruption brought her down with a shock to the scale of the individual.

"I am the concierge," said the man who had addressed her. He had the air of a superior artisan. "It was my wife who spoke to you this afternoon. This," pointing to his companion, "this is the law. I regret it, but …"

The law saluted and shut the front door. Like the concierge, the law emitted an odour—the odour of uncleanliness on a hot August day.

"The rent?" exclaimed Sophia.

"No, madame, not the rent: the furniture!"

Then she learnt the history of the furniture. It had belonged to the concierge, who had acquired it from a previous tenant and sold it on credit to Madame Foucault. Madame Foucault had signed bills and had not met them. She had made promises and broken them. She had done everything except discharge her liabilities. She had been warned and warned again. That day had been fixed as the last limit, and she had solemnly assured her creditor that on that day she would pay. On leaving the house she had stated precisely and clearly that she would return before lunch with all the money. She had made no mention of a sick father.

Sophia slowly perceived the extent of Madame Foucault's duplicity and moral cowardice. No doubt the sick father was an invention. The woman, at the end of a tether which no ingenuity of lies could further lengthen, had probably absented herself solely to avoid the pain of witnessing the seizure. She would do anything, however silly, to avoid an immediate unpleasantness. Or perhaps she had absented herself without any particular aim, but simply in the hope that something fortunate might occur. Perhaps she had hoped that Sophia, taken unawares, would generously pay. Sophia smiled grimly.

"Well," she said. "I can't do anything. I suppose you must do what you have to do. You will let me pack up my own affairs?"

"Perfectly, madame!"

She warned them as to the danger of opening the sealed rooms. The man of the law seemed prepared to stay in the corridor indefinitely. No prospect of delay disturbed him.

Strange and disturbing, the triumph of the concierge! He was a locksmith by trade. He and his wife and their children lived in two little dark rooms by the archway—an insignificant fragment of the house. He was away from home about fourteen hours every day, except Sundays, when he washed the courtyard. All the other duties of the concierge were performed by the wife. The pair always looked poor, untidy, dirty, and rather forlorn. But they were steadily levying toll on everybody in the big house. They amassed money in forty ways. They lived for money, and all men have what they live for. With what arrogant gestures Madame Foucault would descend from a carriage at the great door! What respectful attitudes and tones the ageing courtesan would receive from the wife and children of the concierge! But beneath these conventional fictions the truth was that the concierge held the whip. At last he was using it. And he had given himself a half-holiday in order to celebrate his second acquirement of the ostentatious furniture and the crimson lampshades. This was one of the dramatic crises in his career as a man of substance. The national thrill of victory had not penetrated into the flat with the concierge and the law. The emotions of the concierge were entirely independent of the Napoleonic foreign policy.

As Sophia, sick with a sudden disillusion, was putting her things together, and wondering where she was to go, and whether it would be politic to consult Chirac, she heard a fluster at the front door: cries, protestations, implorings. Her own door was thrust open, and Madame Foucault burst in.

"Save me!" exclaimed Madame Foucault, sinking to the ground.

The feeble theatricality of the gesture offended Sophia's taste. She asked sternly what Madame Foucault expected her to do. Had not Madame Foucault knowingly exposed her, without the least warning, to the extreme annoyance of this visit of the law, a visit which meant practically that Sophia was put into the street?

"You must not be hard!" Madame Foucault sobbed.

Sophia learnt the complete history of the woman's efforts to pay for the furniture: a farrago of folly and deceptions. Madame Foucault confessed too much. Sophia scorned confession for the sake of confession. She scorned the impulse which forces a weak creature to insist on its weakness, to revel in remorse, and to find an excuse for its conduct in the very fact that there is no excuse. She gathered that Madame Foucault had in fact gone away in the hope that Sophia, trapped, would pay; and that in the end, she had not even had the courage of her own trickery, and had run back, driven by panic into audacity, to fall at Sophia's feet, lest Sophia might not have yielded and the furniture have been seized. From, beginning to end the conduct of Madame Foucault had been fatuous and despicable and wicked. Sophia coldly condemned Madame Foucault for having allowed herself to be brought into the world with such a weak and maudlin character, and for having allowed herself to grow old and ugly. As a sight the woman was positively disgraceful.

"Save me!" she exclaimed again. "I did what I could for you!"

Sophia hated her. But the logic of the appeal was irresistible.

"But what can I do?" she asked reluctantly.

"Lend me the money. You can. If you don't, this will be the end for me."

"And a good thing, too!" thought Sophia's hard sense.

"How much is it?" Sophia glumly asked.

"It isn't a thousand francs!" said Madame Foucault with eagerness. "All my beautiful furniture will go for less than a thousand francs! Save me!"

She was nauseating Sophia.

"Please rise," said Sophia, her hands fidgeting undecidedly.

"I shall repay you, surely!" Madame Foucault asseverated. "I swear!"

"Does she take me for a fool?" thought Sophia, "with her oaths!"

"No!" said Sophia. "I won't lend you the money. But I tell you what I will do. I will buy the furniture at that price; and I will promise to re-sell it to you as soon as you can pay me. Like that, you can be tranquil. But I have very little money. I must have a guarantee. The furniture must be mine till you pay me."

"You are an angel of charity!" cried Madame Foucault, embracing Sophia's skirts. "I will do whatever you wish. Ah! You Englishwomen are astonishing."

Sophia was not an angel of charity. What she had promised to do involved sacrifice and anxiety without the prospect of reward. But it was not charity. It was part of the price Sophia paid for the exercise of her logical faculty; she paid it unwillingly. 'I did what I could for you!' Sophia would have died sooner than remind any one of a benefit conferred, and Madame Foucault had committed precisely that enormity. The appeal was inexcusable to a fine mind; but it was effective.

The men were behind the door, listening. Sophia paid out of her stock of notes. Needless to say, the total was more and not less than a thousand francs. Madame Foucault grew rapidly confidential with the man. Without consulting Sophia, she asked the bailiff to draw up a receipt transferring the ownership of all the furniture to Sophia; and the bailiff, struck into obligingness by glimpses of Sophia's beauty, consented to do so. There was much conferring upon forms of words, and flourishing of pens between thick, vile fingers, and scattering of ink.

Before the men left Madame Foucault uncorked a bottle of wine for them, and helped them to drink it. Throughout the evening she was insupportably deferential to Sophia, who was driven to bed. Madame Foucault contentedly went up to the sixth floor to occupy the servant's bedroom. She was glad to get so far away from the sulphur, of which a few faint fumes had penetrated into the corridor.

The next morning, after a stifling night of bad dreams, Sophia was too ill to get up. She looked round at the furniture in the little room, and she imagined the furniture in the other rooms, and dismally thought: "All this furniture is mine. She will never pay me! I am saddled with it."

It was cheaply bought, but she probably could not sell it for even what she had paid. Still, the sense of ownership was reassuring.

The charwoman brought her coffee, and Chirac's newspaper; from which she learnt that the news of the victory which had sent the city mad on the previous day was utterly false. Tears came into her eyes as she gazed absently at all the curtained windows of the courtyard. She had youth and loveliness; according to the rules she ought to have been irresponsible, gay, and indulgently watched over by the wisdom of admiring age. But she felt towards the French nation as a mother might feel towards adorable, wilful children suffering through their own charming foolishness. She saw France personified in Chirac. How easily, despite his special knowledge, he had yielded to the fever! Her heart bled for France and Chirac on that morning of reaction and of truth. She could not bear to recall the scene in the Place de la Concorde. Madame Foucault had not descended.

CHAPTER VI

THE SIEGE
I

Madame Foucault came into Sophia's room one afternoon with a peculiar guilty expression on her large face, and she held her peignoir close to her exuberant body in folds consciously majestic, as though endeavouring to prove to Sophia by her carriage that despite her shifting eyes she was the most righteous and sincere woman that ever lived.

It was Saturday, the third of September, a beautiful day. Sophia, suffering from an unimportant relapse, had remained in a state of inactivity, and had scarcely gone out at all. She loathed the flat, but lacked the energy to leave it every day. There was no sufficiently definite object in leaving it. She could not go out and look for health as she might have looked for flowers. So she remained in the flat, and stared at the courtyard and the continual mystery of lives hidden behind curtains that occasionally moved. And the painted yellow walls of the house, and the papered walls of her room pressed upon her and crushed her. For a few days Chirac had called daily, animated by the most adorable solicitude. Then he had ceased to call. She had tired of reading the journals; they lay unopened. The relations between Madame Foucault and herself, and her status in the flat of which she now legally owned the furniture,—these things were left unsettled. But the question of her board was arranged on the terms that she halved the cost of food and service with Madame Foucault; her expenses were thus reduced to the lowest possible—about eighteen francs a week. An idea hung in the air—like a scientific discovery on the point of being made by several independent investigators simultaneously—that she and Madame Foucault should co-operate in order to let furnished rooms at a remunerative profit. Sophia felt the nearness of the idea and she wanted to be shocked at the notion of any avowed association between herself and Madame Foucault; but she could not be.

"Here are a lady and a gentleman who want a bedroom," began Madame Foucault, "a nice large bedroom, furnished."

"Oh!" said Sophia; "who are they?"

"They will pay a hundred and thirty francs a month, in advance, for the middle bedroom."

"You've shown it to them already?" said Sophia. And her tone implied that somehow she was conscious of a right to overlook the affair of Madame Foucault.

"No," said the other. "I said to myself that first I would ask you for a counsel."

"Then will they pay all that for a room they haven't seen?"

"The fact is," said Madame Foucault, sheepishly. "The lady has seen the room before. I know her a little. It is a former tenant. She lived here some weeks."

"In that room?"

"Oh no! She was poor enough then."

"Where are they?"

"In the corridor. She is very well, the lady. Naturally one must live, she like all the world; but she is veritably well. Quite respectable! One would never say … Then there would be the meals. We could demand one franc for the cafe au lait, two and a half francs for the lunch, and three francs for the dinner. Without counting other things. That would mean over five hundred francs a month, at least. And what would they cost us? Almost nothing! By what appears, he is a plutocrat … I could thus quickly repay you."

"Is it a married couple?"

"Ah! You know, one cannot demand the marriage certificate." Madame Foucault indicated by a gesture that the Rue Breda was not the paradise of saints.

"When she came before, this lady, was it with the same man?" Sophia asked coldly.

"Ah, my faith, no!" exclaimed Madame Foucault, bridling. "It was a bad sort, the other, a…! Ah, no."

"Why do you ask my advice?" Sophia abruptly questioned, in a hard, inimical voice. "Is it that it concerns me?"

Tears came at once into the eyes of Madame Foucault. "Do not be unkind," she implored.

"I'm not unkind," said Sophia, in the same tone.

"Shall you leave me if I accept this offer?"

There was a pause.

"Yes," said Sophia, bluntly. She tried to be large-hearted, large-minded, and sympathetic; but there was no sign of these qualities in her speech.

"And if you take with you the furniture which is yours…!"

Sophia kept silence.

"How am I to live, I demand of you?" Madame Foucault asked weakly.

"By being respectable and dealing with respectable people!" said Sophia, uncompromisingly, in tones of steel.

"I am unhappy!" murmured the elder woman. "However, you are more strong than I!"

She brusquely dabbed her eyes, gave a little sob, and ran out of the room. Sophia listened at the door, and heard her dismiss the would-be tenants of the best bedroom. She wondered that she should possess such moral ascendancy over the woman, she so young and ingenuous! For, of course, she had not meant to remove the furniture. She could hear Madame Foucault sobbing quietly in one of the other rooms; and her lips curled.

Before evening a truly astonishing event happened. Perceiving that Madame Foucault showed no signs of bestirring herself, Sophia, with good nature in her heart but not on her tongue, went to her, and said:

"Shall I occupy myself with the dinner?"

Madame Foucault sobbed more loudly.

"That would be very amiable on your part," Madame Foucault managed at last to reply, not very articulately.

Sophia put a hat on and went to the grocer's. The grocer, who kept a busy establishment at the corner of the Rue Clausel, was a middle-aged and wealthy man. He had sent his young wife and two children to Normandy until victory over the Prussians should be more assured, and he asked Sophia whether it was true that there was a good bedroom to let in the flat where she lived. His servant was ill of smallpox; he was attacked by anxieties and fears on all sides; he would not enter his own flat on account of possible infection; he liked Sophia, and Madame Foucault had been a customer of his, with intervals, for twenty years. Within an hour he had arranged to rent the middle bedroom at eighty francs a month, and to take his meals there. The terms were modest, but the respectability was prodigious. All the glory of this tenancy fell upon Sophia.

Madame Foucault was deeply impressed. Characteristically she began at once to construct a theory that Sophia had only to walk out of the house in order to discover ideal tenants for the rooms. Also she regarded the advent of the grocer as a reward from Providence for her self-denial in refusing the profits of sinfulness. Sophia felt personally responsible to the grocer for his comfort, and so she herself undertook the preparation of the room. Madame Foucault was amazed at the thoroughness of her housewifery, and at the ingenuity of her ideas for the arrangement of furniture. She sat and watched with admiration sycophantic but real.

That night, when Sophia was in bed, Madame Foucault came into the room, and dropped down by the side of the bed, and begged Sophia to be her moral support for ever. She confessed herself generally. She explained how she had always hated the negation of respectability; how respectability was the one thing that she had all her life passionately desired. She said that if Sophia would be her partner in the letting of furnished rooms to respectable persons, she would obey her in everything. She gave Sophia a list of all the traits in Sophia's character which she admired. She asked Sophia to influence her, to stand by her. She insisted that she would sleep on the sixth floor in the servant's tiny room; and she had a vision of three bedrooms let to successful tradesmen. She was in an ecstasy of repentance and good intentions.

Sophia consented to the business proposition; for she had nothing else whatever in prospect, and she shared Madame Foucault's rosy view about the remunerativeness of the bedrooms. With three tenants who took meals the two women would be able to feed themselves for nothing and still make a profit on the food; and the rents would be clear gain.

And she felt very sorry for the ageing, feckless Madame Foucault, whose sincerity was obvious. The association between them would be strange; it would have been impossible to explain it to St. Luke's Square…. And yet, if there was anything at all in the virtue of Christian charity, what could properly be urged against the association?

"Ah!" murmured Madame Foucault, kissing Sophia's hands, "it is to-day, then, that I recommence my life. You will see—you will see! You have saved me!"

It was a strange sight, the time-worn, disfigured courtesan, half prostrate before the beautiful young creature proud and unassailable in the instinctive force of her own character. It was almost a didactic tableau, fraught with lessons for the vicious. Sophia was happier than she had been for years. She had a purpose in existence; she had a fluid soul to mould to her will according to her wisdom; and there was a large compassion to her credit. Public opinion could not intimidate her, for in her case there was no public opinion; she knew nobody; nobody had the right to question her doings.

The next day, Sunday, they both worked hard at the bedrooms from early morning. The grocer was installed in his chamber, and the two other rooms were cleansed as they had never been cleansed. At four o'clock, the weather being more magnificent than ever, Madame Foucault said:

"If we took a promenade on the boulevard?"

Sophia reflected. They were partners. "Very well," she agreed.

The boulevard was crammed with gay, laughing crowds. All the cafes were full. None, who did not know, could have guessed that the news of Sedan was scarcely a day old in the capital. Delirious joy reigned in the glittering sunshine. As the two women strolled along, content with their industry and their resolves, they came to a National Guard, who, perched on a ladder, was chipping away the "N" from the official sign of a court-tradesman. He was exchanging jokes with a circle of open mouths. It was in this way that Madame Foucault and Sophia learnt of the establishment of a republic.

"Vive la republique!" cried Madame Foucault, incontinently, and then apologized to Sophia for the lapse. They listened a long while to a man who was telling strange histories of the Empress.

Suddenly Sophia noticed that Madame Foucault was no longer at her elbow. She glanced about, and saw her in earnest conversation with a young man whose face seemed familiar. She remembered it was the young man with whom Madame Foucault had quarrelled on the night when Sophia found her prone in the corridor; the last remaining worshipper of the courtesan.

The woman's face was quite changed by her agitation. Sophia drew away, offended. She watched the pair from a distance for a few moments, and then, furious in disillusion, she escaped from the fever of the boulevards and walked quietly home. Madame Foucault did not return. Apparently Madame Foucault was doomed to be the toy of chance. Two days later Sophia received a scrawled letter from her, with the information that her lover had required that she should accompany him to Brussels, as Paris would soon be getting dangerous. "He adores me always. He is the most delicious boy. As I have always said, this is the grand passion of my life. I am happy. He would not permit me to come to you. He has spent two thousand francs on clothes for me, since naturally I had nothing." And so on. No word of apology. Sophia, in reading the letter, allowed for a certain exaggeration and twisting of the truth.

"Young fool! Fool!" she burst out angrily. She did not mean herself; she meant the fatuous adorer of that dilapidated, horrible woman. She never saw her again. Doubtless Madame Foucault fulfilled her own prediction as to her ultimate destiny, but in Brussels.

II

Sophia still possessed about a hundred pounds, and had she chosen to leave Paris and France, there was nothing to prevent her from doing so. Perhaps if she had chanced to visit the Gare St. Lazare or the Gare du Nord, the sight of tens of thousands of people flying seawards might have stirred in her the desire to flee also from the vague coming danger. But she did not visit those termini; she was too busy looking after M. Niepce, her grocer. Moreover, she would not quit her furniture, which seemed to her to be a sort of rock. With a flat full of furniture she considered that she ought to be able to devise a livelihood; the enterprise of becoming independent was already indeed begun. She ardently wished to be independent, to utilize in her own behalf the gifts of organization, foresight, commonsense and tenacity which she knew she possessed and which had lain idle. And she hated the idea of flight.

Chirac returned as unexpectedly as he had gone; an expedition for his paper had occupied him. With his lips he urged her to go, but his eyes spoke differently. He had, one afternoon, a mood of candid despair, such as he would have dared to show only to one in whom he felt great confidence. "They will come to Paris," he said; "nothing can stop them. And … then…!" He gave a cynical laugh. But when he urged her to go she said:

"And what about my furniture? And I've promised M. Niepce to look after him."

Then Chirac informed her that he was without a lodging, and that he would like to rent one of her rooms. She agreed.

Shortly afterwards he introduced a middle-aged acquaintance named Carlier, the secretary-general of his newspaper, who wished to rent a bedroom. Thus by good fortune Sophia let all her rooms immediately, and was sure of over two hundred francs a month, apart from the profit on meals supplied. On this latter occasion Chirac (and his companion too) was quite optimistic, reiterating an absolute certitude that Paris could never be invested. Briefly, Sophia did not believe him. She believed the candidly despairing Chirac. She had no information, no wide theory, to justify her pessimism; nothing but the inward conviction that the race capable of behaving as she had seen it behave in the Place de la Concorde, was bound to be defeated. She loved the French race; but all the practical Teutonic sagacity in her wanted to take care of it in its difficulties, and was rather angry with it for being so unfitted to take care of itself.

She let the men talk, and with careless disdain of their discussions and their certainties she went about her business of preparation. At this period, overworked and harassed by novel responsibilities and risks, she was happier, for days together, than she had ever been, simply because she had a purpose in life and was depending upon herself. Her ignorance of the military and political situation was complete; the situation did not interest her. What interested her was that she had three men to feed wholly or partially, and that the price of eatables was rising. She bought eatables. She bought fifty pecks of potatoes at a franc a peck, and another fifty pecks at a franc and a quarter—double the normal price; ten hams at two and a half francs a pound; a large quantity of tinned vegetables and fruits, a sack of flour, rice, biscuits, coffee, Lyons sausage, dried prunes, dried figs, and much wood and charcoal. But the chief of her purchases was cheese, of which her mother used to say that bread and cheese and water made a complete diet. Many of these articles she obtained from her grocer. All of them, except the flour and the biscuits, she stored in the cellar belonging to the flat; after several days' delay, for the Parisian workmen were too elated by the advent of a republic to stoop to labour, she caused a new lock to be fixed on the cellar-door. Her activities were the sensation of the house. Everybody admired, but no one imitated.

One morning, on going to do her marketing, she found a notice across the shuttered windows of her creamery in the Rue Notre Dame de Lorette: "Closed for want of milk." The siege had begun. It was in the closing of the creamery that the siege was figured for her; in this, and in eggs at five sous a piece. She went elsewhere for her milk and paid a franc a litre for it. That evening she told her lodgers that the price of meals would be doubled, and that if any gentleman thought that he could get equally good meals elsewhere, he was at liberty to get them elsewhere. Her position was strengthened by the appearance of another candidate for a room, a friend of Niepce. She at once offered him her own room, at a hundred and fifty francs a month.

"You see," she said, "there is a piano in it."

"But I don't play the piano," the man protested, shocked at the price.

"That is not my fault," she said.

He agreed to pay the price demanded for the room because of the opportunity of getting good meals much cheaper than in the restaurants. Like M. Niepce, he was a 'siege-widower,' his wife having been put under shelter in Brittany. Sophia took to the servant's bedroom on the sixth floor. It measured nine feet by seven, and had no window save a skylight; but Sophia was in a fair way to realize a profit of at least four pounds a week, after paying for everything.

On the night when she installed herself in that chamber, amid a world of domestics and poor people, she worked very late, and the rays of her candles shot up intermittently through the skylight into a black heaven; at intervals she flitted up and down the stairs with a candle. Unknown to her a crowd gradually formed opposite the house in the street, and at about one o'clock in the morning a file of soldiers woke the concierge and invaded the courtyard, and every window was suddenly populated with heads. Sophia was called upon to prove that she was not a spy signalling to the Prussians. Three quarters of an hour passed before her innocence was established and the staircases cleared of uniforms and dishevelled curiosity. The childish, impossible unreason of the suspicion against her completed in Sophia's mind the ruin of the reputation of the French people as a sensible race. She was extremely caustic the next day to her boarders. Except for this episode, the frequency of military uniforms in the streets, the price of food, and the fact that at least one house in four was flying either the ambulance flag or the flag of a foreign embassy (in an absurd hope of immunity from the impending bombardment) the siege did not exist for Sophia. The men often talked about their guard-duty, and disappeared for a day or two to the ramparts, but she was too busy to listen to them. She thought of nothing but her enterprise, which absorbed all her powers. She arose at six a.m., in the dark, and by seven-thirty M. Niepce and his friend had been served with breakfast, and much general work was already done. At eight o'clock she went out to market. When asked why she continued to buy at a high price, articles of which she had a store, she would reply: "I am keeping all that till things are much dearer." This was regarded as astounding astuteness.

On the fifteenth of October she paid the quarter's rent of the flat, four hundred francs, and was accepted as tenant. Her ears were soon quite accustomed to the sound of cannon, and she felt that she had always been a citizeness of Paris, and that Paris had always been besieged. She did not speculate about the end of the siege; she lived from day to day. Occasionally she had a qualm of fear, when the firing grew momentarily louder, or when she heard that battles had been fought in such and such a suburb. But then she said it was absurd to be afraid when you were with a couple of million people, all in the same plight as yourself. She grew reconciled to everything. She even began to like her tiny bedroom, partly because it was so easy to keep warm (the question of artificial heat was growing acute in Paris), and partly because it ensured her privacy. Down in the flat, whatever was done or said in one room could be more or less heard in all the others, owing to the prevalence of doors.

Her existence, in the first half of November, had become regular with a monotony almost absolute. Only the number of meals served to her boarders varied slightly from day to day. All these repasts, save now and then one in the evening, were carried into the bedrooms by the charwoman. Sophia did not allow herself to be seen much, except in the afternoons. Though Sophia continued to increase her prices, and was now selling her stores at an immense profit, she never approached the prices current outside. She was very indignant against the exploitation of Paris by its shopkeepers, who had vast supplies of provender, and were hoarding for the rise. But the force of their example was too great for her to ignore it entirely; she contented herself with about half their gains. Only to M. Niepce did she charge more than to the others, because he was a shopkeeper. The four men appreciated their paradise. In them developed that agreeable feeling of security which solitary males find only under the roof of a landlady who is at once prompt, honest, and a votary of cleanliness. Sophia hung a slate near the frontdoor, and on this slate they wrote their requests for meals, for being called, for laundry-work, etc. Sophia never made a mistake, and never forgot. The perfection of the domestic machine amazed these men, who had been accustomed to something quite different, and who every day heard harrowing stories of discomfort and swindling from their acquaintances. They even admired Sophia for making them pay, if not too high, still high. They thought it wonderful that she should tell them the price of all things in advance, and even show them how to avoid expense, particularly in the matter of warmth. She arranged rugs for each of them, so that they could sit comfortably in their rooms with nothing but a small charcoal heater for the hands. Quite naturally they came to regard her as the paragon and miracle of women. They endowed her with every fine quality. According to them there had never been such a woman in the history of mankind; there could not have been! She became legendary among their friends: a young and elegant creature, surpassingly beautiful, proud, queenly, unapproachable, scarcely visible, a marvellous manager, a fine cook and artificer of strange English dishes, utterly reliable, utterly exact and with habits of order…! They adored the slight English accent which gave a touch of the exotic to her very correct and freely idiomatic French. In short, Sophia was perfect for them, an impossible woman. Whatever she did was right.

And she went up to her room every night with limbs exhausted, but with head clear enough to balance her accounts and go through her money. She did this in bed with thick gloves on. If often she did not sleep well, it was not because of the distant guns, but because of her preoccupation with the subject of finance. She was making money, and she wanted to make more. She was always inventing ways of economy. She was so anxious to achieve independence that money was always in her mind. She began to love gold, to love hoarding it, and to hate paying it away.

One morning her charwoman, who by good fortune was nearly as precise as Sophia herself, failed to appear. When the moment came for serving M. Niepce's breakfast, Sophia hesitated, and then decided to look after the old man personally. She knocked at his door, and went boldly in with the tray and candle. He started at seeing her; she was wearing a blue apron, as the charwoman did, but there could be no mistaking her for the charwoman. Niepce looked older in bed than when dressed. He had a rather ridiculous, undignified appearance, common among old men before their morning toilette is achieved; and a nightcap did not improve it. His rotund paunch lifted the bedclothes, upon which, for the sake of extra warmth, he had spread unmajestic garments. Sophia smiled to herself; but the contempt implied by that secret smile was softened by the thought: "Poor old man!" She told him briefly that she supposed the charwoman to be ill. He coughed and moved nervously. His benevolent and simple face beamed on her paternally as she fixed the tray by the bed. "I really must open the window for one little second," she said, and did so. The chill air of the street came through the closed shutters, and the old man made a noise as of shivering. She pushed back the shutters, and closed the window, and then did the same with the other two windows. It was almost day in the room. "You will no longer need the candle," she said, and came back to the bedside to extinguish it.

The benign and fatherly old man put his arm round her waist. Fresh from the tonic of pure air, and with the notion of his ridiculousness still in her mind, she was staggered for an instant by this gesture. She had never given a thought to the temperament of the old grocer, the husband of a young wife. She could not always imaginatively keep in mind the effect of her own radiance, especially under such circumstances. But after an instant her precocious cynicism, which had slept, sprang up. "Naturally! I might have expected it!" she thought with blasting scorn.

"Take away your hand!" she said bitterly to the amiable old fool. She did not stir.

He obeyed, sheepishly.

"Do you wish to remain with me?" she asked, and as he did not immediately answer, she said in a most commanding tone: "Answer, then!"

"Yes," he said feebly.

"Well, behave properly."

She went towards the door.

"I wished only—" he stammered.

"I do not wish to know what you wished," she said.

Afterwards she wondered how much of the incident had been overheard. The other breakfasts she left outside the respective doors; and in future Niepce's also.

The charwoman never came again. She had caught smallpox and she died of it, thus losing a good situation. Strange to say, Sophia did not replace her; the temptation to save her wages and food was too strong. She could not, however, stand waiting for hours at the door of the official baker and the official butcher, one of a long line of frozen women, for the daily rations of bread and tri-weekly rations of meat. She employed the concierge's boy, at two sous an hour, to do this. Sometimes he would come in with his hands so blue and cold that he could scarcely hold the precious cards which gave the right to the rations and which cost Chirac an hour or two of waiting at the mayoral offices each week. Sophia might have fed her flock without resorting to the official rations, but she would not sacrifice the economy which they represented. She demanded thick clothes for the concierge's boy, and received boots from Chirac, gloves from Carlier, and a great overcoat from Niepce. The weather increased in severity, and provisions in price. One day she sold to the wife of a chemist who lived on the first floor, for a hundred and ten francs, a ham for which she had paid less than thirty francs. She was conscious of a thrill of joy in receiving a beautiful banknote and a gold coin in exchange for a mere ham. By this time her total cash resources had grown to nearly five thousand francs. It was astounding. And the reserves in the cellar were still considerable, and the sack of flour that encumbered the kitchen was still more than half full. The death of the faithful charwoman, when she heard of it, produced but little effect on Sophia, who was so overworked and so completely absorbed in her own affairs that she had no nervous energy to spare for sentimental regrets. The charwoman, by whose side she had regularly passed many hours in the kitchen, so that she knew every crease in her face and fold of her dress, vanished out of Sophia's memory.

Sophia cleaned and arranged two of the bedrooms in the morning, and two in the afternoon. She had stayed in hotels where fifteen bedrooms were in charge of a single chambermaid, and she thought it would be hard if she could not manage four in the intervals of cooking and other work! This she said to herself by way of excuse for not engaging another charwoman. One afternoon she was rubbing the brass knobs of the numerous doors in M. Niepce's room, when the grocer unexpectedly came in.

She glanced at him sharply. There was a self-conscious look in his eye. He had entered the flat noiselessly. She remembered having told him, in response to a question, that she now did his room in the afternoon. Why should he have left his shop? He hung up his hat behind the door, with the meticulous care of an old man. Then he took off his overcoat and rubbed his hands.

"You do well to wear gloves, madame," he said. "It is dog's weather."

"I do not wear them for the cold," she replied. "I wear them so as not to spoil my hands."

"Ah! truly! Very well! Very well! May I demand some wood? Where shall I find it? I do not wish to derange you."

She refused his help, and brought wood from the kitchen, counting the logs audibly before him.

"Shall I light the fire now?" she asked.

"I will light it," he said.

"Give me a match, please."

As she was arranging the wood and paper, he said: "Madame, will you listen to me?"

"What is it?"

"Do not be angry," he said. "Have I not proved that I am capable of respecting you? I continue in that respect. It is with all that respect that I say to you that I love you, madame…. No, remain calm, I implore you!" The fact was that Sophia showed no sign of not remaining calm. "It is true that I have a wife. But what do you wish…? She is far away. I love you madly," he proceeded with dignified respect. "I know I am old; but I am rich. I understand your character. You are a lady, you are decided, direct, sincere, and a woman of business. I have the greatest respect for you. One can talk to you as one could not to another woman. You prefer

220

directness and sincerity. Madame, I will give you two thousand francs a month, and all you require from my shop, if you will be amiable to me. I am very solitary, I need the society of a charming creature who would be sympathetic. Two thousand francs a month. It is money."

He wiped his shiny head with his hand.

Sophia was bending over the fire. She turned her head towards him.

"Is that all?" she said quietly.

"You could count on my discretion," he said in a low voice. "I appreciate your scruples. I would come, very late, to your room on the sixth. One could arrange … You see, I am direct, like you."

She had an impulse to order him tempestuously out of the flat; but it was not a genuine impulse. He was an old fool. Why not treat him as such? To take him seriously would be absurd. Moreover, he was a very remunerative boarder.

"Do not be stupid," she said with cruel tranquillity. "Do not be an old fool."

And the benign but fatuous middle-aged lecher saw the enchanting vision of Sophia, with her natty apron and her amusing gloves, sweep and fade from the room. He left the house, and the expensive fire warmed an empty room.

Sophia was angry with him. He had evidently planned the proposal. If capable of respect, he was evidently also capable of chicane. But she supposed these Frenchmen were all alike: disgusting; and decided that it was useless to worry over a universal fact. They had simply no shame, and she had been very prudent to establish herself far away on the sixth floor. She hoped that none of the other boarders had overheard Niepce's outrageous insolence. She was not sure if Chirac was not writing in his room.

That night there was no sound of cannon in the distance, and Sophia for some time was unable to sleep. She woke up with a start, after a doze, and struck a match to look at her watch. It had stopped. She had forgotten to wind it up, which omission indicated that the grocer had perturbed her more than she thought. She could not be sure how long she had slept. The hour might be two o'clock or it might be six o'clock. Impossible for her to rest! She got up and dressed (in case it should be as late as she feared) and crept down the interminable creaking stairs with the candle. As she descended, the conviction that it was the middle of the night grew upon her, and she stepped more softly. There was no sound save that caused by her footfalls. With her latchkey she cautiously opened the front door of the flat and entered. She could then hear the noisy ticking of the small, cheap clock in the kitchen. At the same moment another door creaked, and Chirac, with hair all tousled, but fully dressed, appeared in the corridor.

"So you have decided to sell yourself to him!" Chirac whispered.

She drew away instinctively, and she could feel herself blushing. She was at a loss. She saw that Chirac was in a furious rage, tremendously moved. He crept towards her, half crouching. She had never seen anything so theatrical as his movement, and the twitching of his face. She felt that she too ought to be theatrical, that she ought nobly to scorn his infamous suggestion, his unwarrantable attack. Even supposing that she had decided to sell herself to the old pasha, did that concern him? A dignified silence, an annihilating glance, were all that he deserved. But she was not capable of this heroic behaviour.

"What time is it?" she added weakly.

"Three o'clock," Chirac sneered.

"I forgot to wind up my watch," she said. "And so I came down to see."

"In effect!" He spoke sarcastically, as if saying: "I've waited for you, and here you are."

She said to herself that she owed him nothing, but all the time she felt that he and she were the only young people in that flat, and that she did owe to him the proof that she was guiltless of the supreme dishonour of youth. She collected her forces and looked at him.

"You should be ashamed," she said. "You will wake the others."

"And M. Niepce—will he need to be wakened?"

"M. Niepce is not here," she said.

Niepce's door was unlatched. She pushed it open, and went into the room, which was empty and bore no sign of having been used.

"Come and satisfy yourself!" she insisted.

Chirac did so. His face fell.

She took her watch from her pocket.

"And now wind my watch, and set it, please."

She saw that he was in anguish. He could not take the watch. Tears came into his eyes. Then he hid his face, and dashed away. She heard a sob-impeded murmur that sounded like, "Forgive me!" and the banging of a

221

door. And in the stillness she heard the regular snoring of M. Carlier. She too cried. Her vision was blurred by a mist, and she stumbled into the kitchen and seized the clock, and carried it with her upstairs, and shivered in the intense cold of the night. She wept gently for a very long time. "What a shame! What a shame!" she said to herself. Yet she did not quite blame Chirac. The frost drove her into bed, but not to sleep. She continued to cry. At dawn her eyes were inflamed with weeping. She was back in the kitchen then. Chirac's door was wide open. He had left the flat. On the slate was written, "I shall not take meals to-day."

III

Their relations were permanently changed. For several days they did not meet at all; and when at the end of the week Chirac was obliged at last to face Sophia in order to pay his bill, he had a most grievous expression. It was obvious that he considered himself a criminal without any defence to offer for his crime. He seemed to make no attempt to hide his state of mind. But he said nothing. As for Sophia, she preserved a mien of amiable cheerfulness. She exerted herself to convince him by her attitude that she bore no resentment, that she had determined to forget the incident, that in short she was the forgiving angel of his dreams. She did not, however, succeed entirely in being quite natural. Confronted by his misery, it would have been impossible for her to be quite natural, and at the same time quite cheerful!

A little later the social atmosphere of the flat began to grow querulous, disputatious and perverse. The nerves of everybody were seriously strained. This applied to the whole city. Days of heavy rains followed the sharp frosts, and the town was, as it were, sodden with woe. The gates were closed. And though nine-tenths of the inhabitants never went outside the gates, the definite and absolute closing of them demoralized all hearts. Gas was no longer supplied. Rats, cats, and thorough-bred horses were being eaten and pronounced 'not bad.' The siege had ceased to be a novelty. Friends did not invite one another to a 'siege-dinner' as to a picnic. Sophia, fatigued by regular overwork, became weary of the situation. She was angry with the Prussians for dilatoriness, and with the French for inaction, and she poured out her English spleen on her boarders. The boarders told each other in secret that the patronne was growing formidable. Chiefly she bore a grudge against the shopkeepers; and when, upon a rumour of peace, the shop-windows one day suddenly blossomed with prodigious quantities of all edibles, at highest prices, thus proving that the famine was artificially created, Sophia was furious. M. Niepce in particular, though he sold goods to her at a special discount, suffered indignities. A few days later that benign and fatherly man put himself lamentably in the wrong by attempting to introduce into his room a charming young creature who knew how to be sympathetic. Sophia, by an accident unfortunate for the grocer, caught them in the corridor. She was beside herself, but the only outward symptoms were a white face and a cold steely voice that grated like a rasp on the susceptibilities of the adherents of Aphrodite. At this period Sophia had certainly developed into a termagant—without knowing it! She would often insist now on talking about the siege, and hearing everything that the men could tell her. Her comments, made without the least regard for the justifiable delicacy of their feelings as Frenchmen, sometimes led to heated exchanges. When all Montmartre and the Quartier Breda was impassioned by the appearance from outside of the Thirty-second battalion, she took the side of the populace, and would not credit the solemn statement of the journalists, proved by documents, that these maltreated soldiers were not cowards in flight. She supported the women who had spit in the faces of the Thirty-second. She actually said that if she had met them, she would have spit too. Really, she was convinced of the innocence of the Thirty-second, but something prevented her from admitting it. The dispute ended with high words between herself and Chirac.

The next day Chirac came home at an unusual hour, knocked at the kitchen door, and said:

"I must give notice to leave you."

"Why?" she demanded curtly.

She was kneading flour and water for a potato-cake. Her potato-cakes were the joy of the household.

"My paper has stopped!" said Chirac.

"Oh!" she added thoughtfully, but not looking at him. "That is no reason why you should leave."

"Yes," he said. "This place is beyond my means. I do not need to tell you that in ceasing to appear the paper has omitted to pay its debts. The house owes me a month's salary. So I must leave."

"No!" said Sophia. "You can pay me when you have money."

He shook his head. "I have no intention of accepting your kindness."

"Haven't you got any money?" she abruptly asked.

222

"None," said he. "It is the disaster—quite simply!"

"Then you will be forced to get into debt somewhere."

"Yes, but not here! Not to you!"

"Truly, Chirac," she exclaimed, with a cajoling voice, "you are not reasonable."

"Nevertheless it is like that!" he said with decision.

"Eh, well!" she turned on him menacingly. "It will not be like that! You understand me? You will stay. And you will pay me when you can. Otherwise we shall quarrel. Do you imagine I shall tolerate your childishness? Just because you were angry last night——"

"It is not that," he protested. "You ought to know it is not that." (She did.) "It is solely that I cannot permit myself to——"

"Enough!" she cried peremptorily, stopping him. And then in a quieter tone, "And what about Carlier? Is he also in the ditch?"

"Ah! he has money," said Chirac, with sad envy.

"You also, one day," said she. "You stop—in any case until after Christmas, or we quarrel. Is it agreed?" Her accent had softened.

"You are too good!" he yielded. "I cannot quarrel with you. But it pains me to accept——"

"Oh!" she snapped, dropping into the vulgar idiom, "you make me sweat with your stupid pride. Is it that that you call friendship? Go away now. How do you wish that I should succeed with this cake while you station yourself there to distract me?"

IV

But in three days' Chirac, with amazing luck, fell into another situation, and on the Journal des Debats. It was the Prussians who had found him a place. The celebrated Payenneville, second greatest chroniqueur of his time, had caught a cold while doing his duty as a national guard, and had died of pneumonia. The weather was severe again; soldiers were being frozen to death at Aubervilliers. Payenneville's position was taken by another man, whose post was offered to Chirac. He told Sophia of his good fortune with unconcealed vanity.

"You with your smile!" she said impatiently. "One can refuse you nothing!"

She behaved just as though Chirac had disgusted her. She humbled him. But with his fellow-lodgers his airs of importance as a member of the editorial staff of the Debats were comical in their ingenuousness. On the very same day Carlier gave notice to leave Sophia. He was comparatively rich; but the habits which had enabled him to arrive at independence in the uncertain vocation of a journalist would not allow him, while he was earning nothing, to spend a sou more than was absolutely necessary. He had decided to join forces with a widowed sister, who was accustomed to parsimony as parsimony is understood in France, and who was living on hoarded potatoes and wine.

"There!" said Sophia, "you have lost me a tenant!"

And she insisted, half jocularly and half seriously, that Carlier was leaving because he could not stand Chirac's infantile conceit. The flat was full of acrimonious words.

On Christmas morning Chirac lay in bed rather late; the newspapers did not appear that day. Paris seemed to be in a sort of stupor. About eleven o'clock he came to the kitchen door.

"I must speak with you," he said. His tone impressed Sophia.

"Enter," said she.

He went in, and closed the door like a conspirator. "We must have a little fete," he said. "You and I."

"Fete!" she repeated. "What an idea! How can I leave?"

If the idea had not appealed to the secrecies of her heart, stirring desires and souvenirs upon which the dust of time lay thick, she would not have begun by suggesting difficulties; she would have begun by a flat refusal.

"That is nothing," he said vigorously. "It is Christmas, and I must have a chat with you. We cannot chat here. I have not had a true little chat with you since you were ill. You will come with me to a restaurant for lunch."

She laughed. "And the lunch of my lodgers?"

"You will serve it a little earlier. We will go out immediately afterwards, and we will return in time for you to prepare dinner. It is quite simple."

She shook her head. "You are mad," she said crossly.

"It is necessary that I should offer you something," he went on scowling. "You comprehend me? I wish you to lunch with me to-day. I demand it, and you are not going to refuse me."

He was very close to her in the little kitchen, and he spoke fiercely, bullyingly, exactly as she had spoken to him when insisting that he should live on credit with her for a while.

"You are very rude," she parried.

"If I am rude, it is all the same to me," he held out uncompromisingly.

"You will lunch with me; I hold to it."

"How can I be dressed?" she protested.

"That does not concern me. Arrange that as you can."

It was the most curious invitation to a Christmas dinner imaginable.

At a quarter past twelve they issued forth side by side, heavily clad, into the mournful streets. The sky, slate-coloured, presaged snow. The air was bitterly cold, and yet damp. There were no fiacres in the little three-cornered place which forms the mouth of the Rue Clausel. In the Rue Notre Dame de Lorette, a single empty omnibus was toiling up the steep glassy slope, the horses slipping and recovering themselves in response to the whip-cracking, which sounded in the streets as in an empty vault. Higher up, in the Rue Fontaine, one of the few shops that were open displayed this announcement: "A large selection of cheeses for New Year's gifts." They laughed.

"Last year at this moment," said Chirac, "I was thinking of only one thing—the masked ball at the opera. I could not sleep after it. This year even the churches, are not open. And you?"

She put her lips together. "Do not ask me," she said.

They proceeded in silence.

"We are triste, we others," he said. "But the Prussians, in their trenches, they cannot be so gay, either! Their families and their Christmas trees must be lacking to them. Let us laugh!"

The Place Blanche and the Boulevard de Clichy were no more lively than the lesser streets and squares. There was no life anywhere, scarcely a sound; not even the sound of cannon. Nobody knew anything; Christmas had put the city into a lugubrious trance of hopelessness. Chirac took Sophia's arm across the Place Blanche, and a few yards up the Rue Lepic he stopped at a small restaurant, famous among the initiated, and known as "The Little Louis." They entered, descending by two steps into a confined and sombrely picturesque interior.

Sophia saw that they were expected. Chirac must have paid a previous visit to the restaurant that morning. Several disordered tables showed that people had already lunched, and left; but in the corner was a table for two, freshly laid in the best manner of such restaurants; that is to say, with a red-and-white checked cloth, and two other red-and-white cloths, almost as large as the table-cloth, folded as serviettes and arranged flat on two thick plates between solid steel cutlery; a salt-cellar, out of which one ground rock-salt by turning a handle, a pepper-castor, two knife-rests, and two common tumblers. The phenomena which differentiated this table from the ordinary table were a champagne bottle and a couple of champagne glasses. Champagne was one of the few items which had not increased in price during the siege.

The landlord and his wife were eating in another corner, a fat, slatternly pair, whom no privations of a siege could have emaciated. The landlord rose. He was dressed as a chef, all in white, with the sacred cap; but a soiled white. Everything in the place was untidy, unkempt and more or less unclean, except just the table upon which champagne was waiting. And yet the restaurant was agreeable, reassuring. The landlord greeted his customers as honest friends. His greasy face was honest, and so was the pale, weary, humorous face of his wife. Chirac saluted her.

"You see," said she, across from the other corner, indicating a bone on her plate. "This is Diane!"

"Ah! the poor animal!" exclaimed Chirac, sympathetically.

"What would you?" said the landlady. "It cost too dear to feed her. And she was so mignonne! One could not watch her grow thin!"

"I was saying to my wife," the landlord put in, "how she would have enjoyed that bone—Diane!" He roared with laughter.

Sophia and the landlady exchanged a curious sad smile at this pleasantry, which had been re-discovered by the landlord for perhaps the thousandth time during the siege, but which he evidently regarded as quite new and original.

"Eh, well!" he continued confidentially to Chirac. "I have found for you something very good—half a duck." And in a still lower tone: "And it will not cost you too dear."

No attempt to realize more than a modest profit was ever made in that restaurant. It possessed a regular clientele who knew the value of the little money they had, and who knew also how to appreciate sincere and accomplished cookery. The landlord was the chef, and he was always referred to as the chef, even by his wife. "How did you get that?" Chirac asked.

"Ah!" said the landlord, mysteriously. "I have one of my friends, who comes from Villeneuve St. Georges— refugee, you know. In fine …" A wave of the fat hands, suggesting that Chirac should not inquire too closely.

"In effect!" Chirac commented. "But it is very chic, that!"

"I believe you that it is chic!" said the landlady, sturdily.

"It is charming," Sophia murmured politely.

"And then a quite little salad!" said the landlord.

"But that—that is still more striking!" said Chirac.

The landlord winked. The fact was that the commerce which resulted in fresh green vegetables in the heart of a beleagured town was notorious.

"And then also a quite little cheese!" said Sophia, slightly imitating the tone of the landlord, as she drew from the inwardness of her cloak a small round parcel. It contained a Brie cheese, in fairly good condition. It was worth at least fifty francs, and it had cost Sophia less than two francs. The landlady joined the landlord in inspecting this wondrous jewel. Sophia seized a knife and cut a slice for the landlady's table.

"Madame is too good!" said the landlady, confused by this noble generosity, and bearing the gift off to her table as a fox-terrier will hurriedly seek solitude with a sumptuous morsel. The landlord beamed. Chirac was enchanted. In the intimate and unaffected cosiness of that interior the vast, stupefied melancholy of the city seemed to be forgotten, to have lost its sway.

Then the landlord brought a hot brick for the feet of madame. It was more an acknowledgment of the slice of cheese than a necessity, for the restaurant was very warm; the tiny kitchen opened directly into it, and the door between the two was open; there was no ventilation whatever.

"It is a friend of mine," said the landlord, proudly, in the way of gossip as he served an undescribed soup, "a butcher in the Faubourg St. Honore, who has bought the three elephants of the Jardin des Plantes for twenty-seven thousand francs."

Eyebrows were lifted. He uncorked the champagne.

As she drank the first mouthful (she had long lost her youthful aversion for wine), Sophia had a glimpse of herself in a tilted mirror hung rather high on the opposite wall. It was several months since she had attired herself with ceremoniousness. The sudden unexpected vision of elegance and pallid beauty pleased her. And the instant effect of the champagne was to renew in her mind a forgotten conception of the goodness of life and of the joys which she had so long missed.

V

At half-past two they were alone in the little salon of the restaurant, and vaguely in their dreamy and feverish minds that were too preoccupied to control with precision their warm, relaxed bodies, there floated the illusion that the restaurant belonged to them and that in it they were at home. It was no longer a restaurant, but a retreat and shelter from hard life. The chef and his wife were dozing in an inner room. The champagne was drunk; the adorable cheese was eaten; and they were sipping Marc de Bourgogne. They sat at right angles to one another, close to one another, with brains aswing; full of good nature and quick sympathy; their flesh content and yet expectant. In a pause of the conversation (which, entirely banal and fragmentary, had seemed to reach the acme of agreeableness), Chirac put his hand on the hand of Sophia as it rested limp on the littered table. Accidentally she caught his eye; she had not meant to do so. They both became self-conscious. His thin, bearded face had more than ever that wistfulness which always softened towards him the uncompromisingness of her character. He had the look of a child. For her, Gerald had sometimes shown the same look. But indeed she was now one of those women for whom all men, and especially all men in a tender mood, are invested with a certain incurable quality of childishness. She had not withdrawn her hand at once, and so she could not withdraw it at all.

He gazed at her with timid audacity. Her eyes were liquid.

"What are you thinking about?" she asked.

"I was asking myself what I should have done if you had refused to come."

"And what SHOULD you have done?"

"Assuredly something terribly inconvenient," he replied, with the large importance of a man who is in the domain of pure supposition. He leaned towards her. "My very dear friend," he said in a different voice, getting bolder.

It was infinitely sweet to her, voluptuously sweet, this basking in the heat of temptation. It certainly did seem to her, then, the one real pleasure in the world. Her body might have been saying to his: "See how ready I am!" Her body might have been saying to his: "Look into my mind. For you I have no modesty. Look and see all that is there." The veil of convention seemed to have been rent. Their attitude to each other was almost that of lover and mistress, between whom a single glance may be charged with the secrets of the past and promises for the future. Morally she was his mistress in that moment.

He released her hand and put his arm round her waist.

"I love thee," he whispered with great emotion.

Her face changed and hardened. "You must not do that," she said, coldly, unkindly, harshly. She scowled. She would not abate one crease in her forehead to the appeal of his surprised glance. Yet she did not want to repulse him. The instinct which repulsed him was not within her control. Just as a shy man will obstinately refuse an invitation which he is hungering to accept, so, though not from shyness, she was compelled to repulse Chirac. Perhaps if her desires had not been laid to sleep by excessive physical industry and nervous strain, the sequel might have been different.

Chirac, like most men who have once found a woman weak, imagined that he understood women profoundly. He thought of women as the Occidental thinks of the Chinese, as a race apart, mysterious but capable of being infallibly comprehended by the application of a few leading principles of psychology. Moreover he was in earnest; he was hard driven, and he was honest. He continued, respectfully obedient in withdrawing his arm: "Very dear friend," he urged with undaunted confidence, "you must know that I love you."

She shook her head impatiently, all the time wondering what it was that prevented her from slipping into his arms. She knew that she was treating him badly by this brusque change of front; but she could not help it. Then she began to feel sorry for him.

"We have been very good friends," he said. "I have always admired you enormously. I did not think that I should dare to love you until that day when I overheard that old villain Niepce make his advances. Then, when I perceived my acute jealousy, I knew that I was loving you. Ever since, I have thought only of you. I swear to you that if you will not belong to me, it is already finished for me! Altogether! Never have I seen a woman like you! So strong, so proud, so kind, and so beautiful! You are astonishing, yes, astonishing! No other woman could have drawn herself out of an impossible situation as you have done, since the disappearance of your husband. For me, you are a woman unique. I am very sincere. Besides, you know it … Dear friend!"

She shook her head passionately.

She did not love him. But she was moved. And she wanted to love him.

She wanted to yield to him, only liking him, and to love afterwards.

But this obstinate instinct held her back. "I do not say, now," Chirac went on. "Let me hope."

The Latin theatricality of his gestures and his tone made her sorrowful for him.

"My poor Chirac!" she plaintively murmured, and began to put on her gloves.

"I shall hope!" he persisted.

She pursed her lips. He seized her violently by the waist. She drew her face away from his, firmly. She was not hard, not angry now. Disconcerted by her compassion, he loosed her.

"My poor Chirac," she said, "I ought not to have come. I must go. It is perfectly useless. Believe me."

"No, no!" he whispered fiercely.

She stood up and the abrupt movement pushed the table gratingly across the floor. The throbbing spell of the flesh was snapped like a stretched string, and the scene over. The landlord, roused from his doze, stumbled in. Chirac had nothing but the bill as a reward for his pains. He was baffled.

They left the restaurant, silently, with a foolish air.

Dusk was falling on the mournful streets, and the lamp-lighters were lighting the miserable oil lamps that had replaced gas. They two, and the lamplighters, and an omnibus were alone in the streets. The gloom was awful; it was desolating. The universal silence seemed to be the silence of despair. Steeped in woe, Sophia thought wearily upon the hopeless problem of existence. For it seemed to her that she and Chirac had created this woe out of nothing, and yet it was an incurable woe!

CHAPTER VII

SUCCESS
I

Sophia lay awake one night in the room lately quitted by Carlier. That silent negation of individuality had come and gone, and left scarcely any record of himself either in his room or in the memories of those who had surrounded his existence in the house. Sophia had decided to descend from the sixth floor, partly because the temptation of a large room, after months in a cubicle, was rather strong; but more because of late she had been obliged to barricade the door of the cubicle with a chest of drawers, owing to the propensities of a new tenant of the sixth floor. It was useless to complain to the concierge; the sole effective argument was the chest of drawers, and even that was frailer than Sophia could have wished. Hence, finally, her retreat.

She heard the front-door of the flat open; then it was shut with nervous violence. The resonance of its closing would have certainly wakened less accomplished sleepers than M. Niepce and his friend, whose snores continued with undisturbed regularity. After a pause of shuffling, a match was struck, and feet crept across the corridor with the most exaggerated precautions against noise. There followed the unintentional bang of another door. It was decidedly the entry of a man without the slightest natural aptitude for furtive irruptions. The clock in M. Niepce's room, which the grocer had persuaded to exact time-keeping, chimed three with its delicate ting.

For several days past Chirac had been mysteriously engaged very late at the bureaux of the Debats. No one knew the nature of his employment; he said nothing, except to inform Sophia that he would continue to come home about three o'clock until further notice. She had insisted on leaving in his room the materials and apparatus for a light meal. Naturally he had protested, with the irrational obstinacy of a physically weak man who sticks to it that he can defy the laws of nature. But he had protested in vain.

His general conduct since Christmas Day had frightened Sophia, in spite of her tendency to stifle facile alarms at their birth. He had eaten scarcely anything at all, and he went about with the face of a man dying of a broken heart. The change in him was indeed tragic. And instead of improving, he grew worse. "Have I done this?" Sophia asked herself. "It is impossible that I should have done this! It is absurd and ridiculous that he should behave so!" Her thoughts were employed alternately in sympathizing with him and in despising him, in blaming herself and in blaming him. When they spoke, they spoke awkwardly, as though one or both of them had committed a shameful crime, which could not even be mentioned. The atmosphere of the flat was tainted by the horror. And Sophia could not offer him a bowl of soup without wondering how he would look at her or avoid looking, and without carefully arranging in advance her own gestures and speech. Existence was a nightmare of self-consciousness.

"At last they have unmasked their batteries!" he had exclaimed with painful gaiety two days after Christmas, when the besiegers had recommenced their cannonade. He tried to imitate the strange, general joy of the city, which had been roused from apathy by the recurrence of a familiar noise; but the effort was a deplorable failure. And Sophia condemned not merely the failure of Chirac's imitation, but the thing imitated. "Childish!" she thought. Yet, despise the feebleness of Chirac's behaviour as she might, she was deeply impressed, genuinely astonished, by the gravity and persistence of the symptoms. "He must have been getting himself into a state about me for a long time," she thought. "Surely he could not have gone mad like this all in a day or two! But I never noticed anything. No; honestly I never noticed anything!" And just as her behaviour in the restaurant had shaken Chirac's confidence in his knowledge of the other sex, so now the singular behaviour of Chirac shook hers. She was taken aback. She was frightened, though she pretended not to be frightened.

She had lived over and over again the scene in the restaurant. She asked herself over and over again if really she had not beforehand expected him to make love to her in the restaurant. She could not decide exactly when she had begun to expect a declaration; but probably a long time before the meal was finished. She had foreseen it, and might have stopped it. But she had not chosen to stop it. Curiosity concerning not merely him, but also herself, had tempted her tacitly to encourage him. She asked herself over and over again why she had repulsed him. It struck her as curious that she had repulsed him. Was it because she was a married woman? Was it because she had moral scruples? Was it at bottom because she did not care for him? Was it because she could not care for anybody? Was it because his fervid manner of love-making offended her English phlegm? And did she feel pleased or displeased by his forbearance in not renewing the assault? She could not answer. She did not know.

227

But all the time she knew that she wanted love. Only, she conceived a different kind of love: placid, regular, somewhat stern, somewhat above the plane of whims, moods, caresses, and all mere fleshly contacts. Not that she considered that she despised these things (though she did)! What she wanted was a love that was too proud, too independent, to exhibit frankly either its joy or its pain. She hated a display of sentiment. And even in the most intimate abandonments she would have made reserves, and would have expected reserves, trusting to a lover's powers of divination, and to her own! The foundation of her character was a haughty moral independence, and this quality was what she most admired in others.

Chirac's inability to draw from his own pride strength to sustain himself against the blow of her refusal gradually killed in her the sexual desire which he had aroused, and which during a few days flickered up under the stimulus of fancy and of regret. Sophia saw with increasing clearness that her unreasoning instinct had been right in saying him nay. And when, in spite of this, regrets still visited her, she would comfort herself in thinking: "I cannot be bothered with all that sort of thing. It is not worth while. What does it lead to? Is not life complicated enough without that? No, no! I will stay as I am. At any rate I know what I am in for, as things are!" And she would reflect upon her hopeful financial situation, and the approaching prospect of a constantly sufficient income. And a little thrill of impatience against the interminable and gigantic foolishness of the siege would take her.

But her self-consciousness in presence of Chirac did not abate.

As she lay in bed she awaited accustomed sounds which should have connoted Chirac's definite retirement for the night. Her ear, however, caught no sound whatever from his room. Then she imagined that there was a smell of burning in the flat. She sat up, and sniffed anxiously, of a sudden wideawake and apprehensive. And then she was sure that the smell of burning was not in her imagination. The bedroom was in perfect darkness. Feverishly she searched with her right hand for the matches on the night-table, and knocked candlestick and matches to the floor. She seized her dressing-gown, which was spread over the bed, and put it on, aiming for the door. Her feet were bare. She discovered the door. In the passage she could discern nothing at first, and then she made out a thin line of light, which indicated the bottom of Chirac's door. The smell of burning was strong and unmistakable. She went towards the faint light, fumbled for the door-handle with her palm, and opened. It did not occur to her to call out and ask what was the matter.

The house was not on fire; but it might have been. She had left on the table at the foot of Chirac's bed a small cooking-lamp, and a saucepan of bouillon. All that Chirac had to do was to ignite the lamp and put the saucepan on it. He had ignited the lamp, having previously raised the double wicks, and had then dropped into the chair by the table just as he was, and sunk forward and gone to sleep with his head lying sideways on the table. He had not put the saucepan on the lamp; he had not lowered the wicks, and the flames, capped with thick black smoke, were waving slowly to and fro within a few inches of his loose hair. His hat had rolled along the floor; he was wearing his great overcoat and one woollen glove; the other glove had lodged on his slanting knee. A candle was also burning.

Sophia hastened forward, as it were surreptitiously, and with a forward-reaching movement turned down the wicks of the lamp; black specks were falling on the table; happily the saucepan was covered, or the bouillon would have been ruined.

Chirac made a heart-rending spectacle, and Sophia was aware of deep and painful emotion in seeing him thus. He must have been utterly exhausted and broken by loss of sleep. He was a man incapable of regular hours, incapable of treating his body with decency. Though going to bed at three o'clock, he had continued to rise at his usual hour. He looked like one dead; but more sad, more wistful. Outside in the street a fog reigned, and his thin draggled beard was jewelled with the moisture of it. His attitude had the unconsidered and violent prostration of an overspent dog. The beaten animal in him was expressed in every detail of that posture. It showed even in his white, drawn eyelids, and in the falling of a finger. All his face was very sad. It appealed for mercy as the undefended face of sleep always appeals; it was so helpless, so exposed, so simple. It recalled Sophia to a sense of the inner mysteries of life, reminding her somehow that humanity walks ever on a thin crust over terrific abysses. She did not physically shudder; but her soul shuddered.

She mechanically placed the saucepan on the lamp, and the noise awakened Chirac. He groaned. At first he did not perceive her. When he saw that some one was looking down at him, he did not immediately realize who this some one was. He rubbed his eyes with his fists, exactly like a baby, and sat up, and the chair cracked.

"What then?" he demanded. "Oh, madame, I ask pardon. What?"

"You have nearly destroyed the house," she said. "I smelt fire, and I came in. I was just in time. There is no danger now. But please be careful." She made as if to move towards the door.

228

"But what did I do?" he asked, his eyelids wavering.

She explained.

He rose from his chair unsteadily. She told him to sit down again, and he obeyed as though in a dream.

"I can go now," she said.

"Wait one moment," he murmured. "I ask pardon. I should not know how to thank you. You are truly too good. Will you wait one moment?"

His tone was one of supplication. He gazed at her, a little dazzled by the light and by her. The lamp and the candle illuminated the lower part of her face, theatrically, and showed the texture of her blue flannel peignoir; the pattern of a part of the lace collar was silhouetted in shadow on her cheek. Her face was flushed, and her hair hung down unconfined. Evidently he could not recover from his excusable astonishment at the apparition of such a figure in his room.

"What is it—now?" she said. The faint, quizzical emphasis which she put on the 'now' indicated the essential of her thought. The sight of him touched her and filled her with a womanly sympathy. But that sympathy was only the envelope of her disdain of him. She could not admire weakness. She could but pity it with a pity in which scorn was mingled. Her instinct was to treat him as a child. He had failed in human dignity. And it seemed to her as if she had not previously been quite certain whether she could not love him, but that now she was quite certain. She was close to him. She saw the wounds of a soul that could not hide its wounds, and she resented the sight. She was hard. She would not make allowances. And she revelled in her hardness. Contempt—a good-natured, kindly, forgiving contempt—that was the kernel of the sympathy which exteriorly warmed her! Contempt for the lack of self-control which had resulted in this swift degeneration of a man into a tortured victim! Contempt for the lack of perspective which magnified a mere mushroom passion till it filled the whole field of life! Contempt for this feminine slavery to sentiment! She felt that she might have been able to give herself to Chirac as one gives a toy to an infant. But of loving him…! No! She was conscious of an immeasurable superiority to him, for she was conscious of the freedom of a strong mind.

"I wanted to tell you," said he, "I am going away."

"Where?" she asked.

"Out of Paris."

"Out of Paris? How?"

"By balloon! My journal…! It is an affair of great importance. You understand. I offered myself. What would you?"

"It is dangerous," she observed, waiting to see if he would put on the silly air of one who does not understand fear.

"Oh!" the poor fellow muttered with a fatuous intonation and snapping of the fingers. "That is all the same to me. Yes, it is dangerous. Yes, it is dangerous!" he repeated. "But what would you…? For me…!"

She wished that she had not mentioned danger. It hurt her to watch him incurring her ironic disdain.

"It will be the night after to-morrow," he said. "In the courtyard of the Gare du Nord. I want you to come and see me go. I particularly want you to come and see me go. I have asked Carlier to escort you."

He might have been saying, "I am offering myself to martyrdom, and you must assist at the spectacle."

She despised him yet more.

"Oh! Be tranquil," he said. "I shall not worry you. Never shall I speak to you again of my love. I know you. I know it would be useless. But I hope you will come and wish me bon voyage."

"Of course, if you really wish it," she replied with cheerful coolness.

He seized her hand and kissed it.

Once it had pleased her when he kissed her hand. But now she did not like it. It seemed hysterical and foolish to her. She felt her feet to be stone-cold on the floor.

"I'll leave you now," she said. "Please eat your soup."

She escaped, hoping he would not espy her feet.

II

The courtyard of the Nord Railway Station was lighted by oil-lamps taken from locomotives; their silvered reflectors threw dazzling rays from all sides on the under portion of the immense yellow mass of the balloon; the upper portion was swaying to and fro with gigantic ungainliness in the strong breeze. It was only a small balloon, as balloons are measured, but it seemed monstrous as it wavered over the human forms that were agitating themselves beneath it. The cordage was silhouetted against the yellow taffetas as high up as the widest diameter of the balloon, but above that all was vague, and even spectators standing at a distance could not clearly separate the summit of the great sphere from the darkly moving sky. The car, held by ropes fastened to stakes, rose now and then a few inches uneasily from the ground. The sombre and severe architecture of the station-buildings enclosed the balloon on every hand; it had only one way of escape. Over the roofs of that architecture, which shut out the sounds of the city, came the irregular booming of the bombardment. Shells were falling in the southern quarters of Paris, doing perhaps not a great deal of damage, but still plunging occasionally into the midst of some domestic interior and making a sad mess of it. The Parisians were convinced that the shells were aimed maliciously at hospitals and museums; and when a child happened to be blown to pieces their unspoken comments upon the Prussian savagery were bitter. Their faces said: "Those barbarians cannot even spare our children!" They amused themselves by creating a market in shells, paying more for a live shell than a dead one, and modifying the tariff according to the supply. And as the cattle-market was empty, and the vegetable-market was empty, and beasts no longer pastured on the grass of the parks, and the twenty-five million rats of the metropolis were too numerous to furnish interest to spectators, and the Bourse was practically deserted, the traffic in shells sustained the starving mercantile instinct during a very dull period. But the effect on the nerves was deleterious. The nerves of everybody were like nothing but a raw wound. Violent anger would spring up magically out of laughter, and blows out of caresses. This indirect consequence of the bombardment was particularly noticeable in the group of men under the balloon. Each behaved as if he were controlling his temper in the most difficult circumstances. Constantly they all gazed upwards into the sky, though nothing could possibly be distinguished there save the blurred edge of a flying cloud. But the booming came from that sky; the shells that were dropping on Montrouge came out of that sky; and the balloon was going up into it; the balloon was ascending into its mysteries, to brave its dangers, to sweep over the encircling ring of fire and savages.

Sophia stood apart with Carlier. Carlier had indicated a particular spot, under the shelter of the colonnade, where he said it was imperative that they should post themselves. Having guided Sophia to this spot, and impressed upon her that they were not to move, he seemed to consider that the activity of his role was finished, and spoke no word. With the very high silk hat which he always wore, and a thin old-fashioned overcoat whose collar was turned up, he made a rather grotesque figure. Fortunately the night was not very cold, or he might have passively frozen to death on the edge of that feverish group. Sophia soon ignored him. She watched the balloon. An aristocratic old man leaned against the car, watch in hand; at intervals he scowled, or stamped his foot. An old sailor, tranquilly smoking a pipe, walked round and round the balloon, staring at it; once he climbed up into the rigging, and once he jumped into the car and angrily threw out of it a bag, which some one had placed in it. But for the most part he was calm. Other persons of authority hurried about, talking and gesticulating; and a number of workmen waited idly for orders.

"Where is Chirac?" suddenly cried the old man with the watch.

Several voices deferentially answered, and a man ran away into the gloom on an errand.

Then Chirac appeared, nervous, self-conscious, restless. He was enveloped in a fur coat that Sophia had never seen before, and he carried dangling in his hand a cage containing six pigeons whose whiteness stirred uneasily within it. The sailor took the cage from him and all the persons of authority gathered round to inspect the wonderful birds upon which, apparently, momentous affairs depended. When the group separated, the sailor was to be seen bending over the edge of the car to deposit the cage safely. He then got into the car, still smoking his pipe, and perched himself negligently on the wicker-work. The man with the watch was conversing with Chirac; Chirac nodded his head frequently in acquiescence, and seemed to be saying all the time: "Yes, sir! Perfectly sir! I understand, sir! Yes, sir!"

Suddenly Chirac turned to the car and put a question to the sailor, who shook his head. Whereupon Chirac gave a gesture of submissive despair to the man with the watch. And in an instant the whole throng was in a ferment.

"The victuals!" cried the man with the watch. "The victuals, name of

God! Must one be indeed an idiot to forget the victuals! Name of

God—of God!"

Sophia smiled at the agitation, and at the inefficient management which had never thought of food. For it appeared that the food had not merely been forgotten; it was a question which had not even been considered. She could not help despising all that crowd of self-important and fussy males to whom the idea had not occurred that even balloonists must eat. And she wondered whether everything was done like that. After a delay that seemed very long, the problem of victuals was solved, chiefly, as far as Sophia could judge, by means of cakes of chocolate and bottles of wine.

"It is enough! It is enough!" Chirac shouted passionately several times to a knot of men who began to argue with him.

Then he gazed round furtively, and with an inflation of the chest and a patting of his fur coat he came directly towards Sophia. Evidently Sophia's position had been prearranged between him and Carlier. They could forget food, but they could think of Sophia's position!

All eyes followed him. Those eyes could not, in the gloom, distinguish Sophia's beauty, but they could see that she was young and slim and elegant, and of foreign carriage. That was enough. The very air seemed to vibrate with the intense curiosity of those eyes. And immediately Chirac grew into the hero of some brilliant and romantic adventure. Immediately he was envied and admired by every man of authority present. What was she? Who was she? Was it a serious passion or simply a caprice? Had she flung herself at him? It was undeniable that lovely creatures did sometimes fling themselves at lucky mediocrities. Was she a married woman? An artiste? A girl? Such queries thumped beneath overcoats, while the correctness of a ceremonious demeanour was strictly observed.

Chirac uncovered, and kissed her hand. The wind disarranged his hair. She saw that his face was very pale and anxious beneath the swagger of a sincere desire to be brave.

"Well, it is the moment!" he said.

"Did you all forget the food?" she asked.

He shrugged his shoulders. "What will you? One cannot think of everything."

"I hope you will have a safe voyage," she said.

She had already taken leave of him once, in the house, and heard all about the balloon and the sailor-aeronaut and the preparations; and now she had nothing to say, nothing whatever.

He shrugged his shoulders again. "I hope so!" he murmured, but in a tone to convey that he had no such hope.

"The wind isn't too strong?" she suggested.

He shrugged his shoulders again. "What would you?"

"Is it in the direction you want?"

"Yes, nearly," he admitted unwillingly. Then rousing himself: "Eh, well, madame. You have been extremely amiable to come. I held to it very much—that you should come. It is because of you I quit Paris."

She resented the speech by a frown.

"Ah!" he implored in a whisper. "Do not do that. Smile on me. After all, it is not my fault. Remember that this may be the last time I see you, the last time I regard your eyes."

She smiled. She was convinced of the genuineness of the emotion which expressed itself in all this flamboyant behaviour. And she had to make excuses to herself on behalf of Chirac. She smiled to give him pleasure. The hard commonsense in her might sneer, but indubitably she was the centre of a romantic episode. The balloon darkly swinging there! The men waiting! The secrecy of the mission! And Chirac, bare-headed in the wind that was to whisk him away, telling her in fatalistic accents that her image had devastated his life, while envious aspirants watched their colloquy! Yes, it was romantic. And she was beautiful! Her beauty was an active reality that went about the world playing tricks in spite of herself. The thoughts that passed through her mind were the large, splendid thoughts of romance. And it was Chirac who had aroused them! A real drama existed, then, triumphing over the accidental absurdities and pettinesses of the situation. Her final words to Chirac were tender and encouraging.

He hurried back to the balloon, resuming his cap. He was received with the respect due to one who comes fresh from conquest. He was sacred.

Sophia rejoined Carlier, who had withdrawn, and began to talk to him with a self-conscious garrulity. She spoke without reason and scarcely noticed what she was saying. Already Chirac was snatched out of her life, as other beings, so many of them, had been snatched. She thought of their first meetings, and of the sympathy which had always united them. He had lost his simplicity, now, in the self-created crisis of his fate, and had sunk in her esteem. And she was determined to like him all the more because he had sunk in her esteem. She wondered whether he really had undertaken this adventure from sentimental disappointment. She wondered whether, if she had not forgotten to wind her watch one night, they would still have been living quietly under the same roof in the Rue Breda.

The sailor climbed definitely into the car; he had covered himself with a large cloak. Chirac had got one leg over the side of the car, and eight men were standing by the ropes, when a horse's hoofs clattered through the

231

guarded entrance to the courtyard, amid an uproar of sudden excitement. The shiny chest of the horse was flecked with the classic foam.

"A telegram from the Governor of Paris!"

As the orderly, checking his mount, approached the group, even the old man with the watch raised his hat. The orderly responded, bent down to make an inquiry, which Chirac answered, and then, with another exchange of salutes, the official telegram was handed over to Chirac, and the horse backed away from the crowd. It was quite thrilling. Carlier was thrilled.

"He is never too prompt, the Governor. It is a quality!" said Carlier, with irony.

Chirac entered the car. And then the old man with the watch drew a black bag from the shadow behind him and entrusted it to Chirac, who accepted it with a profound deference and hid it. The sailor began to issue commands. The men at the ropes were bending down now. Suddenly the balloon rose about a foot and trembled. The sailor continued to shout. All the persons of authority gazed motionless at the balloon. The moment of suspense was eternal.

"Let go all!" cried the sailor, standing up, and clinging to the cordage. Chirac was seated in the car, a mass of dark fur with a small patch of white in it. The men at the ropes were a knot of struggling confused figures. One side of the car tilted up, and the sailor was nearly pitched out.

Three men at the other side had failed to free the ropes.

"Let go, corpses!" the sailor yelled at them.

The balloon jumped, as if it were drawn by some terrific impulse from the skies.

"Adieu!" called Chirac, pulling his cap off and waving it. "Adieu!"

"Bon voyage! Bon voyage!" the little crowd cheered. And then, "Vive la France!" Throats tightened, including Sophia's.

But the top of the balloon had leaned over, destroying its pear-shape, and the whole mass swerved violently towards the wall of the station, the car swinging under it like a toy, and an anchor under the car. There was a cry of alarm. Then the great ball leaped again, and swept over the high glass roof, escaping by inches the spouting. The cheers expired instantly.... The balloon was gone. It was spirited away as if by some furious and mighty power that had grown impatient in waiting for it. There remained for a few seconds on the collective retina of the spectators a vision of the inclined car swinging near the roof like the tail of a kite. And then nothing! Blankness! Blackness! Already the balloon was lost to sight in the vast stormy ocean of the night, a plaything of the winds. The spectators became once more aware of the dull booming of the cannonade. The balloon was already perhaps flying unseen amid the wrack over those guns.

Sophia involuntarily caught her breath. A chill sense of loneliness, of purposelessness, numbed her being. Nobody ever saw Chirac or the old sailor again. The sea must have swallowed them. Of the sixty-five balloons that left Paris during the siege, two were not heard of. This was the first of the two. Chirac had, at any rate, not magnified the peril, though his intention was undoubtedly to magnify it.

III

This was the end of Sophia's romantic adventures in France. Soon afterwards the Germans entered Paris, by mutual agreement, and made a point of seeing the Louvre, and departed, amid the silence of a city. For Sophia the conclusion of the siege meant chiefly that prices went down. Long before supplies from outside could reach Paris, the shop-windows were suddenly full of goods which had arrived from the shopkeepers alone knew where. Sophia, with the stock in her cellar, could have held out for several weeks more, and it annoyed her that she had not sold more of her good things while good things were worth gold. The signing of a treaty at Versailles reduced the value of Sophia's two remaining hams from about five pounds apiece to the usual price of hams. However, at the end of January she found herself in possession of a capital of about eight thousand francs, all the furniture of the flat, and a reputation. She had earned it all. Nothing could destroy the structure of her beauty, but she looked worn and appreciably older. She wondered often when Chirac would return. She might have written to Carlier or to the paper; but she did not. It was Niepce who discovered in a newspaper that Chirac's balloon had miscarried. At the moment the news did not affect her at all; but after several days she began to feel her loss in a dull sort of way; and she felt it more and more, though never acutely. She was perfectly convinced that Chirac could never have attracted her powerfully. She continued to dream, at rare intervals, of the kind of passion that would have satisfied her, glowing but banked down like a fire in some fine chamber of a rich but careful household.

She was speculating upon what her future would be, and whether by inertia she was doomed to stay for ever in the Rue Breda, when the Commune caught her. She was more vexed than frightened by the Commune; vexed that a city so in need of repose and industry should indulge in such antics. For many people the Commune was a worse experience than the siege; but not for Sophia. She was a woman and a foreigner. Niepce was infinitely more disturbed than Sophia; he went in fear of his life. Sophia would go out to market and take her chances. It is true that during one period the whole population of the house went to live in the cellars, and orders to the butcher and other tradesmen were given over the party-wall into the adjoining courtyard, which communicated with an alley. A strange existence, and possibly perilous! But the women who passed through it and had also passed through the siege, were not very much intimidated by it, unless they happened to have husbands or lovers who were active politicians.

Sophia did not cease, during the greater part of the year 1871, to make a living and to save money. She watched every sou, and she developed a tendency to demand from her tenants all that they could pay. She excused this to herself by ostentatiously declaring every detail of her prices in advance. It came to the same thing in the end, with this advantage, that the bills did not lead to unpleasantness. Her difficulties commenced when Paris at last definitely resumed its normal aspect and life, when all the women and children came back to those city termini which they had left in such huddled, hysterical throngs, when flats were re-opened that had long been shut, and men who for a whole year had had the disadvantages and the advantages of being without wife and family, anchored themselves once more to the hearth. Then it was that Sophia failed to keep all her rooms let. She could have let them easily and constantly and at high rents; but not to men without encumbrances. Nearly every day she refused attractive tenants in pretty hats, or agreeable gentlemen who only wanted a room on condition that they might offer hospitality to a dashing petticoat. It was useless to proclaim aloud that her house was 'serious.' The ambition of the majority of these joyous persons was to live in a 'serious' house, because each was sure that at bottom he or she was a 'serious' person, and quite different from the rest of the joyous world. The character of Sophia's flat, instead of repelling the wrong kind of aspirant, infallibly drew just that kind. Hope was inextinguishable in these bosoms. They heard that there would be no chance for them at Sophia's; but they tried nevertheless. And occasionally Sophia would make a mistake, and grave unpleasantness would occur before the mistake could be rectified. The fact was that the street was too much for her. Few people would credit that there was a serious boarding-house in the Rue Breda. The police themselves would not credit it. And Sophia's beauty was against her. At that time the Rue Breda was perhaps the most notorious street in the centre of Paris; at the height of its reputation as a warren of individual improprieties; most busily creating that prejudice against itself which, over thirty years later, forced the authorities to change its name in obedience to the wish of its tradesmen. When Sophia went out at about eleven o'clock in the morning with her reticule to buy, the street was littered with women who had gone out with reticules to buy. But whereas Sophia was fully dressed, and wore headgear, the others were in dressing-gown and slippers, or opera-cloak and slippers, having slid directly out of unspeakable beds and omitted to brush their hair out of their puffy eyes. In the little shops of the Rue Breda, the Rue Notre Dame de Lorette, and the Rue des Martyrs, you were very close indeed to the primitive instincts of human nature. It was wonderful; it was amusing; it was excitingly picturesque; and the universality of the manners rendered moral indignation absurd. But the neighbourhood was certainly not one in which a woman of Sophia's race, training, and character, could comfortably earn a living, or even exist. She could not fight against the entire street. She, and not the street, was out of place and in the wrong. Little wonder that the neighbours lifted their shoulders when they spoke of her! What beautiful woman but a mad Englishwoman would have had the idea of establishing herself in the Rue Breda with the intention of living like a nun and compelling others to do the same?

By dint of continual ingenuity, Sophia contrived to win somewhat more than her expenses, but she was slowly driven to admit to herself that the situation could not last.

Then one day she saw in Galignani's Messenger an advertisement of an English pension for sale in the Rue Lord Byron, in the Champs Elysees quarter. It belonged to some people named Frensham, and had enjoyed a certain popularity before the war. The proprietor and his wife, however, had not sufficiently allowed for the vicissitudes of politics in Paris. Instead of saving money during their popularity they had put it on the back and on the fingers of Mrs. Frensham. The siege and the Commune had almost ruined them. With capital they might have restored themselves to their former pride; but their capital was exhausted. Sophia answered the advertisement. She impressed the Frenshams, who were delighted with the prospect of dealing in business with an honest English face. Like many English people abroad they were most strangely obsessed by the notion that they had quitted an island of honest men to live among thieves and robbers. They always implied that dishonesty was unknown in Britain. They offered, if she would take over the lease, to sell all their furniture and their renown for ten thousand francs. She declined, the price seeming absurd to her. When they asked her to name a price, she said that she preferred not to do so. Upon entreaty, she said four thousand francs. They then allowed her to see that they considered her to have been quite right in hesitating to name a price so ridiculous. And their confidence in the honest English face seemed to have been shocked. Sophia left. When she got back to the Rue Breda she was relieved that the matter had come to nothing. She did not precisely foresee what her future was to be, but at any rate she knew she shrank from the responsibility of the Pension Frensham. The next morning she received a letter offering to accept six thousand. She wrote and declined. She was indifferent and she would not budge from four thousand. The Frenshams gave way. They were pained, but they gave way. The glitter of four thousand francs in cash, and freedom, was too tempting. Thus Sophia became the proprietress of the Pension Frensham in the cold and correct Rue Lord Byron. She made room in it for nearly all her other furniture, so that instead of being under-furnished, as pensions usually are, it was over-furnished. She was extremely timid at first, for the rent alone was four thousand francs a year; and the prices of the quarter were alarmingly different from those of the Rue Breda. She lost a lot of sleep. For some nights, after she had been installed in the Rue Lord Byron about a fortnight, she scarcely slept at all, and she ate no more than she slept. She cut down expenditure to the very lowest, and frequently walked over to the Rue Breda to do her marketing. With the aid of a charwoman at six sous an hour she accomplished everything. And though clients were few, the feat was in the nature of a miracle; for Sophia had to cook. The articles which George Augustus Sala wrote under the title "Paris herself again" ought to have been paid for in gold by the hotel and pension-keepers of Paris. They awakened English curiosity and the desire to witness the scene of terrible events. Their effect was immediately noticeable. In less than a year after her adventurous purchase, Sophia had acquired confidence, and she was employing two servants, working them very hard at low wages. She had also acquired the landlady's manner. She was known as Mrs. Frensham. Across the balconies of two windows the Frenshams had left a gilded sign, "Pension Frensham," and Sophia had not removed it. She often explained that her name was not Frensham; but in vain. Every visitor inevitably and persistently addressed her according to the sign. It was past the general comprehension that the proprietress of the Pension Frensham might bear another name than Frensham. But later there came into being a class of persons, habitues of the Pension Frensham, who knew the real name of the proprietress and were proud of knowing it, and by this knowledge were distinguished from the herd. What struck Sophia was the astounding similarity of her guests. They all asked the same questions, made the same exclamations, went out on the same excursions, returned with the same judgments, and exhibited the same unimpaired assurance that foreigners were really very peculiar people. They never seemed to advance in knowledge. There was a constant stream of explorers from England who had to be set on their way to the Louvre or the Bon Marche. Sophia's sole interest was in her profits. The excellence of her house was firmly established. She kept it up, and she kept the modest prices up. Often she had to refuse guests. She naturally did so with a certain distant condescension. Her manner to guests increased in stiff formality; and she was excessively firm with undesirables. She grew to be seriously convinced that no pension as good as hers existed in the world, or ever had existed, or ever could exist. Hers was the acme of niceness and respectability. Her preference for the respectable rose to a passion. And there were no faults in her establishment. Even the once despised showy furniture of Madame Foucault had mysteriously changed into the best conceivable furniture; and its cracks were hallowed.

She never heard a word of Gerald nor of her family. In the thousands of people who stayed under her perfect roof, not one mentioned Bursley nor disclosed a knowledge of anybody that Sophia had known. Several men had the wit to propose marriage to her with more or less skilfulness, but none of them was skilful enough to perturb her heart. She had forgotten the face of love. She was a landlady. She was THE landlady: efficient, stylish, diplomatic, and tremendously experienced. There was no trickery, no baseness of Parisian life that she was not acquainted with and armed against. She could not be startled and she could not be swindled.

Years passed, until there was a vista of years behind her. Sometimes she would think, in an unoccupied moment, "How strange it is that I should be here, doing what I am doing!" But the regular ordinariness of her existence would instantly seize her again. At the end of 1878, the Exhibition Year, her Pension consisted of two floors instead of one, and she had turned the two hundred pounds stolen from Gerald into over two thousand.

CHAPTER I

FRENSHAM'S

I

Matthew Peel-Swynnerton sat in the long dining-room of the Pension Frensham, Rue Lord Byron, Paris; and he looked out of place there. It was an apartment about thirty feet in length, and of the width of two windows, which sufficiently lighted one half of a very long table with round ends. The gloom of the other extremity was illumined by a large mirror in a tarnished gilt frame, which filled a good portion of the wall opposite the windows. Near the mirror was a high folding-screen of four leaves, and behind this screen could be heard the sound of a door continually shutting and opening. In the long wall to the left of the windows were two doors, one dark and important, a door of state, through which a procession of hungry and a procession of sated solemn self-conscious persons passed twice daily, and the other, a smaller door, glazed, its glass painted with wreaths of roses, not an original door of the house, but a late breach in the wall, that seemed to lead to the dangerous and to the naughty. The wall-paper and the window drapery were rich and forbidding, dark in hue, mysterious of pattern. Over the state-door was a pair of antlers. And at intervals, so high up as to defy inspection, engravings and oil-paintings made oblong patches on the walls. They were hung from immense nails with porcelain heads, and they appeared to depict the more majestic aspect of man and nature. One engraving, over the mantelpiece and nearer earth than the rest, unmistakably showed Louis Philippe and his family in attitudes of virtue. Beneath this royal group, a vast gilt clock, flanked by pendants of the same period, gave the right time—a quarter past seven.

And down the room, filling it, ran the great white table, bordered with bowed heads and the backs of chairs. There were over thirty people at the table, and the peculiarly restrained noisiness of their knives and forks on the plates proved that they were a discreet and a correct people. Their clothes—blouses, bodices, and jackets—did not flatter the lust of the eye. Only two or three were in evening dress. They spoke little, and generally in a timorous tone, as though silence had been enjoined. Somebody would half-whisper a remark, and then his neighbour, absently fingering her bread and lifting gaze from her plate into vacancy, would conscientiously weigh the remark and half-whisper in reply: "I dare say." But a few spoke loudly and volubly, and were regarded by the rest, who envied them, as underbred.

Food was quite properly the chief preoccupation. The diners ate as those eat who are paying a fixed price per day for as much as they can consume while observing the rules of the game. Without moving their heads they glanced out of the corners of their eyes, watching the manoeuvres of the three starched maids who served. They had no conception of food save as portions laid out in rows on large silver dishes, and when a maid bent over them deferentially, balancing the dish, they summed up the offering in an instant, and in an instant decided how much they could decently take, and to what extent they could practise the theoretic liberty of choice. And if the food for any reason did not tempt them, or if it egregiously failed to coincide with their aspirations, they considered themselves aggrieved. For, according to the game, they might not command; they had the right to seize all that was presented under their noses, like genteel tigers; and they had the right to refuse: that was all. The dinner was thus a series of emotional crises for the diners, who knew only that full dishes and clean plates came endlessly from the banging door behind the screen, and that ravaged dishes and dirty plates vanished endlessly through the same door. They were all eating similar food simultaneously; they began together and they finished together. The flies that haunted the paper-bunches which hung from the chandeliers to the level of the flower-vases, were more free. The sole event that chequered the exact regularity of the repast was the occasional arrival of a wine-bottle for one of the guests. The receiver of the wine-bottle signed a small paper in exchange for it and wrote largely a number on the label of the bottle; then, staring at the number and fearing that after all it might be misread by a stupid maid or an unscrupulous compeer, he would re-write the number on another part of the label, even more largely.

Matthew Peel-Swynnerton obviously did not belong to this world. He was a young man of twenty-five or so, not handsome, but elegant. Though he was not in evening dress, though he was, as a fact, in a very light grey suit, entirely improper to a dinner, he was elegant. The suit was admirably cut, and nearly new; but he wore it as though he had never worn anything else. Also his demeanour, reserved yet free from self-consciousness, his method of handling a knife and fork, the niceties of his manner in transferring food from the silver dishes to his plate, the tone in which he ordered half a bottle of wine—all these details infallibly indicated to the company that Matthew Peel-Swynnerton was their superior. Some folks hoped that he was the son of a lord, or even a lord. He happened to be fixed at the end of the table, with his back to the window, and there was a vacant chair on either side of him; this situation favoured the hope of his high rank. In truth, he was the son, the grandson, and several times the nephew, of earthenware manufacturers. He noticed that the large 'compote' (as it was called in his trade) which marked the centre of the table, was the production of his firm. This surprised him, for Peel, Swynnerton and Co., known and revered throughout the Five Towns as 'Peels,' did not cater for cheap markets. A late guest startled the room, a fat, flabby, middle-aged man whose nose would have roused the provisional hostility of those who have convinced themselves that Jews are not as other men. His nose did not definitely brand him as a usurer and a murderer of Christ, but it was suspicious. His clothes hung loose, and might have been anybody's clothes. He advanced with brisk assurance to the table, bowed, somewhat too effusively, to several people, and sat down next to Peel-Swynnerton. One of the maids at once brought him a plate of soup, and he said: "Thank you, Marie," smiling at her. He was evidently a habitue of the house. His spectacled eyes beamed the superiority which comes of knowing girls by their names. He was seriously handicapped in the race for sustenance, being two and a half courses behind, but he drew level with speed and then, having accomplished this, he sighed, and pointedly engaged Peel-Swynnerton with his sociable glance.

"Ah!" he breathed out. "Nuisance when you come in late, sir!"

Peel-Swynnerton gave a reluctant affirmative.

"Doesn't only upset you! It upsets the house! Servants don't like it!"

"No," murmured Peel-Swynnerton, "I suppose not."

"However, it's not often *I'm* late," said the man. "Can't help it sometimes. Business! Worst of these French business people is that they've no notion of time. Appointments…! God bless my soul!"

"Do you come here often?" asked Peel-Swynnerton. He detested the fellow, quite inexcusably, perhaps because his serviette was tucked under his chin; but he saw that the fellow was one of your determined talkers, who always win in the end. Moreover, as being clearly not an ordinary tourist in Paris, the fellow mildly excited his curiosity.

"I live here," said the other. "Very convenient for a bachelor, you know. Have done for years. My office is just close by. You may know my name—Lewis Mardon."

Peel-Swynnerton hesitated. The hesitation convicted him of not 'knowing his Paris' well.

"House-agent," said Lewis Mardon, quickly.

"Oh yes," said Peel-Swynnerton, vaguely recalling a vision of the name among the advertisements on newspaper kiosks.

"I expect," Mr. Mardon went on, "my name is as well-known as anybody's in Paris."

"I suppose so," assented Peel-Swynnerton.

The conversation fell for a few moments.

"Staying here long?" Mr. Mardon demanded, having added up Peel-Swynnerton as a man of style and of means, and being puzzled by his presence at that table.

"I don't know," said Peel-Swynnerton.

This was a lie, justified in the utterer's opinion as a repulse to Mr. Mardon's vulgar inquisitiveness, such inquisitiveness as might have been expected from a fellow who tucked his serviette under his chin. Peel-Swynnerton knew exactly how long he would stay. He would stay until the day after the morrow; he had only about fifty francs in his pocket. He had been making a fool of himself in another quarter of Paris, and he had descended to the Pension Frensham as a place where he could be absolutely sure of spending not more than twelve francs a day. Its reputation was high, and it was convenient for the Galliera Museum, where he was making some drawings which he had come to Paris expressly to make, and without which he could not reputably return to England. He was capable of foolishness, but he was also capable of wisdom, and scarcely any pressure of need would have induced him to write home for money to replace the money spent on making himself into a fool.

Mr. Mardon was conscious of a check. But, being of an accommodating disposition, he at once tried another direction.

"Good food here, eh?" he suggested.

"Very," said Peel-Swynnerton, with sincerity. "I was quite—"

At that moment, a tall straight woman of uncertain age pushed open the principal door and stood for an instant in the doorway. Peel-Swynnerton had just time to notice that she was handsome and pale, and that her hair was black, and then she was gone again, followed by a clipped poodle that accompanied her. She had signed with a brief gesture to one of the servants, who at once set about lighting the gas-jets over the table.

"Who is that?" asked Peel-Swynnerton, without reflecting that it was now he who was making advances to the fellow whose napkin covered all his shirt-front.

"That's the missis, that is," said Mr. Mardon, in a lower and semi-confidential voice.

"Oh! Mrs. Frensham?"

"Yes. But her real name is Scales," said Mr. Mardon, proudly.

"Widow, I suppose?"

"Yes."

"And she runs the whole show?"

"She runs the entire contraption," said Mr. Mardon, solemnly; "and don't you make any mistake!" He was getting familiar.

Peel-Swynnerton beat him off once more, glancing with careful, uninterested nonchalance at the gas-burners which exploded one after another with a little plop under the application of the maid's taper. The white table gleamed more whitely than ever under the flaring gas. People at the end of the room away from the window instinctively smiled, as though the sun had begun to shine. The aspect of the dinner was changed, ameliorated; and with the reiterated statement that the evenings were drawing in though it was only July, conversation became almost general. In two minutes Mr. Mardon was genially talking across the whole length of the table. The meal finished in a state that resembled conviviality.

Matthew Peel-Swynnerton might not go out into the crepuscular delights of Paris. Unless he remained within the shelter of the Pension, he could not hope to complete successfully his re-conversion from folly to wisdom. So he bravely passed through the small rose-embroidered door into a small glass-covered courtyard, furnished with palms, wicker armchairs, and two small tables; and he lighted a pipe and pulled out of his pocket a copy of The Referee. That retreat was called the Lounge; it was the only part of the Pension where smoking was not either a positive crime or a transgression against good form. He felt lonely. He said to himself grimly in one breath that pleasure was all rot, and in the next he sullenly demanded of the universe how it was that pleasure could not go on for ever, and why he was not Mr. Barney Barnato. Two old men entered the retreat and burnt cigarettes with many precautions. Then Mr. Lewis Mardon appeared and sat down boldly next to Matthew, like a privileged friend. After all, Mr. Mardon was better than nobody whatever, and Matthew decided to suffer him, especially as he began without preliminary skirmishing to talk about life in Paris. An irresistible subject! Mr. Mardon said in a worldly tone that the existence of a bachelor in Paris might easily be made agreeable. But that, of course, for himself—well, he preferred, as a general rule, the Pension Frensham sort of thing; and it was excellent for his business. Still he could not … he knew … He compared the advantages of what he called 'knocking about' in Paris, with the equivalent in London. His information about London was out of date, and Peel-Swynnerton was able to set him right on important details. But his information about Paris was infinitely precious and interesting to the younger man, who saw that he had hitherto lived under strange misconceptions.

"Have a whiskey?" asked Mr. Mardon, suddenly. "Very good here!" he added.

"Thanks!" drawled Peel-Swynnerton.

The temptation to listen to Mr. Mardon as long as Mr. Mardon would talk was not to be overcome. And presently, when the old men had departed, they were frankly telling each other stories in the dimness of the retreat. Then, when the supply of stories came to an end, Mr. Mardon smacked his lips over the last drop of whiskey and ejaculated: "Yes!" as if giving a general confirmation to all that had been said.

"Do have one with me," said Matthew, politely. It was the least he could do.

The second supply of whiskies was brought into the Lounge by Mr. Mardon's Marie. He smiled on her familiarly, and remarked that he supposed she would soon be going to bed after a hard day's work. She gave a moue and a flounce in reply, and swished out.

"Carries herself well, doesn't she?" observed Mr. Mardon, as though Marie had been an exhibit at an agricultural show. "Ten years ago she was very fresh and pretty, but of course it takes it out of 'em, a place like this!"

"But still," said Peel-Swynnerton, "they must like it or they wouldn't stay—that is, unless things are very different here from what they are in England."

The conversation seemed to have stimulated him to examine the woman question in all its bearings, with philosophic curiosity.

"Oh! They LIKE it," Mr. Mardon assured him, as one who knew. "Besides, Mrs. Scales treats 'em very well. I know THAT. She's told me. She's very particular"—he looked around to see if walls had ears—"and, by Jove, you've got to be; but she treats 'em well. You'd scarcely believe the wages they get, and pickings. Now at the Hotel Moscow—know the Hotel Moscow?"

Happily Peel-Swynnerton did. He had been advised to avoid it because it catered exclusively for English visitors, but in the Pension Frensham he had accepted something even more exclusively British than the Hotel Moscow. Mr. Mardon was quite relieved at his affirmative.

"The Hotel Moscow is a limited company now," said he; "English."

"Really?"

"Yes. I floated it. It was my idea. A great success! That's how I know all about the Hotel Moscow." He looked at the walls again. "I wanted to do the same here," he murmured, and Peel-Swynnerton had to show that he appreciated this confidence. "But she never would agree. I've tried her all ways. No go! It's a thousand pities."

"Paying thing, eh?"

"This place? I should say it was! And I ought to be able to judge, I reckon. Mrs. Scales is one of the shrewdest women you'd meet in a day's march. She's made a lot of money here, a lot of money. And there's no reason why a place like this shouldn't be five times as big as it is. Ten times. The scope's unlimited, my dear sir. All that's wanted is capital. Naturally she has capital of her own, and she could get more. But then, as she says, she doesn't want the place any bigger. She says it's now just as big as she can handle. That isn't so. She's a woman who could handle anything—a born manager—but even if it was so, all she would have to do would be to retire—only leave us the place and the name. It's the name that counts. And she's made the name of Frensham worth something, I can tell you!"

"Did she get the place from her husband?" asked Peel-Swynnerton. Her own name of Scales intrigued him. Mr. Mardon shook his head. "Bought it on her own, after the husband's time, for a song—a song! I know, because I knew the original Frenshams."

"You must have been in Paris a long time," said Peel-Swynnerton.

Mr. Mardon could never resist an opportunity to talk about himself. His was a wonderful history. And Peel-Swynnerton, while scorning the man for his fatuity, was impressed. And when that was finished—

"Yes!" said Mr. Mardon after a pause, reaffirming everything in general by a single monosyllable.

Shortly afterwards he rose, saying that his habits were regular.

"Good-night," he said with a mechanical smile.

"G-good-night," said Peel-Swynnerton, trying to force the tone of fellowship and not succeeding. Their intimacy, which had sprung up like a mushroom, suddenly fell into dust. Peel-Swynnerton's unspoken comment to Mr. Mardon's back was: "Ass!" Still, the sum of Peel-Swynnerton's knowledge had indubitably been increased during the evening. And the hour was yet early. Half-past ten! The Folies-Marigny, with its beautiful architecture and its crowds of white toilettes, and its frothing of champagne and of beer, and its musicians in tight red coats, was just beginning to be alive—and at a distance of scarcely a stone's-throw! Peel-Swynnerton pictured the terraced, glittering hall, which had been the prime origin of his exceeding foolishness. And he pictured all the other resorts, great and small, garlanded with white lanterns, in the Champs Elysees; and the sombre aisles of the Champs Elysees where mysterious pale figures walked troublingly under the shade of trees, while snatches of wild song or absurd brassy music floated up from the resorts and restaurants. He wanted to go out and spend those fifty francs that remained in his pocket. After all, why not telegraph to England for more money? "Oh, damn it!" he said savagely, and stretched his arms and got up. The Lounge was very small, gloomy and dreary.

One brilliant incandescent light burned in the hall, crudely illuminating the wicker fauteuils, a corded trunk with a blue-and-red label on it, a Fitzroy barometer, a map of Paris, a coloured poster of the Compagnie Transatlantique, and the mahogany retreat of the hall-portress. In that retreat was not only the hall-portress— an aged woman with a white cap above her wrinkled pink face—but the mistress of the establishment. They were murmuring together softly; they seemed to be well disposed to one another. The portress was respectful, but the mistress was respectful also. The hall, with its one light tranquilly burning, was bathed in an honest calm, the calm of a day's work accomplished, of gradual relaxation from tension, of growing expectation of repose. In its simplicity it affected Peel-Swynnerton as a medicine tonic for nerves might have affected him. In that hall, though exterior nocturnal life was but just stirring into activity, it seemed that the middle of the night had come, and that these two women alone watched in a mansion full of sleepers. And all the recitals which Peel-Swynnerton and Mr. Mardon had exchanged sank to the level of pitiably foolish gossip. Peel-Swynnerton felt that his duty to the house was to retire to bed. He felt, too, that he could not leave the house without saying that he was going out, and that he lacked the courage deliberately to tell these two women that he was going out—at that time of night! He dropped into one of the chairs and made a second attempt to peruse The Referee. Useless! Either his mind was outside in the Champs Elysees, or his gaze would wander surreptitiously to the figure of Mrs. Scales. He could not well distinguish her face because it was in the shadow of the mahogany.

Then the portress came forth from her box, and, slightly bent, sped actively across the hall, smiling pleasantly at the guest as she passed him, and disappeared up the stairs. The mistress was alone in the retreat. Peel-Swynnerton jumped up brusquely, dropping the paper with a rustle, and approached her.

"Excuse me," he said deferentially. "Have any letters come for me to-night?"

He knew that the arrival of letters for him was impossible, since nobody knew his address.

"What name?" The question was coldly polite, and the questioner looked him full in the face. Undoubtedly she was a handsome woman. Her hair was greying at the temples, and the skin was withered and crossed with lines. But she was handsome. She was one of those women of whom to their last on earth the stranger will say: "When she was young she must have been worth looking at!"—with a little transient regret that beautiful young women cannot remain for ever young. Her voice was firm and even, sweet in tone, and yet morally harsh from incessant traffic—with all varieties of human nature. Her eyes were the impartial eyes of one who is always judging. And evidently she was a proud, even a haughty creature, with her careful, controlled politeness. Evidently she considered herself superior to no matter what guest. Her eyes announced that she had lived and learnt, that she knew more about life than any one whom she was likely to meet, and that having pre-eminently succeeded in life, she had tremendous confidence in herself. The proof of her success was the unique Frensham's. A consciousness of the uniqueness of Frensham's was also in those eyes. Theoretically Matthew Peel-Swynnerton's mental attitude towards lodging-house keepers was condescending, but here it was not condescending. It had the real respectfulness of a man who for the moment at any rate is impressed beyond his calculations. His glance fell as he said—

"Peel-Swynnerton." Then he looked up again.

He said the words awkwardly, and rather fearfully, as if aware that he was playing with fire. If this Mrs. Scales was the long-vanished aunt of his friend, Cyril Povey, she must know those two names, locally so famous. Did she start? Did she show a sign of being perturbed? At first he thought he detected a symptom of emotion, but in an instant he was sure that he had detected nothing of the sort, and that it was silly to suppose that he was treading on the edge of a romance. Then she turned towards the letter-rack at her side, and he saw her face in profile. It bore a sudden and astonishing likeness to the profile of Cyril Povey; a resemblance unmistakable and finally decisive. The nose, and the curve of the upper lip were absolutely Cyril's. Matthew Peel-Swynnerton felt very queer. He felt like a criminal in peril of being caught in the act, and he could not understand why he should feel so. The landlady looked in the 'P' pigeon-hole, and in the 'S' pigeon-hole.

"No," she said quietly, "I see nothing for you."

Taken with a swift rash audacity, he said: "Have you had any one named Povey here recently?"

"Povey?"

"Yes. Cyril Povey, of Bursley—in the Five Towns."

He was very impressionable, very sensitive, was Matthew Peel-Swynnerton. His voice trembled as he spoke. But hers also trembled in reply.

"Not that I remember! No! Were you expecting him to be here?"

"Well, it wasn't at all sure," he muttered. "Thank you. Good-night."

"Good-night," she said, apparently with the simple perfunctoriness of the landlady who says good-night to dozens of strangers every evening.

He hurried away upstairs, and met the portress coming down. "Well, well!" he thought. "Of all the queer things—!" And he kept nodding his head. At last he had encountered something REALLY strange in the spectacle of existence. It had fallen to him to discover the legendary woman who had fled from Bursley before he was born, and of whom nobody knew anything. What news for Cyril! What a staggering episode! He had scarcely any sleep that night. He wondered whether he would be able to meet Mrs. Scales without self-consciousness on the morrow. However, he was spared the curious ordeal of meeting her. She did not appear at all on the following day; nor did he see her before he left. He could not find a pretext for asking why she was invisible.

II

The hansom of Matthew Peel-Swynnerton drew up in front of No. 26, Victoria Grove, Chelsea; his kit-bag was on the roof of the cab. The cabman had a red flower in his buttonhole. Matthew leaped out of the vehicle, holding his straw hat on his head with one hand. On reaching the pavement he checked himself suddenly and became carelessly calm. Another straw-hatted and grey-clad figure was standing at the side-gate of No. 26 in the act of lighting a cigarette.

"Hello, Matt!" exclaimed the second figure, languidly, and in a veiled voice due to the fact that he was still holding the match to the cigarette and puffing. "What's the meaning of all this fluster? You're just the man I want to see."

He threw away the match with a wave of the arm, and took Matthew's hand for a moment, blowing a double shaft of smoke through his nose.

"I want to see you, too," said Matthew. "And I've only got a minute.

I'm on my way to Euston. I must catch the twelve-five."

He looked at his friend, and could positively see no feature of it that was not a feature of Mrs. Scales's face. Also, the elderly woman held her body in exactly the same way as the young man. It was entirely disconcerting.

"Have a cigarette," answered Cyril Povey, imperturbably. He was two years younger than Matthew, from whom he had acquired most of his vast and intricate knowledge of life and art, with certain leading notions of deportment; whose pupil indeed he was in all the things that matter to young men. But he had already surpassed his professor. He could pretend to be old much more successfully than Matthew could.

The cabman approvingly watched the ignition of the second cigarette, and then the cabman pulled out a cigar, and showed his large, white teeth, as he bit the end off it. The appearance and manner of his fare, the quality of the kit-bag, and the opening gestures of the interview between the two young dukes, had put the cabman in an optimistic mood. He had no apprehensions of miserly and ungentlemanly conduct by his fare upon the arrival at Euston. He knew the language of the tilt of a straw hat. And it was a magnificent day in London. The group of the two elegances dominated by the perfection of the cabman made a striking tableau of triumphant masculinity, content with itself, and needing nothing.

Matthew lightly took Cyril's arm and drew him further down the street, past the gate leading to the studio (hidden behind a house) which Cyril rented.

"Look here, my boy," he began, "I've found your aunt."

"Well, that's very nice of you," said Cyril, solemnly. "That's a friendly act. May I ask what aunt?"

"Mrs. Scales," said Matthew. "You know—"

"Not the—" Cyril's face changed.

"Yes, precisely!" said Matthew, feeling that he was not being cheated of the legitimate joy caused by making a sensation. Assuredly he had made a sensation in Victoria Grove.

When he had related the whole story, Cyril said: "Then she doesn't know you know?"

"I don't think so. No, I'm sure she doesn't. She may guess."

"But how can you be certain you haven't made a mistake? It may be that—"

"Look here, my boy," Matthew interrupted him. "I've not made any mistake."

"But you've no proof."

"Proof be damned!" said Matthew, nettled. "I tell you it's HER!"

"Oh! All right! All right! What puzzles me most is what the devil you were doing in a place like that. According to your description of it, it must be a—"

"I went there because I was broke," said Matthew.

"Razzle?"

Matthew nodded.

"Pretty stiff, that!" commented Cyril, when Matthew had narrated the prologue to Frensham's.

"Well, she absolutely swore she never took less than two hundred francs. And she looked it, too! And she was worth it! I had the time of my life with that woman. I can tell you one thing—no more English for me! They simply aren't in it."

"How old was she?"

Matthew reflected judicially. "I should say she was thirty." The gaze of admiration and envy was upon him. He had the legitimate joy of making a second sensation. "I'll let you know more about that when I come back," he added. "I can open your eyes, my child."

Cyril smiled sheepishly. "Why can't you stay now?" he asked. "I'm going to take the cast of that Verrall girl's arm this afternoon, and I know I can't do it alone. And Robson's no good. You're just the man I want."

"Can't!" said Matthew.

"Well, come into the studio a minute, anyhow."

"Haven't time; I shall miss my train."

"I don't care if you miss forty trains. You must come in. You've got to see that fountain," Cyril insisted crossly.

Matthew yielded. When they emerged into the street again, after six minutes of Cyril's savage interest in his own work, Matthew remembered Mrs. Scales.

"Of course you'll write to your mother?" he said.

"Yes," said Cyril, "I'll write; but if you happen to see her, you might tell her."

"I will," said Matthew. "Shall you go over to Paris?"

"What! To see Auntie?" He smiled. "I don't know. Depends. If the mater will fork out all my exes … it's an idea," he said lightly, and then without any change of tone, "Naturally, if you're going to idle about here all morning you aren't likely to catch the twelve-five."

Matthew got into the cab, while the driver, the stump of a cigar between his exposed teeth, leaned forward and lifted the reins away from the tilted straw hat.

"By-the-by, lend me some silver," Matthew demanded. "It's a good thing I've got my return ticket. I've run it as fine as ever I did in my life."

Cyril produced eight shillings in silver. Secure in the possession of these riches, Matthew called to the driver—

"Euston—like hell!"

"Yes, sir," said the driver, calmly.

"Not coming my way I suppose?" Matthew shouted as an afterthought, just when the cab began to move.

"No. Barber's," Cyril shouted in answer, and waved his hand.

The horse rattled into Fulham Road.

III

Three days later Matthew Peel-Swynnerton was walking along Bursley Market Place when, just opposite the Town Hall, he met a short, fat, middle-aged lady dressed in black, with a black embroidered mantle, and a small bonnet tied with black ribbon and ornamented with jet fruit and crape leaves. As she stepped slowly and carefully forward she had the dignified, important look of a provincial woman who has always been accustomed to deference in her native town, and whose income is ample enough to extort obsequiousness from the vulgar of all ranks. But immediately she caught sight of Matthew, her face changed. She became simple and naive. She blushed slightly, smiling with a timid pleasure. For her, Matthew belonged to a superior race. He bore the almost sacred name of Peel. His family had been distinguished in the district for generations. 'Peel!' You could without impropriety utter it in the same breath with 'Wedgwood.' And 'Swynnerton' stood not much lower. Neither her self-respect, which was great, nor her commonsense, which far exceeded the average, could enable her to extend as far as the Peels the theory that one man is as good as another. The Peels never shopped in St. Luke's Square. Even in its golden days the Square could not have expected such a condescension. The Peels shopped in London or in Stafford; at a pinch, in Oldcastle. That was the distinction for the ageing stout lady in black. Why, she had not in six years recovered from her surprise that her son and Matthew Peel-Swynnerton treated each other rudely as equals! She and Matthew did not often meet, but they liked each other. Her involuntary meekness flattered him. And his rather elaborate homage flattered her. He admired her fundamental goodness, and her occasional raps at Cyril seemed to put him into ecstasies of joy.

"Well, Mrs. Povey," he greeted her, standing over her with his hat raised. (It was a fashion he had picked up in Paris.) "Here I am, you see."

"You're quite a stranger, Mr. Matthew. I needn't ask you how you are.
Have you been seeing anything of my boy lately?"

"Not since Wednesday," said Matthew. "Of course he's written to you?"

"There's no 'of course' about it," she laughed faintly. "I had a short letter from him on Wednesday morning. He said you were in Paris."

"But since that—hasn't he written?"

"If I hear from him on Sunday I shall be lucky, bless ye!" said
Constance, grimly. "It's not letter-writing that will kill Cyril."

"But do you mean to say he hasn't—" Matthew stopped.

"Whatever's amiss?" asked Constance. Matthew was at a loss to know what to do or say. "Oh, nothing."

"Now, Mr. Matthew, do please—" Constance's tone had suddenly quite changed. It had become firm, commanding, and gravely suspicious. The conversation had ceased to be small-talk for her.

Matthew saw how nervous and how fragile she was. He had never noticed before that she was so sensitive to trifles, though it was notorious that nobody could safely discuss Cyril with her in terms of chaff. He was really astounded at that youth's carelessness, shameful carelessness. That Cyril's attitude to his mother was marked by a certain benevolent negligence—this Matthew knew; but not to have written to her with the important news concerning Mrs. Scales was utterly inexcusable; and Matthew determined that he would tell Cyril so. He felt very sorry for Mrs. Povey. She seemed pathetic to him, standing there in ignorance of a tremendous fact which she ought to have been aware of. He was very content that he had said nothing about Mrs. Scales to anybody except his own mother, who had prudently enjoined silence upon him, saying that his one duty, having told Cyril, was to keep his mouth shut until the Poveys talked. Had it not been for his mother's advice he would assuredly have spread the amazing tale, and Mrs. Povey might have first heard of it from a stranger's gossip, which would have been too cruel upon her.

"Oh!" Matthew tried to smile gaily, archly. "You're bound to hear from
Cyril to-morrow."

He wanted to persuade her that he was concealing merely some delightful surprise from her. But he did not succeed. With all his experience of the world and of women he was not clever enough to deceive that simple woman.

"I'm waiting, Mr. Matthew," she said, in a tone that flattened the smile out of Matthew's sympathetic face. She was ruthless. The fact was, she had in an instant convinced herself that Cyril had met some girl and was engaged to be married. She could think of nothing else. "What has Cyril been doing?" she added, after a pause.

"It's nothing to do with Cyril," said he.

"Then what is it?"

"It was about—Mrs. Scales," he murmured, nearly trembling. As she offered no response, merely looking around her in a peculiar fashion, he said: "Shall we walk along a bit?" And he turned in the direction in which she had been going. She obeyed the suggestion.

"What did ye say?" she asked. The name of Scales for a moment had no significance for her. But when she comprehended it she was afraid, and so she said vacantly, as though wishing to postpone a shock: "What did ye say?"

"I said it was about Mrs. Scales. You know I m-met her in Paris." And he was saying to himself: "I ought not to be telling this poor old thing here in the street. But what can I do?"

"Nay, nay!" she muttered.

She stopped and looked at him with a worried expression. Then he observed that the hand that carried her reticule was making strange purposeless curves in the air, and her rosy face went the colour of cream, as though it had been painted with one stroke of an unseen brush. Matthew was very much put about.

"Hadn't you better—" he began.

"Eh," she said; "I must sit me—" Her bag dropped.

He supported her to the door of Allman's shop, the ironmonger's. Unfortunately, there were two steps up into the shop, and she could not climb them. She collapsed like a sack of flour on the first step. Young Edward Allman ran to the door. He was wearing a black apron and fidgeting with it in his excitement.

"Don't lift her up—don't try to lift her up, Mr. Peel-Swynnerton!" he cried, as Matthew instinctively began to do the wrong thing.

Matthew stopped, looking a fool and feeling one, and he and young Allman contemplated each other helpless for a second across the body of Constance Povey. A part of the Market Place now perceived that the unusual was occurring. It was Mr. Shawcross, the chemist next door to Allman's who dealt adequately with the situation. He had seen all, while selling a Kodak to a young lady, and he ran out with salts. Constance recovered very rapidly. She had not quite swooned. She gave a long sigh, and whispered weakly that she was all right. The three men helped her into the lofty dark shop, which smelt of nails and of stove-polish, and she was balanced on a ricketty chair.

"My word!" exclaimed young Allman, in his loud voice, when she could smile and the pink was returning reluctantly to her cheeks. "You mustn't frighten us like that, Mrs. Povey!"

Matthew said nothing. He had at last created a genuine sensation. Once again he felt like a criminal, and could not understand why.

Constance announced that she would walk slowly home, down the Cock-yard and along Wedgwood Street. But when, glancing round in her returned strength, she saw the hedge of faces at the doorway, she agreed with Mr. Shawcross that she would do better to have a cab. Young Allman went to the door and whistled to the unique cab that stands for ever at the grand entrance to the Town Hall.

"Mr. Matthew will come with me," said Constance.

"Certainly, with pleasure," said Matthew.

And she passed through the little crowd of gapers on Mr. Shawcross's arm.

"Just take care of yourself, missis," said Mr. Shawcross to her, through the window of the cab. "It's fainting weather, and we're none of us any younger, seemingly."

She nodded.

"I'm awfully sorry I upset you, Mrs. Povey," said Matthew, when the cab moved.

She shook her head, refusing his apology as unnecessary. Tears filled her eyes. In less than a minute the cab had stopped in front of Constance's light-grained door. She demanded her reticule from Matthew, who had carried it since it fell. She would pay the cabman. Never before had Matthew permitted a woman to pay for a cab in which he had ridden; but there was no arguing with Constance. Constance was dangerous.

Amy Bates, still inhabiting the cave, had seen the cab-wheels through the grating of her window and had panted up the kitchen stairs to open the door ere Constance had climbed the steps. Amy, decidedly over forty, was a woman of authority. She wanted to know what was the matter, and Constance had to tell her that she had 'felt unwell.' Amy took the hat and mantle and departed to prepare a cup of tea. When they were alone Constance said to Matthew:

"Now. Mr. Matthew, will you please tell me?"

"It's only this," he began.

And as he told it, in quite a few words, it indeed had the air of being 'only that.' And yet his voice shook, in sympathy with the ageing woman's controlled but visible emotion. It seemed to him that gladness should have filled the absurd little parlour, but the spirit that presided had no name; it was certainly not joy. He himself felt very sad, desolated. He would have given much money to have been spared the experience. He knew simply that in the memory of the stout, comical, nice woman in the rocking-chair he had stirred old, old things, wakened slumbers that might have been eternal. He did not know that he was sitting on the very spot where the sofa had been on which Samuel Povey lay when a beautiful and shameless young creature of fifteen extracted his tooth. He did not know that Constance was sitting in the very chair in which the memorable Mrs. Baines had sat in vain conflict with that same unconquerable girl. He did not know ten thousand matters that were rushing violently about in the vast heart of Constance.

She cross-questioned him in detail. But she did not put the questions which he in his innocence expected; such as, if her sister looked old, if her hair was grey, if she was stout or thin. And until Amy, mystified and resentful, had served the tea, on a little silver tray, she remained comparatively calm. It was in the middle of a gulp of tea that she broke down, and Matthew had to take the cup from her.

"I can't thank you, Mr. Matthew," she wept. "I couldn't thank you enough."

"But I've done nothing," he protested.

She shook her head. "I never hoped for this. Never hoped for it!" she went on. "It makes me so happy—in a way…. You mustn't take any notice of me. I'm silly. You must kindly write down that address for me. And I must write to Cyril at once. And I must see Mr. Critchlow."

"It's really very funny that Cyril hasn't written to you," said Matthew.

"Cyril has not been a good son," she said with sudden, solemn coldness.

"To think that he should have kept that…!" She wept again.

At length Matthew saw the possibility of leaving. He felt her warm, soft, crinkled hand round his fingers. "You've behaved very nicely over this," she said. "And very cleverly. In EVERY thing—both over there and here. Nobody could have shown a nicer feeling than you've shown. It's a great comfort to me that my son has got you for a friend."

When he thought of his escapades, and of all the knowledge, unutterable in Bursley, fantastically impossible in Bursley, which he had imparted to her son, he marvelled that the maternal instinct should be so deceived. Still, he felt that her praise of him was deserved.

Outside, he gave vent to a 'Phew' of relief. He smiled, in his worldliest manner. But the smile was a sham. A pretence to himself! A childish attempt to disguise from himself how profoundly he had been moved by a natural scene!

IV

On the night when Matthew Peel-Swynnerton spoke to Mrs. Scales, Matthew was not the only person in the Pension Frensham who failed to sleep. When the old portress came downstairs from her errand, she observed that her mistress was leaving the mahogany retreat.

"She is sleeping tranquilly, the poor one!" said the portress, discharging her commission, which had been to learn the latest news of the mistress's indisposed dog, Fossette. In saying this her ancient, vibrant voice was rich with sympathy for the suffering animal. And she smiled. She was rather like a figure out of an almshouse, with her pink, apparently brittle skin, her tight black dress, and frilled white cap. She stooped habitually, and always walked quickly, with her head a few inches in advance of her feet. Her grey hair was scanty. She was old; nobody perhaps knew exactly how old. Sophia had taken her with the Pension, over a quarter of a century before, because she was old and could not easily have found another place. Although the clientele was almost exclusively English, she spoke only French, explaining herself to Britons by means of benevolent smiles.

"I think I shall go to bed, Jacqueline," said the mistress, in reply.

A strange reply, thought Jacqueline. The unalterable custom of Jacqueline was to retire at midnight and to rise at five-thirty. Her mistress also usually retired about midnight, and during the final hour mistress and portress saw a good deal of each other. And considering that Jacqueline had just been sent up into the mistress's own bedroom to glance at Fossette, and that the bulletin was satisfactory, and that madame and Jacqueline had several customary daily matters to discuss, it seemed odd that madame should thus be going instantly to bed. However, Jacqueline said nothing but:

"Very well, madame. And the number 32?"

"Arrange yourself as you can," said the mistress, curtly.

"It is well, madame. Good evening, madame, and a good night."

Jacqueline, alone in the hall, re-entered her box and set upon one of those endless, mysterious tasks which occupied her when she was not rushing to and fro or whistling up the tubes.

Sophia, scarcely troubling even to glance into Fossette's round basket, undressed, put out the light, and got into bed. She felt extremely and inexplicably gloomy. She did not wish to reflect; she strongly wished not to reflect; but her mind insisted on reflection—a monotonous, futile, and distressing reflection. Povey! Povey! Could this be Constance's Povey, the unique Samuel Povey? That is to say, not he, but his son, Constance's son. Had Constance a grown-up son? Constance must be over fifty now, perhaps a grandmother! Had she really married Samuel Povey? Possibly she was dead. Certainly her mother must be dead, and Aunt Harriet and Mr. Critchlow. If alive, her mother must be at least eighty years of age.

The cumulative effect of merely remaining inactive when one ought to be active, was terrible. Undoubtedly she should have communicated with her family. It was silly not to have done so. After all, even if she had, as a child, stolen a trifle of money from her wealthy aunt, what would that have mattered? She had been proud. She was criminally proud. That was her vice. She admitted it frankly. But she could not alter her pride. Everybody had some weak spot. Her reputation for sagacity, for commonsense, was, she knew, enormous; she always felt, when people were talking to her, that they regarded her as a very unusually wise woman. And yet she had been guilty of the capital folly of cutting herself off from her family. She was ageing, and she was alone in the world. She was enriching herself; she had the most perfectly managed and the most respectable Pension in the world (she sincerely believed), and she was alone in the world. Acquaintances she had— French people who never offered nor accepted hospitality other than tea or wine, and one or two members of the English commercial colony—but her one friend was Fossette, aged three years! She was the most solitary person on earth. She had heard no word of Gerald, no word of anybody. Nobody whatever could truly be interested in her fate. This was what she had achieved after a quarter of a century of ceaseless labour and anxiety, during which she had not once been away from the Rue Lord Byron for more than thirty hours at a stretch. It was appalling—the passage of years; and the passage of years would grow more appalling. Ten years hence, where would she be? She pictured herself dying. Horrible!

Of course there was nothing to prevent her from going back to Bursley and repairing the grand error of her girlhood. No, nothing except the fact that her whole soul recoiled from the mere idea of any such enterprise! She was a fixture in the Rue Lord Byron. She was a part of the street. She knew all that happened or could happen there. She was attached to it by the heavy chains of habit. In the chill way of long use she loved it. There! The incandescent gas-burner of the street-lamp outside had been turned down, as it was turned down every night! If it is possible to love such a phenomenon, she loved that phenomenon. That phenomenon was a portion of her life, dear to her.

An agreeable young man, that Peel-Swynnerton! Then evidently, since her days in Bursley, the Peels and the Swynnertons, partners in business, must have intermarried, or there must have been some affair of a will. Did he suspect who she was? He had had a very self-conscious, guilty look. No! He could not have suspected who she was. The idea was ridiculous. Probably he did not even know that her name was Scales. And even if he knew her name, he had probably never heard of Gerald Scales, or the story of her flight. Why, he could not have been born until after she had left Bursley! Besides, the Peels were always quite aloof from the ordinary social life of the town. No! He could not have suspected her identity. It was infantile to conceive such a thing. And yet, she inconsequently proceeded in the tangle of her afflicted mind, supposing he had suspected it! Supposing by some queer chance, he had heard her forgotten story, and casually put two and two together! Supposing even that he were merely to mention in the Five Towns that the Pension Frensham was kept by a Mrs. Scales. 'Scales? Scales?' people might repeat. 'Now, what does that remind me of?' And the ball might roll and roll till Constance or somebody picked it up! And then…

Moreover—a detail of which she had at first unaccountably failed to mark the significance—this Peel-Swynnerton was a friend of the Mr. Povey as to whom he had inquired. In that case it could not be the same Povey. Impossible that the Peels should be on terms of friendship with Samuel Povey or his connections! But supposing after all they were! Supposing something utterly unanticipated and revolutionary had happened in the Five Towns!

She was disturbed. She was insecure. She foresaw inquiries being made concerning her. She foresaw an immense family fuss, endless tomfoolery, the upsetting of her existence, the destruction of her calm. And she sank away from that prospect. She could not face it. She did not want to face it. "No," she cried passionately in her soul, "I've lived alone, and I'll stay as I am. I can't change at my time of life." And her attitude towards a possible invasion of her solitude became one of resentment. "I won't have it! I won't have it! I will be left alone. Constance! What can Constance be to me, or I to her, now?" The vision of any change in her existence was in the highest degree painful to her. And not only painful! It frightened her. It made her shrink. But she could not dismiss it…. She could not argue herself out of it. The apparition of Matthew Peel-Swynnerton had somehow altered the very stuff of her fibres.

And surging on the outskirts of the central storm of her brain were ten thousand apprehensions about the management of the Pension. All was black, hopeless. The Pension might have been the most complete business failure that gross carelessness and incapacity had ever provoked. Was it not the fact that she had to supervise everything herself, that she could depend on no one? Were she to be absent even for a single day the entire structure would inevitably fall. Instead of working less she worked harder. And who could guarantee that her investments were safe?

When dawn announced itself, slowly discovering each object in the chamber, she was ill. Fever seemed to rage in her head. And in and round her mouth she had strange sensations. Fossette stirred in the basket near the large desk on which multifarious files and papers were ranged with minute particularity.

"Fossette!" she tried to call out; but no sound issued from her lips. She could not move her tongue. She tried to protrude it, and could not. For hours she had been conscious of a headache. Her heart sank. She was sick with fear. Her memory flashed to her father and his seizure. She was his daughter! Paralysis! "Ca serait le comble!" she thought in French, horrified. Her fear became abject! "Can I move at all?" she thought, and madly jerked her head. Yes, she could move her head slightly on the pillow, and she could stretch her right arm, both arms. Absurd cowardice! Of course it was not a seizure! She reassured herself. Still, she could not put her tongue out. Suddenly she began to hiccough, and she had no control over the hiccough. She put her hand to the bell, whose ringing would summon the man who slept in a pantry off the hall, and suddenly the hiccough ceased.

Her hand dropped. She was better. Besides, what use in ringing for a man if she could not speak to him through the door? She must wait for Jacqueline. At six o'clock every morning, summer and winter, Jacqueline entered her mistress's bedroom to release the dog for a moment's airing under her own supervision. The clock on the mantelpiece showed five minutes past three. She had three hours to wait. Fossette pattered across the room, and sprang on to the bed and nestled down. Sophia ignored her, but Fossette, being herself unwell and torpid, did not seem to care.

Jacqueline was late. In the quarter of an hour between six o'clock and a quarter past, Sophia suffered the supreme pangs of despair and verged upon insanity. It appeared to her that her cranium would blow off under pressure from within. Then the door opened silently, a few inches. Usually Jacqueline came into the room, but sometimes she stood behind the door and called in her soft, trembling voice, "Fossette! Fossette!" And on this morning she did not come into the room. The dog did not immediately respond. Sophia was in an agony. She marshalled all her volition, all her self-control and strength, to shout:

"Jacqueline!"

It came out of her, a horribly difficult and misshapen birth, but it came. She was exhausted.

"Yes, madame." Jacqueline entered.

As soon as she had a glimpse of Sophia she threw up her hands. Sophia stared at her, wordless.

"I will fetch the doctor—myself," whispered Jacqueline, and fled.

"Jacqueline!" The woman stopped. Then Sophia determined to force herself to make a speech, and she braced her muscles to an unprecedented effort. "Say not a word to the others." She could not bear that the whole household should know of her illness. Jacqueline nodded and vanished, the dog following. Jacqueline understood. She lived in the place with her mistress as with a fellow-conspirator.

Sophia began to feel better. She could get into a sitting posture, though the movement made her dizzy. By working to the foot of the bed she could see herself in the glass of the wardrobe. And she saw that the lower part of her face was twisted out of shape.

The doctor, who knew her, and who earned a lot of money in her house, told her frankly what had happened. Paralysie glosso-labio-laryngee was the phrase he used. She understood. A very slight attack; due to overwork and worry. He ordered absolute rest and quiet.

"Impossible!" she said, genuinely convinced that she alone was indispensable.

"Repose the most absolute!" he repeated.

She marvelled that a few words with a man who chanced to be named Peel-Swynnerton could have resulted in such a disaster, and drew a curious satisfaction from this fearful proof that she was so highly-strung. But even then she did not realize how profoundly she had been disturbed.

V

"My darling Sophia—"

The inevitable miracle had occurred. Her suspicions concerning that Mr. Peel-Swynnerton were well-founded, after all! Here was a letter from Constance! The writing on the envelope was not Constance's; but even before examining it she had had a peculiar qualm. She received letters from England nearly every day asking about rooms and prices (and on many of them she had to pay threepence excess postage, because the writers carelessly or carefully forgot that a penny stamp was not sufficient); there was nothing to distinguish this envelope, and yet her first glance at it had startled her; and when, deciphering the smudged post-mark, she made out the word 'Bursley,' her heart did literally seem to stop, and she opened the letter in quite violent tremulation, thinking to herself: "The doctor would say this is very bad for me." Six days had elapsed since her attack, and she was wonderfully better; the distortion of her face had almost disappeared. But the doctor was grave; he ordered no medicine, merely a tonic; and monotonously insisted on 'repose the most absolute,' on perfect mental calm. He said little else, allowing Sophia to judge from his silences the seriousness of her condition. Yes, the receipt of such a letter must be bad for her!

She controlled herself while she read it, lying in her dressing-gown against several pillows on the bed; a mist did not form in her eyes, nor did she sob, nor betray physically that she was not reading an order for two rooms for a week. But the expenditure of nervous force necessary to self-control was terrific.

Constance's handwriting had changed; it was, however, easily recognizable as a development of the neat calligraphy of the girl who could print window-tickets. The 'S' of Sophia was formed in the same way as she had formed it in the last letter which she had received from her at Axe!

"MY DARLING SOPHIA,

"I cannot tell you how overjoyed I was to learn that after all these years you are alive and well, and doing so well too. I long to see you, my dear sister. It was Mr. Peel-Swynnerton who told me. He is a friend of Cyril's. Cyril is the name of my son. I married Samuel in 1867. Cyril was born in 1874 at Christmas. He is now twenty-two, and doing very well in London as a student of sculpture, though so young. He won a National Scholarship. There were only eight, of which he won one, in all England. Samuel died in 1888. If you read the papers you must have seen about the Povey affair. I mean of course Mr. Daniel Povey, Confectioner. It was that that killed poor Samuel. Poor mother died in 1875. It doesn't seem so long. Aunt Harriet and Aunt Maria are both dead. Old Dr. Harrop is dead, and his son has practically retired. He has a partner, a Scotchman. Mr. Critchlow has married Miss Insull. Did you ever hear of such a thing? They have taken over the shop, and I live in the house part, the other being bricked up. Business in the Square is not what it used to be. The steam trams take all the custom to Hanbridge, and they are talking of electric trams, but I dare say it is only talk. I have a fairly good servant. She has been with me a long time, but servants are not what they were. I keep pretty well, except for my sciatica and palpitation. Since Cyril went to London I have been very lonely. But I try to cheer up and count my blessings. I am sure I have a great deal to be thankful for. And now this news of you! Please write to me a long letter, and tell me all about yourself. It is a long way to Paris. But surely now you know I am still here, you will come and pay me a visit—at least. Everybody would be most glad to see you. And I should be so proud and glad. As I say, I am all alone. Mr. Critchlow says I am to say there is a deal of money waiting for you. You know he is the trustee. There is the half-share of mother's and also of Aunt Harriet's, and it has been accumulating. By the way, they are getting up a subscription for Miss Chetwynd, poor old thing. Her sister is dead, and she is in poverty. I have put myself down for L20. Now, my dear sister, please do write to me at once. You see it is still the old address. I remain, my darling Sophia, with much love, your affectionate sister,

"CONSTANCE POVEY.

"P.S.—I should have written yesterday, but I was not fit. Every time I sat down to write, I cried."

"Of course," said Sophia to Fossette, "she expects me to go to her, instead of her coming to me! And yet who's the busiest?"

But this observation was not serious. It was merely a trifle of affectionate malicious embroidery that Sophia put on the edge of her deep satisfaction. The very spirit of simple love seemed to emanate from the paper on which Constance had written. And this spirit woke suddenly and completely Sophia's love for Constance. Constance! At that moment there was assuredly for Sophia no creature in the world like Constance. Constance personified for her the qualities of the Baines family. Constance's letter was a great letter, a perfect letter, perfect in its artlessness; the natural expression of the Baines character at its best. Not an awkward reference in the whole of it! No clumsy expression of surprise at anything that she, Sophia, had done, or failed to do! No mention of Gerald! Just a sublime acceptance of the situation as it was, and the assurance of undiminished love! Tact? No; it was something finer than tact! Tact was conscious, skilful. Sophia was certain that the notion of tactfulness had not entered Constance's head. Constance had simply written out of her heart. And that was what made the letter so splendid. Sophia was convinced that no one but a Baines could have written such a letter. She felt that she must rise to the height of that letter, that she too must show her Baines blood. And she went primly to her desk, and began to write (on private notepaper) in that imperious large hand of hers that was so different from Constance's. She began a little stiffly, but after a few lines her generous and passionate soul was responding freely to the appeal of Constance. She asked that Mr. Critchlow should pay L20 for her to the Miss Chetwynd fund. She spoke of her Pension and of Paris, and of her pleasure in Constance's letter. But she said nothing as to Gerald, nor as to the possibility of a visit to the Five Towns. She finished the letter in a blaze of love, and passed from it as from a dream to the sterile banality of the daily life of the Pension Frensham, feeling that, compared to Constance's affection, nothing else had any worth. But she would not consider the project of going to Bursley. Never, never would she go to Bursley. If Constance chose to come to Paris and see her, she would be delighted, but she herself would not budge. The mere notion of any change in her existence intimidated her. And as for returning to Bursley itself … no, no! Nevertheless, at the Pension Frensham, the future could not be as the past. Sophia's health forbade that. She knew that the doctor was right. Every time that she made an effort, she knew intimately and speedily that the doctor was right. Only her will-power was unimpaired; the machinery by which will-power is converted into action was mysteriously damaged. She was aware of the fact. But she could not face it yet. Time would have to elapse before she could bring herself to face that fact. She was getting an old woman. She could no longer draw on reserves. Yet she persisted to every one that she was quite recovered, and was abstaining from her customary work simply from an excess of prudence. Certainly her face had recovered. And the Pension, being a machine all of whose parts were in order, continued to run, apparently, with its usual smoothness. It is true that the excellent chef began to peculate, but as his cuisine did not suffer, the result was not noticeable for a long period. The whole staff and many of the guests knew that Sophia had been indisposed; and they knew no more.

When by hazard Sophia observed a fault in the daily conduct of the house, her first impulse was to go to the root of it and cure it, her second was to leave it alone, or to palliate it by some superficial remedy.

Unperceived, and yet vaguely suspected by various people, the decline of the Pension Frensham had set in. The tide, having risen to its highest, was receding, but so little that no one could be sure that it had turned. Every now and then it rushed up again and washed the furthest stone.

Sophia and Constance exchanged several letters. Sophia said repeatedly that she could not leave Paris. At length she roundly asked Constance to come and pay her a visit. She made the suggestion with fear—for the prospect of actually seeing her beloved Constance alarmed her—but she could do no less than make it. And in a few days she had a reply to say that Constance would have come, under Cyril's charge, but that her sciatica was suddenly much worse, and she was obliged to lie down every day after dinner to rest her legs. Travelling was impossible for her. The fates were combining against Sophia's decision.

And now Sophia began to ask herself about her duty to Constance. The truth was that she was groping round to find an excuse for reversing her decision. She was afraid to reverse it, yet tempted. She had the desire to do something which she objected to doing. It was like the desire to throw one's self over a high balcony. It drew her, drew her, and she drew back against it. The Pension was now tedious to her. It bored her even to pretend to be the supervising head of the Pension. Throughout the house discipline had loosened.

She wondered when Mr. Mardon would renew his overtures for the transformation of her enterprise into a limited company. In spite of herself she would deliberately cross his path and give him opportunities to begin on the old theme. He had never before left her in peace for so long a period. No doubt she had, upon his last assault, absolutely convinced him that his efforts had no smallest chance of success, and he had made up his mind to cease them. With a single word she could wind him up again. The merest hint, one day when he was paying his bill, and he would be beseeching her. But she could not utter the word.

Then she began to say openly that she did not feel well, that the house was too much for her, and that the doctor had imperatively commanded rest. She said this to every one except Mardon. And every one somehow persisted in not saying it to Mardon. The doctor having advised that she should spend more time in the open air, she would take afternoon drives in the Bois with Fossette. It was October. But Mr. Mardon never seemed to hear of those drives.

One morning he met her in the street outside the house.

"I'm sorry to hear you're so unwell," he said confidentially, after they had discussed the health of Fossette.

"So unwell!" she exclaimed as if resenting the statement. "Who told you
I was so unwell?"

"Jacqueline. She told me you often said that what you needed was a complete change. And it seems the doctor says so, too."

"Oh! doctors!" she murmured, without however denying the truth of
Jacqueline's assertion. She saw hope in Mr. Mardon's eyes.

"Of course, you know," he said, still more confidentially, "if you SHOULD happen to change your mind, I'm always ready to form a little syndicate to take this"—he waved discreetly at the Pension—"off your hands."

She shook her head violently, which was strange, considering that for weeks she had been wishing to hear such words from Mr. Mardon.

"You needn't give it up altogether," he said. "You could retain your hold on it. We'd make you manageress, with a salary and a share in the profits. You'd be mistress just as much as you are now."

"Oh!" said she carelessly. "IF *I* GAVE IT UP, *I* SHOULD GIVE IT UP
ENTIRELY. No half measures for me."

With the utterance of that sentence, the history of Frensham's as a private understanding was brought to a close. Sophia knew it. Mr. Mardon knew it. Mr. Mardon's heart leapt. He saw in his imagination the formation of the preliminary syndicate, with himself at its head, and then the re-sale by the syndicate to a limited company at a profit. He saw a nice little profit for his own private personal self of a thousand or so—gained in a moment. The plant, his hope, which he had deemed dead, blossomed with miraculous suddenness.

"Well," he said. "Give it up entirely, then! Take a holiday for life. You've deserved it, Mrs. Scales."

She shook her head once again.

"Think it over," he said.

"I gave you my answer years ago," she said obstinately, while fearing lest he should take her at her word.

"Oblige me by thinking it over," he said. "I'll mention it to you again in a few days."

"It will be no use," she said.

He took his leave, waddling down the street in his vague clothes, conscious of his fame as Lewis Mardon, the great house-agent of the Champs Elysees, known throughout Europe and America.

In a few days he did mention it again.

"There's only one thing that makes me dream of it even for a moment," said Sophia. "And that is my sister's health."

"Your sister!" he exclaimed. He did not know she had a sister. Never had she spoken of her family.

"Yes. Her letters are beginning to worry me."

"Does she live in Paris?"

"No. In Staffordshire. She has never left home."

And to preserve her pride intact she led Mr. Mardon to think that Constance was in a most serious way, whereas in truth Constance had nothing worse than her sciatica, and even that was somewhat better.

Thus she yielded.

CHAPTER II

THE MEETING
I

Soon after dinner one day in the following spring, Mr. Critchlow knocked at Constance's door. She was seated in the rocking-chair in front of the fire in the parlour. She wore a large 'rough' apron, and with the outlying parts of the apron she was rubbing the moisture out of the coat of a young wire-haired fox-terrier, for whom no more original name had been found than 'Spot.' It is true that he had a spot. Constance had more than once called the world to witness that she would never have a young dog again, because, as she said, she could not be always running about after them, and they ate the stuffing out of the furniture. But her last dog had lived too long; a dog can do worse things than eat furniture; and, in her natural reaction against age in dogs, and also in the hope of postponing as long as possible the inevitable sorrow and upset which death causes when it takes off a domestic pet, she had not known how to refuse the very desirable fox-terrier aged ten months that an acquaintance had offered to her. Spot's beautiful pink skin could be seen under his disturbed hair; he was exquisitely soft to the touch, and to himself he was loathsome. His eyes continually peeped forth between corners of the agitated towel, and they were full of inquietude and shame.

Amy was assisting at this performance, gravely on the watch to see that Spot did not escape into the coal-cellar. She opened the door to Mr. Critchlow's knock. Mr. Critchlow entered without any formalities, as usual. He did not seem to have changed. He had the same quantity of white hair, he wore the same long white apron, and his voice (which showed however an occasional tendency to shrillness) had the same grating quality. He stood fairly straight. He was carrying a newspaper in his vellum hand.

"Well, missis!" he said.

"That will do, thank you, Amy," said Constance, quietly. Amy went slowly.

"So ye're washing him for her!" said Mr. Critchlow.

"Yes," Constance admitted. Spot glanced sharply at the aged man.

"An' ye seen this bit in the paper about Sophia?" he asked, holding the Signal for her inspection.

"About Sophia?" cried Constance. "What's amiss?"

"Nothing's amiss. But they've got it. It's in the 'Staffordshire day by day' column. Here! I'll read it ye." He drew a long wooden spectacle-case from his waistcoat pocket, and placed a second pair of spectacles on his nose. Then he sat down on the sofa, his knees sticking out pointedly, and read: "'We understand that Mrs. Sophia Scales, proprietress of the famous Pension Frensham in the Rue Lord Byron, Paris'—it's that famous that nobody in th' Five Towns has ever heard of it—'is about to pay a visit to her native town, Bursley, after an absence of over thirty years. Mrs. Scales belonged to the well-known and highly respected family of Baines. She has recently disposed of the Pension Frensham to a limited company, and we are betraying no secret in stating that the price paid ran well into five figures.' So ye see!" Mr. Critchlow commented.

"How do those Signal people find out things?" Constance murmured.

"Eh, bless ye, I don't know," said Mr. Critchlow.

This was an untruth. Mr. Critchlow had himself given the information to the new editor of the Signal, who had soon been made aware of Critchlow's passion for the press, and who knew how to make use of it.

"I wish it hadn't appeared just to-day," said Constance.

"Why?"

"Oh! I don't know, I wish it hadn't."

"Well, I'll be touring on, missis," said Mr. Critchlow, meaning that he would go.

He left the paper, and descended the steps with senile deliberation. It was characteristic that he had shown no curiosity whatever as to the details of Sophia's arrival.

Constance removed her apron, wrapped Spot up in it, and put him in a corner of the sofa. She then abruptly sent Amy out to buy a penny time-table.

"I thought you were going by tram to Knype," Amy observed.

"I have decided to go by train," said Constance, with cold dignity, as if she had decided the fate of nations. She hated such observations from Amy, who unfortunately lacked, in an increasing degree, the supreme gift of unquestioning obedience.

When Amy came breathlessly back, she found Constance in her bedroom, withdrawing crumpled balls of paper from the sleeves of her second-best mantle. Constance scarcely ever wore this mantle. In theory it was destined for chapel on wet Sundays; in practice it had remained long in the wardrobe, Sundays having been obstinately fine for weeks and weeks together. It was a mantle that Constance had never really liked. But she was not going to Knype to meet Sophia in her everyday mantle; and she had no intention of donning her best mantle for such an excursion. To make her first appearance before Sophia in the best mantle she had—this would have been a sad mistake of tactics! Not only would it have led to an anti-climax on Sunday, but it would have given to Constance the air of being in awe of Sophia. Now Constance was in truth a little afraid of Sophia; in thirty years Sophia might have grown into anything, whereas Constance had remained just Constance. Paris was a great place; and it was immensely far off. And the mere sound of that limited company business was intimidating. Imagine Sophia having by her own efforts created something which a real limited company wanted to buy and had bought! Yes, Constance was afraid, but she did not mean to show her fear in her mantle. After all, she was the elder. And she had her dignity too—and a lot of it—tucked away in her secret heart, hidden within the mildness of that soft exterior. So she had decided on the second-best mantle, which, being seldom used, had its sleeves stuffed with paper to the end that they might keep their shape and their 'fall.' The little balls of paper were strewed over the bed.

"There's a train at a quarter to three, gets to Knype at ten minutes past." said Amy. officiously. "But supposing it was only three minutes late and the London train was prompt, then you might miss her. Happen you'd better take the two fifteen to be on the safe side."

"Let me look," said Constance, firmly. "Please put all this paper in the wardrobe."

She would have preferred not to follow Amy's suggestion, but it was so incontestably wise that she was obliged to accept it.

"Unless ye go by tram," said Amy. "That won't mean starting quite so soon."

But Constance would not go by tram. If she took the tram she would be bound to meet people who had read the Signal, and who would say, with their stupid vacuity: "Going to meet your sister at Knype?" And then tiresome conversations would follow. Whereas, in the train, she would choose a compartment, and would be far less likely to encounter chatterers.

There was now not a minute to lose. And the excitement which had been growing in that house for days past, under a pretence of calm, leapt out swiftly into the light of the sun, and was unashamed. Amy had to help her mistress make herself as comely as she could be made without her best dress, mantle, and bonnet. Amy was frankly consulted as to effects. The barrier of class was lowered for a space. Many years had elapsed since

250

Constance had been conscious of a keen desire to look smart. She was reminded of the days when, in full fig for chapel, she would dash downstairs on a Sunday morning, and, assuming a pose for inspection at the threshold of the parlour, would demand of Samuel: "Shall I do?" Yes, she used to dash downstairs, like a child, and yet in those days she had thought herself so sedate and mature! She sighed, half with lancinating regret, and half in gentle disdain of that mercurial creature aged less than thirty. At fifty-one she regarded herself as old. And she was old. And Amy had the tricks and manners of an old spinster. Thus the excitement in the house was an 'old' excitement, and, like Constance's desire to look smart, it had its ridiculous side, which was also its tragic side, the side that would have made a boor guffaw, and a hysterical fool cry, and a wise man meditate sadly upon the earth's fashion of renewing itself.

At half-past one Constance was dressed, with the exception of her gloves. She looked at the clock a second time to make sure that she might safely glance round the house without fear of missing the train. She went up into the bedroom on the second-floor, her and Sophia's old bedroom, which she had prepared with enormous care for Sophia. The airing of that room had been an enterprise of days, for, save by a minister during the sittings of the Wesleyan Methodist Conference at Bursley, it had never been occupied since the era when Maria Insull used occasionally to sleep in the house. Cyril clung to his old room on his visits. Constance had an ample supply of solid and stately furniture, and the chamber destined for Sophia was lightened in every corner by the reflections of polished mahogany. It was also fairly impregnated with the odour of furniture paste—an odour of which no housewife need be ashamed. Further, it had been re-papered in a delicate blue, with one of the new 'art' patterns. It was a 'Baines' room. And Constance did not care where Sophia came from, nor what Sophia had been accustomed to, nor into what limited company Sophia had been transformed—that room was adequate! It could not have been improved upon. You had only to look at the crocheted mats—even those on the washstand under the white-and-gold ewer and other utensils. It was folly to expose such mats to the splashings of a washstand, but it was sublime folly. Sophia might remove them if she cared. Constance was house-proud; house-pride had slumbered within her; now it blazed forth.

A fire brightened the drawing-room, which was a truly magnificent apartment, a museum of valuables collected by the Baines and the Maddack families since the year 1840, tempered by the latest novelties in antimacassars and cloths. In all Bursley there could have been few drawing-rooms to compare with Constance's. Constance knew it. She was not afraid of her drawing-room being seen by anybody.

She passed for an instant into her own bedroom, where Amy was patiently picking balls of paper from the bed.

"Now you quite understand about tea?" Constance asked.

"Oh yes, 'm," said Amy, as if to say: "How much oftener are you going to ask me that question?" "Are you off now, 'm?"

"Yes," said Constance. "Come and fasten the front-door after me."

They descended together to the parlour. A white cloth for tea lay folded on the table. It was of the finest damask that skill could choose and money buy. It was fifteen years old, and had never been spread. Constance would not have produced it for the first meal, had she not possessed two other of equal eminence. On the harmonium were ranged several jams and cakes, a Bursley pork-pie, and some pickled salmon; with the necessary silver. All was there. Amy could not go wrong. And crocuses were in the vases on the mantelpiece. Her 'garden,' in the phrase which used to cause Samuel to think how extraordinarily feminine she was! It was a long time since she had had a 'garden' on the mantelpiece. Her interest in her chronic sciatica and in her palpitations had grown at the expense of her interest in gardens. Often, when she had finished the complicated processes by which her furniture and other goods were kept in order, she had strength only to 'rest.' She was rather a fragile, small, fat woman, soon out of breath, easily marred. This business of preparing for the advent of Sophia had appeared to her genuinely colossal. However, she had come through it very well. She was in pretty good health; only a little tired, and more than a little anxious and nervous, as she gave the last glance.

"Take away that apron, do!" she said to Amy, pointing to the rough apron in the corner of the sofa. "By the way, where is Spot?"

"Spot, m'm?" Amy ejaculated.

Both their hearts jumped. Amy instinctively looked out of the window. He was there, sure enough, in the gutter, studying the indescribabilities of King Street. He had obviously escaped when Amy came in from buying the time-table. The woman's face was guilty.

"Amy, I wonder AT you!" exclaimed Constance, tragically. She opened the door.

"Well, I never did see the like of that dog!" murmured Amy.

"Spot!" his mistress commanded. "Come here at once. Do you hear me?"

Spot turned sharply and gazed motionless at Constance. Then with a toss of the head he dashed off to the corner of the Square, and gazed motionless again. Amy went forth to catch him. After an age she brought him in, squealing. He was in a state exceedingly offensive to the eye and to the nose. He had effectively got rid of the smell of soap, which he loathed. Constance could have wept. It did really appear to her that nothing had gone right that day. And Spot had the most innocent, trustful air. Impossible to make him realize that his aunt Sophia was coming. He would have sold his entire family into servitude in order to buy ten yards of King Street gutter.

"You must wash him in the scullery, that's all there is for it," said
Constance, controlling herself. "Put that apron on, and don't forget
one of your new aprons when you open the door. Better shut him up in
Mr. Cyril's bedroom when you've dried him."

And she went, charged with worries, clasping her bag and her umbrella and smoothing her gloves, and spying downwards at the folds of her mantle.

"That's a funny way to go to Bursley Station, that is," said Amy, observing that Constance was descending King Street instead of crossing it into Wedgwood Street. And she caught Spot 'a fair clout on the head,' to indicate to him that she had him alone in the house now.

Constance was taking a round-about route to the station, so that, if stopped by acquaintances, she should not be too obviously going to the station. Her feelings concerning the arrival of Sophia, and concerning the town's attitude towards it, were very complex.

She was forced to hurry. And she had risen that morning with plans perfectly contrived for the avoidance of hurry. She disliked hurry because it always 'put her about.'

II

The express from London was late, so that Constance had three-quarters of an hour of the stony calmness of Knype platform when it is waiting for a great train. At last the porters began to cry, "Macclesfield, Stockport, and Manchester train;" the immense engine glided round the curve, dwarfing the carriages behind it, and Constance had a supreme tremor. The calmness of the platform was transformed into a melee. Little Constance found herself left on the fringe of a physically agitated crowd which was apparently trying to scale a precipice surmounted by windows and doors from whose apertures looked forth defenders of the train. Knype platform seemed as if it would never be reduced to order again. And Constance did not estimate highly the chances of picking out an unknown Sophia from that welter. She was very seriously perturbed. All the muscles of her face were drawn as her gaze wandered anxiously from end to end of the train.

Presently she saw a singular dog. Other people also saw it. It was of the colour of chocolate; it had a head and shoulders richly covered with hair that hung down in thousands of tufts like the tufts of a modern mop such as is bought in shops. This hair stopped suddenly rather less than halfway along the length of the dog's body, the remainder of which was naked and as smooth as marble. The effect was to give to the inhabitants of the Five Towns the impression that the dog had forgotten an essential part of its attire and was outraging decency. The ball of hair which had been allowed to grow on the dog's tail, and the circles of hair which ornamented its ankles, only served to intensify the impression of indecency. A pink ribbon round its neck completed the outrage. The animal had absolutely the air of a decked trollop. A chain ran taut from the creature's neck into the middle of a small crowd of persons gesticulating over trunks, and Constance traced it to a tall and distinguished woman in a coat and skirt with a rather striking hat. A beautiful and aristocratic woman, Constance thought, at a distance! Then the strange idea came to her: "That's Sophia!" She was sure…. She was not sure…. She was sure. The woman emerged from the crowd. Her eye fell on Constance. They both hesitated, and, as it were, wavered uncertainly towards each other.

"I should have known you anywhere," said Sophia, with apparently careless tranquillity, as she stooped to kiss Constance, raising her veil.

Constance saw that this marvellous tranquillity must be imitated, and she imitated it very well. It was a 'Baines' tranquillity. But she noticed a twitching of her sister's lips. The twitching comforted Constance, proving to her that she was not alone in foolishness. There was also something queer about the permanent lines of Sophia's mouth. That must be due to the 'attack' about which Sophia had written.

"Did Cyril meet you?" asked Constance. It was all that she could think of to say.

"Oh yes!" said Sophia, eagerly. "And I went to his studio, and he saw me off at Euston. He is a VERY nice boy. I love him."

She said 'I love him' with the intonation of Sophia aged fifteen. Her tone and imperious gesture sent Constance flying back to the 'sixties. "She hasn't altered one bit," Constance thought with joy. "Nothing could change Sophia." And at the back of that notion was a more general notion: "Nothing could change a Baines." It was true that Constance's Sophia had not changed. Powerful individualities remain undisfigured by no matter what vicissitudes. After this revelation of the original Sophia, arising as it did out of praise of Cyril, Constance felt easier, felt reassured.

"This is Fossette," said Sophia, pulling at the chain.

Constance knew not what to reply. Surely Sophia could not be aware what she did in bringing such a dog to a place where people were so particular as they are in the Five Towns.

"Fossette!" She repeated the name in an endearing accent, half stooping towards the dog. After all, it was not the dog's fault. Sophia had certainly mentioned a dog in her letters, but she had not prepared Constance for the spectacle of Fossette.

All that happened in a moment. A porter appeared with two trunks belonging to Sophia. Constance observed that they were superlatively 'good' trunks; also that Sophia's clothes, though 'on the showy side,' were superlatively 'good.' The getting of Sophia's ticket to Bursley occupied them next, and soon the first shock of meeting had worn off.

In a second-class compartment of the Loop Line train, with Sophia and Fossette opposite to her, Constance had leisure to 'take in' Sophia. She came to the conclusion that, despite her slenderness and straightness and the general effect of the long oval of her face under the hat, Sophia looked her age. She saw that Sophia must have been through a great deal; her experiences were damagingly printed in the details of feature. Seen at a distance, she might have passed for a woman of thirty, even for a girl, but seen across a narrow railway carriage she was a woman whom suffering had aged. Yet obviously her spirit was unbroken. Hear her tell a doubtful porter that of course she should take Fossette with her into the carriage! See her shut the carriage door with the expressed intention of keeping other people out! She was accustomed to command. At the same time her face had an almost set smile, as though she had said to herself: "I will die smiling." Constance felt sorry for her. While recognizing in Sophia a superior in charm, in experience, in knowledge of the world and in force of personality, she yet with a kind of undisturbed, fundamental superiority felt sorry for Sophia.

"What do you think?" said Sophia, absently fingering Fossette. "A man came up to me at Euston, while Cyril was getting my ticket, and said, 'Eh, Miss Baines, I haven't seen ye for over thirty years, but I know you're Miss Baines, or WERE—and you're looking bonny.' Then he went off. I think it must have been Holl, the grocer."

"Had he got a long white beard?"

"Yes."

"Then it was Mr. Holl. He's been Mayor twice. He's an alderman, you know."

"Really!" said Sophia. "But wasn't it queer?"

"Eh! Bless us!" exclaimed Constance. "Don't talk about queer! It's terrible how time flies."

The conversation stopped, and it refused to start again. Two women who are full of affectionate curiosity about each other, and who have not seen each other for thirty years, and who are anxious to confide in each other, ought to discover no difficulty in talking; but somehow these two could not talk. Constance perceived that Sophia was impeded by the same awkwardness as herself.

"Well I never!" cried Sophia, suddenly. She had glanced out of the window and had seen two camels and an elephant in a field close to the line, amid manufactories and warehouses and advertisements of soap.

"Oh!" said Constance. "That's Barnum's, you know. They have what they call a central depot here, because it's the middle of England." Constance spoke proudly. (After all, there can be only one middle.) It was on her tongue to say, in her 'tart' manner, that Fossette ought to be with the camels, but she refrained. Sophia hit on the excellent idea of noting all the buildings that were new to her and all the landmarks that she remembered. It was surprising how little the district had altered.

"Same smoke!" said Sophia.

"Same smoke!" Constance agreed.

"It's even worse," said Sophia.

"Do you think so?" Constance was slightly piqued. "But they're doing something now for smoke abatement."

"I must have forgotten how dirty it was!" said Sophia. "I suppose that's it. I'd no idea…!"

"Really!" said Constance. Then, in candid admission, "The fact is, it is dirty. You can't imagine what work it makes, especially with window-curtains."

As the train puffed under Trafalgar Road, Constance pointed to a new station that was being built there, to be called 'Trafalgar Road' station.

"Won't it be strange?" said she, accustomed to the eternal sequence of Loop Lane stations—Turnhill, Bursley, Bleakridge, Hanbridge, Cauldon, Knype, Trent Vale, and Longshaw. A 'Trafalgar Road' inserting itself between Bleakridge and Hanbridge seemed to her excessively curious.

"Yes, I suppose it will," Sophia agreed.

"But of course it's not the same to you," said Constance, dashed. She indicated the glories of Bursley Park, as the train slackened for Bursley, with modesty. Sophia gazed, and vaguely recognized the slopes where she had taken her first walk with Gerald Scales.

Nobody accosted them at Bursley Station, and they drove to the Square in a cab. Amy was at the window; she held up Spot, who was in a plenary state of cleanliness, rivalling the purity of Amy's apron.

"Good afternoon, m'm," said Amy, officiously, to Sophia, as Sophia came up the steps.

"Good afternoon, Amy," Sophia replied. She flattered Amy in thus showing that she was acquainted with her name; but if ever a servant was put into her place by mere tone, Amy was put into her place on that occasion. Constance trembled at Sophia's frigid and arrogant politeness. Certainly Sophia was not used to being addressed first by servants. But Amy was not quite the ordinary servant. She was much older than the ordinary servant, and she had acquired a partial moral dominion over Constance, though Constance would have warmly denied it. Hence Constance's apprehension. However, nothing happened. Amy apparently did not feel the snub.

"Take Spot and put him in Mr. Cyril's bedroom," Constance murmured to her, as if implying: "Have I not already told you to do that?" The fact was, she was afraid for Spot's life.

"Now, Fossette!" She welcomed the incoming poodle kindly; the poodle began at once to sniff.

The fat, red cabman was handling the trunks on the pavement, and Amy was upstairs. For a moment the sisters were alone together in the parlour.

"So here I am!" exclaimed the tall, majestic woman of fifty. And her lips twitched again as she looked round the room—so small to her.

"Yes, here you are!" Constance agreed. She bit her lip, and, as a measure of prudence to avoid breaking down, she bustled out to the cabman. A passing instant of emotion, like a fleck of foam on a wide and calm sea!

The cabman blundered up and downstairs with trunks, and saluted Sophia's haughty generosity, and then there was quietness. Amy was already brewing the tea in the cave. The prepared tea-table in front of the fire made a glittering array.

"Now, what about Fossette?" Constance voiced anxieties that had been growing on her.

"Fossette will be quite right with me," said Sophia, firmly.

They ascended to the guest's room, which drew Sophia's admiration for its prettiness. She hurried to the window and looked out into the Square.

"Would you like a fire?" Constance asked, in a rather perfunctory manner. For a bedroom fire, in seasons of normal health, was still regarded as absurd in the Square.

"Oh, no!" said Sophia; but with a slight failure to rebut the suggestion as utterly ridiculous.

"Sure?" Constance questioned.

"Quite, thank you," said Sophia.

"Well, I'll leave you. I expect Amy will have tea ready directly." She went down into the kitchen. "Amy," she said, "as soon as we've finished tea, light a fire in Mrs. Scales's bedroom."

"In the top bedroom, m'm?"

"Yes."

Constance climbed again to her own bedroom, and shut the door. She needed a moment to herself, in the midst of this terrific affair. She sighed with relief as she removed her mantle. She thought: "At any rate we've met, and I've got her here. She's very nice. No, she isn't a bit altered." She hesitated to admit that to her Sophia was the least in the world formidable. And so she said once more: "She's very nice. She isn't a bit altered." And then: "Fancy her being here! She really is here." With her perfect simplicity it did not occur to Constance to speculate as to what Sophia thought of her.

Sophia was downstairs first, and Constance found her looking at the blank wall beyond the door leading to the kitchen steps.

254

"So this is where you had it bricked up?" said Sophia.

"Yes," said Constance. "That's the place."

"It makes me feel like people feel when they have tickling in a limb that's been cut off!" said Sophia.

"Oh, Sophia!"

The tea received a great deal of praise from Sophia, but neither of them ate much. Constance found that Sophia was like herself: she had to be particular about her food. She tasted dainties for the sake of tasting, but it was a bird's pecking. Not the twelfth part of the tea was consumed. They dared not indulge caprices. Only their eyes could feed.

After tea they went up to the drawing-room, and in the corridor had the startling pleasure of seeing two dogs who scurried about after each other in amity. Spot had found Fossette, with the aid of Amy's incurable carelessness, and had at once examined her with great particularity. She seemed to be of an amiable disposition, and not averse from the lighter distractions. For a long time the sisters sat chatting together in the lit drawing-room to the agreeable sound of happy dogs playing in the dark corridor. Those dogs saved the situation, because they needed constant attention. When the dogs dozed, the sisters began to look through photograph albums, of which Constance had several, bound in plush or morocco. Nothing will sharpen the memory, evoke the past, raise the dead, rejuvenate the ageing, and cause both sighs and smiles, like a collection of photographs gathered together during long years of life. Constance had an astonishing menagerie of unknown cousins and their connections, and of townspeople; she had Cyril at all ages; she had weird daguerreotypes of her parents and their parents. The strangest of all was a portrait of Samuel Povey as an infant in arms. Sophia checked an impulse to laugh at it. But when Constance said: "Isn't it funny?" she did allow herself to laugh. A photograph of Samuel in the year before his death was really imposing. Sophia stared at it, impressed. It was the portrait of an honest man.

"How long have you been a widow?" Constance asked in a low voice, glancing at upright Sophia over her spectacles, a leaf of the album raised against her finger.

Sophia unmistakably flushed. "I don't know that I am a widow," said she, with an air. "My husband left me in 1870, and I've never seen nor heard of him since."

"Oh, my dear!" cried Constance, alarmed and deafened as by a clap of awful thunder. "I thought ye were a widow. Mr. Peel-Swynnerton said he was told positively ye were a widow. That's why I never…." She stopped. Her face was troubled.

"Of course I always passed for a widow, over there," said Sophia.

"Of course," said Constance quickly. "I see…."

"And I may be a widow," said Sophia.

Constance made no remark. This was a blow. Bursley was such a particular place. Doubtless, Gerald Scales had behaved like a scoundrel. That was sure!

When, immediately afterwards, Amy opened the drawing-room door (having first knocked—the practice of encouraging a servant to plunge without warning of any kind into a drawing-room had never been favoured in that house) she saw the sisters sitting rather near to each other at the walnut oval table, Mrs. Scales very upright, and staring into the fire, and Mrs. Povey 'bunched up' and staring at the photograph album; both seeming to Amy aged and apprehensive; Mrs. Povey's hair was quite grey, though Mrs. Scales' hair was nearly as black as Amy's own. Mrs. Scales started at the sound of the knock, and turned her head.

"Here's Mr. and Mrs. Critchlow, m'm," announced Amy.

The sisters glanced at one another, with lifted foreheads. Then Mrs. Povey spoke to Amy as though visits at half-past eight at night were a customary phenomenon of the household. Nevertheless, she trembled to think what outrageous thing Mr. Critchlow might say to Sophia after thirty years' absence. The occasion was great, and it might also be terrible.

"Ask them to come up," she said calmly.

But Amy had the best of that encounter. "I have done," she replied, and instantly produced them out of the darkness of the corridor. It was providential: the sisters had made no remark that the Critchlows might not hear.

Then Maria Critchlow, simpering, had to greet Sophia. Mrs. Critchlow was very agitated, from sheer nervousness. She curvetted; she almost pranced; and she made noises with her mouth as though she saw some one eating a sour apple. She wanted to show Sophia how greatly she had changed from the young, timid apprentice. Certainly since her marriage she had changed. As manager of other people's business she had not felt the necessity of being effusive to customers, but as proprietress, anxiety to succeed had dragged her out of her capable and mechanical indifference. It was a pity. Her consistent dullness had had a sort of dignity; but genial, she was merely ridiculous. Animation cruelly displayed her appalling commonness and physical shabbiness. Sophia's demeanour was not chilly; but it indicated that Sophia had no wish to be eyed over as a freak of nature.

Mr. Critchlow advanced very slowly into the room. "Ye still carry your head on a stiff neck," said he, deliberately examining Sophia. Then with great care he put out his long thin arm and took her hand. "Well, I'm rare and glad to see ye!"

Every one was thunderstruck at this expression of joy. Mr. Critchlow had never been known to be glad to see anybody.

"Yes," twittered Maria, "Mr. Critchlow would come in to-night. Nothing would do but he must come in to-night."

"You didn't tell me this afternoon," said Constance, "that you were going to give us the pleasure of your company like this."

He looked momentarily at Constance. "No," he grated, "I don't know as I did."

His gaze flattered Sophia. Evidently he treated this experienced and sad woman of fifty as a young girl. And in presence of his extreme age she felt like a young girl, remembering the while how as a young girl she had hated him. Repulsing the assistance of his wife, he arranged an armchair in front of the fire and meticulously put himself into it. Assuredly he was much older in a drawing-room than behind the counter of his shop. Constance had noticed that in the afternoon. A live coal fell out of the fire. He bent forward, wet his fingers, picked up the coal and threw it back into the fire.

"Well," said Sophia. "I wouldn't have done that."

"I never saw Mr. Critchlow's equal for picking up hot cinders," Maria giggled.

Mr. Critchlow deigned no remark. "When did ye leave this Paris?" he demanded of Sophia, leaning back, and putting his hands on the arms of the chair.

"Yesterday morning," said Sophia,

"And what'n ye been doing with yeself since yesterday morning?"

"I spent last night in London," Sophia replied.

"Oh, in London, did ye?"

"Yes. Cyril and I had an evening together."

"Eh? Cyril! What's yer opinion o' Cyril, Sophia?"

"I'm very proud to have Cyril for a nephew," said Sophia.

"Oh! Are ye?" The old man was obviously ironic.

"Yes I am," Sophia insisted sharply. "I'm not going to hear a word said against Cyril."

She proceeded to an enthusiastic laudation of Cyril which rather overwhelmed his mother. Constance was pleased; she was delighted. And yet somewhere in her mind was an uncomfortable feeling that Cyril, having taken a fancy to his brilliant aunt, had tried to charm her as he seldom or never tried to charm his mother. Cyril and Sophia had dazzled and conquered each other; they were of the same type; whereas she, Constance, being but a plain person, could not glitter.

She rang the bell and gave instructions to Amy about food—fruit cakes, coffee and hot milk, on a tray; and Sophia also spoke to Amy murmuring a request as to Fossette.

"Yes, Mrs. Scales," said Amy, with eager deference.

Mrs. Critchlow smiled vaguely from a low chair near the curtained window. Then Constance lit another burner of the chandelier. In doing so, she gave a little sigh; it was a sigh of relief. Mr. Critchlow had behaved himself. Now that he and Sophia had met, the worst was over. Had Constance known beforehand that he would pay a call, she would have been agonized by apprehensions, but now that he had actually come she was glad he had come.

When he had silently sipped some hot milk, he drew a thick bunch of papers, white and blue, from his bulging breast-pocket.

"Now, Maria Critchlow," he called, edging round his chair slightly.

"Ye'd best go back home."

Maria Critchlow was biting at a bit of walnut cake, while in her right hand, all seamed with black lines, she held a cup of coffee.

"But, Mr. Critchlow——!" Constance protested.

"I've got business with Sophia, and I must get it done. I've got for to render an account of my stewardship to Sophia, under her father's will, and her mother's will, and her aunt's will, and it's nobody's business but mine and Sophia's, I reckon. Now then," he glanced at his wife, "off with ye!"

Maria rose, half-kittenish and half-ashamed.

"Surely you don't want to go into all that to-night," said Sophia. She spoke softly, for she had already fully perceived that Mr. Critchlow must be managed with the tact which the capricious obstinacies of advanced age demanded. "Surely you can wait a day or two. I'm in no hurry."

"HAVEN'T I WAITED LONG ENOUGH?" he retorted fiercely.

There was a pause. Maria Critchlow moved.

"As for you being in no hurry, Sophia," the old man went on, "nobody can say as you've been in a hurry." Sophia had suffered a check. She glanced hesitatingly at Constance.

"Mrs. Critchlow and I will go down into the parlour," said Constance, quickly. "There is a bit of fire there."

"Oh no. I won't hear of such a thing!"

"Yes, we will, won't we, Mrs. Critchlow?" Constance insisted, cheerfully but firmly. She was determined that in her house Sophia should have all the freedom and conveniences that she could have had in her own. If a private room was needed for discussions between Sophia and her trustee, Constance's pride was piqued to supply that room. Further, Constance was glad to get Maria out of Sophia's sight. She was accustomed to Maria; with her it did not matter; but she did not care that the teeth of Sophia should be set on edge by the ridiculous demeanour of Maria. So those two left the drawing-room, and the old man began to open the papers which he had been preparing for weeks.

There was very little fire in the parlour, and Constance, in addition to being bored by Mrs. Critchlow's inane and inquisitive remarks, felt chilly, which was bad for her sciatica. She wondered whether Sophia would have to confess to Mr. Critchlow that she was not certainly a widow. She thought that steps ought to be taken to ascertain, through Birkinshaws, if anything was known of Gerald Scales. But even that course was set with perils. Supposing that he still lived, an unspeakable villain (Constance could only think of him as an unspeakable villain), and supposing that he molested Sophia,—what scenes! What shame in the town! Such frightful thoughts ran endlessly through Constance's mind as she bent over the fire endeavouring to keep alive a silly conversation with Maria Critchlow.

Amy passed through the parlour to go to bed. There was no other way of reaching the upper part of the house.

"Are you going to bed, Amy?"

"Yes'm."

"Where is Fossette?"

"In the kitchen, m'm," said Amy, defending herself. "Mrs. Scales told me the dog might sleep in the kitchen with Spot, as they was such good friends. I've opened the bottom drawer, and Fossit is lying in that."

"Mrs. Scales has brought a dog with her!" exclaimed Maria.

"Yes'm!" said Amy, drily, before Constance could answer. She implied everything in that affirmative.

"You are a family for dogs," said Maria. "What sort of dog is it?"

"Well," said Constance. "I don't know exactly what they call it. It's a French dog, one of those French dogs."

Amy was lingering at the stairfoot. "Good night, Amy, thank you."

Amy ascended, shutting the door.

"Oh! I see!" Maria muttered. "Well, I never!"

It was ten o'clock before sounds above indicated that the first interview between trustee and beneficiary was finished.

"I'll be going on to open our side-door," said Maria. "Say good night to Mrs. Scales for me." She was not sure whether Charles Critchlow had really meant her to go home, or whether her mere absence from the drawing-room had contented him. So she departed. He came down the stairs with the most tiresome slowness, went through the parlour in silence, ignoring Constance, and also Sophia, who was at his heels, and vanished.

As Constance shut and bolted the front-door, the sisters looked at each other, Sophia faintly smiling. It seemed to them that they understood each other better when they did not speak. With a glance, they exchanged their ideas on the subject of Charles Critchlow and Maria, and learnt that their ideas were similar. Constance said nothing as to the private interview. Nor did Sophia. At present, on this the first day, they could only achieve intimacy by intermittent flashes.

"What about bed?" asked Sophia.

"You must be tired," said Constance.

Sophia got to the stairs, which received a little light from the corridor gas, before Constance, having tested the window-fastening, turned out the gas in the parlour. They climbed the lower flight of stairs together.

"I must just see that your room is all right," Constance said.

"Must you?" Sophia smiled.

They climbed the second flight, slowly. Constance was out of breath.

"Oh, a fire! How nice!" cried Sophia. "But why did you go to all that trouble? I told you not to."

"It's no trouble at all," said Constance, raising the gas in the bedroom. Her tone implied that bedroom fires were a quite ordinary incident of daily life in a place like Bursley.

"Well, my dear, I hope you'll find everything comfortable," said
Constance.

"I'm sure I shall. Good night, dear."

"Good night, then."

They looked at each other again, with timid affectionateness. They did not kiss. The thought in both their minds was: "We couldn't keep on kissing every day." But there was a vast amount of quiet, restrained affection, of mutual confidence and respect, even of tenderness, in their tones.

About half an hour later a dreadful hullaballoo smote the ear of Constance. She was just getting into bed. She listened intently, in great alarm. It was undoubtedly those dogs fighting, and fighting to the death. She pictured the kitchen as a battlefield, and Spot slain. Opening the door, she stepped out into the corridor.

"Constance," said a low voice above her. She jumped. "Is that you?"

"Yes."

"Well, don't bother to go down to the dogs; they'll stop in a moment.
Fossette won't bite. I'm so sorry she's upsetting the house."

Constance stared upwards, and discerned a pale shadow. The dogs did soon cease their altercation. This short colloquy in the dark affected Constance strangely.

III

The next morning, after a night varied by periods of wakefulness not unpleasant, Sophia arose and, taking due precautions against cold, went to the window. It was Saturday; she had left Paris on the Thursday. She looked forth upon the Square, holding aside the blind. She had expected, of course, to find that the Square had shrunk in size; but nevertheless she was startled to see how small it was. It seemed to her scarcely bigger than a courtyard. She could remember a winter morning when from the window she had watched the Square under virgin snow in the lamplight, and the Square had been vast, and the first wayfarer, crossing it diagonally and leaving behind him the irregular impress of his feet, had appeared to travel for hours over an interminable white waste before vanishing past Holl's shop in the direction of the Town Hall. She chiefly recalled the Square under snow; cold mornings, and the coldness of the oil-cloth at the window, and the draught of cold air through the ill-fitting sash (it was put right now)! These visions of herself seemed beautiful to her; her childish existence seemed beautiful; the storms and tempests of her girlhood seemed beautiful; even the great sterile expanse of tedium when, after giving up a scholastic career, she had served for two years in the shop—even this had a strange charm in her memory.

And she thought that not for millions of pounds would she live her life over again.

In its contents the Square had not surprisingly changed during the immense, the terrifying interval that separated her from her virginity. On the east side, several shops had been thrown into one, and forced into a semblance of eternal unity by means of a coat of stucco. And there was a fountain at the north end which was new to her. No other constructional change! But the moral change, the sad declension from the ancient proud spirit of the Square—this was painfully depressing. Several establishments lacked tenants, had obviously lacked tenants for a long time; 'To let' notices hung in their stained and dirty upper windows, and clung insecurely to their closed shutters. And on the sign-boards of these establishments were names that Sophia did not know. The character of most of the shops seemed to have worsened; they had become pettifogging little holes, unkempt, shabby, poor; they had no brightness, no feeling of vitality. And the floor of the Square was littered with nondescript refuse. The whole scene, paltry, confined, and dull, reached for her the extreme of provinciality. It was what the French called, with a pregnant intonation, la province. This—being said, there was nothing else to say. Bursley, of course, was in the provinces; Bursley must, in the nature of things, be typically provincial. But in her mind it had always been differentiated from the common province; it had always had an air, a distinction, and especially St. Luke's Square! That illusion was now gone. Still, the alteration was not wholly in herself; it was not wholly subjective. The Square really had changed for the worse; it might not be smaller, but it had deteriorated. As a centre of commerce it had assuredly approached very near to death. On a Saturday morning thirty years ago it would have been covered with linen-roofed

258

stalls, and chattering country-folk, and the stir of bargains. Now, Saturday morning was like any other morning in the Square, and the glass-roof of St. Luke's market in Wedgwood Street, which she could see from her window, echoed to the sounds of noisy commerce. In that instance business had simply moved a few yards to the east; but Sophia knew, from hints in Constance's letters and in her talk, that business in general had moved more than a few yards, it had moved a couple of miles—to arrogant and pushing Hanbridge, with its electric light and its theatres and its big, advertising shops. The heaven of thick smoke over the Square, the black deposit on painted woodwork, the intermittent hooting of steam syrens, showed that the wholesale trade of Bursley still flourished. But Sophia had no memories of the wholesale trade of Bursley; it meant nothing to the youth of her heart; she was attached by intimate links to the retail traffic of Bursley, and as a mart old Bursley was done for.

She thought: "It would kill me if I had to live here. It's deadening. It weighs on you. And the dirt, and the horrible ugliness! And the—way they talk, and the way they think! I felt it first at Knype station. The Square is rather picturesque, but it's such a poor, poor little thing! Fancy having to look at it every morning of one's life! No!" She almost shuddered.

For the time being she had no home. To Constance she was 'paying a visit.'

Constance did not appear to realize the awful conditions of dirt, decay, and provinciality in which she was living. Even Constance's house was extremely inconvenient, dark, and no doubt unhealthy. Cellar-kitchen, no hall, abominable stairs, and as to hygiene, simply mediaeval. She could not understand why Constance had remained in the house. Constance had plenty of money and might live where she liked, and in a good modern house. Yet she stayed in the Square. "I daresay she's got used to it," Sophia thought leniently. "I daresay I should be just the same in her place." But she did not really think so, and she could not understand Constance's state of mind.

Certainly she could not claim to have 'added up' Constance yet. She considered that her sister was in some respects utterly provincial—what they used to call in the Five Towns a 'body.' Somewhat too diffident, not assertive enough, not erect enough; with curious provincial pronunciations, accents, gestures, mannerisms, and inarticulate ejaculations; with a curious narrowness of outlook! But at the same time Constance was very shrewd, and she was often proving by some bit of a remark that she knew what was what, despite her provinciality. In judgments upon human nature they undoubtedly thought alike, and there was a strong natural general sympathy between them. And at the bottom of Constance was something fine. At intervals Sophia discovered herself secretly patronizing Constance, but reflection would always cause her to cease from patronage and to examine her own defences. Constance, besides being the essence of kindness, was no fool. Constance could see through a pretence, an absurdity, as quickly as any one. Constance did honestly appear to Sophia to be superior to any Frenchwoman that she had ever encountered. She saw supreme in Constance that quality which she had recognized in the porters at Newhaven on landing—the quality of an honest and naive goodwill, of powerful simplicity. That quality presented itself to her as the greatest in the world, and it seemed to be in the very air of England. She could even detect it in Mr. Critchlow, whom, for the rest, she liked, admiring the brutal force of his character. She pardoned his brutality to his wife. She found it proper. "After all," she said, "supposing he hadn't married her, what would she have been? Nothing but a slave! She's infinitely better off as his wife. In fact she's lucky. And it would be absurd for him to treat her otherwise than he does treat her." (Sophia did not divine that her masterful Critchlow had once wanted Maria as one might want a star.)

But to be always with such people! To be always with Constance! To be always in the Bursley atmosphere, physical and mental!

She pictured Paris as it would be on that very morning—bright, clean, glittering; the neatness of the Rue Lord Byron, and the magnificent slanting splendour of the Champs Elysees. Paris had always seemed beautiful to her; but the life of Paris had not seemed beautiful to her. Yet now it did seem beautiful. She could delve down into the earlier years of her ownership of the Pension, and see a regular, placid beauty in her daily life there. Her life there, even so late as a fortnight ago, seemed beautiful; sad, but beautiful. It had passed into history. She sighed when she thought of the innumerable interviews with Mardon, the endless formalities required by the English and the French law and by the particularity of the Syndicate. She had been through all that. She had actually been through it and it was over. She had bought the Pension for a song and sold it for great riches. She had developed from a nobody into the desired of Syndicates. And after long, long, monotonous, strenuous years of possession the day had come, the emotional moment had come, when she had yielded up the keys of ownership to Mr. Mardon and a man from the Hotel Moscow, and had paid her servants for the last time and signed the last receipted bill. The men had been very gallant, and had requested her to stay in the Pension as their guest until she was ready to leave Paris. But she had declined that. She could not have borne to remain in the Pension under the reign of another. She had left at once and gone to a hotel with her few goods while finally disposing of certain financial questions. And one evening Jacqueline had come to see her, and had wept.

Her exit from the Pension Frensham struck her now as poignantly pathetic, in its quickness and its absence of ceremonial. Ten steps, and her career was finished, closed. Astonishing with what liquid tenderness she turned and looked back on that hard, fighting, exhausting life in Paris! For, even if she had unconsciously liked it, she had never enjoyed it. She had always compared France disadvantageously with England, always resented the French temperament in business, always been convinced that 'you never knew where you were' with French tradespeople. And now they flitted before her endowed with a wondrous charm; so polite in their lying, so eager to spare your feelings and to reassure you, so neat and prim. And the French shops, so exquisitely arranged! Even a butcher's shop in Paris was a pleasure to the eye, whereas the butcher's shop in Wedgwood Street, which she remembered of old, and which she had glimpsed from the cab—what a bloody shambles! She longed for Paris again. She longed to stretch her lungs in Paris. These people in Bursley did not suspect what Paris was. They did not appreciate and they never would appreciate the marvels that she had accomplished in a theatre of marvels. They probably never realized that the whole of the rest of the world was not more or less like Bursley. They had no curiosity. Even Constance was a thousand times more interested in relating trifles of Bursley gossip than in listening to details of life in Paris. Occasionally she had expressed a mild, vapid surprise at things told to her by Sophia; but she was not really impressed, because her curiosity did not extend beyond Bursley. She, like the rest, had the formidable, thrice-callous egotism of the provinces. And if Sophia had informed her that the heads of Parisians grew out of their navels she would have murmured: "Well, well! Bless us! I never heard of such things! Mrs. Brindley's second boy has got his head quite crooked, poor little fellow!"

Why should Sophia feel sorrowful? She did not know. She was free; free to go where she liked and do what she liked, She had no responsibilities, no cares. The thought of her husband had long ago ceased to rouse in her any feeling of any kind. She was rich. Mr. Critchlow had accumulated for her about as much money as she had herself acquired. Never could she spend her income! She did not know how to spend it. She lacked nothing that was procurable. She had no desires except the direct desire for happiness. If thirty thousand pounds or so could have bought a son like Cyril, she would have bought one for herself. She bitterly regretted that she had no child. In this, she envied Constance. A child seemed to be the one commodity worth having. She was too free, too exempt from responsibilities. In spite of Constance she was alone in the world. The strangeness of the hazards of life overwhelmed her. Here she was at fifty, alone.

But the idea of leaving Constance, having once rejoined her, did not please Sophia. It disquieted her. She could not see herself living away from Constance. She was alone—but Constance was there.

She was downstairs first, and she had a little conversation with Amy. And she stood on the step of the front-door while Fossette made a preliminary inspection of Spot's gutter. She found the air nipping.

Constance, when she descended, saw stretching across one side of the breakfast-table an umbrella, Sophia's present to her from Paris. It was an umbrella such that a better could not be bought. It would have impressed even Aunt Harriet. The handle was of gold, set with a circlet of opalines. The tips of the ribs were also of gold. It was this detail which staggered Constance. Frankly, this development of luxury had been unknown and unsuspected in the Square. That the tips of the ribs should match the handle … that did truly beat everything! Sophia said calmly that the device was quite common. But she did not conceal that the umbrella was strictly of the highest class and that it might be shown to queens without shame. She intimated that the frame (a 'Fox's Paragon'), handle, and tips, would outlast many silks. Constance was childish with pleasure.

They decided to go out marketing together. The unspoken thought in their minds was that as Sophia would have to be introduced to the town sooner or later, it might as well be sooner. Constance looked at the sky. "It can't possibly rain," she said. "I shall take my umbrella."

CHAPTER III

TOWARDS HOTEL LIFE
I

SOPHIA wore list slippers in the morning. It was a habit which she had formed in the Rue Lord Byron—by accident rather than with an intention to utilize list slippers for the effective supervision of servants. These list slippers were the immediate cause of important happenings in St. Luke's Square. Sophia had been with Constance one calendar month—it was, of course, astonishing how quickly the time had passed!—and she had become familiar with the house. Restraint had gradually ceased to mark the relations of the sisters. Constance, in particular, hid nothing from Sophia, who was made aware of the minor and major defects of Amy and all the other creakings of the household machine. Meals were eaten off the ordinary tablecloths, and on the days for 'turning out' the parlour, Constance assumed, with a little laugh, that Sophia would excuse Amy's apron, which she had not had time to change. In brief, Sophia was no longer a stranger, and nobody felt bound to pretend that things were not exactly what they were. In spite of the foulness and the provinciality of Bursley, Sophia enjoyed the intimacy with Constance. As for Constance, she was enchanted. The inflections of their voices, when they were talking to each other very privately, were often tender, and these sudden surprising tendernesses secretly thrilled both of them.

On the fourth Sunday morning Sophia put on her dressing-gown and those list slippers very early, and paid a visit to Constance's bedroom. She was somewhat concerned about Constance, and her concern was pleasurable to her. She made the most of it. Amy, with her lifelong carelessness about doors, had criminally failed to latch the street-door of the parlour on the previous morning, and Constance had only perceived the omission by the phenomenon of frigidity in her legs at breakfast. She always sat with her back to the door, in her mother's fluted rocking-chair; and Sophia on the spot, but not in the chair, occupied by John Baines in the forties, and in the seventies and later by Samuel Povey. Constance had been alarmed by that frigidity. "I shall have a return of my sciatica!" she had exclaimed, and Sophia was startled by the apprehension in her tone. Before evening the sciatica had indeed revisited Constance's sciatic nerve, and Sophia for the first time gained an idea of what a pulsating sciatica can do in the way of torturing its victim. Constance, in addition to the sciatica, had caught a sneezing cold, and the act of sneezing caused her the most acute pain. Sophia had soon stopped the sneezing. Constance was got to bed. Sophia wished to summon the doctor, but Constance assured her that the doctor would have nothing new to advise. Constance suffered angelically. The weak and exquisite sweetness of her smile, as she lay in bed under the stress of twinging pain amid hot-water bottles, was amazing to Sophia. It made her think upon the reserves of Constance's character, and upon the variety of the manifestations of the Baines' blood.

So on the Sunday morning she had arisen early, just after Amy.

She discovered Constance to be a little better, as regards the neuralgia, but exhausted by the torments of a sleepless night. Sophia, though she had herself not slept well, felt somehow conscience-stricken for having slept at all.

"You poor dear!" she murmured, brimming with sympathy. "I shall make you some tea at once, myself."

"Oh, Amy will do it," said Constance.

Sophia repeated with a resolute intonation: "I shall make it myself." And after being satisfied that there was no instant need for a renewal of hot-water bottles, she went further downstairs in those list slippers.

As she was descending the dark kitchen steps she heard Amy's voice in pettish exclamation: "Oh, get out, YOU!" followed by a yelp from Fossette. She had a swift movement of anger, which she controlled. The relations between her and Fossette were not marked by transports, and her rule over dogs in general was severe; even when alone she very seldom kissed the animal passionately, according to the general habit of people owning dogs. But she loved Fossette. And, moreover, her love for Fossette had been lately sharpened by the ridicule which Bursley had showered upon that strange beast. Happily for Sophia's amour propre, there was no means of getting Fossette shaved in Bursley, and thus Fossette was daily growing less comic to the Bursley eye. Sophia could therefore without loss of dignity yield to force of circumstances what she would not have yielded to popular opinion. She guessed that Amy had no liking for the dog, but the accent which Amy had put upon the 'you' seemed to indicate that Amy was making distinctions between Fossette and Spot, and this disturbed Sophia much more than Fossette's yelp.

Sophia coughed, and entered the kitchen.

Spot was lapping his morning milk out of a saucer, while Fossette stood wistfully, an amorphous mass of thick hair, under the table.

"Good morning, Amy," said Sophia, with dreadful politeness.

"Good morning, m'm," said Amy, glumly.

Amy knew that Sophia had heard that yelp, and Sophia knew that she knew. The pretence of politeness was horrible. Both the women felt as though the kitchen was sanded with gunpowder and there were lighted matches about. Sophia had a very proper grievance against Amy on account of the open door of the previous day. Sophia thought that, after such a sin, the least Amy could do was to show contrition and amiability and an anxiety to please: which things Amy had not shown. Amy had a grievance against Sophia because Sophia had recently thrust upon her a fresh method of cooking green vegetables. Amy was a strong opponent of new or foreign methods. Sophia was not aware of this grievance, for Amy had hidden it under her customary cringing politeness to Sophia.

They surveyed each other like opposing armies.

"What a pity you have no gas-stove here! I want to make some tea at once for Mrs. Povey," said Sophia, inspecting the just-born fire.

"Gas-stove, m'm?" said Amy, hostilely. It was Sophia's list slippers which had finally decided Amy to drop the mask of deference.

She made no effort to aid Sophia; she gave no indication as to where the various necessaries for tea were to be found. Sophia got the kettle, and washed it out. Sophia got the smallest tea-pot, and, as the tea-leaves had been left in it, she washed out the teapot also, with exaggerated noise and meticulousness. Sophia got the sugar and the other trifles, and Sophia blew up the fire with the bellows. And Amy did nothing in particular except encourage Spot to drink.

"Is that all the milk you give to Fossette?" Sophia demanded coldly, when it had come to Fossette's turn. She was waiting for the water to boil. The saucer for the bigger dog, who would have made two of Spot, was not half full.

"It's all there is to spare, m'm," Amy rasped.

Sophia made no reply. Soon afterwards she departed, with the tea successfully made. If Amy had not been a mature woman of over forty she would have snorted as Sophia went away. But Amy was scarcely the ordinary silly girl.

Save for a certain primness as she offered the tray to her sister, Sophia's demeanour gave no sign whatever that the Amazon in her was aroused. Constance's eager trembling pleasure in the tea touched her deeply, and she was exceedingly thankful that Constance had her, Sophia, as a succour in time of distress.

A few minutes later, Constance, having first asked Sophia what time it was by the watch in the watch-case on the chest of drawers (the Swiss clock had long since ceased to work), pulled the red tassel of the bell-cord over her bed. A bell tinkled far away in the kitchen.

"Anything I can do?" Sophia inquired.

"Oh no, thanks," said Constance. "I only want my letters, if the postman has come. He ought to have been here long ago." Sophia had learned during her stay that Sunday morning was the morning on which Constance expected a letter from Cyril. It was a definite arrangement between mother and son that Cyril should write on Saturdays, and Constance on Sundays. Sophia knew that Constance set store by this letter, becoming more and more preoccupied about Cyril as the end of the week approached. Since Sophia's arrival Cyril's letter had not failed to come, but once it had been naught save a scribbled line or two, and Sophia gathered that it was never a certainty, and that Constance was accustomed, though not reconciled, to disappointments. Sophia had been allowed to read the letters. They left a faint impression on her mind that her favourite was perhaps somewhat negligent in his relations with his mother.

There was no reply to the bell. Constance rang again without effect.

With a brusque movement Sophia left the bedroom by way of Cyril's room.

"Amy," she called over the banisters, "do you not hear your mistress's bell?"

"I'm coming as quick as I can, m'm." The voice was still very glum.

Sophia murmured something inarticulate, staying till assured that Amy really was coming, and then she passed back into Cyril's bedroom. She waited there, hesitant, not exactly on the watch, not exactly unwilling to assist at an interview between Amy and Amy's mistress; indeed, she could not have surely analyzed her motive for remaining in Cyril's bedroom, with the door ajar between that room and Constance's.

Amy reluctantly mounted the stairs and went into her mistress's bedroom with her chin in the air. She thought that Sophia had gone up to the second storey, where she 'belonged.' She stood in silence by the bed, showing no sympathy with Constance, no curiosity as to the indisposition. She objected to Constance's attack of sciatica, as being a too permanent reproof of her carelessness as to doors.

Constance also waited, for the fraction of a second, as if expectant.

"Well, Amy," she said at length in her voice weakened by fatigue and pain. "The letters?"

"There ain't no letters," said Amy, grimly. "You might have known, if there'd been any, I should have brought 'em up. Postman went past twenty minutes agone. I'm always being interrupted, and it isn't as if I hadn't got enough to do—now!"

She turned to leave, and was pulling the door open.

"Amy!" said a voice sharply. It was Sophia's.

The servant jumped, and in spite of herself obeyed the implicit, imperious command to stop.

"You will please not speak to your mistress in that tone, at any rate while I'm here," said Sophia, icily. "You know she is ill and weak. You ought to be ashamed of yourself."

"I never——" Amy began.

"I don't want to argue," Sophia said angrily. "Please leave the room."

Amy obeyed. She was cowed, in addition to being staggered.

To the persons involved in it, this episode was intensely dramatic. Sophia had surmised that Constance permitted liberties of speech to Amy; she had even guessed that Amy sometimes took licence to be rude. But that the relations between them were such as to allow the bullying of Constance by an Amy downright insolent—this had shocked and wounded Sophia, who suddenly had a vision of Constance as the victim of a reign of terror. "If the creature will do this while I'm here," said Sophia to herself, "what does she do when they are alone together in the house?"

"Well," she exclaimed, "I never heard of such goings-on! And you let her talk to you in that style! My dear Constance!"

Constance was sitting up in bed, the small tea-tray on her knees. Her eyes were moist. The tears had filled them when she knew that there was no letter. Ordinarily the failure of Cyril's letter would not have made her cry, but weakness had impaired her self-control. And the tears having once got into her eyes, she could not dismiss them. There they were!

"She's been with me such a long time," Constance murmured. "She takes liberties. I've corrected her once or twice."

"Liberties!" Sophia repeated the word. "Liberties!"

"Of course I really ought not to allow it," said Constance. "I ought to have put a stop to it long since."

"Well," said Sophia, rather relieved by this symptom of Constance's secret mind, "I do hope you won't think I'm meddlesome, but truly it was too much for me. The words were out of my mouth before I——" She stopped.

"You were quite right, quite right," said Constance, seeing before her in the woman of fifty the passionate girl of fifteen.

"I've had a good deal of experience of servants," said Sophia.

"I know you have," Constance put in.

"And I'm convinced that it never pays to stand any sauce. Servants don't understand kindness and forbearance. And this sort of thing grows and grows till you can't call your soul your own."

"You are quite right," Constance said again, with even more positiveness.

Not merely the conviction that Sophia was quite right, but the desire to assure Sophia that Sophia was not meddlesome, gave force to her utterance. Amy's allusion to extra work shamed Amy's mistress as a hostess, and she was bound to make amends.

"Now as to that woman," said Sophia in a lower voice, as she sat down confidentially on the edge of the bed. And she told Constance about Amy and the dogs, and about Amy's rudeness in the kitchen. "I should never have DREAMT of mentioning such things," she finished. "But under the circumstances I feel it right that you should know. I feel you ought to know."

And Constance nodded her head in thorough agreement. She did not trouble to go into articulate apologies to her guest for the actual misdeeds of her servant. The sisters were now on a plane of intimacy where such apologies would have been supererogatory. Their voices fell lower and lower, and the case of Amy was laid bare and discussed to the minutest detail.

Gradually they realized that what had occurred was a crisis. They were both very excited, apprehensive, and rather too consciously defiant. At the same time they were drawn very close to each other, by Sophia's generous indignation and by Constance's absolute loyalty.

A long time passed before Constance said, thinking about something else:

"I expect it's been delayed in the post."

"Cyril's letter? Oh, no doubt! If you knew the posts in France, my word!"

Then they determined, with little sighs, to face the crisis cheerfully.

In truth it was a crisis, and a great one. The sensation of the crisis affected the atmosphere of the entire house. Constance got up for tea and managed to walk to the drawing-room. And when Sophia, after an absence in her own room, came down to tea and found the tea all served, Constance whispered:

"She's given notice! And Sunday too!"

"What did she say?"

"She didn't say much," Constance replied vaguely, hiding from Sophia that Amy had harped on the too great profusion of mistresses in that house. "After all, it's just as well. She'll be all right. She's saved a good bit of money, and she has friends."

"But how foolish of her to give up such a good place!"

"She simply doesn't care," said Constance, who was a little hurt by Amy's defection. "When she takes a thing into her head she simply doesn't care. She's got no common sense. I've always known that."

"So you're going to leave, Amy?" said Sophia that evening, as Amy was passing through the parlour on her way to bed. Constance was already arranged for the night.

"I am, m'm," answered Amy, precisely.

Her tone was not rude, but it was firm. She had apparently reconnoitred her position in calmness.

"I'm sorry I was obliged to correct you this morning," said Sophia, with cheerful amicableness, pleased in spite of herself with the woman's tone. "But I think you will see that I had reason to."

"I've been thinking it over, m'm," said Amy, with dignity, "and I see as I must leave."

There was a pause.

"Well, you know best…. Good night, Amy."

"Good night, m'm."

"She's a decent woman," thought Sophia, "but hopeless for this place now."

The sisters were fronted with the fact that Constance had a month in which to find a new servant, and that a new servant would have to be trained in well-doing and might easily prove disastrous. Both Constance and Amy were profoundly disturbed by the prospective dissolution of a bond which dated from the seventies. And both were decided that there was no alternative to the dissolution. Outsiders knew merely that Mrs. Povey's old servant was leaving. Outsiders merely saw Mrs. Povey's advertisement in the Signal for a new servant. They could not read hearts. Some of the younger generation even said superiorly that old-fashioned women like Mrs. Povey seemed to have servants on the brain, etc., etc.

II

"Well, have you got your letter?" Sophia demanded cheerfully of
Constance when she entered the bedroom the next morning.
Constance merely shook her head. She was very depressed. Sophia's cheerfulness died out. As she hated to be insincerely optimistic, she said nothing. Otherwise she might have remarked: "Perhaps the afternoon post will bring it." Gloom reigned. To Constance particularly, as Amy had given notice and as Cyril was 'remiss,' it seemed really that the time was out of joint and life unworth living. Even the presence of Sophia did not bring her much comfort. Immediately Sophia left the room Constance's sciatica began to return, and in a severe form. She had regretted this, less for the pain than because she had just assured Sophia, quite honestly, that she was not suffering; Sophia had been sceptical. After that it was of course imperative that Constance should get up as usual. She had said that she would get up as usual. Besides, there was the immense enterprise of obtaining a new servant! Worries loomed mountainous. Suppose Cyril were dangerously ill, and unable to write! Suppose something had happened to him! Supposing she never did obtain a new servant!

Sophia, up in her room, was endeavouring to be philosophical, and to see the world brightly. She was saying to herself that she must take Constance in hand, that what Constance lacked was energy, that Constance must be stirred out of her groove. And in the cavernous kitchen Amy, preparing the nine-o'clock breakfast, was meditating upon the ingratitude of employers and wondering what the future held for her. She had a widowed mother in the picturesque village of Sneyd, where the mortal and immortal welfare of every inhabitant was watched over by God's vicegerent, the busy Countess of Chell; she possessed about two hundred pounds of her own; her mother for years had been begging Amy to share her home free of expense. But nevertheless Amy's mind was black with foreboding and vague dejection. The house was a house of sorrow, and these three women, each solitary, the devotees of sorrow. And the two dogs wandered disconsolate up and down, aware of the necessity for circumspection, never guessing that the highly peculiar state of the atmosphere had been brought about by nothing but a half-shut door and an incorrect tone.

As Sophia, fully dressed this time, was descending to breakfast, she heard Constance's voice, feebly calling her, and found the convalescent still in bed. The truth could not be concealed. Constance was once more in great pain, and her moral condition was not favourable to fortitude.

"I wish you had told me, to begin with," Sophia could not help saying, "then I should have known what to do."

Constance did not defend herself by saying that the pain had only recurred since their first interview that morning. She just wept.

"I'm very low!" she blubbered.

Sophia was surprised. She felt that this was not 'being a Baines.'

During the progress of that interminable April morning, her acquaintance with the possibilities of sciatica as an agent destructive of moral fibre was further increased. Constance had no force at all to resist its activity. The sweetness of her resignation seemed to melt into nullity. She held to it that the doctor could do nothing for her.

About noon, when Sophia was moving anxiously around her, she suddenly screamed.

"I feel as if my leg was going to burst!" she cried.

That decided Sophia. As soon as Constance was a little easier she went downstairs to Amy.

"Amy," she said, "it's a Doctor Stirling that your mistress has when she's ill, isn't it?"

"Yes, m'm."

"Where is his surgery?"

"Well, m'm, he did live just opposite, with Dr. Harrop, but latterly he's gone to live at Bleakridge."

"I wish you would put your things on, and run up there and ask him to call as soon as he can."

"I will, m'm," said Amy, with the greatest willingness. "I thought I heard missis cry out." She was not effusive. She was better than effusive: kindly and helpful with a certain reserve.

"There's something about that woman I like," said Sophia, to herself.

For a proved fool, Amy was indeed holding her own rather well.

Dr. Stirling drove down about two o'clock. He had now been established in the Five Towns for more than a decade, and the stamp of success was on his brow and on the proud forehead of his trotting horse. He had, in the phrase of the Signal, 'identified himself with the local life of the district.' He was liked, being a man of broad sympathies. In his rich Scotch accent he could discuss with equal ability the flavour of whisky or of a sermon, and he had more than sufficient tact never to discuss either whiskies or sermons in the wrong place. He had made a speech (responding for the learned professions) at the annual dinner of the Society for the Prosecution of Felons, and this speech (in which praise of red wine was rendered innocuous by praise of books—his fine library was notorious) had classed him as a wit with the American consul, whose post-prandial manner was modelled on Mark Twain's. He was thirty-five years of age, tall and stoutish, with a chubby boyish face that the razor left chiefly blue every morning.

The immediate effect of his arrival on Constance was miraculous. His presence almost cured her for a moment, just as though her malady had been toothache and he a dentist. Then, when he had finished his examination, the pain resumed its sway over her.

In talking to her and to Sophia, he listened very seriously to all that they said; he seemed to regard the case as the one case that had ever aroused his genuine professional interest; but as it unfolded itself, in all its difficulty and urgency, so he seemed, in his mind, to be discovering wondrous ways of dealing with it; these mysterious discoveries seemed to give him confidence, and his confidence was communicated to the patient by means of faint sallies of humour. He was a highly skilled doctor. This fact, however, had no share in his popularity; which was due solely to his rare gift of taking a case very seriously while remaining cheerful.

He said he would return in a quarter of an hour, and he returned in thirteen minutes with a hypodermic syringe, with which he attacked the pain in its central strongholds.

"What is it?" asked Constance, breathing gratitude for the relief.

He paused, looking at her roguishly from under lowered eyelids.

"I'd better not tell ye," he said. "It might lead ye into mischief."

"Oh, but you must tell me, doctor," Constance insisted, anxious that he should live up to his reputation for Sophia's benefit.

"It's hydrochloride of cocaine," he said, and lifted a finger. "Beware of the cocaine habit. It's ruined many a respectable family. But if I hadn't had a certain amount of confidence in yer strength of character, Mrs. Povey, I wouldn't have risked it."

"He will have his joke, will the doctor!" Constance smiled, in a brighter world.

He said he should come again about half-past five, and he arrived about half-past six, and injected more cocaine. The special importance of the case was thereby established. On this second visit, he and Sophia soon grew rather friendly. When she conducted him downstairs again he stopped chatting with her in the parlour for a long time, as though he had nothing else on earth to do, while his coachman walked the horse to and fro in front of the door.

His attitude to her flattered Sophia, for it showed that he took her for no ordinary woman. It implied a continual assumption that she must be a mine of interest for any one who was privileged to delve into her memory. So far, among Constance's acquaintance, Sophia had met no one who showed more than a perfunctory curiosity as to her life. Her return was accepted with indifference. Her escapade of thirty years ago had entirely lost its dramatic quality. Many people indeed had never heard that she had run away from home to marry a commercial traveller; and to those who remembered, or had been told, it seemed a sufficiently banal exploit—after thirty years! Her fear, and Constance's, that the town would be murmurous with gossip was ludicrously unfounded. The effect of time was such that even Mr. Critchlow appeared to have forgotten even that she had been indirectly responsible for her father's death. She had nearly forgotten it herself; when she happened to think of it she felt no shame, no remorse, seeing the death as purely accidental, and not altogether unfortunate. On two points only was the town inquisitive: as to her husband, and as to the precise figure at which she had sold the pension. The town knew that she was probably not a widow, for she had been obliged to tell Mr. Critchlow, and Mr. Critchlow in some hour of tenderness had told Maria. But nobody had dared to mention the name of Gerald Scales to her. With her fashionable clothes, her striking mien of command, and the legend of her wealth, she inspired respect, if not awe, in the townsfolk. In the doctor's attitude there was something of amaze; she felt it. Though the dull apathy of the people she had hitherto met was assuredly not without its advantageous side for her tranquillity of mind, it had touched her vanity, and the gaze of the doctor soothed the smart. He had so obviously divined her interestingness; he so obviously wanted to enjoy it.

"I've just been reading Zola's 'Downfall,'" he said.

Her mind searched backwards, and recalled a poster.

"Oh!" she replied. "'La Debacle'?"

"Yes. What do ye think of it?" His eyes lighted at the prospect of a talk. He was even pleased to hear her give him the title in French.

"I haven't read it," she said, and she was momentarily sorry that she had not read it, for she could see that he was dashed. The doctor had supposed that residence in a foreign country involved a knowledge of the literature of that country. Yet he had never supposed that residence in England involved a knowledge of English literature. Sophia had read practically nothing since 1870; for her the latest author was Cherbuliez. Moreover, her impression of Zola was that he was not at all nice, and that he was the enemy of his race, though at that date the world had scarcely heard of Dreyfus. Dr. Stirling had too hastily assumed that the opinions of the bourgeois upon art differ in different countries.

"And ye actually were in the siege of Paris?" he questioned, trying again.

"Yes."

"AND the commune?"

"Yes, the commune too."

"Well!" he exclaimed. "It's incredible! When I was reading the 'Downfall' the night before last, I said to myself that you must have been through a lot of all that. I didn't know I was going to have the pleasure of a chat with ye so soon."

She smiled. "But how did you know I was in the siege of Paris?" she asked, curious.

"How do I know? I know because I've seen that birthday card ye sent to Mrs. Povey in 1871, after it was over. It's one of her possessions, that card is. She showed it me one day when she told me ye were coming."

Sophia started. She had quite forgotten that card. It had not occurred to her that Constance would have treasured all those cards that she had despatched during the early years of her exile. She responded as well as she could to his eagerness for personal details concerning the siege and the commune. He might have been disappointed at the prose of her answers, had he not been determined not to be disappointed.

"Ye seem to have taken it all very quietly," he observed.

"Eh yes!" she agreed, not without pride. "But it's a long time since."

Those events, as they existed in her memory, scarcely warranted the tremendous fuss subsequently made about them. What were they, after all? Such was her secret thought. Chirac himself was now nothing but a faint shadow. Still, were the estimate of those events true or false, she was a woman who had been through them, and Dr. Stirling's high appreciation of that fact was very pleasant to her. Their friendliness approached intimacy. Night had fallen. Outside could be heard the champing of a bit.

"I must be getting on," he said at last; but he did not move.

"Then there is nothing else I am to do for my sister?" Sophia inquired.

"I don't think so," said he. "It isn't a question of medicine."

"Then what is it a question of?" Sophia demanded bluntly.

"Nerves," he said. "It's nearly all nerves. I know something about Mrs. Povey's constitution now, and I was hoping that your visit would do her good."

"She's been quite well—I mean what you may call quite well—until the day before yesterday, when she sat in that draught. She was better last night, and then this morning I find her ever so much worse."

"No worries?" The doctor looked at her confidentially.

"What CAN she have in the way of worries?" exclaimed Sophia. "That's to say—real worries."

"Exactly!" the doctor agreed.

"I tell her she doesn't know what worry is," said Sophia.

"So do I!" said the doctor, his eyes twinkling.

"She was a little upset because she didn't receive her usual Sunday letter from Cyril yesterday. But then she was weak and low."

"Clever youth, Cyril!" mused the doctor.

"I think he's a particularly nice boy," said Sophia, eagerly,

"So you've seen him?"

"Of course," said Sophia, rather stiffly. Did the doctor suppose that she did not know her own nephew? She went back to the subject of her sister. "She is also a little bothered, I think, because the servant is going to leave."

"Oh! So Amy is going to leave, is she?" He spoke still lower. "Between you and me, it's no bad thing."

"I'm so glad you think so."

"In another few years the servant would have been the mistress here. One can see these things coming on, but it's so difficult to do anything. In fact ye can't do anything."

"I did something," said Sophia, sharply. "I told the woman straight that it shouldn't go on while I was in the house. I didn't suspect it at first—but when I found it out … I can tell you!" She let the doctor imagine what she could tell him.

He smiled. "No," he said. "I can easily understand that ye didn't suspect anything at first. When she's well and bright Mrs. Povey could hold her own—so I'm told. But it was certainly slowly getting worse."

"Then people talk about it?" said Sophia, shocked.

"As a native of Bursley, Mrs. Scales," said the doctor, "ye ought to know what people in Bursley do!" Sophia put her lips together. The doctor rose, smoothing his waistcoat. "What does she bother with servants at all for?" he burst out. "She's perfectly free. She hasn't got a care in the world, if she only knew it. Why doesn't she go out and about, and enjoy herself? She wants stirring up, that's what your sister wants."

"You're quite right," Sophia burst out in her turn. "That's precisely what I say to myself; precisely! I was thinking it over only this morning. She wants stirring up. She's got into a rut."

"She needs to be jolly. Why doesn't she go to some seaside place, and live in a hotel, and enjoy herself? Is there anything to prevent her?"

"Nothing whatever."

"Instead of being dependent on a servant! I believe in enjoying one's self—when ye've got the money to do it with! Can ye imagine anybody living in Bursley, for pleasure? And especially in St. Luke's Square, right in the thick of it all! Smoke! Dirt! No air! No light! No scenery! No amusements! What does she do it for? She's in a rut."

"Yes, she's in a rut," Sophia repeated her own phrase, which he had copied.

"My word!" said the doctor. "Wouldn't I clear out and enjoy myself if I could! Your sister's a young woman."

"Of course she is!" Sophia concurred, feeling that she herself was even younger. "Of course she is!"

"And except that she's nervously organized, and has certain predispositions, there's nothing the matter with her. This sciatica—I don't say it would be cured, but it might be, by a complete change and throwing off all these ridiculous worries. Not only does she live in the most depressing conditions, but she suffers tortures for it, and there's absolutely no need for her to be here at all."

"Doctor," said Sophia, solemnly, impressed, "you are quite right. I agree with every word you say."

"Naturally she's attached to the place," he continued, glancing round the room. "I know all about that. After living here all her life! But she's got to break herself of her attachment. It's her duty to do so. She ought to show a little energy. I'm deeply attached to my bed in the morning, but I have to leave it."

"Of course," said Sophia, in an impatient tone, as though disgusted with every person who could not perceive, or would not subscribe to, these obvious truths that the doctor was uttering. "Of course!"

"What she needs is the bustle of life in a good hotel, a good hydro, for instance. Among jolly people. Parties! Games! Excursions! She wouldn't be the same woman. You'd see. Wouldn't I do it, if I could? Strathpeffer. She'd soon forget her sciatica. I don't know what Mrs. Povey's annual income is, but I expect that if she took it into her head to live in the dearest hotel in England, there would be no reason why she shouldn't."

Sophia lifted her head and smiled in calm amusement. "I expect so," she said superiorly.

"A hotel—that's the life. No worries. If ye want anything ye ring a bell. If a waiter gives notice, it's some one else who has the worry, not you. But you know all about that, Mrs. Scales."

"No one better," murmured Sophia.

"Good evening," he said abruptly, sticking out his hand. "I'll be down in the morning."

"Did you ever mention this to my sister?" Sophia asked him, rising.

"Yes," said he. "But it's no use. Oh yes, I've told her. But she does really think it's quite impossible. She wouldn't even hear of going to live in London with her beloved son. She won't listen."

"I never thought of that," said Sophia. "Good night."

Their hand-grasp was very intimate and mutually comprehending. He was pleased by the quick responsiveness of her temperament, and the masterful vigour which occasionally flashed out in her replies. He noticed the hardly perceptible distortion of her handsome, worn face, and he said to himself: "She's been through a thing or two," and: "She'll have to mind her p's and q's." Sophia was pleased because he admired her, and because with her he dropped his bedside jocularities, and talked plainly as a sensible man will talk when he meets an uncommonly wise woman, and because he echoed and amplified her own thoughts. She honoured him by standing at the door till he had driven off.

For a few moments she mused solitary in the parlour, and then, lowering the gas, she went upstairs to her sister, who lay in the dark. Sophia struck a match.

"You've been having quite a long chat with the doctor," said Constance.

"He's very good company, isn't he? What did he talk about this time?"

"He wanted to know about Paris and so on," Sophia answered.

"Oh! I believe he's a rare student."

Lying there in the dark, the simple Constance never suspected that those two active and strenuous ones had been arranging her life for her, so that she should be jolly and live for twenty years yet. She did not suspect that she had been tried and found guilty of sinful attachments, and of being in a rut, and of lacking the elements of ordinary sagacity. It had not occurred to her that if she was worried and ill, the reason was to be found in her own blind and stupid obstinacy. She had thought herself a fairly sensible kind of creature.

III

The sisters had an early supper together in Constance's bedroom. Constance was much easier. Having a fancy that a little movement would be beneficial, she had even got up for a few moments and moved about the room. Now she sat ensconced in pillows. A fire burned in the old-fashioned ineffectual grate. From the Sun Vaults opposite came the sound of a phonograph singing an invitation to God to save its gracious queen. This phonograph was a wonderful novelty, and filled the Sun nightly. For a few evenings it had interested the sisters, in spite of themselves, but they had soon sickened of it and loathed it. Sophia became more and more obsessed by the monstrous absurdity of the simple fact that she and Constance were there, in that dark inconvenient house, wearied by the gaiety of public-houses, blackened by smoke, surrounded by mud, instead of being luxuriously installed in a beautiful climate, amid scenes of beauty and white cleanliness. Secretly she became more and more indignant.

268

Amy entered, bearing a letter in her coarse hand. As Amy unceremoniously handed the letter to Constance, Sophia thought: "If she was my servant she would hand letters on a tray." (An advertisement had already been sent to the Signal.)

Constance took the letter trembling. "Here it is at last," she cried.

When she had put on her spectacles and read it, she exclaimed:

"Bless us! Here's news! He's coming down! That's why he didn't write on Saturday as usual."

She gave the letter to Sophia to read. It ran—

"Sunday midnight.

"DEAR MOTHER,

"Just a line to say I am coming down to Bursley on Wednesday, on business with Peels. I shall get to Knype at 5.28, and take the Loop. I've been very busy, and as I was coming down I didn't write on Saturday. I hope you didn't worry. Love to yourself and Aunt Sophia.

"Yours, C."

"I must send him a line," said Constance, excitedly.

"What? To-night?"

"Yes. Amy can easily catch the last post with it. Otherwise he won't know that I've got his letter."

She rang the bell.

Sophia thought: "His coming down is really no excuse for his not writing on Saturday. How could she guess that he was coming down? I shall have to put in a little word to that young man. I wonder Constance is so blind. She is quite satisfied now that his letter has come." On behalf of the elder generation she rather resented Constance's eagerness to write in answer.

But Constance was not so blind. Constance thought exactly as Sophia thought. In her heart she did not at all justify or excuse Cyril. She remembered separately almost every instance of his carelessness in her regard.

"Hope I didn't worry, indeed!" she said to herself with a faint touch of bitterness, apropos of the phrase in his letter.

Nevertheless she insisted on writing at once. And Amy had to bring the writing materials.

"Mr. Cyril is coming down on Wednesday," she said to Amy with great dignity.

Amy's stony calmness was shaken, for Mr. Cyril was a great deal to Amy. Amy wondered how she would be able to look Mr. Cyril in the face when he knew that she had given notice.

In the middle of writing, on her knee, Constance looked up at Sophia, and said, as though defending herself against an accusation: "I didn't write to him yesterday, you know, or to-day."

"No," Sophia murmured assentingly.

Constance rang the bell yet again, and Amy was sent out to the post.

Soon afterwards the bell was rung for a fourth time, and not answered.

"I suppose she hasn't come back yet. But I thought I heard the door.

What a long time she is!"

"What do you want?" Sophia asked.

"I just want to speak to her," said Constance.

When the bell had been rung seven or eight times, Amy at length re-appeared, somewhat breathless.

"Amy," said Constance, "let me examine those sheets, will you?"

"Yes'm," said Amy, apparently knowing what sheets, of all the various and multitudinous sheets in that house.

"And the pillow-cases," Constance added as Amy left the room.

So it continued. The next day the fever heightened. Constance was up early, before Sophia, and trotting about the house like a girl. Immediately after breakfast Cyril's bedroom was invested and revolutionized; not till evening was order restored in that chamber. And on the Wednesday morning it had to be dusted afresh.

Sophia watched the preparations, and the increasing agitation of Constance's demeanour, with an astonishment which she had real difficulty in concealing. "Is the woman absolutely mad?" she asked herself. The spectacle was ludicrous: or it seemed so to Sophia, whose career had not embraced much experience of mothers. It was not as if the manifestations of Constance's anxiety were dignified or original or splendid. They were just silly, ordinary fussinesses; they had no sense in them. Sophia was very careful to make no observation. She felt that before she and Constance were very much older she had a very great deal to do, and that a subtle diplomacy and wary tactics would be necessary. Moreover, Constance's angelic temper was slightly affected by the strain of expectation. She had a tendency to rasp. After the high-tea was set she suddenly sprang on to the sofa and lifted down the 'Stag at Eve' engraving. The dust on the top of the frame incensed her.

"What are you going to do?" Sophia asked, in a final marvel.

"I'm going to change it with that one," said Constance, pointing to another engraving opposite the fireplace. "He said the effect would be very much better if they were changed. And his lordship is very particular."

Constance did not go to Bursley station to meet her son. She explained that it upset her to do so, and that also Cyril preferred her not to come.

"Suppose I go to meet him," said Sophia, at half-past five. The idea had visited her suddenly. She thought: "Then I could talk to him before any one else."

"Oh, do!" Constance agreed.

Sophia put her things on with remarkable expedition. She arrived at the station a minute before the train came in. Only a few persons emerged from the train, and Cyril was not among them. A porter said that there was not supposed to be any connection between the Loop Line trains and the main line expresses, and that probably the express had missed the Loop. She waited thirty-five minutes for the next Loop, and Cyril did not emerge from that train either.

Constance opened the front-door to her, and showed a telegram—

"Sorry prevented last moment. Writing. CYRIL."

Sophia had known it. Somehow she had known that it was useless to wait for the second train. Constance was silent and calm; Sophia also.

"What a shame! What a shame!" thumped Sophia's heart.

It was the most ordinary episode. But beneath her calm she was furious against her favourite. She hesitated.

"I'm just going out a minute," she said.

"Where?" asked Constance. "Hadn't we better have tea? I suppose we must have tea."

"I shan't be long. I want to buy something."

Sophia went to the post-office and despatched a telegram. Then, partially eased, she returned to the arid and painful desolation of the house.

IV

The next evening Cyril sat at the tea-table in the parlour with his mother and his aunt. To Constance his presence there had something of the miraculous in it. He had come, after all! Sophia was in a rich robe, and for ornament wore an old silver-gilt neck-chain, which was clasped at the throat, and fell in double to her waist, where it was caught in her belt. This chain interested Cyril. He referred to it once or twice, and then he said: "Just let me have a LOOK at that chain," and put out his hand; and Sophia leaned forward so that he could handle it. His fingers played with it thus for some seconds; the picture strikingly affected Constance. At length he dropped it, and said: "H'm!" After a pause he said: "Louis Sixteenth, eh?" and Sophia said: "They told me so. But it's nothing; it only cost thirty francs, you know." And Cyril took her up sharply: "What does that matter?" Then after another pause he asked: "How often do you break a link of it?"

"Oh, often," she said. "It's always getting shorter."

And he murmured mysteriously: "H'm!"

He was still mysterious, withdrawn within himself extraordinarily uninterested in his physical surroundings. But that evening he talked more than he usually did. He was benevolent, and showed a particular benevolence towards his mother, apparently exerting himself to answer her questions with fullness and heartiness, as though admitting frankly her right to be curious. He praised the tea; he seemed to notice what he was eating. He took Spot on his knee, and gazed in admiration at Fossette.

"By Jove!" he said, "that's a dog, that is! … All the same…." And he burst out laughing.

"I won't have Fossette laughed at," Sophia warned him.

"No, seriously," he said, in his quality of an amateur of dogs; "she is very fine." Even then he could not help adding: "What you can see of her!"

270

Whereupon Sophia shook her head, deprecating such wit. Sophia was very lenient towards him. Her leniency could be perceived in her eyes, which followed his movements all the time. "Do you think he is like me, Constance?" she asked.

"I wish I was half as good-looking," said Cyril, quickly; and Constance said:

"As a baby he was very like you. He was a handsome baby. He wasn't at all like you when he was at school. These last few years he's begun to be like you again. He's very much changed since he left school; he was rather heavy and clumsy then."

"Heavy and clumsy!" exclaimed Sophia. "Well, I should never have believed it!"

"Oh, but he was!" Constance insisted.

"Now, mater," said Cyril, "it's a pity you don't want that cake cutting into. I think I could have eaten a bit of that cake. But of course if it's only for show…!"

Constance sprang up, seizing a knife.

"You shouldn't tease your mother," Sophia told him. "He doesn't really want any, Constance; he's regularly stuffed himself."

And Cyril agreed, "No, no, mater, don't cut it; I really couldn't. I was only gassing."

But Constance could never clearly see through humour of that sort. She cut three slices of cake, and she held the plate towards Cyril.

"I tell you I really couldn't!" he protested.

"Come!" she said obstinately. "I'm waiting! How much longer must I hold this plate?"

And he had to take a slice. So had Sophia. When she was roused, they both of them had to yield to Constance. With the dogs, and the splendour of the tea-table under the gas, and the distinction of Sophia and Cyril, and the conversation, which on the whole was gay and free, rising at times to jolly garrulity, the scene in her parlour ought surely to have satisfied Constance utterly. She ought to have been quite happy, as her sciatica had raised the siege for a space. But she was not quite happy. The circumstances of Cyril's arrival had disturbed her; they had in fact wounded her, though she would scarcely admit the wound. In the morning she had received a brief letter from Cyril to say that he had not been able to come, and vaguely promising, or half-promising, to run down at a later date. That letter had the cardinal defects of all Cyril's relations with his mother; it was casual, and it was not candid. It gave no hint of the nature of the obstacle which had prevented him from coming. Cyril had always been too secretive. She was gravely depressed by the letter, which she did not show to Sophia, because it impaired her dignity as a mother, and displayed her son in a bad light. Then about eleven o'clock a telegram had come for Sophia.

"That's all right," Sophia had said, on reading it. "He'll be here this evening!" And she had handed over the telegram, which read—

"Very well. Will come same train to-day."

And Constance learned that when Sophia had rushed out just before tea on the previous evening, it was to telegraph to Cyril.

"What did you say to him?" Constance asked.

"Oh!" said Sophia, with a careless air, "I told him I thought he ought to come. After all, you're more important than any business, Constance! And I don't like him behaving like that. I was determined he should come!" Sophia had tossed her proud head.

Constance had pretended to be pleased and grateful. But the existence of a wound was incontestable. Sophia, then, could do more with Cyril than she could! Sophia had only met him once, and could simply twist him round her little finger. He would never have done so much for his mother. A fine sort of an obstacle it must have been, if a single telegram from Sophia could overcome it…! And Sophia, too, was secretive. She had gone out and had telegraphed, and had not breathed a word until she got the reply, sixteen hours later. She was secretive, and Cyril was secretive. They resembled one another. They had taken to one another. But Sophia was a curious mixture. When Constance had asked her if she should go to the station again to meet Cyril, she had replied scornfully: "No, indeed! I've done going to meet Cyril. People who don't arrive must not expect to be met."

When Cyril drove up to the door, Sophia had been in attendance. She hurried down the steps. "Don't say anything about my telegram," she had rapidly whispered to Cyril; there was no time for further explanation. Constance was at the top of the steps. Constance had not heard the whisper, but she had seen it; and she saw a guilty, puzzled look on Cyril's face, afterwards an ineffectively concealed conspiratorial look on both their faces. They had 'something between them,' from which she, the mother, was shut out! Was it not natural that she should be wounded? She was far too proud to mention the telegrams. And as neither Cyril nor Sophia

271

mentioned them, the circumstances leading to Cyril's change of plan were not referred to at all, which was very curious. Then Cyril was more sociable than he had ever been; he was different, under his aunt's gaze. Certainly he treated his mother faultlessly. But Constance said to herself: "It is because she is here that he is so specially nice to me."

When tea was finished and they were going upstairs to the drawing-room, she asked him, with her eye on the 'Stag at Eve' engraving:

"Well, is it a success?"

"What?" His eye followed hers. "Oh, you've changed it! What did you do that for, mater?"

"You said it would be better like that," she reminded him.

"Did I?" He seemed genuinely surprised. "I don't remember. I believe it is better, though," he added. "It might be even better still if you turned it the other way up."

He pulled a face to Sophia, and screwed up his shoulders, as if to indicate: "I've done it, this time!"

"How? The other way up?" Constance queried. Then as she comprehended that he was teasing her, she said: "Get away with you!" and pretended to box his ears. "You were fond enough of that picture at one time!" she said ironically.

"Yes, I was, mater," he submissively agreed. "There's no getting over that." And he pressed her cheeks between his hands and kissed her.

In the drawing-room he smoked cigarettes and played the piano—waltzes of his own composition. Constance and Sophia did not entirely comprehend those waltzes. But they agreed that all were wonderful and that one was very pretty indeed. (It soothed Constance that Sophia's opinion coincided with hers.) He said that that waltz was the worst of the lot. When he had finished with the piano, Constance informed him about Amy.

"Oh! She told me," he said, "when she brought me my water. I didn't mention it because I thought it would be rather a sore subject." Beneath the casualness of his tone there lurked a certain curiosity, a willingness to hear details. He heard them.

At five minutes to ten, when Constance had yawned, he threw a bomb among them on the hearthrug.

"Well," he said, "I've got an appointment with Matthew at the Conservative Club at ten o'clock. I must go. Don't wait up for me."

Both women protested, Sophia the more vivaciously. It was Sophia now who was wounded.

"It's business," he said, defending himself. "He's going away early to-morrow, and it's my only chance." And as Constance did not brighten he went on: "Business has to be attended to. You mustn't think I've got nothing to do but enjoy myself."

No hint of the nature of the business! He never explained. As to business, Constance knew only that she allowed him three hundred a year, and paid his local tailor. The sum had at first seemed to her enormous, but she had grown accustomed to it.

"I should have preferred you to see Mr. Peel-Swynnerton here," said Constance. "You could have had a room to yourselves. I do not like you going out at ten o'clock at night to a club."

"Well, good night, mater," he said, getting up. "See you to-morrow. I shall take the key out of the door. It's true my pocket will never be the same again."

Sophia saw Constance into bed, and provided her with two hot-water bottles against sciatica. They did not talk much.

V

Sophia sat waiting on the sofa in the parlour. It appeared to her that, though little more than a month had elapsed since her arrival in Bursley, she had already acquired a new set of interests and anxieties. Paris and her life there had receded in the strangest way. Sometimes for hours she would absolutely forget Paris. Thoughts of Paris were disconcerting; for either Paris or Bursley must surely be unreal! As she sat waiting on the sofa Paris kept coming into her mind. Certainly it was astonishing that she should be just as preoccupied with her schemes for the welfare of Constance as she had ever been preoccupied with schemes for the improvement of the Pension Frensham. She said to herself: "My life has been so queer—and yet every part of it separately seemed ordinary enough—how will it end?"

Then there were footfalls on the steps outside, and a key was put into the door, which she at once opened.

"Oh!" exclaimed Cyril, startled, and also somewhat out of countenance.

"You're still up! Thanks." He came in, smoking the end of a cigar.

"Fancy having to cart that about!" he murmured, holding up the great old-fashioned key before inserting it in the lock on the inside.

"I stayed up," said Sophia, "because I wanted to talk to you about your mother, and it's so difficult to get a chance."

Cyril smiled, not without self-consciousness, and dropped into his mother's rocking-chair, which he had twisted round with his feet to face the sofa.

"Yes," he said. "I was wondering what was the real meaning of your telegram. What was it?" He blew out a lot of smoke and waited for her reply.

"I thought you ought to come down," said Sophia, cheerfully but firmly. "It was a fearful disappointment to your mother that you didn't come yesterday. And when she's expecting a letter from you and it doesn't come, it makes her ill."

"Oh, well!" he said. "I'm glad it's no worse. I thought from your telegram there was something seriously wrong. And then when you told me not to mention it—when I came in…!"

She saw that he failed to realize the situation, and she lifted her head challengingly.

"You neglect your mother, young man," she said.

"Oh, come now, auntie!" he answered quite gently. "You mustn't talk like that. I write to her every week. I've never missed a week. I come down as often as——"

"You miss the Sunday sometimes," Sophia interrupted him.

"Perhaps," he said doubtfully. "But what——"

"Don't you understand that she simply lives for your letters? And if one doesn't come, she's very upset indeed—can't eat! And it brings on her sciatica, and I don't know what!"

He was taken aback by her boldness, her directness.

"But how silly of her! A fellow can't always——"

"It may be silly. But there it is. You can't alter her. And, after all, what would it cost you to be more attentive, even to write to her twice a week? You aren't going to tell me you're so busy as all that! I know a great deal more about young men than your mother does." She smiled like an aunt.

He answered her smile sheepishly.

"If you'll only put yourself in your mother's place…!"

"I expect you're quite right," he said at length. "And I'm much obliged to you for telling me. How was I to know?" He threw the end of the cigar, with a large sweeping gesture, into the fire.

"Well, anyhow, you know now!" she said curtly; and she thought: "You OUGHT to have known. It was your business to know." But she was pleased with the way in which he had accepted her criticism, and the gesture with which he threw away the cigar-end struck her as very distinguished.

"That's all right!" he said dreamily, as if to say: "That's done with."

And he rose.

Sophia, however, did not stir.

"Your mother's health is not what it ought to be," she went on, and gave him a full account of her conversation with the doctor.

"Really!" Cyril murmured, leaning on the mantel-piece with his elbow and looking down at her. "Stirling said that, did he? I should have thought she would have been better where she is, in the Square."

"Why better in the Square?"

"Oh, I don't know!"

"Neither do I!"

"She's always been here."

"Yes." said Sophia, "she's been here a great deal too long."

"What do YOU suggest?" Cyril asked, with impatience in his voice against this new anxiety that was being thrust upon him.

"Well," said Sophia, "what should you say to her coming to London and living with you?"

Cyril started back. Sophia could see that he was genuinely shocked. "I don't think that would do at all," he said.

"Why?"

"Oh! I don't think it would. London wouldn't suit her. She's not that sort of woman. I really thought she was quite all right down here. She wouldn't like London." He shook his head, looking up at the gas; his eyes had a dangerous glare.

"But supposing she said she did?"

273

"Look here," Cyril began in a new and brighter tone. "Why don't you and she keep house together somewhere? That would be the very—"

He turned his head sharply. There was a noise on the staircase, and the staircase door opened with its eternal creak.

"Yes," said Sophia. "The Champs Elysees begins at the Place de la

Concorde, and ends———. Is that you, Constance?"

The figure of Constance filled the doorway. Her face was troubled. She had heard Cyril in the street, and had come down to see why he remained so long in the parlour. She was astounded to find Sophia with him. There they were, as intimate as cronies, chattering about Paris! Undoubtedly she was jealous! Never did Cyril talk like that to her!

"I thought you were in bed and asleep, Sophia," she said weakly. "It's nearly one o'clock."

"No," said Sophia. "I didn't seem to feel like going to bed; and then

Cyril happened to come in."

But neither she nor Cyril could look innocent. And Constance glanced from one to the other apprehensively. The next morning Cyril received a letter which, he said—with no further explanation—forced him to leave at once. He intimated that there had been danger in his coming just then, and that matters had turned out as he had feared.

"You think over what I said," he whispered to Sophia when they were alone for an instant, "and let me know."

VI

A week before Easter the guests of the Rutland Hotel in the Broad Walk, Buxton, being assembled for afternoon tea in the "lounge" of that establishment, witnessed the arrival of two middle-aged ladies and two dogs. Critically to examine newcomers was one of the amusements of the occupants of the lounge. This apartment, furnished "in the oriental style," made a pretty show among the photographs in the illustrated brochure of the hotel, and, though draughty, it was of all the public rooms the favourite. It was draughty because only separated from the street (if the Broad Walk can be called a street) by two pairs of swinging-doors—in charge of two page-boys. Every visitor entering the hotel was obliged to pass through the lounge, and for newcomers the passage was an ordeal; they were made to feel that they had so much to learn, so much to get accustomed to; like passengers who join a ship at a port of call, they felt that the business lay before them of creating a niche for themselves in a hostile and haughty society. The two ladies produced a fairly favourable impression at the outset by reason of their two dogs. It is not every one who has the courage to bring dogs into an expensive private hotel; to bring one dog indicates that you are not accustomed to deny yourself small pleasures for the sake of a few extra shillings; to bring two indicates that you have no fear of hotel-managers and that you are in the habit of regarding your own whim as nature's law. The shorter and stouter of the two ladies did not impose herself with much force on the collective vision of the Rutland; she was dressed in black, not fashionably, though with a certain unpretending richness; her gestures were timid and nervous; evidently she relied upon her tall companion to shield her in the first trying contacts of hotel life. The tall lady was of a different stamp. Handsome, stately, deliberate, and handsomely dressed in colours, she had the assured hard gaze of a person who is thoroughly habituated to the inspection of strangers. She curtly asked one of the page-boys for the manager, and the manager's wife tripped rapidly down the stairs in response, and was noticeably deferential—Her voice was quiet and commanding, the voice of one who gives orders that are obeyed. The opinion of the lounge was divided as to whether or not they were sisters.

They vanished quietly upstairs in convoy of the manager's wife, and they did not re-appear for the lounge tea, which in any case would have been undrinkably stewed. It then became known, by the agency of one of those guests, to be found in every hotel, who acquire all the secrets of the hotel by the exercise of unabashed curiosity on the personnel, that the two ladies had engaged two bedrooms, Nos. 17 and 18, and the sumptuous private parlour with a balcony on the first floor, styled "C" in the nomenclature of rooms. This fact definitely established the position of the new arrivals in the moral fabric of the hotel. They were wealthy. They had money to throw away. For even in a select hotel like the Rutland it is not everybody who indulges in a private sitting-room; there were only four such apartments in the hotel, as against fifty bedrooms.

At dinner they had a small table to themselves in a corner. The short lady wore a white shawl over her shoulders. Her almost apologetic manner during the meal confirmed the view that she must be a very simple person, unused to the world and its ways. The other continued to be imperial. She ordered half-a-bottle of wine and drank two glasses. She stared about her quite self-unconsciously, whereas the little woman divided her glances between her companion and her plate. They did not talk much. Immediately after dinner they retired. "Widows in easy circumstances" was the verdict; but the contrast between the pair held puzzles that piqued the inquisitive.

Sophia had conquered again. Once more Sophia had resolved to accomplish a thing and she had accomplished it. Events had fallen out thus. The advertisement for a general servant in the Signal had been a disheartening failure. A few answers were received, but of an entirely unsatisfactory character. Constance, a great deal more than Sophia, had been astounded by the bearing and the demands of modern servants. Constance was in despair. If Constance had not had an immense pride she would have been ready to suggest to Sophia that Amy should be asked to 'stay on.' But Constance would have accepted a modern impudent wench first. It was Maria Critchlow who got Constance out of her difficulty by giving her particulars of a reliable servant who was about to leave a situation in which she had stayed for eight years. Constance did not imagine that a servant recommended by Maria Critchlow would suit her, but, being in a quandary, she arranged to see the servant, and both she and Sophia were very pleased with the girl—Rose Bennion by name. The mischief was that Rose would not be free until about a month after Amy had left. Rose would have left her old situation, but she had a fancy to go and spend a fortnight with a married sister at Manchester before settling into new quarters. Constance and Sophia felt that this caprice of Rose's was really very tiresome and unnecessary. Of course Amy might have been asked to 'stay on' just for a month. Amy would probably have volunteered to do so had she been aware of the circumstances. She was not, however, aware of the circumstances. And Constance was determined not to be beholden to Amy for anything. What could the sisters do? Sophia, who conducted all the interviews with Rose and other candidates, said that it would be a grave error to let Rose slip. Besides, they had no one to take her place, no one who could come at once.

The dilemma was appalling. At least, it seemed appalling to Constance, who really believed that no mistress had ever been so 'awkwardly fixed.' And yet, when Sophia first proposed her solution, Constance considered it to be a quite impossible solution. Sophia's idea was that they should lock up the house and leave it on the same day as Amy left it, to spend a few weeks in some holiday resort. To begin with, the idea of leaving the house empty seemed to Constance a mad idea. The house had never been left empty. And then—going for a holiday in April! Constance had never been for a holiday except in the month of August. No! The project was beset with difficulties and dangers which could not be overcome nor provided against. For example, "We can't come back to a dirty house," said Constance. "And we can't have a strange servant coming here before us." To which Sophia had replied: "Then what SHALL you do?" And Constance, after prodigious reflection on the frightful pass to which destiny had brought her, had said that she supposed she would have to manage with a charwoman until Rose's advent. She asked Sophia if she remembered old Maggie. Sophia, of course, perfectly remembered. Old Maggie was dead, as well as the drunken, amiable Hollins, but there was a young Maggie (wife of a bricklayer) who went out charing in the spare time left from looking after seven children. The more Constance meditated upon young Maggie, the more was she convinced that young Maggie would meet the case. Constance felt she could trust young Maggie.

This expression of trust in Maggie was Constance's undoing. Why should they not go away, and arrange with Maggie to come to the house a few days before their return, to clean and ventilate? The weight of reason overbore Constance. She yielded unwillingly, but she yielded. It was the mention of Buxton that finally moved her. She knew Buxton. Her old landlady at Buxton was dead, and Constance had not visited the place since before Samuel's death; nevertheless its name had a reassuring sound to her ears, and for sciatica its waters and climate were admitted to be the best in England. Gradually Constance permitted herself to be embarked on this perilous enterprise of shutting up the house for twenty-five days. She imparted the information to Amy, who was astounded. Then she commenced upon her domestic preparations. She wrapped Samuel's Family Bible in brown paper; she put Cyril's straw-framed copy of Sir Edwin Landseer away in a drawer, and she took ten thousand other precautions. It was grotesque; it was farcical; it was what you please. And when, with the cab at the door and the luggage on the cab, and the dogs chained together, and Maria Critchlow waiting on the pavement to receive the key, Constance put the key into the door on the outside, and locked up the empty house, Constance's face was tragic with innumerable apprehensions. And Sophia felt that she had performed a miracle. She had.

On the whole the sisters were well received in the hotel, though they were not at an age which commands popularity. In the criticism which was passed upon them—the free, realistic and relentless criticism of private hotels—Sophia was at first set down as overbearing. But in a few days this view was modified, and Sophia rose in esteem. The fact was that Sophia's behaviour changed after forty-eight hours. The Rutland Hotel was very good. It was so good as to disturb Sophia's profound beliefs that there was in the world only one truly high-class pension, and that nobody could teach the creator of that unique pension anything about the art of management. The food was excellent; the attendance in the bedrooms was excellent (and Sophia knew how difficult of attainment was excellent bedroom attendance); and to the eye the interior of the Rutland presented a spectacle far richer than the Pension Frensham could show. The standard of comfort was higher. The guests had a more distinguished appearance. It is true that the prices were much higher. Sophia was humbled. She had enough sense to adjust her perspective. Further, she found herself ignorant of many matters which by the other guests were taken for granted and used as a basis for conversation. Prolonged residence in Paris would not justify this ignorance; it seemed rather to intensify its strangeness. Thus, when someone of cosmopolitan experience, having learnt that she had lived in Paris for many years, asked what had been going on lately at the Comedie Francaise, she had to admit that she had not been in a French theatre for nearly thirty years. And when, on a Sunday, the same person questioned her about the English chaplain in Paris, lo! she knew nothing but his name, had never even seen him. Sophia's life, in its way, had been as narrow as Constance's. Though her experience of human nature was wide, she had been in a groove as deep as Constance's. She had been utterly absorbed in doing one single thing.

By tacit agreement she had charge of the expedition. She paid all the bills. Constance protested against the expensiveness of the affair several times, but Sophia quietened her by sheer force of individuality. Constance had one advantage over Sophia. She knew Buxton and its neighbourhood intimately, and she was therefore in a position to show off the sights and to deal with local peculiarities. In all other respects Sophia led.

They very soon became acclimatized to the hotel. They moved easily between Turkey carpets and sculptured ceilings; their eyes grew used to the eternal vision of themselves and other slow-moving dignities in gilt mirrors, to the heaviness of great oil-paintings of picturesque scenery, to the indications of surreptitious dirt behind massive furniture, to the grey-brown of the shirt-fronts of the waiters, to the litter of trays, boots and pails in long corridors; their ears were always awake to the sounds of gongs and bells. They consulted the barometer and ordered the daily carriage with the perfunctoriness of habit. They discovered what can be learnt of other people's needlework in a hotel on a wet day. They performed co-operative outings with fellow-guests. They invited fellow-guests into their sitting-room. When there was an entertainment they did not avoid it. Sophia was determined to do everything that could with propriety be done, partly as an outlet for her own energy (which since she left Paris had been accumulating), but more on Constance's account. She remembered all that Dr. Stirling had said, and the heartiness of her own agreement with his opinions. It was a great day when, under tuition of an aged lady and in the privacy of their parlour, they both began to study the elements of Patience. Neither had ever played at cards. Constance was almost afraid to touch cards, as though in the very cardboard there had been something unrighteous and perilous. But the respectability of a luxurious private hotel makes proper every act that passes within its walls. And Constance plausibly argued that no harm could come from a game which you played by yourself. She acquired with some aptitude several varieties of Patience. She said: "I think I could enjoy that, if I kept at it. But it does make my head whirl."

Nevertheless Constance was not happy in the hotel. She worried the whole time about her empty house. She anticipated difficulties and even disasters. She wondered again and again whether she could trust the second Maggie in her house alone, whether it would not be better to return home earlier and participate personally in the cleaning. She would have decided to do so had it not been that she hesitated to subject Sophia to the inconvenience of a house upside down. The matter was on her mind, always. Always she was restlessly anticipating the day when they would leave. She had carelessly left her heart behind in St. Luke's Square. She had never stayed in a hotel before, and she did not like it. Sciatica occasionally harassed her. Yet when it came to the point she would not drink the waters. She said she never had drunk them, and seemed to regard that as a reason why she never should. Sophia had achieved a miracle in getting her to Buxton for nearly a month, but the ultimate grand effect lacked brilliance.

Then came the fatal letter, the desolating letter, which vindicated Constance's dark apprehensions. Rose Bennion calmly wrote to say that she had decided not to come to St. Luke's Square. She expressed regret for any inconvenience which might possibly be caused; she was polite. But the monstrousness of it! Constance felt that this actually and truly was the deepest depth of her calamities. There she was, far from a dirty home, with no servant and no prospect of a servant! She bore herself bravely, nobly; but she was stricken. She wanted to return to the dirty home at once.

Sophia felt that the situation created by this letter would demand her highest powers of dealing with situations, and she determined to deal with it adequately. Great measures were needed, for Constance's health and happiness were at stake. She alone could act. She knew that she could not rely upon Cyril. She still had an immense partiality for Cyril; she thought him the most charming young man she had ever known; she knew him to be industrious and clever; but in his relations with his mother there was a hardness, a touch of callousness. She explained it vaguely by saying that 'they did not get on well together'; which was strange, considering Constance's sweet affectionateness. Still, Constance could be a little trying—at times. Anyhow, it was soon clear to Sophia that the idea of mother and son living together in London was entirely impracticable. No! If Constance was to be saved from herself, there was no one but Sophia to save her.

After half a morning spent chiefly in listening to Constance's hopeless comments on the monstrous letter, Sophia said suddenly that she must take the dogs for an airing. Constance did not feel equal to walking out, and she would not drive. She did not want Sophia to 'venture,' because the sky threatened. However, Sophia did venture, and she returned a few minutes late for lunch, full of vigour, with two happy dogs. Constance was moodily awaiting her in the dining-room. Constance could not eat. But Sophia ate, and she poured out cheerfulness and energy as from a source inexhaustible. After lunch it began to rain. Constance said she thought she should retire directly to the sitting-room. "I'm coming too," said Sophia, who was still wearing her hat and coat and carried her gloves in her hand. In the pretentious and banal sitting-room they sat down on either side the fire. Constance put a little shawl round her shoulders, pushed her spectacles into her grey hair, folded her hands, and sighed an enormous sigh: "Oh, dear!" She was the tragic muse, aged, and in black silk.

"I tell you what I've been thinking," said Sophia, folding up her gloves.

"What?" asked Constance, expecting some wonderful solution to come out of Sophia's active brain.

"There's no earthly reason why you should go back to Bursley. The house won't run away, and it's costing nothing but the rent. Why not take things easy for a bit?"

"And stay here?" said Constance, with an inflection that enlightened
Sophia as to the intensity of her dislike of the existence at the
Rutland.

"No, not here," Sophia answered with quick deprecation. "There are plenty of other places we could go to."

"I don't think I should be easy in my mind," said Constance. "What with nothing being settled, the house——
"

"What does it matter about the house?"

"It matters a great deal," said Constance, seriously, and slightly hurt. "I didn't leave things as if we were going to be away for a long time. It wouldn't do."

"I don't see that anything could come to any harm, I really don't!" said Sophia, persuasively. "Dirt can always be cleaned, after all. I think you ought to go about more. It would do you good—all the good in the world. And there is no reason why you shouldn't go about. You are perfectly free. Why shouldn't we go abroad together, for instance, you and I? I'm sure you would enjoy it very much."

"Abroad?" murmured Constance, aghast, recoiling from the proposition as from a grave danger.

"Yes," said Sophia, brightly and eagerly. She was determined to take Constance abroad. "There are lots of places we could go to, and live very comfortably among nice English people." She thought of the resorts she had visited with Gerald in the sixties. They seemed to her like cities of a dream. They came back to her as a dream recurs.

"I don't think going abroad would suit me," said Constance.

"But why not? You don't know. You've never tried, my dear." She smiled encouragingly. But Constance did not smile. Constance was inclined to be grim.

"I don't think it would," said she, obstinately. "I'm one of your stay-at-homes. I'm not like you. We can't all be alike," she added, with her 'tart' accent.

Sophia suppressed a feeling of irritation. She knew that she had a stronger individuality than Constance's.

"Well, then," she said, with undiminished persuasiveness, "in England or Scotland. There are several places I should like to visit—Torquay, Tunbridge Wells. I've always under-stood that Tunbridge Wells is a very nice town indeed, with very superior people, and a beautiful climate."

"I think I shall have to be getting back to St. Luke's Square," said Constance, ignoring all that Sophia had said. "There's so much to be done."

Then Sophia looked at Constance with a more serious and resolute air; but still kindly, as though looking thus at Constance for Constance's own good.

"You are making a mistake, Constance," she said, "if you will allow me to say so."

"A mistake!" exclaimed Constance, startled.

"A very great mistake," Sophia insisted, observing that she was creating an effect.

"I don't see how I can be making a mistake," Constance said, gaining confidence in herself, as she thought the matter over.

"No," said Sophia, "I'm sure you don't see it. But you are. You know, you are just a little apt to let yourself be a slave to that house of yours. Instead of the house existing for you, you exist for the house."

"Oh! Sophia!" Constance muttered awkwardly. "What ideas you do have, to be sure!" In her nervousness she rose and picked up some embroidery, adjusting her spectacles and coughing. When she sat down she said: "No one could take things easier than I do as regards housekeeping. I can assure you I let dozens of little matters go, rather than bother myself."

"Then why do you bother now?" Sophia posed her.

"I can't leave the place like that." Constance was hurt.

"There's one thing I can't understand," said Sophia, raising her head and gazing at Constance again, "and that is, why you live in St. Luke's Square at all."

"I must live somewhere. And I'm sure it's very pleasant."

"In all that smoke! And with that dirt! And the house is very old."

"It's a great deal better built than a lot of those new houses by the Park," Constance sharply retorted. In spite of herself she resented any criticism of her house. She even resented the obvious truth that it was old.

"You'll never get a servant to stay in that cellar-kitchen, for one thing," said Sophia, keeping calm.

"Oh! I don't know about that! I don't know about that! That Bennion woman didn't object to it, anyway. It's all very well for you, Sophia, to talk like that. But I know Bursley perhaps better than you do." She was tart again. "And I can assure you that my house is looked upon as a very good house indeed."

"Oh! I don't say it isn't; I don't say it isn't. But you would be better away from it. Every one says that."

"Every one?" Constance looked up, dropping her work. "Who? Who's been talking about me?"

"Well," said Sophia, "the doctor, for instance."

"Dr. Stirling? I like that! He's always saying that Bursley is one of the healthiest climates in England. He's always sticking up for Bursley."

"Dr. Stirling thinks you ought to go away more—not stay always in that dark house." If Sophia had sufficiently reflected she would not have used the adjective 'dark.' It did not help her cause.

"Oh, does he!" Constance fairly snorted. "Well, if it's of any interest to Dr. Stirling, I like my dark house."

"Hasn't he ever told you you ought to go away more?" Sophia persisted.

"He may have mentioned it," Constance reluctantly admitted.

"When he was talking to me he did a good deal more than mention it. And I've a good mind to tell you what he said."

"Do!" said Constance, politely.

"You don't realize how serious it is, I'm afraid," said Sophia. "You can't see yourself." She hesitated a moment. Her blood being stirred by Constance's peculiar inflection of the phrase 'my dark house,' her judgment was slightly obscured. She decided to give Constance a fairly full version of the conversation between herself and the doctor.

"It's a question of your health," she finished. "I think it's my duty to talk to you seriously, and I have done. I hope you'll take it as it's meant."

"Oh, of course!" Constance hastened to say. And she thought: "It isn't yet three months that we've been together, and she's trying already to get me under her thumb."

A pause ensued. Sophia at length said: "There's no doubt that both your sciatica and your palpitations are due to nerves. And you let your nerves get into a state because you worry over trifles. A change would do you a tremendous amount of good. It's just what you need. Really, you must admit, Constance, that the idea of living always in a place like St. Luke's Square, when you are perfectly free to do what you like and go where you like—you must admit it's rather too much."

Constance put her lips together and bent over her embroidery.

"Now, what do you say?" Sophia gently entreated.

"There's some of us like Bursley, black as it is!" said Constance. And Sophia was surprised to detect tears in her sister's voice.

"Now, my dear Constance," she remonstrated.

"It's no use!" cried Constance, flinging away her work, and letting her tears flow suddenly. Her face was distorted. She was behaving just like a child. "It's no use! I've got to go back home and look after things. It's no use. Here we are pitching money about in this place. It's perfectly sinful. Drives, carriages, extras! A shilling a day extra for each dog. I never heard of such goings-on. And I'd sooner be at home. That's it. I'd sooner be at home." This was the first reference that Constance had made for a long time to the question of expense, and incomparably the most violent. It angered Sophia.

"We will count it that you are here as my guest," said Sophia, loftily, "if that is how you look at it."

"Oh no!" said Constance. "It isn't the money I grudge. Oh no, we won't." And her tears were falling thick.

"Yes, we will," said Sophia, coldly. "I've only been talking to you for your own good. I—"

"Well," Constance interrupted her despairingly, "I wish you wouldn't try to domineer over me!"

"Domineer!" exclaimed Sophia, aghast. "Well, Constance, I do think—"

She got up and went to her bedroom, where the dogs were imprisoned. They escaped to the stairs. She was shaking with emotion. This was what came of trying to help other people! Imagine Constance…! Truly Constance was most unjust, and quite unlike her usual self! And Sophia encouraged in her breast the feeling of injustice suffered. But a voice kept saying to her: "You've made a mess of this. You've not conquered this time. You're beaten. And the situation is unworthy of you, of both of you. Two women of fifty quarreling like this! It's undignified. You've made a mess of things." And to strangle the voice, she did her best to encourage the feeling of injustice suffered.

'Domineer!'

And Constance was absolutely in the wrong. She had not argued at all. She had merely stuck to her idea like a mule! How difficult and painful would be the next meeting with Constance, after this grievous miscarriage! As she was reflecting thus the door burst open, and Constance stumbled, as it were blindly, into the bedroom. She was still weeping.

"Sophia!" she sobbed, supplicatingly, and all her fat body was trembling. "You mustn't kill me … I'm like that—you can't alter me. I'm like that. I know I'm silly. But it's no use!" She made a piteous figure.

Sophia was aware of a lump in her throat.

"It's all right, Constance; it's all right. I quite understand. Don't bother any more."

Constance, catching her breath at intervals, raised her wet, worn face and kissed her.

Sophia remembered the very words, 'You can't alter her,' which she had used in remonstrating with Cyril. And now she had been guilty of precisely the same unreason as that with which she had reproached Cyril! She was ashamed, both for herself and for Constance. Assuredly it had not been such a scene as women of their age would want to go through often. It was humiliating. She wished that it could have been blotted out as though it had never happened. Neither of them ever forgot it. They had had a lesson. And particularly Sophia had had a lesson. Having learnt, they left the Rutland, amid due ceremonies, and returned to St. Luke's Square.

CHAPTER IV

END OF SOPHIA
I

The kitchen steps were as steep, dark, and difficult as ever. Up those steps Sophia Scales, nine years older than when she had failed to persuade Constance to leave the Square, was carrying a large basket, weighted with all the heaviness of Fossette. Sophia, despite her age, climbed the steps violently, and burst with equal violence into the parlour, where she deposited the basket on the floor near the empty fireplace. She was triumphant and breathless. She looked at Constance, who had been standing near the door in the attitude of a shocked listener.

"There!" said Sophia. "Did you hear how she talked?"

"Yes," said Constance. "What shall you do?"

"Well," said Sophia. "I had a very good mind to order her out of the house at once. But then I thought I would take no notice. Her time will be up in three weeks. It's best to be indifferent. If once they see they can upset you…. However, I wasn't going to leave Fossette down there to her tender mercies a moment longer. She's simply not looked after her at all."

Sophia went on her knees to the basket, and, pulling aside the dog's hair, round about the head, examined the skin. Fossette was a sick dog and behaved like one. Fossette, too, was nine years older, and her senility was offensive. She was to no sense a pleasant object.

"See here," said Sophia.

279

Constance also knelt to the basket.

"And here," said Sophia. "And here."

The dog sighed, the insincere and pity-seeking sigh of a spoilt animal. Fossette foolishly hoped by such appeals to be spared the annoying treatment prescribed for her by the veterinary surgeon.

While the sisters were coddling her, and protecting her from her own paws, and trying to persuade her that all was for the best, another aged dog wandered vaguely into the room: Spot. Spot had very few teeth, and his legs were stiff. He had only one vice, jealousy. Fearing that Fossette might be receiving the entire attention of his mistresses, he had come to inquire into the situation. When he found the justification of his gloomiest apprehensions, he nosed obstinately up to Constance, and would not be put off. In vain Constance told him at length that he was interfering with the treatment. In vain Sophia ordered him sharply to go away. He would not listen to reason, being furious with jealousy. He got his foot into the basket.

"Will you!" exclaimed Sophia angrily, and gave him a clout on his old head. He barked snappishly, and retired to the kitchen again, disillusioned, tired of the world, and nursing his terrific grievance. "I do declare," said Sophia, "that dog gets worse and worse."

Constance said nothing.

When everything was done that could be done for the aged virgin in the basket, the sisters rose from their knees, stiffly; and they began to whisper to each other about the prospects of obtaining a fresh servant. They also debated whether they could tolerate the criminal eccentricities of the present occupant of the cave for yet another three weeks. Evidently they were in the midst of a crisis. To judge from Constance's face every imaginable woe had been piled on them by destiny without the slightest regard for their powers of resistance. Her eyes had the permanent look of worry, and there was in them also something of the self-defensive. Sophia had a bellicose air, as though the creature in the cave had squarely challenged her, and she was decided to take up the challenge. Sophia's tone seemed to imply an accusation of Constance. The general tension was acute. Then suddenly their whispers expired, and the door opened and the servant came in to lay the supper. Her nose was high, her gaze cruel, radiant, and conquering. She was a pretty and an impudent girl of about twenty-three. She knew she was torturing her old and infirm mistresses. She did not care. She did it purposely. Her motto was: War on employers, get all you can out of them, for they will get all they can out of you. On principle—the sole principle she possessed—she would not stay in a place more than six months. She liked change. And employers did not like change. She was shameless with men. She ignored all orders as to what she was to eat and what she was not to eat. She lived up to the full resources of her employers. She could be to the last degree slatternly. Or she could be as neat as a pin, with an apron that symbolized purity and propriety, as to-night. She could be idle during a whole day, accumulating dirty dishes from morn till eve. On the other hand she could, when she chose, work with astonishing celerity and even thoroughness. In short, she was born to infuriate a mistress like Sophia and to wear out a mistress like Constance. Her strongest advantage in the struggle was that she enjoyed altercation; she revelled in a brawl; she found peace tedious. She was perfectly calculated to convince the sisters that times had worsened, and that the world would never again be the beautiful, agreeable place it once had been.

Her gestures as she laid the table were very graceful, in the pert style. She dropped forks into their appointed positions with disdain; she made slightly too much noise; when she turned she manoeuvred her swelling hips as though for the benefit of a soldier in a handsome uniform.

Nothing but the servant had been changed in that house. The harmonium on which Mr. Povey used occasionally to play was still behind the door; and on the harmonium was the tea-caddy of which Mrs. Baines used to carry the key on her bunch. In the corner to the right of the fireplace still hung the cupboard where Mrs. Baines stored her pharmacopoeia. The rest of the furniture was arranged as it had been arranged when the death of Mrs. Baines endowed Mr. and Mrs. Povey with all the treasures of the house at Axe. And it was as good as ever; better than ever. Dr. Stirling often expressed the desire for a corner cupboard like Mrs. Baines's corner cupboard. One item had been added: the 'Peel' compote which Matthew Peel-Swynnerton had noticed in the dining-room of the Pension Frensham. This majestic piece, which had been reserved by Sophia in the sale of the pension, stood alone on a canterbury in the drawingroom. She had stored it, with a few other trifles, in Paris, and when she sent for it and the packing-case arrived, both she and Constance became aware that they were united for the rest of their lives. Of worldly goods, except money, securities, and clothes, that compote was practically all that Sophia owned. Happily it was a first-class item, doing no shame to the antique magnificence of the drawing-room.

In yielding to Constance's terrible inertia, Sophia had meant nevertheless to work her own will on the interior of the house. She had meant to bully Constance into modernizing the dwelling. She did bully Constance, but the house defied her. Nothing could be done to that house. If only it had had a hall or lobby a complete transformation would have been possible. But there was no access to the upper floor except through the parlour. The parlour could not therefore be turned into a kitchen and the basement suppressed, and the ladies of the house could not live entirely on the upper floor. The disposition of the rooms had to remain exactly as it had always been. There was the same draught under the door, the same darkness on the kitchen stairs, the same difficulties with tradesmen in the distant backyard, the same twist in the bedroom stairs, the same eternal ascending and descending of pails. An efficient cooking-stove, instead of the large and capacious range, alone represented the twentieth century in the fixtures of the house.

Buried at the root of the relations between the sisters was Sophia's grudge against Constance for refusing to leave the Square. Sophia was loyal. She would not consciously give with one hand while taking away with the other, and in accepting Constance's decision she honestly meant to close her eyes to its stupidity. But she could not entirely succeed. She could not avoid thinking that the angelic Constance had been strangely and monstrously selfish in refusing to quit the Square. She marvelled that a woman of Constance's sweet and calm disposition should be capable of so vast and ruthless an egotism. Constance must have known that Sophia would not leave her, and that the habitation of the Square was a continual irk to Sophia. Constance had never been able to advance a single argument for remaining in the Square. And yet she would not budge. It was so inconsistent with the rest of Constance's behaviour. See Sophia sitting primly there by the table, a woman approaching sixty, with immense experience written on the fine hardness of her worn and distinguished face! Though her hair is not yet all grey, nor her figure bowed, you would imagine that she would, in her passage through the world, have learnt better than to expect a character to be consistent. But no! She was ever disappointed and hurt by Constance's inconsistency! And see Constance, stout and bowed, looking more than her age with hair nearly white and slightly trembling hands! See that face whose mark is meekness and the spirit of conciliation, the desire for peace—you would not think that that placid soul could, while submitting to it, inly rage against the imposed weight of Sophia's individuality. "Because I wouldn't turn out of my house to please her," Constance would say to herself, "she fancies she is entitled to do just as she likes." Not often did she secretly rebel thus, but it occurred sometimes. They never quarrelled. They would have regarded separation as a disaster. Considering the difference of their lives, they agreed marvellously in their judgment of things. But that buried question of domicile prevented a complete unity between, them. And its subtle effect was to influence both of them to make the worst, instead of the best, of the trifling mishaps that disturbed their tranquillity. When annoyed, Sophia would meditate upon the mere fact that they lived in the Square for no reason whatever, until it grew incredibly shocking to her. After all it was scarcely conceivable that they should be living in the very middle of a dirty, ugly, industrial town simply because Constance mulishly declined to move. Another thing that curiously exasperated both of them upon occasion was that, owing to a recurrence of her old complaint of dizziness after meals, Sophia had been strictly forbidden to drink tea, which she loved. Sophia chafed under the deprivation, and Constance's pleasure was impaired because she had to drink it alone. While the brazen and pretty servant, mysteriously smiling to herself, dropped food and utensils on to the table, Constance and Sophia attempted to converse with negligent ease upon indifferent topics, as though nothing had occurred that day to mar the beauty of ideal relations between employers and employed. The pretence was ludicrous. The young wench saw through it instantly, and her mysterious smile developed almost into a laugh.

"Please shut the door after you, Maud," said Sophia, as the girl picked up her empty tray.

"Yes, ma'am," replied Maud, politely.

She went out and left the door open.

It was a defiance, offered from sheer, youthful, wanton mischief.

The sisters looked at each other, their faces gravely troubled, aghast, as though they had glimpsed the end of civilized society, as though they felt that they had lived too long into an age of decadence and open shame. Constance's face showed despair—she might have been about to be pitched into the gutter without a friend and without a shilling—but Sophia's had the reckless courage that disaster breeds.

Sophia jumped up, and stepped to the door. "Maud," she called out.

No answer.

"Maud, do you hear me?"

The suspense was fearful.

Still no answer.

Sophia glanced at Constance. "Either she shuts this door, or she leaves this house at once, even if I have to fetch a policeman!"

And Sophia disappeared down the kitchen steps. Constance trembled with painful excitement. The horror of existence closed in upon her. She could imagine nothing more appalling than the pass to which they had been brought by the modern change in the lower classes.

In the kitchen, Sophia, conscious that the moment held the future of at least the next three weeks, collected her forces.

"Maud," she said, "did you not hear me call you?"

Maud looked up from a book—doubtless a wicked book.

"No, ma'am."

"You liar!" thought Sophia. And she said: "I asked you to shut the parlour door, and I shall be obliged if you will do so."

Now Maud would have given a week's wages for the moral force to disobey Sophia. There was nothing to compel her to obey. She could have trampled on the fragile and weak Sophia. But something in Sophia's gaze compelled her to obey. She flounced; she bridled; she mumbled; she unnecessarily disturbed the venerable Spot; but she obeyed. Sophia had risked all, and she had won something.

"And you should light the gas in the kitchen," said Sophia magnificently, as Maud followed her up the steps. "Your young eyes may be very good now, but you are not going the way to preserve them. My sister and I have often told you that we do not grudge you gas."

With stateliness she rejoined Constance, and sat down to the cold supper. And as Maud clicked the door to, the sisters breathed relief. They envisaged new tribulations, but for a brief instant there was surcease.

Yet they could not eat. Neither of them, when it came to the point, could swallow. The day had been too exciting, too distressing. They were at the end of their resources. And they did not hide from each other that they were at the end of their resources. The illness of Fossette, without anything else, had been more than enough to ruin their tranquillity. But the illness of Fossette was as nothing to the ingenious naughtiness of the servant. Maud had a sense of temporary defeat, and was planning fresh operations; but really it was Maud who had conquered. Poor old things, they were in such a 'state' that they could not eat!

"I'm not going to let her think she can spoil my appetite!" said Sophia, dauntless. Truly that woman's spirit was unquenchable.

She cut a couple of slices off the cold fowl; she cut a tomato into slices; she disturbed the butter; she crumbled bread on the cloth, and rubbed bits of fowl over the plates, and dirtied knives and forks. Then she put the slices of fowl and bread and tomato into a piece of tissue paper, and silently went upstairs with the parcel and came down again a moment afterwards empty-handed.

After an interval she rang the bell, and lighted the gas.

"We've finished, Maud. You can clear away."

Constance thirsted for a cup of tea. She felt that a cup of tea was the one thing that would certainly keep her alive. She longed for it passionately. But she would not demand it from Maud. Nor would she mention it to Sophia, lest Sophia, flushed by the victory of the door, should incur new risks. She simply did without. On empty stomachs they tried pathetically to help each other in games of Patience. And when the blithe Maud passed through the parlour on the way to bed, she saw two dignified and apparently calm ladies, apparently absorbed in a delightful game of cards, apparently without a worry in the world. They said "Good night, Maud," cheerfully, politely, and coldly. It was a heroic scene. Immediately afterwards Sophia carried Fossette up to her own bedroom.

II

The next afternoon the sisters, in the drawing-room, saw Dr. Stirling's motor-car speeding down the Square. The doctor's partner, young Harrop, had died a few years before at the age of over seventy, and the practice was much larger than it had ever been, even in the time of old Harrop. Instead of two or three horses, Stirling kept a car, which was a constant spectacle in the streets of the district.

"I do hope he'll call in," said Mrs. Povey, and sighed.

Sophia smiled to herself with a little scorn. She knew that Constance's desire for Dr. Stirling was due simply to the need which she felt of telling some one about the great calamity that had happened to them that morning. Constance was utterly absorbed by it, in the most provincial way. Sophia had said to herself at the beginning of her sojourn in Bursley, and long afterwards, that she should never get accustomed to the exasperating provinciality of the town, exemplified by the childish preoccupation of the inhabitants with their own two-penny affairs. No characteristic of life in Bursley annoyed her more than this. None had oftener caused her to yearn in a brief madness for the desert-like freedom of great cities. But she had got accustomed to it. Indeed, she had almost ceased to notice it. Only occasionally, when her nerves were more upset than usual, did it strike her.

She went into Constance's bedroom to see whether the doctor's car halted in King Street. It did.

"He's here," she called out to Constance.

"I wish you'd go down, Sophia," said Constance. "I can't trust that minx——"

So Sophia went downstairs to superintend the opening of the door by the minx.

The doctor was radiant, according to custom.

"I thought I'd just see how that dizziness was going on," said he as he came up the steps.

"I'm glad you've come," said Sophia, confidentially. Since the first days of their acquaintanceship they had always been confidential. "You'll do my sister good to-day."

Just as Maud was closing the door a telegraph-boy arrived, with a telegram addressed to Mrs. Scales. Sophia read it and then crumpled it in her hand.

"What's wrong with Mrs. Povey to-day?" the doctor asked, when the servant had withdrawn.

"She only wants a bit of your society," said Sophia. "Will you go up?
You know the way to the drawing-room. I'll follow."

As soon as he had gone she sat down on the sofa, staring out of the window. Then with a grunt: "Well, that's no use, anyway!" she went upstairs after the doctor. Already Constance had begun upon her recital.

"Yes," Constance was saying. "And when I went down this morning to keep an eye on the breakfast, I thought Spot was very quiet——" She paused. "He was dead in the drawer. She pretended she didn't know, but I'm sure she did. Nothing will convince me that she didn't poison that dog with the mice-poison we had last year. She was vexed because Sophia took her up sharply about Fossette last night, and she revenged herself on the other dog. It would just be like her. Don't tell me! I know. I should have packed her off at once, but Sophia thought better not. We couldn't prove anything, as Sophia says. Now, what do you think of it, doctor?"

Constance's eyes suddenly filled with tears.

"Ye'd had Spot a long time, hadn't ye?" he said sympathetically.

She nodded. "When I was married," said she, "the first thing my husband did was to buy a fox-terrier, and ever since we've always had a fox-terrier in the house." This was not true, but Constance was firmly convinced of its truth.

"It's very trying," said the doctor. "I know when my Airedale died, I said to my wife I'd never have another dog—unless she could find me one that would live for ever. Ye remember my Airedale?"

"Oh, quite well!"

"Well, my wife said I should be bound to have another one sooner or later, and the sooner the better. She went straight off to Oldcastle and bought me a spaniel pup, and there was such a to-do training it that we hadn't too much time to think about Piper."

Constance regarded this procedure as somewhat callous, and she said so, tartly. Then she recommenced the tale of Spot's death from the beginning, and took it as far as his burial, that afternoon, by Mr. Critchlow's manager, in the yard. It had been necessary to remove and replace paving-stones.

"Of course," said Dr. Stirling, "ten years is a long time. He was an old dog. Well, you've still got the celebrated Fossette." He turned to Sophia.

"Oh yes," said Constance, perfunctorily. "Fossette's ill. The fact is that if Fossette hadn't been ill, Spot would probably have been alive and well now."

Her tone exhibited a grievance. She could not forget that Sophia had harshly dismissed Spot to the kitchen, thus practically sending him to his death. It seemed very hard to her that Fossette, whose life had once been despaired of, should continue to exist, while Spot, always healthy and unspoilt, should die untended, and by treachery. For the rest, she had never liked Fossette. On Spot's behalf she had always been jealous of Fossette. "Probably alive and well now!" she repeated, with a peculiar accent.

Observing that Sophia maintained a strange silence, Dr. Stirling suspected a slight tension in the relations of the sisters, and he changed the subject. One of his great qualities was that he refrained from changing a subject introduced by a patient unless there was a professional reason for changing it.

"I've just met Richard Povey in the town," said he. "He told me to tell ye that he'll be round in about an hour or so to take you for a spin. He was in a new car, which he did his best to sell to me, but he didn't succeed."

"It's very kind of Dick," said Constance. "But this afternoon really we're not—"

"I'll thank ye to take it as a prescription, then," replied the doctor. "I told Dick I'd see that ye went. Splendid June weather. No dust after all that rain. It'll do ye all the good in the world. I must exercise my authority. The truth is, I've gradually been losing all control over ye. Ye do just as ye like."

"Oh, doctor, how you do run on!" murmured Constance, not quite well pleased to-day by his tone.

After the scene between Sophia and herself at Buxton, Constance had always, to a certain extent, in the doctor's own phrase, 'got her knife into him.' Sophia had, then, in a manner betrayed him. Constance and the doctor discussed that matter with frankness, the doctor humorously accusing her of being 'hard' on him. Nevertheless the little cloud between them was real, and the result was often a faint captiousness on Constance's part in judging the doctor's behaviour.

"He's got a surprise for ye, has Dick!" the doctor added.

Dick Povey, after his father's death and his own partial recovery, had set up in Hanbridge as a bicycle agent. He was permanently lamed, and he hopped about with a thick stick. He had succeeded with bicycles and had taken to automobiles, and he was succeeding with automobiles. People were at first startled that he should advertise himself in the Five Towns. There was an obscure general feeling that because his mother had been a drunkard and his father a murderer, Dick Povey had no right to exist. However, when it had recovered from the shock of seeing Dick Povey's announcement of bargains in the Signal, the district most sensibly decided that there was no reason why Dick Povey should not sell bicycles as well as a man with normal parents. He was now supposed to be acquiring wealth rapidly. It was said that he was a marvellous chauffeur, at once daring and prudent. He had one day, several years previously, overtaken the sisters in the rural neighbourhood of Sneyd, where they had been making an afternoon excursion. Constance had presented him to Sophia, and he had insisted on driving the ladies home. They had been much impressed by his cautious care of them, and their natural prejudice against anything so new as a motorcar had been conquered instantly. Afterwards he had taken them out for occasional runs. He had a great admiration for Constance, founded on gratitude to Samuel Povey; and as for Sophia, he always said to her that she would be an ornament to any car.

"You haven't heard his latest, I suppose?" said the doctor, smiling.

"What is it?" Sophia asked perfunctorily.

"He wants to take to ballooning. It seems he's been up once."

Constance made a deprecating noise with her lips.

"However, that's not his surprise," the doctor added, smiling again at the floor. He was sitting on the music-stool, and saying to himself, behind his mask of effulgent good-nature: "It gets more and more uphill work, cheering up these two women. I'll try them on Federation."

Federation was the name given to the scheme for blending the Five Towns into one town, which would be the twelfth largest town in the kingdom. It aroused fury in Bursley, which saw in the suggestion nothing but the extinction of its ancient glory to the aggrandizement of Hanbridge. Hanbridge had already, with the assistance of electric cars that whizzed to and fro every five minutes, robbed Bursley of two-thirds of its retail trade—as witness the steady decadence of the Square!—and Bursley had no mind to swallow the insult and become a mere ward of Hanbridge. Bursley would die fighting. Both Constance and Sophia were bitter opponents of Federation. They would have been capable of putting Federationists to the torture. Sophia in particular, though so long absent from her native town, had adopted its cause with characteristic vigour. And when Dr. Stirling wished to practise his curative treatment of taking the sisters 'out of themselves,' he had only to start the hare of Federation and the hunt would be up in a moment. But this afternoon he did not succeed with Sophia, and only partially with Constance. When he stated that there was to be a public meeting that very night, and that Constance as a ratepayer ought to go to it and vote, if her convictions were genuine, she received his chaff with a mere murmur to the effect that she did not think she should go. Had the man forgotten that Spot was dead? At length he became grave, and examined them both as to their ailments, and nodded his head, and looked into vacancy while meditating upon each case. And then, when he had inquired where they meant to go for their summer holidays, he departed.

"Aren't you going to see him out?" Constance whispered to Sophia, who had shaken hands with him at the drawingroom door. It was Sophia who did the running about, owing to the state of Constance's sciatic nerve. Constance had, indeed, become extraordinarily inert, leaving everything to Sophia.

Sophia shook her head. She hesitated; then approached Constance, holding out her hand and disclosing the crumpled telegram.

"Look at that!" said she.

Her face frightened Constance, who was always expectant of new anxieties and troubles. Constance straightened out the paper with difficulty, and read—

"Mr. Gerald Scales is dangerously ill here. Boldero, 49, Deansgate, Manchester."

All through the inexpressibly tedious and quite unnecessary call of Dr. Stirling—(Why had he chosen to call just then? Neither of them was ill)—Sophia had held that telegram concealed in her hand and its information concealed in her heart. She had kept her head up, offering a calm front to the world. She had given no hint of the terrible explosion—for an explosion it was. Constance was astounded at her sister's self-control, which entirely passed her comprehension. Constance felt that worries would never cease, but would rather go on multiplying until death ended all. First, there had been the frightful worry of the servant; then the extremely distressing death and burial of Spot—and now it was Gerald Scales turning up again! With what violence was the direction of their thoughts now shifted! The wickedness of maids was a trifle; the death of pets was a trifle. But the reappearance of Gerald Scales! That involved the possibility of consequences which could not even be named, so afflictive was the mere prospect to them. Constance was speechless, and she saw that Sophia was also speechless.

Of course the event had been bound to happen. People do not vanish never to be heard of again. The time surely arrives when the secret is revealed. So Sophia said to herself—now!

She had always refused to consider the effect of Gerald's reappearance. She had put the idea of it away from her, determined to convince herself that she had done with him finally and for ever. She had forgotten him. It was years since he had ceased to disturb her thoughts—many years. "He MUST be dead," she had persuaded herself. "It is inconceivable that he should have lived on and never come across me. If he had been alive and learnt that I had made money, he would assuredly have come to me. No, he must be dead!"

And he was not dead! The brief telegram overwhelmingly shocked her. Her life had been calm, regular, monotonous. And now it was thrown into an indescribable turmoil by five words of a telegram, suddenly, with no warning whatever. Sophia had the right to say to herself: "I have had my share of trouble, and more than my share!" The end of her life promised to be as awful as the beginning. The mere existence of Gerald Scales was a menace to her. But it was the simple impact of the blow that affected her supremely, beyond ulterior things. One might have pictured fate as a cowardly brute who had struck this ageing woman full in the face, a felling blow, which however had not felled her. She staggered, but she stuck on her legs. It seemed a shame—one of those crude, spectacular shames which make the blood boil—that the gallant, defenceless creature should be so maltreated by the bully, destiny.

"Oh, Sophia!" Constance moaned. "What trouble is this?"

Sophia's lip curled with a disgusted air. Under that she hid her suffering.

She had not seen him for thirty-six years. He must be over seventy years of age, and he had turned up again like a bad penny, doubtless a disgrace! What had he been doing in those thirty-six years? He was an old, enfeebled man now! He must be a pretty sight! And he lay at Manchester, not two hours away!

Whatever feelings were in Sophia's heart, tenderness was not among them. As she collected her wits from the stroke, she was principally aware of the sentiment of fear. She recoiled from the future.

"What shall you do?" Constance asked. Constance was weeping.

Sophia tapped her foot, glancing out of the window.

"Shall you go to see him?" Constance continued.

"Of course," said Sophia. "I must!"

She hated the thought of going to see him. She flinched from it. She felt herself under no moral obligation to go. Why should she go? Gerald was nothing to her, and had no claim on her of any kind. This she honestly believed. And yet she knew that she must go to him. She knew it to be impossible that she should not go.

"Now?" demanded Constance.

Sophia nodded.

"What about the trains? … Oh, you poor dear!" The mere idea of the journey to Manchester put Constance out of her wits, seeming a business of unparalleled complexity and difficulty.

"Would you like me to come with you?"

"Oh no! I must go by myself."

Constance was relieved by this. They could not have left the servant in the house alone, and the idea of shutting up the house without notice or preparation presented itself to Constance as too fantastic.

By a common instinct they both descended to the parlour.

"Now, what about a time-table? What about a time-table?" Constance mumbled on the stairs. She wiped her eyes resolutely. "I wonder whatever in this world has brought him at last to that Mr. Boldero's in Deansgate?" she asked the walls.

As they came into the parlour, a great motor-car drove up before the door, and when the pulsations of its engine had died away, Dick Povey hobbled from the driver's seat to the pavement. In an instant he was hammering at the door in his lively style. There was no avoiding him. The door had to be opened. Sophia opened it. Dick Povey was over forty, but he looked considerably younger. Despite his lameness, and the fact that his lameness tended to induce corpulence, he had a dashing air, and his face, with its short, light moustache, was boyish. He seemed to be always upon some joyous adventure.

"Well, aunties," he greeted the sisters, having perceived Constance behind Sophia; he often so addressed them. "Has Dr. Stirling warned you that I was coming? Why haven't you got your things on?"

Sophia observed a young woman in the car.

"Yes," said he, following her gaze, "you may as well look. Come down, miss. Come down, Lily. You've got to go through with it." The young woman, delicately confused and blushing, obeyed. "This is Miss Lily Holl," he went on. "I don't know whether you would remember her. I don't think you do. It's not often she comes to the Square. But, of course, she knows you by sight. Granddaughter of your old neighbour, Alderman Holl! We are engaged to be married, if you please."

Constance and Sophia could not decently pour out their griefs on the top of such news. The betrothed pair had to come in and be congratulated upon their entry into the large realms of mutual love. But the sisters, even in their painful quandary, could not help noticing what a nice, quiet, ladylike girl Lily Holl was. Her one fault appeared to be that she was too quiet. Dick Povey was not the man to pass time in formalities, and he was soon urging departure.

"I'm sorry we can't come," said Sophia. "I've got to go to Manchester now. We are in great trouble."

"Yes, in great trouble," Constance weakly echoed.

Dick's face clouded sympathetically. And both the affianced began to see that to which the egotism of their happiness had blinded them. They felt that long, long years had elapsed since these ageing ladies had experienced the delights which they were feeling.

"Trouble? I'm sorry to hear that!" said Dick.

"Can you tell me the trains to Manchester?" asked Sophia.

"No," said Dick, quickly, "But I can drive you there quicker than any train, if it's urgent. Where do you want to go to?"

"Deansgate," Sophia faltered.

"Look here," said Dick, "it's half-past three. Put yourself in my hands; I'll guarantee at Deansgate you shall be before half-past five. I'll look after you."

"But——"

"There isn't any 'but.' I'm quite free for the afternoon and evening."

At first the suggestion seemed absurd, especially to Constance. But really it was too tempting to be declined. While Sophia made ready for the journey, Dick and Lily Holl and Constance conversed in low, solemn tones. The pair were waiting to be enlightened as to the nature of the trouble; Constance, however, did not enlighten them. How could Constance say to them: "Sophia has a husband that she hasn't seen for thirty-six years, and he's dangerously ill, and they've telegraphed for her to go?" Constance could not. It did not even occur to Constance to order a cup of tea.

III

Dick Povey kept his word. At a quarter-past five he drew up in front of No. 49, Deansgate, Manchester. "There you are!" he said, not without pride. "Now, we'll come back in about a couple of hours or so, just to take your orders, whatever they are." He was very comforting, with his suggestion that in him Sophia had a sure support in the background.

Without many words Sophia went straight into the shop. It looked like a jeweller's shop, and a shop for bargains generally. Only the conventional sign over a side-entrance showed that at heart it was a pawnbroker's. Mr. Till Boldero did a nice business in the Five Towns, and in other centres near Manchester, by selling silver-ware second-hand, or nominally second hand, to persons who wished to make presents to other persons or to themselves. He would send anything by post on approval. Occasionally he came to the Five Towns, and he had once, several years before, met Constance. They had talked. He was the son of a cousin of the late great and wealthy Boldero, sleeping partner in Birkinshaws, and Gerald's uncle. It was from

Constance that he had learnt of Sophia's return to Bursley. Constance had often remarked to Sophia what a superior man Mr. Till Boldero was.

The shop was narrow and lofty. It seemed like a menagerie for trapped silver-ware. In glass cases right up to the dark ceiling silver vessels and instruments of all kinds lay confined. The top of the counter was a glass prison containing dozens of gold watches, together with snuff-boxes, enamels, and other antiquities. The front of the counter was also glazed, showing vases and large pieces of porcelain. A few pictures in heavy gold frames were perched about. There was a case of umbrellas with elaborate handles and rich tassels. There were a couple of statuettes. The counter, on the customers' side, ended in a glass screen on which were the words 'Private Office.' On the seller's side the prospect was closed by a vast safe. A tall young man was fumbling in this safe. Two women sat on customers' chairs, leaning against the crystal counter. The young man came towards them from the safe, bearing a tray.

"How much is that goblet?" asked one of the women, raising her parasol dangerously among such fragility and pointing to one object among many in a case high up from the ground.

"That, madam?"

"Yes."

"Thirty-five pounds."

The young man disposed his tray on the counter. It was packed with more gold watches, adding to the extraordinary glitter and shimmer of the shop. He chose a small watch from the regiment.

"Now, this is something I can recommend," he said. "It's made by Cuthbert Butler of Blackburn. I can guarantee you that for five years."

He spoke as though he were the accredited representative of the Bank of England, with calm and absolute assurance.

The effect upon Sophia was mysteriously soothing. She felt that she was among honest men. The young man raised his head towards her with a questioning, deferential gesture.

"Can I see Mr. Boldero?" she asked. "Mrs. Scales."

The young man's face changed instantly to a sympathetic comprehension.

"Yes, madam. I'll fetch him at once," said he, and he disappeared behind the safe. The two customers discussed the watch. Then the door opened in the glass screen, and a portly, middle-aged man showed himself. He was dressed in blue broad-cloth, with a turned-down collar and a small black tie. His waistcoat displayed a plain but heavy gold watch-chain, and his cuff-links were of plain gold. His eye-glasses were gold-rimmed. He had grey hair, beard and moustache, but on the backs of his hands grew a light brown hair. His appearance was strangely mild, dignified, and confidence-inspiring. He was, in fact, one of the most respected tradesmen in Manchester.

He peered forward, looking over his eye-glasses, which he then took off, holding them up in the air by their short handle. Sophia had approached him.

"Mrs. Scales?" he said, in a very quiet, very benevolent voice. Sophia nodded. "Please come this way." He took her hand, squeezing it commiseratingly, and drew her into the sanctum. "I didn't expect you so soon," he said. "I looked up th' trains, and I didn't see how you could get here before six."

Sophia explained.

He led her further, through the private office, into a sort of parlour, and asked her to sit down. And he too sat down. Sophia waited, as it were, like a suitor.

"I'm afraid I've got bad news for you, Mrs. Scales," he said, still in that mild, benevolent voice.

"He's dead?" Sophia asked.

Mr. Till Boldero nodded. "He's dead. I may as well tell you that he had passed away before I telegraphed. It all happened very, very suddenly." He paused. "Very, very suddenly!"

"Yes," said Sophia, weakly. She was conscious of a profound sadness which was not grief, though it resembled grief. And she had also a feeling that she was responsible to Mr. Till Boldero for anything untoward that might have occurred to him by reason of Gerald.

"Yes," said Mr. Till Boldero, deliberately and softly. "He came in last night just as we were closing. We had very heavy rain here. I don't know how it was with you. He was wet, in a dreadful state, simply dreadful. Of course, I didn't recognize him. I'd never seen him before, so far as my recollection goes. He asked me if I was the son of Mr. Till Boldero that had this shop in 1866. I said I was. 'Well,' he says, 'you're the only connection I've got. My name's Gerald Scales. My mother was your father's cousin. Can you do anything for me?' he says. I could see he was ill. I had him in here. When I found he couldn't eat nor drink I thought I'd happen better send for th' doctor. The doctor got him to bed. He passed away at one o'clock this afternoon. I was very sorry my wife wasn't here to look after things a bit better. But she's at Southport, not well at all."

"What was it?" Sophia asked briefly.

Mr. Boldero indicated the enigmatic. "Exhaustion, I suppose," he replied.

"He's here?" demanded Sophia, lifting her eyes to possible bedrooms.

"Yes," said Mr. Boldero. "I suppose you would wish to see him?"

"Yes," said Sophia.

"You haven't seen him for a long time, your sister told me?" Mr. Boldero murmured, sympathetically.

"Not since 'seventy," said Sophia.

"Eh, dear! Eh, dear!" ejaculated Mr. Boldero. "I fear it's been a sad business for ye, Mrs. Scales. Not since 'seventy!" He sighed. "You must take it as well as you can. I'm not one as talks much, but I sympathize, with you. I do that! I wish my wife had been here to receive you."

Tears came into Sophia's eyes.

"Nay, nay!" he said. "You must bear up now!"

"It's you that make me cry," said Sophia, gratefully. "You were very good to take him in. It must have been exceedingly trying for you."

"Oh," he protested, "you mustn't talk like that. I couldn't leave a Boldero on the pavement, and an old man at that! … Oh, to think that if he'd only managed to please his uncle he might ha' been one of the richest men in Lancashire. But then there'd ha' been no Boldero Institute at Strangeways!" he added.

They both sat silent a moment.

"Will you come now? Or will you wait a bit?" asked Mr. Boldero, gently.

"Just as you wish. I'm sorry as my wife's away, that I am!"

"I'll come now," said Sophia, firmly. But she was stricken.

He conducted her up a short, dark flight of stairs, which gave on a passage, and at the end of the passage was a door ajar. He pushed the door open. "I'll leave you for a moment," he said, always in the same very restrained tone. "You'll find me downstairs, there, if you want me." And he moved away with hushed, deliberate tread.

Sophia went into the room, of which the white blind was drawn. She appreciated Mr. Boldero's consideration in leaving her. She was trembling. But when she saw, in the pale gloom, the face of an aged man peeping out from under a white sheet on a naked mattress, she started back, trembling no more—rather transfixed into an absolute rigidity. That was no conventional, expected shock that she had received. It was a genuine unforeseen shock, the most violent that she had ever had. In her mind she had not pictured Gerald as a very old man. She knew that he was old; she had said to herself that he must be very old, well over seventy. But she had not pictured him. This face on the bed was painfully, pitiably old. A withered face, with the shiny skin all drawn into wrinkles! The stretched skin under the jaw was like the skin of a plucked fowl. The cheek-bones stood up, and below them were deep hollows, almost like egg-cups. A short, scraggy white beard covered the lower part of the face. The hair was scanty, irregular, and quite white; a little white hair grew in the ears. The shut mouth obviously hid toothless gums, for the lips were sucked in. The eyelids were as if pasted down over the eyes, fitting them like kid. All the skin was extremely pallid; it seemed brittle. The body, whose outlines were clear under the sheet, was very small, thin, shrunk, pitiable as the face. And on the face was a general expression of final fatigue, of tragic and acute exhaustion; such as made Sophia pleased that the fatigue and exhaustion had been assuaged in rest, while all the time she kept thinking to herself horribly: "Oh! how tired he must have been!"

Sophia then experienced a pure and primitive emotion, uncoloured by any moral or religious quality. She was not sorry that Gerald had wasted his life, nor that he was a shame to his years and to her. The manner of his life was of no importance. What affected her was that he had once been young, and that he had grown old, and was now dead. That was all. Youth and vigour had come to that. Youth and vigour always came to that. Everything came to that. He had ill-treated her; he had abandoned her; he had been a devious rascal; but how trivial were such accusations against him! The whole of her huge and bitter grievance against him fell to pieces and crumbled. She saw him young, and proud, and strong, as for instance when he had kissed her lying on the bed in that London hotel—she forgot the name—in 1866; and now he was old, and worn, and horrible, and dead. It was the riddle of life that was puzzling and killing her. By the corner of her eye, reflected in the mirror of a wardrobe near the bed, she glimpsed a tall, forlorn woman, who had once been young and now was old; who had once exulted in abundant strength, and trodden proudly on the neck of circumstance, and now was old. He and she had once loved and burned and quarrelled in the glittering and scornful pride of

288

youth. But time had worn them out. "Yet a little while," she thought, "and I shall be lying on a bed like that! And what shall I have lived for? What is the meaning of it?" The riddle of life itself was killing her, and she seemed to drown in a sea of inexpressible sorrow.

Her memory wandered hopelessly among those past years. She saw Chirac with his wistful smile. She saw him whipped over the roof of the Gare du Nord at the tail of a balloon. She saw old Niepce. She felt his lecherous arm round her. She was as old now as Niepce had been then. Could she excite lust now? Ah! the irony of such a question! To be young and seductive, to be able to kindle a man's eye—that seemed to her the sole thing desirable. Once she had been so! … Niepce must certainly have been dead for years. Niepce, the obstinate and hopeful voluptuary, was nothing but a few bones in a coffin now!

She was acquainted with affliction in that hour. All that she had previously suffered sank into insignificance by the side of that suffering.

She turned to the veiled window and idly pulled the blind and looked out. Huge red and yellow cars were swimming in thunder along Deansgate; lorries jolted and rattled; the people of Manchester hurried along the pavements, apparently unconscious that all their doings were vain. Yesterday he too had been in Deansgate, hungry for life, hating the idea of death! What a figure he must have made! Her heart dissolved in pity for him. She dropped the blind.

"My life has been too terrible!" she thought. "I wish I was dead. I have been through too much. It is monstrous, and I cannot stand it. I do not want to die, but I wish I was dead."

There was a discreet knock on the door.

"Come in," she said, in a calm, resigned, cheerful voice. The sound had recalled her with the swiftness of a miracle to the unconquerable dignity of human pride.

Mr. Till Boldero entered.

"I should like you to come downstairs and drink a cup of tea," he said. He was a marvel of tact and good nature. "My wife is unfortunately not here, and the house is rather at sixes and sevens; but I have sent out for some tea."

She followed him downstairs into the parlour. He poured out a cup of tea.

"I was forgetting," she said. "I am forbidden tea. I mustn't drink it."

She looked at the cup, tremendously tempted. She longed for tea. An occasional transgression could not harm her. But no! She would not drink it.

"Then what can I get you?"

"If I could have just milk and water," she said meekly.

Mr. Boldero emptied the cup into the slop basin, and began to fill it again.

"Did he tell you anything?" she asked, after a considerable silence.

"Nothing," said Mr. Boldero in his low, soothing tones. "Nothing except that he had come from Liverpool. Judging from his shoes I should say he must have walked a good bit of the way."

"At his age!" murmured Sophia, touched.

"Yes," sighed Mr. Boldero. "He must have been in great straits. You know, he could scarcely talk at all. By the way, here are his clothes. I have had them put aside."

Sophia saw a small pile of clothes on a chair. She examined the suit, which was still damp, and its woeful shabbiness pained her. The linen collar was nearly black, its stud of bone. As for the boots, she had noticed such boots on the feet of tramps. She wept now. These were the clothes of him who had once been a dandy living at the rate of fifty pounds a week.

"No luggage or anything, of course?" she muttered.

"No," said Mr. Boldero. "In the pockets there was nothing whatever but this."

He went to the mantelpiece and picked up a cheap, cracked letter case, which Sophia opened. In it were a visiting card—'Senorita Clemenzia Borja'—and a bill-head of the Hotel of the Holy Spirit, Concepcion del Uruguay, on the back of which a lot of figures had been scrawled.

"One would suppose," said Mr. Boldero, "that he had come from South America."

"Nothing else?"

"Nothing."

Gerald's soul had not been compelled to abandon much in the haste of its flight.

A servant announced that Mrs. Scales's friends were waiting for her outside in the motor-car. Sophia glanced at Mr. Till Boldero with an exacerbated anxiety on her face.

"Surely they don't expect me to go back with them tonight!" she said.

"And look at all there is to be done!"

Mr. Till Boldero's kindness was then redoubled. "You can do nothing for HIM now," he said. "Tell me your wishes about the funeral. I will arrange everything. Go back to your sister to-night. She will be nervous about you. And return tomorrow or the day after…. No! It's no trouble, I assure you!"

She yielded.

Thus towards eight o'clock, when Sophia had eaten a little under Mr. Boldero's superintendence, and the pawnshop was shut up, the motor-car started again for Bursley, Lily Holl being beside her lover and Sophia alone in the body of the car. Sophia had told them nothing of the nature of her mission. She was incapable of talking to them. They saw that she was in a condition of serious mental disturbance. Under cover of the noise of the car, Lily said to Dick that she was sure Mrs. Scales was ill, and Dick, putting his lips together, replied that he meant to be in King Street at nine-thirty at the latest. From time to time Lily surreptitiously glanced at Sophia—a glance of apprehensive inspection, or smiled at her silently; and Sophia vaguely responded to the smile.

In half an hour they had escaped from the ring of Manchester and were on the county roads of Cheshire, polished, flat, sinuous. It was the season of the year when there is no night—only daylight and twilight; when the last silver of dusk remains obstinately visible for hours. And in the open country, under the melancholy arch of evening, the sadness of the earth seemed to possess Sophia anew. Only then did she realize the intensity of the ordeal through which she was passing.

To the south of Congleton one of the tyres softened, immediately after Dick had lighted his lamps. He stopped the car and got down again. They were two miles Astbury, the nearest village. He had just, with the resignation of experience, reached for the tool-bag, when Lily exclaimed: "Is she asleep, or what?" Sophia was not asleep, but she was apparently not conscious.

It was a difficult and a trying situation for two lovers. Their voices changed momentarily to the tone of alarm and consternation, and then grew firm again. Sophia showed life but not reason. Lily could feel the poor old lady's heart.

"Well, there's nothing for it!" said Dick, briefly, when all their efforts failed to rouse her.

"What—shall you do?"

"Go straight home as quick as I can on three tyres. We must get her over to this side, and you must hold her. Like that we shall keep the weight off the other side."

He pitched back the tool-bag into its box. Lily admired his decision.

It was in this order, no longer under the spell of the changing beauty of nocturnal landscapes, that they finished the journey. Constance had opened the door before the car came to a stop in the gloom of King Street. The young people considered that she bore the shock well, though the carrying into the house of Sophia's inert, twitching body, with its hat forlornly awry, was a sight to harrow a soul sturdier than Constance.

When that was done, Dick said curtly: "I'm off. You stay here, of course."

"Where are you going?" asked Lily.

"Doctor!" snapped Dick, hobbling rapidly down the steps.

IV

The extraordinary violence of the turn in affairs was what chiefly struck Constance, though it did not overwhelm her. Less than twelve hours before—nay, scarcely six hours before—she and Sophia had been living their placid and monotonous existence, undisturbed by anything worse than the indisposition or death of dogs, or the perversity of a servant. And now, the menacing Gerald Scales having reappeared, Sophia's form lay mysterious and affrightening on the sofa; and she and Lily Holl, a girl whom she had not met till that day, were staring at Sophia side by side, intimately sharing the same alarm. Constance rose to the crisis. She no longer had Sophia's energy and decisive peremptoriness to depend on, and the Baines in her was awakened. All her daily troubles sank away to their proper scale of unimportance. Neither the young woman nor the old one knew what to do. They could loosen clothes, vainly offer restoratives to the smitten mouth: that was all. Sophia was not unconscious, as could be judged from her eyes; but she could not speak, nor make signs; her body was frequently convulsed. So the two women waited, and the servant waited in the background. The sight of Sophia had effected an astonishing transformation in Maud. Maud was a changed girl. Constance could not recognize, in her eager deferential anxiety to be of use, the pert naughtiness of the minx. She was altered as a wanton of the middle ages would have been altered by some miraculous visitation. It might have been the turning-point in Maud's career!

Doctor Stirling arrived in less than ten minutes. Dick Povey had had the wit to look for him at the Federation meeting in the Town Hall. And the advent of the doctor and Dick, noisily, at breakneck speed in the car, provided a second sensation. The doctor inquired quickly what had occurred. Nobody could tell him anything. Constance had already confided to Lily Holl the reason of the visit to Manchester; but that was the extent of her knowledge. Not a single person in Bursley, except Sophia, knew what had happened in Manchester. But Constance conjectured that Gerald Scales was dead—or Sophia would never have returned so soon. Then the doctor suggested that on the contrary Gerald Scales might be out of danger. And all then pictured to themselves this troubling Gerald Scales, this dark and sinister husband that had caused such a violent upheaval.

Meanwhile the doctor was at work. He sent Dick Povey to knock up Critchlow's, if the shop should be closed, and obtain a drug. Then, after a time, he lifted Sophia, just as she was, like a bundle on his shoulder, and carried her single-handed upstairs to the second floor. He had recently been giving a course of instruction to enthusiasts of the St. John's Ambulance Association in Bursley. The feat had an air of the superhuman. Above all else it remained printed on Constance's mind: the burly doctor treading delicately and carefully on the crooked, creaking stairs, his precautions against damaging Sophia by brusque contacts, his stumble at the two steps in the middle of the corridor; Sophia's horribly limp head and loosened hair; and then the tender placing of her on the bed, and the doctor's long breath and flourish of his large handkerchief, all that under the crude lights and shadows of gas jets! The doctor was nonplussed. Constance gave him a second-hand account of Sophia's original attack in Paris, roughly as she had heard it from Sophia. He at once said that it could not have been what the French doctor had said it was. Constance shrugged her shoulders. She was not surprised. For her there was necessarily something of the charlatan about a French doctor. She said she only knew what Sophia had told her. After a time Dr. Stirling determined to try electricity, and Dick Povey drove him up to the surgery to fetch his apparatus. The women were left alone again. Constance was very deeply impressed by Lily Holl's sensible, sympathetic attitude. "Whatever I should have done without Miss Lily I don't know!" she used to exclaim afterwards. Even Maud was beyond praise. It seemed to be the middle of the night when Dr. Stirling came back, but it was barely eleven o'clock, and people were only just returning from Hanbridge Theatre and Hanbridge Music Hall. The use of the electrical apparatus was a dead spectacle. Sophia's inertness under it was agonizing. They waited, as it were, breathless for the result. And there was no result. Both injections and electricity had entirely failed to influence the paralysis of Sophia's mouth and throat. Everything had failed. "Nothing to do but wait a bit!" said the doctor quietly. They waited in the chamber. Sophia seemed to be in a kind of coma. The distortion of her handsome face was more marked as time passed. The doctor spoke now and then in a low voice. He said that the attack had ultimately been determined by cold produced by rapid motion in the automobile. Dick Povey whispered that he must run over to Hanbridge and let Lily's parents know that there was no cause for alarm on her account, and that he would return at once. He was very devoted. On the landing out-side the bedroom, the doctor murmured to him: "U.P." And Dick nodded. They were great friends.

At intervals the doctor, who never knew when he was beaten, essayed new methods of dealing with Sophia's case. New symptoms followed. It was half-past twelve when, after gazing with prolonged intensity at the patient, and after having tested her mouth and heart, he rose slowly and looked at Constance.

"It's over?" said Constance.

And he very slightly moved his head. "Come downstairs, please," he enjoined her, in a pause that ensued. Constance was amazingly courageous. The doctor was very solemn and very kind; Constance had never before seen him to such heroic advantage. He led her with infinite gentleness out of the room. There was nothing to stay for; Sophia had gone. Constance wanted to stay by Sophia's body; but it was the rule that the stricken should be led away, the doctor observed this classic rule, and Constance felt that he was right and that she must obey. Lily Holl followed. The servant, learning the truth by the intuition accorded to primitive natures, burst into loud sobs, yelling that Sophia had been the most excellent mistress that servant ever had. The doctor angrily told her not to stand blubbering there, but to go into her kitchen and shut the door if she couldn't control herself. All his accumulated nervous agitation was discharged on Maud like a thunderclap. Constance continued to behave wonderfully. She was the admiration of the doctor and Lily Holl. Then Dick Povey came back. It was settled that Lily should pass the night with Constance. At last the doctor and Dick departed together, the doctor undertaking the mortuary arrangements. Maud was hunted to bed.

Early in the morning Constance rose up from her own bed. It was five o'clock, and there had been daylight for two hours already. She moved noiselessly and peeped over the foot of the bed at the sofa. Lily was quietly asleep there, breathing with the softness of a child. Lily would have deemed that she was a very mature woman, who had seen life and much of it. Yet to Constance her face and attitude had the exquisite quality of a child's. She was not precisely a pretty girl, but her features, the candid expression of her disposition, produced an impression that was akin to that of beauty. Her abandonment was complete. She had gone through the night unscathed, and was now renewing herself in calm, oblivious sleep. Her ingenuous girlishness was apparent then. It seemed as if all her wise and sweet behaviour of the evening could have been nothing but so many imitative gestures. It seemed impossible that a being so young and fresh could have really experienced the mood of which her gestures had been the expression. Her strong virginal simplicity made Constance vaguely sad for her.

Creeping out of the room, Constance climbed to the second floor in her dressing-gown, and entered the other chamber. She was obliged to look again upon Sophia's body. Incredible swiftness of calamity! Who could have foreseen it? Constance was less desolated than numbed. She was as yet only touching the fringe of her bereavement. She had not begun to think of herself. She was drenched, as she gazed at Sophia's body, not by pity for herself, but by compassion for the immense disaster of her sister's life. She perceived fully now for the first time the greatness of that disaster. Sophia's charm and Sophia's beauty—what profit had they been to their owner? She saw pictures of Sophia's career, distorted and grotesque images formed in her untravelled mind from Sophia's own rare and compressed recitals. What a career! A brief passion, and then nearly thirty years in a boarding-house! And Sophia had never had a child; had never known either the joy or the pain of maternity. She had never even had a true home till, in all her sterile splendour, she came to Bursley. And she had ended—thus! This was the piteous, ignominious end of Sophia's wondrous gifts of body and soul. Hers had not been a life at all. And the reason? It is strange how fate persists in justifying the harsh generalizations of Puritan morals, of the morals in which Constance had been brought up by her stern parents! Sophia had sinned. It was therefore inevitable that she should suffer. An adventure such as she had in wicked and capricious pride undertaken with Gerald Scales, could not conclude otherwise than it had concluded. It could have brought nothing but evil. There was no getting away from these verities, thought Constance. And she was to be excused for thinking that all modern progress and cleverness was as naught, and that the world would be forced to return upon its steps and start again in the path which it had left.

Up to within a few days of her death people had been wont to remark that Mrs. Scales looked as young as ever, and that she was as bright and as energetic as ever. And truly, regarding Sophia from a little distance— that handsome oval, that erect carriage of a slim body, that challenging eye!—no one would have said that she was in her sixtieth year. But look at her now, with her twisted face, her sightless orbs, her worn skin—she did not seem sixty, but seventy! She was like something used, exhausted, and thrown aside! Yes, Constance's heart melted in an anguished pity for that stormy creature. And mingled with the pity was a stern recognition of the handiwork of divine justice. To Constance's lips came the same phrase as had come to the lips of Samuel Povey on a different occasion: God is not mocked! The ideas of her parents and her grandparents had survived intact in Constance. It is true that Constance's father would have shuddered in Heaven could he have seen Constance solitarily playing cards of a night. But in spite of cards, and of a son who never went to chapel, Constance, under the various influences of destiny, had remained essentially what her father had been. Not in her was the force of evolution manifest. There are thousands such.

Lily, awake, and reclothed with that unreal mien of a grown and comprehending woman, stepped quietly into the room, searching for the poor old thing, Constance. The layer-out had come.

By the first post was delivered a letter addressed to Sophia by Mr. Till Boldero. From its contents the death of Gerald Scales was clear. There seemed then to be nothing else for Constance to do. What had to be done was done for her. And stronger wills than hers put her to bed. Cyril was telegraphed for. Mr. Critchlow called, Mrs. Critchlow following—a fussy infliction, but useful in certain matters. Mr. Critchlow was not allowed to see Constance. She could hear his high grating voice in the corridor. She had to lie calm, and the sudden tranquillity seemed strange after the feverish violence of the night. Only twenty-four hours since, and she had been worrying about the death of a dog! With a body crying for sleep, she dozed off, thoughts of the mystery of life merging into the incoherence of dreams.

The news was abroad in the Square before nine o'clock. There were persons who had witnessed the arrival of the motorcar, and the transfer of Sophia to the house. Untruthful rumours had spread as to the manner of Gerald Scales's death. Some said that he had dramatically committed suicide. But the town, though titillated, was not moved as it would have been moved by a similar event twenty years, or even ten years earlier. Times had changed in Bursley. Bursley was more sophisticated than in the old days.

Constance was afraid lest Cyril, despite the seriousness of the occasion, might exhibit his customary tardiness in coming. She had long since learnt not to rely upon him. But he came the same evening. His behaviour was in every way perfect. He showed quiet but genuine grief for the death of his aunt, and he was a model of consideration for his mother. Further, he at once assumed charge of all the arrangements, in regard both to Sophia and to her husband. Constance was surprised at the ease which he displayed in the conduct of practical affairs, and the assurance with which he gave orders. She had never seen him direct anything before. He said, indeed, that he had never directed anything before, but that there appeared to him to be no difficulties. Whereas Constance had figured a tiresome series of varied complications. As to the burial of Sophia, Cyril was vigorously in favour of an absolutely private funeral; that is to say, a funeral at which none but himself should be present. He seemed to have a passionate objection to any sort of parade. Constance agreed with him. But she said that it would be impossible not to invite Mr. Critchlow, Sophia's trustee, and that if Mr. Critchlow were invited certain others must be invited. Cyril asked: "Why impossible?" Constance said: "Because it would be impossible. Because Mr. Critchlow would be hurt." Cyril asked: "What does it matter if he is hurt?" and suggested that Mr. Critchlow would get over his damage. Constance grew more serious. The discussion threatened to be warm. Suddenly Cyril yielded. "All right, Mrs. Plover, all right! It shall be exactly as you choose," he said, in a gentle, humouring tone. He had not called her 'Mrs. Plover' for years. She thought the hour badly chosen for verbal pleasantry, but he was so kind that she made no complaint. Thus there were six people at Sophia's funeral, including Mr. Critchlow. No refreshments were offered. The mourners separated at the church. When both funerals were accomplished Cyril sat down and played the harmonium softly, and said that it had kept well in tune. He was extraordinarily soothing.

He had now reached the age of thirty-three. His habits were as industrious as ever, his preoccupation with his art as keen. But he had achieved no fame, no success. He earned nothing, living in comfort on an allowance from his mother. He seldom spoke of his plans and never of his hopes. He had in fact settled down into a dilettante, having learnt gently to scorn the triumphs which he lacked the force to win. He imagined that industry and a regular existence were sufficient justification in themselves for any man's life. Constance had dropped the habit of expecting him to astound the world. He was rather grave and precise in manner, courteous and tepid, with a touch of condescension towards his environment; as though he were continually permitting the perspicacious to discern that he had nothing to learn—if the truth were known! His humour had assumed a modified form. He often smiled to himself. He was unexceptionable.

On the day after Sophia's funeral he set to work to design a simple stone for his aunt's tomb. He said he could not tolerate the ordinary gravestone, which always looked, to him, as if the wind might blow it over, thus negativing the idea of solidity. His mother did not in the least understand him. She thought the lettering of his tombstone affected and finicking. But she let it pass without comment, being secretly very flattered that he should have deigned to design a stone at all.

Sophia had left all her money to Cyril, and had made him the sole executor of her will. This arrangement had been agreed with Constance. The sisters thought it was the best plan. Cyril ignored Mr. Critchlow entirely, and went to a young lawyer at Hanbridge, a friend of his and of Matthew Peel-Swynnerton's. Mr. Critchlow, aged and unaccustomed to interference, had to render accounts of his trusteeship to this young man, and was incensed. The estate was proved at over thirty-five thousand pounds. In the main, Sophia had been careful, and had even been parsimonious. She had often told Constance that they ought to spend money much more freely, and she had had a few brief fits of extravagance. But the habit of stern thrift, begun in 1870 and practised without any intermission till she came to England in 1897, had been too strong for her theories. The squandering of money pained her. And she could not, in her age, devise expensive tastes.

Cyril showed no emotion whatever on learning himself the inheritor of thirty-five thousand pounds. He did not seem to care. He spoke of the sum as a millionaire might have spoken of it. In justice to him it is to be said that he cared nothing for wealth, except in so far as wealth could gratify his eye and ear trained to artistic voluptuousness. But, for his mother's sake, and for the sake of Bursley, he might have affected a little satisfaction. His mother was somewhat hurt. His behaviour caused her to revert in meditation again and again to the futility of Sophia's career, and the waste of her attributes. She had grown old and hard in joyless years in order to amass this money which Cyril would spend coldly and ungratefully, never thinking of the immense effort and endless sacrifice which had gone to its collection. He would spend it as carelessly as though he had picked it up in the street. As the days went by and Constance realized her own grief, she also realized more and more the completeness of the tragedy of Sophia's life. Headstrong Sophia had deceived her mother, and for the deception had paid with thirty years of melancholy and the entire frustration of her proper destiny. After haunting Bursley for a fortnight in elegant black, Cyril said, without any warning, one night: "I must go the day after to-morrow, mater." And he told her of a journey to Hungary which he had long since definitely planned with Matthew Peel-Swynnerton, and which could not be postponed, as it comprised 'business.' He had hitherto breathed no word of this. He was as secretive as ever. As to her holiday, he suggested that she should arrange to go away with the Holls and Dick Povey. He approved of Lily Holl and of Dick Povey. Of Dick Povey he said: "He's one of the most remarkable chaps in the Five Towns." And he had the air of having made Dick's reputation. Constance, knowing there was no appeal, accepted the sentence of loneliness. Her health was singularly good.

When he was gone she said to herself: "Scarcely a fortnight and Sophia was here at this table!" She would remember every now and then, with a faint shock, that poor, proud, masterful Sophia was dead.

CHAPTER V

END OF CONSTANCE
I

When, on a June afternoon about twelve months later, Lily Holl walked into Mrs. Povey's drawing-room overlooking the Square, she found a calm, somewhat optimistic old lady—older than her years—which were little more than sixty—whose chief enemies were sciatica and rheumatism. The sciatica was a dear enemy of long standing, always affectionately referred to by the forgiving Constance as 'my sciatica'; the rheumatism was a new-comer, unprivileged, spoken of by its victim apprehensively and yet disdainfully as 'this rheumatism.' Constance was now very stout. She sat in a low easy-chair between the oval table and the window, arrayed in black silk. As the girl Lily came in, Constance lifted her head with a bland smile, and Lily kissed her, contentedly. Lily knew that she was a welcome visitor. These two had become as intimate as the difference between their ages would permit; of the two, Constance was the more frank. Lily as well as Constance was in mourning. A few months previously her aged grandfather, 'Holl, the grocer,' had died. The second of his two sons, Lily's father, had then left the business established by the brothers at Hanbridge in order to manage, for a time, the parent business in St. Luke's Square. Alderman Holl's death had delayed Lily's marriage. Lily took tea with Constance, or at any rate paid a call, four or five times a week. She listened to Constance.

Everybody considered that Constance had 'come splendidly through' the dreadful affair of Sophia's death. Indeed, it was observed that she was more philosophic, more cheerful, more sweet, than she had been for many years. The truth was that, though her bereavement had been the cause of a most genuine and durable sorrow, it had been a relief to her. When Constance was over fifty, the energetic and masterful Sophia had burst in upon her lethargic tranquillity and very seriously disturbed the flow of old habits. Certainly Constance had fought Sophia on the main point, and won; but on a hundred minor points she had either lost or had not fought. Sophia had been 'too much' for Constance, and it had been only by a wearying expenditure of nervous force that Constance had succeeded in holding a small part of her own against the unconscious domination of Sophia. The death of Mrs. Scales had put an end to all the strain, and Constance had been once again mistress in Constance's house. Constance would never have admitted these facts, even to herself; and no one would ever have dared to suggest them to her. For with all her temperamental mildness she had her formidable side. She was slipping a photograph into a plush-covered photograph album.

"More photographs?" Lily questioned. She had almost exactly the same benignant smile that Constance had. She seemed to be the personification of gentleness—one of those feather-beds that some capricious men occasionally have the luck to marry. She was capable, with a touch of honest, simple stupidity. All her character was displayed in the tone in which she said: "More photographs?" It showed an eager responsive sympathy with Constance's cult for photographs, also a slight personal fondness for photographs, also a dim perception that a cult for photographs might be carried to the ridiculous, and a kind desire to hide all trace of this perception. The voice was thin, and matched the pale complexion of her delicate face.

294

Constance's eyes had a quizzical gleam behind her spectacles as she silently held up the photograph for Lily's inspection.

Lily, sitting down, lowered the corners of her soft lips when she beheld the photograph, and nodded her head several times, scarce perceptibly.

"Her ladyship has just given it to me," whispered Constance.

"Indeed!" said Lily, with an extraordinary accent.

'Her ladyship' was the last and best of Constance's servants, a really excellent creature of thirty, who had known misfortune, and who must assuredly have been sent to Constance by the old watchful Providence. They 'got on together' nearly perfectly. Her name was Mary. After ten years of turmoil, Constance in the matter of servants was now at rest.

"Yes," said Constance. "She's named it to me several times—about having her photograph taken, and last week I let her go. I told you, didn't I? I always consider her in every way, all her little fancies and everything. And the copies came to-day. I wouldn't hurt her feelings for anything. You may be sure she'll take a look into the album next time she cleans the room."

Constance and Lily exchanged a glance agreeing that Constance had affably stretched a point in deciding to put the photograph of a servant between the same covers with photographs of her family and friends. It was doubtful whether such a thing had ever been done before.

One photograph usually leads to another, and one photograph album to another photograph album.

"Pass me that album on the second shelf of the Canterbury; my dear," said Constance.

Lily rose vivaciously, as though to see the album on the second shelf of the Canterbury had been the ambition of her life.

They sat side by side at the table, Lily turning over the pages. Constance, for all her vast bulk, continually made little nervous movements. Occasionally she would sniff and occasionally a mysterious noise would occur in her chest; she always pretended that this noise was a cough, and would support the pretence by emitting a real cough immediately after it.

"Why!" exclaimed Lily. "Have I seen that before?"

"I don't know, my dear," said Constance. "HAVE you?"

It was a photograph of Sophia taken a few years previously by 'a very nice gentleman,' whose acquaintance the sisters had made during a holiday at Harrogate. It portrayed Sophia on a knoll, fronting the weather.

"It's Mrs. Scales to the life—I can see that," said Lily.

"Yes," said Constance. "Whenever there was a wind she always stood like that, and took long deep breaths of it."

This recollection of one of Sophia's habits recalled the whole woman to Constance's memory, and drew a picture of her character for the girl who had scarcely known her.

"It's not like ordinary photographs. There's something special about it," said Lily, enthusiastically. "I don't think I ever saw a photograph like that."

"I've got another copy of it in my bedroom," said Constance. "I'll give you this one."

"Oh, Mrs. Povey! I couldn't think—!"

"Yes, yes!" said Constance, removing the photograph from the page.

"Oh, THANK you!" said Lily.

"And that reminds me," said Constance, getting up with great difficulty from her chair.

"Can I find anything for you?" Lily asked.

"No, no!" said Constance, leaving the room.

She returned in a moment with her jewel-box, a receptacle of ebony with ivory ornamentations.

"I've always meant to give you this," said Constance, taking from the box a fine cameo brooch. "I don't seem to fancy wearing it myself. And I should like to see you wearing it. It was mother's. I believe they're coming into fashion again. I don't see why you shouldn't wear it while you're in mourning. They aren't half so strict now about mourning as they used to be."

"Truly!" murmured Lily, ecstatically. They kissed. Constance seemed to breathe out benevolence, as with trembling hands she pinned the brooch at Lily's neck. She lavished the warm treasure of her heart on Lily, whom she regarded as an almost perfect girl, and who had become the idol of her latter years.

"What a magnificent old watch!" said Lily, as they delved together in the lower recesses of the box. "AND the chain to it!"

"That was father's," said Constance. "He always used to swear by it.

When it didn't agree with the Town Hall, he used to say: 'Then th' Town

Hall's wrong.' And it's curious, the Town Hall WAS wrong. You know the Town Hall clock has never been a good timekeeper. I've been thinking of giving that watch and chain to Dick."

"HAVE you?" said Lily.

"Yes. It's just as good as it was when father wore it. My husband never would wear it. He preferred his own. He had little fancies like that. And Cyril takes after his father." She spoke in her 'dry' tone. "I've almost decided to give it to Dick—that is, if he behaves himself. Is he still on with this ballooning?"

Lily Smiled guiltily: "Oh yes!"

"Well," said Constance, "I never heard the like! If he's been up and come down safely, that ought to be enough for him. I wonder you let him do it, my dear."

"But how can I stop him? I've no control over him."

"But do you mean to say that he'd still do it if you told him seriously you didn't want him to?"

"Yes," said Lily; and added: "So I shan't tell him."

Constance nodded her head, musing over the secret nature of men. She remembered too well the cruel obstinacy of Samuel, who had nevertheless loved her. And Dick Povey was a thousand times more bizarre than Samuel. She saw him vividly, a little boy, whizzing down King Street on a boneshaker, and his cap flying off. Afterwards it had been motor-cars! Now it was balloons! She sighed. She was struck by the profound instinctive wisdom just enunciated by the girl.

"Well," she said, "I shall see. I've not made up my mind yet. What's the young man doing this afternoon, by the way?"

"He's gone to Birmingham to try to sell two motor-lorries. He won't be back home till late. He's coming over here to-morrow."

It was an excellent illustration of Dick Povey's methods that at this very moment Lily heard in the Square the sound of a motor-car, which happened to be Dick's car. She sprang up to look.

"Why!" she cried, flushing. "Here he is now!"

"Bless us, bless us!" muttered Constance, closing the box.

When Dick, having left his car in King Street, limped tempestuously into the drawing-room, galvanizing it by his abundant vitality into a new life, he cried joyously: "Sold my lorries! Sold my lorries!" And he explained that by a charming accident he had disposed of them to a chance buyer in Hanbridge, just before starting for Birmingham. So he had telephoned to Birmingham that the matter was 'off,' and then, being 'at a loose end,' he had come over to Bursley in search of his betrothed. At Holl's shop they had told him that she was with Mrs. Povey. Constance glanced at him, impressed by his jolly air of success. He seemed exactly like his breezy and self-confident advertisements in the Signal. He was absolutely pleased with himself. He triumphed over his limp—that ever-present reminder of a tragedy. Who would dream, to look at his blond, laughing, scintillating face, astonishingly young for his years, that he had once passed through such a night as that on which his father had killed his mother while he lay immovable and cursing, with a broken knee, in bed? Constance had heard all about that scene from her husband, and she paused in wonder at the contrasting hazards of existence. Dick Povey brought his hands together with a resounding smack, and then rubbed them rapidly.

"AND a good price, too!" he exclaimed blithely. "Mrs. Povey, I don't mind telling you that I've netted seventy pounds odd this afternoon."

Lily's eyes expressed her proud joy.

"I hope pride won't have a fall," said Constance, with a calm smile out of which peeped a hint of a rebuke.

"That's what I hope. I must just go and see about tea."

"I can't stay for tea—really," said Dick.

"Of course you can," said Constance, positively. "Suppose you'd been at Birmingham? It's weeks since you stayed to tea."

"Oh, well, thanks!" Dick yielded, rather snubbed.

"Can't I save you a journey, Mrs. Povey?" Lily asked, eagerly thoughtful.

"No, thank you, my dear. There are one or two little things that need my attention." And Constance departed with her jewel-box.

Dick, having assured himself that the door was closed, assaulted Lily with a kiss.

"Been here long?" he inquired.

"About an hour and a half."

"Glad to see me?"

"Oh, Dick!" she protested.

"Old lady's in one of her humours, eh?"

"No, no! Only she was just talking about balloons—you know. She's very much up in arms."

"You ought to keep her off balloons. Balloons may be the ruin of her wedding-present to us, my child."

"Dick! How can you talk like that? … It's all very well saying I ought to keep her off balloons. You try to keep her off balloons when once she begins, and see!"

"What started her?"

"She said she was thinking of giving you old Mr. Baines's gold watch and chain—if you behaved yourself."

"Thank you for nothing!" said Dick. "I don't want it."

"Have you seen it?"

"Have I seen it? I should say I had seen it. She's mentioned it once or twice before."

"Oh! I didn't know."

"I don't see myself carting that thing about. I much prefer my own.

What do you think of it?"

"Of course it is rather clumsy," said Lily. "But if she offered it to you, you couldn't refuse it, and you'd simply have to wear it."

"Well, then," said Dick, "I must try to behave myself just badly enough to keep off the watch, but not badly enough to upset her notions about wedding-presents."

"Poor old thing!" Lily murmured, compassionately.

Then Lily put her hand silently to her neck.

"What's that?"

"She's just given it to me."

Dick approached very near to examine the cameo brooch. "Hm!" he murmured. It was an adverse verdict.

And Lily coincided with it by a lift of the eyebrows.

"And I suppose you'll have to wear that!" said Dick.

"She values it as much as anything she's got, poor old thing!" said Lily. "It belonged to her mother. And she says cameos are coming into fashion again. It really is rather good, you know."

"I wonder where she learnt that!" said Dick, drily. "I see you've been suffering from the photographs again."

"Well," said Lily, "I much prefer the photographs to helping her to play Patience. The way she cheats herself—it's too silly! I—"

She stopped. The door which had after all not been latched, was pushed open, and the antique Fossette introduced herself painfully into the room. Fossette had an affection for Dick Povey.

"Well, Methusaleh!" he greeted the animal loudly. She could scarcely wag her tail, nor shake the hair out of her dim eyes in order to look up at him. He stooped to pat her.

"That dog does smell," said Lily, bluntly.

"What do you expect? What she wants is the least dose of prussic acid.

She's a burden to herself."

"It's funny that if you venture to hint to Mrs. Povey that the dog is offensive she gets quite peppery," said Lily.

"Well, that's very simple," said Dick. "Don't hint, that's all! Hold your nose and your tongue too."

"Dick, I do wish you wouldn't be so absurd."

Constance returned into the room, cutting short the conversation.

"Mrs. Povey," said Dick, in a voice full of gratitude, "Lily has just been showing me her brooch—"

He noticed that she paid no heed to him, but passed hurriedly to the window.

"What's amiss in the Square?" Constance exclaimed. "When I was in the parlour just now I saw a man running along Wedgwood Street, and I said to myself, what's amiss?"

Dick and Lily joined her at the window.

Several people were hurrying down the Square, and then a man came running with a doctor from the market-place. All these persons disappeared from view under the window of Mrs. Povey's drawing-room, which was over part of Mrs. Critchlow's shop. As the windows of the shop projected beyond the walls of the house it was impossible, from the drawing-room window, to see the pavement in front of the shop.

"It must be something on the pavement—or in the shop!" murmured
Constance.

"Oh, ma'am!" said a startled voice behind the three. It was Mary, original of the photograph, who had run unperceived into the drawing-room. "They say as Mrs. Critchlow has tried to commit suicide!"

Constance started back. Lily went towards her, with an instinctive gesture of supporting consolation.

"Maria Critchlow tried to commit suicide!" Constance muttered.

"Yes, ma'am! But they say she's not done it."

"By Jove! I'd better go and see if I can help, hadn't I?" cried Dick Povey, hobbling off, excited and speedy. "Strange, isn't it?" he exclaimed afterwards, "how I manage to come in for things? Sheer chance that I was here to-day! But it's always like that! Somehow something extraordinary is always happening where I am." And this too ministered to his satisfaction, and to his zest for life.

II

When, in the evening, after all sorts of comings and goings, he finally returned to the old lady and the young one, in order to report the upshot, his demeanour was suitably toned to Constance's mood. The old lady had been very deeply disturbed by the tragedy, which, as she said, had passed under her very feet while she was calmly talking to Lily.

The whole truth came out in a short space of time. Mrs. Critchlow was suffering from melancholia. It appeared that for long she had been depressed by the failing trade of the shop, which was none of her fault. The state of the Square had steadily deteriorated. Even the 'Vaults' were not what they once were. Four or five shops had been shut up, as it were definitely, the landlords having given up hope of discovering serious tenants. And, of those kept open, the majority were struggling desperately to make ends meet. Only Holl's and a new upstart draper, who had widely advertised his dress-making department, were really flourishing. The confectionery half of Mr. Brindley's business was disappearing. People would not go to Hanbridge for their bread or for their groceries, but they would go for their cakes. These electric trams had simply carried to Hanbridge the cream, and much of the milk, of Bursley's retail trade. There were unprincipled tradesmen in Hanbridge ready to pay the car-fares of any customer who spent a crown in their establishments. Hanbridge was the geographical centre of the Five Towns, and it was alive to its situation. Useless for Bursley to compete! If Mrs. Critchlow had been a philosopher, if she had known that geography had always made history, she would have given up her enterprise a dozen years ago. But Mrs. Critchlow was merely Maria Insull. She had seen Baines's in its magnificent prime, when Baines's almost conferred a favour on customers in serving them. At the time when she took over the business under the wing of her husband, it was still a good business. But from that instant the tide had seemed to turn. She had fought, and she kept on fighting, stupidly. She was not aware that she was fighting against evolution, not aware that evolution had chosen her for one of its victims! She could understand that all the other shops in the Square should fail, but not that Baines's should fail! She was as industrious as ever, as good a buyer, as good a seller, as keen for novelties, as economical, as methodical! And yet the returns dropped and dropped.

She naturally had no sympathy from Charles, who now took small interest even in his own business, or what was left of it, and who was coldly disgusted at the ultimate cost of his marriage. Charles gave her no money that he could avoid giving her. The crisis had been slowly approaching for years. The assistants in the shop had said nothing, or had only whispered among themselves, but now that the crisis had flowered suddenly in an attempted self-murder, they all spoke at once, and the evidences were pieced together into a formidable proof of the strain which Mrs. Critchlow had suffered. It appeared that for many months she had been depressed and irritable, that sometimes she would sit down in the midst of work and declare, with every sign of exhaustion, that she could do no more. Then with equal briskness she would arise and force herself to labour. She did not sleep for whole nights. One assistant related how she had complained of having had no sleep whatever for four nights consecutively. She had noises in the ears and a chronic headache. Never very plump, she had grown thinner and thinner. And she was for ever taking pills: this information came from Charles's manager. She had had several outrageous quarrels with the redoubtable Charles, to the stupefaction of all who heard or saw them…. Mrs. Critchlow standing up to her husband! Another strange thing was that she thought the bills of several of the big Manchester firms were unpaid, when as a fact they had been paid. Even when shown the receipts she would not be convinced, though she pretended to be convinced. She would recommence the next day. All this was sufficiently disconcerting for female assistants in the drapery. But what could they do?

Then Maria Critchlow had gone a step further. She had summoned the eldest assistant to her corner and had informed her, with all the solemnity of a confession made to assuage a conscience which has been tortured too long, that she had on many occasions been guilty of sexual irregularity with her late employer, Samuel Povey. There was no truth whatever in this accusation (which everybody, however, took care not to mention to Constance); it merely indicated, perhaps, the secret aspirations of Maria Insull, the virgin. The assistant was properly scandalized, more by the crudity of Mrs. Critchlow's language than by the alleged sin buried in the past. Goodness knows what the assistant would have done! But two hours later Maria Critchlow tried to commit suicide by stabbing herself with a pair of scissors. There was blood in the shop.

With as little delay as possible she had been driven away to the asylum. Charles Critchlow, enveloped safely in the armour of his senile egotism, had shown no emotion, and very little activity. The shop was closed. And as a general draper's it never opened again. That was the end of Baines's. Two assistants found themselves without a livelihood. The small tumble with the great.

Constance's emotion was more than pardonable; it was justified. She could not eat and Lily could not persuade her to eat. In an unhappy moment Dick Povey mentioned—he never could remember how, afterwards—the word Federation! And then Constance, from a passive figure of grief became a menace. She overwhelmed Dick Povey with her anathema of Federation, for Dick was a citizen of Hanbridge, where this detestable movement for Federation had had its birth. All the misfortunes of St. Luke's Square were due to that great, busy, grasping, unscrupulous neighbour. Had not Hanbridge done enough, without wanting to merge all the Five Towns into one town, of which of course itself would be the centre? For Constance, Hanbridge was a borough of unprincipled adventurers, bent on ruining the ancient 'Mother of the Five Towns' for its own glory and aggrandizement. Let Constance hear no more of Federation! Her poor sister Sophia had been dead against Federation, and she had been quite right! All really respectable people were against it! The attempted suicide of Mrs. Critchlow sealed the fate of Federation and damned it for ever, in Constance's mind. Her hatred of the idea of it was intensified into violent animosity; insomuch that in the result she died a martyr to the cause of Bursley's municipal independence.

III

It was on a muddy day in October that the first great battle for and against Federation was fought in Bursley. Constance was suffering severely from sciatica. She was also suffering from disgust with the modern world. Unimaginable things had happened in the Square. For Constance, the reputation of the Square was eternally ruined. Charles Critchlow, by that strange good fortune which always put him in the right when fairly he ought to have been in the wrong, had let the Baines shop and his own shop and house to the Midland Clothiers Company, which was establishing branches throughout Staffordshire, Warwickshire, Leicestershire, and adjacent counties. He had sold his own chemist's stock and gone to live in a little house at the bottom of Kingstreet. It is doubtful whether he would have consented to retire had not Alderman Holl died earlier in the year, thus ending a long rivalry between the old men for the patriarchate of the Square. Charles Critchlow was as free from sentiment as any man, but no man is quite free from it, and the ancient was in a position to indulge sentiment had he chosen. His business was not a source of loss, and he could still trust his skinny hands and peering eyes to make up a prescription. However, the offer of the Midland Clothiers Company tempted him, and as the undisputed 'father' of the Square he left the Square in triumph.

The Midland Clothiers Company had no sense of the proprieties of trade. Their sole idea was to sell goods. Having possessed themselves of one of the finest sites in a town which, after all was said and done, comprised nearly forty thousand inhabitants, they set about to make the best of that site. They threw the two shops into one, and they caused to be constructed a sign compared to which the spacious old 'Baines' sign was a postcard. They covered the entire frontage with posters of a theatrical description—coloured posters! They occupied the front page of the Signal, and from that pulpit they announced that winter was approaching, and that they meant to sell ten thousand overcoats at their new shop in Bursley at the price of twelve and sixpence each. The tailoring of the world was loudly and coarsely defied to equal the value of those overcoats. On the day of opening they arranged an orchestra or artillery of phonographs upon the leads over the window of that part of the shop which had been Mr. Critchlow's. They also carpeted the Square with handbills, and flew flags from their upper storeys. The immense shop proved to be full of overcoats; overcoats were shown in all the three great windows; in one window an overcoat was disposed as a receptacle for water, to prove that the Midland twelve-and-sixpenny overcoats were impermeable by rain. Overcoats flapped in the two doorways. These devices woke and drew the town, and the town found itself received by bustling male assistants very energetic and rapid, instead of by demure anaemic virgins. At moments towards evening the shop was populous with custom; the number of overcoats sold was prodigious. On another day the Midland sold trousers in a like manner, but without the phonographs. Unmistakably the Midland had shaken the Square and demonstrated that commerce was still possible to fearless enterprise.

299

Nevertheless the Square was not pleased. The Square was conscious of shame, of dignity departed. Constance was divided between pain and scornful wrath. For her, what the Midland had done was to desecrate a shrine. She hated those flags, and those flaring, staring posters on the honest old brick walls, and the enormous gilded sign, and the windows all filled with a monotonous repetition of the same article, and the bustling assistants. As for the phonographs, she regarded them as a grave insult; they had been within twenty feet of her drawing-room window! Twelve-and-sixpenny overcoats! It was monstrous, and equally monstrous was the gullibility of the people. How could an overcoat at twelve and sixpence be 'good.' She remembered the overcoats made and sold in the shop in the time of her father and her husband, overcoats of which the inconvenience was that they would not wear out! The Midland, for Constance, was not a trading concern, but something between a cheap-jack and a circus. She could scarcely bear to walk down the Square, to such a degree did the ignoble frontage of the Midland offend her eye and outrage her ancestral pride. She even said that she would give up her house.

But when, on the twenty-ninth of September, she received six months' notice, signed in Critchlow's shaky hand, to quit the house—it was wanted for the Midland's manager, the Midland having taken the premises on condition that they might eject Constance if they chose—the blow was an exceedingly severe one. She had sworn to go—but to be turned out, to be turned out of the house of her birth and out of her father's home, that was different! Her pride, injured as it was, had a great deal to support. It became necessary for her to recollect that she was a Baines. She affected magnificently not to care. But she could not refrain from telling all her acquaintances that she was being turned out of her house, and asking them what they thought of THAT; and when she met Charles Critchlow in the street she seared him with the heat of her resentment. The enterprise of finding a new house and moving into it loomed before her gigantic, terrible, the idea of it was alone sufficient to make her ill.

Meanwhile, in the matter of Federation, preparations for the pitched battle had been going forward, especially in the columns of the Signal, where the scribes of each one of the Five Towns had proved that all the other towns were in the clutch of unscrupulous gangs of self-seekers. After months of argument and recrimination, all the towns except Bursley were either favourable or indifferent to the prospect of becoming a part of the twelfth largest town in the United Kingdom. But in Bursley the opposition was strong, and the twelfth largest town in the United Kingdom could not spring into existence without the consent of Bursley. The United Kingdom itself was languidly interested in the possibility of suddenly being endowed with a new town of a quarter of a million inhabitants. The Five Towns were frequently mentioned in the London dailies, and London journalists would write such sentences as: "The Five Towns, which are of course, as everybody knows, Hanbridge, Bursley, Knype, Longshaw, and Turnhill…." This was renown at last, for the most maligned district in the country! And then a Cabinet Minister had visited the Five Towns, and assisted at an official inquiry, and stated in his hammering style that he meant personally to do everything possible to accomplish the Federation of the Five Towns: an incautious remark, which infuriated, while it flattered, the opponents of Federation in Bursley. Constance, with many other sensitive persons, asked angrily what right a Cabinet Minister had to take sides in a purely local affair. But the partiality of the official world grew flagrant. The Mayor of Bursley openly proclaimed himself a Federationist, though there was a majority on the Council against him. Even ministers of religion permitted themselves to think and to express opinions. Well might the indignant Old Guard imagine that the end of public decency had come! The Federationists were very ingenious individuals. They contrived to enrol in their ranks a vast number of leading men. Then they hired the Covered Market, and put a platform in it, and put all these leading men on the platform, and made them all speak eloquently on the advantages of moving with the times. The meeting was crowded and enthusiastic, and readers of the Signal next day could not but see that the battle was won in advance, and that anti-Federation was dead. In the following week, however, the anti-Federationists held in the Covered Market an exactly similar meeting (except that the display of leading men was less brilliant), and demanded of a floor of serried heads whether the old Mother of the Five Towns was prepared to put herself into the hands of a crew of highly-paid bureaucrats at Hanbridge, and was answered by a wild defiant "No," that could be heard on Duck Bank. Readers of the Signal next day were fain to see that the battle had not been won in advance. Bursley was lukewarm on the topics of education, slums, water, gas, electricity. But it meant to fight for that mysterious thing, its identity. Was the name of Bursley to be lost to the world? To ask the question was to give the answer.

Then dawned the day of battle, the day of the Poll, when the burgesses were to indicate plainly by means of a cross on a voting paper whether or not they wanted Federation. And on this day Constance was almost incapacitated by sciatica. It was a heroic day. The walls of the town were covered with literature, and the streets dotted with motor-cars and other vehicles at the service of the voters. The greater number of these vehicles bore large cards with the words, "Federation this time." And hundreds of men walked briskly about with circular cards tied to their lapels, as though Bursley had been a race-course, and these cards too had the words, "Federation this time." (The reference was to a light poll which had been taken several years before, when no interest had been aroused and the immature project yet defeated by a six to one majority.) All partisans of Federation sported a red ribbon; all Anti-Federationists sported a blue ribbon. The schools were closed and the Federationists displayed their characteristic lack of scruple in appropriating the children. The Federationists, with devilish skill, had hired the Bursley Town Silver Prize Band, an organization of terrific respectability, and had set it to march playing through the town followed by wagonettes crammed with children, who sang:

Vote, vote, vote for Federation, Don't be stupid, old and slow, We are sure that it will be Good for the communitie, So vote, vote, vote, and make it go.

How this performance could affect the decision of grave burgesses at the polls was not apparent; but the Anti-Federationists feared that it might, and before noon was come they had engaged two bands and had composed in committee, the following lyric in reply to the first one:

Down, down, down, with Federation, As we are we'd rather stay; When the vote on Saturday's read Federation will be dead, Good old Bursley's sure to win the day.

They had also composed another song, entitled "Dear old Bursley," which, however, they made the fatal error of setting to the music of "Auld Lang Syne." The effect was that of a dirge, and it perhaps influenced many voters in favour of the more cheerful party. The Anti-Federationists, indeed, never regained the mean advantage filched by unscrupulous Federationists with the help of the Silver Prize Band and a few hundred infants. The odds were against the Anti-Federationists. The mayor had actually issued a letter to the inhabitants accusing the Anti-Federationists of unfair methods! This was really too much! The impudence of it knocked the breath out of its victims, and breath is very necessary in a polling contest. The Federationists, as one of their prominent opponents admitted, 'had it all their own way,' dominating both the streets and the walls. And when, early in the afternoon, Mr. Dick Povey sailed over the town in a balloon that was plainly decorated with the crimson of Federation, it was felt that the cause of Bursley's separate identity was for ever lost. Still, Bursley, with the willing aid of the public-houses, maintained its gaiety.

IV

Towards dusk a stout old lady, with grey hair, and a dowdy bonnet, and an expensive mantle, passed limping, very slowly, along Wedgwood Street and up the Cock Yard towards the Town Hall. Her wrinkled face had an anxious look, but it was also very determined. The busy, joyous Federationists and Anti-Federationists who knew her not saw merely a stout old lady fussing forth, and those who knew her saw merely Mrs. Povey and greeted her perfunctorily, a woman of her age and gait being rather out of place in that feverish altercation of opposed principles. But it was more than a stout old lady, it was more than Mrs. Povey that waddled with such painful deliberation through the streets—it was a miracle.

In the morning Constance had been partially incapacitated by her sciatica; so much so, at any rate, that she had perceived the advisability of remaining on the bedroom floor instead of descending to the parlour. Therefore Mary had lighted the drawing-room fire, and Constance had ensconced herself by it, with Fossette in a basket. Lily Holl had called early, and had been very sympathetic, but rather vague. The truth was that she was concealing the imminent balloon ascent which Dick Povey, with his instinct for the picturesque, had somehow arranged, in conjunction with a well-known Manchester aeronaut, for the very day of the poll. That was one of various matters that had to be 'kept from' the old lady. Lily herself was much perturbed about the balloon ascent. She had to run off and see Dick before he started, at the Football Ground at Bleakridge, and then she had to live through the hours till she should receive a telegram to the effect that Dick had come down safely or that Dick had broken his leg in coming down, or that Dick was dead. It was a trying time for Lily. She had left Constance after a brief visit, with a preoccupied unusual air, saying that as the day was a special day, she should come in again 'if she could.' And she did not forget to assure Constance that Federation would beyond any question whatever be handsomely beaten at the poll; for this was another matter as to which it was deemed advisable to keep the old lady 'in the dark,' lest the foolish old lady should worry and commit indiscretions.

After that Constance had been forgotten by the world of Bursley, which could pay small heed to sciatical old ladies confined to sofas and firesides. She was in acute pain, as Mary could see when at intervals she hovered round her. Assuredly it was one of Constance's bad days, one of those days on which she felt that the tide of life had left her stranded in utter neglect. The sound of the Bursley Town Silver Prize Band aroused her from her mournful trance of suffering. Then the high treble of children's voices startled her. She defied her sciatica, and, grimacing, went to the window. And at the first glimpse she could see that the Federation Poll was going to be a much more exciting affair than she had imagined. The great cards swinging from the wagonettes showed her that Federation was at all events still sufficiently alive to make a formidable impression on the eye and the ear. The Square was transformed by this clamour in favour of Federation; people cheered, and sang also, as the procession wound down the Square. And she could distinctly catch the tramping, martial syllables, "Vote, vote, vote." She was indignant. The pother, once begun, continued. Vehicles flashed frequently across the Square, most of them in the crimson livery. Little knots and processions of excited wayfarers were a recurring feature of the unaccustomed traffic, and the large majority of them flaunted the colours of Federation. Mary, after some errands of shopping, came upstairs and reported that 'it was simply "Federation" everywhere,' and that Mr. Brindley, a strong Federationist, was 'above a bit above himself'; further, that the interest in the poll was tremendous and universal. She said there were 'crowds and crowds' round the Town Hall. Even Mary, generally a little placid and dull, had caught something of the contagious vivacity. Constance remained at the window till dinner, and after dinner she went to it again. It was fortunate that she did not think of looking up into the sky when Dick's balloon sailed westwards; she would have guessed instantly that Dick was in that balloon, and her grievances would have been multiplied. The vast grievance of the Federation scheme weighed on her to the extremity of her power to bear. She was not a politician; she had no general ideas; she did not see the cosmic movement in large curves. She was incapable of perceiving the absurdity involved in perpetuating municipal divisions which the growth of the district had rendered artificial, vexatious, and harmful. She saw nothing but Bursley, and in Bursley nothing but the Square. She knew nothing except that the people of Bursley, who once shopped in Bursley, now shopped in Hanbridge, and that the Square was a desert infested by cheap-jacks. And there were actually people who wished to bow the neck to Hanbridge, who were ready to sacrifice the very name of Bursley to the greedy humour of that pushing Chicago! She could not understand such people. Did they know that poor Maria Critchlow was in a lunatic asylum because Hanbridge was so grasping? Ah, poor Maria was al-ready forgotten! Did they know that, as a further indirect consequence, she, the daughter of Bursley's chief tradesman, was to be thrown out of the house in which she was born? She wished, bitterly, as she stood there at the window, watching the triumph of Federation, that she had bought the house and shop at the Mericarp sale years ago. She would have shown them, as owner, what was what! She forgot that the property which she already owned in Bursley was a continual annoyance to her, and that she was always resolving to sell it at no matter what loss.

She said to herself that she had a vote, and that if she had been 'at all fit to stir out' she would certainly have voted. She said to herself that it had been her duty to vote. And then by an illusion of her wrought nerves, tightened minute by minute throughout the day, she began to fancy that her sciatica was easier. She said: "If only I could go out!" She might have a cab, of any of the parading vehicles would be glad to take her to the Town Hall, and, perhaps, as a favour, to bring her back again. But no! She dared not go out. She was afraid, really afraid that even the mild Mary might stop her. Otherwise, she could have sent Mary for a cab. And supposing that Lily returned, and caught her going out or coming in! She ought not to go out. Yet her sciatica was strangely better. It was folly to think of going out. Yet…! And Lily did not come. She was rather hurt that Lily had not paid her a second visit. Lily was neglecting her…. She would go out. It was not four minutes' walk for her to the Town Hall, and she was better. And there had been no shower for a long time, and the wind was drying the mud in the roadways. Yes, she would go.

Like a thief she passed into her bedroom and put on her things; and like a thief she crept downstairs, and so, without a word to Mary, into the street. It was a desperate adventure. As soon as she was in the street she felt all her weakness, all the fatigue which the effort had already cost her. The pain returned. The streets were still wet and foul, the wind cold, and the sky menacing. She ought to go back. She ought to admit that she had been a fool to dream of the enterprise. The Town Hall seemed to be miles off, at the top of a mountain. She went forward, however, steeled to do her share in the killing of Federation. Every step caused her a gnashing of her old teeth. She chose the Cock Yard route, because if she had gone up the Square she would have had to pass Holl's shop, and Lily might have spied her.

This was the miracle that breezy politicians witnessed without being aware that it was a miracle. To have impressed them, Constance ought to have fainted before recording her vote, and made herself the centre of a

302

crowd of gapers. But she managed, somehow, to reach home again on her own tortured feet, and an astounded and protesting Mary opened the door to her. Rain was descending. She was frightened, then, by the hardihood of her adventure, and by its atrocious results on her body. An appalling exhaustion rendered her helpless. But the deed was done.

V

The next morning, after a night which she could not have described, Constance found herself lying flat in bed, with all her limbs stretched out straight. She was conscious that her face was covered with perspiration. The bell-rope hung within a foot of her head, but she had decided that, rather than move in order to pull it, she would prefer to wait for assistance until Mary came of her own accord. Her experiences of the night had given her a dread of the slightest movement; anything was better than movement. She felt vaguely ill, with a kind of subdued pain, and she was very thirsty and somewhat cold. She knew that her left arm and leg were extraordinarily tender to the touch. When Mary at length entered, clean and fresh and pale in all her mildness, she found the mistress the colour of a duck's egg, with puffed features, and a strangely anxious expression. "Mary," said Constance, "I feel so queer. Perhaps you'd better run up and tell Miss Holl, and ask her to telephone for Dr. Stirling."

This was the beginning of Constance's last illness. Mary most impressively informed Miss Holl that her mistress had been out on the previous afternoon in spite of her sciatica, and Lily telephoned the fact to the Doctor. Lily then came down to take charge of Constance. But she dared not upbraid the invalid.

"Is the result out?" Constance murmured.

"Oh yes," said Lily, lightly. "There's a majority of over twelve hundred against Federation. Great excitement last night! I told you yesterday morning that Federation was bound to be beaten."

Lily spoke as though the result throughout had been a certainty; her tone to Constance indicated: "Surely you don't imagine that I should have told you untruths yesterday morning merely to cheer you up!" The truth was, however, that towards the end of the day nearly every one had believed Federation to be carried. The result had caused great surprise. Only the profoundest philosophers had not been surprised to see that the mere blind, deaf, inert forces of reaction, with faulty organization, and quite deprived of the aid of logic, had proved far stronger than all the alert enthusiasm arrayed against them. It was a notable lesson to reformers.

"Oh!" murmured Constance, startled. She was relieved; but she would have liked the majority to be smaller. Moreover, her interest in the question had lessened. It was her limbs that pre-occupied her now.

"You look tired," she said feebly to Lily.

"Do I?" said Lily, shortly, hiding the fact that she had spent half the night in tending Dick Povey, who, in a sensational descent near Macclesfield, had been dragged through the tops of a row of elm trees to the detriment of an elbow-joint; the professional aeronaut had broken a leg.

Then Dr. Stirling came.

"I'm afraid my sciatica's worse, Doctor," said Constance, apologetically.

"Did you expect it to be better?" said he, gazing at her sternly. She knew then that some one had saved her the trouble of confessing her escapade.

However, her sciatica was not worse. Her sciatica had not behaved basely. What she was suffering from was the preliminary advances of an attack of acute rheumatism. She had indeed selected the right month and weather for her escapade! Fatigued by pain, by nervous agitation, and by the immense moral and physical effort needed to carry her to the Town Hall and back, she had caught a chill, and had got her feet damp. In such a subject as herself it was enough. The doctor used only the phrase 'acute rheumatism.' Constance did not know that acute rheumatism was precisely the same thing as that dread disease, rheumatic fever, and she was not informed. She did not surmise for a considerable period that her case was desperately serious. The doctor explained the summoning of two nurses, and the frequency of his own visits, by saying that his chief anxiety was to minimise the fearful pain as much as possible, and that this end could only be secured by incessant watchfulness. The pain was certainly formidable. But then Constance was well habituated to formidable pain. Sciatica, at its most active, cannot be surpassed even by rheumatic fever. Constance had been in nearly continuous pain for years. Her friends, however sympathetic, could not appreciate the intensity of her torture. They were just as used to it as she was. And the monotony and particularity of her complaints (slight though the complaints were in comparison with their cause) necessarily blunted the edge of compassion. "Mrs. Povey and her sciatica again! Poor thing, she really is a little tedious!" They were apt not to realise that sciatica is even more tedious than complaints about sciatica.

She asked one day that Dick should come to see her. He came with his arm in a sling, and told her charily that he had hurt his elbow through dropping his stick and slipping downstairs.

"Lily never told me," said Constance, suspiciously.

"Oh, it's simply nothing!" said Dick. Not even the sick room could chasten him of his joy in the magnificent balloon adventure.

"I do hope you won't go running any risks!" said Constance.

"Never you fear!" said he. "I shall die in my bed."

And he was absolutely convinced that he would, and not as the result of any accident, either! The nurse would not allow him to remain in the room.

Lily suggested that Constance might like her to write to Cyril. It was only in order to make sure of Cyril's correct address. He had gone on a tour through Italy with some friends of whom Constance knew nothing. The address appeared to be very uncertain; there were several addresses, poste restante in various towns. Cyril had sent postcards to his mother. Dick and Lily went to the post-office and telegraphed to foreign parts. Though Constance was too ill to know how ill she was, though she had no conception of the domestic confusion caused by her illness, her brain was often remarkably clear, and she could reflect in long, sane meditations above the uneasy sea of her pain. In the earlier hours of the night, after the nurses had been changed, and Mary had gone to bed exhausted with stair-climbing, and Lily Holl was recounting the day to Dick up at the grocer's, and the day-nurse was already asleep, and the night-nurse had arranged the night, then, in the faintly-lit silence of the chamber, Constance would argue with herself for an hour at a time. She frequently thought of Sophia. In spite of the fact that Sophia was dead she still pitied Sophia as a woman whose life had been wasted. This idea of Sophia's wasted and sterile life, and of the far-reaching importance of adhering to principles, recurred to her again and again. "Why did she run away with him? If only she had not run away!" she would repeat. And yet there had been something so fine about Sophia! Which made Sophia's case all the more pitiable! Constance never pitied herself. She did not consider that Fate had treated her very badly. She was not very discontented with herself. The invincible commonsense of a sound nature prevented her, in her best moments, from feebly dissolving in self-pity. She had lived in honesty and kindliness for a fair number of years, and she had tasted triumphant hours. She was justly respected, she had a position, she had dignity, she was well-off. She possessed, after all, a certain amount of quiet self-conceit. There existed nobody to whom she would 'knuckle down,' or could be asked to 'knuckle down.' True, she was old! So were thousands of other people in Bursley. She was in pain. So there were thousands of other people. With whom would she be willing to exchange lots? She had many dissatisfactions. But she rose superior to them. When she surveyed her life, and life in general, she would think, with a sort of tart but not sour cheerfulness: "Well, that is what life is!" Despite her habit of complaining about domestic trifles, she was, in the essence of her character, 'a great body for making the best of things.' Thus she did not unduly bewail her excursion to the Town Hall to vote, which the sequel had proved to be ludicrously supererogatory. "How was I to know?" she said.

The one matter in which she had gravely to reproach herself was her indulgent spoiling of Cyril after the death of Samuel Povey. But the end of her reproaches always was: "I expect I should do the same again! And probably it wouldn't have made any difference if I hadn't spoiled him!" And she had paid tenfold for the weakness. She loved Cyril, but she had no illusions about him; she saw both sides of him. She remembered all the sadness and all the humiliations which he had caused her. Still, her affection was unimpaired. A son might be worse than Cyril was; he had admirable qualities. She did not resent his being away from England while she lay ill. "If it was serious," she said, "he would not lose a moment." And Lily and Dick were a treasure to her. In those two she really had been lucky. She took great pleasure in contemplating the splendour of the gift with which she would mark her appreciation of them at their approaching wedding. The secret attitude of both of them towards her was one of good-natured condescension, expressed in the tone in which they would say to each other, 'the old lady.' Perhaps they would have been startled to know that Constance lovingly looked down on both of them. She had unbounded admiration for their hearts; but she thought that Dick was a little too brusque, a little too clownish, to be quite a gentleman. And though Lily was perfectly ladylike, in Constance's opinion she lacked backbone, or grit, or independence of spirit. Further, Constance considered that the disparity of age between them was excessive. It is to be doubted whether, when all was said, Constance had such a very great deal to learn from the self-confident wisdom of these young things.

After a period of self-communion, she would sometimes fall into a shallow delirium. In all her delirium she was invariably wandering to and fro, lost, in the long underground passage leading from the scullery past the coal-cellar and the cinder-cellar to the backyard. And she was afraid of the vast-obscure of those regions, as she had been in her infancy.

It was not acute rheumatism, but a supervening pericarditis that in a few days killed her. She died in the night, alone with the night-nurse. By a curious chance the Wesleyan minister, hearing that she was seriously ill, had called on the previous day. She had not asked for him; and this pastoral visit, from a man who had always said that the heavy duties of the circuit rendered pastoral visits almost impossible, made her think. In the evening she had requested that Fossette should be brought upstairs.

Thus she was turned out of her house, but not by the Midland Clothiers Company. Old people said to one another: "Have you heard that Mrs. Povey is dead? Eh, dear me! There'll be no one left soon." These old people were bad prophets. Her friends genuinely regretted her, and forgot the tediousness of her sciatica. They tried, in their sympathetic grief, to picture to themselves all that she had been through in her life. Possibly they imagined that they succeeded in this imaginative attempt. But they did not succeed. No one but Constance could realize all that Constance had been through, and all that life had meant to her.

Cyril was not at the funeral. He arrived three days later. (As he had no interest in the love affairs of Dick and Lily, the couple were robbed of their wedding-present. The will, fifteen years old, was in Cyril's favour.) But the immortal Charles Critchlow came to the funeral, full of calm, sardonic glee, and without being asked. Though fabulously senile, he had preserved and even improved his faculty for enjoying a catastrophe. He now went to funerals with gusto, contentedly absorbed in the task of burying his friends one by one. It was he who said, in his high, trembling, rasping, deliberate voice: "It's a pity her didn't live long enough to hear as Federation is going on after all! That would ha' worritted her." (For the unscrupulous advocates of Federation had discovered a method of setting at naught the decisive result of the referendum, and that day's Signal was fuller than ever of Federation.)

When the short funeral procession started, Mary and the infirm Fossette (sole relic of the connection between the Baines family and Paris) were left alone in the house. The tearful servant prepared the dog's dinner and laid it before her in the customary soup-plate in the customary corner. Fossette sniffed at it, and then walked away and lay down with a dog's sigh in front of the kitchen fire. She had been deranged in her habits that day; she was conscious of neglect, due to events which passed her comprehension. And she did not like it. She was hurt, and her appetite was hurt. However, after a few minutes, she began to reconsider the matter. She glanced at the soup-plate, and, on the chance that it might after all contain something worth inspection, she awkwardly balanced herself on her old legs and went to it again.

The Card, A Story Of Adventure
In The Five Towns

THE CARD
CHAPTER I
THE DANCE

I

Edward Henry Machin first saw the smoke on the 27th May 1867, in Brougham Street, Bursley, the most ancient of the Five Towns. Brougham Street runs down from St Luke's Square straight into the Shropshire Union Canal, land consists partly of buildings known as "potbanks" (until they come to be sold by auction, when auctioneers describe them as "extensive earthenware manufactories") and partly of cottages whose highest rent is four-and-six a week. In such surroundings was an extraordinary man born. He was the only anxiety of a widowed mother, who gained her livelihood and his by making up "ladies' own materials" in ladies' own houses. Mrs Machin, however, had a speciality apart from her vocation: she could wash flannel with less shrinking than any other woman in the district, and she could wash fine lace without ruining it; thus often she came to sew and remained to wash. A somewhat gloomy woman; thin, with a tongue! But I liked her. She saved a certain amount of time every day by addressing her son as Denry, instead of Edward Henry.

Not intellectual, not industrious, Denry would have maintained the average dignity of labour on a potbank had he not at the age of twelve won a scholarship from the Board School to the Endowed School. He owed his triumph to audacity rather than learning, and to chance rather than design. On the second day of the examination he happened to arrive in the examination-room ten minutes too soon for the afternoon sitting. He wandered about the place exercising his curiosity, and reached the master's desk. On the desk was a tabulated form with names of candidates and the number of marks achieved by each in each subject of the previous day. He had done badly in geography, and saw seven marks against his name, in the geographical column, out of a possible thirty. The figures had been written in pencil. The pencil lay on the desk. He picked it up, glanced at the door and at the rows of empty desks, and a neat "2" in front of the 7; then he strolled innocently forth and came back late. His trick ought to have been found out—the odds were against him—but it was not found out. Of course it was dishonest. Yes, but I will not agree that Denry was uncommonly vicious. Every schoolboy is dishonest, by the adult standard. If I knew an honest schoolboy I would begin to count my silver spoons as he grew up. All is fair between schoolboys and schoolmasters.

This dazzling feat seemed to influence not only Denry's career but also his character. He gradually came to believe that he had won the scholarship by genuine merit, and that he was a remarkable boy and destined to great ends. His new companions, whose mothers employed Denry's mother, also believed that he was a remarkable boy; but they did not forget, in their gentlemanly way, to call him "washer-woman." Happily Denry did not mind.

He had a thick skin, and fair hair and bright eyes and broad shoulders, and the jolly gaiety of his disposition developed daily. He did not shine at the school; he failed to fulfil the rosy promise of the scholarship; but he was not stupider than the majority; and his opinion of himself, having once risen, remained at "set fair." It was inconceivable that he should work in clay with his hands.

II

When he was sixteen his mother, by operations [**words missing in original] a yard and a half of Brussels point lace, put [**words missing in original] Emery under an obligation. Mrs Emery [**words missing in original] the sister of Mr Duncalf. Mr Duncalf was town Clerk of Bursley, and a solicitor. It is well known that all bureaucracies are honey-combed with intrigue. Denry Machin left school to be clerk to Mr Duncalf, on the condition that within a year he should be able to write shorthand at the rate of a hundred and fifty words a minute. In those days mediocre and incorrect shorthand was not a drug on the market. He complied (more or less, and decidedly less than more) with the condition. And for several years he really thought that he had nothing further to hope for. Then he met the Countess.

The Countess of Chell was born of poor but picturesque parents, and she could put her finger on her great-grandfather's grandfather. Her mother gained her livelihood and her daughter's by allowing herself to be seen a great deal with humbler but richer people's daughters. The Countess was brought up to matrimony. She was aimed and timed to hit a given mark at a given moment. She succeeded. She married the Earl of Chell. She also married about twenty thousand acres in England, about a fifth of Scotland, a house in Piccadilly, seven country seats (including Sneyd), a steam yacht, and five hundred thousand pounds' worth of shares in the Midland Railway. She was young and pretty. She had travelled in China and written a book about China. She sang at charity concerts and acted in private theatricals. She sketched from nature. She was one of the great hostesses of London. And she had not the slightest tendency to stoutness. All this did not satisfy her. She was ambitious! She wanted to be taken seriously. She wanted to enter into the life of the people. She saw in the quarter of a million souls that constitute the Five Towns a unique means to her end, an unrivalled toy. And she determined to be identified with all that was most serious in the social progress of the Five Towns. Hence some fifteen thousand pounds were spent in refurbishing Sneyd Hall, which lies on the edge of the Five Towns, and the Earl and Countess passed four months of the year there. Hence the Earl, a mild, retiring man, when invited by the Town Council to be the ornamental Mayor of Bursley, accepted the invitation. Hence the Mayor and Mayoress gave an immense afternoon reception to practically the entire roll of burgesses. And hence, a little later, the Mayoress let it be known that she meant to give a municipal ball. The news of the ball thrilled Bursley more than anything had thrilled Bursley since the signing of Magna Charta. Nevertheless, balls had been offered by previous mayoresses. One can only suppose that in Bursley there remains a peculiar respect for land, railway stock, steam yachts, and great-grandfathers' grandfathers.

Now, everybody of account had been asked to the reception. But everybody could not be asked to the ball, because not more than two hundred people could dance in the Town Hall. There were nearly thirty-five thousand inhabitants in Bursley, of whom quite two thousand "counted," even though they did not dance.

III

Three weeks and three days before the ball Denry Machin was seated one Monday alone in Mr Duncalf's private offices in Duck Square (where he carried on his practice as a solicitor), when in stepped a tall and pretty young woman, dressed very smartly but soberly in dark green. On the desk in front of Denry were several wide sheets of "abstract" paper, concealed by a copy of that morning's *Athletic News*. Before Denry could even think of reversing the positions of the abstract paper and the *Athletic News* the young woman said "Good-morning!" in a very friendly style. She had a shrill voice and an efficient smile.

"Good-morning, madam," said Denry.

"Mr Duncalf in?" asked the young woman brightly.

(Why should Denry have slipped off his stool? It is utterly against etiquette for solicitors' clerks to slip off their stools while answering inquiries.)

"No, madam; he's across at the Town Hall," said Denry.

The young lady shook her head playfully, with a faint smile.

"I've just been there," she said. "They said he was here."

"I daresay I could find him, madam—if you would——"

She now smiled broadly. "Conservative Club, I suppose?" she said, with an air deliciously confidential.

He, too, smiled.

"Oh, no," she said, after a little pause; "just tell him I've called."

"Certainly, madam. Nothing I can do?"

She was already turning away, but she turned back and scrutinised his face, as Denry thought, roguishly.

"You might just give him this list," she said, taking a paper from her satchel and spreading it. She had come to the desk; their elbows touched. "He isn't to take any notice of the crossings-out in red ink— you understand? Of course, I'm relying on him for the other lists, and I expect all the invitations to be out on Wednesday. Good-morning."

She was gone. He sprang to the grimy window. Outside, in the snow, were a brougham, twin horses, twin men in yellow, and a little crowd of youngsters and oldsters. She flashed across the footpath, and vanished; the door of the carriage banged, one of the twins in yellow leaped up to his brother, and the whole affair dashed dangerously away. The face of the leaping twin was familiar to Denry. The man had, indeed, once inhabited Brougham Street, being known to the street as Jock, and his mother had for long years been a friend of Mrs Machin's.

It was the first time Denry had seen the Countess, save at a distance. Assuredly she was finer even than her photographs. Entirely different from what one would have expected! So easy to talk to! (Yet what had he said to her? Nothing—and everything.)

He nodded his head and murmured, "No mistake about that lot!" Meaning, presumably, that all that one had read about the brilliance of the aristocracy was true, and more than true.

"She's the finest woman that ever came into this town," he murmured.

The truth was that she surpassed his dreams of womanhood. At two o'clock she had been a name to him. At five minutes past two he was in love with her. He felt profoundly thankful that, for a church tea-meeting that evening, he happened to be wearing his best clothes.

It was while looking at her list of invitations to the ball that he first conceived the fantastic scheme of attending the ball himself. Mr Duncalf was, fussily and deferentially, managing the machinery of the ball for the Countess. He had prepared a little list of his own of people who ought to be invited. Several aldermen had been requested to do the same. There were thus about half-a-dozen lists to be combined into one. Denry did the combining. Nothing was easier than to insert the name of E.H. Machin inconspicuously towards the centre of the list! Nothing was easier than to lose the original lists, inadvertently, so that if a question arose as to any particular name, the responsibility for it could not be ascertained without inquiries too delicate to be made. On Wednesday Denry received a lovely Bristol board, stating in copper-plate that the Countess desired the pleasure of his company at the ball; and on Thursday his name was ticked off as one who had accepted.

IV

He had never been to a dance. He had no dress-suit, and no notion of dancing.

He was a strange, inconsequent mixture of courage and timidity. You and I are consistent in character; we are either one thing or the other but Denry Machin had no consistency.

For three days he hesitated, and then, secretly trembling, he slipped into Shillitoe's, the young tailor who had recently set up, and who was gathering together the *jeunesse dorée* of the town.

"I want a dress-suit," he said.

Shillitoe, who knew that Denry only earned eighteen shillings a week, replied with only superficial politeness that a dress-suit was out of the question; he had already taken more orders than he could execute without killing himself. The whole town had uprisen as one man and demanded a dress-suit.

"So you're going to the ball, are you?" said Shillitoe, trying to condescend, but, in fact, slightly impressed.

"Yes," said Denry; "are you?"

Shillitoe started and then shook his head. "No time for balls," said he.

"I can get you an invitation, if you like," said Denry, glancing at the door precisely as he had glanced at the door before adding 2 to 7.

"Oh!" Shillitoe cocked his ears. He was not a native of the town, and had no alderman to protect his legitimate interests.

To cut a shameful story short, in a week Denry was being tried on. Shillitoe allowed him two years' credit.

The prospect of the ball gave an immense impetus to the study of the art of dancing in Bursley, and so put quite a nice sum of money info the pocket of Miss Earp, a young mistress in that art. She was the daughter of a furniture dealer with a passion for the Bankruptcy Court. Miss Earp's evening classes were attended by Denry, but none of his money went into her pocket. She was compensated by an expression of the Countess's desire for the pleasure of her company at the ball.

The Countess had aroused Denry's interest in women as a sex; Ruth Earp quickened the interest. She was plain, but she was only twenty-four, and very graceful on her feet. Denry had one or two strictly private lessons from her in reversing. She said to him one evening, when he was practising reversing and they were entwined in the attitude prescribed by the latest fashion: "Never mind me! Think about yourself. It's the same in dancing as it is in life—the woman's duty is to adapt herself to the man." He did think about himself. He was thinking about himself in the middle of the night, and about her too. There had been something in her tone... her eye... At the final lesson he inquired if she would give him the first waltz at the ball. She paused, then said yes.

V

On the evening of the ball, Denry spent at least two hours in the operation which was necessary before he could give the Countess the pleasure of his company. This operation took place in his minute bedroom at the back of the cottage in Brougham Street, and it was of a complex nature. Three weeks ago he had innocently thought that you had only to order a dress-suit and there you were! He now knew that a dress-suit is merely the beginning of anxiety. Shirt! Collar! Tie! Studs! Cuff-links! Gloves! Handkerchief! (He was very glad to learn authoritatively from Shillitoe that handkerchiefs were no longer worn in the waistcoat opening, and that men who so wore them were barbarians and the truth was not in them. Thus, an everyday handkerchief would do.) Boots!... Boots were the rock on which he had struck. Shillitoe, in addition to being a tailor was a hosier, but by some flaw in the scheme of the universe hosiers do not sell boots. Except boots, Denry could get all he needed on credit; boots he could not get on credit, and he could not pay cash for them. Eventually he decided that his church boots must be dazzled up to the level of this great secular occasion. The pity was that he forgot—not that he was of a forgetful disposition in great matters; he was simply over-excited—he forgot to dazzle them up until after he had fairly put his collar on and his necktie in a bow. It is imprudent to touch blacking in a dress-shirt, so Denry had to undo the past and begin again. This hurried him. He was not afraid of being late for the first waltz with Miss Ruth Earp, but he was afraid of not being out of the house before his mother returned. Mrs Machin had been making up a lady's own materials all day, naturally—the day being what it was! If she had had twelve hands instead of two, she might have made up the own materials of half-a-dozen ladies instead of one, and earned twenty-four shillings instead of four. Denry did not want his mother to see him ere he departed. He had lavished an enormous amount of brains and energy to the end of displaying himself in this refined and novel attire to the gaze of two hundred persons, and yet his secret wish was to deprive his mother of the beautiful spectacle.

However, she slipped in, with her bag and her seamy fingers and her rather sardonic expression, at the very moment when Denry was putting on his overcoat in the kitchen (there being insufficient room in the passage). He did what he could to hide his shirt-front (though she knew all about it), and failed.

"Bless us!" she exclaimed briefly, going to the fire to warm her hands.

A harmless remark. But her tone seemed to strip bare the vanity of human greatness.

"I'm in a hurry," said Denry, importantly, as if he was going forth to sign a treaty involving the welfare of the nations.

"Well," said she, "happen ye are, Denry. But th' kitchen table's no place for boot-brushes."

He had one piece of luck. It froze. Therefore no anxiety about the condition of boots.

VI

The Countess was late; some trouble with a horse. Happily the Earl had been in Bursley all day, and had dressed at the Conservative Club; and his lordship had ordered that the programme of dances should be begun. Denry learned this as soon as he emerged, effulgent, from the gentlemen's cloak-room into the broad red-carpeted corridor which runs from end to end of the ground-floor of the Town Hall. Many important townspeople were chatting in the corridor—the innumerable Swetnam family, the Stanways, the great Etches, the Fearnses, Mrs Clayton Vernon, the Suttons, including Beatrice Sutton. Of course everybody knew him for Duncalf's shorthand clerk and the son of the flannel-washer; but universal white kid gloves constitute a democracy, and Shillitoe could put more style into a suit than any other tailor in the Five Towns.

"How do?" the eldest of the Swetnam boys nodded carelessly.

"How do, Swetnam?" said Denry, with equal carelessness.

The thing was accomplished! That greeting was like a Masonic initiation, and henceforward he was the peer of no matter whom. At first he had thought that four hundred eyes would be fastened on him, their glance saying, "This youth is wearing a dress-suit for the first time, and it is not paid for, either!" But it was not so. And the reason was that the entire population of the Town Hall was heartily engaged in pretending that never in its life had it been seen after seven o'clock of a night apart from a dress-suit. Denry observed with joy that, while numerous middle-aged and awkward men wore red or white silk handkerchiefs in their waistcoats, such people as Charles Fearns, the Swetnams, and Harold Etches did not. He was, then, in the shyness of his handkerchief, on the side of the angels.

He passed up the double staircase (decorated with white or pale frocks of unparalleled richness), and so into the grand hall. A scarlet orchestra was on the platform, and many people strolled about the floor in attitudes of expectation. The walls were festooned with flowers. The thrill of being magnificent seized him, and he was drenched in a vast desire to be truly magnificent himself. He dreamt of magnificence and boot-brushes kept sticking out of this dream like black mud out of snow. In his reverie he looked about for Ruth Earp, but she was invisible. Then he went downstairs again, idly; gorgeously feigning that he spent six evenings a week in ascending and descending monumental staircases, appropriately clad. He was determined to be as sublime as any one.

There was a stir in the corridor, and the sublimest consented to be excited.

The Countess was announced to be imminent. Everybody was grouped round the main portal, careless of temperatures. Six times was the Countess announced to be imminent before she actually appeared, expanding from the narrow gloom of her black carriage like a magic vision. Aldermen received her—and they did not do it with any excess of gracefulness. They seemed afraid of her, as though she was recovering from influenza and they feared to catch it. She had precisely the same high voice, and precisely the same efficient smile, as she had employed to Denry, and these instruments worked marvels on aldermen; they were as melting as salt on snow. The Countess disappeared upstairs in a cloud of shrill apologies and trailing aldermen. She seemed to have greeted everybody except Denry. Somehow he was relieved that she had not drawn attention to him. He lingered, hesitating, and then he saw a being in a long yellow overcoat, with a bit of peacock's feather at the summit of a shiny high hat. This being held a lady's fur mantle. Their eyes met. Denry had to decide instantly. He decided.

"Hello, Jock!" he said.

"Hello, Denry!" said the other, pleased.

"What's been happening?" Denry inquired, friendly.

Then Jock told him about the antics of one of the Countess's horses.

He went upstairs again, and met Ruth Earp coming down. She was glorious in white. Except that nothing glittered in her hair, she looked the very equal of the Countess, at a little distance, plain though her features were.

"What about that waltz?" Denry began informally.

"That waltz is nearly over," said Ruth Earp, with chilliness. "I suppose you've been staring at her ladyship with all the other men."

"I'm awfully sorry," he said. "I didn't know the waltz was——"

"Well, why didn't you look at your programme?"

"Haven't got one," he said naïvely.

He had omitted to take a programme. Ninny! Barbarian!

"Better get one," she said cuttingly, somewhat in her *rôle* of dancing mistress.

"Can't we finish the waltz?" he suggested, crestfallen.

"No!" she said, and continued her solitary way downwards.

She was hurt. He tried to think of something to say that was equal to the situation, and equal to the style of his suit. But he could not. In a moment he heard her, below him, greeting some male acquaintance in the most effusive way.

Yet, if Denry had not committed a wicked crime for her, she could never have come to the dance at all!

He got a programme, and with terror gripping his heart he asked sundry young and middle-aged women whom he knew by sight and by name for a dance. (Ruth had taught him how to ask.) Not one of them had a dance left. Several looked at him as much as to say: "You must be a goose to suppose that my programme is not filled up in the twinkling of my eye!"

Then he joined a group of despisers of dancing near the main door. Harold Etches was there, the wealthiest manufacturer of his years (barely twenty-four) in the Five Towns. Also Shillitoe, cause of another of Denry's wicked crimes. The group was taciturn, critical, and very doggish.

The group observed that the Countess was not dancing. The Earl was dancing (need it be said with Mrs Jos Curtenty, second wife of the Deputy Mayor?), but the Countess stood resolutely smiling, surrounded by aldermen. Possibly she was getting her breath; possibly nobody had had the pluck to ask her. Anyhow, she seemed to be stranded there, on a beach of aldermen. Very wisely she had brought with her no members of a house-party from Sneyd Hall. Members of a house-party, at a municipal ball, invariably operate as a bar between greatness and democracy; and the Countess desired to participate in the life of the people.

"Why don't some of those johnnies ask her?" Denry burst out. He had hitherto said nothing in the group, and he felt that he must be a man with the rest of them.

"Well, *you* go and do it. It's a free country," said Shillitoe.

"So I would, for two pins!" said Denry.

Harold Etches glanced at him, apparently resentful of his presence there. Harold Etches was determined to put the extinguisher on *him*.

"I'll bet you a fiver you don't," said Etches scornfully.

"I'll take you," said Denry, very quickly, and very quickly walked off.

VII

"She can't eat me. She can't eat me!"

This was what he said to himself as he crossed the floor. People seemed to make a lane for him, divining his incredible intention. If he had not started at once, if his legs had not started of themselves, he would never

310

have started; and, not being in command of a fiver, he would afterwards have cut a preposterous figure in the group. But started he was, like a piece of clockwork that could not be stopped! In the grand crises of his life something not himself, something more powerful than himself, jumped up in him and forced him to do things. Now for the first time he seemed to understand what had occurred within him in previous crises.

In a second—so it appeared—he had reached the Countess. Just behind her was his employer, Mr Duncalf, whom Denry had not previously noticed there. Denry regretted this, for he had never mentioned to Mr Duncalf that he was coming to the ball, and he feared Mr Duncalf.

"Could I have this dance with you?" he demanded bluntly, but smiling and showing his teeth.

No ceremonial title! No mention of "pleasure" or "honour." Not a trace of the formula in which Ruth Earp had instructed him! He forgot all such trivialities.

"I've won that fiver, Mr Harold Etches," he said to himself.

The mouths of aldermen inadvertently opened. Mr Duncalf blenched.

"It's nearly over, isn't it?" said the Countess, still efficiently smiling. She did not recognise Denry. In that suit he might have been a Foreign Office attaché.

"Oh! that doesn't matter, I'm sure," said Denry.

She yielded, and he took the paradisaical creature in his arms. It was her business that evening to be universally and inclusively polite. She could not have begun with a refusal. A refusal might have dried up all other invitations whatsoever. Besides, she saw that the aldermen wanted a lead. Besides, she was young, though a countess, and adored dancing.

Thus they waltzed together, while the flower of Bursley's chivalry gazed in enchantment. The Countess's fan, depending from her arm, dangled against Denry's suit in a rather confusing fashion, which withdrew his attention from his feet. He laid hold of it gingerly between two unemployed fingers. After that he managed fairly well. Once they came perilously near the Earl and his partner; nothing else. And then the dance ended, exactly when Denry had begun to savour the astounding spectacle of himself enclasping the Countess.

The Countess had soon perceived that he was the merest boy.

"You waltz quite nicely!" she said, like an aunt, but with more than an aunt's smile.

"Do I?" he beamed. Then something compelled him to say: "Do you know, it's the first time I've ever waltzed in my life, except in a lesson, you know?"

"Really!" she murmured. "You pick things up easily, I suppose?"

"Yes," he said. "Do you?"

Either the question or the tone sent the Countess off into carillons of amusement. Everybody could see that Denry had made the Countess laugh tremendously. It was on this note that the waltz finished. She was still laughing when he bowed to her (as taught by Ruth Earp). He could not comprehend why she had so laughed, save on the supposition that he was more humorous than he had suspected. Anyhow, he laughed too, and they parted laughing. He remembered that he had made a marked effect (though not one of laughter) on the tailor by quickly returning the question, "Are you?" And his unpremeditated stroke with the Countess was similar. When he had got ten yards on his way towards Harold Etches and a fiver he felt something in his hand. The Countess's fan was sticking between his fingers. It had unhooked itself from her chain. He furtively pocketed it.

VIII

"Just the same as dancing with any other woman!" He told this untruth in reply to a question from Shillitoe. It was the least he could do. And any other young man in his place would have said as much or as little.

"What was she laughing at?" somebody asked.

"Ah!" said Denry, judiciously, "wouldn't you like to know?"

"Here you are!" said Etches, with an inattentive, plutocratic gesture handing over a five-pound note. He was one of those men who never venture out of sight of a bank without a banknote in their pockets— "Because you never know what may turn up."

Denry accepted the note with a silent nod. In some directions he was gifted with astounding insight, and he could read in the faces of the haughty males surrounding him that in the space of a few minutes he had risen from nonentity into renown. He had become a great man. He did not at once realise how great, how renowned. But he saw enough in those eyes to cause his heart to glow, and to rouse in his brain those ambitious dreams which stirred him upon occasion. He left the group; he had need of motion, and also of that mental privacy which one may enjoy while strolling about on a crowded floor in the midst of a considerable noise. He noticed that the Countess was now dancing with an alderman, and that the alderman, by an oversight inexcusable in an alderman, was not wearing gloves. It was he, Denry, who had broken the ice, so that the alderman might plunge into the water. He first had danced with the Countess, and had rendered her up to the alderman with delicious gaiety upon her countenance. By instinct he knew Bursley, and he knew that he would be talked of. He knew that, for a time at any rate, he would displace even Jos Curtenty, that almost professional "card" and amuser of burgesses, in the popular imagination. It would not be: "Have ye heard Jos's latest?" It would be: "Have ye heard about young Machin, Duncalf's clerk?"

Then he met Ruth Earp, strolling in the opposite direction with a young girl, one of her pupils, of whom all he knew was that her name was Nellie, and that this was her first ball: a childish little thing with a wistful face. He could not decide whether to look at Ruth or to avoid her glance. She settled the point by smiling at him in a manner that could not be ignored.

"Are you going to make it up to me for that waltz you missed?" said Ruth Earp. She pretended to be vexed and stern, but he knew that she was not. "Or is your programme full?" she added.

"I should like to," he said simply.

"But perhaps you don't care to dance with us poor, ordinary people, now you've danced with the *Countess*!" she said, with a certain lofty and bitter pride.

He perceived that his tone had lacked eagerness.

"Don't talk like that," he said, as if hurt.

"Well," she said, "you can have the supper dance."

He took her programme to write on it.

"Why," he said, "there's a name down here for the supper dance. 'Herbert,' it looks like."

"Oh!" she replied carelessly, "that's nothing. Cross it out."

So he crossed Herbert out.

"Why don't you ask Nellie here for a dance?" said Ruth Earp.

And Nellie blushed. He gathered that the possible honour of dancing with the supremely great man had surpassed Nellie's modest expectations.

"Can I have the next one?" he said.

"Oh, yes!" Nellie timidly whispered.

"It's a polka, and you aren't very good at polking, you know," Ruth warned him. "Still, Nellie will pull you through."

Nellie laughed, in silver. The naïve child thought that Ruth was trying to joke at Denry's expense. Her very manifest joy and pride in being seen with the unique Mr Machin, in being the next after the Countess to dance with him, made another mirror in which Denry could discern the reflection of his vast importance.

At the supper, which was worthy of the hospitable traditions of the Chell family (though served standing-up in the police-court), he learnt all the gossip of the dance from Ruth Earp; amongst other things that more than one young man had asked the Countess for a dance, and had been refused, though Ruth Earp for her part declined to believe that aldermen and councillors had utterly absorbed the Countess's programme. Ruth hinted that the Countess was keeping a second dance open for him, Denry. When she asked him squarely if he meant to request another from the Countess, he said no, positively. He knew when to let well alone, a knowledge which is more precious than a knowledge of geography. The supper was the summit of Denry's triumph. The best people spoke to him without being introduced. And lovely creatures mysteriously and intoxicatingly discovered that programmes which had been crammed two hours before were not, after all, quite full.

"Do tell us what the Countess was laughing at?" This question was shot at him at least thirty times. He always said he would not tell. And one girl who had danced with Mr Stanway, who had danced with the Countess, said that Mr Stanway had said that the Countess would not tell either. Proof, here, that he was being extensively talked about!

Towards the end of the festivity the rumour floated abroad that the Countess had lost her fan. The rumour reached Denry, who maintained a culpable silence. But when all was over, and the Countess was departing, he rushed down after her, and, in a dramatic fashion which demonstrated his genius for the effective, he caught her exactly as she was getting into her carriage.

"I've just picked it up," he said, pushing through the crowd of worshippers.

"On! thank you so much!" she said. And the Earl also thanked Denry. And then the Countess, leaning from the carriage, said, with archness in her efficient smile: "You do pick things up easily, don't you?"

And both Denry and the Countess laughed without restraint, and the pillars of Bursley society were mystified.

Denry winked at Jock as the horses pawed away. And Jock winked back.

The envied of all, Denry walked home, thinking violently. At a stroke he had become possessed of more than he could earn from Duncalf in a month. The faces of the Countess, of Ruth Earp, and of the timid Nellie mingled in exquisite hallucinations before his tired eyes. He was inexpressibly happy. Trouble, however, awaited him.

CHAPTER II
THE WIDOW HULLINS'S HOUSE

I

The simple fact that he first, of all the citizens of Bursley, had asked a countess for a dance (and not been refused) made a new man of Denry Machin. He was not only regarded by the whole town as a fellow wonderful and dazzling, but he so regarded himself. He could not get over it. He had always been cheerful, even to optimism. He was now in a permanent state of calm, assured jollity. He would get up in the morning with song and dance. Bursley and the general world were no longer Bursley and the general world; they had been mysteriously transformed into an oyster; and Denry felt strangely that the oyster-knife was lying about somewhere handy, but just out of sight, and that presently he should spy it and seize it. He waited for something to happen. And not in vain.

A few days after the historic revelry, Mrs Codleyn called to see Denry's employer. Mr Duncalf was her solicitor. A stout, breathless, and yet muscular woman of near sixty, the widow of a chemist and druggist who had made money before limited companies had taken the liberty of being pharmaceutical. The money had been largely invested in mortgage on cottage property; the interest on it had not been paid, and latterly Mrs Codleyn had been obliged to foreclose, thus becoming the owner of some seventy cottages. Mrs Codleyn, though they brought her in about twelve pounds a week gross, esteemed these cottages an infliction, a bugbear, an affront, and a positive source of loss. Invariably she talked as though she would willingly present them to anybody who cared to accept— "and glad to be rid of 'em!" Most owners of property talk thus. She particularly hated paying the rates on them.

Now there had recently occurred, under the direction of the Borough Surveyor, a revaluation of the whole town. This may not sound exciting; yet a revaluation is the most exciting event (save a municipal ball given by a titled mayor) that can happen in any town. If your house is rated at forty pounds a year, and rates are seven shillings in the pound, and the revaluation lifts you up to forty-five pounds, it means thirty-five shillings a year right out of your pocket, which is the interest on thirty-five pounds. And if the revaluation drops you to thirty-five pounds, it means thirty-five shillings *in* your pocket, which is a box of Havanas or a fancy waistcoat. Is not this exciting? And there are seven thousand houses in Bursley. Mrs Codleyn hoped that her rateable value would be reduced. She based the hope chiefly on the fact that she was a client of Mr Duncalf, the Town Clerk. The Town Clerk was not the Borough Surveyor and had nothing to do with the revaluation. Moreover, Mrs Codleyn presumably [Transcriber's note: sic] entrusted him with her affairs because she considered him an honest man, and an honest man could not honestly have sought to tickle the Borough Surveyor out of the narrow path of rectitude in order to oblige a client. Nevertheless, Mrs Codleyn thought that because she patronised the Town Clerk her rates ought to be reduced! Such is human nature in the provinces! So different from human nature in London, where nobody ever dreams of offering even a match to a municipal official, lest the act might be construed into an insult.

It was on a Saturday morning that Mrs Codleyn called to impart to Mr Duncalf the dissatisfaction with which she had learned the news (printed on a bit of bluish paper) that her rateable value, far from being reduced, had been slightly augmented.

The interview, as judged by the clerks through a lath-and-plaster wall and by means of a speaking tube, atoned by its vivacity for its lack of ceremony. When the stairs had finished creaking under the descent of Mrs Codleyn's righteous fury, Mr Duncalf whistled sharply twice. Two whistles meant Denry. Denry picked up his shorthand note-book and obeyed the summons.

"Take this down!" said his master, rudely and angrily.

Just as though Denry had abetted Mrs Codleyn! Just as though Denry was not a personage of high importance in the town, the friend of countesses, and a shorthand clerk only on the surface.

"Do you hear?"

"Yes, sir."

"MADAM"—hitherto it had always been "Dear Madam," or "Dear Mrs Codleyn"—"MADAM,—Of course I need hardly say that if, after our interview this morning, and your extraordinary remarks, you wish to place

313

your interests in other hands, I shall be most happy to hand over all the papers, on payment of my costs. Yours truly ... To Mrs Codleyn."

Denry reflected: "Ass! Why doesn't he let her cool down?" Also: "He's got 'hands' and 'hand' in the same sentence. Very ugly. Shows what a temper he's in!" Shorthand clerks are always like that—hypercritical. Also: "Well, I jolly well hope she does chuck him! Then I shan't have those rents to collect." Every Monday, and often on Tuesday, too, Denry collected the rents of Mrs Codleyn's cottages—an odious task for Denry. Mr Duncalf, though not affected by its odiousness, deducted 7-1/2 per cent. for the job from the rents.

"That'll do," said Mr Duncalf.

But as Denry was leaving the room Mr Duncalf called with formidable brusqueness—

"Machin!"

"Yes, sir?"

In a flash Denry knew what was coming. He felt sickly that a crisis had supervened with the suddenness of a tidal wave. And for one little second it seemed to him that to have danced with a countess while the flower of Bursley's chivalry watched in envious wonder was not, after all, the key to the door of success throughout life. Undoubtedly he had practised fraud in sending to himself an invitation to the ball. Undoubtedly he had practised fraud in sending invitations to his tailor and his dancing-mistress. On the day after the ball, beneath his great glory, he had trembled to meet Mr Duncalf's eye, lest Mr Duncalf should ask him: "Machin, what were *you* doing at the Town Hall last night, behaving as if you were the Shah of Persia, the Prince of Wales, and Henry Irving?" But Mr Duncalf had said nothing, and Mr Duncalf's eye had said nothing, and Denry thought that the danger was past.

Now it surged up. "Who invited you to the Mayor's ball?" demanded Mr Duncalf like thunder.

Yes, there it was! And a very difficult question.

"I did, sir," he blundered out. Transparent veracity. He simply could not think of a lie.

"Why?"

"I thought you'd perhaps forgotten to put my name down on the list of invitations, sir."

"Oh!" This grimly. "And I suppose you thought I'd also forgotten to put down that tailor chap, Shillitoe?"

So it was all out! Shillitoe must have been chattering. Denry remembered that the classic established tailor of the town, Hatterton, whose trade Shillitoe was getting, was a particular friend of Mr Duncalf's. He saw the whole thing.

"Well?" persisted Mr Duncalf, after a judicious silence from Denry.

Denry, sheltered in the castle of his silence, was not to be tempted out.

"I suppose you rather fancy yourself dancing with your betters?" growled Mr Duncalf, menacingly.

"Yes," said Denry. "Do *you*?"

He had not meant to say it. The question slipped out of his mouth. He had recently formed the habit of retorting swiftly upon people who put queries to him: "Yes, are *you*?" or "No, do *you*?" The trick of speech had been enormously effective with Shillitoe, for instance, and with the Countess. He was in process of acquiring renown for it. Certainly it was effective now. Mr Duncalf's dance with the Countess had come to an ignominious conclusion in the middle, Mr Duncalf preferring to dance on skirts rather than on the floor, and the fact was notorious.

"You can take a week's notice," said Mr Duncalf, pompously.

It was no argument. But employers are so unscrupulous in an altercation.

"Oh, very well," said Denry; and to himself he said: "Something *must* turn up, now."

He felt dizzy at being thus thrown upon the world—he who had been meditating the propriety of getting himself elected to the stylish and newly-established Sports Club at Hillport! He felt enraged, for Mr Duncalf had only been venting on Denry the annoyance induced in him by Mrs Codleyn. But it is remarkable that he was not depressed at all. No! he went about with songs and whistling, though he had no prospects except starvation or living on his mother. He traversed the streets in his grand, new manner, and his thoughts ran: "What on earth can I do to live up to my reputation?" However, he possessed intact the five-pound note won from Harold Etches in the matter of the dance.

II

Every life is a series of coincidences. Nothing happens that is not rooted in coincidence. All great changes find their cause in coincidence. Therefore I shall not mince the fact that the next change in Denry's career was due to an enormous and complicated coincidence. On the following morning both Mrs Codleyn and Denry were late for service at St Luke's Church—Mrs Codleyn by accident and obesity, Denry by design. Denry was later than Mrs Codleyn, whom he discovered waiting in the porch. That Mrs Codleyn was waiting is an essential part of the coincidence. Now Mrs Codleyn would not have been waiting if her pew had not been right at the front of the church, near the choir. Nor would she have been waiting if she had been a thin woman and not given to breathing loudly after a hurried walk. She waited partly to get her breath, and partly so that she might take advantage of a hymn or a psalm to gain her seat without attracting attention. If she had not been late, if she had not been stout, if she had not had a seat under the pulpit, if she had not had an objection to making herself conspicuous, she would have been already in the church and Denry would not have had a private colloquy with her.

"Well, you're nice people, I must say!" she observed, as he raised his hat.

She meant Duncalf and all Duncalf's myrmidons. She was still full of her grievance. The letter which she had received that morning had startled her. And even the shadow of the sacred edifice did not prevent her from referring to an affair that was more suited to Monday than to Sunday morning. A little more, and she would have snorted.

"Nothing to do with me, you know!" Denry defended himself.

"Oh!" she said, "you're all alike, and I'll tell you this, Mr Machin, I'd take him at his word if it wasn't that I don't know who else I could trust to collect my rents. I've heard such tales about rent-collectors.... I reckon I shall have to make my peace with him."

"Why," said Denry, "I'll keep on collecting your rents for you if you like."

"You?"

"I've given him notice to leave," said Denry. "The fact is, Mr Duncalf and I don't hit it off together."

Another procrastinator arrived in the porch, and, by a singular simultaneous impulse, Mrs Codleyn and Denry fell into the silence of the overheard and wandered forth together among the graves.

There, among the graves, she eyed him. He was a clerk at eighteen shillings a week, and he looked it. His mother was a sempstress, and he looked it. The idea of neat but shabby Denry and the mighty Duncalf not hitting it off together seemed excessively comic. If only Denry could have worn his dress-suit at church! It vexed him exceedingly that he had only worn that expensive dress-suit once, and saw no faintest hope of ever being able to wear it again.

"And what's more," Denry pursued, "I'll collect 'em for five per cent, instead of seven-and-a-half. Give me a free hand, and see if I don't get better results than *he* did. And I'll settle accounts every month, or week if you like, instead of once a quarter, like *he* does."

The bright and beautiful idea had smitten Denry like some heavenly arrow. It went through him and pierced Mrs Codleyn with equal success. It was an idea that appealed to the reason, to the pocket, and to the instinct of revenge. Having revengefully settled the hash of Mr Duncalf, they went into church.

No need to continue this part of the narrative. Even the text of the rector's sermon has no bearing on the issue.

In a week there was a painted board affixed to the door of Denry's mother:

E.H. MACHIN, *Rent Collector and Estate Agent.*

There was also an advertisement in the *Signal*, announcing that Denry managed estates large or small.

III

The next crucial event in Denry's career happened one Monday morning, in a cottage that was very much smaller even than his mother's. This cottage, part of Mrs Codleyn's multitudinous property, stood by itself in Chapel Alley, behind the Wesleyan chapel; the majority of the tenements were in Carpenter's Square, near to. The neighbourhood was not distinguished for its social splendour, but existence in it was picturesque, varied, exciting, full of accidents, as existence is apt to be in residences that cost their occupiers an average of three shillings a week. Some persons referred to the quarter as a slum, and ironically insisted on its adjacency to the Wesleyan chapel, as though that was the Wesleyan chapel's fault. Such people did not understand life and the joy thereof.

The solitary cottage had a front yard, about as large as a blanket, surrounded by an insecure brick wall and paved with mud. You went up two steps, pushed at a door, and instantly found yourself in the principal reception-room, which no earthly blanket could possibly have covered. Behind this chamber could be seen obscurely an apartment so tiny that an auctioneer would have been justified in terming it "bijou," Furnished simply but practically with a slopstone; also the beginnings of a stairway. The furniture of the reception-room comprised two chairs and a table, one or two saucepans, and some antique crockery. What lay at the upper end of the stairway no living person knew, save the old woman who slept there. The old woman sat at the fireplace, "all bunched up," as they say in the Five Towns. The only fire in the room, however, was in the short clay pipe which she smoked; Mrs Hullins was one of the last old women in Bursley to smoke a cutty; and even then the pipe was considered coarse, and cigarettes were coming into fashion—though not in Chapel Alley. Mrs Hullins smoked her pipe, and thought about nothing in particular. Occasionally some vision of the past floated through her drowsy brain. She had lived in that residence for over forty years. She had brought up eleven children and two husbands there. She had coddled thirty-five grand-children there, and given instruction to some half-dozen daughters-in-law. She had known midnights when she could scarcely move in that residence without disturbing somebody asleep. Now she was alone in it. She never left it, except to fetch water from the pump in the square. She had seen a lot of life, and she was tired.

Denry came unceremoniously in, smiling gaily and benevolently, with his bright, optimistic face under his fair brown hair. He had large and good teeth. He was getting—not stout, but plump.

"Well, mother!" he greeted Mrs Hullins, and sat down on the other chair.

A young fellow obviously at peace with the world, a young fellow content with himself for the moment. No longer a clerk; one of the employed; saying "sir" to persons with no more fingers and toes than he had himself; bound by servile agreement to be in a fixed place at fixed hours! An independent unit, master of his own time and his own movements! In brief, a man! The truth was that he earned now in two days a week slightly more than Mr Duncalf paid him for the labour of five and a half days. His income, as collector of rents and manager of estates large or small, totalled about a pound a week. But, he walked forth in the town, smiled, joked, spoke vaguely, and said, "Do *you*?" to such a tune that his income might have been guessed to be anything from ten pounds a week to ten thousand a year. And he had four days a week in which to excogitate new methods of creating a fortune.

"I've nowt for ye," said the old woman, not moving.

"Come, come, now! That won't do," said Denry. "Have a pinch of my tobacco."

She accepted a pinch of his tobacco, and refilled her pipe, and he gave her a match.

"I'm not going out of this house without half-a-crown at any rate!" said Denry, blithely.

And he rolled himself a cigarette, possibly to keep warm. It was very chilly in the stuffy residence, but the old woman never shivered. She was one of those old women who seem to wear all the skirts of all their lives, one over the other.

"Ye're here for th' better part o' some time, then," observed Mrs Hullins, looking facts in the face. "I've told you about my son Jack. He's been playing [out of work] six weeks. He starts to-day, and he'll gi'me summat Saturday."

"That won't do," said Denry, curtly and kindly.

He then, with his bluff benevolence, explained to Mother Hullins that Mrs Codleyn would stand no further increase of arrears from anybody, that she could not afford to stand any further increase of arrears, that her tenants were ruining her, and that he himself, with all his cheery good-will for the rent-paying classes, would be involved in her fall.

"Six-and-forty years have I been i' this 'ere house!" said Mrs Hullins.

"Yes, I know," said Denry. "And look at what you owe, mother!"

It was with immense good-humoured kindliness that he invited her attention to what she owed. She tacitly declined to look at it.

"Your children ought to keep you," said Denry, upon her silence.

"Them as is dead, can't," said Mrs Hullins, "and them as is alive has their own to keep, except Jack."

"Well, then, it's bailiffs," said Denry, but still cheerfully.

"Nay, nay! Ye'll none turn me out."

Denry threw up his hands, as if to exclaim: "I've done all I can, and I've given you a pinch of tobacco. Besides, you oughtn't to be here alone. You ought to be with one of your children."

There was more conversation, which ended in Denry's repeating, with sympathetic resignation:

"No, you'll have to get out. It's bailiffs."

Immediately afterwards he left the residence with a bright filial smile. And then, in two minutes, he popped his cheerful head in at the door again.

"Look here, mother," he said, "I'll lend you half-a-crown if you like."

Charity beamed on his face, and genuinely warmed his heart.

"But you must pay me something for the accommodation," he added. "I can't do it for nothing. You must pay me back next week and give me threepence. That's fair. I couldn't bear to see you turned out of your house. Now get your rent-book."

And he marked half-a-crown as paid in her greasy, dirty rent-book, and the same in his large book.

"Eh, you're a queer 'un, Mester Machin!" murmured the old woman as he left. He never knew precisely what she meant. Fifteen—twenty—years later in his career her intonation of that phrase would recur to him and puzzle him.

On the following Monday everybody in Chapel Alley and Carpenter's Square seemed to know that the inconvenience of bailiffs and eviction could be avoided by arrangement with Denry the philanthropist. He did quite a business. And having regard to the fantastic nature of the security, he could not well charge less than threepence a week for half-a-crown. That was about 40 per cent. a month and 500 per cent. per annum. The security was merely fantastic, but nevertheless he had his remedy against evil-doers. He would take what they paid him for rent and refuse to mark it as rent, appropriating it to his loans, so that the fear of bailiffs was upon them again. Thus, as the good genius of Chapel Alley and Carpenter's Square, saving the distressed from the rigours of the open street, rescuing the needy from their tightest corners, keeping many a home together when but for him it would have fallen to pieces—always smiling, jolly, sympathetic, and picturesque—Denry at length employed the five-pound note won from Harold Etches. A five-pound note— especially a new and crisp one, as this was—is a miraculous fragment of matter, wonderful in the pleasure which the sight of it gives, even to millionaires; but perhaps no five-pound note was ever so miraculous as Denry's. Ten per cent. per week, compound interest, mounts up; it ascends, and it lifts. Denry never talked precisely. But the town soon began to comprehend that he was a rising man, a man to watch. The town admitted that, so far, he had lived up to his reputation as a dancer with countesses. The town felt that there was something indefinable about Denry.

Denry himself felt this. He did not consider himself clever or brilliant. But he considered himself peculiarly gifted. He considered himself different from other men. His thoughts would run:

"Anybody but me would have knuckled down to Duncalf and remained a shorthand clerk for ever."

"Who but me would have had the idea of going to the ball and asking the Countess to dance?... And then that business with the fan!"

"Who but me would have had the idea of taking his rent-collecting off Duncalf?"

"Who but me would have had the idea of combining these loans with the rent-collecting? It's simple enough! It's just what they want! And yet nobody ever thought of it till I thought of it!"

And he knew of a surety that he was that most admired type in the bustling, industrial provinces—a card.

IV

The desire to become a member of the Sports Club revived in his breast. And yet, celebrity though he was, rising though he was, he secretly regarded the Sports Club at Hillport as being really a bit above him. The Sports Club was the latest and greatest phenomenon of social life in Bursley, and it was emphatically the club to which it behoved the golden youth of the town to belong. To Denry's generation the Conservative Club and the Liberal Club did not seem like real clubs; they were machinery for politics, and membership carried nearly no distinction with it. But the Sports Club had been founded by the most dashing young men of Hillport, which is the most aristocratic suburb of Bursley and set on a lofty eminence. The sons of the wealthiest earthenware manufacturers made a point of belonging to it, and, after a period of disdain, their fathers also made a point of belonging to it. It was housed in an old mansion, with extensive grounds and a pond and tennis courts; it had a working agreement with the Golf Club and with the Hillport Cricket Club. But chiefly it was a social affair. The correctest thing was to be seen there at nights, rather late than early; and an exact knowledge of card games and billiards was worth more in it than prowess on the field.

It was a club in the Pall Mall sense of the word.

And Denry still lived in insignificant Brougham Street, and his mother was still a sempstress! These were apparently insurmountable truths. All the men whom he knew to be members were somehow more dashing than Denry--and it was a question of dash; few things are more mysterious than dash. Denry was unique, knew himself to be unique; he had danced with a countess, and yet... these other fellows!... Yes, there are puzzles, baffling puzzles, in the social career.

In going over on Tuesdays to Hanbridge, where he had a few trifling rents to collect, Denry often encountered Harold Etches in the tramcar. At that time Etches lived at Hillport, and the principal Etches manufactory was at Hanbridge. Etches partook of the riches of his family, and, though a bachelor, was reputed to have the spending of at least a thousand a year. He was famous, on summer Sundays, on the pier at Llandudno, in white flannels. He had been one of the originators of the Sports Club. He spent far more on clothes alone than Denry spent in the entire enterprise of keeping his soul in his body. At their first meeting little was said. They were not equals, and nothing but dress-suits could make them equals. However, even a king could not refuse speech with a scullion whom he had allowed to win money from him.

And Etches and Denry chatted feebly. Bit by bit they chatted less feebly. And once, when they were almost alone on the car, they chatted with vehemence during the complete journey of twenty minutes.

"He isn't so bad," said Denry to himself, of the dashing Harold Etches.

And he took a private oath that at his very next encounter with Etches he would mention the Sports Club—"just to see." This oath disturbed his sleep for several night. But with Denry an oath was sacred. Having sworn that he would mention the club to Etches, he was bound to mention it. When Tuesday came, he hoped that Etches would not be on the tram, and the coward in him would have walked to Hanbridge instead of taking the tram. But he was brave. And he boarded the tram, and Etches was already in it. Now that he looked at it close, the enterprise of suggesting to Harold Etches that he, Denry, would be a suitable member of the Sports Club at Hillport, seemed in the highest degree preposterous. Why! He could not play any games at all! He was a figure only in the streets! Nevertheless—the oath!

He sat awkwardly silent for a few moments, wondering how to begin. And then Harold Etches leaned across the tram to him and said:

"I say, Machin, I've several times meant to ask you. Why don't you put up for the Sports Club? It's really very good, you know."

Denry blushed, quite probably for the last time in his life. And he saw with fresh clearness how great he was, and how large he must loom in the life of the town. He perceived that he had been too modest.

V

You could not be elected to the Sports Club all in a minute. There were formalities; and that these formalities were complicated and took time is simply a proof that the club was correctly exclusive and worth belonging to. When at length Denry received notice from the "Secretary and Steward" that he was elected to the most sparkling fellowship in the Five Towns, he was positively afraid to go and visit the club. He wanted some old and experienced member to lead him gently into the club and explain its usages and introduce him to the chief *habitués*. Or else he wanted to slip in unobserved while the heads of clubmen were turned. And then he had a distressing shock. Mrs Codleyn took it into her head that she must sell her cottage property. Now, Mrs Codleyn's cottage property was the back-bone of Denry's livelihood, and he could by no means be sure that a new owner would employ him as rent-collector. A new owner might have the absurd notion of collecting rents in person. Vainly did Denry exhibit to Mrs Codleyn rows of figures, showing that her income from the property had increased under his control. Vainly did he assert that from no other form of investment would she derive such a handsome interest. She went so far as to consult an auctioneer. The auctioneer's idea of what could constitute a fair reserve price shook, but did not quite overthrow her. At this crisis it was that Denry happened to say to her, in his new large manner: "Why! If I could afford, I'd buy the property off you myself, just to show you...!" (He did not explain, and he did not perhaps know himself, what had to be shown.) She answered that she wished to goodness he would! Then he said wildly that he *would*, in instalments! And he actually did buy the Widow Hullins's half-a-crown-a-week cottage for forty-five pounds, of which he paid thirty pounds in cash and arranged that the balance should be deducted gradually from his weekly commission. He chose the Widow Hullins's because it stood by itself—an odd piece, as it were, chipped off from the block of Mrs Codleyn's realty. The transaction quietened Mrs Codleyn. And Denry felt secure because she could not now dispense with his services without losing her security for fifteen pounds. (He still thought in these small sums instead of thinking in thousands.)

He was now a property owner.

Encouraged by this great and solemn fact, he went up one afternoon to the club at Hillport. His entry was magnificent, superficially. No one suspected that he was nervous under the ordeal. The truth is that no one suspected because the place was empty. The emptiness of the hall gave him pause. He saw a large framed copy of the "Rules" hanging under a deer's head, and he read them as carefully as though he had not got a copy in his pocket. Then he read the notices, as though they had been latest telegrams from some dire seat of war. Then, perceiving a massive open door of oak (the club-house had once been a pretty stately mansion), he passed through it, and saw a bar (with bottles) and a number of small tables and wicker chairs, and on one of the tables an example of the *Staffordshire Signal* displaying in vast letters the fearful question:—"Is your skin troublesome?" Denry's skin was troublesome; it crept. He crossed the hall and went into another room which was placarded "Silence." And silence was. And on a table with copies of *The Potter's World, The British Australasian, The Iron Trades Review*, and the *Golfers' Annual*, was a second copy of the *Signal*, again demanding of Denry in vast letters whether his skin was troublesome. Evidently the reading-room.

He ascended the stairs and discovered a deserted billiard-room with two tables. Though he had never played at billiards, he seized a cue, but when he touched them the balls gave such a resounding click in the hush of the chamber that he put the cue away instantly. He noticed another door, curiously opened it, and started back at the sight of a small room, and eight middle-aged men, mostly hatted, playing cards in two groups. They had the air of conspirators, but they were merely some of the finest solo-whist players in Bursley. (This was before bridge had quitted Pall Mall.) Among them was Mr Duncalf. Denry shut the door quickly. He felt like a wanderer in an enchanted castle who had suddenly come across something that ought not to be come across. He returned to earth, and in the hall met a man in shirt-sleeves—the Secretary and Steward, a nice, homely man, who said, in the accents of ancient friendship, though he had never spoken to Denry before: "Is it Mr Machin? Glad to see you, Mr Machin! Come and have a drink with me, will you? Give it a name." Saying which, the Secretary and Steward went behind the bar, and Denry imbibed a little whisky and much information.

"Anyhow, I've *been!*" he said to himself, going home.

VI

The next night he made another visit to the club, about ten o'clock. The reading-room, that haunt of learning, was as empty as ever; but the bar was full of men, smoke, and glasses. It was so full that Denry's arrival was scarcely observed. However, the Secretary and Steward observed him, and soon he was chatting with a group at the bar, presided over by the Secretary and Steward's shirt-sleeves. He glanced around, and was satisfied. It was a scene of dashing gaiety and worldliness that did not belie the club's reputation. Some of the most important men in Bursley were there. Charles Fearns, the solicitor, who practised at Hanbridge, was arguing vivaciously in a corner. Fearns lived at Bleakridge and belonged to the Bleakridge Club, and his presence at Hillport (two miles from Bleakridge) was a dramatic tribute to the prestige of Hillport's Club.

Fearns was apparently in one of his anarchistic moods. Though a successful business man who voted right, he was pleased occasionally to uproot the fabric of society and rebuild it on a new plan of his own. To-night he was inveighing against landlords—he who by "conveyancing" kept a wife and family, and a French governess for the family, in rather more than comfort. The Fearns's French governess was one of the seven wonders of the Five Towns. Men enjoyed him in these moods; and as he raised his voice, so he enlarged the circle of his audience.

"If the by-laws of this town were worth a bilberry," he was saying, "about a thousand so-called houses would have to come down to-morrow. Now there's that old woman I was talking about just now—Hullins. She's a Catholic—and my governess is always slumming about among Catholics— that's how I know. She's paid half-a-crown a week for pretty near half a century for a hovel that isn't worth eighteen-pence, and now she's going to be pitched into the street because she can't pay any more. And she's seventy if she's a day! And that's the basis of society. Nice refined society, eh?"

"Who's the grasping owner?" some one asked.

"Old Mrs Codleyn," said Fearns.

"Here, Mr Machin, they're talking about you," said the Secretary and Steward, genially. He knew that Denry collected Mrs Codleyn's rents.

"Mrs Codleyn isn't the owner," Denry called out across the room, almost before he was aware what he was doing. There was a smile on his face and a glass in his hand.

"Oh!" said Fearns. "I thought she was. Who is?"

Everybody looked inquisitively at the renowned Machin, the new member.

"I am," said Denry.

He had concealed the change of ownership from the Widow Hullins. In his quality of owner he could not have lent her money in order that she might pay it instantly back to himself.

"I beg your pardon," said Fearns, with polite sincerity. "I'd no idea...!" He saw that unwittingly he had come near to committing a gross outrage on club etiquette.

"Not at all!" said Denry. "But supposing the cottage was *yours*, what would *you* do, Mr Fearns? Before I bought the property I used to lend her money myself to pay her rent."

"I know," Fearns answered, with a certain dryness of tone.

It occurred to Denry that the lawyer knew too much.

"Well, what should you do?" he repeated obstinately.

"She's an old woman," said Fearns. "And honest enough, you must admit. She came up to see my governess, and I happened to see her."

"But what should you do in my place?" Denry insisted.

"Since you ask, I should lower the rent and let her off the arrears," said Fearns.

"And supposing she didn't pay then? Let her have it rent-free because she's seventy? Or pitch her into the street?"

"Oh—Well—"

"Fearns would make her a present of the blooming house and give her a conveyance free!" a voice said humorously, and everybody laughed.

"Well, that's what I'll do," said Denry. "If Mr Fearns will do the conveyance free, I'll make her a present of the blooming house. That's the sort of grasping owner I am."

There was a startled pause. "I mean it," said Denry firmly, even fiercely, and raised his glass. "Here's to the Widow Hullins!"

There was a sensation, because, incredible though the thing was, it had to be believed. Denry himself was not the least astounded person in the crowded, smoky room. To him, it had been like somebody else talking, not himself. But, as always when he did something crucial, spectacular, and effective, the deed had seemed to be done by a mysterious power within him, over which he had no control.

This particular deed was quixotic, enormously unusual; a deed assuredly without precedent in the annals of the Five Towns. And he, Denry, had done it. The cost was prodigious, ridiculously and dangerously beyond his means. He could find no rational excuse for the deed. But he had done it. And men again wondered. Men had wondered when he led the Countess out to waltz. That was nothing to this. What! A smooth-chinned youth giving houses away—out of mere, mad, impulsive generosity.

And men said, on reflection, "Of course, that's just the sort of thing Machin *would* do!" They appeared to find a logical connection between dancing with a Countess and tossing a house or so to a poor widow. And the next morning every man who had been in the Sports Club that night was remarking eagerly to his friends: "I say, have you heard young Machin's latest?"

And Denry, inwardly aghast at his own rashness, was saying to himself: "Well, no one but me would ever have done that!"

He was now not simply a card; he was *the* card.

CHAPTER III
THE PANTECHNICON

I

"How do you do, Miss Earp?" said Denry, in a worldly manner, which he had acquired for himself by taking the most effective features of the manners of several prominent citizens, and piecing them together so that, as a whole, they formed Denry's manner.

"Oh! How do you do, Mr Machin?" said Ruth Earp, who had opened her door to him at the corner of Tudor Passage and St Luke's Square.

It was an afternoon in July. Denry wore a new summer suit, whose pattern indicated not only present prosperity but the firm belief that prosperity would continue. As for Ruth, that plain but piquant girl was in one of her simpler costumes; blue linen; no jewellery. Her hair was in its usual calculated disorder; its outer fleeces held the light. She was now at least twenty-five, and her gaze disconcertingly combined extreme maturity with extreme candour. At one moment a man would be saying to himself: "This woman knows more of the secrets of human nature than I can ever know." And the next he would be saying to himself: "What a simple little thing she is!" The career of nearly every man is marked at the sharp corners with such women. Speaking generally, Ruth Earp's demeanour was hard and challenging. It was evident that she could not be subject to the common weaknesses of her sex. Denry was glad.

A youth of quick intelligence, he had perceived all the dangers of the mission upon which he was engaged, and had planned his precautions.

"May I come in a minute?" he asked in a purely business tone. There was no hint in that tone of the fact that once she had accorded him a supper-dance.

"Please do," said Ruth.

An agreeable flouncing swish of linen skirts as she turned to precede him down the passage! But he ignored it. That is to say, he easily steeled himself against it.

She led him to the large room which served as her dancing academy—the bare-boarded place in which, a year and a half before, she had taught his clumsy limbs the principles of grace and rhythm. She occupied the back part of a building of which the front part was an empty shop. The shop had been tenanted by her father, one of whose frequent bankruptcies had happened there; after which his stock of the latest novelties in inexpensive furniture had been seized by rapacious creditors, and Mr Earp had migrated to Birmingham, where he was courting the Official Receiver anew. Ruth had remained solitary and unprotected, with a considerable amount of household goods which had been her mother's. (Like all professional bankrupts, Mr Earp had invariably had belongings which, as he could prove to his creditors, did not belong to him.) Public opinion had justified Ruth in her enterprise of staying in Bursley on her own responsibility and renting part of the building, in order not to lose her "connection" as a dancing-mistress. Public opinion said that "there would have been no sense in her going dangling after her wastrel of a father."

"Quite a long time since we saw anything of each other," observed Ruth in rather a pleasant style, as she sat down and as he sat down.

It was. The intimate ecstasy of the supper-dance had never been repeated. Denry's exceeding industry in carving out his career, and his desire to graduate as an accomplished clubman, had prevented him from giving to his heart that attention which it deserved, having regard to his tender years.

"Yes, it is, isn't it?" said Denry.

Then there was a pause, and they both glanced vaguely about the inhospitable and very wooden room. Now was the moment for Denry to carry out his pre-arranged plan in all its savage simplicity. He did so. "I've called about the rent, Miss Earp," he said, and by an effort looked her in the eyes.

"The rent?" exclaimed Ruth, as though she had never in all her life heard of such a thing as rent; as though June 24 (recently past) was an ordinary day like any other day.

"Yes," said Denry.

"What rent?" asked Ruth, as though for aught she guessed it might have been the rent of Buckingham Palace that he had called about.

"Yours," said Denry.

"Mine!" she murmured. "But what has my rent got to do with you?" she demanded. And it was just as if she had said, "But what has my rent got to do with you, little boy?"

"Well," he said, "I suppose you know I'm a rent-collector?"

"No, I didn't," she said.

He thought she was fibbing out of sheer naughtiness. But she was not. She did not know that he collected rents. She knew that he was a card, a figure, a celebrity; and that was all. It is strange how the knowledge of even the cleverest woman will confine itself to certain fields.

"Yes," he said, always in a cold, commercial tone, "I collect rents."

"I should have thought you'd have preferred postage-stamps," she said, gazing out of the window at a kiln that was blackening all the sky.

If he could have invented something clever and cutting in response to this sally he might have made the mistake of quitting his *rôle* of hard, unsentimental man of business. But he could think of nothing. So he proceeded sternly:

"Mr Herbert Calvert has put all his property into my hands, and he has given me strict instructions that no rent is to be allowed to remain in arrear."

No answer from Ruth. Mr Calvert was a little fellow of fifty who had made money in the mysterious calling of a "commission agent." By reputation he was really very much harder than Denry could even pretend to be, and indeed Denry had been considerably startled by the advent of such a client. Surely if any man in Bursley were capable of unmercifully collecting rents on his own account, Herbert Calvert must be that man!

"Let me see," said Denry further, pulling a book from his pocket and peering into it, "you owe five quarters' rent—thirty pounds."

He knew without the book precisely what Ruth owed, but the book kept him in countenance, supplied him with needed moral support.

Ruth Earp, without the least warning, exploded into a long peal of gay laughter. Her laugh was far prettier than her face. She laughed well. She might, with advantage to Bursley, have given lessons in laughing as well as in dancing, for Bursley laughs without grace. Her laughter was a proof that she had not a care in the world, and that the world for her was naught but a source of light amusement.

Denry smiled guardedly.

"Of course, with me it's purely a matter of business," said he.

"So that's what Mr Herbert Calvert has done!" she exclaimed, amid the embers of her mirth. "I wondered what he would do! I presume you know all about Mr Herbert Calvert," she added.

321

"No," said Denry, "I don't know anything about him, except that he owns some property and I'm in charge of it. Stay," he corrected himself, "I think I do remember crossing his name off your programme once."

And he said to himself: "That's one for her. If she likes to be so desperately funny about postage-stamps, I don't see why I shouldn't have my turn." The recollection that it was precisely Herbert Calvert whom he had supplanted in the supper-dance at the Countess of Chell's historic ball somehow increased his confidence in his ability to manage the interview with brilliance.

Ruth's voice grew severe and chilly. It seemed incredible that she had just been laughing.

"I will tell you about Mr Herbert Calvert;" she enunciated her words with slow, stern clearness. "Mr Herbert Calvert took advantage of his visits here for his rent to pay his attentions to me. At one time he was so far—well—gone, that he would scarcely take his rent."

"Really!" murmured Denry, genuinely staggered by this symptom of the distance to which Mr Herbert Calvert was once "gone."

"Yes," said Ruth, still sternly and inimically. "Naturally a woman can't make up her mind about these things all of a sudden," she continued. "Naturally!" she repeated.

"Of course," Denry agreed, perceiving that his experience of life, and deep knowledge of human nature were being appealed to.

"And when I did decide definitely, Mr Herbert Calvert did not behave like a gentleman. He forgot what was due to himself and to me. I won't describe to you the scene he made. I'm simply telling you this, so that you may know. To cut a long story short, he behaved in a very vulgar way. And a woman doesn't forget these things, Mr Machin." Her eyes threatened him. "I decided to punish Mr Herbert Calvert. I thought if he wouldn't take his rent before—well, let him wait for it now! I might have given him notice to leave. But I didn't. I didn't see why I should let myself be upset because Mr Herbert Calvert had forgotten that he was a gentleman. I said, 'Let him wait for his rent,' and I promised myself I would just see what he would dare to do."

"I don't quite follow your argument," Denry put in.

"Perhaps you don't," she silenced him. "I didn't expect you would. You and Mr Herbert Calvert...! So he didn't dare to do anything himself, and he's paying you to do his dirty work for him! Very well! Very well!..." She lifted her head defiantly. "What will happen if I don't pay the rent?"

"I shall have to let things take their course," said Denry with a genial smile.

"All right, then," Ruth Earp responded. "If you choose to mix yourself up with people like Mr Herbert Calvert, you must take the consequences! It's all the same to me, after all."

"Then it isn't convenient for you to pay anything on account?" said Denry, more and more affable.

"Convenient!" she cried. "It's perfectly convenient, only I don't care to. I won't pay a penny until I'm forced. Let Mr Herbert Calvert do his worst, and then I'll pay. And not before! And the whole town shall hear all about Mr Herbert Calvert!"

"I see," he laughed easily.

"Convenient! " she reiterated, contemptuously. "I think everybody in Bursley knows how my *clientèle* gets larger and larger every year!... Convenient!"

"So that's final, Miss Earp?"

"Perfectly!" said Miss Earp.

He rose. "Then the simplest thing will be for me to send round a bailiff to-morrow morning, early." He might have been saying: "The simplest thing will be for me to send round a bunch of orchids."

Another man would have felt emotion, and probably expressed it. But not Denry, the rent-collector and manager of estates large and small. There were several different men in Denry, but he had the great gift of not mixing up two different Denrys when he found himself in a complicated situation.

Ruth Earp rose also. She dropped her eyelids and looked at him from under them. And then she gradually smiled.

"I thought I'd just see what you'd do," she said, in a low, confidential voice from which all trace of hostility had suddenly departed. "You're a strange creature," she went on curiously, as though fascinated by the problems presented by his individuality. "Of course, I shan't let it go as far as that. I only thought I'd see what you'd say. I'll write you to-night."

"With a cheque?" Denry demanded, with suave, jolly courtesy. "I don't collect postage-stamps."

(And to himself: "She's got her stamps back.")

She hesitated. "Stay!" she said. "I'll tell you what will be better. Can you call to-morrow afternoon? The bank will be closed now."

"Yes," he said, "I can call. What time?"

"Oh!" she answered, "any time. If you come in about four, I'll give you a cup of tea into the bargain. Though you don't deserve it!" After an instant, she added reassuringly: "Of course I know business is business with you. But I'm glad I've told you the real truth about your precious Mr Herbert Calvert, all the same."

And as he walked slowly home Denry pondered upon the singular, erratic, incalculable strangeness of woman, and of the possibly magic effect of his own personality on women.

II

It was the next afternoon, in July. Denry wore his new summer suit, but with a necktie of higher rank than the previous day's. As for Ruth, that plain but piquant girl was in one of her more elaborate and foamier costumes. The wonder was that such a costume could survive even for an hour the smuts that lend continual interest and excitement to the atmosphere of Bursley. It was a white muslin, spotted with spots of opaque white, and founded on something pink. Denry imagined that he had seen parts of it before—at the ball; and he had; but it was now a tea-gown, with long, languishing sleeves; the waves of it broke at her shoulders, sending lacy surf high up the precipices of Ruth's neck. Denry did not know it was a tea-gown. But he knew that it had a most peculiar and agreeable effect on himself, and that she had promised him tea. He was glad that he had paid her the homage of his best necktie.

Although the month was July, Ruth wore a kind of shawl over the tea-gown. It was not a shawl, Denry noted; it was merely about two yards of very thin muslin. He puzzled himself as to its purpose. It could not be for warmth, for it would not have helped to melt an icicle. Could it be meant to fulfil the same function as muslin in a confectioner's shop? She was pale. Her voice was weak and had an imploring quality.

She led him, not into the inhospitable wooden academy, but into a very small room which, like herself, was dressed in muslin and bows of ribbon. Photographs of amiable men and women decorated the pinkish-green walls. The mantelpiece was concealed in drapery as though it had been a sin. A writing-desk as green as a leaf stood carelessly in one corner; on the desk a vase containing some Cape gooseberries. In the middle of the room a small table, on the table a spirit-lamp in full blast, and on the lamp a kettle practising scales; a tray occupied the remainder of the table. There were two easy chairs; Ruth sank delicately into one, and Denry took the other with precautions.

He was nervous. Nothing equals muslin for imparting nervousness to the naïve. But he felt pleased.

"Not much of the Widow Hullins touch about this!" he reflected privately.

And he wished that all rent-collecting might be done with such ease, and amid such surroundings, as this particular piece of rent-collecting. He saw what a fine thing it was to be a free man, under orders from nobody; not many men in Bursley were in a position to accept invitations to four o'clock tea at a day's notice. Further 5 per cent. on thirty pounds was thirty shillings, so that if he stayed an hour—and he meant to stay an hour—he would, while enjoying himself, be earning money steadily at the rate of sixpence a minute.

It was the ideal of a business career.

When the kettle, having finished its scales, burst into song with an accompaniment of castanets and vapour, and Ruth's sleeves rose and fell as she made the tea, Denry acknowledged frankly to himself that it was this sort of thing, and not the Brougham Street sort of thing, that he was really born for. He acknowledged to himself humbly that this sort of thing was "life," and that hitherto he had had no adequate idea of what "life" was. For, with all his ability as a card and a rising man, with all his assiduous frequenting of the Sports Club, he had not penetrated into the upper domestic strata of Bursley society. He had never been invited to any house where, as he put it, he would have had to mind his p's and q's. He still remained the kind of man whom you familiarly chat with in the street and club, and no more. His mother's fame as a flannel-washer was against him; Brougham Street was against him; and, chiefly, his poverty was against him. True, he had gorgeously given a house away to an aged widow! True, he succeeded in transmitting to his acquaintances a vague idea that he was doing well and waxing financially from strength to strength! But the idea was too vague, too much in the air. And save by a suit of clothes, he never gave ocular proof that he had money to waste. He could not. It was impossible for him to compete with even the more modest of the bloods and the blades. To keep a satisfactory straight crease down the middle of each leg of his trousers was all he could accomplish with the money regularly at his disposal. The town was waiting for him to do something decisive in the matter of what it called "the stuff."

Thus Ruth Earp was the first to introduce him to the higher intimate civilisations, the refinements lurking behind the foul walls of Bursley.

"Sugar?" she questioned, her head on one side, her arm uplifted, her sleeve drooping, and a bit of sugar caught like a white mouse between the claws of the tongs.

Nobody before had ever said "Sugar?" to him like that. His mother never said "Sugar?" to him. His mother was aware that he liked three pieces, but she would not give him more than two. "Sugar?" in that slightly weak, imploring voice seemed to be charged with a significance at once tremendous and elusive.

"Yes, please."

"Another?"

And the "Another?" was even more delicious.

He said to himself: "I suppose this is what they call flirting."

When a chronicler tells the exact truth, there is always a danger that he will not be believed. Yet, in spite of the risk, it must be said plainly that at this point Denry actually thought of marriage. An absurd and childish thought, preposterously rash; but it came into his mind, and—what is more—it stuck there! He pictured marriage as a perpetual afternoon tea alone with an elegant woman, amid an environment of ribboned muslin. And the picture appealed to him very strongly. And Ruth appeared to him in a new light. It was perhaps the change in her voice that did it. She appeared to him at once as a creature very feminine and enchanting, and as a creature who could earn her own living in a manner that was both original and ladylike. A woman such as Ruth would be a delight without being a drag. And, truly, was she not a remarkable woman, as remarkable as he was a man? Here she was living amid the refinements of luxury. Not an expensive luxury (he had an excellent notion of the monetary value of things), but still luxury. And the whole affair was so stylish. His heart went out to the stylish.

The slices of bread-and-butter were rolled up. There, now, was a pleasing device! It cost nothing to roll up a slice of bread-and-butter--her fingers had doubtless done the rolling—and yet it gave quite a different taste to the food.

"What made you give that house to Mrs Hullins?" she asked him suddenly, with a candour that seemed to demand candour.

"Oh," he said, "just a lark! I thought I would. It came to me all in a second, and I did."

She shook her head. "Strange boy!" she observed.

There was a pause.

"It was something Charlie Fearns said, wasn't it?" she inquired.

She uttered the name "Charlie Fearns" with a certain faint hint of disdain, as if indicating to Denry that of course she and Denry were quite able to put Fearns into his proper place in the scheme of things.

"Oh!" he said. "So you know all about it?"

"Well," said she, "naturally it was all over the town. Mrs Fearns's girl, Annunciata—what a name, eh?—is one of my pupils—the youngest, in fact."

"Well," said he, after another pause, "I wasn't going to have Fearns coming the duke over me!" She smiled sympathetically. He felt that they understood each other deeply.

"You'll find some cigarettes in that box," she said, when he had been there thirty minutes, and pointed to the mantelpiece.

"Sure you don't mind?" he murmured.

She raised her eyebrows.

There was also a silver match-box in the larger box. No detail lacked. It seemed to him that he stood on a mountain and had only to walk down a winding path in order to enter the promised land. He was decidedly pleased with the worldly way in which he had said: "Sure you don't mind?"

He puffed out smoke delicately. And, the cigarette between his lips, as with his left hand he waved the match into extinction, he demanded:

"You smoke?"

"Yes," she said, "but not in public. I know what you men are."

This was in the early, timid days of feminine smoking.

"I assure you!" he protested, and pushed the box towards her. But she would not smoke.

"It isn't that I mind *you*," she said, "not at all. But I'm not well. I've got a frightful headache."

He put on a concerned expression.

"I *thought* you looked rather pale," he said awkwardly.

"Pale!" she repeated the word. "You should have seen me this morning: I have fits of dizziness, you know, too. The doctor says it's nothing but dyspepsia. However, don't let's talk about poor little me and my silly complaints. Perhaps the tea will do me good."

He protested again, but his experience of intimate civilisation was too brief to allow him to protest with effectiveness. The truth was, he could not say these things naturally. He had to compose them, and then pronounce them, and the result failed in the necessary air of spontaneity. He could not help thinking what marvellous self-control women had. Now, when he had a headache—which happily was seldom—he could think of nothing else and talk of nothing else; the entire universe consisted solely of his headache. And here she was overcome with a headache, and during more than half-an-hour had not even mentioned it!

She began talking gossip about the Fearnses and the Swetnams, and she mentioned rumours concerning Henry Mynors (who had scruples against dancing) and Anna Tellwright, the daughter of that rich old skinflint Ephraim Tellwright. No mistake; she was on the inside of things in Bursley society! It was just as if she had removed the front walls of every house and examined every room at her leisure, with minute particularity. But of course a teacher of dancing had opportunities.... Denry had to pretend to be nearly as omniscient as she was.

Then she broke off, without warning, and lay back in her chair.

"I wonder if you'd mind going into the barn for me?" she murmured.

She generally referred to her academy as the barn. It had once been a warehouse.

He jumped up. "Certainly," he said, very eager.

"I think you'll see a small bottle of eau-de-Cologne on the top of the piano," she said, and shut her eyes.

He hastened away, full of his mission, and feeling himself to be a terrific cavalier and guardian of weak women. He felt keenly that he must be equal to the situation. Yes, the small bottle of eau-de-Cologne was on the top of the piano. He seized it and bore it to her on the wings of chivalry. He had not been aware that eau-de-Cologne was a remedy for, or a palliative of, headaches.

She opened her eyes, and with a great effort tried to be bright and better. But it was a failure. She took the stopper out of the bottle and sniffed first at the stopper and then at the bottle; then she spilled a few drops of the liquid on her handkerchief and applied the handkerchief to her temples.

"It's easier," she said.

"Sure?" he asked. He did not know what to do with himself—whether to sit down and feign that she was well, or to remain standing in an attitude of respectful and grave anxiety. He thought he ought to depart; yet would it not be ungallant to desert her under the circumstances? She was alone. She had no servant, only an occasional charwoman.

She nodded with brave, false gaiety. And then she had a relapse.

"Don't you think you'd better lie down?" he suggested in more masterful accents. And added; "And I'll go....? You ought to lie down. It's the only thing." He was now speaking to her like a wise uncle.

"Oh no!" she said, without conviction. "Besides, you can't go till I've paid you."

It was on the tip of his tongue to say, "Oh! don't bother about that now!" But he restrained himself. There was a notable core of common-sense in Denry. He had been puzzling how he might neatly mention the rent while departing in a hurry so that she might lie down. And now she had solved the difficulty for him.

She stretched out her arm, and picked up a bunch of keys from a basket on a little table.

"You might just unlock that desk for me, will you?" she said. And, further, as she went through the keys one by one to select the right key: "Each quarter I've put your precious Mr Herbert Calvert's rent in a drawer in that desk. ... Here's the key." She held up the whole ring by the chosen key, and he accepted it. And she lay back once more in her chair, exhausted by her exertions.

"You must turn the key sharply in the lock," she said weakly, as he fumbled at the locked part of the desk.

So he turned the key sharply.

"You'll see a bag in the little drawer on the right," she murmured.

The key turned round and round. It had begun by resisting, but now it yielded too easily.

"It doesn't seem to open," he said, feeling clumsy.

The key clicked and slid, and the other keys rattled together.

"Oh yes," she replied. "I opened it quite easily this morning. It *is* a bit catchy."

The key kept going round and round.

"Here! I'll do it," she said wearily.

"Oh no!" he urged.

But she rose courageously, and tottered to the desk, and took the bunch from him.

"I'm afraid you've broken something in the lock," she announced, with gentle resignation, after she had tried to open the desk and failed.

"Have I?" he mumbled. He knew that he was not shining.

"Would you mind calling in at Allman's," she said, resuming her chair, "and tell them to send a man down at once to pick the lock? There's nothing else for it. Or perhaps you'd better say first thing to-morrow morning.

And then as soon as he's done it I'll call and pay you the money myself. And you might tell your precious Mr Herbert Calvert that next quarter I shall give notice to leave."

"Don't you trouble to call, please," said he. "I can easily pop in here."

She sped him away in an enigmatic tone. He could not be sure whether he had succeeded or failed, in her estimation, as a man of the world and a partaker of delicate teas.

"Don't *forget* Allman's!" she enjoined him as he left the room. He was to let himself out.

III

He was coming home late that night from the Sports Club, from a delectable evening which had lasted till one o'clock in the morning, when just as he put the large door-key into his mother's cottage he grew aware of peculiar phenomena at the top end of Brougham Street, where it runs into St Luke's Square. And then in the gas-lit gloom of the warm summer night he perceived a vast and vague rectangular form in the slow movement towards the slope of Brougham Street.

It was a pantechnicon van.

But the extraordinary thing was, not that it should be a pantechnicon van, but that if should be moving of its own accord and power. For there were no horses in front of it, and Denry saw that the double shafts had been pushed up perpendicularly, after the manner of carmen when they outspan. The pantechnicon was running away. It had perceived the wrath to come and was fleeing. Its guardians had evidently left it imperfectly scotched or braked, and it had got loose.

It proceeded down the first bit of Brougham Street with a dignity worthy of its dimensions, and at the same time with apparently a certain sense of the humour of the situation. Then it seemed to be saying to itself: "Pantechnicons will be pantechnicons." Then it took on the absurd gravity of a man who is perfectly sure that he is not drunk. Nevertheless it kept fairly well to the middle of the road, but as though the road were a tight-rope.

The rumble of it increased as it approached Denry. He withdrew the key from his mother's cottage and put it in his pocket. He was always at his finest in a crisis. And the onrush of the pantechnicon constituted a clear crisis. Lower down the gradient of Brougham Street was more dangerous, and it was within the possibilities that people inhabiting the depths of the street might find themselves pitched out of bed by the sharp corner of a pantechnicon that was determined to be a pantechnicon. A pantechnicon whose ardour is fairly aroused may be capable of surpassing deeds. Whole thoroughfares might crumble before it.

As the pantechnicon passed Denry, at the rate of about three and a half miles an hour, he leaped, or rather he scrambled, on to it, losing nothing in the process except his straw hat, which remained a witness at his mother's door that her boy had been that way and departed under unusual circumstances. Denry had the bright idea of dropping the shafts down to act as a brake. But, unaccustomed to the manipulation of shafts, he was rather slow in accomplishing the deed, and ere the first pair of shafts had fallen the pantechnicon was doing quite eight miles an hour and the steepest declivity was yet to come. Further, the dropping of the left-hand shafts jerked the van to the left, and Denry dropped the other pair only just in time to avoid the sudden uprooting of a lamp-post. The four points of the shafts digging and prodding into the surface of the road gave the pantechnicon something to think about for a few seconds. But unfortunately the precipitousness of the street encouraged its head-strong caprices, and a few seconds later all four shafts were broken, and the pantechnicon seemed to scent the open prairie. (What it really did scent was the canal.) Then Denry discovered the brake, and furiously struggled with the iron handle. He turned it and turned it, some forty revolutions. It seemed to have no effect. The miracle was that the pantechnicon maintained its course in the middle of the street. Presently Denry could vaguely distinguish the wall and double wooden gates of the canal wharf. He could not jump off; the pantechnicon was now an express, and I doubt whether he would have jumped off, even if jumping off had not been madness. His was the kind of perseverance that, for the fun of it, will perish in an attempt. The final fifty or sixty yards of Brougham Street were level, and the pantechnicon slightly abated its haste. Denry could now plainly see, in the radiance of a gas-lamp, the gates of the wharf, and on them the painted letters:—

| SHROPSHIRE | UNION | CANAL | COY., | LTD.. |
| GENERAL | | | | CARRIERS. |

No Admittance except on Business

He was heading straight for those gates, and the pantechnicon evidently had business within. It jolted over the iron guard of the weighing-machine, and this jolt deflected it, so that instead of aiming at the gates it aimed for part of a gate and part of a brick pillar. Denry ground his teeth together and clung to his seat. The gate might have been paper, and the brick pillar a cardboard pillar. The pantechnicon went through them as a sword will go through a ghost, and Denry was still alive. The remainder of the journey was brief and violent, owing partly to a number of bags of cement, and partly to the propinquity of the canal basin. The pantechnicon jumped into the canal like a mastodon, and drank.

Denry, clinging to the woodwork, was submerged for a moment, but, by standing on the narrow platform from which sprouted the splintered ends of the shafts, he could get his waist clear of the water. He was not a swimmer.

All was still and dark, save for the faint stream of starlight on the broad bosom of the canal basin. The pantechnicon had encountered nobody whatever *en route*. Of its strange escapade Denry had been the sole witness.

"Well, I'm dashed!" he murmured aloud.

And a voice replied from the belly of the pantechnicon:

"Who is there?"

All Denry's body shook.

"It's me!" said he.

"Not Mr Machin?" said the voice.

"Yes," said he. "I jumped on as it came down the street—and here we are!"

"Oh!" cried the voice. "I do wish you could get round to me."

Ruth Earp's voice.

He saw the truth in a moment of piercing insight. Ruth had been playing with him! She had performed a comedy for him in two acts. She had meant to do what is called in the Five Towns "a moonlight flit." The pantechnicon (doubtless from Birmingham, where her father was) had been brought to her door late in the evening, and was to have been filled and taken away during the night. The horses had been stabled, probably in Ruth's own yard, and while the carmen were reposing the pantechnicon had got off, Ruth in it. She had no money locked in her unlockable desk. Her reason for not having paid the precious Mr Herbert Calvert was not the reason which she had advanced.

His first staggered thought was:

"She's got a nerve! No mistake!"

Her duplicity, her wickedness, did not shock him. He admired her tremendous and audacious enterprise; it appealed strongly to every cell in his brain. He felt that she and he were kindred spirits.

He tried to clamber round the side of the van so as to get to the doors at the back, but a pantechnicon has a wheel-base which forbids leaping from wheel to wheel, especially, when the wheels are under water. Hence he was obliged to climb on to the roof, and so slide down on to the top of one of the doors, which was swinging loose. The feat was not simple. At last he felt the floor of the van under half a yard of water.

"Where are you?"

"I'm here," said Ruth, very plaintively. "I'm on a table. It was the only thing they had put into the van before they went off to have their supper or something. Furniture removers are always like that. Haven't you got a match?"

"I've got scores of matches," said Denry. "But what good do you suppose they'll be now, all soaked through?

A short silence. He noticed that she had offered no explanation of her conduct towards himself. She seemed to take it for granted that he would understand.

"I'm frightfully bumped, and I believe my nose is bleeding, said Ruth, still more plaintively. "It's a good thing there was a lot of straw and sacks here."

Then, after much groping, his hand touched her wet dress.

"You know you're a very naughty girl," he said.

He heard a sob, a wild sob. The proud, independent creature had broken down under the stress of events. He climbed out of the water on to the part of the table which she was not occupying. And the van was as black as Erebus.

Gradually, out of the welter of sobs, came faint articulations, and little by little he learnt the entire story of her difficulties, her misfortunes, her struggles, and her defeats. He listened to a frank confession of guilt. But what could she do? She had meant well. But what could she do? She had been driven into a corner. And she had her father to think of! Honestly, on the previous day, she had intended to pay the rent, or part of it. But there had been a disappointment! And she had been so unwell. In short...

The van gave a lurch. She clutched at him and he at her. The van was settling down for a comfortable night in the mud.

(Queer that it had not occurred to him before, but at the first visit she had postponed paying him on the plea that the bank was closed, while at the second visit she had stated that the actual cash had been slowly accumulating in her desk! And the discrepancy had not struck him. Such is the influence of a teagown. However, he forgave her, in consideration of her immense audacity.)

"What can we do?" she almost whispered.

Her confidence in him affected him.

"Wait till it gets light," said he.

So they waited, amid the waste of waters. In a hot July it is not unpleasant to dangle one's feet in water during the sultry dark hours. She told him more and more.

When the inspiring grey preliminaries of the dawn began, Denry saw that at the back of the pantechnicon the waste of waters extended for at most a yard, and that it was easy, by climbing on to the roof, to jump therefrom to the wharf. He did so, and then fixed a plank so that Ruth could get ashore. Relieved of their weight the table floated out after them. Denry seized it, and set about smashing it to pieces with his feet.

"What *are* you doing?" she asked faintly. She was too enfeebled to protest more vigorously.

"Leave it to me," said Denry." This table is the only thing that can give your show away. We can't carry it back. We might meet some one."

He tied the fragments of the table together with rope that was afloat in the van, and attached the heavy iron bar whose function was to keep the doors closed. Then he sank the faggot of wood and iron in a distant corner of the basin.

"There!" he said. "Now you understand. Nothing's happened except that a furniture van's run off and fallen into the canal owing to the men's carelessness. We can settle the rest later—I mean about the rent and so on."

They looked at each other.

Her skirts were nearly dry. Her nose showed no trace of bleeding, but there was a bluish lump over her left eye. Save that he was hatless, and that his trousers clung, he was not utterly unpresentable.

They were alone in the silent dawn.

"You'd better go home by Acre Lane, not up Brougham Street, he said. "I'll come in during the morning."

It was a parting in which more was felt than said.

They went one after the other through the devastated gateway, baptising the path as they walked. The Town Hall clock struck three as Denry crept up his mother's stairs. He had seen not a soul.

IV

The exact truth in its details was never known to more than two inhabitants of Bursley. The one thing clear certainly appeared to be that Denry, in endeavouring to prevent a runaway pantechnicon from destroying the town, had travelled with it into the canal. The romantic trip was accepted as perfectly characteristic of Denry. Around this island of fact washed a fabulous sea of uninformed gossip, in which assertion conflicted with assertion, and the names of Denry and Ruth were continually bumping against each other.

Mr Herbert Calvert glanced queerly and perhaps sardonically at Denry when Denry called and handed over ten pounds (less commission) which he said Miss Earp had paid on account.

"Look here," said the little Calvert, his mean little eyes gleaming. "You must get in the balance at once."

"That's all right," said Denry. "I shall."

"Was she trying to hook it on the q.t.?" Calvert demanded.

"Oh, no!" said Denry. "That was a very funny misunderstanding. The only explanation I can think of is that that van must have come to the wrong house."

"Are you engaged to her?" Calvert asked, with amazing effrontery.

Denry paused. "Yes," he said. "Are you?"

Mr Calvert wondered what he meant.

He admitted to himself that the courtship had begun in a manner surpassingly strange.

CHAPTER IV
WRECKING OF A LIFE

I

In the Five Towns, and perhaps elsewhere, there exists a custom in virtue of which a couple who have become engaged in the early summer find themselves by a most curious coincidence at the same seaside resort, and often in the same street thereof, during August. Thus it happened to Denry and to Ruth Earp. There had been difficulties—there always are. A business man who lives by collecting weekly rents obviously cannot go away for an indefinite period. And a young woman who lives alone in the world is bound to respect public opinion. However, Ruth arranged that her girlish friend, Nellie Cotterill, who had generous parents, should accompany her. And the North Staffordshire Railway's philanthropic scheme of issuing four-shilling tourist return tickets to the seaside enabled Denry to persuade himself that he was not absolutely mad in contemplating a fortnight on the shores of England.

Ruth chose Llandudno, Llandudno being more stylish than either Rhyl or Blackpool, and not dearer. Ruth and Nellie had a double room in a boarding-house, No. 26 St Asaph's Road (off the Marine Parade), and Denry had a small single room in another boarding-house, No. 28 St Asaph's Road. The ideal could scarcely have been approached more nearly.

Denry had never seen the sea before. As, in his gayest clothes, he strolled along the esplanade or on the pier between those two girls in their gayest clothes, and mingled with the immense crowd of pleasure-seekers and money-spenders, he was undoubtedly much impressed by the beauty and grandeur of the sea. But what impressed him far more than the beauty and grandeur of the sea was the field for profitable commercial enterprise which a place like Llandudno presented. He had not only his first vision of the sea, but his first genuine vision of the possibilities of amassing wealth by honest ingenuity. On the morning after his arrival he went out for a walk and lost himself near the Great Orme, and had to return hurriedly along the whole length of the Parade about nine o'clock. And through every ground-floor window of every house he saw a long table full of people eating and drinking the same kinds of food. In Llandudno fifty thousand souls desired always to perform the same act at the same time; they wanted to be distracted and they would do anything for the sake of distraction, and would pay for the privilege. And they would all pay at once.

This great thought was more majestic to him than the sea, or the Great Orme, or the Little Orme.

It stuck in his head because he had suddenly grown into a very serious person. He had now something to live for, something on which to lavish his energy. He was happy in being affianced, and more proud than happy, and more startled than proud. The manner and method of his courtship had sharply differed from his previous conception of what such an affair would be. He had not passed through the sensations which he would have expected to pass through. And then this question was continually presenting itself: *What could she see in him?* She must have got a notion that he was far more wonderful than he really was. Could it be true that she, his superior in experience and in splendour of person, had kissed him? *Him!* He felt that it would be his duty to live up to this exaggerated notion which she had of him. But how?

II

They had not yet discussed finance at all, though Denry would have liked to discuss it. Evidently she regarded him as a man of means. This became clear during the progress of the journey to Llandudno. Denry was flattered, but the next day he had slight misgivings, and on the following day he was alarmed; and on the day after that his state resembled terror. It is truer to say that she regarded him less as a man of means than as a magic and inexhaustible siphon of money.

He simply could not stir out of the house without spending money, and often in ways quite unforeseen. Pier, minstrels, Punch and Judy, bathing, buns, ices, canes, fruit, chairs, row-boats, concerts, toffee, photographs, char--bancs: any of these expenditures was likely to happen whenever they went forth for a simple stroll. One might think that strolls were gratis, that the air was free! Error! If he had had the courage he would have left his purse in the house as Ruth invariably did. But men are moral cowards.

He had calculated thus:—Return fare, four shillings a week. Agreed terms at boarding-house, twenty-five shillings a week. Total expenses per week, twenty-nine shillings,—say thirty!

On the first day he spent fourteen shillings on nothing whatever—which was at the rate of five pounds a week of supplementary estimates! On the second day he spent nineteen shillings on nothing whatever, and Ruth insisted on his having tea with herself and Nellie at their boarding-house; for which of course he had to pay, while his own tea was wasting next door. So the figures ran on, jumping up each day. Mercifully, when Sunday dawned the open wound in his pocket was temporarily stanched. Ruth wished him to come in for tea again. He refused—at any rate he did not come—and the exquisite placidity of the stream of their love was slightly disturbed.

Nobody could have guessed that she was in monetary difficulties on her own account. Denry, as a chivalrous lover, had assisted her out of the fearful quagmire of her rent; but she owed much beyond rent. Yet, when some of her quarterly fees had come in, her thoughts had instantly run to Llandudno, joy, and frocks. She did not know what money was, and she never would. This was, perhaps, part of her superior splendour. The gentle, timid, silent Nellie occasionally let Denry see that she, too, was scandalised by her bosom friend's recklessness. Often Nellie would modestly beg for permission to pay her share of the cost of an amusement. And it seemed just to Denry that she should pay her share, and he violently wished to accept her money, but he could not. He would even get quite curt with her when she insisted. From this it will be seen how absurdly and irrationally different he was from the rest of us.

Nellie was continually with them, except just before they separated for the night. So that Denry paid consistently for three. But he liked Nellie Cotterill. She blushed so easily, and she so obviously worshipped Ruth and admired himself, and there was a marked vein of common-sense in her ingenuous composition.

On the Monday morning he was up early and off to Bursley to collect rents and manage estates. He had spent nearly five pounds beyond his expectation. Indeed, if by chance he had not gone to Llandudno with a portion of the previous week's rents in his pockets, he would have been in what the Five Towns call a fix.

While in Bursley he thought a good deal. Bursley in August encourages nothing but thought. His mother was working as usual. His recitals to her of the existence led by betrothed lovers at Llandudno were vague.

On the Tuesday evening he returned to Llandudno, and, despite the general trend of his thoughts, it once more occurred that his pockets were loaded with a portion of the week's rents. He did not know precisely what was going to happen, but he knew that something was going to happen; for the sufficient reason that his career could not continue unless something did happen. Without either a quarrel, an understanding, or a miracle, three months of affianced bliss with Ruth Earp would exhaust his resources and ruin his reputation as one who was ever equal to a crisis.

III

What immediately happened was a storm at sea. He heard it mentioned at Rhyl, and he saw, in the deep night, the foam of breakers at Prestatyn. And when the train reached Llandudno, those two girls in ulsters and caps greeted him with wondrous tales of the storm at sea, and of wrecks, and of lifeboats. And they were so jolly, and so welcoming, so plainly glad to see their cavalier again, that Denry instantly discovered himself to be in the highest spirits. He put away the dark and brooding thoughts which had disfigured his journey, and became the gay Denry of his own dreams. The very wind intoxicated him. There was no rain.

It was half-past nine, and half Llandudno was afoot on the Parade and discussing the storm—a storm unparalleled, it seemed, in the month of August. At any rate, people who had visited Llandudno yearly for twenty-five years declared that never had they witnessed such a storm. The new lifeboat had gone forth, amid cheers, about six o'clock to a schooner in distress near Rhos, and at eight o'clock a second lifeboat (an old one which the new one had replaced and which had been bought for a floating warehouse by an aged fisherman) had departed to the rescue of a Norwegian barque, the *Hjalmar*, round the bend of the Little Orme.

"Let's go on the pier," said Denry. "It will be splendid."

He was not an hour in the town, and yet was already hanging expense!

"They've closed the pier," the girls told him.

But when in the course of their meanderings among the excited crowd under the gas-lamps they arrived at the pier-gates, Denry perceived figures on the pier.

"They're sailors and things, and the Mayor," the girls explained.

"Pooh!" said Denry, fired.

He approached the turnstile and handed a card to the official. It was the card of an advertisement agent of the *Staffordshire Signal*, who had called at Brougham Street in Denry's absence about the renewal of Denry's advertisement.

"Press," said Denry to the guardian at the turnstile, and went through with the ease of a bird on the wing.

"Come along," he cried to the girls.

The guardian seemed to hesitate.

"These ladies are with me," he said.

The guardian yielded.

It was a triumph for Denry. He could read his triumph in the eyes of his companions. When she looked at him like that, Ruth was assuredly marvellous among women, and any ideas derogatory to her marvellousness which he might have had at Bursley and in the train were false ideas.

At the head of the pier beyond the pavilion, there were gathered together some fifty people, and the tale ran that the second lifeboat had successfully accomplished its mission and was approaching the pier.

"I shall write an account of this for the *Signal*," said Denry, whose thoughts were excusably on the Press.

"Oh, do!" exclaimed Nellie.

"They have the *Signal* at all the newspaper shops here," said Ruth.

Then they seemed to be merged in the storm. The pier shook and trembled under the shock of the waves, and occasionally, though the tide was very low, a sprinkle of water flew up and caught their faces. The eyes could see nothing save the passing glitter of the foam on the crest of a breaker. It was the most thrilling situation that any of them had ever been in.

And at last came word from the mouths of men who could apparently see as well in the dark as in daylight, that the second lifeboat was close to the pier. And then everybody momentarily saw it—a ghostly thing that heaved up pale out of the murk for an instant, and was lost again. And the little crowd cheered.

The next moment a Bengal light illuminated the pier, and the lifeboat was silhouetted with strange effectiveness against the storm. And some one flung a rope, and then another rope arrived out of the sea, and fell on Denry's shoulder.

"Haul on there!" yelled a hoarse voice. The Bengal light expired.

Denry hauled with a will. The occasion was unique. And those few seconds were worth to him the whole of Denry's precious life—yes, not excluding the seconds in which he had kissed Ruth and the minutes in which he had danced with the Countess of Chell. Then two men with beards took the rope from his hands. The air was now alive with shoutings. Finally there was a rush of men down the iron stairway to the lower part of the pier, ten feet nearer the water.

"You stay here, you two!" Denry ordered.

"But, Denry—"

"Stay here, I tell you!" All the male in him was aroused. He was off, after the rush of men. "Half a jiffy," he said, coming back. "Just take charge of this, will you?" And he poured into their hands about twelve shillings' worth of copper, small change of rents, from his hip-pocket. "If anything happened, that might sink me," he said, and vanished.

It was very characteristic of him, that effusion of calm sagacity in a supreme emergency.

IV

Beyond getting his feet wet Denry accomplished but little in the dark basement of the pier. In spite of his success in hauling in the thrown rope, he seemed to be classed at once down there by the experts assembled as an eager and useless person who had no right to the space which he occupied. However, he witnessed the heaving arrival of the lifeboat and the disembarking of the rescued crew of the Norwegian barque, and he was more than ever decided to compose a descriptive article for the *Staffordshire Signal*. The rescued and the rescuing crews disappeared in single file to the upper floor of the pier, with the exception of the coxswain, a man with a spreading red beard, who stayed behind to inspect the lifeboat, of which indeed he was the absolute owner. As a journalist Denry did the correct thing and engaged him in conversation. Meanwhile, cheering could be heard above. The coxswain, who stated that his name was Cregeen, and that he was a Manxman, seemed to regret the entire expedition. He seemed to be unaware that it was his duty now to play the part of the modest hero to Denry's interviewing. At every loose end of the chat he would say gloomily:

"And look at her now, I'm telling ye!" Meaning the battered craft, which rose and fell on the black waves.

Denry ran upstairs again, in search of more amenable material. Some twenty men in various sou'-westers and other headgear were eating thick slices of bread and butter and drinking hot coffee, which with foresight had been prepared for them in the pier buffet. A few had preferred whisky. The whole crowd was now under the lee of the pavilion, and it constituted a spectacle which Denry said to himself he should refer to in his article as "Rembrandtesque." For a few moments he could not descry Ruth and Nellie in the gloom. Then he saw the indubitable form of his betrothed at a penny-in-the-slot machine, and the indubitable form of Nellie at another penny-in-the-slot machine. And then he could hear the click-click-click of the machines, working rapidly. And his thoughts took a new direction.

Presently Ruth ran with blithe gracefulness from her machine and commenced a generous distribution of packets to the members of the crews. There was neither calculation nor exact justice in her generosity. She dropped packets on to heroic knees with a splendid gesture of largesse. Some packets even fell on the floor. But she did not mind.

Denry could hear her saying:

"You must eat it. Chocolate is so sustaining. There's nothing like it."

She ran back to the machines, and snatched more packets from Nellie, who under her orders had been industrious; and then began a second distribution.

A calm and disinterested observer would probably have been touched by this spectacle of impulsive womanly charity. He might even have decided that it was one of the most beautifully human things that he had ever seen. And the fact that the hardy heroes and Norsemen appeared scarcely to know what to do with the silver-wrapped bonbons would not have impaired his admiration for these two girlish figures of benevolence. Denry, too, was touched by the spectacle, but in another way. It was the rents of his clients that were being thus dissipated in a very luxury of needless benevolence. He muttered:

"Well, that's a bit thick, that is!" But of course he could do nothing.

As the process continued, the clicking of the machine exacerbated his ears.

"Idiotic!" he muttered.

The final annoyance to him was that everybody except himself seemed to consider that Ruth was displaying singular ingenuity, originality, enterprise, and goodness of heart.

In that moment he saw clearly for the first time that the marriage between himself and Ruth had not been arranged in Heaven. He admitted privately then that the saving of a young woman from violent death in a pantechnicon need not inevitably involve espousing her. She was without doubt a marvellous creature, but it was as wise to dream of keeping a carriage and pair as to dream of keeping Ruth. He grew suddenly cynical. His age leaped to fifty or so, and the curve of his lips changed.

Ruth, spying around, saw him and ran to him him with a glad cry.

"Here!" she said, "take these. They're no good." She held out her hands.

"What are they?" he asked.

"They're the halfpennies."

"So sorry!" he said, with an accent whose significance escaped her, and took the useless coins.

"We've exhausted all the chocolate," said she. "But there's butterscotch left—it's nearly as good—and gold-tipped cigarettes. I daresay some of them would enjoy a smoke. Have you got any more pennies?"

"No!" he replied. "But I've got ten or a dozen half-crowns. They'll work the machine just as well, won't they?"

This time she did notice a certain unusualness in the flavour of his accent. And she hesitated.

"Don't be silly!" she said.

"I'll try not to be," said Denry. So far as he could remember, he had never used such a tone before. Ruth swerved away to rejoin Nellie.

Denry surreptitiously counted the halfpennies. There were eighteen. She had fed those machines, then, with over a hundred and thirty pence.

He murmured, "Thick, thick!"

Considering that he had returned to Llandudno in the full intention of putting his foot down, of clearly conveying to Ruth that his conception of finance differed from hers, the second sojourn had commenced badly. Still, he had promised to marry her, and he must marry her. Better a lifetime of misery and insolvency than a failure to behave as a gentleman should. Of course, if she chose to break it off.... But he must be minutely careful to do nothing which might lead to a breach. Such was Denry's code. The walk home at midnight, amid the reverberations of the falling tempest, was marked by a slight pettishness on the part of Ruth, and by Denry's polite taciturnity.

V

Yet the next morning, as the three companions sat together under the striped awning of the buffet on the pier, nobody could have divined, by looking at them, that one of them at any rate was the most uncomfortable young man in all Llandudno. The sun was hotly shining on their bright attire and on the still turbulent waves. Ruth, thirsty after a breakfast of herrings and bacon, was sucking iced lemonade up a straw. Nellie was eating chocolate, undistributed remains of the night's benevolence. Denry was yawning, not in the least because the proceedings failed to excite his keen interest, but because he had been a journalist till three a.m. and had risen at six in order to despatch a communication to the editor of the *Staffordshire Signal* by train. The girls were very playful. Nellie dropped a piece of chocolate into Ruth's glass, and Ruth fished it out, and bit at it.

"What a jolly taste!" she exclaimed.

And then Nellie bit at it.

"Oh, it's just lovely!" said Nellie, softly.

"Here, dear!" said Ruth, "try it."

And Denry had to try it, and to pronounce it a delicious novelty (which indeed it was) and generally to brighten himself up. And all the time he was murmuring in his heart, "This can't go on."

Nevertheless, he was obliged to admit that it was he who had invited Ruth to pass the rest of her earthly life with him, and not *vice versa.*

"Well, shall we go on somewhere else? " Ruth suggested.

And he paid yet again. He paid and smiled, he who had meant to be the masterful male, he who deemed himself always equal to a crisis. But in this crisis he was helpless.

They set off down the pier, brilliant in the brilliant crowd. Everybody was talking of wrecks and lifeboats. The new lifeboat had done nothing, having been forestalled by the Prestatyn boat; but Llandudno was apparently very proud of its brave old worn-out lifeboat which had brought ashore the entire crew of the *Hjalmar,* without casualty, in a terrific hurricane.

"Run along, child," said Ruth to Nellie, "while uncle and auntie talk to each other for a minute."

Nellie stared, blushed, and walked forward in confusion. She was startled. And Denry was equally startled. Never before had Ruth so brazenly hinted that lovers must be left alone at intervals. In justice to her, it must be said that she was a mirror for all the proprieties. Denry had even reproached her, in his heart, for not sufficiently showing her desire for his exclusive society. He wondered, now, what was to be the next revelation of her surprising character.

"I had our bill this morning," said Ruth.

She leaned gracefully on the handle of her sunshade, and they both stared at the sea. She was very elegant, with an aristocratic air. The bill, as she mentioned it, seemed a very negligible trifle. Nevertheless, Denry's heart quaked.

"Oh!" he said. "Did you pay it?"

"Yes," said she. "The landlady wanted the money, she told me. So Nellie gave me her share, and I paid it at once."

"Oh!" said Denry.

There was a silence. Denry felt as though he were defending a castle, or as though he were in a dark room and somebody was calling him, calling him, and he was pretending not to be there and holding his breath.

"But I've hardly enough money left," said Ruth. "The fact is, Nellie and I spent such a lot yesterday and the day before.... You've no idea how money goes!"

"Haven't I? "said Denry. But not to her—only to his own heart.

To her he said nothing.

"I suppose we shall have to go back home," she ventured lightly. "One can't run into debt here. They'd claim your luggage."

"What a pity!" said Denry, sadly.

Just those few words—and the interesting part of the interview was over! All that followed counted not in the least. She had meant to induce him to offer to defray the whole of her expenses in Llandudno—no doubt in the form of a loan; and she had failed. She had intended him to repair the disaster caused by her chronic extravagance. And he had only said: "What a pity!"

"Yes, it is!" she agreed bravely, and with a finer disdain than ever of petty financial troubles. "Still, it can't be helped."

"No, I suppose not," said Denry.

There was undoubtedly something fine about Ruth. In that moment she had it in her to kill Denry with a bodkin. But she merely smiled. The situation was terribly strained, past all Denry's previous conceptions of a strained situation; but she deviated with superlative *sang-froid* into frothy small talk. A proud and an unconquerable woman! After all, what were men for, if not to pay?

"I think I shall go home to-night," she said, after the excursion into prattle.

"I'm sorry," said Denry.

He was not coming out of his castle.

At that moment a hand touched his shoulder. It was the hand of Cregeen, the owner of the old lifeboat.

"Mister," said Cregeen, too absorbed in his own welfare to notice Ruth. "It's now or never! Five-and-twenty'll buy the *Fleetwing*, if ten's paid down this mornun."

And Denry replied boldly:

"You shall have it in an hour. Where shall you be?"

333

"I'll be in John's cabin, under the pier," said Cregeen, "where ye found me this mornun."

"Right," said Denry.

If Ruth had not been caracoling on her absurdly high horse, she would have had the truth out of Denry in a moment concerning these early morning interviews and mysterious transactions in shipping. But from that height she could not deign to be curious. And so she said naught. Denry had passed the whole morning since breakfast and had uttered no word of pre-prandial encounters with mariners, though he had talked a lot about his article for the *Signal* and of how he had risen betimes in order to despatch it by the first train.

And as Ruth showed no curiosity Denry behaved on the assumption that she felt none. And the situation grew even more strained.

As they walked down the pier towards the beach, at the dinner-hour, Ruth bowed to a dandiacal man who obsequiously saluted her.

"Who's that?" asked Denry, instinctively.

"It's a gentleman that I was once engaged to," answered Ruth, with cold, brief politeness.

Denry did not like this.

The situation almost creaked under the complicated stresses to which it was subject. The wonder was that it did not fly to pieces long before evening.

VI

The pride of the principal actors being now engaged, each person was compelled to carry out the intentions which he had expressed either in words or tacitly. Denry's silence had announced more efficiently than any words that he would under no inducement emerge from his castle. Ruth had stated plainly that there was nothing for it but to go home at once, that very night. Hence she arranged to go home, and hence Denry refrained from interfering with her arrangements. Ruth was lugubrious under a mask of gaiety; Nellie was lugubrious under no mask whatever. Nellie was merely the puppet of these betrothed players, her elders. She admired Ruth and she admired Denry, and between them they were spoiling the little thing's holiday for their own adult purposes. Nellie knew that dreadful occurrences were in the air—occurrences compared to which the storm at sea was a storm in a tea-cup. She knew partly because Ruth had been so queenly polite, and partly because they had come separately to St Asaph's Road and had not spent the entire afternoon together.

So quickly do great events loom up and happen that at six o'clock they had had tea and were on their way afoot to the station. The odd man of No. 26 St Asaph's Road had preceded them with the luggage. All the rest of Llandudno was joyously strolling home to its half-past six high tea— grand people to whom weekly bills were as dust and who were in a position to stop in Llandudno for ever and ever, if they chose! And Ruth and Nellie were conscious of the shame which always afflicts those whom necessity forces to the railway station of a pleasure resort in the middle of the season. They saw omnibuses loaded with luggage and jolly souls were actually *coming*, whose holiday had not yet properly commenced. And this spectacle added to their humiliation and their disgust. They genuinely felt that they belonged to the lower orders.

Ruth, for the sake of effect, joked on the most solemn subjects. She even referred with giggling laughter to the fact that she had borrowed from Nellie in order to discharge her liabilities for the final twenty-four hours at the boarding-house. Giggling laughter being contagious, as they were walking side by side close together, they all laughed. And each one secretly thought how ridiculous was such behaviour, and how it failed to reach the standard of true worldliness.

Then, nearer the station, some sprightly caprice prompted Denry to raise his hat to two young women who were crossing the road in front of them. Neither of the two young women responded to the homage.

"Who are they?" asked Ruth, and the words were out of her mouth before she could remind herself that curiosity was beneath her.

"It's a young lady I was once engaged to," said Denry.

"Which one?" asked the ninny, Nellie, astounded.

"I forget," said Denry.

He considered this to be one of his greatest retorts—not to Nellie, but to Ruth. Nellie naturally did not appreciate its loveliness. But Ruth did. There was no facet of that retort that escaped Ruth's critical notice.

At length they arrived at the station, quite a quarter of an hour before the train was due, and half-an-hour before it came in.

Denry tipped the odd man for the transport of the luggage.

"Sure it's all there?" he asked the girls, embracing both of them in his gaze.

"Yes," said Ruth, "but where's yours?"

"Oh!" he said. "I'm not going to-night. I've got some business to attend to here. I thought you understood. I expect you'll be all right, you two together."

After a moment, Ruth said brightly: "Oh yes! I was quite forgetting about your business." Which was completely untrue, since she knew nothing of his business, and he had assuredly not informed her that he would not return with them.

But Ruth was being very brave, haughty, and queenlike, and for this the precise truth must sometimes be abandoned. The most precious thing in the world to Ruth was her dignity—and who can blame her? She meant to keep it at no matter what costs.

In a few minutes the bookstall on the platform attracted them as inevitably as a prone horse attracts a crowd. Other people were near the bookstall, and as these people were obviously leaving Llandudno, Ruth and Nellie felt a certain solace. The social outlook seemed brighter for them. Denry bought one or two penny papers, and then the newsboy began to paste up the contents poster of the *Staffordshire Signal*, which had just arrived. And on this poster, very prominent, were the words:—"The Great Storm in North Wales. Special Descriptive Report." Denry snatched up one of the green papers and opened it, and on the first column of the news-page saw his wondrous description, including the word "Rembrandtesque." "Graphic Account by a Bursley Gentleman of the Scene at Llandudno," said the sub-title. And the article was introduced by the phrase: "We are indebted to Mr E.H. Machin, a prominent figure in Bursley," etc.

It was like a miracle. Do what he would, Denry could not stop his face from glowing.

With false calm he gave the paper, to Ruth. Her calmness in receiving it upset him.

"We'll read it in the train," she said primly, and started to talk about something else. And she became most agreeable and companionable.

Mixed up with papers and sixpenny novels on the bookstall were a number of souvenirs of Llandudno— paper-knives, pens, paper-weights, watch-cases, pen-cases, all in light wood or glass, and ornamented with coloured views of Llandudno, and also the word "Llandudno" in large German capitals, so that mistakes might not arise. Ruth remembered that she had even intended to buy a crystal paper-weight with a view of the Great Orme at the bottom. The bookstall clerk had several crystal paper-weights with views of the pier, the Hotel Majestic, the Esplanade, the Happy Valley, but none with a view of the Great Orme. He had also paper-knives and watch-cases with a view of the Great Orme. But Ruth wanted a combination of paper-weight and Great Orme, and nothing else would satisfy her. She was like that. The clerk admitted that such a combination existed, but he was sold "out of it."

"Couldn't you get one and send it to me?" said Ruth.

And Denry saw anew that she was incurable.

"Oh yes, miss," said the clerk. "Certainly, miss. To-morrow at latest." And he pulled out a book. "What name?"

Ruth looked at Denry, as women do look on such occasions.

"Rothschild," said Denry.

It may seem perhaps strange that that single word ended their engagement. But it did. She could not tolerate a rebuke. She walked away, flushing. The bookstall clerk received no order. Several persons in the vicinity dimly perceived that a domestic scene had occurred, in a flash, under their noses, on a platform of a railway station. Nellie was speedily aware that something very serious had happened, for the train took them off without Ruth speaking a syllable to Denry, though Denry raised his hat and was almost effusive.

The next afternoon Denry received by post a ring in a box. "I will not submit to insult," ran the brief letter.

"I only said 'Rothschild'! "Denry murmured to himself. "Can't a fellow say 'Rothschild'?"

But secretly he was proud of himself.

CHAPTER V

THE MERCANTILE MARINE

I

THE decisive scene, henceforward historic, occurred in the shanty known as "John's cabin"—John being the unacknowledged leader of the long-shore population under the tail of Llandudno pier. The cabin, festooned with cordage, was lighted by an oil-lamp of a primitive model, and round the orange case on which the lamp was balanced sat Denry, Cregeen, the owner of the lifeboat, and John himself (to give, as it were, a semi-official character to whatever was afoot).

"Well, here you are," said Denry, and handed to Cregeen a piece of paper.

"What's this, I'm asking ye?" said Cregeen, taking the paper in his large fingers and peering at it as though it had been a papyrus.

But he knew quite well what it was. It was a cheque for twenty-five pounds. What he did not know was that, with the ten pounds paid in cash earlier in the day, it represented a very large part indeed of such of Denry's savings as had survived his engagement to Ruth Earp. Cregeen took a pen as though it had been a match-end and wrote a receipt. Then, after finding a stamp in a pocket of his waistcoat under his jersey, he put it in his mouth and lost it there for a long time. Finally Denry got the receipt, certifying that he was the owner of the lifeboat formerly known as *Llandudno*, but momentarily without a name, together with all her gear and sails.

"Are ye going to live in her?" the rather curt John inquired.

"Not in her. On her," said Denry.

And he went out on to the sand and shingle, leaving John and Cregeen to complete the sale to Cregeen of the *Fleetwing*, a small cutter specially designed to take twelve persons forth for "a pleasant sail in the bay." If Cregeen had not had a fancy for the *Fleetwing* and a perfect lack of the money to buy her, Denry might never have been able to induce him to sell the lifeboat.

Under another portion of the pier Denry met a sailor with a long white beard, the aged Simeon, who had been one of the crew that rescued the *Hjalmar*, but whom his colleagues appeared to regard rather as an ornament than as a motive force.

"It's all right," said Denry.

And Simeon, in silence, nodded his head slowly several times.

"I shall give you thirty shilling for the week," said Denry.

And that venerable head oscillated again in the moon-lit gloom and rocked gradually to a stand-still.

Presently the head said, in shrill, slow tones:

"I've seen three o' them Norwegian chaps. Two of 'em can no more speak English than a babe unborn; no, nor understand what ye say to 'em, though I fair bawled in their ear-holes."

"So much the better," said Denry.

"I showed 'em that sovereign," said the bearded head, wagging again.

"Well," said Denry, "you won't forget. Six o'clock to-morrow morning."

"Ye'd better say five, the head suggested. "Quieter like."

"Five, then," Denry agreed.

And he departed to St Asaph's Road burdened with a tremendous thought.

The thought was:

"I've gone and done it this time!"

Now that the transaction was accomplished and could not be undone, he admitted to himself that he had never been more mad. He could scarcely comprehend what had led him to do that which he had done. But he obscurely imagined that his caprice for the possession of sea-going craft must somehow be the result of his singular adventure with the pantechnicon in the canal at Bursley. He was so preoccupied with material interests as to be capable of forgetting, for a quarter of an hour at a stretch, that in all essential respects his life was wrecked, and that he had nothing to hope for save hollow worldly success. He knew that Ruth would return the ring. He could almost see the postman holding the little cardboard cube which would contain the rendered ring. He had loved, and loved tragically. (That was how he put it—in his unspoken thoughts; but the truth was merely that he had loved something too expensive.) Now the dream was done. And a man of disillusion walked along the Parade towards St Asaph's Road among revellers, a man with a past, a man who had probed women, a man who had nothing to learn about the sex. And amid all the tragedy of his heart, and all his apprehensions concerning hollow, worldly success, little thoughts of absurd unimportance kept running about like clockwork mice in his head. Such as that it would be a bit of a bore to have to tell people at Bursley that his engagement, which truly had thrilled the town, was broken off. Humiliating, that! And, after all, Ruth was a glittering gem among women. Was there another girl in Bursley so smart, so effective, so truly ornate? Then he comforted himself with the reflection: "I'm certainly the only man that ever ended an engagement by just saying 'Rothschild!'" This was probably true. But it did not help him to sleep.

II

The next morning at 5.20 the youthful sun was shining on the choppy water of the Irish Sea, just off the Little Orme, to the west of Llandudno Bay. Oscillating on the uneasy waves was Denry's lifeboat, manned by the nodding bearded head, three ordinary British longshoremen, a Norwegian who could speak English of two syllables, and two other Norwegians who by a strange neglect of education could speak nothing but Norwegian.

Close under the headland, near a morsel of beach lay the remains of the *Hjalmar* in an attitude of repose. It was as if the *Hjalmar*, after a long struggle, had lain down like a cab-horse and said to the tempest: "Do what you like now!"

"Yes," the venerable head was piping. "Us can come out comfortable in twenty minutes, unless the tide be setting east strong. And, as for getting back, it'll be the same, other way round, if ye understand me."

There could be no question that Simeon had come out comfortable. But he was the coxswain. The rowers seemed to be perspiringly aware that the boat was vast and beamy.

"Shall we row up to it?" Simeon inquired, pointing to the wreck.

Then a pale face appeared above the gunwale, and an expiring, imploring voice said: "No. We'll go back." Whereupon the pale face vanished again.

Denry had never before been outside the bay. In the navigation of pantechnicons on the squall-swept basins of canals he might have been a great master, but he was unfitted for the open sea. At that moment he would have been almost ready to give the lifeboat and all that he owned for the privilege of returning to land by train. The inward journey was so long that Denry lost hope of ever touching his native island again. And then there was a bump. And he disembarked, with hope burning up again cheerfully in his bosom. And it was a quarter to six. By the first post, which arrived at half-past seven, there came a brown package. "The ring!" he thought, starting horribly. But the package was a cube of three inches, and would have held a hundred rings. He undid the cover, and saw on half a sheet of notepaper the words:—

"Thank you so much for the lovely time you gave me. I hope you will like this, NELLIE."

He was touched. If Ruth was hard, mercenary, costly, her young and ingenuous companion could at any rate be grateful and sympathetic. Yes, he was touched. He had imagined himself to be dead to all human affections, but it was not so. The package contained chocolate, and his nose at once perceived that it was chocolate impregnated with lemon—the surprising but agreeable compound accidentally invented by Nellie on the previous day at the pier buffet. The little thing must have spent a part of the previous afternoon in preparing it, and she must have put the package in the post at Crewe. Secretive and delightful little thing! After his recent experience beyond the bay he had imagined himself to be incapable of ever eating again, but it was not so. The lemon gave a peculiar astringent, appetising, *settling* quality to the chocolate. And he ate even with gusto. The result was that, instead of waiting for the nine o'clock boarding-house breakfast, he hurried energetically into the streets and called on a jobbing printer whom he had seen on the previous evening. As Ruth had said, "There is nothing like chocolate for sustaining you."

III

At ten o'clock two Norwegian sailors, who could only smile in answer to the questions which assailed them, were distributing the following handbill on the Parade:—

WRECK OF THE *HJALMAR*

HEROISM AT LLANDUDNO

Every hour, at 11, 12, 2, 3, 4, 5, and 6 o'oclock, [sic] THE IDENTICAL (guaranteed) LIFEBOAT which rescued the crew of the

HJALMAR

will leave the beach for the scene of the wreck Manned by Simeon Edwards, the oldest boatman in LLANDUDNO, and by members of the rescued crew, genuine Norwegians (guaranteed)
SIMEON EDWARDS, *Coxswain.*
Return Fare, with use of Cork Belt and Life-lines if desired, 2s. 6d. A UNIQUE OPPORTUNITY

A UNIQUE EXPERIENCE

P.S.—The bravery of the lifeboatmen has been the theme of the Press throughout the Principality and neighbouring counties.

E.D. MACHIN.

At eleven o'clock there was an eager crowd down on the beach where, with some planks and a piece of rock, Simeon had arranged an embarkation pier for the lifeboat. One man, in overalls, stood up to his knees in the water and escorted passengers up the planks, while Simeon's confidence-generating beard received them into the broad waist of the boat. The rowers wore sou'westers and were secured to the craft by life-lines, and these conveniences were also offered, with life-belts, to the intrepid excursionists. A paper was pinned in the stern: "Licensed to carry Fourteen." (Denry had just paid the fee.) But quite forty people were anxious to make the first voyage.

"No more," shrilled Simeon, solemnly. And the wader scrambled in and the boat slid away.

"Fares, please!" shrilled Simeon.

He collected one pound fifteen, and slowly buttoned it up in the right-hand pocket of his blue trousers.

"Now, my lads, with a will," he gave the order. And then, with deliberate method, he lighted his pipe. And the lifeboat shot away.

Close by the planks stood a young man in a negligent attitude, and with a look on his face as if to say: "Please do not imagine that I have the slightest interest in this affair." He stared consistently out to sea until the boat had disappeared round the Little Orme, and then he took a few turns on the sands, in and out amid the castles. His heart was beating in a most disconcerting manner. After a time he resumed his perusal of the sea. And the lifeboat reappeared and grew larger and larger, and finally arrived at the spot from which it had departed, only higher up the beach because the tide was rising. And Simeon debarked first, and there was a small blue and red model of a lifeboat in his hand, which he shook to a sound of coins.

"*For* the Lifeboat Fund! *For* the Lifeboat Fund!" he gravely intoned.

Every debarking passenger dropped a coin into the slit.

In five minutes the boat was refilled, and Simeon had put the value of fourteen more half-crowns into his pocket.

The lips of the young man on the beach moved, and he murmured:

"That makes over three pounds! Well, I'm dashed!"

At the hour appointed for dinner he went to St Asaph's Road, but could eat nothing. He could only keep repeating very softly to himself, "Well, I'm dashed!"

Throughout the afternoon the competition for places in the lifeboat grew keener and more dangerous. Denry's craft was by no means the sole craft engaged in carrying people to see the wreck. There were dozens of boats in the business, which had suddenly sprung up that morning, the sea being then fairly inoffensive for the first time since the height of the storm. But the other boats simply took what the lifeboat left. The guaranteed identity of the lifeboat, and of the Norsemen (who replied to questions in gibberish), and of Simeon himself; the sou'westers, the life-belts and the lines; even the collection for the Lifeboat Fund at the close of the voyage: all these matters resolved themselves into a fascination which Llandudno could not resist.

And in regard to the collection, a remarkable crisis arose. The model of a lifeboat became full, gorged to the slot. And the Local Secretary of the Fund had the key. The model was despatched to him by special messenger to open and to empty, and in the meantime Simeon used his sou'-wester as a collecting-box. This contretemps was impressive. At night Denry received twelve pounds odd at the hands of Simeon Edwards. He showered the odd in largesse on his heroic crew, who had also received many tips. By the evening post the fatal ring arrived from Ruth, as he anticipated. He was just about to throw it into the sea, when he thought better of the idea, and stuck it in his pocket. He tried still to feel that his life had been blighted by Ruth. But he could not. The twelve pounds, largely in silver, weighed so heavy in his pocket. He said to himself: "Of course this can't last!"

IV

Then came the day when he first heard some one saying discreetly behind him:

"That's the lifeboat chap!"

Or more briefly:

"That's him!"

Implying that in all Llandudno "him" could mean only one person.

And for a time he went about the streets self-consciously. However, that self-consciousness soon passed off, and he wore his fame as easily as he wore his collar.

338

The lifeboat trips to the *Hjalmar* became a feature of daily life in Llandudno. The pronunciation of the ship's name went through a troublous period. Some said the "j" ought to be pronounced to the exclusion of the "h," and others maintained the contrary. In the end the first two letters were both abandoned utterly, also the last—but nobody had ever paid any attention to the last. The facetious had a trick of calling the wreck *Inkerman*. This definite settlement of the pronunciation of the name was a sign that the pleasure-seekers of Llandudno had definitely fallen in love with the lifeboat-trip habit. Denry's timid fear that the phenomenon which put money into his pocket could not continue, was quite falsified. It continued violently. And Denry wished that the *Hjalmar* had been wrecked a month earlier. He calculated that the tardiness of the *Hjalmar* in wrecking itself had involved him in a loss of some four hundred pounds. If only the catastrophe had happened early in July, instead of early in August, and he had been there. Why, if forty *Hjalmars* had been wrecked, and their forty crews saved by forty different lifeboats, and Denry had bought all the lifeboats, he could have filled them all!

Still, the regularity of his receipts was extremely satisfactory and comforting. The thing had somehow the air of being a miracle; at any rate of being connected with magic. It seemed to him that nothing could have stopped the visitors to Llandudno from fighting for places in his lifeboat and paying handsomely for the privilege. They had begun the practice, and they looked as if they meant to go on with the practice eternally. He thought that the monotony of it would strike them unfavourably. But no! He thought that they would revolt against doing what every one had done. But no! Hundreds of persons arrived fresh from the railway station every day, and they all appeared to be drawn to that lifeboat as to a magnet. They all seemed to know instantly and instinctively that to be correct in Llandudno they must make at least one trip in Denry's lifeboat.

He was pocketing an income which far exceeded his most golden visions. And therefore naturally his first idea was to make that income larger and larger still. He commenced by putting up the price of the afternoon trips. There was a vast deal too much competition for seats in the afternoon. This competition led to quarrels, unseemly language, and deplorable loss of temper. It also led to loss of time. Denry was therefore benefiting humanity by charging three shillings after two o'clock. This simple and benign device equalised the competition throughout the day, and made Denry richer by seven or eight pounds a week.

But his fertility of invention did not stop there. One morning the earliest excursionists saw a sort of Robinson Crusoe marooned on the strip of beach near the wreck. All that heartless fate had left him appeared to be a machine on a tripod and a few black bags. And there was no shelter for him save a shallow cave. The poor fellow was quite respectably dressed. Simeon steered the boat round by the beach, which shelved down sharply, and as he did so the Robinson Crusoe hid his head in a cloth, as though ashamed, or as though he had gone mad and believed himself to be an ostrich. Then apparently he thought the better of it, and gazed boldly forth again. And the boat passed on its starboard side within a dozen feet of him and his machine. Then it put about and passed on the port side. And the same thing occurred on every trip. And the last trippers of the day left Robinson Crusoe on the strip of beach in his solitude.

The next morning a photographer's shop on the Parade pulled down its shutters and displayed posters all over the upper part of its windows. And the lower part of the windows held sixteen different large photographs of the lifeboat broad-side on. The likenesses of over a hundred visitors, many of them with sou'-westers, cork belts, and life-lines, could be clearly distinguished in these picturesque groups. A notice said:—

"Copies of any of these magnificent permanent holographs can be supplied, handsomely mounted, at a charge of two shillings each. Orders executed in rotation, and delivered by post if necessary. It is respectfully requested that cash be paid with order. Otherwise orders cannot be accepted."

Very few of those who had made the trip could resist the fascination of a photograph of themselves in a real lifeboat, manned by real heroes and real Norwegians on real waves, especially if they had worn the gear appropriate to lifeboats. The windows of the shop were beset throughout the day with crowds anxious to see who was in the lifeboat, and who had come out well, and who was a perfect fright. The orders on the first day amounted to over fifteen pounds, for not everybody was content with one photograph. The novelty was acute and enchanting, and it renewed itself each day. "Let's go down and look at the lifeboat photographs," people would say, when they were wondering what to do next. Some persons who had not "taken nicely" would perform a special trip in the lifeboat and would wear special clothes and compose special faces for the ordeal. The Mayor of Ashby-de-la-Zouch for that year ordered two hundred copies of a photograph which showed himself in the centre, for presentation as New Year's cards. On the mornings after very dull days or wet days, when photography had been impossible or unsatisfactory, Llandudno felt that something lacked. Here it may be mentioned that inclement weather (of which, for the rest, there was little) scarcely interfered with Denry's receipts. Imagine a lifeboat being deterred by rain or by a breath of wind! There were tarpaulins. When the tide was strong and adverse, male passengers were allowed to pull, without extra charge, though naturally they would give a trifle to this or that member of the professional crew.

Denry's arrangement with the photographer was so simple that a child could have grasped it. The photographer paid him sixpence on every photograph sold. This was Denry's only connection with the photographer. The sixpences totalled over a dozen pounds a week. Regardless of cost, Denry reprinted his article from the *Staffordshire Signal* descriptive of the night of the wreck, with a photograph of the lifeboat and its crew, and presented a copy to every client of his photographic department.

V

Llandudno was next titillated by the mysterious "Chocolate Remedy," which made its first appearance in a small boat that plied off Robinson Crusoe's strip of beach. Not infrequently passengers in the lifeboat were inconvenienced by displeasing and even distressing sensations, as Denry had once been inconvenienced. He felt deeply for them. The Chocolate Remedy was designed to alleviate the symptoms while captivating the palate. It was one of the most agreeable remedies that the wit of man ever invented. It tasted like chocolate and yet there was an astringent flavour of lemon in it—a flavour that flattered the stomach into a good opinion of itself, and seemed to say, "All's right with the world." The stuff was retailed in sixpenny packets, and you were advised to eat only a very little of it at a time, and not to masticate, but merely to permit melting. Then the Chocolate Remedy came to be sold on the lifeboat itself, and you were informed that if you "took" it before starting on the wave, no wave could disarrange you. And, indeed, many persons who followed this advice suffered no distress, and were proud accordingly, and duly informed the world. Then the Chocolate Remedy began to be sold everywhere. Young people bought it because they enjoyed it, and perfectly ignored the advice against over-indulgence and against mastication. The Chocolate Remedy penetrated like the refrain of a popular song to other seaside places. It was on sale from Morecambe to Barmouth, and at all the landing-stages of the steamers for the Isle of Man and Anglesey. Nothing surprised Denry so much as the vogue of the Chocolate Remedy. It was a serious anxiety to him, and he muddled both the manufacture and distribution of the remedy, from simple ignorance and inexperience. His chief difficulty at first had been to obtain small cakes of chocolate that were not stamped with the maker's name or mark. Chocolate manufacturers seemed to have a passion for imprinting their Quakerly names on every bit of stuff they sold. Having at length obtained a supply, he was silly enough to spend time in preparing the remedy himself in his bedroom! He might as well have tried to feed the British Army from his mother's kitchen. At length he went to a confectioner in Rhyl and a greengrocer in Llandudno, and by giving away half the secret to each, he contrived to keep the whole secret to himself. But even then he was manifestly unequal to the situation created by the demand for the Chocolate Remedy. It was a situation that needed the close attention of half a dozen men of business. It was quite different from the affair of the lifeboat.

One night a man who had been staying a day or two in the boarding-house in St Asaph's Road said to Denry:

"Look here, mister. I go straight to the point. What'll you take?"

And he explained what he meant. What would Denry take for the entire secret and rights of the Chocolate Remedy and the use of the name "Machin" ("without which none was genuine").

"What do you offer?" Denry asked.

"Well, I'll give you a hundred pounds down, and that's my last word."

Denry was staggered. A hundred pounds for simply nothing at all—for dipping bits of chocolate in lemon-juice!

He shook his head.

"I'll take two hundred," he replied.

And he got two hundred. It was probably the worst bargain that he ever made in his life. For the Chocolate Remedy continued obstinately in demand for ten years afterwards. But he was glad to be rid of the thing; it was spoiling his sleep and wearing him out.

He had other worries. The boatmen of Llandudno regarded him as an enemy of the human race. If they had not been nature's gentlemen they would have burned him alive at a stake. Cregeen, in particular, consistently referred to him in terms which could not have been more severe had Denry been the assassin of Cregeen's wife and seven children. In daring to make over a hundred pounds a week out of a ramshackle old lifeboat that Cregeen had sold to him for thirty-five pounds, Denry was outraging Cregeen's moral code. Cregeen had paid thirty-five pounds for the *Fleetwinz*, a craft immeasurably superior to Denry's nameless tub. And was Cregeen

340

making a hundred pounds a week out of it? Not a hundred shillings! Cregeen genuinely thought that he had a right to half Denry's profits. Old Simeon, too, seemed to think that *he* had a right to a large percentage of the same profits. And the Corporation, though it was notorious that excursionists visited the town purposely to voyage in the lifeboat, the Corporation made difficulties—about the embarking and disembarking, about the photographic strip of beach, about the crowds on the pavement outside the photograph shop. Denry learnt that he had committed the sin of not being a native of Llandudno. He was a stranger, and he was taking money out of the town. At times he wished he could have been born again. His friend and saviour was the Local Secretary of the Lifeboat Institution, who happened to be a Town Councillor. This worthy man, to whom Denry paid over a pound a day, was invaluable to him. Further, Denry was invited—nay commanded—to contribute to nearly every church, chapel, mission, and charity in Carnarvonshire, Flintshire, and other counties. His youthfulness was not accepted as an excuse. And as his gross profits could be calculated by any dunce who chose to stand on the beach for half a day, it was not easy for him to pretend that he was on the brink of starvation. He could only ward off attacks by stating with vague, convinced sadness that his expenses were much greater than any one could imagine.

In September, when the moon was red and full, and the sea glassy, he announced a series of nocturnal "Rocket Fêtes." The lifeboat, hung with Chinese lanterns, put out in the evening (charge five shillings) and, followed by half the harbour's fleet of rowing-boats and cutters, proceeded to the neighbourhood of the strip of beach, where a rocket apparatus had been installed by the help of the Lifeboat Secretary. The mortar was trained; there was a flash, a whizz, a line of fire, and a rope fell out of the sky across the lifeboat. The effect was thrilling and roused cheers. Never did the Lifeboat Institution receive such an advertisement as Denry gave it—gratis.

After the rocketing Denry stood alone on the slopes of the Little Orme and watched the lanterns floating home over the water, and heard the lusty mirth of his clients in the still air. It was an emotional experience for him.

"By Jove!" he said, "I've wakened this town up!"

VI

One morning, in the very last sad days of the dying season, when his receipts had dropped to the miserable figure of about fifty pounds a week, Denry had a great and pleasing surprise. He met Nellie on the Parade. It was a fact that the recognition of that innocent, childlike blushing face gave him joy. Nellie was with her father, Councillor Cotterill, and her mother. The Councillor was a speculative builder, who was erecting several streets of British homes in the new quarter above the new municipal park at Bursley. Denry had already encountered him once or twice in the way of business. He was a big and portly man of forty-five, with a thin face and a consciousness of prosperity. At one moment you would think him a jolly, bluff fellow, and at the next you would be disconcerted by a note of cunning or of harshness. Mrs Councillor Cotterill was one of these women who fail to live up to the ever-increasing height of their husbands. Afflicted with an eternal stage-fright, she never opened her close-pressed lips in society, though a few people knew that she could talk as fast and as effectively as any one. Difficult to set in motion, her vocal machinery was equally difficult to stop. She generally wore a low bonnet and a mantle. The Cotterills had been spending a fortnight in the Isle of Man, and they had come direct from Douglas to Llandudno by steamer, where they meant to pass two or three days. They were staying at Craig-y-don, at the eastern end of the Parade.

"Well, young man!" said Councillor Cotterill.

And he kept on young-manning Denry with an easy patronage which Denry could scarcely approve of. "I bet I've made more money this summer than you have with all your jerrying!" said Denry silently to the Councillor's back while the Cotterill family were inspecting the historic lifeboat on the beach. Councillor Cotterill said frankly that one reason for their calling at Llandudno was his desire to see this singular lifeboat, about which there had really been a very great deal of talk in the Five Towns. The admission comforted Denry. Then the Councillor recommended his young-manning.

"Look here," said Denry, carelessly, "you must come and dine with me one night, all of you—will you?"

Nobody who has not passed at least twenty years in a district where people dine at one o'clock, and dining after dark is regarded as a wild idiosyncrasy of earls, can appreciate the effect of this speech.

The Councillor, when he had recovered himself, said that they would be pleased to dine with him; Mrs Cotterill's tight lips were seen to move, but not heard; and Nellie glowed.

"Yes," said Denry, "come and dine with me at the Majestic."

The name of the Majestic put an end to the young-manning. It was the new hotel by the pier, and advertised itself as the most luxurious hotel in the Principality. Which was bold of it, having regard to the magnificence of caravanserais at Cardiff. It had two hundred bedrooms, and waiters who talked English imperfectly; and its prices were supposed to be fantastic.

After all, the most startled and frightened person of the four was perhaps Denry. He had never given a dinner to anybody. He had never even dined at night. He had never been inside the Majestic. He had never had the courage to go inside the Majestic. He had no notion of the mysterious preliminaries to the offering of a dinner in a public place.

But the next morning he contracted to give away the lifeboat to a syndicate of boatmen, headed by John their leader, for thirty-five pounds. And he swore to himself that he would do that dinner properly, even if it cost him the whole price of the boat. Then he met Mrs Cotterill coming out of a shop. Mrs Cotterill, owing to a strange hazard of fate, began talking at once. And Denry, as an old shorthand writer, instinctively calculated that not Thomas Allen Reed himself could have taken Mrs Cotterill down verbatim. Her face tried to express pain, but pleasure shone out of it. For she found herself in an exciting contretemps which she could understand.

"Oh, Mr Machin," she said, "what *do* you think's happened? I don't know how to tell you, I'm sure. Here you've arranged for that dinner to-morrow and it's all settled, and now Miss Earp telegraphs to our Nellie to say she's coming to-morrow for a day or two with us. You know Ruth and Nellie are *such* friends. It's like as if what must be, isn't it? I don't know what to do, I do declare. What *ever* will Ruth say at us leaving her all alone the first night she comes? I really do think she might have———"

"You must bring her along with you," said Denry.

"But won't you—shan't you—won't she—won't it———"

"Not at all," said Denry. "Speaking for myself, I shall be delighted."

"Well, I'm sure you're very sensible," said Mrs Cotterill. "I was but saying to Mr Cotterill over breakfast—I said to him———"

"I shall ask Councillor Rhys-Jones to meet you," said Denry. "He's one of the principal members of the Town Council here; Local Secretary of the Lifeboat Institution. Great friend of mine."

"Oh!" exclaimed Mrs Cotterill, "it'll be quite an affair.

It was.

Denry found to his relief that the only difficult part of arranging a dinner at the Majestic was the steeling of yourself to enter the gorgeous portals of the hotel. After that, and after murmuring that you wished to fix up a little snack, you had nothing to do but listen to suggestions, each surpassing the rest in splendour, and say "Yes." Similarly with the greeting of a young woman who was once to you the jewel of the world. You simply said, "Good-afternoon, how are you?" And she said the same. And you shook hands. And there you were, still alive!

The one defect of the dinner was that the men were not in evening dress. (Denry registered a new rule of life: Never travel without your evening dress, because you never know what may turn up.) The girls were radiantly white. And after all there is nothing like white. Mrs Cotterill was in black silk and silence. And after all there is nothing like black silk. There was champagne. There were ices. Nellie, not being permitted champagne, took her revenge in ice. Denry had found an opportunity to relate to her the history of the Chocolate Remedy. She said, "How wonderful you are!" And he said it was she who was wonderful. Denry gave no information about the Chocolate Remedy to her father. Neither did she. As for Ruth, indubitably she was responsible for the social success of the dinner. She seemed to have the habit of these affairs. She it was who loosed tongues. Nevertheless, Denry saw her now with different eyes, and it appeared incredible to him that he had once mistaken her for the jewel of the world.

At the end of the dinner Councillor Rhys-Jones produced a sensation by rising to propose the health of their host. He referred to the superb heroism of England's lifeboatmen, and in the name of the Institution thanked Denry for the fifty-three pounds which Denry's public had contributed to the funds. He said it was a noble contribution and that Denry was a philanthropist. And he called on Councillor Cotterill to second the toast. Which Councillor Cotterill did, in good set terms, the result of long habit. And Denry stammered that he was much obliged, and that really it was nothing.

But when the toasting was finished, Councillor Cotterill lapsed somewhat into a patronising irony, as if he were jealous of a youthful success. And he did not stop at "young man." He addressed Denry grandiosely as "my boy."

"This lifeboat—it was just an idea, my boy, just an idea," he said.

"Yes," said Denry, "but I thought of it."

"The question is," said the Councillor, "can you think of any more ideas as good?"

"Well," said Denry, "can *you*?"

With reluctance they left the luxury of the private dining-room, and Denry surreptitiously paid the bill with a pile of sovereigns, and Councillor Rhys-Jones parted from them with lively grief. The other five walked in a row along the Parade in the moonlight. And when they arrived in front of Craig-y-don, and the Cotterills were entering, Ruth, who loitered behind, said to Denry in a liquid voice:

"I don't feel a bit like going to sleep. I suppose you wouldn't care for a stroll?"

"Well———"

"I daresay you're very tired," she said.

"No," he replied, "it's this moonlight I'm afraid of."

And their eyes met under the door-lamp, and Ruth wished him pleasant dreams and vanished. It was exceedingly subtle.

VII

The next afternoon the Cotterills and Ruth Earp went home, and Denry with them. Llandudno was just settling into its winter sleep, and Denry's rather complex affairs had all been put in order. Though the others showed a certain lassitude, he himself was hilarious. Among his insignificant luggage was a new hat-box, which proved to be the origin of much gaiety.

"Just take this, will you?" he said to a porter on the platform at Llandudno Station, and held out the new hat-box with an air of calm. The porter innocently took it, and then, as the hat-box nearly jerked his arm out of the socket, gave vent to his astonishment after the manner of porters.

"By gum, mister!" said he, "that's heavy!"

It, in fact, weighed nearly two stone.

"Yes," said Denry, "it's full of sovereigns, of course."

And everybody laughed.

At Crewe, where they had to change, and again at Knype and at Bursley, he produced astonishment in porters by concealing the effort with which he handed them the hat-box, as though its weight was ten ounces. And each time he made the same witticism about sovereigns.

"What *have* you got in that hat-box?" Ruth asked.

"Don't I tell you?" said Denry, laughing. "Sovereigns!"

Lastly, he performed the same trick on his mother. Mrs Machin was working, as usual, in the cottage in Brougham Street. Perhaps the notion of going to Llandudno for a change had not occurred to her. In any case, her presence had been necessary in Bursley, for she had frequently collected Denry's rents for him, and collected them very well. Denry was glad to see her again, and she was glad to see him, but they concealed their feelings as much as possible. When he basely handed her the hat-box she dropped it, and roundly informed him that she was not going to have any of his pranks.

After tea, whose savouriness he enjoyed quite as much as his own state dinner, he gave her a key and asked her to open the hat-box, which he had placed on a chair.

"What is there in it?"

"A lot of jolly fine pebbles that I've been collecting on the beach," he said.

She got the hat-box on to her knee, and unlocked it, and came to a thick cloth, which she partly withdrew, and then there was a scream from Mrs Machin, and the hat-box rolled with a terrific crash to the tiled floor, and she was ankle-deep in sovereigns. She could see sovereigns running about all over the parlour. Gradually even the most active sovereigns decided to lie down and be quiet, and a great silence ensued. Denry's heart was beating.

Mrs Machin merely shook her head. Not often did her son deprive her of words, but this theatrical culmination of his home-coming really did leave her speechless.

Late that night rows of piles of sovereigns decorated the oval table in the parlour.

"A thousand and eleven," said Denry, at length, beneath the lamp. "There's fifteen missing yet. We'll look for 'em to-morrow."

For several days afterwards Mrs Machin was still picking up sovereigns. Two had even gone outside the parlour, and down the two steps into the backyard, and finding themselves unable to get back, had remained there.

And all the town knew that the unique Denry had thought of the idea of returning home to his mother with a hat-box crammed with sovereigns.

This was Denry's "latest," and it employed the conversation of the borough for I don't know how long.

I

The fact that Denry Machin decided not to drive behind his mule to Sneyd Hall showed in itself that the enterprise of interviewing the Countess of Chell was not quite the simple daily trifling matter that he strove to pretend it was.

The mule was a part of his more recent splendour. It was aged seven, and it had cost Denry ten pounds. He had bought it off a farmer whose wife "stood" St Luke's Market. His excuse was that he needed help in getting about the Five Towns in pursuit of cottage rents, for his business of a rent-collector had grown. But for this purpose a bicycle would have served equally well, and would not have cost a shilling a day to feed, as the mule did, nor have shied at policemen, as the mule nearly always did. Denry had bought the mule simply because he had been struck all of a sudden with the idea of buying the mule. Some time previously Jos Curtenty (the Deputy-Mayor, who became Mayor of Bursley on the Earl of Chell being called away to govern an Australian colony) had made an enormous sensation by buying a flock of geese and driving them home himself. Denry did not like this. He was indeed jealous, if a large mind can be jealous. Jos Curtenty was old enough to be his grandfather, and had been a recognised "card" and "character" since before Denry's birth. But Denry, though so young, had made immense progress as a card, and had, perhaps justifiably, come to consider himself as the premier card, the very ace, of the town. He felt that some reply was needed to Curtenty's geese, and the mule was his reply. It served excellently. People were soon asking each other whether they had heard that Denry Machin's "latest" was to buy a mule. He obtained a little old victoria for another ten pounds, and a good set of harness for three guineas. The carriage was low, which enabled him, as he said, to nip in and out much more easily than in and out of a trap. In his business you did almost nothing but nip in and out. On the front seat he caused to be fitted a narrow box of japanned tin, with a formidable lock and slits on the top. This box was understood to receive the rents, as he collected them. It was always guarded on journeys by a cross between a mastiff and something unknown, whose growl would have terrorised a lion-tamer. Denry himself was afraid of Rajah, the dog, but he would not admit it. Rajah slept in the stable behind Mrs Machin's cottage, for which Denry paid a shilling a week. In the stable there was precisely room for Rajah, the mule and the carriage, and when Denry entered to groom or to harness, something had to go out.

The equipage quickly grew into a familiar sight in the streets of the district. Denry said that it was funny without being vulgar. Certainly it amounted to a continual advertisement for him; an infinitely more effective advertisement than, for instance, a sandwichman at eighteen-pence a day, and costing no more, even with the licence and the shoeing. Moreover, a sandwichman has this inferiority to a turnout: when you have done with him you cannot put him up to auction and sell him. Further, there are no sandwichmen in the Five Towns; in that democratic and independent neighbourhood nobody would deign to be a sandwichman.

The mulish vehicular display does not end the tale of Denry's splendour. He had an office in St Luke's Square, and in the office was an office-boy, small but genuine, and a real copying-press, and outside it was the little square signboard which in the days of his simplicity used to be screwed on to his mother's door. His mother's steely firmness of character had driven him into the extravagance of an office. Even after he had made over a thousand pounds out of the Llandudno lifeboat in less than three months, she would not listen to a proposal for going into a slightly larger house, of which one room might serve as an office. Nor would she abandon her own labours as a sempstress. She said that since her marriage she had always lived in that cottage and had always worked, and that she meant to die there, working: and that Denry could do what he chose. He was a bold youth, but not bold enough to dream of quitting his mother; besides, his share of household expenses in the cottage was only ten shillings a week. So he rented the office; and he hired an office-boy, partly to convey to his mother that he *should* do what he chose, and partly for his own private amusement.

He was thus, at an age when fellows without imagination are fraying their cuffs for the enrichment of their elders and glad if they can afford a cigar once a month, in possession of a business, business premises, a clerical staff, and a private carriage drawn by an animal unique in the Five Towns. He was living on less than his income; and in the course of about two years, to a small extent by economies and to a large extent by injudicious but happy investments, he had doubled the Llandudno thousand and won the deference of the manager of the bank at the top of St Luke's Square—one of the most unsentimental men that ever wrote "refer to drawer" on a cheque.

And yet Denry was not satisfied. He had a secret woe, due to the facts that he was gradually ceasing to be a card, and that he was not multiplying his capital by two every six months. He did not understand the money market, nor the stock market, nor even the financial article in the *Signal*; but he regarded himself as a financial genius, and deemed that as a financial genius he was vegetating. And as for setting the town on fire, or painting it scarlet, he seemed to have lost the trick of that.

II

And then one day the populace saw on his office door, beneath his name-board, another sign:

FIVE TOWNS UNIVERSAL THRIFT CLUB. *Secretary and Manager*— E.H. MACHIN.

An idea had visited him.

Many tradesmen formed slate-clubs—goose-clubs, turkey-clubs, whisky-clubs—in the autumn, for Christmas. Their humble customers paid so much a week to the tradesmen, who charged them nothing for keeping it, and at the end of the agreed period they took out the total sum in goods—dead or alive; eatable, drinkable, or wearable. Denry conceived a universal slate-club. He meant it to embrace each of the Five Towns. He saw forty thousand industrial families paying weekly instalments into his slate-club. He saw his slate-club entering into contracts with all the principal tradesmen of the entire district, so that the members of the slate-club could shop with slate-club tickets practically where they chose. He saw his slate-club so powerful that no tradesman could afford not to be in relations with it. He had induced all Llandudno to perform the same act daily for nearly a whole season, and he now wished to induce all the vast Five Towns to perform the same act to his profit for all eternity.

And he would be a philanthropist into the bargain. He would encourage thrift in the working-man and the working-man's wife. He would guard the working-man's money for him; and to save trouble to the working-man he would call at the working-man's door for the working-man's money. Further, as a special inducement and to prove superior advantages to ordinary slate-clubs, he would allow the working man to spend his full nominal subscription to the club as soon as he had actually paid only half of it. Thus, after paying ten shillings to Denry, the working-man could spend a pound in Denry's chosen shops, and Denry would settle with the shops at once, while collecting the balance weekly at the working-man's door. But this privilege of anticipation was to be forfeited or postponed if the working-man's earlier payments were irregular.

And Denry would bestow all these wondrous benefits on the working-man without any charge whatever. Every penny that members paid in, members would draw out. The affair was enormously philanthropic.

Denry's modest remuneration was to come from the shopkeepers upon whom his scheme would shower new custom. They were to allow him at least twopence in the shilling discount on all transactions, which would be more than 16 per cent. on his capital; and he would turn over his capital three times a year. He calculated that out of 50 per cent. per annum he would be able to cover working expenses and a little over.

Of course, he had to persuade the shopkeepers. He drove his mule to Hanbridge and began with Bostocks, the largest but not the most distinguished drapery house in the Five Towns. He succeeded in convincing them on every point except that of his own financial stability. Bostocks indicated their opinion that he looked far too much like a boy to be financially stable. His reply was to offer to deposit fifty pounds with them before starting business, and to renew the sum in advance as quickly as the members of his club should exhaust it. Cheques talk. He departed with Bostocks' name at the head of his list, and he used them as a clinching argument with other shops. But the prejudice against his youth was strong and general. "Yes," tradesmen would answer, "what you say is all right, but you are so young." As if to insinuate that a man must be either a rascal or a fool until he is thirty, just as he must be either a fool or a physician after he is forty. Nevertheless, he had soon compiled a list of several score shops.

His mother said:

"Why don't you grow a beard? Here you spend money on razors, strops, soaps and brushes, besides a quarter of an hour of your time every day, and cutting yourself—all to keep yourself from having something that would be the greatest help to you in business! With a beard you'd look at least thirty-one. Your father had a splendid beard, and so could you if you chose."

This was high wisdom. But he would not listen to it. The truth is, he was getting somewhat dandiacal.

At length his scheme lacked naught but what Denry called a "right-down good starting shove." In a word, a fine advertisement to fire it off. Now, he could have had the whole of the first page of the *Signal* (at that period) for five-and-twenty pounds. But he had been so accustomed to free advertisements of one sort or another that the notion of paying for one was loathsome to him. Then it was that he thought of the Countess of Chell, who happened to be staying at Knype. If he could obtain that great aristocrat, that ex-Mayoress, that lovely witch, that benefactor of the district, to honour his Thrift Club as patroness, success was certain. Everybody in the Five Towns sneered at the Countess and called her a busybody; she was even dubbed "Interfering Iris" (Iris being one of her eleven Christian names); the Five Towns was fiercely democratic—in theory. In practice the Countess was worshipped; her smile was worth at least five pounds, and her invitation to tea was priceless. She could not have been more sincerely adulated in the United States, the home of social equality.

Denry said to himself:

"And why *shouldn't* I get her name as patroness? I will have her name as patroness."

Hence the expedition to Sneyd Hall, one of the ancestral homes of the Earls of Chell.

III

He had been to Sneyd Hall before many times—like the majority of the inhabitants of the Five Towns—for, by the generosity of its owner, Sneyd Park was always open to the public. To picnic in Sneyd Park was one of the chief distractions of the Five Towns on Thursday and Saturday afternoons. But he had never entered the private gardens. In the midst of the private gardens stood the Hall, shut off by immense iron palisades, like a lion in a cage at the Zoo. On the autumn afternoon of his Historic visit, Denry passed with qualms through the double gates of the palisade, and began to crunch the gravel of the broad drive that led in a straight line to the overwhelming Palladian façade of the Hall.

Yes, he was decidedly glad that he had not brought his mule. As he approached nearer and nearer to the Countess's front-door his arguments in favour of the visit grew more and more ridiculous. Useless to remind himself that he had once danced with the Countess at the municipal ball, and amused her to the giggling point, and restored her lost fan to her. Useless to remind himself that he was a quite exceptional young man, with a quite exceptional renown, and the equal of any man or woman on earth. Useless to remind himself that the Countess was notorious for her affability and also for her efforts to encourage the true welfare of the Five Towns. The visit was grotesque.

He ought to have written. He ought, at any rate, to have announced his visit by a note. Yet only an hour earlier he had been arguing that he could most easily capture the Countess by storm, with no warning or preparations of any kind.

Then, from a lateral path, a closed carriage and pair drove rapidly up to the Hall, and a footman bounced off the hammercloth. Denry could not see through the carriage, but under it he could distinguish the skirts of some one who got put of it. Evidently the Countess was just returning from a drive. He quickened his pace, for at heart he was an audacious boy.

"She can't eat me," he said.

This assertion was absolutely irrefutable, and yet there remained in his bold heart an irrational fear that after all she *could* eat him. Such is the extraordinary influence of a Palladian façade!

After what seemed several hours of torture entirely novel in his experience, he skirted the back of the carriage and mounted the steps to the portal. And, although the coachman was innocuous, being apparently carved in stone, Denry would have given a ten-pound note to find himself suddenly in his club or even in church. The masonry of the Hall rose up above him like a precipice. He was searching for the bell-knob in the face of the precipice when a lady suddenly appeared at the doors. At first he thought it was the Countess, and that heart of his began to slip down the inside of his legs. But it was not the Countess.

"Well?" demanded the lady. She was dressed in black.

"Can I see the Countess?" he inquired.

The lady stared at him. He handed her his professional card which lay waiting all ready in his waistcoat pocket.

"I will ask my lady," said the lady in black.

Denry perceived from her accent that she was not English.

She disappeared through a swinging door; and then Denry most clearly heard the Countess's own authentic voice saying in a pettish, disgusted tone:

"Oh! Bother!"

And he was chilled. He seriously wished that he had never thought of starting his confounded Universal Thrift Club.

After some time the carriage suddenly drove off, presumably to the stables. As he was now within the hollow of the porch, a sort of cave at the foot of the precipice, he could not see along the length of the façade. Nobody came to him. The lady who had promised to ask my lady whether the latter could see him did not return. He reflected that she had not promised to return; she had merely promised to ask a question. As the minutes passed he grew careless, or grew bolder, gradually dropping his correct attitude of a man-about-town paying an afternoon call, and peered through the glass of the doors that divided him from the Countess. He could distinguish nothing that had life. One of his preliminary tremors had been caused by a fanciful vision of multitudinous footmen, through a double line of whom he would be compelled to walk in order to reach the Countess.

But there was not even one footman. This complete absence of indoor footmen seemed to him remiss, not in accordance with centuries of tradition concerning life at Sneyd.

Then he caught sight, through the doors, of the back of Jock, the Countess's carriage footman and the son of his mother's old friend. Jock was standing motionless at a half-open door to the right of the space between Denry's double doors and the next pair of double doors. Denry tried to attract his attention by singular movements and strange noises of the mouth. But Jock, like his partner the coachman, appeared to be carven in stone. Denry decided that he would go in and have speech with Jock. They were on Christian-name terms, or had been a few years ago. He unobtrusively pushed at the doors, and at the very same moment Jock, with a start—as though released from some spell—vanished away from the door to the right.

Denry was now within.

"Jock!" He gave a whispering cry, rather conspiratorial in tone. And as Jock offered no response, he hurried after Jock through the door to the right. This door led to a large apartment which struck Denry as being an idealisation of a first-class waiting-room at a highly important terminal station. In a wall to the left was a small door, half open. Jock must have gone through that door. Denry hesitated—he had not properly been invited into the Hall. But in hesitating he was wrong; he ought to have followed his prey without qualms. When he had conquered qualms and reached the further door, his eyes were met, to their amazement, by an immense perspective of great chambers. Denry had once seen a Pullman car, which had halted at Knype Station with a French actress on board. What he saw now presented itself to him as a train of Pullman cars, one opening into the other, constructed for giants. Each car was about as large as the large hall in Bursley Town Hall, and, like that auditorium, had a ceiling painted to represent blue sky, milk-white clouds, and birds. But in the corners were groups of naked Cupids, swimming joyously on the ceiling; in Bursley Town Hall there were no naked Cupids. He understood now that he had been quite wrong in his estimate of the room by which he had come into this Versailles. Instead of being large it was tiny, and instead of being luxurious it was merely furnished with miscellaneous odds and ends left over from far more important furnishings. It was indeed naught but a nondescript box of a hole insignificantly wedged between the state apartments and the outer lobby.

For an instant he forgot that he was in pursuit of Jock. Jock was perfectly invisible and inaudible. He must, however, have gone down the vista of the great chambers, and therefore Denry went down the vista of the great chambers after him, curiously expecting to have a glimpse of his long salmon-tinted coat or his cockaded hat popping up out of some corner. He reached the other end of the vista, having traversed three enormous chambers, of which the middle one was the most enormous and the most gorgeous. There were high windows everywhere to his right, and to his left, in every chamber, double doors with gilt handles of a peculiar shape. Windows and doors, with equal splendour, were draped in hangings of brocade. Through the windows he had glimpses of the gardens in their autumnal colours, but no glimpse of a gardener. Then a carriage flew past the windows at the end of the suite, and he had a very clear though a transient view of two menials on the box-seat; one of those menials he knew must be Jock. Hence Jock must have escaped from the state suite by one of the numerous doors.

Denry tried one door after another, and they were all fastened firmly on the outside. The gilded handles would turn, but the lofty and ornate portals would not yield to pressure. Mystified and startled, he went back to the place from which he had begun his explorations, and was even more seriously startled, and more deeply mystified to find nothing but a blank wall where he had entered. Obviously he could not have penetrated through a solid wall. A careful perusal of the wall showed him that there was indeed a door in it, but that the door was artfully disguised by painting and other devices so as to look like part of the wall. He had never seen such a phenomenon before. A very small glass knob was the door's sole fitting. Denry turned this crystal, but with no useful result. In the brief space of time since his entrance, that door, and the door by which Jock had gone, had been secured by unseen hands. Denry imagined sinister persons bolting all the multitudinous doors, and inimical eyes staring at him through many keyholes. He imagined himself to be the victim of some fearful and incomprehensible conspiracy.

Why, in the sacred name of common-sense, should he have been imprisoned in the state suite? The only answer to the conundrum was that nobody was aware of his quite unauthorised presence in the state suite. But then why should the state suite be so suddenly locked up, since the Countess had just come in from a drive? It then occurred to him that, instead of just coming in, the Countess had been just leaving. The carriage must have driven round from some humbler part of the Hall, with the lady in black in it, and the lady in black— perhaps a lady's-maid—alone had stepped out from it. The Countess had been waiting for the carriage in the porch, and had fled to avoid being forced to meet the unfortunate Denry. (Humiliating thought!) The carriage had then taken her up at a side door. And now she was gone. Possibly she had left Sneyd Hall not to return for months, and that was why the doors had been locked. Perhaps everybody had departed from the Hall save one aged and deaf retainer—he knew, from historical novels which he had glanced at in his youth, that in every Hall that respected itself an aged and deaf retainer was invariably left solitary during the absences of the noble owner. He knocked on the small disguised door. His unique purpose in knocking was naturally to make a noise, but something prevented him from making a noise. He felt that he must knock decently, discreetly; he felt that he must not outrage the conventions.

No result to this polite summoning.

He attacked other doors; he attacked every door he could put his hands on; and gradually he lost his respect for decency and the conventions proper to Halls, knocking loudly and more loudly. He banged. Nothing but sheer solidity stopped his sturdy hands from going through the panels. He so far forgot himself as to shake the doors with all his strength furiously.

And finally he shouted: "Hi there! Hi! Can't you hear?"

Apparently the aged and deaf retainer could not hear. Apparently he was the deafest retainer that a peeress of the realm ever left in charge of a princely pile.

"Well, that's a nice thing!" Denry exclaimed, and he noticed that he was hot and angry. He took a certain pleasure in being angry. He considered that he had a right to be angry.

At this point he began to work himself up into the state of "not caring," into the state of despising Sneyd Hall, and everything for which it stood. As for permitting himself to be impressed or intimidated by the lonely magnificence of his environment, he laughed at the idea; or, more accurately, he snorted at it. Scornfully he tramped up and down those immense interiors, doing the caged lion, and cogitating in quest of the right dramatic, effective act to perform in the singular crisis. Unhappily, the carpets were very thick, so that though he could tramp, he could not stamp; and he desired to stamp. But in the connecting doorways there were expanses of bare, highly-polished oak floor, and here he did stamp.

The rooms were not furnished after the manner of ordinary rooms. There was no round or square table in the midst of each, with a checked cloth on it, and a plant in the centre. Nor in front of each window was there a small table with a large Bible thereupon. The middle parts of the rooms were empty, save for a group of statuary in the largest room. Great arm-chairs and double-ended sofas were ranged about in straight lines, and among these, here and there, were smaller chairs gilded from head to foot. Round the walls were placed long narrow tables with tops like glass-cases, and in the cases were all sorts of strange matters— such as coins, fans, daggers, snuff-boxes. In various corners white statues stood awaiting the day of doom without a rag to protect them from the winds of destiny. The walls were panelled in tremendous panels, and in each panel was a formidable dark oil-painting. The mantelpieces were so preposterously high that not even a giant could have sat at the fireplace and put his feet on them. And if they had held clocks, as mantelpieces do, a telescope would have been necessary to discern the hour. Above each mantelpiece, instead of a looking-glass, was a vast picture. The chandeliers were overpowering in glitter and in dimensions.

Near to a sofa Denry saw a pile of yellow linen things. He picked up the topmost article, and it assumed the form of a chair. Yes, these articles were furniture-covers. The Hall, then, was to be shut up. He argued from the furniture-covers that somebody must enter sooner or later to put the covers on the furniture.

Then he did a few more furlongs up and down the vista, and sat down at the far end, under a window. Anyhow, there were always the windows.

High though they were from the floor, he could easily open one, spring out, and slip unostentatiously away. But he thought he would wait until dusk fell. Prudence is seldom misplaced. The windows, however, held a disappointment for him. A mere bar, padlocked, prevented each one of them from being opened; it was a simple device. He would be under the necessity of breaking a plate-glass pane. For this enterprise he thought he would wait until black night. He sat down again. Then he made a fresh and noisy assault on all the doors. No result. He sat down a third time, and gazed info the gardens where the shadows were creeping darkly. Not a soul in the gardens. Then he felt a draught on the crown of his head, and looking aloft he saw that the summit of the window had a transverse glazed flap, for ventilation, and that this flap had been left open. If he could have climbed up, he might have fallen out on the other side into the gardens and liberty. But the summit of the window was at least sixteen feet from the floor. Night descended.

IV

At a vague hour in the evening a stout woman dressed in black, with a black apron, a neat violet cap on her head, and a small lamp in her podgy hand, unlocked one of the doors giving entry to the state rooms. She was on her nightly round of inspection. The autumn moon, nearly at full, had risen and was shining into the great windows. And in front of the furthest window she perceived in the radiance of the moonshine a pyramidal group, somewhat in the style of a family of acrobats, dangerously arranged on the stage of a music-hall. The base of the pyramid comprised two settees; upon these were several arm-chairs laid flat, and on the arm-chairs two tables covered with cushions and rugs; lastly, in the way of inanimate nature, two gilt chairs. On the gilt chairs was something that unmistakably moved, and was fumbling with the top of the window. Being a stout woman with a tranquil and sagacious mind, her first act was not to drop the lamp. She courageously clung to the lamp.

"Who's there? said a voice from the apex of the pyramid.

Then a subsidence began, followed by a crash and a multitudinous splintering of glass. The living form dropped on to one of the settees, rebounding like a football from its powerful springs. There was a hole as big as a coffin in the window. The living form collected itself, and then jumped wildly through that hole into the gardens.

Denry ran. The moment had not struck him as a moment propitious for explanation. In a flash he had seen the ridiculousness of endeavouring to convince a stout lady in black that he was a gentleman paying a call on the Countess. He simply scrambled to his legs and ran. He ran aimlessly in the darkness and sprawled over a hedge, after crossing various flower-beds. Then he saw the sheen of the moon on Sneyd Lake, and he could take his bearings. In winter all the Five Towns skate on Sneyd Lake if the ice will bear, and the geography of it was quite familiar to Denry. He skirted its east bank, plunged into Great Shendon Wood, and emerged near Great Shendon Station, on the line from Stafford to Knype. He inquired for the next train in the tones of innocency, and in half an hour was passing through Sneyd Station itself. In another fifty minutes he was at home. The clock showed ten-fifteen. His mother's cottage seemed amazingly small. He said that he had been detained in Hanbridge on business, that he had had neither tea nor supper, and that he was hungry. Next morning he could scarcely be sure that his visit to Sneyd Hall was not a dream. In any event, it had been a complete failure.

V

It was on this untriumphant morning that one of the tenants under his control, calling at the cottage to pay some rent overdue, asked him when the Universal Thrift Club was going to commence its operations. He had talked of the enterprise to all his tenants, for it was precisely with his tenants that he hoped to make a beginning. He had there a *clientèle* ready to his hand, and as he was intimately acquainted with the circumstances of each, he could judge between those who would be reliable and those to whom he would be obliged to refuse membership. The tenants, conclaving together of an evening on doorsteps, had come to the conclusion that the Universal Thrift Club was the very contrivance which they had lacked for years. They saw in it a cure for all their economic ills, and the gate to Paradise. The dame who put the question to him on the morning after his defeat wanted to be the possessor of carpets, a new teapot, a silver brooch, and a cookery book; and she was evidently depending upon Denry. On consideration he saw no reason why the Universal Thrift Club should not be allowed to start itself by the impetus of its own intrinsic excellence. The dame was inscribed for three shares, paid eighteen-pence entrance fee, undertook to pay three shillings a week, and received a document entitling her to spend £3, 18s. in sixty-five shops as soon as she had paid £1, 19s. to Denry. It was a marvellous scheme. The rumour of it spread; before dinner Denry had visits from other aspirants to membership, and he had posted a cheque to Bostocks', but more from ostentation than necessity; for no member could possibly go into Bostocks' with his coupons until at least two months had elapsed.

But immediately after dinner, when the posters of the early edition of the *Signal* waved in the streets, he had material for other thought. He saw a poster as he was walking across to his office. The awful legend ran:

ASTOUNDING ATTEMPTED BURGLARY AT SNEYD HALL.

In buying the paper he was afflicted with a kind of ague. And the description of events at Sneyd Hall was enough to give ague to a negro. The account had been taken from the lips of Mrs Gater, housekeeper at Sneyd Hall. She had related to a reporter how, upon going into the state suite before retiring for the night, she had surprised a burglar of Herculean physique and Titanic proportions. Fortunately she knew her duty, and did not blench. The burglar had threatened her with a revolver, and then, finding such bluff futile, had deliberately jumped through a large plate-glass window and vanished. Mrs Gater could not conceive how the fellow had "effected an entrance." (According to the reporter, Mrs Gater said "effected an entrance," not "got in." And here it may be mentioned that in the columns of the *Signal* burglars never get into a residence; without exception they invariably effect an entrance.) Mrs Gater explained further how the plans of the burglar must have been laid with the most diabolic skill; how he must have studied the daily life of the Hall patiently for weeks, if not months; how he must have known the habits and plans of every soul in the place, and the exact instant at which the Countess had arranged to drive to Stafford to catch the London express.

It appeared that save for four maidservants, a page, two dogs, three gardeners, and the kitchen-clerk, Mrs Gater was alone in the Hall. During the late afternoon and early evening they had all been to assist at a rat-catching in the stables, and the burglar must have been aware of this. It passed Mrs Gater's comprehension how the criminal had got clear away out of the gardens and park, for to set up a hue and cry had been with her the work of a moment. She could not be sure whether he had taken any valuable property, but the inventory was being checked. Though surely for her an inventory was scarcely necessary, as she had been housekeeper at Sneyd Hall for six-and-twenty years, and might be said to know the entire contents of the mansion by heart! The police were at work. They had studied footprints and *débris*. There was talk of obtaining detectives from London. Up to the time of going to press, no clue had been discovered, but Mrs Gater was confident that a clue would be discovered, and of her ability to recognise the burglar when he should be caught. His features, as seen in the moonlight, were imprinted on her mind for ever. He was a young man, well dressed. The Earl had telegraphed, offering a reward of £20 for the fellow's capture. A warrant was out.

So it ran on.

Denry saw clearly all the errors of tact which he had committed on the previous day. He ought not to have entered uninvited. But having entered, he ought to have held firm in quiet dignity until the housekeeper came, and then he ought to have gone into full details with the housekeeper, producing his credentials and showing her unmistakably that he was offended by the experience which somebody's gross carelessness had forced upon him.

Instead of all that, he had behaved with simple stupidity, and the result was that a price was upon his head. Far from acquiring moral impressiveness and influential aid by his journey to Sneyd Hall, he had utterly ruined himself as a founder of a Universal Thrift Club. You cannot conduct a thrift club from prison, and a sentence of ten years does not inspire confidence in the ignorant mob. He trembled at the thought of what would happen when the police learned from the Countess that a man with a card on which was the name of Machin had called at Sneyd just before her departure.

However, the police never did learn this from the Countess (who had gone to Rome for the autumn). It appeared that her maid had merely said to the Countess that "a man" had called, and also that the maid had lost the card. Careful research showed that the burglar had been disturbed before he had had opportunity to burgle. And the affair, after raising a terrific bother in the district, died down.

Then it was that an article appeared in the *Signal*, signed by Denry, and giving a full picturesque description of the state apartments at Sneyd Hall. He had formed a habit of occasional contributions to the *Signal*. This article began:—

"The recent sensational burglary at Sneyd Hall has drawn attention to the magnificent state apartments of that unique mansion. As very few but the personal friends of the family are allowed a glimpse of these historic rooms, they being of course quite closed to the public, we have thought that some account of them might interest the readers of the *Signal*. On the occasion of our last visit...," etc.

He left out nothing of their splendour.

The article was quoted as far as Birmingham in the Midlands Press. People recalled Denry's famous waltz with the Countess at the memorable dance in Bursley Town Hall. And they were bound to assume that the relations thus begun had been more or less maintained. They were struck by Denry's amazing discreet self-denial in never boasting of them. Denry rose in the market of popular esteem. Talking of Denry, people talked of the Universal Thrift Club, which went quietly ahead, and they admitted that Denry was of the stuff which succeeds and deserves to succeed.

But only Denry himself could appreciate fully how great Denry was, to have snatched such a wondrous victory out of such a humiliating defeat!

His chin slowly disappeared from view under a quite presentable beard. But whether the beard was encouraged out of respect for his mother's sage advice, or with the object of putting the housekeeper of Sneyd Hall off the scent, if she should chance to meet Denry, who shall say?

CHAPTER VII
THE RESCUER OF DAMES

I

It next happened that Denry began to suffer from the ravages of a malady which is almost worse than failure—namely, a surfeit of success. The success was that of his Universal Thrift Club. This device, by which members after subscribing one pound in weekly instalments could at once get two pounds' worth of goods at nearly any large shop in the district, appealed with enormous force to the democracy of the Five Towns. There was no need whatever for Denry to spend money on advertising. The first members of the club did all the advertising and made no charge for doing it. A stream of people anxious to deposit money with Denry in exchange for a card never ceased to flow Into his little office in St Luke's Square. The stream, indeed, constantly thickened. It was a wonderful invention, the Universal Thrift Club. And Denry ought to have been happy, especially as his beard was growing strongly and evenly, and giving him the desired air of a man of wisdom and stability. But he was not happy. And the reason was that the popularity of the Thrift Club necessitated much book-keeping, which he hated.

He was an adventurer, in the old honest sense, and no clerk. And he found himself obliged not merely to buy large books of account, but to fill them with figures; and to do addition sums from page to page; and to fill up hundreds of cards; and to write out lists of shops, and to have long interviews with printers whose proofs made him dream of lunatic asylums; and to reckon innumerable piles of small coins; and to assist his small office-boy in the great task of licking envelopes and stamps. Moreover, he was worried by shopkeepers; every shopkeeper in the district now wanted to allow him twopence in the shilling on the purchases of club members. And he had to collect all the subscriptions, in addition to his rents; and also to make personal preliminary inquiries as to the reputation of intending members. If he could have risen every day at 4 A.M. and stayed up working every night till 4 A.M. he might have got through most of the labour. He did, as a fact, come very near to this ideal. So near that one morning his mother said to him, at her driest:

"I suppose I may as well sell your bedstead. Denry?"

And there was no hope of improvement; instead of decreasing, the work multiplied.

What saved him was the fortunate death of Lawyer Lawton. The aged solicitor's death put the town into mourning and hung the church with black. But Denry as a citizen bravely bore the blow because he was able to secure the services of Penkethman, Lawyer Lawton's eldest clerk, who, after keeping the Lawton books and writing the Lawton letters for thirty-five years, was dismissed by young Lawton for being over fifty and behind the times. The desiccated bachelor was grateful to Denry. He called Denry "Sir," or rather he called Denry's suit of clothes "Sir," for he had a vast respect for a well-cut suit. On the other hand, he maltreated the little office-boy, for he had always been accustomed to maltreating little office-boys, not seriously, but just enough to give them an interest in life. Penkethman enjoyed desks, ledgers, pens, ink, rulers, and blotting-paper. He could run from bottom to top of a column of figures more quickly than the fire-engine could run up Oldcastle Street; and his totals were never wrong. His gesture with a piece of blotting-paper as he blotted off a total was magnificent. He liked long hours; he was thoroughly used to overtime, and his boredom in his lodgings was such that he would often arrive at the office before the appointed hour. He asked thirty shillings a week, and Denry in a mood of generosity gave him thirty-one. He gave Denry his whole life, and put a meticulous order into the establishment. Denry secretly thought him a miracle, but up at the club at Porthill he was content to call him "the human machine." "I wind him up every Saturday night with a sovereign, half a sovereign, and a shilling," said Denry, "and he goes for a week. Compensated balance adjusted for all temperatures. No escapement. Jewelled in every hole. Ticks in any position. Made in England."

This jocularity of Denry's was a symptom that Denry's spirits were rising. The bearded youth was seen oftener in the streets behind his mule and his dog. The adventurer had, indeed, taken to the road again. After an emaciating period he began once more to stouten. He was the image of success. He was the picturesque card, whom everybody knew and everybody had pleasure in greeting.

In some sort he was rather like the flag on the Town Hall.

And then a graver misfortune threatened.

It arose out of the fact that, though Denry was a financial genius, he was in no sense qualified to be a Fellow of the Institute of Chartered Accountants. The notion that an excess of prosperity may bring ruin had never presented itself to him, until one day he discovered that out of over two thousand pounds there remained less than six hundred to his credit at the bank. This was at the stage of the Thrift Club when the founder of the Thrift Club was bound under the rules to give credit. When the original lady member had paid in her two pounds or so, she was entitled to spend four pounds or so at shops. She did spend four pounds or so at shops. And Denry had to pay the shops. He was thus temporarily nearly two pounds out of pocket, and he had to collect that sum by trifling instalments. Multiply this case by five hundred, and you will understand the drain on Denry's capital. Multiply it by a thousand, and you will understand the very serious peril which overhung Denry. Multiply it by fifteen hundred and you will understand that Denry had been culpably silly to inaugurate a mighty scheme like the Universal Thrift Club on a paltry capital of two thousand pounds. He had. In his simplicity he had regarded two thousand pounds as boundless wealth.

Although new subscriptions poured in, the drain grew more distressing. Yet he could not persuade himself to refuse new members. He stiffened his rules, and compelled members to pay at his office instead of on their own doorsteps; he instituted fines for irregularity. But nothing could stop the progress of the Universal Thrift Club. And disaster approached. Denry felt as though he were being pushed nearer and nearer to the edge of a precipice by a tremendous multitude of people. At length, very much against his inclination, he put up a card in his window that no new members could be accepted until further notice, pending the acquisition of larger offices and other arrangements. For the shrewd, it was a confession of failure, and he knew it.

Then the rumour began to form, and to thicken, and to spread, that Denry's famous Universal Thrift Club was unsound at the core, and that the teeth of those who had bitten the apple would be set on edge.

And Denry saw that something great, something decisive, must be done and done with rapidity.

II

His thoughts turned to the Countess of Chell. The original attempt to engage her moral support in aid of the Thrift Club had ended in a dangerous fiasco. Denry had been beaten by circumstances. And though he had emerged from the defeat with credit, he had no taste for defeat. He disliked defeat even when it was served with jam. And his indomitable thoughts turned to the Countess again. He put it to himself in this way, scratching his head:

"I've got to get hold of that woman, and that's all about it!"

The Countess at this period was busying herself with the policemen of the Five Towns. In her exhaustless passion for philanthropy, bazaars, and platforms, she had already dealt with orphans, the aged, the blind, potter's asthma, crèches, churches, chapels, schools, economic cookery, the smoke-nuisance, country holidays, Christmas puddings and blankets, healthy musical entertainments, and barmaids. The excellent and beautiful creature was suffering from a dearth of subjects when the policemen occurred to her. She made the benevolent discovery that policemen were over-worked, underpaid, courteous and trustworthy public servants, and that our lives depended on them. And from this discovery it naturally followed that policemen deserved her energetic assistance. Which assistance resulted in the erection of a Policemen's Institute at Hanbridge, the chief of the Five Towns. At the Institute policemen would be able to play at draughts, read the papers, and drink everything non-alcoholic at prices that defied competition. And the Institute also conferred other benefits on those whom all the five Mayors of the Five Towns fell into the way of describing as "the stalwart guardians of the law." The Institute, having been built, had to be opened with due splendour and ceremony. And naturally the Countess of Chell was the person to open it, since without her it would never have existed.

The solemn day was a day in March, and the hour was fixed for three o'clock, and the place was the large hall of the Institute itself, behind Crown Square, which is the Trafalgar Square of Hanbridge. The Countess was to drive over from Sneyd. Had the epoch been ten years later she would have motored over. But probably that would not have made any difference to what happened.

In relating what did happen, I confine myself to facts, eschewing imputations. It is a truism that life is full of coincidences, but whether these events comprised a coincidence, or not, each reader must decide for himself, according to his cynicism or his faith in human nature.

The facts are: First, that Denry called one day at the house of Mrs Kemp a little lower down Brougham Street, Mrs Kemp being friendly with Mrs Machin, and the mother of Jock, the Countess's carriage-footman, whom Denry had known from boyhood. Second, that a few days later, when Jock came over to see his mother, Denry was present, and that subsequently Denry and Jock went for a stroll together in the cemetery, the principal resort of strollers in Bursley. Third, that on the afternoon of the opening ceremony the Countess's carriage broke down in Sneyd Vale, two miles from Sneyd and three miles from Hanbridge. Fourth, that five minutes later Denry, all in his best clothes, drove up behind his mule. Fifth, that Denry drove right past the breakdown, apparently not noticing it. Sixth, that Jock, touching his hat to Denry as if to a stranger (for, of course, while on duty a footman must be dead to all humanities), said:

"Excuse me, sir," and so caused Denry to stop.

These are the simple facts.

Denry looked round with that careless half-turn of the upper part of the body which drivers of elegant equipages affect when their attention is called to something trifling behind them. The mule also looked round—it was a habit of the mule's—and if the dog had been there the dog would have shown an even livelier inquisitiveness; but Denry had left the faithful animal at home.

"Good-afternoon, Countess," he said, raising his hat, and trying to express surprise, pleasure, and imperturbability all at once.

The Countess of Chell, who was standing in the road, raised her lorgnon, which was attached to the end of a tortoiseshell pole about a foot long, and regarded Denry. This lorgnon was a new device of hers, and it was already having the happy effect of increasing the sale of long-handled lorgnons throughout the Five Towns.

"Oh! it's you, is it?" said the Countess. "I see you've grown a beard."

It was just this easy familiarity that endeared her to the district. As observant people put it, you never knew what she would say next, and yet she never compromised her dignity.

"Yes," said Denry. "Have you had an accident?"

"No," said the Countess, bitterly: "I'm doing this for idle amusement."

The horses had been taken out, and were grazing by the roadside like common horses. The coachman was dipping his skirts in the mud as he bent down in front of the carriage and twisted the pole to and fro and round about and round about. The footman, Jock, was industriously watching him.

"It's the pole-pin, sir," said Jock.

Denry descended from his own hammercloth. The Countess was not smiling. It was the first time that Denry had ever seen her without an efficient smile on her face.

"Have you got to be anywhere particular?" he asked. Many ladies would not have understood what he meant. But the Countess was used to the Five Towns.

"Yes," said she. "I have got to be somewhere particular. I've got to be at the Police Institute at three o'clock particular, Mr Machin. And I shan't be. I'm late now. We've been here ten minutes."

The Countess was rather too often late for public ceremonies. Nobody informed her of the fact. Everybody, on the contrary, assiduously pretended that she had arrived to the very second. But she was well aware that she had a reputation for unpunctuality. Ordinarily, being too hurried to invent a really clever excuse, she would assert lightly that something had happened to her carriage. And now something in truth had happened to her carriage—but who would believe it at the Police Institute?

"If you'll come with me I'll guarantee to get you there by three o'clock," said Denry.

The road thereabouts was lonely. A canal ran parallel with it at a distance of fifty yards, and on the canal a boat was moving in the direction of Hanbridge at the rate of a mile an hour. Such was the only other vehicle in sight. The outskirts of Knype, the nearest town, did not begin until at least a mile further on; and the Countess, dressed for the undoing of mayors and other unimpressionable functionaries, could not possibly have walked even half a mile in that rich dark mud. She thanked him, and without a word to her servants took the seat beside him.

III

Immediately the mule began to trot the Countess began to smile again. Relief and content were painted upon her handsome features. Denry soon learnt that she knew all about mules—or almost all. She told him how she had ridden hundreds of miles on mules in the Apennines, where there were no roads, and only mules, goats and flies could keep their feet on the steep, stony paths. She said that a good mule was worth forty pounds in the Apennines, more than a horse of similar quality. In fact, she was very sympathetic about mules. Denry saw that he must drive with as much style as possible, and he tried to remember all that he had picked up from a book concerning the proper manner of holding the reins. For in everything that appertained to riding and driving the Countess was an expert. In the season she hunted once or twice a week with the North Staffordshire Hounds, and the *Signal* had stated that she was a fearless horsewoman. It made this statement one day when she had been thrown and carried to Sneyd senseless.

The mule, too, seemingly conscious of its responsibilities and its high destiny, put its best foot foremost and behaved in general like a mule that knew the name of its great-grandfather. It went through Knype in admirable style, not swerving at the steam-cars nor exciting itself about the railway bridge. A photographer who stood at his door manoeuvring a large camera startled it momentarily, until it remembered that it had seen a camera before. The Countess, who wondered why on earth a photographer should be capering round a tripod in a doorway, turned to inspect the man with her lorgnon.

They were now coursing up the Cauldon Bank towards Hanbridge. They were already within the boundaries of Hanbridge, and a pedestrian here and there recognised the Countess. You can hide nothing from the quidnunc of Hanbridge. Moreover, when a quidnunc in the streets of Hanbridge sees somebody famous or striking, or notorious, he does not pretend that he has seen nobody. He points unmistakably to what he has observed, if he has a companion, and if he has no companion he stands still and stares with such honest intensity that the entire street stands and stares too. Occasionally you may see an entire street standing and staring without any idea of what it is staring at. As the equipage dashingly approached the busy centre of Hanbridge, the region of fine shops, public-houses, hotels, halls, and theatres, more and more of the inhabitants knew that Iris (as they affectionately called her) was driving with a young man in a tumble-down little victoria behind a mule whose ears flapped like an elephant's. Denry being far less renowned in Hanbridge than in his native Bursley, few persons recognised him. After the victoria had gone by people who had heard the news too late rushed from shops and gazed at the Countess's back as at a fading dream until the insistent clang of a car-bell made them jump again to the footpath.

At length Denry and the Countess could see the clock of the Old Town Hall in Crown Square and it was a minute to three. They were less than a minute off the Institute.

"There you are!" said Denry, proudly. "Three miles if it's a yard, in seventeen minutes. For a mule it's none so dusty."

And such was the Countess's knowledge of the language of the Five Towns that she instantly divined the meaning of even that phrase, "none so dusty."

They swept into Crown Square grandly.

And then, with no warning, the mule suddenly applied all the automatic brakes which a mule has, and stopped.

"Oh Lor!" sighed Denry. He knew the cause of that arresting.

A large squad of policemen, a perfect regiment of policemen, was moving across the north side of the square in the direction of the Institute. Nothing could have seemed more reassuring, less harmful, than that band of policemen, off duty for the afternoon and collected together for the purpose of giving a hearty and policemanly welcome to their benefactress the Countess. But the mule had his own views about policemen. In the early days of Denry's ownership of him he had nearly always shied at the spectacle of a policemen. He would tolerate steam-rollers, and even falling kites, but a policeman had ever been antipathetic to him. Denry, by patience and punishment, had gradually brought him round almost to the Countess's views of policemen—namely, that they were a courteous and trustworthy body of public servants, not to be treated as scarecrows or the dregs of society. At any rate, the mule had of late months practically ceased to set his face against the policing of the Five Towns. And when he was on his best behaviour he would ignore a policeman completely. But there were several hundreds of policemen in that squad, the majority of all the policemen in the Five Towns. And clearly the mule considered that Denry, in confronting him with several hundred policemen simultaneously, had been presuming upon his good-nature.

The mule's ears were saying agitatedly:

"A line must be drawn somewhere, and I have drawn it where my forefeet now are."

The mule's ears soon drew together a little crowd.

It occurred to Denry that if mules were so wonderful in the Apennines the reason must be that there are no policemen in the Apennines. It also occurred to him that something must be done to this mule.

"Well?" said the Countess, inquiringly.

It was a challenge to him to prove that he and not the mule was in charge of the expedition.

He briefly explained the mule's idiosyncrasy, as it were apologising for its bad taste in objecting to public servants whom the Countess cherished.

"They'll be out of sight in a moment," said the Countess. And both she and Denry tried to look as if the victoria had stopped in that special spot for a special reason, and that the mule was a pattern of obedience. Nevertheless, the little crowd was growing a little larger.

"Now," said the Countess, encouragingly. The tail of the regiment of policemen had vanished towards the Institute.

"Tchk! Tchk!" Denry persuaded the mule.

No response from those forefeet!

"Perhaps I'd better get out and walk," the Countess suggested. The crowd was becoming inconvenient, and had even begun to offer unsolicited hints as to the proper management of mules. The crowd was also saying to itself: "It's her! It's her! It's her!" Meaning that it was the Countess.

"Oh no," said Denry, "it's all right."

And he caught the mule "one" over the head with his whip.

The mule, stung into action, dashed away, and the crowd scattered as if blown to pieces by the explosion of a bomb. Instead of pursuing a right line the mule turned within a radius of its own length, swinging the victoria round after it as though the victoria had been a kettle attached to it with string. And Countess, Denry, and victoria were rapt with miraculous swiftness away—not at all towards the Policemen's Institute, but down Longshaw Road, which is tolerably steep. They were pursued, but ineffectually. For the mule had bolted and was winged. They fortunately came into contact with nothing except a large barrow of carrots, turnips, and cabbages which an old woman was wheeling up Longshaw Road. The concussion upset the barrow, half filled the victoria with vegetables, and for a second stayed the mule; but no real harm seemed to have been done, and the mule proceeded with vigour. Then the Countess noticed that Denry was not using his right arm, which swung about rather uselessly.

"I must have knocked my elbow against the barrow," he muttered. His face was pale.

"Give me the reins," said the Countess.

"I think I can turn the brute up here," he said.

And he did in fact neatly divert the mule up Birches Street, which is steeper even than Longshaw Road. The mule for a few instants pretended that all gradients, up or down, were equal before its angry might. But Birches Street has the slope of a house-roof. Presently the mule walked, and then it stood still. And half Birches Street emerged to gaze, for the Countess's attire was really very splendid.

"I'll leave this here, and we'll walk back," said Denry." You won't be late—that is, nothing to speak of. The Institute is just round the top here."

You don't mean to say you're going to let that mule beat you?" exclaimed the Countess.

"I was only thinking of your being late."

"Oh, bother!" said she. "Your mule may be ruined." The horse-trainer in her was aroused.

"And then my arm?" said Denry.

"Shall I drive back?" the Countess suggested.

"Oh, do," said Denry. "Keep on up the street, and then to the left."

They changed places, and two minutes later she brought the mule to an obedient rest in front of the Police Institute, which was all newly red with terra-cotta. The main body of policemen had passed into the building, but two remained at the door, and the mule haughtily tolerated them. The Countess despatched one to Longshaw Road to settle with the old woman whose vegetables they had brought away with them. The other policeman, who, owing to the Countess's philanthropic energy, had received a course of instruction in first aid, arranged a sling for Denry's arm. And then the Countess said that Denry ought certainly to go with her to the inauguration ceremony. The policeman whistled a boy to hold the mule. Denry picked a carrot out of the complex folds of the Countess's rich costume. And the Countess and her saviour entered the portico and were therein met by an imposing group of important male personages, several of whom wore mayoral chains. Strange tales of what had happened to the Countess had already flown up to the Institute, and the chief expression on the faces of the group seemed to be one of astonishment that she still lived.

IV

Denry observed that the Countess was now a different woman. She had suddenly put on a manner to match her costume, which in certain parts was stiff with embroidery. From the informal companion and the tamer of mules she had miraculously developed into the public celebrity, the peeress of the realm, and the inaugurator-general of philanthropic schemes and buildings. Not one of the important male personages but would have looked down on Denry!

And yet, while treating Denry as a jolly equal, the Countess with all her embroidered and stiff politeness somehow looked down on the important male personages—and they knew it. And the most curious thing was that they seemed rather to enjoy it. The one who seemed to enjoy it the least was Sir Jehoshophat Dain, a white-bearded pillar of terrific imposingness.

Sir Jee—as he was then beginning to be called—had recently been knighted, by way of reward for his enormous benefactions to the community. In the *rôle* of philanthropist he was really much more effective than the Countess. But he was not young, he was not pretty, he was not a woman, and his family had not helped to rule England for generations—at any rate, so far as anybody knew. He had made more money than had ever before been made by a single brain in the manufacture of earthenware, and he had given more money to public causes than a single pocket had ever before given in the Five Towns. He had never sought municipal honours, considering himself to be somewhat above such trifles. He was the first purely local man to be knighted in the Five Towns. Even before the bestowal of the knighthood his sense of humour had been deficient, and immediately afterwards it had vanished entirely. Indeed, he did not miss it. He divided the population of the kingdom into two classes—the titled and the untitled. With Sir Jee, either you were titled, or you weren't. He lumped all the untitled together; and to be just to his logical faculty, he lumped all the titled together. There were various titles—Sir Jee admitted that—but a title was a title, and therefore all titles were practically equal. The Duke of Norfolk was one titled individual, and Sir Jee was another. The fine difference between them might be perceptible to the titled, and might properly be recognised by the titled when the titled were among themselves, but for the untitled such a difference ought not to exist and could not exist.

Thus for Sir Jee there were two titled beings in the group—the Countess and himself. The Countess and himself formed one caste in the group, and the rest another caste. And although the Countess, in her punctilious demeanour towards him, gave due emphasis to his title (he returning more than due emphasis to hers), he was not precisely pleased by the undertones of suave condescension that characterised her greeting of him as well as her greeting of the others. Moreover, he had known Denry as a clerk of Mr Duncalf's, for Mr Duncalf had done a lot of legal work for him in the past. He looked upon Denry as an upstart, a capering mountebank, and he strongly resented Denry's familiarity with the Countess. He further resented Denry's sling, which gave to Denry an interesting romantic aspect (despite his beard), and he more than all resented that Denry should have rescued the Countess from a carriage accident by means of his preposterous mule. Whenever the Countess, in the preliminary chatter, referred to Denry or looked at Denry, in recounting the history of her adventures, Sir Jee's soul squirmed, and his body sympathised with his soul. Something in him that was more powerful than himself compelled him to do his utmost to reduce Denry to a moral pulp, to flatten him, to ignore him, or to exterminate him by the application of ice. This tactic was no more lost on the Countess than it was on Denry. And the Countess foiled it at every instant. In truth, there existed between the Countess and Sir Jee a rather hot rivalry in philanthropy and the cultivation of the higher welfare of the district. He regarded himself, and she regarded herself, as the most brightly glittering star of the Five Towns.

When the Countess had finished the recital of her journey, and the faces of the group had gone through all the contortions proper to express terror, amazement, admiration, and manly sympathy, Sir Jee took the lead, coughed, and said in his elaborate style:

"Before we adjourn to the hall, will not your ladyship take a little refreshment?"

"Oh no, thanks," said the Countess. "I'm not a bit upset." Then she turned to the enslinged Denry and with concern added: "But will *you* have something?"

If she could have foreseen the consequences of her question, she might never have put it. Still, she might have put it just the same.

Denry paused an instant, and an old habit rose up in him.

"Oh no, thanks," he said, and turning deliberately to Sir Jee, he added: "Will *you*?"

This, of course, was mere crude insolence to the titled philanthropic white-beard. But it was by no means the worst of Denry's behaviour. The group—every member of the group—distinctly perceived a movement of Denry's left hand towards Sir Jee. It was the very slightest movement, a wavering, a nothing. It would have had no significance whatever, but for one fact. Denry's left hand still held the carrot.

Everybody exhibited the most marvellous self-control. And everybody except Sir Jee was secretly charmed, for Sir Jee had never inspired love. It is remarkable how local philanthropists are unloved, locally. The Countess, without blenching, gave the signal for what Sir Jee called the "adjournment" to the hall. Nothing might have happened, yet everything had happened.

V

Next, Denry found himself seated on the temporary platform which had been erected in the large games hall of the Policemen's Institute.

The Mayor of Hanbridge was in the chair, and he had the Countess on his right and the Mayoress of Bursley on his left. Other mayoral chains blazed in the centre of the platform, together with fine hats of mayoresses and uniforms of police-superintendents and captains of fire-brigades. Denry's sling also contributed to the effectiveness; he was placed behind the Countess. Policemen (looking strange without helmets) and their wives, sweethearts, and friends, filled the hall to its fullest; enthusiasm was rife and strident; and there was only one little sign that the untoward had occurred. That little sign was an empty chair in the first row near the Countess. Sir Jee, a prey to a sudden indisposition, had departed. He had somehow faded away, while the personages were climbing the stairs. He had faded away amid the expressed regrets of those few who by chance saw him in the act of fading. But even these bore up manfully. The high humour of the gathering was not eclipsed.

Towards the end of the ceremony came the votes of thanks, and the principal of these was the vote of thanks to the Countess, prime cause of the Institute. It was proposed by the Superintendent of the Hanbridge Police. Other personages had wished to propose it, but the stronger right of the Hanbridge Superintendent, as chief officer of the largest force of constables in the Five Towns, could not be disputed. He made a few facetious references to the episode of the Countess's arrival, and brought the house down by saying that if he did his duty he would arrest both the Countess and Denry for driving to the common danger. When he sat down, amid tempestuous applause, there was a hitch. According to the official programme Sir Jehoshophat Dain was to have seconded the vote, and Sir Jee was not there. All that remained of Sir Jee was his chair. The Mayor of Hanbridge looked round about, trying swiftly to make up his mind what was to be done, and Denry heard him whisper to another mayor for advice.

"Shall I do it?" Denry whispered, and by at once rising relieved the Mayor from the necessity of coming to a decision.

Impossible to say why Denry should have risen as he did, without any warning. Ten seconds before, five seconds before, he himself had not the dimmest idea that he was about to address the meeting. All that can be said is that he was subject to these attacks of the unexpected.

Once on his legs he began to suffer, for he had never before been on his legs on a platform, or even on a platform at all. He could see nothing whatever except a cloud that had mysteriously and with frightful suddenness filled the room. And through this cloud he could feel that hundreds and hundreds of eyes were piercingly fixed upon him. A voice was saying inside him— "What a fool you are! What a fool you are! I always told you you were a fool!" And his heart was beating as it had never beat, and his forehead was damp, his throat distressingly dry, and one foot nervously tap-tapping on the floor. This condition lasted for something like ten hours, during which time the eyes continued to pierce the cloud and him with patient, obstinate cruelty.

Denry heard some one talking. It was himself.

The Superintendent had said: "I have very great pleasure in proposing the vote of thanks to the Countess of Chell."

And so Denry heard himself saying: "I have very great pleasure in seconding the vote of thanks to the Countess of Chell."

He could not think of anything else to say. And there was a pause, a real pause, not a pause merely in Denry's sick imagination.

Then the cloud was dissipated. And Denry himself said to the audience of policemen, with his own natural tone, smile and gesture, colloquially, informally, comically:

"Now then! Move along there, please! I'm not going to say any more!"

And for a signal he put his hands in the position for applauding. And sat down.

He had tickled the stout ribs of every bobby in the place. The applause surpassed all previous applause. The most staid ornaments of the platform had to laugh. People nudged each other and explained that it was "that chap Machin from Bursley," as if to imply that that chap Machin from Bursley never let a day pass without doing something striking and humorous. The Mayor was still smiling when he put the vote to the meeting, and the Countess was still smiling when she responded.

Afterwards in the portico, when everything was over, Denry exercised his right to remain in charge of the Countess. They escaped from the personages by going out to look for her carriage and neglecting to return. There was no sign of the Countess's carriage, but Denry's mule and victoria were waiting in a quiet corner.

"May I drive you home?" he suggested.

But she would not. She said that she had a call to pay before dinner, and that her brougham would surely arrive the very next minute.

"Will you come and have tea at the Sub Rosa?" Denry next asked.

"The Sub Rosa?" questioned the Countess.

"Well," said Denry, "that's what we call the new tea-room that's just been opened round here." He indicated a direction. "It's quite a novelty in the Five Towns."

The Countess had a passion for tea.

"They have splendid China tea," said Denry.

"Well," said the Countess, "I suppose I may as well go through with it."

At the moment her brougham drove up. She instructed her coachman to wait next to the mule and victoria. Her demeanour had cast off all its similarity to her dress: it appeared to imply that, as she had begun with a mad escapade, she ought to finish with another one.

Thus the Countess and Denry went to the tea-shop, and Denry ordered tea and paid for it. There was scarcely a customer in the place, and the few who were fortunate enough to be present had not the wit to recognise the Countess. The proprietress did not recognise the Countess. (Later, when it became known that the Countess had actually patronised the Sub Rosa, half the ladies of Hanbridge were almost ill from sheer disgust that they had not heard of it in time. It would have been so easy for them to be there, taking tea at the next table to the Countess, and observing her choice of cakes, and her manner of holding a spoon, and whether she removed her gloves or retained them in the case of a meringue. It was an opportunity lost that would in all human probability never occur again.)

And in the discreet corner which she had selected the Countess fired a sudden shot at Denry.

"How did you get all those details about the state rooms at Sneyd?" she asked.

Upon which opening the conversation became lively.

The same evening Denry called at the *Signal* office and gave an order for a half-page advertisement of the Five Towns Universal Thrift Club— "Patroness, the Countess of Chell." The advertisement informed the public that the club had now made arrangements to accept new members. Besides the order for a half-page advertisement, Denry also gave many interesting and authentic details about the historic drive from Sneyd Vale to Hanbridge. The next day the *Signal* was simply full of Denry and the Countess. It had a large photograph, taken by a photographer on Cauldon Bank, which showed Denry actually driving the Countess, and the Countess's face was full in the picture. It presented, too, an excellently appreciative account of Denry's speech, and it congratulated Denry on his first appearance in the public life of the Five Towns. (In parenthesis it sympathised with Sir Jee in his indisposition.) In short, Denry's triumph obliterated the memory of his previous triumphs. It obliterated, too, all rumours adverse to the Thrift Club. In a few days he had a thousand new members. Of course, this addition only increased his liabilities; but now he could obtain capital on fair terms, and he did obtain it. A company was formed. The Countess had a few shares in this company. So (strangely) had Jock and his companion the coachman. Not the least of the mysteries was that when Denry reached his mother's cottage on the night of the tea with the Countess, his arm was not in a sling, and showed no symptom of having been damaged.

CHAPTER VIII
RAISING A WIGWAM

I

A still young man—his age was thirty—with a short, strong beard peeping out over the fur collar of a vast overcoat, emerged from a cab at the snowy corner of St Luke's Square and Brougham Street, and paid the cabman with a gesture that indicated both wealth and the habit of command. And the cabman, who had driven him over from Hanbridge through the winter night, responded accordingly. Few people take cabs in the Five Towns. There are few cabs to take. If you are going to a party you may order one in advance by telephone, reconciling yourself also in advance to the expense, but to hail a cab in the street without forethought and jump into it as carelessly as you would jump into a tram—this is by very few done. The young man with the beard did it frequently, which proved that he was fundamentally ducal.

He was encumbered with a large and rather heavy parcel as he walked down Brougham Street, and, moreover, the footpath of Brougham Street was exceedingly dirty. And yet no one acquainted with the circumstances of his life would have asked why he had dismissed the cab before arriving at his destination, because every one knew. The reason was that this ducal person, with the gestures of command, dared not drive up to his mother's door in a cab oftener than about once a month. He opened that door with a latch-key (a modern lock was almost the only innovation that he had succeeded in fixing on his mother), and stumbled with his unwieldy parcel into the exceedingly narrow lobby.

"Is that you, Denry?" called a feeble voice from the parlour.

"Yes," said he, and went into the parlour, hat, fur coat, parcel, and all.

Mrs Machin, in a shawl and an antimacassar over the shawl, sat close to the fire and leaning towards it. She looked cold and ill. Although the parlour was very tiny and the fire comparatively large, the structure of the grate made it impossible that the room should be warm, as all the heat went up the chimney. If Mrs Machin had sat on the roof and put her hands over the top of the chimney, she would have been much warmer than at the grate.

"You aren't in bed?" Denry queried.

"Can't ye see?" said his mother. And, indeed, to ask a woman who was obviously sitting up in a chair whether she was in bed, did seem somewhat absurd. She added, less sarcastically: "I was expecting ye every minute. Where have ye had your tea?"

"Oh!" he said lightly, "in Hanbridge."

An untruth! He had not had his tea anywhere. But he had dined richly at the new Hôtel Métropole, Hanbridge.

"What have ye got there?" asked his mother.

"A present for you," said Denry. "It's your birthday to-morrow."

"I don't know as I want reminding of that," murmured Mrs Machin.

But when he had undone the parcel and held up the contents before her, she exclaimed:

"Bless us!"

The staggered tone was an admission that for once in a way he had impressed her.

It was a magnificent sealskin mantle, longer than sealskin mantles usually are. It was one of those articles the owner of which can say: "Nobody can have a better than this—I don't care who she is." It was worth in monetary value all the plain, shabby clothes on Mrs Machin's back, and all her very ordinary best clothes upstairs, and all the furniture in the entire house, and perhaps all Denry's dandiacal wardrobe too, except his fur coat. If the entire contents of the cottage, with the aforesaid exception, had been put up to auction, they would not have realised enough to pay for that sealskin mantle.

Had it been anything but a sealskin mantle, and equally costly, Mrs Machin would have upbraided. But a sealskin mantle is not "showy." It "goes with" any and every dress and bonnet. And the most respectable, the most conservative, the most austere woman may find legitimate pleasure in wearing it. A sealskin mantle is the sole luxurious ostentation that a woman of Mrs Machin's temperament—and there are many such in the Five Towns and elsewhere—will conscientiously permit herself.

"Try it on," said Denry.

She rose weakly and tried it on. It fitted as well as a sealskin mantle can fit.

"My word—it's warm!" she said. This was her sole comment.

"Keep it on," said Denry.

His mother's glance withered the suggestion.

"Where are you going?" he asked, as she left the room.

"To put it away," said she. "I must get some moth-powder to-morrow."

He protested with inarticulate noises, removed his own furs, which he threw down on to the old worn-out sofa, and drew a Windsor chair up to the fire. After a while his mother returned, and sat down in her rocking-chair, and began to shiver again under the shawl and the antimacassar. The lamp on the table lighted up the left side of her face and the right side of his.

"Look here, mother," said he, "you must have a doctor."

"I shall have no doctor."

"You've got influenza, and it's a very tricky business—influenza is; you never know where you are with it."

"Ye can call it influenza if ye like," said Mrs Machin. "There was no influenza in my young days. We called a cold a cold."

"Well," said Denry, "you aren't well, are you?"

"I never said I was," she answered grimly.

"No," said Denry, with the triumphant ring of one who is about to devastate an enemy. "And you never will be in this rotten old cottage."

"This was reckoned a very good class of house when your father and I came into it. And it's always been kept in repair. It was good enough for your father, and it's good enough for me. I don't see myself flitting. But some folks have gotten so grand. As for health, old Reuben next door is ninety-one. How many people over ninety are there in those gimcrack houses up by the Park, I should like to know?"

Denry could argue with any one save his mother. Always, when he was about to reduce her to impotence, she fell on him thus and rolled him in the dust. Still, he began again.

"Do we pay four-and-sixpence a week for this cottage, or don't we?" he demanded.

"And always have done," said Mrs Machin. "I should like to see the landlord put it up," she added, formidably, as if to say: "I'd landlord him, if he tried to put *my* rent up!"

"Well," said Denry, "here we are living in a four-and-six-a-week cottage, and do you know how much I'm making? I'm making two thousand pounds a year. That's what I'm making."

A second wilful deception of his mother! As Managing Director of the Five Towns Universal Thrift Club, as proprietor of the majority of its shares, as its absolute autocrat, he was making very nearly four thousand a year. Why could he not as easily have said four as two to his mother? The simple answer is that he was afraid to say four. It was as if he ought to blush before his mother for being so plutocratic, his mother who had passed most of her life in hard toil to gain a few shillings a week. Four thousand seemed so fantastic! And in fact the Thrift Club, which he had invented in a moment, had arrived at a prodigious success, with its central offices in Hanbridge and its branch offices in the other four towns, and its scores of clerks and collectors presided over by Mr Penkethman. It had met with opposition. The mighty said that Denry was making an unholy fortune under the guise of philanthropy. And to be on the safe side the Countess of Chell had resigned her official patronage of the club and given her shares to the Pirehill Infirmary, which had accepted the high dividends on them without the least protest. As for Denry, he said that he had never set out to be a philanthropist nor posed as one, and that his unique intention was to grow rich by supplying a want, like the rest of them, and that anyhow there was no compulsion to belong to his Thrift Club. Then letters in his defence from representatives of the thousands and thousands of members of the club rained into the columns of the *Signal*, and Denry was the most discussed personage in the county. It was stated that such thrift clubs, under various names, existed in several large towns in Yorkshire and Lancashire. This disclosure rehabilitated Denry completely in general esteem, for whatever obtains in Yorkshire and Lancashire must be right for Staffordshire; but it rather dashed Denry, who was obliged to admit to himself that after all he had not invented the Thrift Club. Finally the hundreds of tradesmen who had bound themselves to allow a discount of twopence in the shilling to the club (sole source of the club's dividends) had endeavoured to revolt. Denry effectually cowed them by threatening to establish co-operative stores—there was not a single co-operative store in the Five Towns. They knew he would have the wild audacity to do it.

Thenceforward the progress of the Thrift Club had been unruffled. Denry waxed amazingly in importance. His mule died. He dared not buy a proper horse and dogcart, because he dared not bring such an equipage to the front door of his mother's four-and-sixpenny cottage. So he had taken to cabs. In all exterior magnificence and lavishness he equalled even the great Harold Etches, of whom he had once been afraid; and like Etches he became a famous *habitué* of Llandudno pier. But whereas Etches lived with his wife in a superb house at Bleakridge, Denry lived with his mother in a ridiculous cottage in ridiculous Brougham Street. He had a regiment of acquaintances and he accepted a lot of hospitality, but he could not return it at Brougham Street. His greatness fizzled into nothing in Brougham Street. It stopped short and sharp at the corner of St Luke's Square, where he left his cabs. He could do nothing with his mother. If she was not still going out as a sempstress the reason was, not that she was not ready to go out, but that her old clients had ceased to send for her. And could they be blamed for not employing at three shillings a day the mother of a young man who wallowed in thousands sterling? Denry had essayed over and over again to instil reason into his mother, and he had invariably failed. She was too independent, too profoundly rooted in her habits; and her character had more force than his. Of course, he might have left her and set up a suitably gorgeous house of his own.

But he would not.

In fact, they were a remarkable pair.

On this eve of her birthday he had meant to cajole her into some step, to win her by an appeal, basing his argument on her indisposition. But he was being beaten off once more. The truth was that a cajoling, caressing tone could not be long employed towards Mrs Machin. She was not persuasive herself, nor; favourable to persuasiveness in others.

"Well," said she, "if you're making two thousand a year, ye can spend it or save it as ye like, though ye'd better save it. Ye never know what may happen in these days. There was a man dropped half-a-crown down a grid opposite only the day before yesterday."

Denry laughed.

"Ay!" she said; "ye can laugh."

"There's no doubt about one thing," he said, "you ought to be in bed. You ought to stay in bed for two or three days at least."

"Yes," she said. "And who's going to look after the house while I'm moping between blankets?"

"You can have Rose Chudd in," he said.

"No," said she. "I'm not going to have any woman rummaging about my house, and me in bed."

"You know perfectly well she's been practically starving since her husband died, and as she's going out charing, why can't you have her and put a bit of bread into her mouth?"

"Because I won't have her! Neither her nor any one. There's naught to prevent you giving her some o' your two thousand a year if you've a mind. But I see no reason for my house being turned upside down by her, even if I *have* got a bit of a cold."

"You're an unreasonable old woman," said Denry.

"Happen I am!" said she. "There can't be two wise ones in a family. But I'm not going to give up this cottage, and as long as I am standing on my feet I'm not going to pay any one for doing what I can do better myself." A pause. "And so you needn't think it! You can't come round me with a fur mantle." She retired to rest. On the following morning he was very glum.

"You needn't be so glum," she said.

But she was rather pleased at his glumness. For in him glumness was a sign that he recognised defeat.

II

The next episode between them was curiously brief. Denry had influenza. He said that naturally he had caught hers.

He went to bed and stayed there. She nursed him all day, and grew angry in a vain attempt to force him to eat. Towards night he tossed furiously on the little bed in the little bedroom, complaining of fearful headaches. She remained by his side most of the night. In the morning he was easier. Neither of them mentioned the word "doctor." She spent the day largely on the stairs. Once more towards night he grew worse, and she remained most of the second night by his side.

In the sinister winter dawn Denry murmured in a feeble tone:

"Mother, you'd better send for him."

"Doctor?" she said. And secretly she thought that she *had* better send for the doctor, and that there must be after all some difference between influenza and a cold.

"No," said Denry; "send for young Lawton."

"Young Lawton!" she exclaimed. "What do you want young Lawton to come *here* for?"

"I haven't made my will," Denry answered.

"Pooh!" she retorted.

Nevertheless she was the least bit in the world frightened. And she sent for Dr Stirling, the aged Harrop's Scotch partner.

Dr Stirling, who was full-bodied and left little space for anybody else in the tiny, shabby bedroom of the man with four thousand a year, gazed at Mrs Machin, and he gazed also at Denry.

"Ye must go to bed this minute," said he.

"But he's *in* bed," cried Mrs Machin.

"I mean yerself," said Dr Stirling.

She was very nearly at the end of her resources. And the proof was that she had no strength left to fight Dr Stirling. She did go to bed. And shortly afterwards Denry got up. And a little later, Rose Chudd, that prim and efficient young widow from lower down the street, came into the house and controlled it as if it had been her own. Mrs Machin, whose constitution was hardy, arose in about a week, cured, and duly dismissed Rose with wages and without thanks. But Rose had been. Like the *Signal's* burglars, she had "effected an entrance." And the house had not been turned upside down. Mrs Machin, though she tried, could not find fault with the result of Rose's uncontrolled activities.

III

One morning—and not very long afterwards, in such wise did Fate seem to favour the young at the expense of the old—Mrs Machin received two letters which alarmed and disgusted her. One was from her landlord, announcing that he had sold the house in which she lived to a Mr Wilbraham of London, and that in future she must pay the rent to the said Mr Wilbraham or his legal representatives. The other was from a firm of London solicitors announcing that their client, Mr Wilbraham, had bought the house, and that the rent must be paid to their agent, whom they would name later.

Mrs Machin gave vent to her emotion in her customary manner: "Bless us!"

And she showed the impudent letters to Denry.

"Oh!" said Denry. "So he has bought them, has he? I heard he was going to."

"Them?," exclaimed Mrs Machin. "What else has he bought?"

361

"I expect he's bought all the five—this and the four below, as far as Downes's. I expect you'll find that the other four have had notices just like these. You know all this row used to belong to the Wilbrahams. You surely must remember that, mother?"

"Is he one of the Wilbrahams of Hillport, then?"

"Yes, of course he is."

"I thought the last of 'em was Cecil, and when he'd beggared himself here he went to Australia and died of drink. That's what I always heard. We always used to say as there wasn't a Wilbraham left."

"He did go to Australia, but he didn't die of drink. He disappeared, and when he'd made a fortune he turned up again in Sydney, so it seems. I heard he's thinking of coming back here to settle. Anyhow, he's buying up a lot of the Wilbraham property. I should have thought you'd have heard of it. Why, lots of people have been talking about it."

"Well," said Mrs Machin, "I don't like it."

She objected to a law which permitted a landlord to sell a house over the head of a tenant who had occupied it for more than thirty years. In the course of the morning she discovered that Denry was right—the other tenants had received notices exactly similar to hers.

Two days later Denry arrived home for tea with a most surprising article of news. Mr Cecil Wilbraham had been down to Bursley from London, and had visited him, Denry. Mr Cecil Wilbraham's local information was evidently quite out of date, for he had imagined Denry to be a rent-collector and estate agent, whereas the fact was that Denry had abandoned this minor vocation years ago. His desire had been that Denry should collect his rents and watch over his growing interests in the district.

"So what did you tell him?" asked Mrs Machin.

"I told him I'd do it." said Denry.

"Why?"

"I thought it might be safer for *you*," said Denry, with a certain emphasis. "And, besides, it looked as if it might be a bit of a lark. He's a very peculiar chap."

"Peculiar?"

"For one thing, he's got the largest moustaches of any man I ever saw. And there's something up with his left eye. And then I think he's a bit mad."

"Mad?"

"Well, touched. He's got a notion about building a funny sort of a house for himself on a plot of land at Bleakridge. It appears he's fond of living alone, and he's collected all kind of dodges for doing without servants and still being comfortable."

"Ay! But he's right there!" breathed Mrs Machin in deep sympathy. As she said about once a week, "She never could abide the idea of servants." "He's not married, then?" she added.

"He told me he'd been a widower three times, but he'd never had any children," said Denry.

"Bless us!" murmured Mrs Machin.

Denry was the one person in the town who enjoyed the acquaintance and the confidence of the thrice-widowed stranger with long moustaches. He had descended without notice on Bursley, seen Denry (at the branch office of the Thrift Club), and then departed. It was understood that later he would permanently settle in the district. Then the wonderful house began to rise on the plot of land at Bleakridge. Denry had general charge of it, but always subject to erratic and autocratic instructions from London. Thanks to Denry, who, since the historic episode at Llandudno, had remained very friendly with the Cotterill family, Mr Cotterill had the job of building the house; the plans came from London. And though Mr Cecil Wilbraham proved to be exceedingly watchful against any form of imposition, the job was a remunerative one for Mr Cotterill, who talked a great deal about the originality of the residence. The town judged of the wealth and importance of Mr Cecil Wilbraham by the fact that a person so wealthy and important as Denry should be content to act as his agent. But then the Wilbrahams had been magnates in the Bursley region for generations, up till the final Wilbraham smash in the late seventies. The town hungered to see those huge moustaches and that peculiar eye. In addition to Denry, only one person had seen the madman, and that person was Nellie Cotterill, who had been viewing the half-built house with Denry one Sunday morning when the madman had most astonishingly arrived upon the scene, and after a few minutes vanished. The building of the house strengthened greatly the friendship between Denry and the Cotterills. Yet Denry neither liked Mr Cotterill nor trusted him. The next incident in these happening was that Mrs Machin received notice from the London firm to quit her four-and-sixpence-a-week cottage. It seemed to her that not merely Brougham Street, but the world, was coming to an end. She was very angry with Denry for not protecting her more successfully. He

362

was Mr Wilbraham's agent, he collected the rent, and it was his duty to guard his mother from unpleasantness. She observed, however, that he was remarkably disturbed by the notice, and he assured her that Mr Wilbraham had not consulted him in the matter at all. He wrote a letter to London, which she signed, demanding the reason of this absurd notice flung at an ancient and perfect tenant. The reply was that Mr Wilbraham intended to pull the houses down, beginning with Mrs Machin's, and rebuild.

"Pooh!" said Denry. "Don't you worry your head, mother; I shall arrange it. He'll be down here soon to see his new house—it's practically finished, and the furniture is coming in—and I'll just talk to him."

But Mr Wilbraham did not come, the explanation doubtless being that he was mad. On the other hand, fresh notices came with amazing frequency. Mrs Machin just handed them over to Denry. And then Denry received a telegram to say that Mr Wilbraham would be at his new house that night and wished to see Denry there. Unfortunately, on the same day, by the afternoon post, while Denry was at his offices, there arrived a sort of supreme and ultimate notice from London to Mrs Machin, and it was on blue paper. It stated, baldly, that as Mrs Machin had failed to comply with all the previous notices, had, indeed, ignored them, she and her goods would now be ejected into the street, according to the law. It gave her twenty-four hours to flit. Never had a respectable dame been so insulted as Mrs Machin was insulted by that notice. The prospect of camping out in Brougham Street confronted her. When Denry reached home that evening, Mrs Machin, as the phrase is, "gave it him."

Denry admitted frankly that he was nonplussed, staggered and outraged. But the thing was simply another proof of Mr Wilbraham's madness. After tea he decided that his mother must put on her best clothes, and go up with him to see Mr Wilbraham and firmly expostulate—in fact, they would arrange the situation between them; and if Mr Wilbraham was obstinate they would defy Mr Wilbraham. Denry explained to his mother that an Englishwoman's cottage was her castle, that a landlord's minions had no right to force an entrance, and that the one thing that Mr Wilbraham could do was to begin unbuilding the cottage from the top outside.... And he would like to see Mr Wilbraham try it on!

So the sealskin mantle (for it was spring again) went up with Denry to Bleakridge.

IV

The moon shone in the chill night. The house stood back from Trafalgar Road in the moonlight—a squarish block of a building.

"Oh!" said Mrs Machin, "it isn't so large."

"No! He didn't want it large. He only wanted it large enough," said Denry, and pushed a button to the right of the front door. There was no reply, though they heard the ringing of the bell inside. They waited. Mrs Machin was very nervous, but thanks to her sealskin mantle she was not cold.

"This is a funny doorstep," she remarked, to kill time.

"It's of marble," said Denry.

"What's that for? " asked his mother.

"So much easier to keep clean," said Denry.

"Well," said Mrs Machin, "it's pretty dirty now, anyway."

It was.

"Quite simple to clean," said Denry, bending down. "You just turn this tap at the side. You see, it's so arranged that it sends a flat jet along the step. Stand off a second."

He turned the tap, and the step was washed pure in a moment.

"How is it that that water steams?" Mrs Machin demanded.

"Because it's hot," said Denry. " Did you ever know water steam for any other reason?"

"Hot water outside?"

"Just as easy to have hot water outside as inside, isn't it?" said Denry.

"Well, I never!" exclaimed Mrs Machin. She was impressed.

"That's how everything's dodged up in this house," said Denry. He shut off the water.

And he rang once again. No answer! No illumination within the abode!

"I'll tell you what I shall do," said Denry at length. "I shall let myself in. I've got a key of the back door."

"Are you sure it's all right?"

"I don't care if it isn't all right," said Denry, defiantly. "He asked me to be up here, and he ought to be here to meet me. I'm not going to stand any nonsense from anybody."

In they went, having skirted round the walls of the house.

Denry closed the door, pushed a switch, and the electric light shone. Electric light was then quite a novelty in Bursley. Mrs Machin had never seen it in action. She had to admit that it was less complicated than oil-lamps.

In the kitchen the electric light blazed upon walls tiled in grey and a floor tiled in black and white. There was a gas range and a marble slopstone with two taps. The woodwork was dark. Earthenware saucepans stood on a shelf. The cupboards were full of gear chiefly in earthenware. Denry began to exhibit to his mother a tank provided with ledges and shelves and grooves, in which he said that everything except knives could be washed and dried automatically.

"Hadn't you better go and find your Mr Wilbraham? she interrupted.

"So I had," said Denry; "I was forgetting him."

She heard him wandering over the house and calling in divers tones upon Mr Wilbraham. But she heard no other voice. Meanwhile she examined the kitchen in detail, appreciating some of its devices and failing to comprehend others.

"I expect he's missed the train," said Denry, coming back. "Anyhow, he isn't here. I may as well show you the rest of the house now."

He led her into the hall, which was radiantly lighted.

"It's quite warm here," said Mrs Machin.

"The whole house is heated by steam," said Denry. "No fireplaces."

"No fireplaces!"

"No! No fireplaces. No grates to polish, ashes to carry down, coals to carry up, mantelpieces to dust, fire-irons to clean, fenders to polish, chimneys to sweep."

"And suppose he wants a bit of fire all of a sudden in summer?"

"Gas stove in every room for emergencies," said Denry.

She glanced into a room.

"But," she cried, "it's all complete, ready! And as warm as toast."

"Yes," said Denry, "he gave orders. I can't think why on earth he isn't here."

At that moment an electric bell rang loud and sharp, and Mrs Machin jumped.

"There he is!" said Denry, moving to the door.

"Bless us! What will he think of us being here like? " Mrs Machin mumbled.

"Pooh!" said Denry, carelessly. And he opened the door.

V

Three persons stood on the newly-washed marble step—Mr and Mrs Cotterill and their daughter.

"Oh! Come in! Come in! Make yourselves quite at home. That's what *we're* doing," said Denry in blithe greeting; and added, "I suppose he's invited you too?"

And it appeared that Mr Cecil Wilbraham had indeed invited them too. He had written from London saying that he would be glad if Mr and Mrs Cotterill would "drop in" on this particular evening. Further, he had mentioned that, as be had already had the pleasure of meeting Miss Cotterill, perhaps she would accompany her parents.

"Well, he isn't here," said Denry, shaking hands. "He must have missed his train or something. He can't possibly be here now till to-morrow. But the house seems to be all ready for him...."

"Yes, my word! And how's yourself, Mrs Cotterill?" put in Mrs Machin.

"So we may as well look over it in its finished state. I suppose that's what he asked us up for," Denry concluded.

Mrs Machin explained quickly and nervously that she had not been comprised in any invitation; that her errand was pure business.

"Come on upstairs," Denry called out, turning switches and adding radiance to radiance.

"Denry!" his mother protested, "I'm sure I don't know what Mr and Mrs Cotterill will think of you! You carry on as if you owned everything in the place. I wonder *at* you!"

"Well," said Denry, "if anybody in this town is the owner's agent I am. And Mr Cotterill has built the blessed house. If Wilbraham wanted to keep his old shanty to himself, he shouldn't send out invitations. It's simple enough not to send out invitations. Now, Nellie!"

He was hanging over the balustrade at the curve of the stairs.

The familiar ease with which he said, "Now, Nellie," and especially the spontaneity of Nellie's instant response, put new thoughts into the mind of Mrs Machin. But she neither pricked up her ears, nor started back, nor accomplished any of the acrobatic feats which an ordinary mother of a wealthy son would have performed under similar circumstances. Her ears did not even tremble. And she just said:

"I like this balustrade knob being of black china."

"Every knob in the house is of black china," said Denry. "Never shows dirt. But if you should take it into your head to clean it, you can do it with a damp cloth in a second."

Nellie now stood beside him. Nellie had grown up since the Llandudno episode. She did not blush at a glance. When spoken to suddenly she could answer without torture to herself. She could, in fact, maintain a conversation without breaking down for a much longer time than, a few years ago, she had been able to skip without breaking down. She no longer imagined that all the people in the street were staring at her, anxious to find faults in her appearance. She had temporarily ruined the lives of several amiable and fairly innocent young men by refusing to marry them. (For she was pretty, and her father cut a figure in the town, though her mother did not.) And yet, despite the immense accumulation of her experiences and the weight of her varied knowledge of human nature, there was something very girlish and timidly roguish about her as she stood on the stairs near Denry, waiting for the elder generation to follow. The old Nellie still lived in her.

The party passed to the first floor.

And the first floor exceeded the ground floor in marvels. In each bedroom two aluminium taps poured hot and cold water respectively into a marble basin, and below the marble basin was a sink. No porterage of water anywhere in the house. The water came to you, and every room consumed its own slops. The bedsteads were of black enamelled iron and very light. The floors were covered with linoleum, with a few rugs that could be shaken with one hand. The walls were painted with grey enamel. Mrs Cotterill, with her all-seeing eye, observed a detail that Mrs Machin had missed. There were no sharp corners anywhere. Every corner, every angle between wall and floor or wall and wall, was rounded, to facilitate cleaning. And every wall, floor, ceiling, and fixture could be washed, and all the furniture was enamelled and could be wiped with a cloth in a moment instead of having to be polished with three cloths and many odours in a day and a half. The bath-room was absolutely waterproof; you could spray it with a hose, and by means of a gas apparatus you could produce an endless supply of hot water independent of the general supply. Denry was apparently familiar with each detail of Mr Wilbraham's manifold contrivances, and he explained them with an enormous gusto.

"Bless us!" said Mrs Machin.

"Bless us!" said Mrs Cotterill (doubtless the force of example).

They descended to the dining-room, where a supper-table had been laid by order of the invisible Mr Cecil Wilbraham. And there the ladies lauded Mr Wilbraham's wisdom in eschewing silver. Everything of the table service that could be of earthenware was of earthenware. The forks and spoons were electro-plate.

"Why," Mrs Cotterill said, "I could run this house without a servant and have myself tidy by ten o'clock in a morning."

And Mrs Machin nodded.

"And then when you want a regular turn-out, as you call it," said Denry, "there's the vacuum-cleaner."

The vacuum-cleaner was at that period the last word of civilisation, and the first agency for it was being set up in Bursley. Denry explained the vacuum-cleaner to the housewives, who had got no further than a Ewbank. And they again called down blessings on themselves.

"What price this supper?" Denry exclaimed. "We ought to eat it. I'm sure he'd like us to eat it. Do sit down, all of you. I'll take the consequences."

Mrs Machin hesitated even more than the other ladies.

"It's really very strange, him not being here." She shook her head.

"Don't I tell you he's quite mad," said Denry.

"I shouldn't think he was so mad as all that," said Mrs Machin, dryly. "This is the most sensible kind of a house I've ever seen."

"Oh! Is it?" Denry answered. "Great Scott! I never noticed those three bottles of wine on the sideboard."

At length he succeeded in seating them at the table. Thenceforward there was no difficulty. The ample and diversified cold supper began to disappear steadily, and the wine with it. And as the wine disappeared so did Mr Cotterill (who had been pompous and taciturn) grow talkative, offering to the company the exact figures of the cost of the house, and so forth. But ultimately the sheer joy of life killed arithmetic.

Mrs Machin, however, could not quite rid herself of the notion that she was in a dream that outraged the proprieties. The entire affair, for an unromantic spot like Bursley, was too fantastically and wickedly romantic.

"We must be thinking about home, Denry," said she.

"Plenty of time," Denry replied. "What! All that wine gone! I'll see if there's any more in the sideboard."

He emerged, with a red face, from bending into the deeps of the enamelled sideboard, and a wine-bottle was in his triumphant hand. It had already been opened.

"Hooray!" he proclaimed, pouring a white wine into his glass and raising the glass: "here's to the health of Mr Cecil Wilbraham."

He made a brave tableau in the brightness of the electric light.

Then he drank. Then he dropped the glass, which broke.

"Ugh! What's that?" he demanded, with the distorted features of a gargoyle.

His mother, who was seated next to him, seized the bottle. Denry's hand, in clasping the bottle, had hidden a small label, which said:

"*POISON—Nettleship's Patent Enamel-Cleaning Fluid. One wipe does it.*"

Confusion! Only Nellie Cotterill seemed to be incapable of realising that a grave accident had occurred. She had laughed throughout the supper, and she still laughed, hysterically, though she had drunk scarcely any wine. Her mother silenced her.

Denry was the first to recover.

"It'll be all right," said he, leaning back in his chair. "They always put a bit of poison in those things. It can't hurt me, really. I never noticed the label."

Mrs Machin smelt at the bottle. She could detect no odour, but the fact that she could detect no odour appeared only to increase her alarm.

"You must have an emetic instantly," she said.

"Oh no!" said Denry. "I shall be all right." And he did seem to be suddenly restored.

"You must have an emetic instantly," she repeated.

"What can I have?" he grumbled. "You can't expect to find emetics here."

"Oh yes, I can," said she. "I saw a mustard tin in a cupboard in the kitchen. Come along now, and don't be silly."

Nellie's hysteric mirth surged up again.

Denry objected to accompanying his mother into the kitchen. But he was forced to submit. She shut the door on both of them. It is probable that during the seven minutes which they spent mysteriously together in the kitchen, the practicability of the kitchen apparatus for carrying off waste products was duly tested. Denry came forth, very pale and very cross, on his mother's arm.

"There's no danger now," said his mother, easily.

Naturally the party was at an end. The Cotterills sympathised, and prepared to depart, and inquired whether Denry could walk home.

Denry replied, from a sofa, in a weak, expiring voice, that he was perfectly incapable of walking home, that his sensations were in the highest degree disconcerting, that he should sleep in that house, as the bedrooms were ready for occupation, and that he should expect his mother to remain also.

And Mrs Machin had to concur. Mrs Machin sped the Cotterills from the door as though it had been her own door. She was exceedingly angry and agitated. But she could not impart her feelings to the suffering Denry. He moaned on a bed for about half-an-hour, and then fell asleep. And in the middle of the night, in the dark, strange house, she also fell asleep.

VI

The next morning she arose and went forth, and in about half-an-hour returned. Denry was still in bed, but his health seemed to have resumed its normal excellence. Mrs Machin burst upon him in such a state of complicated excitement as he had never before seen her in.

"Denry," she cried, "what do you think?"

"What?" said he.

"I've just been down home, and they're—they're pulling the house down. All the furniture's out, and they've got all the tiles off the roof, and the windows out. And there's a regular crowd watching."

Denry sat up.

"And I can tell you another piece of news," said he. "Mr Cecil Wilbraham is dead."

"Dead!" she breathed.

"Yes," said Denry. "*I think he's served his purpose.* As we're here, we'll stop here. Don't forget it's the most sensible kind of a house you've ever seen. Don't forget that Mrs Cotterill could run it without a servant and have herself tidy by ten o'clock in a morning."

Mrs Machin perceived then, in a flash of terrible illumination, that there never had been any Cecil Wilbraham; that Denry had merely invented him and his long moustaches and his wall eye for the purpose of getting the better of his mother. The whole affair was an immense swindle upon her. Not a Mr Cecil Wilbraham, but her own son had bought her cottage over her head and jockeyed her out of it beyond any chance of getting into it

366

again. And to defeat his mother the rascal had not simply perverted the innocent Nellie Cotterill to some co-operation in his scheme, but he had actually bought four other cottages, because the landlord would not sell one alone, and he was actually demolishing property to the sole end of stopping her from re-entering it!

Of course, the entire town soon knew of the upshot of the battle, of the year-long battle, between Denry and his mother, and the means adopted by Denry to win. The town also had been hoodwinked, but it did not mind that. It loved its Denry the more, and seeing that he was now properly established in the most remarkable house in the district, it soon afterwards made him a Town Councillor as some reward for his talent in amusing it.

And Denry would say to himself:

"Everything went like clockwork, except the mustard and water. I didn't bargain for the mustard and water. And yet, if I was clever enough to think of putting a label on the bottle and to have the beds prepared, I ought to have been clever enough to keep mustard out of the house." It would be wrong to mince the unpleasant fact that the sham poisoning which he had arranged to the end that he and his mother should pass the night in the house had finished in a manner much too realistic for Denry's pleasure. Mustard and water, particularly when mixed by Mrs Machin, is mustard and water. She had that consolation.

CHAPTER IX
THE GREAT NEWSPAPER WAR

I

When Denry and his mother had been established a year and a month in the new house at Bleakridge, Denry received a visit one evening which perhaps flattered him more than anything had ever flattered him. The visitor was Mr Myson. Now Mr Myson was the founder, proprietor and editor of the *Five Towns Weekly*, a new organ of public opinion which had been in existence about a year; and Denry thought that Mr Myson had popped in to see him in pursuit of an advertisement of the Thrift Club, and at first he was not at all flattered.

But Mr Myson was not hunting for advertisements, and Denry soon saw him to be the kind of man who would be likely to depute that work to others. Of middle height, well and quietly dressed, with a sober, assured deportment, he spoke in a voice and accent that were not of the Five Towns; they were superior to the Five Towns. And in fact Mr Myson originated in Manchester and had seen London. He was not provincial, and he beheld the Five Towns as part of the provinces; which no native of the Five Towns ever succeeds in doing. Nevertheless, his manner to Denry was the summit of easy and yet deferential politeness.

He asked permission "to put something before" Denry. And when, rather taken aback by such smooth phrases, Denry had graciously accorded the permission, he gave a brief history of the *Five Towns Weekly*, showing how its circulation had grown, and definitely stating that at that moment it was yielding a profit. Then he said:

"Now my scheme is to turn it into a daily."

"Very good notion," said Denry, instinctively.

"I'm glad you think so," said Mr Myson. "Because I've come here in the hope of getting your assistance. I'm a stranger to the district, and I want the co-operation of some one who isn't. So I've come to you. I need money, of course, though I have myself what most people would consider sufficient capital. But what I need more than money is—well—moral support."

"And who put you on to me?" asked Denry.

Mr Myson smiled. "I put myself on to you," said he. "I think I may say I've got my bearings in the Five Towns, after over a year's journalism in it, and it appeared to me that you were the best man I could approach. I always believe in flying high."

Therein was Denry flattered. The visit seemed to him to seal his position in the district in a way in which his election to the Bursley Town Council had failed to do. He had been somehow disappointed with that election. He had desired to display his interest in the serious welfare of the town, and to answer his opponent's arguments with better ones. But the burgesses of his ward appeared to have no passionate love of logic. They just cried "Good old Denry!" and elected him—with a majority of only forty-one votes. He had expected to feel a different Denry when he could put "Councillor" before his name. It was not so. He had been solemnly in the mayoral procession to church, he had attended meetings of the council, he had been nominated to the Watch Committee. But he was still precisely the same Denry, though the youngest member of the council. But now he was being recognised from the outside. Mr Myson's keen Manchester eye, ranging over the quarter of a million inhabitants of the Five Towns in search of a representative individual force, had settled on Denry Machin. Yes, he was flattered. Mr Myson's choice threw a rose-light on all Denry's career: his wealth and its origin; his house and stable, which were the astonishment and the admiration of the town; his Universal Thrift Club; yea, and his councillorship! After all, these *were* marvels. (And possibly the greatest marvel was the resigned presence of his mother in that wondrous house, and the fact that she consented to employ Rose Chudd, the incomparable Sappho of charwomen, for three hours every day.)

In fine, he perceived from Mr Myson's eyes that his position was unique.

And after they had chatted a little, and the conversation had deviated momentarily from journalism to house property, he offered to display Machin House (as he had christened it) to Mr Myson, and Mr Myson was really impressed beyond the ordinary. Mr Myson's homage to Mrs Machin, whom they chanced on in the paradise of the bath-room, was the polished mirror of courtesy. How Denry wished that he could behave like that when he happened to meet countesses.

Then, once more in the drawing-room, they resumed the subject of newspapers.

"You know," said Mr Myson, "it's really a very bad thing indeed for a district to have only one daily newspaper. I've nothing myself to say against *The Staffordshire Signal*, but you'd perhaps be astonished"— this in a confidential tone—"at the feeling there is against the *Signal* in many quarters."

"Really!" said Denry.

"Of course its fault is that it isn't sufficiently interested in the great public questions of the district. And it can't be. Because it can't take a definite side. It must try to please all parties. At any rate it must offend none. That is the great evil of a journalistic monopoly.... Two hundred and fifty thousand people—why! there is an ample public for two first-class papers. Look at Nottingham! Look at Bristol! Look at Leeds! Look at Sheffield!...and*their* newspapers."

And Denry endeavoured to look at these great cities! Truly the Five Towns was just about as big.

The dizzy journalistic intoxication seized him. He did not give Mr Myson an answer at once, but he gave himself an answer at once. He would go into the immense adventure. He was very friendly with the *Signal*people—certainly; but business was business, and the highest welfare of the Five Towns was the highest welfare of the Five Towns.

Soon afterwards all the hoardings of the district spoke with one blue voice, and said that the *Five Towns Weekly*was to be transformed into the *Five Towns Daily*, with four editions, beginning each day at noon, and that the new organ would be conducted on the lines of a first-class evening paper.

The inner ring of knowing ones knew that a company entitled "The Five Towns Newspapers, Limited," had been formed, with a capital of ten thousand pounds, and that Mr Myson held three thousand pounds' worth of shares, and the great Denry Machin one thousand five hundred, and that the remainder were to be sold and allotted as occasion demanded. The inner ring said that nothing would ever be able to stand up against the*Signal*. On the other hand, it admitted that Denry, the most prodigious card ever born into the Five Towns, had never been floored by anything. The inner ring anticipated the future with glee. Denry and Mr Myson anticipated the future with righteous confidence. As for the *Signal*, it went on its august way, blind to sensational hoardings.

II

On the day of the appearance of the first issue of the *Five Towns Daily*, the offices of the new paper at Hanbridge gave proof of their excellent organisation, working in all details with an admirable smoothness. In the basement a Marinoni machine thundered like a sucking dove to produce fifteen thousand copies an hour. On the ground floor ingenious arrangements had been made for publishing the paper; in particular, the iron railings to keep the boys in order in front of the publishing counter had been imitated from the *Signal*. On the first floor was the editor and founder with his staff, and above that the composing department. The number of stairs that separated the composing department from the machine-room was not a positive advantage, but bricks and mortar are inelastic, and one does what one can. The offices looked very well from the outside, and they compared passably with the offices of the *Signal* close by. The posters were duly in the ground-floor windows, and gold signs, one above another to the roof, produced an air of lucrative success.

Denry happened to be in the *Daily* offices that afternoon. He had had nothing to do with the details of organisation, for details of organisation were not his speciality. His speciality was large, leading ideas. He knew almost nothing of the agreements with correspondents and Press Association and Central News, and the racing services and the fiction syndicates, nor of the difficulties with the Compositors' Union, nor of the struggle to lower the price of paper by the twentieth of a penny per pound, nor of the awful discounts allowed to certain advertisers, nor of the friction with the railway company, nor of the sickening adulation that had been lavished on quite unimportant newsagents, nor—worst of all —of the dearth of newsboys. These matters did not attract him. He could not stoop to them. But when Mr Myson, calm and proud, escorted him down to the machine-room, and the Marinoni threw a folded pink *Daily* almost into his hands, and it looked exactly like a real newspaper, and he saw one of his own descriptive articles in it, and he reflected that he was an owner of. it—then Denry was attracted and delighted, and his heart beat. For this pink thing was the symbol and result of the whole affair, and had the effect of a miracle on him.

And he said to himself, never guessing how many thousands of men had said it before him, that a newspaper was the finest toy in the world.

About four o'clock the publisher, in shirt sleeves and an apron, came up to Mr Myson and respectfully asked him to step into the publishing office. Mr Myson stepped into the publishing office and Denry with him, and they there beheld a small ragged boy with a bleeding nose and a bundle of *Dailys* in his wounded hand.

"Yes," the boy sobbed; "and they said they'd cut my eyes out and plee [play] marbles wi' 'em, if they cotched me in Crown Square agen," And he threw down the papers with a final yell.

The two directors learnt that the delicate threat had been uttered by four *Signal* boys, who had objected to any fellow-boys offering any paper other than the *Signal* for sale in Crown Square or anywhere else.

Of course, it was absurd.

Still, absurd as it was, it continued. The central publishing offices of the *Daily* at Hanbridge, and its branch offices in the neighbouring towns, were like military hospitals, and the truth appeared to the directors that while the public was panting to buy copies of the *Daily*, the sale of the *Daily* was being prevented by means of a scandalous conspiracy on the part of *Signal* boys. For it must be understood that in the Five Towns people prefer to catch their newspaper in the street as it flies and cries. The *Signal* had a vast army of boys, to whom every year it gave a great *fête*. Indeed, the *Signal* possessed nearly all the available boys, and assuredly all the most pugilistic and strongest boys. Mr Myson had obtained boys only after persistent inquiry and demand, and such as he had found were not the fittest, and therefore were unlikely to survive. You would have supposed that in a district that never ceases to grumble about bad trade and unemployment, thousands of boys would have been delighted to buy the *Daily* at fourpence a dozen and sell it at sixpence. But it was not so.

On the second day the dearth of boys at the offices of the *Daily* was painful. There was that magnificent, enterprising newspaper waiting to be sold, and there was the great enlightened public waiting to buy; and scarcely any business could be done because the *Signal* boys had established a reign of terror over their puny and upstart rivals!

The situation was unthinkable.

Still, unthinkable as it was, it continued. Mr Myson had thought of everything except this. Naturally it had not occurred to him that an immense and serious effort for the general weal was going to be blocked by a gang of tatterdemalions.

He complained with dignity to the *Signal*, and was informed with dignity by the *Signal* that the *Signal* could not be responsible for the playful antics of its boys in the streets; that, in short, the Five Towns was a free country. In the latter proposition Mr Myson did not concur.

After trouble in the persuasion of parents—astonishing how indifferent the Five Towns' parent was to the loss of blood by his offspring!—a case reached the police-court. At the hearing the *Signal* gave a solicitor a watching brief, and that solicitor expressed the *Signal's* horror of carnage. The evidence was excessively contradictory, and the Stipendiary dismissed the summons with a good joke. The sole definite result was that the boy whose father had ostensibly brought the summons, got his ear torn within a quarter of an hour of leaving the court. Boys will be boys.

Still, the *Daily* had so little faith in human nature that it could not believe that the *Signal* was not secretly encouraging its boys to be boys. It could not believe that the *Signal*, out of a sincere desire for fair play and for the highest welfare of the district, would willingly sacrifice nearly half its circulation and a portion of its advertisement revenue. And the hurt tone of Mr Myson's leading articles seemed to indicate that in Mr Myson's opinion his older rival *ought* to do everything in its power to ruin itself. The *Signal* never spoke of the fight. The*Daily* gave shocking details of it every day.

The struggle trailed on through the weeks.

Then Denry had one of his ideas. An advertisement was printed in the *Daily* for two hundred able-bodied men to earn two shillings for working six hours a day. An address different from the address of the *Daily* was given. By a ruse Denry procured the insertion of the advertisement in the *Signal* also.

"We must expend our capital on getting the paper on to the streets," said Denry. "That's evident. We'll have it sold by men. We'll soon see if the *Signal* ragamuffins will attack *them*. And we won't pay 'em by results; we'll pay 'em a fixed wage; that'll fetch 'em. And a commission on sales into the bargain. Why! I wouldn't mind engaging *five* hundred men. Swamp the streets! That's it! Hang expense. And when we've done the trick, then we can go back to the boys; they'll have learnt their lesson."

And Mr Myson agreed and was pleased that Denry was living up to his reputation.

The state of the earthenware trade was supposed that summer to be worse than it had been since 1869, and the grumblings of the unemployed were prodigious, even seditious. Mr Myson therefore, as a measure of precaution, engaged a couple of policemen to ensure order at the address, and during the hours, named in the advertisement as a rendezvous for respectable men in search of a well-paid job. Having regard to the thousands of perishing families in the Five Towns, he foresaw a rush and a crush of eager breadwinners. Indeed, the arrangements were elaborate.

Forty minutes after the advertised time for the opening of the reception of respectable men in search of money, four men had arrived. Mr Myson, mystified, thought that there had been a mistake in the advertisement, but there was no mistake in the advertisement. A little later two more men came. Of the six, three were tipsy, and the other three absolutely declined to be seen selling papers in the streets. Two were abusive, one facetious. Mr Myson did not know his Five Towns; nor did Denry. A Five Towns' man, when he can get neither bread nor beer, will keep himself and his family on pride and water. The policemen went off to more serious duties.

III

Then came the announcement of the thirty-fifth anniversary of the *Signal*, and of the processional *fête* by which the *Signal* was at once to give itself a splendid spectacular advertisement and to reward and enhearten its boys. The *Signal* meant to liven up the streets of the Five Towns on that great day by means of a display of all the gilt chariots of Snape's Circus in the main thoroughfare. Many of the boys would be in the gilt chariots. Copies of the anniversary number of the *Signal* would be sold from the gilt chariots. The idea was excellent, and it showed that after all the *Signal* was getting just a little more afraid of its young rival than it had pretended to be.

For, strange to say, after a trying period of hesitation, the *Five Towns Daily* was slightly on the upward curve—thanks to Denry. Denry did not mean to be beaten by the puzzle which the *Daily* offered to his intelligence. There the *Daily* was, full of news, and with quite an encouraging show of advertisements, printed on real paper with real ink—and yet it would not "go." Notoriously the *Signal* earned a net profit of at the very least five thousand a year, whereas the *Daily* earned a net loss of at the very least sixty pounds a week—and of that sixty quite a third was Denry's money. He could not explain it. Mr Myson tried to rouse the public by passionately stirring up extremely urgent matters—such as the smoke nuisance, the increase of the rates, the park question, German competition, technical education for apprentices; but the public obstinately would not be roused concerning its highest welfare to the point of insisting on a regular supply of the *Daily*. If a mere five thousand souls had positively demanded daily a copy of the *Daily* and not slept till boys or agents had responded to their wish, the troubles of the *Daily* would soon have vanished. But this ridiculous public did not seem to care which paper was put into its hand in exchange for its halfpenny, so long as the sporting news was put there. It simply was indifferent. It failed to see the importance to such an immense district of having two flourishing and mutually-opposing daily organs. The fundamental boy difficulty remained ever present.

And it was the boy difficulty that Denry perseveringly and ingeniously attacked, until at length the *Daily* did indeed possess some sort of a brigade of its own, and the bullying and slaughter in the streets (so amusing to the inhabitants) grew a little less one-sided.

A week or more before the *Signal's* anniversary day, Denry heard that the *Signal* was secretly afraid lest the *Daily's* brigade might accomplish the marring of its gorgeous procession, and that the *Signal* was ready to do anything to smash the *Daily's* brigade. He laughed; he said he did not mind. About that time hostilities were rather acute; blood was warming, and both papers, in the excitation of rivalry, had partially lost the sense of what was due to the dignity of great organs. By chance a tremendous local football match—Knype v: Bursley—fell on the very Saturday of the procession. The rival arrangements for the reporting of the match were as tremendous as the match itself, and somehow the match seemed to add keenness to the journalistic struggle, especially as the *Daily* favoured Bursley and the *Signal* was therefore forced to favour Knype.

By all the laws of hazard there ought to have been a hitch on that historic Saturday. Telephone or telegraph ought to have broken down, or rain ought to have made play impossible, but no hitch occurred. And at five-thirty o'clock of a glorious afternoon in earliest November the *Daily* went to press with a truly brilliant account of the manner in which Bursley (for the first and last time in its history) had defeated Knype by one goal to none. Mr Myson was proud. Mr Myson defied the *Signal* to beat his descriptive report. As for the *Signal's* procession—well, Mr Myson and the chief sub-editor of the *Daily* glanced at each other and smiled.

And a few minutes later the *Daily* boys were rushing out of the publishing room with bundles of papers—assuredly in advance of the *Signal*.

It was at this juncture that the unexpected began to occur to the *Daily* boys. The publishing door of the *Daily* opened into Stanway Rents, a narrow alley in a maze of mean streets behind Crown Square. In Stanway Rents was a small warehouse in which, according to rumours of the afternoon, a free soup kitchen was to be opened. And just before the football edition of the *Daily* came off the Marinoni, it emphatically was opened, and there issued from its inviting gate an odour—not, to be sure, of soup, but of toasted cheese and hot jam—such an odour as had never before tempted the nostrils of a *Daily* boy; a unique and omnipotent odour. Several boys (who, I may state frankly, were traitors to the *Daily* cause, spies and mischief-makers from elsewhere) raced unhesitatingly in, crying that toasted cheese sandwiches and jam tarts were to be distributed like lightning to all authentic newspaper lads.

The entire gang followed—scores, over a hundred—inwardly expecting to emerge instantly with teeth fully employed, followed like sheep into a fold.

And the gate was shut.

Toasted cheese and hot jammy pastry were faithfully served to the ragged host—but with no breathless haste. And when, loaded, the boys struggled to depart, they were instructed by the kind philanthropist who had fed them to depart by another exit, and they discovered themselves In an enclosed yard, of which the double doors were apparently unyielding. And the warehouse door was shut also. And as the cheese and jam disappeared, shouts of fury arose on the air. The yard was so close to the offices of the *Daily* that the chimneypots of those offices could actually be seen. And yet the shouting brought no answer from the lords of the *Daily*, congratulating themselves up there on their fine account of the football match, and on their celerity in going to press and on the loyalty of their brigade.

The *Signal*, it need not be said, disavowed complicity in this extraordinary entrapping of the *Daily* brigade by means of an odour. Could it be held responsible for the excesses of its disinterested sympathisers?... Still, the appalling trick showed the high temperature to which blood had risen in the genial battle between great rival organs. Persons in the inmost ring whispered that Denry Machin had at length been bested on this critically important day.

IV

Snape's Circus used to be one of the great shining institutions of North Staffordshire, trailing its magnificence on sculptured wheels from town to town, and occupying the dreams of boys from one generation to another. Its headquarters were at Axe, in the Moorlands, ten miles away from Hanbridge, but the riches of old Snape had chiefly come from the Five Towns. At the time of the struggle between the *Signal* and the *Daily* its decline had already begun. The aged proprietor had recently died, and the name, and the horses, and the chariots, and the carefully-repaired tents had been sold to strangers. On the Saturday of the anniversary and the football match (which was also Martinmas Saturday) the circus was set up at Oldcastle, on the edge of the Five Towns, and was giving its final performances of the season. Even boys will not go to circuses in the middle of a Five Towns' winter. The *Signal* people had hired the processional portion of Snape's for the late afternoon and early evening. And the instructions were that the entire *cortège* should be round about the *Signal* offices, in marching order, not later than five o'clock.

But at four o'clock several gentlemen with rosettes in their button-holes and *Signal* posters in their hands arrived important and panting at the fair-ground at Oldcastle, and announced that the programme had been altered at the last moment, in order to defeat certain feared machinations of the unscrupulous *Daily*. The cavalcade was to be split into three groups, one of which, the chief, was to enter Hanbridge by a "back road," and the other two were to go to Bursley and Longshaw respectively. In this manner the forces of advertisement would be distributed, and the chief parts of the district equally honoured.

The special linen banners, pennons, and ribbons—bearing the words—

"*SIGNAL:* THIRTY-FIFTH ANNIVERSARY," &c.

had already been hung and planted and draped about the gilded summits of the chariots. And after some delay the processions were started, separating at the bottom of the Cattle Market. The head of the Hanbridge part of the procession consisted of an enormous car of Jupiter, with six wheels and thirty-six paregorical figures (as the clown used to say), and drawn by six piebald steeds guided by white reins. This coach had a windowed interior (at the greater fairs it sometimes served as a box-office) and in the interior one of the delegates of the *Signal* had fixed himself; from it he directed the paths of the procession.

It would be futile longer to conceal that the delegate of the *Signal* in the bowels of the car of Jupiter was not honestly a delegate of the *Signal* at all. He was, indeed, Denry Machin, and none other. From this single fact it will be seen to what extent the representatives of great organs had forgotten what was due to their dignity and to public decency. Ensconced in his lair Denry directed the main portion of the *Signal's* advertising procession by all manner of discreet lanes round the skirts of Hanbridge and so into the town from the hilly side. And ultimately the ten vehicles halted in Crapper Street, to the joy of the simple inhabitants.

Denry emerged and wandered innocently towards the offices of his paper, which were close by. It was getting late. The first yelling of the imprisoned *Daily* boys was just beginning to rise on the autumn air.

Suddenly Denry was accosted by a young man.

"Hello, Machin!" cried the young man. "What have you shaved your beard off, for? I scarcely knew you."

"I just thought I would, Swetnam," said Denry, who was obviously discomposed.

It was the youngest of the Swetnam boys; he and Denry had taken a sort of curt fancy to one another.

"I say," said Swetnam, confidentially, as if obeying a swift impulse, "I did hear that the *Signal* people meant to collar all your chaps this afternoon, and I believe they have done. Hear that now?" (Swetnam's father was intimate with the *Signal* people.)

"I know," Denry replied.

"But I mean—papers and all."

"I know," said Denry.

"Oh!" murmured Swetnam.

"But I'll tell you a secret," Denry added. "They aren't to-day's papers. They're yesterday's, and last week's and last month's. We've been collecting them specially and keeping them nice and new-looking."

"Well, you're a caution!" murmured Swetnam.

"I am," Denry agreed.

A number of men rushed at that instant with bundles of the genuine football edition from the offices of the *Daily*.

"Come on!" Denry cried to them. "Come on! This way! By-by, Swetnam."

And the whole file vanished round a corner. The yelling of imprisoned cheese-fed boys grew louder.

V

In the meantime at the *Signal* office (which was not three hundred yards away, but on the other side of Crown Square) apprehension had deepened into anxiety as the minutes passed and the Snape Circus procession persisted in not appearing on the horizon of the Oldcastle Road. The *Signal* would have telephoned to Snape's, but for the fact that a circus is never on the telephone. It then telephoned to its Oldcastle agent, who, after a long delay, was able to reply that the cavalcade had left Oldcastle at the appointed hour, with every sign of health and energy. Then the *Signal* sent forth scouts all down the Oldcastle Road to put spurs into the procession, and the scouts returned, having seen nothing. Pessimists glanced at the possibility of the whole procession having fallen into the canal at Cauldon Bridge. The paper was printed, the train-parcels for Knype, Longshaw, Bursley, and Turnhill were despatched; the boys were waiting; the fingers of the clock in the publishing department were simply flying. It had been arranged that the bulk of the Hanbridge edition, and in particular the first copies of it, should be sold by boys from the gilt chariots themselves. The publisher hesitated for an awful moment, and then decided that he could wait no more, and that the boys must sell the papers in the usual way from the pavements and gutters. There was no knowing what the *Daily* might not be doing.

And then *Signal* boys in dozens rushed forth paper-laden, but they were disappointed boys; they had thought to ride in gilt chariots, not to paddle in mud. And almost the first thing they saw in Crown Square was the car of Jupiter in its glory, flying all the *Signal* colours; and other cars behind. They did not rush now; they sprang, as from a catapult; and alighted like flies on the vehicles. Men insisted on taking their papers from them and paying for them on the spot. The boys were startled; they were entirely puzzled; but they had not the habit of refusing money. And off went the procession to the music of its own band down the road to Knype, and perhaps a hundred boys on board, cheering. The men in charge then performed a curious act: they tore down all the *Signal* flagging, and replaced it with the emblem of the *Daily*.

So that all the great and enlightened public wandering home in crowds from the football match at Knype, had the spectacle of a *Daily* procession instead of a *Signal* procession, and could scarce believe their eyes. And *Dailys* were sold in quantities from the cars. At Knype Station the procession curved and returned to Hanbridge, and finally, after a multitudinous triumph, came to a stand with all its *Daily* bunting in front of the *Signal* offices; and Denry appeared from his lair. Denry's men fled with bundles.

"They're an hour and a half late," said Denry calmly to one of the proprietors of the *Signal*, who was on the pavement. "But I've managed to get them here. I thought I'd just look in to thank you for giving such a good feed to our lads."

The telephones hummed with news of similar *Daily* processions in Longshaw and Bursley. And there was not a high-class private bar in the district that did not tinkle with delighted astonishment at the brazen, the inconceivable effrontery of that card, Denry Machin. Many people foresaw law-suits, but it was agreed that the*Signal* had begun the game of impudence in trapping the *Daily* lads so as to secure a holy calm for its much-trumpeted procession.

And Denry had not finished with the *Signal*.

In the special football edition of the *Daily* was an announcement, the first, of special Martinmas *fêtes* organised by the *Five Towns Daily*. And on the same morning every member of the Universal Thrift Club had received an invitation to the said *fêtes*. They were three—held on public ground at Hanbridge, Bursley, and Longshaw. They were in the style of the usual Five Towns "wakes"; that is to say, roundabouts, shows, gingerbread stalls, swings, cocoanut shies. But at each *fête* a new and very simple form of "shy" had been erected. It consisted of a row of small railway signals.

"March up! March up!" cried the shy-men. "Knock down the signal! Knock down the signal! And a packet of Turkish delight is yours. Knock down the signal!"

And when you had knocked down the signal the men cried:

"We wrap it up for you in the special Anniversary Number of the *Signal*."

And they disdainfully tore into suitable fragments copies of the *Signal* which had cost Denry & Co. a halfpenny each, and enfolded the Turkish delight therein, and handed it to you with a smack.

And all the fair-grounds were carpeted with draggled and muddy *Signals*. People were up to the ankles in*Signals*.

The affair was the talk of Sunday. Few matters in the Five Towns have raised more gossip than did that enormous escapade which Denry invented and conducted. The moral damage to the *Signal* was held to approach the disastrous. And now not the possibility but the probability of law-suits was incessantly discussed.

On the Monday both papers were bought with anxiety. Everybody was frothing to know what the respective editors would say.

But in neither sheet was there a single word as to the affair. Both had determined to be discreet; both were afraid. The *Signal* feared lest it might not, if the pinch came, be able to prove its innocence of the crime of luring boys into confinement by means of toasted cheese and hot jam. The *Signal* had also to consider its seriously damaged dignity; for such wounds silence is the best dressing. The *Daily* was comprehensively afraid. It had practically driven its gilded chariots through the entire Decalogue. Moreover, it had won easily in the grand altercation. It was exquisitely conscious of glory.

Denry went away to Blackpool, doubtless to grow his beard.

The proof of the *Daily's* moral and material victory was that soon afterwards there were four applicants, men of substance, for shares in the *Daily* company. And this, by the way, was the end of the tale. For these applicants, who secured options on a majority of the shares, were emissaries of the *Signal*. Armed with the options, the*Signal* made terms with its rival, and then by mutual agreement killed it. The price of its death was no trifle, but it was less than a year's profits of the *Signal*. Denry considered that he had been "done." But in the depths of his heart he was glad that he had been done. He had had too disconcerting a glimpse of the rigours and perils of journalism to wish to continue it. He had scored supremely and, for him, to score was life itself. His reputation as a card was far, far higher than ever. Had he so desired, he could have been elected to the House of Commons on the strength of his procession and *fête*.

Mr Myson, somewhat scandalised by the exuberance of his partner, returned to Manchester.

And the *Signal*, subsequently often referred to as "The Old Lady," resumed its monopolistic sway over the opinions of a quarter of a million of people, and has never since been attacked.

CHAPTER X
HIS INFAMY

I

When Denry at a single stroke "wherreted" his mother and proved his adventurous spirit by becoming the possessor of one of the first motor-cars ever owned in Bursley, his instinct naturally was to run up to Councillor Cotterill's in it. Not that he loved Councillor Cotterill, and therefore wished to make him a partaker in his joy; for he did not love Councillor Cotterill. He had never been able to forgive Nellie's father for those patronising airs years and years before at Llandudno, airs indeed which had not even yet disappeared from Cotterill's attitude towards Denry. Though they were Councillors on the same Town Council, though Denry was getting richer and Cotterill was assuredly not getting richer, the latter's face and tone always seemed to be saying to Denry: "Well, you are not doing so badly for a beginner." So Denry did not care to lose an opportunity of impressing Councillor Cotterill. Moreover, Denry had other reasons for going up to the Cotterills. There existed a sympathetic bond between him and Mrs Cotterill, despite her prim taciturnity and her exasperating habit of sitting with her hands pressed tight against her body and one over the other. Occasionally he teased her—and she liked being teased. He had glimpses now and then of her secret soul; he was perhaps the only person in Bursley thus privileged. Then there was Nellie. Denry and Nellie were great friends. For the rest of the world she had grown up, but not for Denry, who treated her as the chocolate child; while she, if she called him anything, called him respectfully "Mr."

The Cotterills had a fairly large old house with a good garden "up Bycars Lane," above the new park and above all those red streets which Mr Cotterill had helped to bring into being. Mr Cotterill built new houses with terra-cotta facings for others, but preferred an old one in stucco for himself. His abode had been saved from the parcelling out of several Georgian estates. It was dignified. It had a double entrance gate, and from this portal the drive started off for the house door, but deliberately avoided reaching the house door until it had wandered in curves over the entire garden. That was the Georgian touch! The modern touch was shown in Councillor Cotterill's bay windows, bath-room and garden squirter. There was stabling, in which were kept a Victorian dogcart and a Georgian horse, used by the Councillor in his business. As sure as ever his wife or daughter wanted the dogcart, it was either out or just going out, or the Georgian horse was fatigued and needed repose. The man who groomed the Georgian also ploughed the flowerbeds, broke the windows in cleaning them, and put blacking on brown boots. Two indoor servants had differing views as to the frontier between the kingdom of his duties and the kingdom of theirs, in fact, it was the usual spacious household of successful trade in a provincial town.

Denry got to Bycars Lane without a breakdown. This was in the days, quite thirteen years ago, when automobilists made their wills and took food supplies when setting forth. Hence Denry was pleased. The small but useful fund of prudence in him, however, forbade him to run the car along the unending sinuous drive. The May night was fine, and he left the loved vehicle with his new furs in the shadow of a monkey-tree near the gate.

As he was crunching towards the door, he had a beautiful idea: "I'll take 'em all out for a spin. There'll just be room!" he said.

Now even to-day, when the very cabman drives his automobile, a man who buys a motor cannot say to a friend: "I've bought a motor. Come for a spin," in the same self-unconscious accents as he would say: "I've bought a boat. Come for a sail," or "I've bought a house. Come and look at it." Even to-day and in the centre of London there is still something about a motor—well something.... Everybody who has bought a motor, and everybody who has dreamed of buying a motor, will comprehend me. Useless to feign that a motor is the most banal thing imaginable. It is not. It remains the supreme symbol of swagger. If such is the effect of a motor in these days and in Berkeley Square, what must it have been in that dim past, and in that dim town three hours by the fastest express from Euston? The imagination must be forced to the task of answering this question. Then will it be understood that Denry was simply tingling with pride.

"Master in?" he demanded of the servant, who was correctly starched, but unkempt in detail.

"No, sir. He ain't been in for tea."

("I shall take the women out then," said Denry to himself.)

"Come in!. Come in!" cried a voice from the other side of the open door of the drawing-room, Nellie's voice! The manners and state of a family that has industrially risen combine the spectacular grandeur of the caste to which it has climbed with the ease and freedom of the caste which it has quitted.

"Such a surprise!" said the voice. Nellie appeared, rosy.

Denry threw his new motoring cap hastily on to the hall-stand. No! He did not hope that Nellie would see it. He hoped that she would not see it. Now that the moment was really come to declare himself the owner of a motor-car, he grew timid and nervous. He would have liked to hide his hat. But then Denry was quite different from our common humanity. He was capable even of feeling awkward in a new suit of clothes. A singular person.

"Hello!" she greeted him.

"Hello!" he greeted her.

Their hands touched.

"Father hasn't come yet," she added. He fancied she was not quite at ease.

"Well," he said, "what's this surprise."

She motioned him into the drawing-room.

The surprise was a wonderful woman, brilliant in black—not black silk, but a softer, delicate stuff. She reclined in an easy-chair with surpassing grace and self-possession. A black Egyptian shawl, spangled with silver, was slipping off her shoulders. Her hair was dressed—that is to say, it was *dressed*; it was obviously and thrillingly a work of elaborate art. He could see her two feet and one of her ankles. The boots, the open-work stocking—such boots, such an open-work stocking, had never been seen in Bursley, not even at a ball! She was in mourning, and wore scarcely any jewellery, but there was a gleaming tint of gold here and there among the black, which resulted in a marvellous effect of richness.

The least experienced would have said, and said rightly: "This must be a woman of wealth and fashion." It was the detail that finished the demonstration. The detail was incredible. There might have been ten million stitches in the dress. Ten sempstresses might have worked on the dress for ten years. An examination of it under a microscope could but have deepened one's amazement at it.

She was something new in the Five Towns, something quite new.

Denry was not equal to the situation. He seldom was equal to a small situation. And although he had latterly acquired a considerable amount of social *savoir*, he was constantly mislaying it, so that he could not put his hand on it at the moment when he most required it, as now.

"Well, Denry!" said the wondrous creature in black, softly.

And he collected himself as though for a plunge, and said:

"Well, Ruth!"

This was the woman whom he had once loved, kissed, and engaged himself to marry. He was relieved that she had begun with Christian names, because he could not recall her surname. He could not even remember whether he had ever heard it. All he knew was that, after leaving Bursley to join her father in Birmingham, she had married somebody with a double name, somebody well off, somebody older than herself; somebody apparently of high social standing; and that this somebody had died.

She made no fuss. There was no implication in her demeanour that she expected to be wept over as a lone widow, or that because she and he had on a time been betrothed, therefore they could never speak naturally to each other again. She just talked as if nothing had ever happened to her, and as if about twenty-four hours had elapsed since she had last seen him. He felt that she must have picked up this most useful diplomatic calmness in her contacts with her late husband's class. It was a valuable lesson to him: "Always behave as if nothing had happened--no matter what has happened."

To himself he was saying:

"I'm glad I came up in my motor."

He seemed to need something in self-defence against the sudden attack of all this wealth and all this superior social tact, and the motor-car served excellently.

"I've been hearing a great deal about you lately," said she with a soft smile, unobtrusively rearranging a fold of her skirt.

"Well," he replied, "I'm sorry I can't say the same of you."

Slightly perilous perhaps, but still he thought it rather neat.

"Oh!" she said. "You see I've been so much out of England. We were just talking about holidays. I was saying to Mrs Cotterill they certainly ought to go to Switzerland this year for a change."

"Yes, Mrs Capron-Smith was just saying—" Mrs Cotterill put in.

(So that was her name.)

"It would be something too lovely!" said Nellie in ecstasy.

Switzerland! Astonishing how with a single word she had marked the gulf between Bursley people and herself. The Cotterills had never been out of England. Not merely that, but the Cotterills had never dreamt of going out of England. Denry had once been to Dieppe, and had come back as though from Timbuctoo with a traveller's renown. And she talked of Switzerland easily!

"I suppose it is very jolly," he said.

"Yes," she said, "it's splendid in summer. But, of course, *the* time is winter, for the sports. Naturally, when you aren't free to take a bit of a holiday in winter, you must be content with summer, and very splendid it is. I'm sure you'd enjoy it frightfully, Nell."

"I'm sure I should—frightfully!" Nellie agreed. "I shall speak to father. I shall make him—"

"Now, Nellie—" her mother warned her.

"Yes, I shall, mother," Nellie insisted.

"There *is* your father!" observed Mrs Cotterill, after listening.

Footsteps crossed the hall, and died away into the dining-room.

"I wonder why on earth father doesn't come in here. He must have heard us talking," said Nellie, like a tyrant crossed in some trifle.

A bell rang, and then the servant came into the drawing-room and remarked: "If you please, mum," at Mrs Cotterill, and Mrs Cotterill disappeared, closing the door after her.

"What are they up to, between them?" Nellie demanded, and she, too, departed, with wrinkled brow, leaving Denry and Ruth together. It could be perceived on Nellie's brow that her father was going "to catch it."

"I haven't seen Mr Cotterill yet," said Mrs Capron-Smith.

"When did you come?" Denry asked.

"Only this afternoon."

She continued to talk.

As he looked at her, listening and responding intelligently now and then, he saw that Mrs Capron-Smith was in truth the woman that Ruth had so cleverly imitated ten years before. The imitation had deceived him then; he had accepted it for genuine. It would not have deceived him now—he knew that. Oh yes! This was the real article that could hold its own anywhere.... Switzerland! And not simply Switzerland, but a refinement on Switzerland! Switzerland in winter! He divined that in her opinion Switzerland in summer was not worth doing—in the way of correctness. But in winter...

II

Nellie had announced a surprise for Denry as he entered the house, but Nellie's surprise for Denry, startling and successful though it proved, was as naught to the surprise which Mr Cotterill had in hand for Nellie, her mother, Denry, the town of Bursley, and various persons up and down the country.

Mrs Cotterill came hysterically in upon the duologue between Denry and Ruth in the drawing-room. From the activity of her hands, which, instead of being decently folded one over the other, were waving round her head in the strangest way, it was clear that Mrs Cotterill was indeed under the stress of a very unusual emotion.

"It's those creditors—at last! I knew it would be! It's all those creditors! They won't let him alone, and now they've *done* it."

So Mrs Cotterill! She dropped into a chair. She had no longer any sense of shame, of what was due to her dignity. She seemed to have forgotten that certain matters are not proper to be discussed in drawing-rooms. She had left the room Mrs Councillor Cotterill; she returned to it nobody in particular, the personification of defeat. The change had operated in five minutes.

Mrs Capron-Smith and Denry glanced at each other, and even Mrs Capron-Smith was at a loss for a moment. Then Ruth approached Mrs Cotterill and took her hand. Perhaps Mrs Capron-Smith was not so astonished after all. She and Nellie's mother had always been "very friendly." And in the Five Towns "very friendly" means a lot.

"Perhaps if you were to leave us," Ruth suggested, twisting her head to glance at Denry.

It was exactly what he desired to do. There could be no doubt that Ruth was supremely a woman of the world. Her tact was faultless.

He left them, saying to himself: "Well, here's a go!"

In the hall, through an open door, he saw Councillor Cotterill standing against the dining-room mantelpiece.

When Cotterill caught sight of Denry he straightened himself into a certain uneasy perkiness.

"Young man," he said in a counterfeit of his old patronising tone, "come in here. You may as well hear about it. You're a friend of ours. Come in and shut the door."

Nellie was not in view.

Denry went in and shut the door.

"Sit down," said Cotterill.

And it was just as if he had said: "Now, you're a fairly bright sort of youth, and you haven't done so badly in life; and as a reward I mean to admit you to the privilege of hearing about our ill-luck, which for some mysterious reason reflects more credit on me than your good luck reflects on you, young man."

And he stroked his straggling grey beard.

"I'm going to file my petition to-morrow," said he, and gave a short laugh.

"Really!" said Denry, who could think of nothing else to say. His name was not Capron-Smith.

"Yes; they won't leave me any alternative," said Mr Cotterill.

Then he gave a brief history of his late commercial career to the young man. And he seemed to figure it as a sort of tug-of-war between his creditors and his debtors, he himself being the rope. He seemed to imply that he had always done his sincere best to attain the greatest good of the greatest number, but that those wrong-headed creditors had consistently thwarted him.

However, he bore them no grudge. It was the fortune of the tug-of-war. He pretended, with shabby magnificence of spirit, that a bankruptcy at the age of near sixty, in a community where one has cut a figure, is a mere passing episode.

"Are you surprised?" he asked foolishly, with a sheepish smile.

Denry took vengeance for all the patronage that he had received during a decade.

"No!" he said. "Are you?"

Instead of kicking Denry out of the house for an impudent young jackanapes, Mr Cotterill simply resumed his sheepish smile.

Denry had been surprised for a moment, but he had quickly recovered. Cotterill's downfall was one of those events which any person of acute intelligence can foretell after they have happened. Cotterill had run the risks of the speculative builder, built and mortgaged, built and mortgaged, sold at a profit, sold without profit, sold at a loss, and failed to sell; given bills, second mortgages, and third mortgages; and because he was a builder and could do nothing but build, he had continued to build in defiance of Bursley's lack of enthusiasm for his erections. If rich gold deposits had been discovered in Bursley Municipal Park, Cotterill would have owned a mining camp and amassed immense wealth; but unfortunately gold deposits were not discovered in the Park. Nobody knew his position; nobody ever does know the position of a speculative builder. He did not know it himself. There had been rumours, but they had been contradicted in an adequate way. His recent refusal of the mayoral chain, due to lack of spare coin, had been attributed to prudence. His domestic existence had always been conducted on the same moderately lavish scale. He had always paid the baker, the butcher, the tailor, the dressmaker.

And now he was to file his petition in bankruptcy, and to-morrow the entire town would have "been seeing it coming" for years.

"What shall you do?" Denry inquired in amicable curiosity.

"Well," said Cotterill, "that's the point. I've got a brother a builder in Toronto, you know. He's doing very well; building *is* building over there. I wrote to him a bit since, and he replied by the next mail--by the next mail—that what he wanted was just a man like me to overlook things. He's getting an old man now, is John. So, you see, there's an opening waiting for me."

As if to say, "The righteous are never forsaken."

"I tell you all this as you're a friend of the family like," he added.

Then, after an expanse of vagueness, he began hopefully, cheerfully, undauntedly:

"Even *now* if I could get hold of a couple of thousand I could pull through handsome—and there's plenty of security for it."

"Bit late now, isn't it?"

"Not it. If only some one who really knows the town, and has faith in the property market, would come down with a couple of thousand—well, he might double it in five years."

"Really!"

"Yes," said Cotterill. "Look at Clare Street."

Clare Street was one of his terra-cotta masterpieces.

"You, now," said Cotterill, insinuating. "I don't expect anyone can teach *you* much about the value o' property in this town. You know as well as I do. If you happened to have a couple of thousand loose—by gosh! it's a chance in a million."

"Yes," said Denry. "I should say that was just about what it was."

"I put it before you," Cotterill proceeded, gathering way, and missing the flavour of Denry's remark. "Because you're a friend of the family. You're so often here. Why, it's pretty near ten years...."

Denry sighed: "I expect I come and see you all about once a fortnight fairly regular. That makes two hundred and fifty times in ten years. Yes...."

"A couple of thou'," said Cotterill, reflectively.

"Two hundred and fifty into two thousand—eight. Eight pounds a visit. A shade thick, Cotterill, a shade thick. You might be half a dozen fashionable physicians rolled into one."

Never before had he called the Councillor "Cotterill" unadorned. Me Cotterill flushed and rose.

Denry does not appear to advantage in this interview. He failed in magnanimity. The only excuse that can be offered for him is that Mr Cotterill had called him "young man" once or twice too often in the course of ten years. It is subtle.

III

"No," whispered Ruth, in all her wraps. "Don't bring it up to the door. I'll walk down with you to the gate, and get in there."

He nodded.

They were off, together. Ruth, it had appeared, was actually staying at the Five Towns Hotel at Knype, which at that epoch was the only hotel in the Five Towns seriously pretending to be "first-class" in the full-page advertisement sense. The fact that Ruth was staying at the Five Towns Hotel impressed Denry anew. Assuredly she did things in the grand manner. She had meant to walk down by the Park to Bursley Station and catch the last loop-line train to Knype, and when Denry suddenly disclosed the existence of his motor-car, and proposed to see her to her hotel in it, she in her turn had been impressed. The astonishment in her tone as she exclaimed: "Have you got a *motor*?" was the least in the world naïve.

Thus they departed together from the stricken house, Ruth saying brightly to Nellie, who had reappeared in a painful state of demoralisation, that she should return on the morrow.

And Denry went down the obscure drive with a final vision of the poor child, Nellie, as she stood at the door to speed them. It was extraordinary how that child had remained a child. He knew that she must be more than half-way through her twenties, and yet she persisted in being the merest girl. A delightful little thing; but no *savoir vivre*, no equality to a situation, no spectacular pride. Just a nice, bright girl, strangely girlish.... The Cotterills had managed that bad evening badly. They had shown no dignity, no reserve, no discretion; and old Cotterill had been simply fatuous in his suggestion. As for Mrs Cotterill, she was completely overcome, and it was due solely to Ruth's calm, managing influence that Nellie, nervous and whimpering, had wound herself up to come and shut the front door after the guests.

It was all very sad.

When he had successfully started the car, and they were sliding down the Moorthorne hill together, side by side, their shoulders touching, Denry threw off the nightmarish effect of the bankrupt household. After all, there was no reason why he should be depressed. He was not a bankrupt. He was steadily adding riches to riches. He acquired wealth mechanically now. Owing to the habits of his mother, he never came within miles of living up to his income. And Ruth—she, too, was wealthy. He felt that she must be wealthy in the strict significance of the term. And she completed wealth by experience of the world. She was his equal. She understood things in general. She had lived, travelled, suffered, reflected—in short, she was a completed article of manufacture. She was no little, clinging, raw girl. Further, she was less hard than of yore. Her voice and gestures had a different quality. The world had softened her. And it occurred to him suddenly that her sole fault—extravagance— had no importance now that she was wealthy.

He told her all that Mr Cotterill had said about Canada. And she told him all that Mrs Cotterill had said about Canada. And they agreed that Mr Cotterill had got his deserts, and that, in its own interest, Canada was the only thing for the Cotterill family; and the sooner the better. People must accept the consequences of bankruptcy. Nothing could be done.

"I think it's a pity Nellie should have to go," said Denry.

"Oh! *Do* you?" replied Ruth.

"Yes; going out to a strange country like that. She's not what you may call the Canadian kind of girl. If she could only get something to do here. ...If something could be found for her."

"Oh, I don't agree with you at *all*," said Ruth. "Do you really think she ought to leave her parents just *now*? Her place is with her parents. And besides, between you and me, she'll have a much better chance of marrying there than in *this* town—after all this. Of course I shall be very sorry to lose her—and Mrs Cotterill, too. But...."

"I expect you're right," Denry concurred.

And they sped on luxuriously through the lamp-lit night of the Five Towns. And Denry pointed out his house as they passed it. And they both thought much of the security of their positions in the world, and of their incomes, and of the honeyed deference of their bankers; and also of the mistake of being a failure.... You could do nothing with a failure.

IV

On a frosty morning in early winter you might have seen them together in a different vehicle—a first-class compartment of the express from Knype to Liverpool. They had the compartment to themselves, and they were installed therein with every circumstance of luxury. Both were enwrapped in furs, and a fur rug united their knees in its shelter. Magazines and newspapers were scattered about to the value of a labourer's hire for a whole day; and when Denry's eye met the guard's it said "shilling." In short, nobody could possibly be more superb than they were on that morning in that compartment.

The journey was the result of peculiar events.

Mr Cotterill had made himself a bankrupt, and cast away the robe of a Town Councillor. He had submitted to the inquisitiveness of the Official Receiver, and to the harsh prying of those rampant baying beasts, his creditors. He had laid bare his books, his correspondence, his lack of method, his domestic extravagance, and the distressing fact that he had continued to trade long after he knew himself to be insolvent. He had for several months, in the interests of the said beasts, carried on his own business as manager at a nominal salary. And gradually everything that was his had been sold. And during the final weeks the Cotterill family had been obliged to quit their dismantled house and exist in lodgings. It had been arranged that they should go to Canada by way of Liverpool, and on the day before the journey of Denry and Ruth to Liverpool they had departed from the borough of Bursley (which Mr Cotterill had so extensively faced with terra-cotta) unhonoured and unsung. Even Denry, though he had visited them in their lodgings to say good-bye, had not seen them off at the station; but Ruth Capron-Smith had seen them off at the station. She had interrupted a sojourn to Southport in order to come to Bursley, and despatch them therefrom with due friendliness. Certain matters had to be attended to after their departure, and Ruth had promised to attend to them.

Now immediately after seeing them off Ruth had met Denry in the street.

"Do you know," she said brusquely, "those people are actually going steerage? I'd no idea of it. Mr and Mrs Cotterill kept it from me, and I should not have heard of it only from something Nellie said. That's why they've gone to-day. The boat doesn't sail till to-morrow afternoon."

"Steerage?" and Denry whistled.

"Yes," said Ruth. "Nothing but pride, of course. Old Cotterill wanted to have every penny he could scrape, so as to be able to make the least tiny bit of a show when he gets to Toronto, and so—steerage! Just think of Mrs Cotterill and Nellie in the steerage. If I'd known of it I should have altered that, I can tell you, and pretty quickly too; and now it's too late."

"No, it isn't," Denry contradicted her flatly.

"But they've gone."

"I could telegraph to Liverpool for saloon berths—there's bound to be plenty at this time of year—and I could run over to Liverpool to-morrow and catch 'em on the boat, and make 'em change."

She asked him whether he really thought he could, and he assured her.

"Second-cabin berths would be better," said she.

"Why?"

"Well, because of dressing for dinner, and so on. They haven't got the clothes, you know."

"Of course," said Denry.

"Listen," she said, with an enchanting smile. "Let's halve the cost, you and I. And let's go to Liverpool together, and—er—make the little gift, and arrange things. I'm leaving for Southport to-morrow, and Liverpool's on my way."

Denry was delighted by the suggestion, and telegraphed to Liverpool with success.

Thus they found themselves on that morning in the Liverpool express together. The work of benevolence in which they were engaged had a powerful influence on their mood, which grew both intimate and tender. Ruth made no concealment of her regard for Denry; and as he gazed across the compartment at her, exquisitely mature (she was slightly older than himself), dressed to a marvel, perfect in every detail of manner, knowing all that was to be known about life, and secure in a handsome fortune—as he gazed, Denry reflected, joyously, victoriously:

"I've got the dibs, of course. But she's got 'em too—perhaps more. Therefore she must like me for myself alone. This brilliant creature has been everywhere and seen everything, and she comes back to the Five Towns and comes back to *me*."

It was his proudest moment. And in it he saw his future far more glorious than he had dreamt.

"When shall you be out of mourning?" he inquired.

"In two months," said she.

This was not a proposal and acceptance, but it was very nearly one. They were silent, and happy.

Then she said:

"Do you ever have business at Southport?"

And he said, in a unique manner:

"I shall have."

Another silence. This time he felt he *would* marry her.

V

The White Star liner, *Titubic*, stuck out of the water like a row of houses against the landing-stage. There was a large crowd on her promenade-deck, and a still larger crowd on the landing-stage. Above the promenade-deck officers paced on the navigating deck, and above that was the airy bridge, and above that the funnels, smoking, and somewhere still higher a flag or two fluttering in the icy breeze. And behind the crowd on the landing-stage stretched a row of four-wheeled cabs and rickety horses. The landing-stage swayed ever so slightly on the tide. Only the ship was apparently solid, apparently cemented in foundations of concrete.

On the starboard side of the promenade-deck, among a hundred other small groups, was a group consisting of Mr and Mrs Cotterill and Ruth and Denry. Nellie stood a few feet apart, Mrs Cotterill was crying. People naturally thought she was crying because of the adieux; but she was not. She wept because Denry and Ruth, by sheer force of will, had compelled them to come out of the steerage and occupy beautiful and commodious berths in the second cabin, where the manner of the stewards was quite different. She wept because they had been caught in the steerage. She wept because she was ashamed, and because people were too kind. She was at once delighted and desolated. She wanted to outpour psalms of gratitude, and also she wanted to curse.

Mr Cotterill said stiffly that he should repay—and that soon.

An immense bell sounded impatiently.

"We'd better be shunting," said Denry. "That's the second."

In exciting crises he sometimes employed such peculiar language as this. And he was very excited. He had done a great deal of rushing about. The upraising of the Cotterill family from the social Hades of the steerage to the respectability of the second cabin had demanded all his energy, and a lot of Ruth's.

Ruth kissed Mrs Cotterill and then Nellie. And Mrs Cotterill and Nellie acquired rank and importance for the whole voyage by reason of being kissed in public by a woman so elegant and aristocratic as Ruth Capron-Smith.

And Denry shook hands. He looked brightly at the parents, but he could not look at Nellie; nor could she look at him; their handshaking was perfunctory. For months their playful intimacy had been in abeyance.

"Good-bye."

"Good luck."

"Thanks. Good-bye."

"Good-bye."

The horrible bell continued to insist.

"All non-passengers ashore! All ashore!"

The numerous gangways were thronged with people obeying the call, and handkerchiefs began to wave. And there was a regular vibrating tremor through the ship.

Mr and Mrs Cotterill turned away.

Ruth and Denry approached the nearest gangway, and Denry stood aside, and made a place for her to pass. And, as always, a number of women pushed into the gangways immediately after her, and Denry had to wait, being a perfect gentleman.

His eye caught Nellie's. She had not moved.

He felt then as he had never felt in his life. No, absolutely never. Her sad, her tragic glance rendered him so uncomfortable, and yet so deliciously uncomfortable, that the symptoms startled him. He wondered what would happen to his legs. He was not sure that he had legs.

However, he demonstrated the existence of his legs by running up to Nellie. Ruth was by this time swallowed in the crowd on the landing-stage. He looked at Nellie. Nellie looked at him. Her lips twitched.

"What am I doing here?" he asked of his soul.

She was not at all well dressed. She was indeed shabby—in a steerage style. Her hat was awry; her gloves miserable. No girlish pride in her distraught face. No determination to overcome Fate. No consciousness of ability to meet a bad situation. Just those sad eyes and those twitching lips.

"Look here," Denry whispered, "you must come ashore for a second. I've something I want to give you, and I've left it in the cab."

"But there's no time. The bell's..."

"Bosh!" he exclaimed gruffly, extinguishing her timid, childish voice. "You won't go for at least a quarter of an hour. All that's only a dodge to get people off in plenty of time. Come on, I tell you."

And in a sort of hysteria he seized her thin, long hand and dragged her along the deck to another gangway, down whose steep slope they stumbled together. The crowd of sightseers and handkerchief-wavers jostled them. They could see nothing but heads and shoulders, and the great side of the ship rising above. Denry turned her back on the ship.

"This way." He still held her hand.

He struggled to the cab-rank.

"Which one is it?" she asked.

"Any one. Never mind which. Jump in." And to the first driver whose eye met his, he said: "Lime Street Station."

The gangways were being drawn away. A hoarse boom filled the air, and then a cheer.

"But I shall miss the boat," the dazed girl protested.

"Jump in."

He pushed her in.

"But I shall miss the..."

"I know you will," he replied, as if angrily. "Do you suppose I was going to let you go by that steamer? Not much."

"But mother and father..."

"I'll telegraph. They'll get it on landing."

"And where's Ruth?"

"*Be hanged to Ruth!*" he shouted furiously.

As the cab rattled over the cobbles the *Titubic* slipped away from the landing-stage. The irretrievable had happened.

Nellie burst into tears.

"Look here," Denry said savagely. "If you don't dry up, I shall have to cry myself."

"What are you going to do with me?" she whimpered.

"Well, what do *you* think? I'm going to marry you, of course."

His aggrieved tone might have been supposed to imply that people had tried to thwart him, but that he had no intention of being thwarted, nor of asking permissions, nor of conducting himself as anything but a fierce tyrant.

As for Nellie, she seemed to surrender.

Then he kissed her—also angrily. He kissed her several times—yes, even in Lord Street itself—less and less angrily.

"Where are you taking me to?" she inquired humbly, as a captive.

"I shall take you to my mother's," he said.

"Will she like it?"

"She'll either like it or lump it," said Denry. "It'll take a fortnight."

"What?"

"The notice, and things."

In the train, in the midst of a great submissive silence, she murmured:

"It'll be simply awful for father and mother."

"That can't be helped," said he. "And they'll be far too sea-sick to bother their heads about you."

"You can't think how you've staggered me," said she.

"You can't think how I've staggered myself," said he.

"When did you decide to..."

"When I was standing at the gangway, and you looked at me," he answered.

"But..."

"It's no use butting," he said. "I'm like that.... That's me, that is."

It was the bare truth that he had staggered himself. But he had staggered himself into a miraculous, ecstatic happiness. She had no money, no clothes, no style, no experience, no particular gifts. But she was she. And when he looked at her, calmed, he knew that he had done well for himself. He knew that if he had not yielded to that terrific impulse he would have done badly for himself. Mrs Machin had what she called a ticklish night of it.

The next day he received a note from Ruth, dated Southport, inquiring how he came to lose her on the landing-stage, and expressing concern. It took him three days to reply, and even then the reply was a bad one. He had behaved infamously to Ruth; so much could not be denied. Within three hours of practically proposing to her, he had run off with a simple girl, who was not fit to hold a candle to her. And he did not care. That was the worst of it; he did not care.

Of course the facts reached her. The facts reached everybody; for the singular reappearance of Nellie in the streets of Bursley immediately after her departure for Canada had to be explained. Moreover, the infamous Denry was rather proud of the facts. And the town inevitably said: "Machin all over, that! Snatching the girl off the blooming lugger. Machin all over." And Denry agreed privately that it was Machin all over.

"What other chap," he demanded of the air, "would have thought of it? Or had the pluck?..."

It was mere malice on the part of destiny that caused Denry to run across Mrs Capron-Smith at Euston some weeks later. Happily they both had immense nerve.

"Dear me," said she. "What are *you* doing here?"

"Only honeymooning," he said.

CHAPTER XI
IN THE ALPS

Although Denry was extremely happy as a bridegroom, and capable of the most foolish symptoms of affection in private, he said to himself, and he said to Nellie (and she sturdily agreed with him): "We aren't going to be the ordinary silly honeymooners." By which, of course, he meant that they would behave so as to be taken for staid married persons. They failed thoroughly in this enterprise as far as London, where they spent a couple of nights, but on leaving Charing Cross they made a new and a better start, in the light of experience.

Their destination, it need hardly be said, was Switzerland. After Mrs Capron-Smith's remarks on the necessity of going to Switzerland in winter if one wished to respect one's self, there was really no alternative to Switzerland. Thus it was announced in the *Signal* (which had reported the wedding in ten lines, owing to the excessive quietude of the wedding) that Mr and Mrs Councillor Machin were spending a month at Mont Pridoux, sur Montreux, on the Lake of Geneva. And the announcement looked very well.

At Dieppe they got a through carriage. There were several through carriages for Switzerland on the train. In walking through the corridors from one to another Denry and Nellie had their first glimpse of the world which travels and which runs off for a holiday whenever it feels in the mood. The idea of going for a holiday in any month but August seemed odd to both of them. Denry was very bold and would insist on talking in a naturally loud voice. Nellie was timid and clinging. "What do you say?" Denry would roar at her when she half-whispered something, and she had to repeat it so that all could hear. It was part of their plan to address each other curtly, brusquely, and to frown, and to pretend to be slightly bored by each other.

They were outclassed by the world which travels. Try as they might, even Denry was morally intimidated. He had managed his clothes fairly correctly; he was not ashamed of them; and Nellie's were by no means the worst in the compartments; indeed, according to the standard of some of the most intimidating women, Nellie's costume erred in not being quite sufficiently negligent, sufficiently "anyhow." And they had plenty, and ten times plenty of money, and the consciousness of it. Expense was not being spared on that honeymoon. And yet.... Well, all that can be said is that the company was imposing. The company, which was entirely English, seemed to be unaware that any one ever did anything else but travel luxuriously to places mentioned in second-year geographies. It astounded Nellie that there should be so many people in the world with nothing to do but spend. And they were constantly saying the strangest things with an air of perfect calm.

"How much did you pay for the excess luggage?" an untidy young woman asked of an old man.

"Oh! Thirteen pounds," answered the old man, carelessly.

And not long before Nellie had scarcely escaped ten days in the steerage of an Atlantic liner.

After dinner in the restaurant car—no champagne, because it was vulgar, but a good sound, expensive wine—they felt more equal to the situation, more like part-owners of the train. Nellie prudently went to bed ere the triumphant feeling wore off. But Denry stayed up smoking in the corridor. He stayed up very late, being too proud and happy and too avid of new sensations to be able to think of sleep. It was a match which led to a conversation between himself and a thin, drawling, overbearing fellow with an eyeglass. Denry had hated this lordly creature all the way from Dieppe. In presenting him with a match he felt that he was somehow getting the better of him, for the match was precious in the nocturnal solitude of the vibrating corridor. The mere fact that two people are alone together and awake, divided from a sleeping or sleepy population only by a row of closed, mysterious doors, will do much to break down social barriers. The excellence of Denry's cigar also helped. It atoned for the breadth of his accent.

He said to himself:

"I'll have a bit of a chat with this johnny."

And then he said aloud:

"Not a bad train this!"

"No!" the eyeglass agreed languidly. "Pity they give you such a beastly dinner!"

And Denry agreed hastily that it was.

Soon they were chatting of places, and somehow it came out of Denry that he was going to Montreux. The eyeglass professed its indifference to Montreux in winter, but said the resorts above Montreux were all right, such as Caux or Pridoux.

And Denry said:

"Well, of course, shouldn't think of stopping *in* Montreux. Going to try Pridoux."

The eyeglass said it wasn't going so far as Switzerland yet; it meant to stop in the Jura.

"Geneva's a pretty deadly place, ain't it?" said the eyeglass after a pause.

"Ye-es," said Denry.

"Been there since that new esplanade was finished?"

"No," said Denry. "I saw nothing of it."

"When were you there?"

"Oh! A couple of years ago."

"Ah! It wasn't started then. Comic thing! Of course they're awfully proud in Geneva of the view of Mont Blanc."

"Yes," said Denry.

"Ever noticed how queer women are about that view? They're no end keen on it at first, but after a day or two it gets on their nerves."

"Yes," said Denry. "I've noticed that myself. My wife...."

He stopped, because he didn't know what he was going to say. The eyeglass nodded understandingly.

"All alike," it said. "Odd thing!"

When Denry introduced himself into the two-berth compartment which he had managed to secure at the end of the carriage for himself and Nellie, the poor tired child was as wakeful as an owl.

"Who have you been talking to?" she yawned.

"The eyeglass johnny."

"Oh! Really," Nellie murmured, interested and impressed. "With him, have you? I could hear voices. What sort of a man is he?"

"He seems to be an ass," said Denry. "Fearfully haw-haw. Couldn't stand him for long. I've made him believe we've been married for two years."

II

They stood on the balcony of the Hôtel Beau-Site of Mont Pridoux. A little below, to the right, was the other hotel, the Métropole, with the red-and-white Swiss flag waving over its central tower. A little below that was the terminal station of the funicular railway from Montreux. The railway ran down the sheer of the mountain into the roofs of Montreux, like a wire. On it, two toy trains crawled towards each other, like flies climbing and descending a wall. Beyond the fringe of hotels that constituted Montreux was a strip of water, and beyond the water a range of hills white at the top.

"So these are the Alps!" Nellie exclaimed.

She was disappointed; he also. But when Denry learnt from the guide-book and by inquiry that the strip of lake was seven miles across, and the highest notched peaks ten thousand feet above the sea and twenty-five miles off, Nellie gasped and was content.

They liked the Hôtel Beau-Site. It had been recommended to Denry, by a man who knew what was what, as the best hotel in Switzerland. "Don't you be misled by prices," the man had said. And Denry was not. He paid sixteen francs a day for the two of them at the Beau-Site, and was rather relieved than otherwise by the absence of finger-bowls. Everything was very good, except sometimes the hot water. The hot-water cans bore the legend "hot water," but these two words were occasionally the only evidence of heat in the water. On the

383

other hand, the bedrooms could be made sultry by merely turning a handle; and the windows were double. Nellie was wondrously inventive. They breakfasted in bed, and she would save butter and honey from the breakfast to furnish forth afternoon tea, which was not included in the terms. She served the butter freshly with ice by the simple expedient of leaving it outside the window of a night. And Denry was struck by this house-wifery.

The other guests appeared to be of a comfortable, companionable class, with, as Denry said, "no frills." They were amazed to learn that a chattering little woman of thirty-five, who gossiped with everybody, and soon invited Denry and Nellie to have tea in her room, was an authentic Russian Countess, inscribed in the visitors' lists as "Comtesse Ruhl (with maid), Moscow." Her room was the untidiest that Nellie had ever seen, and the tea a picnic. Still, it was thrilling to have had tea with a Russian Countess.... (Plots! Nihilism! Secret police! Marble palaces!).... Those visitors' lists were breath-taking. Pages and pages of them; scores of hotels, thousands of names, nearly all English—and all people who came to Switzerland in winter, having naught else to do. Denry and Nellie bathed in correctness as in a bath.

The only persons in the hotel with whom they did not "get on" nor "hit it off" were a military party, chiefly named Clutterbuck, and presided over by a Major Clutterbuck and his wife. They sat at a large table in a corner—father, mother, several children, a sister-in-law, a sister, a governess—eight heads in all; and while utterly polite they seemed to draw a ring round themselves. They grumbled at the hotel; they played bridge (then a newish game); and once, when Denry and the Countess played with them (Denry being an adept card-player) for shilling points, Denry overheard the sister-in-law say that she was sure Captain Deverax wouldn't play for shilling points. This was the first rumour of the existence of Captain Deverax; but afterwards Captain Deverax began to be mentioned several times a day. Captain Deverax was coming to join them, and it seemed that he was a very particular man. Soon all the rest of the hotel had got its back up against this arriving Captain Deverax. Then a Clutterbuck cousin came, a smiling, hard, fluffy woman, and pronounced definitely that the Hôtel Beau-Site would never do for Captain Deverax. This cousin aroused Denry's hostility in a strange way. She imparted to the Countess (who united all sects) her opinion that Denry and Nellie were on their honeymoon. At night in a corner of the drawing-room the Countess delicately but bluntly asked Nellie if she had been married long. "No," said Nellie. "A month?" asked the Countess, smiling. "N-no," said Nellie.

The next day all the hotel knew. The vast edifice of make-believe that Denry and Nellie had laboriously erected crumbled at a word, and they stood forth, those two, blushing for the criminals they were.

The hotel was delighted. There is more rejoicing in a hotel over one honeymoon couple than over fifty families with children.

But the hotel had a shock the same day. The Clutterbuck cousin had proclaimed that owing to the inadequacy of the bedroom furniture she had been obliged to employ a sofa as a wardrobe. Then there were more references to Captain Deverax. And then at dinner it became known— Heaven knows how!—that the entire Clutterbuck party had given notice and was seceding to the Hotel Métropole. Also they had tried to carry the Countess with them, but had failed.

Now, among the guests of the Hôtel Beau-Site there had always been a professed scorn of the rival Hotel Métropole, which was a franc a day dearer, and famous for its new and rich furniture. The Métropole had an orchestra twice a week, and the English Church services were held in its drawing-room; and it was larger than the Beau-Site. In spite of these facts the clients of the Beau-Site affected to despise it, saying that the food was inferior and that the guests were snobbish. It was an article of faith in the Beau-Site that the Beau-Site was the best hotel on the mountain-side, if not in Switzerland.

The insolence of this defection on the part of the Clutterbucks! How on earth *could* people have the face to go to a landlord and say to him that they meant to desert him in favour of his rival?

Another detail: the secession of nine or ten people from one hotel to the other meant that the Métropole would decidedly be more populous than the Beau-Site, and on the point of numbers the emulation was very keen. "Well," said the Beau-Site, "let 'em go! With their Captain Deverax! We shall be better without 'em!" And that deadliest of all feuds sprang up--a rivalry between the guests of rival hotels. The Métropole had issued a general invitation to a dance, and after the monstrous conduct of the Clutterbucks the question arose whether the Beau-Site should not boycott the dance. However, it was settled that the truly effective course would be to go with critical noses in the air, and emit unfavourable comparisons with the Beau-Site. The Beau-Site suddenly became perfect in the esteem of its patrons. Not another word was heard on the subject of hot water being coated with ice. And the Clutterbucks, with incredible assurance, slid their luggage off in a sleigh to the Métropole, in the full light of day, amid the contempt of the faithful.

III

Under the stars the dancing section of the Beau-Site went off in jingling sleighs over the snow to the ball at the Métropole. The distance was not great, but it was great enough to show the inadequacy of furs against twenty degrees of mountain frost, and it was also great enough to allow the party to come to a general final understanding that its demeanour must be cold and critical in the gilded halls of the Métropole. The rumour ran that Captain Deverax had arrived, and every one agreed that he must be an insufferable booby, except the Countess Ruhl, who never used her fluent exotic English to say ill of anybody.

The gilded halls of the Métropole certainly were imposing. The hotel was incontestably larger than the Beau-Site, newer, more richly furnished. Its occupants, too, had a lordly way with them, trying to others, but inimitable. Hence the visitors from the Beau-Site, as they moved to and fro beneath those crystal chandeliers from Tottenham Court Road, had their work cut out to maintain the mien of haughty indifference. Nellie, for instance, frankly could not do it. And Denry did not do it very well. Denry, nevertheless, did score one point over Mrs Clutterbuck's fussy cousin.

"Captain Deverax has come," said this latter. "He was very late. He'll be downstairs in a few minutes. We shall get him to lead the cotillon."

"Captain Deverax?" Denry questioned.

"Yes. You've heard us mention him," said the cousin, affronted.

"Possibly," said Denry. "I don't remember."

On hearing this brief colloquy the cohorts of the Beau-Site felt that in Denry they possessed the making of a champion.

There was a disturbing surprise, however, waiting for Denry.

The lift descended; and with a peculiar double action of his arms on the doors, like a pantomime fairy emerging from an enchanted castle, a tall thin man stepped elegantly out of the lift and approached the company with a certain mincingness. But before he could reach the company several young women had rushed towards him, as though with the intention of committing suicide by hanging themselves from his neck. He was in an evening suit so perfect in detail that it might have sustained comparison with the costume of the head waiter. And he wore an eyeglass in his left eye. It was the eyeglass that made Denry jump. For two seconds he dismissed the notion.... But another two seconds of examination showed beyond doubt that this eyeglass was the eyeglass of the train. And Denry had apprehensions....

"Captain Deverax!" exclaimed several voices.

The manner in which the youthful and the mature fair clustered around this Captain, aged forty (and not handsome) was really extraordinary, to the males of the Hôtel Beau-Site. Even the little Russian Countess attached herself to him at once. And by reason of her title, her social energy, and her personal distinction, she took natural precedence of the others.

"Recognise him?" Denry whispered to his wife.

Nellie nodded. "He seems rather nice," she said diffidently.

"Nice!" Denry repeated the adjective. "The man's an ass!"

And the majority of the Beau-Site party agreed with Denry's verdict either by word or gesture.

Captain Deverax stared fixedly at Denry; then smiled vaguely and drawled, "Hullo! How d' do?"

And they shook hands.

"So you know him?" some one murmured to Denry.

"Know him?... Since infancy."

The inquirer scented facetiousness, but he was somehow impressed. The remarkable thing was that though he regarded Captain Deverax as a popinjay, he could not help feeling a certain slight satisfaction in the fact that they were in some sort acquaintances.... Mystery of the human heart!... He wished sincerely that he had not, in his conversation with the Captain in the train, talked about previous visits to Switzerland. It was dangerous.

The dance achieved that brightness and joviality which entitle a dance to call itself a success. The cotillon reached brilliance, owing to the captaincy of Captain Deverax. Several score opprobrious epithets were applied to the Captain in the course of the night, but it was agreed *nemine contradicente* that, whatever he would have done in front of a Light Brigade at Balaclava, as a leader of cotillons he was terrific. Many men, however, seemed to argue that if a man who *was* a man led a cotillon, he ought not to lead it too well, on pain of being considered a cox-comb.

At the close, during the hot soup, the worst happened. Denry had known that it would.

Captain Deverax was talking to Nellie, who was respectfully listening, about the scenery, when the Countess came up, plate in hand.

"No, no," the Countess protested. "As for me, I hate your mountains. I was born in the steppe where it is all level—level! Your mountains close me in. I am only here by order of my doctor. Your mountains get on my nerves." She shrugged her shoulders.

Captain Deverax smiled.

"It is the same with you, isn't it?" he said turning to Nellie.

"Oh, no," said Nellie, simply.

"But your husband told me the other day that when you and he were in Geneva a couple of years ago, the view of Mont Blanc used to—er—upset you."

"View of Mont Blanc?" Nellie stammered.

Everybody was aware that she and Denry had never been in Switzerland before, and that their marriage was indeed less than a month old.

"You misunderstood me," said Denry, gruffly. "My wife hasn't been to Geneva."

"Oh!" drawled Captain Deverax.

His "Oh!" contained so much of insinuation, disdain, and lofty amusement that Denry blushed, and when Nellie saw her husband's cheek she blushed in competition and defeated him easily. It was felt that either Denry had been romancing to the Captain, or that he had been married before, unknown to his Nellie, and had been "carrying on" at Geneva. The situation, though it dissolved of itself in a brief space, was awkward. It discredited the Hôtel Beau-Site. It was in the nature of a repulse for the Hôtel Beau-Site (franc a day cheaper than the Métropole) and of a triumph for the popinjay. The fault was utterly Denry's. Yet he said to himself: "I'll be even with that chap."

On the drive home he was silent. The theme of conversation in the sleighs which did not contain the Countess was that the Captain had flirted tremendously with the Countess, and that it amounted to an affair.

IV

Captain Deverax was equally salient in the department of sports. There was a fair sheet of ice, obtained by cutting into the side of the mountain, and a very good tobogganing track, about half a mile in length and full of fine curves, common to the two hotels. Denry's predilection was for the track. He would lie on his stomach on the little contrivance which the Swiss call a luge, and which consists of naught but three bits of wood and two steel-clad runners, and would course down the perilous curves at twenty miles an hour. Until the Captain came, this was regarded as dashing, because most people were content to sit on the luge and travel legs-foremost instead of head-foremost. But the Captain, after a few eights on the ice, intimated that for the rest no sport was true sport save the sport of ski-running. He allowed it to be understood that luges were for infants. He had brought his skis, and these instruments of locomotion, some six feet in length, made a sensation among the inexperienced. For when he had strapped them to his feet the Captain, while stating candidly that his skill was as nothing to that of the Swedish professionals at St Moritz, could assuredly slide over snow in manner prodigious and beautiful. And he was exquisitely clothed for the part. His knickerbockers, in the elegance of their lines, were the delight of beholders. Ski-ing became the rage. Even Nellie insisted on hiring a pair. And the pronunciation of the word "ski" aroused long discussions and was never definitely settled by anybody. The Captain said "skee," but he did not object to "shee," which was said to be the more strictly correct by a lady who knew some one who had been to Norway. People with no shame and no feeling for correctness said brazenly, "sky." Denry, whom nothing could induce to desert his luge, said that obviously "s-k-i" could only spell "planks." And thanks to his inspiration this version was adopted by the majority.

On the second day of Nellie's struggle with her skis she had more success than she either anticipated or desired. She had been making experiments at the summit of the track, slithering about, falling, and being restored to uprightness by as many persons as happened to be near. Skis seemed to her to be the most ungovernable and least practical means of travel that the madness of man had ever concocted. Skates were well-behaved old horses compared to these long, untamed fiends, and a luge was like a tricycle. Then suddenly a friendly starting push drove her a yard or two, and she glided past the level on to the first imperceptible slope of the track. By some hazard her two planks were exactly parallel, as they ought to be, and she glided forward miraculously. And people heard her say:

"How lovely!"

And then people heard her say:

"Oh!... Oh!"

For her pace was increasing. And she dared not strike her pole into the ground. She had, in fact, no control whatever over those two planks to which her feet were strapped. She might have been Mazeppa and they mustangs. She could not even fall. So she fled down the preliminary straight of the track, and ecstatic spectators cried: "Look how *well* Mrs Machin is doing!"

Mrs Machin would have given all her furs to be anywhere off those planks. On the adjacent fields of glittering snow the Captain had been giving his adored Countess a lesson in the use of skis; and they stood together, the Countess somewhat insecure, by the side of the track at its first curve.

Nellie, dumb with excitement and amazement, swept towards them.

"Look out!" cried the Captain.

In vain! He himself might perhaps have escaped, but he could not abandon his Countess in the moment of peril, and the Countess could only move after much thought and many efforts, being scarce more advanced than Nellie. Nellie's wilful planks quite ignored the curve, and, as it were afloat on them, she charged off the track, and into the Captain and the Countess. The impact was tremendous. Six skis waved like semaphores in the air. Then all was still. Then, as the beholders hastened to the scene of the disaster, the Countess laughed and Nellie laughed. The laugh of the Captain was not heard. The sole casualty was a wound about a foot long in the hinterland of the Captain's unique knicker-bockers. And as threads of that beautiful check pattern were afterwards found attached to the wheel of Nellie's pole, the cause of the wound was indisputable. The Captain departed home, chiefly backwards, but with great rapidity.

In the afternoon Denry went down to Montreux and returned with an opal bracelet, which Nellie wore at dinner.

"Oh! What a ripping bracelet!" said a girl.

"Yes," said Nellie. "My husband gave it me only to-day."

"I suppose it's your birthday or something," the inquisitive girl ventured.

"No," said Nellie.

"How nice of him!" said the girl.

The next day Captain Deverax appeared in riding breeches. They were not correct for ski-running, but they were the best he could do. He visited a tailor's in Montreux.

V

The Countess Ruhl had a large sleigh of her own, also a horse; both were hired from Montreux. In this vehicle, sometimes alone, sometimes with a male servant, she would drive at Russian speed over the undulating mountain roads; and for such expeditions she always wore a large red cloak with a hood. Often she was thus seen, in the afternoon; the scarlet made a bright moving patch on the vast expanses of snow. Once, at some distance from the village, two tale-tellers observed a man on skis careering in the neighbourhood of the sleigh. It was Captain Deverax. The flirtation, therefore, was growing warmer and warmer. The hotels hummed with the tidings of it. But the Countess never said anything; nor could anything be extracted from her by even the most experienced gossips. She was an agreeable but a mysterious woman, as befitted a Russian Countess. Again and again were she and the Captain seen together afar off in the landscape. Certainly it was a novelty in flirtations. People wondered what might happen between the two at the fancy-dress ball which the Hôtel Beau-Site was to give in return for the hospitality of the Hôtel Métropole. The ball was offered not in love, but in emulation, almost in hate; for the jealousy displayed by the Beau-Site against the increasing insolence of the Métropole had become acute. The airs of the Captain and his lieges, the Clutterbuck party, had reached the limit of the Beau-Site's endurance. The Métropole seemed to take it for granted that the Captain would lead the cotillon at the Beau-Site's ball as he had led it at the Métropole's.

And then, on the very afternoon of the ball, the Countess received a telegram—it was said from St Petersburg—which necessitated her instant departure. And she went, in an hour, down to Montreux by the funicular railway, and was lost to the Beau-Site. This was a blow to the prestige of the Beau-Site. For the Countess was its chief star, and, moreover, much loved by her fellow-guests, despite her curious weakness for the popinjay, and the mystery of her outings with him.

In the stables Denry saw the Countess's hired sleigh and horse, and in the sleigh her glowing red cloak. And he had one of his ideas, which he executed, although snow was beginning to fall. In ten minutes he and Nellie were driving forth, and Nellie in the red cloak held the reins. Denry, in a coachman's furs, sat behind. They whirled past the Hôtel Métropole. And shortly afterwards, on the wild road towards Attalens, Denry saw a pair of skis scudding as quickly as skis can scud in their rear. It was astonishing how the sleigh, with all the merry jingle of its bells, kept that pair of skis at a distance of about a hundred yards. It seemed to invite the skis to overtake it, and then to regret the invitation and flee further. Up the hills it would crawl, for the skis climbed slowly. Down them it galloped, for the skis slid on the slopes at a dizzy pace. Occasionally a shout came from the skis. And the snow fell thicker and thicker. So for four or five miles. Starlight commenced.

Then the road made a huge descending curve round a hollowed meadow, and the horse galloped its best. But the skis, making a straight line down the snow, acquired the speed of an express, and gained on the sleigh one yard in every three. At the bottom, where the curve met the straight line, was a farmhouse and outbuildings and a hedge and a stone wall and other matters. The sleigh arrived at the point first, but only by a trifle. "Mind your toes," Denry muttered to himself, meaning an injunction to the skis, whose toes were three feet long. The skis, through the eddying snow, yelled frantically to the sleigh to give room. The skis shot up into the road, and in swerving aside swerved into a snow-laden hedge, and clean over it into the farmyard, where they stuck themselves up in the air, as skis will when the person to whose feet they are attached is lying prone. The door of the farm opened and a woman appeared.

She saw the skis at her doorstep. She heard the sleigh-bells, but the sleigh had already vanished into the dusk.

"Well, that was a bit of a lark, that was, Countess!" said Denry to Nellie. "That will be something to talk about. We'd better drive home through Corsier, and quick too! It'll be quite dark soon."

"Supposing he's dead!" Nellie breathed, aghast, reining in the horse.

"Not he!" said Denry. "I saw him beginning to sit up."

"But how will he get home?"

"It looks a very nice farmhouse," said Denry. "I should think he'd be sorry to leave it."

VI

When Denry entered the dining-room of the Beau-Site, which had been cleared for the ball, his costume drew attention not so much by its splendour or ingenuity as by its peculiarity. He wore a short Chinese-shaped jacket, which his wife had made out of blue linen, and a flat Chinese hat to match, which they had constructed together on a basis of cardboard. But his thighs were enclosed in a pair of absurdly ample riding-breeches of an impressive check and cut to a comic exaggeration of the English pattern. He had bought the cloth for these at the tailor's in Montreux. Below them were very tight leggings, also English. In reply to a question as to what or whom he supposed himself to represent, he replied:

"A Captain of Chinese cavalry, of course."

And he put an eyeglass into his left eye and stared.

Now it had been understood that Nellie was to appear as Lady Jane Grey. But she appeared as Little Red Riding-Hood, wearing over her frock the forgotten cloak of the Countess Ruhl.

Instantly he saw her, Denry hurried towards her, with a movement of the legs and a flourish of the eyeglass in his left hand which powerfully suggested a figure familiar to every member of the company. There was laughter. People saw that the idea was immensely funny and clever, and the laughter ran about like fire. At the same time some persons were not quite sure whether Denry had not lapsed a little from the finest taste in this caricature. And all of them were secretly afraid that the uncomfortable might happen when Captain Deverax arrived.

However, Captain Deverax did not arrive. The party from the Métropole came with the news that he had not been seen at the hotel for dinner; it was assumed that he had been to Montreux and missed the funicular back.

"Our two stars simultaneously eclipsed!" said Denry, as the Clutterbucks (representing all the history of England) stared at him curiously.

"Why?" exclaimed the Clutterbuck cousin, "who's the other?"

"The Countess," said Denry. "She went this afternoon—three o'clock."

And all the Métropole party fell into grief.

"It's a world of coincidences," said Denry, with emphasis.

"You don't mean to insinuate," said Mrs Clutterbuck, with a nervous laugh, "that Captain Deverax has—er— gone after the Countess?"

"Oh no!" said Denry, with unction. "Such a thought never entered my head."

"I think you're a very strange man, Mr Machin," retorted Mrs Clutterbuck, hostile and not a bit reassured. "May one ask what that costume is supposed to be?"

"A Captain of Chinese cavalry," said Denry, lifting his eyeglass.

Nevertheless, the dance was a remarkable success, and little by little even the sternest adherents of the absent Captain Deverax deigned to be amused by Denry's Chinese gestures. Also, Denry led the cotillon, and was thereafter greatly applauded by the Beau-Site. The visitors agreed among themselves that, considering that his name was not Deverax, Denry acquitted himself honourably. Later he went to the bureau, and, returning, whispered to his wife:

"It's all right. He's come back safe."

"How do you know?"

"I've just telephoned to ask."

Denry's subsequent humour was wildly gay. And for some reason which nobody could comprehend, he put a sling round his left arm. His efforts to insert the eyeglass into his left eye with his right hand were insistently ludicrous and became a sure source of laughter for all beholders. When the Métropole party were getting into their sleighs to go home—it had ceased snowing—Denry was still trying to insert his eyeglass into his left eye with his right hand, to the universal joy.

VII

But the joy of the night was feeble in comparison with the violent joy of the next morning. Denry was wandering, apparently aimless, between the finish of the tobogganing track and the portals of the Métropole. The snowfall had repaired the defects of the worn track, but it needed to be flattened down by use, and a number of conscientious "lugeurs" were flattening it by frequent descents, which grew faster at each repetition. Other holiday-makers were idling about in the sunshine. A page-boy of the Métropole departed in the direction of the Beau-Site with a note.

At length—the hour was nearing eleven—Captain Deverax, languid, put his head out of the Métropole and sniffed the air. Finding the air sufferable, he came forth on to the steps. His left arm was in a sling. He was wearing the new knickerbockers which he had ordered at Montreux, and which were of precisely the same vast check as had ornamented Denry's legs on the previous night.

"Hullo!" said Denry, sympathetically. "What's this?"

The Captain needed sympathy.

"Ski-ing yesterday afternoon," said he, with a little laugh. "Hasn't the Countess told any of you?"

No," said Denry, "not a word."

The Captain seemed to pause a moment.

"Yes," said he. " A trifling accident. I was ski-ing with the Countess. That is, I was ski-ing and she was in her sleigh."

"Then this is why you didn't turn up at the dance?"

"Yes," said the Captain.

"Well," said Denry, "I hope it's not serious. I can tell you one thing, the cotillon was a most fearful frost without you." The Captain seemed grateful.

They strolled together toward the track.

The first group of people that caught sight of the Captain with his checked legs and his arm in a sling began to smile. Observing this smile, and fancying himself deceived, the Captain attempted to put his eyeglass into his left eye with his right hand, and regularly failed. His efforts towards this feat changed the smiles to enormous laughter.

"I daresay it's awfully funny," said he. "But what can a fellow do with one arm in a sling?"

The laughter was merely intensified. And the group, growing as luge after luge arrived at the end of the track, seemed to give itself up to mirth, to the exclusion of even a proper curiosity about the nature of the Captain's damage. Each fresh attempt to put the eyeglass to his eye was coal on the crackling fire. The Clutterbucks alone seemed glum.

"What on earth is the joke?" Denry asked primly. "Captain Deverax came to grief late yesterday afternoon, ski-ing with the Countess Ruhl. That's why he didn't turn up last night. By the way, where was it, Captain?"

"On the mountain, near Attalens," Deverax answered gloomily. "Happily there was a farmhouse near—it was almost dark."

"With the Countess?" demanded a young impulsive schoolgirl.

"You did say the Countess, didn't you?" Denry asked.

"Why, certainly," said the Captain, testily.

"Well," said the schoolgirl with the nonchalant thoughtless cruelty of youth, "considering that we all saw the Countess off in the funicular at three o'clock, I don't see how you could have been ski-ing with her when it was nearly dark." And the child turned up the hill with her luge, leaving her elders to unknot the situation.

"Oh, yes!" said Denry. "I forgot to tell you that the Countess left yesterday after lunch."

At the same moment the page-boy, reappearing, touched his cap and placed a note in the Captain's only free hand.

"Couldn't deliver it, sir. The Comtesse left early yesterday afternoon."

Convicted of imaginary adventure with noble ladies, the Captain made his retreat, muttering, back to the hotel.

At lunch Denry related the exact circumstances to a delighted table, and the exact circumstances soon reached the Clutterbuck faction at the Métropole. On the following day the Clutterbuck faction and Captain Deverax (now fully enlightened) left Mont Pridoux for some paradise unknown. If murderous thoughts could kill, Denry would have lain dead. But he survived to go with about half the Beau-Site guests to the funicular station to wish the Clutterbucks a pleasant journey. The Captain might have challenged him to a duel but a haughty and icy ceremoniousness was deemed the best treatment for Denry. "Never show a wound" must have been the Captain's motto.

The Beau-Site had scored effectively. And, now that its rival had lost eleven clients by one single train, it beat the Métropole even in vulgar numbers.

Denry had an embryo of a conscience somewhere, and Nellie's was fully developed.

"Well," said Denry, in reply to Nellie's conscience, "it serves him right for making me look a fool over that Geneva business. And besides, I can't stand uppishness, and I won't. I'm from the Five Towns, I am."

Upon which singular utterance the incident closed.

CHAPTER XII
THE SUPREME HONOUR

I

Denry was not as regular in his goings and comings as the generality of business men in the Five Towns; no doubt because he was not by nature a business man at all, but an adventurous spirit who happened to be in a business which was much too good to leave. He was continually, as they say there, "up to something" that caused changes in daily habits. Moreover, the Universal Thrift Club (Limited) was so automatic and self-winding that Denry ran no risks in leaving it often to the care of his highly drilled staff. Still, he did usually come home to his tea about six o'clock of an evening, like the rest, and like the rest, he brought with him a copy of the *Signal* to glance at during tea.

One afternoon in July he arrived thus upon his waiting wife at Machin House, Bleakridge. And she could see that an idea was fermenting in his head. Nellie understood him. One of the most delightful and reassuring things about his married life was Nellie's instinctive comprehension of him. His mother understood him profoundly. But she understood him in a manner sardonic, slightly malicious and even hostile, whereas Nellie understood him with her absurd love. According to his mother's attitude, Denry was guilty till he had proved himself innocent. According to Nellie's, he was always right and always clever in what he did, until he himself said that he had been wrong and stupid—and not always then. Nevertheless, his mother was just as ridiculously proud of him as Nellie was; but she would have perished on the scaffold rather than admit that Denry differed in any detail from the common run of sons. Mrs Machin had departed from Machin House without waiting to be asked. It was characteristic of her that she had returned to Brougham Street and rented there an out-of-date cottage without a single one of the labour-saving contrivances that distinguished the residence which her son had originally built for her.

It was still delicious for Denry to sit down to tea in the dining-room, that miracle of conveniences, opposite the smile of his wife, which told him (*a*) that he was wonderful, (*b*) that she was enchanted to be alive, and (*c*) that he had deserved her particular caressing attentions and would receive them. On the afternoon in July the smile told him (*d*) that he was possessed by one of his ideas.

"Extraordinary how she tumbles to things!" he reflected.

Nellie's new fox-terrier had come in from the garden through the French window, and eaten part of a muffin, and Denry had eaten a muffin and a half, before Nellie, straightening herself proudly and putting her shoulders back (a gesture of hers) thought fit to murmur:

"Well, anything thrilling happened to-day?"

Denry opened the green sheet and read:

"'Sudden death of Alderman Bloor in London.' What price that?"

"Oh!" exclaimed Nellie. "How shocked father will be! They were always rather friendly. By the way, I had a letter from mother this morning. It appears as if Toronto was a sort of paradise. But you can see the old thing prefers Bursley. Father's had a boil on his neck, just at the edge of his collar. He says it's because he's too well. What did Mr Bloor die off?"

"He was in the fashion," said Denry.

"How?"

"Appendicitis, of course. Operation—domino! All over in three days."

"Poor man!" Nellie murmured, trying to feel sad for a change and not succeeding. "And he was to have been mayor in November, wasn't he? How disappointing for him."

"I expect he's got something else to think about," said Denry.

After a pause Nellie asked suddenly:

"Who'll be mayor—now?"

"Well," said Denry, "his Worship Councillor Barlow, J.P., will be extremely cross if *he* isn't."

"How horrid!" said Nellie, frankly. "And he's got nobody at all to be mayoress."

"Mrs Prettyman would be mayoress," said Denry. "When there's no wife or daughter, it's always a sister if there is one."

"But can you *imagine* Mrs Prettyman as mayoress? Why, they say she scrubs her own doorstep—after dark. They ought to make you mayor."

"Do you fancy yourself as mayoress?" he inquired.

"I should be better than Mrs Prettyman, anyhow."

"I believe you'd make an A1 mayoress," said Denry.

"I should be frightfully nervous," she confidentially admitted.

"I doubt it," said he.

The fact was, that since her return to Bursley from the honeymoon, Nellie was an altered woman. She had acquired, as it were in a day, to an astonishing extent, what in the Five Towns is called "a nerve."

"I should like to try it," said she.

One day you'll have to try it, whether you want to or not."

"When will that be?"

"Don't know. Might be next year but one. Old Barlow's pretty certain to be chosen for next November. It's looked on as his turn next. I know there's been a good bit of talk about me for the year after Barlow. Of course, Bloor's death will advance everything by a year. But even if I come next after Barlow it'll be too late."

"Too late? Too late for what?"

"I'll tell you," said Denry. "I wanted to be the youngest mayor that Bursley's ever had. It was only a kind of notion I had a long time ago. I'd given it up, because I knew there was no chance unless I came before Bloor, which of course I couldn't do. Now he's dead. If I could upset old Barlow's apple-cart I should just be the youngest mayor by the skin of my teeth. Huskinson, the mayor in 1884, was aged thirty-four and six months. I've looked it all up this afternoon."

"How lovely if you *could* be the youngest mayor!"

"Yes. I'll tell you how I feel. I feel as though I didn't want to be mayor at all if I can't be the youngest mayor... you know."

She knew.

"Oh!" she cried, "do upset Mr Barlow's apple-cart. He's a horrid old thing. Should I be the youngest mayoress?"

"Not by chalks," said he. "Huskinson's sister was only sixteen."

"But that's only playing at being mayoress!" Nellie protested. "Anyhow, I do think you might be youngest mayor. Who settles it?"

"The Council, of course."

"Nobody likes Councillor Barlow."

"He'll be still less liked when he's wound up the Bursley Football Club."

"Well, urge him on to wind it up, then. But I don't see what football has got to do with being mayor."

She endeavoured to look like a serious politician.

"You are nothing but a cuckoo," Denry pleasantly informed her. "Football has got to do with everything. And it's been a disastrous mistake in my career that I've never taken any interest in football. Old Barlow wants no urging on to wind up the Football Club. He's absolutely set on it. He's lost too much over it. If I could stop him from winding it up, I might...."

"What?"

"I dunno."

She perceived that his idea was yet vague.

II

Not very many days afterwards the walls of Bursley called attention, by small blue and red posters (blue and red being the historic colours of the Bursley Football Club), to a public meeting, which was to be held in the

Town Hall, under the presidency of the Mayor, to consider what steps could be taken to secure the future of the Bursley Football Club.

There were two "great" football clubs in the Five Towns—Knype, one of the oldest clubs in England, and Bursley. Both were in the League, though Knype was in the first division while Bursley was only in the second. Both were, in fact, limited companies, engaged as much in the pursuit of dividends as in the practice of the one ancient and glorious sport which appeals to the reason and the heart of England. (Neither ever paid a dividend.) Both employed professionals, who, by a strange chance, were nearly all born in Scotland; and both also employed trainers who, before an important match, took the teams off to a hydropathic establishment far, far distant from any public-house. (This was called "training.") Now, whereas the Knype Club was struggling along fairly well, the Bursley Club had come to the end of its resources. The great football public had practically deserted it. The explanation, of course, was that Bursley had been losing too many matches. The great football public had no use for anything but victories. It would treat its players like gods—so long as they won. But when they happened to lose, the great football public simply sulked. It did not kick a man that was down; it merely ignored him, well knowing that the man could not get up without help. It cared nothing whatever for fidelity, municipal patriotism, fair play, the chances of war, or dividends on capital. If it could see victories it would pay sixpence, but it would not pay sixpence to assist at defeats.

Still, when at a special general meeting of the Bursley Football Club, Limited, held at the registered office, the Coffee House, Bursley, Councillor Barlow, J.P., Chairman of the Company since the creation of the League, announced that the Directors had reluctantly come to the conclusion that they could not conscientiously embark on the dangerous risks of the approaching season, and that it was the intention of the Directors to wind up the club, in default of adequate public interest— when Bursley read this in the *Signal*, the town was certainly shocked. Was the famous club, then, to disappear for ever, and the football ground to be sold in plots, and the grand stand for firewood? The shock was so severe that the death of Alderman Bloor (none the less a mighty figure in Bursley) had passed as a minor event.

Hence the advertisement of the meeting in the Town Hall caused joy and hope, and people said to themselves: "Something's bound to be done; the old club can't go out like that." And everybody grew quite sentimental. And although nothing is supposed to be capable of filling Bursley Town Hall except a political meeting and an old folk's treat, Bursley Town Hall was as near full as made no matter for the football question. Many men had cheerfully sacrificed a game of billiards and a glass of beer in order to attend it.

The Mayor, in the chair, was a mild old gentleman who knew nothing whatever about football and had probably never seen a football match; but it was essential that the meeting should have august patronage and so the Mayor had been trapped and tamed. On the mere fact that he paid an annual subscription to the golf club, certain parties built up the legend that he was a true sportsman, with the true interests of sport in his soul. He uttered a few phrases, such as "the manly game," "old associations," "bound up with the history of England," "splendid fellows," "indomitable pluck," "dogged by misfortune" (indeed, he produced quite an impression on the rude and grim audience), and then he called upon Councillor Barlow to make a statement.

Councillor Barlow, on the Mayor's right, was a different kind of man from the Mayor. He was fifty and iron-grey, with whiskers, but no moustache; short, stoutish, raspish.

He said nothing about manliness, pluck, history, or Auld Lang Syne.

He said he had given his services as Chairman to the football club for thirteen years; that he had taken up £2000 worth of shares in the Company; and that as at that moment the Company's liabilities would exactly absorb its assets, his £2000 was worth exactly nothing. "You may say," he said, "I've lost that £2000 in thirteen years. That is, it's the same as if I'd been steadily paying three pun' a week out of my own pocket to provide football matches that you chaps wouldn't take the trouble to go and see. That's the straight of it! What have I got for my pains? Nothing but worries and these!" (He pointed to his grey hairs.) "And I'm not alone; there's others; and now I have to come and defend myself at a public meeting. I'm supposed not to have the best interests of football at heart. Me and my co-Directors," he proceeded, with even a rougher raspishness, "have warned the town again and again what would happen if the matches weren't better patronised. And now it's happened, and now it's too late, you want to *do* something! You can't! It's too late. There's only one thing the matter with first-class football in Bursley," he concluded, "and it isn't the players. It's the public—it's yourselves. You're the most craven lot of tom-fools that ever a big football club had to do with. When we lose a match, what do you do? Do you come and encourage us next time? No, you stop away, and leave us fifty or sixty pound out of pocket on a match, just to teach us better! Do you expect us to win every match? Why, Preston North End itself"— here he spoke solemnly, of heroes—"Preston North End itself in its great days didn't win every match—it lost to Accrington. But did the Preston public desert it? No! *You*—you haven't got the pluck of a louse, nor the faithfulness of a cat. You've starved your football club to death, and now you call a meeting to weep and grumble. And you have the insolence to write letters to the *Signal* about bad management, forsooth! If anybody in the hall thinks he can manage this club better than me and my co-Directors have done, I may say that we hold a majority of the shares, and we'll part with the whole show to any clever person or persons who care to take it off our hands at a bargain price. That's talking."

He sat down.

Silence fell. Even in the Five Towns a public meeting is seldom bullied as Councillor Barlow had bullied that meeting. It was aghast. Councillor Barlow had never been popular: he had merely been respected; but thenceforward he became even less popular than before.

"I'm sure we shall all find Councillor Barlow's heat quite excusable—" the Mayor diplomatically began.

"No heat at all," the Councillor interrupted. "Simply cold truth!"

A number of speakers followed, and nearly all of them were against the Directors. Some, with prodigious memories for every combination of players in every match that had ever been played, sought to prove by detailed instances that Councillor Barlow and his co-Directors had persistently and regularly muddled their work during thirteen industrious years. And they defended the insulted public by asserting that no public that respected itself would pay sixpence to watch the wretched football provided by Councillor Barlow. They shouted that the team wanted reconstituting, wanted new blood.

"Yes," shouted Councillor Barlow in reply; "And how are you going to get new blood, with transfer fees as high as they are now? You can't get even an average good player for less than £200. Where's the money to come from? Anybody want to lend a thousand or so on second debentures?"

He laughed sneeringly.

No one showed a desire to invest in second debentures of the Bursley F.C. Ltd.

Still, speakers kept harping on the necessity of new blood in the team, and then others, bolder, harped on the necessity of new blood on the board.

"Shares on sale!" cried the Councillor. "Any buyers? Or," he added, "do you want something for nothing—as usual?"

At length a gentleman rose at the back of the hall.

"I don't pretend to be an expert on football," said he, "though I think it's a great game, but I should like to say a few words as to this question of new blood."

The audience craned its neck.

"Will Mr Councillor Machin kindly step up to the platform?" the Mayor suggested.

And up Denry stepped.

The thought in every mind was: "What's he going to do? What's he got up his sleeve—this time?"

"Three cheers for Machin!" people chanted gaily.

"Order!" said the Mayor.

Denry faced the audience. He was now accustomed to audiences. He said:

"If I'm not mistaken, one of the greatest modern footballers is a native of this town."

And scores of voices yelled: "Ay! Callear! Callear! Greatest centre forward in England!"

"Yes," said Denry. "Callear is the man I mean. Callear left the district, unfortunately for the district, at the age of nineteen for Liverpool. And it was not till after he left that his astounding abilities were perceived. It isn't too much to say that he made the fortune of Liverpool City. And I believe it is the fact that he scored more goals in three seasons than any other player has ever done in the League. Then, York County, which was in a tight place last year, bought him from Liverpool for a high price, and, as all the world knows, Callear had his leg broken in the first match he played for his new club. That just happened to be the ruin of the York Club, which is now quite suddenly in bankruptcy (which happily we are not), and which is disposing of its players. Gentlemen, I say that Callear ought to come back to his native town. He is fitter than ever he was, and his proper place is in his native town."

Loud cheers.

"As captain and centre forward of the club of the Mother of the Five Towns, he would be an immense acquisition and attraction, and he would lead us to victory."

Renewed cheers.

"And how," demanded Councillor Barlow, jumping up angrily, "are we to get him back to his precious native town? Councillor Machin admits that he is not an expert on football. It will probably be news to him that Aston Villa have offered £700 to York for the transfer of Callear, and Blackburn Rovers have offered £750, and they're fighting it out between 'em. Any gentleman willing to put down £800 to buy Callear for Bursley?"

393

he sneered. "I don't mind telling you that steam-engines and the King himself couldn't get Callear into our club."

"Quite finished?" Denry inquired, still standing.

Laughter, overtopped by Councillor Barlow's snort as he sat down.

Denry lifted his voice.

"Mr Callear, will you be good enough to step forward and let us all have a look at you?"

The effect of these apparently simple words surpassed any effect previously obtained by the most complex flights of oratory in that hall. A young, blushing, clumsy, long-limbed, small-bodied giant stumbled along the central aisle and climbed the steps to the platform, where Denry pointed him to a seat. He was recognised by all the true votaries of the game. And everybody said to everybody: "By Gosh! It's him, right enough. It's Callear!" And a vast astonishment and expectation of good fortune filled the hall. Applause burst forth, and though no one knew what the appearance of Callear signified, the applause continued and waxed.

"Good old Callear!" The hoarse shouts succeeded each other. "Good old Machin!"

"Anyhow," said Denry, when the storm was stilled, "we've got him here, without either steam-engines or His Majesty. Will the Directors of the club accept him?"

"And what about the transfer?" Councillor Barlow demanded.

"Would you accept him and try another season if you could get him free?" Denry retorted.

Councillor Barlow always knew his mind, and was never afraid to let other people share that knowledge.

"Yes," he said.

"Then I will see that you have the transfer free."

"But what about York?"

"I have settled with York provisionally," said Denry. "That is my affair. I have returned from York to-day. Leave all that to me. This town has had many benefactors far more important than myself. But I shall be able to claim this originality: I'm the first to make a present of a live man to the town. Gentlemen—Mr Mayor—I venture to call for three cheers for the greatest centre forward in England, our fellow-townsman."

The scene, as the *Signal* said, was unique.

And at the Sports Club and the other clubs afterwards, men said to each other: "No one but him would have thought of bringing Callear over specially and showing him on the platform.... That's cost him above twopence, that has!"

Two days later a letter appeared in the *Signal* (signed "Fiat Justitia"), suggesting that Denry, as some reward for his public spirit, ought to be the next mayor of Bursley, in place of Alderman Bloor deceased. The letter urged that he would make an admirable mayor, the sort of mayor the old town wanted in order to wake it up. And also it pointed out that Denry would be the youngest mayor that Bursley had ever had, and probably the youngest mayor in England that year. The sentiment in the last idea appealed to the town. The town decided that it would positively *like* to have the youngest mayor it had ever had, and probably the youngest mayor in England that year. The *Signal* printed dozens of letters on the subject. When the Council met, more informally than formally, to choose a chief magistrate in place of the dead alderman, several councillors urged that what Bursley wanted was a young and *popular* mayor. And, in fine, Councillor Barlow was shelved for a year. On the choice being published the entire town said: "Now we *shall* have a mayoralty—and don't you forget it!"

And Denry said to Nellie: "You'll be mayoress to the youngest mayor, etc., my child. And it's cost me, including hotel and travelling expenses, eight hundred and eleven pounds six and seven-pence."

III

The rightness of the Council in selecting Denry as mayor was confirmed in a singular manner by the behaviour of the football and of Callear at the opening match of the season.

It was a philanthropic match, between Bursley and Axe, for the benefit of a county orphanage, and, according to the custom of such matches, the ball was formally kicked off by a celebrity, a pillar of society. The ceremony of kicking off has no sporting significance; the celebrity merely with gentleness propels the ball out of the white circle and then flies for his life from the *mêlée*; but it is supposed to add to the moral splendour of the game. In the present instance the posters said: "Kick-off at 3.45 by Councillor E.H. Machin, Mayor-designate." And, indeed, no other celebrity could have been decently selected. On the fine afternoon of the match Denry therefore discovered himself with a new football at his toes, a silk hat on his head, and twenty-two Herculean players menacing him in attitudes expressive of an intention to murder him. Bursley had lost the toss, and hence Denry had to kick towards the Bursley goal. As the *Signal* said, he "despatched the sphere " straight into the keeping of Callear, who as centre forward was facing him, and Callear was dodging down the field with it before the Axe players had finished admiring Denry's effrontery. Every reader will remember with a thrill the historic match in which the immortal Jimmy Brown, on the last occasion when he captained Blackburn Rovers, dribbled the ball himself down the length of the field, scored a goal, and went home with the English Cup under his arm. Callear evidently intended to imitate the feat. He was entirely wrong. Dribbling tactics had been killed for ever, years before, by Preston North End, who invented the "passing" game. Yet Callear went on, and good luck seemed to float over him like a cherub. Finally he shot; a wild, high shot; but there was an adverse wind which dragged the ball down, swept it round, and blew it into the net. The first goal had been scored in twenty seconds! (It was also the last in the match.) Callear's reputation was established. Useless for solemn experts to point out that he had simply been larking for the gallery, and that the result was a shocking fluke—Callear's reputation was established. He became at once the idol of the populace. As Denry walked gingerly off the field to the grand stand he, too, was loudly cheered, and he could not help feeling that, somehow, it was he who had scored that goal. And although nobody uttered the precise thought, most people did secretly think, as they gazed at the triumphant Denry, that a man who triumphed like that, because he triumphed like that, was the right sort of man to be mayor, the kind of man they needed.

Denry became identified with the highest class of local football. This fact led to a curious crisis in the history of municipal manners. On Corporation Sunday the mayor walks to church, preceded by the mace, and followed by the aldermen and councillors, the borough officials, the Volunteers and the Fire Brigade; after all these, in the procession, come individuals known as prominent citizens. Now the first and second elevens of the Bursley Football Club, headed by Callear, expressed their desire to occupy a place in Denry's mayoral procession; they felt that some public acknowledgment was due to the Mayor for his services to the national sport. Denry instantly agreed, with thanks: the notion seemed to him entirely admirable. Then some unfortunately-inspired parson wrote to the *Signal* to protest against professional footballers following the chief magistrate of the borough to church. His arguments were that such a thing was unheard-of, and that football was the cause of a great deal of evil gambling. Some people were inclined to agree with the protest, until Denry wrote to the *Signal* and put a few questions: Was Bursley proud of its football team? Or was Bursley ashamed of its football team? Was the practice of football incompatible with good citizenship? Was there anything dishonourable in playing football? Ought professional footballers to be considered as social pariahs? Was there any class of beings to whom the churches ought to be closed?

The parson foundered in a storm of opprobrium, scorn, and ironic laughter. Though the town laughed, it only laughed to hide its disgust of the parson.

People began to wonder whether the teams would attend in costume, carrying the football between them on a charger as a symbol. No such multitudes ever greeted a mayoral procession in Bursley before. The footballers, however, appeared in ordinary costume (many of them in frock-coats); but they wore neckties of the club colours, a device which was agreed to be in the nicest taste. St Luke's Church was crowded; and, what is stranger, the churchyard was also crowded. The church barely held the procession itself and the ladies who, by influence, had been accommodated with seats in advance. Thousands of persons filled the churchyard, and to prevent them from crushing into the packed fane and bursting it at its weakest point, the apse, the doors had to be locked and guarded. Four women swooned during the service: neither Mrs Machin, senior, nor Nellie, was among the four. It was the first time that any one had been known to swoon at a religious service held in November. This fact alone gave a tremendous prestige to Denry's mayoralty. When, with Nellie on his arm, he emerged from the church to the thunders of the organ, the greeting which he received in the churchyard, though the solemnity of the occasion forbade clapping, lacked naught in brilliance and efficacy.

The real point and delight of that Corporation Sunday was not fully appreciated till later. It had been expected that the collection after the sermon would be much larger than usual, because the congregation was much larger than usual. But the church-wardens were startled to find it four times as large as usual. They were further startled to find only three threepenny-bits among all the coins. This singularity led to comment and to note-comparing. Everybody had noticed for weeks past a growing dearth of threepenny-bits. Indeed, threepenny-bits had practically vanished from circulation in the Five Towns. On the Monday it became known that the clerks of the various branches of the Universal Thrift Club, Limited, had paid into the banks enormous and unparalleled quantities of threepenny-bits, and for at least a week afterwards everybody paid for everything in threepenny-bits. And the piquant news passed from mouth to mouth that Denry, to the simple end of ensuring a thumping collection for charities on Corporation Sunday, had used the vast organisation of the Thrift Club to bring about a famine of threepenny-bits. In the annals of the town that Sunday is referred to as "Threepenny-bit Sunday," because it was so happily devoid of threepenny-bits.

A little group of councillors were discussing Denry.

"What a card!" said one, laughing joyously. "He's a rare 'un, no mistake."

"Of course, this'll make him more popular than ever," said another. "We've never had a man to touch him for that."

"And yet," demanded Councillor Barlow, "what's he done? Has he ever done a day's work in his life? What great cause is he identified with?"

"He's identified," said the speaker, "with the great cause of cheering us all up."

The Grand Babylon Hotel

Chapter One THE MILLIONAIRE AND THE WAITER

'YES, sir?'

Jules, the celebrated head waiter of the Grand Babylon, was bending formally towards the alert, middle-aged man who had just entered the smoking-room and dropped into a basket-chair in the corner by the conservatory. It was 7.45 on a particularly sultry June night, and dinner was about to be served at the Grand Babylon. Men of all sizes, ages, and nationalities, but every one alike arrayed in faultless evening dress, were dotted about the large, dim apartment. A faint odour of flowers came from the conservatory, and the tinkle of a fountain. The waiters, commanded by Jules, moved softly across the thick Oriental rugs, balancing their trays with the dexterity of jugglers, and receiving and executing orders with that air of profound importance of which only really first-class waiters have the secret. The atmosphere was an atmosphere of serenity and repose, characteristic of the Grand Babylon. It seemed impossible that anything could occur to mar the peaceful, aristocratic monotony of existence in that perfectly-managed establishment. Yet on that night was to happen the mightiest upheaval that the Grand Babylon had ever known.

'Yes, sir?' repeated Jules, and this time there was a shade of august disapproval in his voice: it was not usual for him to have to address a customer twice.

'Oh!' said the alert, middle-aged man, looking up at length. Beautifully ignorant of the identity of the great Jules, he allowed his grey eyes to twinkle as he caught sight of the expression on the waiter's face. 'Bring me an Angel Kiss.'

'Pardon, sir?'

'Bring me an Angel Kiss, and be good enough to lose no time.'

'If it's an American drink, I fear we don't keep it, sir.' The voice of Jules fell icily distinct, and several men glanced round uneasily, as if to deprecate the slightest disturbance of their calm. The appearance of the person to whom Jules was speaking, however, reassured them somewhat, for he had all the look of that expert, the travelled Englishman, who can differentiate between one hôtel and another by instinct, and who knows at once where he may make a fuss with propriety, and where it is advisable to behave exactly as at the club. The Grand Babylon was a hôtel in whose smoking-room one behaved as though one was at one's club.

'I didn't suppose you did keep it, but you can mix it, I guess, even in this hôtel.'

'This isn't an American hôtel, sir.' The calculated insolence of the words was cleverly masked beneath an accent of humble submission.

The alert, middle-aged man sat up straight, and gazed placidly at Jules, who was pulling his famous red side-whiskers.

'Get a liqueur glass,' he said, half curtly and half with good-humoured tolerance, 'pour into it equal quantities of maraschino, cream, and crême de menthe. Don't stir it; don't shake it. Bring it to me. And, I say, tell the bar-tender—'

'Bar-tender, sir?'

'Tell the bar-tender to make a note of the recipe, as I shall probably want an Angel Kiss every evening before dinner so long as this weather lasts.'

'I will send the drink to you, sir,' said Jules distantly. That was his parting shot, by which he indicated that he was not as other waiters are, and that any person who treated him with disrespect did so at his own peril.

A few minutes later, while the alert, middle-aged man was tasting the Angel Kiss, Jules sat in conclave with Miss Spencer, who had charge of the bureau of the Grand Babylon. This bureau was a fairly large chamber, with two sliding glass partitions which overlooked the entrance-hall and the smoking-room. Only a small portion of the clerical work of the great hôtel was performed there. The place served chiefly as the lair of Miss Spencer, who was as well known and as important as Jules himself. Most modern hôtels have a male clerk to superintend the bureau. But the Grand Babylon went its own way. Miss Spencer had been bureau clerk almost since the Grand Babylon had first raised its massive chimneys to heaven, and she remained in her place despite the vagaries of other hôtels. Always admirably dressed in plain black silk, with a small diamond brooch, immaculate wrist-bands, and frizzed yellow hair, she looked now just as she had looked an indefinite number of years ago. Her age—none knew it, save herself and perhaps one other, and none cared. The gracious and alluring contours of her figure were irreproachable; and in the evenings she was a useful ornament of which any hôtel might be innocently proud. Her knowledge of Bradshaw, of steamship services, and the programmes of theatres and music-halls was unrivalled; yet she never travelled, she never went to a theatre or a music-hall. She seemed to spend the whole of her life in that official lair of hers, imparting information to guests, telephoning to the various departments, or engaged in intimate conversations with her special friends on the staff, as at present.

'Who's Number 107?' Jules asked this black-robed lady.

Miss Spencer examined her ledgers.

'Mr Theodore Racksole, New York.'

'I thought he must be a New Yorker,' said Jules, after a brief, significant pause, 'but he talks as good English as you or me. Says he wants an "Angel Kiss"—maraschino and cream, if you please—every night. I'll see he doesn't stop here too long.'

Miss Spencer smiled grimly in response. The notion of referring to Theodore Racksole as a 'New Yorker' appealed to her sense of humour, a sense in which she was not entirely deficient. She knew, of course, and she knew that Jules knew, that this Theodore Racksole must be the unique and only Theodore Racksole, the third richest man in the United States, and therefore probably in the world. Nevertheless she ranged herself at once on the side of Jules.

Just as there was only one Racksole, so there was only one Jules, and Miss Spencer instinctively shared the latter's indignation at the spectacle of any person whatsoever, millionaire or Emperor, presuming to demand an 'Angel Kiss', that unrespectable concoction of maraschino and cream, within the precincts of the Grand Babylon. In the world of hôtels it was currently stated that, next to the proprietor, there were three gods at the Grand Babylon—Jules, the head waiter, Miss Spencer, and, most powerful of all, Rocco, the renowned chef, who earned two thousand a year, and had a chalet on the Lake of Lucerne. All the great hôtels in Northumberland Avenue and on the Thames Embankment had tried to get Rocco away from the Grand Babylon, but without success. Rocco was well aware that even he could rise no higher than the maître hôtel of the Grand Babylon, which, though it never advertised itself, and didn't belong to a limited company, stood an easy first among the hôtels of Europe—first in expensiveness, first in exclusiveness, first in that mysterious quality known as 'style'.

Situated on the Embankment, the Grand Babylon, despite its noble proportions, was somewhat dwarfed by several colossal neighbours. It had but three hundred and fifty rooms, whereas there are two hôtels within a quarter of a mile with six hundred and four hundred rooms respectively. On the other hand, the Grand Babylon was the only hôtel in London with a genuine separate entrance for Royal visitors constantly in use. The Grand Babylon counted that day wasted on which it did not entertain, at the lowest, a German prince or the Maharajah of some Indian State. When Felix Babylon—after whom, and not with any reference to London's nickname, the hôtel was christened—when Felix Babylon founded the hôtel in 1869 he had set himself to cater for Royalty, and that was the secret of his triumphant eminence.

The son of a rich Swiss hôtel proprietor and financier, he had contrived to established a connection with the officials of several European Courts, and he had not spared money in that respect. Sundry kings and not a few princesses called him Felix, and spoke familiarly of the hôtel as 'Felix's'; and Felix had found that this was very good for trade. The Grand Babylon was managed accordingly. The 'note' of its policy was discretion, always discretion, and quietude, simplicity, remoteness. The place was like a palace incognito. There was no gold sign over the roof, not even an explanatory word at the entrance. You walked down a small side street off the Strand, you saw a plain brown building in front of you, with two mahogany swing doors, and an official behind each; the doors opened noiselessly; you entered; you were in Felix's. If you meant to be a guest, you, or your courier, gave your card to Miss Spencer. Upon no consideration did you ask for the tariff. It was not good form to mention prices at the Grand Babylon; the prices were enormous, but you never mentioned them. At the conclusion of your stay a bill was presented, brief and void of dry details, and you paid it without a word. You met with a stately civility, that was all. No one had originally asked you to come; no one expressed the hope that you would come again. The Grand Babylon was far above such manoeuvres; it defied competition by ignoring it; and consequently was nearly always full during the season.

If there was one thing more than another that annoyed the Grand Babylon—put its back up, so to speak—it was to be compared with, or to be mistaken for, an American hôtel. The Grand Babylon was resolutely opposed to American methods of eating, drinking, and lodging—but especially American methods of drinking. The resentment of Jules, on being requested to supply Mr Theodore Racksole with an Angel Kiss, will therefore be appreciated.

'Anybody with Mr Theodore Racksole?' asked Jules, continuing his conversation with Miss Spencer. He put a scornful stress on every syllable of the guest's name.

398

'Miss Racksole—she's in No. 111.'

Jules paused, and stroked his left whisker as it lay on his gleaming white collar.

'She's where?' he queried, with a peculiar emphasis.

'No. 111. I couldn't help it. There was no other room with a bathroom and dressing-room on that floor.' Miss Spencer's voice had an appealing tone of excuse.

'Why didn't you tell Mr Theodore Racksole and Miss Racksole that we were unable to accommodate them?'

'Because Babs was within hearing.'

Only three people in the wide world ever dreamt of applying to Mr Felix Babylon the playful but mean abbreviation—Babs: those three were Jules, Miss Spencer, and Rocco. Jules had invented it. No one but he would have had either the wit or the audacity to do so.

'You'd better see that Miss Racksole changes her room to-night,' Jules said after another pause. 'Leave it to me: I'll fix it. Au revoir! It's three minutes to eight. I shall take charge of the dining-room myself to-night.'

And Jules departed, rubbing his fine white hands slowly and meditatively. It was a trick of his, to rub his hands with a strange, roundabout motion, and the action denoted that some unusual excitement was in the air.

At eight o'clock precisely dinner was served in the immense salle manger, that chaste yet splendid apartment of white and gold. At a small table near one of the windows a young lady sat alone. Her frocks said Paris, but her face unmistakably said New York. It was a self-possessed and bewitching face, the face of a woman thoroughly accustomed to doing exactly what she liked, when she liked, how she liked: the face of a woman who had taught hundreds of gilded young men the true art of fetching and carrying, and who, by twenty years or so of parental spoiling, had come to regard herself as the feminine equivalent of the Tsar of All the Russias. Such women are only made in America, and they only come to their full bloom in Europe, which they imagine to be a continent created by Providence for their diversion.

The young lady by the window glanced disapprovingly at the menu card. Then she looked round the dining-room, and, while admiring the diners, decided that the room itself was rather small and plain. Then she gazed through the open window, and told herself that though the Thames by twilight was passable enough, it was by no means level with the Hudson, on whose shores her father had a hundred thousand dollar country cottage. Then she returned to the menu, and with a pursing of lovely lips said that there appeared to be nothing to eat.

'Sorry to keep you waiting, Nella.' It was Mr Racksole, the intrepid millionaire who had dared to order an Angel Kiss in the smoke-room of the Grand Babylon. Nella—her proper name was Helen—smiled at her parent cautiously, reserving to herself the right to scold if she should feel so inclined.

'You always are late, father,' she said.

'Only on a holiday,' he added. 'What is there to eat?'

'Nothing.'

'Then let's have it. I'm hungry. I'm never so hungry as when I'm being seriously idle.'

'Consommé Britannia,' she began to read out from the menu, 'Saumon d'Ecosse, Sauce Genoise, Aspics de Homard. Oh, heavens! Who wants these horrid messes on a night like this?'

'But, Nella, this is the best cooking in Europe,' he protested.

'Say, father,' she said, with seeming irrelevance, 'had you forgotten it's my birthday to-morrow?'

'Have I ever forgotten your birthday, O most costly daughter?'

'On the whole you've been a most satisfactory dad,' she answered sweetly, 'and to reward you I'll be content this year with the cheapest birthday treat you ever gave me. Only I'll have it to-night.'

'Well,' he said, with the long-suffering patience, the readiness for any surprise, of a parent whom Nella had thoroughly trained, 'what is it?'

'It's this. Let's have filleted steak and a bottle of Bass for dinner to-night. It will be simply exquisite. I shall love it.'

'But my dear Nella,' he exclaimed, 'steak and beer at Felix's! It's impossible! Moreover, young women still under twenty-three cannot be permitted to drink Bass.'

'I said steak and Bass, and as for being twenty-three, shall be going in twenty-four to-morrow.'

Miss Racksole set her small white teeth.

There was a gentle cough. Jules stood over them. It must have been out of a pure spirit of adventure that he had selected this table for his own services. Usually Jules did not personally wait at dinner. He merely hovered observant, like a captain on the bridge during the mate's watch. Regular frequenters of the hôtel felt themselves honoured when Jules attached himself to their tables.

Theodore Racksole hesitated one second, and then issued the order with a fine air of carelessness:

399

'Filleted steak for two, and a bottle of Bass.' It was the bravest act of Theodore Racksole's life, and yet at more than one previous crisis a high courage had not been lacking to him.

'It's not in the menu, sir,' said Jules the imperturbable.

'Never mind. Get it. We want it.'

'Very good, sir.'

Jules walked to the service-door, and, merely affecting to look behind, came immediately back again.

'Mr Rocco's compliments, sir, and he regrets to be unable to serve steak and Bass to-night, sir.'

'Mr Rocco?' questioned Racksole lightly.

'Mr Rocco,' repeated Jules with firmness.

'And who is Mr Rocco?'

'Mr Rocco is our chef, sir.' Jules had the expression of a man who is asked to explain who Shakespeare was.

The two men looked at each other. It seemed incredible that Theodore Racksole, the ineffable Racksole, who owned a thousand miles of railway, several towns, and sixty votes in Congress, should be defied by a waiter, or even by a whole hôtel. Yet so it was. When Europe's effete back is against the wall not a regiment of millionaires can turn its flank. Jules had the calm expression of a strong man sure of victory. His face said: 'You beat me once, but not this time, my New York friend!'

As for Nella, knowing her father, she foresaw interesting events, and waited confidently for the steak. She did not feel hungry, and she could afford to wait.

'Excuse me a moment, Nella,' said Theodore Racksole quietly, 'I shall be back in about two seconds,' and he strode out of the salle à manger. No one in the room recognized the millionaire, for he was unknown to London, this being his first visit to Europe for over twenty years. Had anyone done so, and caught the expression on his face, that man might have trembled for an explosion which should have blown the entire Grand Babylon into the Thames.

Jules retired strategically to a corner. He had fired; it was the antagonist's turn. A long and varied experience had taught Jules that a guest who embarks on the subjugation of a waiter is almost always lost; the waiter has so many advantages in such a contest.

Chapter Two HOW MR RACKSOLE OBTAINED HIS DINNER

NEVERTHELESS, there are men with a confirmed habit of getting their own way, even as guests in an exclusive hôtel: and Theodore Racksole had long since fallen into that useful practice—except when his only daughter Helen, motherless but high-spirited girl, chose to think that his way crossed hers, in which case Theodore capitulated and fell back. But when Theodore and his daughter happened to be going one and the same road, which was pretty often, then Heaven alone might help any obstacle that was so ill-advised as to stand in their path. Jules, great and observant man though he was, had not noticed the terrible projecting chins of both father and daughter, otherwise it is possible he would have reconsidered the question of the steak and Bass.

Theodore Racksole went direct to the entrance-hall of the hôtel, and entered Miss Spencer's sanctum.

'I want to see Mr Babylon,' he said, 'without the delay of an instant.'

Miss Spencer leisurely raised her flaxen head.

'I am afraid—,' she began the usual formula. It was part of her daily duty to discourage guests who desired to see Mr Babylon.

'No, no,' said Racksole quickly, 'I don't want any "I'm afraids." This is business. If you had been the ordinary hôtel clerk I should have slipped you a couple of sovereigns into your hand, and the thing would have been done.

As you are not—as you are obviously above bribes—I merely say to you, I must see Mr Babylon at once on an affair of the utmost urgency. My name is Racksole—Theodore Racksole.'

'Of New York?' questioned a voice at the door, with a slight foreign accent.

The millionaire turned sharply, and saw a rather short, French-looking man, with a bald head, a grey beard, a long and perfectly-built frock coat, eye-glasses attached to a minute silver chain, and blue eyes that seemed to have the transparent innocence of a maid's.

'There is only one,' said Theodore Racksole succinctly.

'You wish to see me?' the new-comer suggested.

'You are Mr Felix Babylon?'

The man bowed.

'At this moment I wish to see you more than anyone else in the world,' said Racksole. 'I am consumed and burnt up with a desire to see you, Mr Babylon.

I only want a few minutes' quiet chat. I fancy I can settle my business in that time.'

With a gesture Mr Babylon invited the millionaire down a side corridor, at the end of which was Mr Babylon's private room, a miracle of Louis XV furniture and tapestry: like most unmarried men with large incomes, Mr Babylon had 'tastes' of a highly expensive sort.

The landlord and his guest sat down opposite each other. Theodore Racksole had met with the usual millionaire's luck in this adventure, for Mr Babylon made a practice of not allowing himself to be interviewed by his guests, however distinguished, however wealthy, however pertinacious. If he had not chanced to enter Miss Spencer's office at that precise moment, and if he had not been impressed in a somewhat peculiar way by the physiognomy of the millionaire, not all Mr Racksole's American energy and ingenuity would have availed for a confabulation with the owner of the Grand Babylon Hôtel that night. Theodore Racksole, however, was ignorant that a mere accident had served him. He took all the credit to himself.

'I read in the New York papers some months ago,' Theodore started, without even a clearing of the throat, 'that this hôtel of yours, Mr Babylon, was to be sold to a limited company, but it appears that the sale was not carried out.'

'It was not,' answered Mr Babylon frankly, 'and the reason was that the middle-men between the proposed company and myself wished to make a large secret profit, and I declined to be a party to such a profit. They were firm; I was firm; and so the affair came to nothing.'

'The agreed price was satisfactory?'

'Quite.'

'May I ask what the price was?'

'Are you a buyer, Mr Racksole?'

'Are you a seller, Mr Babylon?'

'I am,' said Babylon, 'on terms. The price was four hundred thousand pounds, including the leasehold and goodwill. But I sell only on the condition that the buyer does not transfer the property to a limited company at a higher figure.'

'I will put one question to you, Mr Babylon,' said the millionaire. 'What have your profits averaged during the last four years?'

'Thirty-four thousand pounds per annum.'

'I buy,' said Theodore Racksole, smiling contentedly; 'and we will, if you please, exchange contract-letters on the spot.'

'You come quickly to a resolution, Mr Racksole. But perhaps you have been considering this question for a long time?'

'On the contrary,' Racksole looked at his watch, 'I have been considering it for six minutes.'

Felix Babylon bowed, as one thoroughly accustomed to eccentricity of wealth.

'The beauty of being well-known,' Racksole continued, 'is that you needn't trouble about preliminary explanations. You, Mr Babylon, probably know all about me. I know a good deal about you. We can take each other for granted without reference. Really, it is as simple to buy an hôtel or a railroad as it is to buy a watch, provided one is equal to the transaction.'

'Precisely,' agreed Mr Babylon smiling. 'Shall we draw up the little informal contract? There are details to be thought of. But it occurs to me that you cannot have dined yet, and might prefer to deal with minor questions after dinner.'

'I have not dined,' said the millionaire, with emphasis, 'and in that connexion will you do me a favour? Will you send for Mr Rocco?'

'You wish to see him, naturally.'

'I do,' said the millionaire, and added, 'about my dinner.'

'Rocco is a great man,' murmured Mr Babylon as he touched the bell, ignoring the last words. 'My compliments to Mr Rocco,' he said to the page who answered his summons, 'and if it is quite convenient I should be glad to see him here for a moment.'

'What do you give Rocco?' Racksole inquired.

'Two thousand a year and the treatment of an Ambassador.'

'I shall give him the treatment of an Ambassador and three thousand.'

'You will be wise,' said Felix Babylon.

At that moment Rocco came into the room, very softly—a man of forty, thin, with long, thin hands, and an inordinately long brown silky moustache.

'Rocco,' said Felix Babylon, 'let me introduce Mr Theodore Racksole, of New York.'

'Sharmed,' said Rocco, bowing. 'Ze—ze, vat you call it, millionaire?'

'Exactly,' Racksole put in, and continued quickly: 'Mr Rocco, I wish to acquaint you before any other person with the fact that I have purchased the Grand Babylon Hôtel. If you think well to afford me the privilege of retaining your services I shall be happy to offer you a remuneration of three thousand a year.'

'Tree, you said?'

'Three.'

'Sharmed.'

'And now, Mr Rocco, will you oblige me very much by ordering a plain beefsteak and a bottle of Bass to be served by Jules—I particularly desire Jules—at table No. 17 in the dining-room in ten minutes from now? And will you do me the honour of lunching with me to-morrow?'

Mr Rocco gasped, bowed, muttered something in French, and departed.

Five minutes later the buyer and seller of the Grand Babylon Hôtel had each signed a curt document, scribbled out on the hôtel note-paper. Felix Babylon asked no questions, and it was this heroic absence of curiosity, of surprise on his part, that more than anything else impressed Theodore Racksole. How many hôtel proprietors in the world, Racksole asked himself, would have let that beef-steak and Bass go by without a word of comment.

'From what date do you wish the purchase to take effect?' asked Babylon.

'Oh,' said Racksole lightly, 'it doesn't matter. Shall we say from to-night?'

'As you will. I have long wished to retire. And now that the moment has come—and so dramatically—I am ready. I shall return to Switzerland. One cannot spend much money there, but it is my native land. I shall be the richest man in Switzerland.' He smiled with a kind of sad amusement.

'I suppose you are fairly well off?' said Racksole, in that easy familiar style of his, as though the idea had just occurred to him.

'Besides what I shall receive from you, I have half a million invested.'

'Then you will be nearly a millionaire?'

Felix Babylon nodded.

'I congratulate you, my dear sir,' said Racksole, in the tone of a judge addressing a newly-admitted barrister. 'Nine hundred thousand pounds, expressed in francs, will sound very nice—in Switzerland.'

'Of course to you, Mr Racksole, such a sum would be poverty. Now if one might guess at your own wealth?' Felix Babylon was imitating the other's freedom.

'I do not know, to five millions or so, what I am worth,' said Racksole, with sincerity, his tone indicating that he would have been glad to give the information if it were in his power.

'You have had anxieties, Mr Racksole?'

'Still have them. I am now holiday-making in London with my daughter in order to get rid of them for a time.'

'Is the purchase of hôtels your notion of relaxation, then?'

Racksole shrugged his shoulders. 'It is a change from railroads,' he laughed.

'Ah, my friend, you little know what you have bought.'

'Oh! yes I do,' returned Racksole; 'I have bought just the first hôtel in the world.'

'That is true, that is true,' Babylon admitted, gazing meditatively at the antique Persian carpet. 'There is nothing, anywhere, like my hôtel. But you will regret the purchase, Mr Racksole. It is no business of mine, of course, but I cannot help repeating that you will regret the purchase.'

'I never regret.'

'Then you will begin very soon—perhaps to-night.'

'Why do you say that?'

'Because the Grand Babylon is the Grand Babylon. You think because you control a railroad, or an iron-works, or a line of steamers, therefore you can control anything. But no. Not the Grand Babylon. There is something about the Grand Babylon—' He threw up his hands.

'Servants rob you, of course.'

'Of course. I suppose I lose a hundred pounds a week in that way. But it is not that I mean. It is the guests. The guests are too—too distinguished.

The great Ambassadors, the great financiers, the great nobles, all the men that move the world, put up under my roof. London is the centre of everything, and my hôtel—your hôtel—is the centre of London. Once I had a King and a Dowager Empress staying here at the same time. Imagine that!'

'A great honour, Mr Babylon. But wherein lies the difficulty?'

'Mr Racksole,' was the grim reply, 'what has become of your shrewdness—that shrewdness which has made your fortune so immense that even you cannot calculate it? Do you not perceive that the roof which habitually shelters all the force, all the authority of the world, must necessarily also shelter nameless and numberless plotters, schemers, evil-doers, and workers of mischief? The thing is as clear as day—and as dark as night. Mr Racksole, I never know by whom I am surrounded. I never know what is going forward.

Only sometimes I get hints, glimpses of strange acts and strange secrets.

You mentioned my servants. They are almost all good servants, skilled, competent. But what are they besides? For anything I know my fourth sub-chef may be an agent of some European Government. For anything I know my invaluable Miss Spencer may be in the pay of a court dressmaker or a Frankfort banker. Even Rocco may be someone else in addition to Rocco.'

'That makes it all the more interesting,' remarked Theodore Racksole.

'What a long time you have been, Father,' said Nella, when he returned to table No. 17 in the salle manger.

'Only twenty minutes, my dove.'

'But you said two seconds. There is a difference.'

'Well, you see, I had to wait for the steak to cook.'

'Did you have much trouble in getting my birthday treat?'

'No trouble. But it didn't come quite as cheap as you said.'

'What do you mean, Father?'

'Only that I've bought the entire hôtel. But don't split.'

'Father, you always were a delicious parent. Shall you give me the hôtel for a birthday present?'

'No. I shall run it—as an amusement. By the way, who is that chair for?'

He noticed that a third cover had been laid at the table.

'That is for a friend of mine who came in about five minutes ago. Of course I told him he must share our steak. He'll be here in a moment.'

'May I respectfully inquire his name?'

'Dimmock—Christian name Reginald; profession, English companion to Prince Aribert of Posen. I met him when I was in St Petersburg with cousin Hetty last fall. Oh; here he is. Mr Dimmock, this is my dear father. He has succeeded with the steak.'

Theodore Racksole found himself confronted by a very young man, with deep black eyes, and a fresh, boyish expression. They began to talk.

Jules approached with the steak. Racksole tried to catch the waiter's eye, but could not. The dinner proceeded.

'Oh, Father!' cried Nella, 'what a lot of mustard you have taken!'

'Have I?' he said, and then he happened to glance into a mirror on his left hand between two windows. He saw the reflection of Jules, who stood behind his chair, and he saw Jules give a slow, significant, ominous wink to Mr Dimmock—Christian name, Reginald.

He examined his mustard in silence. He thought that perhaps he had helped himself rather plenteously to mustard.

Chapter Three AT THREE A.M.

MR REGINALD DIMMOCK proved himself, despite his extreme youth, to be a man of the world and of experiences, and a practised talker. Conversation between him and Nella Racksole seemed never to flag. They chattered about St Petersburg, and the ice on the Neva, and the tenor at the opera who had been exiled to Siberia, and the quality of Russian tea, and the sweetness of Russian champagne, and various other aspects of Muscovite existence. Russia exhausted, Nella lightly outlined her own doings since she had met the young man in the Tsar's capital, and this recital brought the topic round to London, where it stayed till the final piece of steak was eaten. Theodore Racksole noticed that Mr Dimmock gave very meagre information about his own movements, either past or future. He regarded the youth as a typical hanger-on of Courts, and wondered how he had obtained his post of companion to Prince Aribert of Posen, and who Prince Aribert of Posen might be. The millionaire thought he had once heard of Posen, but he wasn't sure; he rather fancied it was one of those small nondescript German States of which five-sixths of the subjects are Palace officials, and the rest charcoal-burners or innkeepers. Until the meal was nearly over, Racksole said little—perhaps his thoughts were too busy with Jules' wink to Mr Dimmock, but when ices had been followed by coffee, he decided that it might be as well, in the interests of the hôtel, to discover something about his daughter's friend. He never for an instant questioned her right to possess her own friends; he had always left her in the most amazing liberty, relying on her inherited good sense to keep her out of mischief; but, quite apart from the wink, he was struck by Nella's attitude towards Mr Dimmock, an attitude in which an amiable scorn was blended with an evident desire to propitiate and please.

'Nella tells me, Mr Dimmock, that you hold a confidential position with Prince Aribert of Posen,' said Racksole. 'You will pardon an American's ignorance, but is Prince Aribert a reigning Prince—what, I believe, you call in Europe, a Prince Regnant?'

'His Highness is not a reigning Prince, nor ever likely to be,' answered Dimmock. 'The Grand Ducal Throne of Posen is occupied by his Highness's nephew, the Grand Duke Eugen.'

'Nephew?' cried Nella with astonishment.

'Why not, dear lady?'

'But Prince Aribert is surely very young?'

'The Prince, by one of those vagaries of chance which occur sometimes in the history of families, is precisely the same age as the Grand Duke. The late Grand Duke's father was twice married. Hence this youthfulness on the part of an uncle.'

'How delicious to be the uncle of someone as old as yourself! But I suppose it is no fun for Prince Aribert. I suppose he has to be frightfully respectful and obedient, and all that, to his nephew?'

'The Grand Duke and my Serene master are like brothers. At present, of course, Prince Aribert is nominally heir to the throne, but as no doubt you are aware, the Grand Duke will shortly marry a near relative of the Emperor's, and should there be a family—' Mr Dimmock stopped and shrugged his straight shoulders. 'The Grand Duke,' he went on, without finishing the last sentence, 'would much prefer Prince Aribert to be his successor. He really doesn't want to marry. Between ourselves, strictly between ourselves, he regards marriage as rather a bore. But, of course, being a German Grand Duke, he is bound to marry. He owes it to his country, to Posen.'

'How large is Posen?' asked Racksole bluntly.

'Father,' Nella interposed laughing, 'you shouldn't ask such inconvenient questions. You ought to have guessed that it isn't etiquette to inquire about the size of a German Dukedom.'

'I am sure,' said Dimmock, with a polite smile, 'that the Grand Duke is as much amused as anyone at the size of his territory. I forget the exact acreage, but I remember that once Prince Aribert and myself walked across it and back again in a single day.'

'Then the Grand Duke cannot travel very far within his own dominions? You may say that the sun does set on his empire?'

'It does,' said Dimmock.

'Unless the weather is cloudy,' Nella put in. 'Is the Grand Duke content always to stay at home?'

'On the contrary, he is a great traveller, much more so than Prince Aribert.

I may tell you, what no one knows at present, outside this hôtel, that his Royal Highness the Grand Duke, with a small suite, will be here to-morrow.'

'In London?' asked Nella.

'Yes.'

'In this hôtel?'

'Yes.'

'Oh! How lovely!'

'That is why your humble servant is here to-night—a sort of advance guard.'

'But I understood,' Racksole said, 'that you were—er—attached to Prince Aribert, the uncle.'

'I am. Prince Aribert will also be here. The Grand Duke and the Prince have business about important investments connected with the Grand Duke's marriage settlement.... In the highest quarters, you understand.'

'For so discreet a person,' thought Racksole, 'you are fairly communicative.' Then he said aloud: 'Shall we go out on the terrace?'

As they crossed the dining-room Jules stopped Mr Dimmock and handed him a letter. 'Just come, sir, by messenger,' said Jules.

Nella dropped behind for a second with her father. 'Leave me alone with this boy a little—there's a dear parent,' she whispered in his ear.

'I am a mere cypher, an obedient nobody,' Racksole replied, pinching her arm surreptitiously. 'Treat me as such. Use me as you like. I will go and look after my hôtel' And soon afterwards he disappeared.

Nella and Mr Dimmock sat together on the terrace, sipping iced drinks. They made a handsome couple, bowered amid plants which blossomed at the command of a Chelsea wholesale florist. People who passed by remarked privately that from the look of things there was the beginning of a romance in that conversation. Perhaps there was, but a more intimate acquaintance with the character of Nella Racksole would have been necessary in order to predict what precise form that romance would take.

Jules himself served the liquids, and at ten o'clock he brought another note. Entreating a thousand pardons, Reginald Dimmock, after he had glanced at the note, excused himself on the plea of urgent business for his Serene master, uncle of the Grand Duke of Posen. He asked if he might fetch Mr Racksole, or escort Miss Racksole to her father. But Miss Racksole said gaily that she felt no need of an escort, and should go to bed. She added that her father and herself always endeavoured to be independent of each other.

Just then Theodore Racksole had found his way once more into Mr Babylon's private room. Before arriving there, however, he had discovered that in some mysterious manner the news of the change of proprietorship had worked its way down to the lowest strata of the hôtel's cosmos. The corridors hummed with it, and even under-servants were to be seen discussing the thing, just as though it mattered to them.

'Have a cigar, Mr Racksole,' said the urbane Mr Babylon, 'and a mouthful of the oldest cognac in all Europe.'

In a few minutes these two were talking eagerly, rapidly. Felix Babylon was astonished at Racksole's capacity for absorbing the details of hôtel management. And as for Racksole he soon realized that Felix Babylon must be a prince of hôtel managers. It had never occurred to Racksole before that to manage an hôtel, even a large hôtel, could be a specially interesting affair, or that it could make any excessive demands upon the brains of the manager; but he came to see that he had underrated the possibilities of an hôtel. The business of the Grand Babylon was enormous. It took Racksole, with all his genius for organization, exactly half an hour to master the details of the hôtel laundry-work. And the laundry-work was but one branch of activity amid scores, and not a very large one at that. The machinery of checking supplies, and of establishing a mean ratio between the raw stuff received in the kitchen and the number of meals served in the salle à manger and the private rooms, was very complicated and delicate. When Racksole had grasped it, he at once suggested some improvements, and this led to a long theoretical discussion, and the discussion led to digressions, and then Felix Babylon, in a moment of absent-mindedness, yawned.

Racksole looked at the gilt clock on the high mantelpiece.

'Great Scott!' he said. 'It's three o'clock. Mr Babylon, accept my apologies for having kept you up to such an absurd hour.'

'I have not spent so pleasant an evening for many years. You have let me ride my hobby to my heart's content. It is I who should apologize.'

Racksole rose.

'I should like to ask you one question,' said Babylon. 'Have you ever had anything to do with hôtels before?'

'Never,' said Racksole.

'Then you have missed your vocation. You could have been the greatest of all hôtel-managers. You would have been greater than me, and I am unequalled, though I keep only one hôtel, and some men have half a dozen. Mr Racksole, why have you never run an hôtel?'

'Heaven knows,' he laughed, 'but you flatter me, Mr Babylon.'

'I? Flatter? You do not know me. I flatter no one, except, perhaps, now and then an exceptionally distinguished guest. In which case I give suitable instructions as to the bill.'

'Speaking of distinguished guests, I am told that a couple of German princes are coming here to-morrow.'

'That is so.'

'Does one do anything? Does one receive them formally—stand bowing in the entrance-hall, or anything of that sort?'

'Not necessarily. Not unless one wishes. The modern hôtel proprietor is not like an innkeeper of the Middle Ages, and even princes do not expect to see him unless something should happen to go wrong. As a matter of fact, though the Grand Duke of Posen and Prince Aribert have both honoured me by staying here before, I have never even set eyes on them. You will find all arrangements have been made.'

They talked a little longer, and then Racksole said good night. 'Let me see you to your room. The lifts will be closed and the place will be deserted.

As for myself, I sleep here,' and Mr Babylon pointed to an inner door.

'No, thanks,' said Racksole; 'let me explore my own hôtel unaccompanied. I believe I can discover my room.'

When he got fairly into the passages, Racksole was not so sure that he could discover his own room. The number was 107, but he had forgotten whether it was on the first or second floor.

Travelling in a lift, one is unconscious of floors. He passed several lift-doorways, but he could see no glint of a staircase; in all self-respecting hôtels staircases have gone out of fashion, and though hôtel architects still continue, for old sakes' sake, to build staircases, they are tucked away in remote corners where their presence is not likely to offend the eye of a spoiled and cosmopolitan public. The hôtel seemed vast, uncanny, deserted. An electric light glowed here and there at long intervals. On the thick carpets, Racksole's thinly-shod feet made no sound, and he wandered at ease to and fro, rather amused, rather struck by the peculiar senses of night and mystery which had suddenly come over him. He fancied he could hear a thousand snores peacefully descending from the upper realms. At length he found a staircase, a very dark and narrow one, and presently he was on the first floor. He soon discovered that the numbers of the rooms on this floor did not get beyond seventy. He encountered another staircase and ascended to the second floor. By the decoration of the walls he recognized this floor as his proper home, and as he strolled through the long corridor he whistled a low, meditative whistle of satisfaction. He thought he heard a step in the transverse corridor, and instinctively he obliterated himself in a recess which held a service-cabinet and a chair. He did hear a step. Peeping cautiously out, he perceived, what he had not perceived previously, that a piece of white ribbon had been tied round the handle of the door of one of the bedrooms. Then a man came round the corner of the transverse corridor, and Racksole drew back. It was Jules—Jules with his hands in his pockets and a slouch hat over his eyes, but in other respects attired as usual.

Racksole, at that instant, remembered with a special vividness what Felix Babylon had said to him at their first interview. He wished he had brought his revolver. He didn't know why he should feel the desirability of a revolver in a London hôtel of the most unimpeachable fair fame, but he did feel the desirability of such an instrument of attack and defence. He privately decided that if Jules went past his recess he would take him by the throat and in that attitude put a few plain questions to this highly dubious waiter. But Jules had stopped. The millionaire made another cautious observation. Jules, with infinite gentleness, was turning the handle of the door to which the white ribbon was attached. The door slowly yielded and Jules disappeared within the room. After a brief interval, the night-prowling Jules reappeared, closed the door as softly as he had opened it, removed the ribbon, returned upon his steps, and vanished down the transverse corridor.

'This is quaint,' said Racksole; 'quaint to a degree!'

It occurred to him to look at the number of the room, and he stole towards it.

'Well, I'm d—d!' he murmured wonderingly.

The number was 111, his daughter's room! He tried to open it, but the door was locked. Rushing to his own room, No. 107, he seized one of a pair of revolvers (the kind that are made for millionaires) and followed after Jules down the transverse corridor. At the end of this corridor was a window; the window was open; and Jules was innocently gazing out of the window. Ten silent strides, and Theodore Racksole was upon him.

'One word, my friend,' the millionaire began, carelessly waving the revolver in the air. Jules was indubitably startled, but by an admirable exercise of self-control he recovered possession of his faculties in a second.

'Sir?' said Jules.

'I just want to be informed, what the deuce you were doing in No. 111 a moment ago.'

'I had been requested to go there,' was the calm response.

'You are a liar, and not a very clever one. That is my daughter's room. Now—out with it, before I decide whether to shoot you or throw you into the street.'

'Excuse me, sir, No. 111 is occupied by a gentleman.'

'I advise you that it is a serious error of judgement to contradict me, my friend. Don't do it again. We will go to the room together, and you shall prove that the occupant is a gentleman, and not my daughter.'

'Impossible, sir,' said Jules.

'Scarcely that,' said Racksole, and he took Jules by the sleeve. The millionaire knew for a certainty that Nella occupied No. 111, for he had examined the room her, and himself seen that her trunks and her maid and herself had arrived there in safety. 'Now open the door,' whispered Racksole, when they reached No.111.

'I must knock.'

'That is just what you mustn't do. Open it. No doubt you have your pass-key.'

Confronted by the revolver, Jules readily obeyed, yet with a deprecatory gesture, as though he would not be responsible for this outrage against the decorum of hôtel life. Racksole entered. The room was brilliantly lighted.

'A visitor, who insists on seeing you, sir,' said Jules, and fled.

Mr Reginald Dimmock, still in evening dress, and smoking a cigarette, rose hurriedly from a table.

'Hello, my dear Mr Racksole, this is an unexpected—ah—pleasure.'

'Where is my daughter? This is her room.'

'Did I catch what you said, Mr Racksole?'

'I venture to remark that this is Miss Racksole's room.'

'My good sir,' answered Dimmock, 'you must be mad to dream of such a thing.

Only my respect for your daughter prevents me from expelling you forcibly, for such an extraordinary suggestion.'

A small spot half-way down the bridge of the millionaire's nose turned suddenly white.

'With your permission,' he said in a low calm voice, 'I will examine the dressing-room and the bath-room.'

'Just listen to me a moment,' Dimmock urged, in a milder tone.

'I'll listen to you afterwards, my young friend,' said Racksole, and he proceeded to search the bath-room, and the dressing-room, without any result whatever. 'Lest my attitude might be open to misconstruction, Mr Dimmock, I may as well tell you that I have the most perfect confidence in my daughter, who is as well able to take care of herself as any woman I ever met, but since you entered it there have been one or two rather mysterious occurrences in this hôtel. That is all.' Feeling a draught of air on his shoulder, Racksole turned to the window. 'For instance,' he added, 'I perceive that this window is broken, badly broken, and from the outside.

Now, how could that have occurred?'

'If you will kindly hear reason, Mr Racksole,' said Dimmock in his best diplomatic manner, 'I will endeavour to explain things to you. I regarded your first question to me when you entered my room as being offensively put, but I now see that you had some justification.' He smiled politely. 'I was passing along this corridor about eleven o'clock, when I found Miss Racksole in a difficulty with the hôtel servants. Miss Racksole was retiring to rest in this room when a large stone, which must have been thrown from the Embankment, broke the window, as you see. Apart from the discomfort of the broken window, she did not care to remain in the room. She argued that where one stone had come another might follow. She therefore insisted on her room being changed. The servants said that there was no other room available with a dressing-room and bath-room attached, and your daughter made a point of these matters. I at once offered to exchange apartments with her. She did me the honour to accept my offer. Our respective belongings were moved—and that is all. Miss Racksole is at this moment, I trust, asleep in No. 124.'

Theodore Racksole looked at the young man for a few seconds in silence.

There was a faint knock at the door.

'Come in,' said Racksole loudly.

Someone pushed open the door, but remained standing on the mat. It was Nella's maid, in a dressing-gown.

'Miss Racksole's compliments, and a thousand excuses, but a book of hers was left on the mantelshelf in this room. She cannot sleep, and wishes to read.'

'Mr Dimmock, I tender my apologies—my formal apologies,' said Racksole, when the girl had gone away with the book. 'Good night.'

'Pray don't mention it,' said Dimmock suavely—and bowed him out.

Chapter Four ENTRANCE OF THE PRINCE

NEVERTHELESS, sundry small things weighed on Racksole's mind. First there was Jules' wink. Then there was the ribbon on the door-handle and Jules' visit to No. 111, and the broken window—broken from the outside. Racksole did not forget that the time was 3 a.m. He slept but little that night, but he was glad that he had bought the Grand Babylon Hôtel. It was an acquisition which seemed to promise fun and diversion.

The next morning he came across Mr Babylon early. 'I have emptied my private room of all personal papers,' said Babylon, 'and it is now at your disposal.

I purpose, if agreeable to yourself, to stay on in the hôtel as a guest for the present. We have much to settle with regard to the completion of the purchase, and also there are things which you might want to ask me. Also, to tell the truth, I am not anxious to leave the old place with too much suddenness. It will be a wrench to me.'

'I shall be delighted if you will stay,' said the millionaire, 'but it must be as my guest, not as the guest of the hôtel.'

'You are very kind.'

'As for wishing to consult you, no doubt I shall have need to do so, but I must say that the show seems to run itself.'

'Ah!' said Babylon thoughtfully. 'I have heard of hôtels that run themselves. If they do, you may be sure that they obey the laws of gravity and run downwards. You will have your hands full. For example, have you yet heard about Miss Spencer?'

'No,' said Racksole. 'What of her?'

'She has mysteriously vanished during the night, and nobody appears to be able to throw any light on the affair. Her room is empty, her boxes gone.

You will want someone to take her place, and that someone will not be very easy to get.'

'H'm!' Racksole said, after a pause. 'Hers is not the only post that falls vacant to-day.'

A little later, the millionaire installed himself in the late owner's private room and rang the bell.

'I want Jules,' he said to the page.

While waiting for Jules, Racksole considered the question of Miss Spencer's disappearance.

'Good morning, Jules,' was his cheerful greeting, when the imperturbable waiter arrived.

'Good morning, sir.'

'Take a chair.'

'Thank you, sir.'

'We have met before this morning, Jules.'

'Yes, sir, at 3 a.m.'

'Rather strange about Miss Spencer's departure, is it not?' suggested Racksole.

'It is remarkable, sir.'

'You are aware, of course, that Mr Babylon has transferred all his interests in this hôtel to me?'

'I have been informed to that effect, sir.'

'I suppose you know everything that goes on in the hôtel, Jules?'

'As the head waiter, sir, it is my business to keep a general eye on things.'

'You speak very good English for a foreigner, Jules.'

'For a foreigner, sir! I am an Englishman, a Hertfordshire man born and bred. Perhaps my name has misled you, sir. I am only called Jules because the head waiter of any really high-class hôtel must have either a French or an Italian name.'

'I see,' said Racksole. 'I think you must be rather a clever person, Jules.'

'That is not for me to say, sir.'

'How long has the hôtel enjoyed the advantage of your services?'

'A little over twenty years.'

'That is a long time to be in one place. Don't you think it's time you got out of the rut? You are still young, and might make a reputation for yourself in another and wider sphere.'

Racksole looked at the man steadily, and his glance was steadily returned.

'You aren't satisfied with me, sir?'

'To be frank, Jules, I think—I think you—er—wink too much. And I think that it is regrettable when a head waiter falls into a habit of taking white ribbons from the handles of bedroom doors at three in the morning.'

Jules started slightly.

'I see how it is, sir. You wish me to go, and one pretext, if I may use the term, is as good as another. Very well, I can't say that I'm surprised. It sometimes happens that there is incompatibility of temper between a hôtel proprietor and his head waiter, and then, unless one of them goes, the hôtel is likely to suffer. I will go, Mr Racksole. In fact, I had already thought of giving notice.'

The millionaire smiled appreciatively. 'What wages do you require in lieu of notice? It is my intention that you leave the hôtel within an hour.'

'I require no wages in lieu of notice, sir. I would scorn to accept anything. And I will leave the hôtel in fifteen minutes.'

'Good-day, then. You have my good wishes and my admiration, so long as you keep out of my hôtel.'

Racksole got up. 'Good-day, sir. And thank you.'

'By the way, Jules, it will be useless for you to apply to any other first-rate European hôtel for a post, because I shall take measures which will ensure the rejection of any such application.'

'Without discussing the question whether or not there aren't at least half a dozen hôtels in London alone that would jump for joy at the chance of getting me,' answered Jules, 'I may tell you, sir, that I shall retire from my profession.'

'Really! You will turn your brains to a different channel.'

'No, sir. I shall take rooms in Albemarle Street or Jermyn Street, and just be content to be a man-about-town. I have saved some twenty thousand pounds—a mere trifle, but sufficient for my needs, and I shall now proceed to enjoy it. Pardon me for troubling you with my personal affairs. And good-day again.'

That afternoon Racksole went with Felix Babylon first to a firm of solicitors in the City, and then to a stockbroker, in order to carry out the practical details of the purchase of the hôtel.

'I mean to settle in England,' said Racksole, as they were coming back. 'It is the only country—' and he stopped.

'The only country?'

'The only country where you can invest money and spend money with a feeling of security. In the United States there is nothing worth spending money on, nothing to buy. In France or Italy, there is no real security.'

'But surely you are a true American?' questioned Babylon.

'I am a true American,' said Racksole, 'but my father, who began by being a bedmaker at an Oxford college, and ultimately made ten million dollars out of iron in Pittsburg—my father took the wise precaution of having me educated in England. I had my three years at Oxford, like any son of the upper middle class! It did me good. It has been worth more to me than many successful speculations. It taught me that the English language is different from, and better than, the American language, and that there is something—I haven't yet found out exactly what—in English life that Americans will never get. Why,' he added, 'in the United States we still bribe our judges and our newspapers. And we talk of the eighteenth century as though it was the beginning of the world. Yes, I shall transfer my securities to London. I shall build a house in Park Lane, and I shall buy some immemorial country seat with a history as long as the A. T. and S. railroad, and I shall calmly and gradually settle down. D'you know—I am rather a good-natured man for a millionaire, and of a social disposition, and yet I haven't six real friends in the whole of New York City. Think of that!'

'And I,' said Babylon, 'have no friends except the friends of my boyhood in Lausanne. I have spent thirty years in England, and gained nothing but a perfect knowledge of the English language and as much gold coin as would fill a rather large box.'

These two plutocrats breathed a simultaneous sigh.

'Talking of gold coin,' said Racksole, 'how much money should you think Jules has contrived to amass while he has been with you?'

'Oh!' Babylon smiled. 'I should not like to guess. He has had unique opportunities—opportunities.'

'Should you consider twenty thousand an extraordinary sum under the circumstances?'

'Not at all. Has he been confiding in you?'

'Somewhat. I have dismissed him.'

'You have dismissed him?'

'Why not?'

'There is no reason why not. But I have felt inclined to dismiss him for the past ten years, and never found courage to do it.'

'It was a perfectly simple proceeding, I assure you. Before I had done with him, I rather liked the fellow.'

'Miss Spencer and Jules—both gone in one day!' mused Felix Babylon.

'And no one to take their places,' said Racksole. 'And yet the hôtel continues its way!'

But when Racksole reached the Grand Babylon he found that Miss Spencer's chair in the bureau was occupied by a stately and imperious girl, dressed becomingly in black.

'Heavens, Nella!' he cried, going to the bureau. 'What are you doing here?'

'I am taking Mis Spencer's place. I want to help you with your hôtel, Dad. I fancy I shall make an excellent hôtel clerk. I have arranged with a Miss Selina Smith, one of the typists in the office, to put me up to all the tips and tricks, and I shall do very well.'

'But look here, Helen Racksole. We shall have the whole of London talking about this thing—the greatest of all American heiresses a hôtel clerk! And I came here for quiet and rest!'

'I suppose it was for the sake of quiet and rest that you bought the hôtel, Papa?'

'You would insist on the steak,' he retorted. 'Get out of this, on the instant.'

'Here I am, here to stay,' said Nella, and deliberately laughed at her parent.

Just then the face of a fair-haired man of about thirty years appeared at the bureau window. He was very well-dressed, very aristocratic in his pose, and he seemed rather angry.

He looked fixedly at Nella and started back.

'Ach!' he exclaimed. 'You!'

'Yes, your Highness, it is indeed I. Father, this is his Serene Highness Prince Aribert of Posen—one of our most esteemed customers.'

'You know my name, Fräulein?' the new-comer murmured in German.

'Certainly, Prince,' Nella replied sweetly. 'You were plain Count Steenbock last spring in Paris—doubtless travelling incognito—'

'Silence,' he entreated, with a wave of the hand, and his forehead went as white as paper.

Chapter Five WHAT OCCURRED TO REGINALD DIMMOCK

IN another moment they were all three talking quite nicely, and with at any rate an appearance of being natural. Prince Aribert became suave, even deferential to Nella, and more friendly towards Nella's father than their respective positions demanded. The latter amused himself by studying this sprig of royalty, the first with whom he had ever come into contact. He decided that the young fellow was personable enough, 'had no frills on him,' and would make an exceptionally good commercial traveller for a first-class firm. Such was Theodore Racksole's preliminary estimate of the man who might one day be the reigning Grand Duke of Posen.

It occurred to Nella, and she smiled at the idea, that the bureau of the hôtel was scarcely the correct place in which to receive this august young man. There he stood, with his head half-way through the bureau window, negligently leaning against the woodwork, just as though he were a stockbroker or the manager of a New York burlesque company.

'Is your Highness travelling quite alone?' she asked.

'By a series of accidents I am,' he said. 'My equerry was to have met me at Charing Cross, but he failed to do so—I cannot imagine why.'

'Mr Dimmock?' questioned Racksole.

'Yes, Dimmock. I do not remember that he ever missed an appointment before.
You know him? He has been here?'

'He dined with us last night,' said Racksole—'on Nella's invitation,' he added maliciously; 'but to-day we have seen nothing of him. I know, however, that he has engaged the State apartments, and also a suite adjoining the State apartments—No. 55. That is so, isn't it, Nella?'

'Yes, Papa,' she said, having first demurely examined a ledger. 'Your Highness would doubtless like to be conducted to your room—apartments I mean.' Then Nella laughed deliberately at the Prince, and said, 'I don't know who is the proper person to conduct you, and that's a fact. The truth is that Papa and I are rather raw yet in the hôtel line. You see, we only bought the place last night.'

'You have bought the hôtel!' exclaimed the Prince.

'That's so,' said Racksole.

'And Felix Babylon has gone?'

'He is going, if he has not already gone.'

'Ah! I see,' said the Prince; 'this is one of your American "strokes". You have bought to sell again, is that not it? You are on your holidays, but you cannot resist making a few thousands by way of relaxation. I have heard of such things.'

'We sha'n't sell again, Prince, until we are tired of our bargain. Sometimes we tire very quickly, and sometimes we don't. It depends—eh? What?'

Racksole broke off suddenly to attend to a servant in livery who had quietly entered the bureau and was making urgent mysterious signs to him.

'If you please, sir,' the man by frantic gestures implored Mr Theodore Racksole to come out.

'Pray don't let me detain you, Mr Racksole,' said the Prince, and therefore the proprietor of the Grand Babylon departed after the servant, with a queer, curt little bow to Prince Aribert.

'Mayn't I come inside?' said the Prince to Nella immediately the millionaire had gone.

'Impossible, Prince,' Nella laughed. 'The rule against visitors entering this bureau is frightfully strict.'

'How do you know the rule is so strict if you only came into possession last night?'

'I know because I made the rule myself this morning, your Highness.'

'But seriously, Miss Racksole, I want to talk to you.'

'Do you want to talk to me as Prince Aribert or as the friend—the acquaintance—whom I knew in Paris last year?'

'As the friend, dear lady, if I may use the term.'

'And you are sure that you would not like first to be conducted to your apartments?'

'Not yet. I will wait till Dimmock comes; he cannot fail to be here soon.'

'Then we will have tea served in father's private room—the proprietor's private room, you know.'

'Good!' he said.

Nella talked through a telephone, and rang several bells, and behaved generally in a manner calculated to prove to Princes and to whomever it might concern that she was a young woman of business instincts and training, and then she stepped down from her chair of office, emerged from the bureau, and, preceded by two menials, led Prince Aribert to the Louis XV chamber in which her father and Felix Babylon had had their long confabulation on the previous evening.

'What do you want to talk to me about?' she asked her companion, as she poured out for him a second cup of tea. The Prince looked at her for a moment as he took the proffered cup, and being a young man of sane, healthy, instincts, he could think of nothing for the moment except her loveliness.

Nella was indeed beautiful that afternoon. The beauty of even the most beautiful woman ebbs and flows from hour to hour. Nella's this afternoon was at the flood. Vivacious, alert, imperious, and yet ineffably sweet, she seemed to radiate the very joy and exuberance of life.

'I have forgotten,' he said.

'You have forgotten! That is surely very wrong of you? You gave me to understand that it was something terribly important. But of course I knew it couldn't be, because no man, and especially no Prince, ever discussed anything really important with a woman.'

'Recollect, Miss Racksole, that this afternoon, here, I am not the Prince.'

'You are Count Steenbock, is that it?'

He started. 'For you only,' he said, unconsciously lowering his voice. 'Miss Racksole, I particularly wish that no one here should know that I was in Paris last spring.'

'An affair of State?' she smiled.

'An affair of State,' he replied soberly. 'Even Dimmock doesn't know. It was strange that we should be fellow guests at that quiet out-of-the-way hôtel—strange but delightful. I shall never forget that rainy afternoon that we spent together in the Museum of the Trocadéro. Let us talk about that.'

'About the rain, or the museum?'

'I shall never forget that afternoon,' he repeated, ignoring the lightness of her question.

'Nor I,' she murmured corresponding to his mood.

'You, too enjoyed it?' he said eagerly.

'The sculptures were magnificent,' she replied, hastily glancing at the ceiling.

'Ah! So they were! Tell me, Miss Racksole, how did you discover my identity.'

'I must not say,' she answered. 'That is my secret. Do not seek to penetrate it. Who knows what horrors you might discover if you probed too far?' She laughed, but she laughed alone. The Prince remained pensive—as it were brooding.

'I never hoped to see you again,' he said.

'Why not?'

'One never sees again those whom one wishes to see.'

'As for me, I was perfectly convinced that we should meet again.'

'Why?'

'Because I always get what I want.'

'Then you wanted to see me again?'

'Certainly. You interested me extremely. I have never met another man who could talk so well about sculpture as the Count Steenbock.'

'Do you really always get what you want, Miss Racksole?'

'Of course.'

'That is because your father is so rich, I suppose?'

'Oh, no, it isn't!' she said. 'It's simply because I always do get what I want. It's got nothing to do with Father at all.'

'But Mr Racksole is extremely wealthy?'

'Wealthy isn't the word, Count. There is no word. It's positively awful the amount of dollars poor Papa makes. And the worst of it is he can't help it.

He told me once that when a man had made ten millions no power on earth could stop those ten millions from growing into twenty. And so it continues.

I spend what I can, but I can't come near coping with it; and of course Papa is no use whatever at spending.'

'And you have no mother?'

'Who told you I had no mother?' she asked quietly.

'I—er—inquired about you,' he said, with equal candour and humility.

'In spite of the fact that you never hoped to see me again?'

'Yes, in spite of that.'

'How funny!' she said, and lapsed into a meditative silence.

'Yours must be a wonderful existence,' said the Prince. 'I envy you.'

'You envy me—what? My father's wealth?'

'No,' he said; 'your freedom and your responsibilities.'

'I have no responsibilities,' she remarked.

'Pardon me,' he said; 'you have, and the time is coming when you will feel them.'

'I'm only a girl,' she murmured with sudden simplicity. 'As for you, Count, surely you have sufficient responsibilities of your own?'

'I?' he said sadly. 'I have no responsibilities. I am a nobody—a Serene Highness who has to pretend to be very important, always taking immense care never to do anything that a Serene Highness ought not to do. Bah!'

'But if your nephew, Prince Eugen, were to die, would you not come to the throne, and would you not then have these responsibilities which you so much desire?'

'Eugen die?' said Prince Aribert, in a curious tone. 'Impossible. He is the perfection of health. In three months he will be married. No, I shall never be anything but a Serene Highness, the most despicable of God's creatures.'

'But what about the State secret which you mentioned? Is not that a responsibility?'

'Ah!' he said. 'That is over. That belongs to the past. It was an accident in my dull career. I shall never be Count Steenbock again.'

'Who knows?' she said. 'By the way, is not Prince Eugen coming here to-day? Mr Dimmock told us so.'

'See!' answered the Prince, standing up and bending over her. 'I am going to confide in you. I don't know why, but I am.'

'Don't betray State secrets,' she warned him, smiling into his face.

But just then the door of the room was unceremoniously opened.

'Go right in,' said a voice sharply. It was Theodore Racksole's. Two men entered, bearing a prone form on a stretcher, and Racksole followed them.

Nella sprang up. Racksole stared to see his daughter.

'I didn't know you were in here, Nell. Here,' to the two men, 'out again.'

'Why!' exclaimed Nella, gazing fearfully at the form on the stretcher, 'it's Mr Dimmock!'

'It is,' her father acquiesced. 'He's dead,' he added laconically. 'I'd have broken it to you more gently had I known. Your pardon, Prince.' There was a pause.

'Dimmock dead!' Prince Aribert whispered under his breath, and he kneeled down by the side of the stretcher. 'What does this mean?'

The poor fellow was just walking across the quadrangle towards the portico when he fell down. A commissionaire who saw him says he was walking very quickly. At first I thought it was sunstroke, but it couldn't have been, though the weather certainly is rather warm. It must be heart disease. But anyhow, he's dead. We did what we could. I've sent for a doctor, and for the police. I suppose there'll have to be an inquest.'

Theodore Racksole stopped, and in an awkward solemn silence they all gazed at the dead youth. His features were slightly drawn, and his eyes closed; that was all. He might have been asleep.

'My poor Dimmock!' exclaimed the Prince, his voice broken. 'And I was angry because the lad did not meet me at Charing Cross!'

'Are you sure he is dead, Father?' Nella said.

'You'd better go away, Nella,' was Racksole's only reply; but the girl stood still, and began to sob quietly. On the previous night she had secretly made fun of Reginald Dimmock. She had deliberately set herself to get information from him on a topic in which she happened to be specially interested and she had got it, laughing the while at his youthful crudities—his vanity, his transparent cunning, his absurd airs. She had not liked him; she had even distrusted him, and decided that he was not 'nice'. But now, as he lay on the stretcher, these things were forgotten. She went so far as to reproach herself for them. Such is the strange commanding power of death.

'Oblige me by taking the poor fellow to my apartments,' said the Prince, with a gesture to the attendants. 'Surely it is time the doctor came.'

Racksole felt suddenly at that moment he was nothing but a mere hôtel proprietor with an awkward affair on his hands. For a fraction of a second he wished he had never bought the Grand Babylon.

A quarter of an hour later Prince Aribert, Theodore Racksole, a doctor, and an inspector of police were in the Prince's reception-room. They had just come from an ante-chamber, in which lay the mortal remains of Reginald Dimmock.

'Well?' said Racksole, glancing at the doctor.

The doctor was a big, boyish-looking man, with keen, quizzical eyes.

'It is not heart disease,' said the doctor.

'Not heart disease?'

'No.'

'Then what is it?' asked the Prince.

'I may be able to answer that question after the post-mortem,' said the doctor. 'I certainly can't answer it now. The symptoms are unusual to a degree.'

The inspector of police began to write in a note-book.

Chapter Six IN THE GOLD ROOM

AT the Grand Babylon a great ball was given that night in the Gold Room, a huge saloon attached to the hôtel, though scarcely part of it, and certainly less exclusive than the hôtel itself. Theodore Racksole knew nothing of the affair, except that it was an entertainment offered by a Mr and Mrs Sampson Levi to their friends. Who Mr and Mrs Sampson Levi were he did not know, nor could anyone tell him anything about them except that Mr Sampson Levi was a prominent member of that part of the Stock Exchange familiarly called the Kaffir Circus, and that his wife was a stout lady with an aquiline nose and many diamonds, and that they were very rich and very hospitable. Theodore Racksole did not want a ball in his hôtel that evening, and just before dinner he had almost a mind to issue a decree that the Gold Room was to be closed and the ball forbidden, and Mr and Mrs Sampson Levi might name the amount of damages suffered by them. His reasons for such a course were threefold—first, he felt depressed and uneasy; second, he didn't like the name of Sampson Levi; and, third, he had a desire to show these so-called plutocrats that their wealth was nothing to him, that they could not do what they chose with Theodore Racksole, and that for two pins Theodore Racksole would buy them up, and the whole Kaffir Circus to boot. But something warned him that though such a high-handed proceeding might be tolerated in America, that land of freedom, it would never be tolerated in England. He felt instinctively that in England there are things you can't do, and that this particular thing was one of them. So the ball went forward, and neither Mr nor Mrs Sampson Levi had ever the least suspicion what a narrow escape they had had of looking very foolish in the eyes of the thousand or so guests invited by them to the Gold Room of the Grand Babylon that evening.

The Gold Room of the Grand Babylon was built for a ballroom. A balcony, supported by arches faced with gilt and lapis-lazulo, ran around it, and from this vantage men and maidens and chaperons who could not or would not dance might survey the scene. Everyone knew this, and most people took advantage of it. What everyone did not know—what no one knew—was that higher up than the balcony there was a little barred

413

window in the end wall from which the hôtel authorities might keep a watchful eye, not only on the dancers, but on the occupants of the balcony itself.

It may seem incredible to the uninitiated that the guests at any social gathering held in so gorgeous and renowned an apartment as the Gold Room of the Grand Babylon should need the observation of a watchful eye. Yet so it was. Strange matters and unexpected faces had been descried from the little window, and more than one European detective had kept vigil there with the most eminently satisfactory results.

At eleven o'clock Theodore Racksole, afflicted by vexation of spirit, found himself gazing idly through the little barred window. Nella was with him.

Together they had been wandering about the corridors of the hôtel, still strange to them both, and it was quite by accident that they had lighted upon the small room which had a surreptitious view of Mr and Mrs Sampson Levi's ball. Except for the light of the chandelier of the ball-room the little cubicle was in darkness. Nella was looking through the window; her father stood behind.

'I wonder which is Mrs Sampson Levi?' Nella said, 'and whether she matches her name. Wouldn't you love to have a name like that, Father—something that people could take hold of—instead of Racksole?'

The sound of violins and a confused murmur of voices rose gently up to them.

'Umph!' said Theodore. 'Curse those evening papers!' he added, inconsequently but with sincerity.

'Father, you're very horrid to-night. What have the evening papers been doing?'

'Well, my young madame, they've got me in for one, and you for another; and they're manufacturing mysteries like fun. It's young Dimmock's death that has started 'em.'

'Well, Father, you surely didn't expect to keep yourself out of the papers. Besides, as regards newspapers, you ought to be glad you aren't in New York. Just fancy what the dear old Herald would have made out of a little transaction like yours of last night.'

'That's true,' assented Racksole. 'But it'll be all over New York to-morrow morning, all the same. The worst of it is that Babylon has gone off to Switzerland.'

'Why?'

'Don't know. Sudden fancy, I guess, for his native heath.'

'What difference does it make to you?'

'None. Only I feel sort of lonesome. I feel I want someone to lean up against in running this hôtel.'

'Father, if you have that feeling you must be getting ill.'

'Yes,' he sighed, 'I admit it's unusual with me. But perhaps you haven't grasped the fact, Nella, that we're in the middle of a rather queer business.'

'You mean about poor Mr Dimmock?'

'Partly Dimmock and partly other things. First of all, that Miss Spencer, or whatever her wretched name is, mysteriously disappears. Then there was the stone thrown into your bedroom. Then I caught that rascal Jules conspiring with Dimmock at three o'clock in the morning. Then your precious Prince Aribert arrives without any suite—which I believe is a most peculiar and wicked thing for a Prince to do—and moreover I find my daughter on very intimate terms with the said Prince. Then young Dimmock goes and dies, and there is to be an inquest; then Prince Eugen and his suite, who were expected here for dinner, fail to turn up at all—'

'Prince Eugen has not come?'

'He has not; and Uncle Aribert is in a deuce of a stew about him, and telegraphing all over Europe. Altogether, things are working up pretty lively.'

'Do you really think, Dad, there was anything between Jules and poor Mr Dimmock?'

'Think! I know! I tell you I saw that scamp give Dimmock a wink last night at dinner that might have meant—well!'

'So you caught that wink, did you, Dad?'

'Why, did you?'

'Of course, Dad. I was going to tell you about it.'

The millionaire grunted.

'Look here, Father,' Nella whispered suddenly, and pointed to the balcony immediately below them. 'Who's that?' She indicated a man with a bald patch on the back of his head, who was propping himself up against the railing of the balcony and gazing immovable into the ball-room.

'Well, who is it?'

'Isn't it Jules?'

'Gemini! By the beard of the prophet, it is!'

'Perhaps Mr Jules is a guest of Mrs Sampson Levi.'

'Guest or no guest, he goes out of this hôtel, even if I have to throw him out myself.'

Theodore Racksole disappeared without another word, and Nella followed him.

But when the millionaire arrived on the balcony floor he could see nothing of Jules, neither there nor in the ball-room itself. Saying no word aloud, but quietly whispering wicked expletives, he searched everywhere in vain, and then, at last, by tortuous stairways and corridors returned to his original post of observation, that he might survey the place anew from the vantage ground. To his surprise he found a man in the dark little room, watching the scene of the ball as intently as he himself had been doing a few minutes before. Hearing footsteps, the man turned with a start.

It was Jules.

The two exchanged glances in the half light for a second.

'Good evening, Mr Racksole,' said Jules calmly. 'I must apologize for being here.'

'Force of habit, I suppose,' said Theodore Racksole drily.

'Just so, sir.'

'I fancied I had forbidden you to re-enter this hôtel?'

'I thought your order applied only to my professional capacity. I am here to-night as the guest of Mr and Mrs Sampson Levi.'

'In your new rôle of man-about-town, eh?'

'Exactly.'

'But I don't allow men-about-town up here, my friend.'

'For being up here I have already apologized.'

'Then, having apologized, you had better depart; that is my disinterested advice to you.'

'Good night, sir.'

'And, I say, Mr Jules, if Mr and Mrs Sampson Levi, or any other Hebrews or Christians, should again invite you to my hôtel you will oblige me by declining the invitation. You'll find that will be the safest course for you.'

'Good night, sir.'

Before midnight struck Theodore Racksole had ascertained that the invitation-list of Mr and Mrs Sampson Levi, though a somewhat lengthy one, contained no reference to any such person as Jules.

He sat up very late. To be precise, he sat up all night. He was a man who, by dint of training, could comfortably dispense with sleep when he felt so inclined, or when circumstances made such a course advisable. He walked to and fro in his room, and cogitated as few people beside Theodore Racksole could cogitate. At 6 a.m. he took a stroll round the business part of his premises, and watched the supplies come in from Covent Garden, from Smithfield, from Billingsgate, and from other strange places. He found the proceedings of the kitchen department quite interesting, and made mental notes of things that he would have altered, of men whose wages he would increase and men whose wages he would reduce. At 7 a.m. he happened to be standing near the luggage lift, and witnessed the descent of vast quantities of luggage, and its disappearance into a Carter Paterson van.

'Whose luggage is that?' he inquired peremptorily.

The luggage clerk, with an aggrieved expression, explained to him that it was the luggage of nobody in particular, that it belonged to various guests, and was bound for various destinations; that it was, in fact, 'expressed' luggage despatched in advance, and that a similar quantity of it left the hôtel every morning about that hour.

Theodore Racksole walked away, and breakfasted upon one cup of tea and half a slice of toast.

At ten o'clock he was informed that the inspector of police desired to see him. The inspector had come, he said, to superintend the removal of the body of Reginald Dimmock to the mortuary adjoining the place of inquest, and a suitable vehicle waited at the back entrance of the hôtel.

The inspector had also brought subpoenas for himself and Prince Aribert of Posen and the commissionaire to attend the inquest.

'I thought Mr Dimmock's remains were removed last night,' said Racksole wearily.

'No, sir. The fact is the van was engaged on another job.'

The inspector gave the least hint of a professional smile, and Racksole, disgusted, told him curtly to go and perform his duties.

In a few minutes a message came from the inspector requesting Mr Racksole to be good enough to come to him on the first floor. Racksole went. In the ante-room, where the body of Reginald Dimmock had originally been placed, were the inspector and Prince Aribert, and two policemen.

415

'Well?' said Racksole, after he and the Prince had exchanged bows. Then he saw a coffin laid across two chairs. 'I see a coffin has been obtained,' he remarked. 'Quite right' He approached it. 'It's empty,' he observed unthinkingly.

'Just so,' said the inspector. 'The body of the deceased has disappeared.

And his Serene Highness Prince Aribert informs me that though he has occupied a room immediately opposite, on the other side of the corridor, he can throw no light on the affair.'

'Indeed, I cannot!' said the Prince, and though he spoke with sufficient calmness and dignity, you could see that he was deeply pained, even distressed.

'Well, I'm—' murmured Racksole, and stopped.

Chapter Seven NELLA AND THE PRINCE

IT appeared impossible to Theodore Racksole that so cumbrous an article as a corpse could be removed out of his hôtel, with no trace, no hint, no clue as to the time or the manner of the performance of the deed. After the first feeling of surprise, Racksole grew coldly and severely angry. He had a mind to dismiss the entire staff of the hôtel. He personally examined the night-watchman, the chambermaids and all other persons who by chance might or ought to know something of the affair; but without avail. The corpse of Reginald Dimmock had vanished utterly—disappeared like a fleshless spirit.

Of course there were the police. But Theodore Racksole held the police in sorry esteem. He acquainted them with the facts, answered their queries with a patient weariness, and expected nothing whatever from that quarter. He also had several interviews with Prince Aribert of Posen, but though the Prince was suavity itself and beyond doubt genuinely concerned about the fate of his dead attendant, yet it seemed to Racksole that he was keeping something back, that he hesitated to say all he knew. Racksole, with characteristic insight, decided that the death of Reginald Dimmock was only a minor event, which had occurred, as it were, on the fringe of some far more profound mystery. And, therefore, he decided to wait, with his eyes very wide open, until something else happened that would throw light on the business. At the moment he took only one measure—he arranged that the theft of Dimmock's body should not appear in the newspapers. It is astonishing how well a secret can be kept, when the possessors of the secret are handled with the proper mixture of firmness and persuasion. Racksole managed this very neatly. It was a complicated job, and his success in it rather pleased him.

At the same time he was conscious of being temporarily worsted by an unknown group of schemers, in which he felt convinced that Jules was an important item. He could scarcely look Nella in the eyes. The girl had evidently expected him to unmask this conspiracy at once, with a single stroke of the millionaire's magic wand. She was thoroughly accustomed, in the land of her birth, to seeing him achieve impossible feats. Over there he was a 'boss'; men trembled before his name; when he wished a thing to happen—well, it happened; if he desired to know a thing, he just knew it. But here, in London, Theodore Racksole was not quite the same Theodore Racksole. He dominated New York; but London, for the most part, seemed not to take much interest in him; and there were certainly various persons in London who were capable of snapping their fingers at him—at Theodore Racksole. Neither he nor his daughter could get used to that fact.

As for Nella, she concerned herself for a little with the ordinary business of the bureau, and watched the incomings and outgoings of Prince Aribert with a kindly interest. She perceived, what her father had failed to perceive, that His Highness had assumed an attitude of reserve merely to hide the secret distraction and dismay which consumed him. She saw that the poor fellow had no settled plan in his head, and that he was troubled by something which, so far, he had confided to nobody. It came to her knowledge that each morning he walked to and fro on the Victoria Embankment, alone, and apparently with no object. On the third morning she decided that driving exercise on the Embankment would be good for her health, and thereupon ordered a carriage and issued forth, arrayed in a miraculous putty-coloured gown. Near Blackfriars Bridge she met the Prince, and the carriage was drawn up by the pavement.

'Good morning, Prince,' she greeted him. 'Are you mistaking this for Hyde Park?'

He bowed and smiled.

'I usually walk here in the mornings,' he said.

'You surprise me,' she returned. 'I thought I was the only person in London who preferred the Embankment, with this view of the river, to the dustiness of Hyde Park. I can't imagine how it is that London will never take exercise anywhere except in that ridiculous Park. Now, if they had Central Park—'

'I think the Embankment is the finest spot in all London,' he said.

She leaned a little out of the landau, bringing her face nearer to his.

'I do believe we are kindred spirits, you and I,' she murmured; and then, 'Au revoir, Prince!'

'One moment, Miss Racksole.' His quick tones had a note of entreaty.

'I am in a hurry,' she fibbed; 'I am not merely taking exercise this morning. You have no idea how busy we are.'

'Ah! then I will not trouble you. But I leave the Grand Babylon to-night.'

'Do you?' she said. 'Then will your Highness do me the honour of lunching with me today in Father's room? Father will be out—he is having a day in the City with some stockbroking persons.'

'I shall be charmed,' said the Prince, and his face showed that he meant it.

Nella drove off.

If the lunch was a success that result was due partly to Rocco, and partly to Nella. The Prince said little beyond what the ordinary rules of the conversational game demanded. His hostess talked much and talked well, but she failed to rouse her guest. When they had had coffee he took a rather formal leave of her.

'Good-bye, Prince,' she said, 'but I thought—that is, no I didn't. Good-bye.'

'You thought I wished to discuss something with you. I did; but I have decided that I have no right to burden your mind with my affairs.'

'But suppose—suppose I wish to be burdened?'

'That is your good nature.'

'Sit down,' she said abruptly, 'and tell me everything; mind, everything. I adore secrets.'

Almost before he knew it he was talking to her, rapidly, eagerly.

'Why should I weary you with my confidences?' he said. 'I don't know, I cannot tell; but I feel that I must. I feel that you will understand me better than anyone else in the world. And yet why should you understand me? Again, I don't know. Miss Racksole, I will disclose to you the whole trouble in a word. Prince Eugen, the hereditary Grand Duke of Posen, has disappeared. Four days ago I was to have met him at Ostend. He had affairs in London. He wished me to come with him. I sent Dimmock on in front, and waited for Eugen. He did not arrive. I telegraphed back to Cologne, his last stopping-place, and I learned that he had left there in accordance with his programme; I learned also that he had passed through Brussels. It must have been between Brussels and the railway station at Ostend Quay that he disappeared. He was travelling with a single equerry, and the equerry, too, has vanished. I need not explain to you, Miss Racksole, that when a person of the importance of my nephew contrives to get lost one must proceed cautiously. One cannot advertise for him in the London Times. Such a disappearance must be kept secret. The people at Posen and at Berlin believe that Eugen is in London, here, at this hôtel; or, rather, they did so believe. But this morning I received a cypher telegram from—from His Majesty the Emperor, a very peculiar telegram, asking when Eugen might be expected to return to Posen, and requesting that he should go first to Berlin. That telegram was addressed to myself. Now, if the Emperor thought that Eugen was here, why should he have caused the telegram to be addressed to me? I have hesitated for three days, but I can hesitate no longer. I must myself go to the Emperor and acquaint him with the facts.'

'I suppose you've just got to keep straight with him?' Nella was on the point of saying, but she checked herself and substituted, 'The Emperor is your chief, is he not? "First among equals", you call him.'

'His Majesty is our over-lord,' said Aribert quietly.

'Why do you not take immediate steps to inquire as to the whereabouts of your Royal nephew?' she asked simply. The affair seemed to her just then so plain and straightforward.

'Because one of two things may have happened. Either Eugen may have been, in plain language, abducted, or he may have had his own reasons for changing his programme and keeping in the background—out of reach of telegraph and post and railways.'

'What sort of reasons?'

'Do not ask me. In the history of every family there are passages—' He stopped.

'And what was Prince Eugen's object in coming to London?'

Aribert hesitated.

'Money,' he said at length. 'As a family we are very poor—poorer than anyone in Berlin suspects.'

'Prince Aribert,' Nella said, 'shall I tell you what I think?' She leaned back in her chair, and looked at him out of half-closed eyes. His pale, thin, distinguished face held her gaze as if by some fascination. There could be no mistaking this man for anything else but a Prince.

'If you will,' he said.

'Prince Eugen is the victim of a plot.'

'You think so?'

'I am perfectly convinced of it.'

'But why? What can be the object of a plot against him?'

'That is a point of which you should know more than me,' she remarked drily.

'Ah! Perhaps, perhaps,' he said. 'But, dear Miss Racksole, why are you so sure?'

'There are several reasons, and they are connected with Mr Dimmock. Did you ever suspect, your Highness, that that poor young man was not entirely loyal to you?'

'He was absolutely loyal,' said the Prince, with all the earnestness of conviction.

'A thousand pardons, but he was not.'

'Miss Racksole, if any other than yourself made that assertion, I would—I would—'

'Consign them to the deepest dungeon in Posen?' she laughed, lightly.

'Listen.' And she told him of the incidents which had occurred in the night preceding his arrival in the hôtel.

'Do you mean, Miss Racksole, that there was an understanding between poor Dimmock and this fellow Jules?'

'There was an understanding.'

'Impossible!'

'Your Highness, the man who wishes to probe a mystery to its root never uses the word "impossible". But I will say this for young Mr Dimmock. I think he repented, and I think that it was because he repented that he—er—died so suddenly, and that his body was spirited away.'

'Why has no one told me these things before?' Aribert exclaimed.

'Princes seldom hear the truth,' she said.

He was astonished at her coolness, her firmness of assertion, her air of complete acquaintance with the world.

'Miss Racksole,' he said, 'if you will permit me to say it, I have never in my life met a woman like you. May I rely on your sympathy—your support?'

'My support, Prince? But how?'

'I do not know,' he replied. 'But you could help me if you would. A woman, when she has brain, always has more brain than a man.'

'Ah!' she said ruefully, 'I have no brains, but I do believe I could help you.'

What prompted her to make that assertion she could not have explained, even to herself. But she made it, and she had a suspicion—a prescience—that it would be justified, though by what means, through what good fortune, was still a mystery to her.

'Go to Berlin,' she said. 'I see that you must do that; you have no alternative. As for the rest, we shall see. Something will occur. I shall be here. My father will be here. You must count us as your friends.'

He kissed her hand when he left, and afterwards, when she was alone, she kissed the spot his lips had touched again and again. Now, thinking the matter out in the calmness of solitude, all seemed strange, unreal, uncertain to her. Were conspiracies actually possible nowadays? Did queer things actually happen in Europe? And did they actually happen in London hôtels? She dined with her father that night.

'I hear Prince Aribert has left,' said Theodore Racksole.

'Yes,' she assented. She said not a word about their interview.

Chapter Eight ARRIVAL AND DEPARTURE OF THE BARONESS

ON the following morning, just before lunch, a lady, accompanied by a maid and a considerable quantity of luggage, came to the Grand Babylon Hôtel. She was a plump, little old lady, with white hair and an old-fashioned bonnet, and she had a quaint, simple smile of surprise at everything in general.

Nevertheless, she gave the impression of belonging to some aristocracy, though not the English aristocracy. Her tone to her maid, whom she addressed in broken English—the girl being apparently English—was distinctly insolent, with the calm, unconscious insolence peculiar to a certain type of Continental nobility. The name on the lady's card ran thus: 'Baroness Zerlinski'. She desired rooms on the third floor. It happened that Nella was in the bureau.

'On the third floor, madam?' questioned Nella, in her best clerkly manner.

'I did say on de tird floor,' said the plump little old lady.

'We have accommodation on the second floor.'

'I wish to be high up, out of de dust and in de light,' explained the Baroness.

'We have no suites on the third floor, madam.'

'Never mind, no mattaire! Have you not two rooms that communicate?'

Nella consulted her books, rather awkwardly.

'Numbers 122 and 123 communicate.'

'Or is it 121 and 122?' the little old lady remarked quickly, and then bit her lip.

'I beg your pardon. I should have said 121 and 122.'

At the moment Nella regarded the Baroness's correction of her figures as a curious chance, but afterwards, when the Baroness had ascended in the lift, the thing struck her as somewhat strange. Perhaps the Baroness Zerlinski had stayed at the hôtel before. For the sake of convenience an index of visitors to the hôtel was kept and the index extended back for thirty years. Nella examined it, but it did not contain the name of Zerlinski. Then it was that Nella began to imagine, what had swiftly crossed her mind when first the Baroness presented herself at the bureau, that the features of the Baroness were remotely familiar to her. She thought, not that she had seen the old lady's face before, but that she had seen somewhere, some time, a face of a similar cast. It occurred to Nella to look at the 'Almanach de Gotha'—that record of all the mazes of Continental blue blood; but the 'Almanach de Gotha' made no reference to any barony of Zerlinski. Nella inquired where the Baroness meant to take lunch, and was informed that a table had been reserved for her in the dining-room, and she at once decided to lunch in the dining-room herself. Seated in a corner, half-hidden by a pillar, she could survey all the guests, and watch each group as it entered or left. Presently the Baroness appeared, dressed in black, with a tiny lace shawl, despite the June warmth; very stately, very quaint, and gently smiling. Nella observed her intently. The lady ate heartily, working without haste and without delay through the elaborate menu of the luncheon. Nella noticed that she had beautiful white teeth. Then a remarkable thing happened. A cream puff was served to the Baroness by way of sweets, and Nella was astonished to see the little lady remove the top, and with a spoon quietly take something from the interior which looked like a piece of folded paper. No one who had not been watching with the eye of a lynx would have noticed anything extraordinary in the action; indeed, the chances were nine hundred and ninety-nine to one that it would pass unheeded. But, unfortunately for the Baroness, it was the thousandth chance that happened. Nella jumped up, and walking over to the Baroness, said to her:

'I'm afraid that the tart is not quite nice, your ladyship.'

'Thanks, it is delightful,' said the Baroness coldly; her smile had vanished. 'Who are you? I thought you were de bureau clerk.'

'My father is the owner of this hôtel. I thought there was something in the tart which ought not to have been there.'

Nella looked the Baroness full in the face. The piece of folded paper, to which a little cream had attached itself, lay under the edge of a plate.

'No, thanks.' The Baroness smiled her simple smile.

Nella departed. She had noticed one trifling thing besides the paper—namely, that the Baroness could pronounce the English 'th' sound if she chose.

That afternoon, in her own room, Nella sat meditating at the window for long time, and then she suddenly sprang up, her eyes brightening.

'I know,' she exclaimed, clapping her hands. 'It's Miss Spencer, disguised!

Why didn't I think of that before?' Her thoughts ran instantly to Prince Aribert. 'Perhaps I can help him,' she said to herself, and gave a little sigh. She went down to the office and inquired whether the Baroness had given any instructions about dinner. She felt that some plan must be formulated. She wanted to get hold of Rocco, and put him in the rack. She knew now that Rocco, the unequalled, was also concerned in this mysterious affair.

'The Baroness Zerlinski has left, about a quarter of an hour ago,' said the attendant.

'But she only arrived this morning.'

'The Baroness's maid said that her mistress had received a telegram and must leave at once. The Baroness paid the bill, and went away in a four-wheeler.'

'Where to?'

'The trunks were labelled for Ostend.'

Perhaps it was instinct, perhaps it was the mere spirit of adventure; but that evening Nella was to be seen of all men on the steamer for Ostend which leaves Dover at 11 p.m. She told no one of her intentions—not even her father, who was not in the hôtel when she left. She had scribbled a brief note to him to expect her back in a day or two, and had posted this at Dover. The steamer was the Marie Henriette, a large and luxurious boat, whose state-rooms on deck vie with the glories of the Cunard and White Star liners. One of these state-rooms, the best, was evidently occupied, for every curtain of its windows was carefully drawn. Nella did not hope that the Baroness was on board; it was quite possible for the Baroness to have caught the eight o'clock steamer, and it was also possible for the Baroness not to have gone to Ostend at all, but to some other place in an entirely different direction. Nevertheless, Nella had a faint hope that the lady who called herself Zerlinski might be in that curtained stateroom, and throughout the smooth moonlit voyage she never once relaxed her observation of its doors and its windows.

The Maria Henriette arrived in Ostend Harbour punctually at 2 a.m. in the morning. There was the usual heterogeneous, gesticulating crowd on the quay.

Nella kept her post near the door of the state-room, and at length she was rewarded by seeing it open. Four middle-aged Englishmen issued from it. From a glimpse of the interior Nella saw that they had spent the voyage in card-playing.

It would not be too much to say that she was distinctly annoyed. She pretended to be annoyed with circumstances, but really she was annoyed with Nella Racksole. At two in the morning, without luggage, without any companionship, and without a plan of campaign, she found herself in a strange foreign port—a port of evil repute, possessing some of the worst-managed hôtels in Europe. She strolled on the quay for a few minutes, and then she saw the smoke of another steamer in the offing. She inquired from an official what that steamer might be, and was told that it was the eight o'clock from Dover, which had broken down, put into Calais for some slight necessary repairs, and was arriving at its destination nearly four hours late. Her mercurial spirits rose again. A minute ago she was regarding herself as no better than a ninny engaged in a wild-goose chase. Now she felt that after all she had been very sagacious and cunning. She was morally sure that she would find the Zerlinski woman on this second steamer, and she took all the credit to herself in advance. Such is human nature.

The steamer seemed interminably slow in coming into harbour. Nella walked on the Digue for a few minutes to watch it the better. The town was silent and almost deserted. It had a false and sinister aspect. She remembered tales which she had heard of this glittering resort, which in the season holds more scoundrels than any place in Europe, save only Monte Carlo. She remembered that the gilded adventurers of every nation under the sun forgathered there either for business or pleasure, and that some of the most wonderful crimes of the latter half of the century had been schemed and matured in that haunt of cosmopolitan iniquity.

When the second steamer arrived Nella stood at the end of the gangway, close to the ticket-collector. The first person to step on shore was—not the Baroness Zerlinski, but Miss Spencer herself! Nella turned aside instantly, hiding her face, and Miss Spencer, carrying a small bag, hurried with assured footsteps to the Custom House. It seemed as if she knew the port of Ostend fairly well. The moon shone like day, and Nella had full opportunity to observe her quarry. She could see now quite plainly that the Baroness Zerlinski had been only Miss Spencer in disguise. There was the same gait, the same movement of the head and of the hips; the white hair was easily to be accounted for by a wig, and the wrinkles by a paint brush and some grease paints. Miss Spencer, whose hair was now its old accustomed yellow, got through the Custom House without difficulty, and Nella saw her call a closed carriage and say something to the driver. The vehicle drove off. Nella jumped into the next carriage—an open one—that came up.

'Follow that carriage,' she said succinctly to the driver in French.

'Bien, madame!' The driver whipped up his horse, and the animal shot forward with a terrific clatter over the cobbles. It appeared that this driver was quite accustomed to following other carriages.

'Now I am fairly in for it!' said Nella to herself. She laughed unsteadily, but her heart was beating with an extraordinary thump.

For some time the pursued vehicle kept well in front. It crossed the town nearly from end to end, and plunged into a maze of small streets far on the south side of the Kursaal. Then gradually Nella's equipage began to overtake it. The first carriage stopped with a jerk before a tall dark house, and Miss Spencer emerged. Nella called to her driver to stop, but he, determined to be in at the death, was engaged in whipping his horse, and he completely ignored her commands. He drew up triumphantly at the tall dark house just at the moment when

Miss Spencer disappeared into it. The other carriage drove away. Nella, uncertain what to do, stepped down from her carriage and gave the driver some money. At the same moment a man reopened the door of the house, which had closed on Miss Spencer.

'I want to see Miss Spencer,' said Nella impulsively. She couldn't think of anything else to say.

'Miss Spencer?'

'Yes; she's just arrived.'

'It's O.K., I suppose,' said the man.

'I guess so,' said Nella, and she walked past him into the house. She was astonished at her own audacity.

Miss Spencer was just going into a room off the narrow hall. Nella followed her into the apartment, which was shabbily furnished in the Belgian lodging-house style.

'Well, Miss Spencer,' she greeted the former Baroness Zerlinski, 'I guess you didn't expect to see me. You left our hôtel very suddenly this afternoon, and you left it very suddenly a few days ago; and so I've just called to make a few inquiries.'

To do the lady justice, Miss Spencer bore the surprising ordeal very well.

She did not flinch; she betrayed no emotion. The sole sign of perturbation was in her hurried breathing.

'You have ceased to be the Baroness Zerlinski,' Nella continued. 'May I sit down?'

'Certainly, sit down,' said Miss Spencer, copying the girl's tone. 'You are a fairly smart young woman, that I will say. What do you want? Weren't my books all straight?'

'Your books were all straight. I haven't come about your books. I have come about the murder of Reginald Dimmock, the disappearance of his corpse, and the disappearance of Prince Eugen of Posen. I thought you might be able to help me in some investigations which I am making.'

Miss Spencer's eyes gleamed, and she stood up and moved swiftly to the mantelpiece.

'You may be a Yankee, but you're a fool,' she said.

She took hold of the bell-rope.

'Don't ring that bell if you value your life,' said Nella.

'If what?' Miss Spencer remarked.

'If you value your life,' said Nella calmly, and with the words she pulled from her pocket a very neat and dainty little revolver.

Chapter Nine TWO WOMEN AND THE REVOLVER

'YOU—you're only doing that to frighten me,' stammered Miss Spencer, in a low, quavering voice.

'Am I?' Nella replied, as firmly as she could, though her hand shook violently with excitement, could Miss Spencer but have observed it. 'Am I? You said just now that I might be a Yankee girl, but I was a fool. Well, I am a Yankee girl, as you call it; and in my country, if they don't teach revolver-shooting in boarding-schools, there are at least a lot of girls who can handle a revolver. I happen to be one of them. I tell you that if you ring that bell you will suffer.'

Most of this was simple bluff on Nella's part, and she trembled lest Miss Spencer should perceive that it was simple bluff. Happily for her, Miss Spencer belonged to that order of women who have every sort of courage except physical courage. Miss Spencer could have withstood successfully any moral trial, but persuade her that her skin was in danger, and she would succumb. Nella at once divined this useful fact, and proceeded accordingly, hiding the strangeness of her own sensations as well as she could.

'You had better sit down now,' said Nella, 'and I will ask you a few questions.'

And Miss Spencer obediently sat down, rather white, and trying to screw her lips into a formal smile.

'Why did you leave the Grand Babylon that night?' Nella began her examination, putting on a stern, barrister-like expression.

'I had orders to, Miss Racksole.'

'Whose orders?'

'Well, I'm—I'm—the fact is, I'm a married woman, and it was my husband's orders.'

'Who is your husband?'

'Tom Jackson—Jules, you know, head waiter at the Grand Babylon.'

'So Jules's real name is Tom Jackson? Why did he want you to leave without giving notice?'

'I'm sure I don't know, Miss Racksole. I swear I don't know. He's my husband, and, of course, I do what he tells me, as you will some day do what your husband tells you. Please heaven you'll get a better husband than mine!'

Miss Spencer showed a sign of tears.

Nella fingered the revolver, and put it at full cock. 'Well,' she repeated, 'why did he want you to leave?' She was tremendously surprised at her own coolness, and somewhat pleased with it, too.

'I can't tell you, I can't tell you.'

'You've just got to,' Nella said, in a terrible, remorseless tone.

'He—he wished me to come over here to Ostend. Something had gone wrong.

Oh! he's a fearful man, is Tom. If I told you, he'd—'

'Had something gone wrong in the hôtel, or over here?'

'Both.'

'Was it about Prince Eugen of Posen?'

'I don't know—that is, yes, I think so.'

'What has your husband to do with Prince Eugen?'

'I believe he has some—some sort of business with him, some money business.'

'And was Mr Dimmock in this business?'

'I fancy so, Miss Racksole. I'm telling you all I know, that I swear.'

'Did your husband and Mr Dimmock have a quarrel that night in Room 111?'

'They had some difficulty.'

'And the result of that was that you came to Ostend instantly?'

'Yes; I suppose so.'

'And what were you to do in Ostend? What were your instructions from this husband of yours?'

Miss Spencer's head dropped on her arms on the table which separated her from Nella, and she appeared to sob violently.

'Have pity on me,' she murmured, 'I can't tell you any more.'

'Why?'

'He'd kill me if he knew.'

'You're wandering from the subject,' observed Nella coldly. 'This is the last time I shall warn you. Let me tell you plainly I've got the best reasons for being desperate, and if anything happens to you I shall say I did it in sell-defence. Now, what were you to do in Ostend?'

'I shall die for this anyhow,' whined Miss Spencer, and then, with a sort of fierce despair, 'I had to keep watch on Prince Eugen.'

'Where? In this house?'

Miss Spencer nodded, and, looking up, Nella could see the traces of tears in her face.

'Then Prince Eugen was a prisoner? Some one had captured him at the instigation of Jules?'

'Yes, if you must have it.'

'Why was it necessary for you specially to come to Ostend?'

'Oh! Tom trusts me. You see, I know Ostend. Before I took that place at the Grand Babylon I had travelled over Europe, and Tom knew that I knew a thing or two.'

'Why did you take the place at the Grand Babylon?'

'Because Tom told me to. He said I should be useful to him there.'

'Is your husband an Anarchist, or something of that kind, Miss Spencer?'

'I don't know. I'd tell you in a minute if I knew. But he's one of those that keep themselves to themselves.'

'Do you know if he has ever committed a murder?'

'Never!' said Miss Spencer, with righteous repudiation of the mere idea.

'But Mr Dimmock was murdered. He was poisoned. If he had not been poisoned why was his body stolen? It must have been stolen to prevent inquiry, to hide traces. Tell me about that.'

'I take my dying oath,' said Miss Spencer, standing up a little way from the table, 'I take my dying oath I didn't know Mr Dimmock was dead till I saw it in the newspaper.'

'You swear you had no suspicion of it?'

'I swear I hadn't.'

Nella was inclined to believe the statement. The woman and the girl looked at each other in the tawdry, frowsy, lamp-lit room. Miss Spencer nervously patted her yellow hair into shape, as if gradually recovering her composure and equanimity. The whole affair seemed like a dream to Nella, a disturbing, sinister nightmare. She was a little uncertain what to say. She felt that she had not yet got hold of any very definite information. 'Where is Prince Eugen now?' she asked at length.

'I don't know, miss.'

'He isn't in this house?'

'No, miss.'

'Ah! We will see presently.'

'They took him away, Miss Racksole.'

'Who took him away? Some of your husband's friends?'

'Some of his—acquaintances.'

'Then there is a gang of you?'

'A gang of us—a gang! I don't know what you mean,' Miss Spencer quavered.

'Oh, but you must know,' smiled Nella calmly. 'You can't possibly be so innocent as all that, Mrs Tom Jackson. You can't play games with me. You've just got to remember that I'm what you call a Yankee girl. There's one thing that I mean to find out, within the next five minutes, and that is—how your charming husband kidnapped Prince Eugen, and why he kidnapped him. Let us begin with the second question. You have evaded it once.'

Miss Spencer looked into Nella's face, and then her eyes dropped, and her fingers worked nervously with the tablecloth.

'How can I tell you,' she said, 'when I don't know? You've got the whip-hand of me, and you're tormenting me for your own pleasure.' She wore an expression of persecuted innocence.

'Did Mr Tom Jackson want to get some money out of Prince Eugen?'

'Money! Not he! Tom's never short of money.'

'But I mean a lot of money—tens of thousands, hundreds of thousands?'

'Tom never wanted money from anyone,' said Miss Spencer doggedly.

'Then had he some reason for wishing to prevent Prince Eugen from coming to London?'

'Perhaps he had. I don't know. If you kill me, I don't know.' Nella stopped to reflect. Then she raised the revolver. It was a mechanical, unintentional sort of action, and certainly she had no intention of using the weapon, but, strange to say, Miss Spencer again cowered before it. Even at that moment Nella wondered that a woman like Miss Spencer could be so simple as to think the revolver would actually be used. Having absolutely no physical cowardice herself, Nella had the greatest difficulty in imagining that other people could be at the mercy of a bodily fear. Still, she saw her advantage, and used it relentlessly, and with as much theatrical gesture as she could command. She raised the revolver till it was level with Miss Spencer's face, and suddenly a new, queer feeling took hold of her. She knew that she would indeed use that revolver now, if the miserable woman before her drove her too far. She felt afraid—afraid of herself; she was in the grasp of a savage, primeval instinct. In a flash she saw Miss Spencer dead at her feet—the police—a court of justice—the scaffold. It was horrible.

'Speak,' she said hoarsely, and Miss Spencer's face went whiter.

'Tom did say,' the woman whispered rapidly, awesomely, 'that if Prince Eugen got to London it would upset his scheme.'

'What scheme? What scheme? Answer me.'

'Heaven help me, I don't know.' Miss Spencer sank into a chair. 'He said Mr Dimmock had turned tail, and he should have to settle him and then Rocco—'

'Rocco! What about Rocco?' Nella could scarcely hear herself. Her grip of the revolver tightened.

Miss Spencer's eyes opened wider; she gazed at Nella with a glassy stare.

'Don't ask me. It's death!' Her eyes were fixed as if in horror.

'It is,' said Nella, and the sound of her voice seemed to her to issue from the lips of some third person.

'It's death,' repeated Miss Spencer, and gradually her head and shoulders sank back, and hung loosely over the chair. Nella was conscious of a sudden revulsion. The woman had surely fainted. Dropping the revolver she ran round the table. She was herself again—feminine, sympathetic, the old Nella. She felt immensely relieved that this had happened. But at the same instant Miss Spencer sprang up from the chair like a cat, seized the revolver, and with a wild movement of the arm flung it against the window. It crashed through the glass, exploding as it went, and there was a tense silence.

'I told you that you were a fool,' remarked Miss Spencer slowly, 'coming here like a sort of female Jack Sheppard, and trying to get the best of me.

We are on equal terms now. You frightened me, but I knew I was a cleverer woman than you, and that in the end, if I kept on long enough, I should win.

Now it will be my turn.'

Dumbfounded, and overcome with a miserable sense of the truth of Miss Spencer's words, Nella stood still. The idea of her colossal foolishness swept through her like a flood. She felt almost ashamed. But even at this juncture she had no fear. She faced the woman bravely, her mind leaping about in search of some plan. She could think of nothing but a bribe—an enormous bribe.

'I admit you've won,' she said, 'but I've not finished yet. Just listen.'

Miss Spencer folded her arms, and glanced at the door, smiling bitterly.

'You know my father is a millionaire; perhaps you know that he is one of the richest men in the world. If I give you my word of honour not to reveal anything that you've told me, what will you take to let me go free?'

'What sum do you suggest?' asked Miss Spencer carelessly.

'Twenty thousand pounds,' said Nella promptly. She had begun to regard the affair as a business operation.

Miss Spencer's lip curled.

'A hundred thousand.'

Again Miss Spencer's lip curled.

'Well, say a million. I can rely on my father, and so may you.'

'You think you are worth a million to him?'

'I do,' said Nella.

'And you think we could trust you to see that it was paid?'

'Of course you could.'

'And we should not suffer afterwards in any way?'

'I would give you my word, and my father's word.'

'Bah!' exclaimed Miss Spencer: 'how do you know I wouldn't let you go free for nothing? You are only a rash, silly girl.'

'I know you wouldn't. I can read your face too well.'

'You are right,' Miss Spencer replied slowly. 'I wouldn't. I wouldn't let you go for all the dollars in America.'

Nella felt cold down the spine, and sat down again in her chair. A draught of air from the broken window blew on her cheek. Steps sounded in the passage; the door opened, but Nella did not turn round. She could not move her eyes from Miss Spencer's. There was a noise of rushing water in her ears. She lost consciousness, and slipped limply to the ground.

Chapter Ten AT SEA

IT seemed to Nella that she was being rocked gently in a vast cradle, which swayed to and fro with a motion at once slow and incredibly gentle. This sensation continued for some time, and there was added to it the sound of a quick, quiet, muffled beat. Soft, exhilarating breezes wafted her forward in spite of herself, and yet she remained in a delicious calm. She wondered if her mother was kneeling by her side, whispering some lullaby in her childish ears. Then strange colours swam before her eyes, her eyelids wavered, and at last she awoke. For a few moments her gaze travelled to and fro in a vain search for some clue to her surroundings, was aware of nothing except sense of repose and a feeling of relief that some mighty and fatal struggle was over; she cared not whether she had conquered or suffered defeat in the struggle of her soul with some other soul; it was finished, done with, and the consciousness of its conclusion satisfied and contented her. Gradually her brain, recovering from its obsession, began to grasp the phenomena of her surroundings, and she saw that she was on a yacht, and that the yacht was moving. The motion of the cradle was the smooth rolling of the vessel; the beat was the beat of its screw; the strange colours were the cloud tints thrown by the sun as it rose over a distant and receding shore in the wake of the yacht; her mother's lullaby was the crooned song of the man at the wheel. Nella all through her life had had many experiences of yachting. From the waters of the River Hudson to those bluer tides of the Mediterranean Sea, she had yachted in all seasons and all weathers. She loved the water, and now it seemed deliciously right and proper that she should be on the water again. She raised her head to look round, and then let it sink back: she was fatigued, enervated; she desired only solitude and calm; she had no care, no anxiety, no responsibility: a hundred years might have passed since her meeting with Miss Spencer, and the memory of that meeting appeared to have faded into the remotest background of her mind.

It was a small yacht, and her practised eye at once told that it belonged to the highest aristocracy of pleasure craft. As she reclined in the deck-chair (it did not occur to her at that moment to speculate as to the identity of the person who had led her therein) she examined all visible details of the vessel. The deck was as white and smooth as her own hand, and the seams ran along its length like blue veins. All the brass-work, from the band round the slender funnel to the concave surface of the binnacle, shone like gold.

The tapered masts stretched upwards at a rakish angle, and the rigging seemed like spun silk. No sails were set; the yacht was under steam, and doing about seven or eight knots. She judged that it was a boat of a hundred tons or so, probably Clyde-built, and not more than two or three years old.

No one was to be seen on deck except the man at the wheel: this man wore a blue jersey; but there was neither name nor initial on the jersey, nor was there a name on the white life-buoys lashed to the main rigging, nor on the polished dinghy which hung on the starboard davits. She called to the man, and called again, in a feeble voice, but the steerer took no notice of her, and continued his quiet song as though nothing else existed in the universe save the yacht, the sea, the sun, and himself.

Then her eyes swept the outline of the land from which they were hastening, and she could just distinguish a lighthouse and a great white irregular dome, which she recognized as the Kursaal at Ostend, that gorgeous rival of the gaming palace at Monte Carlo. So she was leaving Ostend. The rays of the sun fell on her caressingly, like a restorative. All around the water was changing from wonderful greys and dark blues to still more wonderful pinks and translucent unearthly greens; the magic kaleidoscope of dawn was going forward in its accustomed way, regardless of the vicissitudes of mortals.

Here and there in the distance she descried a sail—the brown sail of some Ostend fishing-boat returning home after a night's trawling. Then the beat of paddles caught her ear, and a steamer blundered past, wallowing clumsily among the waves like a tortoise. It was the Swallow from London. She could see some of its passengers leaning curiously over the aft-rail. A girl in a mackintosh signalled to her, and mechanically she answered the salute with her arm. The officer of the bridge of the Swallow hailed the yacht, but the man at the wheel offered no reply. In another minute the Swallow was nothing but a blot in the distance.

Nella tried to sit straight in the deck-chair, but she found herself unable to do so. Throwing off the rug which covered her, she discovered that she had been tied to the chair by means of a piece of broad webbing. Instantly she was alert, awake, angry; she knew that her perils were not over; she felt that possibly they had scarcely yet begun. Her lazy contentment, her dreamy sense of peace and repose, vanished utterly, and she steeled herself to meet the dangers of a grave and difficult situation.

Just at that moment a man came up from below. He was a man of forty or so, clad in irreproachable blue, with a peaked yachting cap. He raised the cap politely.

'Good morning,' he said. 'Beautiful sunrise, isn't it?' The clever and calculated insolence of his tone cut her like a lash as she lay bound in the chair. Like all people who have lived easy and joyous lives in those fair regions where gold smoothes every crease and law keeps a tight hand on disorder, she found it hard to realize that there were other regions where gold was useless and law without power. Twenty-four hours ago she would have declared it impossible that such an experience as she had suffered could happen to anyone; she would have talked airily about civilization and the nineteenth century, and progress and the police. But her experience was teaching her that human nature remains always the same, and that beneath the thin crust of security on which we good citizens exist the dark and secret forces of crime continue to move, just as they did in the days when you couldn't go from Cheapside to Chelsea without being set upon by thieves. Her experience was in a fair way to teach her this lesson better than she could have learnt it even in the bureaux of the detective police of Paris, London, and St Petersburg.

'Good morning,' the man repeated, and she glanced at him with a sullen, angry gaze.

'You!' she exclaimed, 'You, Mr Thomas Jackson, if that is your name! Loose me from this chair, and I will talk to you.' Her eyes flashed as she spoke, and the contempt in them added mightily to her beauty. Mr Thomas Jackson, otherwise Jules, erstwhile head waiter at the Grand Babylon, considered himself a connoisseur in feminine loveliness, and the vision of Nella Racksole smote him like an exquisite blow.

'With pleasure,' he replied. 'I had forgotten that to prevent you from falling I had secured you to the chair'; and with a quick movement he unfastened the band. Nella stood up, quivering with fiery annoyance and scorn.

'Now,' she said, fronting him, 'what is the meaning of this?'

'You fainted,' he replied imperturbably. 'Perhaps you don't remember.'

The man offered her a deck-chair with a characteristic gesture. Nella was obliged to acknowledge, in spite of herself, that the fellow had distinction, an air of breeding. No one would have guessed that for twenty years he had been an hôtel waiter. His long, lithe figure, and easy, careless carriage seemed to be the figure and carriage of an aristocrat, and his voice was quiet, restrained, and authoritative.

'That has nothing to do with my being carried off in this yacht of yours.'

'It is not my yacht,' he said, 'but that is a minor detail. As to the more important matter, forgive me that I remind you that only a few hours ago you were threatening a lady in my house with a revolver.'

'Then it was your house?'

'Why not? May I not possess a house?' He smiled.

'I must request you to put the yacht about at once, instantly, and take me back.' She tried to speak firmly.

'Ah!' he said, 'I am afraid that's impossible. I didn't put out to sea with the intention of returning at once, instantly.' In the last words he gave a faint imitation of her tone.

'When I do get back,' she said, 'when my father gets to know of this affair, it will be an exceedingly bad day for you, Mr Jackson.'

'But supposing your father doesn't hear of it—'

'What?'

'Supposing you never get back?'

'Do you mean, then, to have my murder on your conscience?'

'Talking of murder,' he said, 'you came very near to murdering my friend, Miss Spencer. At least, so she tells me.'

'Is Miss Spencer on board?' Nella asked, seeing perhaps a faint ray of hope in the possible presence of a woman.

'Miss Spencer is not on board. There is no one on board except you and myself and a small crew—a very discreet crew, I may add.'

'I will have nothing more to say to you. You must take your own course.'

'Thanks for the permission,' he said. 'I will send you up some breakfast.'

He went to the saloon stairs and whistled, and a Negro boy appeared with a tray of chocolate. Nella took it, and, without the slightest hesitation, threw it overboard. Mr Jackson walked away a few steps and then returned.

'You have spirit,' he said, 'and I admire spirit. It is a rare quality.'

She made no reply. 'Why did you mix yourself up in my affairs at all?' he went on. Again she made no reply, but the question set her thinking: why had she mixed herself up in this mysterious business? It was quite at variance with the usual methods of her gay and butterfly existence to meddle at all with serious things. Had she acted merely from a desire to see justice done and wickedness punished? Or was it the desire of adventure? Or was it, perhaps, the desire to be of service to His Serene Highness Prince Aribert? 'It is no fault of mine that you are in this fix,' Jules continued. 'I didn't bring you into it. You brought yourself into it. You and your father—you have been moving along at a pace which is rather too rapid.'

'That remains to be seen,' she put in coldly.

'It does,' he admitted. 'And I repeat that I can't help admiring you—that is, when you aren't interfering with my private affairs. That is a proceeding which I have never tolerated from anyone—not even from a millionaire, nor even from a beautiful woman.' He bowed. 'I will tell you what I propose to do. I propose to escort you to a place of safety, and to keep you there till my operations are concluded, and the possibility of interference entirely removed. You spoke just now of murder. What a crude notion that was of yours! It is only the amateur who practises murder—'

'What about Reginald Dimmock?' she interjected quickly.

He paused gravely.

'Reginald Dimmock,' he repeated. 'I had imagined his was a case of heart disease. Let me send you up some more chocolate. I'm sure you're hungry.'

'I will starve before I touch your food,' she said.

'Gallant creature!' he murmured, and his eyes roved over her face. Her superb, supercilious beauty overcame him. 'Ah!' he said, 'what a wife you would make!' He approached nearer to her. 'You and I, Miss Racksole, your beauty and wealth and my brains—we could conquer the world. Few men are worthy of you, but I am one of the few. Listen! You might do worse. Marry me. I am a great man; I shall be greater. I adore you. Marry me, and I will save your life. All shall be well. I will begin again. The past shall be as though there had been no past.'

'This is somewhat sudden—Jules,' she said with biting contempt.

'Did you expect me to be conventional?' he retorted. 'I love you.'

'Granted,' she said, for the sake of the argument. 'Then what will occur to your present wife?'

'My present wife?'

'Yes, Miss Spencer, as she is called.'

'She told you I was her husband?'

'Incidentally she did.'

'She isn't.'

'Perhaps she isn't. But, nevertheless, I think I won't marry you.' Nella stood like a statue of scorn before him.

He went still nearer to her. 'Give me a kiss, then; one kiss—I won't ask for more; one kiss from those lips, and you shall go free. Men have ruined themselves for a kiss. I will.'

'Coward!' she ejaculated.

'Coward!' he repeated. 'Coward, am I? Then I'll be a coward, and you shall kiss me whether you will or not.'

He put a hand on her shoulder. As she shrank back from his lustrous eyes, with an involuntary scream, a figure sprang out of the dinghy a few feet away. With a single blow, neatly directed to Mr Jackson's ear, Mr Jackson was stretched senseless on the deck. Prince Aribert of Posen stood over him with a revolver. It was probably the greatest surprise of Mr Jackson's whole life.

'Don't be alarmed,' said the Prince to Nella, 'my being here is the simplest thing in the world, and I will explain it as soon as I have finished with this fellow.'

Nella could think of nothing to say, but she noticed the revolver in the Prince's hand.

'Why,' she remarked, 'that's my revolver.'

'It is,' he said, 'and I will explain that, too.'

The man at the wheel gave no heed whatever to the scene.

Chapter Eleven THE COURT PAWNBROKER

'MR SAMPSON LEVI wishes to see you, sir.'

These words, spoken by a servant to Theodore Racksole, aroused the millionaire from a reverie which had been the reverse of pleasant. The fact was, and it is necessary to insist on it, that Mr Racksole, owner of the Grand Babylon Hôtel, was by no means in a state of self-satisfaction. A mystery had attached itself to his hôtel, and with all his acumen and knowledge of things in general he was unable to solve that mystery. He laughed at the fruitless efforts of the police, but he could not honestly say that his own efforts had been less barren. The public was talking, for, after all, the disappearance of poor Dimmock's body had got noised abroad in an indirect sort of way, and Theodore Racksole did not like the idea of his impeccable hôtel being the subject of sinister rumours. He wondered, grimly, what the public and the Sunday newspapers would say if they were aware of all the other phenomena, not yet common property: of Miss Spencer's disappearance, of Jules' strange visits, and of the non-arrival of Prince Eugen of Posen. Theodore Racksole had worried his brain without result. He had conducted an elaborate private investigation without result, and he had spent a certain amount of money without result. The police said that they had a clue; but Racksole remarked that it was always the business of the police to have a clue, that they seldom had more than a clue, and that a clue without some sequel to it was a pretty stupid business. The only sure thing in the whole affair was that a cloud rested over his hôtel, his beautiful new toy, the finest of its kind. The cloud was not interfering with business, but, nevertheless, it was a cloud, and he fiercely resented its presence; perhaps it would be more correct to say that he fiercely resented his inability to dissipate it.

'Mr Sampson Levi wishes to see you, sir,' the servant repeated, having received no sign that his master had heard him.

'So I hear,' said Racksole. 'Does he want to see me, personally?'

'He asked for you, sir.'

'Perhaps it is Rocco he wants to see, about a menu or something of that kind?'

'I will inquire, sir,' and the servant made a move to withdraw.

'Stop,' Racksole commanded suddenly. 'Desire Mr Sampson Levi to step this way.'

The great stockbroker of the 'Kaffir Circus' entered with a simple unassuming air. He was a rather short, florid man, dressed like a typical Hebraic financier, with too much watch-chain and too little waistcoat. In his fat hand he held a gold-headed cane, and an absolutely new silk hat—for it was Friday, and Mr Levi purchased a new hat every Friday of his life, holiday times only excepted. He breathed heavily and sniffed through his nose a good deal, as though he had just performed some Herculean physical labour. He glanced at the American millionaire with an expression in which a slight embarrassment might have been detected, but at the same time his round, red face disclosed a certain frank admiration and good nature.

'Mr Racksole, I believe—Mr Theodore Racksole. Proud to meet you, sir.'

Such were the first words of Mr Sampson Levi. In form they were the greeting of a third-rate chimney-sweep, but, strangely enough, Theodore Racksole liked their tone. He said to himself that here, precisely where no one would have expected to find one, was an honest man.

'Good day,' said Racksole briefly. 'To what do I owe the pleasure—'

'I expect your time is limited,' answered Sampson Levi. 'Anyhow, mine is, and so I'll come straight to the point, Mr Racksole. I'm a plain man. I don't pretend to be a gentleman or any nonsense of that kind. I'm a stockbroker, that's what I am, and I don't care who knows it. The other night I had a ball in this hôtel. It cost me a couple of thousand and odd pounds, and, by the way, I wrote out a cheque for your bill this morning. I don't like balls, but they're useful to me, and my little wife likes 'em, and so we give 'em. Now, I've nothing to say against the hôtel management as regards that ball: it was very decently done, very decently, but what I want to know is this—Why did you have a private detective among my guests?'

'A private detective?' exclaimed Racksole, somewhat surprised at this charge.

'Yes,' Mr Sampson Levi said firmly, fanning himself in his chair, and gazing at Theodore Racksole with the direct earnest expression of a man having a grievance. 'Yes; a private detective. It's a small matter, I know, and I dare say you think you've got a right, as proprietor of the show, to do what you like in that line; but I've just called to tell you that I object. I've called as a matter of principle. I'm not angry; it's the principle of the thing.'

'My dear Mr Levi,' said Racksole, 'I assure you that, having let the Gold Room to a private individual for a private entertainment, I should never dream of doing what you suggest.'

'Straight?' asked Mr Sampson Levi, using his own picturesque language.

'Straight,' said Racksole smiling.

'There was a gent present at my ball that I didn't ask. I've got a wonderful memory for faces, and I know. Several fellows asked me afterwards what he was doing there. I was told by someone that he was one of your waiters, but I didn't believe that. I know nothing of the Grand Babylon; it's not quite my style of tavern, but I don't think you'd send one of your own waiters to watch my guests—unless, of course, you sent him as a waiter; and this chap didn't do any waiting, though he did his share of drinking.'

'Perhaps I can throw some light on this mystery,' said Racksole. 'I may tell you that I was already aware that man had attended your ball uninvited.'

'How did you get to know?'

'By pure chance, Mr Levi, and not by inquiry. That man was a former waiter at this hôtel—the head waiter, in fact—Jules. No doubt you have heard of him.'

'Not I,' said Mr Levi positively.

'Ah!' said Racksole, 'I was informed that everyone knew Jules, but it appears not. Well, be that as it may, previously to the night of your ball, I had dismissed Jules. I had ordered him never to enter the Babylon again. But on that evening I encountered him here—not in the Gold Room, but in the hôtel itself. I asked him to explain his presence, and he stated he was your guest. That is all I know of the matter, Mr Levi, and I am extremely sorry that you should have thought me capable of the enormity of placing a private detective among your guests.'

'This is perfectly satisfactory to me,' Mr Sampson Levi said, after a pause.

'I only wanted an explanation, and I've got it. I was told by some pals of mine in the City I might rely on Mr Theodore Racksole going straight to the point, and I'm glad they were right. Now as to that feller Jules, I shall make my own inquiries as to him. Might I ask you why you dismissed him?'

'I don't know why I dismissed him.'

'You don't know? Oh! come now! I'm only asking because I thought you might be able to give me a hint why he turned up uninvited at my ball. Sorry if I'm too inquisitive.'

'Not at all, Mr Levi; but I really don't know. I only sort of felt that he was a suspicious character. I dismissed him on instinct, as it were. See?'

Without answering this question Mr Levi asked another. 'If this Jules is such a well-known person,' he said, 'how could the feller hope to come to my ball without being recognized?'

'Give it up,' said Racksole promptly.

'Well, I'll be moving on,' was Mr Sampson Levi's next remark. 'Good day, and thank ye. I suppose you aren't doing anything in Kaffirs?'

Mr Racksole smiled a negative.

'I thought not,' said Levi. 'Well, I never touch American rails myself, and so I reckon we sha'n't come across each other. Good day.'

'Good day,' said Racksole politely, following Mr Sampson Levi to the door.

With his hand on the handle of the door, Mr Levi stopped, and, gazing at Theodore Racksole with a shrewd, quizzical expression, remarked:

'Strange things been going on here lately, eh?'

The two men looked very hard at each other for several seconds.

'Yes,' Racksole assented. 'Know anything about them?'

'Well—no, not exactly,' said Mr Levi. 'But I had a fancy you and I might be useful to each other; I had a kind of fancy to that effect.'

'Come back and sit down again, Mr Levi,' Racksole said, attracted by the evident straightforwardness of the man's tone. 'Now, how can we be of service to each other? I flatter myself I'm something of a judge of character, especially financial character, and I tell you—if you'll put your cards on the table, I'll do ditto with mine.'

'Agreed,' said Mr Sampson Levi. 'I'll begin by explaining my interest in your hôtel. I have been expecting to receive a summons from a certain Prince Eugen of Posen to attend him here, and that summons hasn't arrived. It appears that Prince Eugen hasn't come to London at all. Now, I could have taken my dying davy that he would have been here yesterday at the latest.'

'Why were you so sure?'

'Question for question,' said Levi. 'Let's clear the ground first, Mr Racksole. Why did you buy this hôtel? That's a conundrum that's been puzzling a lot of our fellows in the City for some days past. Why did you buy the Grand Babylon? And what is the next move to be?'

'There is no next move,' answered Racksole candidly, 'and I will tell you why I bought the hôtel; there need be no secret about it. I bought it because of a whim.' And then Theodore Racksole gave this little Jew, whom he had begun to respect, a faithful account of the transaction with Mr Felix Babylon. 'I suppose,' he added, 'you find a difficulty in appreciating my state of mind when I did the deal.'

'Not a bit,' said Mr Levi. 'I once bought an electric launch on the Thames in a very similar way, and it turned out to be one of the most satisfactory purchases I ever made. Then it's a simple accident that you own this hôtel at the present moment?'

'A simple accident—all because of a beefsteak and a bottle of Bass.'

'Um!' grunted Mr Sampson Levi, stroking his triple chin.

'To return to Prince Eugen,' Racksole resumed. 'I was expecting His Highness here. The State apartments had been prepared for him. He was due on the very afternoon that young Dimmock died. But he never came, and I have not heard why he has failed to arrive; nor have I seen his name in the papers. What his business was in London, I don't know.'

'I will tell you,' said Mr Sampson Levi, 'he was coming to arrange a loan.'

'A State loan?'

'No—a private loan.'

'Whom from?'

'From me, Sampson Levi. You look surprised. If you'd lived in London a little longer, you'd know that I was just the person the Prince would come to. Perhaps you aren't aware that down Throgmorton Street way I'm called "The Court Pawnbroker", because I arrange loans for the minor, second-class Princes of Europe. I'm a stockbroker, but my real business is financing some of the little Courts of Europe. Now, I may tell you that the Hereditary Prince of Posen particularly wanted a million, and he wanted it by a certain date, and he knew that if the affair wasn't fixed up by a certain time here he wouldn't be able to get it by that certain date. That's why I'm surprised he isn't in London.'

'What did he need a million for?'

'Debts,' answered Sampson Levi laconically.

'His own?'

429

'Certainly.'

'But he isn't thirty years of age?'

'What of that? He isn't the only European Prince who has run up a million of debts in a dozen years. To a Prince the thing is as easy as eating a sandwich.'

'And why has he taken this sudden resolution to liquidate them?'

'Because the Emperor and the lady's parents won't let him marry till he has done so! And quite right, too! He's got to show a clean sheet, or the Princess Anna of Eckstein-Schwartzburg will never be Princess of Posen. Even now the Emperor has no idea how much Prince Eugen's debts amount to. If he had—!'

'But would not the Emperor know of this proposed loan?'

'Not necessarily at once. It could be so managed. Twig?' Mr Sampson Levi laughed. 'I've carried these little affairs through before. After marriage it might be allowed to leak out. And you know the Princess Anna's fortune is pretty big! Now, Mr Racksole,' he added, abruptly changing his tone, 'where do you suppose Prince Eugen has disappeared to? Because if he doesn't turn up to-day he can't have that million. To-day is the last day. To-morrow the money will be appropriated, elsewhere. Of course, I'm not alone in this business, and my friends have something to say.'

'You ask me where I think Prince Eugen has disappeared to?'

'I do.'

'Then you think it's a disappearance?'

Sampson Levi nodded. 'Putting two and two together,' he said, 'I do. The Dimmock business is very peculiar—very peculiar, indeed. Dimmock was a left-handed relation of the Posen family. Twig? Scarcely anyone knows that.

He was made secretary and companion to Prince Aribert, just to keep him in the domestic circle. His mother was an Irishwoman, whose misfortune was that she was too beautiful. Twig?' (Mr Sampson Levi always used this extraordinary word when he was in a communicative mood.) 'My belief is that Dimmock's death has something to do with the disappearance of Prince Eugen.

The only thing that passes me is this: Why should anyone want to make Prince Eugen disappear? The poor little Prince hasn't an enemy in the world. If he's been "copped", as they say, why has he been "copped"? It won't do anyone any good.'

'Won't it?' repeated Racksole, with a sudden flash.

'What do you mean?' asked Mr Levi.

'I mean this: Suppose some other European pauper Prince was anxious to marry Princess Anna and her fortune, wouldn't that Prince have an interest in stopping this loan of yours to Prince Eugen? Wouldn't he have an interest in causing Prince Eugen to disappear—at any rate, for a time?'

Sampson Levi thought hard for a few moments.

'Mr Theodore Racksole,' he said at length, 'I do believe you have hit on something.'

Chapter Twelve ROCCO AND ROOM NO. 111

ON the afternoon of the same day—the interview just described had occurred in the morning—Racksole was visited by another idea, and he said to himself that he ought to have thought of it before. The conversation with Mr Sampson Levi had continued for a considerable time, and the two men had exchanged various notions, and agreed to meet again, but the theory that Reginald Dimmock had probably been a traitor to his family—a traitor whose repentance had caused his death—had not been thoroughly discussed; the talk had tended rather to Continental politics, with a view to discovering what princely family might have an interest in the temporary disappearance of Prince Eugen. Now, as Racksole considered in detail the particular affair of Reginald Dimmock, deceased, he was struck by one point especially, to wit: Why had Dimmock and Jules manoeuvred to turn Nella Racksole out of Room No. 111 on that first night? That they had so manoeuvred, that the broken window-pane was not a mere accident, Racksole felt perfectly sure. He had felt perfectly sure all along; but the significance of the facts had not struck him. It was plain to him now that there must be something of extraordinary and peculiar importance about Room No. 111. After lunch he wandered quietly upstairs and looked at Room No. 111; that is to say, he looked at the outside of it; it happened to be occupied, but the guest was leaving that evening. The thought crossed his mind that there could be no object in gazing blankly at the outside of a room; yet he gazed; then he wandered quickly down again to the next floor, and in passing along the corridor of that floor he stopped, and with an involuntary gesture stamped his foot.

'Great Scott!' he said, 'I've got hold of something—No. 111 is exactly over the State apartments.'

He went to the bureau, and issued instructions that No. 111 was not to be re-let to anyone until further orders. At the bureau they gave him Nella's note, which ran thus:

Dearest Papa,—I am going away for a day or two on the trail of a clue.

If I'm not back in three days, begin to inquire for me at Ostend. Till then leave me alone.—Your sagacious daughter, NELL.

These few words, in Nella's large scrawling hand, filled one side of the paper. At the bottom was a P.T.O. He turned over, and read the sentence, underlined, 'P.S.—Keep an eye on Rocco.'

'I wonder what the little creature is up to?' he murmured, as he tore the letter into small fragments, and threw them into the waste-paper basket.

Then, without any delay, he took the lift down to the basement, with the object of making a preliminary inspection of Rocco in his lair. He could scarcely bring himself to believe that this suave and stately gentleman, this enthusiast of gastronomy, was concerned in the machinations of Jules and other rascals unknown. Nevertheless, from habit, he obeyed his daughter, giving her credit for a certain amount of perspicuity and cleverness.

The kitchens of the Grand Babylon Hôtel are one of the wonders of Europe.

Only three years before the events now under narration Felix Babylon had had them newly installed with every device and patent that the ingenuity of two continents could supply. They covered nearly an acre of superficial space.

They were walled and floored from end to end with tiles and marble, which enabled them to be washed down every morning like the deck of a man-of-war.

Visitors were sometimes taken to see the potato-paring machine, the patent plate-dryer, the Babylon-spit (a contrivance of Felix Babylon's own), the silver-grill, the system of connected stock-pots, and other amazing phenomena of the department. Sometimes, if they were fortunate, they might also see the artist who sculptured ice into forms of men and beasts for table ornaments, or the first napkin-folder in London, or the man who daily invented fresh designs for pastry and blancmanges. Twelve chefs pursued their labours in those kitchens, helped by ninety assistant chefs, and a further army of unconsidered menials. Over all these was Rocco, supreme and unapproachable. Half-way along the suite of kitchens, Rocco had an apartment of his own, wherein he thought out those magnificent combinations, those marvellous feats of succulence and originality, which had given him his fame. Visitors never caught a glimpse of Rocco in the kitchens, though sometimes, on a special night, he would stroll nonchalantly through the dining-room, like the great man he was, to receive the compliments of the hôtel habitués—people of insight who recognized his uniqueness.

Theodore Racksole's sudden and unusual appearance in the kitchen caused a little stir. He nodded to some of the chefs, but said nothing to anyone, merely wandering about amid the maze of copper utensils, and white-capped workers. At length he saw Rocco, surrounded by several admiring chefs. Rocco was bending over a freshly-roasted partridge which lay on a blue dish. He plunged a long fork into the back of the bird, and raised it in the air with his left hand. In his right he held a long glittering carving-knife. He was giving one of his world-famous exhibitions of carving. In four swift, unerring, delicate, perfect strokes he cleanly severed the limbs of the partridge. It was a wonderful achievement—how wondrous none but the really skilful carver can properly appreciate. The chefs emitted a hum of applause, and Rocco, long, lean, and graceful, retired to his own apartment. Racksole followed him. Rocco sat in a chair, one hand over his eyes; he had not noticed Theodore Racksole.

'What are you doing, M. Rocco?' the millionaire asked smiling. 'Ah!' exclaimed Rocco, starting up with an apology. 'Pardon! I was inventing a new mayonnaise, which I shall need for a certain menu next week.'

'Do you invent these things without materials, then?' questioned Racksole.

'Certainly. I do dem in my mind. I tink dem. Why should I want materials? I know all flavours. I tink, and tink, and tink, and it is done. I write down.

I give the recipe to my best chef—dere you are. I need not even taste, I know how it will taste. It is like composing music. De great composers do not compose at de piano.'

'I see,' said Racksole.

'It is because I work like dat dat you pay me three thousand a year,' Rocco added gravely.

'Heard about Jules?' said Racksole abruptly.

'Jules?'

'Yes. He's been arrested in Ostend,' the millionaire continued, lying cleverly at a venture. 'They say that he and several others are implicated in a murder case—the murder of Reginald Dimmock.'

'Truly?' drawled Rocco, scarcely hiding a yawn. His indifference was so superb, so gorgeous, that Racksole instantly divined that it was assumed for the occasion.

'It seems that, after all, the police are good for something. But this is the first time I ever knew them to be worth their salt. There is to be a thorough and systematic search of the hôtel to-morrow,' Racksole went on. 'I have mentioned it to you to warn you that so far as you are concerned the search is of course merely a matter of form. You will not object to the detectives looking through your rooms?'

'Certainly not,' and Rocco shrugged his shoulders.

'I shall ask you to say nothing about this to anyone,' said Racksole. 'The news of Jules' arrest is quite private to myself. The papers know nothing of it. You comprehend?'

Rocco smiled in his grand manner, and Rocco's master thereupon went away.

Racksole was very well satisfied with the little conversation. It was perhaps dangerous to tell a series of mere lies to a clever fellow like Rocco, and Racksole wondered how he should ultimately explain them to this great master-chef if his and Nella's suspicions should be unfounded, and nothing came of them. Nevertheless, Rocco's manner, a strange elusive something in the man's eyes, had nearly convinced Racksole that he was somehow implicated in Jules' schemes—and probably in the death of Reginald Dimmock and the disappearance of Prince Eugen of Posen.

That night, or rather about half-past one the next morning, when the last noises of the hôtel's life had died down, Racksole made his way to Room 111 on the second floor. He locked the door on the inside, and proceeded to examine the place, square foot by square foot. Every now and then some creak or other sound startled him, and he listened intently for a few seconds. The bedroom was furnished in the ordinary splendid style of bedrooms at the Grand Babylon Hôtel, and in that respect called for no remark. What most interested Racksole was the flooring. He pulled up the thick Oriental carpet, and peered along every plank, but could discover nothing unusual.

Then he went to the dressing-room, and finally to the bathroom, both of which opened out of the main room. But in neither of these smaller chambers was he any more successful than in the bedroom itself. Finally he came to the bath, which was enclosed in a panelled casing of polished wood, after the manner of baths. Some baths have a cupboard beneath the taps, with a door at the side, but this one appeared to have none. He tapped the panels, but not a single one of them gave forth that 'curious hollow sound' which usually betokens a secret place. Idly he turned the cold-tap of the bath, and the water began to rush in. He turned off the cold-tap and turned on the waste-tap, and as he did so his knee, which was pressing against the panelling, slipped forward. The panelling had given way, and he saw that one large panel was hinged from the inside, and caught with a hasp, also on the inside. A large space within the casing of the end of the bath was thus revealed. Before doing anything else, Racksole tried to repeat the trick with the waste-tap, but he failed; it would not work again, nor could he in any way perceive that there was any connection between the rod of the waste-tap and the hasp of the panel. Racksole could not see into the cavity within the casing, and the electric light was fixed, and could not be moved about like a candle. He felt in his pockets, and fortunately discovered a box of matches. Aided by these, he looked into the cavity, and saw nothing; nothing except a rather large hole at the far end—some three feet from the casing. With some difficulty he squeezed himself through the open panel, and took a half-kneeling, half-sitting posture within. There he struck a match, and it was a most unfortunate thing that in striking, the box being half open, he set fire to all the matches, and was half smothered in the atrocious stink of phosphorus which resulted. One match burned clear on the floor of the cavity, and, rubbing his eyes, Racksole picked it up, and looked down the hole which he had previously descried. It was a hole apparently bottomless, and about eighteen inches square. The curious part about the hole was that a rope-ladder hung down it. When he saw that rope-ladder Racksole smiled the smile of a happy man.

The match went out.

Should he make a long journey, perhaps to some distant corner of the hôtel, for a fresh box of matches, or should he attempt to descend that rope-ladder in the dark? He decided on the latter course, and he was the more strongly moved thereto as he could now distinguish a faint, a very faint tinge of light at the bottom of the hole.

With infinite care he compressed himself into the well-like hole, and descended the latter. At length he arrived on firm ground, perspiring, but quite safe and quite excited. He saw now that the tinge of light came through a small hole in the wood. He put his eye to the wood, and found that he had a fine view of the State bathroom, and through the door of the State bathroom into the State bedroom. At the massive marble-topped washstand in the State bedroom a man was visible, bending over some object which lay thereon.

The man was Rocco!

Chapter Thirteen IN THE STATE BEDROOM

IT was of course plain to Racksole that the peculiar passageway which he had, at great personal inconvenience, discovered between the bathroom of No. 111 and the State bathroom on the floor below must have been specially designed by some person or persons for the purpose of keeping a nefarious watch upon the occupants of the State suite of apartments. It was a means of communication at once simple and ingenious. At that moment he could not be sure of the precise method employed for it, but he surmised that the casing of the waterpipes had been used as a 'well', while space for the pipes themselves had been found in the thickness of the ample brick walls of the Grand Babylon. The eye-hole, through which he now had a view of the bedroom, was a very minute one, and probably would scarcely be noticed from the exterior. One thing he observed concerning it, namely, that it had been made for a man somewhat taller than himself; he was obliged to stand on tiptoe in order to get his eye in the correct position. He remembered that both Jules and Rocco were distinctly above the average height; also that they were both thin men, and could have descended the well with comparative ease. Theodore Racksole, though not stout, was a well-set man with large bones.

These things flashed through his mind as he gazed, spellbound, at the mysterious movements of Rocco. The door between the bathroom and the bedroom was wide open, and his own situation was such that his view embraced a considerable portion of the bedroom, including the whole of the immense and gorgeously-upholstered bedstead, but not including the whole of the marble washstand. He could see only half of the washstand, and at intervals Rocco passed out of sight as his lithe hands moved over the object which lay on the marble. At first Theodore Racksole could not decide what this object was, but after a time, as his eyes grew accustomed to the position and the light, he made it out.

It was the body of a man. Or, rather, to be more exact, Racksole could discern the legs of a man on that half of the table which was visible to him. Involuntarily he shuddered, as the conviction forced itself upon him that Rocco had some unconscious human being helpless on that cold marble surface. The legs never moved. Therefore, the hapless creature was either asleep or under the influence of an anaesthetic—or (horrible thought!) dead.

Racksole wanted to call out, to stop by some means or other the dreadful midnight activity which was proceeding before his astonished eyes; but fortunately he restrained himself.

On the washstand he could see certain strangely-shaped utensils and instruments which Rocco used from time to time. The work seemed to Racksole to continue for interminable hours, and then at last Rocco ceased, gave a sign of satisfaction, whistled several bars from 'Cavalleria Rusticana', and came into the bath-room, where he took off his coat, and very quietly washed his hands. As he stood calmly and leisurely wiping those long fingers of his, he was less than four feet from Racksole, and the cooped-up millionaire trembled, holding his breath, lest Rocco should detect his presence behind the woodwork. But nothing happened, and Rocco returned unsuspectingly to the bedroom. Racksole saw him place some sort of white flannel garment over the prone form on the table, and then lift it bodily on to the great bed, where it lay awfully still. The hidden watcher was sure now that it was a corpse upon which Rocco had been exercising his mysterious and sinister functions.

But whose corpse? And what functions? Could this be a West End hôtel, Racksole's own hôtel, in the very heart of London, the best-policed city in the world? It seemed incredible, impossible; yet so it was. Once more he remembered what Felix Babylon had said to him and realized the truth of the saying anew. The proprietor of a vast and complicated establishment like the Grand Babylon could never know a tithe of the extraordinary and queer occurrences which happened daily under his very nose; the atmosphere of such a caravanserai must necessarily be an atmosphere of mystery and problems apparently inexplicable. Nevertheless, Racksole thought that Fate was carrying things with rather a high hand when she permitted his chef to spend the night hours over a man's corpse in his State bedroom, this sacred apartment which was supposed to be occupied only by individuals of Royal Blood. Racksole would not have objected to a certain amount of mystery, but he decidedly thought that there was a little too much mystery here for his taste. He thought that even Felix Babylon would have been surprised at this.

The electric chandelier in the centre of the ceiling was not lighted; only the two lights on either side of the washstand were switched on, and these did not sufficiently illuminate the features of the man on the bed to enable Racksole to see them clearly. In vain the millionaire strained his eyes; he could only make out that the corpse was probably that of a young man. Just as he was wondering what would be the best course of action to pursue, he saw Rocco with a square-shaped black box in his hand. Then the chef switched off the two electric lights, and the State bedroom was in darkness. In that swift darkness Racksole heard Rocco spring on to the bed. Another half-dozen moments of suspense, and there was a blinding flash of white, which endured for several seconds, and showed Rocco standing like an evil spirit over the corpse, the black box in one hand and a burning piece of aluminium wire in the other. The aluminium wire burnt out, and darkness followed blacker than before.

Rocco had photographed the corpse by flashlight.

But the dazzling flare which had disclosed the features of the dead man to the insensible lens of the camera had disclosed them also to Theodore Racksole. The dead man was Reginald Dimmock!

Stung into action by this discovery, Racksole tried to find the exit from his place of concealment. He felt sure that there existed some way out into the State bathroom, but he sought for it fruitlessly, groping with both hands and feet. Then he decided that he must ascend the rope-ladder, make haste for the first-floor corridor, and intercept Rocco when he left the State apartments. It was a painful and difficult business to ascend that thin and yielding ladder in such a confined space, but Racksole was managing it very nicely, and had nearly reached the top, when, by some untoward freak of chance, the ladder broke above his weight, and he slipped ignominiously down to the bottom of the wooden tube. Smothering an excusable curse, Racksole crouched, baffled. Then he saw that the force of his fall had somehow opened a trap-door at his feet. He squeezed through, pushed open another tiny door, and in another second stood in the State bathroom. He was dishevelled, perspiring, rather bewildered; but he was there. In the next second he had resumed absolute command of all his faculties.

Strange to say, he had moved so quietly that Rocco had apparently not heard him. He stepped noiselessly to the door between the bathroom and the bedroom, and stood there in silence. Rocco had switched on again the lights over the washstand and was busy with his utensils.

Racksole deliberately coughed.

Chapter Fourteen ROCCO ANSWERS SOME QUESTIONS

ROCCO turned round with the swiftness of a startled tiger, and gave Theodore Racksole one long piercing glance.

'D—n!' said Rocco, with as pure an Anglo-Saxon accent and intonation as Racksole himself could have accomplished.

The most extraordinary thing about the situation was that at this juncture Theodore Racksole did not know what to say. He was so dumbfounded by the affair, and especially by Rocco's absolute and sublime calm, that both speech and thought failed him.

'I give in,' said Rocco. 'From the moment you entered this cursed hôtel I was afraid of you. I told Jules I was afraid of you. I knew there would be trouble with a man of your kidney, and I was right; confound it! I tell you I give in. I know when I'm beaten. I've got no revolver and no weapons of any kind. I surrender. Do what you like.'

And with that Rocco sat down on a chair. It was magnificently done. Only a truly great man could have done it. Rocco actually kept his dignity.

For answer, Racksole walked slowly into the vast apartment, seized a chair, and, dragging it up to Rocco's chair, sat down opposite to him. Thus they faced each other, their knees almost touching, both in evening dress. On Rocco's right hand was the bed, with the corpse of Reginald Dimmock. On Racksole's right hand, and a little behind him, was the marble washstand, still littered with Rocco's implements. The electric light shone on Rocco's left cheek, leaving the other side of his face in shadow. Racksole tapped him on the knee twice.

'So you're another Englishman masquerading as a foreigner in my hôtel,' Racksole remarked, by way of commencing the interrogation.

'I'm not,' answered Rocco quietly. 'I'm a citizen of the United States.'

'The deuce you are!' Racksole exclaimed.

'Yes, I was born at West Orange, New Jersey, New York State. I call myself an Italian because it was in Italy that I first made a name as a chef—at Rome. It is better for a great chef like me to be a foreigner. Imagine a great chef named Elihu P. Rucker. You can't imagine it. I changed my nationality for the same reason that my friend and colleague, Jules, otherwise Mr Jackson, changed his.'

'So Jules is your friend and colleague, is he?'

'He was, but from this moment he is no longer. I began to disapprove of his methods no less than a week ago, and my disapproval will now take active form.'

'Will it?' said Racksole. 'I calculate it just won't, Mr Elihu P. Rucker, citizen of the United States. Before you are very much older you'll be in the kind hands of the police, and your activities, in no matter what direction, will come to an abrupt conclusion.'

'It is possible,' sighed Rocco.

'In the meantime, I'll ask you one or two questions for my own private satisfaction. You've acknowledged that the game is up, and you may as well answer them with as much candour as you feel yourself capable of. See?'

'I see,' replied Rocco calmly, 'but I guess I can't answer all questions.

I'll do what I can.'

'Well,' said Racksole, clearing his throat, 'what's the scheme all about? Tell me in a word.'

'Not in a thousand words. It isn't my secret, you know.'

'Why was poor little Dimmock poisoned?' The millionaire's voice softened as he looked for an instant at the corpse of the unfortunate young man.

'I don't know,' said Rocco. 'I don't mind informing you that I objected to that part of the business. I wasn't made aware of it till after it was done, and then I tell you it got my dander up considerable.'

'You mean to say you don't know why Dimmock was done to death?'

'I mean to say I couldn't see the sense of it. Of course he—er—died, because he sort of cried off the scheme, having previously taken a share of it. I don't mind saying that much, because you probably guessed it for yourself. But I solemnly state that I have a conscientious objection to murder.'

'Then it was murder?'

'It was a kind of murder,' Rocco admitted. 'Who did it?'

'Unfair question,' said Rocco.

'Who else is in this precious scheme besides Jules and yourself?'

'Don't know, on my honour.'

'Well, then, tell me this. What have you been doing to Dimmock's body?'

'How long were you in that bathroom?' Rocco parried with sublime impudence.

'Don't question me, Mr Rucker,' said Theodore Racksole. 'I feel very much inclined to break your back across my knee. Therefore I advise you not to irritate me. What have you been doing to Dimmock's body?'

'I've been embalming it.'

'Em—balming it.'

'Certainly; Richardson's system of arterial fluid injection, as improved by myself. You weren't aware that I included the art of embalming among my accomplishments. Nevertheless, it is so.'

'But why?' asked Racksole, more mystified than ever. 'Why should you trouble to embalm the poor chap's corpse?'

'Can't you see? Doesn't it strike you? That corpse has to be taken care of.

It contains, or rather, it did contain, very serious evidence against some person or persons unknown to the police. It may be necessary to move it about from place to place. A corpse can't be hidden for long; a corpse betrays itself. One couldn't throw it in the Thames, for it would have been found inside twelve hours. One couldn't bury it—it wasn't safe. The only thing was to keep it handy and movable, ready for emergencies. I needn't inform you that, without embalming, you can't keep a corpse handy and movable for more than four or five days. It's the kind of thing that won't keep. And so it was suggested that I should embalm it, and I did. Mind you, I still objected to the murder, but I couldn't go back on a colleague, you understand. You do understand that, don't you? Well, here you are, and here it is, and that's all.'

Rocco leaned back in his chair as though he had said everything that ought to be said. He closed his eyes to indicate that so far as he was concerned the conversation was also closed. Theodore Racksole stood up.

435

'I hope,' said Rocco, suddenly opening his eyes, 'I hope you'll call in the police without any delay. It's getting late, and I don't like going without my night's rest.'

'Where do you suppose you'll get a night's rest?' Racksole asked.

'In the cells, of course. Haven't I told you I know when I'm beaten. I'm not so blind as not to be able to see that there's at any rate a prima facie case against me. I expect I shall get off with a year or two's imprisonment as accessory after the fact—I think that's what they call it. Anyhow, I shall be in a position to prove that I am not implicated in the murder of this unfortunate nincompoop.' He pointed, with a strange, scornful gesture of his elbow, to the bed. 'And now, shall we go? Everyone is asleep, but there will be a policeman within call of the watchman in the portico. I am at your service. Let us go down together, Mr Racksole. I give you my word to go quietly.'

'Stay a moment,' said Theodore Racksole curtly; 'there is no hurry. It won't do you any harm to forego another hour's sleep, especially as you will have no work to do to-morrow. I have one or two more questions to put to you.'

'Well?' Rocco murmured, with an air of tired resignation, as if to say, 'What must be must be.'

'Where has Dimmock's corpse been during the last three or four days, since he—died?'

'Oh!' answered Rocco, apparently surprised at the simplicity of the question. 'It's been in my room, and one night it was on the roof; once it went out of the hôtel as luggage, but it came back the next day as a case of Demerara sugar. I forget where else it has been, but it's been kept perfectly safe and treated with every consideration.'

'And who contrived all these manoeuvres?' asked Racksole as calmly as he could.

'I did. That is to say, I invented them and I saw that they were carried out. You see, the suspicions of your police obliged me to be particularly spry.'

'And who carried them out?'

'Ah! that would be telling tales. But I don't mind assuring you that my accomplices were innocent accomplices. It is absurdly easy for a man like me to impose on underlings—absurdly easy.'

'What did you intend to do with the corpse ultimately?' Racksole pursued his inquiry with immovable countenance.

'Who knows?' said Rocco, twisting his beautiful moustache. 'That would have depended on several things— on your police, for instance. But probably in the end we should have restored this mortal clay'—again he jerked his elbow—'to the man's sorrowing relatives.'

'Do you know who the relatives are?'

'Certainly. Don't you? If you don't I need only hint that Dimmock had a Prince for his father.'

'It seems to me,' said Racksole, with cold sarcasm, 'that you behaved rather clumsily in choosing this bedroom as the scene of your operations.'

'Not at all,' said Rocco. 'There was no other apartment so suitable in the whole hôtel. Who would have guessed that anything was going on here? It was the very place for me.'

'I guessed,' said Racksole succinctly.

'Yes, you guessed, Mr Racksole. But I had not counted on you. You are the only smart man in the business. You are an American citizen, and I hadn't reckoned to have to deal with that class of person.'

'Apparently I frightened you this afternoon?'

'Not in the least.'

'You were not afraid of a search?'

'I knew that no search was intended. I knew that you were trying to frighten me. You must really credit me with a little sagacity and insight, Mr Racksole. Immediately you began to talk to me in the kitchen this afternoon I felt you were on the track. But I was not frightened. I merely decided that there was no time to be lost—that I must act quickly. I did act quickly, but, it seems, not quickly enough. I grant that your rapidity exceeded mine. Let us go downstairs, I beg.'

Rocco rose and moved towards the door. With an instinctive action Racksole rushed forward and seized him by the shoulder.

'No tricks!' said Racksole. 'You're in my custody and don't forget it.'

Rocco turned on his employer a look of gentle, dignified scorn. 'Have I not informed you,' he said, 'that I have the intention of going quietly?'

Racksole felt almost ashamed for the moment. It flashed across him that a man can be great, even in crime.

'What an ineffable fool you were,' said Racksole, stopping him at the threshold, 'with your talents, your unique talents, to get yourself mixed up in an affair of this kind. You are ruined. And, by Jove! you were a great man in your own line.'

'Mr Racksole,' said Rocco very quickly, 'that is the truest word you have spoken this night. I was a great man in my own line. And I am an ineffable fool. Alas!' He brought his long arms to his sides with a thud.

'Why did you do it?'

'I was fascinated—fascinated by Jules. He, too, is a great man. We had great opportunities, here in the Grand Babylon. It was a great game. It was worth the candle. The prizes were enormous. You would admit these things if you knew the facts. Perhaps some day you will know them, for you are a fairly clever person at getting to the root of a matter. Yes, I was blinded, hypnotized.'

'And now you are ruined.'

'Not ruined, not ruined. Afterwards, in a few years, I shall come up again. A man of genius like me is never ruined till he is dead. Genius is always forgiven. I shall be forgiven. Suppose I am sent to prison. When I emerge I shall be no gaol-bird. I shall be Rocco—the great Rocco. And half the hôtels in Europe will invite me to join them.'

'Let me tell you, as man to man, that you have achieved your own degradation. There is no excuse.'

'I know it,' said Rocco. 'Let us go.'

Racksole was distinctly and notably impressed by this man—by this master spirit to whom he was to have paid a salary at the rate of three thousand pounds a year. He even felt sorry for him. And so, side by side, the captor and the captured, they passed into the vast deserted corridor of the hôtel.

Rocco stopped at the grating of the first lift.

'It will be locked,' said Racksole. 'We must use the stairs to-night.'

'But I have a key. I always carry one,' said Rocco, and he pulled one out of his pocket, and, unfastening the iron screen, pushed it open. Racksole smiled at his readiness and aplomb.

'After you,' said Rocco, bowing in his finest manner, and Racksole stepped into the lift.

With the swiftness of lighting Rocco pushed forward the iron screen, which locked itself automatically. Theodore Racksole was hopelessly a prisoner within the lift, while Rocco stood free in the corridor.

'Good-bye, Mr Racksole,' he remarked suavely, bowing again, lower than before. 'Good-bye: I hate to take a mean advantage of you in this fashion, but really you must allow that you have been very simple. You are a clever man, as I have already said, up to a certain point. It is past that point that my own cleverness comes in. Again, good-bye. After all, I shall have no rest to-night, but perhaps even that will be better that sleeping in a police cell. If you make a great noise you may wake someone and ultimately get released from this lift. But I advise you to compose yourself, and wait till morning. It will be more dignified. For the third time, good-bye.'

And with that Rocco, without hastening, walked down the corridor and so out of sight.

Racksole said never a word. He was too disgusted with himself to speak. He clenched his fists, and put his teeth together, and held his breath. In the silence he could hear the dwindling sound of Rocco's footsteps on the thick carpet.

It was the greatest blow of Racksole's life.

The next morning the high-born guests of the Grand Babylon were aroused by a rumour that by some accident the millionaire proprietor of the hôtel had remained all night locked up in the lift. It was also stated that Rocco had quarrelled with his new master and incontinently left the place. A duchess said that Rocco's departure would mean the ruin of the hôtel, whereupon her husband advised her not to talk nonsense.

As for Racksole, he sent a message for the detective in charge of the Dimmock affair, and bravely told him the happenings of the previous night.

The narration was a decided ordeal to a man of Racksole's temperament.

'A strange story!' commented Detective Marshall, and he could not avoid a smile. 'The climax was unfortunate, but you have certainly got some valuable facts.'

Racksole said nothing.

'I myself have a clue,' added the detective. 'When your message arrived I was just coming up to see you. I want you to accompany me to a certain spot not far from here. Will you come, now, at once?'

'With pleasure,' said Racksole.

At that moment a page entered with a telegram. Racksole opened it read:

'Please come instantly. Nella. Hôtel Wellington, Ostend.'

He looked at his watch.

'I can't come,' he said to the detective. I'm going to Ostend.'

'To Ostend?'

'Yes, now.'

'But really, Mr Racksole,' protested the detective. 'My business is urgent.'

'So's mine,' said Racksole.

In ten minutes he was on his way to Victoria Station.

Chapter Fifteen END OF THE YACHT ADVENTURE

WE must now return to Nella Racksole and Prince Aribert of Posen on board the yacht without a name. The Prince's first business was to make Jules, otherwise Mr Tom Jackson, perfectly secure by means of several pieces of rope. Although Mr Jackson had been stunned into a complete unconsciousness, and there was a contused wound under his ear, no one could say how soon he might not come to himself and get very violent. So the Prince, having tied his arms and legs, made him fast to a stanchion.

'I hope he won't die,' said Nella. 'He looks very white.'

'The Mr Jacksons of this world,' said Prince Aribert sententiously, 'never die till they are hung. By the way, I wonder how it is that no one has interfered with us. Perhaps they are discreetly afraid of my revolver—of your revolver, I mean.'

Both he and Nella glanced up at the imperturbable steersman, who kept the yacht's head straight out to sea. By this time they were about a couple of miles from the Belgian shore.

Addressing him in French, the Prince ordered the sailor to put the yacht about, and make again for Ostend Harbour, but the fellow took no notice whatever of the summons. The Prince raised the revolver, with the idea of frightening the steersman, and then the man began to talk rapidly in a mixture of French and Flemish. He said that he had received Jules' strict orders not to interfere in any way, no matter what might happen on the deck of the yacht. He was the captain of the yacht, and he had to make for a certain English port, the name of which he could not divulge: he was to keep the vessel at full steam ahead under any and all circumstances. He seemed to be a very big, a very strong, and a very determined man, and the Prince was at a loss what course of action to pursue. He asked several more questions, but the only effect of them was to render the man taciturn and ill-humoured.

In vain Prince Aribert explained that Miss Nella Racksole, daughter of millionaire Racksole, had been abducted by Mr Tom Jackson; in vain he flourished the revolver threateningly; the surly but courageous captain said merely that that had nothing to do with him; he had instructions, and he should carry them out. He sarcastically begged to remind his interlocutor that he was the captain of the yacht.

'It won't do to shoot him, I suppose,' said the Prince to Nella. 'I might bore a hole into his leg, or something of that kind.'

'It's rather risky, and rather hard on the poor captain, with his extraordinary sense of duty,' said Nella. 'And, besides, the whole crew might turn on us. No, we must think of something else.'

'I wonder where the crew is,' said the Prince.

Just then Mr Jackson, prone and bound on the deck, showed signs of recovering from his swoon. His eyes opened, and he gazed vacantly around. At length he caught sight of the Prince, who approached him with the revolver well in view.

'It's you, is it?' he murmured faintly. 'What are you doing on board? Who's tied me up like this?'

'See here!' replied the Prince, 'I don't want to have any arguments, but this yacht must return to Ostend at once, where you will be given up to the authorities.'

'Really!' snarled Mr Tom Jackson. 'Shall I!' Then he called out in French to the man at the wheel, 'Hi André! let these two be put off in the dinghy.'

It was a peculiar situation. Certain of nothing but the possession of Nella's revolver, the Prince scarcely knew whether to carry the argument further, and with stronger measures, or to accept the situation with as much dignity as the circumstances would permit.

'Let us take the dinghy,' said Nella; 'we can row ashore in an hour.'

He felt that she was right. To leave the yacht in such a manner seemed somewhat ignominious, and it certainly involved the escape of that profound villain, Mr Thomas Jackson. But what else could be done? The Prince and Nella constituted one party on the vessel; they knew their own strength, but they did not know the

438

strength of their opponents. They held the hostile ringleader bound and captive, but this man had proved himself capable of giving orders, and even to gag him would not help them if the captain of the yacht persisted in his obstinate course. Moreover, there was a distinct objection to promiscuous shooting. The Prince felt that there was no knowing how promiscuous shooting might end.

'We will take the dinghy,' said the Prince quickly, to the captain.

A bell rang below, and a sailor and the Negro boy appeared on deck. The pulsations of the screw grew less rapid. The yacht stopped. The dinghy was lowered. As the Prince and Nella prepared to descend into the little cock-boat Mr Tom Jackson addressed Nella, all bound as he lay.

'Good-bye,' he said, 'I shall see you again, never fear.'.

In another moment they were in the dinghy, and the dinghy was adrift. The yacht's screw churned the water, and the beautiful vessel slipped away from them. As it receded a figure appeared at the stem. It was Mr Thomas Jackson.

He had been released by his minions. He held a white handkerchief to his ear, and offered a calm, enigmatic smile to the two forlorn but victorious occupants of the dinghy. Jules had been defeated for once in his life; or perhaps it would be more just to say that he had been out-manoeuvred. Men like Jules are incapable of being defeated. It was characteristic of his luck that now, in the very hour when he had been caught red-handed in a serious crime against society, he should be effecting a leisurely escape—an escape which left no clue behind.

The sea was utterly calm and blue in the morning sun. The dinghy rocked itself lazily in the swell of the yacht's departure. As the mist cleared away the outline of the shore became more distinct, and it appeared as if Ostend was distant scarcely a cable's length. The white dome of the great Kursaal glittered in the pale turquoise sky, and the smoke of steamers in the harbour could be plainly distinguished. On the offing was a crowd of brown-sailed fishing luggers returning with the night's catch. The many-hued bathing-vans could be counted on the distant beach. Everything seemed perfectly normal. It was difficult for either Nella or her companion to realize that anything extraordinary had happened within the last hour. Yet there was the yacht, not a mile off, to prove to them that something very extraordinary had, in fact, happened. The yacht was no vision, nor was that sinister watching figure at its stern a vision, either.

'I suppose Jules was too surprised and too feeble to inquire how I came to be on board his yacht,' said the Prince, taking the oars.

'Oh! How did you?' asked Nella, her face lighting up. 'Really, I had almost forgotten that part of the affair.'

'I must begin at the beginning and it will take some time,' answered the Prince. 'Had we not better postpone the recital till we get ashore?'

'I will row and you shall talk,' said Nella. 'I want to know now.'

He smiled happily at her, but gently declined to yield up the oars.

'Is it not sufficient that I am here?' he said.

'It is sufficient, yes,' she replied, 'but I want to know.'

With a long, easy stroke he was pulling the dinghy shorewards. She sat in the stern-sheets.

'There is no rudder,' he remarked, 'so you must direct me. Keep the boat's head on the lighthouse. The tide seems to be running in strongly; that will help us. The people on shore will think that we have only been for a little early morning excursion.'

'Will you kindly tell me how it came about that you were able to save my life, Prince?' she said.

'Save your life, Miss Racksole? I didn't save your life; I merely knocked a man down.'

'You saved my life,' she repeated. 'That villain would have stopped at nothing. I saw it in his eye.'

'Then you were a brave woman, for you showed no fear of death.' His admiring gaze rested full on her. For a moment the oars ceased to move.

She gave a gesture of impatience.

'It happened that I saw you last night in your carriage,' he said. 'The fact is, I had not had the audacity to go to Berlin with my story. I stopped in Ostend to see whether I could do a little detective work on my own account. It was a piece of good luck that I saw you. I followed the carriage as quickly as I could, and I just caught a glimpse of you as you entered that awful house. I knew that Jules had something to do with that house. I guessed what you were doing. I was afraid for you. Fortunately I had surveyed the house pretty thoroughly. There is an entrance to it at the back, from a narrow lane. I made my way there. I got into the yard at the back, and I stood under the window of the room where you had the interview with Miss Spencer. I heard everything that was said. It was a courageous enterprise on your part to follow Miss Spencer from the Grand Babylon to Ostend. Well, I dared not force an entrance, lest I might precipitate matters too suddenly, and involve both of us in a difficulty. I merely kept watch. Ah, Miss Racksole! you were magnificent with Miss Spencer; as I say,

I could hear every word, for the window was slightly open. I felt that you needed no assistance from me. And then she cheated you with a trick, and the revolver came flying through the window. I picked it up, I thought it would probably be useful. There was a silence. I did not guess at first that you had fainted. I thought that you had escaped. When I found out the truth it was too late for me to intervene. There were two men, both desperate, besides Miss Spencer—'

'Who was the other man?' asked Nella.

'I do not know. It was dark. They drove away with you to the harbour. Again I followed. I saw them carry you on board. Before the yacht weighed anchor I managed to climb unobserved into the dinghy. I lay down full length in it, and no one suspected that I was there. I think you know the rest.'

'Was the yacht all ready for sea?'

'The yacht was all ready for sea. The captain fellow was on the bridge, and steam was up.'

'Then they expected me! How could that be?'

'They expected some one. I do not think they expected you.'

'Did the second man go on board?'

'He helped to carry you along the gangway, but he came back again to the carriage. He was the driver.'

'And no one else saw the business?'

'The quay was deserted. You see, the last steamer had arrived for the night.'

There was a brief silence, and then Nella ejaculated, under her breath.

'Truly, it is a wonderful world!'

And it was a wonderful world for them, though scarcely perhaps, in the sense which Nella Racksole had intended. They had just emerged from a highly disconcerting experience. Among other minor inconveniences, they had had no breakfast. They were out in the sea in a tiny boat. Neither of them knew what the day might bring forth. The man, at least, had the most serious anxieties for the safety of his Royal nephew. And yet— and yet—neither of them wished that that voyage of the little boat on the summer tide should come to an end. Each, perhaps unconsciously, had a vague desire that it might last for ever, he lazily pulling, she directing his course at intervals by a movement of her distractingly pretty head. How was this condition of affairs to be explained? Well, they were both young; they both had superb health, and all the ardour of youth; and—they were together.

The boat was very small indeed; her face was scarcely a yard from his. She, in his eyes, surrounded by the glamour of beauty and vast wealth; he, in her eyes, surrounded by the glamour of masculine intrepidity and the brilliance of a throne.

But all voyages come to an end, either at the shore or at the bottom of the sea, and at length the dinghy passed between the stone jetties of the harbour. The Prince rowed to the nearest steps, tied up the boat, and they landed. It was six o'clock in the morning, and a day of gorgeous sunlight had opened. Few people were about at that early hour.

'And now, what next?' said the Prince. 'I must take you to an hôtel.'

'I am in your hands,' she acquiesced, with a smile which sent the blood racing through his veins. He perceived now that she was tired and overcome, suffering from a sudden and natural reaction.

At the Hôtel Wellington the Prince told the sleepy door-keeper that they had come by the early train from Bruges, and wanted breakfast at once. It was absurdly early, but a common English sovereign will work wonders in any Belgian hôtel, and in a very brief time Nella and the Prince were breakfasting on the verandah of the hôtel upon chocolate that had been specially and hastily brewed for them.

'I never tasted such excellent chocolate,' claimed the Prince.

The statement was wildly untrue, for the Hôtel Wellington is not celebrated for its chocolate. Nevertheless Nella replied enthusiastically, 'Nor I.'

Then there was a silence, and Nella, feeling possibly that she had been too ecstatic, remarked in a very matter-of-fact tone: 'I must telegraph to Papa instantly.'

Thus it was that Theodore Racksole received the telegram which drew him away from Detective Marshall.

Chapter Sixteen THE WOMAN WITH THE RED HAT

'THERE is one thing, Prince, that we have just got to settle straight off,' said Theodore Racksole.

They were all three seated—Racksole, his daughter, and Prince Aribert—round a dinner table in a private room at the Hôtel Wellington. Racksole had duly arrived by the afternoon boat, and had been met on the quay by the other two. They had dined early, and Racksole had heard the full story of the adventures by sea and land of Nella and the Prince. As to his own adventure of the previous night he said very little, merely explaining, with as little detail as possible, that Dimmock's body had come to light.

'What is that?' asked the Prince, in answer to Racksole's remark.

'We have got to settle whether we shall tell the police at once all that has occurred, or whether we shall proceed on our own responsibility. There can be no doubt as to which course we ought to pursue. Every consideration of prudence points to the advisability of taking the police into our confidence, and leaving the matter entirely in their hands.'

'Oh, Papa!' Nella burst out in her pouting, impulsive way. 'You surely can't think of such a thing. Why, the fun has only just begun.'

'Do you call last night fun?' questioned Racksole, gazing at her solemnly.

'Yes, I do,' she said promptly. 'Now.'

'Well, I don't,' was the millionaire's laconic response; but perhaps he was thinking of his own situation in the lift.

'Do you not think we might investigate a little further,' said the Prince judiciously, as he cracked a walnut, 'just a little further—and then, if we fail to accomplish anything, there would still be ample opportunity to consult the police?'

'How do you suggest we should begin?' asked Racksole.

'Well, there is the house which Miss Racksole so intrepidly entered last evening'—he gave her the homage of an admiring glance; 'you and I, Mr Racksole, might examine that abode in detail.'

'To-night?'

'Certainly. We might do something.'

'We might do too much.'

'For example?'

'We might shoot someone, or get ourselves mistaken for burglars. If we outstepped the law, it would be no excuse for us that we had been acting in a good cause.'

'True,' said the Prince. 'Nevertheless—' He stopped.

'Nevertheless you have a distaste for bringing the police into the business.

You want the hunt all to yourself. You are on fire with the ardour of the chase. Is not that it? Accept the advice of an older man, Prince, and sleep on this affair. I have little fancy for nocturnal escapades two nights together. As for you, Nella, off with you to bed. The Prince and I will have a yarn over such fluids as can be obtained in this hole.'

'Papa,' she said, 'you are perfectly horrid to-night.'

'Perhaps I am,' he said. 'Decidedly I am very cross with you for coming over here all alone. It was monstrous. If I didn't happen to be the most foolish of parents—There! Good-night. It's nine o'clock. The Prince, I am sure, will excuse you.'

If Nella had not really been very tired Prince Aribert might have been the witness of a good-natured but stubborn conflict between the millionaire and his spirited offspring. As it was, Nella departed with surprising docility, and the two men were left alone.

'Now,' said Racksole suddenly, changing his tone, 'I fancy that after all I'm your man for a little amateur investigation to-night. And, if I must speak the exact truth, I think that to sleep on this affair would be about the very worst thing we could do. But I was anxious to keep Nella out of harm's way at any rate till to-morrow. She is a very difficult creature to manage, Prince, and I may warn you,' he laughed grimly, 'that if we do succeed in doing anything to-night we shall catch it from her ladyship in the morning. Are you ready to take that risk?'

'I am,' the Prince smiled. 'But Miss Racksole is a young lady of quite remarkable nerve.'

'She is,' said Racksole drily. 'I wish sometimes she had less.'

'I have the highest admiration for Miss Racksole,' said the Prince, and he looked Miss Racksole's father full in the face.

'You honour us, Prince,' Racksole observed. 'Let us come to business. Am I right in assuming that you have a reason for keeping the police out of this business, if it can possibly be done?'

'Yes,' said the Prince, and his brow clouded. 'I am very much afraid that my poor nephew has involved himself in some scrape that he would wish not to be divulged.'

'Then you do not believe that he is the victim of foul play?'

'I do not.'

'And the reason, if I may ask it?'

'Mr Racksole, we speak in confidence—is it not so? Some years ago my foolish nephew had an affair—an affair with a feminine star of the Berlin stage. For anything I know, the lady may have been the very pattern of her sex, but where a reigning Prince is concerned scandal cannot be avoided in such a matter. I had thought that the affair was quite at an end, since my nephew's betrothal to Princess Anna of Eckstein-Schwartzburg is shortly to be announced. But yesterday I saw the lady to whom I have referred driving on the Digue. The coincidence of her presence here with my nephew's disappearance is too extraordinary to be disregarded.'

'But how does this theory square with the murder of Reginald Dimmock?'

'It does not square with it. My idea is that the murder of poor Dimmock and the disappearance of my nephew are entirely unconnected—unless, indeed, this Berlin actress is playing into the hands of the murderers. I had not thought of that.'

'Then what do you propose to do to-night?'

'I propose to enter the house which Miss Racksole entered last night and to find out something definite.'

'I concur,' said Racksole. 'I shall heartily enjoy it. But let me tell you, Prince, and pardon me for speaking bluntly, your surmise is incorrect. I would wager a hundred thousand dollars that Prince Eugen has been kidnapped.'

'What grounds have you for being so sure?'

'Ah! said Racksole, 'that is a long story. Let me begin by asking you this.

Are you aware that your nephew, Prince Eugen, owes a million of money?'

'A million of money!' cried Prince Aribert astonished. 'It is impossible!'

'Nevertheless, he does,' said Racksole calmly. Then he told him all he had learnt from Mr Sampson Levi.

'What have you to say to that?' Racksole ended. Prince Aribert made no reply.

'What have you to say to that?' Racksole insisted.

'Merely that Eugen is ruined, even if he is alive.'

'Not at all,' Racksole returned with cheerfulness. 'Not at all. We shall see about that. The special thing that I want to know just now from you is this:

Has any previous application ever been made for the hand of the Princess Anna?'

'Yes. Last year. The King of Bosnia sued for it, but his proposal was declined.'

'Why?'

'Because my nephew was considered to be a more suitable match for her.'

'Not because the personal character of his Majesty of Bosnia is scarcely of the brightest?'

'No. Unfortunately it is usually impossible to consider questions of personal character when a royal match is concerned.'

'Then, if for any reason the marriage of Princess Anna with your nephew was frustrated, the King of Bosnia would have a fair chance in that quarter?'

'He would. The political aspect of things would be perfectly satisfactory.'

'Thanks!' said Racksole. 'I will wager another hundred thousand dollars that someone in Bosnia—I don't accuse the King himself—is at the bottom of this business. The methods of Balkan politicians have always been half-Oriental. Let us go.'

'Where?'

'To this precious house of Nella's adventure.'

'But surely it is too early?'

'So it is,' said Racksole, 'and we shall want a few things, too. For instance, a dark lantern. I think I will go out and forage for a lantern.'

'And a revolver?' suggested Prince Aribert.

'Does it mean revolvers?' The millionaire laughed. 'It may come to that.' 'Here you are, then, my friend,' said Racksole, and he pulled one out of his hip pocket. 'And yours?'

'I,' said the Prince, 'I have your daughter's.'

'The deuce you have!' murmured Racksole to himself.

It was then half past nine. They decided that it would be impolitic to begin their operations till after midnight. There were three hours to spare.

'Let us go and see the gambling,' Racksole suggested. 'We might encounter the Berlin lady.'

The suggestion, in the first instance, was not made seriously, but it appeared to both men that they might do worse than spend the intervening time in the gorgeous saloon of the Kursaal, where, in the season, as much money is won and lost as at Monte Carlo. It was striking ten o'clock as they entered the rooms. There was a large company present—a company which included some of the most notorious persons in Europe. In that multifarious assemblage all were equal. The electric light shone coldly and impartially on the just and on the unjust, on the fool and the knave, on the European and the Asiatic. As usual, women monopolized the best places at the tables.

The scene was familiar enough to Prince Aribert, who had witnessed it frequently at Monaco, but Theodore Racksole had never before entered any European gaming palace; he had only the haziest idea of the rules of play, and he was at once interested. For some time they watched the play at the table which happened to be nearest to them. Racksole never moved his lips.

With his eyes glued on the table, and ears open for every remark, of the players and the croupier, he took his first lesson in roulette. He saw a mere youth win fifteen thousand francs, which were stolen in the most barefaced manner by a rouged girl scarcely older than the youth; he saw two old gamesters stake their coins, and lose, and walk quietly out of the place; he saw the bank win fifty thousand francs at a single turn.

'This is rather good fun,' he said at length, 'but the stakes are too small to make it really exciting. I'll try my luck, just for the experience. I'm bound to win.'

'Why?' asked the Prince.

'Because I always do, in games of chance,' Racksole answered with gay confidence. 'It is my fate. Then to-night, you must remember, I shall be a beginner, and you know the tyro's luck.'

In ten minutes the croupier of that table was obliged to suspend operations pending the arrival of a further supply of coin.

'What did I tell you?' said Racksole, leading the way to another table further up the room. A hundred curious glances went after him. One old woman, whose gay attire suggested a false youthfulness, begged him in French to stake a five-franc piece for her. She offered him the coin. He took it, and gave her a hundred-franc note in exchange. She clutched the crisp rustling paper, and with hysterical haste scuttled back to her own table.

At the second table there was a considerable air of excitement. In the forefront of the players was a woman in a low-cut evening dress of black silk and a large red picture hat. Her age appeared to be about twenty-eight; she had dark eyes, full lips, and a distinctly Jewish nose. She was handsome, but her beauty was of that forbidding, sinister order which is often called Junoesque. This woman was the centre of attraction. People said to each other that she had won a hundred and sixty thousand francs that day at the table.

'You were right,' Prince Aribert whispered to Theodore Racksole; 'that is the Berlin lady.'

'The deuce she is! Has she seen you? Will she know you?'

'She would probably know me, but she hasn't looked up yet.'

'Keep behind her, then. I propose to find her a little occupation.' By dint of a carefully-exercised diplomacy, Racksole manoeuvred himself into a seat opposite to the lady in the red hat. The fame of his success at the other table had followed him, and people regarded him as a serious and formidable player. In the first turn the lady put a thousand francs on double zero; Racksole put a hundred on number nineteen and a thousand on the odd numbers.

Nineteen won. Racksole received four thousand four hundred francs. Nine times in succession Racksole backed number nineteen and the odd numbers; nine times the lady backed double zero. Nine times Racksole won and the lady lost. The other players, perceiving that the affair had resolved itself into a duel, stood back for the most part and watched those two. Prince Aribert never stirred from his position behind the great red hat. The game continued. Racksole lost trifles from time to time, but ninety-nine hundredths of the luck was with him. As an English spectator at the table remarked, 'he couldn't do wrong.' When midnight struck the lady in the red hat was reduced to a thousand francs. Then she fell into a winning vein for half an hour, but at one o'clock her resources were exhausted. Of the hundred and sixty thousand francs which she was reputed to have had early in the evening, Racksole held about ninety thousand, and the bank had the rest.

It was a calamity for the Juno of the red hat. She jumped up, stamped her foot, and hurried from the room. At a discreet distance Racksole and the Prince pursued her.

'It might be well to ascertain her movements,' said Racksole.

Outside, in the glare of the great arc lights, and within sound of the surf which beats always at the very foot of the Kursaal, the Juno of the red hat summoned a fiacre and drove rapidly away. Racksole and the Prince took an open carriage and started in pursuit. They had not, however, travelled more than half a mile when Prince Aribert stopped the carriage, and, bidding Racksole get out, paid the driver and dismissed him.

'I feel sure I know where she is going,' he explained, 'and it will be better for us to follow on foot.'

'You mean she is making for the scene of last night's affair?' said Racksole.

'Exactly. We shall—what you call, kill two birds with one stone.'

Prince Aribert's guess was correct. The lady's carriage stopped in front of the house where Nella Racksole and Miss Spencer had had their interview on the previous evening, and the lady vanished into the building just as the two men appeared at the end of the street. Instead of proceeding along that street, the Prince led Racksole to the lane which gave on to the backs of the houses, and he counted the houses as they went up the lane. In a few minutes they had burglariously climbed over a wall, and crept, with infinite caution, up a long, narrow piece of ground—half garden, half paved yard, till they crouched under a window—a window which was shielded by curtains, but which had been left open a little.

'Listen,' said the Prince in his lightest whisper, 'they are talking.'

'Who?'

'The Berlin lady and Miss Spencer. I'm sure it's Miss Spencer's voice.'

Racksole boldly pushed the french window a little wider open, and put his ear to the aperture, through which came a beam of yellow light.

'Take my place,' he whispered to the Prince, 'they're talking German. You'll understand better.'

Silently they exchanged places under the window, and the Prince listened intently.

'Then you refuse?' Miss Spencer's visitor was saying.

There was no answer from Miss Spencer.

'Not even a thousand francs? I tell you I've lost the whole twenty-five thousand.'

Again no answer.

'Then I'll tell the whole story,' the lady went on, in an angry rush of words. 'I did what I promised to do. I enticed him here, and you've got him safe in your vile cellar, poor little man, and you won't give me a paltry thousand francs.'

'You have already had your price.' The words were Miss Spencer's. They fell cold and calm on the night air.

'I want another thousand.'

'I haven't it.'

'Then we'll see.'

Prince Aribert heard a rustle of flying skirts; then another movement—a door banged, and the beam of light through the aperture of the window suddenly disappeared. He pushed the window wide open. The room was in darkness, and apparently empty.

'Now for that lantern of yours,' he said eagerly to Theodore Racksole, after he had translated to him the conversation of the two women, Racksole produced the dark lantern from the capacious pocket of his dust coat, and lighted it. The ray flashed about the ground.

'What is it?' exclaimed Prince Aribert with a swift cry, pointing to the ground. The lantern threw its light on a perpendicular grating at their feet, through which could be discerned a cellar. They both knelt down, and peered into the subterranean chamber. On a broken chair a young man sat listlessly with closed eyes, his head leaning heavily forward on his chest.

In the feeble light of the lantern he had the livid and ghastly appearance of a corpse.

'Who can it be?' said Racksole.

'It is Eugen,' was the Prince's low answer.

Chapter Seventeen THE RELEASE OF PRINCE EUGEN

'EUGEN,' Prince Aribert called softly. At the sound of his own name the young man in the cellar feebly raised his head and stared up at the grating which separated him from his two rescuers. But his features showed no recognition. He gazed in an aimless, vague, silly manner for a few seconds, his eyes blinking under the glare of the lantern, and then his head slowly drooped again on to his chest. He was dressed in a dark tweed travelling suit, and Racksole observed that one sleeve—the left—was torn across the upper part of the cuff, and that there were stains of dirt on the left shoulder. A soiled linen collar, which had lost all its starch and was half unbuttoned, partially encircled the captive's neck; his brown boots were unlaced; a cap, a handkerchief, a portion of a watch-chain, and a few gold coins lay on the floor. Racksole flashed the lantern into the corners of the cellar, but he could discover no other furniture except the chair on which the Hereditary Prince of Posen sat and a small deal table on which were a plate and a cup.

'Eugen,' cried Prince Aribert once more, but this time his forlorn nephew made no response whatever, and then Aribert added in a low voice to Racksole: 'Perhaps he cannot see us clearly.'

'But he must surely recognize your voice,' said Racksole, in a hard, gloomy tone. There was a pause, and the two men above ground looked at each other hesitatingly. Each knew that they must enter that cellar and get Prince Eugen out of it, and each was somehow afraid to take the next step.

'Thank God he is not dead!' said Aribert.

'He may be worse than dead!' Racksole replied.

'Worse than—What do you mean?'

'I mean—he may be mad.'

'Come,' Aribert almost shouted, with a sudden access of energy—a wild impulse for action. And, snatching the lantern from Racksole, he rushed into the dark room where they had heard the conversation of Miss Spencer and the lady in the red hat. For a moment Racksole did not stir from the threshold of the window. 'Come,' Prince Aribert repeated, and there was an imperious command in his utterance. 'What are you afraid of?'

'I don't know,' said Racksole, feeling stupid and queer; 'I don't know.'

Then he marched heavily after Prince Aribert into the room. On the mantelpiece were a couple of candles which had been blown out, and in a mechanical, unthinking way, Racksole lighted them, and the two men glanced round the room. It presented no peculiar features: it was just an ordinary room, rather small, rather mean, rather shabby, with an ugly wallpaper and ugly pictures in ugly frames. Thrown over a chair was a man's evening-dress jacket. The door was closed. Prince Aribert turned the knob, but he could not open it.

'It's locked,' he said. 'Evidently they know we're here.'

'Nonsense,' said Racksole brusquely; 'how can they know?' And, taking hold of the knob, he violently shook the door, and it opened. 'I told you it wasn't locked,' he added, and this small success of opening the door seemed to steady the man. It was a curious psychological effect, this terrorizing (for it amounted to that) of two courageous full-grown men by the mere apparition of a helpless creature in a cellar. Gradually they both recovered from it. The next moment they were out in the passage which led to the front door of the house. The front door stood open. They looked into the street, up and down, but there was not a soul in sight. The street, lighted by three gas-lamps only, seemed strangely sinister and mysterious.

'She has gone, that's clear,' said Racksole, meaning the woman with the red hat.

'And Miss Spencer after her, do you think?' questioned Aribert.

'No. She would stay. She would never dare to leave. Let us find the cellar steps.'

The cellar steps were happily not difficult to discover, for in moving a pace backwards Prince Aribert had a narrow escape of precipitating himself to the bottom of them. The lantern showed that they were built on a curve.

Silently Racksole resumed possession of the lantern and went first, the Prince close behind him. At the foot was a short passage, and in this passage crouched the figure of a woman. Her eyes threw back the rays of the lantern, shining like a cat's at midnight. Then, as the men went nearer, they saw that it was Miss Spencer who barred their way. She seemed half to kneel on the stone floor, and in one hand she held what at first appeared to be a dagger, but which proved to be nothing more romantic than a rather long bread-knife.

'I heard you, I heard you,' she exclaimed. 'Get back; you mustn't come here.'

There was a desperate and dangerous look on her face, and her form shook with scarcely controlled passionate energy.

'Now see here, Miss Spencer,' Racksole said calmly, 'I guess we've had enough of this fandango. You'd better get up and clear out, or we'll just have to drag you off.'

He went calmly up to her, the lantern in his hand. Without another word she struck the knife into his arm, and the lantern fell extinguished. Racksole gave a cry, rather of angry surprise than of pain, and retreated a few steps. In the darkness they could still perceive the glint of her eyes.

'I told you you mustn't come here,' the woman said. 'Now get back.'

Racksole positively laughed. It was a queer laugh, but he laughed, and he could not help it. The idea of this woman, this bureau clerk, stopping his progress and that of Prince Aribert by means of a bread-knife aroused his sense of humour. He struck a match, relighted the candle, and faced Miss Spencer once more.

'I'll do it again,' she said, with a note of hard resolve.

'Oh, no, you won't, my girl,' said Racksole; and he pulled out his revolver, cocked it, raised his hand.

'Put down that plaything of yours,' he said firmly.

'No,' she answered.

'I shall shoot.'

She pressed her lips together.

'I shall shoot,' he repeated. 'One—two—three.'

Bang, bang! He had fired twice, purposely missing her. Miss Spencer never blenched. Racksole was tremendously surprised—and he would have been a thousandfold more surprised could he have contrasted her behaviour now with her abject terror on the previous evening when Nella had threatened her.

'You've got a bit of pluck,' he said, 'but it won't help you. Why won't you let us pass?'

As a matter of fact, pluck was just what she had not, really; she had merely subordinated one terror to another. She was desperately afraid of Racksole's revolver, but she was much more afraid of something else.

'Why won't you let us pass?'

'I daren't,' she said, with a plaintive tremor; 'Tom put me in charge.'

That was all. The men could see tears running down her poor wrinkled face.

Theodore Racksole began to take off his light overcoat.

'I see I must take my coat off to you,' he said, and he almost smiled. Then, with a quick movement, he threw the coat over Miss Spencer's head and flew at her, seizing both her arms, while Prince Aribert assisted.

Her struggles ceased—she was beaten.

'That's all right,' said Racksole: 'I could never have used that revolver—to mean business with it, of course.'

They carried her, unresisting, upstairs and on to the upper floor, where they locked her in a bedroom. She lay in the bed as if exhausted.

'Now for my poor Eugen,' said Prince Aribert.

'Don't you think we'd better search the house first?' Racksole suggested; 'it will be safer to know just how we stand. We can't afford any ambushes or things of that kind, you know.'

The Prince agreed, and they searched the house from top to bottom, but found no one. Then, having locked the front door and the french window of the sitting-room, they proceeded again to the cellar.

Here a new obstacle confronted them. The cellar door was, of course, locked; there was no sign of a key, and it appeared to be a heavy door. They were compelled to return to the bedroom where Miss Spencer was incarcerated, in order to demand the key of the cellar from her. She still lay without movement on the bed.

'Tom's got it,' she replied, faintly, to their question: 'Tom's got it, I swear to you. He took it for safety.'

'Then how do you feed your prisoner?' Racksole asked sharply.

'Through the grating,' she answered.

Both men shuddered. They felt she was speaking the truth. For the third time they went to the cellar door. In vain Racksole thrust himself against it; he could do no more than shake it.

'Let's try both together,' said Prince Aribert. 'Now!' There was a crack.

'Again,' said Prince Aribert. There was another crack, and then the upper hinge gave way. The rest was easy. Over the wreck of the door they entered Prince Eugen's prison.

The captive still sat on his chair. The terrific noise and bustle of breaking down the door seemed not to have aroused him from his lethargy, but when Prince Aribert spoke to him in German he looked at his uncle.

'Will you not come with us, Eugen?' said Prince Aribert; 'you needn't stay here any longer, you know.'

'Leave me alone,' was the strange reply; 'leave me alone. What do you want?'

'We are here to get you out of this scrape,' said Aribert gently. Racksole stood aside.

'Who is that fellow?' said Eugen sharply.

'That is my friend Mr Racksole, an Englishman—or rather, I should say, an American—to whom we owe a great deal. Come and have supper, Eugen.'

'I won't,' answered Eugen doggedly. 'I'm waiting here for her. You didn't think anyone had kept me here, did you, against my will? I tell you I'm waiting for her. She said she'd come.'

'Who is she?' Aribert asked, humouring him.

'She! Why, you know! I forgot, of course, you don't know. You mustn't ask.

Don't pry, Uncle Aribert. She was wearing a red hat.'

'I'll take you to her, my dear Eugen.' Prince Aribert put his hands on the other's shoulder, but Eugen shook him off violently, stood up, and then sat down again.

Aribert looked at Racksole, and they both looked at Prince Eugen. The latter's face was flushed, and Racksole observed that the left pupil was more dilated than the right. The man started, muttered odd, fragmentary scraps of sentences, now grumbling, now whining.

'His mind is unhinged,' Racksole whispered in English.

'Hush!' said Prince Aribert. 'He understands English.' But Prince Eugen took no notice of the brief colloquy.

'We had better get him upstairs, somehow,' said Racksole.

'Yes,' Aribert assented. 'Eugen, the lady with the red hat, the lady you are waiting for, is upstairs. She has sent us down to ask you to come up. Won't you come?'

'Himmel!' the poor fellow exclaimed, with a kind of weak anger. 'Why did you not say this before?'

He rose, staggered towards Aribert, and fell headlong on the floor. He had swooned. The two men raised him, carried him up the stone steps, and laid him with infinite care on a sofa. He lay, breathing queerly through the nostrils, his eyes closed, his fingers contracted; every now and then a convulsion ran through his frame.

'One of us must fetch a doctor,' said Prince Aribert.

'I will,' said Racksole. At that moment there was a quick, curt rap on the french window, and both Racksole and the Prince glanced round startled. A girl's face was pressed against the large window-pane. It was Nella's. Racksole unfastened the catch, and she entered.

'I have found you,' she said lightly; 'you might have told me. I couldn't sleep. I inquired from the hôtel-folks if you had retired, and they said no; so I slipped out. I guessed where you were.' Racksole interrupted her with a question as to what she meant by this escapade, but she stopped him with a careless gesture. 'What's this?' She pointed to the form on the sofa.

'That is my nephew, Prince Eugen,' said Aribert.

'Hurt?' she inquired coldly. 'I hope not.'

'He is ill,' said Racksole, 'his brain is turned.'

Nella began to examine the unconscious Prince with the expert movements of a girl who had passed through the best hospital course to be obtained in New York.

'He has got brain fever,' she said. 'That is all, but it will be enough. Do you know if there is a bed anywhere in this remarkable house?'

Chapter Eighteen IN THE NIGHT-TIME

'HE must on no account be moved,' said the dark little Belgian doctor, whose eyes seemed to peer so quizzically through his spectacles; and he said it with much positiveness.

That pronouncement rather settled their plans for them. It was certainly a professional triumph for Nella, who, previous to the doctor's arrival, had told them the very same thing. Considerable argument had passed before the doctor was sent for. Prince Aribert was for keeping the whole affair a deep secret among their three selves. Theodore Racksole agreed so far, but he suggested further that at no matter what risk they should transport the patient over to England at once. Racksole had an idea that he should feel safer in that hôtel of his, and better able to deal with any situation that might arise. Nella scorned the idea. In her quality of an amateur nurse, she assured them that Prince Eugen was much more seriously ill than either of them suspected, and she urged that they should take absolute possession of the house, and keep possession till Prince Eugen was convalescent.

'But what about the Spencer female?' Racksole had said.

'Keep her where she is. Keep her a prisoner. And hold the house against all comers. If Jules should come back, simply defy him to enter—that is all.

There are two of you, so you must keep an eye on the former occupiers, if they return, and on Miss Spencer, while I nurse the patient. But first, you must send for a doctor.'

'Doctor!' Prince Aribert had said, alarmed. 'Will it not be necessary to make some awkward explanation to the doctor?'

'Not at all!' she replied. 'Why should it be? In a place like Ostend doctors are far too discreet to ask questions; they see too much to retain their curiosity. Besides, do you want your nephew to die?'

Both the men were somewhat taken aback by the girl's sagacious grasp of the situation, and it came about that they began to obey her like subordinates.

She told her father to sally forth in search of a doctor, and he went. She gave Prince Aribert certain other orders, and he promptly executed them.

By the evening of the following day, everything was going smoothly. The doctor came and departed several times, and sent medicine, and seemed fairly optimistic as to the issue of the illness. An old woman had been induced to come in and cook and clean. Miss Spencer was kept out of sight on the attic floor, pending some decision as to what to do with her. And no one outside the house had asked any questions. The inhabitants of that particular street must have been accustomed to strange behaviour on the part of their neighbours, unaccountable appearances and disappearances, strange flittings and arrivals. This strong-minded and active trio—Racksole, Nella, and Prince Aribert—might have been the lawful and accustomed tenants of the house, for any outward evidence to the contrary.

On the afternoon of the third day Prince Eugen was distinctly and seriously worse. Nella had sat up with him the previous night and throughout the day.

Her father had spent the morning at the hôtel, and Prince Aribert had kept watch. The two men were never absent from the house at the same time, and one of them always did duty as sentinel at night. On this afternoon Prince Aribert and Nella sat together in the patient's bedroom. The doctor had just left. Theodore Racksole was downstairs reading the New York Herald. The Prince and Nella were near the window, which looked on to the back-garden.

It was a queer shabby little bedroom to shelter the august body of a European personage like Prince Eugen of Posen. Curiously enough, both Nella and her father, ardent democrats though they were, had been somehow impressed by the royalty and importance of the fever-stricken Prince—impressed as they had never been by Aribert. They had both felt that here, under their care, was a species of individuality quite new to them, and different from anything they had previously encountered. Even the gestures and tones of his delirium had an air of abrupt yet condescending command—an imposing mixture of suavity and haughtiness. As for Nella, she had been first struck by the beautiful 'E' over a crown on the sleeves of his linen, and by the signet ring on his pale, emaciated hand. After all, these trifling outward signs are at least as effective as others of deeper but less obtrusive significance. The Racksoles, too, duly marked the attitude of Prince Aribert to his nephew: it was at once paternal and reverential; it disclosed clearly that Prince Aribert continued, in spite of everything, to regard his nephew as his sovereign lord and master, as a being surrounded by a natural and inevitable pomp and awe. This attitude, at the beginning, seemed false and unreal to the Americans; it seemed to them to be assumed; but gradually they came to perceive that they were mistaken, and that though America might have cast out 'the monarchial superstition', nevertheless that 'superstition' had vigorously survived in another part of the world.

'You and Mr Racksole have been extraordinarily kind to me,' said Prince Aribert very quietly, after the two had sat some time in silence.

'Why? How?' she asked unaffectedly. 'We are interested in this affair ourselves, you know. It began at our hôtel—you mustn't forget that, Prince.'

'I don't,' he said. 'I forget nothing. But I cannot help feeling that I have led you into a strange entanglement. Why should you and Mr Racksole be here—you who are supposed to be on a holiday!—hiding in a strange house in a foreign country, subject to all sorts of annoyances and all sorts of risks, simply because I am anxious to avoid scandal, to avoid any sort of talk, in connection with my misguided nephew? It is nothing to you that the Hereditary Prince of Posen should be liable to a public disgrace. What will it matter to you if the throne of Posen becomes the laughing-stock of Europe?'

'I really don't know, Prince,' Nella smiled roguishly. 'But we Americans have, a habit of going right through with anything we have begun.'

'Ah!' he said, 'who knows how this thing will end? All our trouble, our anxieties, our watchfulness, may come to nothing. I tell you that when I see Eugen lying there, and think that we cannot learn his story until he recovers, I am ready to go mad. We might be arranging things, making matters smooth, preparing for the future, if only we knew—knew what he can tell us. I tell you that I am ready to go mad. If anything should happen to you, Miss Racksole, I would kill myself.'

'But why?' she questioned. 'Supposing, that is, that anything could happen to me—which it can't.'

'Because I have dragged you into this,' he replied, gazing at her. 'It is nothing to you. You are only being kind.'

'How do you know it is nothing to me, Prince?' she asked him quickly.

Just then the sick man made a convulsive movement, and Nella flew to the bed and soothed him. From the head of the bed she looked over at Prince Aribert, and he returned her bright, excited glance. She was in her travelling-frock, with a large white Belgian apron tied over it. Large dark circles of fatigue and sleeplessness surrounded her eyes, and to the Prince her cheek seemed hollow and thin; her hair lay thick over the temples, half covering the ears. Aribert gave no answer to her query—merely gazed at her with melancholy intensity.

'I think I will go and rest,' she said at last. 'You will know all about the medicine.'

'Sleep well,' he said, as he softly opened the door for her. And then he was alone with Eugen. It was his turn that night to watch, for they still half-expected some strange, sudden visit, or onslaught, or move of one kind or another from Jules. Racksole slept in the parlour on the ground floor.

Nella had the front bedroom on the first floor; Miss Spencer was immured in the attic; the last-named lady had been singularly quiet and incurious, taking her food from Nella and asking no questions, the old woman went at nights to her own abode in the purlieus of the harbour. Hour after hour Aribert sat silent by his nephew's bed-side, attending mechanically to his wants, and every now and then gazing hard into the vacant, anguished face, as if trying to extort from that mask the secrets which it held. Aribert was tortured by the idea that if he could have only half an hour's, only a quarter of an hour's, rational speech with Prince Eugen, all might be cleared up and put right, and by the fact that that rational talk was absolutely impossible on Eugen's part until the fever had run its course. As the minutes crept on to midnight the watcher, made nervous by the intense, electrical atmosphere which seems always to surround a person who is dangerously ill, grew more and more a prey to vague and terrible apprehensions. His mind dwelt hysterically on the most fatal possibilities.

He wondered what would occur if by any ill-chance Eugen should die in that bed—how he would explain the affair to Posen and to the Emperor, how he would justify himself. He saw himself being tried for murder, sentenced (him—a Prince of the blood!), led to the scaffold... a scene unparalleled in Europe for over a century! ... Then he gazed anew at the sick man, and thought he saw death in every drawn feature of that agonized face. He could have screamed aloud. His ears heard a peculiar resonant boom. He started—it was nothing but the city clock striking twelve. But there was another sound—a mysterious shuffle at the door. He listened; then jumped from his chair. Nothing now! Nothing! But still he felt drawn to the door, and after what seemed an interminable interval he went and opened it, his heart beating furiously. Nella lay in a heap on the door mat. She was fully dressed, but had apparently lost consciousness. He clutched at her slender body, picked her up, carried her to the chair by the fire-place, and laid her in it. He had forgotten all about Eugen.

'What is it, my angel?' he whispered, and then he kissed her—kissed her twice. He could only look at her; he did not know what to do to succour her.

At last she opened her eyes and sighed.

'Where am I?' she asked vaguely, in a tremulous tone as she recognized him. 'Is it you? Did I do anything silly? Did I faint?'

'What has happened? Were you ill?' he questioned anxiously. He was kneeling at her feet, holding her hand tight.

'I saw Jules by the side of my bed,' she murmured; 'I'm sure I saw him; he laughed at me. I had not undressed. I sprang up, frightened, but he had gone, and then I ran downstairs—to you.'

'You were dreaming,' he soothed her.

'Was I?'

'You must have been. I have not heard a sound. No one could have entered.

But if you like I will wake Mr Racksole.'

'Perhaps I was dreaming,' she admitted. 'How foolish!'

'You were over-tired,' he said, still unconsciously holding her hand. They gazed at each other. She smiled at him.

'You kissed me,' she said suddenly, and he blushed red and stood up before her. 'Why did you kiss me?'

'Ah! Miss Racksole,' he murmured, hurrying the words out. 'Forgive me. It is unforgivable, but forgive me. I was overpowered by my feelings. I did not know what I was doing.'

'Why did you kiss me?' she repeated.

'Because—Nella! I love you. I have no right to say it.'

'Why have you no right to say it?'

'If Eugen dies, I shall owe a duty to Posen—I shall be its ruler.'

'Well!' she said calmly, with an adorable confidence. 'Papa is worth forty millions. Would you not abdicate?'

'Ah!' he gave a low cry. 'Will you force me to say these things? I could not shirk my duty to Posen, and the reigning Prince of Posen can only marry a Princess.'

'But Prince Eugen will live,' she said positively, 'and if he lives—'

'Then I shall be free. I would renounce all my rights to make you mine, if—if—'

'If what, Prince?'

'If you would deign to accept my hand.'

'Am I, then, rich enough?'

'Nella!' He bent down to her.

Then there was a crash of breaking glass. Aribert went to the window and opened it. In the starlit gloom he could see that a ladder had been raised against the back of the house. He thought he heard footsteps at the end of the garden.

'It was Jules,' he exclaimed to Nella, and without another word rushed upstairs to the attic. The attic was empty. Miss Spencer had mysteriously vanished.

Chapter Nineteen ROYALTY AT THE GRAND BABYLON

THE Royal apartments at the Grand Babylon are famous in the world of hôtels, and indeed elsewhere, as being, in their own way, unsurpassed. Some of the palaces of Germany, and in particular those of the mad Ludwig of Bavaria, may possess rooms and saloons which outshine them in gorgeous luxury and the mere wild fairy-like extravagance of wealth; but there is nothing, anywhere, even on Eighth Avenue, New York, which can fairly be called more complete, more perfect, more enticing, or—not least important—more comfortable.

The suite consists of six chambers—the ante-room, the saloon or audience chamber, the dining-room, the yellow drawing-room (where Royalty receives its friends), the library, and the State bedroom—to the last of which we have already been introduced. The most important and most impressive of these is, of course, the audience chamber, an apartment fifty feet long by forty feet broad, with a superb outlook over the Thames, the Shot Tower, and the higher signals of the South-Western Railway. The decoration of this room is mainly in the German taste, since four out of every six of its Royal occupants are of Teutonic blood; but its chief glory is its French ceiling, a masterpiece by Fragonard, taken bodily from a certain famous palace on the Loire. The walls are of panelled oak, with an eight-foot dado of Arras cloth imitated from unique Continental examples. The carpet, woven in one piece, is an antique specimen of the finest Turkish work, and it was obtained, a bargain, by Felix Babylon, from an impecunious Roumanian Prince. The silver candelabra, now fitted with electric light, came from the Rhine, and each had a separate history. The Royal chair—it is not etiquette to call it a throne, though it amounts to a throne—was looted by Napoleon from an Austrian city, and bought by Felix Babylon at the sale of a French collector. At each corner of the room stands a gigantic grotesque vase of German faïence of the sixteenth century. These were presented to Felix Babylon by William the First of Germany, upon the conclusion of his first incognito visit to London in connection with the French trouble of 1875.

There is only one picture in the audience chamber. It is a portrait of the luckless but noble Dom Pedro, Emperor of the Brazils. Given to Felix Babylon by Dom Pedro himself, it hangs there solitary and sublime as a reminder to Kings and Princes that Empires may pass away and greatness fall. A certain Prince who was occupying the suite during the Jubilee of 1887—when the Grand Babylon had seven persons of Royal blood under its roof—sent a curt message to Felix that the portrait must be removed. Felix respectfully declined to remove it, and the Prince left for another hôtel, where he was robbed of two thousand pounds' worth of jewellery. The Royal audience chamber of the Grand Babylon, if people only knew it, is one of the sights of London, but it is never shown, and if you ask the hôtel servants about its wonders they will tell you only foolish facts concerning it, as that the Turkey carpet costs fifty pounds to clean, and that one of the great vases is cracked across the pedestal, owing to the rough treatment accorded to it during a riotous game of Blind Man's Buff, played one night by four young Princesses, a Balkan King, and his aides-de-camp.

In one of the window recesses of this magnificent apartment, on a certain afternoon in late July, stood Prince Aribert of Posen. He was faultlessly dressed in the conventional frock-coat of English civilization, with a gardenia in his button-hole, and the indispensable crease down the front of the trousers. He seemed to be fairly amused, and also to expect someone, for at frequent intervals he looked rapidly over his shoulder in the direction of the door behind the Royal chair. At last a little wizened, stooping old man, with a distinctly German cast of countenance, appeared through the door, and laid some papers on a small table by the side of the chair.

'Ah, Hans, my old friend!' said Aribert, approaching the old man. 'I must have a little talk with you about one or two matters. How do you find His Royal Highness?'

The old man saluted, military fashion. 'Not very well, your Highness,' he answered. 'I've been valet to your Highness's nephew since his majority, and I was valet to his Royal father before him, but I never saw—' He stopped, and threw up his wrinkled hands deprecatingly.

'You never saw what?' Aribert smiled affectionately on the old fellow. You could perceive that these two, so sharply differentiated in rank, had been intimate in the past, and would be intimate again.

'Do you know, my Prince,' said the old man, 'that we are to receive the financier, Sampson Levi—is that his name?—in the audience chamber? Surely, if I may humbly suggest, the library would have been good enough for a financier?'

'One would have thought so,' agreed Prince Aribert, 'but perhaps your master has a special reason. Tell me,' he went on, changing the subject quickly, 'how came it that you left the Prince, my nephew, at Ostend, and returned to Posen?'

'His orders, Prince,' and old Hans, who had had a wide experience of Royal whims and knew half the secrets of the Courts of Europe, gave Aribert a look which might have meant anything. 'He sent me back on an—an errand, your Highness.'

'And you were to rejoin him here?'

'Just so, Highness. And I did rejoin him here, although, to tell the truth, I had begun to fear that I might never see my master again.'

'The Prince has been very ill in Ostend, Hans.'

'So I have gathered,' Hans responded drily, slowly rubbing his hands together. 'And his Highness is not yet perfectly recovered.'

'Not yet. We despaired of his life, Hans, at one time, but thanks to an excellent constitution, he came safely through the ordeal.'

'We must take care of him, your Highness.'

'Yes, indeed,' said Aribert solemnly, 'his life is very precious to Posen.'

At that moment, Eugen, Hereditary Prince of Posen, entered the audience chamber. He was pale and languid, and his uniform seemed to be a trouble to him. His hair had been slightly ruffled, and there was a look of uneasiness, almost of alarmed unrest, in his fine dark eyes. He was like a man who is afraid to look behind him lest he should see something there which ought not to be there. But at the same time, here beyond doubt was Royalty. Nothing could have been more striking than the contrast between Eugen, a sick man in the shabby house at Ostend, and this Prince Eugen in the Royal apartments of the Grand Babylon Hôtel, surrounded by the luxury and pomp which modern civilization can offer to those born in high places. All the desperate episode of Ostend was now hidden, passed over. It was supposed never to have occurred. It existed only like a secret shame in the hearts of those who had witnessed it. Prince Eugen had recovered; at any rate, he was convalescent, and he had been removed to London, where he took up again the dropped thread of his princely life. The lady with the red hat, the incorruptible and savage Miss Spencer, the unscrupulous and brilliant Jules, the dark, damp cellar, the horrible little bedroom—these things were over. Thanks to Prince Aribert and the Racksoles, he had emerged from them in safety. He was able to resume his public and official career. The Emperor had been informed of his safe arrival in London, after an unavoidable delay in Ostend; his name once more figured in the Court chronicle of the newspapers. In short, everything was smothered over. Only—only Jules, Rocco, and Miss Spencer were still at large; and the body of Reginald Dimmock lay buried in the domestic mausoleum of the palace at Posen; and Prince Eugen had still to interview Mr Sampson Levi.

That various matters lay heavy on the mind of Prince Eugen was beyond question. He seemed to have withdrawn within himself. Despite the extraordinary experiences through which he had recently passed, events which called aloud for explanations and confidence between the nephew and the uncle, he would say scarcely a word to Prince Aribert. Any allusion, however direct, to the days at Ostend, was ignored by him with more or less ingenuity, and Prince Aribert was really no nearer a full solution of the mystery of Jules' plot than he had been on the night when he and Racksole visited the gaming tables at Ostend. Eugen was well aware that he had been kidnapped through the agency of the woman in the red hat, but, doubtless ashamed at having been her dupe, he would not proceed in any way with the clearing-up of the matter.

'You will receive in this room, Eugen?' Aribert questioned him.

'Yes,' was the answer, given pettishly. 'Why not? Even if I have no proper retinue here, surely that is no reason why I should not hold audience in a proper manner?... Hans, you can go.' The old valet promptly disappeared.

'Aribert,' the Hereditary Prince continued, when they were alone in the chamber, 'you think I am mad.'

'My dear Eugen,' said Prince Aribert, startled in spite of himself. 'Don't be absurd.'

'I say you think I am mad. You think that that attack of brain fever has left its permanent mark on me. Well, perhaps I am mad. Who can tell? God knows that I have been through enough lately to drive me mad.'

Aribert made no reply. As a matter of strict fact, the thought had crossed his mind that Eugen's brain had not yet recovered its normal tone and activity. This speech of his nephew's, however, had the effect of immediately restoring his belief in the latter's entire sanity. He felt convinced that if only he could regain his nephew's confidence, the old brotherly confidence which had existed between them since the years when they played together as boys, all might yet be well. But at present there appeared to be no sign that Eugen meant to give his confidence to anyone.

The young Prince had come up out of the valley of the shadow of death, but some of the valley's shadow had clung to him, and it seemed he was unable to dissipate it.

'By the way,' said Eugen suddenly, 'I must reward these Racksoles, I suppose. I am indeed grateful to them. If I gave the girl a bracelet, and the father a thousand guineas—how would that meet the case?'

'My dear Eugen!' exclaimed Aribert aghast. 'A thousand guineas! Do you know that Theodore Racksole could buy up all Posen from end to end without making himself a pauper. A thousand guineas! You might as well offer him sixpence.'

'Then what must I offer?'

'Nothing, except your thanks. Anything else would be an insult. These are no ordinary hôtel people.'

'Can't I give the little girl a bracelet?' Prince Eugen gave a sinister laugh.

Aribert looked at him steadily. 'No,' he said.

'Why did you kiss her—that night?' asked Prince Eugen carelessly.

'Kiss whom?' said Aribert, blushing and angry, despite his most determined efforts to keep calm and unconcerned.

'The Racksole girl.'

'When do you mean?'

'I mean,' said Prince Eugen, 'that night in Ostend when I was ill. You thought I was in a delirium. Perhaps I was. But somehow I remember that with extraordinary distinctness. I remember raising my head for a fraction of an instant, and just in that fraction of an instant you kissed her. Oh, Uncle Aribert!'

'Listen, Eugen, for God's sake. I love Nella Racksole. I shall marry her.'

'You!' There was a long pause, and then Eugen laughed. 'Ah!' he said. 'They all talk like that to start with. I have talked like that myself, dear uncle; it sounds nice, and it means nothing.'

'In this case it means everything, Eugen,' said Aribert quietly. Some accent of determination in the latter's tone made Eugen rather more serious.

'You can't marry her,' he said. 'The Emperor won't permit a morganatic marriage.'

'The Emperor has nothing to do with the affair. I shall renounce my rights.

I shall become a plain citizen.'

'In which case you will have no fortune to speak of.'

'But my wife will have a fortune. Knowing the sacrifices which I shall have made in order to marry her, she will not hesitate to place that fortune in my hands for our mutual use,' said Aribert stiffly.

'You will decidedly be rich,' mused Eugen, as his ideas dwelt on Theodore Racksole's reputed wealth. 'But have you thought of this,' he asked, and his mild eyes glowed again in a sort of madness. 'Have you thought that I am unmarried, and might die at any moment, and then the throne will descend to you—to you, Aribert?'

'The throne will never descend to me, Eugen,' said Aribert softly, 'for you will live. You are thoroughly convalescent. You have nothing to fear.'

'It is the next seven days that I fear,' said Eugen.

'The next seven days! Why?'

'I do not know. But I fear them. If I can survive them—'

'Mr Sampson Levi, sire,' Hans announced in a loud tone.

PRINCE EUGEN started. 'I will see him,' he said, with a gesture to Hans as if to indicate that Mr Sampson Levi might enter at once.

'I beg one moment first,' said Aribert, laying a hand gently on his nephew's arm, and giving old Hans a glance which had the effect of precipitating that admirably trained servant through the doorway.

'What is it?' asked Prince Eugen crossly. 'Why this sudden seriousness? Don't forget that I have an appointment with Mr Sampson Levi, and must not keep him waiting. Someone said that punctuality is the politeness of princes.'

'Eugen,' said Aribert, 'I wish you to be as serious as I am. Why cannot we have faith in each other? I want to help you. I have helped you. You are my titular Sovereign; but on the other hand I have the honour to be your uncle:

I have the honour to be the same age as you, and to have been your companion from youth up. Give me your confidence. I thought you had given it me years ago, but I have lately discovered that you had your secrets, even then. And now, since your illness, you are still more secretive.'

'What do you mean, Aribert?' said Eugen, in a tone which might have been either inimical or friendly. 'What do you want to say?'

'Well, in the first place, I want to say that you will not succeed with the estimable Mr Sampson Levi.'

'Shall I not?' said Eugen lightly. 'How do you know what my business is with him?'

'Suffice it to say that I know. You will never get that million pounds out of him.'

Prince Eugen gasped, and then swallowed his excitement. 'Who has been talking? What million?' His eyes wandered uneasily round the room. 'Ah!' he said, pretending to laugh. 'I see how it is. I have been chattering in my delirium. You mustn't take any notice of that, Aribert. When one has a fever one's ideas become grotesque and fanciful.'

'You never talked in your delirium,' Aribert replied; 'at least not about yourself. I knew about this projected loan before I saw you in Ostend.'

'Who told you?' demanded Eugen fiercely.

'Then you admit that you are trying to raise a loan?'

'I admit nothing. Who told you?'

'Theodore Racksole, the millionaire. These rich men have no secrets from each other. They form a coterie, closer than any coterie of ours. Eugen, and far more powerful. They talk, and in talking they rule the world, these millionaires. They are the real monarchs.'

'Curse them!' said Eugen.

'Yes, perhaps so. But let me return to your case. Imagine my shame, my disgust, when I found that Racksole could tell me more about your affairs than I knew myself. Happily, he is a good fellow; one can trust him; otherwise I should have been tempted to do something desperate when I discovered that all your private history was in his hands. Eugen, let us come to the point; why do you want that million? Is it actually true that you are so deeply in debt? I have no desire to improve the occasion. I merely ask.'

'And what if I do owe a million?' said Prince Eugen with assumed valour.

'Oh, nothing, my dear Eugen, nothing. Only it is rather a large sum to have scattered in ten years, is it not? How did you manage it?'

'Don't ask me, Aribert. I've been a fool. But I swear to you that the woman whom you call "the lady in the red hat" is the last of my follies. I am about to take a wife, and become a respectable Prince.'

'Then the engagement with Princess Anna is an accomplished fact?'

'Practically so. As soon as I have settled with Levi, all will be smooth.

Aribert, I wouldn't lose Anna for the Imperial throne. She is a good and pure woman, and I love her as a man might love an angel.'

'And yet you would deceive her as to your debts, Eugen?'

'Not her, but her absurd parents, and perhaps the Emperor. They have heard rumours, and I must set those rumours at rest by presenting to them a clean sheet.'

'I am glad you have been frank with me, Eugen,' said Prince Aribert, 'but I will be plain with you. You will never marry the Princess Anna.'

'And why?' said Eugen, supercilious again.

'Because her parents will not permit it. Because you will not be able to present a clean sheet to them. Because this Sampson Levi will never lend you a million.'

'Explain yourself.'

'I propose to do so. You were kidnapped—it is a horrid word, but we must use it—in Ostend.'

'True.'

'Do you know why?'

'I suppose because that vile old red-hatted woman and her accomplices wanted to get some money out of me. Fortunately, thanks to you, they didn't.'

'Not at all,' said Aribert. 'They wanted no money from you. They knew well enough that you had no money. They knew you were the naughty schoolboy among European Princes, with no sense of responsibility or of duty towards your kingdom. Shall I tell you why they kidnapped you?'

'When you have done abusing me, my dear uncle.'

'They kidnapped you merely to keep you out of England for a few days, merely to compel you to fail in your appointment with Sampson Levi. And it appears to me that they succeeded. Assuming that you don't obtain the money from Levi, is there another financier in all Europe from whom you can get it—on such strange security as you have to offer?'

'Possibly there is not,' said Prince Eugen calmly. 'But, you see, I shall get it from Sampson Levi. Levi promised it, and I know from other sources that he is a man of his word. He said that the money, subject to certain formalities, would be available till—'

'Till?'

'Till the end of June.'

'And it is now the end of July.'

'Well, what is a month? He is only too glad to lend the money. He will get excellent interest. How on earth have you got into your sage old head this notion of a plot against me? The idea is ridiculous. A plot against me? What for?'

'Have you ever thought of Bosnia?' asked Aribert coldly.

'What of Bosnia?'

'I need not tell you that the King of Bosnia is naturally under obligations to Austria, to whom he owes his crown. Austria is anxious for him to make a good influential marriage.'

'Well, let him.'

'He is going to. He is going to marry the Princess Anna.'

'Not while I live. He made overtures there a year ago, and was rebuffed.'

'Yes; but he will make overtures again, and this time he will not be rebuffed. Oh, Eugen! can't you see that this plot against you is being engineered by some persons who know all about your affairs, and whose desire is to prevent your marriage with Princess Anna? Only one man in Europe can have any motive for wishing to prevent your marriage with Princess Anna, and that is the man who means to marry her himself.' Eugen went very pale.

'Then, Aribert, do you mean to convey to me that my detention in Ostend was contrived by the agents of the King of Bosnia?'

'I do.'

'With a view to stopping my negotiations with Sampson Levi, and so putting an end to the possibility of my marriage with Anna?'

Aribert nodded.

'You are a good friend to me, Aribert. You mean well. But you are mistaken. You have been worrying about nothing.'

'Have you forgotten about Reginald Dimmock?'

'I remember you said that he had died.'

'I said nothing of the sort. I said that he had been assassinated. That was part of it, my poor Eugen.'

'Pooh!' said Eugen. 'I don't believe he was assassinated. And as for Sampson Levi, I will bet you a thousand marks that he and I come to terms this morning, and that the million is in my hands before I leave London.'

Aribert shook his head.

'You seem to be pretty sure of Mr Levi's character. Have you had much to do with him before?'

'Well,' Eugen hesitated a second, 'a little. What young man in my position hasn't had something to do with Mr Sampson Levi at one time or another?'

'I haven't,' said Aribert.

'You! You are a fossil.' He rang a silver bell. 'Hans! I will receive Mr Sampson Levi.'

Whereupon Aribert discreetly departed, and Prince Eugen sat down in the great velvet chair, and began to look at the papers which Hans had previously placed upon the table.

'Good morning, your Royal Highness,' said Sampson Levi, bowing as he entered. 'I trust your Royal Highness is well.'

'Moderately, thanks,' returned the Prince.

In spite of the fact that he had had as much to do with people of Royal blood as any plain man in Europe, Sampson Levi had never yet learned how to be at ease with these exalted individuals during the first few minutes of an interview. Afterwards, he resumed command of himself and his faculties, but at the beginning he was invariably flustered, scarlet of face, and inclined to perspiration.

'We will proceed to business at once,' said Prince Eugen. 'Will you take a seat, Mr Levi?'

'I thank your Royal Highness.'

'Now as to that loan which we had already practically arranged—a million, I think it was,' said the Prince airily.

'A million,' Levi acquiesced, toying with his enormous watch chain.

'Everything is now in order. Here are the papers and I should like to finish the matter up at once.'

'Exactly, your Highness, but—'

'But what? You months ago expressed the warmest satisfaction at the security, though I am quite prepared to admit that the security, is of rather an unusual nature. You also agreed to the rate of interest. It is not everyone, Mr Levi, who can lend out a million at 5-1/2 per cent. And in ten years the whole amount will be paid back. I—er—I believe I informed you that the fortune of Princess Anna, who is about to accept my hand, will ultimately amount to something like fifty millions of marks, which is over two million pounds in your English money.' Prince Eugen stopped. He had no fancy for talking in this confidential manner to financiers, but he felt that circumstances demanded it.

'You see, it's like this, your Royal Highness,' began Mr Sampson Levi, in his homely English idiom. 'It's like this. I said I could keep that bit of money available till the end of June, and you were to give me an interview here before that date. Not having heard from your Highness, and not knowing your Highness's address, though my German agents made every inquiry, I concluded, that you had made other arrangements, money being so cheap this last few months.'

'I was unfortunately detained at Ostend,' said Prince Eugen, with as much haughtiness as he could assume, 'by—by important business. I have made no other arrangements, and I shall have need of the million. If you will be so good as to pay it to my London bankers—'

'I'm very sorry,' said Mr Sampson Levi, with a tremendous and dazzling air of politeness, which surprised even himself, 'but my syndicate has now lent the money elsewhere. It's in South America—I don't mind telling your Highness that we've lent it to the Chilean Government.'

'Hang the Chilean Government, Mr Levi,' exclaimed the Prince, and he went white. 'I must have that million. It was an arrangement.'

'It was an arrangement, I admit,' said Mr Sampson Levi, 'but your Highness broke the arrangement.'

There was a long silence.

'Do you mean to say,' began the Prince with tense calmness, 'that you are not in a position to let me have that million?'

'I could let your Highness have a million in a couple of years' time.'

The Prince made a gesture of annoyance. 'Mr Levi,' he said, 'if you do not place the money in my hands to-morrow you will ruin one of the oldest of reigning families, and, incidentally, you will alter the map of Europe. You are not keeping faith, and I had relied on you.'

'Pardon me, your Highness,' said little Levi, rising in resentment, 'it is not I who have not kept faith. I beg to repeat that the money is no longer at my disposal, and to bid your Highness good morning.'

And Mr Sampson Levi left the audience chamber with an awkward, aggrieved bow. It was a scene characteristic of the end of the nineteenth century—an overfed, commonplace, pursy little man who had been born in a Brixton semi-detached villa, and whose highest idea of pleasure was a Sunday up the river in an expensive electric launch, confronting and utterly routing, in a hôtel belonging to an American millionaire, the representative of a race of men who had fingered every page of European history for centuries, and who still, in their native castles, were surrounded with every outward circumstance of pomp and power.

'Aribert,' said Prince Eugen, a little later, 'you were right. It is all over. I have only one refuge—'

'You don't mean—' Aribert stopped, dumbfounded.

'Yes, I do,' he said quickly. 'I can manage it so that it will look like an accident.'

Chapter Twenty-One THE RETURN OF FÉLIX BABYLON

ON the evening of Prince Eugen's fateful interview with Mr Sampson Levi, Theodore Racksole was wandering somewhat aimlessly and uneasily about the entrance hail and adjacent corridors of the Grand Babylon. He had returned from Ostend only a day or two previously, and had endeavoured with all his might to forget the affair which had carried him there—to regard it, in fact, as done with. But he found himself unable to do so. In vain he remarked, under his breath, that there were some things which were best left alone: if his experience as a manipulator of markets, a contriver of gigantic schemes in New York, had taught him anything at all, it should surely have taught him that. Yet he could not feel reconciled to such a position. The mere presence of the princes in his hôtel roused the fighting instincts of this man, who had never in his whole career been beaten. He had, as it were, taken up arms on their side, and if the princes of Posen would not continue their own battle, nevertheless he, Theodore Racksole, wanted to continue it for them. To a certain extent, of course, the battle had been won, for Prince Eugen had been rescued from an extremely difficult and dangerous position, and the enemy—consisting of Jules, Rocco, Miss Spencer, and perhaps others—had been put to flight. But that, he conceived, was not enough; it was very far from being enough. That the criminals, for criminals they decidedly were, should still be at large, he regarded as an absurd anomaly. And there was another point: he had said nothing to the police of all that had occurred. He disdained the police, but he could scarcely fail to perceive that if the police should by accident gain a clue to the real state of the case he might be placed rather awkwardly, for the simple reason that in the eyes of the law it amounted to a misdemeanour to conceal as much as he had concealed. He asked himself, for the thousandth time, why he had adopted a policy of concealment from the police, why he had become in any way interested in the Posen matter, and why, at this present moment, he should be so anxious to prosecute it further? To the first two questions he replied, rather lamely, that he had been influenced by Nella, and also by a natural spirit of adventure; to the third he replied that he had always been in the habit of carrying things through, and was now actuated by a mere childish, obstinate desire to carry this one through. Moreover, he was splendidly conscious of his perfect ability to carry it through. One additional impulse he had, though he did not admit it to himself, being by nature adverse to big words, and that was an abstract love of justice, the Anglo-Saxon's deep-found instinct for helping the right side to conquer, even when grave risks must thereby be run, with no corresponding advantage.

He was turning these things over in his mind as he walked about the vast hôtel on that evening of the last day in July. The Society papers had been stating for a week past that London was empty, but, in spite of the Society papers, London persisted in seeming to be just as full as ever. The Grand Babylon was certainly not as crowded as it had been a month earlier, but it was doing a very passable business. At the close of the season the gay butterflies of the social community have a habit of hovering for a day or two in the big hôtels before they flutter away to castle and country-house, meadow and moor, lake and stream. The great basket-chairs in the portico were well filled by old and middle-aged gentlemen engaged in enjoying the varied delights of liqueurs, cigars, and the full moon which floated so serenely above the Thames. Here and there a pretty woman on the arm of a cavalier in immaculate attire swept her train as she turned to and fro in the promenade of the terrace. Waiters and uniformed commissionaires and gold-braided doorkeepers moved noiselessly about; at short intervals the chief of the doorkeepers blew his shrill whistle and hansoms drove up with tinkling bell to take away a pair of butterflies to some place of amusement or boredom; occasionally a private carriage drawn by expensive and self-conscious horses put the hansoms to shame by its mere outward glory. It was a hot night, a night for the summer woods, and save for the vehicles there was no rapid movement of any kind. It seemed as though the world—the world, that is to say, of the Grand Babylon—was fully engaged in the solemn processes of digestion and small-talk. Even the long row of the Embankment gas-lamps, stretching right and left, scarcely trembled in the still, warm, caressing air. The stars overhead looked down with many blinkings upon the enormous pile of the Grand Babylon, and the moon regarded it with bland and changeless face; what they thought of it and its inhabitants cannot, unfortunately, be recorded. What Theodore Racksole thought of the moon can be recorded: he thought it was a nuisance. It somehow fascinated his gaze with its silly stare, and so interfered with his complex meditations. He glanced round at the well-dressed and satisfied people—his guests, his customers. They appeared to ignore him absolutely.

Probably only a very small percentage of them had the least idea that this tall spare man, with the iron-grey hair and the thin, firm, resolute face, who wore his American-cut evening clothes with such careless ease, was the sole proprietor of the Grand Babylon, and possibly the richest man in Europe. As has already been stated, Racksole was not a celebrity in England.

The guests of the Grand Babylon saw merely a restless male person, whose restlessness was rather a disturber of their quietude, but with whom, to judge by his countenance, it would be inadvisable to remonstrate. Therefore Theodore Racksole continued his perambulations unchallenged, and kept saying to himself, 'I must do something.' But what? He could think of no course to pursue.

At last he walked straight through the hôtel and out at the other entrance, and so up the little unassuming side street into the roaring torrent of the narrow and crowded Strand. He jumped on a Putney bus, and paid his fair to Putney, fivepence, and then, finding that the humble occupants of the vehicle stared at the spectacle of a man in evening dress but without a dustcoat, he jumped off again, oblivious of the fact that the conductor jerked a thumb towards him and winked at the passengers as who should say, 'There goes a lunatic.' He went into a tobacconist's shop and asked for a cigar. The shopman mildly inquired what price.

'What are the best you've got?' asked Theodore Racksole.

'Five shillings each, sir,' said the man promptly.

'Give me a penny one,' was Theodore Racksole's laconic request, and he walked out of the shop smoking the penny cigar. It was a new sensation for him.

He was inhaling the aromatic odours of Eugène Rimmel's establishment for the sale of scents when a gentleman, walking slowly in the opposite direction, accosted him with a quiet, 'Good evening, Mr Racksole.' The millionaire did not at first recognize his interlocutor, who wore a travelling overcoat, and was carrying a handbag. Then a slight, pleased smile passed over his features, and he held out his hand.

'Well, Mr Babylon,' he greeted the other, 'of all persons in the wide world you are the man I would most have wished to meet.'

'You flatter me,' said the little Anglicized Swiss.

'No, I don't,' answered Racksole; 'it isn't my custom, any more than it's yours. I wanted to have a real good long yarn with you, and lo! here you are! Where have you sprung from?'

'From Lausanne,' said Felix Babylon. 'I had finished my duties there, I had nothing else to do, and I felt homesick. I felt the nostalgia of London, and so I came over, just as you see,' and he raised the handbag for Racksole's notice. 'One toothbrush, one razor, two slippers, eh?' He laughed. 'I was wondering as I walked along where I should stay—me, Felix Babylon, homeless in London.'

'I should advise you to stay at the Grand Babylon,' Racksole laughed back.

'It is a good hôtel, and I know the proprietor personally.'

'Rather expensive, is it not?' said Babylon.

'To you, sir,' answered Racksole, 'the inclusive terms will be exactly half a crown a week. Do you accept?'

'I accept,' said Babylon, and added, 'You are very good, Mr Racksole.'

They strolled together back to the hôtel, saying nothing in particular, but feeling very content with each other's company.

'Many customers?' asked Felix Babylon.

'Very tolerable,' said Racksole, assuming as much of the air of the professional hôtel proprietor as he could. 'I think I may say in the storekeeper's phrase, that if there is any business about I am doing it.

To-night the people are all on the terrace in the portico—it's so confoundedly hot—and the consumption of ice is simply enormous—nearly as large as it would be in New York.'

'In that case,' said Babylon politely, 'let me offer you another cigar.'

'But I have not finished this one.'

'That is just why I wish to offer you another one. A cigar such as yours, my good friend, ought never to be smoked within the precincts of the Grand Babylon, not even by the proprietor of the Grand Babylon, and especially when all the guests are assembled in the portico. The fumes of it would ruin any hôtel.'

Theodore Racksole laughingly lighted the Rothschild Havana which Babylon gave him, and they entered the hôtel arm in arm. But no sooner had they mounted the steps than little Felix became the object of numberless greetings. It appeared that he had been highly popular among his quondam guests. At last they reached the managerial room, where Babylon was regaled on a chicken, and Racksole assisted him in the consumption of a bottle of Heidsieck Monopole, Carte d'Or.

'This chicken is almost perfectly grilled,' said Babylon at length. 'It is a credit to the house. But why, my dear Racksole, why in the name of Heaven did you quarrel with Rocco?'

457

'Then you have heard?'

'Heard! My dear friend, it was in every newspaper on the Continent. Some journals prophesied that the Grand Babylon would have to close its doors within half a year now that Rocco had deserted it. But of course I knew better. I knew that you must have a good reason for allowing Rocco to depart, and that you must have made arrangements in advance for a substitute.'

'As a matter of fact, I had not made arrangements in advance,' said Theodore Racksole, a little ruefully; 'but happily we have found in our second sous-chef an artist inferior only to Rocco himself. That, however, was mere good fortune.'

'Surely,' said Babylon, 'it was indiscreet to trust to mere good fortune in such a serious matter?'

'I didn't trust to mere good fortune. I didn't trust to anything except Rocco, and he deceived me.'

'But why did you quarrel with him?'

'I didn't quarrel with him. I found him embalming a corpse in the State bedroom one night—'

'You what?' Babylon almost screamed.

'I found him embalming a corpse in the State bedroom,' repeated Racksole in his quietest tones.

The two men gazed at each other, and then Racksole replenished Babylon's glass.

'Tell me,' said Babylon, settling himself deep in an easy chair and lighting a cigar.

And Racksole thereupon recounted to him the whole of the Posen episode, with every circumstantial detail so far as he knew it. It was a long and complicated recital, and occupied about an hour. During that time little Felix never spoke a word, scarcely moved a muscle; only his small eyes gazed through the bluish haze of smoke. The clock on the mantelpiece tinkled midnight.

'Time for whisky and soda,' said Racksole, and got up as if to ring the bell; but Babylon waved him back.

'You have told me that this Sampson Levi had an audience of Prince Eugen to-day, but you have not told me the result of that audience,' said Babylon.

'Because I do not yet know it. But I shall doubtless know to-morrow. In the meantime, I feel fairly sure that Levi declined to produce Prince Eugen's required million. I have reason to believe that the money was lent elsewhere.'

'H'm!' mused Babylon; and then, carelessly, 'I am not at all surprised at that arrangement for spying through the bathroom of the State apartments.'

'Why are you not surprised?'

'Oh!' said Babylon, 'it is such an obvious dodge—so easy to carry out. As for me, I took special care never to involve myself in these affairs. I knew they existed; I somehow felt that they existed. But I also felt that they lay outside my sphere. My business was to provide board and lodging of the most sumptuous kind to those who didn't mind paying for it; and I did my business. If anything else went on in the hôtel, under the rose, I long determined to ignore it unless it should happen to be brought before my notice; and it never was brought before my notice. However, I admit that there is a certain pleasurable excitement in this kind of affair and doubtless you have experienced that.'

'I have,' said Racksole simply, 'though I believe you are laughing at me.'

'By no means,' Babylon replied. 'Now what, if I may ask the question, is going to be your next step?'

'That is just what I desire to know myself,' said Theodore Racksole.

'Well,' said Babylon, after a pause, 'let us begin. In the first place, it is possible you may be interested to hear that I happened to see Jules to-day.'

'You did!' Racksole remarked with much calmness. 'Where?'

'Well, it was early this morning, in Paris, just before I left there. The meeting was quite accidental, and Jules seemed rather surprised at meeting me. He respectfully inquired where I was going, and I said that I was going to Switzerland. At that moment I thought I was going to Switzerland. It had occurred to me that after all I should be happier there, and that I had better turn back and not see London any more. However, I changed my mind once again, and decided to come on to London, and accept the risks of being miserable there without my hôtel. Then I asked Jules whither he was bound, and he told me that he was off to Constantinople, being interested in a new French hôtel there. I wished him good luck, and we parted.'

'Constantinople, eh!' said Racksole. 'A highly suitable place for him, I should say.'

'But,' Babylon resumed, 'I caught sight of him again.'

'Where?'

'At Charing Cross, a few minutes before I had the pleasure of meeting you.

Mr Jules had not gone to Constantinople after all. He did not see me, or I should have suggested to him that in going from Paris to Constantinople it is not usual to travel via London.'

'The cheek of the fellow!' exclaimed Theodore Racksole. 'The gorgeous and colossal cheek of the fellow!'

Chapter Twenty-Two IN THE WINE CELLARS OF THE GRAND BABYLON

'DO you know anything of the antecedents of this Jules,' asked Theodore Racksole, helping himself to whisky. 'Nothing whatever,' said Babylon. 'Until you told me, I don't think I was aware that his true name was Thomas Jackson, though of course I knew that it was not Jules. I certainly was not aware that Miss Spencer was his wife, but I had long suspected that their relations were somewhat more intimate than the nature of their respective duties in the hôtel absolutely demanded. All that I do know of Jules—he will always be called Jules—is that he gradually, by some mysterious personal force, acquired a prominent position in the hôtel. Decidedly he was the cleverest and most intellectual waiter I have ever known, and he was specially skilled in the difficult task of retaining his own dignity while not interfering with that of other people.

I'm afraid this information is a little too vague to be of any practical assistance in the present difficulty.'

'What is the present difficulty?' Racksole queried, with a simple air.

'I should imagine that the present difficulty is to account for the man's presence in London.'

'That is easily accounted for,' said Racksole.

'How? Do you suppose he is anxious to give himself up to justice, or that the chains of habit bind him to the hôtel?'

'Neither,' said Racksole. 'Jules is going to have another try—that's all.'

'Another try at what?'

'At Prince Eugen. Either at his life or his liberty. Most probably the former this time; almost certainly the former. He has guessed that we are somewhat handicapped by our anxiety to keep Prince Eugen's predicament quite quiet, and he is taking advantage, of that fact. As he already is fairly rich, on his own admission, the reward which has been offered to him must be enormous, and he is absolutely determined to get it. He has several times recently proved himself to be a daring fellow; unless I am mistaken he will shortly prove himself to be still more daring.'

'But what can he do? Surely you don't suggest that he will attempt the life of Prince Eugen in this hôtel?'

'Why not? If Reginald Dimmock fell on mere suspicion that he would turn out unfaithful to the conspiracy, why not Prince Eugen?'

'But it would be an unspeakable crime, and do infinite harm to the hôtel!'

'True!' Racksole admitted, smiling. Little Felix Babylon seemed to brace himself for the grasping of his monstrous idea.

'How could it possibly be done?' he asked at length.

'Dimmock was poisoned.'

'Yes, but you had Rocco here then, and Rocco was in the plot. It is conceivable that Rocco could have managed it—barely conceivable. But without Rocco I cannot think it possible. I cannot even think that Jules would attempt it. You see, in a place like the Grand Babylon, as probably I needn't point out to you, food has to pass through so many hands that to poison one person without killing perhaps fifty would be a most delicate operation. Moreover, Prince Eugen, unless he has changed his habits, is always served by his own attendant, old Hans, and therefore any attempt to tamper with a cooked dish immediately before serving would be hazardous in the extreme.'

'Granted,' said Racksole. 'The wine, however, might be more easily got at.

Had you thought of that?'

'I had not,' Babylon admitted. 'You are an ingenious theorist, but I happen to know that Prince Eugen always has his wine opened in his own presence. No doubt it would be opened by Hans. Therefore the wine theory is not tenable, my friend.'

'I do not see why,' said Racksole. 'I know nothing of wine as an expert, and I very seldom drink it, but it seems to me that a bottle of wine might be tampered with while it was still in the cellar, especially if there was an accomplice in the hôtel.'

'You think, then, that you are not yet rid of all your conspirators?'

'I think that Jules might still have an accomplice within the building.'

'And that a bottle of wine could be opened and recorked without leaving any trace of the operation?' Babylon was a trifle sarcastic.

'I don't see the necessity of opening the bottle in order to poison the wine,' said Racksole. 'I have never tried to poison anybody by means of a bottle of wine, and I don't lay claim to any natural talent as a poisoner, but I think I could devise several ways of managing the trick. Of course, I admit I may be entirely mistaken as to Jules' intentions.'

'Ah!' said Felix Babylon. 'The wine cellars beneath us are one of the wonders of London. I hope you are aware, Mr Racksole, that when you bought the Grand Babylon you bought what is probably the finest stock of wines in England, if not in Europe. In the valuation I reckoned them at sixty thousand pounds. And I may say that I always took care that the cellars were properly guarded. Even Jules would experience a serious difficulty in breaking into the cellars without the connivance of the wine-clerk, and the wine-clerk is, or was, incorruptible.'

'I am ashamed to say that I have not yet inspected my wines,' smiled Racksole; 'I have never given them a thought. Once or twice I have taken the trouble to make a tour of the hôtel, but I omitted the cellars in my excursions.'

'Impossible, my dear fellow!' said Babylon, amused at such a confession, to him—a great connoisseur and lover of fine wines—almost incredible. 'But really you must see them to-morrow. If I may, I will accompany you.'

'Why not to-night?' Racksole suggested, calmly.

'To-night! It is very late: Hubbard will have gone to bed.'

'And may I ask who is Hubbard? I remember the name but dimly.'

'Hubbard is the wine-clerk of the Grand Babylon,' said Felix, with a certain emphasis. 'A sedate man of forty. He has the keys of the cellars. He knows every bottle of every bin, its date, its qualities, its value. And he's a teetotaler. Hubbard is a curiosity. No wine can leave the cellars without his knowledge, and no person can enter the cellars without his knowledge. At least, that is how it was in my time,' Babylon added.

'We will wake him,' said Racksole.

'But it is one o'clock in the morning,' Babylon protested.

'Never mind—that is, if you consent to accompany me. A cellar is the same by night as by day. Therefore, why not now?'

Babylon shrugged his shoulders. 'As you wish,' he agreed, with his indestructible politeness.

'And now to find this Mr Hubbard, with his key of the cupboard,' said Racksole, as they walked out of the room together. Although the hour was so late, the hôtel was not, of course, closed for the night. A few guests still remained about in the public rooms, and a few fatigued waiters were still in attendance. One of these latter was despatched in search of the singular Mr Hubbard, and it fortunately turned out that this gentleman had not actually retired, though he was on the point of doing so. He brought the keys to Mr Racksole in person, and after he had had a little chat with his former master, the proprietor and the ex-proprietor of the Grand Babylon Hôtel proceeded on their way to the cellars.

These cellars extend over, or rather under, quite half the superficial areas of the whole hôtel—the longitudinal half which lies next to the Strand.

Owing to the fact that the ground slopes sharply from the Strand to the river, the Grand Babylon is, so to speak, deeper near the Strand than it is near the Thames. Towards the Thames there is, below the entrance level, a basement and a sub-basement. Towards the Strand there is basement, sub-basement, and the huge wine cellars beneath all. After descending the four flights of the service stairs, and traversing a long passage running parallel with the kitchen, the two found themselves opposite a door, which, on being unlocked, gave access to another flight of stairs. At the foot of this was the main entrance to the cellars. Outside the entrance was the wine-lift, for the ascension of delicious fluids to the upper floors, and, opposite, Mr Hubbard's little office. There was electric light everywhere.

Babylon, who, as being most accustomed to them, held the bunch of keys, opened the great door, and then they were in the first cellar—the first of a suite of five. Racksole was struck not only by the icy coolness of the place, but also by its vastness. Babylon had seized a portable electric handlight, attached to a long wire, which lay handy, and, waving it about, disclosed the dimensions of the place. By that flashing illumination the subterranean chamber looked unutterably weird and mysterious, with its rows of numbered bins, stretching away into the distance till the radiance was reduced to the occasional far gleam of the light on the shoulder of a bottle. Then Babylon switched on the fixed electric lights, and Theodore Racksole entered upon a personally-conducted tour of what was quite the most interesting part of his own property.

460

To see the innocent enthusiasm of Felix Babylon for these stores of exhilarating liquid was what is called in the North 'a sight for sair een'.

He displayed to Racksole's bewildered gaze, in their due order, all the wines of three continents—nay, of four, for the superb and luscious Constantia wine of Cape Colony was not wanting in that most catholic collection of vintages. Beginning with the unsurpassed products of Burgundy, he continued with the clarets of Médoc, Bordeaux, and Sauterne; then to the champagnes of Ay, Hautvilliers, and Pierry; then to the hocks and moselles of Germany, and the brilliant imitation champagnes of Main, Neckar, and Naumburg; then to the famous and adorable Tokay of Hungary, and all the Austrian varieties of French wines, including Carlowitz and Somlauer; then to the dry sherries of Spain, including purest Manzanilla, and Amontillado, and Vino de Pasto; then to the wines of Malaga, both sweet and dry, and all the 'Spanish reds' from Catalonia, including the dark 'Tent' so often used sacramentally; then to the renowned port of Oporto. Then he proceeded to the Italian cellar, and descanted upon the excellence of Barolo from Piedmont, of Chianti from Tuscany, of Orvieto from the Roman States, of the 'Tears of Christ' from Naples, and the commoner Marsala from Sicily. And so on, to an extent and with a fullness of detail which cannot be rendered here.

At the end of the suite of cellars there was a glazed door, which, as could be seen, gave access to a supplemental and smaller cellar, an apartment about fifteen or sixteen feet square.

'Anything special in there?' asked Racksole curiously, as they stood before the door, and looked within at the seined ends of bottles.

'Ah!' exclaimed Babylon, almost smacking his lips, 'therein lies the cream of all.'

'The best champagne, I suppose?' said Racksole.

'Yes,' said Babylon, 'the best champagne is there—a very special Sillery, as exquisite as you will find anywhere. But I see, my friend, that you fall into the common error of putting champagne first among wines. That distinction belongs to Burgundy. You have old Burgundy in that cellar, Mr Racksole, which cost me—how much do you think?—eighty pounds a bottle.

Probably it will never be drunk,' he added with a sigh. 'It is too expensive even for princes and plutocrats.'

'Yes, it will,' said Racksole quickly. 'You and I will have a bottle up to-morrow.'

'Then,' continued Babylon, still riding his hobby-horse, 'there is a sample of the Rhine wine dated 1706 which caused such a sensation at the Vienna Exhibition of 1873. There is also a singularly glorious Persian wine from Shiraz, the like of which I have never seen elsewhere. Also there is an unrivalled vintage of Romanée-Conti, greatest of all modern Burgundies. If I remember right Prince Eugen invariably has a bottle when he comes to stay here. It is not on the hôtel wine list, of course, and only a few customers know of it. We do not precisely hawk it about the dining-room.'

'Indeed!' said Racksole. 'Let us go inside.'

They entered the stone apartment, rendered almost sacred by the preciousness of its contents, and Racksole looked round with a strangely intent and curious air. At the far side was a grating, through which came a feeble light.

'What is that?' asked the millionaire sharply.

'That is merely a ventilation grating. Good ventilation is absolutely essential.'

'Looks broken, doesn't it?' Racksole suggested and then, putting a finger quickly on Babylon's shoulder, 'there's someone in the cellar. Can't you hear breathing, down there, behind that bin?'

The two men stood tense and silent for a while, listening, under the ray of the single electric light in the ceiling. Half the cellar was involved in gloom. At length Racksole walked firmly down the central passage-way between the bins and turned to the corner at the right.

'Come out, you villain!' he said in a low, well-nigh vicious tone, and dragged up a cowering figure.

He had expected to find a man, but it was his own daughter, Nella Racksole, upon whom he had laid angry hands.

Chapter Twenty-Three FURTHER EVENTS IN THE CELLAR

'WELL, Father,' Nella greeted her astounded parent. 'You should make sure that you have got hold of the right person before you use all that terrible muscular force of yours. I do believe you have broken my shoulder bone.' She rubbed her shoulder with a comical expression of pain, and then stood up before the two men. The skirt of her dark grey dress was torn and dirty, and the usually trim Nella looked as though she had been shot down a canvas fire-escape. Mechanically she smoothed her frock, and gave a straightening touch to her hair.

'Good evening, Miss Racksole,' said Felix Babylon, bowing formally. 'This is an unexpected pleasure.' Felix's drawing-room manners never deserted him upon any occasion whatever.

'May I inquire what you are doing in my wine cellar, Nella Racksole?' said the millionaire a little stiffly He was certainly somewhat annoyed at having mistaken his daughter for a criminal; moreover, he hated to be surprised, and upon this occasion he had been surprised beyond any ordinary surprise; lastly, he was not at all pleased that Nella should be observed in that strange predicament by a stranger.

'I will tell you,' said Nella. 'I had been reading rather late in my room—the night was so close. I heard Big Ben strike half-past twelve, and then I put the book down, and went out on to the balcony of my window for a little fresh air before going to bed. I leaned over the balcony very quietly—you will remember that I am on the third floor now—and looked down below into the little sunk yard which separates the wall of the hôtel from Salisbury Lane. I was rather astonished to see a figure creeping across the yard. I knew there was no entrance into the hôtel from that yard, and besides, it is fifteen or twenty feet below the level of the street. So I watched. The figure went close up against the wall, and disappeared from my view. I leaned over the balcony as far as I dared, but I couldn't see him. I could hear him, however.'

'What could you hear?' questioned Racksole sharply.

'It sounded like a sawing noise,' said Nella; 'and it went on for quite a long time—nearly a quarter of an hour, I should think—a rasping sort of noise.'

'Why on earth didn't you come and warn me or someone else in the hôtel?' asked Racksole.

'Oh, I don't know, Dad,' she replied sweetly. 'I had got interested in it, and I thought I would see it out myself. Well, as I was saying, Mr. Babylon,' she continued, addressing her remarks to Felix, with a dazzling smile, 'that noise went on for quite a long time. At last it stopped, and the figure reappeared from under the wall, crossed the yard, climbed up the opposite wall by some means or other, and so over the railings into Salisbury Lane. I felt rather relieved then, because I knew he hadn't actually broken into the hôtel. He walked down Salisbury Lane very slowly. A policeman was just coming up. "Goodnight, officer," I heard him say to the policeman, and he asked him for a match. The policeman supplied the match, and the other man lighted a cigarette, and proceeded further down the lane. By cricking your neck from my window, Mr Babylon, you can get a glimpse of the Embankment and the river. I saw the man cross the Embankment, and lean over the river wall, where he seemed to be talking to some one. He then walked along the Embankment to Westminster and that was the last I saw of him. I waited a minute or two for him to come back, but he didn't come back, and so I thought it was about time I began to make inquiries into the affair. I went downstairs instantly, and out of the hôtel, through the quadrangle, into Salisbury Lane, and I looked over those railings. There was a ladder on the other side, by which it was perfectly easy—once you had got over the railings—to climb down into the yard. I was horribly afraid lest someone might walk up Salisbury Lane and catch me in the act of negotiating those railings, but no one did, and I surmounted them, with no worse damage than a torn skirt. I crossed the yard on tiptoe, and I found that in the wall, close to the ground and almost exactly under my window, there was an iron grating, about one foot by fourteen inches. I suspected, as there was no other ironwork near, that the mysterious visitor must have been sawing at this grating for private purposes of his own. I gave it a good shake, and I was not at all surprised that a good part of it came off in my hand, leaving just enough room for a person to creep through. I decided that I would creep through, and now wish I hadn't. I don't know, Mr Babylon, whether you have ever tried to creep through a small hole with a skirt on. Have you?'

'I have not had that pleasure,' said little Felix, bowing again, and absently taking up a bottle which lay to his hand.

'Well, you are fortunate,' the imperturbable Nella resumed. 'For quite three minutes I thought I should perish in that grating, Dad, with my shoulder inside and the rest of me outside. However, at last, by the most amazing and agonizing efforts, I pulled myself through and fell into this extraordinary cellar more dead than alive. Then I wondered what I should do next. Should I wait for the mysterious visitor to return, and stab him with my pocket scissors if he tried to enter, or should I raise an alarm? First of all I replaced the broken grating, then I struck a match, and I saw that I had got landed in a wilderness of bottles. The match went out, and I hadn't another one. So I sat down in the corner to think. I had just decided to wait and see if the visitor returned, when I heard footsteps, and then voices; and then you came in. I must say I was rather taken aback, especially as I recognized the voice of Mr Babylon. You see, I didn't want to frighten you.

If I had bobbed up from behind the bottles and said "Booh!" you would have had a serious shock. I wanted to think of a way of breaking my presence gently to you. But you saved me the trouble, Dad. Was I really breathing so loudly that you could hear me?'

The girl ended her strange recital, and there was a moment's silence in the cellar. Racksole merely nodded an affirmative to her concluding question.

'Well, Nell, my girl,' said the millionaire at length, 'we are much obliged for your gymnastic efforts—very much obliged. But now, I think you had better go off to bed. There is going to be some serious trouble here, I'll lay my last dollar on that?'

'But if there is to be a burglary I should so like to see it, Dad,' Nella pleaded. 'I've never seen a burglar caught red-handed.'

'This isn't a burglary, my dear. I calculate it's something far worse than a burglary.'

'What?' she cried. 'Murder? Arson? Dynamite plot? How perfectly splendid!'

'Mr Babylon informs me that Jules is in London,' said Racksole quietly.

'Jules!' she exclaimed under her breath, and her tone changed instantly to the utmost seriousness. 'Switch off the light, quick!' Springing to the switch, she put the cellar in darkness.

'What's that for?' said her father.

'If he comes back he would see the light, and be frightened away,' said Nella. 'That wouldn't do at all.'

'It wouldn't, Miss Racksole,' said Babylon, and there was in his voice a note of admiration for the girl's sagacity which Racksole heard with high paternal pride.

'Listen, Nella,' said the latter, drawing his daughter to him in the profound gloom of the cellar. 'We fancy that Jules may be trying to tamper with a certain bottle of wine—a bottle which might possibly be drunk by Prince Eugen. Now do you think that the man you saw might have been Jules?'

'I hadn't previously thought of him as being Jules, but immediately you mentioned the name I somehow knew that he was. Yes, I am sure it was Jules.'

'Well, just hear what I have to say. There is no time to lose. If he is coming at all he will be here very soon—and you can help.' Racksole explained what he thought Jules' tactics might be. He proposed that if the man returned he should not be interfered with, but merely watched from the other side of the glass door.

'You want, as it were, to catch Mr Jules alive?' said Babylon, who seemed rather taken aback at this novel method of dealing with criminals. 'Surely,' he added, 'it would be simpler and easier to inform the police of your suspicion, and to leave everything to them.'

'My dear fellow,' said Racksole, 'we have already gone much too far without the police to make it advisable for us to call them in at this somewhat advanced stage of the proceedings. Besides, if you must know it, I have a particular desire to capture the scoundrel myself. I will leave you and Nella here, since Nella insists on seeing everything, and I will arrange things so that once he has entered the cellar Jules will not get out of it again—at any rate through the grating. You had better place yourselves on the other side of the glass door, in the big cellar; you will be in a position to observe from there, I will skip off at once. All you have to do is to take note of what the fellow does. If he has any accomplices within the hôtel we shall probably be able by that means to discover who the accomplice is.'

Lighting a match and shading it with his hands, Racksole showed them both out of the little cellar. 'Now if you lock this glass door on the outside he can't escape this way: the panes of glass are too small, and the woodwork too stout. So, if he comes into the trap, you two will have the pleasure of actually seeing him frantically writhe therein, without any personal danger; but perhaps you'd better not show yourselves.'

In another moment Felix Babylon and Nella were left to themselves in the darkness of the cellar, listening to the receding footfalls of Theodore Racksole. But the sound of these footfalls had not died away before another sound greeted their ears—the grating of the small cellar was being removed.

'I hope your father will be in time,' whispered Felix

'Hush!' the girl warned him, and they stooped side by side in tense silence.

A man cautiously but very neatly wormed his body through the aperture of the grating. The watchers could only see his form indistinctly in the darkness.

Then, being fairly within the cellar, he walked without the least hesitation to the electric switch and turned on the light. It was unmistakably Jules, and he knew the geography of the cellar very well. Babylon could with difficulty repress a start as he saw this bold and unscrupulous ex-waiter moving with such an air of assurance and determination about the precious cellar. Jules went directly to a small bin which was numbered 17, and took there from the topmost bottle.

'The Romanee-Conti—Prince Eugen's wine!' Babylon exclaimed under his breath.

Jules neatly and quickly removed the seal with an instrument which he had clearly brought for the purpose. He then took a little flat box from his pocket, which seemed to contain a sort of black salve. Rubbing his finger in this, he smeared the top of the neck of the bottle with it, just where the cork came against the glass. In another instant he had deftly replaced the seal and restored the bottle to its position. He then turned off the light, and made for the aperture. When he was half-way through Nella exclaimed, 'He will escape, after all. Dad has not had time—we must stop him.'

But Babylon, that embodiment of caution, forcibly, but nevertheless politely, restrained this Yankee girl, whom he deemed so rash and imprudent, and before she could free herself the lithe form of Jules had disappeared.

Chapter Twenty-Four THE BOTTLE OF WINE

AS regards Theodore Racksole, who was to have caught his man from the outside of the cellar, he made his way as rapidly as possible from the wine-cellars, up to the ground floor, out of the hôtel by the quadrangle, through the quadrangle, and out into the top of Salisbury Lane. Now, owing to the vastness of the structure of the Grand Babylon, the mere distance thus to be traversed amounted to a little short of a quarter of a mile, and, as it included a number of stairs, about two dozen turnings, and several passages which at that time of night were in darkness more or less complete, Racksole could not have been expected to accomplish the journey in less than five minutes. As a matter of fact, six minutes had elapsed before he reached the top of Salisbury Lane, because he had been delayed nearly a minute by some questions addressed to him by a muddled and whisky-laden guest who had got lost in the corridors. As everybody knows, there is a sharp short bend in Salisbury Lane near the top. Racksole ran round this at good racing speed, but he was unfortunate enough to run straight up against the very policeman who had not long before so courteously supplied Jules with a match. The policeman seemed to be scarcely in so pliant a mood just then.

'Hullo!' he said, his naturally suspicious nature being doubtless aroused by the spectacle of a bareheaded man in evening dress running violently down the lane. 'What's this? Where are you for in such a hurry?' and he forcibly detained Theodore Racksole for a moment and scrutinized his face.

'Now, officer,' said Racksole quietly, 'none of your larks, if you please.
I've no time to lose.'

'Beg your pardon, sir,' the policeman remarked, though hesitatingly and not quite with good temper, and Racksole was allowed to proceed on his way. The millionaire's scheme for trapping Jules was to get down into the little sunk yard by means of the ladder, and then to secrete himself behind some convenient abutment of brickwork until Mr Tom Jackson should have got into the cellar. He therefore nimbly surmounted the railings—the railings of his own hôtel—and was gingerly descending the ladder, when lo! a rough hand seized him by the coat-collar and with a ferocious jerk urged him backwards. The fact was, Theodore Racksole had counted without the policeman. That guardian of the peace, mistrusting Racksole's manner, quietly followed him down the lane. The sight of the millionaire climbing the railings had put him on his mettle, and the result was the ignominious capture of Racksole. In vain Theodore expostulated, explained, anathematized. Only one thing would satisfy the stolid policeman—namely, that Racksole should return with him to the hôtel and there establish his identity. If Racksole then proved to be Racksole, owner of the Grand Babylon, well and good—the policeman promised to apologize. So Theodore had no alternative but to accept the suggestion. To prove his identity was, of course, the work of only a few minutes, after which Racksole, annoyed, but cool as ever, returned to his railings, while the policeman went off to another part of his beat, where he would be likely to meet a comrade and have a chat.

In the meantime, our friend Jules, sublimely unconscious of the altercation going on outside, and of the special risk which he ran, was of course actually in the cellar, which he had reached before Racksole got to the railings for the first time. It was, indeed, a happy chance for Jules that his exit from the cellar coincided with the period during which Racksole was absent from the railings. As Racksole came down the lane for the second time, he saw a figure walking about fifty yards in front of him towards the Embankment. Instantly he divined that it was Jules, and that the policeman had thrown him just too late. He ran, and Jules, hearing the noise of pursuit, ran also. The ex-waiter was fleet; he made direct for a certain spot in the Embankment wall, and, to the intense astonishment of Racksole, jumped clean over the wall, as it seemed, into the river. 'Is he so desperate as to commit suicide?' Racksole exclaimed as he ran, but a second later the puff and snort of a steam launch told him that Jules was not quite driven to suicide. As the millionaire crossed the Embankment roadway he saw the funnel of the launch move out from under the river-wall. It swerved into midstream and headed towards London Bridge. There was a silent mist over the river. Racksole was helpless....

Although Racksole had now been twice worsted in a contest of wits within the precincts of the Grand Babylon, once by Rocco and once by Jules, he could not fairly blame himself for the present miscarriage of his plans—a miscarriage due to the meddlesomeness of an extraneous person, combined with pure ill-fortune. He did not, therefore, permit the accident to interfere with his sleep that night.

On the following day he sought out Prince Aribert, between whom and himself there now existed a feeling of unmistakable, frank friendship, and disclosed to him the happenings of the previous night, and particularly the tampering with the bottle of Romanée-Conti.

'I believe you dined with Prince Eugen last night?'

'I did. And curiously enough we had a bottle of Romanée-Conti, an admirable wine, of which Eugen is passionately fond.'

'And you will dine with him to-night?'

'Most probably. To-day will, I fear, be our last day here. Eugen wishes to return to Posen early to-morrow.'

'Has it struck you, Prince,' said Racksole, 'that if Jules had succeeded in poisoning your nephew, he would probably have succeeded also in poisoning you?'

'I had not thought of it,' laughed Aribert, 'but it would seem so. It appears that so long as he brings down his particular quarry, Jules is careless of anything else that may be accidentally involved in the destruction. However, we need have no fear on that score now. You know the bottle, and you can destroy it at once.'

'But I do not propose to destroy it,' said Racksole calmly. 'If Prince Eugen asks for Romanée-Conti to be served to-night, as he probably will, I propose that that precise bottle shall be served to him—and to you.'

'Then you would poison us in spite of ourselves?'

'Scarcely,' Racksole smiled. 'My notion is to discover the accomplices within the hôtel. I have already inquired as to the wine-clerk, Hubbard. Now does it not occur to you as extraordinary that on this particular day Mr Hubbard should be ill in bed? Hubbard, I am informed, is suffering from an attack of stomach poisoning, which has supervened during the night. He says that he does not know what can have caused it. His place in the wine cellars will be taken to-day by his assistant, a mere youth, but to all appearances a fairly smart youth. I need not say that we shall keep an eye on that youth.'

'One moment,' Prince Aribert interrupted. 'I do not quite understand how you think the poisoning was to have been effected.'

'The bottle is now under examination by an expert, who has instructions to remove as little as possible of the stuff which Jules put on the rim of the mouth of it. It will be secretly replaced in its bin during the day. My idea is that by the mere action of pouring out the wine takes up some of the poison, which I deem to be very strong, and thus becomes fatal as it enters the glass.'

'But surely the servant in attendance would wipe the mouth of the bottle?'

'Very carelessly, perhaps. And moreover he would be extremely unlikely to wipe off all the stuff; some of it has been ingeniously placed just on the inside edge of the rim. Besides, suppose he forgot to wipe the bottle?'

'Prince Eugen is always served at dinner by Hans. It is an honour which the faithful old fellow reserves for himself.'

'But suppose Hans—' Racksole stopped.

'Hans an accomplice! My dear Racksole, the suggestion is wildly impossible.'

That night Prince Aribert dined with his august nephew in the superb dining-room of the Royal apartments. Hans served, the dishes being brought to the door by other servants. Aribert found his nephew despondent and taciturn. On the previous day, when, after the futile interview with Sampson Levi, Prince Eugen had despairingly threatened to commit suicide, in such a manner as to make it 'look like an accident', Aribert had compelled him to give his word of honour not to do so.

'What wine will your Royal Highness take?' asked old Hans in his soothing tones, when the soup was served.

'Sherry,' was Prince Eugen's curt order.

'And Romanée-Conti afterwards?' said Hans. Aribert looked up quickly.

'No, not to-night. I'll try Sillery to-night,' said Prince Eugen.

'I think I'll have Romanée-Conti, Hans, after all,' he said. 'It suits me better than champagne.'

The famous and unsurpassable Burgundy was served with the roast. Old Hans brought it tenderly in its wicker cradle, inserted the corkscrew with mathematical precision, and drew the cork, which he offered for his master's inspection. Eugen nodded, and told him to put it down. Aribert watched with intense interest. He could not for an instant believe that Hans was not the very soul of fidelity, and yet, despite himself, Racksole's words had caused him a certain uneasiness. At that moment Prince Eugen murmured across the table:

'Aribert, I withdraw my promise. Observe that, I withdraw it.' Aribert shook his head emphatically, without removing his gaze from Hans. The white-haired servant perfunctorily dusted his napkin round the neck of the bottle of Romanée-Conti, and poured out a glass. Aribert trembled from head to foot.

Eugen took up the glass and held it to the light.

'Don't drink it,' said Aribert very quietly. 'It is poisoned.'

'Poisoned!' exclaimed Prince Eugen.

'Poisoned, sire!' exclaimed old Hans, with an air of profound amazement and concern, and he seized the glass. 'Impossible, sire. I myself opened the bottle. No one else has touched it, and the cork was perfect.'

'I tell you it is poisoned,' Aribert repeated.

'Your Highness will pardon an old man,' said Hans, 'but to say that this wine is poison is to say that I am a murderer. I will prove to you that it is not poisoned. I will drink it.' And he raised the glass to his trembling lips. In that moment Aribert saw that old Hans, at any rate, was not an accomplice of Jules. Springing up from his seat, he knocked the glass from the aged servitor's hands, and the fragments of it fell with a light tinkling crash partly on the table and partly on the floor. The Prince and the servant gazed at one another in a distressing and terrible silence.

There was a slight noise, and Aribert looked aside. He saw that Eugen's body had slipped forward limply over the left arm of his chair; the Prince's arms hung straight and lifeless; his eyes were closed; he was unconscious.

'Hans!' murmured Aribert. 'Hans! What is this?'

Chapter Twenty-Five THE STEAM LAUNCH

MR TOM JACKSON's notion of making good his escape from the hôtel by means of a steam launch was an excellent one, so far as it went, but Theodore Racksole, for his part, did not consider that it went quite far enough.

Theodore Racksole opined, with peculiar glee, that he now had a tangible and definite clue for the catching of the Grand Babylon's ex-waiter. He knew nothing of the Port of London, but he happened to know a good deal of the far more complicated, though somewhat smaller, Port of New York, and he was sure there ought to be no extraordinary difficulty in getting hold of Jules' steam launch. To those who are not thoroughly familiar with it the River Thames and its docks, from London Bridge to Gravesend, seems a vast and uncharted wilderness of craft—a wilderness in which it would be perfectly easy to hide even a three-master successfully. To such people the idea of looking for a steam launch on the river would be about equivalent to the idea of looking for a needle in a bundle of hay. But the fact is, there are hundreds of men between St Katherine's Wharf and Blackwall who literally know the Thames as the suburban householder knows his back-garden—who can recognize thousands of ships and put a name to them at a distance of half a mile, who are informed as to every movement of vessels on the great stream, who know all the captains, all the engineers, all the lightermen, all the pilots, all the licensed watermen, and all the unlicensed scoundrels from the Tower to Gravesend, and a lot further. By these experts of the Thames the slightest unusual event on the water is noticed and discussed—a wherry cannot change hands but they will guess shrewdly upon the price paid and the intentions of the new owner with regard to it. They have a habit of watching the river for the mere interest of the sight, and they talk about everything like housewives gathered of an evening round the cottage door. If the first mate of a Castle Liner gets the sack they will be able to tell you what he said to the captain, what the old man said to him, and what both said to the Board, and having finished off that affair they will cheerfully turn to discussing whether Bill Stevens sank his barge outside the West Indian No.2 by accident or on purpose.

Theodore Racksole had no satisfactory means of identifying the steam launch which carried away Mr Tom Jackson. The sky had clouded over soon after midnight, and there was also a slight mist, and he had only been able to make out that it was a low craft, about sixty feet long, probably painted black. He had personally kept a watch all through the night on vessels going upstream, and during the next morning he had a man to take his place who warned him whenever a steam launch went towards Westminster. At noon, after his conversation with Prince Aribert, he went down the river in a hired row-boat as far as the Custom House, and poked about everywhere, in search of any vessel which could by any possibility be the one he was in search of.

But he found nothing. He was, therefore, tolerably sure that the mysterious launch lay somewhere below the Custom House. At the Custom House stairs, he landed, and asked for a very high official—an official inferior only to a Commissioner—whom he had entertained once in New York, and who had met him in London on business at Lloyd's. In the large but dingy office of this great man a long conversation took place—a conversation in which Racksole had to exercise a certain amount of persuasive power, and which ultimately ended in the high official ringing his bell.

'Desire Mr Hazell—room No. 332—to speak to me,' said the official to the boy who answered the summons, and then, turning to Racksole: 'I need hardly repeat, my dear Mr Racksole, that this is strictly unofficial.'

'Agreed, of course,' said Racksole.

Mr Hazell entered. He was a young man of about thirty, dressed in blue serge, with a pale, keen face, a brown moustache and a rather handsome brown beard.

'Mr Hazell,' said the high official, 'let me introduce you to Mr Theodore Racksole—you will doubtless be familiar with his name. Mr Hazell,' he went on to Racksole, 'is one of our outdoor staff—what we call an examining officer. Just now he is doing night duty. He has a boat on the river and a couple of men, and the right to board and examine any craft whatever. What Mr Hazell and his crew don't know about the Thames between here and Gravesend isn't knowledge.'

'Glad to meet you, sir,' said Racksole simply, and they shook hands.

Racksole observed with satisfaction that Mr Hazell was entirely at his ease.

'Now, Hazell,' the high official continued, 'Mr Racksole wants you to help in a little private expedition on the river to-night. I will give you a night's leave. I sent for you partly because I thought you would enjoy the affair and partly because I think I can rely on you to regard it as entirely unofficial and not to talk about it. You understand? I dare say you will have no cause to regret having obliged Mr Racksole.'

'I think I grasp the situation,' said Hazell, with a slight smile.

'And, by the way,' added the high official, 'although the business is unofficial, it might be well if you wore your official overcoat. See?'

'Decidedly,' said Hazell; 'I should have done so in any case.'

'And now, Mr Hazell,' said Racksole, 'will you do me the pleasure of lunching with me? If you agree, I should like to lunch at the place you usually frequent.'

So it came to pass that Theodore Racksole and George Hazell, outdoor clerk in the Customs, lunched together at 'Thomas's Chop-House', in the city of London, upon mutton-chops and coffee. The millionaire soon discovered that he had got hold of a keen-witted man and a person of much insight.

'Tell me,' said Hazell, when they had reached the cigarette stage, 'are the magazine writers anything like correct?'

'What do you mean?' asked Racksole, mystified.

'Well, you're a millionaire—"one of the best", I believe. One often sees articles on and interviews with millionaires, which describe their private railroad cars, their steam yachts on the Hudson, their marble stables, and so on, and so on. Do you happen to have those things?'

'I have a private car on the New York Central, and I have a two thousand ton schooner-yacht—though it isn't on the Hudson. It happens just now to be on East River. And I am bound to admit that the stables of my uptown place are fitted with marble.' Racksole laughed.

'Ah!' said Hazell. 'Now I can believe that I am lunching with a millionaire.

It's strange how facts like those—unimportant in themselves—appeal to the imagination. You seem to me a real millionaire now. You've given me some personal information; I'll give you some in return. I earn three hundred a year, and perhaps sixty pounds a year extra for overtime. I live by myself in two rooms in Muscovy Court. I've as much money as I need, and I always do exactly what I like outside office. As regards the office, I do as little work as I can, on principle—it's a fight between us and the Commissioners who shall get the best. They try to do us down, and we try to do them down—it's pretty even on the whole. All's fair in war, you know, and there ain't no ten commandments in a Government office.'

Racksole laughed. 'Can you get off this afternoon?' he asked.

'Certainly,' said Hazell; 'I'll get one of my pals to sign on for me, and then I shall be free.'

'Well,' said Racksole, 'I should like you to come down with me to the Grand Babylon. Then we can talk over my little affair at length. And may we go on your boat? I want to meet your crew.'

'That will be all right,' Hazell remarked. 'My two men are the idlest, most soul-less chaps you ever saw. They eat too much, and they have an enormous appetite for beer; but they know the river, and they know their business, and they will do anything within the fair game if they are paid for it, and aren't asked to hurry.'

That night, just after dark, Theodore Racksole embarked with his new friend George Hazell in one of the black-painted Customs wherries, manned by a crew of two men—both the later freemen of the river, a distinction which carries with it certain privileges unfamiliar to the mere landsman. It was a cloudy and oppressive evening, not a star showing to illumine the slow tide, now just past its flood. The vast forms of steamers at anchor—chiefly those of the General Steam Navigation and the Aberdeen Line—heaved themselves high out of the water, straining sluggishly at their mooring buoys. On either side the naked walls of warehouses rose like grey precipices from the stream, holding forth quaint arms of steam-cranes. To the west the Tower Bridge spanned the river with its formidable arch, and above that its suspended footpath—a hundred and fifty feet from earth.

Down towards the east and the Pool of London a forest of funnels and masts was dimly outlined against the sinister sky. Huge barges, each steered by a single man at the end of a pair of giant oars, lumbered and swirled down-stream at all angles. Occasionally a tug snorted busily past, flashing its red and green signals and dragging an unwieldy tail of barges in its wake. Then a Margate passenger steamer, its electric lights gleaming from every porthole, swerved round to anchor, with its load of two thousand fatigued excursionists. Over everything brooded an air of mystery—a spirit and feeling of strangeness, remoteness, and the inexplicable. As the broad flat little boat bobbed its way under the shadow of enormous hulks, beneath stretched hawsers, and past buoys covered with green slime, Racksole could scarcely believe that he was in the very heart of London—the most prosaic city in the world. He had a queer idea that almost anything might happen in this seeming waste of waters at this weird hour of ten o'clock. It appeared incredible to him that only a mile or two away people were sitting in theatres applauding farces, and that at Cannon Street Station, a few yards off, other people were calmly taking the train to various highly respectable suburbs whose names he was gradually learning. He had the uplifting sensation of being in another world which comes to us sometimes amid surroundings violently different from our usual surroundings. The most ordinary noises—of men calling, of a chain running through a slot, of a distant siren—translated themselves to his ears into terrible and haunting sounds, full of portentous significance. He looked over the side of the boat into the brown water, and asked himself what frightful secrets lay hidden in its depth. Then he put his hand into his hip-pocket and touched the stock of his Colt revolver—that familiar substance comforted him.

The oarsmen had instructions to drop slowly down to the Pool, as the wide reach below the Tower is called. These two men had not been previously informed of the precise object of the expedition, but now that they were safely afloat Hazell judged it expedient to give them some notion of it. 'We expect to come across a rather suspicious steam launch,' he said. 'My friend here is very anxious to get a sight of her, and until he has seen her nothing definite can be done.'

'What sort of a craft is she, sir?' asked the stroke oar, a fat-faced man who seemed absolutely incapable of any serious exertion.

'I don't know,' Racksole replied; 'but as near as I can judge, she's about sixty feet in length, and painted black. I fancy I shall recognize her when I see her.'

'Not much to go by, that,' exclaimed the other man curtly. But he said no more. He, as well as his mate, had received from Theodore Racksole one English sovereign as a kind of preliminary fee, and an English sovereign will do a lot towards silencing the natural sarcastic tendencies and free speech of a Thames waterman.

'There's one thing I noticed,' said Racksole suddenly, 'and I forgot to tell you of it, Mr Hazell. Her screw seemed to move with a rather irregular, lame sort of beat.'

Both watermen burst into a laugh.

'Oh,' said the fat rower, 'I know what you're after, sir—it's Jack Everett's launch, commonly called "Squirm". She's got a four-bladed propeller, and one blade is broken off short.'

'Ay, that's it, sure enough,' agreed the man in the bows. 'And if it's her you want, I seed her lying up against Cherry Gardens Pier this very morning.'

'Let us go to Cherry Gardens Pier by all means, as soon as possible,'

Racksole said, and the boat swung across stream and then began to creep down by the right bank, feeling its way past wharves, many of which, even at that hour, were still busy with their cranes, that descended empty into the bellies of ships and came up full. As the two watermen gingerly manoeuvred the boat on the ebbing tide, Hazell explained to the millionaire that the 'Squirm' was one of the most notorious craft on the river. It appeared that when anyone had a nefarious or underhand scheme afoot which necessitated river work Everett's launch was always available for a suitable monetary consideration. The 'Squirm' had got itself into a thousand scrapes, and out of those scrapes again with safety, if not precisely with honour. The river police kept a watchful eye on it, and the chief marvel about the whole thing was that old Everett, the owner, had never yet been seriously compromised in any illegal escapade. Not once had the officer of the law been able to prove anything definite against the proprietor of the 'Squirm', though several of its quondam hirers were at that very moment in various of Her Majesty's prisons throughout the country. Latterly, however, the launch, with its damaged propeller, which Everett consistently refused to have repaired, had acquired an evil reputation, even among evil-doers, and this fraternity had gradually come to abandon it for less easily recognizable craft.

'Your friend, Mr Tom Jackson,' said Hazell to Racksole, 'committed an error of discretion when he hired the "Squirm". A scoundrel of his experience and calibre ought certainly to have known better than that. You cannot fail to get a clue now.'

By this time the boat was approaching Cherry Gardens Pier, but unfortunately a thin night-fog had swept over the river, and objects could not be discerned with any clearness beyond a distance of thirty yards. As the Customs boat scraped down past the pier all its occupants strained eyes for a glimpse of the mysterious launch, but nothing could be seen of it. The boat continued to float idly down-stream, the men resting on their oars.

Then they narrowly escaped bumping a large Norwegian sailing vessel at anchor with her stem pointing down-stream. This ship they passed on the port side. Just as they got clear of her bowsprit the fat man cried out excitedly, 'There's her nose!' and he put the boat about and began to pull back against the tide. And surely the missing 'Squirm' was comfortably anchored on the starboard quarter of the Norwegian ship, hidden neatly between the ship and the shore. The men pulled very quietly alongside.

Chapter Twenty-Six THE NIGHT CHASE AND THE MUDLARK

'I'LL board her to start with,' said Hazell, whispering to Racksole. 'I'll make out that I suspect they've got dutiable goods on board, and that will give me a chance to have a good look at her.'

Dressed in his official overcoat and peaked cap, he stepped, rather jauntily as Racksole thought, on to the low deck of the launch. 'Anyone aboard?'

Racksole heard him cry out, and a woman's voice answered. 'I'm a Customs examining officer, and I want to search the launch,' Hazell shouted, and then disappeared down into the little saloon amidships, and Racksole heard no more. It seemed to the millionaire that Hazell had been gone hours, but at length he returned.

'Can't find anything,' he said, as he jumped into the boat, and then privately to Racksole: 'There's a woman on board. Looks as if she might coincide with your description of Miss Spencer. Steam's up, but there's no engineer. I asked where the engineer was, and she inquired what business that was of mine, and requested me to get through with my own business and clear off. Seems rather a smart sort. I poked my nose into everything, but I saw no sign of any one else. Perhaps we'd better pull away and lie near for a bit, just to see if anything queer occurs.'

'You're quite sure he isn't on board?' Racksole asked.

'Quite,' said Hazell positively: 'I know how to search a vessel. See this,' and he handed to Racksole a sort of steel skewer, about two feet long, with a wooden handle. 'That,' he said, 'is one of the Customs' aids to searching.'

'I suppose it wouldn't do to go on board and carry off the lady?' Racksole suggested doubtfully.

'Well,' Hazell began, with equal doubtfulness, 'as for that—'

'Where's 'e orf?' It was the man in the bows who interrupted Hazell.

Following the direction of the man's finger, both Hazell and Racksole saw with more or less distinctness a dinghy slip away from the forefoot of the Norwegian vessel and disappear downstream into the mist.

'It's Jules, I'll swear,' cried Racksole. 'After him, men. Ten pounds apiece if we overtake him!'

'Lay down to it now, boys!' said Hazell, and the heavy Customs boat shot out in pursuit.

'This is going to be a lark,' Racksole remarked.

'Depends on what you call a lark,' said Hazell; 'it's not much of a lark tearing down midstream like this in a fog. You never know when you mayn't be in kingdom come with all these barges knocking around. I expect that chap hid in the dinghy when he first caught sight of us, and then slipped his painter as soon as I'd gone.'

The boat was moving at a rapid pace with the tide. Steering was a matter of luck and instinct more than anything else. Every now and then Hazell, who held the lines, was obliged to jerk the boat's head sharply round to avoid a barge or an anchored vessel. It seemed to Racksole that vessels were anchored all over the stream. He looked about him anxiously, but for a long time he could see nothing but mist and vague nautical forms. Then suddenly he said, quietly enough, 'We're on the right road; I can see him ahead. We're gaining on him.' In another minute the dinghy was plainly visible, not twenty yards away, and the sculler—sculling frantically now—was unmistakably Jules—Jules in a light tweed suit and a bowler hat.

'You were right,' Hazell said; 'this is a lark. I believe I'm getting quite excited. It's more exciting than playing the trombone in an orchestra. I'll run him down, eh?—and then we can drag the chap in from the water.'

Racksole nodded, but at that moment a barge, with her red sails set, stood out of the fog clean across the bows of the Customs boat, which narrowly escaped instant destruction. When they got clear, and the usual interchange of calm, nonchalant swearing was over, the dinghy was barely to be discerned in the mist, and the fat man was breathing in such a manner that his sighs might almost have been heard on the banks. Racksole wanted violently to do something, but there was nothing to do; he could only sit supine by Hazell's side in the stern-sheets. Gradually they began again to overtake the dinghy, whose one-man crew was evidently tiring. As they came up, hand over fist, the dinghy's nose swerved aside, and the tiny craft passed down a water-lane between two anchored mineral barges, which lay black and deserted about fifty yards from the Surrey shore. 'To starboard,' said Racksole. 'No, man!'

Hazell replied; 'we can't get through there. He's bound to come out below; it's only a feint. I'll keep our nose straight ahead.'

And they went on, the fat man pounding away, with a face which glistened even in the thick gloom. It was an empty dinghy which emerged from between the two barges and went drifting and revolving down towards Greenwich.

The fat man gasped a word to his comrade, and the Customs boat stopped dead.

"E's all right,' said the man in the bows. 'If it's 'im you want, 'e's on one o' them barges, so you've only got to step on and take 'im orf.'

'That's all,' said a voice out of the depths of the nearest barge, and it was the voice of Jules, otherwise known as Mr Tom Jackson.

"Ear 'im?' said the fat man smiling. "E's a good 'un, 'e is. But if I was you, Mr Hazell, or you, sir, I shouldn't step on to that barge so quick as all that.'

They backed the boat under the stem of the nearest barge and gazed upwards.

'It's all right,' said Racksole to Hazell; 'I've got a revolver. How can I clamber up there?'

'Yes, I dare say you've got a revolver all right,' Hazell replied sharply.

'But you mustn't use it. There mustn't be any noise. We should have the river police down on us in a twinkling if there was a revolver shot, and it would be the ruin of me. If an inquiry was held the Commissioners wouldn't take any official notice of the fact that my superior officer had put me on to this job, and I should be requested to leave the service.'

'Have no fear on that score,' said Racksole. 'I shall, of course, take all responsibility.'

'It wouldn't matter how much responsibility you took,' Hazell retorted; 'you wouldn't put me back into the service, and my career would be at an end.'

'But there are other careers,' said Racksole, who was really anxious to lame his ex-waiter by means of a judiciously-aimed bullet. 'There are other careers.'

'The Customs is my career,' said Hazell, 'so let's have no shooting. We'll wait about a bit; he can't escape. You can have my skewer if you like'—and he gave Racksole his searching instrument. 'And you can do what you please, provided you do it neatly and don't make a row over it.'

For a few moments the four men were passive in the boat, surrounded by swirling mist, with black water beneath them, and towering above them a half-loaded barge with a desperate and resourceful man on board. Suddenly the mist parted and shrivelled away in patches, as though before the breath of some monster. The sky was visible; it was a clear sky, and the moon was shining. The transformation was just one of those meteorological quick-changes which happen most frequently on a great river.

'That's a sight better,' said the fat man. At the same moment a head appeared over the edge of the barge. It was Jules' face—dark, sinister and leering.

'Is it Mr Racksole in that boat?' he inquired calmly; 'because if so, let Mr Racksole step up. Mr Racksole has caught me, and he can have me for the asking. Here I am.' He stood up to his full height on the barge, tall against the night sky, and all the occupants of the boat could see that he held firmly clasped in his right hand a short dagger. 'Now, Mr Racksole, you've been after me for a long time,' he continued; 'here I am. Why don't you step up? If you haven't got the pluck yourself, persuade someone else to step up in your place ... the same fair treatment will be accorded to all.' And Jules laughed a low, penetrating laugh.

He was in the midst of this laugh when he lurched suddenly forward.

'What'r' you doing of aboard my barge? Off you goes!' It was a boy's small shrill voice that sounded in the night. A ragged boy's small form had appeared silently behind Jules, and two small arms with a vicious shove precipitated him into the water. He fell with a fine gurgling splash. It was at once obvious that swimming was not among Jules' accomplishments. He floundered wildly and sank. When he reappeared he was dragged into the Customs boat. Rope was produced, and in a minute or two the man lay ignominiously bound in the bottom of the boat. With the aid of a mudlark—a mere barge boy, who probably had no more right on the barge than Jules himself—Racksole had won his game. For the first time for several weeks the millionaire experienced a sensation of equanimity and satisfaction. He leaned over the prostrate form of Jules, Hazell's professional skewer in his hand.

'What are you going to do with him now?' asked Hazell.

'We'll row up to the landing steps in front of the Grand Babylon. He shall be well lodged at my hôtel, I promise him.'

Jules spoke no word.

Before Racksole parted company with the Customs man that night Jules had been safely transported into the Grand Babylon Hôtel and the two watermen had received their £10 apiece.

'You will sleep here?' said the millionaire to Mr George Hazell. 'It is late.'

'With pleasure,' said Hazell. The next morning he found a sumptuous breakfast awaiting him, and in his table-napkin was a Bank of England note for a hundred pounds. But, though he did not hear of them till much later, many things had happened before Hazell consumed that sumptuous breakfast.

Chapter Twenty-Seven THE CONFESSION OF MR TOM JACKSON

IT happened that the small bedroom occupied by Jules during the years he was head-waiter at the Grand Babylon had remained empty since his sudden dismissal by Theodore Racksole. No other head-waiter had been formally appointed in his place; and, indeed, the absence of one man—even the unique Jules—could scarcely have been noticed in the enormous staff of a place like the Grand Babylon. The functions of a head-waiter are generally more ornamental, spectacular, and morally impressive than useful, and it was so at the great hôtel on the Embankment. Racksole accordingly had the excellent idea of transporting his prisoner, with as much secrecy as possible, to this empty bedroom. There proved to be no difficulty in doing so; Jules showed himself perfectly amenable to a show of superior force.

Racksole took upstairs with him an old commissionaire who had been attached to the outdoor service of the hôtel for many years—a grey-haired man, wiry as a terrier and strong as a mastiff. Entering the bedroom with Jules, whose hands were bound, he told the commissionaire to remain outside the door.

Jules' bedroom was quite an ordinary apartment, though perhaps slightly superior to the usual accommodation provided for servants in the caravanserais of the West End. It was about fourteen by twelve. It was furnished with a bedstead, a small wardrobe, a—mall washstand and dressing-table, and two chairs. There were two hooks behind the door, a strip of carpet by the bed, and some cheap ornaments on the iron mantelpiece. There was also one electric light. The window was a little square one, high up from the floor, and it looked on the inner quadrangle.

The room was on the top storey—the eighth—and from it you had a view sheer to the ground. Twenty feet below ran a narrow cornice about a foot wide; three feet or so above the window another and wider cornice jutted out, and above that was the high steep roof of the hôtel, though you could not see it from the window. As Racksole examined the window and the outlook, he said to himself that Jules could not escape by that exit, at any rate. He gave a glance up the chimney, and saw that the flue was far too small to admit a man's body.

Then he called in the commissionaire, and together they bound Jules firmly to the bedstead, allowing him, however, to lie down. All the while the captive never opened his mouth—merely smiled a smile of disdain. Finally Racksole removed the ornaments, the carpet, the chairs and the hooks, and wrenched away the switch of the electric light. Then he and the commissionaire left the room, and Racksole locked the door on the outside and put the key in his pocket.

'You will keep watch here,' he said to the commissionaire, 'through the night. You can sit on this chair. Don't go to sleep. If you hear the slightest noise in the room blow your cab-whistle; I will arrange to answer the signal. If there is no noise do nothing whatever. I don't want this talked about, you understand. I shall trust you; you can trust me.'

'But the servants will see me here when they get up to-morrow,' said the commissionaire, with a faint smile, 'and they will be pretty certain to ask what I'm doing of up here. What shall I say to 'em?'

'You've been a soldier, haven't you?' asked Racksole.

'I've seen three campaigns, sir,' was the reply, and, with a gesture of pardonable pride, the grey-haired fellow pointed to the medals on his breast.

'Well, supposing you were on sentry duty and some meddlesome person in camp asked you what you were doing—what should you say?'

'I should tell him to clear off or take the consequences, and pretty quick too.'

'Do that to-morrow morning, then, if necessary,' said Racksole, and departed.

It was then about one o'clock a.m. The millionaire retired to bed—not his own bed, but a bed on the seventh storey. He did not, however, sleep very long. Shortly after dawn he was wide awake, and thinking busily about Jules.

He was, indeed, very curious to know Jules' story, and he determined, if the thing could be done at all, by persuasion or otherwise, to extract it from him. With a man of Theodore Racksole's temperament there is no time like the present, and at six o'clock, as the bright morning sun brought gaiety into the window, he dressed and went upstairs again to the eighth storey. The commissionaire sat stolid, but alert on his chair, and, at the sight of his master, rose and saluted.

'Anything happened?' Racksole asked.

'Nothing, sir.'

'Servants say anything?'

'Only a dozen or so of 'em are up yet, sir. One of 'em asked what I was playing at, and so I told her I was looking after a bull bitch and a litter of pups that you was very particular about, sir.'

'Good,' said Racksole, as he unlocked the door and entered the room. All was exactly as he had left it, except that Jules who had been lying on his back, had somehow turned over and was now lying on his face. He gazed silently, scowling at the millionaire. Racksole greeted him and ostentatiously took a revolver from his hip-pocket and laid it on the dressing-table. Then he seated himself on the dressing-table by the side of the revolver, his legs dangling an inch or two above the floor.

'I want to have a talk to you, Jackson,' he began.

'You can talk to me as much as you like,' said Jules. 'I shan't interfere, you may bet on that.'

'I should like you to answer some questions.'

'That's different,' said Jules. 'I'm not going to answer any questions while I'm tied up like this. You may bet on that, too.'

'It will pay you to be reasonable,' said Racksole.

'I'm not going to answer any questions while I'm tied up.'

'I'll unfasten your legs, if you like,' Racksole suggested politely, 'then you can sit up. It's no use you pretending you've been uncomfortable, because I know you haven't. I calculate you've been treated very handsomely, my son. There you are!' and he loosened the lower extremities of his prisoner from their bonds. 'Now I repeat you may as well be reasonable. You may as well admit that you've been fairly beaten in the game and act accordingly. I was determined to beat you, by myself, without the police, and I've done it.'

'You've done yourself,' retorted Jules. 'You've gone against the law. If you'd had any sense you wouldn't have meddled; you'd have left everything to the police. They'd have muddled about for a year or two, and then done nothing. Who's going to tell the police now? Are you? Are you going to give me up to 'em, and say, "Here, I've caught him for you". If you do they'll ask you to explain several things, and then you'll look foolish. One crime doesn't excuse another, and you'll find that out.'

With unerring insight, Jules had perceived exactly the difficulty of Racksole's position, and it was certainly a difficulty which Racksole did not attempt to minimize to himself. He knew well that it would have to be faced. He did not, however, allow Jules to guess his thoughts.

'Meanwhile,' he said calmly to the other, 'you're here and my prisoner.

You've committed a variegated assortment of crimes, and among them is murder. You are due to be hung. You know that. There is no reason why I should call in the police at all. It will be perfectly easy for me to finish you off, as you deserve, myself. I shall only be carrying out justice, and robbing the hangman of his fee. Precisely as I brought you into the hôtel, I can take you out again. A few days ago you borrowed or stole a steam yacht at Ostend. What you have done with it I don't know, nor do I care. But I strongly suspect that my daughter had a narrow escape of being murdered on your steam yacht. Now I have a steam yacht of my own. Suppose I use it as you used yours! Suppose I smuggle you on to it, steam out to sea, and then ask you to step off it into the ocean one night. Such things have been done.

Such things will be done again. If I acted so, I should at least, have the satisfaction of knowing that I had relieved society from the incubus of a scoundrel.'

'But you won't,' Jules murmured.

'No,' said Racksole steadily, 'I won't—if you behave yourself this morning. But I swear to you that if you don't I will never rest till you are dead, police or no police. You don't know Theodore Racksole.'

'I believe you mean it,' Jules exclaimed, with an air of surprised interest, as though he had discovered something of importance.

'I believe I do,' Racksole resumed. 'Now listen. At the best, you will be given up to the police. At the worst, I shall deal with you myself. With the police you may have a chance—you may get off with twenty years' penal servitude, because, though it is absolutely certain that you murdered Reginald Dimmock, it would be a little difficult to prove the case against you. But with me you would have no chance whatever. I have a few questions to put to you, and it will depend on how you answer them whether I give you up to the police or take the law into my own hands. And let me tell you that the latter course would be much simpler for me. And I would take it, too, did I not feel that you were a very clever and exceptional man; did I not have a sort of sneaking admiration for your detestable skill and ingenuity.'

'You think, then, that I am clever?' said Jules. 'You are right. I am. I should have been much too clever for you if luck had not been against me.

You owe your victory, not to skill, but to luck.'

'That is what the vanquished always say. Waterloo was a bit of pure luck for the English, no doubt, but it was Waterloo all the same.'

Jules yawned elaborately. 'What do you want to know?' he inquired, with politeness.

'First and foremost, I want to know the names of your accomplices inside this hôtel.'

'I have no more,' said Jules. 'Rocco was the last.'

'Don't begin by lying to me. If you had no accomplice, how did you contrive that one particular bottle of Romanée-Conti should be served to his Highness Prince Eugen?'

'Then you discovered that in time, did you?' said Jules. 'I was afraid so.

Let me explain that that needed no accomplice. The bottle was topmost in the bin, and naturally it would be taken. Moreover, I left it sticking out a little further than the rest.'

'You did not arrange, then, that Hubbard should be taken ill the night before last?'

'I had no idea,' said Jules, 'that the excellent Hubbard was not enjoying his accustomed health.'

'Tell me,' said Racksole, 'who or what is the origin of your vendetta against the life of Prince Eugen?'

'I had no vendetta against the life of Prince Eugen,' said Jules, 'at least, not to begin with. I merely undertook, for a consideration, to see that Prince Eugen did not have an interview with a certain Mr Sampson Levi in London before a certain date, that was all. It seemed simple enough. I had been engaged in far more complicated transactions before. I was convinced that I could manage it, with the help of Rocco and Em—and Miss Spencer.'

'Is that woman your wife?'

'She would like to be,' he sneered. 'Please don't interrupt. I had completed my arrangements, when you so inconsiderately bought the hôtel. I don't mind admitting now that from the very moment when you came across me that night in the corridor I was secretly afraid of you, though I scarcely admitted the fact even to myself then. I thought it safer to shift the scene of our operations to Ostend. I had meant to deal with Prince Eugen in this hôtel, but I decided, then, to intercept him on the Continent, and I despatched Miss Spencer with some instructions. Troubles never come singly, and it happened that just then that fool Dimmock, who had

473

been in the swim with us, chose to prove refractory. The slightest hitch would have upset everything, and I was obliged to—to clear him off the scene. He wanted to back out—he had a bad attack of conscience, and violent measures were essential. I regret his untimely decease, but he brought it on himself. Well, everything was going serenely when you and your brilliant daughter, apparently determined to meddle, turned up again among us at Ostend. Only twenty-four hours, however, had to elapse before the date which had been mentioned to me by my employers. I kept poor little Eugen for the allotted time, and then you managed to get hold of him. I do not deny that you scored there, though, according to my original instructions, you scored too late. The time had passed, and so, so far as I knew, it didn't matter a pin whether Prince Eugen saw Mr Sampson Levi or not. But my employers were still uneasy. They were uneasy even after little Eugen had lain ill in Ostend for several weeks. It appears that they feared that even at that date an interview between Prince Eugen and Mr Sampson Levi might work harm to them. So they applied to me again. This time they wanted Prince Eugen to be—em—finished off entirely. They offered high terms.'

'What terms?'

'I had received fifty thousand pounds for the first job, of which Rocco had half. Rocco was also to be made a member of a certain famous European order, if things went right. That was what he coveted far more than the money—the vain fellow! For the second job I was offered a hundred thousand. A tolerably large sum. I regret that I have not been able to earn it.'

'Do you mean to tell me,' asked Racksole, horror-struck by this calm confession, in spite of his previous knowledge, 'that you were offered a hundred thousand pounds to poison Prince Eugen?'

'You put it rather crudely,' said Jules in reply. 'I prefer to say that I was offered a hundred thousand pounds if Prince Eugen should die within a reasonable time.'

'And who were your damnable employers?'

'That, honestly, I do not know.'

'You know, I suppose, who paid you the first fifty thousand pounds, and who promised you the hundred thousand.'

'Well,' said Jules, 'I know vaguely. I know that he came via Vienna from—em—Bosnia. My impression was that the affair had some bearing, direct or indirect, on the projected marriage of the King of Bosnia. He is a young monarch, scarcely out of political leading-strings, as it were, and doubtless his Ministers thought that they had better arrange his marriage for him. They tried last year, and failed because the Princess whom they had in mind had cast her sparkling eyes on another Prince. That Prince happened to be Prince Eugen of Posen. The Ministers of the King of Bosnia knew exactly the circumstances of Prince Eugen. They knew that he could not marry without liquidating his debts, and they knew that he could only liquidate his debts through this Jew, Sampson Levi. Unfortunately for me, they ultimately wanted to make too sure of Prince Eugen. They were afraid he might after all arrange his marriage without the aid of Mr Sampson Levi, and so—well, you know the rest.... It is a pity that the poor little innocent King of Bosnia can't have the Princess of his Ministers' choice.'

'Then you think that the King himself had no part in this abominable crime?'

'I think decidedly not.'

'I am glad of that,' said Racksole simply. 'And now, the name of your immediate employer.'

'He was merely an agent. He called himself Sleszak—S-l-e-s-z-a-k. But I imagine that that wasn't his real name. I don't know his real name. An old man, he often used to be found at the Hôtel Ritz, Paris.'

'Mr Sleszak and I will meet,' said Racksole.

'Not in this world,' said Jules quickly. 'He is dead. I heard only last night—just before our little tussle.'

There was a silence.

'It is well,' said Racksole at length. 'Prince Eugen lives, despite all plots. After all, justice is done.'

'Mr Racksole is here, but he can see no one, Miss.' The words came from behind the door, and the voice was the commissionaire's. Racksole started up, and went towards the door.

'Nonsense,' was the curt reply, in feminine tones. 'Move aside instantly.'

The door opened, and Nella entered. There were tears in her eyes.

'Oh! Dad,' she exclaimed, 'I've only just heard you were in the hôtel. We looked for you everywhere. Come at once, Prince Eugen is dying—' Then she saw the man sitting on the bed, and stopped.

Later, when Jules was alone again, he remarked to himself, 'I may get that hundred thousand.'

Chapter Twenty-Eight THE STATE BEDROOM ONCE MORE

WHEN, immediately after the episode of the bottle of Romanée-Conti in the State dining-room, Prince Aribert and old Hans found that Prince Eugen had sunk in an unconscious heap over his chair, both the former thought, at the first instant, that Eugen must have already tasted the poisoned wine. But a moment's reflection showed that this was not possible. If the Hereditary Prince of Posen was dying or dead, his condition was due to some other agency than the Romanée-Conti. Aribert bent over him, and a powerful odour from the man's lips at once disclosed the cause of the disaster: it was the odour of laudanum. Indeed, the smell of that sinister drug seemed now to float heavily over the whole table. Across Aribert's mind there flashed then the true explanation. Prince Eugen, taking advantage of Aribert's attention being momentarily diverted; and yielding to a sudden impulse of despair, had decided to poison himself, and had carried out his intention on the spot.

The laudanum must have been already in his pocket, and this fact went to prove that the unfortunate Prince had previously contemplated such a proceeding, even after his definite promise. Aribert remembered now with painful vividness his nephew's words: 'I withdraw my promise. Observe that—I withdraw it.' It must have been instantly after the utterance of that formal withdrawal that Eugen attempted to destroy himself.

'It's laudanum, Hans,' Aribert exclaimed, rather helplessly.

'Surely his Highness has not taken poison?' said Hans. 'It is impossible!'

'I fear it is only too possible,' said the other. 'It's laudanum. What are we to do? Quick, man!'

'His Highness must be roused, Prince. He must have an emetic. We had better carry him to the bedroom.'

They did, and laid him on the great bed; and then Aribert mixed an emetic of mustard and water, and administered it, but without any effect. The sufferer lay motionless, with every muscle relaxed. His skin was ice-cold to the touch, and the eyelids, half-drawn, showed that the pupils were painfully contracted.

'Go out, and send for a doctor, Hans. Say that Prince Eugen has been suddenly taken ill, but that it isn't serious. The truth must never be known.'

'He must be roused, sire,' Hans said again, as he hurried from the room.

Aribert lifted his nephew from the bed, shook him, pinched him, flicked him cruelly, shouted at him, dragged him about, but to no avail. At length he desisted, from mere physical fatigue, and laid the Prince back again on the bed. Every minute that elapsed seemed an hour. Alone with the unconscious organism in the silence of the great stately chamber, under the cold yellow glare of the electric lights, Aribert became a prey to the most despairing thoughts. The tragedy of his nephew's career forced itself upon him, and it occurred to him that an early and shameful death had all along been inevitable for this good-natured, weak-purposed, unhappy child of a historic throne. A little good fortune, and his character, so evenly balanced between right and wrong, might have followed the proper path, and Eugen might have figured at any rate with dignity on the European stage. But now it appeared that all was over, the last stroke played. And in this disaster Aribert saw the ruin of his own hopes. For Aribert would have to occupy his nephew's throne, and he felt instinctively that nature had not cut him out for a throne. By a natural impulse he inwardly rebelled against the prospect of monarchy. Monarchy meant so much for which he knew himself to be entirely unfitted. It meant a political marriage, which means a forced marriage, a union against inclination. And then what of Nella—Nella!

Hans returned. 'I have sent for the nearest doctor, and also for a specialist,' he said.

'Good,' said Aribert. 'I hope they will hurry.' Then he sat down and wrote a card. 'Take this yourself to Miss Racksole. If she is out of the hôtel, ascertain where she is and follow her. Understand, it is of the first importance.'

Hans bowed, and departed for the second time, and Aribert was alone again.

He gazed at Eugen, and made another frantic attempt to rouse him from the deadly stupor, but it was useless. He walked away to the window: through the opened casement he could hear the tinkle of passing hansoms on the Embankment below, whistles of door-keepers, and the hoot of steam tugs on the river. The world went on as usual, it appeared. It was an absurd world.

He desired nothing better than to abandon his princely title, and live as a plain man, the husband of the finest woman on earth.... But now!...

Pah! How selfish he was, to be thinking of himself when Eugen lay dying. Yet—Nella!

The door opened, and a man entered, who was obviously the doctor. A few curt questions, and he had grasped the essentials of the case. 'Oblige me by ringing the bell, Prince. I shall want some hot water, and an able-bodied man and a nurse.'

'Who wants a nurse?' said a voice, and Nella came quietly in. 'I am a nurse,' she added to the doctor, 'and at your orders.'

The next two hours were a struggle between life and death. The first doctor, a specialist who followed him, Nella, Prince Aribert, and old Hans formed, as it were, a league to save the dying man. None else in the hôtel knew the real seriousness of the case. When a Prince falls ill, and especially by his own act, the precise truth is not issued broadcast to the universe.

According to official intelligence, a Prince is never seriously ill until he is dead. Such is statecraft.

The worst feature of Prince Eugen's case was that emetics proved futile.

Neither of the doctors could explain their failure, but it was only too apparent. The league was reduced to helplessness. At last the great specialist from Manchester Square gave it out that there was no chance for Prince Eugen unless the natural vigour of his constitution should prove capable of throwing off the poison unaided by scientific assistance, as a drunkard can sleep off his potion. Everything had been tried, even to artificial respiration and the injection of hot coffee. Having emitted this pronouncement, the great specialist from Manchester Square left. It was one o'clock in the morning. By one of those strange and futile coincidences which sometimes startle us by their subtle significance, the specialist met Theodore Racksole and his captive as they were entering the hôtel. Neither had the least suspicion of the other's business.

In the State bedroom the small group of watchers surrounded the bed. The slow minutes filed away in dreary procession. Another hour passed. Then the figure on the bed, hitherto so motionless, twitched and moved; the lips parted.

'There is hope,' said the doctor, and administered a stimulant which was handed to him by Nella.

In a quarter of an hour the patient had regained consciousness. For the ten thousandth time in the history of medicine a sound constitution had accomplished a miracle impossible to the accumulated medical skill of centuries.

In due course the doctor left, saying that Prince Eugen was 'on the high road to recovery,' and promising to come again within a few hours. Morning had dawned. Nella drew the great curtains, and let in a flood of sunlight.

Old Hans, overcome by fatigue, dozed in a chair in a far corner of the room.

The reaction had been too much for him. Nella and Prince Aribert looked at each other. They had not exchanged a word about themselves, yet each knew what the other had been thinking. They clasped hands with a perfect understanding. Their brief love-making had been of the silent kind, and it was silent now. No word was uttered. A shadow had passed from over them, but only their eyes expressed relief and joy.

'Aribert!' The faint call came from the bed. Aribert went to the bedside, while Nella remained near the window.

'What is it, Eugen?' he said. 'You are better now.'

'You think so?' murmured the other. 'I want you to forgive me for all this, Aribert. I must have caused you an intolerable trouble. I did it so clumsily; that is what annoys me. Laudanum was a feeble expedient; but I could think of nothing else, and I daren't ask anyone for advice. I was obliged to go out and buy the stuff for myself. It was all very awkward.

But, thank goodness, it has not been ineffectual.'

'What do you mean, Eugen? You are better. In a day or so you will be perfectly recovered.'

'I am dying,' said Eugen quietly. 'Do not be deceived. I die because I wish to die. It is bound to be so. I know by the feel of my heart. In a few hours it will be over. The throne of Posen will be yours, Aribert. You will fill it more worthily than I have done. Don't let them know over there that I poisoned myself. Swear Hans to secrecy; swear the doctors to secrecy; and breathe no word yourself. I have been a fool, but I do not wish it to be known that I was also a coward. Perhaps it is not cowardice; perhaps it is courage, after all—courage to cut the knot. I could not have survived the disgrace of any revelations, Aribert, and revelations would have been sure to come. I have made a fool of myself, but I am ready to pay for it. We of Posen—we always pay—everything except our debts. Ah! those debts! Had it not been for those I could have faced her who was to have been my wife, to have shared my throne. I could have hidden my past, and begun again. With her help I really could have begun again. But Fate has been against me—always! always! By the way, what was that plot against me, Aribert? I forget, I forget.'

His eyes closed. There was a sudden noise. Old Hans had slipped from his chair to the floor. He picked himself up, dazed, and crept shamefacedly out of the room.

Aribert took his nephew's hand.

'Nonsense, Eugen! You are dreaming. You will be all right soon. Pull yourself together.'

'All because of a million,' the sick man moaned. 'One miserable million English pounds. The national debt of Posen is fifty millions, and I, the Prince of Posen, couldn't borrow one. If I could have got it, I might have held my head up again. Good-bye, Aribert.... Who is that girl?'

Aribert looked up. Nella was standing silent at the foot of the bed, her eyes moist. She came round to the bedside, and put her hand on the patient's heart. Scarcely could she feel its pulsation, and to Aribert her eyes expressed a sudden despair.

At that moment Hans re-entered the room and beckoned to her.

'I have heard that Herr Racksole has returned to the hôtel,' he whispered, 'and that he has captured that man Jules, who they say is such a villain.'

Several times during the night Nella inquired for her father, but could gain no knowledge of his whereabouts. Now, at half-past six in the morning, a rumour had mysteriously spread among the servants of the hôtel about the happenings of the night before. How it had originated no one could have determined, but it had originated.

'Where is my father?' Nella asked of Hans.

He shrugged his shoulders, and pointed upwards. 'Somewhere at the top, they say.'

Nella almost ran out of the room. Her interruption of the interview between Jules and Theodore Racksole has already been described. As she came downstairs with her father she said again, 'Prince Eugen is dying—but I think you can save him.'

'I?' exclaimed Theodore.

'Yes,' she repeated positively. 'I will tell you what I want you to do, and you must do it.'

Chapter Twenty-Nine THEODORE IS CALLED TO THE RESCUE

AS Nella passed downstairs from the top storey with her father—the lifts had not yet begun to work—she drew him into her own room, and closed the door.

'What's this all about?' he asked, somewhat mystified, and even alarmed by the extreme seriousness of her face.

'Dad,' the girl began, 'you are very rich, aren't you? very, very rich?' She smiled anxiously, timidly. He did not remember to have seen that expression on her face before. He wanted to make a facetious reply, but checked himself.

'Yes,' he said, 'I am. You ought to know that by this time.'

'How soon could you realize a million pounds?'

'A million—what?' he cried. Even he was staggered by her calm reference to this gigantic sum. 'What on earth are you driving at?'

'A million pounds, I said. That is to say, five million dollars. How soon could you realize as much as that?'

'Oh!' he answered, 'in about a month, if I went about it neatly enough. I could unload as much as that in a month without scaring Wall Street and other places. But it would want some arrangement.'

'Useless!' she exclaimed. 'Couldn't you do it quicker, if you really had to?'

'If I really had to, I could fix it in a week, but it would make things lively, and I should lose on the job.'

'Couldn't you,' she persisted, 'couldn't you go down this morning and raise a million, somehow, if it was a matter of life and death?'

He hesitated. 'Look here, Nella,' he said, 'what is it you've got up your sleeve?'

'Just answer my question, Dad, and try not to think that I'm a stark, staring lunatic.'

'I rather expect I could get a million this morning, even in London. But it would cost pretty dear. It might cost me fifty thousand pounds, and there would be the dickens of an upset in New York—a sort of grand universal slump in my holdings.'

'Why should New York know anything about it?'

'Why should New York know anything about it!' he repeated. 'My girl, when anyone borrows a million sovereigns the whole world knows about it. Do you reckon that I can go up to the Governors of the Bank of

England and say, "Look here, lend Theodore Racksole a million for a few weeks, and he'll give you an IOU and a covering note on stocks"?'

'But you could get it?' she asked again.

'If there's a million in London I guess I could handle it,' he replied.

'Well, Dad,' and she put her arms round his neck, 'you've just got to go out and fix it. See? It's for me. I've never asked you for anything really big before. But I do now. And I want it so badly.'

He stared at her. 'I award you the prize,' he said, at length. 'You deserve it for colossal and immense coolness. Now you can tell me the true inward meaning of all this rigmarole. What is it?'

'I want it for Prince Eugen,' she began, at first hesitatingly, with pauses.

'He's ruined unless he can get a million to pay off his debts. He's dreadfully in love with a Princess, and he can't marry her because of this.

Her parents wouldn't allow it. He was to have got it from Sampson Levi, but he arrived too late—owing to Jules.'

'I know all about that—perhaps more than you do. But I don't see how it affects you or me.'

'The point is this, Dad,' Nella continued. 'He's tried to commit suicide—he's so hipped. Yes, real suicide. He took laudanum last night. It didn't kill him straight off—he's got over the first shock, but he's in a very weak state, and he means to die. And I truly believe he will die. Now, if you could let him have that million, Dad, you would save his life.'

Nella's item of news was a considerable and disconcerting surprise to Racksole, but he hid his feelings fairly well.

'I haven't the least desire to save his life, Nell. I don't overmuch respect your Prince Eugen. I've done what I could for him—but only for the sake of seeing fair play, and because I object to conspiracies and secret murders.

It's a different thing if he wants to kill himself. What I say is: Let him.

Who is responsible for his being in debt to the tune of a million pounds? He's only got himself and his bad habits to thank for that. I suppose if he does happen to peg out, the throne of Posen will go to Prince Aribert. And a good thing, too! Aribert is worth twenty of his nephew.'

'That's just it, Dad,' she said, eagerly following up her chance. 'I want you to save Prince Eugen just because Aribert—Prince Aribert—doesn't wish to occupy the throne. He'd much prefer not to have it.'

'Much prefer not to have it! Don't talk nonsense. If he's honest with himself, he'll admit that he'll be jolly glad to have it. Thrones are in his blood, so to speak.'

'You are wrong, Father. And the reason is this: If Prince Aribert ascended the throne of Posen he would be compelled to marry a Princess.'

'Well! A Prince ought to marry a Princess.'

'But he doesn't want to. He wants to give up all his royal rights, and live as a subject. He wants to marry a woman who isn't a Princess.'

'Is she rich?'

'Her father is,' said the girl. 'Oh, Dad! can't you guess? He—he loves me.' Her head fell on Theodore's shoulder and she began to cry.

The millionaire whistled a very high note. 'Nell!' he said at length. 'And you? Do you sort of cling to him?'

'Dad,' she answered, 'you are stupid. Do you imagine I should worry myself like this if I didn't?' She smiled through her tears. She knew from her father's tone that she had accomplished a victory.

'It's a mighty queer arrangement,' Theodore remarked. 'But of course if you think it'll be of any use, you had better go down and tell your Prince Eugen that that million can be fixed up, if he really needs it. I expect there'll be decent security, or Sampson Levi wouldn't have mixed himself up in it.'

'Thanks, Dad. Don't come with me; I may manage better alone.'

She gave a formal little curtsey and disappeared. Racksole, who had the talent, so necessary to millionaires, of attending to several matters at once, the large with the small, went off to give orders about the breakfast and the remuneration of his assistant of the evening before, Mr George Hazell. He then sent an invitation to Mr Felix Babylon's room, asking that gentleman to take breakfast with him. After he had related to Babylon the history of Jules' capture, and had a long discussion with him upon several points of hôtel management, and especially as to the guarding of wine-cellars, Racksole put on his hat, sallied forth into the Strand, hailed a hansom, and was driven to the City. The order and nature of his operations there were too complex and technical to be described here.

When Nella returned to the State bedroom both the doctor and the great specialist were again in attendance. The two physicians moved away from the bedside as she entered, and began to talk quietly together in the embrasure of the window.

'A curious case!' said the specialist.

'Yes. Of course, as you say, it's a neurotic temperament that's at the bottom of the trouble. When you've got that and a vigorous constitution working one against the other, the results are apt to be distinctly curious. Do you consider there is any hope, Sir Charles?'

'If I had seen him when he recovered consciousness I should have said there was hope. Frankly, when I left last night, or rather this morning, I didn't expect to see the Prince alive again—let alone conscious, and able to talk. According to all the rules of the game, he ought to get over the shock to the system with perfect ease and certainty. But I don't think he will. I don't think he wants to. And moreover, I think he is still under the influence of suicidal mania. If he had a razor he would cut his throat. You must keep his strength up. Inject, if necessary. I will come in this afternoon. I am due now at St James's Palace.' And the specialist hurried away, with an elaborate bow and a few hasty words of polite reassurances to Prince Aribert.

When he had gone Prince Aribert took the other doctor aside. 'Forget everything, doctor,' he said, 'except that I am one man and you are another, and tell me the truth. Shall you be able to save his Highness? Tell me the truth.'

'There is no truth,' was the doctor's reply. 'The future is not in our hands, Prince.'

'But you are hopeful? Yes or no.'

The doctor looked at Prince Aribert. 'No!' he said shortly. 'I am not. I am never hopeful when the patient is not on my side.'

'You mean—?'

'I mean that his Royal Highness has no desire to live. You must have observed that.'

'Only too well,' said Aribert.

'And you are aware of the cause?'

Aribert nodded an affirmative.

'But cannot remove it?'

'No,' said Aribert. He felt a touch on his sleeve. It was Nella's finger.

With a gesture she beckoned him towards the ante-room.

'If you choose,' she said, when they were alone, 'Prince Eugen can be saved. I have arranged it.'

'You have arranged it?' He bent over her, almost with an air of alarm. 'Go and tell him that the million pounds which is so necessary to his happiness will be forthcoming. Tell him that it will be forthcoming today, if that will be any satisfaction to him.'

'But what do you mean by this, Nella?'

'I mean what I say, Aribert,' and she sought his hand and took it in hers. 'Just what I say. If a million pounds will save Prince Eugen's life, it is at his disposal.'

'But how—how have you managed it? By what miracle?'

'My father,' she replied softly, 'will do anything that I ask him. Do not let us waste time. Go and tell Eugen it is arranged, that all will be well. Go!'

'But we cannot accept this—this enormous, this incredible favour. It is impossible.'

'Aribert,' she said quickly, 'remember you are not in Posen holding a Court reception. You are in England and you are talking to an American girl who has always been in the habit of having her own way.'

The Prince threw up his hands and went back in to the bedroom. The doctor was at a table writing out a prescription. Aribert approached the bedside, his heart beating furiously. Eugen greeted him with a faint, fatigued smile.

'Eugen,' he whispered, 'listen carefully to me. I have news. With the assistance of friends I have arranged to borrow that million for you. It is quite settled, and you may rely on it. But you must get better. Do you hear me?'

Eugen almost sat up in bed. 'Tell me I am not delirious,' he exclaimed.

'Of course you aren't,' Aribert replied. 'But you mustn't sit up. You must take care of yourself.'

'Who will lend the money?' Eugen asked in a feeble, happy whisper.

'Never mind. You shall hear later. Devote yourself now to getting better.'

The change in the patient's face was extraordinary. His mind seemed to have put on an entirely different aspect. The doctor was startled to hear him murmur a request for food. As for Aribert, he sat down, overcome by the turmoil of his own thoughts. Till that moment he felt that he had never appreciated the value and the marvellous power of mere money, of the lucre which philosophers pretend to despise and men sell their souls for. His heart almost burst in its admiration for that extraordinary Nella, who by mere personal force had raised two men out of the deepest slough of despair to the blissful heights of hope and happiness. 'These Anglo-Saxons,' he said to himself, 'what a race!'

By the afternoon Eugen was noticeably and distinctly better. The physicians, puzzled for the third time by the progress of the case, announced now that all danger was past. The tone of the announcement seemed to Aribert to imply that the fortunate issue was due wholly to unrivalled medical skill, but perhaps Aribert was mistaken. Anyhow, he was in a most charitable mood, and prepared to forgive anything.

'Nella,' he said a little later, when they were by themselves again in the ante-chamber, 'what am I to say to you? How can I thank you? How can I thank your father?'

'You had better not thank my father,' she said. 'Dad will affect to regard the thing as a purely business transaction, as, of course, it is. As for me, you can—you can—'

'Well?'

'Kiss me,' she said. 'There! Are you sure you've formally proposed to me, mon prince?'

'Ah! Nell!' he exclaimed, putting his arms round her again. 'Be mine! That is all I want!'

'You'll find,' she said, 'that you'll want Dad's consent too!'

'Will he make difficulties? He could not, Nell—not with you!'

'Better ask him,' she said sweetly.

A moment later Racksole himself entered the room. 'Going on all right?' he enquired, pointing to the bedroom.

'Excellently,' the lovers answered together, and they both blushed.

'Ah!' said Racksole. 'Then, if that's so, and you can spare a minute, I've something to show you, Prince.'

Chapter Thirty CONCLUSION

'I'VE a great deal to tell you, Prince,' Racksole began, as soon as they were out of the room, 'and also, as I said, something to show you. Will you come to my room? We will talk there first. The whole hôtel is humming with excitement.'

'With pleasure,' said Aribert.

'Glad his Highness Prince Eugen is recovering,' Racksole said, urged by considerations of politeness.

'Ah! As to that—' Aribert began. 'If you don't mind, we'll discuss that later, Prince,' Racksole interrupted him. They were in the proprietor's private room.

'I want to tell you all about last night,' Racksole resumed, 'about my capture of Jules, and my examination of him this morning.' And he launched into a full account of the whole thing, down to the least details. 'You see,' he concluded, 'that our suspicions as to Bosnia were tolerably correct. But as regards Bosnia, the more I think about it, the surer I feel that nothing can be done to bring their criminal politicians to justice.'

'And as to Jules, what do you propose to do?'

'Come this way,' said Racksole, and led Aribert to another room. A sofa in this room was covered with a linen cloth. Racksole lifted the cloth—he could never deny himself a dramatic moment—and disclosed the body of a dead man.

It was Jules, dead, but without a scratch or mark on him.

'I have sent for the police—not a street constable, but an official from Scotland Yard,' said Racksole.

'How did this happen?' Aribert asked, amazed and startled. 'I understood you to say that he was safely immured in the bedroom.'

'So he was,' Racksole replied. 'I went up there this afternoon, chiefly to take him some food. The commissionaire was on guard at the door. He had heard no noise, nothing unusual. Yet when I entered the room Jules was gone.

He had by some means or other loosened his fastenings; he had then managed to take the door off the wardrobe. He had moved the bed in front of the window, and by pushing the wardrobe door three parts out of the window and lodging the inside end of it under the rail at the head of the bed, he had provided himself with a sort of insecure platform outside the window. All this he did without making the least sound. He must then have got through the window, and stood on the little platform. With his fingers he would just be able to reach the outer edge of the wide cornice under the roof of the hôtel. By main strength of arms he had swung himself on to this cornice, and so got on to the roof proper. He would then have the run of the whole roof.

At the side of the building facing Salisbury Lane there is an iron fire-escape, which runs right down from the ridge of the roof into a little sunk yard level with the cellars. Jules must have thought that his escape was accomplished. But it unfortunately happened that one rung in the iron escape-ladder had rusted rotten through being badly painted. It gave way, and Jules, not expecting anything of the kind, fell to the ground. That was the end of all his cleverness and ingenuity.'

As Racksole ceased, speaking he replaced the linen cloth with a gesture from which reverence was not wholly absent.

When the grave had closed over the dark and tempestuous career of Tom Jackson, once the pride of the Grand Babylon, there was little trouble for the people whose adventures we have described. Miss Spencer, that yellow-haired, faithful slave and attendant of a brilliant scoundrel, was never heard of again. Possibly to this day she survives, a mystery to her fellow-creatures, in the pension of some cheap foreign boarding-house. As for Rocco, he certainly was heard of again. Several years after the events set down, it came to the knowledge of Felix Babylon that the unrivalled Rocco had reached Buenos Aires, and by his culinary skill was there making the fortune of a new and splendid hôtel. Babylon transmitted the information to Theodore Racksole, and Racksole might, had he chosen, have put the forces of the law in motion against him. But Racksole, seeing that everything pointed to the fact that Rocco was now pursuing his vocation honestly, decided to leave him alone. The one difficulty which Racksole experienced after the demise of Jules—and it was a difficulty which he had, of course, anticipated—was connected with the police. The police, very properly, wanted to know things. They desired to be informed what Racksole had been doing in the Dimmock affair, between his first visit to Ostend and his sending for them to take charge of Jules' dead body. And Racksole was by no means inclined to tell them everything. Beyond question he had transgressed the laws of England, and possibly also the laws of Belgium; and the moral excellence of his motives in doing so was, of course, in the eyes of legal justice, no excuse for such conduct. The inquest upon Jules aroused some bother; and about ninety-and-nine separate and distinct rumours. In the end, however, a compromise was arrived at. Racksole's first aim was to pacify the inspector whose clue, which by the way was a false one, he had so curtly declined to follow up. That done, the rest needed only tact and patience. He proved to the satisfaction of the authorities that he had acted in a perfectly honest spirit, though with a high hand, and that substantial justice had been done. Also, he subtly indicated that, if it came to the point, he should defy them to do their worst. Lastly, he was able, through the medium of the United States Ambassador, to bring certain soothing influences to bear upon the situation.

One afternoon, a fortnight after the recovery of the Hereditary Prince of Posen, Aribert, who was still staying at the Grand Babylon, expressed a wish to hold converse with the millionaire. Prince Eugen, accompanied by Hans and some Court officials whom he had sent for, had departed with immense éclat, armed with the comfortable million, to arrange formally for his betrothal.

Touching the million, Eugen had given satisfactory personal security, and the money was to be paid off in fifteen years.

'You wish to talk to me, Prince,' said Racksole to Aribert, when they were seated together in the former's room.

'I wish to tell you,' replied Aribert, 'that it is my intention to renounce all my rights and titles as a Royal Prince of Posen, and to be known in future as Count Hartz—a rank to which I am entitled through my mother.

Also that I have a private income of ten thousand pounds a year, and a château and a town house in Posen. I tell you this because I am here to ask the hand of your daughter in marriage. I love her, and I am vain enough to believe that she loves me. I have already asked her to be my wife, and she has consented. We await your approval.'

'You honour us, Prince,' said Racksole with a slight smile, 'and in more ways than one. May I ask your reason for renouncing your princely titles?'

'Simply because the idea of a morganatic marriage would be as repugnant to me as it would be to yourself and to Nella.'

'That is good.' The Prince laughed. 'I suppose it has occurred to you that ten thousand pounds per annum, for a man in your position, is a somewhat small income. Nella is frightfully extravagant. I have known her to spend sixty thousand dollars in a single year, and have nothing to show for it at the end. Why! she would ruin you in twelve months.'

'Nella must reform her ways,' Aribert said.

'If she is content to do so,' Racksole went on, 'well and good! I consent.'

'In her name and my own, I thank you,' said Aribert gravely.

'And,' the millionaire continued, 'so that she may not have to reform too fiercely, I shall settle on her absolutely, with reversion to your children, if you have any, a lump sum of fifty million dollars, that is to say, ten million pounds, in sound, selected railway stock. I reckon that is about half my fortune. Nella and I have always shared equally.'

Aribert made no reply. The two men shook hands in silence, and then it happened that Nella entered the room.

That night, after dinner, Racksole and his friend Felix Babylon were walking together on the terrace of the Grand Babylon Hôtel.

Felix had begun the conversation.

'I suppose, Racksole,' he had said, 'you aren't getting tired of the Grand Babylon?'

'Why do you ask?'

'Because I am getting tired of doing without it. A thousand times since I sold it to you I have wished I could undo the bargain. I can't bear idleness. Will you sell?'

'I might,' said Racksole, 'I might be induced to sell.'

'What will you take, my friend?' asked Felix

'What I gave,' was the quick answer.

'Eh!' Felix exclaimed. 'I sell you my hôtel with Jules, with Rocco, with Miss Spencer. You go and lose all those three inestimable servants, and then offer me the hôtel without them at the same price! It is monstrous.' The little man laughed heartily at his own wit. 'Nevertheless,' he added, 'we will not quarrel about the price. I accept your terms.'

And so was brought to a close the complex chain of events which had begun when Theodore Racksole ordered a steak and a bottle of Bass at the table d'hôte of the Grand Babylon Hôtel.

Anna of the Five Towns

CHAPTER I

THE KINDLING OF LOVE

The yard was all silent and empty under the burning afternoon heat, which had made its asphalt springy like turf, when suddenly the children threw themselves out of the great doors at either end of the Sunday-school—boys from the right, girls from the left—in two howling, impetuous streams, that widened, eddied, intermingled and formed backwaters until the whole quadrangle was full of clamour and movement. Many of the scholars carried prize-books bound in vivid tints, and proudly exhibited these volumes to their companions and to the teachers, who, tall, languid, and condescending, soon began to appear amid the restless throng. Near the left-hand door a little girl of twelve years, dressed in a cream coloured frock, with a wide and heavy straw hat, stood quietly kicking her foal-like legs against the wall. She was one of those who had won a prize, and once or twice she took the treasure from under her arm to glance at its frontispiece with a vague smile of satisfaction. For a time her bright eyes were fixed expectantly on the doorway; then they would wander, and she started to count the windows of the various Connexional buildings which on three sides enclosed the yard—chapel, school, lecture-hall, and chapel-keeper's house. Most of the children had already squeezed through the narrow iron gate into the street beyond, where a steam-car was rumbling and clattering up Duck Bank, attended by its immense shadow. The teachers remained a little behind. Gradually dropping the pedagogic pose, and happy in the virtuous sensation of duty accomplished, they forgot the frets and fatigues of the day, and grew amiably vivacious among themselves. With an instinctive mutual complacency the two sexes mixed again after separation. Greetings and pleasantries were exchanged, and intimate conversations begun; and then, dividing into small familiar groups, the young men and women slowly followed their pupils out of the gate. The chapel-keeper, who always had an injured expression, left the white step of his residence, and, walking with official dignity across the yard, drew down the side-windows of the chapel one after another. As he approached the little solitary girl in his course he gave her a reluctant acid recognition; then he returned to his hearth. Agnes was alone.

'Well, young lady?'

She looked round with a jump, and blushed, smiling and screwing up her little shoulders, when she recognised the two men who were coming towards her from the door of the lecture-hall. The one who had called out was Henry Mynors, morning superintendent of the Sunday-school and conductor of the men's Bible-class held in the lecture-hall on Sunday afternoons. The other was William Price, usually styled Willie Price, secretary of the same Bible-class, and son of Titus Price, the afternoon superintendent.

'I'm sure you don't deserve that prize. Let me see if it isn't too good for you.' Mynors smiled playfully down upon Agnes Tellwright as he idly turned the leaves of the book which she handed to him. 'Now, do you deserve it? Tell me honestly.'

She scrutinised those sparkling and vehement black eyes with the fearless calm of infancy. 'Yes, I do,' $he answered in her high, thin voice, having at length decided within herself that Mr. Mynors was joking.

'Then I suppose you must have it,' he admitted, with a fine air of giving way.

As Agnes took the volume from him she thought how perfect a man Mr. Mynors was. His eyes, so kind and sincere, and that mysterious, delicious, inexpressible something which dwelt behind his eyes: these constituted an ideal for her.

Willie Price stood somewhat apart, grinning, and pulling a thin honey-coloured moustache. He was at the uncouth, disjointed age, twenty-one, and nine years younger than Henry Mynors. Despite a continual effort after ease of manner, he was often sheepish and self-conscious, even, as now, when he could discover no reason for such a condition of mind. But Agnes liked him too. His simple, pale blue eyes had a wistfulness which made her feel towards him as she felt towards her doll when she happened to find it lying neglected on the floor.

'Your big sister isn't out of school yet?' Mynors remarked.

Agnes shook her head. 'I've been waiting ever so long,' she said plaintively.

At that moment a grey-haired woman with a benevolent but rather pinched face emerged with much briskness from the girls' door. This was Mrs. Sutton, a distant relative of Mynors'—his mother had been her second cousin. The men raised their hats.

'I've just been down to make sure of some of you slippery folks for the sewing-meeting,' she said, shaking hands with Mynors, and including both him and Willie Price in an embracing maternal smile. She was short-sighted and did not perceive Agnes, who had fallen back.

'Had a good class this afternoon, Henry?' Mrs. Sutton's breathing was short and quick.

'Oh, yes,' he said, 'very good indeed.'

'You're doing a grand work.'

'We had over seventy present,' he added.

'Eh!' she said, 'I make nothing of numbers. Henry. I meant a *good* class. Doesn't it say—Where *two or three* are gathered together...? But I must be getting on. The horse will be restless. I've to go up to Hillport before tea. Mrs. Clayton Vernon is ill.'

Scarcely having stopped in her active course, Mrs. Sutton drew the men along with her down the yard, she and Mynors in rapid talk: Willie Price fell a little to the rear, his big hands half-way into his pockets and his eyes diffidently roving. It appeared as though he could not find courage to take a share in the conversation, yet was anxious to convince himself of his right to do so.

Mynors helped Mrs. Sutton into her carriage, which had been drawn up outside the gate of the school yard. Only two families of the Bursley Wesleyan Methodists kept a carriage, the Suttons and the Clayton Vernons. The latter, boasting lineage and a large house in the aristocratic suburb of Hillport, gave to the society monetary aid and a gracious condescension. But though indubitably above the operation of any unwritten sumptuary law, even the Clayton Vernons ventured only in wet weather to bring their carriage to chapel. Yet Mrs. Sutton, who was a plain woman, might with impunity use her equipage on Sundays. This license granted by Connexional opinion was due to the fact that she so obviously regarded her carriage, not as a carriage, but as a contrivance on four wheels for enabling an infirm creature to move rapidly from place to place. When she got into it she had exactly the air of a doctor on his rounds. Mrs. Sutton's bodily frame had long ago proved inadequate to the ceaseless demands of a spirit indefatigably altruistic, and her continuance in activity was a notable illustration of the dominion of mind over matter. Her husband, a potter's valuer and commission agent, made money with facility in that lucrative vocation, and his wife's charities were famous, notwithstanding her attempts to hide them. Neither husband nor wife had allowed riches to put a factitious gloss upon their primal simplicity. They were as they were, save that Mr. Sutton had joined the Five Towns Field Club and acquired some of the habits of an archaeologist. The influence of wealth on manners was to be observed only in their daughter Beatrice, who, while favouring her mother, dressed at considerable expense, and at intervals gave much time to the arts of music and painting. Agnes watched the carriage drive away, and then turned to look up the stairs within the school doorway. She sighed, scowled, and sighed again, murmured something to herself, and finally began to read her book.

'Not come out yet?' Mynors was at her side once more, alone this time.

'No, not yet,' said Agnes, wearied. 'Yes. Here she is. Anna, what ages you've been!'

Anna Tellwright stood motionless for a second in the shadow of the doorway. She was tall, but not unusually so, and sturdily built up. Her figure, though the bust was a little flat, had the lenient curves of absolute maturity. Anna had been a woman since seventeen, and she was now on the eve of her twenty-first birthday. She wore a plain, home-made light frock checked with brown and edged with brown velvet, thin cotton gloves of cream colour, and a broad straw hat like her sister's. Her grave face, owing to the prominence of the cheekbones and the width of the jaw, had a slight angularity; the lips were thin, the brown eyes rather large, the eyebrows level, the nose fine and delicate; the ears could scarcely be seen for the dark brown hair which was brushed diagonally across the temples, leaving of the forehead only a pale triangle. It seemed a face for the cloister, austere in contour, fervent in expression, the severity of it mollified by that resigned and spiritual melancholy peculiar to women who through the error of destiny have been born into a wrong environment.

As if charmed forward by Mynors' compelling eyes, Anna stepped into the sunlight, at the same time putting up her parasol. 'How calm and stately she is,' he thought, as she gave him her cool hand and murmured a reply to his salutation. But even his aquiline gaze could not surprise the secrets of that concealing breast: this was one of the three great tumultuous moments of her life—she realised for the first time that she was loved.

'You are late this afternoon, Miss Tellwright,' Mynors began, with the easy inflections of a man well accustomed to prominence in the society of women. Little Agnes seized Anna's left arm, silently holding up the prize, and Anna nodded appreciation.

'Yes,' she said as they walked across the yard, 'one of my girls has been doing wrong. She stole a Bible from another girl, so of course I had to mention it to the superintendent. Mr. Price gave her a long lecture, and now she is waiting upstairs till he is ready to go with her to her home and talk to her parents. He says she must be dismissed.'

'Dismissed!'

Anna's look flashed a grateful response to him. By the least possible emphasis he had expressed a complete disagreement with his senior colleague which etiquette forbade him to utter in words.

'I think it's a very great pity,' Anna said firmly. 'I rather like the girl,' she ventured in haste; 'you might speak to Mr. Price about it.'

'If he mentions it to me.'

'Yes, I meant that. Mr. Price said—if it had been anything else but a *Bible*——'

'Um!' he murmured very low, but she caught the significance of his intonation. They did not glance at each other: it was unnecessary. Anna felt that comfortable easement of the spirit which springs from the recognition of another spirit capable of understanding without explanations and of sympathising without a phrase. Under that calm mask a strange and sweet satisfaction thrilled through her as her precious instinct of common sense—rarest of good qualities, and pining always for fellowship—found a companion in his own. She had dreaded the overtures which for a fortnight past she had foreseen were inevitably to come from Mynors: he was a stranger, whom she merely respected. Now in a sudden disclosure she knew him and liked him. The dire apprehension of those formal 'advances' which she had watched other men make to other women faded away. It was at once a release and a reassurance.

They were passing through the gate, Agnes skipping round her sister's skirts, when Willie Price reappeared front the direction of the chapel.

'Forgotten something?' Mynors inquired of him blandly.

'Ye-es,' he stammered, clumsily raising his hat to Anna. She thought of him exactly as Agnes had done. He hesitated for a fraction of time, and then went up the yard-towards the lecture-hall.

'Agnes has been showing me her prize,' said Mynors, as the three stood together outside the gate. 'I ask her if she thinks she really deserves it, and she says she does. What do you think, Miss Big Sister?'

Anna gave the little girl an affectionate smile of comprehension. 'What is it called, dear?'

'"Janey's Sacrifice or the Spool of Cotton, and other stories for children,"' Agnes read out in a monotone: then she clutched Anna's elbow and aimed a whisper at her ear.

'Very well, dear,' Anna answered loud, 'but we must be back by a quarter-past four.' And turning to Mynors: 'Agnes wants to go up to the Park to hear the band play.'

'I'm going up there, too,' he said. 'Come along, Agnes, take my arm and show me the way.' Shyly Agnes left her sister's side and put a pink finger into Mynors' hand.

Moor Road, which climbs over the ridge to the mining village of Moorthorne and passes the new Park on its way, was crowded with people going up to criticise and enjoy this latest outcome of municipal enterprise in Bursley: sedate elders of the borough who smiled grimly to see one another on Sunday afternoon in that undignified, idly curious throng; white-skinned potters, and miners with the swarthy pallor of subterranean toil; untidy Sabbath loafers whom neither church nor chapel could entice, and the primly-clad respectable who had not only clothes but a separate deportment for the seventh day; house-wives whose pale faces, as of prisoners free only for a while, showed a naïve and timorous pleasure in the unusual diversion; young women made glorious by richly-coloured stuffs and carrying themselves with the defiant independence of good wages earned in warehouse or painting-shop; youths oppressed by stiff new clothes bought at Whitsuntide, in which the bright necktie and the nosegay revealed a thousand secret aspirations; young children running and yelling with the marvellous energy of their years; here and there a small well-dressed group whose studious repudiation of the crowd betrayed a conscious eminence of rank; louts, drunkards, idiots, beggars, waifs, outcasts, and every oddity of the town: all were more or less under the influence of a new excitement, and all with the same face of pleased expectancy looked towards the spot where, half-way up the hill, a denser mass of sightseers indicated the grand entrance to the Park.

'What stacks of folks!' Agnes exclaimed. 'It's like going to a football match.'

'Do you go to football matches, Agnes?' Mynors asked. The child gave a giggle.

Anna was relieved when these two began to chatter. She had at once, by a firm natural impulse, subdued the agitation which seized her when she found Mynors waiting with such an obvious intention at the school door; she had conversed with him in tones of quiet ease; his attitude had even enabled her in a few moments to establish a pleasant familiarity with him. Nevertheless, as they joined the stream of people in Moor Road, she longed to be at home, in her kitchen, in order to examine herself and the new situation thus created by Mynors. And yet also she was glad that she must remain at his side, but it was a fluttered joy that his presence gave her, too strange for immediate appreciation. As her eye, without directly looking at him, embraced the suave and admirable male creature within its field of vision, she became aware that he was quite inscrutable to her. What were his inmost thoughts, his ideals, the histories of his heart? Surely it was impossible that she should ever know these secrets! He—and she: they were utterly foreign to each other. So the primary dissonances of sex vibrated within her, and her own feelings puzzled her. Still, there was an instant pleasure, delightful, if disturbing and inexplicable. And also there was a sensation of triumph, which, though she tried to scorn it, she could not banish. That a man and a woman should saunter together on that road was nothing; but the circumstance acquired tremendous importance when the man happened to be Henry Mynors and the woman Anna Tellwright. Mynors—handsome, dark, accomplished, exemplary and prosperous—had walked for ten years circumspect and unscathed amid the glances of a whole legion of maids. As for Anna, the peculiarity of her position had always marked her for special attention: ever since her father settled in Bursley, she had felt herself to be the object of an interest in which awe and pity were equally mingled. She guessed that the fact of her going to the Park with Mynors that afternoon would pass swiftly from mouth to mouth like the rumour of a decisive event. She had no friends; her innate reserve had been misinterpreted, and she was not popular among the Wesleyan community. Many people would say, and more would think, that it was her money which was drawing Mynors from the narrow path of his celibate discretion. She could imagine all the innuendoes, the expressive nods, the pursing of lips, the lifting of shoulders and of eyebrows. 'Money 'll do owt': that was the proverb. But she cared not. She had the just and unshakable self-esteem which is fundamental in all strong and righteous natures; and she knew beyond the possibility of doubt that, though Mynors might have no incurable aversion to a fortune, she herself, the spirit and body of her, had been the sole awakener of his desire.

By a common instinct, Mynors and Anna made little Agnes the centre of attraction. Mynors continued to tease her, and Agnes growing courageous, began to retort. She was now walking between them, and the other two smiled to each other at the child's sayings over her head, interchanging thus messages too subtle and delicate for the coarse medium of words.

As they approached the Park the bandstand came into sight over the railway cutting, and they could hear the music of 'The Emperor's Hymn.' The crude, brazen sounds were tempered in their passage through the warm, still air, and fell gently on the ear in soft waves, quickening every heart to unaccustomed emotions. Children leaped forward, and old people unconsciously assumed a lightsome vigour. The Park rose in terraces from the railway station to a street of small villas almost on the ridge of the hill. From its gilded gates to its smallest geranium-slips it was brand-new, and most of it was red. The keeper's house, the bandstand, the kiosks, the balustrades, the shelters—all these assailed the eye with a uniform redness of brick and tile which nullified the pallid greens of the turf and the frail trees. The immense crowd, in order to circulate, moved along in tight processions, inspecting one after another the various features of which they had read full descriptions in the 'Staffordshire Signal'—waterfall, grotto, lake, swans, boat, seats, faience, statues—and scanning with interest the names of the donors so clearly inscribed on such objects of art and craft as from divers motives had been presented to the town by its citizens. Mynors, as he manoeuvred a way for the two girls through the main avenue up to the topmost terrace, gravely judged each thing upon its merits, approving this, condemning that. In deciding that under all the circumstances the Park made a very creditable appearance he only reflected the best local opinion. The town was proud of its achievement, and it had the right to be; for, though this narrow pleasaunce was in itself unlovely, it symbolised the first faint renascence of the longing for beauty in a district long given up to unredeemed ugliness.

At length, Mynors having encountered many acquaintances, they got past the bandstand and stood on the highest terrace, which was almost deserted. Beneath them, in front, stretched a maze of roofs, dominated by the gold angel of the Town Hall spire. Bursley, the ancient home of the potter, has an antiquity of a thousand years. It lies towards the north end of an extensive valley, which must have been one of the fairest spots in Alfred's England, but which is now defaced by the activities of a quarter of a million of people. Five contiguous towns—Turnhill, Bursley, Hanbridge, Knype, and Longshaw—united by a single winding thoroughfare some eight miles in length, have inundated the valley like a succession of great lakes. Of these five Bursley is the mother, but Hanbridge is the largest. They are mean and forbidding of aspect—sombre, hard-featured, uncouth; and the vaporous poison of their ovens and chimneys has soiled and shrivelled the surrounding country till there is no village lane within a league but what offers a gaunt and ludicrous travesty of rural charms. Nothing could be more prosaic than the huddled, red-brown streets; nothing more seemingly remote from romance. Yet be it said that romance is even here—the romance which, for those who have an eye to perceive it, ever dwells amid the seats of industrial manufacture, softening the coarseness, transfiguring the squalor, of these mighty alchemic operations. Look down into the valley from this terrace-height where love is kindling, embrace the whole smoke-girt amphitheatre in a glance, and it may be that you will suddenly comprehend the secret and superb significance of the vast Doing which goes forward below. Because they seldom think, the townsmen take shame when indicted for having disfigured half a county in order to live. They have not understood that this disfigurement is merely an episode in the unending warfare of man and nature, and calls for no contrition. Here, indeed, is nature repaid for some of her notorious cruelties. She imperiously bids man sustain and reproduce himself, and this is one of the places where in the very act of obedience he wounds and maltreats her. Out beyond the municipal confines, where the subsidiary industries of coal and iron prosper amid a wreck of verdure, the struggle is grim, appalling, heroic—so ruthless is his havoc of her, so indomitable her ceaseless recuperation. On the one side is a wresting from nature's own bowels of the means to waste her; on the other, an undismayed, enduring fortitude. The grass grows; though it is not green, it grows. In the very heart of the valley, hedged about with furnaces, a farm still stands, and at harvest-time the sooty sheaves are gathered in.

The band stopped playing. A whole population was idle in the Park, and it seemed, in the fierce calm of the sunlight, that of all the strenuous weekday vitality of the district only a murmurous hush remained. But everywhere on the horizon, and nearer, furnaces cast their heavy smoke across the borders of the sky: the Doing was never suspended.

'Mr. Mynors,' said Agnes, still holding his hand, when they had been silent a moment, 'when do those furnaces go out?'

'They don't go out,' he answered, 'unless there is a strike. It costs hundreds and hundreds of pounds to light them again.'

'Does it?' she said vaguely. 'Father says it's the smoke that stops my gilliflowers from growing.'

Mynors turned to Anna. 'Your father seems the picture of health. I saw him out this morning at a quarter to seven, as brisk as a boy. What a constitution!'

'Yes,' Anna replied, 'he is always up at six.'

'But you aren't, I suppose?'

'Yes, I too.'

'And me too,' Agnes interjected.

'And how does Bursley compare with Hanbridge?' Mynors continued. Anna paused before replying.

'I like it better,' she said. 'At first—last year—I thought I shouldn't.'

'By the way, your father used to preach in Hanbridge circuit——'

'That was years ago,' she said quickly.

'But why won't he preach here? I dare say you know that we are rather short of local preachers—good ones, that is.'

'I can't say why father doesn't preach now:' Anna flushed as she spoke. 'You had better ask him that.'

'Well, I will do,' he laughed. 'I am coming to see him soon—perhaps one night next week.'

Anna looked at Henry Mynors as he uttered the astonishing words. The Tellwrights had been in Bursley a year, but no visitor had crossed their doorsteps except the minister, once, and such poor defaulters as came, full of excuse and obsequious conciliation, to pay rent overdue.

'Business, I suppose?' she said, and prayed that he might not be intending to make a mere call of ceremony.

'Yes, business,' he answered lightly. 'But you will be in?'

'I am always in,' she said. She wondered what the business could be, and felt relieved to know that his visit would have at least some assigned pretext; but already her heart beat with apprehensive perturbation at the thought of his presence in their household.

'See!' said Agnes, whose eyes were everywhere, 'There's Miss Sutton.'

Both Mynors and Anna looked sharply round. Beatrice Sutton was coming towards them along the terrace. Stylishly clad in a dress of pink muslin, with harmonious hat, gloves, and sunshade, she made an agreeable and rather effective picture, despite her plain, round face and stoutish figure. She had the air of being a leader. Grafted on to the original simple honesty of her eyes there was the unconsciously-acquired arrogance of one who had always been accustomed to deference. Socially, Beatrice had no peer among the young women who were active in the Wesleyan Sunday-school. Beatrice had been used to teach in the afternoon school, but she had recently advanced her labours from the afternoon to the morning in response to a hint that if she did so the force of her influence and example might lessen the chronic dearth of morning teachers.

'Good afternoon, Miss Tellwright,' Beatrice said as she came up. 'So you have come to look at the Park.'

'Yes,' said Anna, and then stopped awkwardly. In the tone of each there was an obscure constraint, and something in Mynors' smile of salute to Beatrice showed that he too shared it.

'Seen you before,' Beatrice said to him familiarly, without taking his hand; then she bent down and kissed Agnes.

'What are you doing here, mademoiselle?' Mynors asked her.

'Father's just down below, near the lake. He caught sight of you, and sent me up to say that you were to be sure to come in to supper to-night. You will, won't you?'

'Yes, thanks. I had meant to.'

Anna knew that they were related, and also that Mynors was constantly at the Suttons' house, but the close intimacy between these two came nevertheless like a shock to her. She could not conquer a certain resentment of it, however absurd such a feeling might seem to her intelligence. And this attitude extended not only to the intimacy, but to Beatrice's handsome clothes and facile urbanity, which by contrast emphasised her own poor little frock and tongue-tied manner. The mere existence of Beatrice so near to Mynors was like an affront to her. Yet at heart, and even while admiring this shining daughter of success, she was conscious within herself of a fundamental superiority. The soul of her condescended to the soul of the other one.

They began to discuss the Park.

'Papa says it will send up the value of that land over there enormously,' said Beatrice, pointing with her ribboned sunshade to some building plots which lay to the north, high up the hill. 'Mr. Tellwright owns most of that, doesn't he?' she added to Anna.

'I dare say he does,' said Anna. It was torture to her to refer to her father's possessions.

'Of course it will be covered with streets in a few months. Will he build himself, or will he sell it?'

'I haven't the least idea,' Anna answered, with an effort after gaiety of tone, and then turned aside to look at the crowd. There, close against the bandstand, stood her father, a short, stout, ruddy, middle-aged man in a shabby brown suit. He recognised her, stared fixedly, and nodded with his grotesque and ambiguous grin. Then he sidled off towards the entrance of the Park. None of the others had seen him. 'Agnes dear,' she said abruptly, 'we must go now, or we shall be late for tea.'

As the two women said good-bye their eyes met, and in the brief second of that encounter each tried to wring from the other the true answer to a question which lay unuttered in her heart. Then, having bidden adieu to Mynors, whose parting glance sang its own song to her, Anna took Agnes by the hand and left him and Beatrice together.

CHAPTER II

THE MISER'S DAUGHTER

Anna sat in the bay-window of the front parlour, her accustomed place on Sunday evenings in summer, and watched Mr. Tellwright and Agnes disappear down the slope of Trafalgar Road on their way to chapel. Trafalgar Road is the long thoroughfare which, under many aliases, runs through the Five Towns from end to end, uniting them as a river might unite them. Ephraim Tellwright could remember the time when this part of it was a country lane, flanked by meadows and market gardens. Now it was a street of houses up to and beyond Bleakridge, where the Tellwrights lived; on the other side of the hill the houses came only in patches until the far-stretching borders of Hanbridge were reached. Within the municipal limits Bleakridge was the pleasantest quarter of Bursley—Hillport, abode of the highest fashion, had its own government and authority—and to reside 'at the top of Trafalgar Road' was still the final ambition of many citizens, though the natural growth of the town had robbed Bleakridge of some of that exclusive distinction which it once possessed. Trafalgar Road, in its journey to Bleakridge from the centre of the town, underwent certain changes of character. First came a succession of manufactories and small shops; then, at the beginning of the rise, a quarter of a mile of superior cottages; and lastly, on the brow, occurred the houses of the comfortable-detached, semi-detached, and in terraces, with rentals from 25*l.* to 60*l.* a year. The Tellwrights lived in Manor Terrace (the name being a last reminder of the great farmstead which formerly occupied the western hill side):

their house, of light yellow brick, was two-storied, with a long narrow garden behind, and the rent 30*l*. Exactly opposite was an antique red mansion, standing back its own ground—home of the Mynors family for two generations, but now a school, the Mynors family being extinct in the district save for one member. Somewhat higher up, still on the opposite side to Manor Terrace, came an imposing row of four new houses, said to be the best planned and best built in the town, each erected separately and occupied by its owner. The nearest of these four was Councillor Sutton's, valued at 60*l*. a year. Lower down, below Manor Terrace and on the same side, lived the Wesleyan superintendent minister, the vicar of St. Luke's Church, an alderman, and a doctor.

It was nearly six o'clock. The sun shone, but gentlier; and the earth lay cooling in the mild, pensive effulgence of a summer evening. Even the onrush of the steam-car, as it swept with a gay load of passengers to Hanbridge, seemed to be chastened; the bell of the Roman Catholic chapel sounded like the bell of some village church heard in the distance; the quick but sober tramp of the chapel-goers fell peacefully on the ear. The sense of calm increased, and, steeped in this meditative calm, Anna from the open window gazed idly down the perspective of the road, which ended a mile away in the dim concave forms of ovens suffused in a pale mist. A book from the Free Library lay on her lap; she could not read it. She was conscious of nothing save the quiet enchantment of reverie. Her mind, stimulated by the emotions of the afternoon, broke the fetters of habitual self-discipline, and ranged voluptuously free over the whole field of recollection and anticipation. To remember, to hope: that was sufficient joy.

In the dissolving views of her own past, from which the rigour and pain seemed to have mysteriously departed, the chief figure was always her father—that sinister and formidable individuality, whom her mind hated but her heart disobediently loved. Ephraim Tellwright[1] was one of the most extraordinary and most mysterious men in the Five Towns. The outer facts of his career were known to all, for his riches made him notorious; but of the secret and intimate man none knew anything except Anna, and what little Anna knew had come to her by divination rather than discernment. A native of Hanbridge, he had inherited a small fortune from his father, who was a prominent Wesleyan Methodist. At thirty, owing mainly to investments in property which his calling of potter's valuer had helped him to choose with advantage, he was worth twenty thousand pounds, and he lived in lodgings on a total expenditure of about a hundred a year. When he was thirty-five he suddenly married, without any perceptible public wooing, the daughter of a wood merchant at Oldcastle, and shortly after the marriage his wife inherited from her father a sum of eighteen thousand pounds. The pair lived narrowly in a small house up at Pireford, between Hanbridge and Oldcastle. They visited no one, and were never seen together except on Sundays. She was a rosy-cheeked, very unassuming and simple woman, who smiled easily and talked with difficulty, and for the rest lived apparently a servile life of satisfaction and content. After five years Anna was born, and in another five years Mrs. Tellwright died of erysipelas. The widower engaged a housekeeper: otherwise his existence proceeded without change. No stranger visited the house, the housekeeper never gossiped; but tales will spread, and people fell into the habit of regarding Tellwright's child and his housekeeper with commiseration.

During all this period he was what is termed 'a good Wesleyan,' preaching and teaching, and spending himself in the various activities of Hanbridge chapel. For many years he had been circuit treasurer. Among Anna's earliest memories was a picture of her father arriving late for supper one Sunday night in autumn after an anniversary service, and pouring out on the white tablecloth the contents of numerous chamois-leather money-bags. She recalled the surprising dexterity with which he counted the coins, the peculiar smell of the bags, and her mother's bland exclamation, 'Eh, Ephraim!' Tellwright belonged by birth to the Old Guard of Methodism; there was in his family a tradition of holy valour for the pure doctrine: his father, a Bursley man, had fought in the fight which preceded the famous Primitive Methodist Secession of 1808 at Bursley, and had also borne a notable part in the Warren affrays of '28, and the disastrous trouble of the Fly-Sheets in '49, when Methodism lost a hundred thousand members. As for Ephraim, he expounded the mystery of the Atonement in village conventicles and grew garrulous with God at prayer-meetings in the big Bethesda chapel; but he did these things as routine, without skill and without enthusiasm, because they gave him an unassailable position within the central group of the society. He was not, in fact, much smitten with either the doctrinal or the spiritual side of Methodism. His chief interest lay in those fiscal schemes of organisation without whose aid no religious propaganda can possibly succeed. It was in the finance of salvation that he rose supreme—the interminable alternation of debt-raising and new liability which provides a lasting excitement for Nonconformists. In the negotiation of mortgages, the artful arrangement of appeals, the planning of anniversaries and of mighty revivals, he was an undisputed leader. To him the circuit was a 'going concern,' and he kept it in motion, serving the Lord in committee and over statements of account. The minister by his pleading might bring sinners to the penitent form, but it was Ephraim Tellwright who reduced the cost per head of souls saved, and so widened the frontiers of the Kingdom of Heaven.

Three years after the death of his first wife it was rumoured that he would marry again, and that his choice had fallen on a young orphan girl, thirty years his junior, who 'assisted' at the stationer's shop where he bought his daily newspaper. The rumour was well-founded. Anna, then eight years of age, vividly remembered the home-coming of the pale wife, and her own sturdy attempts to explain, excuse, or assuage to this wistful and fragile creature the implacable harshness of her father's temper. Agnes was born within a year, and the pale girl died of puerperal fever. In that year lay a whole tragedy, which could not have been more poignant in its perfection if the year had been a thousand years. Ephraim promptly re-engaged the old housekeeper, a course which filled Anna with secret childish revolt, for Anna was now nine, and accomplished in all domesticity. In another seven years the housekeeper died, a gaunt grey ruin, and Anna at sixteen became mistress of the household, with a small sister to cherish and control. About this time Anna began to perceive that her father was generally regarded as a man of great wealth, having few rivals in the entire region of the Five Towns. Definite knowledge, however, she had none: he never spoke of his affairs; she knew only that he possessed houses and other property in various places, that he always turned first to the money article in the newspaper, and that long envelopes arrived for him by post almost daily. But she had once heard the surmise that he was worth sixty thousand of his own, apart from the fortune of his first wife, Anna's mother. Nevertheless, it did not occur to her to think of her father, in plain terms, as a miser, until one day she happened to read in the 'Staffordshire Signal' some particulars of the last will and testament of William Wilbraham, J.P., who had just died. Mr. Wilbraham had been a famous magnate and benefactor of the Five Towns; his revered name was in every mouth; he had a fine seat, Hillport House, at Hillport; and his superb horses were constantly seen, winged and nervous, in the streets of Bursley and Hanbridge. The 'Signal' said that the net value of his estate was sworn at fifty-nine thousand pounds. This single fact added a definite and startling significance to figures which had previously conveyed nothing to Anna except an idea of vastness. The crude contrast between the things of Hillport House and the things of the six-roomed abode in Manor Terrace gave food for reflection, silent but profound.

Tellwright had long ago retired from business, and three years after the housekeeper died he retired, practically, from religious work, to the grave detriment of the Hanbridge circuit. In reply to sorrowful questioners, he said merely that he was getting old and needed rest, and that there ought to be plenty of younger men to fill his shoes. He gave up everything except his pew in the chapel. The circuit was astounded by this sudden defection of a class-leader, a local preacher, and an officer. It was an inexplicable fall from grace. Yet the solution of the problem was quite simple. Ephraim had lost interest in his religious avocations; they had ceased to amuse him, the old ardour had cooled. The phenomenon is a common enough experience with men who have passed their fiftieth year—men, too, who began with the true and sacred zeal, which Tellwright never felt. The difference in Tellwright's case was that, characteristically, he at once yielded to the new instinct, caring naught for public opinion. Soon afterwards, having purchased a lot of cottage property in Bursley, he decided to migrate to the town of his fathers. He had more than one reason for doing so, but perhaps the chief was that he found the atmosphere of Hanbridge Wesleyan chapel rather uncongenial. The exodus from it was his silent and malicious retort to a silent rebuke.

He appeared now to grow younger, discarding in some measure a certain morose taciturnity which had hitherto marked his demeanour. He went amiably about in the manner of a veteran determined to enjoy the brief existence of life's winter. His stout, stiff, deliberate yet alert figure became a familiar object to Bursley: that ruddy face, with its small blue eyes, smooth upper lip, and short grey beard under the smooth chin, seemed to pervade the streets, offering everywhere the conundrum of its vague smile. Though no friend ever crossed his doorstep, he had dozens of acquaintances of the footpath. He was not, however, a facile talker, and he seldom gave an opinion; nor were his remarks often noticeably shrewd. He existed within himself, unrevealed. To the crowd, of course, he was a marvellous legend, and moving always in the glory of that legend he received their wondering awe—an awe tinged with contempt for his lack of ostentation and public splendour. Commercial men with whom he had transacted business liked to discuss his abilities, thus disseminating that solid respect for him which had sprung from a personal experience of those abilities, and which not even the shabbiness of his clothes could weaken.

Anna was disturbed by the arrival at the front door of the milk-girl. Alternately with her father, she stayed at home on Sunday evenings, partly to receive the evening milk and partly to guard the house. The Persian cat with one ear preceded her to the door as soon as he heard the clatter of the can. The stout little milk-girl dispensed one pint of milk into Anna's jug, and spilt an eleemosynary supply on the step for the cat. 'He does like it fresh, Miss,' said the milk-girl, smiling at the greedy cat, and then, with a 'Lovely evenin',' departed down the street, one fat red arm stretched horizontally out to balance the weight of the can in the other. Anna leaned idly against the doorpost, waiting while the cat finished, until at length the swaying figure of the milk-girl disappeared in the dip of the road. Suddenly she darted within, shutting the door, and stood on the hall-mat in a startled attitude of dismay. She had caught sight of Henry Mynors in the distance, approaching the house. At that moment the kitchen clock struck seven, and Mynors, according to the rule of a lifetime, should have been in his place in the 'orchestra' (or, as some term it, the 'singing-seat') of the chapel, where he was an admired baritone. Anna dared not conjecture what impulse had led him into this extraordinary, incredible deviation. She dared not conjecture, but despite herself she knew, and the knowledge shocked her sensitive and peremptory conscience. Her heart began to beat rapidly; she was in distress. Aware that her father and sister had left her alone, did he mean to call? It was absolutely impossible, yet she feared it, and blushed, all solitary there in the passage, for shame. Now she heard his sharp, decided footsteps, and through the glazed panels of the door she could see the outline of his form. He stopped; his hand was on the gate, and she ceased to breathe. He pushed the gate open, and then, at the whisper of some blessed angel, he closed it again and continued his way up the street. After a few moments Anna carried the milk into the kitchen, and stood by the dresser, moveless, each muscle braced in the intensity of profound contemplation. Gradually the tears rose to her eyes and fell; they were the tincture of a strange and mystic joy, too poignant to be endured. As it were under compulsion she ran outside, and down the garden path to the low wall which looked over the grey fields of the valley up to Hillport. Exactly opposite, a mile and a half away, on the ridge, was Hillport Church, dark and clear against the orange sky. To the right, and nearer, lay the central masses of the town, tier on tier of richly-coloured ovens and chimneys. Along the field-paths couples moved slowly. All was quiescent, languorous, beautiful in the glow of the sun's stately declension. Anna put her arms on the wall. Far more impressively than in the afternoon she realised that this was the end of one epoch in her career and the beginning of another. Enthralled by austere traditions and that stern conscience of hers, she had never permitted herself to dream of the possibility of an escape from the parental servitude. She had never looked beyond the horizons of her present world, but had sought spiritual satisfaction in the ideas of duty and sacrifice. The worst tyrannies of her father never dulled the sense of her duty to him; and, without perhaps being aware of it, she had rather despised love and the dalliance of the sexes. In her attitude towards such things there had been not only a little contempt but also some disapproval, as though man were destined for higher ends. Now she saw, in a quick revelation, that it was the lovers, and not she, who had the right to scorn. She saw how miserably narrow, tepid, and trickling the stream of her life had been, and had threatened to be. Now it gushed forth warm, impetuous, and full, opening out new and delicious vistas. She lived; and she was finding the sight to see, the courage to enjoy. Now, as she leaned over the wall, she would not have cared if Henry Mynors indeed had called that night. She perceived something splendid and free in his abandonment of habit and discretion at the bidding of a desire. To be the magnet which could draw that pattern and exemplar of seemliness from the strict orbit of virtuous custom! It was she, the miser's shabby daughter, who had caused this amazing phenomenon. The thought intoxicated her. Without the support of the wall she might have fallen. In a sort of trance she murmured these words: 'He loves me.'

This was Anna Tellwright, the ascetic, the prosaic, the impassive.

After an interval which to her was as much like a minute as a century, she went back into the house. As she entered by the kitchen she heard an impatient knocking at the front door.

'At last,' said her father grimly, when she opened the door. In two words he had resumed his terrible sway over her. Agnes looked timidly from one to the other and slipped past them into the house.

'I was in the garden,' Anna explained. 'Have you been here long?' She tried to smile apologetically.

'Only about a quarter of an hour,' he answered, with a grimness still more portentous.

'He won't speak again to-night,' she thought fearfully. But she was mistaken. After he had carefully hung his best hat on the hat-rack, he turned towards her, and said, with a queer smile:

'Ye've been day-dreaming, eh, Sis?'

'Sis' was her pet name, used often by Agnes, but by her father only at the very rarest intervals. She was staggered at this change of front, so unaccountable in this man, who, when she had unwittingly annoyed him, was capable of keeping an awful silence for days together. What did he know? What had those old eyes seen?

'I forgot,' she stammered, gathering herself together happily, 'I forgot the time.' She felt that after all there was a bond between them which nothing could break—the tie of blood. They were father and daughter, united by sympathies obscure but fundamental. Kissing was not in the Tellwright blood, but she had a fleeting wish to hug the tyrant.

[1] Tellwright: tile-wright, a name specially characteristic of, and possibly originating in, this clay-manufacturing district.

CHAPTER III

THE BIRTHDAY

The next morning there was no outward sign that anything unusual had occurred. As the clock in the kitchen struck eight Anna carried to the back parlour a tray on which were a dish of bacon and a coffee-pot. Breakfast was already laid for three. She threw a housekeeper's glance over the table, and called: 'Father!' Mr. Tellwright was re-setting some encaustic tiles in the lobby. He came in, coatless, and, dropping a trowel on the hearth, sat down at the end of the table nearest the fireplace. Anna sat opposite to him, and poured out the coffee.

On the dish were six pieces of bacon. He put one piece on a plate, and set it carefully in front of Agnes's vacant chair, two he passed to Anna, three he kept for himself.

'Where's Agnes?' he inquired.

'Coming—she's finishing her arithmetic.'

In the middle of the table was an unaccustomed small jug containing gilly-flowers. Mr. Tellwright noticed it instantly.

'What an we gotten here?' he said, indicating the jug.

'Agnes gave me them first thing when she got up. She's grown them herself, you know,' Anna said, and then added: 'It's my birthday.'

'Ay!' he exclaimed, with a trace of satire in his voice. 'Thou'rt a woman now, lass.'

No further remark on that matter was made during the meal.

Agnes ran in, all pinafore and legs. With a toss backwards of her light golden hair she slipped silently into her seat, cautiously glancing at the master of the house. Then she began to stir her coffee.

'Now, young woman,' Tellwright said curtly.

She looked a startled interrogative.

'We're waiting,' he explained.

'Oh!' said Agnes, confused. 'I thought you'd said it. "God sanctify this food to our use and us to His service for Christ's sake, Amen."'

The breakfast proceeded in silence. Breakfast at eight, dinner at noon, tea at four, supper at eight: all the meals in this house occurred with absolute precision and sameness. Mr. Tellwright seldom spoke, and his example imposed silence on the girls, who felt as nuns feel when assisting at some grave but monotonous and perfunctory rite. The room was not a cheerful one in the morning, since the window was small and the aspect westerly. Besides the table and three horse-hair chairs, the furniture consisted of an arm-chair, a bent-wood rocking chair, and a sewing-machine. A fatigued Brussels carpet covered the floor. Over the mantelpiece was an engraving of 'The Light of the World,' in a frame of polished brown wood. On the other walls were some family photographs in black frames. A two-light chandelier hung from the ceiling, weighed down on one side by a patent gas-saving mantle and a glass shade; over this the ceiling was deeply discoloured. On either side of the chimney-breast were cupboards about three feet high; some cardboard boxes, a work-basket, and Agnes's school books lay on the tops of these cupboards. On the window-sill was a pot of mignonette in a saucer. The window was wide open, and flies buzzed to and fro, constantly rebounding from the window panes with terrible thuds. In the blue-paved yard beyond the cat was licking himself in the sunlight with an air of being wholly absorbed in his task.

Mr. Tellwright demanded a second and last cup of coffee, and having drunk it pushed away his plate as a sign that he had finished. Then he took from the mantelpiece at his right hand a bundle of letters and opened them methodically. When he had arranged the correspondence in a flattened pile, he put on his steel-rimmed spectacles and began to read.

'Can I return thanks, father?' Agnes asked, and he nodded, looking at her fixedly over his spectacles.

'Thank God for our good breakfast, Amen.'

In two minutes the table was cleared, and Mr. Tellwright was alone. As he read laboriously through communications from solicitors, secretaries of companies, and tenants, he could hear his daughters talking together in the kitchen. Anna was washing the breakfast things while Agnes wiped. Then there were flying steps across the yard: Agnes had gone to school.

After he had mastered his correspondence, Mr. Tellwright took up the trowel again and finished the tile-setting in the lobby. Then he resumed his coat, and, gathering together the letters from the table in the back parlour, went into the front parlour and shut the door. This room was his office. The principal things in it were an old oak bureau and an old oak desk-chair which had come to him from his first wife's father; on the walls were some sombre landscapes in oil, received from the same source; there was no carpet on the floor, and only one other chair. A safe stood in the corner opposite the door. On the mantelpiece were some books— Woodfall's 'Landlord and Tenant,' Jordan's 'Guide to Company Law,' Whitaker's Almanack, and a Gazetteer of the Five Towns. Several wire files, loaded with papers, hung from the mantelpiece. With the exception of a mahogany what-not with a Bible on it, which stood in front of the window, there was nothing else whatever in the room. He sat down to the bureau and opened it, and took from one of the pigeon-holes a packet of various documents: these he examined one by one, from time to time referring to a list. Then he unlocked the safe and extracted from it another bundle of documents which had evidently been placed ready. With these in his hand, he opened the door, and called out:

'Anna.'

'Yes, father;' her voice came from the kitchen.

'I want ye.'

'In a minute. I'm peeling potatoes.'

When she came in, she found him seated at the bureau as usual. He did not look round.

'Yes, father.'

She stood there in her print dress and white apron, full in the eye of the sun, waiting for him. She could not guess what she had been summoned for. As a rule, she never saw her father between breakfast and dinner. At length he turned.

'Anna,' he said in his harsh, abrupt tones, and then stopped for a moment before continuing. His thick, short fingers held the list which he had previously been consulting. She waited in bewilderment. 'It's your birthday, ye told me. I hadna' forgotten. Ye're of age to-day, and there's summat for ye. Your mother had a fortune of her own, and under your grandfeyther's will it comes to you when you're twenty-one. I'm the trustee. Your mother had eighteen thousand pounds i' Government stock.' He laid a slight sneering emphasis on the last two words. 'That was near twenty-five year ago. I've nigh on trebled it for ye, what wi' good investments and interest accumulating. Thou'rt worth'—here he changed to the second personal singular, a habit with him— 'thou'rt worth this day as near fifty thousand as makes no matter, Anna. And that's a tidy bit.'

'Fifty thousand—*pounds*!' she exclaimed aghast.

'Ay, lass.'

She tried to speak calmly. 'Do you mean it's mine, father?'

'It's thine, under thy grandfeyther's will—haven't I told thee? I'm bound by law for to give it to thee this day, and thou mun give me a receipt in due form for the securities. Here they are, and here's the list. Tak' the list, Anna, and read it to me while I check off.'

She mechanically took the blue paper and read: 'Toft End Colliery and Brickworks Limited, five hundred shares of ten pounds.'

'They paid ten per cent. last year,' he said, 'and with coal up as it is they'll pay fiftane this. Let's see what thy arithmetic is worth, lass. How much is fiftane per cent. on five thousand pun?'

'Seven hundred and fifty pounds,' she said, getting the correct answer by a superhuman effort worthy of that occasion.

'Right,' said her father, pleased. 'Recollect that's more till two pun a day. Go on.'

'North Staffordshire Railway Company ordinary stock, ten thousand and two hundred pounds.'

'Right. Th' owd North Stafford's getting up i' th' world. It'll be a five per cent. line yet. Then thou mun sell out.'

She had only a vague idea of his meaning, and continued: 'Five Towns Waterworks Company Limited consolidated stock, eight thousand five hundred pounds.'

493

'That's a tit-bit, lass,' he interjected, looking absently over his spectacles at something outside in the road. 'You canna' pick that up on shardrucks.'

'Norris's Brewery Limited, six hundred ordinary shares of ten pounds.'

'Twenty per cent.,' said the old man. 'Twenty per cent. regular.' He made no attempt to conceal his pride in these investments. And he had the right to be proud of them. They were the finest in the market, the aristocracy of investments, based on commercial enterprises of which every business man in the Five Towns knew the entire soundness. They conferred distinction on the possessor, like a great picture or a rare volume. They stifled all questions and insinuations. Put before any jury of the Five Towns as evidence of character, they would almost have exculpated a murderer.

Anna continued reading the list, which seemed endless: long before she had reached the last item her brain was a menagerie of monstrous figures. The list included, besides all sorts of shares English and American, sundry properties in the Five Towns, and among these was the earthenware manufactory in Edward Street occupied by Titus Price, the Sunday-school superintendent. Anna was a little alarmed to find herself the owner of this works; she knew that her father had had some difficult moments with Titus Price, and that the property was not without grave disadvantages.

'That all!' Tellwright asked, at length.

'That's all.'

'Total face value,' he went on, 'as I value it, forty-eight thousand and fifty pounds, producing a net annual income of three thousand two hundred and ninety pounds or thereabouts. There's not many in this district as 'as gotten that to their names, Anna—no, nor half that—let 'em be who they will.'

Anna had sensations such as a child might have who has received a traction-engine to play with in a back yard. 'What am I to do with it?' she asked plaintively.

'Do wi' it?' he repeated, and stood up and faced her, putting his lips together: 'Do wi' it, did ye say?'

'Yes.'

'Tak' care on it, my girl. Tak' care on it. And remember it's thine. Thou mun sign this list, and all these transfers and fal-lals, and then thou mun go to th' Bank, and tell Mester Lovatt I've sent thee. There's four hundred pound there. He'll give thee a cheque-book. I've told him all about it. Thou'll have thy own account, and be sure thou keeps it straight.'

'I shan't know a bit what to do, father, and so it's no use talking,' she said quietly.

'I'll learn ye,' he replied. 'Here, tak' th' pen, and let's have thy signature.'

She signed her name many times and put her finger on many seals. Then Tellwright gathered up everything into a bundle, and gave it to her to hold.

'That's the lot,' he said. 'Have ye gotten 'em?'

'Yes,' she said.

They both smiled, self-consciously. As for Tellwright, he was evidently impressed by the grandeur of this superb renunciation on his part. 'Shall I keep 'em for ye?'

'Yes, please.'

'Then give 'em me.'

He took back all the documents.

'When shall I call at the Bank, father?'

'Better call this afternoon—afore three, mind ye.'

'Very well. But I shan't know what to do.'

'You've gotten a tongue in that noddle of yours, haven't ye?' he said. 'Now go and get along wi' them potatoes.'

Anna returned to the kitchen. She felt no elation or ferment of any kind; she had not begun to realise the significance of what had occurred. Like the soldier whom a bullet has struck, she only knew vaguely that something had occurred. She peeled the potatoes with more than her usual thrifty care; the peel was so thin as to be almost transparent. It seemed to her that she could not arrange or examine her emotions until after she had met Henry Mynors again. More than anything else she wished to see him: it was as if out of the mere sight of him something definite might emerge, as if when her eyes had rested on him, and not before, she might perceive some simple solution of the problems which she had obscurely discerned ahead of her.

During dinner a boy brought a note for her father. He read it, snorted, and threw it across the table to Anna.

'Here,' he said, 'that's your affair.'

The letter was from Titus Price: it said that he was sorry to be compelled to break his promise, but it was quite impossible for him to pay twenty pounds on account of rent that day; he would endeavour to pay at least twenty pounds in a week's time.

'You'd better call there, after you've been to th' Bank,' said Tellwright, 'and get summat out of him, if it's only ten pun.'

'Must I go to Edward Street?'

'Yes.'

'What am I to say? I've never been there before.'

'Well, it's high time as ye began to look after your own property. You mun see owd Price, and tell him ye canna accept any excuses.'

'How much does he owe?'

'He owes ye a hundred and twenty-five pun altogether—he's five quarters in arrear.'

'A hundred and——! Well, I never!' Anna was aghast. The sum appeared larger to her than all the thousands and tens of thousands which she had received in the morning. She reflected that the weekly bills of the household amounted to about a sovereign, and that the total of this debt of Price's would therefore keep them in food for two years. The idea of being in debt was abhorrent to her. She could not conceive how a man who was in debt could sleep at nights. 'Mr. Price ought to be ashamed of himself,' she said warmly. 'I'm sure he's quite able to pay.' The image of the sleek and stout superintendent of the Sunday-school, arrayed in his rich, almost voluptuous, broadcloth, offended her profoundly. That he, debtor and promise-breaker, should have the effrontery to pray for the souls of children, to chastise their petty furtive crimes, was nearly incredible.

'Oh! Price is all *right*,' her father remarked, with an apparent benignity which surprised her. 'He'll pay when he can.'

'I think it's a shame,' she repeated emphatically.

Agnes looked with a mystified air from one to the other, instinctively divining that something very extraordinary had happened during her absence at school.

'Ye mun'na be too hard, Anna,' said Tellwright. 'Supposing ye sold owd Titus up? What then? D'ye reckon ye'd get a tenant for them ramshackle works? A thousand pound spent wouldn't 'tice a tenant. That Edward Street property was one o' ye grandfeyther's specs; 'twere none o' mine. You'd best tak' what ye can get.'

Anna felt a little ashamed of herself, not because of her bad policy, but because she saw that Mr. Price might have been handicapped by the faults of her property.

That afternoon it was a shy and timid Anna who swung back the heavy polished and glazed portals of the Bursley branch of the Birmingham, Sheffield and district Bank, the opulent and spacious erection which stands commandingly at the top of St. Luke's Square. She looked about her, across broad counters, enormous ledgers, and rows of bent heads, and wondered whom she should address. Then a bearded gentleman, who was weighing gold in a balance, caught sight of her: he slid the gold into a drawer, and whisked round the end of the counter with a celerity which was, at any rate, not born of practice, for he, the cashier, had not done such a thing for years.

'Good afternoon, Miss Tellwright.'

'Good afternoon. I——'

'May I trouble you to step into the manager's room?' and he drew her forward, while every clerk's eye watched. Anna tried not to blush, but she could feel the red mounting even to her temples.

'Delightful weather we're having. But of course we've the right to expect it at this time of year.' He opened a door on the glass of which was painted 'Manager,' and bowed. 'Mr. Lovatt—Miss Tellwright.'

Mr. Lovatt greeted his new customer with a formal and rather fatigued politeness, and invited her to sit in a large leather armchair in front of a large table; on this table lay a large open book. Anna had once in her life been to the dentist's; this interview reminded her of that experience.

'Your father told me I might expect you to-day,' said Mr. Lovatt in his high-pitched, perfunctory tones. Richard Lovatt was probably the most influential man in Bursley. Every Saturday morning he irrigated the whole town with fertilising gold. By a single negative he could have ruined scores of upright merchants and manufacturers. He had only to stop a man in the street and murmur, 'By the way, your overdraft——,' in order to spread discord and desolation through a refined and pious home. His estimate of human nature was falsified by no common illusions; he had the impassive and frosty gaze of a criminal judge. Many men deemed they had cause to hate him, but no one did hate him: all recognised that he was set far above hatred.

'Kindly sign your full name here,' he said, pointing to a spot on the large open page of the book, 'and your ordinary signature, which you will attach to cheques, here.'

Anna wrote, but in doing so she became aware that she had no ordinary signature; she was obliged to invent one.

'Do you wish to draw anything out now? There is already a credit of four hundred and twenty pounds in your favour,' said Mr. Lovatt, after he had handed her a cheque-book, a deposit-book, and a pass-book.

'Oh, no, thank you,' Anna answered quickly. She keenly desired some money, but she well knew that courage would fail her to demand it without her father's consent; moreover, she was in a whirl of uncertainty as to the uses of the three books, though Mr. Lovatt had expounded them severally to her in simple language.

'Good-day.'

'Good-day, Miss Tellwright.'

'My compliments to your father.'

His final glance said half cynically, half in pity: 'You are naïve and unspoilt now, but these eyes will see yours harden like the rest. Wretched victim of gold, you are only one in a procession, after all.'

Outside, Anna thought that everyone had been very agreeable to her. Her complacency increased at a bound. She no longer felt ashamed of her shabby cotton dress. She surmised that people would find it convenient to ignore any difference which might exist between her costume and that of other girls.

She went on to Edward Street, a short steep thoroughfare at the eastern extremity of the town, leading into a rough road across unoccupied land dotted with the mouths of abandoned pits: this road climbed up to Toft End, a mean annexe of the town about half a mile east of Bleakridge. From Toft End, lying on the highest hill in the district, one had a panoramic view of Hanbridge and Bursley, with Hillport to the west, and all the moorland and mining villages to the north and north-east. Titus Price and his son lived in what had once been a farm-house at Toft End; every morning and evening they traversed the desolate and featureless grey road between their dwelling and the works.

Anna had never been in Edward Street before. It was a miserable quarter—two rows of blackened infinitesimal cottages, and her manufactory at the end—a frontier post of the town. Price's works was small, old-fashioned, and out of repair—one of those properties which are forlorn from the beginning, which bring despair into the hearts of a succession of owners, and which, being ultimately deserted, seem to stand for ever in pitiable ruin. The arched entrance for carts into the yard was at the top of the steepest rise of the street, when it might as well have been at the bottom; and this was but one example of the architect's fine disregard for the principle of economy in working—that principle to which in the scheming of manufactories everything else is now so strictly subordinated. Ephraim Tellwright used to say (but not to Titus Price) that the situation of that archway cost five pounds a year in horseflesh, and that five pounds was the interest on a hundred. The place was badly located, badly planned and badly constructed. Its faults defied improvement. Titus Price remained in it only because he was chained there by arrears of rent; Tellwright hesitated to sell it only because the rent was a hundred a year, and the whole freehold would not have fetched eight hundred. He promised repairs in exchange for payment of arrears which he knew would never be paid, and his policy was to squeeze the last penny out of Price without forcing him into bankruptcy. Such was the predicament when Anna assumed ownership. As she surveyed the irregular and huddled frontage from the opposite side of the street, her first feeling was one of depression at the broken and dirty panes of the windows. A man in shirt-sleeves was standing on the weighing platform under the archway; his back was towards her, but she could see the smoke issuing in puffs from his pipe. She crossed the road. Hearing her footfalls, the man turned round: it was Titus Price himself. He was wearing an apron, but no cap; the sleeves of his shirt were rolled up, exposing forearms covered with auburn hair. His puffed, heavy face, and general bigness and untidiness, gave the idea of a vast and torpid male slattern. Anna was astounded by the contrast between the Titus of Sunday and the Titus of Monday: a single glance compelled her to readjust all her notions of the man. She stammered a greeting, and he replied, and then they were both silent for a moment: in the pause Mr. Price thrust his pipe between apron and waistcoat.

'Come inside, Miss Tellwright,' he said, with a sickly, conciliatory smile. 'Come into the office, will ye?'

She followed him without a word through the archway. To the right was an open door into the packing-house, where a man surrounded by straw was packing basins in a crate: with swift, precise movements, twisting straw between basin and basin, he forced piles of ware into a space inconceivably small. Mr. Price lingered to watch him for a few seconds, and passed on. They were in the yard, a small quadrangle paved with black, greasy mud. In one corner a load of coal had been cast; in another lay a heap of broken saggars. Decrepit doorways led to the various 'shops' on the ground floor; those on the upper floor were reached by narrow wooden stairs, which seemed to cling insecurely to the exterior walls. Up one of these stairways Mr. Price climbed with heavy, elephantine movements: Anna prudently waited till he had reached the top before beginning to ascend. He pushed open a flimsy door, and with a nod bade her enter. The office was a long narrow room, the dirtiest that Anna had ever seen. If such was the condition of the master's quarters, she thought, what must the workshops be like? The ceiling, which bulged downwards, was as black as the floor, which sank away in the middle till it was hollow like a saucer. The revolution of an engine somewhere below shook everything with a periodic muffled thud. A greyish light came through one small window. By the window was a large double desk, with chairs facing each other. One of these chairs was occupied by Willie Price. The youth did not observe at first that another person had come in with his father. He was casting up figures in an account book, and murmuring numbers to himself. He wore an office coat, short at the wrists and torn at the elbows, and a battered felt hat was thrust far back over his head so that the brim rested on his dirty collar. He turned round at length, and, on seeing Anna, blushed brilliant crimson, and rose, scraping the legs of his chair horribly across the floor. Tall, thin, and ungainly in every motion, he had the look of a ninny: it was the fact that at school all the boys by a common instinct had combined to tease him, and that on the works the young paintresses continually made private sport of him. Anna, however, had not the least impulse to mock him in her thoughts. For her there was nothing in his blue eyes but simplicity and good intentions. Beside him she felt old, sagacious, crafty: it seemed to her that some one ought to shield that transparent and confiding soul from his father and the intriguing world.

He spoke to her and lifted his hat, holding it afterwards in his great bony hand.

'Get down to th' entry, Will,' said his father, and Willie, with an apologetic sort of cough, slipped silently away through the door.

'Sit down, Miss Tellwright,' said old Price, and she took the Windsor chair that had been occupied by Willie. Her tenant fell into the seat opposite—a leathern chair from which the stuffing had exuded, and with one of its arms broken. 'I hear as ye father is going into partnership with young Mynors—Henry Mynors.'

Anna started at this surprising item of news, which was entirely fresh to her. 'Father has said nothing to me about it,' she replied, coldly.

'Oh! Happen I've said too much. If so, you'll excuse me, Miss. A smart fellow, Mynors. Now you should see *his* little works: not very much bigger than this, but there's everything you can think of there—all the latest machinery and dodges, and not over-rented, I'm told. The biggest fool i' Bursley couldn't help but make money there. This 'ere works 'ere, Miss Tellwright, wants mendin' with a new 'un.'

'It looks very dirty, I must say,' said Anna.

'Dirty!' he laughed—a short, acrid laugh—'I suppose you've called about the rent.'

'Yes, father asked me to call.'

'Let me see, this place belongs to you i' your own right, doesn't it, Miss?'

'Yes,' said Anna. 'It's mine—from my grandfather, you know.'

'Ah! Well, I'm sorry for to tell ye as I can't pay anything now—no, not a cent. But I'll pay twenty pounds in a week. Tell ye father I'll pay twenty pound in a week.'

'That's what you said last week,' Anna remarked, with more brusqueness than she had intended. At first she was fearful at her own temerity in thus addressing a superintendent of the Sunday-school; then, as nothing happened, she felt reassured, and strong in the justice of her position.

'Yes,' he admitted obsequiously. 'But I've been disappointed. One of our best customers put us off, to tell ye the truth. Money's tight, very tight. It's got to be give and take in these days, as ye father knows. And I may as well speak plain to ye, Miss Tellwright. We canna' stay here; we shall be compelled to give ye notice. What's amiss with this bank[1] is that it wants pullin' down.' He went off into a rapid enumeration of ninety-and-nine alterations and repairs that must be done without the loss of a moment, and concluded: 'You tell ye father what I've told ye, and say as I'll send up twenty pounds next week. I can't pay anything now; I've nothing by me at all.'

'Father said particularly I was to be sure and get something on account.' There was a flinty hardness in her tone which astonished herself perhaps more than Titus Price. A long pause followed, and then Mr. Price drew a breath, seeming to nerve himself to a tremendous sacrificial deed.

'I tell ye what I'll do. I'll give ye ten pounds now, and I'll do what I can next week. I'll do what I can. There!'

'Thank you,' said Anna. She was amazed at her success.

He unlocked the desk, and his head disappeared under the lifted lid. Anna gazed through the window. Like many women, and not a few men, in the Five Towns, she was wholly ignorant of the staple manufacture. The interior of a works was almost as strange to her as it would have been to a farm-hand from Sussex. A girl came out of a door on the opposite side of the quadrangle: the creature was clothed in clayey rags, and carried on her right shoulder a board laden with biscuit[2] cups. She began to mount one of the wooden stairways, and as she did so the board, six feet in length, swayed alarmingly to and fro. Anna expected to see it fall with a destructive crash, but the girl went up in safety, and with a nonchalant jerk of the shoulder aimed the end of the board through another door and vanished from sight. To Anna it was a thrilling feat, but she noticed that a man who stood in the yard did not even turn his head to watch it. Mr. Price recalled her to the business of her errand.

'Here's two fives,' he said, shutting down the desk with the sigh of a crocodile.

'Liar! You said you had nothing!' her unspoken thought ran, and at the same instant the Sunday-school and everything connected with it grievously sank in her estimation; she contrasted this scene with that on the previous day with the peccant schoolgirl: it was an hour of disillusion. Taking the notes, she gave a receipt and rose to go.

'Tell ye father'—it seemed to Anna that this phrase was always on his lips—'tell ye father he must come down and look at the state this place is in,' said Mr. Price, enheartened by the heroic payment of ten pounds. Anna said nothing; she thought a fire would do more good than anything else to the foul, squalid buildings: the passing fancy coincided with Mr. Price's secret and most intense desire.

Outside she saw Willie Price superintending the lifting of a crate on to a railway lorry. After twirling in the air, the crate sank safely into the waggon. Young Price was perspiring.

'Warm afternoon, Miss Tellwright,' he called to her as she passed, with his pleasant bashful smile. She gave an affirmative. Then he came to her, still smiling, his face full of an intention to say something, however insignificant.

'I suppose you'll be at the Special Teachers' Meeting to-morrow night,' he remarked.

'I hope to be,' she said. That was all: William had achieved his small-talk: they parted.

'So father and Mr. Mynors are going into partnership,' she kept saying to herself on the way home.

[1] Bank: manufactory.
[2] Biscuit: a term applied to ware which has been fired only once.

CHAPTER IV

A VISIT

The Special Teachers' Meeting to which Willie Price had referred was one of the final preliminaries to a Revival—that is, a revival of godliness and Christian grace—about to be undertaken by the Wesleyan Methodist Society in Bursley. Its object was to arrange for a personal visitation of the parents of Sunday-school scholars in their homes. Hitherto Anna had felt but little interest in the Revival: it had several times been brought indirectly before her notice, but she had regarded it as a phenomenon which recurred at intervals in the cycle of religious activity, and as not in any way affecting herself. The gradual centring of public interest, however—that mysterious movement which, defying analysis, gathers force as it proceeds, and ends by coercing the most indifferent—had already modified her attitude towards this forthcoming event. It got about that the preacher who had been engaged, a specialist in revivals, was a man of miraculous powers: the number of souls which he had snatched from eternal torment was precisely stated, and it amounted to tens of thousands. He played the cornet to the glory of God, and his cornet was of silver: his more distant past had been ineffably wicked, and the faint rumour of that dead wickedness clung to his name like a piquant odour. As Anna walked up Trafalgar Road from Price's she observed that the hoardings had been billed with great posters announcing the Revival and the revivalist, who was to commence his work on Friday night.

During tea Mr. Tellwright interrupted his perusal of the evening 'Signal' to give utterance to a rather remarkable speech.

'Bless us!' he said. 'Th' old trumpeter 'll turn the town upside down!'

'Do you mean the revivalist, father?' Anna asked.

'Ay!'

'He's a beautiful man,' Agnes exclaimed with enthusiasm. 'Our teacher showed us his portrait after school this afternoon. I never saw such a beautiful man.'

Her father gazed hard at the child for an instant, cup in hand, and then turned to Anna with a slightly sardonic air.

'What are you doing i' this Revival, Anna?'

'Nothing,' she said. 'Only there's a teachers' meeting about it to-morrow night, and I have to go to that. Young Mr. Price mentioned it to me specially to-day.'

A pause followed.

'Didst get anything out o' Price?' Tellwright asked.

'Yes; he gave me ten pounds. He wants you to go and look over the works—says they're falling to pieces.'

'Cheque, I reckon?'

She corrected the surmise.

'Better give me them notes, Anna,' he said after tea. 'I'm going to th' Bank i' th' morning, and I'll pay 'em in to your account.'

There was no reason why she should not have suggested the propriety of keeping at least one of the notes for her private use. But she dared not. She had never any money of her own, not a penny; and the effective possession of five pounds seemed far too audacious a dream. She hesitated to imagine her father's reply to such a request, even to frame the request to herself. The thing, viewed close, was utterly impossible. And when she relinquished the notes she also, without being asked, gave up her cheque-book, deposit-book, and pass-book. She did this while ardently desiring to refrain from doing it, as it were under the compulsion of an invincible instinct. Afterwards she felt more at ease, as though some disturbing question had been settled once and for all.

During the whole of that evening she timorously expected Mynors, saying to herself however that he certainly would not call before Thursday. On Tuesday evening she started early for the teachers' meeting. Her intention was to arrive among the first and to choose a seat in obscurity, since she knew well that every eye would be upon her. She was divided between the desire to see Mynors and the desire to avoid the ordeal of being seen by her colleagues in his presence. She trembled lest she should be incapable of commanding her mien so as to appear unconscious of this inspection by curious eyes.

The meeting was held in a large class-room, furnished with wooden seats, a chair and a small table. On the grey distempered walls hung a few Biblical cartoons depicting scenes in the life of Joseph and his brethren—but without reference to Potiphar's wife. From the whitewashed ceiling depended a T-shaped gas-fitting, one burner of which showed a glimmer, though the sun had not yet set. The evening was oppressively warm, and through the wide-open window came the faint effluvium of populous cottages and the distant but raucous cries of children at play. When Anna entered a group of young men were talking eagerly round the table; among these was Willie Price, who greeted her. No others had come: she sat down in a corner by the door, invisible except from within the room. Gradually the place began to fill. Then at last Mynors entered: Anna recognised his authoritative step before she saw him. He walked quickly to the chair in front of the table, and, including all in a friendly and generous smile, said that in the absence of Mr. Titus Price it fell to him to take the chair; he was glad that so many had made a point of being present. Everyone sat down. He gave out a hymn, and led the singing himself, attacking the first note with an assurance born of practice. Then he prayed, and as he prayed Anna gazed at him intently. He was standing up, the ends of his fingers pressed against the top of the table. Very carefully dressed as usual, he wore a brilliant new red necktie, and a gardenia in his button-hole. He seemed happy, wholesome, earnest, and unaffected. He had the elasticity of youth with the firm wisdom of age. And it was as if he had never been younger and would never grow older, remaining always at just thirty and in his prime. Incomparable to the rest, he was clearly born to lead. He fulfilled his functions with tact, grace, and dignity. In such an affair as this present he disclosed the attributes of the skilled workman, whose easy and exact movements are a joy and wonder to the beholder. And behind all was the man, his excellent and strong nature, his kindliness, his sincerity. Yes, to Anna, Mynors was perfect that night; the reality of him exceeded her dreamy meditations. Fearful on the brink of an ecstatic bliss, she could scarcely believe that from the enticements of a thousand woman this paragon had been preserved for her. Like most of us, she lacked the high courage to grasp happiness boldly and without apprehension; she had not learnt that nothing is too good to be true.

Mynors' prayer was a cogent appeal for the success of the Revival. He knew what he wanted, and confidently asked for it, approaching God with humility but with self-respect. The prayer was punctuated by Amens from various parts of the room. The atmosphere became suddenly fervent, emotional and devout. Here was lofty

499

endeavour, idealism, a burning spirituality; and not all the pettinesses unavoidable in such an organisation as a Sunday-school could hide the difference between this impassioned altruism and the ignoble selfishness of the worldly. Anna felt, as she had often felt before, but more acutely now, that she existed only on the fringe of the Methodist society. She had not been converted; technically she was a lost creature: the converted knew it, and in some subtle way their bearing towards her, and others in her case, always showed that they knew it. Why did she teach? Not from the impulse of religious zeal. Why was she allowed to have charge of a class of immortal souls? The blind could not lead the blind, nor the lost save the lost. These considerations troubled her. Conscience pricked, accusing her of a continual pretence. The *rôle* of professing Christian, through false shame, had seemed distasteful to her: she had said that she could never stand up and say, 'I am for Christ,' without being uncomfortable. But now she was ashamed of her inability to profess Christ. She could conceive herself proud and happy in the very part which formerly she had despised. It was these believers, workers, exhorters, wrestlers with Satan, who had the right to disdain; not she. At that moment, as if divining her thoughts, Mynors prayed for those among them who were not converted. She blushed, and when the prayer was finished she feared lest every eye might seek hers in inquiry; but no one seemed to notice her.

Mynors sat down, and, seated, began to explain the arrangements for the Revival. He made it plain that prayers without industry would not achieve success. His remarks revealed the fact that underneath the broad religious structure of the enterprise, and supporting it, there was a basis of individual diplomacy and solicitation. The town had been mapped out into districts, and each of these was being importuned, as at an election: by the thoroughness and instancy of this canvass, quite as much as by the intensity of prayerful desire, would Christ conquer. The affair was a campaign before it was a prostration at the Throne of Grace. He spoke of the children, saying that in connection with these they, the teachers, had at once the highest privilege and the most sacred responsibility. He told of a special service for the children, and the need of visiting them in their homes and inviting the parents also to this feast of God. He wished every teacher during to-morrow and the next day and the next day to go through the list of his or her scholars' names, and call if possible at every house. There must be no shirking. 'Will you ladies do that?' he exclaimed with an appealing, serious smile. 'Will you, Miss Dickinson? Will you, Miss Machin? Will you, Mrs. Salt? Will you, Miss Sutton? Will you——' Until at last it came: 'Will you, Miss Tellwright?' 'I will,' she answered, with averted eyes. 'Thank you. Thank you all.'

Some others spoke, hopefully, enthusiastically, and one or two prayed. Then Mynors rose: 'May the blessing of God the Father, the Son, and the Holy Ghost rest upon us now and for ever.' 'Amen,' someone ejaculated. The meeting was over.

Anna passed rapidly out of he door, down the Quadrangle, and into Trafalgar Road. She was the first to leave, daring not to stay in the room a moment. She had seen him; he had not altered since Sunday; there was no disillusion, but a deepening of the original impression. Caught up by the soaring of his spirit, her spirit lifted, and she was conscious of vague but intense longing skyward. She could not reason or think in that dizzying hour, but she made resolutions which had no verbal form, yielding eagerly to his influence and his appeal. Not till she had reached the bottom of Duck Bank and was breasting the first rise towards Bleakridge did her pace slacken. Then a voice called to her from behind. She recognised it, and turned sharply beneath the shock. Mynors raised his hat and greeted her.

'I'm coming to see your father,' he said.

'Yes?' she said, and gave him her hand.

'It was a very satisfactory meeting to-night,' he began, and in a moment they were talking seriously of the Revival. With the most oblique delicacy, the most perfect assumption of equality between them, he allowed her to perceive his genuine and profound anxiety for her spiritual welfare. The atmosphere of the meeting was still round about him, the divine fire still uncooled. 'I hope you will come to the first service on Friday night,' he pleaded.

'I must,' she replied. 'Oh, yes. I shall come.'

'That is good,' he said. 'I particularly wanted your promise.'

They were at the door of the house. Agnes, obviously expectant and excited, answered the bell. With an effort Anna and Mynors passed into a lighter mood.

'Father said you were coming, Mr. Mynors,' said Agnes, and, turning to Anna, 'I've set supper all myself.'

'Have you?' Mynors laughed. 'Capital! You must let me give you a kiss for that.' He bent down and kissed her, she holding up her face to his with no reluctance. Anna looked on, smiling.

Mr. Tellwright sat near the window of the back parlour, reading the paper. Twilight was at hand. He lowered his head as Mynors entered with Agnes in train, so as to see over his spectacles, which were half-way down his nose.

'How d'ye do, Mr. Mynors? I was just going to begin my supper. I don't wait, you know,' and he glanced at the table.

'Quite right,' said Mynors, 'so long as you wouldn't eat it all. Would he have eaten it all, Agnes, do you think?' Agnes pressed her head against Mynors' arm and laughed shyly. The old man sardonically chuckled.

Anna, who was still in the passage, wondered what could be on the table. If it was only the usual morsel of cheese she felt that she should expire of mortification. She peeped: the cheese was at one end, and at the other a joint of beef, scarcely touched.

'Nay, nay,' said Tellwright, as if he had been engaged some seconds upon the joke, 'I'd have saved ye the bone.'

Anna went upstairs to take off her hat, and immediately Agnes flew after her. The child was breathless with news.

'Oh, Anna! As soon as you'd gone out father told me that Mr. Mynors was coming for supper. Did you know before?'

'Not till Mr. Mynors told me, dear.' It was characteristic of her father to say nothing until the last moment.

'Yes, and he told me to put an extra plate, and I asked him if I had better put the beef on the table, and first he said "No," cross—you know—and then he said I could please myself, so I put it on. Why has Mr. Mynors come, Anna?'

'How should I know? Some business between him and father, I expect.'

'It's very *queer*,' said Agnes positively, with the child's aptitude for looking a fact squarely in the face.

'Why "queer"?'

'You know it is, Anna,' she frowned, and then breaking into a joyous anile: 'But isn't he nice? I think he's lovely.'

'Yes,' Anna assented coldly.

'But really?' Agnes persisted.

Anna brushed her hair and determined not to put on the apron which she usually wore in the house.

'Am I tidy, Anna?'

'Yes. Run downstairs now. I am coming directly.'

'I want to wait for you,' Agnes pouted.

'Very well, dear.'

They entered the parlour together, and Henry Mynors jumped up from his chair, and would not sit at table until they were seated. Then Mr. Tellwright carved the beef, giving each of them a very small piece, and taking only cheese for himself. Agnes handed the water-jug and the bread. Mynors talked about nothing in especial, but he talked and laughed the whole time; he even made the old man laugh, by a comical phrase aimed at Agnes's mad passion for gilly-flowers. He seemed not to have detected any shortcomings in the table appointments—the coarse cloth and plates, the chipped tumblers, the pewter cruet, and the stumpy knives—which caused anguish in the heart of the housewife. He might have sat at such a table every night of his life.

'May I trouble you for a little more beef?' he asked presently, and Anna fancied a shade of mischief in his tone as he thus forced the old man into a tardy hospitality. 'Thanks. *And* a morsel of fat.'

She wondered whether he guessed that she was worth fifty thousand pounds, and her father worth perhaps more.

But on the whole Anna enjoyed the meal. She was sorry when they had finished and Agnes had thanked God for the beef. It was not without considerable reluctance that she rose and left the side of the man whose arm she could have touched at any time during the previous twenty minutes. She had felt happy and perturbed in being so near to him, so intimate and free; already she knew his face by heart. The two girls carried the plates and dishes into the kitchen, Agnes making the last journey with the tablecloth, which Mynors had assisted her to fold.

'Shut the door, Agnes,' said the old man, getting up to light the gas. It was an order of dismissal to both his daughters. 'Let me light that,' Mynors exclaimed, and the gas was lighted before Mr. Tellwright had struck a match. Mynors turned on the full force of gas. Then Mr. Tellwright carefully lowered it. The summer quarter's gas-bill at that house did not exceed five shillings.

Through the open windows of the kitchen and parlour, Anna could hear the voices of the two men in conversation, Mynors' vivacious and changeful, her father's monotonous, curt, and heavy. Once she caught the

501

old man's hard dry chuckle. The washing-up was done, Agnes had accomplished her home-lessons; the grandfather's clock chimed the half-hour after nine.

'You must go to bed, Agnes.'

'Mustn't I say good-night to him?'

'No, I will say good-night for you.'

'Don't forget to. I shall ask you in the morning.'

The regular sound of talk still came from the parlour. A full moon passed along the cloudless sky. By its light and that of a glimmer of gas, Anna sat cleaning silver, or rather nickel, at the kitchen table. The spoons and forks were already clean, but she felt compelled to busy herself with something. At length the talk stopped and she heard the scraping of chair-legs. Should she return to the parlour? Or should she——? Even while she hesitated, the kitchen door opened.

'Excuse me coming in here,' said Mynors. 'I wanted to say good-night to you.'

She sprang up and he took her hand. Could he feel the agitation of that hand?

'Good-night.'

'Good-night.' He said it again.

'And Agnes wished me to say good-night to you for her.'

'Did she?' He smiled; till then his face had been serious. 'You won't forget Friday?'

'As if I could!' she murmured after he had gone.

CHAPTER V

THE REVIVAL

Anna spent the two following afternoons in visiting the houses of her school-children. She had no talent for such work, which demands the vocal rather than the meditative temperament, and the apparent futility of her labours would have disgusted and disheartened her had she not been sustained and urged forward by the still active influence of Mynors and the teachers' meeting. There were fifteen names in her class-book, and she went to each house, except four whose tenants were impeccable Wesleyan families and would have considered themselves insulted by a quasi-didactic visit from an upstart like Anna. Of the eleven, some parents were rude to her; others begged, and she had nothing to give; others made perfunctory promises; only two seemed to regard her as anything but a somewhat tiresome impertinence. The fault was doubtless her own. Nevertheless she found joy in the uncongenial and ill-performed task—the cold, fierce joy of the nun in her penance. When it was done she said 'I have done it,' as one who has sworn to do it come what might, yet without quite expecting to succeed.

On the Friday afternoon, during tea, a boy brought up a large foolscap packet addressed to Mr. Tellwright. 'From Mr. Mynors,' the boy said. Tellwright opened it leisurely after the boy had gone, and took out some sheets covered with figures which he carefully examined. 'Anna,' he said, as she was clearing away the tea things, 'I understand thou'rt going to the Revival meeting to-night. I shall have a message as thou mun give to Mr. Mynors.'

When she went upstairs to dress, she saw the Suttons' landau standing outside their house on the opposite side of the road. Mrs. Sutton came down the front steps and got into the carriage, and was followed by a little restless, nervous, alert man who carried in his hand a black case of peculiar form. 'The Revivalist!' Anna exclaimed, remembering that he was to stay with the Suttons during the Revival week. Then this was the renowned crusader, and the case held his renowned cornet! The carriage drove off down Trafalgar Road, and Anna could see that the little man was talking vehemently and incessantly to Mrs. Sutton, who listened with evident interest; at the same time the man's eyes were everywhere, absorbing all details of the street and houses with unquenchable curiosity.

'What is the message for Mr. Mynors, father?' she asked in the parlour, putting on her cotton gloves.

'Oh!' he said, and then paused. 'Shut th' door, lass.'

She shut it, not knowing what this cautiousness foreshadowed. Agnes was in the kitchen.

'It's o' this'n,' Tellwright began. 'Young Mynors wants a partner wi' a couple o' thousand pounds, and he come to me. Ye understand; 'tis what they call a sleeping partner he's after. He'll give a third share in his concern for two thousand pound now. I've looked into it and there's money in it. He's no fool and he's gotten hold of a good thing. He sent me up his stock-taking and balance sheet to-day, and I've been o'er the place mysen. I'm telling thee this, lass, because I have na' two thousand o' my own idle just now, and I thought as thou might happen like th' investment.'

'But father——'

'Listen. I know as there's only four hundred o' thine in th' Bank now, but next week 'll see the beginning o' July and dividends coming in. I've reckoned as ye'll have nigh on fourteen hundred i' dividends and interests, and I can lend ye a couple o' hundred in case o' necessity. It's a rare chance; thou's best tak' it.'

'Of course, if you think it's all right, father, that's enough,' she said without animation.

'Am' na I telling thee I think it's all right?' he remarked sharply. 'You mun tell Mynors as I say it's satisfactory. Tell him that, see? I say it's satisfactory. I shall want for to see him later on. He told me he couldna' come up any night next week, so ask him to make it the week after. There's no hurry. Dunna' forget.'

What surprised Anna most in the affair was that Henry Mynors should have been able to tempt her father into a speculation. Ephraim Tellwright the investor was usually as shy as a well-fed trout, and this capture of him by a youngster only two years established in business might fairly be regarded as a prodigious feat. It was indeed the highest distinction of Mynors' commercial career. Henry was so prominently active in the Wesleyan Society that the members of that society, especially the women, were apt to ignore the other side of his individuality. They knew him supreme as a religious worker; they did not realise the likelihood of his becoming supreme in the staple manufacture. Left an orphan at seventeen, Mynors belonged to a family now otherwise extinct in the Five Towns—one of those families which by virtue of numbers, variety, and personal force seem to permeate a whole district, to be a calculable item of it, an essential part of its identity. The elders of the Mynors blood had once occupied the red house opposite Tellwright's, now used as a school, and had there reared many children: the school building was still known as 'Mynors's' by old-fashioned people. Then the parents died in middle age: one daughter married in the North, another in the South; a third went to China as a missionary and died of fever; the eldest son died; the second had vanished into Canada and was reported a scapegrace; the third was a sea-captain. Henry (the youngest) alone was left, and of all the family Henry was the only one to be connected with the earthenware trade. There was no inherited money, and during ten years he had worked for a large firm in Turnhill, as clerk, as traveller, and last as manager, living always quietly in lodgings. In the fullness of time he gave notice to leave, was offered a partnership, and refused it. Taking a newly erected manufactory in Bursley near the canal, he started in business for himself, and it became known that, at the age of twenty-eight, he had saved fifteen hundred pounds. Equally expert in the labyrinths of manufacture and in the niceties of the markets (he was reckoned a peerless traveller), Mynors inevitably flourished. His order-books were filled and flowing over at remunerative prices, and insufficiency of capital was the sole peril to which he was exposed. By the raising of a finger he could have had a dozen working and moneyed partners, but he had no desire for a working partner. What he wanted was a capitalist who had confidence in him, Mynors. In Ephraim Tellwright he found the man. Whether it was by instinct, good luck, or skilful diplomacy that Mynors secured this invaluable prize no one could positively say, and perhaps even he himself could not have catalogued all the obscure motives that had guided him to the shrewd miser of Manor Terrace.

Anna had meant to reach chapel before the commencement of the meeting, but the interview with her father threw her late. As she entered the porch an officer told her that the body of the chapel was quite full and that she should go into the gallery, where a few seats were left near the choir. She obeyed: pew-holders had no rights at that service. The scene in the auditorium astonished her, effectually putting an end to the worldly preoccupation caused by her father's news. The historic chapel was crowded almost in every part, and the congregation—impressed, excited, eager—sang the opening hymn with unprecedented vigour and sincerity; above the rest could be heard the trained voices of a large choir, and even the choir, usually perfunctory, seemed to share the general fervour. In the vast mahogany pulpit the Reverend Reginald Banks, the superintendent minister, a stout pale-faced man with pendent cheeks and cold grey eyes, stood impassively regarding the assemblage, and by his side was the revivalist, a manikin in comparison with his colleague; on the broad balustrade of the pulpit lay the cornet. The fiery and inquisitive eyes of the revivalist probed into the furthest corners of the chapel; apparently no detail of any single face or of the florid decoration escaped him, and as Anna crept into a small empty pew next to the east wall she felt that she too had been separately observed. Mr. Banks gave out the last verse of the hymn, and simultaneously with the leading chord from the organ the revivalist seized his cornet and joined the melody. Massive yet exultant, the tones rose clear over the mighty volume of vocal sound, an incitement to victorious effort. The effect was instant: an ecstatic tremor seemed to pass through the congregation, like wind through ripe corn, and at the close of the hymn it was not until the revivalist had put down his cornet that the people resumed their seats. Amid the *frou-frou* of dresses and subdued clearing of throats, Mr. Banks retired softly to the back of the pulpit, and the revivalist, mounting a stool, suddenly dominated the congregation. His glance swept masterfully across the chapel and round the gallery. He raised one hand with the stilling action of a mesmerist, and the people, either kneeling or inclined against the front of the pews, hid their faces from those eyes. It was as though the man had in a moment measured their iniquities, and had courageously resolved to intercede for them with God, but was not very sanguine as to the result. Everyone except the organist, who was searching his tune-book for the next tune, seemed to feel humbled, bitterly ashamed, as it were caught in the act of sin. There was a solemn and terrible pause.

Then the revivalist began:

'Behold us, O dread God, suppliants for Thy mercy—'

His voice was rich and full, but at the same time sharp and decisive. The burning eyes were shut tight, and Anna, who had a profile view of his face, saw that every muscle of it was drawn tense. The man possessed an extraordinary histrionic gift, and he used it with imagination. He had two audiences, God and the congregation. God was not more distant from him than the congregation, or less real to him, or less a heart to be influenced. Declamatory and full of effects carefully calculated—a work of art, in fact—his appeal showed no error of discretion in its approach to the Eternal. There was no minimising of committed sin, nor yet an insincere and grovelling self-accusation. A tyrant could not have taken offence at its tone, which seemed to pacify God while rendering the human audience still more contrite. The conclusion of the catalogue of wickedness and swift confident turn to Christ's Cross was marvellously impressive. The congregation burst out into sighs, groans, blessings, and Amens; and the pillars of distant rural conventicles who had travelled from the confines of the circuit to its centre in order to partake of this spiritual excitation began to feel that they would not be disappointed.

'Let the Holy Ghost descend upon us now,' the revivalist pleaded with restrained passion; and then, opening his eyes and looking at the clock in front of the gallery, he repeated, 'Now, now, at twenty-one minutes past seven.' Then his eyes, without shifting, seemed to ignore the clock, to gaze through it into some unworldly dimension, and he murmured in a soft dramatic whisper: 'I see the Divine Dove!——'

The doors, closed during prayer, were opened, and more people entered. A youth came into Anna's pew.

The superintendent minister gave out another hymn, and when this was finished the revivalist, who had been resting in a chair, came forward again. 'Friends and fellow-sinners,' he said, 'a lot of you, fools that you are, have come here to-night to hear me play my cornet. Well, you have heard me. I have played the cornet, and I will play it again. I would play it on my head if by so doing I could bring sinners to Christ. I have been called a mountebank. I am one. I glory in it. I am God's mountebank, doing God's precious business in my own way. But God's precious business cannot be carried on, even by a mountebank, without money, and there will be a collection towards the expenses of the Revival. During the collection we will sing "Rock of Ages," and you shall hear my cornet again. If you feel willing to give us your sixpences, give; but if you resent a collection,' here he adopted a tone of ferocious sarcasm, 'keep your miserable sixpences and get sixpenny-worth of miserable enjoyment out of them elsewhere.'

As the meeting proceeded, submitting itself more and more to the imperious hypnotism of the revivalist, Anna gradually became oppressed by a vague sensation which was partly sorrow and partly an inexplicable dull anger—anger at her own penitence. She felt as if everything was wrong and could never by any possibility be righted. After two exhortations, from the minister and the revivalist, and another hymn, the revivalist once more prayed, and as he did so Anna looked stealthily about in a sick, preoccupied way. The youth at her side stared glumly in front of him. In the orchestra Henry Mynors was whispering to the organist. Down in the body of the chapel the atmosphere was electric, perilous, overcharged with spiritual emotion. She was glad she was not down there. The voice of the revivalist ceased, but he kept the attitude of supplication. Sobs were heard in various quarters, and here and there an elder of the chapel could be seen talking quietly to some convicted sinner. The revivalist began softly to sing 'Jesu, lover of my soul,' and most of the congregation, standing up, joined him; but the sinners stricken of the Spirit remained abjectly bent, tortured by conscience, pulled this way by Christ and that by Satan. A few rose and went to the Communion rails, there to kneel in the sight of all. Mr. Banks descended from the pulpit and opening the wicket which led to the Communion table spoke to these over the rails, reassuringly, as a nurse to a child. Other sinners, desirous of fuller and more intimate guidance, passed down the aisles and so into the preacher's vestry at the eastern end of the chapel, and were followed thither by class-leaders and other proved servants of God: among these last were Titus Price and Mr. Sutton.

'The blood of Christ atones,' said the revivalist solemnly at the end of the hymn. 'The spirit of Christ is working among us. Let us engage in private prayer. Let us drive the devil out of this chapel.'

More sighs and groans followed. Then someone cried out in sharp, shrill tones, 'Praise Him;' and another cried, 'Praise Him;' and an old woman's quavering voice sang the words, 'I know that my Redeemer liveth.' Anna was in despair at her own predicament, and the sense of sin was not more strong than the sense of being confused and publicly shamed. A man opened the pew-door, and sitting down by the youth's side began to talk with him. It was Henry Mynors. Anna looked steadily away, at the wall, fearful lest he should address her too. Presently the youth got up with a frenzied gesture and walked out of the gallery, followed by Mynors. In a moment she saw the youth stepping awkwardly along the aisle beneath, towards the inquiry room, his head forward, and the lower lip hanging as though he were sulky.

Anna was now in the profoundest misery. The weight of her sins, of her ingratitude to God, lay on her like a physical and intolerable load, and she lost all feeling of shame, as a sea-sick voyager loses shame after an hour of nausea. She knew then that she could no longer go on living as aforetime. She shuddered at the thought of her tremendous responsibility to Agnes—Agnes who took her for perfection. She recollected all her sins individually—lies, sloth, envy, vanity, even theft in her infancy. She heaped up all the wickedness of a lifetime, hysterically augmented it, and found a horrid pleasure in the exaggeration. Her virtuous acts shrank into nothingness.

A man, and then another, emerged from the vestry door with beaming, happy face. These were saved; they had yielded to Christ's persuasive invitation. Anna tried to imagine herself converted, or in the process of being converted. She could not. She could only sit moveless, dull, and abject. She did not stir, even when the congregation rose for another hymn. In what did conversion consist? Was it to say the words, 'I believe'? She repeated to herself softly, 'I believe; I believe.' But nothing happened. Of course she believed. She had never doubted, or dreamed of doubting, that Jesus died on the Cross to save her soul—*her* soul—from eternal damnation. She was probably unaware that any person in Christendom had doubted that fact so fundamental to her. What, then, was lacking? What was belief? What was faith?

A venerable class-leader came from the vestry, and, slowly climbing the pulpit stairs, whispered in the ear of the revivalist. The latter faced the congregation with a cry of joy. 'Lord,' he exclaimed, 'we bless Thee that seventeen souls have found Thee! Lord, let the full crop be gathered, for the fields are white unto harvest.' There was an exuberant chorus of praise to God.

The door of the pew was opened gently, and Anna started to see Mrs. Sutton at her side. She at once guessed that Mynors had sent to her this angel of consolation.

'Are you near the light, dear Anna?' Mrs. Sutton began.

Anna searched for an answer. She now sat huddled up in the corner of the pew, her face partially turned towards Mrs. Sutton, who looked mildly into her eyes. 'I don't know,' Anna stammered, feeling like a naughty school-girl. A doubt whether the whole affair was not after all absurd flashed through her, and was gone.

'But it is quite simple,' said Mrs. Sutton. 'I cannot tell you anything that you do not know. Cast out pride. Cast out pride—that is it. Nothing but earthly pride prevents you from realising the saving power of Christ. You are afraid, Anna, afraid to be humble. Be brave. It is so simple, so easy. If one will but submit.'

Anna said nothing, had nothing to say, was conscious of nothing save excessive discomfort.

'Where do you feel your difficulty to be?' asked Mrs. Sutton.

'I don't know,' she answered wearily.

'The happiness that awaits you is unspeakable. I have followed Christ for nearly fifty years, and my happiness increases daily. Sometimes I do not know how to contain it all. It surges above all the trials and disappointments of this world. Oh, Anna, if you will but believe!'

The ageing woman's thin, distinguished face, crowned with abundant grey hair, glistened with love and compassion, and as Anna's eyes rested upon it Anna felt that here was something tangible, something to lay hold on.

'I think I do believe,' she said weakly.

'You "think"? Are you sure? Are you not deceiving yourself? Belief is not with the lips: it is with the heart.'

There was a pause. Mr. Banks could be heard praying.

'I will go home,' Anna whispered at length, 'and think it out for myself.'

'Do, my dear girl, and God will help you.'

Mrs. Sutton bent and kissed Anna affectionately, and then hurried away to offer her ministrations elsewhere. As Anna left the chapel, she encountered the chapel-keeper pacing regularly to and fro across the length of the broad steps. In the porch was a notice that cabinet photographs of the revivalist could be purchased on application, at one shilling each.

CHAPTER VI

WILLIE

Anna closed the bedroom door softly; through the open window came the tones of Cauldon Church clock, famous for their sonority, and richness, announcing eleven. Agnes lay asleep under the blue-and-white counterpane, on the side of the bed next the wall, the bed-clothes pushed down and disclosing the upper half of her night-gowned figure. She slept in absolute repose, with flushed cheek and every muscle lax, her hair by some chance drawn in a perfect straight line diagonally across the pillow. Anna glanced at her sister, the image of physical innocence and childish security, and then, depositing the candle, went to the window and looked out.

The bedroom was over the kitchen and faced south. The moon was hidden by clouds, but clear stretches of sky showed thick-studded clusters of stars brightly winking. To the far right across the fields the silhouette of Hillport Church could just be discerned on the ridge. In front, several miles away, the blast-furnaces of Cauldon Bar Ironworks shot up vast wreaths of yellow flame with canopies of tinted smoke. Still more distant were a thousand other lights crowning chimney and kiln, and nearer, on the waste lands west of Bleakridge, long fields of burning ironstone glowed with all the strange colours of decadence. The entire landscape was illuminated and transformed by these unique pyrotechnics of labour atoning for its grime, and dull, weird sounds, as of the breathings and sighings of gigantic nocturnal creatures, filled the enchanted air, It was a romantic scene, a romantic summer night, balmy, delicate, and wrapped in meditation. But Anna saw nothing there save the repulsive evidences of manufacture, had never seen anything else.

She was still horribly, acutely miserable, exhausted by the fruitless search for some solution of the enigma of sin—her sin in particular—and of redemption. She had cogitated in a vain circle until she was no longer capable of reasoned ideas. She gazed at the stars and into the illimitable spaces beyond them, and thought of life and its inconceivable littleness, as millions had done before in the presence of that same firmament. Then, after a time, her brain resumed its nightmare-like task. She began to probe herself anew. Would it have availed if she had walked publicly to the penitential form at the Communion rail, and, ranging herself with the working men and women, proved by that overt deed the sincerity of her contrition? She wished ardently that she had done so, yet knew well that such an act would always be impossible for her, even though the evasion of it meant eternal torture. Undoubtedly, as Mrs. Sutton had implied, she was proud, stiff-necked, obstinate in iniquity.

Agnes stirred slightly in her sleep, and Anna, aroused, dropped the blind, turned towards the room and began to undress, slowly, with reflective pauses. Her melancholy became grim, sardonic; if she was doomed to destruction, so let it be. Suddenly, half-glad, she knelt down and prayed, prayed that pride might be cast out, burying her face in the coverlet and caging the passionate effusion in a whisper lest Agnes should be disturbed. Having prayed, she still knelt quiescent; her eyes were dry and burning. The last car thundered up the road, shaking the house, and she rose, finished undressing, blew out the candle, and slipped into bed by Agnes's side.

She could not sleep, did not attempt to sleep, but abandoned herself meekly to despair. Her thoughts covered again the interminable round, and again, and yet again. In the twilight of the brief summer night her accustomed eyes could distinguish every object in the room, all the bits of furniture which had been bought from Hanbridge and with which she had been familiar since her memory began: everything appeared mean, despicable, cheerless; there was nothing to inspire. She dreamed impossibly of a high spirituality which should metamorphose all, change her life, lend glamour to the most pitiful surroundings, ennoble the most ignominious burdens—a spirituality never to be hers.

At any rate she would tell her father in the morning that she was convicted of sin, and, however hopelessly, seeking salvation; she would tell both her father and Agnes at breakfast. The task would be difficult, but she swore to do it. She resolved, she endeavoured to sleep, and did sleep uneasily for a short period. When she woke the great business of the dawn had begun. She left the bed, and drawing up the blind looked forth. The furnace fires were paling; a few milky clouds sailed in the vast pallid blue. It was cool just then, and she shivered. She went to the glass, and examined her face carefully, but it gave no signs whatever of the inward warfare. She saw her plain and mended night-gown. Suppose she were married to Mynors! Suppose he lay asleep in the bed where Agnes lay asleep! Involuntarily she glanced at Agnes to certify that the child and none else was indeed there, and got into bed hurriedly and hid herself because she was ashamed to have had such a fancy. But she continued to think of Mynors. She envied him for his cheerfulness, his joy, his goodness, his dignity, his tact, his sex. She envied every man. Even in the sphere of religion, men were not fettered like women. No man, she thought, would acquiesce in the futility to which she was already half resigned; a man would either wring salvation from the heavenly powers or race gloriously to hell. Mynors—Mynors was a god!

She recollected her resolution to speak to her father and Agnes at breakfast, and shudderingly confirmed it, but less stoutly than before. Then an announcement made by Mr. Banks in chapel on the previous evening presented itself, as though she was listening to it for the first time. It was the announcement of a prayer-meeting for workers in the Revival, to be held that (Saturday) morning at seven o'clock. She instantly decided to go to the meeting, and the decision seemed to give her new hope. Perhaps there she might find peace. On that faint expectancy she fell asleep again and did not wake till half-past six, after her usual hour. She heard noises in the yard; it was her father going towards the garden with a wheelbarrow. She dressed quickly, and when she had pinned on her hat she woke Agnes.

'Going out, Sis?' the child asked sleepily, seeing her attire.

'Yes, dear. I am going to the seven o'clock prayer-meeting. And you must get breakfast. You can—can't you?' The child assented, glad of the chance.

'But what are you going to the prayer-meeting for?'

Anna hesitated. Why not confess? No. 'I must go,' she said quietly at length. 'I shall be back before eight.'

'Does father know?' Agnes enquired apprehensively.

'No, dear.'

Anna shut the door quickly, went softly downstairs and along the passage, and crept into the street like a thief. Men and women and boys and girls were on their way to work, with hurried clattering steps, some munching thick pieces of bread as they went, all self-centred, apparently morose and not quite awake. The dust lay thick in the arid gutters, and in drifts across the pavement; as the night-wind had blown it. Vehicular traffic had not begun, and blinds were still drawn; and though the footpaths were busy the street had a deserted and forlorn aspect. Anna walked hastily down the road, avoiding the glances of such as looked at her, but peering furtively at the faces of those who ignored her. All seemed callous—hoggishly careless of the everlasting verities. At first it appeared strange to her that the potent revival in the Wesleyan chapel had produced no effect on these preoccupied people. Bursley, then, continued its dull and even course. She wondered whether any of them guessed that she was going to the prayer-meeting and secretly sneered at her therefore.

When she had climbed Duck Bank she found to her surprise that the doors of the chapel were fast closed, though it was ten minutes past seven. Was there to be no prayer-meeting? A momentary sensation of relief flashed through her, and then she saw that the gate of the school-yard was open. She should have known that early morning prayers were never offered up in the chapel, but in the lecture-hall. She crossed the quadrangle with beating heart, feeling now that she had embarked on a frightful enterprise. The door of the lecture-hall was ajar; she pushed it and went in. At the other end of the hall a meagre handful of worshippers were collected, and on the raised platform stood Mr. Banks, vapid, perfunctory and fatigued. He gave out a verse, and pitched the tune—too high, but the singers with a heroic effect accomplished the verse without breaking down. The singing was thin and feeble, and the eagerness of one or two voices seemed strained, as though with a determination to make the best of things. Mynors was not present, and Anna did not know whether to be sorry or glad at this. She recognised that save herself all present were old believers, tried warriors of the Lord. There was only one other woman, Miss Sarah Vodrey, an aged spinster who kept house for Titus Price and his son, and found her sole diversion in the variety of her religious experiences. Before the hymn was finished a young man joined the assembly; it was the youth who had sat near Anna on the previous night, an ecstatic and naïve bliss shone from his face. In his prayer the minister drew the attention of the Deity to the fact that although a score or more of souls had been ingathered at the first service, the Methodists of Bursley were by no means satisfied. They wanted more; they wanted the whole of Bursley; and they would be content with no less. He begged that their earnest work might not be shamed before the world by a partial success. In conclusion he sought the blessing of God on the revivalist and asked that this tireless enthusiast might be led to husband his strength: at which there was a fervent Amen.

Several men prayed, and a pause ensued, all still kneeling.

Then the minister said in a tone of oily politeness:

'Will a sister pray?'

Another pause followed.

'Sister Tellwright?'

Anna would have welcomed death and damnation. She clasped her hands tightly, and longed for the endless moment to pass. At last Sarah Vodrey gave a preliminary cough. Miss Vodrey was always happy to pray aloud, and her invocations usually began with the same phrase: 'Lord, we thank Thee that this day finds us with our bodies out of the grave and our souls out of hell.'

Afterwards the minister gave out another hymn, and as soon as the singing commenced Anna slipped away. Once in the yard, she breathed a sigh of relief. Peace at the prayer-meeting? It was like coming out of prison. Peace was farther off than ever. Nay, she had actually forgotten her soul in the sensations of shame and discomfort. She had contrived only to make herself ridiculous, and perhaps the pious at their breakfast-tables would discuss her and her father, and their money, and the queer life they led.

If Mynors had but been present!

She walked out into the street. It was twenty minutes to eight by the town-hall clock. The last workmen's car of the morning was just leaving Bursley: it was packed inside and outside, and the conductor hung insecurely on the step. At the gates of the manufactory opposite the chapel, a man in a white smock stood placidly smoking a pipe. A prayer-meeting was a little thing, a trifle in the immense and regular activity of the town: this thought necessarily occurred to Anna. She hurried homewards, wondering what her father would say about that morning's unusual excursion. A couple of hundred yards distant from home she saw, to her astonishment, Agnes emerging from the front-door of the house. The child ran rapidly down the street, not observing Anna till they were close upon each other.

'Oh, Anna! You forgot to buy the bacon yesterday. There isn't a *scrap*, and father's fearfully angry. He gave me sixpence, and I'm going down to Leal's to get some as quick as ever I can.'

It was a thunderbolt to Anna, this seemingly petty misadventure. As she entered the house she felt a tear on her cheek. She was ashamed to weep, but she wept. This, after the fiasco of the prayer-meeting, was a climax of woe; it overtopped and extinguished all the rest; her soul was nothing to her now. She quickly took off her hat and ran to the kitchen. Agnes had put the breakfast-things on the tray ready for setting; the bread was cut, the coffee portioned into the jug; the fire burned bright, and the kettle sang. Anna took the cloth from the drawer in the oak dresser, and went to the parlour to lay the table. Mr. Tellwright was at the end of the garden, pointing the wall, his back to the house. The table set, Anna observed that the room was only partly dusted: there was a duster on the mantelpiece; she seized it to finish, and at that moment the kitchen clock struck eight. Simultaneously Mr. Tellwright dropped his trowel, and came towards the house. She doggedly dusted one chair, and then, turning coward, flew away upstairs; the kitchen was barred to her since her father would enter by the kitchen door.

She had forgotten to buy bacon, and breakfast would be late: it was a calamity unique in, her experience! She stood at the door of her bedroom, and waited, vehemently, for Agnes's return. At last the child raced breathlessly in; Anna flew to meet her. With incredible speed the bacon was whipped out of its wrapper, and Anna picked up the knife. At the first stroke she cut herself, and Agnes was obliged to bind the finger with rag. The clock struck the half-hour like a knell. It was twenty minutes to nine, forty minutes behind time, when the two girls hurried into the parlour, Anna bearing the bacon and hot plates, Agnes the bread and coffee. Mr. Tellwright sat upright and ferocious in his chair, the image of offence and wrath. Instead of reading his letters he had fed full of this ineffable grievance. The meal began in a desolating silence. The male creature's terrible displeasure permeated the whole room like an ether, invisible but carrying vibrations to the heart. Then, when he had eaten one piece of bacon, and cut his envelopes, the miser began to empty himself of some of his anger in stormy tones that might have uprooted trees. Anna ought to feel thoroughly ashamed. He could not imagine what she had been thinking of. Why didn't she tell him she was going to the prayer-meeting? Why did she go to the prayer-meeting, disarranging the whole household? How came she to forget the bacon? It was gross carelessness. A pretty example to her little sister! The fact was that *since her birthday* she had gotten above hersen. She was careless and extravagant. Look how thick the bacon was cut.

He should not stand it much longer. And her finger all red, and the blood dropping on the cloth: a nice sight at a meal! Go and tie it up again.

Without a word she left the room to obey. Of course she had no defence. Agnes, her tears falling, pecked her food timidly like a bird, not daring to stir from her chair, even to assist at the finger.

'What did Mr. Mynors say?' Tellwright inquired fiercely when Anna had come back into the room.

'Mr. Mynors?' she murmured, at a loss, but vaguely apprehending further trouble.

'Did ye see him?'

'Yes, father.'

'Did ye give him my message?'

'I forgot it.' God in heaven! She had forgotten the message!

With a devastating grunt Mr. Tellwright walked speechless out of the room. The girls cleared the table, exchanging sympathy with a single mute glance. Anna's one satisfaction was that, even if she had remembered the message, she could not possibly have delivered it.

Ephraim Tellwright stayed in the front parlour till half-past ten o'clock, unseen but felt, like an angry god behind a cloud. The consciousness that he was there, unappeased and dangerous, remained uppermost in the minds of the two girls during the morning. At half-past ten he opened the door.

'Agnes!' he commanded, and Agnes ran to him from the kitchen with the speed of propitiation.

'Yes, father.'

'Take this note down to Price's, and don't wait for an answer.'

'Yes, father.'

She was back in twenty minutes. Anna was sweeping the lobby.

'If Mr. Mynors calls while I'm out, you mun tell him to wait,' Mr. Tellwright said to Agnes, pointedly ignoring Anna's presence. Then, having brushed his greenish hat on his sleeve he went off towards town to buy meat and vegetables. He always did Saturday's marketing himself. At the butcher's and in the St. Luke's covered market he was a familiar and redoubtable figure. Among the salespeople who stood the market was a wrinkled, hardy old potato-woman from the other side of Moorthorne: every Saturday the miser bested her in their higgling-match, and nearly every Saturday she scornfully threw at him the same joke: 'Get thee along to th' post-office, Master Terrick:[1] happen they'll give thee sixpenn'orth o' stamps for fivepence ha'penny.' He seldom failed to laugh heartily at this.

At dinner the girls could perceive that the shadow of his displeasure had slightly lifted, though he kept a frowning silence. Expert in all the symptoms of his moods, they knew that in a few hours he would begin to talk again, at first in monosyllables, and then in short detached sentences. An intimation of relief diffused itself through the house like a hint of spring in February.

These domestic upheavals followed always the same course, and Anna had learnt to suffer the later stages of them with calmness and even with impassivity. Henry Mynors had not called. She supposed that her father had expected him to call for the answer which she had forgotten to give him, and she had a hope that he would come in the afternoon: once again she had the idea that something definite and satisfactory might result if she could only see him—that she might, as it were, gather inspiration from the mere sight of his face. After dinner, while the girls were washing the dinner things in the scullery, Agnes's quick ear caught the sound of voices in the parlour. They listened. Mynors had come. Mr. Tellwright must have seen him from the front window and opened the door to him before he could ring.

'It's him,' said Agnes, excited.

'Who?' Anna asked, self-consciously.

'Mr. Mynors, of course,' said the child sharply, making it quite plain that this affectation could not impose on her for a single instant.

'Anna!' It was Mr. Tellwright's summons, through the parlour window. She dried her hands, doffed her apron, and went to the parlour, animated by a thousand fears and expectations. Why was she to be included in the colloquy?

Mynors rose at her entrance and greeted her with conspicuous deference, a deference which made her feel ashamed.

'Hum!' the old man growled, but he was obviously content. 'I gave Anna a message for ye yesterday, Mr. Mynors, but her forgot to deliver it, wench-like. Ye might ha' been saved th' trouble o' calling. Now as ye're here, I've summat for tell ye. It 'll be Anna's money as 'll go into that concern o' yours. I've none by me; in fact, I'm a'most fast for brass, but her 'll have as near two thousand as makes no matter in a month's time, and her says her 'll go in wi' you on th' strength o' my recommendation.'

This speech was evidently a perfect surprise for Henry Mynors. For a moment he seemed to be at a loss; then his face gave candid expression to a feeling of intense pleasure.

'You know all about this business then, Miss Tellwright?'

She blushed. 'Father has told me something about it.'

'And are you willing to be my partner?'

'Nay, I did na' say that,' Tellwright interrupted. 'It 'll be Anna's money, but i' my name.'

'I see,' said Mynors gravely. 'But if it is Miss Anna's money, why should not she be the partner?' He offered one of his courtly diplomatic smiles.

'Oh—but——' Anna began in deprecation.

Tellwright laughed. 'Ay!' he said, 'why not? It 'll be experience for th' lass.'

'Just so,' said Mynors.

Anna stood silent, like a child who is being talked about. There was a pause.

'Would you care for that arrangement, Miss Tellwright?'

'Oh, yes,' she said.

'I shall try to justify your confidence. I needn't say that I think you and your father will have no reason to be disappointed. Two thousand pounds is of course only a trifle to you, but it is a great deal to me, and—and——' He hesitated. Anna did not surmise that he was too much moved by the sight of her, and the situation, to continue, but this was the fact.

'There's nobbut one point, Mr. Mynors,' Tellwright said bluntly, 'and that's the interest on th' capital, as must be deducted before reckoning profits. Us must have six per cent.'

'But I thought we had settled it at five,' said Mynors with sudden firmness.

'We 'n settled as you shall have five on your fifteen hundred,' the miser replied with imperturbable audacity, 'but us mun have our six.'

'I certainly thought we had thrashed that out fully, and agreed that the interest should be the same on each side.' Mynors was alert and defensive.

'Nay, young man. Us mun have our six. We're takkin' a risk.'

Mynors pressed his lips together. He was taken at a disadvantage. Mr. Tellwright, with unscrupulous cleverness, had utilized the effect on Mynors of his daughter's presence to regain a position from which the younger man had definitely ousted him a few days before. Mynors was annoyed, but he gave no sign of his annoyance.

'Very well,' he said at length, with a private smile at Anna to indicate that it was out of regard for her that he yielded.

Mr. Tellwright made no pretence of concealing his satisfaction. He, too, smiled at Anna, sardonically: the last vestige of the morning's irritation vanished in a glow of triumph.

'I'm afraid I must go,' said Mynors, looking at his watch. 'There is a service at chapel at three. Our Revivalist came down with Mrs. Sutton to look over the works this morning, and I told him I should be at the service. So I must. You coming, Mr. Tellwright?'

'Nay, my lad. I'm owd enough to leave it to young uns.'

Anna forced her courage to the verge of rashness, moved by a swift impulse.

'Will you wait one minute?' she said to Mynors. 'I am going to the service. If I'm late back, father, Agnes will see to the tea. Don't wait for me.' She looked him straight in the face. It was one of the bravest acts of her life. After the episode of breakfast, to suggest a procedure which might entail any risk upon another meal was absolutely heroic. Tellwright glanced away from his daughter, and at Mynors. Anna hurried upstairs.

'Who's thy lawyer, Mr. Mynors?' Tellwright asked.

'Dane,' said Mynors.

'That 'll be convenient. Dane does my bit o' business, too. I'll see him, and make a bargain wi' him for th' partnership deed. He always works by contract for me. I've no patience wi' six-and-eight-pences.'

Mynors assented.

'You must come down some afternoon and look over the works,' he said to Anna as they were walking down Trafalgar Road towards chapel.

'I should like to,' Anna replied. 'I've never been over a works in my life.'

'No? You are going to be a partner in the best works of its size in Bursley,' Mynors said enthusiastically.

'I'm glad of that,' she smiled, 'for I do believe I own the worst.'

'What—Price's do you mean?'

She nodded.

'Ah!' he exclaimed, and seemed to be thinking. 'I wasn't sure whether that belonged to you or your father. I'm afraid it isn't quite the best of properties. But perhaps I'd better say nothing about that. We had a grand meeting last night. Our little cornet-player quite lived up to his reputation, don't you think?'

'Quite,' she said faintly.

'You enjoyed the meeting?'

'No,' she blurted out, dismayed but resolute to be honest.

There was a silence.

'But you were at the early prayer-meeting this morning, I hear.'

She said nothing while they took a dozen paces, and then murmured, 'Yes.'

Their eyes met for a second, hers full of trouble.

'Perhaps,' he said at length, 'perhaps—excuse me saying this—but you may be expecting too much——'

'Well?' she encouraged him, prepared now to finish what had been begun.

'I mean,' he said, earnestly, 'that I—we—cannot promise you any sudden change of feeling, any sudden relief and certainty, such as some people experience. At least, I never had it. What is called conversion can happen in various ways. It is a question of living, of constant endeavour, with the example of Christ always before us. It need not always be a sudden wrench, you know, from the world. Perhaps you have been expecting too much,' he repeated, as though offering balm with that phrase.

She thanked him sincerely, but not with her lips, only with the heart. He had revealed to her an avenue of release from a situation which had seemed on all sides fatally closed. She sprang eagerly towards it. She realised afresh how frightful was the dilemma from which there was now a hope of escape, and she was grateful accordingly. Before, she had not dared steadily to face its terrors. She wondered that even her father's displeasure or the project of the partnership had been able to divert her from the plight of her soul. Putting these mundane things firmly behind her, she concentrated the activities of her brain on that idea of Christ-like living, day by day, hour by hour, of a gradual aspiration towards Christ and thereby an ultimate arrival at the state of being saved. This she thought she might accomplish; this gave opportunity of immediate effort, dispensing with the necessity of an impossible violent spiritual metamorphosis. They did not speak again until they had reached the gates of the chapel, when Mynors, who had to enter the choir from the back, bade her a quiet adieu. Anna enjoyed the service, which passed smoothly and uneventfully. At a Revival, night is the time of ecstasy and fervour and salvation; in the afternoon one must be content with preparatory praise and prayer.

That evening, while father and daughters sat in the parlour after supper, there was a ring at the door. Agnes ran to open, and found Willie Price. It had begun to rain, and the visitor, his jacket-collar turned up, was wet and draggled. Agnes left him on the mat and ran back to the parlour.

'Young Mr. Price wants to see you, father.'

Tellwright motioned to her to shut the door.

'You'd best see him, Anna,' he said. 'It's none my business.'

'But what has he come about, father?'

'That note as I sent down this morning. I told owd Titus as he mun pay us twenty pun' on Monday morning certain, or us should distrain. Them as can pay ten pun, especially in bank notes, can pay twenty pun, and thirty.'

'And suppose he says he can't?'

'Tell him he must. I 've figured it out and changed my mind about that works. Owd Titus isna' done for yet, though he's getting on that road. Us can screw another fifty out o' him, that 'll only leave six months rent owing; then us can turn him out. He'll go bankrupt; us can claim for our rent afore th' other creditors, and us 'll have a hundred or a hundred and twenty in hand towards doing the owd place up a bit for a new tenant.'

'Make him bankrupt, father?' Anna exclaimed. It was the only part of the ingenious scheme which she had understood.

'Ay!' he said laconically.

'But——' (Would Christ have driven Titus Price into the bankruptcy court?)

'If he pays, well and good.'

'Hadn't you better see Mr. William, father?'

'Whose property is it, mine or thine?' Tellwright growled. His good humour was still precarious, insecurely re-established, and Anna obediently left the room. After all, she said to herself, a debt is a debt, and honest people pay what they owe.

It was in an uncomplaisant tone that Anna invited Willie Price to the front parlour: nervousness always made her seem harsh and moreover she had not the trick of hiding firmness under suavity.

'Will you come this way, Mr. Price?'

'Yes,' he said with ingratiating, eager compliance. Dusk was falling, and the room in shadow. She forgot to ask him to take a chair, so they both stood up during the interview.

'A grand meeting we had last night,' he began, twisting his hat. 'I saw you there, Miss Tellwright.'

'Yes.'

'Yes. There was a splendid muster of teachers. I wanted to be at the prayer-meeting this morning, but couldn't get away. Did you happen to go, Miss Tellwright?'

She saw that he knew that she had been present, and gave him another curt monosyllable. She would have liked to be kind to him, to reassure him, to make him happy and comfortable, so ludicrous and touching were his efforts after a social urbanity which should appease; but, just as much as he, she was unskilled in the subtle arts of converse.

'Yes,' he continued, 'and I was anxious to be at to-night's meeting, but the dad asked me to come up here. He said I'd better.' That term, 'the dad,' uttered in William's slow, drawling voice, seemed to show Titus Price in a new light to Anna, as a human creature loved, not as a mere gross physical organism: the effect was quite surprising. William went on: 'Can I see your father, Miss Tellwright?'

'Is it about the rent?'

'Yes,' he said.

'Well, if you will tell me——'

'Oh! I beg pardon,' he said quickly. 'Of course I know it's your property, but I thought Mr. Tellwright always saw after it for you. It was he that wrote that letter this morning, wasn't it?'

'Yes,' Anna replied. 'She did not explain the situation.

'You insist on another twenty pounds on Monday?'

'Yes,' she said.

'We paid ten last Monday.'

'But there is still over a hundred owing.'

'I know, but—oh, Miss Tellwright, you mustn't be hard on us. Trade's bad.'

'It says in the "Signal" that trade is improving,' she interrupted sharply.

'Does it?' he said. 'But look at prices; they're cut till there's no profit left. I assure you, Miss Tellwright, my father and me are having a hard struggle. Everything's against us, and the works in particular, as you know.'

His tone was so earnest, so pathetic, that tears of compassion almost rose to her eyes as she looked at those simple naïve blue eyes of his. His lanky figure and clumsily-fitting clothes, his feeble placatory smile, the twitching movements of his long red hands, all contributed to the effect of his defencelessness. She thought of the test: 'Blessed are the meek,' and saw in a flash the deep truth of it. Here were she and her father, rich, powerful, autocratic; and there were Willie Price and his father, commercial hares hunted by hounds of creditors, hares that turned in plaintive appeal to those greedy jaws for mercy. And yet, she, a hound, envied at that moment the hares. Blessed are the meek, blessed are the failures, blessed are the stupid, for they, unknown to themselves, have a grace which is denied to the haughty, the successful, and the wise. The very repulsiveness of old Titus, his underhand methods, his insincerities, only served to increase her sympathy for the pair. How could Titus help being himself any more than Henry Mynors could help being himself? And that idea led her to think of the prospective partnership, destined by every favourable sign to brilliant success, and to contrast it with the ignoble and forlorn undertaking in Edward Street.

She tried to discover some method of soothing the young man's fears, of being considerate to him without injuring her father's scheme.

'If you will pay what you owe,' she said, 'we will spend it all, every penny, on improving the works.'

'Miss Tellwright,' he answered with fatal emphasis, 'we cannot pay.'

Ah! She wished to follow Christ day by day, hour by hour—constantly to endeavour after saintliness. What was she to do now? Left to herself, she might have said in a burst of impulsive generosity, 'I forgive you all arrears. Start afresh.' But her father had to be reckoned with.......

'How much do you think you can pay on Monday?' she asked coldly.

At that moment her father entered the room. His first act was to light the gas. Willie Price's eyes blinked at the glare, as though he were trembling before the anticipated decree of this implacable old man. Anna's heart beat with sympathetic apprehension. Tellwright shook hands grimly with the youth, who re-stated hurriedly what he had said to Anna.

'It's o' this'n,' the old man began with finality, and stopped. Anna caught a glance from him dismissing her. She went out in silence. On the Monday Titus Price paid another twenty pounds.

[1] *Terrick*: a corruption of Tellwright.

CHAPTER VII

THE SEWING MEETING

On an afternoon ten days later, Mr. Sutton's coachman, Barrett by name, arrived at Ephraim Tellwright's back-door with a note. The Tellwrights were having tea. The note could be seen in his enormous hand, and Agnes went out.

'An answer, if you please, Miss,' he said to her, touching his hat, and giving a pull to the leathern belt which, surrounding his waist, alone seemed to hold his frame together. Agnes, much impressed, took the note. She had never before seen that resplendent automaton apart from the equipage which he directed. Always afterwards, Barrett formally saluted her in the streets, affording her thus, every time, a thrilling moment of delicious joy.

'A letter, and there's an answer, and he's waiting,' she cried, running into the parlour.

'Less row!' said her father. 'Here, give it me.'

'It's for Miss Tellwright—that's Anna, isn't it? Oh! Scent!' She put the grey envelope to her nose like a flower.

Anna, secretly as excited as her sister, opened the note and read:—'Lansdowne House, Wednesday. Dear Miss Tellwright,—Mother gives tea to the Sunday-school Sewing Meeting here *to-morrow*. Will you give us the pleasure of your company? I do not think you have been to any of the S.S.S. meetings yet, but we should all be glad to see you and have your assistance. Everyone is working very hard for the Autumn Bazaar, and mother has set her mind on the Sunday-school stall being the best. Do come, will you? Excuse this short notice. Yours sincerely, BEATRICE SUTTON. P.S.—We begin at 3.30.'

'They want me to go to their sewing meeting to-morrow,' she exclaimed timidly to her father, pushing the note towards him across the table. 'Must I go, father?'

'What dost ask me for? Please thysen. I've nowt do wi' it.'

'I don't want to go——'

'Oh! Sis, do go,' Agnes pleaded.

'Perhaps I'd better,' she agreed, but with the misgivings of diffidence. 'I haven't a rag to wear. I really must have a new dress, father, at once.'

'Hast forgotten as that there coachman's waiting?' he remarked curtly.

'Shall I run and tell him you'll go?' Agnes suggested. 'It 'll be splendid for you.'

'Don't be silly, dear. I must write.'

'Well, write then,' said the child energetically. 'I'll get you the ink and paper.' She flew about and hovered over Anna while the answer to the invitation was being written. Anna made her reply as short and simple as possible, and then tendered it for her father's inspection. 'Will that do?'

He pretended to be nonchalant, but in fact he was somewhat interested.

'Thou's forgotten to put th' date in,' was all his comment, and he threw the note back.

'I've put Wednesday.'

'That's not the date.'

'Does it matter? Beatrice Sutton only puts Wednesday.'

His response was to walk out of the room.

'Is he vexed?' Agnes asked anxiously. There had been a whole week of almost perfect amenity.

The next day at half-past three Anna, having put on her best clothes, was ready to start. She had seen almost nothing of social life, and the prospect of taking part in this entertainment of the Suttons filled her with trepidation. Should she arrive early, in which case she would have to talk more, or late, in which case there would be the ordeal of entering a crowded room? She could not decide. She went into her father's bedroom, whose window overlooked Trafalgar Road, and saw from behind a curtain that small groups of ladies were continually passing up the street to disappear into Alderman Sutton's house. Most of the women she recognised; others she knew but vaguely by sight. Then the stream ceased, and suddenly she heard the kitchen clock strike four. She ran downstairs—Agnes, swollen by importance, was carrying her father's tea into the parlour—and hastened out the back way. In another moment she was at the Suttons' front-door. A servant in black alpaca, with white wristbands, cap, streams, and embroidered apron (each article a *dernier cri* from Bostock's great shop at Hanbridge), asked her in a subdued and respectful tone to step within. Externally there had been no sign of the unusual, but once inside the house Anna found it a humming hive of activity. Women laden with stuffs and implements were crossing the picture-hung hall, their footsteps noiseless on the thick rugs which lay about in rich confusion. On either hand was an open door, and from each door came the sound of many eager voices. Beyond these doors a broad staircase rose majestically to unseen heights, closing the vista of the hall. As the servant was demanding Anna's name, Beatrice Sutton, radiant and gorgeous, came with a rush out of the room to the left, the dining-room, and, taking her by both hands, kissed her.

'My dear, we thought you were never coming. Everyone's here, except the men, of course. Come along upstairs and take your things off. I'm so glad you've kept your promise.'

'Did you think I should break it?' said Anna, as they ascended the easy gradient of the stairs.

'Oh, no, my dear. But you're such a shy little bird.'

The conception of herself as a shy little bird amused Anna. By a curious chain of ideas she came to wonder who could clean those stairs the better, she or this gay and flitting butterfly in a pale green tea-gown. Beatrice led the way to a large bedroom, crammed with furniture and knick-knacks. There were three mirrors in this spacious apartment—one in the wardrobe, a cheval-glass, and a third over the mantelpiece; the frame of the last was bordered with photographs.

'This is my room,' said Beatrice. 'Will you put your things on the bed?' The bed was already laden with hats, bonnets, jackets, and wraps.

'I hope your mother won't give me anything fancy to do,' Anna said. 'I'm no good at anything except plain sewing.'

'Oh, that's all right,' Beatrice answered carelessly. 'It's all plain sewing.' She drew a cardboard box from her pocket, and offered it to Anna. 'Here, have one.' They were chocolate creams.

'Thanks,' said Anna, taking one. 'Aren't they very expensive? I've never seen any like these before.'

'Oh! Just ordinary. Four shillings a pound. Papa buys them for me: I simply dote on them. I love to eat them in bed, if I can't sleep.' Beatrice made these statements with her mouth full. 'Don't you adore chocolates?' she added.

'I don't know,' Anna lamely replied. 'Yes, I like them.' She only adored her sister, and perhaps God; and this was the first time she had tasted chocolate.

'I couldn't live without them,' said Beatrice. 'Your hair is lovely. I never saw such a brown. What wash do you use?'

'Wash?' Anna repeated.

'Yes, don't you put anything on it?'

'No, never.'

'Well! Take care you don't lose it, that's all. Now, will you come and have just a peep at my studio—where I paint, you know? I'd like you to see it before we go down.'

They proceeded to a small room on the second floor, with a sloping ceiling and a dormer window.

'I'm obliged to have this room,' Beatrice explained, 'because it's the only one in the house with a north light, and of course you can't do without that. How do you like it?'

Anna said that she liked it very much.

The walls of the room were hung with various odd curtains of Eastern design. Attached somehow to these curtains some coloured plates, bits of pewter, and a few fans were hung high in apparently precarious suspense. Lower down on the walls were pictures and sketches, chiefly unframed, of flowers, fishes, loaves of bread, candlesticks, mugs, oranges and tea-trays. On an immense easel in the middle of the room was an unfinished portrait of a man.

'Who's that?' Anna asked, ignorant of those rules of caution which are observed by the practised frequenter of studios.

'Don't you know?' Beatrice exclaimed, shocked. 'That's papa; I'm doing his portrait; he sits in that chair there. The silly old master at the school won't let me draw from life yet—he keeps me to the antique—so I said to myself I would study the living model at home. I'm dreadfully in earnest about it, you know—I really am. Mother says I work far too long up here.'

Anna was unable to perceive that the picture bore any resemblance to Alderman Sutton, except in the matter of the aldermanic robe, which she could now trace beneath the portrait's neck. The studies on the walls pleased her much better. Their realism amazed her. One could make out not only that here for instance, was a fish—there was no doubt that it was a halibut; the solid roundness of the oranges and the glitter on the tea-trays seemed miraculously achieved. 'Have you actually done all these?' she asked, in genuine admiration. 'I think they're splendid.'

'Oh, yes, they're all mine; they're only still-life studies,' Beatrice said contemptuously of them, but she was nevertheless flattered.

'I see now that that is Mr. Sutton,' Anna said, pointing to the easel picture.

'Yes, it's pa right enough. But I'm sure I'm boring you. Let's go down now, or perhaps we shall catch it from mother.'

As Anna, in the wake of Beatrice, entered the drawing-room, a dozen or more women glanced at her with keen curiosity, and the even flow of conversation ceased for a moment, to be immediately resumed. In the centre of the room, with her back to the fire-place, Mrs. Sutton was seated at a square table, cutting out. Although the afternoon was warm she had a white woollen wrap over her shoulders; for the rest she was attired in plain black silk, with a large stuff apron containing a pocket for scissors and chalk. She jumped up with the activity of which Beatrice had inherited a part, and greeted Anna, kissing her heartily.

'How are you, my dear? So pleased you have come.' The time-worn phrases came from her thin, nervous lips full of sincere and kindly welcome. Her wrinkled face broke into a warm, life-giving smile. 'Beatrice, find Miss Anna a chair.' There were two chairs in the bay of the window, and one of them was occupied by Miss Dickinson, whom Anna slightly knew. The other, being empty, was assigned to the late-comer.

'Now you want something to do, I suppose,' said Beatrice.'

'Please.'

'Mother, let Miss Tellwright have something to get on with at once. She has a lot of time to make up.'

Mrs. Sutton, who had sat down again, smiled across at Anna. 'Let me see, now, what can we give her?'

'There's several of those boys' nightgowns ready tacked,' said Miss Dickinson, who was stitching at a boy's nightgown. 'Here's one half-finished,' and she picked up an inchoate garment from the floor. 'Perhaps Miss Tellwright wouldn't mind finishing it.'

'Yes, I will do my best at it,' said Anna.

The thoughtless girl had arrived at the sewing meeting without needles or thimble or scissors, but one lady or another supplied these deficiencies, and soon she was at work. She stitched her best and her hardest, with head bent, and all her wits concentrated on the task. Most of the others seemed to be doing likewise, though not to the detriment of conversation. Beatrice sank down on a stool near her mother, and, threading a needle with coloured silk, took up a long piece of elaborate embroidery.

The general subjects of talk were the Revival, now over, with a superb record of seventy saved souls, the school-treat shortly to occur, the summer holidays, the fashions, and the change of ministers which would take place in August. The talkers were the wives and daughters of tradesmen and small manufacturers, together with a few girls of a somewhat lower status, employed in shops: it was for the sake of these latter that the sewing meeting was always fixed for the weekly half-holiday. The splendour of Mrs. Sutton's drawing-room was a little dazzling to most of the guests, and Mrs. Sutton herself seemed scarcely of a piece with it. The fact was that the luxury of the abode was mainly due to Alderman Sutton's inability to refuse anything to his daughter, whose tastes lay in the direction of rich draperies, large or quaint chairs, occasional tables, dwarf screens, hand-painted mirrors, and an opulence of bric-à-brac. The hand of Beatrice might be perceived everywhere, even in the position of the piano, whose back, adorned with carelessly-flung silks and photographs, was turned away from the wall. The pictures on the walls had been acquired gradually by Mr. Sutton at auction sales: it was commonly held that he had an excellent taste in pictures, and that his daughter's aptitude for the arts came from him, and not from her mother. The gilt clock and side pieces on the mantelpiece were also peculiarly Mr. Sutton's, having been publicly presented to him by the directors of a local building society of which he had been chairman for many years.

Less intimidated by all this unexampled luxury than she was reassured by the atmosphere of combined and homely effort, the lowliness of several of her companions, and the kind, simple face of Mrs. Sutton, Anna quickly began to feel at ease. She paused in her work, and, glancing around her, happened to catch the eye of Miss Dickinson, who offered a remark about the weather. Miss Dickinson was head-assistant at a draper's in St. Luke's Square, and a pillar of the Sunday-school, which Sunday by Sunday and year by year had watched her develop from a rosy-cheeked girl into a confirmed spinster with sallow and warted face. Miss Dickinson supported her mother, and was a pattern to her sex. She was lovable, but had never been loved. She would have made an admirable wife and mother, but fate had decided that this material was to be wasted. Miss Dickinson found compensation for the rigour of destiny in gossip, as innocent as indiscreet. It was said that she had a tongue.

'I hear,' said Miss Dickinson, lowering her contralto voice to a confidential tone, 'that you are going into partnership with Mr. Mynors, Miss Tellwright.'

The suddenness of the attack took Anna by surprise. Her first defensive impulse was boldly to deny the statement, or at the least to say that it was premature. A fortnight ago, under similar circumstances, she would not have hesitated to do so. But for more than a week Anna had been 'leading a new life,' which chiefly meant a meticulous avoidance of the sins of speech. Never to deviate from the truth, never to utter an unkind or a thoughtless word, under whatever provocation: these were two of her self-imposed rules. 'Yes,' she answered Miss Dickinson, 'I am.'

'Rather a novelty, isn't it?' Miss Dickinson smiled amiably.

'I don't know,' said Anna. 'It's only a business arrangement; father arranged it. Really I have nothing to do with it, and I had no idea that people were talking about it.'

'Oh! Of course *I* should never breathe a syllable,' Miss Dickinson said with emphasis. 'I make a practice of never talking about other people's affairs. I always find that best, don't you? But I happened to hear it mentioned in the shop.'

'It's very funny how things get abroad, isn't it?' said Anna.

'Yes, indeed,' Miss Dickinson concurred. 'Mr. Mynors hasn't been to our sewing meetings for quite a long time, but I expect he'll turn up to-day.'

Anna took thought. 'Is this a sort of special meeting, then?'

'Oh, not at all. But we all of us said just now, while you were upstairs, that he would be sure to come,' Miss Dickinson's features, skilled in innuendo, conveyed that which was too delicate for utterance. Anna said nothing.

'You see a good deal of him at your house, don't you?' Miss Dickinson continued.

'He comes sometimes to see father on business,' Anna replied sharply, breaking one of her rules.

'Oh! Of course I meant that. You didn't suppose I meant anything else, did you?' Miss Dickinson smiled pleasantly. She was thirty-five years of age. Twenty of those years she had passed in a desolating routine; she had existed in the midst of life and never lived; she knew no finer joy than that which she at that moment experienced.

Again Anna offered no reply. The door opened, and every eye was centred on the stately Mrs. Clayton Vernon, who, with Mrs. Banks, the minister's wife, was in charge of the other half of the sewing party in the dining-room. Mrs. Clayton Vernon had heroic proportions, a nose which everyone admitted to be aristocratic, exquisite tact, and the calm consciousness of social superiority. In Bursley she was a great lady: her instincts were those of a great lady; and she would have been a great lady no matter to what sphere her God had called her. She had abundant white hair, and wore a flowered purple silk, in the antique taste.

'Beatrice, my dear,' she began, 'you have deserted us.'

'Have I, Mrs. Vernon?' the girl answered with involuntary deference. 'I was just coming in.'

'Well, I am sent as a deputation from the other room to ask you to sing something.'

'I'm very busy, Mrs. Vernon. I shall never get this mantel-cloth finished in time.'

'We shall all work better for a little music,' Mrs. Clayton Vernon urged. 'Your voice is a precious gift, and should be used for the benefit of all. We entreat, my dear girl.'

Beatrice arose from the footstool and dropped her embroidery.

'Thank you,' said Mrs. Clayton Vernon. 'If both doors are left open we shall hear nicely.'

'What would you like?' Beatrice asked.

'I once heard you sing "Nazareth," and I shall never forget it. Sing that. It will do us all good.'

Mrs. Clayton Vernon departed with the large movement of an argosy, and Beatrice sat down to the piano and removed her bracelets. 'The accompaniment is simply frightful towards the end,' she said, looking at Anna with a grimace. 'Excuse mistakes.'

During the song, Mrs. Sutton beckoned with her finger to Anna to come and occupy the stool vacated by Beatrice. Glad to leave the vicinity of Miss Dickinson, Anna obeyed, creeping on tiptoe across the intervening space. 'I thought I would like to have you near me, my dear,' she whispered maternally. When Beatrice had sung the song and somehow executed that accompaniment which has terrorised whole multitudes of drawing-room pianists, there was a great deal of applause from both rooms. Mrs. Sutton bent down and whispered in Anna's ear: 'Her voice has been very well trained, has it not?' 'Yes, very,' Anna replied. But, though 'Nazareth' had seemed to her wonderful, she had neither understood it nor enjoyed it. She tried to like it, but the effect of it on her was bizarre rather than pleasing.

Shortly after half-past five the gong sounded for tea, and the ladies, bidden by Mrs. Sutton, unanimously thronged into the hall and towards a room at the back of the house. Beatrice came and took Anna by the arm. As they were crossing the hall there was a ring at the door. 'There's father—and Mr. Banks, too,' Beatrice exclaimed, opening to them. Everyone in the vicinity, animated suddenly by this appearance of the male sex, turned with welcoming smiles. 'A greeting to you all,' the minister ejaculated with formal suavity as he removed his low hat. The Alderman beamed a rather absent-minded goodwill on the entire company, and said: 'Well! I see we're just in time for tea.' Then he kissed his daughter, and she accepted from him his hat and stick. 'Miss Tellwright, pa,' Beatrice said, drawing Anna forward: he shook hands with her heartily, emerging for a moment from the benignant dream in which he seemed usually to exist.

That air of being rapt by some inward vision, common in very old men, probably signified nothing in the case of William Sutton: it was a habitual pose into which he had perhaps unconsciously fallen. But people connected it with his humble archæological, geological, and zoological hobbies, which had sprung from his membership of the Five Towns Field Club, and which most of his acquaintances regarded with amiable secret disdain. At a school-treat once, held at a popular rural resort, he had taken some of the teachers to a cave, and pointing out the wave-like formation of its roof had told them that this peculiar phenomenon had actually been caused by waves of the sea. The discovery, valid enough and perfectly substantiated by an inquiry into the levels, was extremely creditable to the amateur geologist, but it seriously impaired his reputation among the Wesleyan community as a shrewd man of the world. Few believed the statement, or even tried to believe it, and nearly all thenceforth looked on him as a man who must be humoured in his harmless hallucinations and inexplicable curiosities. On the other hand, the collection of arrowheads, Roman pottery, fossils and birds' eggs which he had given to the Museum in the Wedgwood Institution was always viewed with municipal pride.

The tea-room opened by a large French window into a conservatory, and a table was laid down the whole length of the room and the conservatory. Mr. Sutton sat at one end and the minister at the other, but neither Mrs. Sutton nor Beatrice occupied a distinctive place. The ancient clumsy custom of having tea-urns on the table itself had been abolished by Beatrice, who had read in a paper that carving was now never done at table, but by a neatly-dressed parlour-maid at the sideboard. Consequently the tea-urns were exiled to the sideboard, and the tea dispensed by a couple of maids. Thus, as Beatrice had explained to her mother, the hostess was left free to devote herself to the social arts. The board was richly spread with fancy breads and cakes, jams of Mrs. Sutton's own celebrated preserving, diverse sandwiches compiled by Beatrice, and one or two large examples of the famous Bursley pork-pie. Numerous as the company was, several chairs remained empty after everyone was seated. Anna found herself again next to Miss Dickinson, and five places from the minister, in the conservatory. Beatrice and her mother were higher up, in the room. Grace was sung, by request of Mrs. Sutton. At first, silence prevailed among the guests, and the inquiries of the maids about milk and sugar were almost painfully audible. Then Mr. Banks, glancing up the long vista of the table and pretending to descry some object in the distance, called out:

'Worthy host, I doubt not you are there, but I can only see you with the eye of faith.'

At this all laughed, and a natural ease was established. The minister and Mrs. Clayton Vernon, who sat on his right, exchanged badinage on the merits and demerits of pork-pies, and their neighbours formed an appreciative audience. Then there was a sharp ring at the front door, and one of the maids went out.

'Didn't I tell you?' Miss Dickinson whispered to Anna.

'What?' asked Anna.

'That he would come to-day—Mr. Mynors, I mean.'

'Who can that be?' Mrs. Sutton's voice was heard from the room.

'I dare say it's Henry, mother,' Beatrice answered.

Mynors entered, joyous and self-possessed, a white rose in his coat: he shook hands with Mr. and Mrs. Sutton, sent a greeting down the table to Mr. Banks and Mrs. Clayton Vernon, and offered a general apology for being late.

'Sit here,' said Beatrice to him, sharply, indicating a chair between Mrs. Banks and herself. 'Mrs. Banks has a word to say to you about the singing of that anthem last Sunday.'

Mynors made some laughing rejoinder, and the voices sank so that Anna could not catch what was said.

'That's a new frock that Miss Sutton is wearing to-day,' Miss Dickinson remarked in an undertone.

'It looks new,' Anna agreed.

'Do you like it?'

'Yes. Don't you?'

'Hum! Yes. It was made at Brunt's at Hanbridge. It's quite the fashion to go there now,' said Miss Dickinson, and added, almost inaudibly, 'She's put it on for Mr. Mynors. You saw how she saved that chair for him.'

Anna made no reply.

'Did you know they were engaged once?' Miss Dickinson resumed.

'No,' said Anna.

'At least people said they were. It was all over the town—oh! let me see, three years ago.'

'I had not heard,' said Anna.

During the rest of the meal she said little. On some natures Miss Dickinson's gossip had the effect of bringing them to silence. Anna had not seen Mynors since the previous Sunday, and now she was apparently unperceived by him. He talked gaily with Beatrice and Mrs. Banks: that group was a centre of animation. Anna envied their ease of manner, their smooth and sparkling flow of conversation. She had the sensation of feeling vulgar, clumsy, tongue-tied; Mynors and Beatrice possessed something which she would never possess. So they had been engaged! But had they? Or was it an idle rumour, manufactured by one who spent her life in such creations? Anna was conscious of misgivings. She had despised Beatrice once, but now it seemed that after all Beatrice was the natural equal of Henry Mynors. Was it more likely that Mynors or she, Anna, should be mistaken in Beatrice? That Beatrice had generous instincts she was sure. Anna lost confidence in herself; she felt humbled, out-of-place, and shamed.

'If our hostess and the company will kindly excuse me,' said the minister with a pompous air, looking at his watch, 'I must go. I have an important appointment, or an appointment which some people think is important.'

He got up and made various adieux. The elaborate meal, complex with fifty dainties each of which had to be savoured, was not nearly over. The parson stopped in his course up the room to speak with Mrs. Sutton. After he had shaken hands with her, he caught the admired violet eyes of his slim wife, a lady of independent fortune whom the wives of circuit stewards found it difficult to please in the matter of furniture, and who despite her forty years still kept something of the pose of a spoiled beauty. As a minister's spouse this languishing but impeccable and invariably correct dame was unique even in the experience of Mrs. Clayton Vernon.

'Shall you not be home early, Rex?' she asked in the tone of a young wife lounging amid the delicate odours of a boudoir.

'My love,' he replied with the stern fixity of a histrionic martyr, 'did you ever know me have a free evening?'

The Alderman accompanied his pastor to the door.

After tea, Mynors was one of the first to leave the room, and Anna one of the last, but he accosted her in the hall, on the way back to the drawing-room, and asked how she was, and how Agnes was, with such deference and sincerity of regard for herself and everything that was hers that she could not fail to be impressed. Her sense of humiliation and of uncertainty was effaced by a single word, a single glance. Uplifted by a delicious reassurance, she passed into the drawing-room, expecting him to follow: strange to say, he did not do so. Work was resumed, but with less ardour than before. It was in fact impossible to be strenuously diligent after one of Mrs. Sutton's teas, and in every heart, save those which beat over the most perfect and vigorous digestive organs, there was a feeling of repentance. The building-society's clock on the mantel-piece intoned seven: all expressed surprise at the lateness of the hour, and Mrs. Clayton Vernon, pleading fatigue after her recent indisposition, quietly departed. As soon as she was gone, Anna said to Mrs. Sutton that she too must go.

'Why, my dear?' Mrs. Sutton asked.

'I shall be needed at home,' Anna replied.

'Ah! In that case—— I will come upstairs with you, my dear,' said Mrs. Sutton.

When they were in the bedroom, Mrs. Sutton suddenly clasped her hand. 'How is it with you, dear Anna?' she said, gazing anxiously into the girl's eyes. Anna knew what she meant, but made no answer. 'Is it well?' the earnest old woman asked.

'I hope so,' said Anna, averting her eyes, 'I am trying.'

Mrs. Sutton kissed her almost passionately. 'Ah! my dear,' she exclaimed with an impulsive gesture, 'I am glad, so glad. I did so want to have a word with you. You must "lean hard," as Miss Havergal says. "Lean hard" on Him. Do not be afraid.' And then, changing her tone: 'You are looking pale, Anna. You want a holiday. We shall be going to the Isle of Man in August or September. Would your father let you come with us?'

'I don't know,' said Anna. She knew, however, that he would not. Nevertheless the suggestion gave her much pleasure.

'We must see about that later,' said Mrs. Sutton, and they went downstairs.

'I must say good-bye to Beatrice. Where is she?' Anna said in the hall. One of the servants directed them to the dining-room. The Alderman and Henry Mynors were looking together at a large photogravure of Sant's 'The Soul's Awakening,' which Mr. Sutton had recently bought, and Beatrice was exhibiting her embroidery to a group of ladies: sundry stitchers were scattered about, including Miss Dickinson.

'It is a great picture—a picture that makes you think,' Henry was saying, seriously, and the Alderman, feeling as the artist might have felt, was obviously flattered by this sagacious praise.

Anna said good-night to Miss Dickinson and then to Beatrice. Mynors, hearing the words, turned round. 'Well, I must go. Good evening,' he said suddenly to the astonished Alderman.

'What? Now?' the latter inquired, scarcely pleased to find that Mynors could tear himself away from the picture with so little difficulty.

'Yes.'

'Good-night, Mr. Mynors,' said Anna.

'If I may I will walk down with you,' Mynors imperturbably answered.

It was one of those dramatic moments which arrive without the slightest warning. The gleam of joyous satisfaction in Miss Dickinson's eyes showed that she alone had foreseen this declaration. For a declaration it was, and a formal declaration. Mynors stood there calm, confident with masculine superiority, and his glance seemed to say to those swiftly alert women, whose faces could not disguise a thrilling excitation: 'Yes. Let all know that I, Henry Mynors, the desired of all, am honourably captive to this shy and perfect creature who is blushing because I have said what I have said.' Even the Alderman forgot his photogravure. Beatrice hurriedly resumed her explanation of the embroidery.

'How did you like the sewing meeting?' Mynors asked Anna when they were on the pavement.

Anna paused. 'I think Mrs. Sutton is simply a splendid woman,' she said enthusiastically.

When, in a moment far too short, they reached Tellwright's house, Mynors, obeying a mutual wish to which neither had given expression, followed Anna up the side entry, and so into the yard, where they lingered for a few seconds. Old Tellwright could be seen at the extremity of the long narrow garden—a garden which consisted chiefly of a grass-plot sown with clothes-props and a narrow bordering of flower beds without flowers. Agnes was invisible. The kitchen-door stood ajar, and as this was the sole means of ingress from the yard Anna, humming an air, pushed it open and entered, Mynors in her wake. They stood on the threshold, happy, hesitating, confused, and looked at the kitchen as at something which they had not seen before. Anna's kitchen was the only satisfactory apartment in the house. Its furniture included a dresser of the simple and dignified kind which is now assiduously collected by amateurs of old oak. It had four long narrow shelves holding plates and saucers; the cups were hung in a row on small brass hooks screwed into the fronts of the shelves. Below the shelves were three drawers in a line, with brass handles, and below the drawers was a large recess which held stone jars, a copper preserving-saucepan, and other receptacles. Seventy years of continuous polishing by a dynasty of priestesses of cleanliness had given to this dresser a rich ripe tone which the cleverest trade-trickster could not have imitated. In it was reflected the conscientious labour of generations. It had a soft and assuaged appearance, as though it had never been new and could never have been new. All its corners and edges had long lost the asperities of manufacture, and its smooth surfaces were marked by slight hollows similar in spirit to those worn by the naked feet of pilgrims into the marble steps of a shrine. The flat portion over the drawers was scarred with hundreds of scratches, and yet even all these seemed to be incredibly ancient, and in some distant past to have partaken of the mellowness of the whole. The dark woodwork formed an admirable background for the crockery on the shelves, and a few of the old plates, hand-painted according to some vanished secret in pigments which time could only improve, had the look of relationship by birth to the dresser. There must still be thousands of exactly similar dressers in the kitchens of the people, but they are gradually being transferred to the dining rooms of curiosity-hunters. To Anna this piece of furniture, which would have made the most taciturn collector vocal with joy, was merely 'the dresser.' She had always lamented that it contained no cupboard. In front of the fireless range was an old steel kitchen fender with heavy fire-irons. It had in the middle of its flat top a circular lodgment for saucepans, but on this polished disc no saucepan was ever placed. The fender was perhaps as old as the dresser, and the profound depths of its polish served to mitigate somewhat the newness of the patent coal-economising range which Tellwright had had put in when he took the house. On the high mantelpiece were four tall brass candlesticks which, like the dresser, were silently awaiting their apotheosis at the hands of some collector. Beside these were two or three common mustard tins, polished to counterfeit silver, containing spices; also an abandoned coffee-mill and two flat-irons. A grandfather's clock of oak to match the dresser stood to the left of the fireplace; it had a very large white dial with a grinning face in the centre. Though it would only run for twenty-four hours, its leisured movement seemed to have the certainty of a natural law, especially to Agnes, for Mr. Tellwright never forgot to wind it before going to bed. Under the window was a plain deal table, with white top and stained legs. Two Windsor chairs completed the catalogue of furniture. The glistening floor was of red and black tiles, and in front of the fender lay a list hearthrug made by attaching innumerable bits of black cloth to a canvas base. On the painted walls were several grocers' almanacs, depicting sailors in the arms of lovers, children crossing brooks, or monks swelling themselves with Gargantuan repasts. Everything in this kitchen was absolutely bright and spotless, as clean as a cat in pattens, except the ceiling, darkened by fumes of gas. Everything was in perfect order, and had the humanised air of use and occupation which nothing but use and occupation can impart to senseless objects. It was a kitchen where, in the housewife's phrase, you might eat off the floor, and to any Bursley matron it would have constituted the highest possible certificate of Anna's character, not only as housewife but as elder sister—for in her absence Agnes had washed the tea-things and put them away.

'This is the nicest room, I know,' said Mynors at length.

'Whatever do you mean?' Anna smiled, incapable of course of seeing the place with his eye.

'I mean there is nothing to beat a clean, straight kitchen,' Mynors replied, 'and there never will be. It wants only the mistress in a white apron to make it complete. Do you know, when I came in here the other night, and you were sitting at the table there, I thought the place was like a picture.'

'How funny!' said Anna, puzzled but well satisfied. 'But won't you come into the parlour?'

The Persian with one ear met them in the lobby, his tail flying, but cautiously sidled upstairs at sight of Mynors. When Anna opened the door of the parlour she saw Agnes seated at the table over her lessons, frowning and preoccupied. Tears were in her eyes.

'Why, what's the matter, Agnes?' she exclaimed.

'Oh! Go away,' said the child crossly. 'Don't bother.'

'But what's the matter? You're crying.'

'No, I'm not. I'm doing my sums, and I can't get it—can't——' The child burst into tears just as Mynors entered. His presence was a complete surprise to her. She hid her face in her pinafore, ashamed to be thus caught.

'Where is it?' said Mynors. 'Where is this sum that won't come right?' He picked up the slate and examined it while Agnes was finding herself again. 'Practice!' he exclaimed. 'Has Agnes got as far as practice?' She gave him an instant's glance and murmured 'Yes.' Before she could shelter her face he had kissed her. Anna was enchanted by his manner, and as for Agnes, she surrendered happily to him at once. He worked the sum, and she copied the figures into her exercise-book. Anna sat and watched.

'Now I must go,' said Mynors.

'But surely you'll stay and see father,' Anna urged.

'No. I really had not meant to call. Good-night, Agnes.' In a moment he was gone out of the room and the house. It was as if, in obedience to a sudden impulse, he had forcibly torn himself away.

'Was *he* at the sewing meeting?' Agnes asked, adding in parenthesis, 'I never dreamt he was here, and I was frightfully vexed. I felt such a baby.'

'Yes. At least, he came for tea.'

'Why did he call here like that?'

'How can I tell?' Anna said. The child looked at her.

'It's awfully queer, isn't it?' she said slowly. 'Tell me all about the sewing meeting. Did they have cakes or was it a plain tea? And did you go into Beatrice Sutton's bedroom?'

CHAPTER VIII

ON THE BANK

Anna began to receive her July interest and dividends. During a fortnight remittances, varying from a few pounds to a few hundred of pounds, arrived by post almost daily. They were all addressed to her, since the securities now stood in her own name; and upon her, under the miser's superintendence, fell the new task of entering them in a book and paying them into the Bank. This mysterious begetting of money by money—a strange process continually going forward for her benefit, in various parts of the world, far and near, by means of activities of which she was completely ignorant and would always be completely ignorant—bewildered her and gave her a feeling of its unreality. The elaborate mechanism by which capital yields interest without suffering diminution from its original bulk is one of the commonest phenomena of modern life, and one of the least understood. Many capitalists never grasp it, nor experience the slightest curiosity about it until the mechanism through some defect ceases to revolve. Tellwright was of these; for him the interval between the outlay of capital and the receipt of interest was nothing but an efflux of time: he planted capital as a gardener plants rhubarb, tolerably certain of a particular result, but not dwelling even in thought on that which is hidden. The productivity of capital was to him the greatest achievement of social progress—indeed, the social organism justified its existence by that achievement; nothing could be more equitable than this productivity, nothing more natural. He would as soon have inquired into it as Agnes would have inquired into the ticking of the grandfather's clock. But to Anna, who had some imagination, and whose imagination had been stirred by recent events, the arrival of moneys out of space, unearned, unasked, was a disturbing experience, affecting her as a conjuring trick affects a child, whose sensations hesitate between pleasure and apprehension. Practically, Anna could not believe that she was rich; and in fact she was not rich—she was merely a fixed point through which moneys that she was unable to arrest passed with the rapidity of trains. If money is a token, Anna was denied the satisfaction of fingering even the token: drafts and cheques were all that she touched (touched only to abandon)—the doubly tantalising and insubstantial tokens of a token. She wanted to test the actuality of this apparent dream by handling coin and causing it to vanish over counters and into the palms of the necessitous. And moreover, quite apart from this curiosity, she really needed money for pressing requirements of Agnes and herself. They had yet had no new summer clothes, and Whitsuntide, the time prescribed by custom for the refurnishing of wardrobes, was long since past. The intercourse with Henry Mynors, the visit to the Suttons, had revealed to her more plainly than ever the intolerable shortcomings of her wardrobe, and similar imperfections. She was more painfully awake to these, and yet, by an unhappy paradox, she was even less in a position to remedy them, than in previous years. For now, she possessed her own fortune; to ask her father's bounty was therefore, she divined, a sure way of inviting a rebuff. But, even if she had dared, she might not use the income that was privately hers, for was not every penny of it already allocated to the partnership with Mynors! So it happened that she never once mentioned the matter to her father; she lacked the courage, since by whatever avenue she approached it circumstances would add an illogical and adventitious force to the brutal snubs which he invariably dealt out when petitioned for money. To demand his money, having fifty thousand of her own! To spend her own in the face of that agreement with Mynors! She could too easily guess his bitter and humiliating retorts to either proposition, and she kept silence, comforting herself with timid visions of a far distant future. The balance at the bank crept up to sixteen hundred pounds. The deed of partnership was drawn; her father pored over the blue draft, and several times Mynors called and the two men discussed it together. Then one morning her father summoned her into the front parlour, and handed to her a piece of parchment on which she dimly deciphered her own name coupled with that of Henry Mynors, in large letters.

'You mun sign, seal, and deliver this,' he said, putting a pen in her hand.

She sat down obediently to write, but he stopped her with a scornful gesture.

'Thou 'lt sign blind then, eh? Just like a woman!'

'I left it to you,' she said.

'Left it to me! Read it.'

She read through the deed, and after she had accomplished the feat one fact only stood clear in her mind, that the partnership was for seven years, a period extensible by consent of both parties to fourteen or twenty-one years. Then she affixed her signature, the pen moving awkwardly over the rough surface of the parchment.

'Now put thy finger on that bit o' wax, and say; "I deliver this as my act and deed."'

'I deliver this as my act and deed.'

The old man signed as witness. 'Soon as I give this to Lawyer Dane,' he remarked, 'thou'rt bound, willy-nilly. Law's law, and thou'rt bound.'

On the following day she had to sign a cheque which reduced her bank-balance to about three pounds. Perhaps it was the knowledge of this reduction that led Ephraim Tellwright to resume at once and with fresh rigour his new policy of 'squeezing the last penny' out of Titus Price (despite the fact that the latter had already achieved the incredible by paying thirty pounds in little more than a month), thus causing the catastrophe which soon afterwards befell. What methods her father was adopting Anna did not know, since he said no word to her about the matter: she only knew that Agnes had twice been dispatched with notes to Edward Street. One day, about noon, a clay-soiled urchin brought a letter addressed to herself: she guessed that it was some appeal for mercy from the Prices, and wished that her father had been at home. The old man was away for the whole day, attending a sale of property at Axe, the agricultural town in the north of the county, locally styled 'the metropolis of the moorlands.' Anna read:—'My dear Miss Tellwright,—Now that our partnership is an accomplished fact, will you not come and look over the works? I should much like you to do so. I shall be passing your house this afternoon about two, and will call on the chance of being able to take you down with me to the works. If you are unable to come no harm will be done, and some other day can be arranged; but of course I shall be disappointed.—Believe me, yours most sincerely, HY. MYNORS.'

She was charmed with the idea—to her so audacious—and relieved that the note was not after all from Titus or Willie Price: but again she had to regret that her father was not at home. He would be capable of thinking and saying that the projected expedition was a truancy, contrived to occur in his absence. He might grumble at the house being left without a keeper. Moreover, according to a tacit law, she never departed from the fixed routine of her existence without first obtaining Ephraim's approval, or at least being sure that such a departure would not make him violently angry. She wondered whether Mynors knew that her father was away, and, if so, whether he had chosen that afternoon purposely. She did not care that Mynors should call for her—it made the visit seem so formal; and as in order to reach the works, down at Shawport by the canal-side, they would necessarily go through the middle of the town, she foresaw infinite gossip and rumour as one result. Already, she knew, the names of herself and Mynors were everywhere coupled, and she could not even enter a shop without being made aware, more or less delicately, that she was an object of piquant curiosity. A woman is profoundly interesting to women at two periods only—before she is betrothed and before she becomes the mother of her firstborn. Anna was in the first period; her life did not comprise the second. When Agnes came home to dinner from school, Anna said nothing of Mynors' note until they had begun to wash up the dinner-things, when she suggested that Agnes should finish this operation alone.

'Yes,' said Agnes, ever compliant. 'But why?'

'I'm going out, and I must get ready.'

'Going out? And shall you leave the house all empty? What will father say? Where are you going to?'

Agnes's tendency to anticipate the worst, and never to blink their father's tyranny, always annoyed Anna, and she answered rather curtly: 'I'm going to the works—Mr. Mynors' works. He's sent word he wants me to.' She despised herself for wishing to hide anything, and added, 'He will call here for me about two o'clock.'

'Mr. Mynors! How splendid!' And then Agnes's face fell somewhat. 'I suppose he won't call before two? If he doesn't, I shall be gone to school.'

'Do you want to see him?'

'Oh, no! I don't want to see him. But—I suppose you'll be out a long time, and he'll bring you back.'

'Of course he won't, you silly girl. And I shan't be out long. I shall be back for tea.'

Anna ran upstairs to dress. At ten minutes to two she was ready. Agnes usually left at a quarter to two, but the child had not yet gone. At five minutes to two, Anna called downstairs to her to ask her when she meant to depart.

'I'm just going now,' Agnes shouted back. She opened the front door and then returned to the foot of the stairs. 'Anna, if I meet him down the road shall I tell him you're ready waiting for him?'

'Certainly not. Whatever are you dreaming of?' the elder sister reproved. 'Besides, he isn't coming from the town.'

'Oh! All right. Good-bye.' And the child at last went.

It was something after two—every siren and hooter had long since finished the summons to work—when Mynors rang the bell. Anna was still upstairs. She examined herself in the glass, and then descended slowly.

'Good afternoon,' he said. 'I see you are ready to come. I'm very glad. I hope I haven't inconvenienced you, but just this afternoon seemed to be a good opportunity for you to see the works, and, you know, you ought to see it. Father in?'

'No,' she said. 'I shall leave the house to take care of itself. Do you want to see him?'

'Not specially,' he replied. 'I think we have settled everything.'

She banged the door behind her, and they started. As he held open the gate for her exit, she could not ignore the look of passionate admiration on his face. It was a look disconcerting by its mere intensity. The man could control his tongue, but not his eyes. His demeanour, as she viewed it, aggravated her self-consciousness as they braved the streets. But she was happy in her perturbation. When they reached Duck Bank, Mynors asked her whether they should go through the market-place or along King Street, by the bottom of St. Luke's Square. 'By the market-place,' she said. The shop where Miss Dickinson was employed was at the bottom of St. Luke's Square, and all the eyes of the marketplace was preferable to the chance of those eyes.

Probably no one in the Five Towns takes a conscious pride in the antiquity of the potter's craft, nor in its unique and intimate relation to human life, alike civilised and uncivilised. Man hardened clay into a bowl before he spun flax and made a garment, and the last lone man will want an earthen vessel after he has abandoned his ruined house for a cave, and his woven rags for an animal's skin. This supremacy of the most ancient of crafts is in the secret nature of things, and cannot be explained. History begins long after the period when Bursley was first the central seat of that honoured manufacture: it is the central seat still—'the mother of the Five Towns,' in our local phrase—and though the townsmen, absorbed in a strenuous daily struggle, may forget their heirship to an unbroken tradition of countless centuries, the seal of their venerable calling is upon their foreheads. If no other relic of an immemorial past is to be seen in these modernised sordid streets, there is at least the living legacy of that extraordinary kinship between workman and work, that instinctive mastery of clay which the past has bestowed upon the present. The horse is less to the Arab than clay is to the Bursley man. He exists in it and by it; it fills his lungs and blanches his cheek; it keeps him alive and it kills him. His fingers close round it as round the hand of a friend. He knows all its tricks and aptitudes; when to coax and when to force it, when to rely on it and when to distrust it. The weavers of Lancashire have dubbed him with an obscene epithet on account of it, an epithet whose hasty use has led to many a fight, but nothing could be more illuminatively descriptive than that epithet, which names his vocation in terms of another vocation. A dozen decades of applied science have of course resulted in the interposition of elaborate machinery between the clay and the man; but no great vulgar handicraft has lost less of the human than potting. Clay is always clay, and the steam-driven contrivance that will mould a basin while a man sits and watches has yet to be invented. Moreover, if in some coarser process the hands are superseded, the number of processes has been multiplied tenfold: the ware in which six men formerly collaborated is now produced by sixty; and thus, in one sense, the touch of finger on clay is more pervasive than ever before.

Mynors' works was acknowledged to be one of the best, of its size, in the district—a model three-oven bank, and it must be remembered that of the hundreds of banks in the Five Towns the vast majority are small, like this: the large manufactory with its corps of jacket-men,[1] one of whom is detached to show visitors round so much of the works as is deemed advisable for them to see, is the exception. Mynors paid three hundred pounds a year in rent, and produced nearly three hundred pounds worth of work a week. He was his own manager, and there was only one jacket-man on the place, a clerk at eighteen shillings. He employed about a hundred hands, and devoted all his ingenuity to prevent that wastage which is at once the easiest to overlook and the most difficult to check, the wastage of labour. No pains were spared to keep all departments in full and regular activity, and owing to his judicious firmness the feast of St. Monday, that canker eternally eating at the root of the prosperity of the Five Towns, was less religiously observed on his bank than perhaps anywhere else in Bursley. He had realised that when a workshop stands empty the employer has not only ceased to make money, but has begun to lose it. The architect of 'Providence Works' (Providence stands godfather to many commercial enterprises in the Five Towns) knew his business and the business of the potter, and he had designed the works with a view to the strictest economy of labour. The various shops were so arranged that in the course of its metamorphosis the clay travelled naturally in a circle from the slip-house by the canal to the packing-house by the canal: there was no carrying to and fro. The steam installation was complete: steam once generated had no respite; after it had exhausted itself in vitalising fifty machines, it was killed by inches in order to dry the unfired ware and warm the dinners of the workpeople.

Henry took Anna to the canal-entrance, because the buildings looked best from that side.

'Now how much is a crate worth?' she asked, pointing to a crate which was being swung on a crane direct from the packing-house into a boat.

'That?' Mynors answered. 'A crateful of ware may be worth anything. At Minton's I have seen a crate worth three hundred pounds. But that one there is only worth eight or nine pounds. You see you and I make cheap stuff.'

'But don't you make any really good pots—are they all cheap?'

'All cheap,' he said.

'I suppose that's business?' He detected a note of regret in her voice.

'I don't know,' he said, with the slightest impatient warmth. 'We make the stuff as good as we can for the money. We supply what everyone wants. Don't you think it's better to please a thousand folks than to please ten? I like to feel that my ware is used all over the country and the colonies. I would sooner do as I do than make swagger ware for a handful of rich people.'

'Oh, yes,' she exclaimed, eagerly accepting the point of view, 'I quite agree with you.' She had never heard him in that vein before, and was struck by his enthusiasm. And Mynors was in fact always very enthusiastic concerning the virtues of the general markets. He had no sympathy with specialities, artistic or otherwise. He found his satisfaction in honestly meeting the public taste. He was born to be a manufacturer of cheap goods on a colossal scale. He could dream of fifty ovens, and his ambition blinded him to the present absurdity of talking about a three-oven bank spreading its productions all over the country and the colonies; it did not occur to him that there were yet scarcely enough plates to go round.

'I suppose we had better start at the start,' he said, leading the way to the slip-house. He did not need to be told that Anna was perfectly ignorant of the craft of pottery, and that every detail of it, so stale to him, would acquire freshness under her naïve and inquiring gaze.

In the slip-house begins the long manipulation which transforms raw porous friable clay into the moulded, decorated and glazed vessel. The large whitewashed place was occupied by ungainly machines and receptacles through which the four sorts of clay used in the common 'body'—ball clay, China clay, flint clay and stone clay—were compelled to pass before they became a white putty-like mixture meet for shaping by human hands. The blunger crushed the clay, the sifter extracted the iron from it by means of a magnet, the press expelled the water, and the pug-mill expelled the air. From the last reluctant mouth slowly emerged a solid stream nearly a foot in diameter, like a huge white snake. Already the clay had acquired the uniformity characteristic of a manufactured product.

Anna moved to touch the bolts of the enormous twenty-four-chambered press.

'Don't stand there,' said Mynors. 'The pressure is tremendous, and if the thing were to burst——'

She fled hastily. 'But isn't it dangerous for the workmen?' she asked.

Eli Machin, the engineman, the oldest employee on the works, a moneyed man and the pattern of reliability, allowed a vague smile to flit across his face at this remark. He had ascended from the engine-house below in order to exhibit the tricks of the various machines, and that done he disappeared. Anna was awed by the sensation of being surrounded by terrific forces always straining for release and held in check by the power of a single wall.

'Come and see a plate made: that is one of the simplest things, and the batting-machine is worth looking at,' said Mynors, and they went into the nearest shop, a hot interior in the shape of four corridors round a solid square middle. Here men and women were working side by side, the women subordinate to the men. All were preoccupied, wrapped up in their respective operations, and there was the sound of irregular whirring movements from every part of the big room. The air was laden with whitish dust, and clay was omnipresent— on the floor, the walls, the benches, the windows, on clothes, hands and faces. It was in this shop, where both hollow-ware pressers and flat pressers were busy as only craftsmen on piecework can be busy, that more than anywhere else clay was to be seen 'in the hand of the potter.' Near the door a stout man with a good-humoured face flung some clay on to a revolving disc, and even as Anna passed a jar sprang into existence. One instant the clay was an amorphous mass, the next it was a vessel perfectly circular, of a prescribed width and a prescribed depth; the flat and apparently clumsy fingers of the craftsman had seemed to lose themselves in the clay for a fraction of time, and the miracle was accomplished. The man threw these vessels with the rapidity of a Roman candle throwing off coloured stars, and one woman was kept busy in supplying him with material and relieving his bench of the finished articles. Mynors drew Anna along to the batting-machines for plate makers, at that period rather a novelty and the latest invention of the dead genius whose brain has reconstituted a whole industry on new lines. Confronted with a piece of clay, the batting-machine descended upon it with the ferocity of a wild animal, worried it, stretched it, smoothed it into the width and thickness of a plate, and then desisted of itself and waited inactive for the flat presser to remove its victim to his more exact shaping machine. Several men were producing plates, but their rapid labours seemed less astonishing than the preliminary feat of the batting-machine. All the ware as it was moulded disappeared into the vast cupboards occupying the centre of the shop, where Mynors showed Anna innumerable rows of shelves full of pots in process of steam-drying. Neither time nor space nor material was wasted in this ant-heap of industry. In order to move to and fro, the women were compelled to insinuate themselves past the stationary bodies of the men. Anna marvelled at the careless accuracy with which they fed the batting-machines with lumps precisely calculated to form a plate of a given diameter. Everyone exerted himself as though the salvation of the world hung on the production of so much stuff by a certain hour; dust, heat, and the presence of a stranger were alike unheeded in the mad creative passion.

'Now,' said Mynors the cicerone, opening another door which gave into the yard, 'when all that stuff is dried and fettled—smoothed, you know—it goes into the biscuit oven: that's the first firing. There's the biscuit oven, but we can't inspect it because it's just being drawn.'

He pointed to the oven near by, in whose dark interior the forms of men, naked to the waist, could dimly be seen struggling with the weight of saggars[2] full of ware. It seemed like some release of martyrs, this unpacking of the immense oven, which, after being flooded with a sea of flame for fifty-four hours, had cooled for two days, and was yet hotter than the Equator. The inertness and pallor of the saggers seemed to be the physical result of their fiery trial, and one wondered that they should have survived the trial. Mynors went into the place adjoining the oven and brought back a plate out of an open sagger; it was still quite warm. It had the *matt*surface of a biscuit, and adhered slightly to the fingers: it was now a 'crook'; it had exchanged malleability for brittleness, and nothing mortal could undo what the fire had done. Mynors took the plate with him to the biscuit-warehouse, a long room where one was forced to keep to narrow alleys amid parterres of pots. A solitary biscuit-warehouseman was examining the ware in order to determine the remuneration of the pressers.

They climbed a flight of steps to the printing-shop, where, by means of copper-plates, printing-presses, mineral colours, and transfer-papers, most of the decoration was done. The room was filled by a little crowd of people—oldish men, women and girls, divided into printers, cutters, transferors and apprentices. Each interminably repeated some trifling process, and every article passed through a succession of hands until at length it was washed in a tank and rose dripping therefrom with its ornament of flowers and scrolls fully revealed. The room smelt of oil and flannel and humanity; the atmosphere was more languid, more like that of a family party, than in the pressers' shop: the old women looked stern and shrewish, the pretty young women pert and defiant, the younger girls meek. The few men seemed out of place. By what trick had they crept into the very centre of that mass of femineity? It seemed wrong, scandalous that they should remain. Contiguous with the printing-shop was the painting-shop, in which the labours of the former were taken to a finish by the brush of the paintress, who filled in outlines with flat colour, and thus converted mechanical printing into handiwork. The paintresses form the *noblesse* of the banks. Their task is a light one, demanding deftness first of all; they have delicate fingers, and enjoy a general reputation for beauty: the wages they earn may be estimated from their finery on Sundays. They come to business in cloth jackets, carry dinner in little satchels; in the shop they wear white aprons, and look startlingly neat and tidy. Across the benches over which they bend their coquettish heads gossip flies and returns like a shuttle; they are the source of a thousand intrigues, and one or other of them is continually getting married or omitting to get married. On the bank they constitute 'the sex.' An infinitesimal proportion of them, from among the branch known as ground-layers, die of lead-poisoning—a fact which adds pathos to their frivolous charm. In a subsidiary room off the painting-shop a single girl was seated at a revolving table actuated by a treadle. She was doing the 'band-and-line' on the rims of saucers. Mynors and Anna watched her as with her left hand she flicked saucer after saucer into the exact centre of the table, moved the treadle, and, holding a brush firmly against the rim of the piece, produced with infallible exactitude the band and the line. She was a brunette, about twenty-eight: she had a calm, vacuously contemplative face; but God alone knew whether she thought. Her work represented the summit of monotony; the regularity of it hypnotised the observer, and Mynors himself was impressed by this stupendous phenomenon of absolute sameness, involuntarily assuming towards it the attitude of a showman.

525

'She earns as much as eighteen shillings a week sometimes,' he whispered.

'May I try?' Anna timidly asked of a sudden, curious to experience what the trick was like.

'Certainly,' said Mynors, in eager assent. 'Priscilla, let this lady have your seat a moment, please.'

The girl got up, smiling politely. Anna took her place.

'Here, try on this,' said Mynors, putting on the table the plate which he still carried.

'Take a full brush,' the paintress suggested, not attempting to hide her amusement at Anna's unaccustomed efforts. 'Now push the treadle. There! It isn't in the middle yet. Now!'

Anna produced a most creditable band, and a trembling but passable line, and rose flushed with the small triumph.

'You have the gift,' said Mynors; and the paintress respectfully applauded.

'I felt I could do it,' Anna responded. 'My mother's mother was a paintress, and it must be in the blood.'

Mynors smiled indulgently. They descended again to the ground floor, and following the course of manufacture came to the 'hardening-on' kiln, a minor oven where for twelve hours the oil is burnt out of the colour in decorated ware. A huge, jolly man in shirt and trousers, with an enormous apron, was in the act of drawing the kiln, assisted by two thin boys. He nodded a greeting to Mynors and exclaimed, 'Warm!' The kiln was nearly emptied. As Anna stopped at the door, the man addressed her.

'Step inside, miss, and try it.'

'No, thanks!' she laughed.

'Come now,' he insisted, as if despising this hesitation. 'An ounce of experience——' The two boys grinned and wiped their foreheads with their bare skeleton-like arms. Anna, challenged by the man's look, walked quickly into the kiln. A blasting heat seemed to assault her on every side, driving her back; it was incredible that any human being could support such a temperature.

'There!' said the jovial man, apparently summing her up with his bright, quizzical eyes. 'You know summat as you didn't know afore, miss. Come along, lads,' he added with brisk heartiness to the boys, and the drawing of the kiln proceeded.

Next came the dipping-house, where a middle-aged woman, enveloped in a protective garment from head to foot, was dipping jugs into a vat of lead-glaze, a boy assisting her. The woman's hands were covered with the grey, slimy glaze. She alone of all the employees appeared to be cool.

'That is the last stage but one,' said Mynors. 'There is only the glost-firing,' and they passed out into the yard once more. One of the glost-ovens was empty; they entered it and peered into the lofty inner chamber, which seemed like the cold crater of an exhausted volcano, or like a vault, or like the ruined seat of some forgotten activity. The other oven was firing, and Anna could only look at its exterior, catching glimpses of the red glow at its twelve mouths, and guess at the Tophet, within, where the lead was being fused into glass.

'Now for the glost-warehouse, and you will have seen all,' said Mynors, 'except the mould-shop, and that doesn't matter.'

The warehouse was the largest place on the works, a room sixty-feet long and twenty broad, low, whitewashed, bare and clean. Piles of ware occupied the whole of the walls and of the immense floorspace, but there was no trace here of the soilure and untidiness incident to manufacture; all processes were at an end, clay had vanished into crock: and the calmness and the whiteness atoned for the disorder, noise and squalor which had preceded. Here was a sample of the total and final achievement towards which the thousands of small, disjointed efforts that Anna had witnessed, were directed. And it seemed a miraculous, almost impossible, result; so definite, precise and regular after a series of acts apparently variable, inexact and casual; so inhuman after all that intensely inhuman labour; so vast in comparison with the minuteness of the separate endeavours. As Anna looked, for instance, at a pile of tea-sets, she found it difficult even to conceive that, a fortnight or so before, they had been nothing but lumps of dirty clay. No stage of the manufacture was incredible by itself, but the result was incredible. It was the result that appealed to the imagination, authenticating the adage that fools and children should never see anything till it is done.

Anna pondered over the organising power, the forethought, the wide vision, and the sheer ingenuity and cleverness which were implied by the contents of this warehouse. 'What brains!' she thought, of Mynors; 'what quantities of all sorts of things he must know!' It was a humble and deeply-felt admiration.

Her spoken words gave no clue to her thoughts. 'You seem to make a fine lot of tea-sets,' she remarked.

'Oh, no,' he said carelessly. 'These few that you see here are a special order. I don't go in much for tea-sets: they don't pay; we lose fifteen per cent. of the pieces in making. It's toilet-ware that pays, and that is our leading line.' He waved an arm vaguely towards rows and rows of ewers and basins in the distance. They walked to the end of the warehouse, glancing at everything.

'See here,' said Mynors, 'isn't that pretty?' He pointed through the last window to a view of the canal, which could be seen thence in perspective, finishing in a curve. On one side, close to the water's edge, was a ruined and fragmentary building, its rich browns reflected in the smooth surface of the canal. On the other side were a few grim, grey trees bordering the towpath. Down the vista moved a boat steered by a woman in a large mob-cap. 'Isn't that picturesque?' he said.

'Very,' Anna assented willingly. 'It's really quite strange, such a scene right in the middle of Bursley.'

'Oh! There are others,' he said. 'But I always take a peep at that whenever I come into the warehouse.'

'I wonder you find time to notice it—with all this place to see after,' she said. 'It's a splendid works!'

'It will do—to be going on with,' he answered, satisfied. 'I'm very glad you've been down. You must come again. I can see you would be interested in it, and there are plenty of things you haven't looked at yet, you know.'

He smiled at her. They were alone in the warehouse.

'Yes,' she said; 'I expect so. Well, I must go, at once; I'm afraid it's very late now. Thank you for showing me round, and explaining, and—I'm frightfully stupid and ignorant. Good-bye.'

Vapid and trite phrases: what unimaginable messages the hearer heard in you!

Anna held out her hand, and he seized it almost convulsively, his incendiary eyes fastened on her face.

'I must see you out,' he said, dropping that ungloved hand.

It was ten o'clock that night before Ephraim Tellwright returned home from Axe. He appeared to be in a bad temper. Agnes had gone to bed. His supper of bread-and-cheese and water was waiting for him, and Anna sat at the table while he consumed it. He ate in silence, somewhat hungrily, and she did not deem the moment propitious for telling him about her visit to Mynors' works.

'Has Titus Price sent up?' he asked at length, gulping down the last of the water.

'Sent up?'

'Yes. Art fond, lass? I told him as he mun send up some more o' thy rent to-day—twenty-five pun. He's not sent?'

'I don't know,' she said timidly. 'I was out this afternoon.'

'Out, wast?'

'Mr. Mynors sent word to ask me to go down and look over the works; so I went. I thought it would be all right.'

'Well, it was'na all right. And I'd like to know what business thou hast gadding out, as soon as my back's turned. How can I tell whether Price sent up or not? And what's more, thou know's as th' house hadn't ought to be left.'

'I'm sorry,' she said pleasantly, with a determination to be meek and dutiful.

He grunted. 'Happen he didna' send. And if he did, and found th' house locked up, he should ha' sent again. Bring me th' inkpot, and I'll write a note as Agnes must take when her goes to school to-morrow morning.'

Anna obeyed. 'They'll never be able to pay twenty-five pounds, father,' she ventured. 'They've paid thirty already, you know.'

'Less gab,' he said shortly, taking up the pen. 'Here—write it thysen.' He threw the pen towards her. 'Tell Titus if he doesn't pay five-and-twenty this wik, us'll put bailiffs in.'

'Won't it come better from you, father?' she pleaded.

'Whose property is it?' The laconic question was final. She knew she must obey, and began to write. But, realising that she would perforce meet both Titus Price and Willie on Sunday, she merely demanded the money, omitting the threat. Her hand trembled as she passed the note to him to read.

'Will that do?'

His reply was to tear the paper across. 'Put down what I tell ye,' he ordered, 'and don't let's have any more paper wasted.' Then he dictated a letter which was an ultimatum in three lines. 'Sign it,' he said.

She signed it, weeping. She could see the wistful reproach in Willie Price's eyes.

'I suppose,' her father said, when she bade him 'Good-night,' 'I suppose if I hadn't asked, I should ha' heard nowt o' this gadding-about wi' Mynors?'

'I was going to tell you I had been to the works, father,' she said.

'Going to!' That was his final blow, and having delivered it, he loosed the victim. 'Go to bed,' he said.

She went upstairs, resolutely read her Bible, and resolutely prayed.

[1] *Jacket-man*: the artisan's satiric term for anyone who does not work in shirt-sleeves, who is not actually a producer, such as a clerk or a pretentious foreman.

[2] *Saggars*: large oval receptacles of coarse clay, in which the ware is placed for firing.

CHAPTER IX

THE TREAT

This surly and terrorising ferocity of Tellwright's was as instinctive as the growl and spring of a beast of prey. He never considered his attitude towards the women of his household as an unusual phenomenon which needed justification, or as being in the least abnormal. The women of a household were the natural victims of their master: in his experience it had always been so. In his experience the master had always, by universal consent, possessed certain rights over the self-respect, the happiness and the peace of the defenceless souls set under him—rights as unquestioned as those exercised by Ivan the Terrible. Such rights were rooted in the secret nature of things. It was futile to discuss them, because their necessity and their propriety were equally obvious. Tellwright would not have been angry with any man who impugned them: he would merely have regarded the fellow as a crank and a born fool, on whom logic or indignation would be entirely wasted. He did as his father and uncles had done. He still thought of his father as a grim customer, infinitely more redoubtable than himself. He really believed that parents spoiled their children nowadays: to be knocked down by a single blow was one of the punishments of his own generation. He could recall the fearful timidity of his mother's eyes without a trace of compassion. His treatment of his daughters was no part of a system, nor obedient to any defined principles, nor the expression of a brutal disposition, nor the result of gradually-acquired habit. It came to him like eating, and like parsimony. He belonged to the great and powerful class of house-tyrants, the backbone of the British nation, whose views on income-tax cause ministries to tremble. If you had talked to him of the domestic graces of life, your words would have conveyed to him no meaning. If you had indicted him for simple unprovoked rudeness, he would have grinned, well knowing that, as the King can do no wrong, so a man cannot be rude in his own house. If you had told him that he inflicted purposeless misery not only on others but on himself, he would have grinned again, vaguely aware that he had not tried to be happy, and rather despising happiness as a sort of childish gewgaw. He had, in fact, never been happy at home: he had never known that expansion of the spirit which is called joy; he existed continually under a grievance. The atmosphere of Manor Terrace afflicted him, too, with a melancholy gloom—him, who had created it. Had he been capable of self-analysis, he would have discovered that his heart lightened whenever he left the house, and grew dark whenever he returned; but he was incapable of the feat. His case, like every similar case, was irremediable.

The next morning his preposterous displeasure lay like a curse on the house; Anna was silent, and Agnes moved on timid feet. In the afternoon Willie Price called in answer to the note. The miser was in the garden, and Agnes at school. Willie's craven and fawning humility was inexpressibly touching and shameful to Anna. She longed to say to him, as he stood hesitant and confused in the parlour: 'Go in peace. Forget this despicable rent. It sickens me to see you so.' She foresaw, as the effect of her father's vindictive pursuit of her tenants, an interminable succession of these mortifying interviews.

'You're rather hard on us,' Willie Price began, using the old phrases, but in a tone of forced and propitiatory cheerfulness, as though he feared to bring down a storm of anger which should ruin all. 'You'll not deny that we've been doing our best.'

'The rent is due, you know, Mr. William,' she replied, blushing.

'Oh, yes,' he said quickly. 'I don't deny that. I admit that. I—did you happen to see Mr. Tellwright's postscript to your letter?'

'No,' she answered, without thinking.

He drew the letter, soiled and creased, from his pocket, and displayed it to her. At the foot of the page she read, in Ephraim's thick and clumsy characters: 'P.S. This is final.'

'My father,' said Willie, 'was a little put about. He said he'd never received such a letter before in the whole of his business career. It isn't as if——'

'I needn't tell you,' she interrupted, with a sudden determination to get to the worst without more suspense, 'that of course I am in father's hands.'

'Oh! Of course, Miss Tellwright; we quite understand that—quite. It's just a matter of business. We owe a debt and we must pay it. All we want is time.' He smiled piteously at her, his blue eyes full of appeal. She was obliged to gaze at the floor.

'Yes,' she said, tapping her foot on the rug. 'But father means what he says.' She looked up at him again, trying to soften her words by means of something more subtle than a smile.

'He means what he says,' Willie agreed; 'and I admire him for it.'

The obsequious, truckling lie was odious to her.

'Perhaps I could see him,' he ventured.

'I wish you would,' Anna said, sincerely. 'Father, you're wanted,' she called curtly through the window.

'I've got a proposal to make to him,' Price continued, while they awaited the presence of the miser, 'and I can't hardly think he'll refuse it.'

'Well, young sir,' Tellwright said blandly, with an air almost insinuating, as he entered. Willie Price, the simpleton, was deceived by it, and, taking courage, adopted another line of defence. He thought the miser was a little ashamed of his postscript.

'About your note, Mr. Tellwright; I was just telling Miss Tellwright that my father said he had never received such a letter in the whole of his business career.' The youth assumed a discreet indignation.

'Thy feyther's had dozens o' such letters, lad,' the miser said with cold emphasis, 'or my name's not Tellwright. Dunna tell me as Titus Price's never heard of a bumbailiff afore.'

Willie was crushed at a blow, and obliged to retreat. He smiled painfully. 'Come, Mr. Tellwright. Don't talk like that. All we want is time.'

'Time is money,' said Tellwright, 'and if us give you time us give you money. 'Stead o' that, it's you as mun give us money. That's right reason.'

Willie laughed with difficulty. 'See here, Mr. Tellwright. To cut a long story short, it's like this. You ask for twenty-five pounds. I've got in my pocket a bill of exchange drawn by us on Mr. Sutton and endorsed by him, for thirty pounds, payable in three months. Will you take that? Remember it's for thirty, and you only ask for twenty-five.'

'So Mr. Sutton has dealings with ye, eh?' Tellwright remarked.

'Oh, yes,' Willie answered proudly. 'He buys off us regularly. We've done business for years.'

'And pays i' bills at three months, eh?' The miser grinned.

'Sometimes,' said Willie.

'Let's see it,' said the miser.

'What—the bill?'

'Ay!'

'Oh! The bill's all right.' Willie took it from his pocket, and opening out the blue paper, gave it to old Tellwright. Anna perceived the anxiety on the youth's face. He flushed and his hand trembled. She dared not speak, but she wished to tell him to be at ease. She knew from infallible signs that her father would take the bill. Ephraim gazed at the stamped paper as at something strange and unprecedented in his experience.

'Father would want you not to negotiate that bill,' said Willie. 'The fact is, we promised Mr. Sutton that that particular bill should not leave our hands—unless it was absolutely necessary. So father would like you not to discount it, and he will redeem it before it matures. You quite understand—we don't care to offend an old customer like Mr. Sutton.'

'Then this bit o' paper's worth nowt for welly[1] three months?' the old man said, with an affectation of bewildered simplicity.

Happily inspired for once, Willie made no answer, but put the question: 'Will you take it?'

'Ay! Us'll tak' it,' said Tellwright, 'though it is but a promise.' He was well pleased.

Young Price's face showed his relief. It was now evident that he had been passing through an ordeal. Anna guessed that perhaps everything had depended on the acceptance by Tellwright of that bill. Had he refused it, Prices, she thought, might have come to sudden disaster. She felt glad and disburdened for the moment; but immediately it occurred to her that her father would not rest satisfied for long; a few weeks, and he would give another turn to the screw.

The Tellwrights were destined to have other visitors that afternoon. Agnes, coming from school, was accompanied by a lady. Anna, who was setting the tea-table, saw a double shadow pass the window, and heard voices. She ran into the kitchen, and found Mrs. Sutton seated on a chair, breathing quickly.

'You'll excuse me coming in so unceremoniously, Anna,' she said, after having kissed her heartily. 'But Agnes said that she always came in by the back way, so I came that way too. Now I'm resting a minute. I've had to walk to-day. Our horse has gone lame.'

This kind heart radiated a heavenly goodwill, even in the most ordinary phrases. Anna began to expand at once.

'Now do come into the parlour,' she said, 'and let me make you comfortable.'

'Just a minute, my dear,' Mrs. Sutton begged, fanning herself with her handkerchief, 'Agnes's legs are so long.'

'Oh, Mrs. Sutton,' Agnes protested, laughing, 'how can you? I could scarcely keep up with you!'

'Well, my dear, I never could walk slowly. I'm one of them that go till they drop. It's very silly.' She smiled, and the two girls smiled happily in return.

'Agnes,' said the housewife, 'set another cup and saucer and plate.' Agnes threw down her hat and satchel of books, eager to show hospitality.

'It still keeps very warm,' Anna remarked, as Mrs. Sutton was silent.

'It's beautifully cool here,' said Mrs. Sutton. 'I see you've got your kitchen like a new pin, Anna, if you'll excuse me saying so. Henry was very enthusiastic about this kitchen the other night, at our house.'

'What! Mr. Mynors?' Anna reddened to the eyes.

'Yes, my dear; and he's a very particular young man, you know.'

The kettle conveniently boiled at that moment, and Anna went to the range to make the tea.

'Tea is all ready, Mrs. Sutton,' she said at length. 'I'm sure you could do with a cup.'

'That I could,' said Mrs. Sutton. 'It's what I've come for.'

'We have tea at four. Father will be glad to see you.' The clock struck, and they went into the parlour, Anna carrying the tea-pot and the hot-water jug. Agnes had preceded them. The old man was sitting expectant in his chair.

'Well, Mr. Tellwright,' said the visitor, 'you see I've called to see you, and to beg a cup of tea. I overtook Agnes coming home from school—overtook her, mind—me, at my age!' Ephraim rose slowly and shook hands.

'You're welcome,' he said curtly, but with a kindliness that amazed Anna. She was unaware that in past days he had known Mrs. Sutton as a young and charming girl, a vision that had stirred poetic ideas in hundreds of prosaic breasts, Tellwright's included. There was scarcely a middle-aged male Wesleyan in Bursley and Hanbridge who had not a peculiar regard for Mrs. Sutton, and who did not think that he alone truly appreciated her.

'What an' you bin tiring yourself with this afternoon?' he asked, when they had begun tea, and Mrs. Sutton had refused a second piece of bread-and-butter.

'What have I been doing? I've been seeing to some inside repairs to the superintendent's house. Be thankful you aren't a circuit-steward's wife, Anna.'

'Why, does she have to see to the repairs of the minister's house?' Anna asked, surprised.

'I should just think she does. She has to stand between the minister's wife and the funds of the society. And Mrs. Reginald Banks has been used to the very best of everything. She's just a bit exacting, though I must say she's willing enough to spend her own money too. She wants a new boiler in the scullery now, and I'm sure her boiler is a great deal better than ours. But we must try to please her. She isn't used to us rough folks and our ways. Mr. Banks said to me this afternoon that he tried always to shield her from the worries of this world.' She smiled almost imperceptibly.

There was a ring at the bell, and Agnes, much perturbed by the august arrival, let in Mr. Banks himself.

'Shall I enter, my little dear?' said Mr. Banks. 'Your father, your sister, in?'

'It ne'er rains but it pours,' said Tellwright, who had caught the minister's voice.

'Speak of angels——' said Mrs. Sutton, laughing quietly.

The minister came grandly into the parlour. 'Ah! How do you do, brother Tellwright, and you, Miss Tellwright? Mrs. Sutton, we two seem happily fated to meet this afternoon. Don't let me disturb you, I beg—I cannot stay. My time is very limited. I wish I could call oftener, brother Tellwright; but really the new *régime* leaves no time for pastoral visits. I was saying to my wife only this morning that I haven't had a free afternoon for a month.' He accepted a cup of tea.

'Us'n have a tea-party this afternoon,' said Tellwright *quasi*-privately to Mrs. Sutton.

'And now,' the minister resumed, 'I've come to beg. The special fund, you know, Mr. Tellwright, to clear off the debt on the new school-buildings. I referred to it from the pulpit last Sabbath. It's not in my province to go round begging, but someone must do it.'

'Well, for me, I'm beforehand with you, Mr. Banks,' said Mrs. Sutton, 'for it's on that very errand I've called to see Mr. Tellwright this afternoon. His name is on my list.'

'Ah! Then I leave our brother to your superior persuasions.'

'Come, Mr. Tellwright,' said Mrs. Sutton, 'you're between two fires, and you'll get no mercy. What will you give?'

The miser foresaw a probable discomfiture, and sought for some means of escape.

'What are others giving?' he asked.

'My husband is giving fifty pounds, and you could buy him up, lock, stock, and barrel.'

'Nay, nay!' said Tellwright, aghast at this sum. He had underrated the importance of the Building Fund.

'And I,' said the parson solemnly, 'I have but fifty pounds in the world, but I am giving twenty to this fund.'

'Then you're giving too much,' said Tellwright with quick brusqueness. 'You canna' afford it.'

'The Lord will provide,' said the parson.

'Happen He will, happen not. It's as well you've gotten a rich wife, Mr. Banks.'

The parson's dignity was obviously wounded, and Anna wondered timidly what would occur next. Mrs. Sutton interposed. 'Come now, Mr. Tellwright,' she said again, 'to the point: what will you give?'

'I'll think it over and let you hear,' said Ephraim.

'Oh, no! That won't do at all, will it, Mr. Banks? I, at any rate, am not going away without a definite promise. As an old and good Wesleyan, of course you will feel it your duty to be generous with us.'

'You used to be a pillar of the Hanbridge circuit—was it not so?' said Mr. Banks to the miser, recovering himself.

'So they used to say,' Tellwright replied grimly. 'That was because I cleared 'em of debt in ten years. But they've slipped into th' ditch again sin' I left 'em.'

'But if I am right, you do not meet[2] with us,' the minister pursued imperturbably.

'No.'

'My own class is at three on Saturdays,' said the minister. 'I should be glad to see you.'

'I tell you what I'll do,' said the miser to Mrs. Sutton. 'Titus Price is a big man at th' Sunday-school. I'll give as much as he gives to th' school buildings. That's fair.'

'Do you know what Mr. Price is giving?' Mrs. Sutton asked the minister.

'I saw Mr. Price yesterday. He is giving twenty-five pounds.'

'Very well, that's a bargain,' said Mrs. Sutton, who had succeeded beyond her expectations.

Ephraim was the dupe of his own scheming. He had made sure that Price's contribution would be a small one. This ostentatious munificence on the part of the beggared Titus filled him with secret anger. He determined to demand more rent at a very early date.

'I'll put you down for twenty-five pounds as a first subscription,' said the minister, taking out a pocket-book. Perhaps you will give Mrs. Sutton or myself the cheque to-day?'

'Has Mr. Price paid?' the miser asked, warily.

'Not yet.'

'Then come to me when he has.' Ephraim perceived the way of escape.

When the minister was gone, as Mrs. Sutton seemed in no hurry to depart, Anna and Agnes cleared the table.

'I've just been telling your father, Anna,' said Mrs. Sutton, when Anna returned to the room, 'that Mr. Sutton and myself and Beatrice are going to the Isle of Man soon for a fortnight or so, and we should very much like you to come with us.'

Anna's heart began to beat violently, though she knew there was no hope for her. This, then, doubtless, was the main object of Mrs. Sutton's visit! 'Oh! But I couldn't, really!' said Anna, scarcely aware what she did say.

'Why not?' asked Mrs. Sutton.

'Well—the house.'

'The house? Agnes could see to what little housekeeping your father would want. The schools will break up next week.'

'What do these young folks want holidays for?' Tellwright inquired with philosophic gruffness. 'I never had one. And what's more, I wouldn't thank ye for one. I'll pig on at Bursley. When ye've gotten a roof of your own, where's the sense o' going elsewhere and pigging?'

'But we really want Anna to go,' Mrs. Sutton went on. 'Beatrice is very anxious about it. Beatrice is very short of suitable friends.'

'I should na' ha' thought it,' said Tellwright. 'Her seems to know everyone.'

'But she is,' Mrs. Sutton insisted.

'I think as you'd better leave Anna out this year,' said the miser stubbornly.

Anna wished profoundly that Mrs. Sutton would abandon the futile attempt. Then she perceived that the visitor was signalling to her to leave the room. Anna obeyed, going into the kitchen to give an eye to Agnes, who was washing up.

'It's all right,' said Mrs. Sutton contentedly, when Anna returned to the parlour. 'Your father has consented to your going with us. It is very kind of him, for I'm sure he'll miss you.'

Anna sat down, limp, speechless. She could not believe the news.

'You are awfully good,' she said to Mrs. Sutton in the lobby, as the latter was leaving the house. 'I'm ever so grateful—you can't think.' And she threw her arms round Mrs. Sutton's neck.

Agnes ran up to say good-bye.

Mrs. Sutton kissed the child. 'Agnes will be the little housekeeper, eh?' The little housekeeper was almost as pleased at the prospect of housekeeping as if she too had been going to the Isle of Man. 'You'll both be at the school-treat next Tuesday,' suppose,' Mrs. Sutton said, holding Agnes by the hand. Agnes glanced at her sister in inquiry.

'I don't know,' Anna replied. 'We shall see.'

The truth was, that not caring to ask her father for the money for the tickets, she had given no thought to the school-treat.

'Did I tell you that Henry Mynors will most likely come with us to the Isle of Man?' said Mrs. Sutton from the gate.

Anna retired to her bedroom to savour an astounding happiness in quietude. At supper the miser was in a mood not unbenevolent. She expected a reaction the next morning, but Ephraim, strange to say, remained innocuous. She ventured to ask him for the money for the treat tickets, two shillings. He made no immediate reply. Half an hour afterwards, he ejaculated: 'What i' th' name o' fortune dost thee want wi' school-treats?'

'It's Agnes,' she answered; 'of course Agnes can't go alone.'

In the end he threw down a florin. He became perilous for the rest of the day, but the florin was an indisputable fact in Anna's pocket.

The school-treat was held in a twelve-acre field near Sneyd, the seat of a marquis, and a Saturday afternoon resort very popular in the Five Towns. The children were formed at noon on Duck Bank into a procession, which marched to the railway station to the singing of 'Shall we gather at the river?' Thence a special train carried them, in seething compartments, excited and strident, to Sneyd, where there had been two sharp showers in the morning, the procession was reformed along a country road, and the vacillating sky threatened more rain; but because the sun had shone dazzlingly at eleven o'clock all the women and girls, too easily tempted by the glory of the moment, blossomed forth in pale blouses and parasols. The chattering crowd, bright and defenceless as flowers, made at Sneyd a picture at once gay and pathetic. It had rained there at half-past twelve; the roads were wet; and among the two hundred and fifty children and thirty teachers there were less than a score umbrellas. The excursion was theoretically in charge of Titus Price, the Senior Superintendent, but this dignitary had failed to arrive on Duck Bank, and Mynors had taken his place. In the train Anna heard that some one had seen Mr. Price, wearing a large grey wide-awake, leap into the guard's van at the very instant of departure. He had not been at school on the previous Sunday, and Anna was somewhat perturbed at the prospect of meeting the man who had defined her letter to him as unique in the whole of his business career. She caught a glimpse of the grey wideawake on the platform at Sneyd, and steered her own scholars so as to avoid its vicinity. But on the march to the field Titus reviewed the procession, and she was obliged to meet his eyes and return his salutation. The look of the man was a shock to her. He seemed thinner, nervous, restless, preoccupied, and terribly careworn; except the new brilliant hat, all his summer clothes were soiled and shabby. It was as though he had forced himself, out of regard for appearances, to attend the fête, but had left his thoughts in Edward Street. His uneasy and hollow cheerfulness was painful to watch. Anna realised the intensity of the crisis through which Mr. Price was passing. She perceived in a single glance, more clearly than she could have done after a hundred interviews with the young and unresponsible William—however distressing these might be—that Titus must for weeks have been engaged in a truly frightful struggle. His face was a proof of the tragic sincerity of William's appeals to herself and to her father. That Price should have contrived to pay seventy pounds of rent in a little more than a month seemed to her, imperfectly acquainted alike with Ephraim's ruthless compulsions and with the financial jugglery often practised by hard-pressed debtors, to be an almost miraculous effort after honesty. Her conscience smote her for conniving at which she now saw to be a persecution. She felt as sorry for Titus as she had felt for his son. The obese man, with his reputation in rags about him, was acutely wistful in her eyes, as a child might have been.

A carriage rolled by, raising the dust in places where the strong sun had already dried the road. It was Mr. Sutton's landau, driven by Barrett. Beatrice, in white, sat solitary amid cushions, while two large hampers occupied most of the coachman's box. The carriage seemed to move with lordly ease and rapidity, and the teachers, already weary and fretted by the endless pranks of the children, bitterly envied the enthroned maid who nodded and smiled to them with such charming condescension. It was a social triumph for Beatrice. She disappeared ahead like a goddess in a cloud, and scarcely a woman who saw her from the humble level of the roadway but would have married a satyr to be able to do as Beatrice did. Later, when the field was reached, and the children bursting through the gate had spread like a flood over the daisied grass, the landau was to be seen drawn up near the refreshment tent; Barrett was unpacking the hampers, which contained delicate creamy confectionery for the teachers' tea; Beatrice explained that these were her mother's gift, and that she had driven down in order to preserve the fragile pasties from the risks of a railway journey. Gratitude became vocal, and Beatrice's success was perfected.

Then the more conscientious teachers set themselves seriously to the task of amusing the smaller children, and the smaller children consented to be amused according to the recipes appointed by long custom for school-treats. Many round-games, which invariably comprised singing or kissing, being thus annually resuscitated by elderly people from the deeps of memory, were preserved for a posterity which otherwise would never have known them. Among these was Bobby-Bingo. For twenty-five years Titus Price had played at Bobby-Bingo with the infant classes at the school-treat, and this year he was bound by the expectations of all to continue the practice. Another diversion which he always took care to organise was the three-legged race for boys. Also, he usually joined in the tut-ball, a quaint game which owes its surprising longevity to the fact that it is equally proper for both sexes. Within half an hour the treat was in full career; football, cricket, rounders, tick, leap-frog, prison-bars, and round-games, transformed the field into a vast arena of complicated struggles and emulations. All were occupied, except a few of the women and older girls, who strolled languidly about in the *rôle* of spectators. The sun shone generously on scores of vivid and frail toilettes, and parasols made slowly-moving hemispheres of glowing colour against the rich green of the grass. All around were yellow cornfields, and meadows where cows of a burnished brown indolently meditated upon the phenomena of a school-treat. Every hedge and ditch and gate and stile was in that ideal condition of plenary correctness which denotes that a great landowner is exhibiting the beauties of scientific farming for the behoof of his villagers. The sky, of an intense blue, was a sea in which large white clouds sailed gently but capriciously; on the northern horizon a low range of smoke marked the sinister region of the Five Towns.

'Will you come and help with the bags and cups?' Henry Mynors asked Anna. She was standing by herself, watching Agnes at play with some other girls. Mynors had evidently walked across to her from the refreshment tent, which was at the opposite extremity of the field. In her eyes he was once more the exemplar of style. His suit of grey flannel, his white straw hat, became him to admiration. He stood at ease with his hands in his coat-pockets, and smiled contentedly.

'After all,' he said, 'the tea is the principal thing, and, although it wants two hours to tea-time yet, it's as well to be beforehand.'

'I should like something to do,' Anna replied.

'How are you?' he said familiarly, after this abrupt opening, and then shook hands. They traversed the field together, with many deviations to avoid trespassing upon areas of play.

The flapping refreshment tent seemed to be full of piles of baskets and piles of bags and piles of cups, which the contractor had brought in a waggon. Some teachers were already beginning to put the paper bags into the baskets; each bag contained bread-and-butter, currant cake, an Eccles-cake, and a Bath-bun. At the far end of the tent Beatrice Sutton was arranging her dainties on a small trestle-table.

'Come along quick, Anna,' she exclaimed, 'and taste my tarts, and tell me what you think of them. I do hope the good people will enjoy them.' And then, turning to Mynors, 'Hello! Are you seeing after the bags and things? I thought that was always Willie Price's favourite job!'

'So it is,' said Mynors. 'But, unfortunately, he isn't here to-day.'

'How's that, pray? I never knew him miss a school-treat before.'

'Mr. Price told me they couldn't both be away from the works just now. Very busy, I suppose.'

'Well, William would have been more use than his father, anyhow.'

'Hush, hush!' Mynors murmured with a subdued laugh.

Beatrice was in one of her 'downright' moods, as she herself called them.

Mynors's arrangements for the prompt distribution of tea at the appointed hour were very minute, and involved a considerable amount of back bending and manual labour. But, though they were enlivened by frequent intervals of gossip, and by excursions into the field to observe this and that amusing sight, all was finished half an hour before time.

'I will go and warn Mr. Price,' said Mynors. 'He is quite capable of forgetting the clock.' Mynors left the tent, and proceeded to the scene of an athletic meeting, at which Titus Price, in shirt-sleeves, was distributing prizes of sixpences and pennies. The famous three-legged race had just been run. Anna followed at a saunter, and shortly afterwards Beatrice overtook her.

'The great Titus looks better than he did when he came on the field,' Beatrice remarked. And indeed the superintendent had put on quite a merry appearance—flushed, excited, and jocular in his elephantine way—it seemed as if he had not a care in the world. The boys crowded appreciatively round him. But this was his last hour of joy.

'Why! Willie Price *is* here,' Anna exclaimed, perceiving William in the fringe of the crowd. The lanky fellow stood hesitatingly, his left hand busy with his moustache.

'So he is,' said Beatrice. 'I wonder what that means.'

Titus had not observed the newcomer, but Henry Mynors saw William, and exchanged a few words with him. Then Mr. Mynors advanced into the crowd and spoke to Mr. Price, who glanced quickly round at his son. The girls, at a distance of forty yards, could discern the swift change in the man's demeanour. In a second he had reverted to the deplorable Titus of three hours ago. He elbowed his way roughly to William, getting into his coat as he went. The pair talked, William glanced at his watch, and in another moment they were leaving the field. Henry Mynors had to finish the prize distribution. So much Anna and Beatrice plainly saw. Others, too, had not been blind to this sudden and dramatic departure. It aroused universal comment among the teachers.

'Something must be wrong at Price's works,' Beatrice said, 'and Willie has had to fetch his papa.' This was the conclusion of all the gossips. Beatrice added: 'Dad has mentioned Price's several times lately, now I think of it.'

Anna grew extremely self-conscious and uncomfortable. She felt as though all were saying of her: 'There goes the oppressor of the poor!' She was fairly sure, however, that her father was not responsible for this particular incident. There must, then, be other implacable creditors. She had been thoroughly enjoying the afternoon, but now her pleasure ceased.

The treat ended disastrously. In the middle of the children's meal, while yet the enormous double-handled tea-cans were being carried up and down the thirsty rows, and the boys were causing their bags to explode with appalling detonations, it began to rain sharply. The fickle sun withdrew his splendour from the toilettes, and was seen no more for a week afterwards. 'It's come at last,' ejaculated Mynors, who had watched the sky with anxiety for an hour previously. He mobilised the children and ranked them under a row of elms. The teachers, running to the tent for their own tea, said to one another that the shower could only be a brief one. The wish was father to the thought, for they were a little ashamed to be under cover while their charges precariously sheltered beneath dripping trees—yet there was nothing else to be done; the men took turns in the rain to keep the children in their places. The sky was completely overcast. 'It's set in for a wet evening, and so we may as well make the best of it,' Beatrice said grimly, and she sent the landau home empty. She was right. A forlorn and disgusted snake of a procession crawled through puddles to the station. The platform resounded with sneezes. None but a dressmaker could have discovered a silver lining to the black and all-pervading cloud which had ruined so many dozens of fair costumes. Anna, melancholy and taciturn, exerted herself to minimise the discomfort of her scholars. A word from Mynors would have been balm to her; but Mynors, the general of a routed army, was parleying by telephone with the traffic-manager of the railway for the expediting of the special train.

CHAPTER X

THE ISLE

About this time Anna was not seeing very much of Henry Mynors. At twenty a man is rash in love, and again, perhaps, at fifty; a man of middle-age enamoured of a young girl is capable of sublime follies. But the man of thirty who loves for the first time is usually the embodiment of cautious discretion. He does not fall in love with a violent descent, but rather lets himself gently down, continually testing the rope. His social value, especially if he have achieved worldly success, is at its highest, and, without conceit, he is aware of it. He has lost many illusions concerning women; he has seen more than one friend wrecked in the sea of foolish marriage; he knows the joys of a bachelor's freedom, without having wearied of them; he perceives risks where the youth perceives only ecstasy, and the oldster only a blissful release from solitude. Instead of searching, he is sought for; accordingly he is selfish and exacting. All these things, combine to tranquillize passion at thirty. Mynors was in love with Anna, and his love had its ardent moments; but in the main it was a temperate affection, an affection that walked circumspectly, with its eyes open, careful of its dignity, too proud to seem in a hurry; if, by impulse, it chanced now and then to leap forward, the involuntary movement was mastered and checked. Mynors called at Manor Terrace once a week, never on the same day of the week, nor without discussing business with the miser. Occasionally he accompanied Anna from school or chapel. Such methods were precisely to Anna's taste. Like him, she loved prudence and decorum, preferring to make haste slowly. Since the Revival, they had only once talked together intimately; on that sole occasion Henry had suggested to her that she might care to join Mrs. Sutton's class, which met on Monday nights; she accepted the hint with pleasure, and found a well of spiritual inspiration in Mrs. Sutton's modest and simple yet fervent homilies. Mynors was not guilty of blowing both hot and cold. She was sure of him. She waited calmly for events, existing, as her habit was, in the future.

The future, then, meant the Isle of Man. Anna dreamed of an enchanted isle and hours of unimaginable rapture. For a whole week after Mrs. Sutton had won Ephraim's consent, her vision never stooped to practical details. Then Beatrice called to see her; it was the morning after the treat, and Anna was brushing her muddy frock; she wore a large white apron, and held a cloth-brush in her hand as she opened the door.

'You're busy?' said Beatrice.

'Yes,' said Anna, 'but come in. Come into the kitchen—do you mind?'

Beatrice was covered from neck to heel with a long mackintosh, which she threw off when entering the kitchen.

'Anyone else in the house?' she asked.

'No,' said Anna, smiling, as Beatrice seated herself, with a sigh of content, on the table.

'Well, let's talk, then.' Beatrice drew from her pocket the indispensable chocolates and offered them to Anna. 'I say, wasn't last night perfectly awful? Henry got wet through in the end, and mother made him stop at our house, as he was at the trouble to take me home. Did you see him go down this morning?'

'No; why?' said Anna, stiffly.

'Oh—no reason. Only I thought perhaps you did. I simply can't tell you how glad I am that you're coming with us to the Isle of Man; we shall have rare fun. We go every year, you know—to Port Erin, a lovely little fishing village. All the fishermen know us there. Last year Henry hired a yacht for the fortnight, and we all went mackerel-fishing, every day; except sometimes Pa. Now and then Pa had a tendency to go fiddling in caves and things. I do hope it will be fine weather again by then, don't you?'

'I'm looking forward to it, I can tell you,' Anna said. 'What day are we supposed to start?'

'Saturday week.'

'So soon?' Anna was surprised at the proximity of the event.

535

'Yes; and quite late enough, too. We should start earlier, only the Dad always makes out he can't. Men always pretend to be so frightfully busy, and I believe it's all put on.' Beatrice continued to chat about the holiday, and then of a sudden she asked: 'What are you going to wear?'

'Wear!' Anna repeated; and added, with hesitation: 'I suppose one will want some new clothes?'

'Well, just a few! Now let me advise you. Take a blue serge skirt. Sea-water won't harm it, and if it's dark enough it will look well to any mortal blouse. Secondly, you can't have too many blouses; they're always useful at the seaside. Plain straw-hats are my tip. A coat for nights, and thick boots. There! Of course no one ever *dresses* at Port Erin. It isn't like Llandudno, and all that sort of thing. You don't have to meet your young man on the pier, because there isn't a pier.'

There was a pause. Anna did not know what to say. At length she ventured: 'I'm not much for clothes, as I dare say you've noticed.'

'I think you always look nice, my dear,' Beatrice responded. Nothing was said as to Anna's wealth, no reference made as to the discrepancy between that and the style of her garments. By a fiction, there was supposed to be no discrepancy.

'Do you make your own frocks?' Beatrice asked, later.

'Yes.'

'Do you know I thought you did. But they do you great credit. There's few people can make a plain frock look decent.'

This conversation brought Anna with a shock to the level of earth. She perceived—only too well—a point which she had not hitherto fairly faced in her idyllic meditations: that her father was still a factor in the case. Since Mrs. Sutton's visit both Anna and the miser avoided the subject of the holiday. 'You can't have too many blouses.' Did Beatrice, then, have blouses by the dozen? A coat, a serge skirt, straw hats (how many?)—the catalogue frightened her. She began to suspect that she would not be able to go to the Isle of Man.

'About me going with Suttons to the Isle of Man?' she accosted her father, in the afternoon, outwardly calm, but with secret trembling.

'Well?' he exclaimed savagely.

'I shall want some money—a little.' She would have given much not to have added that 'little,' but it came out of itself.

'It's a waste o' time and money—that's what I call it. I can't think why Suttons asked ye. Ye aren't ill, are ye?' His savagery changed to sullenness.

'No, father; but as it's arranged, I suppose I shall have to go.'

'Well, I'm none so set up with the idea mysen.'

'Shan't you be all right with Agnes?'

'Oh, yes. *I* shall be all right. *I* don't want much. *I*'ve no fads and fal-lals. How long art going to be away?'

'I don't know. Didn't Mrs. Sutton tell you? You arranged it.'

'That I didna'. Her said nowt to me.'

'Well, anyhow I shall want some clothes.'

'What for? Art naked?'

'I must have some money.' Her voice shook, She was getting near tears.

'Well, thou's gotten thy own money, hast na'?'

'All I want is that you shall let me have some of my own money. There's forty odd pounds now in the bank.'

'Oh!' he repeated, sneering, 'all ye want is as I shall let thee have some o' thy own money. And there's forty odd pound i' the bank. Oh!'

'Will you give me my cheque-book out of the bureau? And I'll draw a cheque; I know how to.' She had conquered the instinct to cry, and unwillingly her tones became somewhat peremptory. Ephraim seized the chance.

'No, I won't give ye the cheque-book out o' th' bureau,' he said flatly. 'And I'll thank ye for less sauce.'

That finished the episode. Proudly she took an oath with herself not to re-open the question, and resolved to write a note to Mrs. Sutton saying that on consideration she found it impossible to go to the Isle of Man.

The next morning there came to Anna a letter from the secretary of a limited company enclosing a post-office order for ten pounds. Some weeks previously her father had discovered an error of that amount in the deduction of income-tax from the dividend paid by this company, and had instructed Anna to demand the sum. She had obeyed, and then forgotten the affair. Here was the answer. Desperate at the thought of missing the holiday, she cashed the order, bought and made her clothes in secret, and then, two days before the arranged date of departure told her father what she had done. He was enraged; but since his anger was too illogical to be rendered effectively coherent in words, he had the wit to keep silence. With bitterness Anna reflected that she owed her holiday to the merest accident—for if the remittance had arrived a little earlier or a little later, or in the form of a cheque, she could not have utilised it.

It was an incredible day, the following Saturday, a warm and benign day of earliest autumn. The Suttons, in a hired cab, called for Anna at half-past eight, on the way to the main line station at Shawport. Anna's tin box was flung on to the roof of the cab amid the trunks and portmanteaux already there.

'Why should not Agnes ride with us to the station?' Beatrice suggested.

'Nay, nay; there's no room,' said Tellwright, who stood at the door, impelled by an unacknowledged awe of Mrs. Sutton thus to give official sanction to Anna's departure.

'Yes, yes,' Mrs. Sutton exclaimed. 'Let the little thing come, Mr. Tellwright.'

Agnes, far more excited than any of the rest, seized her straw hat, and slipping the elastic under her small chin, sprang into the cab, and found a haven between Mr. Sutton's short, fat legs. The driver drew his whip smartly across the aged neck of the cream mare. They were off. What a rumbling, jolting, delicious journey, down the first hill, up Duck Bank, through the market-place, and down the steep declivity of Oldcastle Street! Silent and shy, Agnes smiled ecstatically at the others. Anna answered remarks in a dream. She was conscious only of present happiness and happy expectation. All bitterness had disappeared. At least thirty thousand Bursley folk were not going to the Isle of Man that day—their preoccupied and cheerless faces swam in a continuous stream past the cab window—and Anna sympathised with every unit of them. Her spirit overflowed with universal compassion. What haste and exquisite confusion at the station! The train was signalled, and the porter, crossing the line with the luggage, ran his truck perilously under the very buffers of the incoming engine. Mynors was awaiting them, admirably attired as a tourist. He had got the tickets, and secured a private compartment in the through-coach for Liverpool; and he found time to arrange with the cabman to drive Agnes home on the box-seat. Certainly there was none like Mynors. From the footboard of the carriage Anna bent down to kiss Agnes. The child had been laughing and chattering. Suddenly, as Anna's lips touched hers, she burst into tears, sobbed passionately as though overtaken by some terrible and unexpected misfortune. Tears stood also in Anna's eyes. The sisters had never been parted before.

'Poor little thing!' Mrs. Sutton murmured; and Beatrice told her father to give Agnes a shilling to buy chocolates at Stevenson's in St. Luke's Square, that being the best shop. The shilling fell between the footboard and the platform. A scream from Beatrice! The attendant porter promised to rescue the shilling in due course. The engine whistled, the silver-mounted guard asserted his authority, Mynors leaped in, and amid laughter and tears the brief and unique joy of Anna's life began.

In a moment, so it seemed, the train was thundering through the mile of solid rock which ends at Lime Street Station, Liverpool. Thenceforward, till she fell asleep that night, Anna existed in a state of blissful bewilderment, stupefied by an overdose of novel and wondrous sensations. They lunched in amazing magnificence at the Bear's Paw, and then walked through the crowded and prodigious streets to Prince's landing-stage. The luggage had disappeared by some mysterious agency—Mynors said that they would find it safe at Douglas; but Anna could not banish the fear that her tin box had gone for ever.

The great, wavy river, churned by thousands of keels; the monstrous steamer—the 'Mona's Isle'—whose side rose like solid wall out of the water; the vistas of its decks; its vast saloons, story under story, solid and palatial (could all this float?); its high bridge; its hawsers as thick as trees; its funnels like sloping towers; the multitudes of passengers; the whistles, hoots, cries; the far-stretching panorama of wharves and docks; the squat ferry-craft carrying horses and carts, and no one looking twice at the feat—it was all too much, too astonishing, too lovely. She had not guessed at this.

'They call Liverpool the slum of Europe,' said Mynors.

'How can you!' she exclaimed, shocked.

Beatrice, seeing her radiant and rapt face, walked to and fro with Anna, proud of the effect produced on her friend's inexperience by these sights. One might have thought that Beatrice had built Liverpool and created its trade by her own efforts.

Suddenly the landing-stage and all the people on it moved away bodily from the ship; there was green water between; a tremor like that of an earthquake ran along the deck; handkerchiefs were waved. The voyage had

537

commenced. Mynors found chairs for all the Suttons, and tucked them up on the lee-side of a deck-house; but Anna did not stir. They passed New Brighton, Seaforth, and the Crosby and Formby lightships.

'Come and view the ship,' said Mynors, at her side. 'Suppose we go round and inspect things a bit?'

'It's a very big one, isn't it?' she asked.

'Pretty big,' he said; 'of course not as big as the Atlantic liners—I wonder we didn't meet one in the river—but still pretty big. Three hundred and twenty feet over all. I sailed on her last year on her maiden voyage. She was packed, and the weather very bad.'

'Will it be rough to-day?' Anna inquired timidly.

'Not if it keeps like this,' he laughed. 'You don't feel queer, do you?'

'Oh, no. It's as firm as a house. No one could be ill with this?'

'Couldn't they?' he exclaimed. 'Beatrice could be.'

They descended into the ship, and he explained all its internal economy, with a knowledge that seemed to her encyclopædic. They stayed a long time watching the engines, so Titanic, ruthless, and deliberate; even the smell of the oil was pleasant to Anna. When they came on deck again the ship was at sea. For the first time Anna beheld the ocean. A strong breeze blew from prow to stern, yet the sea was absolutely calm, the unruffled mirror of effulgent sunlight. The steamer moved alone on the waters, exultantly, leaving behind it an endless track of white froth in the green, and the shadow of its smoke. The sun, the salt breeze, the living water, the proud gaiety of the ship, produced a feeling of intense, inexplicable joy, a profound satisfaction with the present, and a negligence of past and future. To exist was enough, then. As Anna and Henry leaned over the starboard quarter and watched the torrent of foam rush madly and ceaselessly from under the paddle-box to be swallowed up in the white wake, the spectacle of the wild torrent almost hypnotised them, destroying thought and reason, and all sense of their relation to other things. With difficulty Anna raised her eyes, and perceived the dim receding line of the Lancashire coast.

'Shall we get quite out of sight of land?' she asked.

'Yes, for a little while, about half an hour or so. Just as much out of sight of land as if we were in the middle of the Atlantic.'

'I can scarcely believe it.'

'Believe what?'

'Oh! The idea of that—of being out of sight of land—nothing but sea.'

When at last it occurred to them to reconnoitre the Suttons, they found all three still in their deck-chairs, enwrapped and languid. Mr. Sutton and Beatrice were apparently dozing. This part of the deck was occupied by somnolent, basking figures.

'Don't wake them,' Mrs. Sutton enjoined, whispering out of her hood. Anna glanced curiously at Beatrice's yellow face.

'Go away, do,' Beatrice exclaimed, opening her eyes and shutting them again, wearily.

So they went away, and discovered two empty deck-chairs on the fore-deck. Anna was innocently vain of her immunity from malaise. Mynors appeared to appoint himself little errands about the deck, returning frequently to his chair. 'Look over there. Can you see anything?'

Anna ran to the rail, with the infantile idea of getting nearer, and Mynors followed, laughing. What looked like a small slate-coloured cloud lay on the horizon.

'I seem to see something,' she said.

'That is the Isle of Man.'

By insensible gradations the contours of the land grew clearer in the afternoon haze.

'How far are we off now?'

'Perhaps twenty miles.'

Twenty miles of uninterrupted flatness, and the ship steadily invading that separating solitude, yard by yard, furlong by furlong! The conception awed her. There, a morsel in the waste of the deep, a speck under the infinite sunlight, lay the island, mysterious, enticing, enchanted, a glinting jewel on, the sea's bosom, a remote entity fraught with strange secrets. It was all unspeakable.

'Anna, you have covered yourself with glory,' said Mrs. Sutton, when they were in the diminutive and absurd train which by breathless plunges annihilates the sixteen miles between Douglas and Port Erin in sixty-five minutes.

'Have I?' she answered. 'How?'

'By not being ill.'

'That's always the beginner's luck,' said Beatrice, pale and dishevelled. They all relapsed into the silence of fatigue. It was growing dusk when the train stopped at the tiny terminus. The station was a hive of bustling activity, the arrival of this train being the daily event at that end of the world. Mynors and the Suttons were greeted familiarly by several sailors, and one of these, Tom Kelly, a tall, middle-aged man, with grey beard, small grey eyes, a wrinkled skin of red mahogany, and an enormous fist, was introduced to Anna. He raised his cap, and shook hands. She was touched by the sad, kind look on his face, the melancholy impress of the sea. Then they drove to their lodging, and here again the party was welcomed as being old and tried friends. A fire was burning in the parlour. Throwing herself down in front of it, Mrs. Sutton breathed, 'At last! Oh, for some tea.' Through the window, Anna had a glimpse of a deeply indented bay at the foot of cliffs below them, with a bold headland to the right. Fishing vessels with flat red sails seemed to hang undecided just outside the bay. From cottage chimneys beneath the road blue smoke softly ascended.

All went early to bed, for the weariness of Mr. and Mrs. Sutton seemed to communicate itself to the three young people, who might otherwise have gone forth into the village in search of adventures. Anna and Beatrice shared a room. Each inspected the other's clothes, and Beatrice made Anna try on the new serge skirt. Through the thin wall came the sound of Mr. and Mrs. Sutton talking, a high voice, then a bass reply, in continual alternation. Beatrice said that these two always discussed the day's doings in such manner. In a few moments Beatrice was snoring; she had the subdued but steady and serious snore characteristic of some muscular men. Anna felt no inclination to sleep. She lived again hour by hour through the day, and beneath Beatrice's snore her ear caught the undertone of the sea.

The next morning was as lovely as the last. It was Sunday, and every activity of the village was stilled. Sea and land were equally folded in a sunlit calm. During breakfast—a meal abundant in fresh herrings, fresh eggs and fresh rolls, eaten with the window wide open—Anna was puzzled by the singular amenity of her friends to one another and to her. They were as polite as though they had been strangers; they chatted amiably, were full of goodwill, and as anxious to give happiness as to enjoy it. She thought at first, so unusual was it to her as a feature of domestic privacy, that this demeanour was affected, or at any rate a somewhat exaggerated punctilio due to her presence; but she soon came to see that she was mistaken. After breakfast Mr. Sutton suggested that they should attend the Wesleyan Chapel on the hill leading to the Chasms. Here they met the sailors of the night before, arrayed now in marvellous blue Melton coats with velveteen collars. Tom Kelly walked back with them to the beach, and showed them the yacht 'Fay' which Mynors had arranged to hire for mackerel-fishing; it lay on the sands speckless in new white paint. All the afternoon they dozed on the cliffs, doing nothing whatever, for this Sunday was tacitly regarded, not as part of the holiday, but as a preparation for the holiday; all felt that the holiday, with its proper exertions and appointed delights, would really begin on Monday morning.

'Let us go for a walk,' said Mynors, after tea, to Beatrice and Anna. They stood at the gate of the lodging-house. The old people were resting within.

'You two go,' Beatrice replied, looking at Anna. 'You know I hate walking, Henry. I'll stop with mother and dad.'

Throughout the day Anna had been conscious of the fact that all the Suttons showed a tendency, slight but perceptible, to treat Henry and herself as a pair desirous of opportunities for being alone together. She did not like it. She flushed under the passing glance with which Beatrice accompanied the words: 'You two go.' Nevertheless, when Mynors placidly remarked: 'Very well,' and his eyes sought hers for a consent, she could not refuse it. One part of her nature would have preferred to find an excuse for staying at home; but another, and a stronger, part insisted on seizing this offered joy.

They walked straight up out of the village toward the high coast-range which stretches peak after peak from Port Erin to Peel. The stony and devious lanes wound about the bleak hillside, passing here and there small, solitary cottages of whitewashed stone, with children, fowls, and dogs at the doors, all embowered in huge fuchsia trees. Presently they had surmounted the limit of habitation and were on the naked flank of Bradda, following a narrow track which crept upwards amid short mossy turf of the most vivid green. Nothing seemed to flourish on this exposed height except bracken, sheep, and boulders that, from a distance, resembled sheep; there was no tree, scarcely a shrub; the immense contours, stark, grim, and unrelieved, rose in melancholy and defiant majesty against the sky: the hand of man could coax no harvest from these smooth but obdurate slopes; they had never relented, and they would never relent. The spirit was braced by the thought that here, to the furthest eternity of civilisation more and more intricate, simple and strong souls would always find solace and repose.

Mynors bore to the left for a while, striking across the moor in the direction of the sea. Then he said:

'Look down, now.'

The little bay lay like an oblong swimming-bath five hundred feet below them. The surface of the water was like glass; the strand, with its phalanx of boats drawn up in Sabbath tidiness, glittered like marble in the living light, and over this marble black dots moved slowly two and fro; behind the boats were the houses—dolls' houses—each with a curling wisp of smoke; further away the railway and the high road ran out in a black and white line to Port St. Mary; the sea, a pale grey, encompassed all; the southern sky had a faint sapphire tinge, rising to delicate azure. The sight of this haven at rest, shut in by the restful sea and by great moveless hills, a calm within a calm, aroused profound emotion.

'It's lovely,' said Anna, as they stood gazing. Tears came to her eyes and hung there. She wondered that scenery should cause tears, felt ashamed, and turned her face so that Mynors should not see. But he had seen.

'Shall we go on to the top?' he suggested, and they set their faces northwards to climb still higher. At length they stood on the rocky summit of Bradda, seven hundred feet from the sea. The Hill of the Night Watch lifted above them to the north, but on east, south, and west, the prospect was bounded only by the ocean. The coast-line was revealed for thirty miles, from Peel to Castletown. Far to the east was Castletown Bay, large, shallow and inhospitable, its floor strewn with a thousand unseen wrecks; the lighthouse at Scarlet Point flashed dimly in the dusk; thence the beach curved nearer in an immense arc, without a sign of life, to the little cove of Port St. Mary, and jutted out again into a tongue of land at the end of which lay the Calf of Man with its single white cottage and cart-track. The dangerous Calf Sound, where the vexed tide is forced to run nine hours one way and three the other, seemed like a grey ribbon, and the Chicken Rock like a tiny pencil on a vast slate. Port Erin was hidden under their feet. They looked westward. The darkening sky was a labyrinth of purple and crimson scarves drawn pellucid, as though by the finger of God, across a sheet of pure saffron. These decadent tints of the sunset faded in every direction to the same soft azure which filled the south, and one star twinkled in the illimitable field. Thirty miles off, on the horizon, could be discerned the Mourne Mountains of Ireland.

'See!' Mynors exclaimed, touching her arm.

The huge disc of the moon was rising in the east, and as this mild lamp passed up the sky, the sense of universal quiescence increased. Lovely, Anna had said. It was the loveliest sight her eyes had ever beheld, a panorama of pure beauty transcending all imagined visions. It overwhelmed her, thrilled her to the heart, this revelation of the loveliness of the world. Her thoughts went back to Hanbridge and Bursley and her life there; and all the remembered scenes, bathed in the glow of a new ideal, seemed to lose their pain. It was as if she had never been really unhappy, as if there was no real unhappiness on the whole earth. She perceived that the monotony, the austerity, the melancholy of her existence had been sweet and beautiful of its kind, and she recalled, with a sort of rapture, hours of companionship with the beloved Agnes, when her father was equable and pacific. Nothing was ugly nor mean. Beauty was everywhere, in everything.

In silence they began to descend, perforce walking quickly because of the steep gradient. At the first cottage they saw a little girl in a mob-cap playing with two kittens.

'How like Agnes!' Mynors said.

'Yes. I was just thinking so,' Anna answered.

'I thought of her up on the hill,' he continued. 'She will miss you, won't she?'

'I know she cried herself to sleep last night. You mightn't guess it, but she is extremely sensitive.'

'Not guess it? Why not? I am sure she is. Do you know—I am very fond of your sister. She's a simply delightful child. And there's a lot in her, too. She's so quick and bright, and somehow like a little woman.'

'She's exactly like a woman sometimes,' Anna agreed. 'Sometimes I fancy she's a great deal older than I am.'

'Older than any of us,' he corrected.

'I'm glad you like her,' Anna said, content. 'She thinks all the world of you.' And she added: 'My word, wouldn't she be vexed if she knew I had told you that!'

This appreciation of Agnes brought them into closer intimacy, and they talked the more easily of other things.

'It will freeze to-night,' Mynors said; and then, suddenly looking at her in the twilight: 'You are feeling chill.'

'Oh, no!' she protested.

'But you are. Put this muffler round your neck.' He took a muffler from his pocket.

'Oh, no, really! You will need it yourself.' She drew a little away from him, as if to avoid the muffler. 'Please take it.'

She did so, and thanked him, tying it loosely and untidily round her throat. That feeling of the untidiness of the muffler, of its being something strange to her skin, something with the rough virtue of masculinity, which no one could detect in the gloom, was in itself pleasant.

'I wager Mrs. Sutton has a good fire burning when we get in,' he said.

She thought with joyous anticipation of the warm, bright, sitting-room, the supper, and the vivacious good-natured conversation. Though the walk was nearly at an end, other delights were in store. Of the holiday, thirteen complete days yet remained, each to be as happy as the one now closing. It was an age! At last they entered the human cosiness of the village. As they walked up the steps of their lodging and he opened the door for her, she quickly drew off the muffler and returned it to him with a word of thanks.

On Monday morning, when Beatrice and Anna came downstairs, they found the breakfast odorously cooling on the table, and nobody in the room.

'Where are they all, I wonder. Any letters?' Beatrice said.

'There's your mother, out on the front—and Mr. Mynors too.'

Beatrice threw up the window, and called: 'Come along, Henry; come along, mother. Everything's going cold.'

'Is it?' Mynors cheerfully replied. 'Come out here, both of you, and begin the day properly with a dose of ozone.'

'I loathe cold bacon,' said Beatrice, glancing at the table, and they went out into the road, where Mrs. Sutton kissed them with as much fervour as if they had arrived from a long journey.

'You look pale, Anna,' she remarked.

'Do I?' said Anna, 'I don't feel pale.'

'It's that long walk last night,' Beatrice put in. 'Henry always goes too far.'

'I don't——' Anna began; but at that moment Mr. Sutton, lumbering and ponderous, joined the party.

'Henry,' he said, without greeting anyone, 'hast noticed those half-finished houses down the road yonder by the "Falcon"? I've been having a chat with Kelly, and he tells me the fellow that was building them has gone bankrupt, and they're at a stand-still. The Receiver wants to sell 'em. In fact Kelly says they're going cheap. I believe they'd be a good spec.'

'Eh, dear!' Mrs. Sutton interrupted him. 'Father, I wish you would leave your specs alone when you're on your holiday.'

'Now, missis!' he affectionately protested, and continued: 'They're fairly well built, seemingly, and the rafters are on the roof. Anna,' he turned to her quickly, as if counting on her sympathy, 'you must come with me and look at 'em after breakfast. Happen they might suit your father—or you. I know your father's fond of a good spec.'

She assented with a ready smile. This was the beginning of a fancy which the Alderman always afterwards showed for Anna.

After breakfast Mrs. Sutton, Beatrice, and Anna arranged to go shopping:

'Father—brass,' Mrs. Sutton ejaculated in two monosyllables to her husband.

'How much will content ye?' he asked mildly.

'Give me five or ten pounds to go on with.'

He opened the left-hand front pocket of his trousers—a pocket which fastened with a button; and leaning back in his chair drew out a fat purse, and passed it to his wife with a preoccupied air. She helped herself, and then Beatrice intercepted the purse and lightened it of half a sovereign.

'Pocket-money,' Beatrice said; 'I'm ruined.'

The Alderman's eyes requested Anna to observe how he was robbed. At last the purse was safely buttoned up again.

Mrs. Sutton's purchases of food at the three principal shops of the village seemed startlingly profuse to Anna, but gradually she became accustomed to the scale, and to the amazing habit of always buying the very best of everything, from beefsteak to grapes. Anna calculated that the housekeeping could not cost less than six pounds a week for the five. At Manor Terrace three people existed on a pound. With her half-sovereign Beatrice bought a belt and a pair of sand-shoes, and some cigarettes for Henry. Mrs. Sutton bought a pipe with a nickel cap, such as is used by sailors. When they returned to the house, Mr. Sutton and Henry were smoking on the front. All five walked in a row down to the harbour, the Alderman giving an arm each to Beatrice and Anna. Near the 'Falcon' the procession had to be stopped in order to view the unfinished houses. Tom Kelly had a cabin partly excavated out of the rock behind the little quay. Here they found him entangled amid nets, sails, and oars. All crowded into the cabin and shook hands with its owner, who remarked with severity on their pallid faces, and insisted that a change of complexion must be brought about. Mynors offered him his tobacco-pouch, but on seeing the light colour of the tobacco he shook his head and refused it, at the same time taking from within his jersey a lump of something that resembled leather.

'Give him this, Henry,' Mrs. Sutton whispered, handing Mynors the pipe which she had bought.

'Mrs. Sutton wishes you to accept this,' said Mynors.

'Eh, thank ye,' he exclaimed. 'There's a leddy that knows my taste.' He cut some shreds from his plug with a clasp-knife and charged and lighted the pipe, filling the cabin with asphyxiating fumes.

'I don't know how you can smoke such horrid, nasty stuff,' said Beatrice, coughing.

He laughed condescendingly at Beatrice's petulant manner. 'That stuff of Henry's is boy's tobacco,' he said shortly.

It was decided that they should go fishing in the 'Fay.' There was a light southerly breeze, a cloudy sky, and smooth water. Under charge of young Tom Kelly, a sheepish lad of sixteen, with his father's smile, they all got into an inconceivably small dinghy, loading it down till it was almost awash. Old Tom himself helped Anna to embark, told her where to tread, and forced her gently into a seat at the stern. No one else seemed to be disturbed, but Anna was in a state of desperate fear. She had never committed herself to a boat before, and the little waves spat up against the sides in a most alarming way as young Tom jerked the dinghy along with the short sculls. She went white, and clung in silence fiercely to the gunwale. In a few moments they were tied up to the 'Fay,' which seemed very big and safe in comparison with the dinghy. They clambered on board, and in the deep well of the two-ton yacht Anna contrived to collect her wits. She was reassured by the painted legend in the well, 'Licensed to carry eleven.' Young Tom and Henry busied themselves with ropes, and suddenly a huge white sail began to ascend the mast; it flapped like thunder in the gentle breeze. Tom pulled up the anchor, curling the chain round and round on the forward deck, and then Anna noticed that, although the wind was scarcely perceptible, they were gliding quickly past the embankment. Henry was at the tiller. The next minute Tom had set the jib, and by this time the 'Fay' was approaching the breakwater at a great pace. There was no rolling or pitching, but simply a smooth, swift progression over the calm surface. Anna thought it the ideal of locomotion. As soon as they were beyond the breakwater and the sails caught the breeze from the Sound, the 'Fay' lay over as if shot, and a little column of green water flung itself on the lee coaming of the well. Anna screamed as she saw the water and felt the angle of the floor suddenly change, but when everyone laughed, she laughed too. Henry, noticing the whiteness of her knuckles as she gripped the coaming, explained the disconcerting phenomena. Anna tried to be at ease, but she was not. She could not for a long time dismiss the suspicion that all these people were foolishly blind to a peril which she alone had the sagacity to perceive.

They cruised about while Tom prepared the lines. The short waves chopped cheerfully against the carvel sides of the yacht; the clouds were breaking at a hundred points; the sea grew lighter in tone; gaiety was in the air; no one could possibly be indisposed in that innocuous weather. At length the lines were ready, but Tom said the yacht was making at least a knot too much for serious fishing, so Henry took a reef in the mainsail, showing Anna how to tie the short strings. The Alderman, lying on the fore-deck, was placidly smoking. The lines were thrown out astern, and Mrs. Sutton and Beatrice each took one. But they had no success; young Tom said it was because the sun had appeared.

'Caught anything?' Mr. Sutton inquired at intervals. After a time he said:

'Suppose Anna and I have a try?'

It was agreed.

'What must I do?' asked Anna, brave now.

'You just hold the line—so. And if you feel a little jerk-jerk, that's a mackerel.' These were the instructions of Beatrice. Anna was becoming excited. She had not held the line ten seconds before she cried out:

'I've got one.'

'Nonsense,' said Beatrice. 'Everyone thinks at first that the motion of the waves against the line is a fish.'

'Well,' said Henry, giving the tiller to young Tom. 'Let's haul in and see, anyway.' Before doing so he held the line for a moment, testing it, and winked at Anna. While Anna and Henry were hauling in, the Alderman, dropping his pipe, began also to haul in his own line with great fury.

'Got one, father?' Mrs. Sutton asked.

'Ay!'

Both lines came in together, and on each was a pounder. Anna saw her fish gleam and flash like silver in the clear water as it neared the surface. Henry held the line short, letting the mackerel plunge and jerk, and then seized and unhooked the catch.

'How cruel!' Anna cried, startled at the nearness of the two fish as they sprang about in an old sugar box at her feet. Young Tom laughed loud at her exclamation. 'They cairn't feel, miss,' he sniggered. Anna wondered that a mouth so soft and kind could utter such heartless words.

In an hour the united efforts of the party had caught nine mackerel; it was not a multitude, but the sun, in perfecting the weather, had spoilt the sport. Anna had ceased to commiserate the captured fish. She was obliged, however, to avert her head when Tom cut some skin from the side of one of the mackerel to provide fresh bait; this device seemed to her the extremest refinement of cruelty. Beatrice grew ominously silent and inert, and Mrs. Sutton glanced first at her daughter and then at her husband; the latter nodded.

'We'd happen better be getting back, Henry,' said the Alderman.

The 'Fay' swept home like a bird. They were at the quay, and Kelly was dragging them one by one from the black dinghy on to what the Alderman called *terra-firma*. Henry had the fish on a string.

'How many did ye catch, Miss Tellwright?' Kelly asked benevolently.

'I caught four,' Anna replied. Never before had she felt so proud, elated, and boisterous. Never had the blood so wildly danced in her veins. She looked at her short blue skirt which showed three inches of ankle, put forward her brown-shod foot like a vain coquette, and darted a covert look at Henry. When he caught it she laughed instead of blushing.

'Ye're doing well,' Tom Kelly approved. 'Ye'll make a famous mackerel-fisher.'

Five of the mackerel were given to young Tom, the other four preceded a fowl in the menu of dinner. They were called Anna's mackerel, and all the diners agreed that better mackerel had never been lured out of the Irish Sea.

In the afternoon the Alderman and his wife slept as usual, Mr. Sutton with a bandanna handkerchief over his face. The rest went out immediately; the invitation of the sun and the sea was far too persuasive to be resisted.

'I'm going to paint,' said Beatrice, with a resolute mien. 'I want to paint Bradda Head frightfully. I tried last year, but I got it too dark, somehow. I've improved since then. What are you going to do?'

'We'll come and watch you,' said Henry.

'Oh, no, you won't. At least you won't; you're such a critic. Anna can if she likes.'

'What! And me be left all afternoon by myself?'

'Well, suppose you go with him, Anna, just to keep him from being bored?'

Anna hesitated. Once more she had the uncomfortable suspicion that Mynors and herself were being manoeuvred.

'Look here,' said Mynors to Beatrice. 'Have you decided absolutely to paint?'

'Absolutely.' The finality of the answer seemed to have a touch of resentment.

'Then'—he turned to Anna—'let's go and get that dinghy and row about the bay. Eh?'

She could offer no rational objection, and they were soon putting off from the jetty, impelled seaward by a mighty push from Kelly's arm. It was very hot. Mynors wore white flannels. He removed his coat, and turned up his sleeves, showing thick, hairy arms. He sculled in a manner almost dramatic, and the dinghy shot about like a water-spider on a brook. Anna had nothing to do except to sit still and enjoy. Everything was drowned in dazzling sunlight, and both Henry and Anna could feel the process of tanning on their faces. The bay shimmered with a million diamond points; it was impossible to keep the eyes open without frowning, and soon Anna could see the beads of sweat on Henry's crimson brow.

'Warm?' she said. This was the first word of conversation. He merely smiled in reply. Presently they were at the other side of the bay, in a cave whose sandy and rock-strewn floor trembled clear under a fathom of blue water. They landed on a jutting rock; Henry pushed his straw hat back, and wiped his forehead. 'Glorious! glorious!' he exclaimed. 'Do you swim? No? You should get Beatrice to teach you. I swam out here this morning at seven o'clock. It was chilly enough then. Oh! I forgot, I told you at breakfast.'

She could see him in the translucent water, swimming with long, powerful strokes. Dozens of boats were moving lazily in the bay, each with a cargo of parasols.

'There's a good deal of the sunshade afloat,' he remarked. 'Why haven't you got one? You'll get as brown as Tom Kelly.'

'That's what I want,' she said.

'Look at yourself in the water there,' he said, pointing to a little pool left on the top of the rock by the tide. She did so, and saw two fiery cheeks, and a forehead divided by a horizontal line into halves of white and crimson; the tip of the nose was blistered.

'Isn't it disgraceful?' he suggested.

'Why,' she exclaimed, 'they'll never know me when I get home!'

It was in such wise that they talked, endlessly exchanging trifles of comment. Anna thought to herself: 'Is this love-making?' It could not be, she decided; but she infinitely preferred it so. She was content. She wished for nothing better than this apparently frivolous and irresponsible dalliance. She felt that if Mynors were to be tender, sentimental, and serious, she would become wretchedly self-conscious.

They re-embarked, and, skirting the shore, gradually came round to the beach. Up above them, on the cliffs, they could discern the industrious figure of Beatrice, with easel and sketching-umbrella, and all the panoply of the earnest amateur.

'Do you sketch?' she asked him.

'Not I!' he said scornfully.

'Don't you believe in that sort of thing, then?'

'It's all right for professional artists,' he said; 'people who can paint. But—— Well, I suppose it's harmless for the amateurs—finds them something to do.'

'I wish I could paint, anyway,' she retorted.

'I'm glad you can't,' he insisted.

When they got back to the cliffs, towards tea-time, Beatrice was still painting, but in a new spot. She seemed entirely absorbed in her work, and did not hear their approach.

'Let's creep up and surprise her,' Mynors whispered. 'You go first, and put your hands over her eyes.'

'Oh!' exclaimed Beatrice, blindfolded; 'how horrid you are, Henry! I know who it is—I know who it is.'

'You just don't, then,' said Henry, now in front of her. Anna removed her hands.

'Well, you told her to do it, I'm sure of that. And I was getting on so splendidly! I shan't do another stroke now.'

'That's right,' said Henry. 'You've wasted quite enough time as it is.'

Beatrice pouted. She was evidently annoyed with both of them. She looked from one to the other, jealous of their mutual understanding and agreement. Mr. and Mrs. Sutton issued from the house, and the five stood chatting till tea was ready; but the shadow remained on Beatrice's face. Mynors made several attempts to laugh it away, and at dusk these two went for a stroll to Port St. Mary. They returned in a state of deep intimacy. During supper Beatrice was consciously and elaborately angelic, and there was that in her voice and eyes, when sometimes she addressed Mynors, which almost persuaded Anna that he might once have loved his cousin. At night, in the bedroom, Anna imagined that she could detect in Beatrice's attitude the least shade of condescension. She felt hurt, and despised herself for feeling hurt.

So the days passed, without much variety, for the Suttons were not addicted to excursions. Anna was profoundly happy; she had forgotten care. She agreed to every suggestion for amusement; each moment had its pleasure, and this pleasure was quite independent of the thing done; it sprang from all activities and idlenesses. She was at special pains to fraternise with Mr. Sutton. He made an interesting companion, full of facts about strata, outcrops, and breaks, his sole weakness being the habit of quoting extremely sentimental scraps of verse when walking by the sea-shore. He frankly enjoyed Anna's attention to him, and took pride in her society. Mrs. Sutton, that simple heart, devoted herself to the attainment of absolute quiescence. She had come for a rest, and she achieved her purpose. Her kindliness became for the time passive instead of active. Beatrice was a changing quantity in the domestic equation. Plainly her parents had spoiled their only child, and she had frequent fits of petulance, particularly with Mynors; but her energy and spirits atoned well for these. As for Mynors, he behaved exactly as on the first Monday. He spent many hours alone with Anna— (Beatrice appeared to insist on leaving them together, even while showing a faint resentment at the loneliness thus entailed on herself)—and his attitude was such as Anna, ignorant of the ways of brothers, deemed a brother might adopt.

On the second Monday an incident occurred. In the afternoon Mr. Sutton had asked Beatrice to go with him to Port St. Mary, and she had refused on the plea that the light was of a suitable grey for painting. Mr. Sutton had slipped off alone, unseen by Anna and Henry, who had meant to accompany him in place of Beatrice. Before tea, while Anna, Beatrice and Henry were awaiting the meal in the parlour, Mynors referred to the matter.

'I hope you've done some decent work this afternoon,' he said to Beatrice.

'I haven't,' she replied shortly; 'I haven't done a stroke.'

'But you said you were going to paint hard!'

'Well, I didn't.'

'Then why couldn't you have gone to Port St. Mary, instead of breaking your fond father's heart by a refusal?'

'He didn't want me, really.'

Anna interjected: 'I think he did, Bee.'

'You, know you're very self-willed, not to say selfish,' Mynors said.

'No, I'm not,' Beatrice protested seriously. 'Am I, Anna?'

'Well——' Anna tried to think of a diplomatic pronouncement. Beatrice took offence at the hesitation.

'Oh! You two are bound to agree, of course. You're as thick as thieves.'

She gazed steadily out of the window, and there was a silence. Mynors' lip curled.

'Oh! There's the loveliest yacht just coming into the bay,' Beatrice cried suddenly, in a tone of affected enthusiasm. 'I'm going out to sketch it.' She snatched up her hat and sketching-block, and ran hastily from the room. The other two saw her sitting on the grass, sharpening a pencil. The yacht, a large and luxurious craft, had evidently come to anchor for the night.

Mrs. Sutton arrived from her bedroom, and then Mr. Sutton also came in. Tea was served. Mynors called to Beatrice through the window and received no reply. Then Mrs. Sutton summoned her.

'Go on with your tea,' Beatrice shouted, without turning her head. 'Don't wait for me. I'm bound to finish this now.'

'Fetch her, Anna dear,' said Mrs. Sutton after another interval. Anna rose to obey, half-fearful.

'Aren't you coming in, Bee?' She stood by the sketcher's side, and observed nothing but a few meaningless lines on the block.

'Didn't you hear what I said to mother?'

Anna retired in discomfiture.

Tea was finished. They went out, but kept at a discreet distance from the artist, who continued to use her pencil until dusk had fallen. Then they returned to the sitting-room, where a fire had been lighted, and Beatrice at length followed. As the others sat in a circle round the fire, Beatrice, who occupied the sofa in solitude, gave a shiver.

'Beatrice, you've taken cold,' said her mother, sitting out there like that.'

'Oh, nonsense, mother—what a fidget you are!'

'A fidget I certainly am not, my darling, and that you know very well. As you've had no tea, you shall have some gruel at once, and go to bed and get warm.'

'Oh no, mother!' But Mrs. Sutton was resolved, and in half an hour she had taken Beatrice to bed and tucked her up.

When Anna went to the bedroom Beatrice was awake.

'Can't you sleep?' she inquired kindly.

'No,' said Beatrice, in a feeble voice, 'I'm restless, somehow.'

'I wonder if it's influenza,' said Mrs. Sutton, on the following morning, when she learnt from Anna that Beatrice had had a bad night, and would take breakfast in bed. She carried the invalid's food upstairs herself. 'I hope it isn't influenza,' she said later. 'The girl is very hot.'

'You haven't a clinical thermometer?' Mynors suggested.

'Go, see if you can buy one at the little chemist's,' she replied eagerly. In a few minutes he came back with the instrument.

'She's at over a hundred,' Mrs. Sutton reported, having used the thermometer. 'What do you say, father? Shall we send for a doctor? I'm not so set up with doctors as a general rule,' she added, as if in defence, to Anna. 'I brought Beatrice through measles and scarlet fever without a doctor—we never used to think of having a doctor in those days for ordinary ailments; but influenza—that's different. Eh, I dread it; you never know how it will end. And poor Beatrice had such a bad attack last Martinmas.'

'If you like, I'll run for a doctor now,' said Mynors.

'Let be till to-morrow,' the Alderman decided. 'We'll see how she goes on. Happen it's nothing but a cold.'

'Yes,' assented Mrs. Sutton; 'it's no use crying out before you're hurt.'

Anna was struck by the placidity with which they covered their apprehension. Towards noon, Beatrice, who said that she felt better, insisted on rising. A fire was lighted at once in the parlour, and she sat in front of it till tea-time, when she was obliged to go to bed again. On the Wednesday morning, after a night which had been almost sleepless for both girls, her temperature stood at 103°, and Henry fetched the doctor, who pronounced it a case of influenza, severe, demanding very careful treatment. Instantly the normal movement of the household was changed. The sickroom became a mysterious centre round which everything revolved, and the parlour, without the alteration of a single chair, took on a deserted, forlorn appearance. Meals were eaten like the passover, with loins girded for any sudden summons. Mrs. Sutton and Anna, as nurses, grew important in the eyes of the men, who instinctively effaced themselves, existing only like messenger-boys whose business it is to await a call. Yet there was no alarm, flurry, nor excitement. In the evening the doctor returned. The patient's temperature had not fallen. It was part of the treatment that a medicine should be administered every two hours with absolute regularity, and Mrs. Sutton said that she should sit up through the night.

'I shall do that,' said Anna.

'Nay, I won't hear of it,' Mrs. Sutton replied, smiling.

But the three men (the doctor had remained to chat in the parlour), recognising Anna's capacity and reliability, and perhaps impressed also by her business-like appearance as, arrayed in a white apron, she stood with firm lips before them, gave a unanimous decision against Mrs. Sutton.

'We'st have you ill next, lass,' said the Alderman to his wife; 'and that'll never do.'

'Well,' Mrs. Sutton surrendered, 'if I can leave her to anyone, it's Anna.'

Mynors smiled appreciatively.

On the Thursday morning there was still no sign of recovery. The temperature was 104°, and the patient slightly delirious. Anna left the sickroom at eight o'clock to preside at breakfast, and Mrs. Sutton took her place.

'You look tired, my dear,' said the Alderman affectionately.

'I feel perfectly well,' she replied with cheerfulness.

'And you aren't afraid of catching it?' Mynors asked.

'Afraid?' she said; 'there's no fear of me catching it.'

'How do you know?'

'I know, that's all. I'm never ill.'

'That's the right way to keep well,' the Alderman remarked.

The quiet admiration of these two men was very pleasant to her. She felt that she had established herself for ever in their esteem. After breakfast, in obedience to them, she slept for several hours on Mrs. Sutton's bed. In the afternoon Beatrice was worse. The doctor called, and found her temperature at 105.9.

'This can't last,' he remarked briefly.

'Well, Doctor,' Mr. Sutton said, 'it's i' your hands.'

'Nay,' Mrs. Sutton murmured with a smile, 'I've left it with God. It's with Him.'

This was the first and only word of religion, except grace at table, that Anna heard from the Suttons during her stay in the Isle of Man. She had feared lest vocal piety might form a prominent feature of their daily life, but her fear had proved groundless. She, too, from reason rather than instinct, had tried to pray for Beatrice's recovery. She had, however, found much more satisfaction in the activity of nursing.

Again that night she sat up, and on the Friday morning Beatrice was better. At noon all immediate danger was past; the patient slept; her temperature was almost correct. Anna went to bed in the afternoon and slept soundly till supper-time, when she awoke very hungry. For the first time in three days Beatrice could be left alone. The other four had supper together, cheerful and relieved after the tension.

'She'll be as right as a trivet in a few days,' said the Alderman.

'A few weeks,' said Mrs. Sutton.

'Of course,' said Mynors, 'you'll stay on here, now?'

'We shall stay until Beatrice is quite fit to travel,' Mr. Sutton answered. 'I might have to run over to th' Five Towns for a day or two middle of next week, but I can come back immediately.'

'Well, I must go tomorrow,' Mynors sighed.

'Surely you can stay over Sunday, Henry?'

'No; I've no one to take my place at school.'

'And I must go to-morrow, too,' said Anna suddenly.

'Fiddle-de-dee, Anna!' the Alderman protested.

'I must,' she insisted. 'Father will expect me. You know I came for a fortnight. Besides, there's Agnes.'

'Agnes will be all right.'

'I must go.' They saw that she was fixed.

'Won't a short walk do you good?' Mynors suggested to her, with singular gravity, after supper. 'You've not been outside for two days.'

She looked inquiringly at Mrs. Sutton.

'Yes, take her, Henry; she'll sleep better for it. Eh, Anna, but it's a shame to send you home with those rings round your eyes.'

She went upstairs for a jacket. Beatrice was awake. 'Anna,' she exclaimed in a weak voice, without any preface, 'I was awfully silly and cross the other afternoon, before all this business. Just now, when you came into the room, I was feeling quite ashamed.'

'Oh! Bee!' she answered, bending over her, 'what nonsense! Now go off to sleep at once.' She was very happy. Beatrice, victim of a temperament which had the childishness and the impulsiveness of the artist without his higher and sterner traits, sank back in facile content.

The night was still and very dark. When Anna and Mynors got outside they could distinguish neither the sky nor the sea; but the faint, restless murmur of the sea came up the cliffs. Only the lights of the houses disclosed the direction of the road.

'Suppose we go down to the jetty, and then along as far as the breakwater?' he said, and she concurred. 'Won't you take my muffler—again?' he added, pulling this ever-present article from his pocket.

'No, thanks,' she said, almost coldly, 'it's really quite warm.' She regarded the offer of the muffler as an indiscretion—his sole indiscretion during their acquaintance. As they walked down the hill to the shore she though how Beatrice's illness had sharply interrupted their relations. If she had come to the Isle of Man with a vague idea that he would possibly propose to her, the expectation was disappointed; but she felt no disappointment. She felt that events had lifted her to a higher plane than that of love-making. She was filled with the proud satisfaction of a duty accomplished. She did not seek to minimise to herself the fact that she had been of real value to her friends in the last few days, had probably saved Mrs. Sutton from illness, had certainly laid them all under an obligation. Their gratitude, unexpressed, but patent on each face, gave her infinite pleasure. She had won their respect by the manner in which she had risen to the height of an emergency that demanded more than devotion. She had proved, not merely to them but to herself, that she could be calm under stress, and could exert moral force when occasion needed. Such were the joyous and exultant reflections which passed through her brain—unnaturally active in the factitious wakefulness caused by excessive fatigue. She was in an extremely nervous and excitable condition—and never guessed it, fancying indeed that her emotions were exceptionally tranquil that night. She had not begun to realise the crisis through which she had just lived.

The uneven road to the ruined breakwater was quite deserted. Having reached the limit of the path, they stood side by side, solitary, silent, gazing at the black and gently heaving surface of the sea. The eye was foiled by the intense gloom; the ear could make nothing of the strange night-noises of the bay and the ocean beyond; but the imagination was stimulated by the appeal of all this mystery and darkness. Never had the water seemed so wonderful, terrible, and austere.

'We are going away to-morrow,' he said at length.

Anna started and shook with apprehension at the tremor in his voice. She had read that a woman was always well warned by her instincts when a man meant to propose to her. But here was the proposal imminent, and she had not suspected. In a flash of insight she perceived that the very event which had separated them for three days had also impelled the lover forward in his course. It was the thought of her vigils, her fortitude, her compassion, that had fanned the flame. She was not surprised, only made uncomfortable, when he took her hand.

'Anna,' he said, 'it's no use making a long story of it. I'm tremendously in love with you; you know I am.'

He stepped back, still holding her hand. She could say nothing.

'Well?' he ventured. 'Didn't you know?'

'I thought—I thought,' she murmured stupidly, 'I thought you liked me.'

'I can't tell you how I admire you. I'm not going to praise you to your face, but I simply never met anyone like you. From the very first moment I saw you, it was the same. It's something in your face, Anna—— Anna, will you be my wife?'

The actual question was put in a precise, polite, somewhat conventional tone. To Anna he was never more himself than at that moment.

She could not speak; she could not analyse her feelings; she could not even think. She was adrift. At last she stammered: 'We've only known each other——'

'Oh, dear,' he exclaimed masterfully, 'what does that matter? If it had been a dozen years instead of one, that would have made no difference.' She drew her hand timidly away, but he took it again. She felt that he dominated her and would decide for her. 'Say yes.'

'Yes,' she said.

547

She saw pictures of her career as his wife, and resolved that one of the first acts of her freedom should be to release Agnes from the more ignominious of her father's tyrannies.

They walked home almost in silence. She was engaged, then. Yet she experienced no new sensation. She felt as she had felt on the way down, except that she was sorely perturbed. There was no ineffable rapture, no ecstatic bliss. Suddenly the prospect of happiness swept over her like a flood.

At the gate she wished to make a request to him, but hesitated, because she could not bring herself to use his Christian name. It was proper for her to use his Christian name, however, and she would do so, or perish.

'Henry,' she said, 'don't tell anyone here.' He merely kissed her once more. She went straight upstairs.

CHAPTER XI

THE DOWNFALL

In order to catch the Liverpool steamer at Douglas it was necessary to leave Port Erin at half-past six in the morning. The freshness of the morning, and the smiles of the Alderman and his wife as they waved God-speed from the doorstep, filled Anna with a serene content which she certainly had not felt during the wakeful night. She forgot, then, the hours passed with her conscience in realising how serious and solemn a thing was this engagement, made in an instant on the previous evening. All that remained in her mind, as she and Henry walked quickly down the road, was the tonic sensation of high resolves to be a worthy wife. The duties, rather than the joys, of her condition, had lain nearest her heart until that moment of setting out, giving her an anxious and almost worried mien which at breakfast neither Henry nor the Suttons could quite understand. But now the idea of duty ceased for a time to be paramount, and she loosed herself to the pleasures of the day in store. The harbour was full of low wandering mists, through which the brown sails of the fishing-smacks played at hide-and-seek. High above them the round forms of immense clouds were still carrying the colours of sunrise. The gentle salt wind on the cheek was like the touch of a life-giver. It was impossible, on such a morning, not to exult in life, not to laugh childishly from irrational glee, not to dismiss the memory of grief and the apprehension of grief as morbid hallucinations. Mynor's face expressed the double happiness of present and anticipated pleasure. He had once again succeeded, he who had never failed; and the voyage back to England was for him a triumphal progress. Anna responded eagerly to his mood. The day was an ecstasy, a bright expanse unstained. To Anna in particular it was a unique day, marking the apogee of her existence. In the years that followed she could always return to it and say to herself: 'That day I was happy, foolishly, ignorantly, but utterly. And all that I have since learnt cannot alter it—I was happy.'

When they reached Shawport Station a cab was waiting for Anna. Unknown to her, Henry had ordered it by telegraph. This considerateness was of a piece, she thought, with his masterly conduct of the entire journey—on the steamer, at Liverpool, in the train; nothing that an experienced traveller could devise had been lacking to her comfort. She got into the cab alone, while Mynors, followed by a boy and his bag, walked to his rooms in Mount Street. It had been arranged, at Anna's wish, that he should not appear at Manor Terrace till supper-time. Ephraim opened for her the door of her home. It seemed to her that he was pleased.

'Well, father, here I am again, you see.'

'Ay, lass.' They shook hands, and she indicated to the cabman where to deposit her tin-box. She was glad and relieved to be back. Nothing had changed, except herself, and this absolute sameness was at once pleasant and pathetic to her.

'Where's Agnes?' she asked, smiling at her father. In the glow of arrival she had a vague notion that her relations with him had been permanently softened by absence.

'I see thou's gotten into th' habit o' flitting about in cabs,' he said, without answering her question.

'Well, father,' she said, smiling yet, 'there was the box. I couldn't carry the box.'

'I reckon thou couldst ha' hired a lad to carry it for sixpence.'

She did not reply. The cabman had gone to his vehicle.

'Art'na going to pay th' cabby?'

'I've paid him, father.'

'How much?'

She paused. 'Eighteen-pence, father.' It was a lie; she had paid two shillings.

She went eagerly into the kitchen, and then into the parlour, where tea was set for one. Agnes was not there. 'Her's upstairs,' Ephraim said, meeting Anna as she came into the lobby again. She ran softly upstairs, and into the bedroom. Agnes was replacing ornaments on the mantelpiece with mathematical exactitude; under her arm was a duster. The child turned, startled, and gave a little shriek.

'Eh, I didn't know you'd come. How early you are!'

They rushed towards each other, embraced, and kissed. Anna was overcome by the pathos of her sister's loneliness in that grim house for fourteen days, while she, the elder, had been absorbed in selfish gaiety. The pale face, large, melancholy eyes, and long, thin arms, were a silent accusation. She wondered that she could ever have brought herself to leave Agnes even for a day. Sitting down on the bed, she drew the child on her knee in a fury of love, and kissed her again, weeping. Agnes cried too, for sympathy.

'Oh, my dear, dear Anna, I'm so glad you've come back!' She dried her eyes, and in quite a different tone of voice asked: 'Has Mr. Mynors proposed to you?'

Anna could not avoid a blush at this simple and astounding query. She said: 'Yes.' It was the one word of which she was capable, under the circumstances. That was not the moment to tax Agnes with too much precocity and abruptness.

'You're engaged, then? Oh, Anna, does it feel nice? It must. I knew you would be!'

'How did you know, Agnes?'

'I mean I knew he would ask you, some time. All the girls at school knew too.'

'I hope you didn't talk about it,' said the elder sister.

'Oh, no! But they did; they were always talking about it.'

'You never told me that.'

'I—I didn't like to. Anna, shall I have to call him Henry now?'

'Yes, of course. When we're married he will be your brother-in-law.'

'Shall you be married soon, Anna?'

'Not for a very long time.'

'When you are—shall I keep house alone? I can, you know—— I shall never dare to call him Henry. But he's awfully nice; isn't he, Anna? Yes, when you are married, I shall keep house here, but I shall come to see you every day. Father will have to let me do that. Does father know you're engaged?'

'Not yet. And you mustn't say anything. Henry is coming for supper. And then father will be told.'

'Did he kiss you, Anna?'

'Who—father?'

'No, silly! Henry, of course—I mean when he'd asked you?'

'I think you are asking all the questions. Suppose I ask you some now. How have you managed with father? Has he been nice?'

'Some days—yes,' said Agnes, after thinking a moment. 'We have had some new cups and saucers up from Mr. Mynors works. And father has swept the kitchen chimney. And, oh Anna! I asked him to-day if I'd kept house well, and he said "Pretty well," and he gave me a penny. Look! It's the first money I've ever had, you know. I wanted you at nights, Anna—and all the time, too. I've been frightfully busy. I cleaned silvers all afternoon. Anna, I *have* tried—— And I've got some tea for you. I'll go down and make it. Now you mustn't come into the kitchen. I'll bring it to you in the parlour.'

'I had my tea at Crewe,' Anna was about to say, but refrained, in due course drinking the cup prepared by Agnes. She felt passionately sorry for Agnes, too young to feel the shadow which overhung her future. Anna would marry into freedom, but Agnes would remain the serf. Would Agnes marry? Could she? Would her father allow it? Anna had noticed that in families the youngest, petted in childhood, was often sacrificed in maturity. It was the last maid who must keep her maidenhood, and, vicariously filial, pay out of her own life the debt of all the rest.

'Mr. Mynors is coming up for supper to-night. He wants to see you;' Anna said to her father, as calmly as she could. The miser grunted. But at eight o'clock, the hour immutably fixed for supper, Henry had not arrived. The meal proceeded, of course, without him. To Anna his absence was unaccountable and disturbing, for none could be more punctilious than he in the matter of appointments. She expected him every moment, but he did not appear. Agnes, filled full of the great secret confided to her, was more openly impatient than her sister. Neither of them could talk, and a heavy silence fell upon the family group, a silence which her father, on that particular evening of Anna's return, resented.

'You dunna' tell us much,' he remarked, when the supper was finished.

She felt that the complaint was a just one. Even before supper, when nothing had occurred to preoccupy her, she had spoken little. There had seemed so much to tell—at Port Erin, and now there seemed nothing to tell. She ventured into a flaccid, perfunctory account of Beatrice's illness, of the fishing, of the unfinished houses which had caught the fancy of Mr. Sutton; she said the sea had been smooth, that they had had something to eat at Liverpool, that the train for Crewe was very prompt; and then she could think of no more. Silence fell again. The supper-things were cleared away and washed up. At a quarter-past nine, Agnes, vainly begging permission to stay up in order to see Mr. Mynors, was sent to bed, only partially comforted by a clothes-brush, long desired, which Anna had brought for her as a present from the Isle of Man.

'Shall you tell father yourself, now Henry hasn't come?' the child asked Anna, who had gone upstairs to unpack her box.

'Yes,' said Anna, briefly.

'I wonder what he'll say,' Agnes reflected, with that habit, always annoying to Anna, of meeting trouble half-way.

At a quarter to ten Anna ceased to expect Mynors, and finally braced herself to the ordeal of a solemn interview with her father, well knowing that she dared not leave him any longer in ignorance of her engagement. Already the old man was locking and bolting the door; he had wound up the kitchen clock. When he came back to the parlour to extinguish the gas she was standing by the mantelpiece.

'Father,' she began, 'I've something I must tell you.'

'Eh, what's that ye say?' his hand was on the gas-tap. He dropped it, examining her face curiously.

'Mr. Mynors has asked me to marry him; he asked me last night. We settled he should come up to-night to see you—I can't think why he hasn't. It must be something very unexpected and important, or he'd have come.' She trembled, her heart beat violently; but the words were out, and she thanked God.

'Asked ye to marry him, did he?' The miser gazed at her quizzically out of his small blue eyes.

'Yes, father.'

'And what didst say?'

'I said I would.'

'Oh! Thou saidst thou wouldst! I reckon it was for thatten as thou must go gadding off to seaside, eh?'

'Father, I never dreamt of such a thing when Suttons asked me to go. I do wish Henry'—the cost of that Christian name!—'had come. He quite meant to come to-night.' She could not help insisting on the propriety of Henry's intentions.

'Then I am for be consulted, eh?'

'Of course, father.'

'Ye've soon made it up, between ye.'

His tone was, at the best, brusque; but she breathed more easily, divining instantly from his manner that he meant to offer no violent objection to the engagement. She knew that only tact was needed now. The miser had, indeed, foreseen the possibility of this marriage for months past, and had long since decided in his own mind that Henry would make a satisfactory son-in-law. Ephraim had no social ambitions—with all his meanness, he was above them; he had nothing but contempt for rank, style, luxury, and 'the theory of what it is to be a lady and a gentleman.' Yet, by a curious contradiction, Henry's smartness of appearance—the smartness of an unrivalled commercial traveller—pleased him. He saw in Henry a young and sedate man of remarkable shrewdness, a man who had saved money, had made money for others, and was now making it for himself; a man who could be trusted absolutely to perform that feat of 'getting on'; a 'safe' and profoundly respectable man, at the same time audacious and imperturbable. He was well aware that Henry had really fallen in love with Anna, but nothing would have convinced him that Anna's money was not the primal cause of Henry's genuine passion for Anna's self.

'You like Henry, don't you, father?' Anna said. It was a failure in the desired tact, for Ephraim had never been known to admit that he liked anyone or anything. Such natures are capable of nothing more positive than toleration.

'He's a hard-headed chap, and he knows the value o' money. Ay! that he does; he knows which side his bread's buttered on.' A sinister emphasis marked the last sentence.

Instead of remaining silent, Anna, in her nervousness, committed another imprudence. 'What do you mean, father?' she asked, pretending that she thought it impossible he could mean what he obviously did mean.

'Thou knows what I'm at, lass. Dost think he isna' marrying thee for thy brass? Dost think as he canna' make a fine guess what thou'rt worth? But that wunna' bother thee as long as thou'st hooked a good-looking chap.'

'Father!'

'Ay! thou mayst bridle; but it's true. Dunna' tell me.'

Securely conscious of the perfect purity of Mynors' affection, she was not in the least hurt. She even thought that her father's attitude was not quite sincere, an attitude partially due to mere wilful churlishness. 'Henry has never even mentioned money to me,' she said mildly.

'Happen not; he isna' such a fool as that.' He paused, and continued: 'Thou'rt free to wed, for me. Lasses will do it, I reckon, and thee among th' rest.' She smiled, and on that smile he suddenly turned out the gas. Anna was glad that the colloquy had ended so well. Congratulations, endearments, loving regard for her welfare: she had not expected these things, and was in no wise grieved by their absence. Groping her way towards the lobby, she considered herself lucky, and only wished that nothing had happened to keep Mynors away. She wanted to tell him at once that her father had proved tractable.

The next morning, Tellwright, whose attendance at chapel was losing the strictness of its old regularity, announced that he should stay at home. Sunday's dinner was to be a cold repast, and so Anna and Agnes went to chapel. Anna's thoughts were wholly occupied with the prospect of seeing Mynors, and hearing the explanation of his absence on Saturday night.

'There he is!' Agnes exclaimed loudly, as they were approaching the chapel.

'Agnes,' said Anna, 'when will you learn to behave in the street?'

Mynors stood at the chapel-gates; he was evidently awaiting them. He looked grave, almost sad. He raised his hat and shook hands, with a particular friendliness for Agnes, who was speculating whether he would kiss Anna, as his betrothed, or herself, as being only a little girl, or both or neither of them. Her eyes already expressed a sort of ownership in him.

'I should like to speak to you a moment,' Henry said. 'Will you come into the school-yard?'

'Agnes, you had better go straight into chapel,' said Anna. It was an ignominious disaster to the child, but she obeyed.

'I didn't give you up last night till nearly ten o'clock,' Anna remarked as they passed into the school-yard. She was astonished to discover in herself an inclination to pout, to play the offended fair one, because Mynors had failed in his appointment. Contemptuously she crushed it.

'Have you heard about Mr. Price?' Mynors began.

'No. What about him? Has anything happened?'

'A very sad thing has happened. Yes——' He stopped, from emotion. 'Our superintendent has committed suicide!'

'Killed himself?' Anna gasped.

'He hanged himself yesterday afternoon at Edward Street, in the slip-house after the works were closed. Willie had gone home, but he came back, when his father didn't turn up for dinner, and found him. Mr. Price was quite dead. He ran in to my place to fetch me just as I was getting my tea. That was why I never came last night.'

Anna was speechless.

'I thought I would tell you myself,' Henry resumed. 'It's an awful thing for the Sunday-school, and the whole society, too. He, a prominent Wesleyan, a worker among us! An awful thing!' he repeated, dominated by the idea of the blow thus dealt to the Methodist connexion by the man now dead.

'Why did he do it?' Anna demanded, curtly.

Mynors shrugged his shoulders, and ejaculated: 'Business troubles, I suppose; it couldn't be anything else. At school this morning I simply announced that he was dead.' Henry's voice broke, but he added, after a pause: 'Young Price bore himself splendidly last night.'

Anna turned away in silence. 'I shall come up for tea, if I may,' Henry said, and then they parted, he to the singing-seat, she to the portico of the chapel. People were talking in groups on the broad steps and in the vestibule. All knew of the calamity, and had received from it a new interest in life. The town was aroused as if from a lethargy. Consternation and eager curiosity were on every face. Those who arrived in ignorance of the event were informed of it in impressive tones, and with intense satisfaction to the informer; nothing of equal importance had happened in the society for decades. Anna walked up the aisle to her pew, filled with one thought:

'We drove him to it, father and I.'

Her fear was that the miser had renewed his terrible insistence during the previous fortnight. She forgot that she had disliked the dead man, that he had always seemed to her mean, pietistic, and two-faced. She forgot that in pressing him for rent many months overdue she and her father had acted within their just rights—acted as Price himself would have acted in their place. She could think only of the strain, the agony, the despair that must have preceded the miserable tragedy. Old Price had atoned for all in one sublime sin, the sole deed that could lend dignity and repose to such a figure as his. Anna's feverish imagination reconstituted the scene in the slip-house: she saw it as something grand, accusing, and unanswerable; and she could not dismiss a feeling of acute remorse that she should have been engaged in pleasure at that very hour of death. Surely some instinct should have warned her that the hare which she had helped to hunt was at its last gasp!

Mr. Sargent, the newly-appointed second minister, was in the pulpit—a little, earnest bachelor, who emphasised every sentence with a continual tremor of the voice. 'Brethren,' he said, after the second hymn— and his tones vibrated with a singular effect through the half-empty building: 'Before I proceed to my sermon I have one word to say in reference to the awful event which is doubtless uppermost in the minds of all of you. It is not for us to judge the man who is now gone from us, ushered into the dread presence of his Maker with the crime of self-murder upon his soul. I say it is not for us to judge him. The ways of the Almighty are past finding out. Therefore at such a moment we may fitly humble ourselves before the Throne, and while prostrate there let us intercede for the poor young man who is left behind, bereft, and full of grief and shame. We will engage in silent prayer.' He lifted his hand, and closed his eyes, and the congregation leaned forward against the fronts of the pews. The appealing face of Willie presented itself vividly to Anna.

'Who is it?' Agnes asked, in a whisper of appalling distinctness. Anna frowned angrily, and gave no reply.

While the last hymn was being sung, Anna signed to Agnes that she wished to leave the chapel. Everyone would be aware that she was among Price's creditors, and she feared that if she stayed till the end of the service some chatterer might draw her into a distressing conversation. The sisters went out, and Agnes's burning curiosity was at length relieved.

'Mr. Price has hanged himself,' Anna said to her father when they reached home.

The miser looked through the window for a moment. 'I am na' surprised,' he said. 'Suicide's i' that blood. Titus's uncle 'Lijah tried to kill himself twice afore he died o' gravel. Us'n have to do summat wi' Edward Street at last.'

She wanted to ask Ephraim if he had been demanding more rent lately, but she could not find courage to do so.

Agnes had to go to Sunday-school alone that afternoon. Without saying anything to her father, Anna decided to stay at home. She spent the time in her bedroom, idle, preoccupied; and did not come downstairs till half-past three. Ephraim had gone out. Agnes presently returned, and then Henry came in with Mr. Tellwright. They were conversing amicably, and Anna knew that her engagement was finally and satisfactorily settled. During tea no reference was made to it, nor to the suicide. Mynors' demeanour was quiet but cheerful. He had partly recovered from the morning's agitation, and gave Ephraim and Agnes a vivacious account of the attractions of Port Erin. Anna noticed the amusement in his eyes when Agnes, reddening, said to him: 'Will you have some more bread-and-butter, Henry?' It seemed to be tacitly understood afterwards that Agnes and her father would attend chapel, while Henry and Anna kept house. No one was ingenious enough to detect an impropriety in the arrangement. For some obscure reason, immediately upon the departure of the chapel-goers, Anna went into the kitchen, rattled some plates, stroked her hair mechanically, and then stole back again to the parlour. It was a chilly evening, and instead of walking up and down the strip of garden the betrothed lovers sat together under the window. Anna wondered whether or not she was happy. The presence of Mynors was, at any rate, marvellously soothing.

'Did your father say anything about the Price affair?' he began, yielding at once to the powerful hypnotism of the subject which fascinated the whole town that night, and which Anna could bear neither to discuss nor to ignore.

'Not much,' she said, and repeated to him her father's remark.

Mynors told her all he knew; how Willie had discovered his father with his toes actually touching the floor, leaning slightly forward, quite dead; how he had then cut the rope and fetched Mynors, who went with him to the police-station; how they had tied up the head of the corpse, and then waited till night to wheel the body on a hand-cart from Edward Street to the mortuary chamber at the police-station; how the police had telephoned to the coroner, and settled at once that the inquest should be held on Tuesday in the court-room at the town-hall; and how quiet, self-contained, and dignified Willie had been, surprising everyone by this new-found manliness. It all seemed hideously real to Anna, as Henry added detail to detail.

'I think I ought to tell you,' she said very calmly, when he had finished the recital, 'that I—I'm dreadfully upset over it. I can't help thinking that I—that father and I, I mean—are somehow partly responsible for this.'

'For Price's death? How?'

'We have been so hard on him for his rent lately, you know.'

My dearest girl! What next?' He took her hand in his. 'I assure you the idea is absurd. You've only got it because you're so sensitive and high-strung. I undertake to say Price was stuck fast everywhere—every where—hadn't a chance.'

'Me high-strung!' she exclaimed. He kissed her lovingly. But, beneath the feeling of reassurance, which by superior force he had imposed on her, there lay a feeling that she was treated like a frightened child who must be tranquillized in the night. Nevertheless, she was grateful for his kindness, and when she went to bed she obtained relief from the returning obsession of the suicide by making anew her vows to him.

As a theatrical effect the death of Titus Price could scarcely have been surpassed. The town was profoundly moved by the spectacle of this abject yet heroic surrender of all those pretences by which society contrives to tolerate itself. Here was a man whom no one respected, but everyone pretended to respect—who knew that he was respected by none, but pretended that he was respected by all; whose whole career was made up of dissimulations: religious, moral, and social. If any man could have been trusted to continue the decent sham to the end, and so preserve the general self-esteem, surely it was this man. But no! Suddenly abandoning all imposture, he transgresses openly, brazenly; and, snatching a bit of hemp cries: 'Behold me; this is real human nature. This is the truth; the rest was lies. I lied; you lied. I confess it, and you shall confess it.' Such a thunderclap shakes the very base of the microcosm. The young folk in particular could with difficulty believe their ears. It seemed incredible to them that Titus Price, the Methodist, the Sunday-school superintendent, the loud champion of the highest virtues, should commit the sin of all sins—murder. They were dazed. The remembrance of his insincerity did nothing to mitigate the blow. In their view it was perhaps even worse that he had played false to his own falsity. The elders were a little less disturbed. The event was not unique in their experience. They had lived longer and felt these seismic shocks before. They could go back into the past and find other cases where a swift impulse had shattered the edifice of a lifetime. They knew that the history of families and of communities is crowded with disillusion. They had discovered that character is changeless, irrepressible, incurable. They were aware of the astonishing fact, which takes at least thirty years to learn, that a Sunday-school superintendent is a man. And the suicide of Titus Price, when they had realised it, served but to confirm their most secret and honest estimate of humanity, that estimate which they never confided to a soul. The young folk thought the Methodist Society shamed and branded by the tragic incident, and imagined that years must elapse before it could again hold up its head in the town. The old folk were wiser, foreseeing with certainty that in only a few days this all-engrossing phenomenon would lose its significance, and be as though it had never been. Even in two days, time had already begun its work, for by Tuesday morning the interest of the affair—on Sunday at the highest pitch—had waned so much that the thought of the inquest was capable of reviving it. Although everyone knew that the case presented no unusual features, and that the coroner's inquiry would be nothing more than a formal ceremony, the almost greedy curiosity of Methodist circles lifted it to the level of a *cause célèbre*. The court was filled with irreproachable respectability when the coroner drove into the town, and each animated face said to its fellow: 'So you're here, are you?' Late comers of the official world—councillors, guardians of the poor, members of the school board, and one or two of their ladies, were forced to intrigue for room with the police and the town-hall keeper, and, having succeeded, sank into their narrow seats with a sigh of expectancy and triumph. Late comers with less influence had to retire, and by a kind of sinister fascination were kept wandering about the corridor before they could decide to go home. The market-place was occupied by hundreds of loafers, who seemed to find a mystic satisfaction in beholding the coroner's dogcart and the exterior of the building which now held the corpse.

It was by accident that Anna was in the town. She knew that the inquest was to occur that morning, but had not dreamed of attending it. When, however, she saw the stir of excitement in the market-place, and the police guarding the entrances of the town-hall, she walked directly across the road, past the two officers at the east door, and into the dark main corridor of the building, which was dotted with small groups idly conversing. She was conscious of two things: a vehement curiosity, and the existence somewhere in the precincts of a dead body, unsightly, monstrous, calm, silent, careless—the insensible origin of all this simmering ferment which disgusted her even while she shared in it. At a small door, half hidden by a curtain, she was startled to see Mynors.

'You here!' he exclaimed, as if painfully surprised, and shook hands with a preoccupied air. 'They are examining Willie. I came outside while he was in the witness-box.'

'Is the inquest going on in there?' she asked, pointing to the door. Each appeared to be concealing a certain resentment against the other; but this appearance was due only to nervous agitation.

A policeman down the corridor called: 'Mr. Mynors, a moment.' Henry hurried away, answering Anna's question as he went: 'Yes, in there. That's the witnesses' and jurors' door; but please don't go in. I don't like you to, and it is sure to upset you.'

She opened the door and went in. None said nay, and she found a few inches of standing-room behind the jury-box. A terrible stench nauseated her; the chamber was crammed, and not a window open. There was silence in the court—no one seemed to be doing anything; but at last she perceived that the coroner, enthroned on the bench justice was writing in a book with blue leaves. In the witness-box stood William Price, dressed in black, with kid gloves, not lounging in an ungainly attitude, as might have been expected, but perfectly erect; he kept his eyes fixed on the coroner's head. Sarah Vodrey, Price's aged housekeeper, sat on a chair near the witness-box, weeping into a black-bordered handkerchief; at intervals she raised her small, wrinkled, red face, with its glistening, inflamed eyes, and then buried it again in the handkerchief. The members of the jury, whom Anna could see only in profile, shuffled to and fro on their long, pew-like seats—they were mostly working men, shabbily clothed; but the foreman was Mr. Leal, the provision dealer, a freemason, and a sidesman at the parish church. The general public sat intent and vacuous; their minds gaped, if not their mouths; occasionally one whispered inaudibly to another; the jury, conscious of an official status, exchanged remarks in a whisper courageously loud. Several tall policemen, helmet in hand, stood in various corners of the room, and the coroner's officer sat near the witness-box to administer the oath. At length the coroner lifted his head. He was rather a young man, with a large, intelligent face; he wore eyeglasses, and his chin was covered with a short, wavy beard. His manner showed that, while secretly proud of his supreme position in that assemblage, he was deliberately trying to make it appear that this exercise of judicial authority was nothing to him, that in truth these eternal inquiries, which interested others so deeply, were to him a weariness conscientiously endured.

'Now, Mr. Price,' the coroner said blandly, and it was plain that he was being ceremoniously polite to an inferior, in obedience to the rules of good form, 'I must ask you some more questions. They may be inconvenient, even painful; but I am here simply as the instrument of the law, and I must do my duty. And these gentlemen here,' he waved a hand in the direction of the jury, 'must be told the whole facts of the case. We know, of course, that the deceased committed suicide—that has been proved beyond doubt; but, as I say, we have the right to know more.' He paused, well satisfied with the sound of his voice, and evidently thinking that he had said something very weighty and impressive.

'What do you want to know?' Willie Price demanded, his broad Five Towns speech contrasting with the Kensingtonian accents of the coroner. The latter, who came originally from Manchester, was irritated by the brusque interruption; but he controlled his annoyance, at the same time glancing at the public as if to signify to them that he had learnt not to take too seriously the unintentional rudeness characteristic of their district.

'You say it was probably business troubles that caused your late father to commit the rash act?'

'Yes.'

'You are sure there was nothing else?'

'What else could there be?'

'Your late father was a widower?'

'Yes.'

'Now as to these business troubles—what were they?'

'We were being pressed by creditors.'

'Were you a partner with your late father?'

'Yes.'

'Oh! You were a partner with him!'

The jury seemed surprised, and the coroner wrote again: 'What was your share in the business?'

'I don't know.'

'You don't know? Surely that is rather singular?'

'My father took me in Co. not long since. We signed a deed, but I forget what was in it. My place was principally on the bank, not in the office.'

'And so you were being pressed by creditors?'

'Yes. And we were behind with the rent.'

'Was the landlord pressing you, too?'

Anna lowered her eyes, fearful lest every head had turned towards her.

'Not then; he had been—she, I mean.'

'The landlord is a lady?' Here the coroner faintly smiled. 'Then, as regards the landlord, the pressure was less than it had been?'

'Yes; we had paid some rent, and settled some other claims.'

'Does it not seem strange——?' the coroner began, with a suave air of suggesting an idea.

'If you must know,' Willie surprisingly burst out, 'I believe it was the failure of a firm in London that owed us money that caused father to hang himself.'

'Ah!' exclaimed the coroner. 'When did you hear of that failure?'

'By second post on Friday. Eleven in the morning.'

'I think we have heard enough, Mr. Coroner,' said Leal, standing up in the jury-box. 'We have decided on our verdict.'

'Thank you, Mr. Price,' said the coroner, dismissing Willie. He added, in a tone of icy severity to the foreman: 'I had concluded my examination of the witness.' Then he wrote further in his book.

'Now, gentlemen of the jury,' the coroner resumed, having first cleared his throat; 'I think you will agree with me that this is a peculiarly painful case. Yet at the same time——'

Anna hastened from the court as impulsively as she had entered it. She could think of nothing but the quiet, silent, pitiful corpse; and all this vapid mouthing exasperated her beyond sufferance.

On the Thursday afternoon, Anna was sitting alone in the house, with the Persian cat and a pile of stockings on her knee, darning. Agnes had with sorrow returned to school; Ephraim was out. The bell sounded violently, and Anna, thinking that perhaps for some reason her father had chosen to enter by the front door, ran to open it. The visitor was Willie Price; he wore the new black suit which had figured in the coroner's court. She invited him to the parlour and they both sat down, tongue-tied. Now that she had learnt from his evidence given at the inquest that Ephraim had not been pressing for rent during her absence in the Isle of Man, she felt less like a criminal before Willie than she would have felt without that assurance. But at the best she was nervous, self-conscious, and shamed. She supposed that he had called to make some arrangement with reference to the tenure of the works, or, more probably, to announce a bankruptcy and stoppage.

'Well, Miss Tellwright,' Willie began, 'I've buried him. He's gone.'

The simple and profound grief, and the restrained bitterness against all the world, which were expressed in these words—the sole epitaph of Titus Price—nearly made Anna cry. She would have cried, if the cat had not opportunely jumped on her knee again; she controlled herself by dint of stroking it. She sympathised with him more intensely in that first moment of his loneliness than she had ever sympathised with anyone, even Agnes. She wished passionately to shield, shelter, and comfort him, to do something, however small, to diminish his sorrow and humiliation; and this despite his size, his ungainliness, his coarse features, his rough voice, his lack of all the conventional refinements. A single look from his guileless and timid eyes atoned for every shortcoming. Yet she could scarcely open her mouth. She knew not what to say. She had no phrases to soften the frightful blow which Providence had dealt him.

'I'm very sorry,' she said. 'You must be relieved it's all over.'

If she could have been Mrs. Sutton for half an hour! But she was Anna, and her feelings could only find outlet in her eyes. Happily young Price was of those meek ones who know by instinct the language of the eyes.

'You've come about the works, I suppose?' she went on.

'Yes,' he said. 'Is your father in? I want to see him very particular.'

'He isn't in now,' she replied: 'but he will be back by four o'clock.'

'That's an hour. You don't know where he is?'

She shook her head. 'Well,' he continued, 'I must tell you, then. I've come up to do it, and do it I must. I can't come up again; neither can I wait. You remember that bill of exchange as we gave you some weeks back towards rent?'

'Yes,' she said. There was a pause. He stood up, and moved to the mantelpiece. Her gaze followed him intently, but she had no idea what he was about to say.

'It's forged, Miss Tellwright.' He sat down again, and seemed calmer, braver, ready to meet any conceivable set of consequences.

'Forged!' she repeated, not immediately grasping the significance of the avowal.

'Mr. Sutton's name is forged on it. So I came to tell your father; but you'll do as well. I feel as if I should like to tell you all about it,' he said, smiling sadly. 'Mr. Sutton had really given us a bill for thirty pounds, but we'd paid that away when Mr. Tellwright sent word down—you remember—that he should put bailiffs in if he didn't have twenty-five pounds next day. We were just turning the corner then, father said to me. There was a goodish sum due to us from a London firm in a month's time, and if we could only hold out till then, father said he could see daylight for us. But he knew as there'd be no getting round Mr. Tellwright. So he had the idea of using Mr. Sutton's name—just temporary like. He sent me to the post-office to buy a bill stamp, and he wrote out the bill all but the name. "You take this up to Tellwright's," he says, "and ask 'em to take it and hold it, and we'll redeem it, and that'll be all right. No harm done there, Will!" he says. Then he tries Sutton's name on the back of an envelope. It's an easy signature, as you know; but he couldn't do it. "Here, Will," he says, "my old hand shakes; you have a go," and he gives me a letter of Sutton's to copy from. I did it easy enough after a try or two. "That'll be all right, Will," he says, and I put my hat on and brought the bill up here. That's the truth, Miss Tellwright. It was the smash of that London firm that finished my poor old father off.'

Her one feeling was the sense of being herself a culprit. After all, it was her father's action, more than anything else, that had led to the suicide, and he was her agent.

'Oh, Mr. Price,' she said foolishly, 'whatever shall you do?'

'There's nothing to be done,' he replied. 'It was bound to be. It's our luck. We'd no thought but what we should bring you thirty pound in cash and get that bit of paper back, and rip it up, and no one the worse. But we were always unlucky, me and him. All you've got to do is just to tell your father, and say I'm ready to go to the police-station when he gives the word. It's a bad business, but I'm ready for it.'

'Can't we do something?' she naïvely inquired, with a vision of a trial and sentence, and years of prison.

'Your father keeps the bill, doesn't he? Not you?'

'I could ask him to destroy it.'

'He wouldn't,' said Willie. 'You'll excuse me saying that, Miss Tellwright, but he wouldn't.'

He rose as if to go, bitterly. As for Anna, she knew well that her father would never permit the bill to be destroyed. But at any cost she meant to comfort him then, to ease his lot, to send him away less grievous than he came.

'Listen!' she said, standing up, and abandoning the cat, 'I will see what can be done. Yes. Something *shall* be done—something or other. I will come and see you at the works to-morrow afternoon. You may rely on me.'

She saw hope brighten his eyes at the earnestness and resolution of her tone, and she felt richly rewarded. He never said another word, but gripped her hand with such force that she flinched in pain. When he had gone, she perceived clearly the dire dilemma; but cared nothing, in the first bliss of having reassured him.

During tea it occurred to her that as soon as Agnes had gone to bed she would put the situation plainly before her father, and, for the first and last time in her life, assert herself. She would tell him that the affair was, after all, entirely her own, she would firmly demand possession of the bill of exchange, and she would insist on it being destroyed. She would point out to the old man that, her promise having been given to Willie Price, no other course than this was possible. In planning this night-surprise on her father's obstinacy, she found argument after argument auspicious of its success. The formidable tyrant was at last to meet his equal, in force, in resolution, and in pugnacity. The swiftness of her onrush would sweep him, for once, off his feet. At whatever cost, she was bound to win, even though victory resulted in eternal enmity between father and daughter. She saw herself towering over him, morally, with blazing eye and scornful nostril. And, thus meditating on the grandeur of her adventure, she fed her courage with indignation. By the act of death, Titus Price had put her father for ever in the wrong. His corpse accused the miser, and Anna, incapable now of seeing aught save the pathos of suicide, acquiesced in the accusation with all the strength of her remorse. She did not reason—she felt; reason was shrivelled up in the fire of emotion. She almost trembled with the urgency of her desire to protect from further shame the figure of Willie Price, so frank, simple, innocent, and big; and to protect also the lifeless and dishonoured body of his parent. She reviewed the whole circumstances again and again, each time finding less excuse for her father's implacable and fatal cruelty.

So her thoughts ran until the appointed hour of Agnes's bedtime. It was always necessary to remind Agnes of that hour; left to herself, the child would have stayed up till the very Day of Judgment. The clock struck, but

Anna kept silence. To utter the word 'bedtime' to Agnes was to open the attack on her father, and she felt as the conductor of an opera feels before setting in motion a complicated activity which may end in either triumph or an unspeakable fiasco. The child was reading; Anna looked and looked at her, and at length her lips were set for the phrase, 'Now Agnes,' when, suddenly, the old man forestalled her:

'Is that wench going for sit here all night?' he asked of Anna, menacingly.

Agnes shut her book and crept away.

This accident was the ruin of Anna's scheme. Her father, always the favourite of circumstance, had by chance struck the first blow; ignorant of the battle that awaited him, he had unwittingly won it by putting her in the wrong, as Titus Price had put him in the wrong. She knew in a flash that her enterprise was hopeless; she knew that her father's position in regard to her was impregnable, that no moral force, no consciousness of right, would avail to overthrow that authority which she had herself made absolute by a life-long submission; she knew that face to face with her father she was, and always would be, a coward. And now, instead of finding arguments for success, she found arguments for failure. She divined all the retorts that he would fling at her. What about Mr. Sutton—in a sense the victim of this fraud? It was not merely a matter of thirty pounds. A man's name had been used. Was he, Ephraim Tellwright, and she, his daughter, to connive at a felony? The felony was done, and could not be undone. Were they to render themselves liable, even in theory, to a criminal prosecution? If Titus Price had killed himself, what of that? If Willie Price was threatened with ruin, what of that? Them as made the bed must lie on it. At the best, and apart from any forgery, the Prices had swindled their creditors; even in dying, old Price had been guilty of a commercial swindle. And was the fact that father and son between them had committed a direct and flagrant crime to serve as an excuse for sympathising with the survivor? Why was Anna so anxious to shield the forger? What claim had he? A forger was a forger, and that was the end of it.

She went to bed without opening her mouth. Irresolute, shamed, and despairing, she tried to pray for guidance, but she could bring no sincerity of appeal into this prayer; it seemed an empty form. Where, indeed, was her religion? She was obliged to acknowledge that the fervour of her aspirations had been steadily cooling for weeks. She was not a whit more a true Christian now than she had been before the Revival; it appeared that she was incapable of real religion, possibly one of those souls foreordained to damnation. This admission added to the general sense of futility, and increased her misery. She lay awake for hours, confronting her deliberate promise to Willie Price. *Something shall be done. Rely on me.* He was relying on her, then. But on whom could she rely? To whom could she turn? It is significant that the idea of confiding in Henry Mynors did not present itself for a single moment as practical. Mynors had been kind to Willie in his trouble, but Anna almost resented this kindness on account of the condescending superiority which she thought she detected therein. It was as though she had overheard Mynors saying to himself: 'Here is this poor, crushed worm. It is my duty as a Christian to pity and succour him. I will do so. I am a righteous man.' The thought of anyone stooping to Willie was hateful to her. She felt equal with him, as a mother feels equal with her child when it cries and she soothes it. And she felt, in another way, that he was equal with her, as she thought of his sturdy and simple confession, and of the loyal love in his voice when he spoke of his father. She liked him for hurting her hand, and for refusing to snatch at the slender chance of her father's clemency. She could never reveal Willie's sin, if it was a sin, to Henry Mynors—that symbol of correctness and of success. She had fraternised with sinners, like Christ; and, with amazing injustice, she was capable of deeming Mynors a Pharisee because she could not find fault with him, because he lived and loved so impeccably and so triumphantly. There was only one person from whom she could have asked advice and help, and that wise and consoling heart was far away in the Isle of Man.

'Why won't father give up the bill?' she demanded, half aloud, in sullen wrath. She could not frame the answer in words, but nevertheless she knew it and felt it. Such an act of grace would have been impossible to her father's nature—that was all.

Suddenly the expression of her face changed from utter disgust into a bitter and proud smile. Without thinking further, without daring to think, she rose out of bed and, night-gowned and bare-footed, crept with infinite precaution downstairs. The oilcloth on the stairs froze her feet; a cold, grey light issuing through the glass square over the front door showed that dawn was beginning. The door of the front-parlour was shut; she opened it gently, and went within. Every object in the room was faintly visible, the bureau, the chair, the files of papers, the pictures, the books on the mantelshelf, and the safe in the corner. The bureau, she knew, was never locked; fear of their father had always kept its privacy inviolate from Anna and Agnes, without the aid of a key. As Anna stood in front of it, a shaking figure with hair hanging loose, she dimly remembered having one day seen a blue paper among white in the pigeon-holes. But if the bill was not there she vowed that she would steal her father's keys while he slept, and force the safe. She opened the bureau, and at once saw the edge of a blue paper corresponding with her recollection. She pulled it forth and scanned it. 'Three months after date pay to our order ... Accepted payable, *William Sutton.*' So here was the forgery, here the two words for which Willie Price might have gone to prison! What a trifle! She tore the flimsy document to bits, and crumpled the bits into a little ball. How should she dispose of the ball? After a moment's reflection she went into the kitchen, stretched on tiptoe to reach the match-box from the high mantelpiece, struck a match, and burnt the ball in the grate. Then, with a restrained and sinister laugh, she ran softly upstairs.

'What's the matter, Anna?' Agnes was sitting up in bed, wide awake.

'Nothing; go to sleep, and don't bother,' Anna angrily whispered.

Had she closed the lid of the bureau? She was compelled to return in order to make sure. Yes, it was closed. When at length she lay in bed, breathless, her heart violently beating, her feet like icicles, she realised what she had done. She had saved Willie Price, but she had ruined herself with her father. She knew well that he would never forgive her.

On the following afternoon she planned to hurry to Edward Street and back while Ephraim and Agnes were both out of the house. But for some reason her father sat persistently after dinner, conning a sale catalogue. At a quarter to three he had not moved. She decided to go at any risks. She put on her hat and jacket, and opened the front door. He heard her.

'Anna!' he called sharply. She obeyed the summons in terror. 'Art going out?'

'Yes, father.'

'Where to?'

'Down town to buy some things.'

'Seems thou'rt always buying.'

That was all; he let her free. In an unworthy attempt to appease her conscience she did in fact go first into the town; she bought some wool; the trick was despicable. Then she hastened to Edward Street. The decrepit works seemed to have undergone no change. She had expected the business would be suspended, and Willie Price alone on the bank; but manufacture was proceeding as usual. She went direct to the office, fancying, as she climbed the stairs, that every window of all the workshops was full of eyes to discern her purpose. Without knocking, she pushed against the unlatched door and entered. Willie was lolling in his father's chair, gloomy, meditative, apparently idle. He was coatless, and wore a dirty apron; a battered hat was at the back of his head, and his great hands which lay on the desk in front of him, were soiled. He sprang up, flushing red, and she shut the door; they were alone together.

'I'm all in my dirt,' he murmured apologetically. Simple and silly creature, to imagine that she cared for his dirt!

'It's all right,' she said; 'you needn't worry any more. It's all right.' They were glorious words for her, and her face shone.

'What do you mean?' he asked gruffly.

'Why,' she smiled, full of happiness, 'I got that paper and burnt it!'

He looked at her exactly as if he had not understood. 'Does your father know?'

She still smiled at him happily. 'No; but I shall tell him this afternoon. It's all right. I've burnt it.'

He sank down in the chair, and, laying his head on the desk, burst into sobbing tears. She stood over him, and put a hand on the sleeve of his shirt. At that touch he sobbed more violently.

'Mr. Price, what is it?' She asked the question in a calm, soothing tone.

He glanced up at her, his face wet, yet apparently not shamed by the tears. She could not meet his gaze without herself crying, and so she turned her head. 'I was only thinking,' he stammered, 'only thinking—what an angel you are.'

Only the meek, the timid, the silent, can, in moments of deep feeling, use this language of hyperbole without seeming ridiculous.

He was her great child, and she knew that ha worshipped her. Oh, ineffable power, that out of misfortune canst create divine happiness!

Later, he remarked in his ordinary tone: 'I was expecting your father here this afternoon about the lease. There is to be a deed of arrangement with the creditors.'

'My father!' she exclaimed, and she bade him good-bye.

As she passed under the archway she heard a familiar voice: 'I reckon I shall find young Mester Price in th' office?' Ephraim, who had wandered into the packing-house, turned and saw her through the doorway; a second's delay, and she would have escaped. She stood waiting the storm, and then they walked out into the road together.

'Anna, what art doing here?'

She did not know what to say.

'What art doing here?' he repeated coldly.

'Father, I—was just going back home.'

He hesitated an instant. 'I'll go with thee,' he said. They walked back to Manor Terrace in silence. They had tea in silence; except that Agnes, with dreadful inopportuneness, continually worried her father for a definite promise that she might leave school at Christmas. The idea was preposterous; but Agnes, fired by her recent success as a housekeeper, clung to it. Ignorant of her imminent danger, and misinterpreting the signs of his face, she at last pushed her insistence too far.

'Get to bed, this minute,' he said, in a voice suddenly terrible. She perceived her error then, but it was too late. Looking wistfully at Anna, the child fled.

'I was told this morning, miss,' Ephraim began, as soon as Agnes was gone, 'that young Price had bin seen coming to this house 'ere yesterday afternoon. I thought as it was strange as thoud'st said nowt about it to thy feyther; but I never suspected as a daughter o' mine was up to any tricks. There was a hang-dog look on thy face this afternoon when I asked where thou wast going, but I didna' think thou wast lying to me.'

'I wasn't,' she began, and stopped.

'Thou wast! Now, what is it? What's this carrying-on between thee and Will Price? I'll have it out of thee.'

'There is no carrying-on, father.'

'Then why hast thou gotten secrets? Why dost go sneaking about to see him—sneaking, creeping, like any brazen moll?'

The miser was wounded in the one spot where there remained to him any sentiment capable of being wounded: his faith in the irreproachable, absolute chastity, in thought and deed, of his womankind.

'Willie Price came in here yesterday,' Anna began, white and calm, 'to see you. But you weren't in. So he saw me. He told me that bill of exchange, that blue paper, for thirty pounds, was forged. He said he had forged Mr. Sutton's name on it.' She stopped, expecting the thunder.

'Get on with thy tale,' said Ephraim, breathing loudly.

'He said he was ready to go to prison as soon as you gave the word. But I told him, "No such thing!" I said it must be settled quietly. I told him to leave it to me. He was driven to the forgery, and I thought——'

'Dost mean to say,' the miser shouted, 'as that blasted scoundrel came here and told thee he'd forged a bill, and thou told him to leave it to thee to settle?' Without waiting for an answer, he jumped up and strode to the door, evidently with the intention of examining the forged document for himself.

'It isn't there—it isn't there!' Anna called to him wildly.

'What isna' there?'

'The paper. I may as well tell you, father. I got up early this morning and burnt it.'

The man was staggered at this audacious and astounding impiety.

'It was mine, really,' she continued; 'and I thought——'

'Thou thought!'

Agnes, upstairs, heard that passionate and consuming roar. 'Shame on thee, Anna Tellwright! Shame on thee for a shameless hussy! A daughter o' mine, and just promised to another man! Thou'rt an accomplice in forgery. Thou sees the scamp on the sly! Thou——' He paused, and then added, with furious scorn: 'Shalt speak o' this to Henry Mynors?'

'I will tell him if you like,' she said proudly.

'Look thee here!' he hissed, 'if thou breathes a word o' this to Henry Mynors, or any other man, I'll cut thy tongue out. A daughter o' mine! If thou breathes a word——'

'I shall not, father.'

It was finished; grey with frightful anger, Ephraim left the room.

CHAPTER XII

AT THE PRIORY

She was not to be pardoned: the offence was too monstrous, daring, and final. At the same time, the unappeasable ire of the old man tended to weaken his power over her. All her life she had been terrorised by the fear of a wrath which had never reached the superlative degree until that day. Now that she had seen and felt the limit of his anger, she became aware that she could endure it; the curse was heavy, and perhaps more irksome than heavy, but she survived; she continued to breathe, eat, drink, and sleep; her father's power stopped short of annihilation. Here, too, was a satisfaction: that things could not be worse. And still greater comfort lay in the fact that she had not only accomplished the deliverance of Willie Price, but had secured absolute secrecy concerning the episode.

The next day was Saturday, when, after breakfast, it was Ephraim's custom to give Anna the weekly sovereign for housekeeping.

'Here, Agnes,' he said, turning in his armchair to face the child, and drawing a sovereign from his waistcoat-pocket, 'take charge o' this, and mind ye make it go as far as ye can.' His tone conveyed a subsidiary message: 'I am terribly angry, but I am not angry with you. However, behave yourself.'

The child mechanically took the coin, scared by this proof of an unprecedented domestic convulsion. Anna, with a tightening of the lips, rose and went into the kitchen. Agnes followed, after a discreet interval, and in silence gave up the sovereign.

'What is it all about, Anna?' she ventured to ask that night.

'Never mind,' said Anna curtly.

The question had needed some courage, for, at certain times, Agnes would as easily have trifled with her father as with Anna. From that moment, with the passive fatalism characteristic of her years, Agnes' spirits began to rise again to the normal level. She accepted the new situation, and fitted herself into it with a child's adaptability. If Anna naturally felt a slight resentment against this too impartial and apparently callous attitude on the part of the child, she never showed it.

Nearly a week later, Anna received a postcard from Beatrice announcing her complete recovery, and the immediate return of her parents and herself to Bursley. That same afternoon, a cab encumbered with much luggage passed up the street as Anna was fixing clean curtains in her father's bedroom. Beatrice, on the look-out, waved a hand and smiled, and Anna responded to the signals. She was glad now that the Suttons had come back, though for several days she had almost forgotten their existence. On the Saturday afternoon, Mynors called. Anna was in the kitchen; she heard him scuffling with Agnes in the lobby, and then talking to her father. Three times she had seen him since her disgrace, and each time the secret bitterness of her soul, despite conscientious effort to repress it, had marred the meeting—it had been plain, indeed, that she was profoundly disturbed; he had affected at first not to observe the change in her, and she, anticipating his questions, hinted briefly that the trouble was with her father, and had no reference to himself, and that she preferred not to discuss it at all; reassured, and too young in courtship yet to presume on a lover's rights, he respected her wish, and endeavoured by every art to restore her to equanimity. This time, as she went to greet him in the parlour, she resolved that he should see no more of the shadow. He noticed instantly the difference in her face.

'I've come to take you into Sutton's for tea—and for the evening,' he said eagerly. 'You must come. They are very anxious to see you. I've told your father,' he added. Ephraim had vanished into his office.

'What did he say, Henry?' she asked timidly.

'He said you must please yourself, of course. Come along, love. Mustn't she, Agnes?'

Agnes concurred, and said that she would get her father's tea, and his supper too.

'You will come,' he urged. She nodded, smiling thoughtfully, and he kissed her, for the first time in front of Agnes, who was filled with pride at this proof of their confidence in her.

'I'm ready, Henry,' Anna said, a quarter of an hour later, and they went across to Sutton's.

'Anna, tell me all about it,' Beatrice burst out when she and Anna had fled to her bedroom. 'I'm so glad. Do you love him really—truly? He's dreadfully fond of you. He told me so this morning; we had quite a long chat in the market. I think you're both very lucky, you know.' She kissed Anna effusively for the third time. Anna looked at her smiling but silent.

'Well?' Beatrice said.

'What do you want me to say?'

'Oh! You are the funniest girl, Anna, I ever met. "What do you want me to say," indeed!' Beatrice added in a different tone: 'Don't imagine this affair was the least bit of a surprise to us. It wasn't. The fact is, Henry had— oh! well, never mind. Do you know, mother and dad used to think there was something between Henry and me. But there wasn't, you know—not really. I tell you that, so that you won't be able to say you were kept in the dark. When shall you be married, Anna?'

'I haven't the least idea,' Anna replied, and began to question Beatrice about her convalescence.

'I'm perfectly well,' Beatrice said. 'It's always the same. If I catch anything I catch it bad and get it over quickly.'

'Now, how long are you two chatterboxes going to stay here?' It was Mrs. Sutton who came into the room. 'Bee, you've got those sewing-meeting letters to write. Eh, Anna, but I'm glad of this. You'll make him a good wife. You two'll just suit each other.'

Anna could not but be impressed by this unaffected joy of her friends in the engagement. Her spirits rose, and once more she saw visions of future happiness. At tea, Alderman Sutton added his felicitations to the rest, with that flattering air of intimate sympathy and comprehension which some middle-aged men can adopt towards young girls. The tea, made specially magnificent in honour of the betrothal, was such a meal as could only have been compassed in Staffordshire or Yorkshire—a high tea of the last richness and excellence, exquisitely gracious to the palate, but ruthless in its demands on the stomach. At one end of the table, which glittered with silver, glass, and Longshaw china, was a fowl which had been boiled for four hours; at the other, a hot pork-pie, islanded in liquor, which might have satisfied a regiment. Between these two dishes were all the delicacies which differentiate high tea from tea, and on the quality of which the success of the meal really depends; hot pikelets, hot crumpets, hot toast, sardines with tomatoes, raisin-bread, current-bread, seed-cake, lettuce, home-made marmalade and home-made jams. The repast occupied over an hour, and even then not a quarter of the food was consumed. Surrounded by all that good fare and good-will, with the Alderman on her left, Henry on her right, and a bright fire in front of her, Anna quickly caught the gaiety of the others. She forgot everything but the gladness of reunion, the joy of the moment, the luxurious comfort of the house. Conversation was busy with the doings of the Suttons at Port Erin after Anna and Henry had left. A listener would have caught fragments like this:—'You know such-and-such a point.... No, not there, over the hill. Well, we hired a carriage and drove.... The weather was simply.... Tom Kelly said he'd never.... And that little guard on the railway came all the way down to the steamer.... Did you see anything in the "Signal" about the actress being drowned? Oh! It was awfully sad. We saw the corpse just after.... Beatrice, will you hush?'

'Wasn't it terrible about Titus Price?' Beatrice exclaimed.

'Eh, my!' sighed Mrs. Sutton, glancing at Anna. 'You can never tell what's going to happen next. I'm always afraid to go away for fear of something happening.'

A silence followed. When tea was finished Beatrice was taken away by her mother to write the letters concerning the immediate resumption of sewing-meetings, and for a little time Anna was left in the drawing-room alone with the two men, who began to talk about the affairs of the Prices. It appeared that Mr. Sutton had been asked to become trustee for the creditors under a deed of arrangement, and that he had hopes of being able to sell the business as a going concern. In the meantime it would need careful management.

'Will Willie Price manage it?' Anna inquired. The question seemed to divert Henry and the Alderman, to afford them a contemptuous and somewhat inimical amusement at the expense of Willie.

'No,' said the Alderman, quietly, but emphatically.

'Master William is fairly good on the works,' said Henry; 'but in the office, I imagine, he is worse than useless.'

Grieved and confused, Anna bent down and moved a hassock in order to hide her face. The attitude of these men to Willie Price, that victim of circumstances and of his own simplicity, wounded Anna inexpressibly. She perceived that they could see in him only a defaulting debtor, that his misfortune made no appeal to their charity. She wondered that men so warm-hearted and kind in some relations could be so hard in others.

'I had a talk with your father at the creditors' meeting yesterday,' said the Alderman. 'You won't lose much. Of course you've got a preferential claim for six months' rent.' He said this reassuringly, as though it would give satisfaction. Anna did not know what a preferential claim might be, nor was she aware of any creditors' meeting. She wished ardently that she might lose as much as possible—hundreds of pounds. She was relieved when Beatrice swept in, her mother following.

'Now, your worship,' said Beatrice to her father, 'seven stamps for these letters, please.' Anna glanced up inquiringly on hearing the form of address. 'You don't mean to say that you didn't know that father is going to be mayor this year?' Beatrice asked, as if shocked at this ignorance of affairs. 'Yes, it was all settled rather late, wasn't it, dad? And the mayor-elect pretends not to care much, but actually he is filled with pride, isn't he, dad? As for the mayoress——?'

'Eh, Bee!' Mrs. Sutton stopped her, smiling; 'you'll tumble over that tongue of yours some day.'

'Mother said I wasn't to mention it,' said Beatrice, 'lest you should think we were putting on airs.'

'Nay, not I!' Mrs. Sutton protested. 'I said no such thing. Anna knows us too well for that. But I'm not so set up with this mayor business as some people will think I am.'

'Or as Beatrice is,' Mynors added.

At half-past eight, and again at nine, Anna said that she must go home; but the Suttons, now frankly absorbed in the topic of the mayoralty, their secret preoccupation, would not spoil the confidential talk which had ensued by letting the lovers depart. It was nearly half-past nine before Anna and Henry stood on the pavement outside, and Beatrice, after facetious farewells, had shut the door.

'Let us just walk round by the Manor Farm,' Henry pleaded. 'It won't take more than a quarter of an hour or so.'

She agreed dutifully. The footpath ran at right angles to Trafalgar Road, past a colliery whose engine-fires glowed in the dark, moonless, autumn night, and then across a field. They stood on a knoll near the old farmstead, that extraordinary and pathetic survival of a vanished agriculture. Immediately in front of them stretched acres of burning ironstone—a vast tremulous carpet of flame woven in red, purple, and strange greens. Beyond were the skeleton-like silhouettes of pit-heads, and the solid forms of furnace and chimney-shaft. In the distance a canal reflected the gigantic illuminations of Cauldon Bar Ironworks. It was a scene mysterious and romantic enough to kindle the raptures of love, but Anna felt cold, melancholy, and apprehensive of vague sorrows. 'Why am I so?' she asked herself, and tried in vain to shake off the mood.

'What will Willie Price do if the business is sold?' she questioned Mynors suddenly.

'Surely,' he said to soothe her, 'you aren't still worrying about that misfortune. I wish you had never gone near the inquest; the thing seems to have got on your mind.'

'Oh, no!' she protested, with an air of cheerfulness. 'But I was just wondering.'

'Well, Willie will have to do the best he can. Get a place somewhere, I suppose. It won't be much, at the best.'

Had he guessed what perhaps hung on that answer, Mynors might have given it in a tone less callous and perfunctory. Could he have seen the tightening of her lips, he might even afterwards have repaired his error by some voluntary assurance that Willie Price should be watched over with a benevolent eye and protected with a strong arm. But how was he to know that in misprizing Willie Price before her, he was misprizing a child to its mother? He had done something for Willie Price, and considered mat he had done enough. His thoughts, moreover, were on other matters.

'Do you remember that day we went up to the park?' he murmured fondly; 'that Sunday? I have never told you that that evening I came out of chapel after the first hymn, when I noticed you weren't there, and walked up past your house. I couldn't help it. Something drew me. I nearly called in to see you. Then I thought I had better not.'

'I saw you,' she said calmly. His warmth made her feel sad. 'I saw you stop at the gate.'

'You did? But you weren't at the window?'

'I saw you through the glass of the front-door.' Her voice grew fainter, more reluctant.

'Then you were watching?' In the dark he seized her with such violence, and kissed her so vehemently, that she was startled out of herself.

'Oh! Henry!' she exclaimed.

'Call me Harry,' he entreated, his arm still round her waist; 'I want you to call me Harry. No one else does or ever has done, and no one shall, now.'

'Harry,' she said deliberately, bracing her mind to a positive determination. She must please him, and she said it again: 'Harry; yes, it has a nice sound.'

Ephraim sat reading the 'Signal' in the parlour when she arrived home at five minutes to ten. Imbued then with ideas of duty, submission, and systematic kindliness, she had an impulse to attempt a reconciliation with her father.

'Good-night, father,' she said, 'I hope I've not kept you up.'

He was deaf.

She went to bed resigned; sad, but not gloomy. It was not for nothing that during all her life she had been accustomed to infelicity. Experience had taught her this: to be the mistress of herself. She knew that she could face any fact—even the fact of her dispassionate frigidity under Mynors' caresses. It was on the firm, almost rapturous resolve to succour Willie Price, if need be, that she fell asleep.

562

The engagement, which had hitherto been kept private, became the theme of universal gossip immediately upon the return of the Suttons from the Isle of Man. Two words let fall by Beatrice in the St. Luke's covered market on Saturday morning had increased and multiplied till the whole town echoed with the news. Anna's private fortune rose as high as a quarter of a million. As for Henry Mynors, it was said that Henry Mynors knew what he was about. After all, he was like the rest. Money, money! Of course it was inconceivable that a fine, prosperous figure of a man, such as Mynors, would have made up to *her*, if she had not been simply rolling in money. Well, there was one thing to be said for young Mynors, he would put money to good use; you might rely he would not hoard it up same as it had been hoarded up. However, the more saved, the more for young Mynors, so he needn't grumble. It was to be hoped he would make her dress herself a bit better—though indeed it hadn't been her fault she went about so shabby; the old skinflint would never allow her a penny of her own. So tongues wagged.

The first Sunday was a tiresome ordeal for Anna, both at school and at chapel. 'Well, I never!' seemed to be written like a note of exclamation on every brow; the monotony of the congratulations fatigued her as much as her involuntary efforts to grasp what each speaker had left unsaid of innuendo, malice, envy or sycophancy. Even the people in the shops, during the next few days, could not serve her without direct and curious reference to her private affairs. The general opinion that she was a cold and bloodless creature was strengthened by her attitude at this period. But the apathy which she displayed was neither affected nor due to an excessive diffidence. As she seemed, so she felt. She often wondered what would have happened to her if that vague 'something' between Henry and Beatrice, to which Beatrice had confessed, had ever taken definite shape.

'Hancock came back from Lancashire last night,' said Mynors, when he arrived at Manor Terrace on the next Saturday afternoon. Ephraim was in the room, and Henry, evidently joyous and triumphant, addressed both him and Anna.

'Is Hancock the commercial traveller?' Anna asked. She knew that Hancock was the commercial traveller, but she experienced a nervous compulsion to make idle remarks in order to hide the breach of intercourse between her father and herself.

'Yes,' said Mynors; 'he's had a magnificent journey.'

'How much?' asked the miser.

Henry named the amount of orders taken in a fortnight's journey.

'Humph!' the miser ejaculated. 'That's better than a bat in the eye with a burnt stick.' From him, this was the superlative of praise. 'You're making good money at any rate?'

'We are,' said Mynors.

'That reminds me,' Ephraim remarked gruffly. 'When dost think o' getting wed? I'm not much for long engagements, and so I tell ye.' He threw a cold glance sideways at Anna. The idea penetrated her heart like a stab: 'He wants to get me out of the house!'

'Well,' said Mynors, surprised at the question and the tone, and, looking at Anna as if for an explanation: 'I had scarcely thought of that. What does Anna say?'

'I don't know,' she murmured; and then, more bravely, in a louder voice, and with a smile: 'The sooner the better.' She thought, in her bitter and painful resentment: 'If he wants me to go, go I will.'

Henry tactfully passed on to another phase of the subject: 'I met Mr. Sutton yesterday, and he was telling me of Price's house up at Toft End. It belonged to Mr. Price, but of course it was mortgaged up to the hilt. The mortgagees have taken possession, and Mr. Sutton said it would be to let cheap at Christmas. Of course Willie and old Sarah Vodrey, the housekeeper, will clear out. I was thinking it might do for us. It's not a bad sort of house, or, rather, it won't be when it's repaired.'

'What will they ask for it?' Ephraim inquired.

'Twenty-five or twenty-eight. It's a nice large house—four bedrooms, and a very good garden.'

'Four bedrooms!' the miser exclaimed. 'What dost want wi' four bedrooms? You'd have for keep a servant.'

'Naturally we should keep a servant,' Mynors said, with calm politeness.

'You could get one o' them new houses up by th' park for fifteen pounds as would do you well enough'; the miser protested against these dreams of extravagance.

'I don't care for that part of the town,' said Mynors. 'It's too new for my taste.'

After tea, when Henry and Anna went out for the Saturday evening stroll, Mynors suddenly suggested: 'Why not go up and look through that house of Price's?'

'Won't it seem like turning them out if we happen to take it?' she asked.

'Turning them out! Willie is bound to leave it. What use is it to him? Besides, it's in the hands of the mortgagees now. Why shouldn't we take it just as well as anybody else, if it suits us?'

Anna had no reply, and she surrendered herself placidly enough to his will; nevertheless she could not entirely banish a misgiving that Willie Price was again to be victimised. Infinitely more disturbing than this illogical sensation, however, was the instinctive and sure knowledge, revealed in a flash, that her father wished to be rid of her. So implacable, then, was his animosity against her! Never, never had she been so deeply hurt. The wound, in fact, was so severe that at first she felt only a numbness that reduced everything to unimportance, robbing her of volition. She walked up to Toft End as if walking in her sleep.

Price's house, sometimes called Priory House, in accordance with a legend that a priory had once occupied the site, stood in the middle of the mean and struggling suburb of Toft End, which was flung up the hillside like a ragged scarf. Built of red brick, towards the end of the eighteenth century, double-fronted, with small, evenly disposed windows, and a chimney stack at either side, it looked westward over the town smoke towards a horizon of hills. It had a long, narrow garden, which ran parallel with the road. Behind it, adjoining, was a small, disused potworks, already advanced in decay. On the north side, and enclosed by a brick wall which surrounded also the garden, was a small orchard of sterile and withered fruit trees. In parts the wall had crumpled under the assaults of generations of boys, and from the orchard, through the gaps, could be seen an expanse of grey-green field, with a few abandoned pit-shafts scattered over it. These shafts, imperfectly protected by ruinous masonry, presented an appearance strangely sinister and forlorn, raising visions in the mind of dark and mysterious depths peopled with miserable ghosts of those who had toiled there in the days when to be a miner was to be a slave. The whole place, house and garden, looked ashamed and sad, with a shabby mournfulness acquired gradually from its inmates during many years. But, nevertheless, the house was substantial, and the air on that height fresh and pure.

Mynors rang in vain at the front door, and then they walked round the house to the orchard, and discovered Sarah Vodrey taking in clothes from a line—a diminutive and wasted figure, with scanty, grey hair, a tiny face permanently soured, and bony hands contorted by rheumatism.

'My rheumatism's that bad,' she said in response to greetings, 'I can scarce move about, and this house is a regular barracks to keep clean. No; Willie's not in. He's at th' works, as usual—Saturday like any other day. I'm by myself here all day and every day. But I reckon us'n be flitting soon, and me lived here eight-and-twenty year! Praise God, there's a mansion up there for me at last. And not sorry shall I be when He calls.'

'It must be very lonely for you, Miss Vodrey,' said Mynors. He knew exactly how to speak to this dame who lived her life like a fly between two panes of glass, and who could find room in her head for only three ideas, namely: that God and herself were on terms of intimacy; that she was, and had always been, indispensable to the Price family; and that her social status was far above that of a servant. 'It's a pity you never married,' Mynors added.

'Me, marry! What would *they* ha' done without me? No, I'm none for marriage and never was. I'd be shamed to be like some o' them spinsters down at chapel, always hanging round chapel-yard on the off-chance of a service, to catch that there young Mr. Sargent, the new minister. It's a sign of a hard winter, Miss Terrick, when the hay runs after the horse, that's what I say.'

'Miss Tellwright and myself are in search of a house,' Mynors gently interrupted the flow, and gave her a peculiar glance which she appreciated. 'We heard you and Willie were going to leave here, and so we came up just to look over the place, if it's quite convenient to you.'

'Eh, I understand ye,' she said; 'come in. But ye mun tak' things as ye find 'em, Miss Terrick.'

Dismal and unkempt, the interior of the house matched the exterior. The carpets were threadbare, the discoloured wall-papers hung loose on the walls, the ceilings were almost black, the paint had nearly been rubbed away from the woodwork; the exhausted furniture looked as if it would fall to pieces in despair if compelled to face the threatened ordeal of an auction-sale. But to Anna the rooms were surprisingly large, and there seemed so many of them! It was as if she were exploring an immense abode, like a castle, with odd chambers continually showing themselves in unexpected places. The upper story was even less inviting than the ground-floor—barer, more chill, utterly comfortless.

'This is the best bedroom,' said Miss Vodrey. 'And a rare big room too! It's not used now. *He* slept here. Willie sleeps at back.'

'A very nice room,' Mynors agreed blandly, and measured it, as he had done all the others, with a two-foot, entering the figures in his pocket-book.

Anna's eye wandered uneasily across the room, with its dismantled bed and decrepit mahogany suite.

'I'm glad he hanged himself at the works, and not here,' she thought. Then she looked out at the window. 'What a splendid view!' she remarked to Mynors.

She saw that he had taken a fancy to the house. The sagacious fellow esteemed it, not as it was, but as it would be, re-papered, re-painted, re-furnished, the outer walls pointed, the garden stocked; everything cleansed, brightened, renewed. And there was indeed much to be said for his fancy. The house was large, with plenty of ground; the boundary wall secured that privacy which young husbands and young wives instinctively demand; the outlook was unlimited, the air the purest in the Five Towns. And the rent was low, because the great majority of those who could afford such a house would never deign to exist in a quarter so poverty-stricken and unfashionable.

After leaving the house they continued their walk up the hill, and then turned off to the left on the high road from Hanbridge to Moorthorne. The venerable but not dignified town lay below them, a huddled medley of brown brick under a thick black cloud of smoke. The gold angel of the town-hall gleamed in the evening light, and the dark, squat tower of the parish church, sole relic of the past stood out grim and obdurate amid the featureless buildings which surrounded it. To the north and east miles of moorland, defaced by collieries and murky hamlets, ran to the horizon. Across the great field at their feet a figure slouched along, past the abandoned pit-shafts. They both recognised the man.

'There's Willie Price going home!' said Mynors.

'He looks tired,' she said. She was relieved that they had not met him at the house.

'I say,' Mynors began earnestly, after a pause, 'why shouldn't we get married soon, since the old gentleman seems rather to expect it? He's been rather awkward lately, hasn't he?'

This was the only reference made by Mynors to her father's temper. She nodded. 'How soon? she asked.

'Well, I was just thinking. Suppose, for the sake of argument, this house turns out all right. I couldn't get it thoroughly done up much before the middle of January—couldn't begin till these people had moved. Suppose we said early in February?'

'Yes!'

'Could you be ready by that time?'

'Oh, yes,' she answered, 'I could be ready.'

'Well, why shouldn't we fix February, then?'

'There's the question of Agnes,' she said.

'Yes; and there will always be the question of Agnes. Your father will have to get a housekeeper. You and I will be able to see after little Agnes, never fear.' So, with tenderness in his voice, he reassured her on that point.

'Why not February?' she reflected. 'Why not to-morrow, as father wants me out of the house?'

It was agreed.

'I've taken the Priory, subject to your approval,' Henry said, less than a fortnight later. From that time he invariably referred to the place as the Priory.

It was on the very night after this eager announcement that the approaching tragedy came one step nearer. Beatrice, in a modest evening-dress, with a white cloak—excited, hurried, and important—ran in to speak to Anna. The carriage was waiting outside. She and her father and mother had to attend a very important dinner at the mayor's house at Hillport, in connection with Mr. Sutton's impending mayoralty. Old Sarah Vodrey had just sent down a girl to say that she was unwell, and would be grateful if Mrs. Sutton or Beatrice would visit her. It was a most unreasonable time for such a summons, but Sarah was a fidgety old crotchet, and knew how frightfully good-natured Mrs. Sutton was. Would Anna mind going up to Toft End? And would Anna come out to the carriage and personally assure Mrs. Sutton that old Sarah should be attended to? If not, Beatrice was afraid her mother would take it into her head to do something stupid.

'It's very good of you, Anna,' said Mrs. Sutton, when Anna went outside with Beatrice. 'But I think I'd better go myself. The poor old thing may feel slighted if I don't, and Beatrice can well take my place at this affair at Hillport, which I've no mind for.' She was already half out of the carriage.

'Nothing of the kind,' said Anna firmly, pushing her back. 'I shall be delighted to go and do what I can.'

'That's right, Anna,' said the Alderman from the darkness of the carriage, where his shirt-front gleamed; 'Bee said you'd go, and we're much obliged to ye.'

'I expect it will be nothing,' said Beatrice, as the vehicle drove off; 'Sarah has served mother this trick before now.'

As Anna opened the garden-gate of the Priory she discerned a figure amid the rank bushes, which had been allowed to grow till they almost met across the narrow path leading to the front door of the house.

It was a thick and mysterious night—such a night as death chooses; and Anna jumped in vague terror at the apparition.

'Who's there?' said a voice sharply.

'It's me,' said Anna. 'Miss Vodrey sent down to ask Mrs. Sutton to come up and see her, but Mrs. Sutton had an engagement, so I came instead.'

The figure moved forward; it was Willie Price.

He peered into her face, and she could see the mortal pallor of his cheeks.

'Oh!' he exclaimed, 'it's Miss Tellwright, is it? Will ye come in, Miss Tellwright?'

She followed him with beating heart, alarmed, apprehensive. The front door stood wide open, and at the far end of the gloomy passage a faint light shone from the open door of the kitchen. 'This way,' he said. In the large, bare, stone-floored kitchen Sarah Vodrey sat limp and with closed eyes in an old rocking-chair close to the fireless range. The window, which gave on to the street, was open; through that window Sarah, in her extremity, had called the child who ran down to Mrs. Sutton's. On the deal table were a dirty cup and saucer, a tea-pot, bread, butter, and a lighted candle—sole illumination of the chamber.

'I come home, and I find this,' he said.

Daunted for a moment by the scene of misery, Anna could say nothing.

'I find this,' he repeated, as if accusing God of spitefulness; and he lifted the candle to show the apparently insensible form of the woman. Sarah's wrinkled and seamed face had the flush of fever, and the features were drawn into the expression of a terrible anxiety; her hands hung loose; she breathed like a dog after a run.

'I wanted her to have the doctor yesterday,' he said, 'but she wouldn't. Ever since you and Mr. Mynors called she's been cleaning the house down. She said you'd happen be coming again soon, and the place wasn't fit to be seen. No use me arguing with her.'

'You had better run for a doctor,' Anna said.

'I was just going off when you came. She's been complaining more of her rheumatism, and pain in her hips, lately.'

'Go now; fetch Mr. Macpherson, and call at our house and say I shall stay here all night. Wait a moment.' Seeing that he was exhausted from lack of food, she cut a thick piece of bread-and-butter. 'Eat this as you go,' she said.

'I can't eat; it'll choke me.'

'Let it choke you,' she said. 'You've got to swallow it.'

Child of a hundred sorrows, he must be treated as a child. As soon as Willie was gone she took off her hat and jacket, and lit a lamp; there was no gas in the kitchen.

'What's that light?' the old woman asked peevishly, rousing herself and sitting up. 'I doubt I'll be late with Willie's tea. Eh, Miss Terrick, what's amiss?'

'You're not quite well, Miss Vodrey,' Anna answered. 'If you'll show me your room, I'll see you into bed.' Without giving her a moment for hesitation, Anna seized the feeble creature under the arms, and so, coaxing, supporting, carrying, got her to bed. At length she lay on the narrow mattress, panting, exhausted. It was Sarah's final effort.

Anna lit fires in the kitchen and in the bedroom, and when Willie returned with Dr. Macpherson, water was boiling and tea made.

'You'd better get a woman in,' said the doctor curtly, in the kitchen, when he had finished his examination of Sarah. 'Some neighbour for to-night, and I'll send a nurse up from the cottage-hospital early to-morrow morning. Not that it will be the least use. She must have been dying for the last two days at least. She's got pericarditis and pleurisy. She's breathing I don't know how many to the minute, and her temperature is just about as high as it can be. It all follows from rheumatism, and then taking cold. Gross carelessness and neglect all through! I've no patience with such work.' He turned angrily to Willie. 'I don't know what on earth you were thinking of, Mr. Price, not to send for me earlier.'

Willie, abashed and guilty, found nothing to say. His eye had the meek wistfulness of Holman Hunt's 'Scapegoat.'

'Mr. Price wanted her to have the doctor,' said Anna, defending him with warmth; 'but she wouldn't. He is out at the works all day till late at night. How was he to know how she was? She could walk about.'

The tall doctor glanced at Anna in surprise, and at once modified his tone. 'Yes,' he said, 'that's the curious thing. It passes me how she managed to get about. But there is no knowing what an obstinate woman won't force herself to do. I'll send the medicine up to-night, and come along myself with the nurse early to-morrow. Meantime, keep carefully to my instructions.'

That night remains for ever fixed in Anna's memory: the grim rooms, echoing and shadowy; the countless journeys up and down dark stairs and passages; Willie sitting always immovable in the kitchen, idle because there was nothing for him to do; Sarah incessantly panting on the truckle-bed; the hired woman from up the street, buxom, kindly, useful, but fatuous in the endless monotony of her commiserations.

Towards morning, Sarah Vodrey gave sign of a desire to talk.

'I've fought the fight,' she murmured to Anna, who alone was in the bedroom with her, 'I've fought the fight; I've kept the faith. In that box there ye'll see a purse. There's seventeen pounds six in it. That will pay for the funeral, and Willie must have what's over. There would ha' been more for the lad, but he never paid me no wages this two years past. I never troubled him.'

'Don't tell Willie that,' Anna said impetuously.

'Eh, bless ye, no!' said the dying drudge, and then seemed to doze.

Anna went to the kitchen, and sent the woman upstairs.

'How is she?' asked Willie, without stirring. Anna shook her head. 'Neither her nor me will be here much longer, I'm thinking,' he said, smiling wearily.

'What?' she exclaimed, startled.

'Mr. Sutton has arranged to sell our business as a going-concern—some people at Turnhill are buying it. I shall go to Australia; there's no room for me here. The creditors have promised to allow me twenty-five pounds, and I can get an assisted passage. Bursley'll know me no more. But—but—I shall always remember you and what you've done.'

She longed to kneel at his feet, and to comfort him, and to cry: 'It is I who have ruined you—driven your father to cheating his servant, to crime, to suicide; driven you to forgery, and turned you out of your house which your old servant killed herself in making clean for me. I have wronged you, and I love you like a mother because I have wronged you and because I saved you from prison.'

But she said nothing except: 'Some of us will miss you.'

The next day Sarah Vodrey died—she who had never lived save in the fetters of slavery and fanaticism. After fifty years of ceaseless labour, she had gained the affection of one person, and enough money to pay for her own funeral. Willie Price took a cheap lodging with the woman who had been called in on the night of Sarah's collapse. Before Christmas he was to sail for Melbourne. The Priory, deserted, gave up its rickety furniture to a van from Hanbridge, where, in an auction-room, the frail sticks lost their identity in a medley of other sticks, and ceased to be. Then the bricklayer, the plasterer, the painter, and the paper-hanger came to the Priory, and whistled and sang in it.

CHAPTER XIII

THE BAZAAR

The Wesleyan Bazaar, the greatest undertaking of its kind ever known in Bursley, gradually became a cloud which filled the entire social horizon. Mrs. Sutton, organiser of the Sunday-school stall, pressed all her friends into the service, and a fortnight after the death of Sarah Vodrey, Anna and even Agnes gave much of their spare time to the work, which was carried on under pressure increasing daily as the final moments approached. This was well for Anna, in that it diverted her thoughts by keeping her energies fully engaged. One morning, however, it occurred to Mrs. Sutton to reflect that Anna, at such a period of life, should be otherwise employed. Anna had called at the Suttons' to deliver some finished garments.

'My dear,' she said, 'I am very much obliged to you for all this industry. But I've been thinking that as you are to be married in February you ought to be preparing your things.'

'My things!' Anna repeated idly; and then she remembered Mynors' phrase, on the hill, 'Can you be ready by that time?'

'Yes,' said Mrs. Sutton; 'but possibly you've been getting forward with them on the quiet.'

'Tell me,' said Anna, with an air of interest; 'I've meant to ask you before: Is it the bride's place to provide all the house-linen, and that sort of thing?'

'It was in my day; but those things alter so. The bride took all the house-linen to her husband, and as many clothes for herself as would last a year; that was the rule. We used to stitch everything at home in those days—everything; and we had what we called a "bottom drawer" to store them in. As soon as a girl passed her fifteenth birthday, she began to sew for the "bottom drawer." But all those things change so, I dare say it's different now.'

'How much will it cost to buy everything, do you think?' Anna asked.

Just then Beatrice entered the room.

'Beatrice, Anna is inquiring how much it will cost to buy her trousseau, and the house-linen. What do you say?'

'Oh!' Beatrice replied, without any hesitation, 'a couple of hundred at least.'

Mrs. Sutton, reading Anna's face, smiled reassuringly. 'Nonsense, Bee! I dare say you could do it on a hundred with care, Anna.'

'Why should Anna want to do it with care?' Beatrice asked curtly.

Anna went straight across the road to her father, and asked him for a hundred pounds of her own money. She had not spoken to him, save under necessity, since the evening spent at the Suttons'.

'What's afoot now?' he questioned savagely.

'I must buy things for the wedding—clothes and things, father.'

'Ay! clothes! clothes! What clothes dost want? A few pounds will cover them.'

'There'll be all the linen for the house.'

'Linen for—— It's none thy place for buy that.'

'Yes, father, it is.'

'I say it isna',' he shouted.

'But I've asked Mrs. Sutton, and she says it is.'

'What business an' ye for go blabbing thy affairs all over Bosley? I say it isna' thy place for buy linen, and let that be sufficient. Go and get dinner. It's nigh on twelve now.'

That evening, when Agnes had gone to bed, she resumed the struggle.

'Father, I must have that hundred pounds. I really must. I mean it.'

'*Thou means it*! What?'

'I mean I must have a hundred pounds.'

'I'd advise thee to tak' care o' thy tongue, my lass. *Thou means it*!'

'But you needn't give it me all at once,' she pursued.

He gazed at her, glowering.

'I shanna' give it thee. It's Henry's place for buy th' house-linen.'

'Father, it isn't.' Her voice broke, but only for an instant. 'I'm asking you for my own money. You seem to want to make me miserable just before my wedding.'

'I wish to God thou 'dst never seen Henry Mynors. It's given thee pride and made thee undutiful.'

'I'm only asking you for my own money.'

Her calm insistence maddened him. Jumping up from his chair, he stamped out of the room, and she heard him strike a match in his office. Presently he returned, and threw angrily on to the table in front of her a cheque-book and pass-book. The deposit-book she had always kept herself for convenience of paying into the bank.

'Here,' he said scornfully, 'tak' thy traps and ne'er speak to me again. I wash my hands of ye. Tak' 'em and do what ye'n a mind. Chuck thy money into th' cut[1] for aught I care.'

The next evening Henry came up. She observed that his face had a grave look, but intent on her own difficulties she did not remark on it, and proceeded at once to do what she resolved to do. It was a cold night in November, yet the miser, wrathfully sullen, chose to sit in his office without a fire. Agnes was working sums in the kitchen.

'Henry,' Anna began, 'I've had a difficulty with father, and I must tell you.'

'Not about the wedding, I hope,' he said.

'It was about money. Of course, Henry, I can't get married without a lot of money.'

'Why not?' he inquired.

'I've my own things to get,' she said, 'and I've all the house-linen to buy.'

'Oh! You buy the house-linen, do you?' She saw that he was relieved by that information.

'Of course. Well, I told father I must have a hundred pounds, and he wouldn't give it me. And when I stuck to him he got angry—you know he can't bear to see money spent—and at last he get a little savage and gave me my bank-books, and said he'd have nothing more to do with my money.'

Henry's face broke into a laugh, and Anna was obliged to smile. 'Capital!' he said. 'Couldn't be better.'

'I want you to tell me how much I've got in the bank,' she said. 'I only know I'm always paying in odd cheques.'

He examined the three books. 'A very tidy bit,' he said; 'something over two hundred and fifty pounds. So you can draw cheques at your ease.'

'Draw me a cheque for twenty pounds,' she said; and then, while he wrote: 'Henry, after we're married, I shall want you to take charge of all this.'

'Yes, of course; I will do that, dear. But your money will be yours. There ought to be a settlement on you. Still, if your father says nothing, it is not for me to say anything.'

'Father will say nothing—now,' she said. 'You've never shown any interest in it, Henry; but as we're talking of money, I may as well tell you that father says I'm worth fifty thousand pounds.'

The man of business was astonished and enraptured beyond measure. His countenance shone with delight.

'Surely not!' he protested formally.

'That's what father told me, and he made me read a list of shares, and so on.'

'We will go slow, to begin with,' said Mynors solemnly. He had not expected more than fifteen, or twenty thousand pounds, and even this sum had dazzled his imagination. He was glad that he had only taken the house at Toft End on a yearly tenancy. He now saw himself the dominant figure in all the Five Towns.

Later in the evening he disclosed, perfunctorily, the matter which had been a serious weight on his mind when he entered the house, but which this revelation of vast wealth had diminished to a trifle. Titus Price had been the treasurer of the building fund which the bazaar was designed to assist. Mynors had assumed the position of the dead man, and that day, in going through the accounts, he had discovered that a sum of fifty pounds was missing.

'It's a dreadful thing for Willie, if it gets about,' he said; 'a tale of that sort would follow him to Australia.'

'Oh, Henry, it is!' she exclaimed, sorrow-stricken, 'but we mustn't let it get about. Let us pay the money ourselves. You must enter it in the books and say nothing.'

'That is impossible,' he said firmly. 'I can't alter the accounts. At least I can't alter the bank-book and the vouchers. The auditor would detect it in a minute. Besides, I should not be doing my duty if I kept a thing like this from the Superintendent-minister. He, at any rate, must know, and perhaps the stewards.'

'But you can urge them to say nothing. Tell them that you will make it good. I will write a cheque at once.'

'I had meant to find the fifty myself,' he said. It was a peddling sum to him now.

'Let me pay half, then,' she asked.

'If you like,' he urged, smiling faintly at her eagerness. 'The thing is bound to be kept quiet—it would create such a frightful scandal. Poor old chap!' he added, carelessly, 'I suppose he was hard run, and meant to put it back—as they all do mean.'

But it was useless for Mynors to affect depression of spirits, or mournful sympathy with the errors of a dead sinner. The fifty thousand danced a jig in his brain that night.

Anna was absorbed in contemplating the misfortune of Willie Price. She prayed wildly that he might never learn the full depth of his father's fall. The miserable robbery of Sarah's wages was buried for evermore, and this new delinquency, which all would regard as flagrant sacrilege, must be buried also. A soul less loyal than Anna's might have feared that Willie, a self-convicted forger, had been a party to the embezzlement; but Anna knew that it could not be so.

It was characteristic of Mynors' cautious prudence that, the first intoxication having passed, he made no further reference of any kind to Anna's fortune. The arrangements for their married life were planned on a scale which ignored the fifty thousand pounds. For both their sakes he wished to avoid all friction with the miser, at any rate until his status as Anna's husband would enable him to enforce her rights, if that should be necessary, with dignity and effectiveness. He did not precisely anticipate trouble, but the fact had not escaped him that Ephraim still held the whole of Anna's securities. He was in no hurry to enlarge his borders. He knew that there were twenty-four hours in every day, three hundred and sixty-five days in every year, and thirty good years in life still left to him; and therefore that there would be ample time, after the wedding, for the execution of his purposes in regard to that fifty thousand pounds. Meanwhile, he told Anna that he had set aside two hundred pounds for the purchase of furniture for the Priory—a modest sum; but he judged it sufficient. His method was to buy a piece at a time, always second-hand, but always good. The bargain-hunt was up, and Anna soon yielded to its mild satisfactions. In the matter of her trousseau and the house-linen, Anna, having obtained the needed money—at so dear a cost—found yet another obstacle in the imminent bazaar, which occupied Mrs. Sutton and Beatrice so completely that they could not contrive any opportunity to assist her in shopping. It was decided between them that every article should be bought ready-made and seamed, and that the first week of the New Year, if indeed Mrs. Sutton survived the bazaar, should be entirely and absolutely devoted to Anna's business.

At nights, when she had leisure to think, Anna was astonished how during the day she had forgotten her preoccupations in the activities precendent to the bazaar, or in choosing furniture with Mynors. But she never slept without thinking of Willie Price, and hoping that no further disaster might overtake him. The incident of the embezzled fifty pounds had been closed, and she had given a cheque for twenty-five pounds to Mynors. He had acquainted the minister with the facts, and Mr. Banks had decided that the two circuit stewards must be informed. Beyond these the scandalous secret was not to go. But Anna wondered whether a secret shared by five persons could long remain a secret.

The bazaar was a triumphant and unparalleled success, and, of the seven stalls, the Sunday-school stall stood first each night in the nightly returns. The scene in the town-hall, on the fourth and final night, a Saturday, was as delirious and gay as a carnival. Four hundred and twenty pounds had been raised up to tea-time, and it was the impassioned desire of everyone to achieve five hundred. The price of admission had been reduced to threepence, in order that the artisan might enter and spend his wages in an excellent cause. The seven stalls, ranged round the room like so many bowers of beauty, draped and frilled and floriated, and still laden with countless articles of use and ornament, were continually reinforced with purchasers by emissaries canvassing the crowd which filled the middle of the paper-strewn floor. The horse was not only taken to the water, but compelled to drink; and many a man who, outside, would have laughed at the risk of being robbed, was robbed openly, shamelessly, under the gaze of ministers and class-leaders. Bouquets were sold at a shilling each, and at the refreshment stall a glass of milk cost sixpence. The noise rivalled that of a fair; there was no quiet anywhere, save in the farthest recess of each stall, where the lady in supreme charge of it, like a spider in the middle of its web, watched customers and cash-box with equal cupidity.

Mrs. Sutton, at seven o'clock, had not returned from tea, and Anna and Beatrice, who managed the Sunday-school stall in her absence, feared that she had at last succumbed under the strain. But shortly afterwards she hurried back breathless to her place.

'See that, Anna? It will be reckoned in our returns,' she said, exhibiting a piece of paper. It was Ephraim's cheque for twenty-five pounds promised months ago, but on a condition which had not been fulfilled.

'She has the secret of persuading him,' thought Anna. 'Why have I never found it?'

Then Agnes, in a new white frock, came up with three shillings, proceeds of bouquets.

'But you must take that to the flower-stall, my pet,' said Mrs. Sutton.

'Can't I give it to you?' the child pleaded. 'I want your stall to be the best.'

Mynors arrived next, with something concealed in tissue-paper. He removed the paper, and showed, in a frame of crimson plush, a common white plate decorated with a simple band and line, and a monogram in the centre—'A.T.' Anna blushed, recognising the plate which she had painted that afternoon in July at Mynors' works.

'Can you sell this?' Mynors asked Mrs. Sutton.

'I'll try to,' said Mrs. Sutton doubtfully—not in the secret. 'What's it meant for?'

'Try to sell it to me,' said Mynors.

'Well,' she laughed, 'what will you give?'

'A couple of sovereigns.'

'Make it guineas.'

He paid the money, and requested Anna to keep the plate for him.

At nine o'clock it was announced that, though raffling was forbidden, the bazaar would be enlivened by an auction. A licensed auctioneer was brought, and the sale commenced. The auctioneer, however, failed to attune himself to the wild spirit of the hour, and his professional efforts would have resulted in a fiasco had not Mynors, perceiving the danger, leaped to the platform and masterfully assumed the hammer. Mynors surpassed himself in the kind of wit that amuses an excited crowd, and the auction soon monopolised the attention of the room; it was always afterwards remembered as the crowning success of the bazaar. The incredible man took ten pounds in twenty minutes. During this episode Anna, who had been left alone in the stall, first noticed Willie Price in the room. His ship sailed on the Monday, but steerage passengers had to be aboard on Sunday, and he was saying good-bye to a few acquaintances. He seemed quite cheerful, as he walked about with his hands in his pockets, chatting with this one and that; it was the false and hysterical gaiety that precedes a final separation. As soon as he saw Anna he came towards her.

'Well, good-bye, Miss Tellwright,' he said jauntily. 'I leave for Liverpool to-morrow morning. Wish me luck.' Nothing more; no word, no accent, to recall the terrible but sublime past.

'I do,' she answered. They shook hands. Others approaching, he drifted away. Her glance followed him like a beneficent influence.

For three days she had carried in her pocket an envelope containing a bank-note for a hundred pounds, intending by some device to force it on him as a parting gift. Now the last chance was lost, and she had not even attempted this difficult feat of charity. Such futility, she reflected, self-scorning, was of a piece with her life. 'He hasn't really gone. He hasn't really gone,' she kept repeating, and yet knew well that he had gone.

'Do you know what they are saying, Anna?' said Beatrice, when, after eleven o'clock, the bazaar was closed to the public, and the stall-holders and their assistants were preparing to depart, their movements hastened by the stern aspect of the town-hall keeper.

'No. What?' said Anna; and in the same moment guessed.

'They say old Titus Price embezzled fifty pounds from the building fund, and Henry made it up, privately, so that there shouldn't be a scandal. Just fancy! Do you believe it?'

The secret was abroad. She looked round the room, and saw it in every face.

'Who says?' Anna demanded fiercely.

'It's all over the place. Miss Dickinson told me.'

'You will be glad to know, ladies,' Mynors' voice sang out from the platform, 'that the total proceeds, so far as we can calculate them now, exceed five hundred and twenty-five pounds.'

There was clapping of hands, which died out suddenly.

'Now Agnes,' Anna called, 'come along, quick; you're as white as a sheet. Good-night, Mrs. Sutton; good-night, Bee.'

Mynors was still occupied on the platform.

The town-hall keeper extinguished some of the lights. The bazaar was over.

[1] *Cut*: canal.

CHAPTER XIV

END OF A SIMPLE SOUL

The next morning, at half-past seven, Anna was standing in the garden-doorway of the Priory. The sun had just risen, the air was cold; roof and pavement were damp; rain had fallen, and more was to fall. A door opened higher up the street, and Willie Price came out, carrying a small bag. He turned to speak to some person within the house, and then stepped forward. As he passed Anna she sprang forth.

'Oh!' she cried, 'I had just come up here to see if the workmen had locked up properly. We have some of our new furniture in the house, you know.' She was as red as the sun over Hillport.

He glanced at her. 'Have *you* heard?' he asked simply.

'About what?' she whispered.

'About my poor old father.'

'Yes. I was hoping—hoping you would never know.'

By a common impulse they went into the garden of the Priory, and he shut the door.

'Never know?' he repeated. 'Oh! they took care to tell me.'

A silence followed.

'Is that your luggage?' she inquired. He lifted up the handbag, and nodded.

'All of it?'

'Yes,' he said. 'I'm only an emigrant.'

'I've got a note here for you,' she said. 'I should have posted it to the steamer; but now you can take it yourself. I want you not to read it till you get to Melbourne.'

'Very well,' he said, and crumpled the proffered envelope into his pocket. He was not thinking of the note at all. Presently he asked: 'Why didn't you tell me about my father? If I had to hear it, I'd sooner have heard it from you.'

'You must try to forget it,' she urged him. 'You are not your father.'

'I wish I had never been born,' he said. 'I wish I'd gone to prison.'

Now was the moment when, if ever, the mother's influence should be exerted.

'Be a man,' she said softly. 'I did the best I could for you. I shall always think of you, in Australia, getting on.' She put a hand on his shoulder. 'Yes,' she said again, passionately: 'I shall always remember you—always.'

The hand with which he touched her arm shook like an old man's hand. As their eyes met in an intense and painful gaze, to her, at least, it was revealed that they were lovers. What he had learnt in that instant can only be guessed from his next action....

Anna ran out of the garden into the street, and so home, never looking behind to see if he pursued his way to the station.

Some may argue that Anna, knowing she loved another man, ought not to have married Mynors. But she did not reason thus; such a notion never even occurred to her. She had promised to marry Mynors, and she married him. Nothing else was possible. She who had never failed in duty did not fail then. She who had always submitted and bowed the head, submitted and bowed the head then. She had sucked in with her mother's milk the profound truth that a woman's life is always a renunciation, greater or less. Hers by chance was greater. Facing the future calmly and genially, she took oath with herself to be a good wife to the man whom, with all his excellences, she had never loved. Her thoughts often dwelt lovingly on Willie Price, whom she deemed to be pursuing in Australia an honourable and successful career, quickened at the outset by her hundred pounds. This vision of him was her stay. But neither she nor anyone in the Five Towns or elsewhere ever heard of Willie Price again. And well might none hear! The abandoned pitshaft does not deliver up its secret. And so—the Bank of England is the richer by a hundred pounds unclaimed, and the world the poorer by a simple and meek soul stung to revolt only in its last hour.

CPSIA information can be obtained at www.ICGtesting.com
Printed in the USA
BVOW06s0611121214

379084BV00018B/129/P